T0189065

Lecture Notes in Computer Science　　9912

Commenced Publication in 1973
Founding and Former Series Editors:
Gerhard Goos, Juris Hartmanis, and Jan van Leeuwen

More information about this series at http://www.springer.com/series/7412

Bastian Leibe · Jiri Matas
Nicu Sebe · Max Welling (Eds.)

Computer Vision – ECCV 2016

14th European Conference
Amsterdam, The Netherlands, October 11–14, 2016
Proceedings, Part VIII

 Springer

Editors
Bastian Leibe
RWTH Aachen
Aachen
Germany

Jiri Matas
Czech Technical University
Prague 2
Czech Republic

Nicu Sebe
University of Trento
Povo - Trento
Italy

Max Welling
University of Amsterdam
Amsterdam
The Netherlands

ISSN 0302-9743   ISSN 1611-3349 (electronic)
Lecture Notes in Computer Science
ISBN 978-3-319-46483-1   ISBN 978-3-319-46484-8   (eBook)
DOI 10.1007/978-3-319-46484-8

Library of Congress Control Number: 2016951693

LNCS Sublibrary: SL6 – Image Processing, Computer Vision, Pattern Recognition, and Graphics

Printed on acid-free paper

This Springer imprint is published by Springer Nature
The registered company is Springer International Publishing AG
The registered company address is: Gewerbestrasse 11, 6330 Cham, Switzerland

Foreword

Welcome to the proceedings of the 2016 edition of the European Conference on Computer Vision held in Amsterdam! It is safe to say that the European Conference on Computer Vision is one of the top conferences in computer vision. It is good to reiterate the history of the conference to see the broad base the conference has built in its 13 editions. First held in 1990 in Antibes (France), it was followed by subsequent conferences in Santa Margherita Ligure (Italy) in 1992, Stockholm (Sweden) in 1994, Cambridge (UK) in 1996, Freiburg (Germany) in 1998, Dublin (Ireland) in 2000, Copenhagen (Denmark) in 2002, Prague (Czech Republic) in 2004, Graz (Austria) in 2006, Marseille (France) in 2008, Heraklion (Greece) in 2010, Florence (Italy) in 2012, and Zürich (Switzerland) in 2014.

For the 14th edition, many people worked hard to provide attendees with a most warm welcome while enjoying the best science. The Program Committee, Bastian Leibe, Jiri Matas, Nicu Sebe, and Max Welling, did an excellent job. Apart from the scientific program, the workshops were selected and handled by Hervé Jégou and Gang Hua, and the tutorials by Jacob Verbeek and Rita Cucchiara. Thanks for the great job. The coordination with the subsequent ACM Multimedia offered an opportunity to expand the tutorials with an additional invited session, offered by the University of Amsterdam and organized together with the help of ACM Multimedia.

Of the many people who worked hard as local organizers, we would like to single out Martine de Wit of the UvA Conference Office, who delicately and efficiently organized the main body. Also the local organizers Hamdi Dibeklioglu, Efstratios Gavves, Jan van Gemert, Thomas Mensink, and Mihir Jain had their hands full. As a venue, we chose the Royal Theatre Carré located on the canals of the Amstel River in downtown Amsterdam. Space in Amsterdam is sparse, so it was a little tighter than usual. The university lent us their downtown campuses for the tutorials and the workshops. A relatively new thing was the industry and the sponsors for which Ronald Poppe and Peter de With did a great job, while Andy Bagdanov and John Schavemaker arranged the demos. Michael Wilkinson took care to make Yom Kippur as comfortable as possible for those for whom it is an important day. We thank Marc Pollefeys, Alberto del Bimbo, and Virginie Mes for their advice and help behind the scenes. We thank all the anonymous volunteers for their hard and precise work. We also thank our generous sponsors. Their support is an essential part of the program. It is good to see such a level of industrial interest in what our community is doing!

Amsterdam does not need any introduction. Please emerge yourself but do not drown in it, have a nice time.

October 2016

Theo Gevers
Arnold Smeulders

Preface

Welcome to the proceedings of the 2016 European Conference on Computer Vision (ECCV 2016) held in Amsterdam, The Netherlands. We are delighted to present this volume reflecting a strong and exciting program, the result of an extensive review process. In total, we received 1,561 paper submissions. Of these, 81 violated the ECCV submission guidelines or did not pass the plagiarism test and were rejected without review. We employed the iThenticate software (www.ithenticate.com) for plagiarism detection. Of the remaining papers, 415 were accepted (26.6 %): 342 as posters (22.6 %), 45 as spotlights (2.9 %), and 28 as oral presentations (1.8 %). The spotlights – short, five-minute podium presentations – are novel to ECCV and were introduced after their success at the CVPR 2016 conference. All orals and spotlights are presented as posters as well. The selection process was a combined effort of four program co-chairs (PCs), 74 area chairs (ACs), 1,086 Program Committee members, and 77 additional reviewers.

As PCs, we were primarily responsible for the design and execution of the review process. Beyond administrative rejections, we were involved in acceptance decisions only in the very few cases where the ACs were not able to agree on a decision. PCs, as is customary in the field, were not allowed to co-author a submission. General co-chairs and other co-organizers played no role in the review process, were permitted to submit papers, and were treated as any other author.

Acceptance decisions were made by two independent ACs. There were 74 ACs, selected by the PCs according to their technical expertise, experience, and geographical diversity (41 from European, five from Asian, two from Australian, and 26 from North American institutions). The ACs were aided by 1,086 Program Committee members to whom papers were assigned for reviewing. There were 77 additional reviewers, each supervised by a Program Committee member. The Program Committee was selected from committees of previous ECCV, ICCV, and CVPR conferences and was extended on the basis of suggestions from the ACs and the PCs. Having a large pool of Program Committee members for reviewing allowed us to match expertise while bounding reviewer loads. Typically five papers, but never more than eight, were assigned to a Program Committee member. Graduate students had a maximum of four papers to review.

The ECCV 2016 review process was in principle double-blind. Authors did not know reviewer identities, nor the ACs handling their paper(s). However, anonymity becomes difficult to maintain as more and more submissions appear concurrently on arXiv.org. This was not against the ECCV 2016 double submission rules, which followed the practice of other major computer vision conferences in the recent past. The existence of arXiv publications, mostly not peer-reviewed, raises difficult problems with the assessment of unpublished, concurrent, and prior art, content overlap, plagiarism, and self-plagiarism. Moreover, it undermines the anonymity of submissions. We found that not all cases can be covered by a simple set of rules. Almost all controversies during the review process were related to the arXiv issue. Most of the reviewer inquiries were resolved by giving the benefit of the doubt to ECCV authors. However, the problem will have to be discussed by the community so that consensus is found on how to handle the issues brought by publishing on arXiv.

Particular attention was paid to handling conflicts of interest. Conflicts of interest between ACs, Program Committee members, and papers were identified based on the authorship of ECCV 2016 submissions, on the home institutions, and on previous collaborations of all researchers involved. To find institutional conflicts, all authors, Program Committee members, and ACs were asked to list the Internet domains of their current institutions. To find collaborators, the Researcher.cc database (http://researcher.cc/), funded by the Computer Vision Foundation, was used to find any co-authored papers in the period 2012–2016. We pre-assigned approximately 100 papers to each AC, based on affinity scores from the Toronto Paper Matching System. ACs then bid on these, indicating their level of expertise. Based on these bids, and conflicts of interest, approximately 40 papers were assigned to each AC. The ACs then suggested seven reviewers from the pool of Program Committee members for each paper, in ranked order, from which three were chosen automatically by CMT (Microsofts Academic Conference Management Service), taking load balancing and conflicts of interest into account.

The initial reviewing period was five weeks long, after which reviewers provided reviews with preliminary recommendations. With the generous help of several last-minute reviewers, each paper received three reviews. Submissions with all three reviews suggesting rejection were independently checked by two ACs and if they agreed, the manuscript was rejected at this stage ("early rejects"). In total, 334 manuscripts (22.5 %) were early-rejected, reducing the average AC load to about 30.

Authors of the remaining submissions were then given the opportunity to rebut the reviews, primarily to identify factual errors. Following this, reviewers and ACs discussed papers at length, after which reviewers finalized their reviews and gave a final recommendation to the ACs. Each manuscript was evaluated independently by two ACs who were not aware of each others, identities. In most of the cases, after extensive discussions, the two ACs arrived at a common decision, which was always adhered to by the PCs. In the very few borderline cases where an agreement was not reached, the PCs acted as tie-breakers. Owing to the rapid expansion of the field, which led to an unexpectedly large increase in the number of submissions, the size of the venue became a limiting factor and a hard upper bound on the number of accepted papers had to be imposed. We were able to increase the limit by replacing one oral session by a poster session. Nevertheless, this forced the PCs to reject some borderline papers that could otherwise have been accepted.

We want to thank everyone involved in making the ECCV 2016 possible. First and foremost, the success of ECCV 2016 depended on the quality of papers submitted by the authors, and on the very hard work of the ACs, the Program Committee members, and the additional reviewers. We are particularly grateful to Rene Vidal for his continuous support and sharing experience from organizing ICCV 2015, to Laurent Charlin for the use of the Toronto Paper Matching System, to Ari Kobren for the use of the Researcher.cc tools, to the Computer Vision Foundation (CVF) for facilitating the use of the iThenticate plagiarism detection software, and to Gloria Zen and Radu-Laurentiu Vieriu for setting up CMT and managing the various tools involved. We also owe a debt of gratitude for the support of the Amsterdam local organizers, especially Hamdi Dibeklioglu for keeping the website always up to date. Finally, the preparation of these proceedings would not have been possible without the diligent effort of the publication chairs, Albert Ali Salah and Robby Tan, and of Anna Kramer from Springer.

October 2016

Bastian Leibe
Jiri Matas
Nicu Sebe
Max Welling

Organization

General Chairs

Theo Gevers	University of Amsterdam, The Netherlands
Arnold Smeulders	University of Amsterdam, The Netherlands

Program Committee Co-chairs

Bastian Leibe	RWTH Aachen, Germany
Jiri Matas	Czech Technical University, Czech Republic
Nicu Sebe	University of Trento, Italy
Max Welling	University of Amsterdam, The Netherlands

Honorary Chair

Jan Koenderink   Delft University of Technology, The Netherlands and KU Leuven, Belgium

Advisory Program Chair

Luc van Gool   ETH Zurich, Switzerland

Advisory Workshop Chair

Josef Kittler   University of Surrey, UK

Advisory Conference Chair

Alberto del Bimbo   University of Florence, Italy

Local Arrangements Chairs

Hamdi Dibeklioglu	Delft University of Technology, The Netherlands
Efstratios Gavves	University of Amsterdam, The Netherlands
Jan van Gemert	Delft University of Technology, The Netherlands
Thomas Mensink	University of Amsterdam, The Netherlands
Michael Wilkinson	University of Groningen, The Netherlands

Workshop Chairs

Hervé Jégou   Facebook AI Research, USA
Gang Hua   Microsoft Research Asia, China

Tutorial Chairs

Jacob Verbeek   Inria Grenoble, France
Rita Cucchiara   University of Modena and Reggio Emilia, Italy

Poster Chairs

Jasper Uijlings   University of Edinburgh, UK
Roberto Valenti   Sightcorp, The Netherlands

Publication Chairs

Albert Ali Salah   Boğaziçi University, Turkey
Robby T. Tan   Yale-NUS College and National University
                               of Singapore, Singapore

Video Chair

Mihir Jain   University of Amsterdam, The Netherlands

Demo Chairs

John Schavemaker   Twnkls, The Netherlands
Andy Bagdanov   University of Florence, Italy

Social Media Chair

Efstratios Gavves   University of Amsterdam, The Netherlands

Industrial Liaison Chairs

Ronald Poppe   Utrecht University, The Netherlands
Peter de With   Eindhoven University of Technology, The Netherlands

Conference Coordinator, Accommodation, and Finance

Conference Office
Martine de Wit   University of Amsterdam, The Netherlands
Melanie Venverloo   University of Amsterdam, The Netherlands
Niels Klein   University of Amsterdam, The Netherlands

Area Chairs

Radhakrishna Achanta	Ecole Polytechnique Fédérale de Lausanne, Switzerland
Antonis Argyros	FORTH and University of Crete, Greece
Michael Bronstein	Universitá della Svizzera Italiana, Switzerland
Gabriel Brostow	University College London, UK
Thomas Brox	University of Freiburg, Germany
Barbara Caputo	Sapienza University of Rome, Italy
Miguel Carreira-Perpinan	University of California, Merced, USA
Ondra Chum	Czech Technical University, Czech Republic
Daniel Cremers	Technical University of Munich, Germany
Rita Cucchiara	University of Modena and Reggio Emilia, Italy
Trevor Darrell	University of California, Berkeley, USA
Andrew Davison	Imperial College London, UK
Fernando de la Torre	Carnegie Mellon University, USA
Piotr Dollar	Facebook AI Research, USA
Vittorio Ferrari	University of Edinburgh, UK
Charless Fowlkes	University of California, Irvine, USA
Jan-Michael Frahm	University of North Carolina at Chapel Hill, USA
Mario Fritz	Max Planck Institute, Germany
Pascal Fua	Ecole Polytechnique Fédérale de Lausanne, Switzerland
Juergen Gall	University of Bonn, Germany
Peter Gehler	University of Tübingen — Max Planck Institute, Germany
Andreas Geiger	Max Planck Institute, Germany
Ross Girshick	Facebook AI Research, USA
Kristen Grauman	University of Texas at Austin, USA
Abhinav Gupta	Carnegie Mellon University, USA
Hervé Jégou	Facebook AI Research, USA
Fredrik Kahl	Lund University, Sweden
Iasonas Kokkinos	Ecole Centrale Paris, France
Philipp Krähenbühl	University of California, Berkeley, USA
Pawan Kumar	University of Oxford, UK
Christoph Lampert	Institute of Science and Technology Austria, Austria
Hugo Larochelle	Université de Sherbrooke, Canada
Neil Lawrence	University of Sheffield, UK
Svetlana Lazebnik	University of Illinois at Urbana-Champaign, USA
Honglak Lee	Stanford University, USA
Kyoung Mu Lee	Seoul National University, Republic of Korea
Vincent Lepetit	Graz University of Technology, Austria
Hongdong Li	Australian National University, Australia
Julien Mairal	Inria, France
Yasuyuki Matsushita	Osaka University, Japan
Nassir Navab	Technical University of Munich, Germany

Sebastian Nowozin	Microsoft Research, Cambridge, UK
Tomas Pajdla	Czech Technical University, Czech Republic
Maja Pantic	Imperial College London, UK
Devi Parikh	Virginia Tech, USA
Thomas Pock	Graz University of Technology, Austria
Elisa Ricci	FBK Technologies of Vision, Italy
Bodo Rosenhahn	Leibniz-University of Hannover, Germany
Stefan Roth	Technical University of Darmstadt, Germany
Carsten Rother	Technical University of Dresden, Germany
Silvio Savarese	Stanford University, USA
Bernt Schiele	Max Planck Institute, Germany
Konrad Schindler	ETH Zürich, Switzerland
Cordelia Schmid	Inria, France
Cristian Sminchisescu	Lund University, Sweden
Noah Snavely	Cornell University, USA
Sabine Süsstrunk	Ecole Polytechnique Fédérale de Lausanne, Switzerland
Qi Tian	University of Texas at San Antonio, USA
Antonio Torralba	Massachusetts Institute of Technology, USA
Zhuowen Tu	University of California, San Diego, USA
Raquel Urtasun	University of Toronto, Canada
Joost van de Weijer	Universitat Autònoma de Barcelona, Spain
Laurens van der Maaten	Facebook AI Research, USA
Nuno Vasconcelos	University of California, San Diego, USA
Andrea Vedaldi	University of Oxford, UK
Xiaogang Wang	Chinese University of Hong Kong, Hong Kong, SAR China
Jingdong Wang	Microsoft Research Asia, China
Lior Wolf	Tel Aviv University, Israel
Ying Wu	Northwestern University, USA
Dong Xu	University of Sydney, Australia
Shuicheng Yan	National University of Singapore, Singapore
MingHsuan Yang	University of California, Merced, USA
Ramin Zabih	Cornell NYC Tech, USA
Larry Zitnick	Facebook AI Research, USA

Technical Program Committee

Austin Abrams	Pulkit Agrawal	Andrea Albarelli
Supreeth Achar	Jorgen Ahlberg	Alexandra Albu
Tameem Adel	Haizhou Ai	Saad Ali
Khurrum Aftab	Zeynep Akata	Daniel Aliaga
Lourdes Agapito	Ijaz Akhter	Marina Alterman
Sameer Agarwal	Karteek Alahari	Hani Altwaijry
Aishwarya Agrawal	Xavier Alameda-Pineda	Jose M. Alvarez

Mitsuru Ambai
Mohamed Amer
Senjian An
Cosmin Ancuti
Juan Andrade-Cetto
Marco Andreetto
Elli Angelopoulou
Relja Arandjelovic
Helder Araujo
Pablo Arbelaez
Chetan Arora
Carlos Arteta
Kalle Astroem
Nikolay Atanasov
Vassilis Athitsos
Mathieu Aubry
Yannis Avrithis
Hossein Azizpour
Artem Babenko
Andrew Bagdanov
Yuval Bahat
Xiang Bai
Lamberto Ballan
Arunava Banerjee
Adrian Barbu
Nick Barnes
Peter Barnum
Jonathan Barron
Adrien Bartoli
Dhruv Batra
Eduardo
  Bayro-Corrochano
Jean-Charles Bazin
Paul Beardsley
Vasileios Belagiannis
Ismail Ben Ayed
Boulbaba Benamor
Abhijit Bendale
Rodrigo Benenson
Fabian Benitez-Quiroz
Ohad Ben-Shahar
Dana Berman
Lucas Beyer
Subhabrata Bhattacharya
Binod Bhattarai
Arnav Bhavsar

Simone Bianco
Hakan Bilen
Horst Bischof
Tom Bishop
Arijit Biswas
Soma Biswas
Marten Bjoerkman
Volker Blanz
Federica Bogo
Xavier Boix
Piotr Bojanowski
Terrance Boult
Katie Bouman
Thierry Bouwmans
Edmond Boyer
Yuri Boykov
Hakan Boyraz
Steven Branson
Mathieu Bredif
Francois Bremond
Stefan Breuers
Michael Brown
Marcus Brubaker
Luc Brun
Andrei Bursuc
Zoya Bylinskii
Daniel Cabrini Hauagge
Deng Cai
Jianfei Cai
Simone Calderara
Neill Campbell
Octavia Camps
Liangliang Cao
Xiaochun Cao
Xun Cao
Gustavo Carneiro
Dan Casas
Tom Cashman
Umberto Castellani
Carlos Castillo
Andrea Cavallaro
Jan Cech
Ayan Chakrabarti
Rudrasis Chakraborty
Krzysztof Chalupka
Tat-Jen Cham

Antoni Chan
Manmohan Chandraker
Sharat Chandran
Hong Chang
Hyun Sung Chang
Jason Chang
Ju Yong Chang
Xiaojun Chang
Yu-Wei Chao
Visesh Chari
Rizwan Chaudhry
Rama Chellappa
Bo Chen
Chao Chen
Chao-Yeh Chen
Chu-Song Chen
Hwann-Tzong Chen
Lin Chen
Mei Chen
Terrence Chen
Xilin Chen
Yunjin Chen
Guang Chen
Qifeng Chen
Xinlei Chen
Jian Cheng
Ming-Ming Cheng
Anoop Cherian
Guilhem Cheron
Dmitry Chetverikov
Liang-Tien Chia
Naoki Chiba
Tat-Jun Chin
Margarita Chli
Minsu Cho
Sunghyun Cho
TaeEun Choe
Jongmoo Choi
Seungjin Choi
Wongun Choi
Wen-Sheng Chu
Yung-Yu Chuang
Albert Chung
Gokberk Cinbis
Arridhana Ciptadi
Javier Civera

James Clark
Brian Clipp
Michael Cogswell
Taco Cohen
Toby Collins
John Collomosse
Camille Couprie
David Crandall
Marco Cristani
James Crowley
Jinshi Cui
Yin Cui
Jifeng Dai
Qieyun Dai
Shengyang Dai
Yuchao Dai
Zhenwen Dai
Dima Damen
Kristin Dana
Kostas Danilidiis
Mohamed Daoudi
Larry Davis
Teofilo de Campos
Marleen de Bruijne
Koichiro Deguchi
Alessio Del Bue
Luca del Pero
Antoine Deleforge
Hervé Delingette
David Demirdjian
Jia Deng
Joachim Denzler
Konstantinos Derpanis
Frederic Devernay
Hamdi Dibeklioglu
Santosh Kumar Divvala
Carl Doersch
Weisheng Dong
Jian Dong
Gianfranco Doretto
Alexey Dosovitskiy
Matthijs Douze
Bruce Draper
Tom Drummond
Shichuan Du
Jean-Luc Dugelay

Enrique Dunn
Zoran Duric
Pinar Duygulu
Alexei Efros
Carl Henrik Ek
Jan-Olof Eklundh
Jayan Eledath
Ehsan Elhamifar
Ian Endres
Aykut Erdem
Anders Eriksson
Sergio Escalera
Victor Escorcia
Francisco Estrada
Bin Fan
Quanfu Fan
Chen Fang
Tian Fang
Masoud Faraki
Ali Farhadi
Giovanni Farinella
Ryan Farrell
Raanan Fattal
Michael Felsberg
Jiashi Feng
Michele Fenzi
Andras Ferencz
Basura Fernando
Sanja Fidler
Mario Figueiredo
Michael Firman
Robert Fisher
John Fisher III
Alexander Fix
Boris Flach
Matt Flagg
Francois Fleuret
Wolfgang Foerstner
David Fofi
Gianluca Foresti
Per-Erik Forssen
David Fouhey
Jean-Sebastien Franco
Friedrich Fraundorfer
Oren Freifeld
Simone Frintrop

Huazhu Fu
Yun Fu
Jan Funke
Brian Funt
Ryo Furukawa
Yasutaka Furukawa
Andrea Fusiello
David Gallup
Chuang Gan
Junbin Gao
Jochen Gast
Stratis Gavves
Xin Geng
Bogdan Georgescu
David Geronimo
Bernard Ghanem
Riccardo Gherardi
Golnaz Ghiasi
Soumya Ghosh
Andrew Gilbert
Ioannis Gkioulekas
Georgia Gkioxari
Guy Godin
Roland Goecke
Boqing Gong
Shaogang Gong
Yunchao Gong
German Gonzalez
Jordi Gonzalez
Paulo Gotardo
Stephen Gould
Venu M. Govindu
Helmut Grabner
Etienne Grossmann
Chunhui Gu
David Gu
Sergio Guadarrama
Li Guan
Matthieu Guillaumin
Jean-Yves Guillemaut
Guodong Guo
Ruiqi Guo
Yanwen Guo
Saurabh Gupta
Pierre Gurdjos
Diego Gutierrez

Abner Guzman Rivera
Christian Haene
Niels Haering
Ralf Haeusler
David Hall
Peter Hall
Onur Hamsici
Dongfeng Han
Mei Han
Xufeng Han
Yahong Han
Ankur Handa
Kenji Hara
Tatsuya Harada
Mehrtash Harandi
Bharath Hariharan
Tal Hassner
Soren Hauberg
Michal Havlena
Tamir Hazan
Junfeng He
Kaiming He
Lei He
Ran He
Xuming He
Zhihai He
Felix Heide
Janne Heikkila
Jared Heinly
Mattias Heinrich
Pierre Hellier
Stephane Herbin
Isabelle Herlin
Alexander Hermans
Anders Heyden
Adrian Hilton
Vaclav Hlavac
Minh Hoai
Judy Hoffman
Steven Hoi
Derek Hoiem
Seunghoon Hong
Byung-Woo Hong
Anthony Hoogs
Yedid Hoshen
Winston Hsu

Changbo Hu
Wenze Hu
Zhe Hu
Gang Hua
Dong Huang
Gary Huang
Heng Huang
Jia-Bin Huang
Kaiqi Huang
Qingming Huang
Rui Huang
Xinyu Huang
Weilin Huang
Zhiwu Huang
Ahmad Humayun
Mohamed Hussein
Wonjun Hwang
Juan Iglesias
Nazli Ikizler-Cinbis
Evren Imre
Eldar Insafutdinov
Catalin Ionescu
Go Irie
Hossam Isack
Phillip Isola
Hamid Izadinia
Nathan Jacobs
Varadarajan Jagannadan
Aastha Jain
Suyog Jain
Varun Jampani
Jeremy Jancsary
C.V. Jawahar
Dinesh Jayaraman
Ian Jermyn
Hueihan Jhuang
Hui Ji
Qiang Ji
Jiaya Jia
Kui Jia
Yangqing Jia
Hao Jiang
Tingting Jiang
Yu-Gang Jiang
Zhuolin Jiang
Alexis Joly

Shantanu Joshi
Frederic Jurie
Achuta Kadambi
Samuel Kadoury
Yannis Kalantidis
Amit Kale
Sebastian Kaltwang
Joni-Kristian Kamarainen
George Kamberov
Chandra Kambhamettu
Martin Kampel
Kenichi Kanatani
Atul Kanaujia
Melih Kandemir
Zhuoliang Kang
Mohan Kankanhalli
Abhishek Kar
Leonid Karlinsky
Andrej Karpathy
Zoltan Kato
Rei Kawakami
Kristian Kersting
Margret Keuper
Nima Khademi Kalantari
Sameh Khamis
Fahad Khan
Aditya Khosla
Hadi Kiapour
Edward Kim
Gunhee Kim
Hansung Kim
Jae-Hak Kim
Kihwan Kim
Seon Joo Kim
Tae Hyun Kim
Tae-Kyun Kim
Vladimir Kim
Benjamin Kimia
Akisato Kimura
Durk Kingma
Thomas Kipf
Kris Kitani
Martin Kleinsteuber
Laurent Kneip
Kevin Koeser
Effrosyni Kokiopoulou

Piotr Koniusz
Theodora Kontogianni
Sanjeev Koppal
Dimitrios Kosmopoulos
Adriana Kovashka
Adarsh Kowdle
Michael Kramp
Josip Krapac
Jonathan Krause
Pavel Krsek
Hilde Kuehne
Shiro Kumano
Avinash Kumar
Sebastian Kurtek
Kyros Kutulakos
Suha Kwak
In So Kweon
Roland Kwitt
Junghyun Kwon
Junseok Kwon
Jan Kybic
Jorma Laaksonen
Alexander Ladikos
Florent Lafarge
Pierre-Yves Laffont
Wei-Sheng Lai
Jean-Francois Lalonde
Michael Langer
Oswald Lanz
Agata Lapedriza
Ivan Laptev
Diane Larlus
Christoph Lassner
Olivier Le Meur
Laura Leal-Taixé
Joon-Young Lee
Seungkyu Lee
Chen-Yu Lee
Andreas Lehrmann
Ido Leichter
Frank Lenzen
Matt Leotta
Stefan Leutenegger
Baoxin Li
Chunming Li
Dingzeyu Li

Fuxin Li
Hao Li
Houqiang Li
Qi Li
Stan Li
Wu-Jun Li
Xirong Li
Xuelong Li
Yi Li
Yongjie Li
Wei Li
Wen Li
Yeqing Li
Yujia Li
Wang Liang
Shengcai Liao
Jongwoo Lim
Joseph Lim
Di Lin
Weiyao Lin
Yen-Yu Lin
Min Lin
Liang Lin
Haibin Ling
Jim Little
Buyu Liu
Miaomiao Liu
Risheng Liu
Si Liu
Wanquan Liu
Yebin Liu
Ziwei Liu
Zhen Liu
Sifei Liu
Marcus Liwicki
Roberto Lopez-Sastre
Javier Lorenzo
Christos Louizos
Manolis Lourakis
Brian Lovell
Chen-Change Loy
Cewu Lu
Huchuan Lu
Jiwen Lu
Le Lu
Yijuan Lu

Canyi Lu
Jiebo Luo
Ping Luo
Siwei Lyu
Zhigang Ma
Chao Ma
Oisin Mac Aodha
John MacCormick
Vijay Mahadevan
Dhruv Mahajan
Aravindh Mahendran
Mohammed Mahoor
Michael Maire
Subhransu Maji
Aditi Majumder
Atsuto Maki
Yasushi Makihara
Alexandros Makris
Mateusz Malinowski
Clement Mallet
Arun Mallya
Dixit Mandar
Junhua Mao
Dmitrii Marin
Elisabeta Marinoiu
Renaud Marlet
Ricardo Martin
Aleix Martinez
Jonathan Masci
David Masip
Diana Mateus
Markus Mathias
Iain Matthews
Kevin Matzen
Bruce Maxwell
Stephen Maybank
Scott McCloskey
Ted Meeds
Christopher Mei
Tao Mei
Xue Mei
Jason Meltzer
Heydi Mendez
Thomas Mensink
Michele Merler
Domingo Mery

Ajmal Mian
Tomer Michaeli
Ondrej Miksik
Anton Milan
Erik Miller
Gregor Miller
Majid Mirmehdi
Ishan Misra
Anurag Mittal
Daisuke Miyazaki
Hossein Mobahi
Pascal Monasse
Sandino Morales
Vlad Morariu
Philippos Mordohai
Francesc Moreno-Noguer
Greg Mori
Bryan Morse
Roozbeh Mottaghi
Yadong Mu
Yasuhiro Mukaigawa
Lopamudra Mukherjee
Joseph Mundy
Mario Munich
Ana Murillo
Vittorio Murino
Naila Murray
Damien Muselet
Sobhan Naderi Parizi
Hajime Nagahara
Nikhil Naik
P.J. Narayanan
Fabian Nater
Jan Neumann
Ram Nevatia
Shawn Newsam
Bingbing Ni
Juan Carlos Niebles
Jifeng Ning
Ko Nishino
Masashi Nishiyama
Shohei Nobuhara
Ifeoma Nwogu
Peter Ochs
Jean-Marc Odobez
Francesca Odone

Iason Oikonomidis
Takeshi Oishi
Takahiro Okabe
Takayuki Okatani
Carl Olsson
Vicente Ordonez
Ivan Oseledets
Magnus Oskarsson
Martin R. Oswald
Matthew O'Toole
Wanli Ouyang
Andrew Owens
Mustafa Ozuysal
Jason Pacheco
Manohar Paluri
Gang Pan
Jinshan Pan
Yannis Panagakis
Sharath Pankanti
George Papandreou
Hyun Soo Park
In Kyu Park
Jaesik Park
Seyoung Park
Omkar Parkhi
Ioannis Patras
Viorica Patraucean
Genevieve Patterson
Vladimir Pavlovic
Kim Pedersen
Robert Peharz
Shmuel Peleg
Marcello Pelillo
Otavio Penatti
Xavier Pennec
Federico Pernici
Adrian Peter
Stavros Petridis
Vladimir Petrovic
Tomas Pfister
Justus Piater
Pedro Pinheiro
Bernardo Pires
Fiora Pirri
Leonid Pishchulin
Daniel Pizarro

Robert Pless
Tobias Pltz
Yair Poleg
Gerard Pons-Moll
Jordi Pont-Tuset
Ronald Poppe
Andrea Prati
Jan Prokaj
Daniel Prusa
Nicolas Pugeault
Guido Pusiol
Guo-Jun Qi
Gang Qian
Yu Qiao
Novi Quadrianto
Julian Quiroga
Andrew Rabinovich
Rahul Raguram
Srikumar Ramalingam
Deva Ramanan
Narayanan Ramanathan
Vignesh Ramanathan
Sebastian Ramos
Rene Ranftl
Anand Rangarajan
Avinash Ravichandran
Ramin Raziperchikolaei
Carlo Regazzoni
Christian Reinbacher
Michal Reinstein
Emonet Remi
Fabio Remondino
Shaoqing Ren
Zhile Ren
Jerome Revaud
Hayko Riemenschneider
Tobias Ritschel
Mariano Rivera
Patrick Rives
Antonio Robles-Kelly
Jason Rock
Erik Rodner
Emanuele Rodola
Mikel Rodriguez
Antonio
    Rodriguez Sanchez

Gregory Rogez
Marcus Rohrbach
Javier Romero
Matteo Ronchi
German Ros
Charles Rosenberg
Guy Rosman
Arun Ross
Paolo Rota
Samuel Rota Bulò
Peter Roth
Volker Roth
Brandon Rothrock
Anastasios Roussos
Amit Roy-Chowdhury
Ognjen Rudovic
Daniel Rueckert
Christian Rupprecht
Olga Russakovsky
Bryan Russell
Emmanuel Sabu
Fereshteh Sadeghi
Hideo Saito
Babak Saleh
Mathieu Salzmann
Dimitris Samaras
Conrad Sanderson
Enver Sangineto
Aswin Sankaranarayanan
Imari Sato
Yoichi Sato
Shin'ichi Satoh
Torsten Sattler
Bogdan Savchynskyy
Yann Savoye
Arman Savran
Harpreet Sawhney
Davide Scaramuzza
Walter Scheirer
Frank Schmidt
Uwe Schmidt
Dirk Schnieders
Johannes Schönberger
Florian Schroff
Samuel Schulter
William Schwartz

Alexander Schwing
Stan Sclaroff
Nicu Sebe
Ari Seff
Anita Sellent
Giuseppe Serra
Laura Sevilla-Lara
Shishir Shah
Greg Shakhnarovich
Qi Shan
Shiguang Shan
Jing Shao
Ling Shao
Xiaowei Shao
Roman Shapovalov
Nataliya Shapovalova
Ali Sharif Razavian
Gaurav Sharma
Pramod Sharma
Viktoriia Sharmanska
Eli Shechtman
Alexander Shekhovtsov
Evan Shelhamer
Chunhua Shen
Jianbing Shen
Li Shen
Xiaoyong Shen
Wei Shen
Yu Sheng
Jianping Shi
Qinfeng Shi
Yonggang Shi
Baoguang Shi
Kevin Shih
Nobutaka Shimada
Ilan Shimshoni
Koichi Shinoda
Takaaki Shiratori
Jamie Shotton
Matthew Shreve
Abhinav Shrivastava
Nitesh Shroff
Leonid Sigal
Nathan Silberman
Tomas Simon
Edgar Simo-Serra

Dheeraj Singaraju
Gautam Singh
Maneesh Singh
Richa Singh
Saurabh Singh
Vikas Singh
Sudipta Sinha
Josef Sivic
Greg Slabaugh
William Smith
Patrick Snape
Jan Sochman
Kihyuk Sohn
Hyun Oh Song
Jingkuan Song
Qi Song
Shuran Song
Xuan Song
Yale Song
Yi-Zhe Song
Alexander
    Sorkine Hornung
Humberto Sossa
Aristeidis Sotiras
Richard Souvenir
Anuj Srivastava
Nitish Srivastava
Michael Stark
Bjorn Stenger
Rainer Stiefelhagen
Martin Storath
Joerg Stueckler
Hang Su
Hao Su
Jingyong Su
Shuochen Su
Yu Su
Ramanathan Subramanian
Yusuke Sugano
Akihiro Sugimoto
Libin Sun
Min Sun
Qing Sun
Yi Sun
Chen Sun
Deqing Sun

Ganesh Sundaramoorthi	Yi-Hsuan Tsai	Chaohui Wang
Jinli Suo	Gavriil Tsechpenakis	Gang Wang
Supasorn Suwajanakorn	Chourmouzios Tsiotsios	Heng Wang
Tomas Svoboda	Stavros Tsogkas	Lei Wang
Chris Sweeney	Kewei Tu	Linwei Wang
Paul Swoboda	Shubham Tulsiani	Liwei Wang
Raza Syed Hussain	Tony Tung	Ping Wang
Christian Szegedy	Pavan Turaga	Qi Wang
Yuichi Taguchi	Matthew Turk	Qian Wang
Yu-Wing Tai	Tinne Tuytelaars	Shenlong Wang
Hugues Talbot	Oncel Tuzel	Song Wang
Toru Tamaki	Georgios Tzimiropoulos	Tao Wang
Mingkui Tan	Norimichi Ukita	Yang Wang
Robby Tan	Osman Ulusoy	Yu-Chiang Frank Wang
Xiaoyang Tan	Martin Urschler	Zhaowen Wang
Masayuki Tanaka	Arash Vahdat	Simon Warfield
Meng Tang	Michel Valstar	Yichen Wei
Siyu Tang	Ernest Valveny	Philippe Weinzaepfel
Ran Tao	Jan van Gemert	Longyin Wen
Dacheng Tao	Kiran Varanasi	Tomas Werner
Makarand Tapaswi	Mayank Vatsa	Aaron Wetzler
Jean-Philippe Tarel	Javier Vazquez-Corral	Yonatan Wexler
Camillo Taylor	Ramakrishna Vedantam	Michael Wilber
Christian Theobalt	Ashok Veeraraghavan	Kyle Wilson
Diego Thomas	Olga Veksler	Thomas Windheuser
Rajat Thomas	Jakob Verbeek	David Wipf
Xinmei Tian	Francisco Vicente	Paul Wohlhart
Yonglong Tian	Rene Vidal	Christian Wolf
YingLi Tian	Jordi Vitria	Kwan-Yee Kenneth Wong
Yonghong Tian	Max Vladymyrov	John Wright
Kinh Tieu	Christoph Vogel	Jiajun Wu
Joseph Tighe	Carl Vondrick	Jianxin Wu
Radu Timofte	Sven Wachsmuth	Tianfu Wu
Massimo Tistarelli	Toshikazu Wada	Yang Wu
Sinisa Todorovic	Catherine Wah	Yi Wu
Giorgos Tolias	Jacob Walker	Zheng Wu
Federico Tombari	Xiaolong Wang	Stefanie Wuhrer
Akihiko Torii	Wei Wang	Jonas Wulff
Andrea Torsello	Limin Wang	Rolf Wurtz
Du Tran	Liang Wang	Lu Xia
Quoc-Huy Tran	Hua Wang	Tao Xiang
Rudolph Triebel	Lijun Wang	Yu Xiang
Roberto Tron	Naiyan Wang	Lei Xiao
Leonardo Trujillo	Xinggang Wang	Yang Xiao
Eduard Trulls	Yining Wang	Tong Xiao
Tomasz Trzcinski	Baoyuan Wang	Wenxuan Xie

Lingxi Xie
Pengtao Xie
Saining Xie
Yuchen Xie
Junliang Xing
Bo Xiong
Fei Xiong
Jia Xu
Yong Xu
Tianfan Xue
Toshihiko Yamasaki
Takayoshi Yamashita
Junjie Yan
Rong Yan
Yan Yan
Keiji Yanai
Jian Yang
Jianchao Yang
Jiaolong Yang
Jie Yang
Jimei Yang
Michael Ying Yang
Ming Yang
Ruiduo Yang
Yi Yang
Angela Yao
Cong Yao
Jian Yao
Jianhua Yao
Jinwei Ye
Shuai Yi
Alper Yilmaz
Lijun Yin
Zhaozheng Yin

Xianghua Ying
Kuk-Jin Yoon
Chong You
Aron Yu
Felix Yu
Fisher Yu
Lap-Fai Yu
Stella Yu
Jing Yuan
Junsong Yuan
Lu Yuan
Xiao-Tong Yuan
Alan Yuille
Xenophon Zabulis
Stefanos Zafeiriou
Sergey Zagoruyko
Amir Zamir
Andrei Zanfir
Mihai Zanfir
Lihi Zelnik-Manor
Xingyu Zeng
Josiane Zerubia
Changshui Zhang
Cheng Zhang
Guofeng Zhang
Jianguo Zhang
Junping Zhang
Ning Zhang
Quanshi Zhang
Shaoting Zhang
Tianzhu Zhang
Xiaoqun Zhang
Yinda Zhang
Yu Zhang

Shiliang Zhang
Lei Zhang
Xiaoqin Zhang
Shanshan Zhang
Ting Zhang
Bin Zhao
Rui Zhao
Yibiao Zhao
Enliang Zheng
Wenming Zheng
Yinqiang Zheng
Yuanjie Zheng
Yin Zheng
Wei-Shi Zheng
Liang Zheng
Dingfu Zhou
Wengang Zhou
Tinghui Zhou
Bolei Zhou
Feng Zhou
Huiyu Zhou
Jun Zhou
Kevin Zhou
Kun Zhou
Xiaowei Zhou
Zihan Zhou
Jun Zhu
Jun-Yan Zhu
Zhenyao Zhu
Zeeshan Zia
Henning Zimmer
Karel Zimmermann
Wangmeng Zuo

Additional Reviewers

Felix Achilles
Sarah Adel Bargal
Hessam Bagherinezhad
Qinxun Bai
Gedas Bertasius
Michal Busta
Erik Bylow
Marinella Cadoni

Dan Andrei Calian
Lilian Calvet
Federico Camposeco
Olivier Canevet
Anirban Chakraborty
Yu-Wei Chao
Sotirios Chatzis
Tatjana Chavdarova

Jimmy Chen
Melissa Cote
Berkan Demirel
Zhiwei Deng
Guy Gilboa
Albert Gordo
Daniel Gordon
Ankur Gupta

Kun He
Yang He
Daniel Holtmann-Rice
Xun Huang
Liang Hui
Drew Jaegle
Cijo Jose
Marco Karrer
Mehran Khodabandeh
Anna Khoreva
Hyo-Jin Kim
Theodora Kontogianni
Pengpeng Liang
Shugao Ma
Ludovic Magerand
Francesco Malapelle
Julio Marco
Vlad Morariu

Rajitha Navarathna
Junhyuk Oh
Federico Perazzi
Marcel Piotraschke
Srivignesh Rajendran
Joe Redmon
Helge Rhodin
Anna Rohrbach
Beatrice Rossi
Wolfgang Roth
Pietro Salvagnini
Hosnieh Sattar
Ana Serrano
Zhixin Shu
Sven Sickert
Jakub Simanek
Ramprakash Srinivasan
Oren Tadmor

Xin Tao
Lucas Teixeira
Mårten Wädenback
Qing Wang
Yaser Yacoob
Takayoshi Yamashita
Huiyuan Yang
Ryo Yonetani
Sejong Yoon
Shaodi You
Xu Zhan
Jianming Zhang
Richard Zhang
Xiaoqun Zhang
Xu Zhang
Zheng Zhang

Contents – Part VIII

Poster Session 8 (Continued)

Query-Focused Extractive Video Summarization

Aidean Sharghi$^{(\boxtimes)}$, Boqing Gong, and Mubarak Shah

Center for Research in Computer Vision, University of Central Florida, Orlando, USA
aidean.sharghi@knights.ucf.edu, {bgong,shah}@crcv.ucf.edu

Abstract. Video data is explosively growing. As a result of the "big video data", intelligent algorithms for automatic video summarization have (re-)emerged as a pressing need. We develop a probabilistic model, Sequential and Hierarchical Determinantal Point Process (SH-DPP), for **query-focused** extractive video summarization. Given a user query and a long video sequence, our algorithm returns a summary by selecting key shots from the video. The decision to include a shot in the summary depends on the shot's relevance to the user query and importance in the context of the video, jointly. We verify our approach on two densely annotated video datasets. The query-focused video summarization is particularly useful for search engines, e.g., to display snippets of videos.

1 Introduction

Video data is explosively growing as a result of the ubiquitous acquisition capabilities. The videos captured by UAVs and/or drones, from ground surveillance, and by body-worn cameras can easily reach the scale of gigabytes per day. About 300 h of videos are uploaded per minute to Youtube. While the "big video data" is a great source for information discovery, the computational challenges are unparalleled. In such context, intelligent algorithms for automatic video summarization (and retrieval, recognition, etc.) (re-)emerge as a pressing need.

In this paper we focus on *extractive* video summarization, which generates a concise summary of a video by selecting from it key frames or shots[1]. The key frames/shots are expected to be (1) individually important—otherwise they should not be selected, and (2) collectively diverse—otherwise one can remove some of them without losing much information. These two principles are employed in most of the existing works on extractive video summarization [4], and yet implemented by different decision choices. Some earlier works define the importance of key frames by low-level appearance and/or motion cues [5–10]. Contextual information of a key frame is often modeled by graphs [11–13]. We

---

[1] It is also appealing to have the summary as a spatial-temporal synopsis or mosaic *composed* of multiple frames. However, the *compositional* summarization is challenging and has achieved some success in only well-controlled environments [1–3].

Electronic supplementary material The online version of this chapter (doi:10. 1007/978-3-319-46484-8_1) contains supplementary material, which is available to authorized users.

© Springer International Publishing AG 2016
B. Leibe et al. (Eds.): ECCV 2016, Part VIII, LNCS 9912, pp. 3–19, 2016.
DOI: 10.1007/978-3-319-46484-8_1

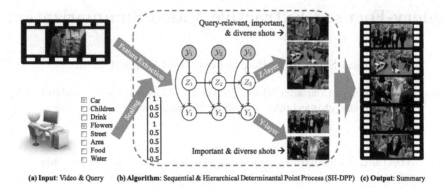

(a) **Input**: Video & Query   (b) **Algorithm**: Sequential & Hierarchical Determinantal Point Process (SH-DPP)   (c) **Output**: Summary

Fig. 1. Query-focused video summarization and our approach to this problem.

note that the system developers play a vital role in this cohort of works; most decisions on how to measure the importance and diversity are handcrafted by the system developers using the low-level cues.

Recently, we see a paradigm shift in some sort: more high-level supervised information is introduced to video summarization than ever before. Rich Web images and videos provide (weak) priors for defining user-oriented importance of the visual content in a video [14–17]. For instance, the CAR images on the Web reveal the canonical views of the cars, which should thus be given special attentions in video summarization. The texts associated with videos are undoubtedly good sources for inferring the semantic importance of video frames [18,19]. Category-specific and domain-specific video summarization approaches are developed in [20,21]. Some other high-level factors include gaze [22], interestingness [23], influence [24], tracking of salient objects [25,26], and so forth.

What are the advantages of leveraging high-level supervised information in video summarization over merely low-level cues? We believe the main advantage is that the system developers are able to better infer the system *users*' needs. After all, video summarization is a subjective process. Comparing to designing the system from the experts' own intuitions, it is more desirable to design a system based on the crowd or average users such that the system's states approach the users' internal ones, which are often semantic and high-level.

What is the best supervision for a video summarization system? We have seen many types of supervision used in the above-mentioned works, such as Web images, texts, and categories. However, we argue that the best supervision, for the purpose of developing video summarization approaches, is the video summaries directly provided by users. In [27], which is the first supervised video summarization work as far as we know, Gong et al. showed that there exists a high inter-annotator agreement in the summaries of the same videos given by distinct users. They proposed a supervised video summarization model, sequential determinantal point process (seqDPP), and train seqDPP by the "oracle" summaries that agree the most with different user summaries. Gygli et al. gave another supervised method using submodular functions [28].

From the low-level visual and motion cues to the high-level (indirect) supervised information, and to the (direct) supervised user summaries, video summarization works become more and more **user-oriented**. Though the two principles, importance and diversity, remain the same, the detailed implementation choices have significantly shifted from the system developers' to the users'; users can essentially teach the system how to summarize videos in [27,28].

In respect to the recent progress, the goal of this paper is to further advance the user-oriented video summarization by modeling user input, or more precisely user intentions, in the summarization process. Figure 1 illustrates our main idea. We name it **query-focused** (extractive) video summarization, in accordance with the query-focused document summarization [29] in NLP. A query refers to one or more concepts (e.g., CAR, FLOWERS) that are both user-nameable and machine-detectable. More generic queries are left for the future work.

Towards the goal of query-focused video summarization, we develop a probabilistic model, Sequential and Hierarchical Determinantal Point Process (SH-DPP). It has two layers of random variables, each of which serves for subset selection from a ground set of video shots (see Fig. 2). The first layer is mainly used to select the shots relevant to the user queries, and the second layer models the importance of the shots in the context of the videos. We condition the second layer on the first layer so that we can automatically balance the two strengths by learning from user labeled summaries. The determinantal point process (DPP) [30] is employed to account for the diversity of the summary.

A key feature in our work is that the decision to include a video shot in the summary is jointly dependent on the shot's relevance to the query and representativeness in the video. Instead of handcrafting any criteria, we use SH-DPP to automatically learn from the user summaries (and the corresponding user queries and video sequences). In a sharp contrast to [27,28] which model average users, our work closely tracks individual users' intentions from their input queries, and thus has greater potential to satisfy various user needs: distinct personal preferences (e.g., a patient user prefers more detailed and lengthy summaries than an impatient user), different interests over time even about the same video (e.g., a party versus a particular person in the party), etc. Finally, we note that our work is especially useful for search engines to produce snippets of videos.

Our main contribution is on the query-focused video summarization. Querying videos is not only an appealing functionality to the users but also an effective communication channel for the system to capture a user' intention. Besides, we develop a novel probabilistic model, SH-DPP. Similarly to the sequential DPP (seqDPP) [27], SH-DPP is efficient in modeling extremely lengthy videos and capable of producing summaries on the fly. Additionally, SH-DPP explicitly accounts for the user input queries. Extensive experiments on the UT Egocentric [31] and TV episodes [32] datasets verify the effectiveness of SH-DPP. To our knowledge, our work is the first on query-focused video summarization.

2   Related Work and Background

In this section, we mainly discuss some related works on query-focused document summarization and some earlier works on interactive video summarization in the multimedia community. We will then describe some variations of DPP and contrast them to our SH-DPP.

Query-focused document summarization has been a long-standing track in the Text Retrieval Conference (http://trec.nist.gov/) and the Document Understanding Conference (DUC) (http://duc.nist.gov/). In DUC 2005, participants were asked to summarize a cluster of documents given a user's query describing the information needs. Some representative approaches to this problem include BAYESUM [33], FASTSUM [34], and log-likelihood based method [35] among others. Behind the vast research in this topic is the strong motivations by popular search engines and human-machine interactions. However, the counterpart in vision, query-focused video summarization, has not been well formulated yet. We make some preliminary efforts toward it through this work.

Interactive video summarization shares some spirits with our query-focused video summarization. The system in [36] allows users to interactively select some video shots to the summary while the system summarizes the remaining video. In contrast, in our system the users can use concept-based queries to influence the summaries without actually watching the videos. Besides, our approach is supervised and trained by user annotations, not handcrafted by the system developers. There are some other works involving users for thumbnail selection [19] and storyline-based video representation [37]. Our work instead involves user input in the video summarization.

Determinantal point process (DPP) [30] is employed in our SH-DPP to model the diversity in the desired video summaries. We give it a brief overview and also contrast SH-DPP to various DPP models.

Denote by $\mathcal{Y} = \{1, 2, \ldots, N\}$ the ground set. A (L-ensemble) DPP defines a discrete probability distribution over a subset selection variable Y,

$$P(Y = y) = \det(\mathbf{L}_y)/\det(\mathbf{L} + \mathbf{I}), \quad \forall y \subseteq \mathcal{Y}, \tag{1}$$

where $\mathbf{I}$ is an identity matrix, $\mathbf{L} \in \mathbb{S}^{N \times N}$ is a positive semidefinite kernel matrix and is the distribution parameter, and $\mathbf{L}_y$ is a squared sub-matrix with rows and columns corresponding to the indices $y \subseteq \mathcal{Y}$. By default $\det(\mathbf{L}_\emptyset) = 1$.

DPP is good for modeling summarization because it integrates the two principles of individual importance and collective diversity. By the definition (Eq. (1)), the importance of an item is represented by $P(i \in Y) = \mathbf{K}_{ii}$ and the repulsion of any two items is captured by $P(i, j \in Y) = P(i \in Y)P(j \in Y) - \mathbf{K}_{ij}^2$, where $\mathbf{K} = \mathbf{L}(\mathbf{L} + \mathbf{I})^{-1}$. In other words, the model parameter $\mathbf{L}$ is sufficient to describe both the importance and diversity of the items being selected by Y. The readers are referred to Theorem 2.2 in [30] for more derivations.

A vanilla DPP gave rise to state-of-the-art performance on document summarization [38,39]. Its variation, Markov DPP [40], was used to maintain the diversity between multiple draws from the ground set. A sequential DPP (seqDPP) [27] was proposed for video summarization. Our SH-DPP brings a hierarchy to seqDPP and uses the first layer to take account of the user queries in the summarization (subset selection) process.

3 Approach

Our approach takes as input a user query q (i.e., concepts) and a long video $\mathcal{Y}$, and outputs a query-focused short summary $y(q, \mathcal{Y})$,

$$y(q, \mathcal{Y}) \leftarrow \underset{y \subseteq \mathcal{Y}}{\operatorname{argmax}} \ P(Y = y | q, \mathcal{Y}), \tag{2}$$

which consists of some shots of the video. We desire **four major properties** from the distribution $P(Y = y | q, \mathcal{Y})$. (i) It models the subset selection variable Y. (ii) It promotes diversity among the items selected by Y. (iii) It works efficiently given very long (e.g., egocentric) or endlessly streaming (e.g., surveillance) videos. (iv) It has some mechanism for accepting the user input q. Together, the properties motivate a Sequential and Hierarchical DPP (SH-DPP) as our implementation to $P(Y = y | q, \mathcal{Y})$. As below, we firstly discuss some related methods—especially seqDPP, how they meet some of the **properties** but not all, and then present the details of SH-DPP.

3.1 Sequential DPP (seqDPP) with User Queries

In order to satisfy **properties** (i) and (ii), one can use a vanilla DPP (cf. Eq. (1)) to extract a diverse subset of shots as a video summary. Though this works well for multi-document summarization [38], it is unappealing in our context mainly due to two reasons. First, DPP sees the ground set (i.e., all shots in a video) as a bag, in which the permutation of the items has no effect on the output. In other words, the temporal flow of the video is totally ignored by DPP; it returns the same summary even if the shots are randomly shuffled. Second, the inference (Eq. (2)) cost is extremely high when the video is long, no matter by exhaustive search among all possible subsets $y \subseteq \mathcal{Y}$ or greedy search [30]. We note that the submodular functions also suffer from the same drawbacks [22,28].

The seqDPP method [27] meets **properties** (i)–(iii) and solves the problems described above. It partitions a video into T consecutive disjoint segments, $\cup_{t=1}^{T} \mathcal{Y}_t = \mathcal{Y}$, where $\mathcal{Y}_t$ represents a set consisting of only a few shots and stands as the ground set of time step t. The model is defined as follows (see the left panel of Fig. 2 for the graphical model),

$$P_{\mathrm{SEQ}}(Y | \mathcal{Y}) = P(Y_1 | \mathcal{Y}_1) \prod_{t=2}^{T} P(Y_t | Y_{t-1}, \mathcal{Y}_t), \quad \mathcal{Y} = \cup_{t=1}^{T} \mathcal{Y}_t \tag{3}$$

where $P(Y_t | Y_{t-1}, \mathcal{Y}_t) \propto \det \mathbf{\Omega}_{Y_{t-1} \cup Y_t}$ is a conditional DPP to ensure diversity between the items selected at time step t (by Y_t) and those of the previous time

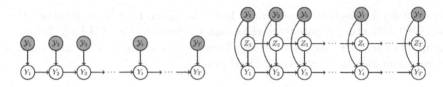

Fig. 2. The graphical models of seqDPP [27] (left) and our SH-DPP (right).

step (by Y_{t-1}). Similarly to the vanilla DPP (cf. Eq. (1)), here the conditional DPP is also associated with a kernel matrix Ω. In [27], this matrix is parameterized by $\Omega_{ij} = \boldsymbol{f}_i^T W^T W \boldsymbol{f}_j$, where $\boldsymbol{f}_i$ is a feature vector of the i-th video shot and W is learned from the user summaries. Note that the seqDPP summarizer $P_{\text{SEQ}}(Y|\mathcal{Y})$ does not account for any user input. It is learned from "oracle" summaries in the hope of reaching a good compromise between distinct users.

In this paper, we instead aim to infer individual users' preferences over the video summaries, through the information conveyed by the user queries. To this end, a simple extension to seqDPP is to engineer query-dependent feature vectors $\boldsymbol{f}(q)$ of the video shots—see Sect. 4.4. We consider this seqDPP variation as our baseline. It is indeed responsive to the queries through the query-dependent features, but it is limited in modeling the query-relevant summaries, in which the importance of a video shot is jointly determined by its relevance to the query and its representativeness in the context. The seqDPP offers no explicit treatment to the two types of interplayed strengths; the user may expect different levels of diversity from the query relevant shots and irrelevant ones, but the single DPP kernel in seqDPP fails to offer such flexibility.

Our SH-DPP possesses all of the four **properties**. It is developed upon seqDPP in order to take advantage of seqDPP's nice properties (i)–(iii), and yet rectifies its downside (mainly on **property** (iv)) by a two-layer hierarchy.

3.2 Sequential and Hierarchical DPP (SH-DPP)

The right panel of Fig. 2 depicts the graphical model of SH-DPP, reading as,

$$P_{\text{SH}}(\{Y_1, Z_1\}, ..., \{Y_T, Z_T\}|q, \mathcal{Y})$$
$$=P(Z_1|q, \mathcal{Y}_1)P(Y_1|Z_1, \mathcal{Y}_1)\prod_{t=2}^{T} P(Z_t|q, Z_{t-1}, \mathcal{Y}_t)P(Y_t|Z_t, Y_{t-1}, \mathcal{Y}_t). \quad (4)$$

Query q is omitted from Fig. 2 for clarity. The shaded nodes represent video segments $\{\mathcal{Y}_t\}$ (i.e., consecutive and disjoint shots). We first use the subset selection variables Z_t to select the query-relevant video shots. Note that Z_t will return empty if the segment $\mathcal{Y}_t$ does not contain any visual content related to the query. Depending on the results of Z_t (and Y_{t-1}), the variable Y_t selects video shots to further summarize the remaining content in the video segment $\mathcal{Y}_t$. The arrows in each layer impose diversity by DPP between the shots selected from two adjacent video segments—we thus have Markov diversity, in contrast to global diversity, in order to allow two (or more) visually similar shots to be simultaneously sampled to the summary if they appear at far-apart time steps (e.g., a man left home in the morning and returned home in the afternoon).

We define two types of DPPs for the two layers of SH-DPP, respectively.

Z-Layer to Summarize Query-Relevant Shots. We apply a conditional DPP $P(Z_t|q, Z_{t-1}, \mathcal{Y}_t)$ at each time step t over the ground set $\mathcal{Y}_t \cup \{Z_{t-1} = z_{t-1}\}$, where $\mathcal{Y}_t$ consists of all the shots in partition t and z_{t-1} are the shots selected by Z_{t-1}. In other words, the DPP here is conditioned on the selected items z_{t-1} of the previous time step, enforcing Markov diversity between two consecutive time steps,

$$P(Z_t = z_t|q, Z_{t-1} = z_{t-1}, \mathcal{Y}_t) = \frac{\det \mathbf{\Omega}_{z_{t-1} \cup z_t}}{\det(\mathbf{\Omega}_{z_{t-1} \cup \mathcal{Y}_t} + I_t)} \tag{5}$$

where I_t is the same as an identity matrix except that its diagonal values are zeros at the entries indexed by z_{t-1}.

Different from seqDPP, we dedicate the Z-layer to query-relevant shots only. This is achieved by how we train SH-DPP (Sect. 3.3) and the way we parameterize the DPP kernel matrix,

$$\mathbf{\Omega}_{ij} = [\mathbf{f}_i(q)]^T W^T W [\mathbf{f}_j(q)] \tag{6}$$

where $\mathbf{f}(q)$ is a query-dependent feature vector of a shot (Sect. 4.4). In testing, the Z-layer only selects shots that are relevant to the user query q, and leaves all the unselected shots to the Y-layer for further summarization.

Y-Layer to Summarize the Remaining Shots. The decision to include a shot in the query-focused video summarization is driven by two interplayed forces: the shot's relevance to the query and its representativeness in the context. Given a user query q (e.g., CAR+FLOWER) and a long video $\mathcal{Y}$, likely many video shots are irrelevant to the query. As a result, we need another Y-layer to compensate the query-relevant shots selected by the Z-layer. In particular, we define the conditional probability distribution for the Y-layer variables as,

$$P(Y_t = y_t|Y_{t-1} = y_{t-1}, Z_t = z_t, \mathcal{Y}_t) = \frac{\det \mathbf{\Upsilon}_{y_{t-1} \cup z_t \cup y_t}}{\det(\mathbf{\Upsilon}_{y_{t-1} \cup \mathcal{Y}_t} + I'_t)} \tag{7}$$

where y_{t-1} is the selected subset in previous time step at the Y-layer, z_t is the selected subset of query-relevant shots in current time step by the Z-layer, and I'_t is a diagonal matrix with ones indexed by $\mathcal{Y}_t \setminus z_t$ and zeros everywhere else.

Conditioning the Y-layer on the Z-layer has two advantages. First, no redundant information that is already selected by Z-layer is added by the Y-layer again to the summary, i.e., the shots selected by Y-layer are diverse from those by Z-layer. Second, Y-layer can, to some extent, compensate the missed query-relevant shots by Z-layer that were supposed to be selected.

Note that the Y-layer involves a new DPP kernel $\mathbf{\Upsilon}$, different from that used for the Z-layer. The reason is twofold: first, two layers of variables serve to select different (query relevant or important) types of shots, and second, the user may expect various levels of diversity from the summary. When a user searches for CAR+FLOWER, s/he probably would like to see more details in the shots of wedding car than in the shots of police, making it necessary to have two types of DPP kernels. The Y-layer kernel is parameterized by:

$$\Upsilon_{ij} = f_i^T V^T V f_j \tag{8}$$

and we will discuss how to extract features f from a shot in Sect. 4.4.

3.3   Training and Testing SH-DPP

The training data in our experiments are in the form of $(q, \mathcal{Y}, z^q, y^q)$, where z^q and y^q respectively denote the query relevant and irrelevant shots in the summary. We learn the model parameters W and V of SH-DPP by maximum likelihood estimation (MLE):

$$\max_{W,V} \sum_q \sum_{\mathcal{Y}} \log P_{\text{SH}}(\{y_1, z_1\}, \cdots, \{y_T, z_T\} | q, \mathcal{Y}) - \lambda_1 \|W\|_F^2 - \lambda_2 \|V\|_F^2, \tag{9}$$

where $\| \cdot \|_F^2$ is the squared Frobenius norm. We tune the hyper-parameters λ_1 and λ_2 by a leaving-one-video-out strategy, and optimize the above problem by gradient descent (cf. Supplement Material for more details on optimization).

After obtaining the local optimum W^* and V^* from the training, we need to know how to maximize the SH-DPP $P_{\text{SH}}(y|q, \mathcal{Y})$ for the testing stage (cf. Eq. (2)). However, the maximization remains a computationally extensive combinatorial problem. We thus follow [27] to have an approximate online inference procedure:

$$z_1^* = \operatorname*{argmax}_{z \in \mathcal{Y}_1} P(Z_1 = z | q, \mathcal{Y}_1), \qquad y_1^* = \operatorname*{argmax}_{y \in \mathcal{Y}_1 \setminus z_1^*} P(Y_1 = y | z_1^*, \mathcal{Y}_1)$$

$$z_t^* = \operatorname*{argmax}_{z \in \mathcal{Y}_t} P(Z_t | q, z_{t-1}^*, \mathcal{Y}_t), \quad y_t^* = \operatorname*{argmax}_{y \in \mathcal{Y}_t \setminus z_t^*} P(Y_t | z_t^*, y_{t-1}^*, \mathcal{Y}_t), \quad t \geq 2 \tag{10}$$

where we exhaustively search for z_t^* and y_t^* from $\mathcal{Y}_t$ at each time step. Thanks to the online inference, SH-DPP can readily handle endlessly streaming videos.

4   Experiment Setup

In this section, we describe the datasets, features of a video shot, user queries, query-focused video summaries for training/evaluation, and finally, metrics to evaluate our learned video summarizer SH-DPP.

4.1   Datasets

We use the UT Egocentric (UTE) dataset [31] and TV episodes [32] whose dense user annotations are provided in [32]. The UTE dataset includes four daily life egocentric videos, each 3–5 h long, and the TV episodes contain four videos, each roughly 45 min long. These two datasets are very different in nature. The videos in UTE are long and recorded in an uncontrolled environment from the first-person view. As a result, many of the visual scenes are repetitive and likely unwanted in the user summaries. In contrast, the TV videos are episodes of TV series from the third person's viewpoint; the scenes are hence controlled and concise. A good summarizer should be able to work/learn well in both scenarios.

In [32], all the UTE/TV videos are partitioned to 5/10-second shots, respectively, and for each shot a textual description is provided by a human subject. Additionally, for each video, 3 reference summaries are also provided each as a subset of the textual annotations. Using dense text annotations, we are able to derive from the text both user queries and two types of query-focused video summaries, respectively, for patient and impatient users.

4.2 User Queries

In this paper, a user query comprises one or more noun concepts (e.g., CAR, FLOWER, KID); more generic queries are left for future research. There are many nouns in the text annotations of the video shots, but are they all useful for users to construct queries? Likely no. Any useful nouns have to be machine-detectable so that the system can "understand" the user queries. To this end, we construct a lexicon of concepts by overlapping all the nouns in the annotations with the nouns in SentiBank [41], which is a large collection of visual concepts and corresponding detectors. This results in a lexicon of 70/52 concepts for the UTE/TV dataset (see Table 1 in the supplementary material). Each pair of concepts is considered as a user query for both training and testing our SH-DPP video summarizer. Besides, at the testing phase, we also examine novel queries—all the triples of concepts.

4.3 Query-Focused Video Summaries

For each input query and video, we need to know the "groundtruth" video summary for training and evaluating SH-DPP. We construct such summaries based on the "oracle" summaries introduced in [27].

Oracle Summary. As mentioned earlier in Sect. 4.1, there are three human-annotated summaries $y^u, u = 1, 2, 3$ for each video $\mathcal{Y}$. An "oracle" summary y^o has the maximum agreement with all of the three annotated summaries, and can be understood as the summary by an "average" user. Such a summary is found by a greedy algorithm [38]. Initialize $y^o = \emptyset$. In each iteration, the set y^o increases by one video shot i which gives rise to the largest marginal gain $G(i)$,

$$y^o \leftarrow y^o \cup \operatorname*{argmax}_{i \in \mathcal{Y}} G(i), \quad G(i) = \sum_u \text{F-score}(y^o \cup i, y_u) - \text{F-score}(y^o, y_u) \quad (11)$$

where the F-score follows [32] and is explained in Sect. 4.5. The algorithm stops when there is no such shot that the gain $G(i)$ is greater than 0. Note that thus far the oracle summary is independent of the user query.

Query-Focused Video Summary. We consider two types of users. A **patient user** would like to watch all the shots relevant to the query in addition to the summary of the other visual content of the video. For example, all the shots whose textual descriptions have the word CAR should be included in the summary if CAR shows up in the query. We union such shots with the oracle summary to have the query-focused summary for the patient user. On the other extreme, an **impatient user** may only want to check the existence of the relevant shots, in contrast to watching all of them. To conduct experiments for the impatient users, we overlap the concepts in the oracle summary with the concept lexicon (cf. Sect. 4.2), and generate all possible bi-concept queries from the survived concepts. Note that the oracle summaries are thus the gold standards for training video summarizers for the impatient users.

4.4   Features

We extract high-level concept-oriented features h and contextual features l for a video shot. For each concept in the lexicon (of size 70/52 for the UTE/TV dataset), we firstly use its corresponding SentiBank detector(s) [41] to obtain the detection scores of the key frames, and then average them within each shot. Some of the concepts each maps to more than one detectors. For instance, there are beautiful SKY, clear SKY, and sunny SKY detectors for the concept SKY. We max-pool their shot-level scores, so there is always one detection score, which is between 0 and 1, for each concept. The resultant high-level concept-oriented feature vector h is 70D/52D for a shot of a UTE/TV video. We ℓ_2 normalize it.

Furthermore, we design some contextual features l for a video shot based on the low-level features that SentiBank uses as input to its classifiers. This set of low-level features includes color histogram, GIST [42], LBP [43], Bag-of-Words descriptor, and an attribute feature [44]. With these features, we put a temporal window around each frame, and compute the mean-correlation as a contextual feature for the frame. The mean-correlation shows how well the frame is representative of the other frames in the temporal window. By varying the window size from 5 to 15 with step size 2, we obtain a 6D feature vector. Again we average pool them within each shot, followed by ℓ_2 normalization, to have the shot-level contextual feature vector l.

The concept-oriented and contextual features are concatenated as the overall shot-level feature vector $f \equiv [h; l]$ for parameterizing the DPP kernel of the Y-layer (Eq. (8)). The Z-layer kernel calls for query-dependent features $f(q)$ (Eq. (6)). For this purpose, we scale the concept-oriented features according to the query: $f(q) \equiv h \circ \alpha(q)$, where $\circ$ is the element-wise product between two vectors, and the scaling factors $\alpha(q)$ are 1 for the concepts shown in the query and 0.5 otherwise (see Fig. 1(a, b) for an example). Though we may employ more sophisticated query-dependent features, the simple features scaled by the query perform well in our experiments. The simplicity also enables us to feed the same features to vanilla and sequential DPPs for fair comparison.

4.5 Evaluation

We evaluate a system generated video summary by contrasting it against the "groundtruth" summary. The comparison is based on the dense text annotations [32]. In particular, the video summaries are mapped to text paragraphs and then compared by the ROUGE-SU metric [45]. We report the precision, recall, F-score returned by ROUGE-SU.

In addition, we also introduce a new metric, called *hitting recall*, to evaluate the system summaries from the query-focused perspective. Given the input query q and long video $\mathcal{Y}$, denote by S^q the shots relevant to the query in the "groundtruth" summary, and S^q_{SYSTEM} the query-relevant shots hit by a video summarizer. The hitting recall is calculated by $\text{HR} = |S^q_{\text{SYSTEM}}|/|S^q|$, where $|\cdot|$ is the cardinality of a set. For our SH-DPP model, we report the hitting recalls for both the overall summaries and those by the Z-layer only.

Table 1. Results of query-focused video summarization with **bi-concept** queries.

Patient users	UTE (%)					TV episodes (%)				
	F	Prec	Recall	HR	HR$_Z$	F	Prec	Recall	HR	HR$_Z$
Sampling	**22.12**	**35.07**	17.11	23.61	n/a	27.99	34.75	24.36	16.00	n/a
Ranking	20.66	24.35	18.38	22.05	n/a	32.19	39.96	32.19	16.61	n/a
SubMod [28]	20.98	31.40	26.99	30.10	n/a	32.19	**41.59**	27.01	21.69	n/a
Quasi [46]	12.45	19.47	13.14	14.95	n/a	31.88	27.49	41.69	19.67	n/a
DPP [38]	15.7	19.22	32.08	30.94	n/a	29.62	35.26	34.00	21.29	n/a
seqDPP [27]	18.85	20.59	35.83	31.91	n/a	27.96	23.80	35.62	14.08	n/a
SH-DPP (ours)	21.27	17.87	**41.65**	**38.26**	**36.92**	**37.02**	38.41	**36.82**	**23.76**	20.35
Impatient users	UTE (%)					TV episodes (%)				
	F	P	R	HR	HR$_Z$	F	P	R	HR	HR$_Z$
Sampling	25.44	44.16	18	6.48	n/a	33.74	**41.03**	28.8	13.03	n/a
Ranking	17.92	21.86	15.46	4.4	n/a	29.67	37.56	24.72	15.43	n/a
SubMod [28]	**27.10**	**51.79**	18.85	8.05	n/a	29.41	38.51	23.85	8.65	n/a
Quasi [46]	11.52	42.32	7.06	1.63	n/a	25.09	27.25	23.71	17.06	n/a
DPP [38]	14.36	30.9	16.18	12.54	n/a	26.01	28.85	39.15	**18.86**	n/a
seqDPP [27]	12.93	7.89	43.39	12.68	n/a	23.35	16.60	39.69	12.56	n/a
SH-DPP (ours)	25.56	18.51	**45.21**	**22.91**	11.57	**35.36**	30.94	**42.02**	17.07	17.07

4.6 Implementation Details

Here we report some details in our implementation of SH-DPP. Out of the four videos in either UTE or TV, we use three videos for training and the remaining one for testing. Each video is taken for testing once and then the averaged results are reported. In the training phase, there are two hyper-parameters in our approach: λ_1 and λ_2 (cf. Eq. (9)). We choose their values by the leave-one-video-out strategy (over the training videos only). The lower-dimensions of **W** and **V** are both fixed to 10, the same as used in seqDPP [27]. Varying this number has little effect to the results and we leave the study about it to the Supplementary Material. We put 10 shots in the ground set $\mathcal{Y}_t$ at each time step, and also examine the ground sets of the other sizes in the experiments.

We train our model SH-DPP using bi-concept queries. However, we test it using not only the bi-concept queries but also novel three-concept queries.

5   Experimental Results

This section presents the comparison results of our approach and some competitive baselines, effect of the ground set size, and finally qualitative results.

5.1   Comparison Results

Table 1 shows the results of different summarizers for the query-focused video summarization when the patient and impatient users supply **bi-concept** queries, while Table 2 includes the results for novel **three-concept** queries. Note that only bi-concept queries are used to train the summarizers. We report the results on both UTE and TV datasets, and contrast our SH-DPP to the following methods: (1) uni-

Table 2. Results of query-focused video summarization with novel **three-concept** queries.

Patient users	UTE (%)			TV episodes (%)		
	F	HR	HR$_Z$	F	HR	HR$_Z$
DPP	20.7	38.53	n/a	29.84	21.68	n/a
seqDPP	18.03	30.3	n/a	24.29	14.15	n/a
SH-DPP (ours)	**24.54**	**41.23**	40.43	**36.3**	**24.73**	21.71
Impatient users	UTE (%)			TV episodes (%)		
	F	HR	HR$_Z$	F	HR	HR$_Z$
DPP	14.77	17.28	n/a	24.71	**18.31**	n/a
seqDPP	19.4	19.17	n/a	29.31	10.09	n/a
SH-DPP (ours)	**29.59**	**25.82**	15.36	**33.94**	17.39	12.33

formly sampling K shots, (2) ranking, where for each query we apply the corresponding concept detectors to the shots, assign to a shot a ranking score as the maximum detection score, and then keep the top K shots, (3) vanilla DPP [38], where we remove the dependency between adjacent subset selection variables in Fig. 2(a), (4) seqDPP [27], (5) SubMod [28], where convex combination of a set of objectives is learned from user summaries, and (6) Quasi [46] which is an unsupervised method based on group sparse coding. We let K be the number of shots in the groundtruth summary; therefore, such privileged information makes (1), (2), and (5) actually strong baselines. We use the same ground sets, whose sizes are fixed to 10 for DPP, seqDPP, and our SH-DPP. All the results are evaluated by the F-score, Precision, and Recall of ROUGE-SU, as well as the hitting recall (HR) (cf. Sect. 4.5).

Interesting insights can be inferred from Tables 1 and 2. An immediate observation is that our SH-DPP is able to generate better overall summaries as our average F-scores are higher than the others'. Furthermore, our method is able to adapt itself to two essentially different datasets, the UTE daily life egocentric videos and TV episodes.

On UTE, we expect both SH-DPP and seqDPP to outperform vanilla DPP, because the egocentric videos are very long and include many unwanted scenes, making the dependency between different subset selection variables essential for eliminating repetitions. In contrast, as mentioned in Sect. 4.1, the TV episodes are from the world of professional recording, and the scenes rapidly change from shots to shots. Therefore, in this case, the dependency is weak and DPP may be able to catch up seqDPP's performance. These hypotheses are verified in the results, if we compare DPP with seqDPP in Tables 1 and 2.

Another important observation is that in 6 out of the 8 experiments: {patient and impatient users} on {UTE and TV datasets} by {bi-concept and novel three-concept queries}, the proposed SH-DPP has better hitting recalls than the other methods, indicating a better response to the user queries. Moreover, the hitting recalls are mainly captured by the Z-layer—the columns HR$_Z$ are the hitting recalls of the shots selected by the Z-layer only of SH-DPP.

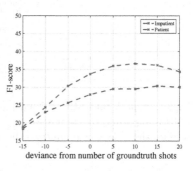

Fig. 3. The effect of number of selected shots on the performance of uniform sampling.

As it can be noticed from Table 1, uniform sampling has competitive performance compared to the other baselines and even outperforms SH-DPP in one scenario. The relatively good performance of random sampling can be explained by looking into the evaluation metric. ROUGE essentially evaluates the summaries by common word/phrase count and penalizing long or short summaries. Thus, accessing the number of groundtruth shots gives an advantage to Sampling. Figure 3 illustrates the change of performance when we deviate from the number of shots in groundtruth summary. This figure was generated using the TV Episodes dataset for both patient and impatient user cases.

5.2   A Peek into the SH-DPP Summarizer

Figure 4 is an exemplar summary for the query FLOWERS+WALL by SH-DPP. For each shot in the summary, we show the middle frame of that shot and the corresponding textual description. The groundtruth summary is also included at the bottom half of the figure. We can see that some query-relevant shots are successfully selected by the Z-layer. Conditioning on those, the Y-layer summarizes the remaining video. We highlight the text descriptions (in the blue color) that have exact matches in the groundtruth. However, please note that the other sentences are also highly correlated with some groundtruth sentences, for instance, *"I looked at flowers at the booth"* selected by the Z-layer versus *"my friend and I looked at flowers at the booth"* in the groundtruth summary.

One may wonder why the top-right shot is selected by the Z-layer, since it is visually not relevant to either FLOWERS or WALL . Inspection tells that it is due to the failure of the concept detectors; the detection scores are 0.86 and 0.65 out of 1 for FLOWERS and WALL , respectively. We may improve our SH-DPP for the query-focused video summarization by using better concept detectors.

Fig. 4. A peek into SH-DPP. Given the query FLOWERS+WALL, the Z-layer of SH-DPP is supposed to summarize the shots relevant to the query. Conditioning on those results, the Y-layer summarizes the remaining video. (Color figure online)

In the Supplementary Material: We first show all the concepts used in our experiments. Also, we describe the detailed training algorithm for SH-DPP using gradient descent. The resultant optimization problem is non-convex; we explain how to choose the initializations by the leaving-one-video-out strategy. We also show that the SH-DPP results remain stable for different lower-dimensions of **W** and **V**. Furthermore, we show how changing the groundset size affects the performance of SH-DPP. Finally, more qualitative results are included in the Supplementary Material.

6   Conclusions

In this paper, we examined a query-focused video summarization problem, in which the decision to select a video shot to the summary depends on both (1) the relevance between the shot and the query and (2) the importance of the shot in the context of the video. To tackle this problem, we developed a probabilistic model, Sequential and Hierarchical Determinantal Point Process (SH-DPP), as well as efficient learning and inference algorithms for it. Our SH-DPP summarizer can conveniently handle extremely long videos or online streaming videos. On two benchmark datasets for video summarization, our approach significantly outperforms some competing baselines. To the best of our knowledge, ours is the first work on query-focused video summarization, and has a great potential to be used in search engines, e.g., to display snippets of videos.

Acknowledgements. A.S. & B.G. are supported in part by NSF IIS #1566511. M.S. is partially supported by NIJ W911NF-14-1-0294.

References

1. Pritch, Y., Rav-Acha, A., Gutman, A., Peleg, S.: Webcam synopsis: peeking around the world. In: IEEE 11th International Conference on Computer Vision 2007, ICCV 2007, pp. 1–8. IEEE (2007)
2. Pal, C., Jojic, N.: Interactive montages of sprites for indexing and summarizing security video. In: IEEE Computer Society Conference on CVPR 2005, vol. 2. IEEE (2005)
3. Kang, H.W., Matsushita, Y., Tang, X., Chen, X.Q.: Space-time video montage. In: IEEE Computer Society Conference on CVPR 2006, vol. 2. IEEE (2006)
4. Jiang, R.M., Sadka, A.H., Crookes, D.: Advances in video summarization and skimming. In: Grgic, M., Delac, K., Ghanbari, M. (eds.) Recent Advances in Multimedia Signal Processing and Communications. SCI, vol. 231, pp. 27–50. Springer, Heidelberg (2009)
5. Rav-Acha, A., Pritch, Y., Peleg, S.: Making a long video short: dynamic video synopsis. In: 2006 IEEE Computer Society Conference on CVPR, vol. 1. IEEE (2006)
6. Goldman, D.B., Curless, B., Salesin, D., Seitz, S.M.: Schematic storyboarding for video visualization and editing. ACM Trans. Graph. (TOG) **25**, 862–871 (2006). ACM
7. Liu, T., Kender, J.R.: Optimization algorithms for the selection of key frame sequences of variable length. In: Heyden, A., Sparr, G., Nielsen, M., Johansen, P. (eds.) ECCV 2002. LNCS, vol. 2353, pp. 403–417. Springer, Heidelberg (2002)
8. Aner, A., Kender, J.R.: Video summaries through mosaic-based shot and scene clustering. In: Heyden, A., Sparr, G., Nielsen, M., Johansen, P. (eds.) ECCV 2002. LNCS, vol. 2353, pp. 388–402. Springer, Heidelberg (2002)
9. Vasconcelos, N., Lippman, A.: A spatiotemporal motion model for video summarization. In: Proceedings of IEEE Computer Society Conference on CVPR 1998, pp. 361–366. IEEE (1998)
10. Wolf, W.: Key frame selection by motion analysis. In: Proceedings of 1996 IEEE International Conference on Acoustics, Speech, and Signal Processing, ICASSP 1996, vol. 2, pp. 1228–1231. IEEE (1996)
11. Lee, K.M., Kwon, J.: A unified framework for event summarization and rare event detection. In: 2012 IEEE Conference on CVPR. IEEE (2012)
12. Cong, Y., Yuan, J., Luo, J.: Towards scalable summarization of consumer videos via sparse dictionary selection. IEEE Trans. Multimedia **14**(1), 66–75 (2012)
13. Ngo, C., Ma, Y., Zhang, H.: Automatic video summarization by graph modeling. In: Proceedings of the Ninth IEEE International Conference on Computer Vision 2003. IEEE (2003)
14. Khosla, A., Hamid, R., Lin, C.J., Sundaresan, N.: Large-scale video summarization using web-image priors. In: Proceedings of the IEEE Conference on CVPR (2013)
15. Kim, G., Sigal, L., Xing, E.: Joint summarization of large-scale collections of web images and videos for storyline reconstruction. In: Proceedings of the IEEE Conference on CVPR (2014)
16. Xiong, B., Grauman, K.: Detecting snap points in egocentric video with a web photo prior. In: Fleet, D., Pajdla, T., Schiele, B., Tuytelaars, T. (eds.) ECCV 2014, Part V. LNCS, vol. 8693, pp. 282–298. Springer, Heidelberg (2014)
17. Chu, W.S., Song, Y., Jaimes, A.: Video co-summarization: video summarization by visual co-occurrence. In: Proceedings of the IEEE Conference on CVPR (2015)

18. Song, Y., Vallmitjana, J., Stent, A., Jaimes, A.: TVSum: summarizing web videos using titles. In: Proceedings of the IEEE Conference on CVPR (2015)
19. Liu, W., Mei, T., Zhang, Y., Che, C., Luo, J.: Multi-task deep visual-semantic embedding for video thumbnail selection. In: Proceedings of the IEEE Conference on CVPR (2015)
20. Potapov, D., Douze, M., Harchaoui, Z., Schmid, C.: Category-specific video summarization. In: Fleet, D., Pajdla, T., Schiele, B., Tuytelaars, T. (eds.) ECCV 2014, Part VI. LNCS, vol. 8694, pp. 540–555. Springer, Heidelberg (2014)
21. Sun, M., Farhadi, A., Seitz, S.: Ranking domain-specific highlights by analyzing edited videos. In: Fleet, D., Pajdla, T., Schiele, B., Tuytelaars, T. (eds.) ECCV 2014, Part I. LNCS, vol. 8689, pp. 787–802. Springer, Heidelberg (2014)
22. Xu, J., Mukherjee, L., Li, Y., Warner, J., Rehg, J.M., Singh, V.: Gaze-enabled egocentric video summarization via constrained submodular maximization. In: Proceedings of the IEEE Conference on CVPR (2015)
23. Gygli, M., Grabner, H., Riemenschneider, H., Van Gool, L.: Creating summaries from user videos. In: Fleet, D., Pajdla, T., Schiele, B., Tuytelaars, T. (eds.) ECCV 2014, Part VII. LNCS, vol. 8695, pp. 505–520. Springer, Heidelberg (2014)
24. Lu, Z., Grauman, K.: Story-driven summarization for egocentric video. In: Proceedings of the IEEE Conference on CVPR (2013)
25. Lee, Y.J., Grauman, K.: Predicting important objects for egocentric video summarization. Int. J. Comput. Vis. 114(1), 38–55 (2015)
26. Liu, D., Hua, G., Chen, T.: A hierarchical visual model for video object summarization. IEEE Trans. Pattern Anal. Mach. Intell. 32(12), 2178–2190 (2010)
27. Gong, B., Chao, W.L., Grauman, K., Sha, F.: Diverse sequential subset selection for supervised video summarization. In: Advances in Neural Information Processing Systems, pp. 2069–2077 (2014)
28. Gygli, M., Grabner, H., Van Gool, L.: Video summarization by learning submodular mixtures of objectives. In: Proceedings of the IEEE Conference on CVPR (2015)
29. Nenkova, A., McKeown, K.: A survey of text summarization techniques. In: Aggarwal, C.C., Zhai, C.X. (eds.) Mining Text Data, pp. 43–76. Springer, Heidelberg (2012)
30. Kulesza, A., Taskar, B.: Determinantal point processes for machine learning. arXiv preprint arXiv:1207.6083 (2012)
31. Ghosh, J., Lee, Y.J., Grauman, K.: Discovering important people and objects for egocentric video summarization. In: 2012 IEEE Conference on CVPR. IEEE (2012)
32. Yeung, S., Fathi, A., Fei-Fei, L.: Videoset: Video summary evaluation through text. arXiv preprint arXiv:1406.5824 (2014)
33. Daumé III., H., Marcu, D.: Bayesian query-focused summarization. In: Proceedings of the 21st International Conference on Computational Linguistics and the 44th Annual Meeting of the Association for Computational Linguistics. Association for Computational Linguistics (2006)
34. Schilder, F., Kondadadi, R.: Fastsum: fast and accurate query-based multi-document summarization. In: Proceedings of the 46th Annual Meeting of the Association for Computational Linguistics on Human Language Technologies: Short Papers, pp. 205–208. Association for Computational Linguistics (2008)
35. Gupta, S., Nenkova, A., Jurafsky, D.: Measuring importance and query relevance in topic-focused multi-document summarization. In: Proceedings of the 45th Annual Meeting of the ACL on Interactive Poster and Demonstration Sessions. Association for Computational Linguistics, pp. 193–196 (2007)

36. Ellouze, M., Boujemaa, N., Alimi, A.M.: IM(S)^2: interactive movie summarization system. J. Vis. Commun. Image Represent. **21**(4), 283–294 (2010)
37. Xiong, B., Kim, G., Sigal, L.: Storyline representation of egocentric videos with an applications to story-based search. In: Proceedings of the IEEE International CVPR (2015)
38. Kulesza, A., Taskar, B.: Learning determinantal point processes. arXiv preprint arXiv:1202.3738 (2012)
39. Chao, W.L., Gong, B., Grauman, K., Sha, F.: Large-margin determinantal point processes. In: Proceedings of the Conference on Uncertainty in Artificial Intelligence (UAI) (2015)
40. Affandi, R.H., Kulesza, A., Fox, E.B.: Markov determinantal point processes. arXiv preprint arXiv:1210.4850 (2012)
41. Borth, D., Chen, T., Ji, R., Chang, S.F.: Sentibank: large-scale ontology and classifiers for detecting sentiment and emotions in visual content. In: Proceedings of the 21st ACM International Conference on Multimedia. ACM (2013)
42. Oliva, A., Torralba, A.: Modeling the shape of the scene: a holistic representation of the spatial envelope. Int. J. Comput. Vsion **42**(3), 145–175 (2001)
43. Ojala, T., Pietikäinen, M., Mäenpää, T.: Multiresolution gray-scale and rotation invariant texture classification with local binary patterns. IEEE Trans. Pattern Anal. Mach. Intell. **24**(7), 971–987 (2002)
44. Yu, F., Cao, L., Feris, R., Smith, J., Chang, S.F.: Designing category-level attributes for discriminative visual recognition. In: Proceedings of the IEEE Conference on CVPR (2013)
45. Lin, C.Y.: Rouge: A package for automatic evaluation of summaries. In: Proceedings of the ACL-04 Workshop, Text Summarization Branches Out, vol. 8 (2004)
46. Zhao, B., Xing, E.: Quasi real-time summarization for consumer videos. In: Proceedings of the IEEE Conference on CVPR (2014)

Temporal Segment Networks: Towards Good Practices for Deep Action Recognition

Limin Wang[1]([✉]), Yuanjun Xiong[2], Zhe Wang[3], Yu Qiao[3], Dahua Lin[2],
Xiaoou Tang[2], and Luc Van Gool[1]

[1] Computer Vision Lab, ETH Zurich, Zurich, Switzerland
07wanglimin@gmail.com
[2] Department of Information Engineering, The Chinese University of Hong Kong,
Hong Kong, China
[3] Shenzhen Institutes of Advanced Technology, CAS, Shenzhen, China

Abstract. Deep convolutional networks have achieved great success for visual recognition in still images. However, for action recognition in videos, the advantage over traditional methods is not so evident. This paper aims to discover the principles to design effective ConvNet architectures for action recognition in videos and learn these models given limited training samples. Our first contribution is temporal segment network (TSN), a novel framework for video-based action recognition. which is based on the idea of long-range temporal structure modeling. It combines a sparse temporal sampling strategy and video-level supervision to enable efficient and effective learning using the whole action video. The other contribution is our study on a series of good practices in learning ConvNets on video data with the help of temporal segment network. Our approach obtains the state-the-of-art performance on the datasets of HMDB51 (69.4%) and UCF101 (94.2%). We also visualize the learned ConvNet models, which qualitatively demonstrates the effectiveness of temporal segment network and the proposed good practices (Models and code at https://github.com/yjxiong/temporal-segment-networks).

Keywords: Action recognition · Temporal segment networks · Good practices · ConvNets

1 Introduction

Video-based action recognition has drawn a significant amount of attention from the academic community [1–6], owing to its applications in many areas like security and behavior analysis. In action recognition, there are two crucial and complementary aspects: appearances and dynamics. The performance of a recognition system depends, to a large extent, on whether it is able to extract

---

Electronic supplementary material The online version of this chapter (doi:10.1007/978-3-319-46484-8_2) contains supplementary material, which is available to authorized users.

© Springer International Publishing AG 2016
B. Leibe et al. (Eds.): ECCV 2016, Part VIII, LNCS 9912, pp. 20–36, 2016.
DOI: 10.1007/978-3-319-46484-8_2

and utilize relevant information therefrom. However, extracting such information is non-trivial due to a number of complexities, such as scale variations, view point changes, and camera motions. Thus it becomes crucial to design effective representations that can deal with these challenges while preserve categorical information of action classes. Recently, Convolutional Networks (ConvNets) [7] have witnessed great success in classifying images of objects, scenes, and complex events [8–11]. ConvNets have also been introduced to solve the problem of video-based action recognition [1,12–14]. Deep ConvNets come with great modeling capacity and are capable of learning discriminative representation from raw visual data with the help of large-scale supervised datasets. However, unlike image classification, end-to-end deep ConvNets remain unable to achieve significant advantage over traditional hand-crafted features for video-based action recognition.

In our view, the application of ConvNets in video-based action recognition is impeded by two major obstacles. *First*, long-range temporal structure plays an important role in understanding the dynamics in action videos [15–18]. However, mainstream ConvNet frameworks [1,13] usually focus on appearances and short-term motions, thus lacking the capacity to incorporate long-range temporal structure. Recently there are a few attempts [4,19,20] to deal with this problem. These methods mostly rely on dense temporal sampling with a pre-defined sampling interval. This approach would incur excessive computational cost when applied to long video sequences, which limits its application in real-world practice and poses a risk of missing important information for videos longer than the maximal sequence length. *Second*, in practice, training deep ConvNets requires a large volume of training samples to achieve optimal performance. However, due to the difficulty in data collection and annotation, publicly available action recognition datasets (e.g. UCF101 [21], HMDB51 [22]) remain limited, in both size and diversity. Consequently, very deep ConvNets [9,23], which have attained remarkable success in image classification, are confronted with high risk of overfitting.

These challenges motivate us to study two problems: *(1) how to design an effective and efficient video-level framework for learning video representation that is able to capture long-range temporal structure; (2) how to learn the ConvNet models given limited training samples.* In particular, we build our method on top of the successful two-stream architecture [1] while tackling the problems mentioned above. In terms of temporal structure modeling, a key observation is that consecutive frames are highly redundant. Therefore, dense temporal sampling, which usually results in highly similar sampled frames, is unnecessary. Instead a sparse temporal sampling strategy will be more favorable in this case. Motivated by this observation, we develop a video-level framework, called *temporal segment network* (TSN). This framework extracts short snippets over a long video sequence with a sparse sampling scheme, where the samples distribute uniformly along the temporal dimension. Thereon, a segmental structure is employed to aggregate information from the sampled snippets. In this sense, temporal segment networks are capable of modeling long-range temporal structure over the whole video. Moreover, this sparse sampling strategy preserves relevant information with dramatically lower cost, thus enabling end-to-end learning over long video sequences under a reasonable budget in both time and computing resources.

To unleash the full potential of temporal segment network framework, we adopt very deep ConvNet architectures [9,23] introduced recently, and explored a number of good practices to overcome the aforementioned difficulties caused by the limited number of training samples, including (1) cross-modality pre-training; (2) regularization; (3) enhanced data augmentation. Meanwhile, to fully utilize visual content from videos, we empirically study four types of input modalities to two-stream ConvNets, namely a single RGB image, stacked RGB difference, stacked optical flow field, and stacked warped optical flow field.

We perform experiments on two challenging action recognition datasets, namely UCF101 [21] and HMDB51 [22], to verify the effectiveness of our method. In experiments, models learned using the temporal segment network significantly outperform the state of the art on these two challenging action recognition datasets. We also visualize the our learned two-stream models trying to provide some insights for future action recognition research.

2 Related Works

Action recognition has been extensively studied in past few years [2,18,24–26]. Previous works related to ours fall into two categories: (1) convolutional networks for action recognition, (2) temporal structure modeling.

Convolutional Networks for Action Recognition. Several works have been trying to design effective ConvNet architectures for action recognition in videos [1,12,13,27,28]. Karpathy *et al.* [12] tested ConvNets with deep structures on a large dataset (Sports-1M). Simonyan *et al.* [1] designed two-stream ConvNets containing spatial and temporal net by exploiting ImageNet dataset for pre-training and calculating optical flow to explicitly capture motion information. Tran *et al.* [13] explored 3D ConvNets [27] on the realistic and large-scale video datasets, where they tried to learn both appearance and motion features with 3D convolution operations. Sun *et al.* [28] proposed a factorized spatio-temporal ConvNets and exploited different ways to decompose 3D convolutional kernels. Recently, several works focused on modeling long-range temporal structure with ConvNets [4,19,20]. However, these methods directly operated on a longer continuous video streams. Limited by computational cost these methods usually process sequences of fixed lengths ranging from 64 to 120 frames. It is non-trivial for these methods to learn from entire video due to their limited temporal coverage. Our method differs from these end-to-end deep ConvNets by its novel adoption of a sparse temporal sampling strategy, which enables efficient learning using the entire videos without the limitation of sequence length.

Temporal Structure Modeling. Many research works have been devoted to modeling the temporal structure for action recognition [15–18,29,30].

Gaidon *et al.* [16] annotated each atomic action for each video and proposed Actom Sequence Model (ASM) for action detection. Niebles *et al.* [15] proposed to use latent variables to model the temporal decomposition of complex actions, and resorted to the Latent SVM [31] to learn the model parameters in an iterative approach. Wang *et al.* [17] and Pirsiavash *et al.* [29] extended the temporal decomposition of complex action into a hierarchical manner using Latent Hierarchical Model (LHM) and Segmental Grammar Model (SGM), respectively. Wang *et al.* [30] designed a sequential skeleton model (SSM) to capture the relations among dynamic-poselets, and performed spatio-temporal action detection. Fernando [18] modeled the temporal evolution of BoVW representations for action recognition. These methods, however, remain unable to assemble an end-to-end learning scheme for modeling the temporal structure. The proposed temporal segment network, while also emphasizing this principle, is the first framework for end-to-end temporal structure modeling on the entire videos.

3   Action Recognition with Temporal Segment Networks

In this section, we give detailed descriptions of performing action recognition with temporal segment networks. Specifically, we first introduce the basic concepts in the framework of temporal segment network. Then, we study the good practices in learning two-stream ConvNets within the temporal segment network framework. Finally, we describe the testing details of the learned two-stream ConvNets.

3.1   Temporal Segment Networks

As we discussed in Sect. 1, an obvious problem of the two-stream ConvNets in their current forms is their inability in modeling long-range temporal structure. This is mainly due to their limited access to temporal context as they are designed to operate only on a single frame (spatial networks) or a single stack of frames in a short snippet (temporal network). However, complex actions, such as sports action, comprise multiple stages spanning over a relatively long time. It would be quite a loss failing to utilize long-range temporal structures in these actions into ConvNet training. To tackle this issue, we propose temporal segment network, a video-level framework as shown in Fig. 1, to enable to model dynamics throughout the whole video.

Specifically, our proposed temporal segment network framework, aiming to utilize the visual information of entire videos to perform video-level prediction, is also composed of spatial stream ConvNets and temporal stream ConvNets. Instead of working on single frames or frame stacks, temporal segment networks operate on a sequence of short snippets sparsely sampled from the entire video. Each snippet in this sequence will produce its own preliminary prediction of the action classes. Then a consensus among the snippets will be derived as the video-level prediction. In the learning process, the loss values of video-level predictions, other than those of snippet-level predictions which were used in two-stream ConvNets, are optimized by iteratively updating the model parameters.

Formally, given a video V, we divide it into K segments $\{S_1, S_2, \cdots, S_K\}$ of equal durations. Then, the temporal segment network models a sequence of snippets as follows:

$$\text{TSN}(T_1, T_2, \cdots, T_K) = \mathcal{H}(\mathcal{G}(\mathcal{F}(T_1; \mathbf{W}), \mathcal{F}(T_2; \mathbf{W}), \cdots, \mathcal{F}(T_K; \mathbf{W}))). \quad (1)$$

Here $(T_1, T_2, \cdots, T_K)$ is a sequence of snippets. Each snippet T_k is randomly sampled from its corresponding segment S_k. $\mathcal{F}(T_k; \mathbf{W})$ is the function representing a ConvNet with parameters $\mathbf{W}$ which operates on the short snippet T_k and produces class scores for all the classes. The segmental consensus function $\mathcal{G}$ combines the outputs from multiple short snippets to obtain a consensus of class hypothesis among them. Based on this consensus, the prediction function $\mathcal{H}$ predicts the probability of each action class for the whole video. Here we choose the widely used Softmax function for $\mathcal{H}$. Combining with standard categorical cross-entropy loss, the final loss function regarding the segmental consensus $\mathbf{G} = \mathcal{G}(\mathcal{F}(T_1; \mathbf{W}), \mathcal{F}(T_2; \mathbf{W}), \cdots, \mathcal{F}(T_K; \mathbf{W}))$ is formed as

$$\mathcal{L}(y, \mathbf{G}) = -\sum_{i=1}^{C} y_i \left(G_i - \log \sum_{j=1}^{C} \exp G_j \right), \quad (2)$$

where C is the number of action classes and y_i the groundtruth label concerning class i. In experiments, the number of snippets K is set to 3 according to previous works on temporal modeling [16,17]. The form of consensus function $\mathcal{G}$ remains an open question. In this work we use the simplest form of $\mathcal{G}$, where $G_i = g(\mathcal{F}_i(T_1), \ldots, \mathcal{F}_i(T_K))$. Here a class score G_i is inferred from the scores of the same class on all the snippets, using an aggregation function g. We empirically evaluated several different forms of the aggregation function g, including evenly averaging, maximum, and weighted averaging in our experiments. Among them, evenly averaging is used to report our final recognition accuracies.

This temporal segment network is differentiable or at least has subgradients, depending on the choice of g. This allows us to utilize the multiple snippets to jointly optimize the model parameters $\mathbf{W}$ with standard back-propagation algorithms. In the back-propagation process, the gradients of model parameters $\mathbf{W}$ with respect to the loss value $\mathcal{L}$ can be derived as

$$\frac{\partial \mathcal{L}(y, \mathbf{G})}{\partial \mathbf{W}} = \frac{\partial \mathcal{L}}{\partial \mathbf{G}} \sum_{k=1}^{K} \frac{\partial \mathcal{G}}{\partial \mathcal{F}(T_k)} \frac{\partial \mathcal{F}(T_k)}{\partial \mathbf{W}}, \quad (3)$$

where K is number of segments temporal segment network uses.

When we use a gradient-based optimization method, like stochastic gradient descent (SGD), to learn the model parameters, Eq. (3) guarantees that the parameter updates are utilizing the segmental consensus $\mathbf{G}$ derived from all snippet-level prediction. Optimized in this manner, temporal segment network can learn model parameters from the entire video rather than a short snippet.

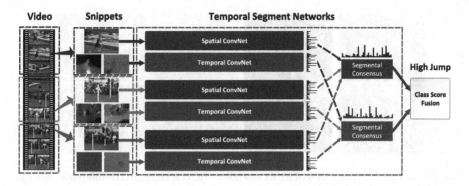

Fig. 1. Temporal segment network: One input video is divided into K segments and a short snippet is randomly selected from each segment. The class scores of different snippets are fused by an the segmental consensus function to yield segmental consensus, which is a video-level prediction. Predictions from all modalities are then fused to produce the final prediction. ConvNets on all snippets share parameters

Meanwhile, by fixing K for all videos, we assemble a sparse temporal sampling strategy, where the sampled snippets contain only a small portion of the frames. It drastically reduces the computational cost for evaluating ConvNets on the frames, compared with previous works using densely sampled frames [4,19,20].

3.2 Learning Temporal Segment Networks

Temporal segment network provides a solid framework to perform video-level learning, but to achieve optimal performance, a few practical concerns have to be taken care of, for example the limited numberof training samples. To this end, we study a series of good practices in training deep ConvNets on video data, which are also directly applicable in learning temporal segment networks.

Network Architectures. Network architecture is an important factor in neural network design. Several works have shown that deeper structures improve object recognition performance [9,10]. However, the original two-stream ConvNets [1] employed a relatively shallow network structure (ClarifaiNet [32]). In this work, we choose the Inception with Batch Normalization (BN-Inception) [23] as building block, due to its good balance between accuracy and efficiency. We adapt the original BN-Inception architecture to the design of two-stream ConvNets. Like in the original two-stream ConvNets [1], the spatial stream ConvNet operates on a single RGB images, and the temporal stream ConvNet takes a stack of consecutive optical flow fields as input.

Network Inputs. We are also interested in exploring more input modalities to enhance the discriminative power of temporal segment networks. Originally, the two-stream ConvNets used RGB images for the spatial stream and stacked optical flow fields for the temporal stream. Here, we propose to study two extra modalities, namely *RGB difference* and *warped optical flow fields*.

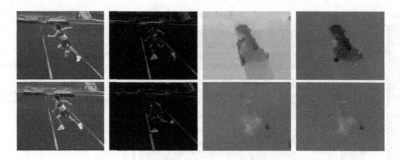

Fig. 2. Examples of four types of input modality: RGB images, RGB difference, optical flow fields (x,y directions), and warped optical flow fields (x,y directions)

A single RGB image usually encodes static appearance at a specific time point and lacks the contextual information about previous and next frames. As shown in Fig. 2, RGB difference between two consecutive frames describe the appearance change, which may correspond to the motion salient region. Inspired by [28], We experiment with adding stacked RGB difference as another input modality and investigate its performance in action recognition.

The temporal stream ConvNets take optical flow field as input and aim to capture the motion information. In realistic videos, however, there usually exists camera motion, and optical flow fields may not concentrate on the human action. As shown in Fig. 2, a remarkable amount of horizontal movement is highlighted in the background due to the camera motion. Inspired by the work of improved dense trajectories [2], we propose to take warped optical flow fields as additional input modality. Following [2], we extract the warped optical flow by first estimating homography matrix and then compensating camera motion. As shown in Fig. 2, the warped optical flow suppresses the background motion and makes motion concentrate on the actor.

Network Training. As the datasets for action recognition are relatively small, training deep ConvNets is challenged by the risk of over-fitting. To mitigate this problem, we design several strategies for training the ConvNets in temporal segment networks as follows.

Cross Modality Pre-training. Pre-training has turned out to be an effective way to initialize deep ConvNets when the target dataset does not have enough training samples [1]. As spatial networks take RGB images as input, it is natural to exploit models trained on the ImageNet [33] as initialization. For other modalities such as optical flow field and RGB difference, they essentially capture different visual aspects of video data and their distributions are different from that of RGB images. We come up with a cross modality pre-training technique in which we utilize RGB models to initialize the temporal networks. First, we discretize optical flow fields into the interval from 0 to 255 by a linear transformation. This step makes the range of optical flow fields to be the same with RGB images. Then, we modify the weights of first convolution layer of RGB models to handle the input of optical flow fields. Specifically, we average the weights across the RGB channels and replicate this average by the channel number of temporal network input. This initialization method works pretty well for temporal networks and reduce the effect of over-fitting in experiments.

Regularization Techniques. Batch Normalization [23] is an important component to deal with the problem of covariate shift. In the learning process, batch normalization will estimate the activation mean and variance within each batch and use them to transform these activation values into a standard Gaussian distribution. This operation speeds up the convergence of training but also leads to over-fitting in the transferring process, due to the biased estimation of activation distributions from limited number of training samples. Therefore, after initialization with pre-trained models, we choose to freeze the mean and variance parameters of all Batch Normalization layers except the first one. As the distribution of optical flow is different from the RGB images, the activation value of first convolution layer will have a different distribution and we need to re-estimate the mean and variance accordingly. We call this strategy **partial BN**. Meanwhile, we add a extra **dropout** layer after the global pooling layer in BN-Inception architecture to further reduce the effect of over-fitting. The dropout ratio is set as 0.8 for spatial stream ConvNets and 0.7 for temporal stream ConvNets.

Data Augmentation. Data augmentation can generate diverse training samples and prevent severe over-fitting. In the original two-stream ConvNets, random cropping and horizontal flipping are employed to augment training samples. We exploit two new data augmentation techniques: corner cropping and scale-jittering. In corner cropping technique, the extracted regions are only selected from the corners or the center of the image to avoid implicitly focusing on the center area of a image. In multi-scale cropping technique, we adapt the scale jittering technique [9] used in ImageNet classification to action recognition. We present an efficient implementation of scale jittering. We fix the size of input image or optical flow fields as 256×340, and the width and height of cropped region are randomly selected from $\{256, 224, 192, 168\}$. Finally, these cropped regions will be resized to 224×224 for network training. In fact, this implementation not only contains scale jittering, but also involves aspect ratio jittering.

3.3 Testing Temporal Segment Networks

Finally, we present our testing method for temporal segment networks. Due to the fact that all snippet-level ConvNets share the model parameters in temporal segment networks, the learned models can perform frame-wise evaluation as normal ConvNets. This allows us to carry out fair comparison with models learned without the temporal segment network framework. Specifically, we follow the testing scheme of the original two-stream ConvNets [1], where we sample 25 RGB frames or optical flow stacks from the action videos. Meanwhile, we crop 4 corners and 1 center, and their horizontal flipping from the sampled frames to evaluate the ConvNets. For the fusion of spatial and temporal stream networks, we take a weighted average of them. When learned within the temporal segment networkframework, the performance gap between spatial stream ConvNets and temporal stream ConvNets is much smaller than that in the original two-stream ConvNets. Based on this fact, we give more credits to the spatial stream by setting its weight as 1 and that of temporal stream as 1.5. When both normal and warped optical flow fields are used, the weight of temporal stream is divided to 1 for optical flow and 0.5 for warped optical flow. It is described in Sect. 3.1 that the segmental consensus function is applied before the Softmax normalization. To test the models in compliance with their training, we fuse the prediction scores of 25 frames and different streams before Softmax normalization.

4   Experiments

In this section, we first introduce the evaluation datasets and the implementation details of our approach. Then, we explore the proposed good practices for learning temporal segment networks. After this, we demonstrate the importance of modeling long-term temporal structures by applying the temporal segment network framework. We also compare the performance of our method with the state of the art. Finally, we visualize our learned ConvNet models.

4.1   Datasets and Implementation Details

We conduct experiments on two large action datasets, namely HMDB51 [22] and UCF101 [21]. The UCF101 dataset contains 101 action classes and 13, 320 video clips. We follow the evaluation scheme of the THUMOS13 challenge [34] and adopt the three training/testing splits for evaluation. The HMDB51 dataset is a large collection of realistic videos from various sources, such as movies and web videos. The dataset is composed of 6, 766 video clips from 51 action categories. Our experiments follow the original evaluation scheme using three training/testing splits and report average accuracy over these splits.

We use the mini-batch stochastic gradient descent algorithm to learn the network parameters, where the batch size is set to 256 and momentum set to 0.9. We initialize network weights with pre-trained models from ImageNet [33]. We set a smaller learning rate in our experiments. For spatial networks, the learning rate is initialized as 0.001 and decreases to its $\frac{1}{10}$ every 2, 000 iterations. The whole training procedure stops at 4, 500 iterations. For temporal networks, we initialize the learning rate as 0.005, which reduces to its $\frac{1}{10}$ after 12, 000 and 18, 000 iterations. The maximum iteration is set as 20, 000. Concerning data augmentation, we use the techniques of location jittering, horizontal flipping, corner cropping, and scale jittering, as specified in Sect. 3.2. For the extraction of optical flow and warped optical flow, we choose the TVL1 optical flow algorithm [35] implemented in OpenCV with CUDA. To speed up training, we employ a data-parallel strategy with multiple GPUs, implemented with our modified version of Caffe [36] and OpenMPI[1]. The whole training time on UCF101 is around 2 h for spatial TSNs and 9 h for temporal TSNs with 4 TITANX GPUs.

---

[1] https://github.com/yjxiong/caffe.

4.2 Exploration Study

In this section, we focus on the investigation the good practices described in Sect. 3.2, including the training strategies and the input modalities. In this exploration study, we use the two-stream ConvNets with very deep architecture adapted from [23] and perform all experiments on the split 1 of UCF101 dataset.

We propose two training strategies in Sect. 3.2, namely cross modality pre-training and partial BN with dropout. Specifically, we compare four settings: (1) training from scratch, (2) only pre-train spatial stream as in [1], (3) with cross modality pre-training, (4) combination of cross modality pre-training and partial BN with dropout. The results are summarized in Table 1. First, we see that the performance of training from scratch is much worse than that of the original two-stream ConvNets (baseline), which implies carefully designed learning strategy is necessary to reduce the risk of over-fitting, especially for spatial networks. Then, We resort to the pre-training of the spatial stream and cross modality pre-training of the temporal stream to help initialize two-stream ConvNets and it achieves better performance than the baseline. We further utilize the partial BN with dropout to regularize the training procedure, which boosts the recognition performance to 92.0 %.

Table 1. Exploration of different training strategies for two-stream ConvNets on the UCF101 dataset (split 1).

Training setting	Spatial ConvNets	Temporal ConvNets	Two-Stream
Baseline [1]	72.7 %	81.0 %	87.0 %
From scratch	48.7 %	81.7 %	82.9 %
Pre-train spatial (same as [1])	84.1 %	81.7 %	90.0 %
+Cross modality pre-training	84.1 %	86.6 %	91.5 %
+Partial BN with dropout	84.5 %	87.2 %	92.0 %

We propose two new types of modalities in Sect. 3.2: RGB difference and warped optical flow fields. Results on comparing the performance of different modalities are reported in Table 2. These experiments are carried out with all the good practices verified in Table 1. We first observe that the combination of RGB images and RGB differences boosts the recognition performance to 87.3 %. This result indicates that RGB images and RGB difference may encode complementary information. Then it is shown that optical flow and warped optical flow yield quite similar performance (87.2 % vs. 86.9 %) and the fusion of them can improve the performance to 87.8 %. Combining all of four modalities leads to an accuracy of 91.7 %. As RGB difference may describe similar but unstable motion patterns, we also evaluate the performance of combining the other three modalities and this brings better recognition accuracy (92.3 % vs 91.7 %). We conjecture that the optical flow is better at capturing motion information and sometimes RGB difference may be unstable for describing motions. On the

Table 2. Exploration of different input modalities for two-stream ConvNets on the UCF101 dataset (split 1).

Modality	Performance
RGB image	84.5 %
RGB difference	83.8 %
RGB image+RGB difference	87.3 %
Optical flow	87.2 %
Warped flow	86.9 %
Optical flow+Warped flow	87.8 %
Optical flow+Warped flow+RGB	**92.3 %**
All modalities	91.7 %

Table 3. Exploration of different segmental consensus functions for temporal segment networks on the UCF101 dataset (split 1).

Consensus function	Spatial ConvNets	Temporal ConvNets	Two-Stream
Max	85.0 %	86.0 %	91.6 %
Average	85.7 %	87.9 %	**93.5 %**
Weighted average	86.2 %	87.7 %	92.4 %

other hand, RGB difference may serve as a low-quality, high-speed alternative for motion representations.

4.3   Evaluation of Temporal Segment Networks

In this subsection, we focus on the study of the temporal segment network framework. We first study the effect of segmental consensus function and then compare different ConvNet architectures on the split 1 of UCF101 dataset. For fair comparison, we only use RGB images and optical flow fields for input modalities in this exploration. As mentioned in Sect. 3.1, the number of segments K is set to 3.

In Eq. (1), a segmental consensus function is defined by its aggregation function g. Here we evaluate three candidates: (1) max pooling, (2) average pooling, (3) weighted average, for the form of g. The experimental results are summarized in Table 3. We see that average pooling function achieves the best performance. So in the following experiments, we choose average pooling as the default aggregation function. Then we compare the performance of different network architectures and the results are summarized in Table 4. Specifically, we compare three very deep architectures: BN-Inception [23], GoogLeNet [10], and VGGNet-16 [9], all these architectures are trained with the good practices aforementioned. Among the compared architectures, the very deep two-stream ConvNets adapted from BN-Inception [23] achieves the best accuracy of 92.0 %. This is in

Table 4. Exploration of different very deep ConvNet architectures on the UCF101 dataset (split 1). "BN-Inception+TSN" refers to the setting where the temporal segment networkframework is applied on top of the best performing BN-Inception [23] architecture.

Training setting	Spatial ConvNets	Temporal ConvNets	Two-Stream
Clarifai [1]	72.7 %	81.0 %	87.0 %
GoogLeNet	77.1 %	83.9 %	89.0 %
VGGNet-16	79.8 %	85.7 %	90.9 %
BN-Inception	84.5 %	87.2 %	92.0 %
BN-Inception+TSN	85.7 %	87.9 %	**93.5 %**

Table 5. Component analysis of the proposed method on the UCF101 dataset (split 1). From left to right we add the components one by one. BN-Inception [23] is used as the ConvNet architecture.

Component	Basic Two-stream [1]	Cross-Modality pre-training	Partial BN with dropout	Temporal segment networks
Accuracy	90.0 %	91.5	92.0 %	93.5 %

accordance with its better performance in the image classification task. So we choose BN-Inception [23] as the ConvNet architecture for temporal segment networks.

With all the design choices set, we now apply the temporal segment network (TSN) to the action recognition. The result is illustrated in Table 4. A component-wise analysis of the components in terms of the recognition accuracies is also presented in Table 5. We can see that temporal segment networkis able to boost the performance of the model even when all the discussed good practices are applied. This corroborates that modeling long-term temporal structures is crucial for better understanding of action in videos. And it is achieved by temporal segment networks.

4.4 Comparison with the State of the Art

After exploring of the good practices and understanding the effect of temporal segment network, we are ready to build up our final action recognition method. Specifically, we assemble three input modalities and all the techniques described as our final recognition approach, and test it on two challenging datasets: HMDB51 and UCF101. The results are summarized in Table 6, where we compare our method with both traditional approaches such as improved trajectories (iDTs) [2], MoFAP representations [39], and deep learning representations, such as 3D convolutional networks (C3D) [13], trajectory-pooled deep-convolutional descriptors (TDD) [5], factorized spatio-temporal convolutional networks ($F_{ST}CN$) [28], long term convolution networks (LTC) [19], and key volume mining framework (KVMF) [41]. Our best result outperforms other

Table 6. Comparison of our method based on temporal segment network(TSN) with other state-of-the-art methods. We separately present the results of using two input modalities (RGB+Flow) and three input modalities (RGB+Flow+Warped Flow).

HMDB51		UCF101	
DT+MVSV [37]	55.9 %	DT+MVSV [37]	83.5 %
iDT+FV [2]	57.2 %	iDT+FV [38]	85.9 %
iDT+HSV [25]	61.1 %	iDT+HSV [25]	87.9 %
MoFAP [39]	61.7 %	MoFAP [39]	88.3 %
Two stream [1]	59.4 %	Two Stream [1]	88.0 %
VideoDarwin [18]	63.7 %	C3D (3 nets) [13]	85.2 %
MPR [40]	65.5 %	Two stream+LSTM [4]	88.6 %
F_{ST}CN (SCI fusion) [28]	59.1 %	F_{ST}CN (SCI fusion) [28]	88.1 %
TDD+FV [5]	63.2 %	TDD+FV [5]	90.3 %
LTC [19]	64.8 %	LTC [19]	91.7 %
KVMF [41]	63.3 %	KVMF [41]	93.1 %
TSN (2 modalities)	68.5 %	TSN (2 modalities)	94.0 %
TSN (3 modalities)	**69.4** %	TSN (3 modalities)	**94.2** %

methods by 3.9 % on the HMDB51 dataset, and 1.1 % on the UCF101 dataset. The superior performance of our methods demonstrates the effectiveness of temporal segment networkand justifies the importance of long-term temporal modeling.

4.5 Model Visualization

Besides recognition accuracies, we would like to attain further insight into the learned ConvNet models. In this sense, we adopt the DeepDraw [42] toolbox. This tool conducts iterative gradient ascent on input images with only white noises. Thus the output after a number of iterations can be considered as class visualization based solely on class knowledge inside the ConvNet model. The original version of the tool only deals with RGB data. To conduct visualization on optical flow based models, we adapt the tool to work with our temporal ConvNets. As a result, we for the first time visualize interesting class information in action recognition ConvNet models. We randomly pick five classes from the UCF101 dataset, *Taichi*, *Punch*, *Diving*, *Long Jump*, and *Biking* for visualization. The results are shown in Fig. 3. For both RGB and optical flow, we visualize the ConvNet models learned with following three settings: (1) without pre-training; (2) only with pre-training; (3) with temporal segment network.

Generally speaking, models with pre-training are more capable of representing visual concepts than those without pre-training. One can see that both spatial and temporal models without pre-training can barely generate any meaningful

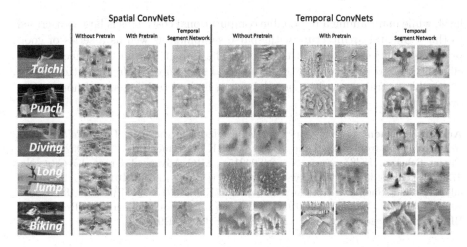

Fig. 3. Visualization of ConvNet models for action recognition using DeepDraw [42]. We compare three settings: (1) without pre-train; (2) with pre-train; (3) with temporal segment network. For spatial ConvNets, we plot three generated visualization as color images. For temporal ConvNets, we plot the flow maps of x (left) and y (right) directions in gray-scales. Note all these images are generated from purely random pixels

visual structure. With the knowledge transferred from the pre-training process, the spatial and temporal models are able to capture structured visual patterns.

It is also easy to notice that the models, trained with only short-term information such as single frames, tend to mistake the scenery patterns and objects in the videos as significant evidences for action recognition. For example, in the class "Diving", the single-frame spatial stream ConvNet mainly looks for water and diving platforms, other than the person performing diving. Its temporal stream counterpart, working on optical flow, tends to focus on the motion caused by waves of surface water. With long-term temporal modeling introduced by temporal segment network, it becomes obvious that learned models focus more on humans in the videos, and seem to be modeling the long-range structure of the action class. Still consider "Diving" as the example, the spatial ConvNet with temporal segment networknow generate a image that human is the major visual information. And different poses can be identified in the image, depicting various stages of one diving action. This suggests that models learned with the proposed method may perform better, which is well reflected in our quantitative experiments. We refer the reader to supplementary materials for visualization of more action classes and more details on the visualization process.

5   Conclusions

In this paper, we presented the Temporal Segment Network (TSN), a video-level framework that aims to model long-term temporal structure. As demonstrated on two challenging datasets, this work has brought the state of the art to a new level, while maintaining a reasonable computational cost. This is largely ascribed to the segmental architecture with sparse sampling, as well as a series of good practices that we explored in this work. The former provides an effective and efficient way to capture long-term temporal structure, while the latter makes it possible to train very deep networks on a limited training set without severe overfitting.

Acknowledgments. This work was supported by the *Big Data Collaboration Research* grant from SenseTime Group (CUHK Agreement No. TS1610626), Early Career Scheme (ECS) grant (No. 24204215), ERC Advanced Grant *VarCity* (No. 273940), Guangdong Innovative Research Program (2015B010129013, 2014B050 505017), and Shenzhen Research Program (KQCX2015033117354153, JSGG2015 0925164740726, CXZZ20150930104115529), and External Cooperation Program of BIC, Chinese Academy of Sciences (172644KYSB20150019).

References

1. Simonyan, K., Zisserman, A.: Two-stream convolutional networks for action recognition in videos. In: NIPS, pp. 568–576 (2014)
2. Wang, H., Schmid, C.: Action recognition with improved trajectories. In: ICCV, pp. 3551–3558 (2013)
3. Wang, L., Qiao, Y., Tang, X.: Motionlets: mid-level 3D parts for human motion recognition. In: CVPR, pp. 2674–2681 (2013)
4. Ng, J.Y.H., Hausknecht, M., Vijayanarasimhan, S., Vinyals, O., Monga, R., Toderici, G.: Beyond short snippets: deep networks for video classification. In: CVPR, pp. 4694–4702 (2015)
5. Wang, L., Qiao, Y., Tang, X.: Action recognition with trajectory-pooled deep-convolutional descriptors. In: CVPR, pp. 4305–4314 (2015)
6. Gan, C., Wang, N., Yang, Y., Yeung, D.Y., Hauptmann, A.G.: Devnet: a deep event network for multimedia event detection and evidence recounting. In: CVPR, pp. 2568–2577 (2015)
7. LeCun, Y., Bottou, L., Bengio, Y., Haffner, P.: Gradient-based learning applied to document recognition. Proc. IEEE **86**(11), 2278–2324 (1998)
8. Krizhevsky, A., Sutskever, I., Hinton, G.E.: ImageNet classification with deep convolutional neural networks. In: NIPS, pp. 1106–1114 (2012)
9. Simonyan, K., Zisserman, A.: Very deep convolutional networks for large-scale image recognition. In: ICLR, pp. 1–14 (2015)
10. Szegedy, C., Liu, W., Jia, Y., Sermanet, P., Reed, S., Anguelov, D., Erhan, D., Vanhoucke, V., Rabinovich, A.: Going deeper with convolutions. In: CVPR, pp. 1–9 (2015)
11. Xiong, Y., Zhu, K., Lin, D., Tang, X.: Recognize complex events from static images by fusing deep channels. In: CVPR, pp. 1600–1609 (2015)
12. Karpathy, A., Toderici, G., Shetty, S., Leung, T., Sukthankar, R., Fei-Fei, L.: Large-scale video classification with convolutional neural networks. In: CVPR, pp. 1725–1732 (2014)
13. Tran, D., Bourdev, L.D., Fergus, R., Torresani, L., Paluri, M.: Learning spatiotemporal features with 3D convolutional networks. In: ICCV, pp. 4489–4497 (2015)
14. Zhang, B., Wang, L., Wang, Z., Qiao, Y., Wang, H.: Real-time action recognition with enhanced motion vector CNNs. In: CVPR, pp. 2718–2726 (2016)

15. Niebles, J.C., Chen, C.-W., Fei-Fei, L.: Modeling temporal structure of decomposable motion segments for activity classification. In: Daniilidis, K., Maragos, P., Paragios, N. (eds.) ECCV 2010, Part II. LNCS, vol. 6312, pp. 392–405. Springer, Heidelberg (2010)
16. Gaidon, A., Harchaoui, Z., Schmid, C.: Temporal localization of actions with actoms. IEEE Trans. Pattern Anal. Mach. Intell. **35**(11), 2782–2795 (2013)
17. Wang, L., Qiao, Y., Tang, X.: Latent hierarchical model of temporal structure for complex activity classification. IEEE Trans. Image Process. **23**(2), 810–822 (2014)
18. Fernando, B., Gavves, E., O., MJ, Ghodrati, A., Tuytelaars, T.: Modeling video evolution for action recognition. In: CVPR, pp. 5378–5387 (2015)
19. Varol, G., Laptev, I., Schmid, C.: Long-term temporal convolutions for action recognition. CoRR abs/1604.04494 (2016)
20. Donahue, J., Anne Hendricks, L., Guadarrama, S., Rohrbach, M., Venugopalan, S., Saenko, K., Darrell, T.: Long-term recurrent convolutional networks for visual recognition and description. In: CVPR, pp. 2625–2634 (2015)
21. Soomro, K., Zamir, A.R., Shah, M.: UCF101: a dataset of 101 human actions classes from videos in the wild. CoRR abs/1212.0402 (2012)
22. Kuehne, H., Jhuang, H., Garrote, E., Poggio, T.A., Serre, T.: HMDB: a large video database for human motion recognition. In: ICCV, pp. 2556–2563 (2011)
23. Ioffe, S., Szegedy, C.: Batch normalization: accelerating deep network training by reducing internal covariate shift. In: ICML, pp. 448–456 (2015)
24. Gan, C., Yao, T., Yang, K., Yang, Y., Mei, T.: You lead, we exceed: labor-free video concept learning by jointly exploiting web videos and images. In: CVPR, pp. 923–932 (2016)
25. Peng, X., Wang, L., Wang, X., Qiao, Y.: Bag of visual words and fusion methods for action recognition: comprehensive study and good practice. Comput. Vis. Image Underst. **150**, 109–125 (2016)
26. Gan, C., Yang, Y., Zhu, L., Zhao, D., Zhuang, Y.: Recognizing an action using its name: a knowledge-based approach. Int. J. Comput. Vis. **120**(1), 61–77 (2016)
27. Ji, S., Xu, W., Yang, M., Yu, K.: 3D convolutional neural networks for human action recognition. IEEE Trans. Pattern Anal. Mach. Intell. **35**(1), 221–231 (2013)
28. Sun, L., Jia, K., Yeung, D., Shi, B.E.: Human action recognition using factorized spatio-temporal convolutional networks. In: ICCV, pp. 4597–4605 (2015)
29. Pirsiavash, H., Ramanan, D.: Parsing videos of actions with segmental grammars. In: CVPR, pp. 612–619 (2014)
30. Wang, L., Qiao, Y., Tang, X.: Video action detection with relational dynamic-poselets. In: Fleet, D., Pajdla, T., Schiele, B., Tuytelaars, T. (eds.) ECCV 2014, Part V. LNCS, vol. 8693, pp. 565–580. Springer, Heidelberg (2014)
31. Felzenszwalb, P.F., Girshick, R.B., McAllester, D.A., Ramanan, D.: Object detection with discriminatively trained part-based models. IEEE Trans. Pattern Anal. Mach. Intell. **32**(9), 1627–1645 (2010)
32. Zeiler, M.D., Fergus, R.: Visualizing and understanding convolutional networks. In: Fleet, D., Pajdla, T., Schiele, B., Tuytelaars, T. (eds.) ECCV 2014, Part I. LNCS, vol. 8689, pp. 818–833. Springer, Heidelberg (2014)
33. Deng, J., Dong, W., Socher, R., Li, L., Li, K., Li, F.: ImageNet: a large-scale hierarchical image database. In: CVPR, pp. 248–255 (2009)
34. Jiang, Y.G., Liu, J., Roshan Zamir, A., Laptev, I., Piccardi, M., Shah, M., Sukthankar, R.: THUMOS challenge: action recognition with a large number of classes (2013)

35. Zach, C., Pock, T., Bischof, H.: A duality based approach for realtime TV-L^1 optical flow. In: Hamprecht, F.A., Schnörr, C., Jähne, B. (eds.) DAGM 2007. LNCS, vol. 4713, pp. 214–223. Springer, Heidelberg (2007)
36. Jia, Y., Shelhamer, E., Donahue, J., Karayev, S., Long, J., Girshick, R.B., Guadarrama, S., Darrell, T.: Caffe: convolutional architecture for fast feature embedding. CoRR abs/1408.5093
37. Cai, Z., Wang, L., Peng, X., Qiao, Y.: Multi-view super vector for action recognition. In: CVPR, pp. 596–603 (2014)
38. Wang, H., Schmid, C.: LEAR-INRIA submission for the thumos workshop. In: ICCV Workshop on THUMOS Challenge, pp. 1–3 (2013)
39. Wang, L., Qiao, Y., Tang, X.: MoFAP: a multi-level representation for action recognition. Int. J. Comput. Vis. **119**(3), 254–271 (2016)
40. Ni, B., Moulin, P., Yang, X., Yan, S.: Motion part regularization: improving action recognition via trajectory group selection. In: CVPR, pp. 3698–3706 (2015)
41. Zhu, W., Hu, J., Sun, G., Cao, X., Qiao, Y.: A key volume mining deep framework for action recognition. In: CVPR, pp. 1991–1999 (2016)
42. GitHub: Deep draw. https://github.com/auduno/deepdraw

PlaNet - Photo Geolocation with Convolutional Neural Networks

Tobias Weyand[1(✉)], Ilya Kostrikov[2], and James Philbin[3]

[1] Google, Los Angeles, USA
weyand@google.com
[2] RWTH Aachen University, Aachen, Germany
ilya.kostrikov@rwth-aachen.de
[3] Zoox, Menlo Park, USA
philbinj@gmail.com

Abstract. Is it possible to determine the location of a photo from just its pixels? While the general problem seems exceptionally difficult, photos often contain cues such as landmarks, weather patterns, vegetation, road markings, or architectural details, which in combination allow to infer where the photo was taken. Previously, this problem has been approached using image retrieval methods. In contrast, we pose the problem as one of classification by subdividing the surface of the earth into thousands of multi-scale geographic cells, and train a deep network using millions of geotagged images. We show that the resulting model, called *PlaNet*, outperforms previous approaches and even attains superhuman accuracy in some cases. Moreover, we extend our model to photo albums by combining it with a long short-term memory (LSTM) architecture. By learning to exploit temporal coherence to geolocate uncertain photos, this model achieves a 50 % performance improvement over the single-image model.

1 Introduction

Photo geolocation is an extremely challenging task since many photos offer only few, possibly ambiguous, cues about their location. For instance, an image of a beach could be taken on many coasts across the world. Even when landmarks are present there can still be ambiguity: a photo of the Rialto Bridge could be taken either at its original location in Venice, Italy, or in Las Vegas which has a replica of the bridge! In the absence of discriminative landmarks, humans can fall back on their world knowledge and use cues like the language of street signs or the driving direction of cars to infer the location of a photo. Traditional computer vision algorithms typically lack this kind of world knowledge, relying on the features provided to them during training. Most previous work has therefore focused on restricted subsets of the problem, like landmark buildings [2,40,59], cities where street view imagery is available [10,29,57], or places with enough

---

I. Kostrikov and J. Philbin—Work done while at Google.

B. Leibe et al. (Eds.): ECCV 2016, Part VIII, LNCS 9912, pp. 37–55, 2016.
DOI: 10.1007/978-3-319-46484-8_3

photos to build structure-from-motion reconstructions that are used for pose estimation [34,44]. In contrast, our goal is to localize any type of photo taken at any location using just its pixels. Only few other works have addressed this task [19,20].

We treat the task of geolocation as a classification problem and subdivide the surface of the earth into a set of geographical cells which make up the target classes. We then train a convolutional neural network (CNN) [49] using millions of geotagged photos. Given a query photo, our model outputs a discrete probability distribution over the earth, assigning each geographical cell a likelihood that the input photo was taken inside it. The resulting model, which we call *PlaNet*, is capable of localizing a large variety of photos. Besides landmark buildings and street scenes, PlaNet can often predict the location of nature scenes like mountains, waterfalls or beaches, with surprising accuracy. In cases of ambiguity, it will often output a distribution with multiple modes corresponding to plausible locations (Fig. 1). Despite being a much simpler and less resource-intensive approach, PlaNet delivers comparable performance to Im2GPS [19,20] which shares a similar goal. A small-scale experiment shows that PlaNet even reaches superhuman performance at the task of geolocating street view scenes. Moreover, we show that the features learned by PlaNet can be used for image retrieval and achieve state-of-the-art results on the INRIA Holidays dataset [25]. Finally, we show that combining PlaNet with an LSTM approach enables it to use context to predict the locations of ambiguous photos, increasing its accuracy on photo albums by 50 %.

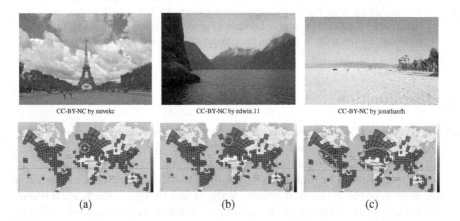

CC-BY-NC by stevekc   CC-BY-NC by edwin.11   CC-BY-NC by jonathanfh

(a)   (b)   (c)

Fig. 1. Given a query photo (top), PlaNet outputs a probability distribution over the surface of the earth (bottom). Viewing the task as a classification problem allows PlaNet to express its uncertainty about a photo. While the Eiffel Tower (a) is confidently assigned to Paris, the model believes that the fjord photo (b) could be taken in either New Zealand or Norway. For the beach photo (c), PlaNet assigns the highest probability to southern California (correct), but some probability is also assigned to places with similar beaches, like Mexico and the Mediterranean. (For visualization purposes we use a model with a much lower spatial resolution than our full model)

2 Related Work

Im2GPS [19,20] (*cf.* Sect. 3) matches a query photo against millions of geo-tagged Flickr photos using global image descriptors and assigns it the location of the closest match. Because photo coverage in rural areas is sparse, [35,36] make additional use of satellite *aerial imagery*. [36] use CNNs to learn a joint embedding for ground and aerial images and localize a query image by matching it against a database of aerial images. [53] take a similar approach and use a CNN to transform ground-level features to the feature space of aerial images. Local feature based *image retrieval* [38,48] is effective at matching buildings, but requires more space and lacks the invariance to match, *e.g.*, natural scenes or articulated objects. Most local feature based approaches therefore focus on local-ization within cities, using photos from photo sharing websites [8,39] or street view [4,10,29,30,46,56,57]. Skyline2GPS [41] matches the skyline captured by an upward-facing camera against a 3D model of the city. While matching against geotagged images can provide the rough location of a query photo, *pose estima-tion* approaches determine the exact 6-dof camera pose of a query image by registering it to a structure-from-motion model [8,23,33,34,43,45]. PoseNet [28] is a CNN that regresses from a query image to its 6-dof pose. However, because a structure-from-motion reconstruction is required for generating its training data, it is restricted to areas with dense enough photo coverage. *Landmark recognition systems* [2,16,24,40,59] construct a database of landmark buildings by cluster-ing internet photo collections and recognize the landmark in a query image using image retrieval. Instead, [7,32] recognize landmarks using SVMs trained on bags-of-visual-words of landmark clusters. [18] perform image geolocation by training one exemplar SVM for each image in a dataset of street view images. CNNs have previously been shown to work well for *scene recognition*. On the SUN database [54], Overfeat [47], a CNN trained on ImageNet [12], consistently outperforms other approaches, including global descriptors like GIST and local descriptors like SIFT, and training on the task-specific Places Database [60] yields another significant boost.

In Sect. 4, we extend PlaNet to geolocate sequences of images using LSTMs. [9,32] address this problem by first clustering the photo collection into landmarks and then learning to predict the sequence of landmarks in a photo sequence. While [9] estimate travel priors on a dataset of photo albums and use a Hidden Markov Model (HMM) to infer the location sequence, [32] train a structured SVM that uses temporal information as an additional feature. [27] also use an HMM, but instead of landmarks, their classes are a set of geographical cells par-titioning the surface of the earth, which is similar to our approach. [31] train a CNN on a large collection of geotagged Flickr photos to predict geographical attributes like "population", "elevation" or "household income". In summary, with few exceptions [19,20,35,36,53] most previous approaches to photo geolo-cation are restricted to urban areas which are densely covered by street view imagery and tourist photos. Prior work has shown that CNNs are well-suited for scene classification [54] and geographical attribute prediction [31], but to our knowledge ours is the first method that directly takes a classification approach to geolocation using CNNs.

3   Image Geolocation with CNNs

We pose the task of image geolocation as a classification problem and subdivide the earth into a set of geographical cells making up the target classes. The training input to the CNN are the image pixels and the target output is a one-hot vector encoding the cell containing the image. Given a test image, the output of this model is a probability distribution over the world. The advantage of this formulation over a regression from pixels to geo-coordinates is that the model can express its uncertainty about an image by assigning each cell a confidence. A regression model would be forced to pinpoint a single location and would have no natural way of expressing uncertainty, especially in the presence of multi-modal answers (as are expected in this task).

Adaptive Partitioning using S2 Cells. We use Google's open source S2 geometry library[1] to partition the surface of the earth into non-overlapping cells that define the classes of our model. The S2 library defines a hierarchical partitioning of the surface of a sphere by projecting the surfaces of an enclosing cube on it. The six sides of the cube are subdivided hierarchically by six quad-trees. A node in a quad-tree defines a region on the sphere called an S2 cell. Figure 4 illustrates this in 2D. We chose this subdivision scheme over a simple subdivision of lat/lon coordinates, because (i) lat/lon regions get elongated near the poles while S2 cells keep a close-to-quadratic shape, and (ii) S2 cells have mostly uniform size (the ratio between the largest and smallest S2 cell is 2.08).

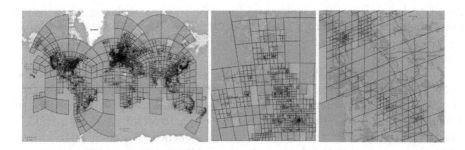

Fig. 2. Left: Adaptive partitioning of the world into 26,263 S2 cells. Middle, Right: Detail views of Great Britain and Ireland and the San Francisco bay area

A naive approach to define a tiling of the earth would use all S2 cells at a certain fixed depth in the hierarchy, resulting in a set of roughly equally sized cells (see Fig. 1). However, this would produce a very imbalanced class distribution since the geographical distribution of photos has strong peaks in densely

---
[1] https://code.google.com/p/s2-geometry-library/, https://goo.gl/vKikP6.

populated areas. We therefore perform adaptive subdivision based on the photos' geotags: starting at the roots, we recursively descend each quad-tree and subdivide cells until no cell contains more than a certain fixed number t_1 of photos. This way, sparsely populated areas are covered by larger cells and densely populated areas are covered by finer cells. Then, we discard all cells containing less than a minimum of t_2 photos. Therefore, PlaNet does not cover areas where photos are very unlikely to be taken, such as oceans or poles. We remove all images from the training set that are in any of the discarded cells. This adaptive tiling has several advantages over a uniform one: (i) training classes are more balanced, (ii) it makes effective use of the parameter space because more model capacity is spent on densely populated areas, (iii) the model can reach up to street-level accuracy in city areas where cells are small. Figure 2 shows the S2 partitioning for our dataset.

CNN Training. We train a CNN based on the Inception architecture [49] with batch normalization [22]. The SoftMax output layer has one output for each S2 cell in the partitioning. We set the target output to 1.0 for the S2 cell containing the training image and set all others to 0.0. We initialize the model weights with random values and train to minimize the cross-entropy loss using AdaGrad [14] with a learning rate of 0.045.

Our dataset consists of 126M photos with Exif geolocations mined from all over the web. We applied very little filtering, only excluding images that are non-photos (like diagrams, clip-art, etc.) and porn. Our dataset is therefore extremely noisy, including indoor photos, portraits, photos of pets, food, products and other photos not indicative of location. Moreover, the Exif geolocations may be incorrect by several hundred meters due to noise. We split the dataset into 91M training images and 34M validation images.

For the adaptive S2 cell partitioning (Sect. 3) we set $t_1 = 10,000$ and $t_2 = 50$, resulting in $26,263$ S2 cells (Fig. 2). Our Inception model has a total of 97,321,048 parameters. We train the model for 2.5 months on 200 CPU cores using the DistBelief framework [11] until the accuracy on the validation set converges. The long training time is due to the large variety of the training data and the large number of classes.

To ensure that none of the test sets we use in this paper have any ll(near-) duplicate images in the training set, we use a CNN trained on near-duplicate images to compute a binary embedding for each training and test image and then remove test images whose Hamming distance to a training image is below an aggressively chosen threshold.

Geolocation Accuracy. We collected a test dataset of 2.3M geotagged Flickr photos from across the world. Other than selecting geotagged images with 1 to 5 textual tags, we did not apply any filtering. Therefore, most of the images have little to no cues about their location. Figure 5 shows example images that illustrate how challenging this benchmark is. We measure localization error as the distance between the center of the predicted S2 cell to the original photo location. We note that this error measure is pessimistic, because even if the ground truth location is within the predicted cell, the error can still be large

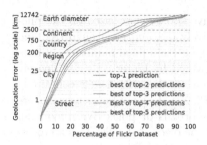

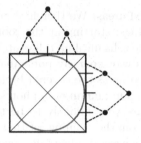

Fig. 3. Geolocation accuracy of the top-k most confident predictions on 2.3M Flickr photos. (Lower right is best) (Color figure online)

Fig. 4. S2 cell quantization in 2D. The sides of the square are subdivided recursively and projected onto the circle

Fig. 5. Example images drawn randomly from the Flickr test set

depending on the cell size. Figure 3 shows what fraction of this dataset was localized within a certain geographical distance of the ground truth locations. The blue curve shows the performance for the most confident prediction, and the other curves show the performance for the best of the top-{2,3,4,5} predictions per image. Following [20], we added approximate geographical scales of streets, cities, regions, countries and continents. Despite the difficulty of the data, PlaNet is able to localize 3.6 % of the images at street-level accuracy and 10.1 % at city-level accuracy. 28.4 % of the photos are correctly localized at country level and 48.0 % at continent level. When considering the best of the top-5 predictions, the model localizes roughly twice as many images correctly at street, city, region and country level.

Qualitative Results. An important advantage of our localization-as-classification paradigm is that the model output is a probability distribution over the globe. This way, even if an image cannot be confidently localized, the model outputs confidences for possible locations. To illustrate this, we trained a smaller model using only S2 cells at level 4 in the S2 hierarchy, resulting in a total of only 354 S2 cells. Figure 1 shows the predictions of this model for test images with different levels of geographical ambiguity.

Figure 6 shows examples of the different types of images PlaNet can localize. Besides landmarks, which can also be recognized by landmark recognition engines [2,40,59], PlaNet can often correctly localize street scenes, landscapes, buildings of characteristic architecture, locally typical objects like red phone booths, and even some plants and animals. Figure 7 shows some failure modes. Misclassifications often occur due to ambiguity, *e.g.*, because certain landscapes

Fig. 6. Examples of images PlaNet localizes correctly. Our model is capable of localizing photos of famous landmarks (top row), but often yields surprisingly accurate results for images with more subtle geographical cues. The model learns to recognize locally typical landscapes, objects, architectural styles and even plants and animals (Color figure online)

or objects occur in multiple places, or are more typical for a certain place than the one the photo was taken (*e.g.*, the Chevrolet Fleetmaster in the first image is mostly found in Cuba nowadays). To give a visual impression of the representations PlaNet has learned for individual S2 cells, Fig. 8 shows the test images that the model assigns to a given cell with the highest confidence. The model learns a very diverse visual representation of each place, assigning highest confidence to the landmarks, landscapes, or animals that are typical for a specific region.

Comparison to Im2GPS. One of the few approaches that, like ours, aims at geolocating arbitrary photos is Im2GPS [19,20]. However, instead of classification, Im2GPS is based on nearest neighbor matching. The original Im2GPS approach [19] matches the query image against a database of 6.5M Flickr images and returns the geolocation of the closest matching image. Images are represented by a combination of six different global image descriptors. The data was collected by downloading Flickr images that have GPS coordinates and whose

Fig. 7. Examples of incorrectly localized images

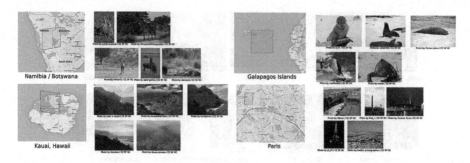

Fig. 8. The top-5 most confident images from the Flickr dataset for the S2 cells on the left, showing the diverse visual representation of places that PlaNet learns

tags contain certain geographic keywords including city, country, territory and continent names. To filter out irrelevant content, images tagged with keywords such as "birthday" or "concert" were removed.

A recent extension of Im2GPS [20] uses both an improved image representation and a more sophisticated localization technique. It estimates a per-pixel probability of being "ground", "vertical", "sky", or "porous" and computes color and texture histograms for each of these classes. Additionally, bag-of-visual-word vectors of length 1k and 50k based on SIFT features are computed for each image. The geolocation of a query is estimated by retrieving nearest neighbors, geo-clustering them with mean shift, training 1-vs.-all SVMs for each resulting cluster, and finally picking the average GPS coordinate of the cluster whose SVM gives the query image the highest positive score.

In contrast, PlaNet is a much simpler pipeline. We performed only little filtering to create our input dataset (see above), localization is performed as a straightforward n-way classification, and image features are jointly learned with the classifier parameters during the training process instead of being hand-engineered.

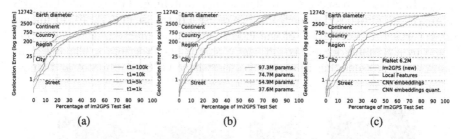

Fig. 9. (a) Performance for different resolutions of S2 discretization representing different tradeoffs between the number of classes and the number of training images per class (Table 1b). (b) Performance for different numbers of model parameters. The full model has 97.3M parameters. (c) Comparison of PlaNet with image retrieval based on local features and CNN embeddings

Table 1. (a) Comparison of PlaNet with Im2GPS. Percentages are the fraction of images from the Im2GPS test set that were localized within the given radius. (Numbers for the original Im2GPS are approximate as they were extracted from a plot in the paper.) (b) Parameters of PlaNet models with different spatial resolutions

(a)

Method	Street 1 km	City 25 km	Region 200 km	Country 750 km	Continent 2500 km
Im2GPS (orig) [19]		12.0 %	15.0 %	23.0 %	47.0 %
Im2GPS (new) [20]	2.5 %	21.9 %	32.1 %	35.4 %	51.9 %
PlaNet (900k)	0.4 %	3.8 %	7.6 %	21.6 %	43.5 %
PlaNet (6.2M)	6.3 %	18.1 %	30.0 %	45.6 %	65.8 %
PlaNet (91M)	**8.4 %**	**24.5 %**	**37.6 %**	**53.6 %**	**71.3 %**

(b)

t_1	#classes	med. imgs per class	#model
100k	214	21,039	23.9M
10k	2,056	2,140	29.1M
5k	3,852	1,225	34.2M
1k	16,307	320	69.3M

We evaluate PlaNet on the Im2GPS test dataset [19] that consists of 237 geotagged photos from Flickr, curated such that most photos contain at least a few geographical cues. Table 1a compares the performance of three versions of PlaNet trained with different amounts of training data to both versions of Im2GPS. The new Im2GPS version is a significant improvement over the old one. However, the full PlaNet model outperforms even the new version with a considerable margin. In particular, PlaNet localizes 236 % more images accurately at street level. The gap narrows at coarser scales, but even at country level PlaNet still localizes 51 % more images accurately. The 'PlaNet 6.2M' model is more directly comparable to Im2GPS, which uses a database of 6.5M images. While Im2GPS wins on city and region levels, 'PlaNet 6.2M' still outperforms Im2GPS on street, country and continent levels. Using similar amounts of input data, PlaNet shows performance comparable to Im2GPS. However, we note that Im2GPS has an advantage over PlaNet in this experiment, because PlaNet's training set comes from random websites and is thus much more noisy and of lower quality than the Flickr images Im2GPS uses (Flickr is targeted at amateur and professional photographers and thus hosts mainly high quality images). Moreover, because Im2GPS is based on Flickr photos, it has an advantage on this test set which is also mined from Flickr. PlaNet's training data are general web photos which have a different geographical distribution and a higher fraction of irrelevant images with no geographical cues (Fig. 5).

Regardless of accuracy, PlaNet has several advantages over Im2GPS: PlaNet is a single model trained end-to-end, while Im2GPS is a manually engineered pipeline that uses a carefully selected set of features. Furthermore, PlaNet uses much less resources than Im2GPS: Since the Im2GPS feature vectors have a dimensionality of 100,000, Im2GPS would require 8.3 TB to represent our corpus of 91M training examples (577 GB for 6.2M images), assuming one byte per descriptor dimension. In contrast, PlaNet uses only 377 MB, which even fits into the memory of a smartphone.

Effect of S2 Discretization. An important meta-parameter of PlaNet is the resolution of the S2 cell discretization. A finer discretization means that the number of target classes increases, while the number of training examples per class decreases. At the same time, the number of model parameters increases due to the final fully-connected layer. We trained models with different levels of discretization by varying the t_1 parameter that determines the maximum number of images in a cell, while leaving t_2 fixed at 50 images. We used the same subset of 6.2M training images we used above for comparability with Im2GPS. Table 1b shows the parameters of the different models used and Fig. 9a shows the results. As expected, the lower the resolution, the fewer images can be localized at street accuracy. Interestingly, while the 1k model performs similar to the 5k model at region level and above, it performs significantly better at street level, localizing 4.2 % of the images correctly, while the 5k model only localizes 1.3 % of images at street level. This is surprising since this model has the highest number of parameters and the lowest number of training images per class, making it prone to overfitting. However, it still performs well since the images it can localize at street level are from dense city centers with a fine S2 discretization, where sufficient training examples exist.

Effect of Model Size. To analyze how many model parameters are required, we trained models with reduced numbers of parameters. As Fig. 9b shows, a model with 74.7M parameters performs almost as well as the full model which has 97.3M parameters, but when reducing the number of parameters further, performance starts to degrade.

(a)   (b)   (c)

Fig. 10. Left: Input image, right: Heatmap of the probability of the correct class when sliding an occluding window over the image [58]. (a) Grand Canyon - Occluding the region containing the distinctive mountain formation makes the confidence in the correct location drop the most. (b) Norway - The snowy mountain range on the left is the most important cue. (c) Hong Kong - Confidence in the correct location *increases* if the palm trees in the foreground are covered since they are not typical for Hong Kong

Comparison to Image Retrieval. We compare the PlaNet 6.2M model with two image retrieval baselines that assign each query photo the location of the closest matching image from the PlaNet 6.2M training data (Fig. 9c). *'Local Features'* retrieves images using an inverted index and spatially verifies tentative matches [39,48]. *'CNN embeddings'* represents each image as a 256 byte vector extracted with a CNN trained on a landmark dataset using the triplet loss [52]. Matching is performed w.r.t. the L_2 distance. 'Local Features' work well on rigid objects like landmarks, but fail to match, similar scenes, causing its low recall. 'CNN embeddings' outperform PlaNet at street level (9.28 % vs. 6.33 %), but fall behind at region level (23.63 % vs. 29.96 %) and above. PlaNet's disadvantage on street level is that its geolocations are quantized into cells, while the retrieval model can use the exact geolocations. Using the same quantization for retrieval (*'CNN embeddings quant.'*) has the same performance as PlaNet on street and city level. This suggests that both retrieval and classification are well-suited for recognizing specific locations inside cities, but classification seems more suitable for recognizing generic scenes and subtle location cues. We also note that the embeddings use 1.5 GB for 6.2M images and would use 21.7 GB for the full 91M images while the PlaNet model uses only 377 MB regardless of the amount of training data.

Model Analysis. To analyze which parts of the input image are most important for the classifier's decision, we employ a method introduced by Zeiler *et al.* [58]. We plot an activation map where the value of each pixel is the classifier's confidence in the ground truth geolocation if the corresponding part of the image is occluded by a gray box (Fig. 10). The first two examples show that the image regions that would be most useful for a human are also most important for the decision of the model. However, as the last example shows, the model can also be fooled by misleading cues.

Comparison to Human Performance. To find out how PlaNet compares with human intuition, we let it compete against 10 well-traveled human subjects in a game of Geoguessr (www.geoguessr.com). Geoguessr presents the player with a random street view panorama (sampled from all street view panoramas across the world) and asks them to place a marker on a map at the panorama' location. We used the game's "challenge mode" where two players are shown the same set of 5 panoramas. We entered the PlaNet guesses manually by running inference on a screenshot of the view presented by the game and entering the center of the highest confidence S2 cell as its guess. We did not allow the human players to pan, zoom or navigate, so they did not use more information than the model. For each player we used a different set of panoramas, so humans and PlaNet played a total of 50 different rounds. PlaNet won 28 of the 50 rounds with a median localization error of 1131.7 km, while the median human localization error was 2320.75 km. Neither humans nor PlaNet were able to localize photos below street or city level, showing that this task was even harder than the Flickr dataset and the Im2GPS dataset. PlaNet was able to localize twice as many photos at region level (4 vs. 2), 1.54× as many photos at country level (17 vs. 11), and 1.23× as many photos at continent level (32 vs. 26). Figure 11 shows example panoramas with the guessed locations. Most panoramas were taken in rural areas containing little to no geographical cues.

When asked what cues they used, human subjects said they looked for any type of signs, the types of vegetation, the architectural style, the color of lane

Fig. 11. Top: GeoGuessr panorama, Bottom: Ground truth location (yellow), human guess (green), PlaNet guess (blue) (Color figure online)

markings and the direction of traffic on the street. Furthermore, humans knew that street view is not available in certain countries such as China allowing them to further narrow down their guesses. One would expect that these cues, especially street signs, together with world knowledge and common sense should give humans an unfair advantage over PlaNet, which was trained solely on images and geolocations. Yet, PlaNet was able to outperform humans by a considerable margin. For example, PlaNet localized 17 panoramas at country granularity (750 km) while humans only localized 11 panoramas within this radius. We think PlaNet has an advantage over humans because it has seen many more places than any human can ever visit and has learned subtle cues of different scenes that are even hard for a well-traveled human to distinguish.

Features for Image Retrieval. A recent study [42] showed that the activations of Overfeat [47], a CNN trained on ImageNet [12] can serve as powerful features for several computer vision tasks, including image retrieval. Since PlaNet was trained for location recognition, its features should be particularly suited for image retrieval of touristic photos. To test this, we evaluate the PlaNet features on the INRIA Holidays dataset [25], consisting of 1,491 personal holiday photos, including landmarks, cities and natural scenes and the and Oxford5k dataset [39], consisting of 5,062 images of historic buildings in Oxford. We extract image embeddings from the final layer below the SoftMax layer (a 2048-dim. vector) and rank images by the L_2 distance between their embedding vectors. As can be seen in Table 2a, the PlaNet features outperform the Overfeat features. Using the *spatial search* and *augmentation* techniques described in [42], PlaNet even outperforms state-of-the-art local feature based image retrieval approaches on the Holidays dataset. PlaNet is not as competitive on Oxford since the query images of this dataset are small cut-out image regions, requiring highly scale-invariant matching, which gives local feature based approaches an advantage. We note that the Euclidean distance between these image embeddings is not necessarily meaningful as PlaNet was trained for classification. We expect Euclidean embeddings trained for image retrieval using a triplet loss [52] to deliver even higher mAP.

Table 2. (a) Image retrieval mAP using PlaNet features compared to other methods. (b) Results of PlaNet LSTM on Google+ photo albums. Percentages are the fraction of images in the dataset localized within the respective distance

(a)

Method	Holidays	Oxford
BoVW	57.2 [26]	38.4 [26]
Hamming Embedding	77.5 [26]	56.1 [26]
Fine Vocabulary	74.9 [37]	74.2 [37]
ASMK+MA	82.2 [51]	**81.7** [51]
GIST	37.6 [13]	
Overfeat	64.2 [42]	32.2 [42]
Overfeat+aug+ss	84.3 [42]	68.0 [42]
AlexNet+LM Retraining	79.3 [6]	54.5 [6]
CNN+aug+ss	**90.0** [3]	79.0 [3]
Aggr. local CNN features	80.2 [5]	58.9 [5]
Pooled CNN features+QE		66.9 [50]
NetVLAD	83.1 [1]	71.6 [1]
NBNN on CNN features	88.7 [55]	
PlaNet (this work)	73.3	34.9
PlaNet+aug+ss	89.9	

(b)

Method	Street 1 km	City 25 km	Region 200 km	Country 750 km	Continent 2500 km
PlaNet	14.9 %	20.3 %	27.4 %	42.0 %	61.8 %
PlaNet avg	22.2 %	35.6 %	51.4 %	68.6 %	82.7 %
PlaNet HMM	23.3 %	34.3 %	47.1 %	63.2 %	79.5 %
LSTM	32.0 %	42.1 %	57.9 %	75.5 %	87.9 %
LSTM off1	30.9 %	41.0 %	56.9 %	74.5 %	85.4 %
LSTM off2	29.9 %	40.0 %	55.8 %	73.4 %	85.9 %
LSTM rep	**34.5 %**	**45.6 %**	**62.6 %**	**79.3 %**	**90.5 %**
LSTM rep 25	28.3 %	37.5 %	49.9 %	68.9 %	82.0 %
BLSTM 25	**33.0 %**	**43.0 %**	**56.7 %**	**73.2 %**	**86.1 %**

4   Sequence Geolocation with LSTMs

While PlaNet is capable of localizing a large variety of images, many images are ambiguous or do not contain enough information that would allow to localize them. However we can exploit the fact that photos naturally occur in sequences, *e.g.*, photo albums, with a high geographical correlation. Intuitively, if we can confidently localize some of the photos in an album, we can use this information to also localize the photos with uncertain location. Assigning each photo in an album a location is a sequence-to-sequence problem which requires a model that accumulates a state from previously seen examples and makes the decision for the current example based on both the state and the current example. Therefore, long-short term memory (LSTM) architectures [21] seem like a good fit for this task. Moreover, using LSTMs allows us to express the entire pipeline as a single neural network. While previous works [9,27] have used HMMs, our results indicate that LSTMs are better suited for this problem.

Training Data and Model Architecture. We collected a dataset of 29.7M public photo albums with geotags from Google+, which we split into 23.5M training albums (490M images) and 6.2M testing albums (126M) images. We use the S2 quantization scheme from the previous section. The basic structure of our model is as follows (Fig. 12a): Given an image, we extract an embedding vector from the final layer before the SoftMax layer in PlaNet. This vector is fed into the LSTM unit. The output vector of the LSTM is then fed into a SoftMax layer that performs the classification into S2 cells. We feed the images of an album into the model in chronological order. For the Inception part, we re-use the parameters of the single-image model. During training, we keep the Inception part fixed and only train the LSTM units and the SoftMax layer.

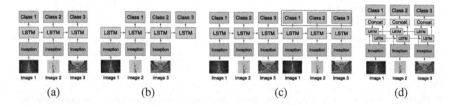

(a)   (b)   (c)   (d)

Fig. 12. Time-unrolled diagrams of the PlaNet LSTM models. (a) Basic model. (b) Label offset. (c) Repeated sequence. The first pass is used to generate the state inside the LSTM, so we only use the predictions of the second pass (red box). (d) Bi-directional LSTM (Color figure online)

Results. We compare our LSTM results to three baselines: *'PlaNet'* is our single-image model, *'PlaNet avg'* assigns each image in the album the average of the confidences of the single-image model, *'PlaNet HMM'* is a Hidden Markov Model on top of PlaNet. Like [9,27], we estimate the HMM class priors and transition probabilities by counting and compute the emission probabilities by applying Bayes' rule to the class posterior probabilities of PlaNet. Unlike [27], we do not incorporate time or distance into the transition probability, but use a much finer spatial resolution (26,263 bins vs. 3,186 bins). We determine the maximum likelihood state sequence using the Viterbi algorithm.

The results are shown in Table 2b. 'PlaNet avg' already yields a significant improvement over single-image PlaNet (49.0 % relative on street level), since it transfers more confident predictions to ambiguous images. Interestingly, the HMM does not perform much better than the simple averaging approach. This is surprising since 'PlaNet avg' predicts the same location for all images. However, its advantage over HMMs is that it sees the whole sequence, while the HMM only uses the images before the current one.

The LSTM model clearly outperforms the averaging and HMM (44.1 % and 37.3 % relative improvement over single-image on the street level, respectively).

Visual inspection of results showed that if an image with high location confidence is followed by several images with lower location confidence, the LSTM model assigns the low-confidence images locations close to the high-confidence image. Thus, while the original PlaNet model tends to "jump around", the LSTM model tends to predict close-by locations unless there is strong evidence of a location change. The LSTM model outperforms the averaging baseline because averaging assigns all images in an album the same confidences and can thus not produce accurate predictions for albums that include different locations (such as albums of trips). The LSTM model outperforms the HMM model, because it is able to capture long-term relationships. For example, at a given photo, HMMs will assign high transition probabilities to all neighboring locations due to the Markov assumption, while LSTMs are capable of learning specific tourist routes conditioned on previous locations. A problem with this simple LSTM model is that many albums contain a number of images in the beginning that contain no helpful visual information. Due to its unidirectional nature, this model cannot fix wrong predictions that occur in the beginning of the sequence after observing a photo with a confident location. For this reason, we now evaluate a model where the LSTM ingests multiple photos from the album before making its first prediction.

Label Offset. The idea of this model is to shift the labels such that inference is postponed for several time steps (Fig. 12b) The main motivation under this idea is that this model can accumulate information from several images in a sequence before making predictions. Nevertheless, we found that using offsets does not improve localization accuracy (Table 2b, LSTM off1, LSTM off2). We assume this is because the mapping from input image to output labels becomes more complex, making prediction more difficult for all photos, while improving predictions just for a limited amount of photos. Moreover, this approach does not solve the problem universally: For example, if we offset the label by 2 steps, but the first image with high location confidence occurs only after 3 steps, the prediction for the first image will likely still be wrong. To fix this, we now consider models that condition their predictions on all images in the sequence instead of only previous ones.

Repeated Sequences. We first evaluate a model that was trained on sequences that had been constructed by concatenating two instances of the same sequence (Fig. 12c) For this model, we take predictions only for the images from the second half of the sequence (*i.e.* the repeated part). Thus, all predictions are conditioned on observations from all images. At inference time, passing the sequence to the model for the first time can be viewed as an *encoding* stage where the LSTM builds up an internal state based on the images. The second pass is the *decoding* stage where the LSTM makes predictions based on its state and the current image. Results show that this approach outperforms the single-pass LSTMs (Table 2b, 'LSTM rep'), achieving a 7.8 % relative improvement at street level, at the cost of a twofold increase in inference time. However, visual inspection showed a problem with this approach: if there are low-confidence images at the beginning of the sequence, they tend to get assigned to the last confident location in the sequence, because the model learns to rely on its previous prediction. Therefore, predictions from the end of the sequence get carried over to the beginning.

Bi-directional LSTM. A well-known neural network architecture that conditions the predictions on the whole sequence are bi-directional LSTM (BLSTM) [17]. This model can be seen as a concatenation of two LSTM models, where the first one does a forward pass, while the second does a backward pass on a sequence (Fig. 12d). Bi-directional LSTMs cannot be trained with truncated back-propagation through time [15] and thus require to unroll the LSTMs to the full length of the sequence. To reduce the computational cost of training, we had to limit the length of the sequences to 25 images. This causes a decrease in total accuracy since longer albums typically yield higher accuracy than shorter ones. Since our experiments on this data are not directly comparable to the previous ones, we also evaluate the repeated LSTM model on sequences truncated to 25 images. As the results show (Table 2b: 'LSTM rep 25', 'BLSTM 25'), BLSTMs clearly outperform repeated LSTMs (16.6 % relative improvement on street level). However, because they are not tractable for long sequences, the repeated model might still be preferable in practice.

5   Conclusion

We presented PlaNet, a CNN for image geolocation. Regarding the problem as one of classification, PlaNet produces a probability distribution over the globe. This allows it to express its uncertainty about the location of a photo and assign probability mass to potential locations. While previous work mainly focused on photos taken inside cities, PlaNet is able to localize landscapes, locally typical objects, and even plants and animals. Our experiments show that PlaNet far outperforms other methods for geolocation of generic photos and even reaches superhuman performance. We further extended PlaNet to photo album geolocation by combining it with LSTMs, achieving 50 % higher performance than the single-image model.

References

1. Arandjelovic, R., Gronat, P., Torii, A., Pajdla, T., Sivic, J.: NetVLAD: CNN architecture for weakly supervised place recognition. In: CVPR (2016)
2. Avrithis, Y., Kalantidis, Y., Tolias, G., Spyrou, E.: Retrieving landmark and non-landmark images from community photo collections. In: ACM Multimedia, pp. 153–162 (2010)
3. Azizpour, H., Razavian, A.S., Sullivan, J., Maki, A., Carlsson, S.: From generic to specific deep representations for visual recognition. In: CVPR DeepVision Workshop (2015)
4. Baatz, G., Köser, K., Chen, D., Grzeszczuk, R., Pollefeys, M.: Handling urban location recognition as a 2D homothetic problem. In: Daniilidis, K., Maragos, P., Paragios, N. (eds.) ECCV 2010, Part VI. LNCS, vol. 6316, pp. 266–279. Springer, Heidelberg (2010)

5. Babenko, A., Lempitsky, V.: Aggregating local deep features for image retrieval. In: ICCV (2015)
6. Babenko, A., Slesarev, A., Chigorin, A., Lempitsky, V.: Neural codes for image retrieval. In: Fleet, D., Pajdla, T., Schiele, B., Tuytelaars, T. (eds.) ECCV 2014, Part I. LNCS, vol. 8689, pp. 584–599. Springer, Heidelberg (2014)
7. Bergamo, A., Sinha, S.N., Torresani, L.: Leveraging structure from motion to learn discriminative codebooks for scalable landmark classification. In: CVPR, pp. 763–770 (2013)
8. Cao, S., Snavely, N.: Graph-based discriminative learning for location recognition. IJCV **112**(2), 239–254 (2015)
9. Chen, C.Y., Grauman, K.: Clues from the beaten path: location estimation with bursty sequences of tourist photos. In: CVPR (2011)
10. Chen, D., Baatz, G., Köser, K., Tsai, S., Vedantham, R., Pylvänäinen, T., Roimela, K., Chen, X., Bach, J., Pollefeys, M., Girod, B., Grzeszczuk, R.: City-scale landmark identification on mobile devices. In: CVPR, pp. 737–744 (2011)
11. Dean, J., Corrado, G.S., Monga, R., Chen, K., Devin, M., Le, Q.V., Mao, M.Z., Ranzato, M., Senior, A., Tucker, P., Yang, K., Ng, A.Y.: Large scale distributed deep networks. In: NIPS (2012)
12. Deng, J., Dong, W., Socher, R., Li, L.J., Li, K., Fei-Fei, L.: ImageNet: a large-scale hierarchical image database. In: CVPR (2009)
13. Douze, M., Jégou, H., Harsimrat, S., Amsaleg, L., Schmid, C.: Evaluation of GIST descriptors for web-scale image search. In: CIVR (2009)
14. Duchi, J., Hazan, E., Singer, Y.: Adaptive subgradient methods for online learning and stochastic optimization. JMLR **12**, 2121–2159 (2011)
15. Elman, J.: Finding structure in time. Cogn. Sci. **14**(2), 179–211 (1990)
16. Gammeter, S., Quack, T., Van Gool, L.: I know what you did last summer: object-level auto-annotation of holiday snaps. In: ICCV, pp. 614–621 (2009)
17. Graves, A., Schmidthuber, J.: Framewise phoneme classification with bidirectional LSTM and other neural network architectures. Neural Netw. **18**(5–6), 602–610 (2005)
18. Gronat, P., Obozinski, G., Sivic, J., Pajdla, T.: Learning per-location classifiers for visual place recognition. In: CVPR (2013)
19. Hays, J., Efros, A.: IM2GPS: estimating geographic information from a single image. In: CVPR (2008)
20. Hays, J., Efros, A.: Large-scale image geolocalization. In: Choi, J., Friedland, G. (eds.) Multimodal Location Estimation of Videos and Images, pp. 41–62. Springer, Cham (2014)
21. Hochreiter, S., Schmidthuber, J.: Long short-term memory. Neural Comput. **9**(8), 1735–1780 (1997)
22. Ioffe, S., Szegedy, C.: Batch normalization: accelerating deep network training by reducing internal covariate shift. In: ICML (2015)
23. Irschara, A., Zach, C., Frahm, J.M., Bischof, H.: From structure-from-motion point clouds to fast location recognition. In: CVPR (2009)
24. Johns, E., Yang, G.Z.: From images to scenes: compressing an image cluster into a single scene model for place recognition. In: ICCV, pp. 874–881 (2011)
25. Jegou, H., Douze, M., Schmid, C.: Hamming embedding and weak geometric consistency for large scale image search. In: Forsyth, D., Torr, P., Zisserman, A. (eds.) ECCV 2008, Part I. LNCS, vol. 5302, pp. 304–317. Springer, Heidelberg (2008)
26. Jégou, H., Douze, M., Schmid, C.: Improving bag-of-features for large scale image search. IJCV **87**(3), 316–336 (2010)

27. Kalogerakis, E., Vesselova, O., Hays, J., Efros, A., Hertzmann, A.: Image sequence geolocation with human travel priors. In: ICCV (2009)
28. Kendall, A., Grimes, M., Cipolla, R.: PoseNet: a convolutional network for real-time 6-DOF camera relocalization. In: ICCV (2015)
29. Kim, H.J., Dunn, E., Frahm, J.M.: Predicting good features for image geo-localization using per-bundle VLAD. In: ICCV (2015)
30. Knopp, J., Sivic, J., Pajdla, T.: Avoiding confusing features in place recognition. In: Daniilidis, K., Maragos, P., Paragios, N. (eds.) ECCV 2010, Part I. LNCS, vol. 6311, pp. 748–761. Springer, Heidelberg (2010)
31. Lee, S., Zhang, H., Crandall, D.J.: Predicting geo-informative attributes in large-scale image collections using convolutional neural networks. In: WACV (2015)
32. Li, Y., Crandall, D.J., Huttenlocher, D.P.: Landmark classification in large-scale image collections. In: ICCV, pp. 1957–1964 (2009)
33. Li, Y., Snavely, N., Huttenlocher, D.P.: Location recognition using prioritized feature matching. In: Daniilidis, K., Maragos, P., Paragios, N. (eds.) ECCV 2010, Part II. LNCS, vol. 6312, pp. 791–804. Springer, Heidelberg (2010)
34. Li, Y., Snavely, N., Huttenlocher, D., Fua, P.: Worldwide pose estimation using 3D point clouds. In: Fitzgibbon, A., Lazebnik, S., Perona, P., Sato, Y., Schmid, C. (eds.) ECCV 2012, Part I. LNCS, vol. 7572, pp. 15–29. Springer, Heidelberg (2012)
35. Lin, T.Y., Belongie, S., Hays, J.: Cross-view image geolocalization. In: CVPR (2013)
36. Lin, T.Y., Cui, Y., Belongie, S., Hays, J.: Learning deep representations for ground-to-aerial geolocalization. In: CVPR (2015)
37. Mikulík, A., Perdoch, M., Chum, O., Matas, J.: Learning a fine vocabulary. In: Daniilidis, K., Maragos, P., Paragios, N. (eds.) ECCV 2010. LNCS, vol. 6313, pp. 1–14. Springer, Heidelberg (2010). doi:10.1007/978-3-642-15558-1_1
38. Nistér, D., Stewénius, H.: Scalable recognition with a vocabulary tree. In: CVPR, pp. 2161–2168 (2006)
39. Philbin, J., Chum, O., Isard, M., Sivic, J., Zisserman, A.: Object retrieval with large vocabularies and fast spatial matching. In: CVPR (2007)
40. Quack, T., Leibe, B., Van Gool, L.: World-scale mining of objects and events from community photo collections. In: CIVR, pp. 47–56 (2008)
41. Ramalingam, S., Bouaziz, S., Sturm, P., Brand, M.: SKYLINE2GPS: localization in urban canyons using omni-skylines. In: IROS (2010)
42. Razavian, A.S., Azizpour, H., Sullivan, J., Carlsson, S.: CNN features off-the-shelf: an astounding baseline for recognition. In: CVPR 2014 DeepVision Workshop (2014)
43. Sattler, T., Leibe, B., Kobbelt, L.: Fast image-based localization using direct 2d-to-3d matching. In: ICCV, pp. 667–674 (2011)
44. Sattler, T., Leibe, B., Kobbelt, L.: Improving image-based localization by active correspondence search. In: Fitzgibbon, A., Lazebnik, S., Perona, P., Sato, Y., Schmid, C. (eds.) ECCV 2012, Part I. LNCS, vol. 7572, pp. 752–765. Springer, Heidelberg (2012)
45. Sattler, T., Weyand, T., Leibe, B., Kobbelt, L.: Image retrieval for image-based localization revisited. In: BMVC, pp. 76.1–76.12 (2012)
46. Schindler, G., Brown, M., Szeliski, R.: City-scale location recognition. In: CVPR (2007)
47. Sermanet, P., Eigen, D., Zhang, X., Mathieu, M., Fergus, R., LeCun, Y.: OverFeat: integrated recognition, localization and detection using convolutional networks. In: ICLR (2014)

48. Sivic, J., Zisserman, A.: Video Google: a text retrieval approach to object matching in videos. In: ICCV, vol. 2, pp. 1470–1477 (2003)
49. Szegedy, C., Liu, W., Jia, Y., Sermanet, P., Reed, S., Anguelov, D., Erhan, D., Vanhoucke, V., Rabinovich, A.: Going deeper with convolutions. In: CVPR (2015)
50. Tolias, G., Sicre, R., Jegou, H.: Particular object retrieval with integral max-pooling of CNN activations. In: ICLR (2016)
51. Tolias, G., Avrithis, Y., Jegou, H.: To aggregate or not to aggregate: selective matchkernels for image search. In: ICCV (2013)
52. Wang, J., Song, Y., Leung, T., Rosenberg, C., Wang, J., Philbin, J., Chen, B., Wu, Y.: Learning fine-grained image similarity with deep ranking. In: CVPR (2014)
53. Workman, S., Souvenir, R., Jacobs, N.: Wide-area image geolocalization with aerial reference imagery. In: ICCV (2015)
54. Xiao, J., Ehinger, K.A., Hays, J., Torralba, A., Oliva, A.: SUN database: exploring a large collection of scene categories. IJCV (2014)
55. Xie, L., Hong, R., Zhang, B., Tian, Q.: Image classification and retrieval are ONE. In: ICMR (2015)
56. Zamir, A.R., Shah, M.: Accurate image localization based on Google maps street view. In: Daniilidis, K., Maragos, P., Paragios, N. (eds.) ECCV 2010, Part IV. LNCS, vol. 6314, pp. 255–268. Springer, Heidelberg (2010)
57. Zamir, A.R., Shah, M.: Image geo-localization based on multiple nearest neighbor feature matching using generalized graphs. PAMI **36**(8), 1546–1558 (2014)
58. Zeiler, M.D., Fergus, R.: Visualizing and understanding convolutional networks. In: Fleet, D., Pajdla, T., Schiele, B., Tuytelaars, T. (eds.) ECCV 2014, Part I. LNCS, vol. 8689, pp. 818–833. Springer, Heidelberg (2014)
59. Zheng, Y.T., Zhao, M., Song, Y., Adam, H., Buddemeier, U., Bissacco, A., Brucher, F., Chua, T.S., Neven, H.: Tour the world: building a web-scale landmark recognition engine. In: CVPR, pp. 961–962 (2009)
60. Zhou, B., Lapedriza, A., Xiao, J., Torralba, A., Oliva, A.: Learning deep features for scene recognition using places database. In: NIPS (2014)

Detecting Text in Natural Image
with Connectionist Text Proposal Network

Zhi Tian[1], Weilin Huang[1,2(✉)], Tong He[1], Pan He[1], and Yu Qiao[1,3]

[1] Shenzhen Key Lab of Computer Vision and Pattern Recognition,
Shenzhen Institutes of Advanced Technology,
Chinese Academy of Sciences, Shenzhen, China
[2] University of Oxford, Oxford, UK
[3] The Chinese University of Hong Kong, Sha Tin, Hong Kong
{zhi.tian,wl.huang,tong.he,pan.he,yu.qiao}@siat.ac.cn

Abstract. We propose a novel Connectionist Text Proposal Network (CTPN) that *accurately* localizes text lines in natural image. The CTPN detects a text line in a sequence of fine-scale text proposals directly in convolutional feature maps. We develop a vertical anchor mechanism that jointly predicts location and text/non-text score of each fixed-width proposal, considerably improving localization accuracy. The sequential proposals are naturally connected by a recurrent neural network, which is seamlessly incorporated into the convolutional network, resulting in an end-to-end trainable model. This allows the CTPN to explore rich context information of image, making it powerful to detect extremely ambiguous text. The CTPN works reliably on multi-scale and multi-language text without further post-processing, departing from previous bottom-up methods requiring multi-step post filtering. It achieves 0.88 and 0.61 F-measure on the ICDAR 2013 and 2015 benchmarks, surpassing recent results [8,35] by a large margin. The CTPN is computationally efficient with 0.14 s/image, by using the very deep VGG16 model [27]. Online demo is available: http://textdet.com/.

Keywords: Scene text detection · Convolutional network · Recurrent neural network · Anchor mechanism

1   Introduction

Reading text in natural image has recently attracted increasing attention in computer vision [1,8–11,14,15,28,32,35]. This is due to its numerous practical applications such as image OCR, multi-language translation, image retrieval, etc. It includes two sub tasks: text detection and recognition. This work focus on the detection task [1,14,28,32], which is more challenging than recognition task carried out on a well-cropped word image [9,15]. Large variance of text patterns and highly cluttered background pose main challenge of *accurate* text localization.

© Springer International Publishing AG 2016
B. Leibe et al. (Eds.): ECCV 2016, Part VIII, LNCS 9912, pp. 56–72, 2016.
DOI: 10.1007/978-3-319-46484-8_4

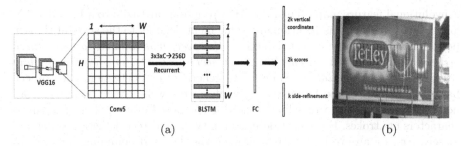

(a)   (b)

Fig. 1. (a) Architecture of the Connectionist Text Proposal Network (CTPN). We densely slide a 3×3 spatial window through the last convolutional maps (*conv5*) of the VGG16 model [27]. The sequential windows in each row are recurrently connected by a Bi-directional LSTM (BLSTM) [7], where the convolutional feature (3×3×C) of each window is used as input of the 256D BLSTM (including two 128D LSTMs). The RNN layer is connected to a 512D fully-connected layer, followed by the output layer, which jointly predicts text/non-text scores, y-axis coordinates and side-refinement offsets of k anchors. (b) The CTPN outputs sequential fixed-width fine-scale text proposals. Color of each box indicates the text/non-text score. Only the boxes with positive scores are presented.

Current approaches for text detection mostly employ a bottom-up pipeline [1,14,28,32,33]. They commonly start from low-level character or stroke detection, which is typically followed by a number of subsequent steps: non-text component filtering, text line construction and text line verification. These multi-step bottom-up approaches are generally complicated with less robustness and reliability. Their performance heavily rely on the results of character detection, and connected-components methods or sliding-window methods have been proposed. These methods commonly explore low-level features (e.g., based on SWT [3,13], MSER [14,23,33], or HoG [28]) to distinguish text candidates from background. However, they are not robust by identifying individual strokes or characters separately, without context information. For example, it is more confident for people to identify a sequence of characters than an individual one, especially when a character is extremely ambiguous. These limitations often result in a large number of non-text components in character detection, causing main difficulties for handling them in following steps. Furthermore, these false detections are easily accumulated sequentially in bottom-up pipeline, as pointed out in [28]. To address these problems, we exploit strong deep features for detecting text information directly in convolutional maps. We develop text anchor mechanism that *accurately* predicts text locations in fine scale. Then, an in-network recurrent architecture is proposed to connect these fine-scale text proposals in sequences, allowing them to encode rich context information.

Deep Convolutional Neural Networks (CNN) have recently advanced general object detection substantially [5,6,25]. The state-of-the-art method is Faster Region-CNN (R-CNN) system [25] where a Region Proposal Network (RPN) is proposed to generate high-quality class-agnostic object proposals directly from convolutional feature maps. Then the RPN proposals are fed into a Fast R-CNN [5] model for further classification and refinement, leading to the state-of-the-art performance on generic object detection. *However, it is difficult to apply these general object detection systems directly to scene text detection, which generally requires a higher localization accuracy.* In generic object detection, each object has a well-defined closed boundary [2], while such a well-defined boundary may not exist in text, since a text line or word is composed of a number of separate characters or strokes. For object detection, a typical correct detection is defined loosely, e.g., by an overlap of >0.5 between the detected bounding box and its ground truth (e.g., the PASCAL standard [4]), since people can recognize an object easily from major part of it. By contrast, reading text comprehensively is a fine-grained recognition task which requires a correct detection that covers a full region of a text line or word. Therefore, text detection generally requires a more *accurate* localization, leading to a different evaluation standard, e.g., the Wolf's standard [30] which is commonly employed by text benchmarks [19,21].

In this work, we fill this gap by extending the RPN architecture [25] to *accurate* text line localization. We present several technical developments that tailor generic object detection model elegantly towards our problem. We strive for a further step by proposing an in-network recurrent mechanism that allows our model to detect text sequence directly in the convolutional maps, avoiding further post-processing by an additional costly CNN detection model.

1.1   Contributions

We propose a novel Connectionist Text Proposal Network (CTPN) that directly localizes text sequences in convolutional layers. This overcomes a number of main limitations raised by previous bottom-up approaches building on character detection. We leverage the advantages of strong deep convolutional features and sharing computation mechanism, and propose the CTPN architecture which is described in Fig. 1. It makes the following major contributions:

First, we cast the problem of text detection into localizing a sequence of fine-scale text proposals. We develop an anchor regression mechanism that jointly predicts vertical location and text/non-text score of each text proposal, resulting in an excellent localization accuracy. This departs from the RPN prediction of a whole object, which is difficult to provide a satisfied localization accuracy.

Second, we propose an in-network recurrence mechanism that elegantly connects sequential text proposals in the convolutional feature maps. This connection allows our detector to explore meaningful context information of text line, making it powerful to detect extremely challenging text reliably.

Third, both methods are integrated seamlessly to meet the nature of text sequence, resulting in a unified end-to-end trainable model. Our method is able to handle multi-scale and multi-lingual text in a single process, avoiding further post filtering or refinement.

Fourth, our method achieves new state-of-the-art results on a number of benchmarks, significantly improving recent results (e.g., 0.88 F-measure over 0.83 in [8] on the ICDAR 2013, and 0.61 F-measure over 0.54 in [35] on the ICDAR

2015). Furthermore, it is computationally efficient, resulting in a 0.14 s/image running time (on the ICDAR 2013) by using the very deep VGG16 model [27].

2 Related Work

Text detection. Past works in scene text detection have been dominated by bottom-up approaches which are generally built on stroke or character detection. They can be roughly grouped into two categories, connected-components (CCs) based approaches and sliding-window based methods. The CCs based approaches discriminate text and non-text pixels by using a fast filter, and then text pixels are greedily grouped into stroke or character candidates, by using low-level properties, e.g., intensity, color, gradient, etc. [3,13,14,32,33]. The sliding-window based methods detect character candidates by densely moving a multi-scale window through an image. The character or non-character window is discriminated by a pre-trained classifier, by using manually-designed features [28,29], or recent CNN features [16]. However, both groups of methods commonly suffer from poor performance of character detection, causing accumulated errors in following component filtering and text line construction steps. Furthermore, robustly filtering out non-character components or confidently verifying detected text lines are even difficult themselves [1,14,33]. Another limitation is that the sliding-window methods are computationally expensive, by running a classifier on a huge number of the sliding windows.

Object detection. Convolutional Neural Networks (CNN) have recently advanced general object detection substantially [5,6,25]. A common strategy is to generate a number of object proposals by employing inexpensive low-level features, and then a strong CNN classifier is applied to further classify and refine the generated proposals. Selective Search (SS) [4] which generates class-agnostic object proposals, is one of the most popular methods applied in recent leading object detection systems, such as Region CNN (R-CNN) [6] and its extensions [5]. Recently, Ren *et al.* [25] proposed a Faster R-CNN system for object detection. They proposed a Region Proposal Network (RPN) that generates high-quality class-agnostic object proposals directly from the convolutional feature maps. The RPN is fast by sharing convolutional computation. However, the RPN proposals are not discriminative, and require a further refinement and classification by an additional costly CNN model, e.g., the Fast R-CNN model [5]. More importantly, text is different significantly from general objects, making it difficult to directly apply general object detection system to this highly domain-specific task.

3 Connectionist Text Proposal Network

This section presents details of the Connectionist Text Proposal Network (CTPN). It includes three key contributions that make it reliable and accurate for text localization: detecting text in fine-scale proposals, recurrent connectionist text proposals, and side-refinement.

3.1 Detecting Text in Fine-Scale Proposals

Similar to Region Proposal Network (RPN) [25], the CTPN is essentially a fully convolutional network that allows an input image of arbitrary size. It detects a text line by densely sliding a small window in the convolutional feature maps, and outputs a sequence of fine-scale (e.g., fixed 16-pixel width) text proposals, as shown in Fig. 1(b).

We take the very deep 16-layer vggNet (VGG16) [27] as an example to describe our approach, which is readily applicable to other deep models. Architecture of the CTPN is presented in Fig. 1(a). We use a small spatial window, 3 × 3, to slide the feature maps of last convolutional layer (e.g., the *conv5* of the VGG16). The size of *conv5* feature maps is determined by the size of input image, while the total stride and receptive field are fixed as 16 and 228 pixels, respectively. Both the total stride and receptive field are fixed by the network architecture. Using a sliding window in the convolutional layer allows it to share convolutional computation, which is the key to reduce computation of the costly sliding-window based methods.

Generally, sliding-window methods adopt multi-scale windows to detect objects of different sizes, where one window scale is fixed to objects of similar size. In [25], Ren *et al.* proposed an efficient anchor regression mechanism that allows the RPN to detect multi-scale objects with a single-scale window. The key insight is that a single window is able to predict objects in a wide range of scales and aspect ratios, by using a number of flexible anchors. We wish to extend this efficient anchor mechanism to our text task. However, text differs from generic objects substantially, which generally have a well-defined enclosed boundary and center, allowing inferring whole object from even a part of it [2]. Text is a sequence which does not have an obvious closed boundary. It may include multi-level components, such as stroke, character, word, text line and text region, which are not distinguished clearly between each other. Text detection is defined in word or text line level, so that it may be easy to make an incorrect detection by defining it as a single object, e.g., detecting part of a word. Therefore, directly predicting the location of a text line or word may be difficult or unreliable, making it hard to get a satisfied accuracy. An example is shown in Fig. 2, where the RPN is directly trained for localizing text lines in an image.

We look for a unique property of text that is able to generalize well to text components in all levels. We observed that word detection by the RPN is difficult

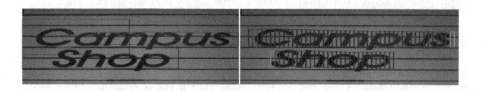

Fig. 2. Left: RPN proposals. **Right**: Fine-scale text proposals.

to accurately predict the horizontal sides of words, since each character within a word is isolated or separated, making it confused to find the start and end locations of a word. Obviously, a text line is a sequence which is the main difference between text and generic objects. It is natural to consider a text line as a sequence of fine-scale text proposals, where each proposal generally represents a small part of a text line, e.g., a text piece with 16-pixel width. Each proposal may include a single or multiple strokes, a part of a character, a single or multiple characters, etc. We believe that it would be more accurate to just predict the vertical location of each proposal, by fixing its horizontal location which may be more difficult to predict. This reduces the search space, compared to the RPN which predicts 4 coordinates of an object. We develop a vertical anchor mechanism that simultaneously predicts a text/non-text score and y-axis location of each fine-scale proposal. It is also more reliable to detect a general fixed-width text proposal than identifying an isolate character, which is easily confused with part of a character or multiple characters. Furthermore, detecting a text line in a sequence of fixed-width text proposals also works reliably on text of multiple scales and multiple aspect ratios.

To this end, we design the fine-scale text proposal as follow. Our detector investigates each spatial location in the *conv5* densely. A text proposal is defined to have a fixed width of 16 pixels (in the input image). This is equal to move the detector densely through the *conv5* maps, where the total stride is exactly 16 pixels. Then we design k vertical anchors to predict y-coordinates for each proposal. The k anchors have a same horizontal location with a fixed width of 16 pixels, but their vertical locations are varied in k different heights. In our experiments, we use ten anchors for each proposal, $k = 10$, whose heights are varied from 11 to 273 pixels (by $\div 0.7$ each time) in the input image. The explicit vertical coordinates are measured by the height and y-axis center of a proposal bounding box. We compute relative predicted vertical coordinates ($\mathbf{v}$) with respect to the bounding box location of an anchor as,

$$v_c = (c_y - c_y^a)/h^a, \qquad v_h = \log(h/h^a) \tag{1}$$
$$v_c^* = (c_y^* - c_y^a)/h^a, \qquad v_h^* = \log(h^*/h^a) \tag{2}$$

where $\mathbf{v} = \{v_c, v_h\}$ and $\mathbf{v}^* = \{v_c^*, v_h^*\}$ are the relative predicted coordinates and ground truth coordinates, respectively. c_y^a and h^a are the center (y-axis) and height of the anchor box, which can be pre-computed from an input image. c_y and h are the predicted y-axis coordinates in the input image, while c_y^* and h^* are the ground truth coordinates. Therefore, each predicted text proposal has a bounding box with size of $h \times 16$ (in the input image), as shown in Fig. 1(b) and Fig. 2(right). Generally, an text proposal is largely smaller than its effective receptive field which is 228×228.

The detection processing is summarised as follow. Given an input image, we have $W \times H \times C$ *conv5* features maps (by using the VGG16 model), where C is the number of feature maps or channels, and $W \times H$ is the spatial arrangement. When our detector is sliding a 3×3 window densely through the conv5, each sliding-window takes a convolutional feature of $3 \times 3 \times C$ for producing the prediction. For each prediction, the horizontal location (x-coordinates) and k-anchor locations are fixed, which can be pre-computed by mapping the spatial window location in the *conv5* onto the input image. Our detector outputs the text/non-text scores and the predicted y-coordinates ($\mathbf{v}$) for k anchors at each window location. The detected text proposals are generated from the anchors having a text/non-text score of >0.7 (with non-maximum suppression). By the designed vertical anchor and fine-scale detection strategy, our detector is able to handle text lines in a wide range of scales and aspect ratios by using a single-scale image. This further reduces its computation, and at the same time, predicting accurate localizations of the text lines. Compared to the RPN or Faster R-CNN system [25], our fine-scale detection provides more detailed supervised information that naturally leads to a more accurate detection.

3.2   Recurrent Connectionist Text Proposals

To improve localization accuracy, we split a text line into a sequence of fine-scale text proposals, and predict each of them separately. Obviously, it is not robust to regard each isolated proposal independently. This may lead to a number of false detections on non-text objects which have a similar structure as text patterns, such as windows, bricks, leaves, etc. (referred as text-like outliers in [13]). It is also possible to discard some ambiguous patterns which contain weak text information. Several examples are presented in Fig. 3 (top). Text have strong sequential characteristics where the sequential context information is crucial to make a reliable decision. This has been verified by recent work [9] where a recurrent neural network (RNN) is applied to encode this context information for text recognition. Their results have shown that the sequential context information is greatly facilitate the recognition task on cropped word images.

Fig. 3. Top: CTPN without RNN. **Bottom**: CTPN with RNN connection.

Motivated from this work, we believe that this context information may also be of importance for our detection task. Our detector should be able to explore this important context information to make a more reliable decision, when it works on each individual proposal. Furthermore, we aim to encode this information directly in the convolutional layer, resulting in an elegant and seamless in-network connection of the fine-scale text proposals. RNN provides a natural choice for encoding this information recurrently using its hidden layers. To this end, we propose to design a RNN layer upon the *conv5*, which takes the convolutional feature of each window as sequential inputs, and updates its internal state recurrently in the hidden layer, H_t,

$$H_t = \varphi(H_{t-1}, X_t), \qquad t = 1, 2, ..., W \tag{3}$$

where $X_t \in R^{3 \times 3 \times C}$ is the input *conv5* feature from t-th sliding-window (3 × 3). The sliding-window moves densely from left to right, resulting in $t = 1, 2, ..., W$ sequential features for each row. W is the width of the *conv5*. H_t is a recurrent internal state that is computed jointly from both current input (X_t) and previous states encoded in H_{t-1}. The recurrence is computed by using a nonlinear function φ, which defines exact form of the recurrent model. We exploit the long short-term memory (LSTM) architecture [12] for our RNN layer. The LSTM was proposed specially to address vanishing gradient problem, by introducing three additional multiplicative gates: the *input gate, forget gate* and *output gate*. Details can be found in [12]. Hence the internal state in RNN hidden layer accesses the sequential context information scanned by all previous windows through the recurrent connection. We further extend the RNN layer by using a bi-directional LSTM, which allows it to encode the recurrent context in both directions, so that the connectionist receipt field is able to cover the whole image width, e.g., 228 × width. We use a 128D hidden layer for each LSTM, resulting in a 256D RNN hidden layer, $H_t \in R^{256}$.

The internal state in H_t is mapped to the following FC layer, and output layer for computing the predictions of the t-th proposal. Therefore, our integration with the RNN layer is elegant, resulting in an efficient model that is end-to-end trainable without additional cost. The efficiency of the RNN connection is demonstrated in Fig. 3. Obviously, it reduces false detections considerably, and at the same time, recovers many missed text proposals which contain very weak text information.

3.3   Side-Refinement

The fine-scale text proposals are detected accurately and reliably by our CTPN. Text line construction is straightforward by connecting continuous text proposals whose text/non-text score is >0.7. Text lines are constructed as follow. First, we define a paired neighbour (B_j) for a proposal B_i as $B_j- > B_i$, when (i) B_j is the nearest horizontal distance to B_i, and (ii) this distance is less than 50 pixels, and (iii) their vertical overlap is >0.7. Second, two proposals are grouped into a pair, if $B_j- > B_i$ and $B_i- > B_j$. Then a text line is constructed by sequentially connecting the pairs having a same proposal.

The fine-scale detection and RNN connection are able to predict accurate localizations in vertical direction. In horizontal direction, the image is divided

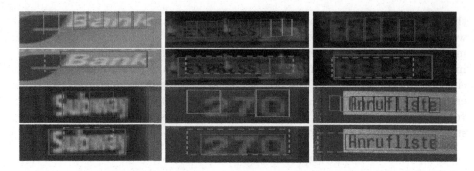

Fig. 4. CTPN detection with (red box) and without (yellow dashed box) the side-refinement. Color of fine-scale proposal box indicate a text/non-text score. (Color figure online)

into a sequence of equal 16-pixel width proposals. This may lead to an inaccurate localization when the text proposals in both horizontal sides are not exactly covered by a ground truth text line area, or some side proposals are discarded (e.g., having a low text score), as shown in Fig. 4. This inaccuracy may be not crucial in generic object detection, but should not be ignored in text detection, particularly for those small-scale text lines or words. To address this problem, we propose a side-refinement approach that accurately estimates the offset for each anchor/proposal in both left and right horizontal sides (referred as side-anchor or side-proposal). Similar to the y-coordinate prediction, we compute relative offset as,

$$o = (x_{side} - c_x^a)/w^a, \quad o^* = (x_{side}^* - c_x^a)/w^a \qquad (4)$$

where x_{side} is the predicted x-coordinate of the nearest horizontal side (e.g., left or right side) to current anchor. x_{side}^* is the ground truth (GT) side coordinate in x-axis, which is pre-computed from the GT bounding box and anchor location. c_x^a is the center of anchor in x-axis. w^a is the width of anchor, which is fixed, $w^a = 16$. The side-proposals are defined as the start and end proposals when we connect a sequence of detected fine-scale text proposals into a text line. We only use the offsets of the side-proposals to refine the final text line bounding box. Several detection examples improved by side-refinement are presented in Fig. 4. The side-refinement further improves the localization accuracy, leading to about 2 % performance improvements on the SWT and Multi-Lingual datasets. Notice that the offset for side-refinement is predicted simultaneously by our model, as shown in Fig. 1. It is not computed from an additional post-processing step.

3.4   Model Outputs and Loss Functions

The proposed CTPN has three outputs which are jointly connected to the last FC layer, as shown in Fig. 1(a). The three outputs simultaneously predict text/non-text scores (**s**), vertical coordinates (**v** = $\{v_c, v_h\}$ in Eq. (2)) and side-refinement offset (**o**). We explore k anchors to predict them on each spatial location in the *conv5*, resulting in $2k$, $2k$ and k parameters in the output layer, respectively.

We employ multi-task learning to jointly optimize model parameters. We introduce three loss functions, L_s^{cl}, L_v^{re} and l_o^{re}, which compute errors of text/non-text score, coordinate and side-refinement, respectively. With these considerations, we follow the multi-task loss applied in [5,25], and minimize an overall objective function (L) for an image as,

$$L(\mathbf{s}_i, \mathbf{v}_j, \mathbf{o}_k) = \frac{1}{N_s} \sum_i L_s^{cl}(\mathbf{s}_i, \mathbf{s}_i^*) + \frac{\lambda_1}{N_v} \sum_j L_v^{re}(\mathbf{v}_j, \mathbf{v}_j^*) + \frac{\lambda_2}{N_o} \sum_k L_o^{re}(\mathbf{o}_k, \mathbf{o}_k^*) \quad (5)$$

where each anchor is a training sample, and i is the index of an anchor in a mini-batch. $\mathbf{s}_i$ is the predicted probability of anchor i being a true text. $\mathbf{s}_i^* = \{0, 1\}$ is the ground truth. j is the index of an anchor in the set of valid anchors for y-coordinates regression, which are defined as follow. A valid anchor is a defined positive anchor ($\mathbf{s}_j^* = 1$, described below), or has an Intersection-over-Union (IoU) >0.5 overlap with a ground truth text proposal. $\mathbf{v}_j$ and $\mathbf{v}_j^*$ are the prediction and ground truth y-coordinates associated with the j-th anchor. k is the index of a side-anchor, which is defined as a set of anchors within a horizontal distance (e.g., 32-pixel) to the left or right side of a ground truth text line bounding box. $\mathbf{o}_k$ and $\mathbf{o}_k^*$ are the predicted and ground truth offsets in x-axis associated to the k-th anchor. L_s^{cl} is the classification loss which we use Softmax loss to distinguish text and non-text. L_v^{re} and L_o^{re} are the regression loss. We follow previous work by using the smooth L_1 function to compute them [5,25]. λ_1 and λ_2 are loss weights to balance different tasks, which are empirically set to 1.0 and 2.0. N_s N_v and N_o are normalization parameters, denoting the total number of anchors used by L_s^{cl}, L_v^{re} and L_o^{re}, respectively.

3.5   Training and Implementation Details

The CTPN can be trained end-to-end by using the standard back-propagation and stochastic gradient descent (SGD). Similar to RPN [25], training samples are the anchors, whose locations can be pre computed in input image, so that the training labels of each anchor can be computed from corresponding GT box.

Training Labels. For text/non-text classification, a binary label is assigned to each positive (text) or negative (non-text) anchor. It is defined by computing the IoU overlap with the GT bounding box (divided by anchor location). A positive anchor is defined as: (i) an anchor that has an >0.7 IoU overlap with any GT box; *or* (ii) the anchor with the highest IoU overlap with a GT box. *By the condition (ii), even a very small text pattern can assign a positive anchor. This is crucial to detect small-scale text patterns, which is one of key advantages of the CTPN.* This is different from generic object detection where the impact of condition (ii) may be not significant. The negative anchors are defined as <0.5 IoU overlap with all GT boxes. The training labels for the y-coordinate regression ($\mathbf{v}^*$) and offset regression ($\mathbf{o}^*$) are computed as Eqs. (2) and (4) respectively.

Training Data. In the training process, each mini-batch samples are collected randomly from a single image. The number of anchors for each mini-batch is fixed to $N_s = 128$, with 1:1 ratio for positive and negative samples. A mini-patch is pad with negative samples if the number of positive ones is fewer than 64. Our model was trained on 3,000 natural images, including 229 images from the ICDAR 2013 training set. We collected the other images ourselves and manually labelled them with text line bounding boxes. All self-collected training images are not overlapped with any test image in all benchmarks. The input image is resized by setting its short side to 600 for training, while keeping its original aspect ratio.

Implementation Details. We follow the standard practice, and explore the very deep VGG16 model [27] pre-trained on the ImageNet data [26]. We initialize the new layers (e.g., the RNN and output layers) by using random weights with Gaussian distribution of 0 mean and 0.01 standard deviation. The model was trained end-to-end by fixing the parameters in the first two convolutional layers. We used 0.9 momentum and 0.0005 weight decay. The learning rate was set to 0.001 in the first 16 K iterations, followed by another 4 K iterations with 0.0001 learning rate. Our model was implemented in Caffe framework [17].

4   Experimental Results and Discussions

We evaluate the CTPN on five text detection benchmarks, namely the ICDAR 2011 [21], ICDAR 2013 [19], ICDAR 2015 [18], SWT [3], and Multilingual dataset [24]. In our experiments, we first verify the efficiency of each proposed component individually, e.g., the fine-scale text proposal detection or in-network recurrent connection. The ICDAR 2013 is used for this component evaluation.

4.1   Benchmarks and Evaluation Metric

The ICDAR 2011 dataset [21] consists of 229 training images and 255 testing ones, where the images are labelled in word level. *The ICDAR 2013* [19] is similar as the ICDAR 2011, and has in total 462 images, including 229 images and 233 images for training and testing, respectively. *The ICDAR 2015* (Incidental Scene Text - Challenge 4) [18] includes 1,500 images which were collected by using the Google Glass. The training set has 1,000 images, and the remained 500 images are used for test. This dataset is more challenging than previous ones by including arbitrary orientation, very small-scale and low resolution text. *The Multilingual* scene text dataset is collected by [24]. It contains 248 images for training and 239 for testing. The images include multi-languages text, and the ground truth is labelled in text line level. Epshtein *et al.* [3] introduced *the SWT* dataset containing 307 images which include many extremely small-scale text.

We follow previous work by using standard evaluation protocols which are provided by the dataset creators or competition organizers. For the ICDAR 2011 we use the standard protocol proposed by [30], the evaluation on the ICDAR 2013 follows the standard in [19]. For the ICDAR 2015, we used the online evaluation system provided by the organizers as in [18]. The evaluations on the SWT and Multilingual datasets follow the protocols defined in [3,24] respectively.

4.2   Fine-Scale Text Proposal Network with Faster R-CNN

We first discuss our fine-scale detection strategy against the RPN and Faster R-CNN system [25]. As can be found in Table 1(left), the individual RPN is difficult to perform accurate text localization, by generating a large amount of false detections (low precision). By refining the RPN proposals with a Fast R-CNN detection model [5], the Faster R-CNN system improves localization accuracy considerably, with a F-measure of 0.75. One observation is that the Faster R-CNN also increases the recall of original RPN. This may benefit from joint bounding box regression mechanism of the Fast R-CNN, which improves the accuracy of a predicted bounding box. The RPN proposals may roughly localize a major part of a text line or word, but they are not accurate enough by the ICDAR 2013 standard. Obviously, the proposed fine-scale text proposal network (FTPN) improves the Faster R-CNN remarkably in both precision and recall, suggesting that the FTPN is more accurate and reliable, by predicting a sequence of fine-scale text proposals rather than a whole text line.

4.3   Recurrent Connectionist Text Proposals

We discuss impact of recurrent connection on our CTPN. As shown in Fig. 3, the context information is greatly helpful to reduce false detections, such as text-like outliers. It is of great importance for recovering highly ambiguous text (e.g., extremely small-scale ones), which is one of main advantages of our CTPN, as demonstrated in Fig. 6. These appealing properties result in a significant performance boost. As shown in Table 1(left), with our recurrent connection, the CTPN improves the FTPN substantially from a F-measure of 0.80 to 0.88.

Running time. The implementation time of our CTPN (for whole detection processing) is about 0.14 s per image with a fixed short side of 600, by using a single GPU. The CTPN without the RNN connection takes about 0.13 s/image GPU time. Therefore, the proposed in-network recurrent mechanism increase model computation marginally, with considerable performance gain obtained.

Table 1. Component evaluation on the ICDAR 2013, and state-of-the-art results on the SWT and MULTILINGUAL.

Components on ICDAR 2013				SWT				MULTILINGUAL			
Method	P	R	F	Method	P	R	F	Method	P	R	F
RPN	0.17	0.63	0.27	Epshtein [3]	0.54	0.42	0.47	Pan [24]	0.65	0.66	0.66
Faster R-CNN	0.79	0.71	0.75	Mao [20]	0.58	0.41	0.48	Yin [33]	0.83	0.68	0.75
FTPN (no RNN)	0.83	0.78	0.80	Zhang [34]	**0.68**	0.53	0.60	Tian [28]	**0.85**	0.78	0.81
CTPN	**0.93**	**0.83**	**0.88**	CTPN	**0.68**	**0.65**	**0.66**	CTPN	0.84	**0.80**	**0.82**

4.4   Comparisons with State-of-the-art Results

Our detection results on several challenging images are presented in Fig. 5. As can be found, the CTPN works perfectly on these challenging cases, some of which are difficult for many previous methods. It is able to handle multi-scale and multi-language efficiently (e.g., Chinese and Korean).

Fig. 5. CTPN detection results several challenging images, including multi-scale and multi-language text lines. Yellow boxes are the ground truth. (Color figure online)

The full evaluation was conducted on five benchmarks. Image resolution is varied significantly in different datasets. We set short side of images to 2000 for the SWT and ICDAR 2015, and 600 for the other three. We compare our performance against recently published results in [1, 28, 34]. As shown in Tables 1 and 2, our CTPN achieves the best performance on all five datasets. On the SWT, our improvements are significant on both recall and F-measure, with marginal gain on precision. Our detector performs favourably against the TextFlow on the Multilingual, suggesting that our method generalize well to various languages. On

Table 2. State-of-the-art results on the ICDAR 2011, 2013 and 2015.

ICDAR 2011				ICDAR 2013					ICDAR 2015			
Method	P	R	F	Method	P	R	F	T(s)	Method	P	R	F
Huang [13]	0.82	0.75	0.73	Yin [33]	0.88	0.66	0.76	0.43	CNN Pro	0.35	0.34	0.35
Yao [31]	0.82	0.66	0.73	Neumann [22]	0.82	0.72	0.77	0.40	Deep2Text	0.50	0.32	0.39
Huang [14]	0.88	0.71	0.78	Neumann [23]	0.82	0.71	0.76	0.40	HUST	0.44	0.38	0.41
Yin [33]	0.86	0.68	0.76	FASText [1]	0.84	0.69	0.77	0.15	AJOU	0.47	0.47	0.47
Zhang [34]	0.84	0.76	0.80	Zhang [34]	0.88	0.74	0.80	60.0	NJU-Text	0.70	0.36	0.47
TextFlow [28]	0.86	0.76	0.81	TextFlow [28]	0.85	0.76	0.80	0.94	StradVision1	0.53	0.46	0.50
Text-CNN [11]	0.91	0.74	0.82	Text-CNN [11]	0.93	0.73	0.82	4.6	StradVision2	0.77	0.37	0.50
Gupta [8]	**0.92**	0.75	0.82	Gupta [8]	0.92	0.76	0.83	**0.07**	Zhang [35]	0.71	0.43	0.54
CTPN	0.89	**0.79**	**0.84**	CTPN	**0.93**	**0.83**	**0.88**	0.14 *	CTPN	**0.74**	**0.52**	**0.61**

Fig. 6. CTPN detection results on extremely small-scale cases (in red boxes), where some ground truth boxes are missed. Yellow boxes are the ground truth. (Color figure online)

the ICDAR 2013, it outperforms recent TextFlow [28] and FASText [1] remarkably by improving the F-measure from 0.80 to 0.88. The gains are considerable in both precision and recall, with more than +5 % and +7 % improvements, respectively. In addition, we further compare our method against [8, 11, 35], which were published after our initial submission. It consistently obtains substantial improvements on F-measure and recall. This may due to strong capability of CTPN for detecting extremely challenging text, e.g., very small-scale ones, some of which are even difficult for human. As shown in Fig. 6, those challenging ones are detected correctly by our detector, but some of them are even missed by the GT labelling, which may reduce our precision in evaluation.

We further investigate running time of various methods, as compared in Table 2. FASText [1] achieves 0.15 s/image CPU time. Our method is slightly faster than it by obtaining 0.14 s/image, but in GPU time. Though it is not fair to compare them directly, the GPU computation has become mainstream with recent great success of deep learning approaches on object detection [5, 6, 25]. Regardless of running time, our method outperforms the FASText substantially with 11 % improvement on F-measure. Our time can be reduced by using a smaller image scale. By using the scale of 450, it is reduced to 0.09 s/image, while obtaining P/R/F of 0.92/0.77/0.84 on the ICDAR 2013, which are compared competitively against Gupta *et al.*'s approach [8] using 0.07 s/image with GPU.

5   Conclusions

We have presented a Connectionist Text Proposal Network (CTPN) - an efficient text detector that is end-to-end trainable. The CTPN detects a text line in a sequence of fine-scale text proposals directly in convolutional maps. We develop vertical anchor mechanism that jointly predicts precise location and text/non-text score for each proposal, which is the key to realize *accurate* localization of text. We propose an in-network RNN layer that connects sequential text proposals elegantly, allowing it to explore meaningful context information. These key technical developments result in a powerful ability to detect highly challenging text, with less false detections. The CTPN is efficient by achieving new state-of-the-art performance on five benchmarks, with 0.14 s/image running time.

Acknowledgments. This work was supported in part by the National Natural Science Foundation of China (61503367), the Science and Technology Planning Project of Guangdong Province (2015A030310289, 2014B050505017, 2015B010129013), Shenzhen Research Program (KQCX2015033117354153, JSGG20150925164740726, CXZZ201-50930104115529, JCYJ20150925163005055), and External Cooperation Program of BIC, Chinese Academy of Sciences (172644KYSB20150019).

References

1. Busta, M., Neumann, L., Matas, J.: FasText: efficient unconstrained scene text detector. In: IEEE International Conference on Computer Vision (ICCV) (2015)
2. Cheng, M., Zhang, Z., Lin, W., Torr, P.: BING: binarized normed gradients for objectness estimation at 300 fps. In: IEEE Computer Vision and Pattern Recognition (CVPR) (2014)
3. Epshtein, B., Ofek, E., Wexler, Y.: Detecting text in natural scenes with stroke width transform. In: IEEE Computer Vision and Pattern Recognition (CVPR) (2010)
4. Everingham, M., Gool, L.V., Williams, C.K.I., Winn, J., Zisserman, A.: The pascal visual object classes (VOC) challenge. Int. J. Comput.Vis. (IJCV) **88**(2), 303–338 (2010)
5. Girshick, R.: Fast R-CNN. In: IEEE International Conference on Computer Vision (ICCV)(2015)
6. Girshick, R., Donahue, J., Darrell, T., Malik, J.: Rich feature hierarchies for accurate object detection and semantic segmentation. In: IEEE Computer Vision and Pattern Recognition (CVPR) (2014)
7. Graves, A., Schmidhuber, J.: Framewise phoneme classification with bidirectional lstm and other neural network architectures. Neural Netw. **18**(5), 602–610 (2005)
8. Gupta, A., Vedaldi, A., Zisserman, A.: Synthetic data for text localisation in natural images. In: IEEE Conference on Computer Vision and Pattern Recognition (CVPR) (2016)
9. He, P., Huang, W., Qiao, Y., Loy, C.C., Tang, X.: Reading scene text in deep convolutional sequences. In: The 30th AAAI Conference on Artificial Intelligence (AAAI-16) (2016)
10. He, T., Huang, W., Qiao, Y., Yao, J.: Accurate text localization in natural image with cascaded convolutional text network (2016). arXiv:1603.09423
11. He, T., Huang, W., Qiao, Y., Yao, J.: Text-attentional convolutional neural networks for scene text detection. IEEE Trans. Image Processing (TIP) **25**, 2529–2541 (2016)
12. Hochreiter, S., Schmidhuber, J.: Long short-term memory. Neural Netw. **9**(8), 1735–1780 (1997)
13. Huang, W., Lin, Z., Yang, J., Wang, J.: Text localization in natural images using stroke feature transform and text covariance descriptors. In: IEEE International Conference on Computer Vision (ICCV) (2013)
14. Huang, W., Qiao, Y., Tang, X.: Robust scene text detection with convolutional neural networks induced mser trees. In: European Conference on Computer Vision (ECCV) (2014)

15. Jaderberg, M., Simonyan, K., Vedaldi, A., Zisserman, A.: Reading text in the wild with convolutional neural networks. Int. J. Comput. Vis. (IJCV) **116**(1), 1–20 (2016)
16. Jaderberg, M., Vedaldi, A., Zisserman, A.: Deep features for text spotting. In: Fleet, D., Pajdla, T., Schiele, B., Tuytelaars, T. (eds.) ECCV 2014, Part IV. LNCS, vol. 8692, pp. 512–528. Springer, Heidelberg (2014)
17. Jia, Y., Shelhamer, E., Donahue, J., Karayev, S., Long, J., Girshick, R., Guadarrama, S., Darrell, T.: Caffe: convolutional architecture for fast feature embedding. In: ACM International Conference on Multimedia (ACM MM) (2014)
18. Karatzas, D., Gomez-Bigorda, L., Nicolaou, A., Ghosh, S., Bagdanov, A., Iwamura, M., Matas, J., Neumann, L., Chandrasekhar, V.R., Lu, S., Shafait, F., Uchida, S., Valveny, E.: ICDAR 2015 competition on robust reading. In: International Conference on Document Analysis and Recognition (ICDAR)(2015)
19. Karatzas, D., Shafait, F., Uchida, S., Iwamura, M., i Bigorda, L.G., Mestre, S.R., Mas, J., Mota, D.F., Almazan, J.A., de las Heras., L.P.: ICDAR 2013 robust reading competition. In: International Conference on Document Analysis and Recognition (ICDAR) (2013)
20. Mao, J., Li, H., Zhou, W., Yan, S., Tian, Q.: Scale based region growing for scene text detection. In: ACM International Conference on Multimedia (ACM MM) (2013)
21. Minetto, R., Thome, N., Cord, M., Fabrizio, J., Marcotegui, B.: Snoopertext: a multiresolution system for text detection in complex visual scenes. In: IEEE International Conference on Pattern Recognition (ICIP) (2010)
22. Neumann, L., Matas, J.: Efficient scene text localization and recognition with local character refinement. In: International Conference on Document Analysis and Recognition (ICDAR) (2015)
23. Neumann, L., Matas, J.: Real-time lexicon-free scene text localization and recognition. In: IEEE Transaction on Pattern Analysis and Machine Intelligence (TPAMI) (2015)
24. Pan, Y., Hou, X., Liu, C.: Hybrid approach to detect and localize texts in natural scene images. IEEE Trans. Image Process. (TIP) **20**, 800–813 (2011)
25. Ren, S., He, K., Girshick, R., Sun, J.: Faster R-CNN: towards real-time object detection with region proposal networks. In: Neural Information Processing Systems (NIPS) (2015)
26. Russakovsky, O., Deng, J., Su, H., Krause, J., Satheesh, S., Ma, S., Huang, Z., Karpathy, A., Khosla, A., Bernstein, M., Berg, A.C., Li, F.: ImageNet large scale visual recognition challenge. Int. J. Comput. Vis. (IJCV) **115**(3), 211–252 (2015)
27. Simonyan, K., Zisserman, A.: Very deep convolutional networks for large-scale image recognition. In: International Conference on Learning Representation (ICLR) (2015)
28. Tian, S., Pan, Y., Huang, C., Lu, S., Yu, K., Tan, C.L.: Text flow: a unified text detection system in natural scene images. In: IEEE International Conference on Computer Vision (ICCV) (2015)
29. Wang, K., Babenko, B., Belongie, S.: End-to-end scene text recognition. In: IEEE International Conference on Computer Vision (ICCV) (2011)
30. Wolf, C., Jolion, J.: Object count / area graphs for the evaluation of object detection and segmentation algorithms. Int. J. Doc. Anal. **8**, 280–296 (2006)
31. Yao, C., Bai, X., Liu, W.: A unified framework for multioriented text detection and recognition. IEEE Trans. Image Process. (TIP) **23**(11), 4737–4749 (2014)

32. Yin, X.C., Pei, W.Y., Zhang, J., Hao, H.W.: Multi-orientation scene text detection with adaptive clustering. IEEE Trans. Pattern Anal. Mach. Intell. (TPAMI) **37**(9), 1930–1937 (2015)
33. Yin, X.C., Yin, X., Huang, K., Hao, H.W.: Robust text detection in natural scene images. IEEE Trans. Pattern Anal. Mach. Intell. (TPAMI) **36**(4), 970–983 (2014)
34. Zhang, Z., Shen, W., Yao, C., Bai, X.: Symmetry-based text line detection in natural scenes. In: IEEE Computer Vision and Pattern Recognition (CVPR) (2015)
35. Zhang, Z., Zhang, C., Shen, W., Yao, C., Liu, W., Bai, X.: Multi-oriented text detection with fully convolutional networks. In: IEEE Conference on Computer Vision and Pattern Recognition (CVPR)(2016)

Face Recognition Using a Unified 3D Morphable Model

Guosheng Hu[1,2]($\boxtimes$), Fei Yan[2], Chi-Ho Chan[2], Weihong Deng[3],
William Christmas[2], Josef Kittler[2], and Neil M. Robertson[1,4]

[1] Anyvision, Queen's Road, Belfast BT39DT, UK
guosheng.hu@anyvision.co
[2] CVSSP, University of Surrey, Guildford GU27XH, UK
[3] Beijing University of Posts and Telecommunications, Beijing 100876, China
[4] ECIT, Queen's University of Belfast, Belfast BT39DT, UK
http://www.anyvision.co

Abstract. We address the problem of 3D-assisted 2D face recognition in scenarios when the input image is subject to degradations or exhibits intra-personal variations not captured by the 3D model. The proposed solution involves a novel approach to learn a subspace spanned by perturbations caused by the missing modes of variation and image degradations, using 3D face data reconstructed from 2D images rather than 3D capture. This is accomplished by modelling the difference in the texture map of the 3D aligned input and reference images. A training set of these texture maps then defines a perturbation space which can be represented using PCA bases. Assuming that the image perturbation subspace is orthogonal to the 3D face model space, then these additive components can be recovered from an unseen input image, resulting in an improved fit of the 3D face model. The linearity of the model leads to efficient fitting. Experiments show that our method achieves very competitive face recognition performance on Multi-PIE and AR databases. We also present baseline face recognition results on a new data set exhibiting combined pose and illumination variations as well as occlusion.

Keywords: 3D morphable model · Face recognition

1 Introduction

3D-assisted 2D face recognition has been attracting increasing attention because it can be used for pose-invariant face matching. This requires fitting a 3D face model to the input image, and using the fitted model to align the input and reference images for matching. As 3D facial shapes are intrinsically invariant to pose and illumination, the fitted shape also provides an invariant representation that can be used directly for recognition. The use of a face prior has been demonstrated to offer impressive performance on images of faces subject to a wide pose variations, even outperforming deep learning [1,2].

© Springer International Publishing AG 2016
B. Leibe et al. (Eds.): ECCV 2016, Part VIII, LNCS 9912, pp. 73–89, 2016.
DOI: 10.1007/978-3-319-46484-8_5

Most popular are 3D morphable face models which represent 3D face images in a PCA subspace. 3D face models proposed in the literature can capture and represent different modes of variations. Some focus solely on 3D shape (3DSM) [3–6]. Others (3DMM) model also the skin texture [7–9], or even face expression (E-3DMM) [10,11]. When fitting 3DMM to an input image, it is essential to estimate the scene illumination, as skin texture and lighting are intrinsically entwined, and need to be separated.

The problem of 3D model to the 2D image fitting becomes challenging when the input image exhibits intra-personal variations not captured by the 3D model, or the image is corrupted in some way. In this work, we use the term 'intra-personal' to represent any variations which are not inter-personal ones (facial shape and texture). We assume that fitting the shape would be affected to a lesser extent if the automatic landmarking procedure used is robust to shape variations and to occlusion. However, fitting the skin texture using 3DMM or E-3DMM would become problematic if the domain of the input data has changed. The problem associated with the missing modes of variation could be rectified by enhancing the 3D face model. However this would require collecting relevant 3D face data, a labour-intensive task which would often be impractical. In any case, this approach would not be appropriate for dealing with other image degradation effects, such as occlusion or image compression artefacts.

The aim of this paper is to develop techniques that can harness the benefits of 3D models in 2D face recognition when the input image is corrupted, e.g. by occlusion, or when it exhibits intra-personal variations which cannot be explicitly synthesised by the models. We address the problem by learning directly from 2D face data the subspace spanned by the missing modes of variation in the surface texture space superimposed on the 3D face shape structure. This is accomplished by estimating the pose of the input image and the face shape from the detected landmarks. The difference of the aligned input and reference images is used to construct a surface texture map. A training set of these texture maps then defines the perturbation space which can be represented using PCA bases. Assuming that the image perturbation subspace is orthogonal to the 3D face model space, then these additive components can be recovered from an unseen input image, resulting in an improved fit of the 3D face model.

We refer to this proposed method as the unified 3DMM (U-3DMM). Unlike the existing 3DMMs, U-3DMM models additional modes of variations in a unified linear framework, which can generalise also to occlusion. In addition, fitting U-3DMM to 2D images is very efficient. It involves first estimating the perturbation component of the input image. Once this component is removed, the core 3D face model fitting is a linear estimation problem. Last, the training set for U-3DMM is much easier to collect than that for 3DMMs.

We conduct an extensive evaluation of U-3DMM on databases which contain diverse modes of variation and perturbation. Experiments show the face recognition rates of U-3DMM are very competitive to state-of-the-art methods. We also present baseline face recognition results on a new dataset including combined pose, illumination and occlusion variations. The datasets and features extracted by U-3DMM will be made publicly available.

The contributions can be summarised as:

- U-3DMM augments the core 3D face model by an additional PCA subspace, a perturbation subspace. Specifically, we project 2D images to 3D space via geometric fitting. Then, in the 3D space, the difference of two images (one being a reference and the other exhibiting additional variations) works as a training sample to learn the perturbation part of U-3DMM. This process is detailed in Sect. 4.3 and Fig. 4. The linear model of these supplementary variations is generic. The framework can model any variation(s), e.g. occlusion, if appropriate training data is available.
- It is an open problem to achieve an accurate and efficient fitting for 3DMMs. Unlike non-linear models such as Phong illumination model used by 3DMMs, the linear perturbation model of U-3DMM can be fitted very efficiently.
- Large number of 3D faces used to train inter- and intra-personal variations are expensive to collect. In comparison, the proposed method uses 2D images, which are much cheaper and easier to acquire, to train diverse variations in the U-3DMM framework.

The paper is organised as follows. In Sect. 2, we present the related work. The 3DMM and its fitting problem are formulated in Sect. 3. Section 4 details our methodology. The proposed algorithm is evaluated in Sect. 5. Section 6 draws conclusions.

2   Related Work

In this section, we discuss the current state-of-the-art. We first introduce various 3D models and fitting strategies, then the motivation of this work is discussed.

2.1   3D Face Models

3D face modeling is an active research field with many applications. The biometrics community uses 3D models to improve face recognition performance. In the graphics and animation community, 3D models are used to reconstruct facial details such as wrinkles. In this work, we mainly focus on the 3D models used for biometrics, namely face recognition. These 3D models are classified into three categories: 3D shape model (3DSM), 3D Morphable Model (3DMM) and extended 3DMM (E-3DMM).

3DSM solves the pose problem using either pose normalisation (PN) [6] or pose synthesis (PS) [3–5]. For the PN method, input images of arbitrary poses are converted to a canonical (frontal) view via a 3D model, then traditional 2D face matchers are used for recognition. On the other hand, PS methods synthesise multiple virtual images with different poses for each gallery image. Only virtual images with similar pose to the probe are chosen for matching. However, these models can only explicitly model one intra-personal variation (pose).

Unlike the 3DSM, the 3D morphable model (3DMM) [7,12] consists of not only a shape model but a texture model learned from a set of 3D exemplar faces. The traditional 3DMMs [7,12] can explicitly model pose and illumination variations. Pose is estimated by either a perspective camera [7,12] or an affine camera [8,13], and illumination is modelled by either Phong model [7,12] or Spherical Harmonic model [8,13].

In addition to pose and illumination variations, the extended 3DMM [10,11, 14,15] (E-3DMM) can model facial expressions. Specifically, the authors collected large number of 3D scans with diverse expressions to train a shape model which can capture both facial shape and expression variations. Experiments show E-3DMM achieves promising face recognition performance in the presence of pose and expression variations. The very recent work [14] uses E-3DMM to improve the accuracy of the facial landmark detection.

2.2   Fitting

3DMM and E-3DMM can recover the pose, shape, facial texture and illumination from a single image via a fitting process. The fitting is mainly conducted by minimising the RGB value differences over all the pixels in the facial area between the input image and its model-based reconstruction. As the fitting is an ill-posed problem, it is difficult to achieve an efficient and accurate fitting. To improve the fitting performance, many methods have been proposed.

The first fitting method is a Stochastic Newton Optimisation (SNO) [7]. To reduce the computational cost, SNO randomly samples a small subset of the model vertices to construct the fitting cost function. However this small subset does not capture enough information of the whole face, leading to inferior fitting. The Inverse Compositional Image Alignment (ICIA) algorithm [16,17], a gradient-based method, modifies the cost function so that the Jacobian matrix becomes constant. Thus, the Jacobian matrix does not need to be updated in every iteration, improving the efficiency. The efficiency is also the driver behind the linear shape and texture fitting algorithm (List) [18]. List constructs linear systems for shape and texture optimisations, and it uses gradient-based methods to optimise pose and illumination. Multi-Feature Fitting (MFF) [19] is an accurate fitting strategy. MFF extracts many complementary features, such as edge and specular highlight, from the input image to constrain the fitting, leading to a smoother cost function. A recent work [8] is an efficient fitting strategy. Specifically, a probabilistic model [8] incorporating model generalisation error is used to estimate shape. To model specularity reflectance, [8] first projects the fitting cost function into a specularity-free space to model diffuse light. After that, the results are projected back to the original RGB colour space to model specularity. Two more recent works [20,21] use image local image features for fitting, achieving promising results.

2.3   Motivation

Although 3DMM and its variants (3DSM and E-3DMM) model pose, illumination and expression, they do not explicitly model other intra-personal variations, which limits their applications. Many of the existing 3DMMs model the intra-personal variations in a non-linear fashion, making the fitting a difficult problem. In comparison, we propose a unified linear framework which can model many more intra-personal variations. In addition, the linearity nature of our framework leads to a very efficient and accurate fitting.

3   Traditional 3D Morphable Model

In this section, the traditional 3DMMs [7,12] and the fitting problem are formulated. To construct a 3DMM, the registered 3D facial scans including shape and texture are needed. Let the ith vertex of a registered face be located at (x_i, y_i, z_i) and have grey value g_i. Then the shape and texture can be represented as $\mathbf{s}' = (x_1, y_1, z_1, ..., x_n, y_n, z_n)^T$ and $\mathbf{t}' = (g_1, g_2, ..., g_n)^T$, respectively. Symbol n is the number of vertices of a registered face. PCA is then applied to m example faces $\mathbf{s}'$ and $\mathbf{t}'$ separately to express shape $\mathbf{s}$ and texture $\mathbf{t}$ as:

$$\mathbf{s} = \mathbf{s}_0 + \mathbf{S}\boldsymbol{\alpha}, \quad \mathbf{t} = \mathbf{t}_0 + \mathbf{T}\boldsymbol{\beta} \qquad (1)$$

where $\mathbf{s} \in \mathbb{R}^{3n}$ and $\mathbf{t} \in \mathbb{R}^n$. $\mathbf{s}_0$ and $\mathbf{t}_0$ are the mean shape and texture of m training faces respectively. The columns of $\mathbf{S}$ and $\mathbf{T}$ are eigenvectors of shape and texture covariance matrices respectively. The free coefficients $\boldsymbol{\alpha}$ and $\boldsymbol{\beta}$ constitute low-dimension codings of $\mathbf{s}$ and $\mathbf{t}$, respectively.

3DMM can recover the 3D shape, texture, pose, and illumination from a single image via a fitting process. The fitting is conducted by minimising the intensity differences between the input and model reconstructed images. To perform such a minimisation, the 3DMM has to be aligned to the input image by projecting the 3D vertices of $\mathbf{s}(\boldsymbol{\alpha})$ to a 2D image plane via a camera model parameterised by ρ. Then we define $\mathbf{a}^M$ and $\mathbf{a}^I$: (1) $\mathbf{a}^M$ is a vector concatenating the pixel values generated by the vertices of a 3DMM. The value of $\mathbf{a}^M$ is determined by facial texture and illumination. In common with [7,19], the texture is represented by $\mathbf{t}(\boldsymbol{\beta})$ and the illumination is modelled by the Phong reflection with parameter μ. (2) Based on the current alignment determined by $\boldsymbol{\alpha}$ and ρ, the vertices of a 3DMM find the nearest corresponding pixels of a 2D input image. The corresponding pixel values are concatenated as a vector $\mathbf{a}^I$. Therefore, $\mathbf{a}^M$ and $\mathbf{a}^I$ depend on $\{\boldsymbol{\beta}, \mu\}$ and $\{\boldsymbol{\alpha}, \rho\}$, respectively. The fitting can be formulated:

$$\min_{\boldsymbol{\alpha}, \rho, \boldsymbol{\beta}, \mu} \|\mathbf{a}^I(\boldsymbol{\alpha}, \rho) - \mathbf{a}^M(\boldsymbol{\beta}, \mu)\|^2 \qquad (2)$$

In common with [7,12], $\mathbf{a}^M$ is formulated as:

$$\mathbf{a}^M = \underbrace{(\mathbf{t}_0 + \mathbf{T}\boldsymbol{\beta})}_{inter-personal} \, .* \, \underbrace{(l_a\mathbf{I} + l_d\mathbf{N}\mathbf{d})}_{illumination} + \mathbf{e} \qquad (3)$$

where $.*$ denotes element-wise multiplication; l_a and l_d are the strengths of ambient and directed light; $\mathbf{I}$ is a vector with all entries equal to 1; $\mathbf{N} \in \mathbb{R}^{n \times 3}$ is stacked by the surface normal at each vertex; $\mathbf{d} \in \mathbb{R}^3$ denotes light direction; $\mathbf{e}$ is stacked by the specular reflectance e of every vertex: $e = k_s \langle \mathbf{v}, \mathbf{r} \rangle^\tau$. k_s is a constant for specularity; $\mathbf{v}$ and $\mathbf{r}$ denote the viewing and reflection directions respectively. τ denotes the coefficient of shininess. Then Eq. (2) can be rewritten as:

$$\min_\phi \| \underbrace{\mathbf{a}^I(\boldsymbol{\alpha}, \rho)}_{input} - \underbrace{((\mathbf{t}_0 + \mathbf{T}\boldsymbol{\beta}).*(l_a\mathbf{I} + l_d\mathbf{N}\mathbf{d}) + \mathbf{e})}_{reconstruction} \|^2 \tag{4}$$

where $\phi = \{\boldsymbol{\alpha}, \rho, \boldsymbol{\beta}, l_a, l_d, \mathbf{d}, \tau\}$. This is a difficult non-linear optimisation problem due to (1) the exponential form of e and (2) the element-wise multiplication. For different optimisation strategies, refer to Sect. 2.2.

4   Unified 3D Morphable Model (U-3DMM)

We propose a unified 3D morphable model (U-3DMM), which linearly models inter- and intra-personal variations. Inter-personal variations, which are usually used to model identity, are discriminate between different people. In comparison, intra-personal variations are caused by various other random factors such as illumination and occlusion. Inter- and intra-personal variations jointly determine the observed images as shown in Fig. 1. In this section, first, the construction of our U-3DMM is described. Next, an efficient fitting strategy is detailed. Finally, we propose a method to train intra-personal variations using 2D images. In this work, the 3D model used is Surrey Face Model [22].

4.1   Model

Like 3DMM, U-3DMM consists of shape and texture models. The shape model is exactly the same as $\mathbf{s}$ in Eq. (1). Here we only focus on the texture part of U-3DMM.

Motivation and Assumption. The existing 3DMMs model the relationship between inter- and intra-personal variations in a non-linear fashion, for example, the element-wise multiplication operation between inter-personal and illumination in Eq. (3). There are two weaknesses of this nonlinear relationship: (1) it does not generalise well because different relationships should be found to handle different intra-personal variations. For example, the Phong model can only model illumination. (2) The non-linearity causes difficulties of optimisation. To solve these two problems, we

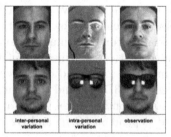

Fig. 1. Intra- and inter-personal variations. The images in the 2nd column are obtained by subtracting the ones in the 3rd column from those in the 1st column with an offset 128

assume an input face is equal to the sum of inter- and intra-personal variations following [23, 24]:

$$\mathbf{a} = \mathbf{a}^{inter} + \mathbf{a}^{intra} \tag{5}$$

where $\mathbf{a}$ is a face, i.e. either $\mathbf{a}^M$ or $\mathbf{a}^I$. $\mathbf{a}^{inter}$ and $\mathbf{a}^{intra}$ are the inter- and intra-peronal parts respectively. The effectiveness of this assumption has been validated in [23, 24]. Specifically, this assumption is successfully used for metric learning in [23] and sparse representation-based classification [24]. The former greatly improves the generalisation capacity of the learned metric and the latter solves the single training sample problem. In the field of 3D modeling, this assumption enables 3DMM to model various intra-personal variations in a unified framework. In addition, it leads to an efficient and accurate fitting detailed in Sect. 4.2.

Modeling. Instead of a non-linear relationship in Eq. (3), the reconstructed texture of U-3DMM is linearly modelled as the sum of two parts in Eq. (5). Each part is modelled linearly. To train these two parts separately, training data $\mathbf{t}'$ and $\mathbf{u}'$ are used: $\mathbf{t}'$, which is the same as in Sect. 3, captures the identity facial texture information; $\mathbf{u}'$ represents one training sample of texture in 3D that captures intra-personal variation such as expression. $\mathbf{u}'$ has the same dimension as $\mathbf{t}'$ and it is organised in the same order in 3D space as $\mathbf{t}'$. $\mathbf{u}'$ can be any type of intra-personal variation. The generation of $\mathbf{u}'$ will be detailed in Sect. 4.3. PCA is applied to m samples $\mathbf{t}'$ and p samples $\mathbf{u}'$ separately to generate the inter- and intra-personal subspaces $\mathbf{T}$ and $\mathbf{U}$ respectively. Thus the U-3DMM reconstructed texture $\mathbf{a}^M$ is formulated as:

$$\mathbf{a}^M = \underbrace{\mathbf{t}_0 + \mathbf{T}\boldsymbol{\beta}}_{inter-personal} + \underbrace{\mathbf{U}\boldsymbol{\gamma}}_{intra-personal} \tag{6}$$

$\mathbf{T}, \mathbf{t}_0$ and $\boldsymbol{\beta}$ have the same meaning as in Eq. (1). The inter-personal part is the same as that of 3DMM in Eq. (3). The columns of $\mathbf{U} \in \mathbb{R}^{n \times p}$ are the eigenvectors of the intra-personal variation covariance matrix. $\boldsymbol{\gamma}$ is a free parameter that determines the intra-personal variations. It is assumed that $\boldsymbol{\beta}$ and $\boldsymbol{\gamma}$ have Gaussian distributions:

$$p(\boldsymbol{\beta}) \sim \mathcal{N}(0, \boldsymbol{\sigma}_t) \tag{7}$$

$$p(\boldsymbol{\gamma}) \sim \mathcal{N}(\boldsymbol{\gamma}_0, \boldsymbol{\sigma}_u) \tag{8}$$

where the value of $\boldsymbol{\gamma}_0$ is computed by projecting the mean of all the training samples $\mathbf{u}'$ to PCA space $\mathbf{U}$, $\boldsymbol{\sigma}_t = (\sigma_{1,t}, ..., \sigma_{m-1,t})^T$, $\boldsymbol{\sigma}_u = (\sigma_{1,u}, ..., \sigma_{p,u})^T$, and $\sigma_{i,t}^2$ and $\sigma_{i,u}^2$ are the ith eigenvalues of inter- and intra-personal variation covariance matrices respectively.

Advantages. The main advantage of U-3DMM is that it can generalise well to diverse intra-personal variations. Table 1 shows that U-3DMM has better generalisation capacity than the existing 3D models. This advantage results from the

Table 1. Generalisation capacity of 3D models

Method	Pose	Illumination	Expression	Occlusion	Other
3DSM [3,6]	✓				
3DMM [7,8]	✓	✓			
E-3DMM [10,11]	✓	✓	✓		
U-3DMM	✓	✓	✓	✓	✓

unified intra-personal part in Eq. (6) which can model more intra-personal variations than the existing 3D models. In addition, compared with the complicated non-linear inter-personal and illumination modeling in Eq. (3), we explicitly linearise the inter- and intra-personal parts in two PCA spaces.

4.2 Fitting

By virtue of a fitting process, U-3DMM can recover the pose, 3D facial shape, facial texture and intra-personal variations from an input image as shown in Fig. 2. Linearly separating intra- and inter-personal parts allows us to achieve an efficient fitting. Based on Eq. (6), the fitting problem of U-3DMM is formulated as:

$$\min_{\alpha,\rho,\beta,\gamma} \| \underbrace{\mathbf{a}^I(\alpha,\rho)}_{input} - \underbrace{(\mathbf{t}_0 + \mathbf{T}\beta + \mathbf{U}\gamma)}_{reconstruction} \|^2 \tag{9}$$

Compared with Eq. (4), clearly, the reconstruction part is linear. To solve this fitting problem, we propose a fitting strategy, which sequentially optimises pose (ρ), shape (α), intra-personal (γ) and facial texture (β) parameters in four separate steps. Closed-form solutions can be obtained for each of these steps. These parameters are optimised by iterating two sequences of steps in turn as shown in Fig. 3. In each step, only one group of parameters are estimated, and the others are regarded as constant.

Pose and Shape Estimations. In the first two steps, pose (ρ) and shape (α) are optimised by solving linear systems using the method in [8]. Specifically, motivated by the fact that the pose and shape variations cause the facial landmarks

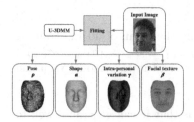

Fig. 2. Input and output of a fitting

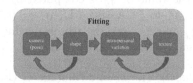

Fig. 3. Topology of fitting algorithm

to shift, ρ and $\boldsymbol{\alpha}$ are estimated by minimising the distance between the landmarks of the input images and those reconstructed from the model. The cost functions for ρ and $\boldsymbol{\alpha}$ are linear [8], thus ρ and $\boldsymbol{\alpha}$ have closed-form solutions. Once ρ and $\boldsymbol{\alpha}$ are estimated, the correspondence between the vertices of the model and pixels of the input images is established.

Intra-personal Variation Estimation. The cost function in Eq. (9) is used to estimate $\boldsymbol{\gamma}$. In this step, $\mathbf{a}^I(\boldsymbol{\alpha}, \rho)$ in Eq. (9) is constant since ρ and $\boldsymbol{\alpha}$ have already been recovered in the first two steps. To avoid over-fitting, a regularisation term based on Eq. (8) is used to constrain the optimisation. Therefore, the optimisation problem is defined as:

$$\min_{\boldsymbol{\gamma}} \|(\mathbf{a}^I - \mathbf{t}_0 - \mathbf{T}\boldsymbol{\beta}) - \mathbf{U}\boldsymbol{\gamma}\|^2 + \lambda_1 \|(\boldsymbol{\gamma} - \boldsymbol{\gamma}_0)./\boldsymbol{\sigma}_u\|^2 \qquad (10)$$

The closed-form solution is $\boldsymbol{\gamma} = (\mathbf{U}^T\mathbf{U} + \boldsymbol{\Sigma}_u)^{-1}(\mathbf{U}^T(\mathbf{a}^I - \mathbf{t}_0 - \mathbf{T}\boldsymbol{\beta}) + \lambda_1(\boldsymbol{\gamma}_0./\boldsymbol{\sigma}_u^2))$ where $\boldsymbol{\Sigma}_u = \mathrm{diag}(\lambda_1/\sigma_{1,u}^2, ..., \lambda_1/\sigma_{p,u}^2)$, ./ denotes element-wise division, and λ_1 is a weighting parameter for the regularisation term. Note that $\boldsymbol{\beta}$ is set to $\mathbf{0}$ in the first iteration: in other words the mean facial texture $\mathbf{t}_0$ is used as the initial estimate of the reconstructed image. In subsequent iterations, $\boldsymbol{\beta}$ is replaced by the estimate recovered in the previous iteration.

Facial Texture Estimation. Having obtained an estimate of $\{\rho, \boldsymbol{\alpha}, \boldsymbol{\gamma}\}$, $\boldsymbol{\beta}$ can be recovered in the final step. Similar to Eq. (10), the cost function for estimating $\boldsymbol{\beta}$ is defined as:

$$\min_{\boldsymbol{\beta}} \|(\mathbf{a}^I - \mathbf{t}_0 - \mathbf{U}\boldsymbol{\gamma}) - \mathbf{T}\boldsymbol{\beta}\|^2 + \lambda_2 \|\boldsymbol{\beta}./\boldsymbol{\sigma}_t\|^2 \qquad (11)$$

The closed-form solution is: $\boldsymbol{\beta} = (\mathbf{T}^T\mathbf{T} + \boldsymbol{\Sigma}_t)^{-1}\mathbf{T}^T(\mathbf{a}^I - \mathbf{t}_0 - \mathbf{U}\boldsymbol{\gamma})$, where λ_2 is a free weighting parameter and $\boldsymbol{\Sigma}_t = \mathrm{diag}(\lambda_2/\sigma_{1,t}^2, ..., \lambda_2/\sigma_{m-1,t}^2)$

4.3   Intra-personal Variation Data Collection

An important prerequisite of building the U-3DMM is to collect intra-personal variation data, i.e. $\mathbf{u}'$. The straightforward approach would be to collect enough 3D scans to capture all types of intra-personal variations. However, such 3D data collection is very expensive. In comparison, it is much easier and cheaper to collect 2D image data which covers such variations. Motivated by this, we propose a method to use 2D images to generate 3D intra-personal variation $\mathbf{u}'$.

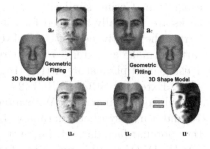

Fig. 4. 3D intra-personal variation data generation. $\mathbf{a}_c$ and $\mathbf{a}_e$ are one 2D image pair without and with intra-personal variation; They are projected to 3D space to reconstruct $\mathbf{u}_c$ and $\mathbf{u}_e$; $\mathbf{u}'$ is the generated 3D data.

The outline of our method is illustrated in Fig. 4. Assume that we have two facial images of the *same* person: one without intra-personal variations $\mathbf{a}_c$ and the other $\mathbf{a}_e$ with such variation, e.g. illumination variation in Fig. 4. In the real world, it is easy to collect this type of image pairs from the internet or from publicly available face databases. To project $\mathbf{a}_e$ and $\mathbf{a}_c$ to 3D space, the correspondence between them and the shape model of U-3DMM has to be created first. Like Sect. 4.2, such a correspondence can be created via geometric fitting, i.e. the pose and shape fitting. By virtue of this correspondence, the intensities of $\mathbf{a}_e$ and $\mathbf{a}_c$ can be associated with the 3D vertices of the shape model, generating 3D data $\mathbf{u}_e$ and $\mathbf{u}_c$.. In Eq. (6), the reconstructed image is computed as a sum of inter- and intra-personal variations. We then define the intra-personal variation $\mathbf{u}'$ as the difference between $\mathbf{u}_e$ and $\mathbf{u}_c$:

$$\mathbf{u}' = \mathbf{u}_e - \mathbf{u}_c \tag{12}$$

The samples of $\mathbf{u}'$ are projected to PCA space to obtain $\mathbf{U}$ of Eq. (6).

Invisible Regions. Due to self-occlusions and pose variations, some facial parts of the 2D images ($\mathbf{a}_e$ and $\mathbf{a}_c$) are not visible. In this work, the pixel values of $\mathbf{u}_e$ and $\mathbf{u}_c$ corresponding to the self-occluded parts of $\mathbf{a}_e$ and $\mathbf{a}_c$ are set to 0. Although those invisible parts are set to 0 for some training images, the same parts are visible for some other training images under different poses. Therefore, training images of different poses are complementary to model the intra-personal variation part.

5   Experiments

Face recognition aims to reduce the impact of intra-personal variations but keep the discriminative inter-personal information. Thus, we remove the intra-personal variations estimated during fitting and keep the shape and texture for face recognition.

In common with [7,8,18], α and β are concatenated as a facial feature for face recognition. Cosine similarity and nearest neighbour classifier are used. Landmarks are manually assigned for the initialisation of U-3DMM fitting. To demonstrate the effectiveness of U-3DMM, we compare U-3DMM with the state of the art. To make an extensive comparison, we implemented a very effective 3DMM using multiple feature fitting [19], Sparse Representation Classification (SRC) [25], Extended SRC (ESRC) [24]. The recognition rates of other methods are cited from their papers. We evaluated these methods on Multi-PIE [26], AR [27], and a new synthetic database. Labeled Faces in the Wild (LFW) [28] is another popular face dataset, however, most subjects in LFW have only one image. As U-3DMM needs image pairs of the same subject to train intra-personal term, LFW is not appropriate to evaluate our method and is not used in our experiment.

5.1   Pose, Occlusion and Illumination Variations

U-3DMM is the first 3D approach to explicitly model combined pose, occlusion and illumination variations. In this section, U-3DMM is compared with state-of-the-art.

Database and Protocol. To our knowledge, there is no database containing large pose, occlusion and illumination variations. Nevertheless, the Multi-PIE database [26] contains two out of three variations, i.e. pose and illumination. We add random occlusions to Multi-PIE images to synthesise a dataset containing all these variations. To simulate real occlusions, the synthetic ones have various sizes and locations within a face.

We generate random occlusions on the facial images. First, we detect the facial area, the width and height of which are denoted as $\mathbf{W}$ and $\mathbf{H}$. Then, a uniformly distributed random coordinate (x, y) in the facial area is generated. Last, the width and height (w and h) of the occlusion are produced by $\{w, h\} = \{\mathbf{W}, \mathbf{H}\} \times rand(0.2, 0.5)$, where $rand$ denotes a uniformly distributed random number generator. $(0.2, 0.5)$ is the range of the random numbers. Hence, the occlusion area of one image can be represented as (x, y, w, h).

A subset of Multi-PIE containing four typical illuminations and four typical poses is used. The four illuminations are left, frontal and right lighting, and ambient lighting (no directed lighting) with lighting IDs 02, 07, 12 and 00. The four poses are frontal and left-rotated by angles $15°$, $30°$, $45°$ with pose IDs 051, 140, 130 and 080. Random occlusions are applied to these images. To train the intra-personal variation part of U-3DMM, a subset of 37 identities (from ID-251 to ID-292) in session II is used. The test set contains all the subjects (from ID-001 to ID-250) in session I. In the test set, the frontal images with ambient lighting and without occlusion are the gallery images and the others are the probe. Both training and test sets contain various pose, illumination and occlusion variations.

Results. Both 3D shape and texture parameters ($\boldsymbol{\alpha}$ and $\boldsymbol{\beta}$) of U-3DMM are discriminative. It is interesting to explore the impact of them on the performance. From Table 2, the face recognition rates when using texture information only is much higher than that when using shape only, indicating that texture is more discriminative than shape. For different illuminations, the performance when using shape does not vary greatly, compared with using texture only. Clearly, facial texture is more sensitive to illumination variations than shape. It is also observed that combining shape and texture by concatenating $\boldsymbol{\alpha}$ and $\boldsymbol{\beta}$ consistently outperforms either one of them. In all the following evaluations, we use both shape and texture.

We compare qualitatively the reconstruction performance of 3DMM and U-3DMM. Facial textures reconstructed by $\boldsymbol{\beta}$ are shown in Fig. 5. As is shown, 3DMM suffers from the over-fitting problem caused by occlusion while U-3DMM can reconstruct the facial features more accurately.

To demonstrate the effectiveness of U-3DMM, it is compared with state-of-the-art methods: SRC [25], ESRC [24] and 3DMM [19]. Figure 6 illustrates

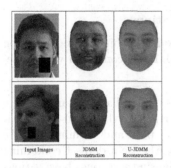

| Input Images | 3DMM Reconstruction | U-3DMM Reconstruction |

Fig. 5. Frontal texture reconstructions

Table 2. Average recognition rate (%) of U-3DMM over all the poses and occlusions per illumination

Parameter	Ambient light	Left light	Frontal light	Right light
Shape (α)	32.1	31.3	31.2	32.1
Texture (β)	59.6	43.4	27.9	48.2
Shape + texture	64.2	48.5	33.9	53.3

how the recognition performance varies with illumination over poses and occlusions. Our U-3DMM outperforms the other three methods because U-3DMM can effectively handle pose, illumination and occlusion simultaneously. By comparison, SRC and ESRC do not handle the pose problem and 3DMM does not explicitly model occlusion. SRC is worst because it suffers from the problem of having just 'a single image per subject in gallery' [24,25]. In the case of 'frontal light', all the methods work worse than the other three illuminations. The inferior performance results from the fact that the illumination effects between the gallery (ambient lighting) and probe (frontal lighting) are larger than the other illumination conditions.

Figure 7 shows how recognition rates, averaged over illuminations and occlusions, vary with pose. All the face recognition rates decrease with the increase of pose variations, showing that pose variations present a challenging problem. U-3DMM works much better than the others due to its strong intra-personal variation modeling capacity. In the case of frontal pose (rotation angle is $0°$) which means only illumination and occlusion are presented, ESRC achieves promising recognition rates because it can explicitly model illumination and occlusion. U-3DMM outperforms ESRC because U-3DMM can extract discriminative shape information for recognition while ESRC cannot.

5.2 Pose and Illumination Variations

Face recognition in the presence of pose variation (PFR) and combining pose and illumination variations (PIFR) is very challenging. Extensive research has been conducted to solve PFR and PIFR problems. In this section, U-3DMM is compared with state-of-the-art methods on Multi-PIE database.

Database and Protocol. Following the existing work, two settings (*Setting*-I and *Setting*-II) are used for PFR and PIFR respectively. *Setting*-I uses a subset in session 01 consisting of 249 subjects with 7 poses and 20 illumination variations. The images of the first 100 subjects constitute the training set. The remaining 149 subjects form the test set. In the test set, the frontal images under neutral

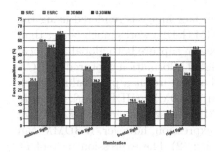

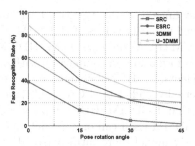

Fig. 6. Average recognition rate over all the poses and occlusions per illumination

Fig. 7. Average recognition rate over all the illuminations and occlusions per pose

illumination work as the gallery and the remaining are probe images. *Setting*-II uses the images of all the 4 sessions (01–04) under 7 poses and only neutral illumination. The images from the first 200 subjects are used for training and the remaining 137 subjects for testing. In the test set, the frontal images from the earliest session work as gallery, and the others are probes.

Pose-Robust Face Recognition. Table 3 compares our U-3DMM with the state-of-the-art. SPAE [31] works best among all the 2D methods due to its strong non-linear modeling capacity. E-3DMM [15] and U-3DMM outperform another two 3D methods ([6] and [32]), as E-3DMM [15] and U-3DMM can model both pose and facial shape rather than pose only by [6,32]. E-3DMM only reports the results using High-Dimensional gabor Feature (HDF) [33] rather than PCA coefficients (α and β). For fair comparison, we also extracted HDF feature from pose-normalised rendered images as follows: First, an input image is aligned to U-3DMM via geometric fitting. Second, the intensity value of each vertex of U-3DMM is assigned by the value of the corresponding pixel of the input image. The values of invisible parts of U-3DMM are assigned with the values

Table 3. Recognition rate (%) across poses on Multi-PIE

Method		$-45°$	$-30°$	$-15°$	$+15°$	$+30°$	$+45°$	Avg.
2D	GMA [29]	75.0	74.5	82.7	92.6	87.5	65.2	79.6
	DAE [30]	69.9	81.2	91.0	91.9	86.5	74.3	82.5
	SPAE [31]	84.9	92.6	96.3	95.7	94.3	84.4	91.4
3D	Asthana [6]	74.1	91.0	95.7	95.7	89.5	74.8	86.8
	MDF [32]	78.7	94.0	99.0	98.7	92.2	81.8	90.7
	E-3DMM (HDF) [15]	97.4	99.5	99.5	99.7	99.0	96.7	**98.6**
	U-3DMM (PCA)	91.2	95.7	96.8	96.9	95.3	90.9	94.5
	U-3DMM (HDF)	96.5	98.4	99.2	98.9	97.9	96.1	**97.8**

from symmetry visible vertices. Last, a frontal face image is rendered using the obtained intensity values of U-3DMM. U-3DMM (HDF) works much better than U-3DMM (PCA) because (1) the HDF feature can capture both global and local facial information, in comparison with only global information captured by PCA coefficients; (2) HDF uses more invariant Gabor feature than pixel values which are actually coded by PCA coefficients. Our U-3DMM (HDF) works slightly worse than E-3DMM (HDF), however, U-3DMM has advantages over E-3DMM: (1) E-3DMM itself can only model pose and expression, however, U-3DMM can explicitly model more intra-personal variations; (2) The expression part of E-3DMM is trained using 3D faces with various expressions, while U-3DMM is trained using easily-collected 2D images; (3) E-3DMM estimates the depth of background, leading to extra computational costs but being useless for improving face recognition rates; while U-3DMM does not.

Pose- and Illumination-Robust Face Recognition. As shown in Table 4, the subspace method [34] works much worse than the others. The deep learning methods, i.e. FIP (face identity-preserving) [2], RL (FIP reconstructed features) [2] and MVP (multi-view perceptron) [35], achieve promising results. U-3DMM outperforms deep learning methods (RL, FIP, and MVP) because 3D methods intrinsically model pose and illumination. Apart from worse performance, deep learning methods share the difficulty of designing a 'good' architecture because (1) there is no theoretical guide and (2) the large number of free parameters are hard to tune.

Table 4. Recognition rate (%) averaging 20 illuminations on Multi-PIE

Method		$-45°$	$-30°$	$-15°$	$0°$	$+15°$	$+30°$	$+45°$	Avg.
Subspace learning	Li [34]	63.5	69.3	79.7	N/A	75.6	71.6	54.6	69.1
Deep learning	RL [2]	66.1	78.9	91.4	94.3	90.0	82.5	62.0	80.7
	FIP [2]	63.6	77.5	90.5	94.3	89.8	80.0	59.5	79.3
	MVP [35]	75.2	83.4	93.3	95.7	92.2	83.9	70.6	84.9
3D method	U-3DMM	73.1	86.9	93.3	99.7	91.3	81.2	69.7	**85.0**

5.3 Other Intra-personal Variations

To further validate the effectiveness of U-3DMM, we evaluate it on the AR database [27].

Database and Protocol. The AR database contains more than 4000 frontal images of 126 subjects with variations in expressions, illuminations and occlusions. To train the intra-personal component of U-3DMM, we use 10 randomly chosen subjects (5 male and 5 female) in Session 1 and with 13 images per subject. Following [10], we randomly chose 100 subjects in Session 1 for testing. In the test set, the neutral images work as gallery and the others are probe.

Table 5. Recognition rate (%) evaluated on AR database

Method	Expression	Illumination	Occlusion	Illu. + Occl	Time
SRC [25]	80.7	71.3	42.5	23.5	-
ESRC [24]	94.3	98.7	80.5	74.5	-
E-3DMM [10]	99.0	-	-	-	slow[a]
3DMM [19]	89.3	99.1	74.5	71.8	23s
U-3DMM	95.3	98.7	92.0	85.5	0.98

[a]The computational complexity of E-3DMM is the same as 3DMM

Results. We compare U-3DMM with 3DMM, E-3DMM [10], SRC, and ESRC. In the presence of illumination, occlusion or both, U-3DMM works much better than SRC and ESRC. This conclusion is consistent with that drawn in Sect. 5.1. For expression variations, our U-3DMM outperforms SRC and ESRC, but works worse than E-3DMM. Note that E-3DMM uses a commercial SDK to extract facial feature and the authors [10] do not report face recognition rates using only shape and texture coefficients that our U-3DMM uses. In addition, our U-3DMM has two advantages over E-3DMM [10]: (1) U-3DMM can potentially model any variations, while E-3DMM is designed specifically to capture pose and expression variations; (2) U-3DMM is more efficient than E-3DMM (Table 5).

6 Conclusions

We propose the U-3DMM, which provides a generic linear framework to model complicated intra-personal variations. The linearity of U-3DMM leads to an efficient and accurate fitting. The experimental results demonstrate that U-3DMM achieves very competitive face recognition rates against the state-of-the-art.

Acknowledgments. This work was sponsored by EPSRC project 'Signal processing in a networked battlespace' under contract EP/K014307/1, 'FACER2VM' under EP/N007743/1, NSFC project under Grant 61375031 and 61573068. The support from EPSRC and the MOD University Defence Research Collaboration (UDRC) in Signal Processing is gratefully acknowledged.

References

1. Hu, G., Chan, C.H., Yan, F., Christmas, W., Kittler, J.: Robust face recognition by an Albedo based 3D morphable model. In: 2014 IEEE International Joint Conference on Biometrics (IJCB), pp. 1–8. IEEE (2014)
2. Zhu, Z., Luo, P., Wang, X., Tang, X.: Deep learning identity preserving face space. In: Proceedings of ICCV, vol. 1, p. 2 (2013)
3. Niinuma, K., Han, H., Jain, A.K.: Automatic multi-view face recognition via 3D model based pose regularization. In: 2013 IEEE Sixth International Conference on Biometrics: Theory, Applications and Systems (BTAS), pp. 1–8. IEEE (2013)

4. Prabhu, U., Heo, J., Savvides, M.: Unconstrained pose-invariant face recognition using 3D generic elastic models. IEEE Trans. Pattern Anal. Mach. Intell. **33**(10), 1952–1961 (2011)
5. Zhang, X., Gao, Y., Leung, M.K.: Recognizing rotated faces from frontal and side views: an approach toward effective use of mugshot databases. IEEE Trans. Inf. Forensics Secur. **3**(4), 684–697 (2008)
6. Asthana, A., Marks, T.K., Jones, M.J., Tieu, K.H., Rohith, M.: Fully automatic pose-invariant face recognition via 3D pose normalization. In: 2011 IEEE International Conference on Computer Vision (ICCV), pp. 937–944. IEEE (2011)
7. Blanz, V., Vetter, T.: Face recognition based on fitting a 3D morphable model. IEEE Trans. Pattern Anal. Mach. Intell., **25**(9), 1063–1074 (2003)
8. Aldrian, O., Smith, W.A.: Inverse rendering of faces with a 3D morphable model. IEEE Trans. Pattern Anal. Mach. Intell. **35**(5), 1080–1093 (2013)
9. Rodriguez, J.T.: 3D face modelling for 2D+3D face recognition. Ph.D. thesis. Surrey University, Guildford, UK (2007)
10. Chu, B., Romdhani, S., Chen, L.: 3D-aided face recognition robust to expression and pose variations. In: 2014 IEEE Conference on Computer Vision and Pattern Recognition (CVPR), pp. 1907–1914. IEEE (2014)
11. Amberg, B., Knothe, R., Vetter, T.: Expression invariant 3D face recognition with a morphable model. In: 8th IEEE International Conference on Automatic Face and Gesture Recognition, FG 2008, pp. 1–6. IEEE (2008)
12. Blanz, V., Vetter, T.: A morphable model for the synthesis of 3D faces. In: Proceedings of the 26th Annual Conference on Computer Graphics and Interactive Techniques, pp. 187–194 (1999)
13. Zhang, L., Samaras, D.: Face recognition from a single training image under arbitrary unknown lighting using spherical harmonics. IEEE Trans. Pattern Anal. Mach. Intell. **28**(3), 351–363 (2006)
14. Zhu, X., Lei, Z., Liu, X., Shi, H., Li, S.Z.: Face alignment across large poses: a 3D solution. arXiv preprint arXiv:1511.07212 (2015)
15. Zhu, X., Lei, Z., Yan, J., Yi, D., Li, S.Z.: High-fidelity pose and expression normalization for face recognition in the wild. In: Proceedings of the IEEE Conference on Computer Vision and Pattern Recognition, pp. 787–796 (2015)
16. Romdhani, S., Vetter, T.: Efficient, robust and accurate fitting of a 3D morphable model. In: Proceedings of 9th IEEE International Conference on Computer Vision, pp. 59–66. IEEE (2003)
17. Kang, B., Byun, H., Kim, D.: Multi-resolution 3D morphable models and its matching method. In: 19th International Conference on Pattern Recognition, pp. 1–4. IEEE (2008)
18. Romdhani, S., Blanz, V., Vetter, T.: Face identification by fitting a 3D morphable model using linear shape and texture error functions. In: Heyden, A., Sparr, G., Nielsen, M., Johansen, P. (eds.) ECCV 2002, Part IV. LNCS, vol. 2353, pp. 3–19. Springer, Heidelberg (2002)
19. Romdhani, S., Vetter, T.: Estimating 3D shape and texture using pixel intensity, edges, specular highlights, texture constraints and a prior. In: IEEE Computer Society Conference on Computer Vision and Pattern Recognition, CVPR 2005, vol. 2, pp. 986–993. IEEE (2005)
20. Huber, P., Feng, Z.H., Christmas, W., Kittler, J., Rätsch, M.: Fitting 3D morphable models using local features. In: ICIP (2015)
21. Zhu, X., Yan, J., Yi, D., Lei, Z., Li, S.Z.: Discriminative 3D morphable model fitting. In: 2015 11th IEEE International Conference and Workshops on Automatic Face and Gesture Recognition (FG), vol. 1, pp. 1–8. IEEE (2015)

22. Huber, P., Hu, G., Tena, R., Mortazavian, P., Koppen, W.P., Christmas, W.J., Rtsch, M., Kittler, J.: A multi resolution 3D morphable face model and fitting framework. In: Proceedings of the 11th Joint Conference on Computer Vision, Imaging and Computer Graphics Theory and Applications,pp. 79–86 (2016)

23. Chen, D., Cao, X., Wang, L., Wen, F., Sun, J.: Bayesian face revisited: a joint formulation. In: Fitzgibbon, A., Lazebnik, S., Perona, P., Sato, Y., Schmid, C. (eds.) ECCV 2012, Part III. LNCS, vol. 7574, pp. 566–579. Springer, Heidelberg (2012)

24. Deng, W., Hu, J., Guo, J.: Extended SRC: undersampled face recognition via intraclass variant dictionary. IEEE Trans. Pattern Anal. Mach. Intell. **34**(9), 1864–1870 (2012)

25. Wright, J., Yang, A.Y., Ganesh, A., Sastry, S.S., Ma, Y.: Robust face recognition via sparse representation. IEEE Trans. Pattern Anal. Mach. Intell. **31**(2), 210–227 (2009)

26. Gross, R., Matthews, I., Cohn, J., Kanade, T., Baker, S.: Multi-pie. Image Vis. Comput. **28**(5), 807–813 (2010)

27. Martinez, A.M.: The AR face database. CVC Technical report 24 (1998)

28. Huang, G.B., Ramesh, M., Berg, T., Learned-Miller, E.: Labeled faces in the wild: a database for studying face recognition in unconstrained environments. Technical report 07–49. University of Massachusetts, Amherst (2007)

29. Sharma, A., Kumar, A., Daume, H., Jacobs, D.W.: Generalized multiview analysis: a discriminative latent space. In: 2012 IEEE Conference on Computer Vision and Pattern Recognition (CVPR), pp. 2160–2167. IEEE (2012)

30. Bengio, Y.: Learning deep architectures for AI. Found. Trends Mach. Learn. **2**(1), 1–127 (2009)

31. Kan, M., Shan, S., Chang, H., Chen, X.: Stacked progressive auto-encoders (spae) for face recognition across poses. In: Proceedings of the IEEE Conference on Computer Vision and Pattern Recognition, pp. 1883–1890 (2013)

32. Li, S., Liu, X., Chai, X., Zhang, H., Lao, S., Shan, S.: Morphable displacement field based image matching for face recognition across pose. In: Fitzgibbon, A., Lazebnik, S., Perona, P., Sato, Y., Schmid, C. (eds.) ECCV 2012, Part I. LNCS, vol. 7572, pp. 102–115. Springer, Heidelberg (2012)

33. Chen, D., Cao, X., Wen, F., Sun, J.: Blessing of dimensionality: high-dimensional feature and its efficient compression for face verification. In: Proceedings of the IEEE Conference on Computer Vision and Pattern Recognition, pp. 3025–3032 (2013)

34. Li, A., Shan, S., Gao, W.: Coupled bias-variance tradeoff for cross-pose face recognition. IEEE Trans. Image Process. **21**(1), 305–315 (2012)

35. Zhu, Z., Luo, P., Wang, X., Tang, X.: Deep learning multi-view representation for face recognition. arXiv preprint arXiv:1406.6947 (2014)

Augmented Feedback in Semantic Segmentation Under Image Level Supervision

Xiaojuan Qi[1]($\boxtimes$), Zhengzhe Liu[1], Jianping Shi[2],
Hengshuang Zhao[1], and Jiaya Jia[1]

[1] The Chinese University of Hong Kong, Shatin, Hong Kong
{xjqi,zzliu,hszhao,leojia}@cse.cuhk.edu.hk
[2] Sense Time Group Limited, Beijing, China
shijianping@sensetime.com

Abstract. Training neural networks for semantic segmentation is data hungry. Meanwhile annotating a large number of pixel-level segmentation masks needs enormous human effort. In this paper, we propose a framework with only image-level supervision. It unifies semantic segmentation and object localization with important proposal aggregation and selection modules. They greatly reduce the notorious error accumulation problem that commonly arises in weakly supervised learning. Our proposed training algorithm progressively improves segmentation performance with augmented feedback in iterations. Our method achieves decent results on the PASCAL VOC 2012 segmentation data, outperforming previous image-level supervised methods by a large margin.

Keywords: Weakly supervised learning · Semantic segmentation · Image-level supervision · Proposal aggregation

1 Introduction

Great improvement was made for semantic segmentation [1–6] based on deep *convolutional neural networks* (DCNNs). The success largely depends on the amount of training data with accurate pixel-level supervision [7–9]. It is well known in this community that collecting accurate annotation in a large quantity is very labor intensive. In our experience, to label a good-quality segmentation map from one image with resolution 400×600, 5–8 min are needed even for an experienced user. It seriously hinders producing a very large set of training data with full labels.

Compared to labor-costly annotation for each pixel, image-level annotation only gives each image several object labels. It is probably the simplest supervision for segmentation, since each image only needs seconds of manual work regardless of its resolution. Compared to the traditional way for segment labeling, image-level supervision can easily scale training data up for hundreds or thousands of times with the same amount of total manual work. This motivates us to conduct research on this topic.

© Springer International Publishing AG 2016
B. Leibe et al. (Eds.): ECCV 2016, Part VIII, LNCS 9912, pp. 90–105, 2016.
DOI: 10.1007/978-3-319-46484-8_6

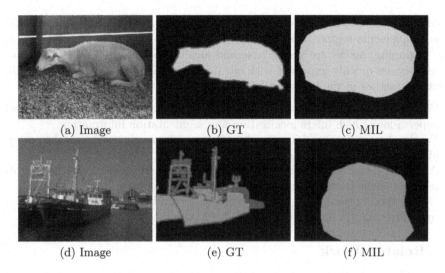

<table>
<tr><td>(a) Image</td><td>(b) GT</td><td>(c) MIL</td></tr>
<tr><td>(d) Image</td><td>(e) GT</td><td>(f) MIL</td></tr>
</table>

Fig. 1. Illustration of MIL prediction. (a) and (d) are the original images. (b) and (e) are the corresponding segmentation ground-truth. (c) and (f) are the corresponding MIL prediction [11]. They are coarse where localization accuracy is not high.

Previous CNN-based image-label supervised segmentation approaches [10–14] can be coarsely cast into two categories. The first line utilizes *multiple instance learning* (MIL) to directly predict pixel labels [10,11,13,14]. Under this setting, each image is viewed as a bag of superpixels/pixels. It is positive when at least one superpixel/pixel is positive. The bag-level image prediction is aggregated by the latent variables, i.e., superpixel/pixel prediction. Since there is no direct pixel-wise supervision from low-level clues during training, this strategy is vulnerable to location variation of objects. One example is shown in Fig. 1, where (c) and (f) are prediction results. Also, MIL heavily relies on good initialization [15–17].

Another stream [12] is based on *Expectation-Maximization* (EM). It iterates between generating temporary segmentation masks and learning with interim supervision. These methods benefit from pixel-level supervision; but errors easily accumulate in iterations.

In this paper, we propose a learning framework that enjoys the benefit from interim pixel-wise supervision. Meanwhile, it suppresses error accumulation in iterations. Instead of obtaining pixel labels solely from previous-round segmentation prediction [12], we introduce an object localization branch to assist supervision generation. This localization branch functions as an object detector, which classifies region proposals to adjust output from the segmentation branch. After localizing the objects, proposals are combined to form a segmentation mask, which also improves segmentation in the other branch.

Our segmentation and localization modules form augmented feedback in the unified training procedure. Prediction of segmentation can help select confident object proposals to supervise training of localization. The result of localization also supplements segmentation to pull results out of local optima. Although in the beginning, masks are very coarse and localization information is not accurate, they are quickly improved with our iterative training procedure. Our main contribution lies in the following folds.

- We propose a new framework for semantic segmentation under image-level supervision, which infers localization and segmentation information.
- We develop an aggregation procedure to generate segmentation masks on top of interim object proposals.
- An effective training method was adopted to make our segmentation and localization benefit from each other with augmented feedback.
- Our method outperforms previous work under similar image-level supervision by a large margin on PASCAL VOC 2012 data.

2 Related Work

2.1 Strongly Supervised Semantic Segmentation

DCNNs have greatly boosted the performance of semantic segmentation [1, 4, 5, 18–20] in the strong supervision setting. The methods fall into two broad categories. One utilizes DCNNs to classify object proposals [4, 5, 18, 20]. The other class adopts fully convolutional networks [1] to make dense prediction. CRF models are applied as post-processing [2] or inside the network to refine prediction [3, 19].

Weakly Supervised Semantic Segmentation. Semantic segmentation under weak supervision is practical due to the heavy burden of annotating pixelwise ground truth. Various forms were proposed [6, 12, 21]. In [6, 12], bounding boxes are used in annotation. Papandreou et al. [12] estimated segmentation with the CRF [22] model. Dai et al. [6] transferred segmentation mask estimation to a proposal selection problem, which achieves good performance. Russakovsky et al. [21] utilized instance points as supervision. To further facilitate annotation, Lin et al. [23] used scribbles, which are more natural for human to draw especially for irregular object shapes. Bounding boxes, points and scribbles are different ways to simplify supervision for users to quickly manipulate images.

Without requiring to draw anything in images, image-level labels were used with *multiple instance learning* (MIL) [10, 11, 13, 14, 24]. Each image is viewed as a bag of pixels (or superpixels). Prediction is taken as latent variables while the image result is accomplished by aggregation. The MIL methods generate coarse prediction because the algorithms generally do not use low-level cues.

Papandreou et al. [12] adopted an *Expectation-Maximization* (EM) approach for image-level supervision. It iterates between segment mask generation and neural network training. Wei et al. [25] used the self-paced learning strategy, initially trained with saliency maps of simple images. It progressively includes more difficult examples. The results update according to output of previous iterations.

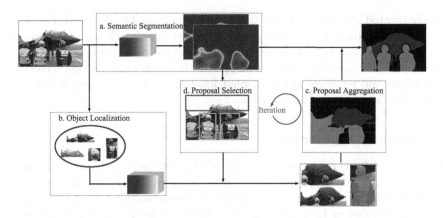

Fig. 2. Overview of our framework with four parts. Part (a) is the fully convolutional segmentation network. Part (b) is the object localization network. Part (c) is the proposal aggregation module. It aggregates the proposal localization result for segmentation training. Part (d) is the proposal selection module. It selects positive and negative proposals for training of the object localization branch. Our network is updated iteratively. In part (d), the green and red bounding boxes mark positive and negative samples. (Color figure online)

Weakly Supervised Localization. Weakly supervised localization uses image-level labels to train detection or localization, which is also related to our task. Part of prior work uses multiple instance learning (MIL) [16,17,26–28]. If an image is positively labeled, at least one region is positive. Contrarily, the image is negative if all regions are negative. The learning process alternates between selecting regions corresponding to the object and estimating the object model. The algorithm relies on the learned model for object region selection. This kind of dependency makes algorithms sensitive to initialization quality [27]. Our localization branch differs from these approaches fundamentally. Our region selection procedure is guided by the segmentation branch, which can effectively correct errors of localization.

3   Our Architecture with Augmented Feedback

Our architecture for weakly-supervised semantic segmentation is illustrated in Fig. 2. It has four main components. Briefly, semantic segmentation and object localization are linked by the aggregation and proposal selection components. The two branches provide augmented feedback to each other to correct errors progressively during training. It is distinct from previous EM/MIL frameworks [12] that only take feedback from the network itself in past iterations.

More specifically, our segmentation branch predicts pixel-wise labels. The per-category scores are clustered into foreground and background as shown in (a). This piece of information is then combined with previous-round object localization prediction to select corresponding positive and negative object proposals for current iteration supervision, as shown in (d). Major errors can be quickly spotted and removed with this type of augmented feedback. Intriguingly, object localization finds objects by classifying proposals. Through aggregation shown in (c), it can tell to an extend whether current segmentation is reasonable or not. This strategy makes it possible to improve segmentation quality by estimating good reference maps. In what follows, we explain these modules and verify their necessity and effectiveness.

3.1 Semantic Segmentation

We adopt a fully convolutional network for the segmentation part [1,2] corresponding to component (a) in our architecture shown in Fig. 2. This part takes an image as input, and generates a per-class score map through down- and up-sampling, denoted as $\{s_c | c = 0, 1, 2, ...C\}$. Where C is the number of categories and class 0 corresponds to background. Each s_c is with the same size of the image. Since this part is almost standard and does not form our main contribution, we refer readers to previous papers [1,2] for more details.

3.2 Object Localization

We resort to bottom-up object proposal generation [29–31] to obtain a set of mask candidates initially. Object localization are obtained with VGG16 [32]. They turn object localization to the task of proposal classification by predicting semantic probability of a proposal belonging to a class. We adopt the sigmoid cross-entropy loss to predict each class. This process is also common now. Each proposal is with a score $\{p^c | c = 1, 2, ..., C\}$ where C is the number of categories.

4 Important Proposal Aggregation and Sample Selection

As aforesaid, our major contribution includes proposal aggregation and selection modules. They provide effective augmented feedback to improve semantic segmentation with only image-level labels.

4.1 Proposal Aggregation

Prediction of localization is inevitably erroneous in the beginning of training. As shown in Fig. 3(c)–(e), birds are mostly mislabeled even with high-confidence localization estimates. This problem is prevalent in weakly supervised localization. Note the results shown in (c)–(e) could significantly degrade learning performance, making parameters stuck at mistaken points.

Our aggregation process is operated independently for each class c. First, we keep useful proposals with proposal score p^c larger than 0.5. For every pixel i in the image, its aggregation score a^i is calculated as sum of all proposal scores p_j^c, i.e., $a^i = \sum_j p_j^c$ where proposals j cover this pixel. If pixel i is not within any proposal, $a^i = 0$.

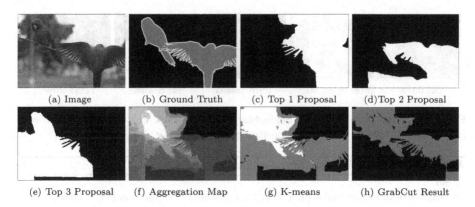

| (a) Image | (b) Ground Truth | (c) Top 1 Proposal | (d)Top 2 Proposal |

| (e) Top 3 Proposal | (f) Aggregation Map | (g) K-means | (h) GrabCut Result |

Fig. 3. Low-level vision cues to update localization scores. (a) Input image. (c)–(e) Top-3 scored proposals for "bird" and their masks generated by MCG [30]. (f) Aggregation map. (g) Clusters by K-means. Since medium-score pixels are ambiguous, we apply graph cuts to determine a partitioning map, which considers image structures. The result is shown in (h).

The resulting aggregation score map is denoted as S_0 as illustrated in Fig. 3(f). It is not accurate initially. To combine information from the two branches, S_0 is then fused with previous-round segmentation score map s_c by element-wise score multiplication. The resulting map is denoted as S.

We group S into three clusters with respect to the high, medium, and low scores. They indicate highly-confidence object, ambiguous, and high-confidence background pixels. The image is accordingly partitioned into three clusters by K-means (Fig. 3(g)). Top and bottom-score pixels are regarded as object and background seeds. Finally, we use GrabCut [33] to partition ambiguous pixels in (g) into objects and background considering image edges. This step makes use of low-level vision cues. In the first pass, the cut result, as shown in Fig. 3(h), is still noisy because of highly inaccurate localization. We will explain in Sect. 5.1 and show in Fig. 5 that it becomes much more reasonable with iteratively improved localization and segmentation with augmented feedback in our framework.

With the above procedure, multiple objects map are generated separately regarding each class. Our final segmentation map is constructed by only assigning each pixel the class with the highest score in S.

4.2 Positive and Negative Sample Selection

To train the localization branch, we need to generate positive and negative samples. These samples are collected by a new strategy by combining segmentation and localization results produced in previous round. Since there are already scores s_c output from the segmentation branch, we collect and group pixels by applying K-means again with cluster number 2. Only the pixels with larger scores are kept. In image space, there can be multiple regions formed for the remaining pixels as shown in Fig. 4(d), corresponding to different objects. We consider

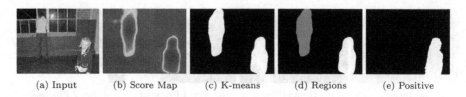

(a) Input	(b) Score Map	(c) K-means	(d) Regions	(e) Positive

Fig. 4. Proposal selection. (b) Segmentation score map. (c) Clusters by scores. (d) Confident regions. (e) Selected positive proposal mask.

Algorithm 1. Positive and Negative Sample Selection

Input:

Segmentation score maps $\{s_c|c = 1, 2, ...C\}$ where C is the number of classes;
Proposal scores $\{p_j^c|j = 1, 2, ...J, c = 1, 2, ..., C\}$ where J is the number of proposals;
IoU thresholds γ_1 and γ_2, where $\gamma_1 > \gamma_2$ for selecting samples;
Proposal score thresholds η_1 and η_2 where $\eta_1 > \eta_2$.

Procedure:

1: **for** $c \in [1, C]$ **do**
2:    **if** Image does not contain object in class c **then**
3:        Continue.
4:    **end if**
5:    Cluster segmentation score map s_c into R_1 and R_2 for confident and ambiguous regions respectively.
6:    **for** $j \in [1, J]$ **do**
7:        Calculate IoU values between the mask of proposal j and all regions in R_1.
8:        Label proposal as positive if its highest IoU $> \gamma_1$ and $p_j^c > \eta_1$.
9:        Label proposal as hard negative if the highest IoU $\leq \gamma_2$ and $p_j^c > \eta_1$.
10:       Label proposal as negative if its highest IoU $\leq \gamma_2$ and $p_j^c \leq \eta_2$.
11:   **end for**
12: **end for**

Output: positive, negative and hard negative samples.

---

their intersection-over-union (IoU) score with the proposal masks. A large score indicates good chance to be an object.

To reduce the influence of incorrect prediction from current segmentation, we consider previous-round proposal score p_j^c for each proposal j to perform positive and negative sample selection. We assign a positive label to proposal j when the IoU overlap with any above mentioned confident segmentation region is higher than a threshold γ_1 and its current proposal score p_j^c is higher than a threshold η_1. We assign it a negative label contrarily when the IoU overlap is lower than a threshold γ_2 with any confident segment region and either of the following conditions is satisfied: (1) its previous-pass proposal score p_j^c is lower than η_2; (2) its previous-pass proposal score is higher than η_1. And the latter are regarded as hard negatives. The selection procedure is summarized in Algorithm 1.

To train the localization branch, positive and negative samples are used. Proposals neither positive nor negative are omitted accordingly. Since positive

---

Algorithm 2. Our Complete Network System with Augmented Feedback

---

Input:
    Input image set; proposal set; maximum iteration number T;
Procedure:
1: Initialize the proposal score with the classification network [32, 35];
2: **for** $i \in [1, T]$ **do**
3:    Aggregate proposals to generate segmentation masks (described in Sect. 4.1);
4:    Train semantic segmentation branch;
5:    Select positive and negative samples (described in Sect. 4.2);
6:    Train object localization branch;
7:    Re-localize object proposals using the trained localization branch;
8: **end for**
Output: Semantic segmentation model.

---

samples are generally much less than negative ones, to balance the learning process, we adopt a random sampling strategy. For each batch, we randomly sample negatives to make the numbers of positive and negative samples around 1 : 3 [34]. Hard negative samples provided in Algorithm 1 are with the highest priority to be kept for training. Specifically, when sampling negative training data, we first consider the hard negatives. If their total number is not large enough for final ratio 1 : 3, we include other negative ones.

4.3 Training Algorithm

We adopt an iterative optimization scheme. The training procedure begins with classifying proposals using the network of [35]. In each pass, we train the segmentation branch with supervision of the segmentation mask produced in previous round. The available prediction scores of both branches are used to select positive and negative samples, which was described in Sect. 4.2. Then we train the object localization branch, which are followed by re-localizing object proposals.

Finally, we aggregate the re-localized object proposals using the method presented in Sect. 4.1, generating semantic segmentation masks. These steps iterate in a few passes until no obvious change on results can be observed. The process is summarized in Algorithm 2.

5 Experiments

Our method is evaluated on the PASCAL VOC 2012 segmentation benchmark dataset [7]. This dataset has 20 object categories and 1,464 images for training. Following the procedure of [2,6,12] to increase image variety, the training data is augmented to 10,582 images. In our experiments, we only use image-level labels. The result is evaluated on the PASCAL VOC validation and test sets, which contain 1,449 and 1,456 images respectively. The performance is evaluated regarding Intersection over union (IoU). We adopt Deeplab-largeFOV [2] as the baseline network. 100 held-out random validation images are used for cross-validation to set hyper-parameters.

5.1   Training Strategy

The network is trained as shown in Algorithm 2. Our optimization alternates between semantic segmentation and object localization training. We use the Caffe framework [36]. Parameters of the segmentation branch are initialized with the model provided in [2,12]. In the training phase, a min-batch size of 8 images is adopted and 321×321 image patches are randomly cropped following the procedure of [2,12] as the network input. The initial learning rate is 0.001. It is divided by 10 after every 2 epochs. Training terminates after 8,000 iterations.

The localization branch is initialized with VGG16 [32,35]. For its training, 30 proposals randomly sampled from one image with positive-negative ratio 1 : 3 form a mini-batch. They are all resized to resolution 224×224. The initial learning rate is 0.0001. It is divided by 10 for every epoch. Training terminates after 15,000 iterations. Momentum and weight decay are set to 0.9 and 0.0005 for both branches.

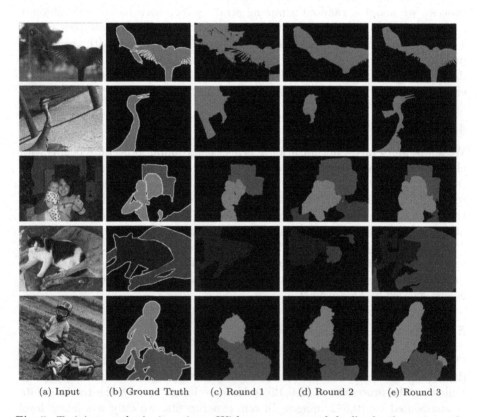

(a) Input   (b) Ground Truth   (c) Round 1   (d) Round 2   (e) Round 3

Fig. 5. Training masks in iterations. With our augmented feedback, the estimated segmentation mask gets improved. The first-row example corresponds to that in Fig. 4, which shows how the segmentation estimate is updated in iterations.

Table 1. Comparison with our baseline model. Results are evaluated on the PASCAL VOC 2012 segmentation validation dataset. Results from different iterations are listed.

Methods	Mean IoU %
WSSL [12]	35.60
Classification network baseline	38.63
Ours (Round 1)	47.40
Ours (Round 2)	48.12
Ours (Round 3)	**50.41**

Table 2. Results on PASCAL VOC 2012 segmentation validation dataset.

Methods	mAP%@0.5
Classification-net baseline [35]	5.71
RMI [26]	12.02
Single-branch baseline	16.75
Ours	**28.25**

5.2 Evaluation of the Two-Branch Framework

We use the classification network finely tuned on VOC 2012 dataset [35] to predict scores of object proposals and aggregate the result to generate the first-iteration segmentation mask, which is our training baseline. Then our training procedure proceeds as depicted in Algorithm 2. In each iteration, the estimated masks get more accurate as shown in Fig. 5. This process benefits from object localization with our proposal aggregation module. The performance on the VOC 2012 validation set of the iterative training procedure is summarized in Table 1.

More than 11 % performance improvement is yielded using our learning procedure. Compared with WSSL [12], which uses the trained semantic segmentation model to perform next-round segmentation mask estimation, our method outperforms it with about 15 % higher mean IoU. The intuitive explanation is that positive feedback is much augmented with our proposal aggregation and selection strategies in iterations. The statistics manifest that our method does not easily accumulate errors in iterations.

5.3 Evaluation of the Localization Branch

We evaluate localization performance in terms of bounding box mAP (mean average precision) [7] on the PASCAL VOC 2012 segmentation validation set with IoU threshold 0.5. The object proposals are obtained from the MCG [30] method. The initial classification network [35] serves as our baseline. We also compare with weakly-supervised object localization method RMI [26] and our own constructed single-model baseline that uses only the object localization branch to

Table 3. Results evaluated on PASCAL VOC 2012 validation set. * denotes utilizing CRF [22] in the testing phase as post processing.

Proposal generation methods	Mean IoU%
SS	46.98
SS*	51.62
MCG	50.41
MCG*	**54.34**

perform positive and negative sample selection. To compare with RMI [26], we extract the VGG16 [32] `fc7` feature and conduct SVM classification following the procedure of [26]. The performance is summarized in Table 2.

Our method outperforms the baseline classification network by a large margin, which shows the effectiveness of our method in terms of localization with the iterative update. Compared to RMI [26] and our own single-branch baseline, the two-branch architecture iteratively and stably provides more and more accurate samples especially in later passes with the effective selection procedure.

5.4   Using Different Object Proposal Generation Strategies

We compare different object proposal generation strategies, including selective search (SS) [29] and MCG [30] for our framework. Segmentation performance with these strategies is listed in Table 3. MCG [30] achieves higher accuracy when training the semantic segmentation module. This is because the segmentation quality of MCG is higher than selective search while our estimated semantic mask is aggregated from the proposal mask where a high-quality contour would be helpful. We note, during testing, our method does not rely on object proposals. So the higher accuracy of MCG makes our network benefit from better segmentation mask. When CRF [22] is applied in post-processing in the segmentation testing phase, the performance difference reduced to 2 %.

Visual quality of the four strategies is compared in Fig. 6. Using MCG proposal masks, the learned network predicts semantic segmentation results with reasonable contours. With CRF, the object contour becomes even clearer.

5.5   Comparison Regarding Different Weak Annotation Strategies

We compare with other weakly-supervised methods using different ways of annotation. The results are listed in Table 4. This is to demonstrate the performance gap among strategies using image-level annotation and other strategies with more information for supervision. The comparison with that of [10] is not that fair because the network deployed in this method uses the overfeat [37] architecture. Moreover, This method uses 700k images to train the network, while all others take only 10k images.

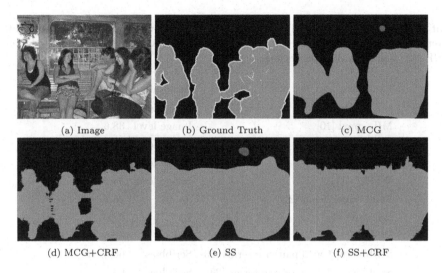

Fig. 6. Results of using different proposal generation methods. (c) and (e) are results using the MCG and selective search proposal masks respectively. (d) and (f) are the corresponding results incorporating CRF [22] post-processing in the testing phase.

Except for [10], all other networks are built on top of VGG-16 [32]. Our method outperforms all other image-level weak supervision methods [10,11,27] with more than 10 % mean IoU difference. Our method even performs better than the method with point supervision, which needs extra point annotation. Compared with the box supervised methods [6,11] and scribble supervised method [23], our method degrades gracefully with regard to the annotation effort needed for getting bounding boxes or scribbles. Nevertheless, image level labels are the easiest to obtain without any image touch-up.

5.6   More Comparison Regarding Image-Level Supervision

We provide more comparison with other image-level weakly-supervised semantic segmentation solutions. Performance was evaluated on the PASCAL VOC 2012 *test* set. Results are listed in Table 5. WSSL [12] and MIL-FCN [11] are built on VGG16 [32]. Our method performs better by a large margin of 15 %, which shows the effectiveness of utilizing object localization to provide extra information during training.

Our method does not have the issues of the EM based method [12] since we utilize two branches to get extra supervision for next round optimization. Our process can be fairly effective by enjoying possible pixel-level information. Our method behaves on par with the transferable learning method [39], which uses 60k images with pixel-level annotation to learn the transferable knowledge. We show our result on Pascal VOC 2012 validation set in Fig. 7. The figure shows that our network can well capture the shape of objects. By using CRF [22] in the testing phase, more details along boundaries are revealed.

Table 4. Comparison of weakly-supervised semantic segmentation methods using different ways for annotation on the PASCAL VOC 2012 validation dataset. * denotes CRF [22] applied in post-processing.

Methods	Annotation	Mean IoU%
MIL-FCN [27]	Image level	25.1
MIL-sppxl [10]	Image level	38.6
MIL-obj [10]	Image level	37.8
MIL-seg [10]	Image level	42.0
WSSL* [11]	Image level	38.2
Point supervision [21]	Spot	46.1
BoxSup* [6]	Bx	62.0
WSSL* [11]	Box	60.6
Scribblesup* w/o pairwise terms [23]	Scribbles	60.5
Scribblesup* w/ pairwise terms [23]	Scribbles	63.1
Ours+ss	Image level	46.98
Ours+mcg	Image level	50.41
Ours+ss*	Image level	52.62
Ours+mcg*	Image level	54.34

Table 5. Comparison with state-of-the-art weakly supervised methods on the PASCAL VOC 2012 test set. * denotes CRF [22] used in post-processing in the testing phase.

Methods	Annotation	Mean IoU%
MIL-sppxl [10]	Image level 700k	35.8
MIL-obj [10]	Image level 700k	37.0
MIL-seg [10]	Image level 700k	40.6
MIL-FCN [11]	Image level 10k	24.9
WSSL* [12]	Image level 10k	39.6
CCNN [14]	Image level 10k	35.6
CCNN+size [14]	Image level 10k+size	43.3
CCNN+size* [14]	Image level 10k +size	45.1
SN_B [38]	Image level 10k	43.2
STC* [25]	Image level 60k	51.2
TransferNet [39]	Image level 10k +pixel level 60k	51.2
Ours+ss	Image level 10k	47.8
Ours+mcg	Image level 10k	50.6
Ours+ss*	Image level 10k	52.7
Ours+mcg*	Image level 10k	**55.5**

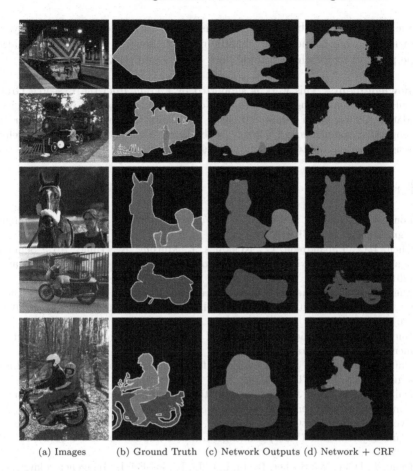

(a) Images   (b) Ground Truth   (c) Network Outputs (d) Network + CRF

Fig. 7. Our network result is the output from the semantic segmentation branch up-sampled to the original image resolution. Network+CRF means utilizing CRF [22] in post processing.

6   Conclusion and Future Work

We have proposed a weakly supervised method for semantic segmentation under image-level supervision. Our method includes the semantic segmentation and object localization branches in a unified framework, in which the two branches profit each other. With our designed object proposal aggregation and proposal selection modules, the positive feedback from the two branches can be augmented. Such augmented positive feedback greatly improve the image level weakly supervised semantic segmentation task. As a byproduct, object localization performance gets also improved. In future work, we will exploit the framework for other weakly supervised learning tasks, e.g. simultaneous segmentation and detection [18], and extend our method to the semi-supervised setting. Further, since our annotation is economical, scaling our segmentation method up to include thousands of object categories is also a target to pursue. Finally, we plan to extend our framework to handle more challenging context segmentation (scene parsing) tasks which include both objects and stuff.

Acknowledgments. This work is supported by a grant from the Research Grants Council of the Hong Kong SAR (project No. 2150760) and by the National Science Foundation China, under Grant 61133009. We thank the anonymous reviewers for their suggestive comments and valuable feedback, and Mr. Zhuotun Zhu for the helpful discussion regarding the topic of multiple instance learning.

References

1. Long, J., Shelhamer, E., Darrell, T.: Fully convolutional networks for semantic segmentation. In: CVPR (2015)
2. Chen, L.C., Papandreou, G., Kokkinos, I., Murphy, K., Yuille, A.L.: Semantic image segmentation with deep convolutional nets and fully connected CRFs. arXiv (2014)
3. Zheng, S., Jayasumana, S., Romera-Paredes, B., Vineet, V., Su, Z., Du, D., Huang, C., Torr, P.H.: Conditional random fields as recurrent neural networks. In: ICCV (2015)
4. Hariharan, B., Arbeláez, P., Girshick, R., Malik, J.: Hypercolumns for object segmentation and fine-grained localization. In: CVPR (2015)
5. Dai, J., He, K., Sun, J.: Convolutional feature masking for joint object and stuff segmentation. In: CVPR (2015)
6. Dai, J., He, K., Sun, J.: Boxsup: exploiting bounding boxes to supervise convolutional networks for semantic segmentation. In: ICCV (2015)
7. Everingham, M., Van Gool, L., Williams, C.K., Winn, J., Zisserman, A.: The pascal visual object classes (VOC) challenge. Int. J. Comput. Vis. IJCV **88**(2), 303–338 (2010)
8. Deng, J., Dong, W., Socher, R., Li, L.J., Li, K., Fei-Fei, L.: Imagenet: a large-scale hierarchical image database. In: CVPR (2009)
9. Lin, T.-Y., Maire, M., Belongie, S., Hays, J., Perona, P., Ramanan, D., Dollár, P., Zitnick, C.L.: Microsoft COCO: common objects in context. In: Fleet, D., Pajdla, T., Schiele, B., Tuytelaars, T. (eds.) ECCV 2014, Part V. LNCS, vol. 8693, pp. 740–755. Springer, Heidelberg (2014)
10. Pinheiro, P.O., Collobert, R.: From image-level to pixel-level labeling with convolutional networks. In: CVPR (2015)
11. Pathak, D., Shelhamer, E., Long, J., Darrell, T.: Fully convolutional multi-class multiple instance learning. arXiv (2014)
12. Papandreou, G., Chen, L.C., Murphy, K., Yuille, A.L.: Weakly-and semi-supervised learning of a DCNN for semantic image segmentation. arXiv (2015)
13. Xu, J., Schwing, A.G., Urtasun, R.: Learning to segment under various forms of weak supervision. In: CVPR (2015)
14. Pathak, D., Krahenbuhl, P., Darrell, T.: Constrained convolutional neural networks for weakly supervised segmentation. In: ICCV (2015)
15. Song, H.O., Girshick, R., Jegelka, S., Mairal, J., Harchaoui, Z., Darrell, T.: On learning to localize objects with minimal supervision. arXiv (2014)
16. Kumar, M.P., Packer, B., Koller, D.: Self-paced learning for latent variable models. In: NIPS (2010)

17. Deselaers, T., Alexe, B., Ferrari, V.: Localizing objects while learning their appearance. In: Daniilidis, K., Maragos, P., Paragios, N. (eds.) ECCV 2010, Part IV. LNCS, vol. 6314, pp. 452–466. Springer, Heidelberg (2010)
18. Hariharan, B., Arbeláez, P., Girshick, R., Malik, J.: Simultaneous detection and segmentation. In: Fleet, D., Pajdla, T., Schiele, B., Tuytelaars, T. (eds.) ECCV 2014, Part VII. LNCS, vol. 8695, pp. 297–312. Springer, Heidelberg (2014)
19. Liu, Z., Li, X., Luo, P., Loy, C.C., Tang, X.: Semantic image segmentation via deep parsing network. In: ICCV (2015)
20. Noh, H., Hong, S., Han, B.: Learning deconvolution network for semantic segmentation. In: ICCV (2015)
21. Russakovsky, O., Bearman, A.L., Ferrari, V., Li, F.F.: What's the point: semantic segmentation with point supervision. arXiv (2015)
22. Krähenbühl, P., Koltun, V.: Efficient inference in fully connected crfs with gaussian edge potentials. arXiv (2012)
23. Lin, D., Dai, J., Jia, J., He, K., Sun, J.: Scribblesup: scribble-supervised convolutional networks for semantic segmentation. In: CVPR (2016)
24. Vezhnevets, A., Buhmann, J.M.: Towards weakly supervised semantic segmentation by means of multiple instance and multitask learning. In: CVPR (2010)
25. Wei, Y., Liang, X., Chen, Y., Shen, X., Cheng, M.M., Zhao, Y., Yan, S.: STC: a simple to complex framework for weakly-supervised semantic segmentation. arXiv (2015)
26. Wang, X., Zhu, Z., Yao, C., Bai, X.: Relaxed multiple-instance svm with application to object discovery. In: ICCV (2015)
27. Cinbis, R.G., Verbeek, J., Schmid, C.: Weakly supervised object localization with multi-fold multiple instance learning. arXiv (2015)
28. Song, H.O., Lee, Y.J., Jegelka, S., Darrell, T.: Weakly-supervised discovery of visual pattern configurations. In: NIPS (2014)
29. Uijlings, J.R., van de Sande, K.E., Gevers, T., Smeulders, A.W.: Selective search for object recognition. Int. J. Comput. Vis. (IJCV) 104(2), 154–171 (2013)
30. Arbeláez, P., Pont-Tuset, J., Barron, J., Marques, F., Malik, J.: Multiscale combinatorial grouping. In: CVPR (2014)
31. Carreira, J., Sminchisescu, C.: Constrained parametric min-cuts for automatic object segmentation. In: CVPR (2010)
32. Simonyan, K., Zisserman, A.: Very deep convolutional networks for large-scale image recognition. arXiv (2014)
33. Rother, C., Kolmogorov, V., Blake, A.: Grabcut: interactive foreground extraction using iterated graph cuts. ACM Trans. Graph. (TOG) 23(3), 309–314 (2004)
34. Girshick, R., Donahue, J., Darrell, T., Malik, J.: Rich feature hierarchies for accurate object detection and semantic segmentation. In: CVPR (2014)
35. Hong, S., Noh, H., Han, B.: Decoupled deep neural network for semi-supervised semantic segmentation. In: NIPS (2015)
36. Jia, Y., Shelhamer, E., Donahue, J., Karayev, S., Long, J., Girshick, R., Guadarrama, S., Darrell, T.: Caffe: convolutional architecture for fast feature embedding. In: Multimedia (2014)
37. Sermanet, P., Eigen, D., Zhang, X., Mathieu, M., Fergus, R., LeCun, Y.: Overfeat: Integrated recognition, localization and detection using convolutional networks. arXiv (2013)
38. Wei, Y., Liang, X., Chen, Y., Jie, Z., Xiao, Y., Zhao, Y., Yan, S.: Learning to segment with image-level annotations. PR (2016)
39. Hong, S., Oh, J., Han, B., Lee, H.: Learning transferrable knowledge for semantic segmentation with deep convolutional neural network. arXiv (2015)

Poster Session 9

Linear Depth Estimation from an Uncalibrated, Monocular Polarisation Image

William A.P. Smith[1(✉)], Ravi Ramamoorthi[2], and Silvia Tozza[3]

[1] University of York, York, UK
william.smith@york.ac.uk
[2] UC San Diego, San Diego, USA
ravir@cs.ucsd.edu
[3] Sapienza - Università di Roma, Rome, Italy
tozza@mat.uniroma1.it

Abstract. We present a method for estimating surface height directly from a single polarisation image simply by solving a large, sparse system of linear equations. To do so, we show how to express polarisation constraints as equations that are linear in the unknown depth. The ambiguity in the surface normal azimuth angle is resolved globally when the optimal surface height is reconstructed. Our method is applicable to objects with uniform albedo exhibiting diffuse and specular reflectance. We extend it to an uncalibrated scenario by demonstrating that the illumination (point source or first/second order spherical harmonics) can be estimated from the polarisation image, up to a binary convex/concave ambiguity. We believe that our method is the first monocular, passive shape-from-x technique that enables well-posed depth estimation with only a single, uncalibrated illumination condition. We present results on glossy objects, including in uncontrolled, outdoor illumination.

Keywords: Polarisation · Shape-from-x · Bas-relief ambiguity

1 Introduction

When unpolarised light is reflected by a surface it becomes partially polarised [1]. The degree to which the reflected light is polarised conveys information about the surface orientation and, therefore, provides a cue for shape recovery. There are a number of attractive properties to this 'shape-from-polarisation' (SfP) cue. It requires only a single viewpoint and illumination environment, it is invariant to illumination and surface albedo and it provides information about both the zenith and azimuth angle of the surface normal. Like photometric stereo, shape estimates are dense (the surface normal is estimated at every pixel so resolution is limited only by the sensor) and, since it does not rely on detecting or matching features, it is applicable to smooth, featureless surfaces.

Electronic supplementary material The online version of this chapter (doi:10. 1007/978-3-319-46484-8_7) contains supplementary material, which is available to authorized users.

© Springer International Publishing AG 2016
B. Leibe et al. (Eds.): ECCV 2016, Part VIII, LNCS 9912, pp. 109–125, 2016.
DOI: 10.1007/978-3-319-46484-8_7

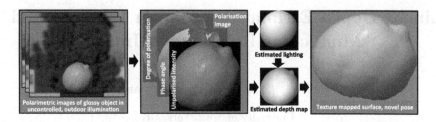

Fig. 1. Overview of method: from a single polarisation image of a homogenous, glossy object in uncontrolled (possibly outdoor) illumination, we estimate lighting and compute depth directly.

However, there are a number of drawbacks to using SfP in a practical setting. The polarisation cue alone provides only ambiguous estimates of surface orientation. Hence, previous work focuses on developing heuristics to locally disambiguate the surface normals. Even having done so, surface orientation is only a 2.5D shape cue and so the estimated normal field must be integrated in order to recover surface depth [2] or used to refine a depth map captured using other cues [3]. This two step approach of disambiguation followed by integration means that the surface integrability constraint is not enforced during disambiguation and also that errors accumulate over the two steps. In this paper, we propose a SfP method (see Fig. 1 for an overview) with the following novel ingredients:

1. In contrast to prior work, we compute SfP in the depth, as opposed to the surface normal, domain. Instead of disambiguating the polarisation normals, we defer resolution of the ambiguity until surface height is computed. To do so, we express the azimuthal ambiguity as a collinearity condition that is satisfied by either interpretation of the polarisation measurements.
2. We express polarisation and shading constraints as linear equations in the unknown depth enabling efficient and globally optimal depth estimation.
3. We use a novel hybrid diffuse/specular polarisation and shading model, allowing us to handle glossy surfaces.
4. We show that illumination can be determined from the ambiguous normals and unpolarised intensity up to a binary ambiguity (a particular generalised Bas-relief [4] transformation: the convex/concave ambiguity). This means that our method can be applied in an uncalibrated scenario and we consider both point source and 1st/2nd order spherical harmonic (SH) illumination.

1.1   Related Work

Previous SfP methods can be categorised into two groups, those that: 1. use only a single polarisation image, and 2. combine a polarisation image with additional cues. The former group (of which our method is a member) can be considered 'single shot' methods (single shot capture devices exist using polarising beam-splitters [25] or CMOS sensors with micropolarising filters [26]). More commonly, a polarisation image is obtained by capturing a sequence of images in which a linear polarising filter is rotated in front of the camera (possibly with unknown rotation angles [5]). SfP methods can also be classified according to the polarisation model used (dielectric versus metal, diffuse, specular or hybrid models) and if they compute shape in the surface normal or surface height domain.

Single polarisation image. The earliest work focussed on capture, decomposition and visualisation of polarisation images [6]. Both Miyazaki et al. [2] and Atkinson and Hancock [7] used a diffuse polarisation model and, under an assumption of object convexity, propagate disambiguation of the surface normal inwards from the boundary. This greedy approach will not produce globally optimal results, limits application to objects with a visible occluding boundary and does not consider integrability. Morel et al. [8] took a similar approach but used a specular polarisation model suitable for metallic surfaces. Huynh et al. [9] also assumed convexity to disambiguate the polarisation normals; however, their approach also estimates refractive index. As in our method, Mahmoud et al. [10] exploited the unpolarised intensity via a shading cue. Assuming Lambertian reflectance and known lighting direction and albedo, the surface normal ambiguity can be resolved. We avoid all of these assumptions and, by strictly enforcing integrability, improve robustness to noise.

Polarisation with additional cues. Rahmann and Canterakis [11] combined a specular polarisation model with stereo cues. Similarly, Atkinson and Hancock [12] used polarisation normals to segment an object into patches, simplifying stereo matching. Huynh et al. [13] extended their earlier work to use multispectral measurements to estimate both shape and refractive index. There have been a number of attempts to augment polarisation cues with calibrated, Lambertian photometric stereo, e.g. [14]. Drbohlav and Sara [15] showed how the Bas-relief ambiguity [4] in uncalibrated photometric stereo could be resolved using polarisation. However, this approach requires a polarised light source. Recently, Ngo et al. [16] derived constraints that allowed surface normals, light directions and refractive index to be estimated from polarisation images under varying lighting. However, this approach requires at least 4 light directions in contrast to the single direction required by our method. Very recently, Kadambi et al. [3] proposed an interesting approach in which a single polarisation image is combined with a depth map obtained by an RGBD camera. The depth map is used to disambiguate the normals and provide a base surface for integration.

2   Problem Formulation and Polarisation Theory

We make the following assumptions (more general than much previous work in the area): **1.** Dielectric (i.e. non-metallic) material with uniform (but unknown) albedo. **2.** Orthographic projection. **3.** The refractive index of the surface is known, though dependency on this quantity is weak and we fix it to a constant value for all of our experiments. **4.** Pixels can be classified as either diffuse dominant or specular dominant. **5.** The object surface is smooth (i.e. C^2 continuous).

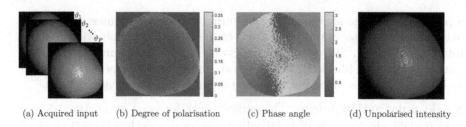

(a) Acquired input   (b) Degree of polarisation   (c) Phase angle   (d) Unpolarised intensity

Fig. 2. Polarimetric capture (a) and decomposition to polarisation image (b–d).

We parameterise surface height by the function $z(\mathbf{u})$, where $\mathbf{u} = (x, y)$ is an image point. Foreground pixels belonging to the surface are represented by the set $\mathcal{F}$, $|\mathcal{F}| = K$. The unit surface normal can be expressed in spherical world coordinates as:

$$\mathbf{n}(\mathbf{u}) = [n_x(\mathbf{u}) \ n_y(\mathbf{u}) \ n_z(\mathbf{u})]^T = [\sin\alpha(\mathbf{u})\sin\theta(\mathbf{u}) \ \cos\alpha(\mathbf{u})\sin\theta(\mathbf{u}) \ \cos\theta(\mathbf{u})]^T, \quad (1)$$

and formulated via the surface gradient as follows

$$\mathbf{n}(\mathbf{u}) = \frac{[-p(\mathbf{u}) \ -q(\mathbf{u}) \ 1]^T}{\sqrt{p(\mathbf{u})^2 + q(\mathbf{u})^2 + 1}}, \quad (2)$$

where $p(\mathbf{u}) = \partial_x z(\mathbf{u})$ and $q(\mathbf{u}) = \partial_y z(\mathbf{u})$, so that $\nabla z(\mathbf{u}) = [p(\mathbf{u}) \ q(\mathbf{u})]^T$.

2.1 Polarisation Image

When unpolarised light is reflected from a surface, it becomes partially polarised. There are a number of mechanisms by which this process occurs. The two models that we use are described in Sect. 2.2 and are suitable for dielectric materials. A *polarisation image* (Fig. 2b–d) can be estimated by capturing a sequence of images (Fig. 2a) in which a linear polarising filter in front of the camera is rotated through a sequence of $P \geq 3$ different angles ϑ_j, $j \in \{1, \ldots, P\}$. The intensity at a pixel varies sinusoidally between $I_{\min}$ and $I_{\max}$ with the polariser angle:

$$i_{\vartheta_j}(\mathbf{u}) = \frac{I_{\max}(\mathbf{u}) + I_{\min}(\mathbf{u})}{2} + \frac{I_{\max}(\mathbf{u}) - I_{\min}(\mathbf{u})}{2} \cos[2\vartheta_j - 2\phi(\mathbf{u})]. \quad (3)$$

The polarisation image is obtained by decomposing the sinusoid at every pixel into three quantities [6]. These are the *phase angle*, $\phi(\mathbf{u})$, the *degree of polarisation*, $\rho(\mathbf{u})$, and the *unpolarised intensity*, $i_{\mathrm{un}}(\mathbf{u})$, where:

$$\rho(\mathbf{u}) = \frac{I_{\max}(\mathbf{u}) - I_{\min}(\mathbf{u})}{I_{\max}(\mathbf{u}) + I_{\min}(\mathbf{u})} \quad \text{and} \quad i_{\mathrm{un}}(\mathbf{u}) = \frac{I_{\max}(\mathbf{u}) + I_{\min}(\mathbf{u})}{2}. \quad (4)$$

The parameters of the sinusoid can be estimated from the captured image sequence using nonlinear least squares [7], linear methods [9] or via a closed form solution [6] for the specific case of $P = 3$, $\vartheta \in \{0°, 45°, 90°\}$. See supplementary material for details of our sinusoid fitting scheme.

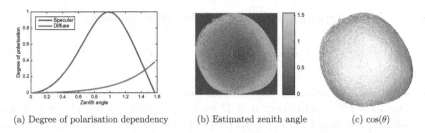

(a) Degree of polarisation dependency   (b) Estimated zenith angle   (c) $\cos(\theta)$

Fig. 3. (a) Relationship between degree of polarisation and zenith angle, for specular and diffuse dielectric reflectance with $\eta = 1.5$. (b) Estimated zenith angle from degree of polarisation in Fig. 2b. (c) Visualisation of estimated zenith angle. (Color figure online)

2.2 Polarisation Models

A polarisation image provides a constraint on the surface normal direction at each pixel. The exact nature of the constraint depends on the polarisation model used. We assume that the object under study is composed of a dielectric material exhibiting both diffuse reflection (due to subsurface scattering) and specular reflection (due to direct reflection at the air/surface interface). We make use of both types of reflection. This model is particularly suitable for smooth, glossy materials such as porcelain, skin, plastic and surfaces finished with gloss paint. We follow recent works [3,17] and assume that reflection from a point can be classified as diffuse dominant or specular dominant (see supplementary material for our classification scheme). Hence, a pixel $\mathbf{u}$ belongs either to the set of diffuse pixels, $\mathcal{D}$, or the set of specular pixels, $\mathcal{S}$, with $\mathcal{F} = \mathcal{D} \cup \mathcal{S}$.

Diffuse polarisation model. For diffuse reflection, the degree of polarisation is related (Fig. 3a, red curve) to the zenith angle $\theta(\mathbf{u}) \in [0, \frac{\pi}{2}]$ of the normal in viewer-centred coordinates (i.e. the angle between the normal and viewer):

$$\rho(\mathbf{u}) = \frac{\sin\left(\theta(\mathbf{u})\right)^2 \left(\eta - \frac{1}{\eta}\right)^2}{4\cos\left(\theta(\mathbf{u})\right)\sqrt{\eta^2 - \sin\left(\theta(\mathbf{u})\right)^2} - \sin\left(\theta(\mathbf{u})\right)^2 \left(\eta + \frac{1}{\eta}\right)^2 + 2\eta^2 + 2}, \quad (5)$$

where η is the refractive index. The dependency on η is weak and typical values for dielectrics range between 1.4 and 1.6. We assume $\eta = 1.5$ for the rest of this paper. This expression can be rearranged to give a closed form solution for the zenith angle in terms of a function, $f(\rho(\mathbf{u}), \eta)$, that depends on the measured degree of polarisation and the refractive index:

$$\cos(\theta(\mathbf{u})) = \mathbf{n}(\mathbf{u}) \cdot \mathbf{v} = f(\rho(\mathbf{u}), \eta)$$

$$= \sqrt{\frac{2\rho + 2\eta^2\rho - 2\eta^2 + \eta^4 + \rho^2 + 4\eta^2\rho^2 - \eta^4\rho^2 - 4\eta^3\rho\sqrt{-(\rho-1)(\rho+1)} + 1}{\eta^4\rho^2 + 2\eta^4\rho + \eta^4 + 6\eta^2\rho^2 + 4\eta^2\rho - 2\eta^2 + \rho^2 + 2\rho + 1}} \quad (6)$$

where we drop the dependency of ρ on $\mathbf{u}$ for brevity. Since we work in a viewer-centred coordinate system, the viewing direction is $\mathbf{v} = [0\ 0\ 1]^T$ and we have simply: $n_z(\mathbf{u}) = f(\rho(\mathbf{u}), \eta)$, or, in terms of the surface gradient,

$$\frac{1}{\sqrt{p(\mathbf{u})^2 + q(\mathbf{u})^2 + 1}} = f(\rho(\mathbf{u}), \eta). \tag{7}$$

The phase angle determines the azimuth angle of the surface normal $\alpha(\mathbf{u}) \in [0, 2\pi]$ up to a $180°$ ambiguity: $\mathbf{u} \in \mathcal{D} \Rightarrow \alpha(\mathbf{u}) = \phi(\mathbf{u})$ or $(\phi(\mathbf{u}) + \pi)$. Hence, for a diffuse pixel $\mathbf{u} \in \mathcal{D}$, this means that the surface normal is given (up to an ambiguity) by either $\mathbf{n}(\mathbf{u}) = \bar{\mathbf{n}}(\mathbf{u})$ or $\mathbf{n}(\mathbf{u}) = \mathbf{T}\bar{\mathbf{n}}(\mathbf{u})$ where

$$\bar{\mathbf{n}}(\mathbf{u}) = \begin{bmatrix} \sin\phi(\mathbf{u})\sin\theta(\mathbf{u}) \\ \cos\phi(\mathbf{u})\sin\theta(\mathbf{u}) \\ \cos\theta(\mathbf{u}) \end{bmatrix} \text{ and } \mathbf{T} = \mathbf{R}_z(180°) = \begin{bmatrix} -1 & 0 & 0 \\ 0 & -1 & 0 \\ 0 & 0 & 1 \end{bmatrix}. \tag{8}$$

Specular polarisation model. For specular reflection, the degree of polarisation is again related to the zenith angle (Fig. 3a, blue curve):

$$\rho_s(\mathbf{u}) = \frac{2\sin(\theta(\mathbf{u}))^2 \cos(\theta(\mathbf{u}))\sqrt{\eta^2 - \sin(\theta(\mathbf{u}))^2}}{\eta^2 - \sin(\theta(\mathbf{u}))^2 - \eta^2 \sin(\theta(\mathbf{u}))^2 + 2\sin(\theta(\mathbf{u}))^4}. \tag{9}$$

This expression is problematic for two reasons: 1. it cannot be analytically inverted to solve for zenith angle, 2. there are two solutions. The first problem is overcome simply by using a lookup table and interpolation. The second problem is not an issue in practice. Specular reflections occur when the surface normal is approximately halfway between the viewer and light source directions. We assume that the light source $\mathbf{s}$ is positioned in the same hemisphere as the viewer, i.e. $\mathbf{v}\cdot\mathbf{s} > 0$. In this configuration, specular pixels will never have a zenith angle $> \sim 45°$. Hence, we can restrict (9) to this range and, therefore, a single solution.

In contrast to diffuse reflection, the azimuth angle of the surface normal is perpendicular to the phase of the specular polarisation [18] leading to a $\frac{\pi}{2}$ shift: $\mathbf{u} \in \mathcal{S} \Rightarrow \alpha(\mathbf{u}) = (\phi(\mathbf{u}) - \pi/2)$ or $(\phi(\mathbf{u}) + \pi/2)$.

Figure 3b shows zenith angle estimates using the diffuse/specular model on $\mathcal{D}/\mathcal{S}$ respectively. In Fig. 3c we show the cosine of the estimated zenith angle, a visualisation corresponding to a Lambertian rendering with frontal lighting.

2.3 Shading Constraint

The unpolarised intensity provides an additional constraint on the surface normal direction via an appropriate reflectance model. We assume that, for diffuse-labelled pixels, light is reflected according to the Lambertian model. We also assume that albedo is uniform and factor it into the light source vector $\mathbf{s}$. Hence, unpolarised intensity is related to the surface normal by:

$$\mathbf{u} \in \mathcal{D} \Rightarrow i_{\text{un}}(\mathbf{u}) = \cos(\theta_i(\mathbf{u})) = \mathbf{n}(\mathbf{u}) \cdot \mathbf{s}, \tag{10}$$

where $\theta_i(\mathbf{u})$ is the angle of incidence (angle between light source and surface normal). In terms of the surface gradient, this becomes:

$$i_{\text{un}}(\mathbf{u}) = \frac{-p(\mathbf{u})s_x - q(\mathbf{u})s_y + s_z}{\sqrt{p(\mathbf{u})^2 + q(\mathbf{u})^2 + 1}}. \tag{11}$$

Note that if the light source and viewer direction coincide (a configuration that is physically impossible to achieve precisely) then this equation provides no more information than the degree of polarisation. Hence, we assume that the light source direction is different from the viewing direction, i.e. $\mathbf{s} \neq \mathbf{v}$.

For specular pixels, we do not use the unpolarised intensity directly (though it is used in the labelling of specular pixels - see supplementary material). Instead, we assume simply that the normal is approximately equal to the halfway vector:

$$\mathbf{u} \in \mathcal{S} \Rightarrow \mathbf{n}(\mathbf{u}) \approx \mathbf{h} = (\mathbf{s} + \mathbf{v})/\|\mathbf{s} + \mathbf{v}\|. \tag{12}$$

3 Linear Depth Estimation with Known Illumination

We now show that the polarisation shape cues can be expressed as per pixel equations that are linear in terms of the surface gradient. By using finite difference approximations to the surface gradient, this allows us to write the problem of depth estimation in terms of a large system of linear equations. This means that depth estimation is both efficient and certain to obtain the global optimum. In this section we assume that the lighting and albedo are known. However, in the following section we describe how they can be estimated from the polarisation image, allowing depth recovery with uncalibrated illumination.

3.1 Polarisation Constraints as Linear Equations

First, we note that the phase angle constraint can be written as a collinearity condition. This condition is satisfied by either of the two possible azimuth angles implied by the phase angle measurement. Writing it in this way is advantageous because it means we do not have to disambiguate the surface normals explicitly. Instead, when we solve the linear system for depth, the azimuthal ambiguities are resolved in a globally optimal way. Specifically, for diffuse pixels we require the projection of the surface normal into the x-y plane, $[n_x\ n_y]$, and a vector in the image plane pointing in the phase angle direction, $[\sin(\phi)\ \cos(\phi)]$, to be collinear. These two vectors are collinear when the following condition is satisfied:

$$\mathbf{n}(\mathbf{u}) \cdot [\cos(\phi(\mathbf{u}))\ -\sin(\phi(\mathbf{u}))\ 0]^T = 0. \tag{13}$$

Substituting (2) into (13) and noting that the nonlinear term in (2) is always $\neq 0$ we obtain the first linear equation in the surface gradient:

$$-p(\mathbf{u})\cos(\phi(\mathbf{u})) + q(\mathbf{u})\sin(\phi(\mathbf{u})) = 0. \tag{14}$$

A similar expression can be obtained for specular pixels, substituting in the $\frac{\pi}{2}$-shifted phase angles. This condition exhibits a natural weighting that is useful in practice. The phase angle estimates are more reliable when the zenith angle is large (i.e. when the degree of polarisation is high and so the signal to noise ratio is high). When the zenith angle is large, the magnitude of the surface gradient is large, meaning that disagreement with the estimated phase angle is penalised more heavily than for a small zenith angle where the gradient magnitude is small.

The second linear constraint has two different forms for diffuse and specular pixels. The diffuse constraint is obtained by combining the expressions for the unpolarised intensity and the degree of polarisation. To do so, we take a ratio between (11) and (7) which cancels the nonlinear normalisation factor:

$$\frac{i_{\mathrm{un}}(\mathbf{u})}{f(\rho(\mathbf{u}), \eta)} = -p(\mathbf{u})s_x - q(\mathbf{u})s_y + s_z, \tag{15}$$

yielding our second linear equation in the surface gradient. For specular pixels, we express (12) in terms of the surface gradient as:

$$p(\mathbf{u}) = -h_x/h_z \text{ and } q(\mathbf{u}) = -h_y/h_z. \tag{16}$$

3.2   Linear Height Recovery

The surface gradient in (2) can be approximated numerically from the discretised surface height function using finite differences. To reduce sensitivity to noise and improve robustness, where possible we use a smoothed central difference approximation. Such an approximation is obtained by convolving the surface height function with Sobel operators $\mathbf{G}_x, \mathbf{G}_y \in \mathbb{R}^{3 \times 3}$: $\partial_x z \approx z * \mathbf{G}_x$ and $\partial_y z \approx z * \mathbf{G}_y$. At the boundary of the image or the foreground mask, not all neighbours may be available for a given pixel. In this case, we use unsmoothed central differences (where both horizontal or both vertical neighbours are available) or, where only a single neighbour is available, single forward/backward differences.

Substituting these finite differences into (14), (15) and (16) therefore leads to linear equations with between 3 and 8 unknown values of z (depending on which combination of numerical gradient approximations are used). Of course, the surface height function is unknown. So, we seek the surface height function whose finite difference gradients solve the system of linear equations over all pixels. Due to noise, we do not expect an exact solution. Hence, for an image with K foreground pixels, we can solve in a least squares sense the system of $2K$ linear equations in the K unknown height values. In order to resolve the unknown constant of integration (i.e. applying an arbitrary offset to z does not affect its orthographic images), we add an additional linear equation to set the height of one pixel to zero. We end up with the linear least squares problem $\min_z \|\mathbf{Az} - \mathbf{b}\|^2$, where $\mathbf{A}$ has $2K + 1$ rows, K columns and is sparse (each row has at most 8 non-zero values). This can be solved efficiently. Note: this is a system of linear equations in depth. It is not a partial differential equation. Hence, we do not require boundary conditions to be specified.

We also find it advantageous (though not essential) to include two priors on the surface height: 1. Laplacian smoothness, 2. convexity. Both are expressed as linear equations in the surface height. See supplementary material for details.

4   Illumination Estimation from a Polarisation Image

The method described above enables linear depth recovery from a single polarisation image when the illumination direction is known. In this section, we describe how to use the polarisation image to estimate illumination, prior to depth estimation, so that the method above can be applied in an uncalibrated scenario. First, we show that the problem of light source estimation is ambiguous. Second, we derive a method to compute the light source direction (up to the binary ambiguity) from ambiguous normals using the minimum possible number of observations. Third, we extend this to an efficient least squares optimisation that uses the whole image and is applicable to noisy data. Finally, we relax the lighting assumptions to allow more flexible 1st and 2nd order SH illumination.

We consider only diffuse pixels for illumination estimation, since specular pixels are sparse and we wish to avoid estimating the parameters of a particular assumed specular reflectance model. Hence, the unpolarised intensity is assumed to follow a Lambertian model with uniform albedo, as in (11). For the true $\mathbf{s}$, $i_{\text{un}}(\mathbf{u}) = \bar{\mathbf{n}}(\mathbf{u})^T\mathbf{s} \vee i_{\text{un}}(\mathbf{u}) = (\mathbf{T}\bar{\mathbf{n}}(\mathbf{u}))^T\mathbf{s}$. Hence, a single pixel restricts the light source to two planes.

4.1   Relationship to the Bas-Relief Ambiguity

For an image with K diffuse pixels, there are 2^K possible disambiguations of the polarisation normals. Suppose that we know the correct disambiguation of the normals and that we stack them to form the matrix $\mathbf{N}_{\text{true}} \in \mathbb{R}^{K \times 3}$ and stack the unpolarised intensities in the vector $\mathbf{i} = [i_{\text{un}}(\mathbf{u}_1) \ \ldots \ i_{\text{un}}(\mathbf{u}_K)]^T$. In this case, the light source $\mathbf{s}$ that satisfies $\mathbf{N}_{\text{true}}\mathbf{s} = \mathbf{i}$ is given by the pseudo-inverse:

$$\mathbf{s} = \mathbf{N}_{\text{true}}^{+}\mathbf{i}. \tag{17}$$

However, for any invertible 3×3 linear transform $\mathbf{A} \in GL(3)$, it is also true that $\mathbf{N}_{\text{true}}\mathbf{A}^{-1}\mathbf{A}\mathbf{s} = \mathbf{i}$, and so $\mathbf{A}\mathbf{s}$ is also a solution using the transformed normals $\mathbf{N}_{\text{true}}\mathbf{A}^{-1}$. However, the only such $\mathbf{A}$ where $\mathbf{N}_{\text{true}}\mathbf{A}^{-1}$ is consistent with the polarisation image is $\mathbf{A} = \mathbf{T}$, i.e. where the azimuth angle of each normal is shifted by π. Hence, if $\mathbf{s}$ is a solution with normals $\mathbf{N}_{\text{true}}$ then $\mathbf{T}\mathbf{s}$ is also a solution with normals $\mathbf{N}_{\text{true}}\mathbf{T}$. Note that $\mathbf{T}$ is a generalised Bas-relief (GBR) transformation [4] with parameters $\mu = 0$, $\nu = 0$ and $\lambda = \pm 1$, i.e. the binary convex/concave ambiguity. Hence, from a polarisation image with unknown lighting, we will be unable to distinguish the true normals and lighting from those transformed by $\mathbf{T}$. Since $\mathbf{T}$ is a GBR transformation, the transformed normals remain integrable and correspond to the true surface negated in depth (see Fig. 4).

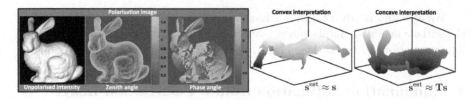

Fig. 4. A polarisation image of a diffuse object enables uncalibrated surface reconstruction up to a convex/concave ambiguity. Both interpretations are consistent with the polarisation image.

4.2 Minimal Solutions

Suppose that $\mathbf{N} \in \mathbb{R}^{K \times 3}$ contains one of the 2^K possible disambiguations of the K surface normals, i.e. $\mathbf{N}_j = \bar{\mathbf{n}}(\mathbf{u}_j)$ or $\mathbf{N}_j = \mathbf{T}\bar{\mathbf{n}}(\mathbf{u}_j)$. If $\mathbf{N}$ is a valid disambiguation, then (with no noise) we expect: $\mathbf{N}\mathbf{N}^+\mathbf{i} = \mathbf{i}$. We can see in a straightforward way that three pixels will be insufficient to distinguish a valid from an invalid disambiguation. When $K = 3$, $\mathbf{N}^+ = \mathbf{N}^{-1}$ and so $\mathbf{N}\mathbf{N}^+ = \mathbf{I}$ and hence the condition is satisfied by any combination of disambiguations. The reason for this is that, apart from degenerate cases, any three planes will intersect at a point so any combination of transformed or untransformed normals will allow an $\mathbf{s}$ to be found that satisfies all three equations.

However, the problem becomes well-posed for $K > 3$. The system of linear equations must be consistent and have a unique solution. If some, but not all, of the normals are transformed from their true direction then the system of equations will be inconsistent. By the Rouché–Capelli theorem [19], consistency and uniqueness require $\text{rank}(\mathbf{N}) = \text{rank}([\mathbf{N} \ \mathbf{i}]) = 3$. So, we could try each possible combination of disambiguated normals and check whether the rank condition is satisfied. Note that we only need consider half of the possible disambiguations. We can divide the 2^K disambiguations into 2^{K-1} pairs differing by a global transformation and only need consider one of each of the pairs. So, for the minimal case of $K = 4$, we construct the 8 possible normal matrices $\mathbf{N}$, with the first row fixed to $\mathbf{N}_1 = \bar{\mathbf{n}}(\mathbf{u}_1)$, and find the one satisfying the rank condition. For this $\mathbf{N}$ we find $\mathbf{s}$ by (17) and the solution is either $(\mathbf{N}, \mathbf{s})$ or $(\mathbf{NT}, \mathbf{Ts})$.

4.3 Alternating Optimisation

In practice, we expect the ambiguous normals and unpolarised intensities to be noisy. Therefore, a least squares solution over all observed pixels is preferable. Since the unknown illumination is only 3D and we have a polarisation observation for every pixel, the problem is highly overconstrained. Following the combinatorial approach above, we could build all 2^K possible systems of linear equations, solve them in a least squares sense and take the one with minimal residual as the solution. However, this is NP-hard and impractical for any non-trivial value of K. Instead, we can write an optimisation problem to find $\mathbf{s}$:

$$\mathbf{s}^* = \arg \min_{\mathbf{s} \in \mathbb{R}^3} \sum_{j \in \mathcal{D}} \min \left([\bar{\mathbf{n}}(\mathbf{u}_j) \cdot \mathbf{s} - i_{un}(\mathbf{u}_j)]^2, [\mathbf{T}\bar{\mathbf{n}}(\mathbf{u}_j) \cdot \mathbf{s} - i_{un}(\mathbf{u}_j)]^2 \right). \quad (18)$$

This is non-convex since the minimum of two convex functions is not convex [20]. However, (18) can be efficiently optimised using alternating assignment and optimisation. In practice, we find that this almost always converges to the global minimum even with a random initialisation. In the assignment step, given an estimate for the light source at iteration t, $\mathbf{s}^{(t)}$, we choose from each ambiguous pair of normals the one that yields minimal error under illumination $\mathbf{s}^{(t)}$:

$$\mathbf{N}_j^{(t)} := \begin{cases} \bar{\mathbf{n}}(\mathbf{u}_j) & \text{if } \left[\bar{\mathbf{n}}(\mathbf{u}_j) \cdot \mathbf{s}^{(t)} - i_{un}(\mathbf{u}_j) \right]^2 < \left[\mathbf{T}\bar{\mathbf{n}}(\mathbf{u}_j) \cdot \mathbf{s}^{(t)} - i_{un}(\mathbf{u}_j) \right]^2 \\ \mathbf{T}\bar{\mathbf{n}}(\mathbf{u}_j) & \text{otherwise.} \end{cases} \quad (19)$$

At the optimisation step, we use the selected normals to compute the new light source by solving the linear least squares system: $\mathbf{s}^{(t+1)} := (\mathbf{N}^{(t)})^+\mathbf{i}$. These two steps are iterated to convergence. In all our experiments, this process converged in fewer than 10 iterations. To resolve the ambiguity in our experimental results, we always take the light source estimate that gives the maximal surface.

4.4   Extension to 1st and 2nd Order Spherical Harmonic Lighting

Using a first or second order SH diffuse lighting model [21,22], the binary ambiguity in the surface normal leads to a binary ambiguity in the SH basis vector at each pixel. Specifically, a first order SH lighting model introduces a constant term: $i_{un}(\mathbf{u}) = \mathbf{b}_4(\mathbf{u})^T \mathbf{s}_4$ with basis vector $\mathbf{b}_4(\mathbf{u}) = \begin{bmatrix} n_x(\mathbf{u}) & n_y(\mathbf{u}) & n_z(\mathbf{u}) & 1 \end{bmatrix}^T$. With ambiguous normals, the basis vector is known up to a binary ambiguity: $\mathbf{b}_4(\mathbf{u}) = \bar{\mathbf{b}}_4(\mathbf{u})$ or $\mathbf{b}_4(\mathbf{u}) = \mathbf{T}_4 \bar{\mathbf{b}}_4(\mathbf{u})$ with $\bar{\mathbf{b}}_4(\mathbf{u}) = \begin{bmatrix} \bar{n}_x(\mathbf{u}) & \bar{n}_y(\mathbf{u}) & \bar{n}_z(\mathbf{u}) & 1 \end{bmatrix}^T$ and the transformation given by: $\mathbf{T}_4 = \text{diag}(-1, -1, 1, 1)$. Solving for $\mathbf{s}_4$ is the same problem as solving for a point source, leading to the same ambiguity. If $\mathbf{s}_4$ is a solution with minimal residual then $\mathbf{T}_4\mathbf{s}_4$ is also an optimal solution and the transformation of the normals corresponds to a GBR convex/concave transformation. Similarly, a second order SH lighting model: $i_{un}(\mathbf{u}) = \mathbf{b}_9(\mathbf{u})^T \mathbf{s}_9$ with basis vector $\mathbf{b}_9 = \begin{bmatrix} 1 & n_x & n_y & n_z & 3n_z^2-1 & n_x n_y & n_x n_z & n_y n_z & n_x^2-n_y^2 \end{bmatrix}^T$, can be handled in exactly the same way with the appropriate transformation matrix given by: $\mathbf{T}_9 = \text{diag}(1, -1, -1, 1, 1, 1, -1, -1, 1)$. For shape estimation, we compute the 4D or 9D lighting vector, subtract from the diffuse intensity the zeroth and second order appearance contributions and then run the same algorithm as for point source illumination using only the first order appearance.

5   Experimental Results

We begin with a quantitative evaluation on synthetic data. We render images of the Stanford bunny with Blinn-Phong reflectance under point source illumination (Fig. 5a). We simulate polarisation according to (3), (5) and (9) with varying polariser angle, add Gaussian noise of standard deviation σ and quantise to 8 bits. We vary light source direction over $\theta_l \in \{15°, 30°, 60°\}$ and $\alpha_l \in \{0°, 90°, 180°, 270°\}$. We estimate a polarisation image for each $(\sigma, \theta_l, \alpha_l)$ and use this as input. For comparison, we implemented the only previous methods applicable to a single polarisation image: 1. boundary propagation [2,7] and 2. Lambertian shading disambiguation [10]. The second method requires known lighting and albedo. For both this and our method, we provide results with ground truth lighting/albedo (superscript "gt") and lighting/albedo estimated using the method in Sect. 4.3 (superscript "est"). For the comparison methods, we compute a depth map using least squares integration, as in [23]. For our method, we compute surface normals using a bicubic fit to the estimated depth.

(a) Input   (b) True normals   (c) Our method   (d) [2,7]   (e) [10]

Fig. 5. Typical surface normal estimates (c–e) from noisy synthetic data (a). The inset sphere in (b) shows how surface orientation is visualised as a colour. (Color figure online)

We show typical results in Fig. 5c-e and quantitative results in Table 1 (RMS depth error and mean angular surface normal error averaged over α_l and 100 repeats for each setting; best result for each setting emboldened). The boundary propagation method [2,7] assumes convexity, meaning that internal concavities are incorrectly recovered. The Lambertian method [10] exhibits high frequency noise since solutions are purely local. Both methods also contain errors in specular regions and propagate errors from normal estimation into the integrated surface. Our solution is smoother and more stable in specular regions yet still recovers fine surface detail. Note however that the simple constraint in (12) encourages all specular normals to point in the same direction, leading to over-flattening of specular regions. Quantitatively, our method offers the best performance across all settings. In many cases, the result with estimated lighting is better than with ground truth. We believe that this is because it enables the method to partially compensate for noise. In Table 2 we show the quantitative accuracy of our lighting estimate. We use the same point source directions as above. When the lighting is within 15° of the viewing direction, the error is less than 1°. For order 1 and 2 SH lighting, we use the same order 1 components as the point source directions and randomly generate the order 0 and 2 components.

In order to evaluate our method on real world images, we capture two datasets using a Canon EOS-1D X and vary a linear polarising filter over 180° in 10° increments. The first dataset is captured in a dark room using a Lowel Prolight

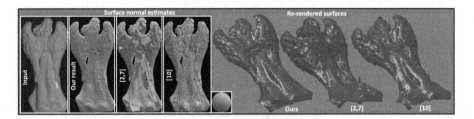

Fig. 6. Qualitative comparison on real world data. Light source direction = [2 0 7].

Table 1. Depth and surface normal estimation errors on synthetic data.

θ_l	Method	$\sigma = 0\%$		$\sigma = 0.5\%$		$\sigma = 1\%$		$\sigma = 2\%$	
		Depth (pixels)	Normal (degrees)	Depth (pixels)	Normal (degrees)	Depth (pixels)	Normal (degrees)	Depth (pixels)	Normal (degrees)
15°	Ours[gt]	**3.65**	**3.30**	5.68	5.39	16.09	9.59	16.96	16.19
	Ours[est]	3.75	3.36	**5.60**	**5.35**	**15.77**	**9.44**	**16.80**	**16.01**
	[10][gt]	11.46	4.43	51.78	8.07	173.89	13.37	92.73	22.78
	[10][est]	11.64	4.86	51.69	8.10	173.83	13.34	92.08	22.71
	[2,7]	17.96	12.19	55.51	9.69	180.02	13.20	90.64	17.59
30°	Ours[gt]	**3.67**	**4.68**	15.42	7.00	10.20	10.06	16.84	16.14
	Ours[est]	6.07	7.57	**14.89**	**6.83**	**9.43**	**9.75**	**16.25**	**15.67**
	[10][gt]	14.22	6.00	780.40	8.69	203.68	13.19	286.65	21.29
	[10][est]	16.34	10.90	780.55	9.21	203.76	13.97	286.15	22.23
	[2,7]	20.68	15.96	798.36	15.90	208.59	18.92	286.51	25.80
60°	Ours[gt]	**7.57**	**11.05**	13.70	**14.22**	**67.62**	**17.81**	21.62	**23.25**
	Ours[est]	12.49	13.91	**12.06**	14.89	76.82	19.22	**20.94**	24.96
	[10][gt]	17.50	14.83	1355.47	20.88	7028.37	26.68	940.74	34.30
	[10][est]	20.90	20.82	1356.00	24.37	7014.33	30.12	936.88	37.53
	[2,7]	22.80	23.74	1376.83	30.25	6468.54	35.32	956.13	41.13

to approximate a point source. We experiment with both known and unknown lighting. For known lighting, the approximate position of the light source is measured and to calibrate for unknown light source intensity and surface albedo, we use the method in Sect. 4.3 to compute the length of the light source vector, fixing its direction to the measured one. The second dataset is captured outdoors on a sunny day using natural illumination. We use an order 1 SH lighting model.

We show a qualitative comparison between our method and the two reference methods in Fig. 6 using known lighting (see supplementary material for more comparative results). The comparison methods exhibit the same artefacts as on synthetic data. Some of the noise in the normals is removed by the smoothing effect of surface integration but concave/convex errors in [2,7] grossly distort the overall shape, while the surface details of the wings are lost by [10]. In Fig. 7 we show qualitative results of our method on a range of material types, under a variety of known or estimated illumination conditions (both indoor point source and outdoor uncontrolled). Note that the recovered surface of the angel remains stable even with estimated illumination (compared to known illumination in

Table 2. Quantitative light source estimation results on synthetic data.

θ_l	Point source err = $\arccos(\mathbf{s} \cdot \mathbf{s}^{est})$				Order 1 SH err = $\|\mathbf{s} - \mathbf{s}^{est}\|$				Order 2 SH err = $\|\mathbf{s} - \mathbf{s}^{est}\|$			
	$\sigma = 0\%$	$\sigma = 0.5\%$	$\sigma = 1\%$	$\sigma = 2\%$	$\sigma = 0\%$	$\sigma = 0.5\%$	$\sigma = 1\%$	$\sigma = 2\%$	$\sigma = 0\%$	$\sigma = 0.5\%$	$\sigma = 1\%$	$\sigma = 2\%$
15°	0.045°	0.069°	0.20°	0.56°	0.0040	0.0040	0.0031	0.0041	0.0007	0.0013	0.0024	0.0035
30°	0.084°	0.33°	0.88°	2.42°	0.0046	0.0047	0.0059	0.0041	0.0006	0.0036	0.0025	0.013
60°	0.81°	3.44°	7.83°	15.97°	0.0062	0.0084	0.0060	0.0060	0.0012	0.0025	0.0091	0.0052

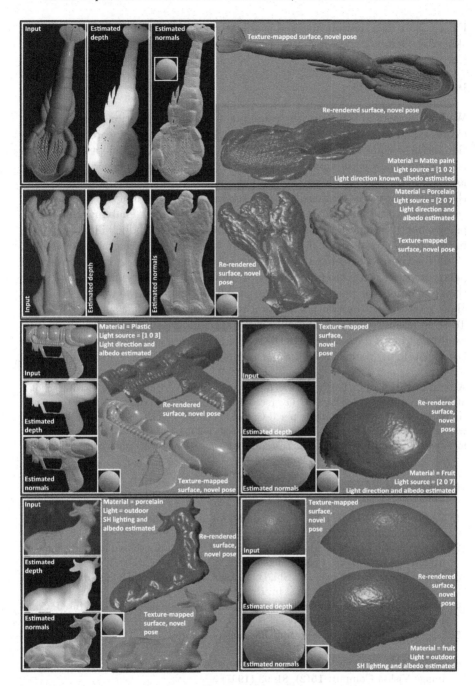

Fig. 7. Qualitative results on a variety of material types. The first three rows show results captured in dark room conditions with a point light source. The two panels in the final row show results in outdoor, uncontrolled illumination. Depth maps are encoded as brighter = closer. The first row shows a result with known lighting direction, all others are estimated.

Fig. 6). Note also that our method is able to recover the fine surface detail of the skin of the lemon and orange under both point source and natural illumination.

6 Conclusions

We have presented the first SfP technique in which polarisation constraints are expressed directly in terms of surface depth. Moreover, through careful construction of these equations, we ensure that they are linear and so depth estimation is simply a linear least squares problem. The SfP cue is often described as being locally ambiguous. We have shown that, in fact, even with unknown lighting the diffuse unpolarised intensity image restricts the uncertainty to a global convex/concave ambiguity. Our method is practically useful, enabling monocular, passive depth estimation even in outdoor lighting. For reproducibility, we make a full implementation of our method and the two comparison methods available[1].

In future, we would like to relax the assumptions in Sect. 2. From a practical perspective, the most useful would be to allow spatially-varying albedo. Rather than assuming that pixels are specular or diffuse dominant, we would also like to allow mixtures of the two polarisation models and to exploit specular shading. To do so would require an assumption of a specular BRDF model. An alternative would be to fit a data-driven BRDF model [24] directly to the ambiguous polarisation normals, potentially allowing single shot BRDF and shape estimation.

Acknowledgments. This work was undertaken while W. Smith was a visiting scholar at UCSD, supported by EPSRC Overseas Travel Grant EP/N028481/1. S. Tozza was supported by Gruppo Nazionale per il Calcolo Scientifico (GNCS-INdAM). This work was supported in part by ONR grant N00014-15-1-2013 and the UC San Diego Center for Visual Computing. We thank Zak Murez for assistance with data collection.

References

1. Wolff, L.B., Boult, T.E.: Constraining object features using a polarization reflectance model. IEEE Trans. Pattern Anal. Mach. Intell. **13**(7), 635–657 (1991)
2. Miyazaki, D., Tan, R.T., Hara, K., Ikeuchi, K.: Polarization-based inverse rendering from a single view. In: Proceedings of ICCV, pp. 982–987 (2003)
3. Kadambi, A., Taamazyan, V., Shi, B., Raskar, R.: Polarized 3D: high-quality depth sensing with polarization cues. In: Proceedings of ICCV (2015)
4. Belhumeur, P.N., Kriegman, D.J., Yuille, A.: The Bas-relief ambiguity. Int. J. Comput. Vis. **35**(1), 33–44 (1999)
5. Schechner, Y.Y.: Self-calibrating imaging polarimetry. In: Proceedings of ICCP (2015)
6. Wolff, L.B.: Polarization vision: a new sensory approach to image understanding. Image Vision Comput. **15**(2), 81–93 (1997)
7. Atkinson, G.A., Hancock, E.R.: Recovery of surface orientation from diffuse polarization. IEEE Trans. Image Process. **15**(6), 1653–1664 (2006)

---

[1] https://github.com/waps101/depth-from-polarisation.

8. Morel, O., Meriaudeau, F., Stolz, C., Gorria, P.: Polarization imaging applied to 3D reconstruction of specular metallic surfaces. In: Proceedings of EI 2005, pp. 178–186 (2005)
9. Huynh, C.P., Robles-Kelly, A., Hancock, E.: Shape and refractive index recovery from single-view polarisation images. In: Proceedings of CVPR, pp. 1229–1236 (2010)
10. Mahmoud, A.H., El-Melegy, M.T., Farag, A.A.: Direct method for shape recovery from polarization and shading. In: Proceedings of ICIP, pp. 1769–1772 (2012)
11. Rahmann, S., Canterakis, N.: Reconstruction of specular surfaces using polarization imaging. In: Proceedings of CVPR (2001)
12. Atkinson, G.A., Hancock, E.R.: Shape estimation using polarization and shading from two views. IEEE Trans. Pattern Anal. Mach. Intell. **29**(11), 2001–2017 (2007)
13. Huynh, C.P., Robles-Kelly, A., Hancock, E.R.: Shape and refractive index from single-view spectro-polarimetric images. Int. J. Comput. Vis. **101**(1), 64–94 (2013)
14. Atkinson, G.A., Hancock, E.R.: Surface reconstruction using polarization and photometric stereo. In: Kropatsch, W.G., Kampel, M., Hanbury, A. (eds.) CAIP 2007. LNCS, vol. 4673, pp. 466–473. Springer, Heidelberg (2007). doi:10.1007/978-3-540-74272-2_58
15. Drbohlav, O., Šára, R.: Unambiguous determination of shape from photometric stereo with unknown light sources. In: Proceedings of ICCV, pp. 581–586 (2001)
16. Ngo, T.T., Nagahara, H., Taniguchi, R.: Shape and light directions from shading and polarization. In: Proceedings of CVPR, pp. 2310–2318 (2015)
17. Tozza, S., Mecca, R., Duocastella, M., Bue Del, A.: Direct differential photometric stereo shape recovery of diffuse and specular surfaces. JMIV **56**(1), 57–76 (2016)
18. Robles-Kelly, A., Huynh, C.P.: Imaging Spectroscopy for Scene Analysis, p. 219. Springer, London (2013)
19. Carpinteri, A.: Structural Mechanics, p. 74. Taylor and Francis, London (1997)
20. Grant, M., Boyd, S., Ye, Y.: Disciplined convex programming. In: Liberti, L., Maculan, N. (eds.) Global Optimization: From Theory to Implementation, pp. 155–210. Springer, New York (2006)
21. Ramamoorthi, R., Hanrahan, P.: On the relationship between radiance and irradiance: determining the illumination from images of a convex Lambertian object. JOSA A **18**(10), 2448–2459 (2001)
22. Basri, R., Jacobs, D.W.: Lambertian reflectance and linear subspaces. IEEE Trans. Pattern Anal. Mach. Intell. **25**(2), 218–233 (2003)
23. Nehab, D., Rusinkiewicz, S., Davis, J., Ramamoorthi, R.: Efficiently combining positions and normals for precise 3D geometry. ACM Trans. Graph. **24**(3), 536–543 (2005)
24. Nielsen, J.B., Jensen, H.W., Ramamoorthi, R.: On optimal, minimal BRDF sampling for reflectance acquisition. ACM Trans. Graph. **34**(6), 1–11 (2015)
25. http://www.fluxdata.com/imaging-polarimeters
26. https://www.ricoh.com/technology/tech/051_polarization.html

Online Variational Bayesian Motion Averaging

Guillaume Bourmaud$^{(\boxtimes)}$

Toshiba Research Europe, Cambridge, UK
guillaume.bourmaud@crl.toshiba.co.uk

Abstract. In this paper, we propose a novel algorithm dedicated to *online motion averaging for large scale problems*. To this end, we design a filter that continuously approximates the posterior distribution of the estimated transformations. In order to deal with large scale problems, we associate a *variational Bayesian approach* with a *relative parametrization of the absolute transformations*. Such an association allows our algorithm to simultaneously possess two features that are essential for an algorithm dedicated to large scale online motion averaging: (1) a low computational time, (2) the ability to detect wrong loop closure measurements. We extensively demonstrate on several applications (binocular SLAM, monocular SLAM and video mosaicking) that our approach not only exhibits a low computational time and detects wrong loop closures but also significantly outperforms the state of the art algorithm in terms of RMSE.

Keywords: Variational Bayes · Motion averaging · Pose-graph · Lie group · Filtering · Relative parametrization · Large scale · Visual SLAM

1 Introduction

The motion averaging problem, also called "multiple rotation averaging" when dealing with 3D rotations or "pose-graph inference" when applied to camera poses, has been studied for more than fifteen years [6,14,16–19,24,31,32] and is still a very active area of research [4,5,7,8,10,12,20,29]. This generic problem arises in a large number of applications, such as video mosaicking [6,24], reconstruction of 3D scenes [10,27] or visual SLAM [13,14], where *only* the considered group of transformations changes: $SE(3)$ for 3D euclidean motions, $SL(3)$ for homographies, $Sim(3)$ for 3D similarities. In fact, in all these applications, the task consists in estimating absolute transformations, between a "world" coordinate system and local coordinate systems, given noisy measurements corresponding to relative transformations between pairs of local coordinate systems.

The noisy relative transformation measurements are usually obtained by processing a video stream, coming from an RGB or RGB-D camera, with two different modules:

Electronic supplementary material The online version of this chapter (doi:10. 1007/978-3-319-46484-8_8) contains supplementary material, which is available to authorized users.

© Springer International Publishing AG 2016
B. Leibe et al. (Eds.): ECCV 2016, Part VIII, LNCS 9912, pp. 126–142, 2016.
DOI: 10.1007/978-3-319-46484-8_8

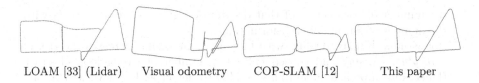

LOAM [33] (Lidar)   Visual odometry   COP-SLAM [12]   This paper

Fig. 1. Results for monocular visual SLAM ($Sim(3)$) on sequence KITTI 13. The ground truth is not available for that sequence. Thus, we reported the best result obtained using a Lidar [33].

- a *visual odometry module* that continuously computes the transformation between the current and the previous local coordinate system of the camera;
- a *loop closure module* that detects when the camera comes back in a previously visited area and computes a relative transformation.

The odometry measurements and loop closure measurements are essentially of the same nature, however, in practice the loop closure module might produce erroneous measurements because of some *perceptual aliasing* (two different places can be very similar), while the visual odometry module usually produces outlier free measurements.

Since the input data is a video stream, most of the applications require an *online estimation* of the absolute transformations. However, the majority of the state of the art approaches do not take that constraint into account in their initial specifications. They usually design a batch algorithm which is applied each time a new measurement is received, using a generic optimization tool-box such as GTSAM [11], g^{2}o [21] or Google Ceres Solver [2]. These toolboxes are highly optimized and able to provide an online estimation with a reasonable computational time for small or medium sized problems, nevertheless, their computational time becomes prohibitive for large scale problems (see [12]).

The purpose of this paper is to present a novel approach specifically designed to operate *online on large scale problems*.

Requirements and Contributions Besides trying to be as accurate as possible, an algorithm dedicated to online motion averaging for large scale problems should also satisfy the following specifications:

(1) Computational efficiency: As it was recently pointed out in [12], minimizing a criterion involving all the past measurements each time a new measurement is received is not suitable for the problem we consider. In order to achieve a low computational time, it is compulsory to *perform filtering*, i.e. to process the measurements one by one;

(2) Memory efficiency: Nevertheless, to perform filtering is not sufficient to obtain an efficient algorithm. For instance, applying a Kalman filter, as proposed in [5], leads to maintaining a covariance matrix whose size grows quadratically with the number of absolute transformations. Hence, such a filter becomes impractical for large scale problems. One way to get a filter able to deal with large scale problems is to seek to continuously approximate the posterior distribution of the estimated transformations, such that

the number of parameters of that distribution grows *at most linearly* with the number of estimated transformations;

(3) <u>Robustness</u>: Finally, dealing with large scale problems increases the risk of *perceptual aliasing* and consequently the number of wrong loop closures. Hence, our approach should also be able to detect and remove wrong loop closures.

As we will see, taking into account the constraints previously described will lead us to considering mathematical tools, such as variational Bayesian approximations, that have not been applied to motion averaging yet. Using these tools, we show that it is possible to obtain a highly efficient and robust online motion averaging algorithm that significantly outperforms the state of the art algorithm [12] (see Fig. 1).

Outline of the paper: The rest of the paper is organized as follows: The mathematical notations and models are presented in Sect. 2. In Sect. 3 we discuss work related to our novel approach. Section 4 deals with the specific case of motion averaging from odometry measurements and a single loop closure. Based on the analysis performed in Sect. 4, we derive a novel motion averaging algorithm in Sect. 5 which is evaluated experimentally in Sect. 6. Finally, a conclusion and future work directions are provided in Sect. 7.

2   Models and Notations

Let us now introduce the notations and mathematical models that are used throughout the paper.

2.1   Lie Group Notations

The theory we develop in the paper can be applied to any matrix Lie group (typically $SE(3)$, $SL(3)$, $Sim(3)$, etc.), which turns out to be very convenient in practice since it allows to apply our algorithm to various applications (see Sect. 6). For a detailed description of Lie groups the reader is referred to [9]. Throughout the paper, we will use the following notations: $G \subset \mathbb{R}^{n \times n}$ is a matrix Lie group of intrinsic dimension p (i.e. $p = 6$ if $G = SE(3) \subset \mathbb{R}^{4 \times 4}$, $p = 8$ if $G = SL(3) \subset \mathbb{R}^{3 \times 3}$, etc.); $\exp_G^\wedge (\cdot) : \mathbb{R}^p \to G$ and $\log_G^\vee (\cdot) : G \to \mathbb{R}^p$ correspond to the exponential and logarithm maps of G respectively; $T_{ij} \in G$ is a matrix representing the transformation from the coordinate system j to the coordinate system i, thus in our notations $T_{ij}T_{jk} = T_{ik}$ and $T_{ij}^{-1} = T_{ji}$.

Another important operator that we will employ is the adjoint representation of G, $\mathrm{Ad}_G (\cdot) : G \to \mathbb{R}^{p \times p}$, which allows to transport an element $\delta_{ij} \in \mathbb{R}^p$, acting initially on T_{ij} through left multiplication, onto the right side of T_{ij} such that $\exp_G^\wedge (\delta_{ij}) T_{ij} = T_{ij}\exp_G^\wedge (\mathrm{Ad}_G (T_{ji}) \delta_{ij})$. Finally, we introduce the notation for a Gaussian distribution on G:

$$\mathcal{N}_G \left(T_{ij}; \overline{T}_{ij}, P_{ij}\right) \propto e^{-\frac{1}{2}\left\|\log_G^\vee \left(T_{ij}\overline{T}_{ij}^{-1}\right)\right\|_{P_{ij}}^2} \iff \begin{array}{l} T_{ij} = \exp_G^\wedge (\epsilon_{ij}) \overline{T}_{ij} \\ \text{where } \epsilon_{ij} \sim \mathcal{N}_{\mathbb{R}^p} (\epsilon_{ij}; \mathbf{0}, P_{ij}) \end{array} \tag{1}$$

where $\|\cdot\|^2$ stands for the squared Mahalanobis distance while $\overline{T}_{ij}$ and P_{ij} are the mean and the covariance of the random variable T_{ij} respectively.

2.2 Measurement Models

In order to tackle the motion averaging problem, two different parametrizations of the absolute transformations are commonly used: the relative parametrization and the absolute parametrization. Of course, different parametrizations lead to different measurement models and consequently to algorithms having different computational complexities and posterior distributions having different shapes. In this paper, we employ the relative parametrization. This choice is motivated in Sect. 4. Here we simply introduce the notations and the measurement models for this parametrization.

Table 1. Odometry measurement model and loop closure measurement model using a relative parametrization of the absolute transformations

Odometry likelihood	Loop closure likelihood
$p\left(Z_{n(n+1)}\vert T_{n(n+1)}\right)$ $= \mathcal{N}_G\left(Z_{n(n+1)}; T_{n(n+1)}, \Sigma_{n(n+1)}\right)$ (2)	$p\left(Z_{mn}\vert \left\{T_{i(i+1)}\right\}_{i=m,\dots,n-1}\right)$ $= \mathcal{N}_G\left(Z_{mn}; \prod_{i=m}^{n-1} T_{i(i+1)}, \Sigma_{mn}\right)$ (3)

Let us first define our notations for the measurements. An odometry measurement, which we denote $Z_{n(n+1)} \in G$, is a noisy transformation between two temporally *consecutive* local coordinate systems. A loop closure measurement, which we denote $Z_{mn} \in G$ where $n \neq m+1$, is a noisy transformation between two temporally *nonconsecutive* local coordinate systems. Moreover, in this work we assume the noises on the measurements to be *mutually independent*.

The relative parametrization consists in estimating transformations of the form $T_{(k-1)k}$ where k is the local coordinate system of the camera at time instant k. Thus, at time instant k, the set of estimated transformations is $\left\{T_{i(i+1)}\right\}_{i=1,\dots,k-1}$. Let us note that the absolute transformation T_{1k} can be obtained simply by composing the estimated relative transformations i.e. $T_{1k} = T_{12}T_{23}\cdots T_{(k-1)k} = \prod_{i=1}^{k-1} T_{i(i+1)}$. The likelihood for an odometry measurement and a loop closure are assumed to be Gaussian and are given in Table 1, Eq. (2) and Eq. (3), respectively.

3   Related Work

In this section, we describe the most recent state of the art approaches and how they are related to the novel method we propose in this paper.

The current workhorse for motion averaging is the Gauss-Newton (GN) algorithm. In fact, this algorithm has been employed for more than a decade to tackle the motion averaging problem (the seminal work of [17] was already proposing to use it). In this context, both relative and absolute parametrizations of the absolute transformations have been employed.

The most widely used is the *absolute parametrization* [13]. The main reason why people tend to use this parametrization is that it leads to solving, at each iteration of the GN, a *sparse* linear system. Even if the size of this linear system is proportional to the number of absolute transformations, its sparsity is usually exploited in solvers such as g²o, resulting in an algorithm with a reasonable computational time for a small or medium sized problem. Using this formalism, several algorithms have been recently proposed to perform robust motion averaging (i.e. when loop closures contain erroneous measurements): [1,8] proposed re-weighted schemes; [10,28] introduced auxiliary variables that in fact correspond to using a robust kernel as it was recently shown in [30] in the context of bundle adjustment; [22] proposed a consensus based algorithm which optimizes clusters of loop closures with a GN and checks their consistency with statistical tests. None of these approaches fulfill our first two requirements (Computational efficiency and Memory efficiency). However, in order to demonstrate the ability of our novel algorithm to detect wrong loop closures, we will compare its results against the Dynamic Covariance Scaling (DCS) [1].

The *relative parametrization* was initially used in [14] for the specific case of planar motions and was then extended to general matrix Lie groups in [25]. Each iteration of these algorithms corresponds to a GN step, even if it is not presented as such. Employing the relative parametrization leads to solving, at each iteration of the GN, a *dense* linear system whose size is proportional to the number of loop closure measurements. Consequently, the approach proposed in [25] is highly efficient when the number of loop closures is small but impractical for large scale problems. At first sight, the relative parametrization does not seem very attractive for our problem since we are mostly interested in large scale problems. However, we will see that, using this parametrization, the posterior distribution of the relative transformations has a specific shape that can be approximated with few parameters.

To the best of our knowledge, the most closely related approaches to the one we propose in this paper are the filters proposed in [5,12]. The algorithm proposed in [5] uses a Kalman filter to estimate absolute transformations using an absolute parametrization and validation gating to detect wrong loop closures. However, their approximation of the posterior distribution is a multivariate Gaussian distribution whose covariance matrix grows quadratically with the number of absolute transformations. Consequently, this filter is impractical for large scale problems. On the contrary, the authors of [12] use a relative parametrization and propose a novel closed-form way to process each loop closure using the concept of trajectory bending. This leads to a highly efficient filter which does not explicitly try to approximate the posterior distribution of the relative transformations but estimates the uncertainty of each transformation with a single scalar. Consequently, this filter also fulfills our "memory efficiency" requirement. However, this approach assumes that the loop closure measurements do not contain outliers.

Table 2. Comparison of state of the art approaches dedicated to motion averaging

	Ours	[12]	[5]	[1]
Computational efficiency	✓	✓	✓	×
Memory efficiency	✓	✓	×	×
Robustness	✓	×	✓	✓

Contrary to these methods, in this paper, we propose a novel filter based on a variational Bayesian approximation of the posterior distribution of the relative transformations which allows to fulfill our three requirements (see Table 2) while being almost as accurate as a batch approach.

4   The Case of a Single Loop

In this paper, we are interested in designing a Bayesian filter which, by definition, has to process the measurements sequentially in order to approximate the posterior distribution of the estimated transformations. However, as we have already seen, two parametrizations of the absolute transformations are possible. In this section, we motivate our choice of employing the relative parametrization on the simpler problem of motion averaging from odometry measurements and a single loop closure (see Fig. 2(a)).

In fact, we consider a loop of length N_L, where we are given $N_L - 1$ odometry measurements $\left\{Z_{i(i+1)}\right\}_{i=1,\dots,N_L-1}$ and a single loop closure Z_{1N_L} between the local coordinate systems 1 and N_L.

Using the likelihoods defined in Eqs. 2 and 3, we wish to minimize the following criterion w.r.t the relative transformations $\left\{T_{i(i+1)}\right\}_{i=1,\dots,N_L-1}$:

$$- 2\ln\left(p\left(\left\{T_{i(i+1)}\right\}_{i=1,\dots,N_L-1} | Z_{1N_L}, \left\{Z_{i(i+1)}\right\}_{i=1,\dots,N_L-1}\right)\right)$$

$$= \left\|\log_G^\vee\left(Z_{1N_L}\left(\prod_{i=1}^{N_L-1} T_{i(i+1)}\right)^{-1}\right)\right\|_{\Sigma_{1N_L}}^2 + \sum_{i=1}^{N_L-1}\left\|\log_G^\vee\left(T_{i(i+1)}Z_{i(i+1)}^{-1}\right)\right\|_{\Sigma_{i(i+1)}}^2 + \text{cst} \quad (4)$$

One way to minimize this criterion is to apply a Gauss-Newton algorithm where the relative transformations are jointly refined iteratively as follows (the superscript stands for the iteration):

$$T_{i(i+1)}^{(l)} = \exp_G^\wedge\left(\delta_{i(i+1)}^{(l/l-1)}\right) T_{i(i+1)}^{(l-1)} \quad \text{for} \quad i = 1 \dots N_L - 1. \quad (5)$$

The increments $\left\{\delta_{i(i+1)}^{(l/l-1)}\right\}_{i=1,\ldots,N_L-1}$ are obtained at each iteration by solving the following (dense) linear system of size $p \times N_L$:

$$
\begin{bmatrix} \delta_{12}^{(l/l-1)} \\ \vdots \\ \delta_{(N_L-1)N_L}^{(l/l-1)} \end{bmatrix} = \left(\left(J_{rel}^{(l)}\right)^T \Lambda J_{rel}^{(l)}\right)^{-1} \left(J_{rel}^{(l)}\right)^T \Lambda \begin{bmatrix} r_{12}^{(l-1)} \\ \vdots \\ r_{(N_L-1)N_L}^{(l-1)} \\ r_{1N_L}^{(l-1)} \end{bmatrix} \tag{6}
$$

where $J_{rel}^{(l)}$ is the Jacobian matrix of the system (see Fig. 2(b)), Λ is a block diagonal matrix concatenating the inverse of the covariance matrices of the measurements, $r_{1N_L}^{(l-1)} = \log_G^\vee\left(Z_{1N_L}\left(\prod_{i=1}^{N_L-1} T_{i(i+1)}^{(l-1)}\right)^{-1}\right)$ and $r_{i(i+1)}^{(l-1)} = \log_G^\vee\left(T_{i(i+1)}^{(l-1)}Z_{i(i+1)}^{-1}\right)$.

At first sight, the relative parametrization does not seem very interesting compared to the absolute parametrization since it requires to solve a dense linear system (in Fig. 2(b) the pseudo-Hessian $J_{rel}^T \Lambda J_{rel}$ is completely dense) instead of a sparse one in the absolute parametrization case[1] (in Fig. 2(b) the pseudo-Hessian $J_{abs}^T \Lambda J_{abs}$ is extremely sparse). However, as proven in the supplementary material, by initializing $T_{i(i+1)}^{(0)} = Z_{i(i+1)}$ for $i = 1 \ldots N_L - 1$, using the Woodbury formula and exploiting the structure of the problem, it is possible to show that

$$
\begin{bmatrix} \delta_{12}^{(l/l-1)} \\ \vdots \\ \delta_{(N_L-1)N_L}^{(l/l-1)} \end{bmatrix} \simeq \begin{bmatrix} \Sigma_{12} & & 0 \\ & \ddots & \\ 0 & & \Sigma_{(N_L-1)N_L} \end{bmatrix} \left(J_{LC}^{(l)}\right)^T \left(\Sigma_{1N_L} + \sum_{i=1}^{N_L-1} J_{1i}^{(l)} \Sigma_{i(i+1)} \left(J_{1i}^{(l)}\right)^T\right)^{-1}
$$
$$
\cdot \left(r_{1N_L}^{(l-1)} + J_{LC}^{(l)} \sum_{n=1}^{l-1} \begin{bmatrix} \delta_{12}^{(n/n-1)} \\ \vdots \\ \delta_{(N_L-1)N_L}^{(n/n-1)} \end{bmatrix}\right) - \sum_{n=1}^{l-1} \begin{bmatrix} \delta_{12}^{(n/n-1)} \\ \vdots \\ \delta_{(N_L-1)N_L}^{(n/n-1)} \end{bmatrix} \tag{7}
$$

where $J_{LC}^{(l)} = \left[J_{11}^{(l)} \cdots J_{1(N_L-1)}^{(l)}\right]$ is the Jacobian of the loop closure error and $J_{1n}^{(l)} \simeq \mathrm{Ad}_G\left(\prod_{i=1}^{n-1} T_{i(i+1)}^{(l-1)}\right)$. In this case, only a linear system of size p (i.e. independent of the length of the loop) has to be solved, making the algorithm highly efficient to close a single loop (in practice, $p = 6$ for $G = SE(3)$, $p = 8$ for $G = SL(3)$, etc.). Moreover, the inverse of the pseudo-Hessian $\left(J_{rel}^T \Lambda J_{rel}\right)^{-1}$ (see Fig. 2(b)), which represents (once the algorithm has reached convergence) the covariance matrix of the posterior distribution under a linear approximation, exhibits very small correlations between the transformations. Therefore, a block diagonal approximation of that covariance matrix seems to be a reasonable approximation that would allow us to derive a filter being able to deal with large

---

[1] Inference in the case of a single loop using the absolute parametrization is detailed in the supplementary material.

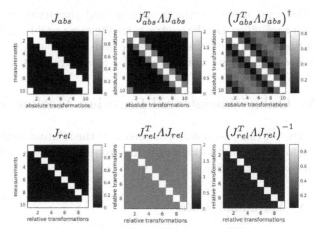

(a) Illustration of a perfect loop of length 10, where a cone represents a camera pose (camera 1 is black camera 10 is blue). The (noiseless) odometry measurements are plotted as solid blue lines while the (noiseless) loop closure measurement is shown as a dashed red line.

(b) Jacobian, pseudo-Hessian and inverse pseudo-Hessian for absolute and relative parametrizations (only the magnitude of the coefficients is shown).

Fig. 2. Illustration of the motion averaging problem on $SE(3)$ for a single loop. Using an absolute parametrization, the inverse pseudo-Hessian exhibits very strong correlations between the absolute transformations. On the contrary, using a relative parametrization, the inverse pseudo-Hessian has very small correlations (not null but close to zero) between the relative transformations, motivating our variational Bayesian approximation of the posterior distribution which assumes independent relative transformations (see text for details). (a) Illustration of a perfect loop of length 10, where a cone represents a camera pose (camera 1 is black camera 10 is blue). The (noiseless) odometry measurements are plotted as solid blue lines while the (noiseless) loop closure measurement is shown as a dashed red line. (b) Jacobian, pseudo-Hessian and inverse pseudo-Hessian for absolute and relative parametrizations (only the magnitude of the coefficients is shown). (Color figure online)

scale problems very efficiently. On the contrary, when using the absolute parametrization, the (pseudo-)inverse of the pseudo-Hessian $\left(J_{abs}^T \Lambda J_{abs}\right)^\dagger$ manifests very strong correlations, making any approximation of that matrix difficult.

From this point of view, the relative parametrization seems to be much more attractive than the absolute parametrization, at least for online inference.

Consequently, when designing our filter, we will employ a relative parametrization. Loop closure measurements will be processed sequentially using this highly efficient GN which only requires to solve a linear system of size p at each iteration. After having processed a loop closure, the covariance matrix of the posterior distribution will be approximated with a block diagonal covariance matrix using a variational Bayesian approximation. All these steps are detailed in Sect. 5.

Let us note that, since our approach employs a GN to process loop closures sequentially, it is optimal for *any* problem (i.e. any matrix Lie group G with anisotropic noises on the measurements) *containing loops that do not interact with each other*. On the contrary, for the same problems, COP-SLAM [12] is only optimal when the noise is isotropic and the logarithm map of G is related to a bi-invariant metric which in practice is usually not true, except for $SO(3)$.

5   Online Variational Bayesian Motion Averaging

In the previous Section, we showed that the relative parametrization was appealing for the online motion averaging problem. We now derive our novel filter using this parametrization.

5.1   Estimated State

At time instant $k-1$ (where $k > 2$), the estimated state consists in all the relative transformations $\mathcal{X}_{k-1} = \{T_{i(i+1)}\}_{i=1,\dots,k-2}$. More specifically, at time instant $k-1$, the posterior distribution of the state is assumed to have the following factorized form:

$$p\left(\mathcal{X}_{k-1}|\mathcal{D}_{odo,k-1},\mathcal{D}_{LC,k-1}\right) = Q_{k-1}(\mathcal{X}_{k-1}) = \prod_{i=1}^{k-2}\mathcal{N}_G\left(T_{i(i+1)};\overline{T}_{i(i+1)},P_{i(i+1)}\right)$$

$$(8)$$

where $\mathcal{D}_{odo,k-1} = \{Z_{i(i+1)}\}_{i=1,\dots,k-2}$ and $\mathcal{D}_{LC,k-1} = \{Z_{ij}\}_{1\leq i<j-1<k-1}$.

5.2   Processing of a New Odometry Measurement

At time instant k, when the new odometry measurement $Z_{(k-1)k}$ (with known covariance $\Sigma_{(k-1)k}$) is available, the estimated state simply augments, i.e. $\mathcal{X}_k = \{T_{i(i+1)}\}_{i=1,\dots,k-1}$. Consequently, the posterior distribution of the state remains factorized and has the following form:

$$p\left(\mathcal{X}_k|\mathcal{D}_{odo,k},\mathcal{D}_{LC,k-1}\right) = Q_k^{odo}\left(\mathcal{X}_k\right) = \prod_{i=1}^{k-1}\mathcal{N}_G\left(T_{i(i+1)};\overline{T}_{i(i+1)},P_{i(i+1)}\right) \quad (9)$$

where $\mathcal{D}_{odo,k} = \{Z_{i(i+1)}\}_{i=1,\dots,k-1}$, $\overline{T}_{(k-1)k} = Z_{(k-1)k}$ and $P_{(k-1)k} = \Sigma_{(k-1)k}$.

5.3   Processing of a New Loop Closure Measurement

At time instant k, after having received the odometry measurement $Z_{(k-1)k}$, a new loop closure measurement Z_{lk} (with known covariance Σ_{lk}) may be available (where $l < k$). In fact, multiple loop closures may be available, however, in order to keep the notations uncluttered, we only describe how to deal with one loop closure. In practice, the processing is applied sequentially to each loop closure as it is described in the pseudo-code presented in the supplementary material.

When a new loop closure measurement Z_{lk} is available, we would like to take into account the information coming from that observation in order to refine our current estimate of the state. However, the observation model Eq. 3 creates dependencies between all the relative transformations involved in the loop, and, therefore, the posterior distribution $p\left(\mathcal{X}_k|\mathcal{D}_{odo,k}, \mathcal{D}_{LC,k-1}, Z_{lk}\right)$ is not factorized anymore. Thus, the number of parameters required to describe that non-factorized posterior distribution becomes huge (typically in $O\left(k^2\right)$ using a linear approximation, see [5]), especially for large scale problems.

In order for our filter to be able to operate online on large scale problems, we propose to approximate that posterior distribution with a factorized distribution, whose number of parameters will be in $O\left(k\right)$. Such an approximation is motivated by our analysis of the single loop case (see Fig. 2). One way to find a factorized distribution "similar" to the true posterior distribution is to minimize the Kullback-Leibler divergence

$$D_{KL}\left(Q_{VB}\left(\mathcal{X}_k\right)\|p\left(\mathcal{X}_k|\mathcal{D}_{odo,k}, \mathcal{D}_{LC,k-1}, Z_{lk}\right)\right) \text{ with } Q_{VB}\left(\mathcal{X}_k\right) = \prod_{i=1}^{k-1} q_{VB}\left(T_{i(i+1)}\right). \quad (10)$$

This approach is usually called "variational Bayesian approximation" in the literature [3] and sometimes "Structured Mean Field" since we do not assume a fully factorized distribution but only the relative transformations to be mutually independent.

Variational Bayesian Approximation. Minimizing the KL divergence in (10) w.r.t $\mathcal{X}_k$ corresponds to maximizing the lower bound

$$\mathcal{L}\left(Q_{VB}\left(\mathcal{X}_k\right)\right) = \int Q_{VB}\left(\mathcal{X}_k\right) \ln\left(\frac{p\left(\mathcal{X}_k, \mathcal{D}_{odo,k}, \mathcal{D}_{LC,k-1}, Z_{lk}\right)}{Q_{VB}\left(\mathcal{X}_k\right)}\right) d\mathcal{X}_k. \quad (11)$$

In our case the (log)-joint distribution of all the random variables has the form:

$$\ln\left(p\left(\mathcal{X}_k, \mathcal{D}_{odo,k}, \mathcal{D}_{LC,k-1}, Z_{lk}\right)\right) = \ln\left(p\left(Z_{lk}|\left\{T_{i(i+1)}\right\}_{i=l,\ldots,k-1}\right) Q_k^{odo}\left(\mathcal{X}_k\right)\right)$$

$$= -\frac{1}{2}\left\|\log_G^{\vee}\left(Z_{lk}\left(\prod_{i=l}^{k-1} T_{i(i+1)}\right)^{-1}\right)\right\|_{\Sigma_{lk}}^2 - \frac{1}{2}\sum_{i=1}^{k-1}\left\|\log_G^{\vee}\left(T_{i(i+1)}\overline{T}_{i(i+1)}^{-1}\right)\right\|_{P_{i(i+1)}}^2 + \text{cst} \quad (12)$$

However, because of the curvature of the Lie group, the terms inside the norms in (12) are not linear in the transformations. One way to apply a variational Bayesian approach in this case is to linearize the terms inside the norms.

At this point, we find it convenient to define the variables involved in the linearization step:

$$T_{i(i+1)} = \exp_G^{\wedge}\left(\epsilon_{i(i+1)}\right)\check{T}_{i(i+1)} \quad \text{for} \quad i = 1\ldots k-1 \quad (13)$$

where $\check{T}_{i(i+1)}$ is the (fixed) linearization point for the relative transformation $T_{i(i+1)}$ and $\epsilon_{i(i+1)}$ is a random variable. This linearization point is quite important and its value is discussed at the end of the section. After linearization, the log-joint distribution becomes:

$$\ln\left(p\left(\{\epsilon_{i(i+1)}\}_{i=1,\dots,k-1}, \mathcal{D}_{odo,k}, \mathcal{D}_{LC,k-1}, Z_{lk}\right)\right)$$

$$= -\frac{1}{2}\left\|r_{lk} - \sum_{i=l}^{k-1} J_{li}\epsilon_{i(i+1)}\right\|_{\Sigma_{lk}}^2 - \frac{1}{2}\sum_{i=1}^{k-1}\left\|r_{i(i+1)} + \epsilon_{i(i+1)}\right\|_{P_{i(i+1)}}^2 + \text{cst} \quad (14)$$

where we approximated the Jacobian of $\log_G^\vee$ by the identity, $J_{li} \simeq \text{Ad}_G\left(\prod_{j=l}^{i-1}\breve{T}_{j(j+1)}\right)$ for $i > l$, $J_{ll} \simeq Id$, $r_{lk} = \log_G^\vee\left(Z_{lk}\left(\prod_{i=l}^{k-1}\breve{T}_{i(i+1)}\right)^{-1}\right)$ and $r_{i(i+1)} = \log_G^\vee\left(\breve{T}_{i(i+1)}\overline{T}_{i(i+1)}^{-1}\right)$.

Given the log-joint distribution (14), the objective is now to maximize the lower bound (11) where $\mathcal{X}_k$ is now replaced with $\{\epsilon_{i(i+1)}\}_{i=1,\dots,k-1}$ because of the linearization step. Here:

$$Q_{VB}\left(\{\epsilon_{i(i+1)}\}_{i=1,\dots,k-1}\right) = \prod_{i=1}^{k-1} q_{VB}\left(\epsilon_{i(i+1)}\right). \quad (15)$$

In fact, it is possible to show that (see [3] pp. 446), for each variable $\epsilon_{i(i+1)}$, the best approximated distribution is given by the following expression:

$$\ln\left(q_{VB}^*\left(\epsilon_{i(i+1)}\right)\right)$$

$$= \mathbb{E}_{Q_{VB}\backslash q_{VB}^*(\epsilon_{i(i+1)})}\left[\ln\left(p\left(\{\epsilon_{i(i+1)}\}_{i=1,\dots,k-1}, \mathcal{D}_{odo,k}, \mathcal{D}_{LC,k-1}, Z_{lk}\right)\right)\right] + \text{cst}$$

$$(16)$$

where $\mathbb{E}_{Q_{VB}\backslash q_{VB}^*(\epsilon_{i(i+1)})}$ stands for the conditional expectation w.r.t all the variables except $\epsilon_{i(i+1)}$. Thus, from (16) and (14), we obtain

$$\ln\left(q_{VB}^*\left(\epsilon_{i(i+1)}\right)\right) = -\frac{1}{2}\left(\epsilon_{i(i+1)} - \mu_{i(i+1)}\right)^T \Xi_{i(i+1)}^{-1}\left(\epsilon_{i(i+1)} - \mu_{i(i+1)}\right) + \text{cst} \quad (17)$$

where

$$\Xi_{i(i+1)} = \left(J_{li}^T \Sigma_{lk}^{-1} J_{li} + P_{i(i+1)}^{-1}\right)^{-1} \quad (18)$$

and

$$\mu_{i(i+1)} = \Xi_{i(i+1)}^{-1}\left(J_{li}^T \Sigma_{lk}^{-1} e_{lk,i} - P_{i(i+1)}^{-1} r_{i(i+1)}\right) \quad (19)$$

with $e_{lk,i} = r_{lk} - \left(\sum_{j=l,j\neq i}^{k-1} J_{lj}\mu_{j(j+1)}\right)$. Therefore, for each random variable $\epsilon_{i(i+1)}$ $(i = 1,\dots,k-1)$, the best approximated distribution is a Gaussian of the form:

$$q_{VB}^*\left(\epsilon_{i(i+1)}\right) = \mathcal{N}_{\mathbb{R}^p}\left(\epsilon_{i(i+1)}; \mu_{i(i+1)}, \Xi_{i(i+1)}\right) \quad \text{for} \quad i = 1,\dots,k-1 \quad (20)$$

Let us note that if $i < l$, i.e. if the relative transformation $T_{i(i+1)}$ is not involved in the loop closure Z_{lk}, then

$$q_{VB}^* \left(\epsilon_{i(i+1)} \right) = \mathcal{N}_{\mathbb{R}^p} \left(\epsilon_{i(i+1)}; \mathbf{0}, \Xi_{i(i+1)} = P_{i(i+1)} \right) \quad \text{for} \quad i < l \qquad (21)$$

making our algorithm very efficient since a loop closure will only modify the relative transformations involved in that loop.

In theory, in order to obtain the values of $\left\{ \mu_{i(i+1)} \right\}_{i=l, \ldots, k-1}$ we should cycle through (19) for each relative transformation involved in the loop until convergence. However, if the linearization step (see Eq. (13)) is performed around the maximizer of (12), then $\mu_{i(i+1)} = \mathbf{0}$ for $i = l, \ldots, k-1$. Thus in practice, for each new loop closure measurement, we first apply, the Gauss-Newton algorithm described in Sect. 4[2] in order to find the maximizer of (12) very efficiently. Then we only have to compute the covariances $\Xi_{i(i+1)}$ (see Eq. (18)) for $i = l, \ldots, k-1$.

Finally, for each relative transformation, $q_{VB}^* \left(\epsilon_{i(i+1)} \right)$ is a Gaussian with zero mean. Therefore, from Eq. (13), one can see that (up to a linear approximation) $q_{VB}^* \left(T_{i(i+1)} \right)$ is a Gaussian distribution on Lie group (see Eq. (1)) of the form $\mathcal{N}_G \left(T_{i(i+1)}; \check{T}_{i(i+1)}, \Xi_{i(i+1)} \right)$. Consequently, after having processed a new loop closure, our factorized approximation of the posterior has the following form:

$$p \left(\mathcal{X}_k | \mathcal{D}_{odo,k}, \mathcal{D}_{LC,k-1}, Z_{lk} \right) \approx Q_{VB} \left(\mathcal{X}_k \right) = \prod_{i=1}^{k-1} \mathcal{N}_G \left(T_{i(i+1)}; \check{T}_{i(i+1)}, \Xi_{i(i+1)} \right) \tag{22}$$

Detection of Outlier Loop Closure Through Validation Gating. So far, we have proposed an efficient way to process a new loop closure measurement assuming it was following the generative model 3. However, in practice, two places being perceived as the same usually produce a wrong loop closure. Consequently, detecting and removing these wrong loop closure measurements is crucial in order to perform motion averaging, especially for large scale problems where wrong loop closures are very likely to occur.

Since we continuously maintain an approximation of the posterior distribution, it is possible to detect wrong loop closure measurements through validation gating [26]. This approach consists in first computing the mean $\overline{Z}_{lk}$ and covariance $\overline{\Sigma}_{lk}$ parameters of the following distribution:

$$p \left(Z_{lk} | \mathcal{D}_{odo,k}, \mathcal{D}_{LC,k-1} \right) \approx \mathcal{N}_G \left(Z_{lk}; \overline{Z}_{lk} = \prod_{i=l}^{k-1} \check{T}_{i(i+1)}, \overline{\Sigma}_{lk} = \Sigma_{lk} + \sum_{i=l}^{k-1} J_{li} P_{i(i+1)} J_{li}^T \right) \tag{23}$$

and then testing w.r.t a threshold t whether or not the received measurement is likely to be an inlier:

$$\left\| \log_G^{\vee} \left(Z_{lk} \overline{Z}_{lk}^{-1} \right) \right\|_{\overline{\Sigma}_{lk}}^2 < t \tag{24}$$

---

[2] Equation (12) has the same form (up to a sign) as the cost function (4). Consequently, the highly efficient GN described in Sect. 4 can be applied to maximize (12).

In theory, t should be based on the p-value of the Chi-squared distribution. However, as we will see in the experiments, such a theoretical value is sometimes too restrictive, especially when processing real data where the covariance of the odometry and loop closure measurements are not very accurate and the assumption of mutually independent noises might be violated.

6   Experiments

We now evaluate experimentally, both on synthetic and real datasets, our novel online variational Bayesian motion averaging algorithm (a pseudo-code is proposed in supplementary material) against the state of the art algorithms LG-IEKF [5], COP-SLAM [12] and DCS [1] (which uses g^2o). To do so, we first compare both the accuracy and the computational time of these approaches on datasets which do not contain wrong loop closures, since COP-SLAM is not able to detect and remove wrong loop closures. The robustness of the different approaches is evaluated separately on datasets specifically dedicated to this task (see [23]). We finally present qualitative results on monocular visual SLAM and video mosaicking applications. In all these experiments, when dealing with synthetic datasets, the threshold t of the validation gating stage of our algorithm has been set to the $\mathcal{X}^2$ value with p degrees of freedom given by a p-value of 0.001. Otherwise, when dealing with real data, we empirically defined $t = 900$, which is much higher that the theoretical $\mathcal{X}^2$ value since the covariance of the odometry and loop closure measurements are usually not very accurate in this case and the assumption of mutually independent noises might be violated.

6.1   Evaluation of the Accuracy and the Computational Time

In this experiment, we consider a binocular 6D SLAM application (Lie group $SE(3)$) and use one synthetic sequence (Sphere) and two real sequences (originally from the KITTI dataset [15]) provided by the authors of [12]. The results for this experiment are given in Table 3 where we reported both the Root Mean Squared Error (RMSE) for the absolute positions as well as the computational time for our approach, COP-SLAM, LG-IEKF and g^2o. We provide the computational time both in C++ and Matlab because only a Matlab implementation of LG-IEKF is available.

Let us first note that we should not expect the RMSE of COP-SLAM and our approach to be as low as the RMSE of LG-IEKF and g^2o because these approaches do not try to summarize the past information with a small number of parameters at each time instant but keep all the past information (g^2o keeps all the past measurements while LG-IEKF maintains a full covariance matrix). However, one can see that our approach remains very accurate. Indeed, on the KITTI 02 sequence, our approach even obtains the same RMSE as LG-IEKF. On the contrary, COP-SLAM obtains much higher RMSE than our approach on every sequence. From the computational time point of view, as expected, both our approach and COP-SLAM are orders of magnitude faster than LG-IEKF

Table 3. Results for binocular 6D SLAM ($SE(3)$): In terms of RMSE (for the position), our approach is much closer to the solutions of both g^{2}o and LG-IEKF [5], compared to COP-SLAM [12]. In terms of computational time, our approach is orders of magnitude faster than both g^{2}o and LG-IEKF, while being only slightly slower than COP-SLAM. *Remark: for these experiments, wrong loop closures have been removed since COP-SLAM cannot cope with them. The robustness of our method w.r.t wrong loop closures is evaluated against LG-IEKF [5] and DCS [1] (which uses g^{2}o) in Sect. 6.2.*

	RMSE position (m)			Time (ms): C++ (left) & Matlab (right)					
	Sphere	KITTI 00	KITTI 02	Sphere		KITTI 00		KITTI 02	
Ours	**2.1**	**2.7**	**13.6**	971	136 000	65	8 000	29	4 000
[12]	6.0	3.8	19.7	**350**	N/a	**7**	N/a	**2**	N/a
[5]	0.8	2.0	13.6	N/a	3 340 000	N/a	80 000	N/a	52 000
g^{2}o	0.2	2.4	13.8	40 000	N/a	1336	N/a	693	N/a

and g^{2}o. Moreover, our approach is only slightly slower than COP-SLAM which is largely compensated by the fact that our approach has a much lower RMSE.

6.2 Evaluation of the Robustness

In this experiment, we employ the dataset provided by the authors of [23] which allows to evaluate the robustness of an approach to wrong loop closures on a planar visual SLAM application (Lie group $SE(2)$). The results and details regarding this experiment are provided in the supplementary material. Our approach surprisingly achieved exactly the same precision and recall as both LG-IEKF and DCS. This is a remarkable result since these two algorithms are not designed to perform online large scale estimation and are consequently much slower than our approach (see Table 3).

6.3 Additional Experiments

In Fig. 1, we present results for monocular visual SLAM (Lie group $Sim(3)$) on sequence 13 of the KITTI dataset. The details regarding this experiment are provided in the supplementary material. However, one can see that the trajectory estimated with our approach is visually much closer to the result of [33] (which employs a Lidar) than the trajectory estimated with COP-SLAM. Results on sequence 15 of the KITTI dataset as well as results for video mosaicking (Lie group $Sim(3)$) are also provided as supplementary material.

7 Conclusion and Future Work

In this paper, we proposed a novel filter dedicated to online motion averaging for large scale problems. We have shown that using a relative parametrization of the absolute transformations produces a posterior distribution that can be efficiently approximated assuming independent relative transformations. Based on this representation, we demonstrated that it is possible to obtain an accurate, efficient and robust filter by employing a variational Bayesian approach.

The performances of our novel algorithm were extensively evaluated against the state of the art algorithm COP-SLAM [12]. Actually, our approach achieved a significantly lower RMSE than COP-SLAM while being only slightly slower.

Since COP-SLAM cannot detect wrong loop closures, we also compared the robustness of our filter against LG-IEKF [5] and DCS [1]. In this context, our approach surprisingly achieved the same robustness as these algorithms. This is a remarkable result since our approach is designed to perform online large scale estimation and, consequently, is orders of magnitude faster than both LG-IEKF and DCS.

As future work, we plan to exploit the high efficiency of our filter to build a multi-hypothesis filter. This would prevent failures, such as those described in the supplementary material, to which LG-IEKF, DCS and the approach presented in this paper are prone due to the fact that they are forced to take a decision when a loop closure measurement is available and cannot wait until new evidence is received.

Acknowledgments. The author would like to thank the reviewers and Cornelia Vacar for their valuable help as well as Christopher Zach for fruitful discussions and feedback.

References

1. Agarwal, P., Tipaldi, G.D., Spinello, L., Stachniss, C., Burgard, W.: Robust map optimization using dynamic covariance scaling. In: 2013 IEEE International Conference on Robotics and Automation (ICRA), pp. 62–69. IEEE (2013)
2. Agarwal, S., Mierle, K., et al.: Ceres solver. http://ceres-solver.org
3. Bishop, C.: Pattern Recognition and Machine Learning. Springer, New York (2006)
4. Boumal, N., Singer, A., Absil, P.A.: Robust estimation of rotations from relative measurements by maximum likelihood. In: Proceedings of the 52nd Conference on Decision and Control, CDC (2013)
5. Bourmaud, G., Mégret, R., Giremus, A., Berthoumieu, Y.: Global motion estimation from relative measurements in the presence of outliers. In: Cremers, D., Reid, I., Saito, H., Yang, M.-H. (eds.) ACCV 2014. LNCS, vol. 9007, pp. 366–381. Springer, Heidelberg (2015)
6. Caballero, F., Merino, L., Ferruz, J., Ollero, A.: Homography based Kalman filter for mosaic building. applications to UAV position estimation. In: 2007 IEEE International Conference on Robotics and Automation, pp. 2004–2009. IEEE (2007)
7. Carlone, L., Aragues, R., Castellanos, J.A., Bona, B.: A fast and accurate approximation for planar pose graph optimization. Int. J. Robot. Res. (2014)
8. Chatterjee, A., Govindu, V.: Efficient and robust large-scale rotation averaging. In: Proceedings of the IEEE International Conference on Computer Vision, pp. 521–528 (2013)
9. Chirikjian, G.S.: Stochastic Models, Information Theory, and Lie Groups, vol. 2. Springer, Boston (2012)

10. Choi, S., Zhou, Q.Y., Koltun, V.: Robust reconstruction of indoor scenes. In: 2015 IEEE Conference on Computer Vision and Pattern Recognition (CVPR), pp. 5556–5565. IEEE (2015)
11. Dellaert, F.: GTSAM - The Georgia Tech Smoothing and Mapping Library. https://collab.cc.gatech.edu/borg/gtsam/
12. Dubbelman, G., Browning, B.: COP-SLAM: closed-form online pose-chain optimization for visual SLAM. IEEE Trans. Robot. **31**(5), 1194–1213 (2015)
13. Engel, J., Schöps, T., Cremers, D.: LSD-SLAM: large-scale direct monocular SLAM. In: Fleet, D., Pajdla, T., Schiele, B., Tuytelaars, T. (eds.) ECCV 2014, Part II. LNCS, vol. 8690, pp. 834–849. Springer, Heidelberg (2014)
14. Estrada, C., Neira, J., Tardós, J.D.: Hierarchical SLAM: real-time accurate mapping of large environments. IEEE Trans. Robot. **21**(4), 588–596 (2005)
15. Geiger, A., Lenz, P., Stiller, C., Urtasun, R.: Vision meets robotics: the KITTI dataset. Int. J. Robot. Res. (IJRR) (2013)
16. Govindu, V.M.: Combining two-view constraints for motion estimation. In: Proceedings of the 2001 IEEE Computer Society Conference on Computer Vision and Pattern Recognition, CVPR 2001, vol. 2, pp. 218–225. IEEE (2001)
17. Govindu, V.M.: Lie-algebraic averaging for globally consistent motion estimation. In: Proceedings of the 2004 IEEE Computer Society Conference on Computer Vision and Pattern Recognition, CVPR 2004, vol. 1, pp. 684–691. IEEE (2004)
18. Govindu, V.M.: Robustness in motion averaging. In: Narayanan, P.J., Nayar, S.K., Shum, H.-Y. (eds.) ACCV 2006. LNCS, vol. 3852, pp. 457–466. Springer, Heidelberg (2006)
19. Grisetti, G., Stachniss, C., Burgard, W.: Nonlinear constraint network optimization for efficient map learning. IEEE Trans. Intell. Transp. Syst. **10**(3), 428–439 (2009)
20. Hartley, R., Trumpf, J., Dai, Y., Li, H.: Rotation averaging. Int. J. Comput. Vis. **103**(3), 267–305 (2013)
21. Kümmerle, R., Grisetti, G., Strasdat, H., Konolige, K., Burgard, W.: g2o: a general framework for graph optimization. In: 2011 IEEE International Conference on Robotics and Automation (ICRA), pp. 3607–3613. IEEE (2011)
22. Latif, Y., Cadena, C., Neira, J.: Robust loop closing over time for pose graph SLAM. Int. J. Robot. Res. (2013)
23. Latif, Y., Cadena, C., Neira, J.: Robust graph slam back-ends: a comparative analysis. In: 2014 IEEE/RSJ International Conference on Intelligent Robots and Systems (IROS 2014), pp. 2683–2690. IEEE (2014)
24. Meidow, J.: Efficient video mosaicking by multiple loop closing. In: Stilla, U., Rottensteiner, F., Mayer, H., Jutzi, B., Butenuth, M. (eds.) PIA 2011. LNCS, vol. 6952, pp. 1–12. Springer, Heidelberg (2011). doi:10.1007/978-3-642-24393-6_1
25. Meidow, J.: Efficient multiple loop adjustment for computer vision tasks. Photogrammetrie-Fernerkundung-Geoinformation **2012**(5), 501–510 (2012)
26. Ramachandra, K.: Kalman Filtering Techniques for Radar Tracking. CRC Press, Boca Raton (2000)
27. Roberts, R., Sinha, S.N., Szeliski, R., Steedly, D.: Structure from motion for scenes with large duplicate structures. In: 2011 IEEE Conference on Computer Vision and Pattern Recognition (CVPR), pp. 3137–3144. IEEE (2011)
28. Sünderhauf, N., Protzel, P.: Switchable constraints for robust pose graph SLAM. In:2012 IEEE/RSJ International Conference on Intelligent Robots and Systems (IROS), pp. 1879–1884. IEEE (2012)

29. Tron, R., Daniilidis, K.: Statistical pose averaging with non-isotropic and incomplete relative measurements. In: Fleet, D., Pajdla, T., Schiele, B., Tuytelaars, T. (eds.) ECCV 2014, Part V. LNCS, vol. 8693, pp. 804–819. Springer, Heidelberg (2014)

30. Zach, C.: Robust bundle adjustment revisited. In: Fleet, D., Pajdla, T., Schiele, B., Tuytelaars, T. (eds.) ECCV 2014, Part V. LNCS, vol. 8693, pp. 772–787. Springer, Heidelberg (2014)

31. Zach, C., Irschara, A., Bischof, H.: What can missing correspondences tell us about 3D structure and motion? In: IEEE Conference on Computer Vision and Pattern Recognition, CVPR 2008, pp. 1–8. IEEE (2008)

32. Zach, C., Klopschitz, M., Pollefeys, M.: Disambiguating visual relations using loop constraints. In: 2010 IEEE Conference on Computer Vision and Pattern Recognition (CVPR), pp. 1426–1433. IEEE (2010)

33. Zhang, J., Singh, S.: LOAM: lidar odometry and mapping in real-time. In: Robotics: Science and Systems Conference (RSS), Berkeley, CA, July 2014

Unified Depth Prediction and Intrinsic Image Decomposition from a Single Image via Joint Convolutional Neural Fields

Seungryong Kim[1], Kihong Park[1], Kwanghoon Sohn[1(✉)], and Stephen Lin[2]

[1] Yonsei University, Seoul, South Korea
{srkim89,khpark7727,khsohn}@yonsei.ac.kr
[2] Microsoft Research, Redmond, USA
stevelin@microsoft.com

Abstract. We present a method for jointly predicting a depth map and intrinsic images from single-image input. The two tasks are formulated in a synergistic manner through a joint conditional random field (CRF) that is solved using a novel convolutional neural network (CNN) architecture, called the joint convolutional neural field (JCNF) model. Tailored to our joint estimation problem, JCNF differs from previous CNNs in its sharing of convolutional activations and layers between networks for each task, its inference in the gradient domain where there exists greater correlation between depth and intrinsic images, and the incorporation of a gradient scale network that learns the confidence of estimated gradients in order to effectively balance them in the solution. This approach is shown to surpass state-of-the-art methods both on single-image depth estimation and on intrinsic image decomposition.

Keywords: Single-image depth estimation · Intrinsic image decomposition · Conditional random field · Convolutional neural networks

1 Introduction

Perceiving the physical properties of a scene undoubtedly plays a fundamental role in understanding real-world imagery. Such inherent properties include the 3-D geometric configuration, the illumination or shading, and the reflectance or albedo of each scene surface. Depth prediction and intrinsic image decomposition, which aims to recover shading and albedo, are thus two fundamental yet challenging tasks in computer vision. While they address different aspects of scene understanding, there exist strong consistencies among depth and intrinsic

S. Kim—This work was done while Seungryong Kim was an intern at Microsoft Research.

Electronic supplementary material The online version of this chapter (doi:10. 1007/978-3-319-46484-8_9) contains supplementary material, which is available to authorized users.

B. Leibe et al. (Eds.): ECCV 2016, Part VIII, LNCS 9912, pp. 143–159, 2016.
DOI: 10.1007/978-3-319-46484-8_9

images, such that information about one provides valuable prior knowledge for recovering the other.

In the intrinsic image decomposition literature, several works have exploited measured depth information to make the decomposition problem more tractable [1-5]. These techniques have all demonstrated better performance than using RGB images alone. On the other hand, in the literature for single-image depth prediction, illumination-invariant features have been utilized for greater robustness in depth inference [6,7], and shading discontinuities have been used to detect surface boundaries [8], suggesting that intrinsic images can be employed to enhance depth prediction performance. Although the two tasks are mutually beneficial, most previous research have solved for them only in sequence, by using estimated intrinsic images to constrain depth prediction [8], or vice versa [9]. We propose in this paper to instead jointly predict depth and intrinsic images in a manner where the two complementary tasks can assist each other.

We address this joint prediction problem using convolutional neural networks (CNNs), which have yielded state-of-the-art performance for the individual problems of single-image depth prediction [6,7] and intrinsic image decomposition [9-11], but are hampered by ambiguity issues that arise from limited training sets. In our work, the two tasks are formulated synergistically in a joint conditional random field (CRF) that is solved using a novel CNN architecture, called the joint convolutional neural field (JCNF) model. This architecture differs from previous CNNs in several ways tailored to our particular problem. One is the sharing of convolutional activations and layers between networks for each task, which allows each network to account for inferences made in other networks. Another is to perform learning in the gradient domain, where there exist stronger correlations between depth and intrinsic images than in the image value domain, which helps to deal with the ambiguity problem from limited training sets. A third is the incorporation of a gradient scale network which jointly learns the confidence of the estimated gradients, to more robustly balance them in the solution. These networks of the JCNF model are iteratively learned in a piece-wise manner using a unified energy function in a joint CRF.

Within this system, depth, shading and albedo are predicted in a coarse-to-fine manner that yields more globally consistent results. Our experiments show that this joint prediction outperforms existing depth prediction methods and intrinsic image decomposition techniques on various benchmarks.

2   Related Work

Depth Prediction from a Single Image. Traditional methods for this task have formulated the depth prediction as a Markov random field (MRF) learning problem [12-14]. As exact MRF learning and inference are intractable in general, most of these approaches employ approximation methods, such as through linear regression of depth with image features [12], learning image-depth correlation with a non-linear kernel function [13], and training category-adaptive model parameters [14]. Although these parametric models infer plausible depth maps to some extent, they cannot estimate the depth of natural scenes reliably due to their limited learning capability.

By leveraging the availability of large RGB-D databases, data-driven approaches have been actively researched [15,16]. Konrad *et al.* [15] proposed a depth fusion scheme to infer the depth map by retrieving the nearest images in the dataset, followed by an aggregation via weighted median filtering. Karsch *et al.* [16] presented the depth transfer (DT) approach which retrieves the nearest similar images and warps their depth maps using dense SIFT flow. Inspired by this method, Choi *et al.* [17] proposed the depth analogy (DA) approach that transfers depth gradients from the nearest images, demonstrating the effectiveness of gradient domain learning. Although these methods can extract reliable depth for certain scenes, there exist many others for which the nearest images are dissimilar and unsuitable. Recently, Kong *et al.* [8] extended the DT approach [16] by using albedo and shading for image matching as well as for detecting contours at surface boundaries. In contrast to our approach, the intrinsic images are estimated independently from the depth prediction.

More recently, methods have been proposed based on CNNs. Eigen *et al.* [6] proposed multi-scale CNNs (MS-CNNs) for predicting depth maps directly from a single image. Other CNN models were later proposed for depth estimation [18], including a deep convolutional neural field (DCNF) by Fayao *et al.* [7] that estimates depth on each superpixel while enforcing smoothness within a CRF. CNN-based methods clearly outperform conventional techniques, and we aim to elevate the performance further by accounting for intrinsic image information.

Intrinsic Image Decomposition. The notion of intrinsic images was first introduced in [19]. Conventional methods are largely based on Retinex theory [20–22], which attributes large image gradients to albedo changes, and smaller gradients to shading. More recent approaches have employed a variety of techniques, based on gradient distribution priors [23], dense CRFs [24], and hybrid L_2-L_p optimization to separate albedo and shading gradients [25]. These single-image based methods, however, are inherently limited by the fundamental ill-posedness of the problem. To partially alleviate this limitation, several approaches have utilized additional input, such as multiple images [26–28], user interaction [29,30], and measured depth maps [1–5]. The use of additional data such as measured depth clearly increases performance but reduces their applicability.

Related to our work is the method of Barron and Malik [31], which estimates object shape in addition to intrinsic images. To regularize the estimation, the method utilizes statistical priors on object shape and albedo which are not generally applicable to images of full scenes.

More recently, intrinsic image decomposition has been addressed using CNNs [9–11]. Zhou *et al.* [10] proposed a multi-stream CNN to predict the relative reflectance ordering between image patches from large-scale human annotations. Narihira *et al.* [11] learned a CNN that directly predicts albedo and shading from an RGB image patch. Shelhamer *et al.* [9] estimated depth through a fully convolutional network and used it to constrain the intrinsic image decomposition. Unlike our approach, the depth and intrinsic images are estimated sequentially.

3 Formulation

3.1 Problem Statement and Model Architecture

Let us define a color image I such that $I_p : \mathcal{I} \to \mathbb{R}^3$ for pixel p, where $\mathcal{I} \subset \mathbb{N}^2$ is a discrete image domain. Similarly, depth, albedo and shading can be defined as $D_p : \mathcal{I} \to \mathbb{R}$ and $A_p, S_p : \mathcal{I} \to \mathbb{R}^3$. All of these image quantities are defined in the log domain. Given a training set of color, depth, albedo, and shading images denoted by $\mathcal{C} = \{(I^i, D^i, A^i, S^i) \,|\, i = 1, 2, ..., \mathcal{N_C}\}$, where $\mathcal{N_C}$ is the number of training images, we first aim to learn a prediction model that approximates depth D^i, albedo A^i, and shading S^i from each color image $I^i \in \mathcal{C}$. This prediction model will then be used to infer reliable depth D, albedo A, and shading S simultaneously from a single query image I.

We specifically learn the joint prediction model in the gradient domain, where depth and intrinsic images generally exhibit stronger correlation than in the value domain, as exemplified in Fig. 1. This greater correlation and reduced discrepancy among ∇D, ∇A, and ∇S facilitate joint learning of the two tasks by allowing them to better leverage information from each other[1]. We therefore formulate our model to predict the depth, albedo, and shading gradient fields from the color image. Our method additionally learns the confidence of predicted gradients based on their consistency among one another in the training set.

We formulate this joint prediction using convolutional neural networks (CNNs) in a joint conditional random field (CRF). Our system architecture is structured as three cooperating networks, namely a depth prediction network, an intrinsic prediction network, and a gradient scale network. The depth prediction network is modeled by two feed-forward processes $\mathcal{F}(I^i; \mathbf{w}_{\mathcal{F}}^D)$ and $\mathcal{F}(I^i; \mathbf{w}_{\mathcal{F}}^{\nabla D})$, where $\mathbf{w}_{\mathcal{F}}^D$ and $\mathbf{w}_{\mathcal{F}}^{\nabla D}$ represent the network parameters for depth and depth gradients. The intrinsic prediction network is similarly modeled by feed-forward processes $\mathcal{F}(I^i; \mathbf{w}_{\mathcal{F}}^{\nabla A})$ and $\mathcal{F}(I^i; \mathbf{w}_{\mathcal{F}}^{\nabla S})$, where $\mathbf{w}_{\mathcal{F}}^{\nabla A}$ and $\mathbf{w}_{\mathcal{F}}^{\nabla S}$ represent the network parameters for albedo gradients and shading gradients. The gradient scale network learns the confidence of depth, albedo and shading gradients using a feed-forward process for each, denoted by $\mathcal{G}(\nabla I^i, \nabla A^i, \nabla S^i; \mathbf{w}_{\mathcal{G}}^{\nabla D})$, $\mathcal{G}(\nabla I^i, \nabla D^i, \nabla S^i; \mathbf{w}_{\mathcal{G}}^{\nabla A})$, and $\mathcal{G}(\nabla I^i, \nabla D^i, \nabla A^i; \mathbf{w}_{\mathcal{G}}^{\nabla S})$, where $\mathbf{w}_{\mathcal{G}}^{\nabla D}$, $\mathbf{w}_{\mathcal{G}}^{\nabla A}$, and $\mathbf{w}_{\mathcal{G}}^{\nabla S}$ are their respective network parameters. The three networks in our system are jointly learned in a manner where each can leverage information from the other networks.

3.2 Joint Conditional Random Field

The networks in our model are jointly learned by minimizing the energy function of a joint CRF. The joint CRF is formulated so that each task can leverage

---

[1] ∇ is a differential operator defined in the **x**- and **y**-direction such that $\nabla = [\nabla_{\mathbf{x}}, \nabla_{\mathbf{y}}]$.

(a)   (b)   (c)   (d)

Fig. 1. For an example from the MPI-SINTEL dataset [32], its (a) color image I, (b) depth D, (c) albedo A, (d) shading S, and their corresponding gradient fields ∇I, ∇D, ∇A, and ∇S shown below. Compared to quantities in the value domain, correlations are stronger among gradient fields, such that estimates of one may help in learning others. Furthermore, the gradient consistency between ∇I, ∇D, ∇A, and ∇S can be used to estimate the confidence of each gradient.

information from the other complementary task, leading to improved prediction in comparison to separate estimation models. Our energy function $\mathbf{E}(D, A, S | I)$ is defined as unary potentials $\mathbf{E}_u$ and pairwise potentials $\mathbf{E}_s$ for each task:

$$
\begin{aligned}
\mathbf{E}(D, A, S | I) = {} & \mathbf{E}_u(D | I) + \mathbf{E}_u(A, S | I) \\
& + \lambda_D \mathbf{E}_s(D | I, A, S) + \lambda_A \mathbf{E}_s(A | I, D, S) + \lambda_S \mathbf{E}_s(S | I, D, A),
\end{aligned}
\tag{1}
$$

where λ_D, λ_A, and λ_S are weights for each pairwise potential. In the training procedure, this energy function is minimized over all the training images, *i.e.*, by minimizing $\sum_i \mathbf{E}(D^i, A^i, S^i | I^i)$. For testing, given a query image I and the learned network parameters, the final solutions of D, A, and S are estimated by minimizing the energy function $\mathbf{E}(D, A, S | I)$.

Unary Potentials. The unary potentials consist of two energy functions, $\mathbf{E}_u(D | I)$ and $\mathbf{E}_u(A, S | I)$. The depth unary function $\mathbf{E}_u(D | I)$ is formulated as

$$
\mathbf{E}_u(D | I) = \sum_p \left(D_p - \mathcal{F}(I_{\mathcal{P}}; \mathbf{w}_{\mathcal{F}}^D) \right)^2,
\tag{2}
$$

which represents the squared differences between depths D_p and predicted depths from $\mathcal{F}(I_{\mathcal{P}}; \mathbf{w}_{\mathcal{F}}^D)$, where $\mathcal{P}$ is the local neighborhood[2] for pixel p. It can be considered as a Dirichlet boundary condition for depth pairwise potentials, which will be described shortly.

The unary function $\mathbf{E}_u(A, S | I)$ for intrinsic images is used in minimizing the reconstruction errors of color image I from albedo A and shading S:

$$
\mathbf{E}_u(A, S | I) = \sum_p \left(L_p (I_p - A_p - S_p) \right)^2,
\tag{3}
$$

where $L_p = \mathrm{lum}(I_p) + \varepsilon$, and $\mathrm{lum}(I)$ denotes the luminance of I with $\varepsilon = 0.001$. It has been noted that processing of luminance balances out the influence of the

---

[2] It is defined as the receptive field through the CNNs for pixel p [33].

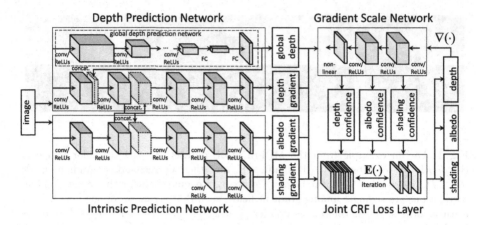

Fig. 2. Network architecture of the JCNF model. It consists of a depth prediction network, an intrinsic prediction network, and a gradient scale network. These networks are learned by minimizing a joint CRF loss function.

unary potential across the image [1, 28], and that treating the image formation equation (*i.e.*, $I_p = A_p + S_p$) as a soft constraint can bring greater stability in optimization [25], especially for dark pixels whose chromaticity can be greatly distorted by sensor noise.

Pairwise Potentials. The pairwise potentials, which include $\mathbf{E}_s(D|I, A, S)$, $\mathbf{E}_s(A|I, D, S)$, and $\mathbf{E}_s(S|I, D, A)$, represent differences between gradients and estimated gradients in the depth, albedo, and shading images. The pairwise potential $\mathbf{E}_s(D|I, A, S)$ for depth gradients is defined as

$$\mathbf{E}_s(D|I, A, S) = \sum_p \|\nabla D_p - \mathcal{G}(\nabla I_\mathcal{P}, \nabla A_\mathcal{P}, \nabla S_\mathcal{P}; \mathbf{w}_\mathcal{G}^{\nabla D}) \circ \mathcal{F}(I_\mathcal{P}; \mathbf{w}_\mathcal{F}^{\nabla D})\|^2, \quad (4)$$

where $\circ$ denotes the Hadamard product, and the estimated depth gradients of $\mathcal{F}(I_p; \mathbf{w}_\mathcal{F}^{\nabla D})$ provide a guidance gradient field for depth, similar to a Poisson equation [34, 35]. They are weighted by a confidence factor $\mathcal{G}(\nabla I_\mathcal{P}, \nabla A_\mathcal{P}, \nabla S_\mathcal{P}; \mathbf{w}_\mathcal{G}^{\nabla D})$ learned in the gradient scale network to reduce the impact of erroneous gradients. This gradient scale is similar to the derivative-level confidence employed in [36] for image restoration, except that our gradient scale is learned non-locally with CNNs and different types of guidance images, as later described in Sect. 3.4. The pairwise potentials for albedo gradients $\mathbf{E}_s(A|I, D, S)$ and shading gradients $\mathbf{E}_s(S|I, D, A)$ are defined in the same manner. Since the gradient scales are jointly estimated with each other task, these pairwise potentials are computed within an iterative solver, which will be described in Sect. 4.1.

3.3   Joint Depth and Intrinsic Prediction Network

Our joint depth and intrinsic prediction network utilizes the aforementioned energy function to predict D, ∇D, ∇A, and ∇S from a single image I.

The joint network consists of a depth prediction network for D and ∇D, and an intrinsic prediction network for ∇A and ∇S. In contrast to previous methods for single-image depth prediction [6,11,37], our system jointly estimates the gradient fields ∇D, ∇A, and ∇S, which are used to reduce ambiguity in the solution and obtain more edge-preserved results. To allow the different estimation tasks to leverage information from one another, we design the depth and intrinsic networks to share concatenated convolutional activations, and share convolutional layers between albedo and shading networks, as illustrated in Fig. 2.

Depth Prediction Network. The depth prediction network consists of a global depth network and a depth gradient network. For the global depth network, we learn its parameters $\mathbf{w}_{\mathcal{F}}^{D}$ for predicting an overall depth map from the entire image structure. Similar to [6,11,37], it provides coarse, spatially-varying depth that may be lacking in fine detail. This coarse depth will later be refined using the output of the depth gradient network.

The global depth network consists of five convolutional layers, three pooling layers, six non-linear activation layers, and two fully-connected (FC) layers. For the first five layers, the pre-trained parameters from the AlexNet architecture [38] are employed, and fine-tuning for the dataset is done. Rectified linear units (ReLUs) are used for the non-linear layers, and the pooling layers employ max pooling. The first FC layer encodes the network responses into fixed-dimensional features, and the second FC layer infers a coarse global depth map at 1/16-scale of the original depth map.

The depth gradient network predicts fine-detail depth gradients for each pixel. Its parameters $\mathbf{w}_{\mathcal{F}}^{\nabla D}$ are learned using an end-to-end patch-level scheme inspired by [35,39], where the network input is an image patch and the output is a depth gradient patch. For inference of depth gradients at the pixel level, the depth gradient network consists of five convolutional networks followed by ReLUs, without stride convolutions or pooling layers. The first convolutional layer is identical to the first convolutional layer in the AlexNet architecture [38]. Four additional convolutional layers are also used as shown in Fig. 2. The depth gradient patches that are output by this network will be used for depth reconstruction in Sect. 4.2. Note that in the testing procedure, the depth gradient network is applied to overlapping patches over the entire image, which are aggregated in the last convolutional layer to yield the full gradient field.

Intrinsic Prediction Network. The intrinsic prediction network has a structure similar to the depth gradient prediction network. The network parameters $\mathbf{w}_{\mathcal{F}}^{\nabla A}$ and $\mathbf{w}_{\mathcal{F}}^{\nabla S}$ are learned for predicting the albedo and shading gradients at each pixel. To jointly infer the depth and intrinsic image gradients, the second convolutional activations for each task are concatenated and passed to their third convolutional layers as shown in Fig. 2. In the training procedure, the depth and intrinsic networks are iteratively learned, which enables each task to benefit from each other's activations to provide more reliable estimates. Furthermore, similar to [11], the albedo and shading gradient networks share their first three convolutional layers, while the last two are separate. Since the albedo and shading images have related properties, these shared convolutional layers benefit their estimation. Details on kernel sizes and the number of channels for each layer are provided in the supplemental material for all the networks.

3.4   Gradient Scale Network

The estimated gradients from the depth and intrinsic prediction networks might contain errors due to the ill-posed nature of their problems. To help in identifying such errors, our system additionally learns the confidence of estimated gradients, specifically, whether a gradient exists at a particular location or not. The basic idea is to learn from the training data about the consistencies that exist among the different types of gradients given their local neighborhood $\mathcal{P}$. From this, we can determine the confidence of a gradient (*e.g.*, a depth gradient), based on the other estimated gradients (*e.g.*, the albedo, shading, and image gradients). This confidence is modeled as a gradient scale that is similar to the scale map used in [36] to model derivative-level confidence for image restoration. It can be noted that in some depth and intrinsic image decomposition methods [1,4,7], the solutions are filtered with fixed parameters using the color image as guidance. Our system instead learns a network for defining the parameters, using not only a color image but also depth and intrinsic images as guidance.

The gradient scale network consists of three convolutional layers and one non-linear activation layer. For the case of depth gradients, the output of the gradient scale network $\mathcal{G}(\nabla I_{\mathcal{P}}, \nabla A_{\mathcal{P}}, \nabla S_{\mathcal{P}}; \mathbf{w}_{\mathcal{G}}^{\nabla D})$ is estimated as the convolution between $\mathbf{w}_{\mathcal{G}}^{\nabla D}$ and $(|\nabla I_{\mathcal{P}}|^2, |\nabla A_{\mathcal{P}}|^2, |\nabla S_{\mathcal{P}}|^2)$, followed by a non-linear activation *i.e.*, $f(\cdot) = (1 - \exp(1 - \cdot))/(1 + \exp(1 - \cdot))$, which is defined within $[-1, 1]$. Here, $|\cdot|^2$ for a vector of gradients denotes a vector of the gradient magnitudes. Thus, in the gradient scale network, the network parameters are convolved with the gradient magnitudes. With the learned parameters $\mathbf{w}_{\mathcal{G}}^{\nabla D}$, the confidence of ∇D_p is estimated from $\nabla I_{\mathcal{P}}, \nabla A_{\mathcal{P}}, \nabla S_{\mathcal{P}}$. This can alternatively be viewed as a guidance filtering weight for D with guidance images I, A, and S. $\mathcal{G}(\nabla I_{\mathcal{P}}, \nabla D_{\mathcal{P}}, \nabla S_{\mathcal{P}}; \mathbf{w}_{\mathcal{G}}^{\nabla A})$ and $\mathcal{G}(\nabla I_{\mathcal{P}}, \nabla D_{\mathcal{P}}, \nabla A_{\mathcal{P}}; \mathbf{w}_{\mathcal{G}}^{\nabla S})$ are also similarly defined.

Some properties of gradient scales are as follows. A gradient scale can be either positive or negative. A large positive value indicates high confidence in the presence of a gradient. A large negative value also indicates high confidence, but for the reversed gradient direction. In addition, when a gradient field contains extra erroneous regions, gradient scales of value 0 can help to disregard them.

4   Unified Depth and Intrinsic Image Prediction

4.1   Training

The energy function $\mathbf{E}(D, A, S|I)$ from (1) is used to simultaneously learn the depth and intrinsic network parameters $(\mathbf{w}_{\mathcal{F}}^D, \mathbf{w}_{\mathcal{F}}^{\nabla D}, \mathbf{w}_{\mathcal{F}}^{\nabla A}, \mathbf{w}_{\mathcal{F}}^{\nabla S})$ and the gradient scale network parameters $(\mathbf{w}_{\mathcal{G}}^{\nabla D}, \mathbf{w}_{\mathcal{G}}^{\nabla A}, \mathbf{w}_{\mathcal{G}}^{\nabla S})$. Although the overall form of the energy is non-quadratic, it has a quadratic form with respect to each of its terms. The energy function can thus be minimized by alternating among its terms.

Loss Functions. For the global depth unary potential of (2), the global depth network parameters $\mathbf{w}_{\mathcal{F}}^{D}$ can be solved by minimizing the following loss function

$$\mathcal{L}(\mathbf{w}_{\mathcal{F}}^{D}) = \sum\nolimits_{\{i,p\}} \left(D_p^i - \mathcal{F}(I_{\mathcal{P}}^i; \mathbf{w}_{\mathcal{F}}^{D})\right)^2. \tag{5}$$

We note that the intrinsic image unary term does not contain network parameters to be learned, so it is used only in the testing procedure.

The pairwise potentials each incorporate two networks, namely the gradient prediction network and gradient scale network, so they are iteratively trained. The loss function for the depth gradient pairwise potential of (4) is defined as

$$\mathcal{L}(\mathbf{w}_{\mathcal{G}}^{\nabla D}, \mathbf{w}_{\mathcal{F}}^{\nabla D}) = \sum\nolimits_{\{i,p\}} \|\nabla D_p^i - \mathcal{G}(\nabla I_{\mathcal{P}}^i, \nabla A_{\mathcal{P}}^i, \nabla S_{\mathcal{P}}^i; \mathbf{w}_{\mathcal{G}}^{\nabla D}) \circ \mathcal{F}(I_{\mathcal{P}}^i; \mathbf{w}_{\mathcal{F}}^{\nabla D})\|^2. \tag{6}$$

The loss functions for the pairwise potentials of the albedo gradients $\mathcal{L}(\mathbf{w}_{\mathcal{G}}^{\nabla A}, \mathbf{w}_{\mathcal{F}}^{\nabla A})$ and shading gradients $\mathcal{L}(\mathbf{w}_{\mathcal{G}}^{\nabla S}, \mathbf{w}_{\mathcal{F}}^{\nabla S})$ are similarly defined.

These loss functions are minimized using stochastic gradient descent with the standard back-propagation [40]. First, $\mathbf{w}_{\mathcal{F}}^{D}$ is estimated through $\partial\mathcal{L}(\mathbf{w}_{\mathcal{F}}^{D})/\partial\mathbf{w}_{\mathcal{F}}^{D}$. Then $\mathbf{w}_{\mathcal{G}}^{\nabla D}$ and $\mathbf{w}_{\mathcal{F}}^{\nabla D}$ are iteratively estimated through $\partial\mathcal{L}(\mathbf{w}_{\mathcal{G}}^{\nabla D}, \mathbf{w}_{\mathcal{F}}^{\nabla D})/\partial\mathbf{w}_{\mathcal{G}}^{\nabla D}$ and $\partial\mathcal{L}(\mathbf{w}_{\mathcal{G}}^{\nabla D}, \mathbf{w}_{\mathcal{F}}^{\nabla D})/\partial\mathbf{w}_{\mathcal{F}}^{\nabla D}$. In each iteration, the loss functions are differently defined according to the other network outputs, where the network parameters are initialized with the values obtained from the previous iteration. In this way, the networks account for the improving outputs of the other networks.

4.2   Testing

Iterative Joint Prediction. In the testing procedure, the outputs D, ∇D, ∇A and ∇S for a given input image I are predicted by minimizing the energy function $\mathbf{E}(D, A, S|I)$ from (1) with constraints from the estimates computed using the learned network parameters and forward-propagation. Similar to the training procedure, we minimize $\mathbf{E}(D, A, S|I)$ with an iterative scheme due to its non-quadratic form, where $\mathbf{E}(D|I)$ and $\mathbf{E}(A, S|I)$ are minimized in alternation.

For the depth prediction, $\mathbf{E}(D|I)$ is defined as a data term for global depth and a pairwise term for depth gradients:

$$\mathbf{E}(D|I) = \sum\nolimits_p \left(D_p - D_p^*\right)^2 + \lambda_D \sum\nolimits_p \|\nabla D_p - C(\nabla D_p^*) \circ \nabla D_p^*\|^2, \tag{7}$$

where $*$ denotes network outputs, and $C(\nabla D_p^*)$ is the gradient scale of ∇D_p^* derived from $\mathcal{G}(\nabla I_{\mathcal{P}}^*, \nabla A_{\mathcal{P}}^*, \nabla S_{\mathcal{P}}^*; \mathbf{w}_{\mathcal{G}}^{\nabla D})$. We note that since $C(\nabla D_p^*)$ is computed with $\nabla I_{\mathcal{P}}^*$, $\nabla A_{\mathcal{P}}^*$, and $\nabla S_{\mathcal{P}}^*$, all of the predictions need to be iteratively estimated.

For the intrinsic prediction, $\mathbf{E}(A, S|I)$ is also defined as data and pairwise terms, with the image formation equation and the albedo and shading gradients:

$$\mathbf{E}(A, S|I) = \sum_p (L_p(I_p - A_p - S_p))^2$$
$$+ \sum_p \lambda_A \|\nabla A_p - C(\nabla A_p^*) \circ \nabla A_p^*\|^2 + \lambda_S \|\nabla S_p - C(\nabla S_p^*) \circ \nabla S_p^*\|^2, \tag{8}$$

where $C(\nabla A_p^*)$ and $C(\nabla S_p^*)$ are defined similarly to $C(\nabla D_p^*)$. This energy function can be optimized with an existing linear solver [1]. These two energy functions $\mathbf{E}(D|I)$ and $\mathbf{E}(A, S|I)$ are iteratively minimized while providing information in the form of depth, albedo, and shading gradients to each other.

Coarse-to-Fine Joint Prediction. In estimating depth and intrinsic images, enforcing a degree of global consistency can lead to performance gains [1,5]. For greater global consistency, we apply our joint prediction model in a coarse-to-fine manner, where color images I^l are constructed at $\mathcal{N}_L$ image pyramid levels $l = \{1, ..., \mathcal{N}_L\}$, and the depth D^l and intrinsic images A^l and S^l are predicted from I^l. Coarser scale results are then used as guidance for finer levels.

Specifically, we reformulate $\mathbf{E}(D|I)$ as $\mathbf{E}(D^l|I^l, I^{l-1})$:

$$\mathbf{E}(D^l|I^l, I^{l-1}) = \sum_p \left(D_p^l - D_p^{l,*}\right)^2 + \sum_p \left(D_p^l - D_p^{l-1}\right)^2$$
$$+ \lambda_D \sum_p \|\nabla D_p^l - C(\nabla D_p^{l,*}) \circ \nabla D_p^{l,*}\|^2. \tag{9}$$

Similarly, $\mathbf{E}(A, S|I)$ is reformulated as $E(A^l, S^l|I^l, I^{l-1})$:

$$E(A^l, S^l|I^l, I^{l-1}) = \sum_p (L_p^l(I_p^l - A_p^l - S_p^l))^2 + (A_p^l - A_p^{l-1})^2 + (S_p^l - S_p^{l-1})^2$$
$$+ \sum_p \lambda_A \|\nabla A_p^l - C(\nabla A_p^{l,*}) \circ \nabla A_p^{l,*}\|^2 + \lambda_S \|\nabla S_p^l - C(\nabla S_p^{l,*}) \circ \nabla S_p^{l,*}\|^2, \tag{10}$$

where the multi-scale unary functions lead to more reliable solutions and faster convergence. The high-level algorithm for the training and testing procedures is provided in the supplemental material.

5   Experimental Results

For our experiments, we implemented the JCNF model using the VLFeat Mat-ConvNet toolbox [40]. The energy function weights were set to $\{\lambda_D, \lambda_A, \lambda_S\} = \{1, 0.1, 0.1\}$ by cross-validation. The filter weights of each network layer were initialized by drawing randomly from a Gaussian distribution with zero mean and a standard deviation of 0.001. The network learning rates were set to 10^{-4}, except for the final layer of the gradient networks where it was set to 10^{-5}.

We additionally augmented the training data by applying random transforms to it, including scalings in the range $[0.8, 1.2]$, in-plane rotations in the range $[-15, 15]$, translations, RGB scalings, image flips, and different gammas.

Table 1. Quantitative results on MPI SINTEL [41] for depth prediction. DCNF-FCSP (NYU) [7] and JCNF(NYU) predict the depth by pre-training on NYU v2 [42].

Methods	Error				Accuracy		
	rel	$\log_{10}$	rms	$rms_{\log}$	$\delta < 1.25$	$\delta < 1.25^2$	$\delta < 1.25^3$
Depth transfer [16]	0.448	0.193	9.242	3.121	0.524	0.712	0.735
Depth analogy [17]	0.432	0.167	8.421	2.741	0.621	0.799	0.812
DCNF-FCSP(NYU) [7]	0.424	0.164	8.112	2.421	0.652	0.782	0.824
JCNF(NYU)	**0.293**	**0.131**	**7.421**	**1.812**	**0.715**	**0.812**	**0.831**
JCNF wo/jnl	**0.292**	**0.138**	**7.471**	**1.973**	**0.714**	**0.783**	**0.839**
JCNF wo/gsn	**0.271**	**0.119**	**7.451**	**1.921**	**0.724**	**0.793**	**0.893**
JCNF wo/ctf	**0.252**	**0.101**	**7.233**	**1.622**	**0.729**	**0.812**	**0.878**
JCNF	**0.183**	**0.097**	**6.118**	**1.037**	**0.823**	**0.834**	**0.902**

In the following, we evaluated our system through comparisons to state-of-the-art depth prediction and intrinsic image decomposition methods on the MPI SINTEL [41], NYU v2 [42], and Make3D [43] benchmarks. We additionally examined the performance contributions of the joint network learning (wo/jnl), the gradient scale network (wo/gsn), and the coarse-to-fine scheme (wo/ctf). The experimental details are provided in the supplemental material.

5.1 MPI SINTEL Benchmark

We evaluated our JCNF model on both depth prediction and intrinsic image decomposition on the MPI SINTEL benchmark [41], which consists of 890 images from 18 scenes with 50 frames each. For a fair evaluation, we followed the same experimental protocol as in [1,11], with their two-fold cross-validation and training/testing image splits. Figures 3 and 4 exhibit predicted depth and intrinsic images from a single image, respectively. Tables 1 and 2 are quantitative evaluations for both tasks using a variety of metrics, including average relative difference (rel), average $\log_{10}$ error ($\log_{10}$), root-mean-squared error (rms), its log version ($rms_{\log}$), and accuracy with thresholds $\delta = \{1.25, 1.25^2, 1.25^3\}$ [7]. For quantitatively evaluating intrinsic image decomposition performance, we used mean-squared error (MSE), local mean-squared error (LMSE), and the dissimilarity version of the structural similarity index (DSSIM) [11].

For the depth prediction task, data-driven approaches (DT [16] and DA [17]) provided limited performance due to their low learning capacity. CNN-based depth prediction (DCNF-FCSP [7]) using a pre-trained model from NYU v2 [42] showed better performance, but is restricted by depth ambiguity problems. Our JCNF model achieved the best results both quantitatively and qualitatively, whether pre-trained using MPI SINTEL or NYU v2 datasets. Furthermore, it is shown that omitting the gradient scale network, coarse-to-fine processing, or joint learning significantly reduced depth prediction performances.

In intrinsic image decomposition, existing single-image based methods [22–24,30,44] produced the lowest quality results as they do not benefit from any

Table 2. Quantitative results on MPI SINTEL [41] for intrinsic decomposition using methods based on single images, RGB-D, CNNs, and our JCNF model.

Methods	MSE			LMSE			DSSIM		
	Albedo	Shading	Avg.	Albedo	Shading	Avg.	Albedo	Shading	Avg.
Retinex [44]	0.053	0.049	0.051	0.033	0.028	0.031	0.214	0.206	0.210
Li et al. [23]	0.042	0.041	0.037	0.024	0.031	0.034	0.242	0.224	0.194
Shen et al. [30]	0.043	0.039	0.048	0.028	0.027	0.032	0.221	0.210	0.232
Zhao et al. [22]	0.047	0.041	0.031	0.028	0.029	0.031	0.210	0.257	0.214
IIW [24]	0.041	0.032	0.041	0.032	0.031	0.027	0.281	0.241	0.284
SIRFS [31]	0.042	0.047	0.043	0.029	0.026	0.028	0.210	0.206	0.208
Jeon et al. [4]	0.042	0.033	0.032	0.021	0.021	0.023	0.204	0.181	0.193
Chen et al. [1]	0.031	0.028	0.029	0.019	0.019	0.019	0.196	0.165	0.181
MSCR [11]	0.020	0.017	0.021	0.016	0.011	0.011	0.201	0.150	0.176
JCNF wo/jnl	0.012	0.015	0.016	0.014	0.010	0.010	0.149	0.123	0.141
JCNF wo/gsn	0.008	0.011	0.011	0.010	0.009	0.008	0.146	0.112	0.132
JCNF wo/ctf	0.008	0.012	0.010	0.009	0.008	0.008	0.127	0.110	0.119
JCNF	**0.007**	**0.009**	**0.007**	**0.006**	**0.007**	**0.007**	**0.092**	**0.101**	**0.097**

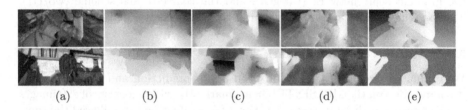

(a)   (b)   (c)   (d)   (e)

Fig. 3. Qualitative results on MPI SINTEL [41] for depth prediction. (a) color image, (b) DA [17], (c) DCNF-FCSP(NYU) [7], (d) JCNF, and (e) ground truth.

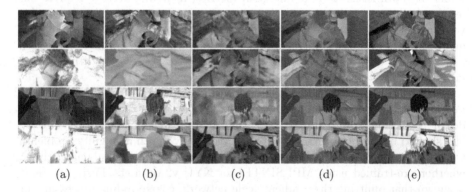

(a)   (b)   (c)   (d)   (e)

Fig. 4. Qualitative results on MPI SINTEL [41] for intrinsic decomposition of Fig. 3. (a) Shen et al. [30], (b) SIRFS [31], (c) MSCR [11], (d) JCNF, and (e) ground truth.

Table 3. Quantitative results on the NYU v2 dataset [42] for depth prediction.

Methods	Error				Accuracy		
	rel	$\log_{10}$	rms	$\text{rms}_{\log}$	$\delta < 1.25$	$\delta < 1.25^2$	$\delta < 1.25^3$
Make3D [12]	0.349	-	1.214	0.409	0.447	0.745	0.897
Depth transfer [16]	0.350	0.134	1.1	0.378	0.460	0.742	0.893
Depth analogy [17]	0.328	0.132	1.31	0.392	0.471	0.799	0.891
MS-CNNs [6]	0.228	-	0.901	0.293	0.611	0.873	0.961
DCNF-FCSP [7]	0.221	0.095	0.760	0.281	0.604	0.885	0.974
JCNF(MPI)	**0.214**	**0.093**	**0.716**	**0.241**	**0.677**	**0.879**	**0.927**
JCNF wo/jnl	**0.216**	**0.101**	**0.753**	**0.241**	**0.625**	**0.896**	**0.925**
JCNF wo/gsn	**0.210**	**0.091**	**0.728**	**0.254**	**0.621**	**0.890**	**0.975**
JCNF wo/ctf	**0.208**	**0.106**	**0.708**	**0.237**	**0.681**	**0.901**	**0.972**
JCNF	**0.201**	**0.077**	**0.711**	**0.212**	**0.690**	**0.910**	**0.979**

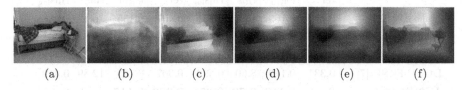

(a)   (b)   (c)   (d)   (e)   (f)

Fig. 5. Qualitative results on NYU v2 [42] for depth prediction. (a) color image, (b) MS-CNNs [6], (c) DCNF-FCSP [7], (d) JCNF(MPI), (e) JCNF, and (f) ground truth.

additional information. RGB-D based methods [1,4,5] performed better with measured depth as input. CNN-based intrinsic decomposition [11] surpassed RGB-D based techniques even without having depth as an input, but its results exhibit some blur, likely due to ambiguity from limited training datasets. Thanks to its gradient domain learning and leverage of estimated depth information, our JCNF model provides more accurate and edge-preserved results, with the best qualitative and quantitative performance.

5.2   NYU v2 RGB-D Benchmark

For further evaluation, we obtained a set of RGB, depth, and intrinsic images by applying RGB-D based intrinsic image decomposition methods [1,4] on the NYU v2 RGB-D database [42]. Of its 1449 RGB-D images of indoor scenes, we used 795 for training and 654 for testing, which is the standard training/testing split for the dataset.

For depth prediction, comparisons are made to the ground truth depth in Fig. 5 and Table 2 using the same experimental settings as in [7]. The state-of-the-art CNN-based methods [6,7] clearly outperformed other previous methods. The performance of our JCNF model was even higher, with pre-training on either MPI SINTEL or NYU v2. Our depth prediction network is similar to [6], but it

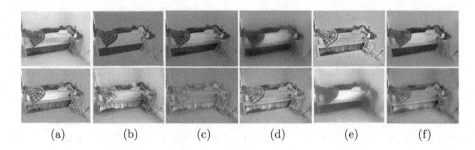

(a)   (b)   (c)   (d)   (e)   (f)

Fig. 6. Qualitative results on NYU v2 [42] for intrinsic decomposition of Fig. 5. (a) Li *et al.* [23], (b) IIW [24], (c) Jeon *et al.* [4], (d) JCNF learned using [4], (e) Chen *et al.* [1], and (f) JCNF learned using [1].

Table 4. Quantitative results on the Make3D dataset [43] for depth prediction.

Methods	Error (C1)				Error (C2)			
	rel	$\log_{10}$	rms	$\text{rms}_{\log}$	rel	$\log_{10}$	rms	$\text{rms}_{\log}$
Make3D [12]	0.412	0.165	11.1	0.451	0.407	0.155	16.1	0.486
Depth transfer [16]	0.355	0.127	9.20	0.421	0.438	0.161	14.81	0.461
Depth analogy [17]	0.371	0.121	8.11	0.381	0.410	0.144	14.52	0.479
DCNF-FCSP [7]	0.331	0.119	8.60	0.392	0.307	0.125	12.89	0.412
JCNF(MPI)	**0.273**	**0.110**	**7.70**	**0.351**	**0.263**	**0.117**	**8.62**	**0.347**
JCNF(NYU)	**0.274**	**0.097**	**7.22**	**0.352**	**0.287**	**0.127**	**8.22**	**0.341**
JCNF	**0.262**	**0.092**	**6.61**	**0.321**	**0.243**	**0.091**	**6.34**	**0.302**

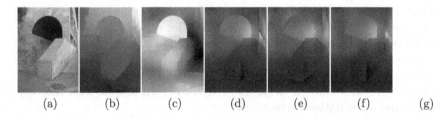

(a)   (b)   (c)   (d)   (e)   (f)   (g)

Fig. 7. Qualitative results on Make3D [42] for depth prediction. (a) color image, (b) DA [17], (c) DCNF-FCSP [7], (d) JCNF(MPI), (e) JCNF(NYU), (f) JCNF, and (g) ground truth.

additionally predicts depth gradients and leverages intrinsic image estimates to elevate performance.

In intrinsic image decomposition of Fig. 6, RGB-D based methods [1,4] are used as ground truth for training. It is seen that our JCNF more closely resembles that assumed ground truth than single-image based methods [23,24].

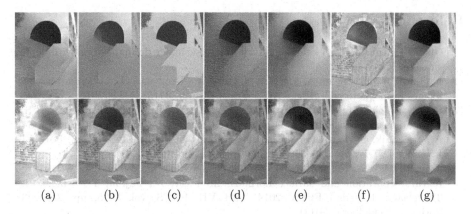

Fig. 8. Qualitative results on Make3D [43] for intrinsic decomposition of Fig. 7. (a) Li *et al.* [23], (b) Zhao *et al.* [22], (c) IIW [24], (d) Jeon *et al.* [4], (e) JCNF learned using [4], (f) Chen *et al.* [1], and (g) JCNF learned using [1].

5.3   Make3D RGB-D Benchmark

We also evaluated our JCNF model on the Make3D dataset [43], which contains 534 images depicting outdoor scenes (with 400 used for training and 134 for testing). To account for a limitation of this dataset [7,12,45], we calculate depth errors in two ways [7,45]: on only regions with ground truth depth less than 70 m (denoted by C1), and over the entire image (C2). From the depth prediction results in Fig. 7 and Table 4, our JCNF model is found to yield the highest accuracy, even when pretrained on MPI SINTEL [41] or NYU v2 [42] (*i.e.*, JCNF(MPI) and JCNF(NYU)). For the intrinsic image decomposition results given in Fig. 8, JCNF also outperforms the comparison techniques.

6   Conclusion

We presented Joint Convolutional Neural Fields (JCNF) for jointly predicting depth, albedo and shading maps from a single input image. Its high performance can be attributed to its sharing network architecture, its gradient domain inference, and the incorporation of gradient scale network. It is shown through extensive experimentation that synergistically solving for these physical scene properties through the JCNF leads to state-of-the-art results in both single-image depth prediction and intrinsic image decomposition. In future work, JCNF can potentially benefit shape refinement and image relighting from a single image.

Acknowledgement. This research was supported by the MSIP (The Ministry of Science, ICT and Future Planning), Korea and Microsoft Research, under ICT/SW Creative research program supervised by the IITP(Institute for Information & Communications Technology Promotion) (IITP-2015-R2212-15-0008).

References

1. Chen, Q., Koltun, V.: A simple model for intrinsic image decomposition with depth cues. In: ICCV (2013)
2. Laffont, P.Y., Bousseau, A., Paris, S., Durand, F., Drettakis, G.: Coherent intrinsic images from photo collections. ACM Trans. Graph. **31**(6), 1–11 (2012)
3. Lee, K.J., Zhao, Q., Tong, X., Gong, M., Izadi, S., Lee, S.U., Tan, P., Lin, S.: Estimation of intrinsic image sequences from image+depth video. In: Fitzgibbon, A., Lazebnik, S., Perona, P., Sato, Y., Schmid, C. (eds.) ECCV 2012, Part VI. LNCS, vol. 7577, pp. 327–340. Springer, Heidelberg (2012)
4. Jeon, J., Cho, S., Tong, X., Lee, S.: Intrinsic image decomposition using structure-texture separation and surface normals. In: Fleet, D., Pajdla, T., Schiele, B., Tuytelaars, T. (eds.) ECCV 2014, Part VII. LNCS, vol. 8695, pp. 218–233. Springer, Heidelberg (2014)
5. Barron, J.T., Malik, J.: intrinsic scene properties from a single RGB-D image. In: CVPR (2013)
6. Eigen, D., Puhrsch, C., Ferus, R.: Depth map prediction from a single image using a multi-scale deep network. In: NIPS (2014)
7. Fayao, L., Chunhua, S., Guosheng, L.: Deep convolutional neural fields for depth estimation from a single images. In: CVPR (2015)
8. Kong, N., Black, M.J.: Intrinsic depth: Improving depth transfer with intrinsic images. In: ICCV (2015)
9. Shelhamer, E., Barron, J., Darrell, T.: Scene intrinsics and depth from a single image. In: ICCV Workshop (2015)
10. Zhou, T., Krahenbuhl, P., Efors, A.A.: Learning data-driven reflectnace priors for intrinsic image decomposition. In: ICCV (2015)
11. Narihira, T., Maire, M., Yu, S.X.: Direct intrinsics: learning albedo-shading decomposition by convolutional regression. In: ICCV (2015)
12. Saxena, A., Sun, M., Andrew, Y.: Make3D learning 3D scene structure from a single still image. IEEE Trans. PAMI **31**(5), 824–840 (2009)
13. Wang, Y., Wang, R., Dai, Q.: A parametric model for describing the correlation between single color images and depth maps. IEEE SPL **21**(7), 800–803 (2014)
14. Li, X., Qin, H., Wang, Y., Zhang, Y., Dai, Q.: DEPT: depth estimation by parameter transfer for single still images. In: Cremers, D., Reid, I., Saito, H., Yang, M.-H. (eds.) ACCV 2014. LNCS, vol. 9004, pp. 45–58. Springer, Heidelberg (2015). doi:10.1007/978-3-319-16808-1_4
15. Konrad, J., Wang, M., Ishwar, P., Wu, C., Mukherjee, D.: Learning-based, automatic 2D-to-3D image and video conversion. IEEE Trans. IP **22**(9), 3485–3496 (2013)
16. Karsch, K., Liu, C., Kang, S.B.: Depth transfer: depth extraction from video using non-parametric sampling. IEEE Trans. PAMI **32**(11), 2144–2158 (2014)
17. Choi, S., Min, D., Ham, B., Kim, Y., Oh, C., Sohn, K.: Depth analogy: data-driven approach for single image depth estimation using gradient samples. IEEE Trans. IP **24**(12), 5953–5966 (2015)
18. Wang, P., Shen, X., Lin, Z., Cohen, S., Price, B., Yuille, A.: Towards unified depth and semantic prediction from a single image. In: CVPR (2015)
19. Barrow, H.G., Tenenbaum, J.M.: Recovering intrinsic scene characteristics from images. In: CVS (1978)
20. Land, E.H., Mccann, J.J.: Lightness and retinex theory. JOSA **61**(1), 1–11 (1971)

21. Shen, J., Tan, P., Lin, S.: Intrinsic image decomposition with non-local texture cues. In: CVPR (2008)
22. Zhao, Q., Tan, P., Dai, Q., SHen, L., Wu, E., Lin, S.: A closed-form solution to retinex with non-local texture constraints. IEEE Trans. PAMI **34**(7), 1437–1444 (2012)
23. Li, Y., Brown, M.S.: Single image layer separation using relative smoothness. In: CVPR (2004)
24. Bell, S., Bala, K., Snavely, N.: Intrinsic images in the wild. ACM Trans. Graph. TOG **33**(4), 159 (2014)
25. Bonneel, N., Sunkavalli, K., Tompkin, J., Sun, D., Paris, S., Pfister, H.: Interactive intrinsic video editing. ACM Trans. Graph. (SIGGRAPH ASIA) **33**(6), 197 (2014)
26. Wiess, Y.: Deriving intrinsic images from image sequences. In: ICCV (2001)
27. Laffont, P.Y., Bousseau, A., Drettakis, G.: Rich intrinsic image decomposition of outdoor scenes from multiple views. IEEE TVCG **19**(2), 1–11 (2013)
28. Kong, N., Gehler, P.V., Black, M.J.: Intrinsic video. In: Fleet, D., Pajdla, T., Schiele, B., Tuytelaars, T. (eds.) ECCV 2014, Part II. LNCS, vol. 8690, pp. 360–375. Springer, Heidelberg (2014)
29. Bousseau, A., Paris, S., Durand, F.: User-assisted intrinsic images. ACM TOG **28**(5), 1–11 (2009)
30. Shen, J., Yang, X., Jia, Y.: Intrinsic image using optimization. In: CVPR (2011)
31. Barron, J., Malik, J.: Shape, albedo, and illumination from a single image of an unknown object. In: CVPR (2012)
32. Butler, D.J., Wulff, J., Stanley, G.B., Black, M.J.: A naturalistic open source movie for optical flow evaluation. In: Fitzgibbon, A., Lazebnik, S., Perona, P., Sato, Y., Schmid, C. (eds.) ECCV 2012, Part VI. LNCS, vol. 7577, pp. 611–625. Springer, Heidelberg (2012)
33. He, K., Zhang, X., Ren, S., Sun, J.: Spatial pyramid pooling in deep convolutional networks for visual recognition. IEEE Trans. PAMI **37**(9), 1904–1916 (2015)
34. Perez, P., Gangnet, M., Blake, A.: Poisson image editing. ACM TOG **22**(3), 313–318 (2003)
35. Xu, L., Ren, J., Yan, Q., Liao, R., Jia, J.: Deep edge-aware filters. In: ICML (2015)
36. Shen, X., Yan, Q., Xu, L., Ma, L., Jia, J.: Multispectral joint image restoration via optimizing a scale map. IEEE Trans. PAMI **31**(9), 1582–1599 (2015)
37. Eigen, D., R, F.: Predicting depth, surface normals and semantic labels with a common multi-scale convolutional architecture. In: ICCV (2015)
38. Alex, K., Ilya, S., E, H.: Imagenet classification with deep convolutional neural networks. In: NIPS (2012)
39. Dong, C., Loy, C.C., He, K., Tang, X.: Image super-resolution using deep convolutional networks. IEEE Trans. PAMI **37**(3), 597–610 (2015)
40. Online: http://www.vlfeat.org/matconvnet/
41. Online: http://sintel.is.tue.mpg.de/
42. Online: http://cs.nyu.edu/silberman/datasets/
43. Online: http://make3d.cs.cornell.edu/
44. Grosse, R., Johnson, M.K., Adelson, E.H., Freeman, W.T.: Ground truth and baseline evaluations for intrinsic image algorithms. In: ICCV (2009)
45. Liu, M., Salzmann, M., He, X.: Discrete-continuous depth estimation from a single image. In: CVPR (2014)

ObjectNet3D: A Large Scale Database
for 3D Object Recognition

Yu Xiang$^{(\boxtimes)}$, Wonhui Kim, Wei Chen, Jingwei Ji, Christopher Choy,
Hao Su, Roozbeh Mottaghi, Leonidas Guibas, and Silvio Savarese

Stanford University, Stanford, USA
yuxiang@cs.standford.edu

Abstract. We contribute a large scale database for 3D object recognition, named ObjectNet3D, that consists of 100 categories, 90,127 images, 201,888 objects in these images and 44,147 3D shapes. Objects in the 2D images in our database are aligned with the 3D shapes, and the alignment provides both accurate 3D pose annotation and the closest 3D shape annotation for each 2D object. Consequently, our database is useful for recognizing the 3D pose and 3D shape of objects from 2D images. We also provide baseline experiments on four tasks: region proposal generation, 2D object detection, joint 2D detection and 3D object pose estimation, and image-based 3D shape retrieval, which can serve as baselines for future research using our database. Our database is available online at http://cvgl.stanford.edu/projects/objectnet3d.

Keywords: Database construction · 3D object recognition

1 Introduction

Recognizing 3D properties of objects from 2D images, such as 3D location, 3D pose and 3D shape, is a central problem in computer vision that has wide applications in different scenarios including robotics, autonomous driving and augmented reality. In recent years, remarkable progress has been achieved on 3D object recognition (e.g. [9,15,24,33,39,42]), as the field has benefited from the introduction of several important databases that provide 3D annotations to 2D objects. For example, the NYU Depth dataset [29] associates depth to 2D images; the KITTI dataset for autonomous driving [10] aligns 2D images with 3D point clouds, and the PASCAL3D+ dataset [40] aligns 2D objects in images with 3D CAD models. With the provided 3D information, supervised learning techniques can be applied to recognize 3D properties of objects. In addition, these datasets serve as benchmarks for comparing different approaches.

However, the existing databases with 3D annotations are limited in scale, either in the number of object categories or in the number of images. At least,

Electronic supplementary material The online version of this chapter (doi:10.1007/978-3-319-46484-8_10) contains supplementary material, which is available to authorized users.

© Springer International Publishing AG 2016
B. Leibe et al. (Eds.): ECCV 2016, Part VIII, LNCS 9912, pp. 160–176, 2016.
DOI: 10.1007/978-3-319-46484-8_10

they are not comparable to large scale 2D image databases such as ImageNet [1] or Microsoft COCO [21]. After witnessing the progress on image classification, 2D object detection and segmentation with the advance of such large scale 2D image databases, we believe that a large scale database with 3D annotations would significantly benefit 3D object recognition.

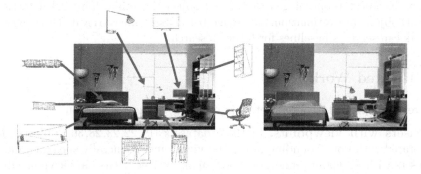

Fig. 1. An example image in our database with 2D objects aligned with 3D shapes. The alignment enables us to project each 3D shape to the image where its projection overlaps with the 2D object as shown in the image on the right

In this work, we contribute a large scale database for 3D object recognition, named ObjectNet3D, that consists of 100 object categories, 90,127 2D images, 201,888 objects in these images and 44,147 3D shapes. The images in our database are collected from the ImageNet repository [1], while the 3D shapes are from the ShapeNet repository [4]. In addition to 2D bounding box annotations for objects of interest, a key aspect of our new database is that each object in an image is aligned with a 3D shape. The alignment enables us to project the 3D shape to the image, where the projection of the 3D shape matches the corresponding 2D object in the image (see an example in Fig. 1). The alignment between 2D and 3D provides 3D annotations to objects in 2D images, i.e., the 3D pose annotation and the closest 3D shape annotation for a 2D object. As a result, our database is useful for 3D object recognition from 2D images. Projection of the 3D shape also produces segmentation boundaries of the object. In addition, we can render an arbitrary number of synthetic images from the 3D shapes. The rendered images can also be used to help 3D object recognition in real images as demonstrated by [34].

The task of aligning a 2D object with a 3D shape is non-trivial. First, we need to select a 3D shape that is similar to the given 2D object from hundreds or thousands of 3D shapes. It is not feasible to ask annotators to go through all the 3D shapes one by one. Second, orienting the pose of the 3D shape for alignment is error-prone, so it is not easy to control the quality of the alignment. (i) To facilitate the selection of 3D shapes, we have applied the deep metric learning method [31] to learn a feature embedding of the 3D shapes using their rendered images. Given a 2D object in an image, our method is able to retrieve top ranked similar 3D shapes using the learned embedding. Then we ask annotators to select the best one among the top K returned 3D shapes. (ii) To guarantee the quality of the alignment, we have designed an annotation tool to align the 3D shape with the 2D object. Our annotation interface allows annotators to interactively find a set of camera parameters for each object that produce good alignment.

We have conducted baseline experiments on the following tasks using our database: object proposal generation, 2D object detection, joint 2D detection and 3D object pose estimation, and image-based 3D shape retrieval. These experiments can serve as baselines for future research.

2   Related Work

We review representative datasets related to 3D object recognition.

Datasets with viewpoints. In these datasets [19,22,23,28,36], objects are annotated with both bounding boxes and viewpoints. Generally speaking, most datasets with viewpoint annotations are small in scale, coarse in viewpoint discretization and simple in scene context. For example, the 3DObject dataset [28] provides viewpoint annotation for 10 everyday object classes such as car, iron and stapler, with 10 instances per category observed from varying viewpoints. The EPFL Car dataset [23] consists of 2,299 images of 20 car instances at multiple azimuth angles, with almost identical elevation. Compared to these datasets, we provide continuous viewpoint annotation to realistic images from the web.

Datasets with depths or 3D points. Datasets in which 2D images are registered with depth or 3D points are introduced. The RGB-D Object dataset [18] provides RGBD images of 300 common household objects organized in 51 categories which are captured from a turntable. The NYU depth dataset [29] contains 1,449 densely labeled pairs of aligned RGB and depth images, where objects from 894 categories are labeled. The SUN RGB-D dataset [32] has 10K RGBD images and provides 2D polygons, 3D bounding boxes with orientations and 3D room layout annotations. The KITTI dataset [10] proposed for autonomous driving registers images with 3D point clouds from a 3D laser scanner. Compared to these datasets, we align a 3D shape to each 2D object and provide 3D shape annotation to objects, which is richer information than depth or 3D points and allows us to transfer meta-data from the 3D shape back to the image.

Datasets with 2D-3D alignments. An influential work in building datasets with 2D-3D alignment is LabelMe3D [27] that estimates the 3D scene structure based on user annotations. Recently, a few datasets were introduced that align 2D objects in images with 3D shapes. The IKEA dataset [20] provides 759 images aligned with 213 3D shapes which are IKEA 3D models from Trimble 3D Warehouse [5]. [17] introduces a new dataset for 2D-3D deformable shape matching. PASCAL3D+ [40] provides 2D-3D alignments to 12 rigid categories in PASCAL VOC 2012 [8]. Although PASCAL3D+ contains 30,899 images, it is still limited in the number of object classes (12 in total) and the number of 3D shapes (79 in total), so it is insufficient to cover the variations of common object

Table 1. Comparison between representative datasets with 3D annotations

	# categories	# images	# 3D shapes	3D annotation type
3DObject [28]	10	6,675	N/A	Discretized view
EPFL Car [23]	1	2,299	N/A	Continuous view
NYU Depth [29]	894	1,449	N/A	Depth
SUN RGB-D [32]	∼ 800	10,335	N/A	Depth
KITTI [10]	2	14,999	N/A	3D point
IKEA [20]	11	759	213	2D-3D alignment
PASCAL3D+ [40]	12	30,899	79	2D-3D alignment
ObjectNet3D (Ours)	100	90,127	44,161	2D-3D alignment

categories and their geometry variability. We contribute a large-scale 3D object dataset with more object categories, more 3D shapes per class and accurate image-shape correspondences. Table 1 compares our dataset to representative datasets in the literature with 3D annotations.

3 Database Construction

Our goal is to build a large scale database for 3D object recognition. We resort to images in existing image repositories and propose an approach to align 3D shapes (which are available from existing 3D shape repositories) to the objects in these images. In this way, we have successfully built the ObjectNet3D database.

3.1 Object Categories

We aim at building a database for object category recognition, so the first step is to decide what categories to work on. Since we are going to utilize 3D object shapes to provide 3D annotations to objects in 2D images, we consider only rigid object categories in this work, where we can collect a large number of 3D shapes for these categories from the web. For deformable and articulated objects such as animals, deformation and articulation of a 3D shape is required in order to align the shape with the corresponding object in a 2D image. We consider the extension to non-rigid object categories as a future work. Table 2 lists all 100 object categories in our database. These categories cover most of the rigid categories in the commonly used object recognition datasets, such as the 12 rigid categories in PASCAL VOC [8] and the 9 rigid categories in [28], but our dataset is one order of magnitude larger in terms of the number of categories.

3.2 2D Image Acquisition

After finalizing the object categories in the database, we collect images for each object category from the ImageNet database [1]. ImageNet organizes images according to the WordNet hierarchy. Each node in the hierarchy is named a

Table 2. 100 object categories in our database

Aeroplane	Camera	Eraser	Jar	Pencil	Shovel	Toothbrush
Ashtray	Can	Eyeglasses	Kettle	Piano	Sign	Train
Backpack	Cap	Fan	Key	Pillow	Skate	Trash bin
Basket	Car	Faucet	Keyboard	Plate	Skateboard	Trophy
Bed	Cellphone	Filing cabinet	Knife	Pot	Slipper	Tub
Bench	Chair	Fire extinguisher	Laptop	Printer	Sofa	Tvmonitor
Bicycle	Clock	Fish tank	Lighter	Racket	Speaker	Vending machine
Blackboard	Coffee maker	Flashlight	Mailbox	Refrigerator	Spoon	Washing machine
Boat	Comb	Fork	Microphone	Remote control	Stapler	Watch
Bookshelf	Computer	Guitar	Microwave	Rifle	Stove	Wheelchair
Bottle	Cup	Hair dryer	Motorbike	Road pole	Suitcase	
Bucket	Desk lamp	Hammer	Mouse	Satellite dish	Teapot	
Bus	Diningtable	Headphone	Paintbrush	Scissors	Telephone	
Cabinet	Dishwasher	Helmet	Pan	Screwdriver	Toaster	
Calculator	Door	Iron	Pen	Shoe	Toilet	

synset that corresponds to a noun (e.g., car, boat, chair, etc.), and each synset contains images depicting the concept. For each object category in our database, we first find its corresponding synset in ImageNet, then we download images in the synset. For can, desk lamp and trophy, we did not find the corresponding synsets in ImageNet. For fork and iron, there are a limited number of images in ImageNet. Thus, we crawl images for these 5 categories using Google Image Search. Figure 2 displays some images from different object categories in our database. For most of these images, there are salient objects from the corresponding category in the image. Some objects tend to appear together, such as teapot and cup, bed and pillow, keyboard and mouse, and so on. Some objects may appear in complex scenes, for instance, a car in a street scene or a bed in an indoor scene.

3.3   3D Shape Acquisition

In order to provide 3D annotations to objects in 2D images, we collect 3D shapes for the object categories in our database. First, we manually select representative 3D shapes for each category from Trimble 3D Warehouse [5]. These 3D shapes are selected to cover different "subcategories". For example, we collect 3D shapes of sedans, SUVs, vans, trucks, etc., for the car category. Figure 3(a)

Fig. 2. Example images in our database

Fig. 3. Examples of the 3D shapes for bench in our database. (a) 3D shapes manually selected from Trimble 3D Warehouse. (b) 3D Shapes collected from ShapeNet

shows the seven 3D shapes we collected for bench, where they represent different types of benches. These 3D shapes have been aligned according to the main axis of the category (e.g., front view of bench), with their sizes normalized to fit into a unit sphere. In addition, we have manually selected key points on each 3D shape as illustrated by the red dots in Fig. 3(a), which can be used for key point recognition in images or in 3D shapes. There are 783 3D shapes in total that are collected from Trimble 3D Warehouse in this way, which cover all the 100 categories.

Second, to increase the number of 3D shapes in our database, we download 3D shapes from the ShapeNet repository [4]. Similar to ImageNet, ShapeNet organizes 3D shapes according to the WordNet hierarchy. We use the ShapeNet-Core subset [7] since all models are single 3D objects with manually verified category annotations and alignment. ShapeNetCore covers 55 object categories, among which 42 categories overlap with the 100 categories in our database. So we download 3D shapes from these 42 categories in ShapeNetCore contributing additional 43,364 3D shapes to our database. Figure 3(b) shows some 3D shapes of benches from the ShapeNetCore repository. These 3D models are valuable since they capture more shape variations and have rich texture/material information.

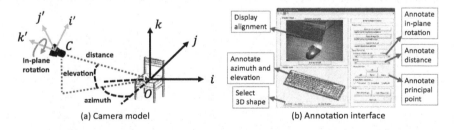

Fig. 4. Illustration of the camera model in our database (a) and the annotation interface for 2D-3D alignment (b)

3.4   Camera Model

After collecting the images and the 3D shapes, our next step is to align an object in an image with a 3D shape. We describe the camera model we use for the alignment as illustrated in Fig. 4(a).

First, the world coordinate system O is defined on the center of the 3D shape, with the three axes (i, j, k) aligned with the dominating directions of the 3D shape. Second, the camera coordinate system C is denoted by (i', j', k'), and we assume that the camera is facing the negative direction of the k' axis towards the origin of the world coordinate system. In this case, the rotation transformation between the two coordinate systems can be defined by three variables: azimuth a, elevation e and in-plane rotation θ. Let's denote the rotation matrix by $R(a, e, \theta)$. The translation vector of the camera center in the world coordinate system can be defined by azimuth, elevation and distance d as $T(a, e, d)$. R and T determine the extrinsic parameters of our camera model. Third, for the intrinsic parameters of the camera, we use a virtual focus length f that is fixed as one. We define the viewport size as $\alpha = 2000$ (i.e., unit one in the world coordinate system corresponds to 2,000 pixels in the image), and denote the principal point as (u, v) (i.e., the projection of the world coordinate origin in the image). Finally, the projection matrix M of our camera model is

$$
M = \underbrace{\begin{bmatrix} \alpha f & 0 & u \\ 0 & \alpha f & v \\ 0 & 0 & 1 \end{bmatrix}}_{\text{intrinsic parameters}} \underbrace{\left[R(a, e, \theta) \; T(a, e, d) \right]}_{\text{extrinsic parameters}}. \tag{1}
$$

By fixing the focal length f and the viewport α, we have 6 variables to be estimated: azimuth a, elevation e, in-plane rotation θ, distance d and principal point (u, v), which define the alignment between the 3D shape and the 2D object.

3.5   Annotation Process

We describe our annotation process to provide 3D annotations to objects in 2D images. (i) We label the 2D bounding box of every object in the images that

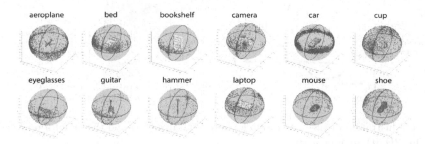

Fig. 5. Viewpoint distributions of different categories in our database. We visualize the camera position as a point on the unit sphere (red points: in-plane rotation $< 15°$; green points: in-plane rotation $> 15°$). See [3] for more plots (Color figure online)

belong to the 100 categories in our database. Occluded objects and truncated objects are also labeled. (ii) Given an object indicated by its bounding box, we associate it to the most similar 3D shape among those downloaded from Trimble 3D Warehouse (Fig. 3(a)). That is, an annotator is asked to select the most similar 3D shape from 7.8 3D shapes for each object on average. (iii) We align the selected 3D shape to the 2D object using the camera model described in Sect. 3.4. For the alignment, we have developed an annotation interface as illustrated in Fig. 4(b). Objects are shown one by one in the annotation tool, and annotators can modify the camera parameters via the interface to align the objects. Annotators have full control of all the 6 camera parameters using the interface: azimuth, elevation, distance, in-plane rotation and principal point. Whenever these parameters are changed, we re-project the 3D shape to the image and display the overlap, which is helpful for the annotator to find a set of camera parameters that align the 3D shape with the 2D object well. Our criterion for the alignment is maximizing the intersection over union between the projection of the 3D shape and the 2D object. Figure 4(b) shows the finished alignment for a computer keyboard. Figure 5 illustrates the viewpoint distribution of several categories in our database.

3.6 3D Shape Retrieval

In our annotation process, we have manually associated every object in the 100 categories to a 3D shape among these 3D models from Trimble 3D Warehouse, where we have around 7 or 8 3D shapes per category. For 42 object categories among the 100 categories, we have additional 3D shapes from ShapeNetCore (Fig. 3(b)). In this case, it is not feasible to manually select the most similar 3D shape among thousands of 3D shapes. So we develop a 3D shape retrieval method by learning feature embeddings with rendered images, and we use this method to retrieve the closest 3D shapes for objects in the 42 object categories.

Specifically, given a 2D object o and a set of N 3D shapes $\mathcal{S} = \{S_1, \ldots, S_N\}$, our goal is to rank the N 3D shapes according to their similarity with the 2D object. We formulate it as a metric learning problem, where the task is to learn a distance metric between a 2D object and a 3D shape: $D(o, S)$. To bridge the two different domains, we use rendered images to represent a 3D shape: $S = \{s_1, \ldots, s_n\}$, where s_i denotes the ith rendered image from the 3D shape S and n is the number of rendered images ($n = 100$ in our experiments). Then we define the distance between a 2D object and a 3D shape as the mean distance between the 2D object and the rendered images from the 3D shape: $D(o, S) = \frac{1}{n}\sum_{i=1}^{n} D(o, s_i)$. Now, the task converts to learning the distance metric $D(o, s_i)$ between 2D images, which is an active research field in the literature.

We apply the lifted structured feature embedding method [31] to learn the distance metric between images, which achieves better performance than contrastive embedding [13] and triplet embedding [38]. The training is conducted with rendered images only, where images rendered from the same 3D shape are considered to be in the same class. As a result, the learned feature embedding will group images from the same shape together. In testing, given a 2D object

o, we compute its euclidean distance $D(o, s_i)$ with each rendered image s_i in the embedding space, and average them to compute its distances with 3D shapes. In order to minimize the gap between rendered images and real test images, we add backgrounds to rendered images and vary their lighting conditions as in [34].

4   Baseline Experiments

In this section, we provide baseline experimental results on four different tasks: object proposal generating, 2D object detection, joint 2D detection and 3D pose estimation, and image-based 3D shape retrieval. We split the images in our dataset into a training/validation (trainval) set with 45,440 images, and a test set with 44,687 images. In the following experiments, training is performed on the trainval set, while testing is conducted on the test set.

4.1   Object Proposal Generation

Recent progress in object recognition can largely be attributed to the advance of Deep Neural Networks (DNNs). Region proposals are widely used in different DNN-based object recognition methods [12] as a preprocessing step to reduce the search space on images. The main idea is to generate a few hundreds or thousands of regions per image that are likely to be objects, then these regions are classified with a DNN. We first apply four different region proposal methods to our dataset and evaluate their performances: SelectiveSearch [37], EdgeBoxes [43], Multiscale Combinatorial Grouping (MCG) [6] and Region Proposal Network (RPN) [25].

We use detection recall to evaluate the region proposal performance. It is defined as the percentage of Ground Truth (GT) object boxes that are correctly covered by the region proposals, and we say a GT box is correctly covered if its Intersection over Union (IoU) with one of the region proposals is larger than some threshold. Figure 6 presents the detection recall of these four region proposal

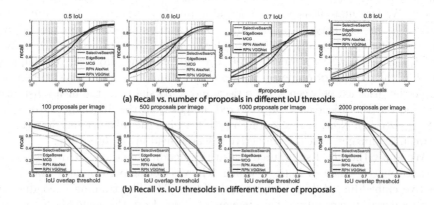

Fig. 6. Evaluation of four different object proposal method on our dataset: SelectiveSearch [37], EdgeBoxes [43], MCG [6] and RPN [25]

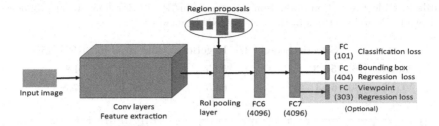

Fig. 7. Illustration of the network architecture based on Fast R-CNN [11] for object detection and pose estimation

methods on our test set according to different number of object proposals per image and different IoU thresholds. For the RPN in [25], we experiment with two network architectures, i.e., AlexNet [16] and VGGNet [30] (VGG16), where we fine-tune their pre-trained networks on ImageNet [26] with our trainval set for region proposal generation. First, we can see that, by using around 1000 proposals, all the four methods achieve recall more than 90 % with 0.5 IoU threshold. The state-of-the-art region proposal methods work well on our dataset. Second, it is interesting to note that the recall of RPN drops significantly when an IoU threshold larger than 0.7 is used. This is because the RPNs are trained with 0.7 IoU threshold, i.e., all proposals with IoU larger than 0.7 are treated as positive examples equally. There is no constraint in the RPN training to ensure that proposals with larger IoU threshold are preferred. Third, RPN with VGGNet achieves the best recall with IoU threshold from 0.5 to 0.7, while MCG performs consistently well across different IoU thresholds.

4.2 2D Object Detection

We evaluate the 2D object detection performance on our dataset using the Fast R-CNN framework [11] which is considered to be a state-of-the-art object detection method. We fine-tune two CNN architectures pre-trained on the ImageNet dataset [26] for the 2D detection task: AlexNet [16] and VGGNet [30] (VGG16). Figure 7 illustrates the network architecture used in Fast R-CNN for object detection. First, an input image is fed into a sequence of convolutional layers to compute a feature map of the image. Then, given a region proposal, the RoI pooling layer extracts a feature vector for the region proposal from the feature map. The feature vector is then processed by two Fully Connected (FC) layers, i.e., FC6 and FC7 each with dimension 4096. Finally, the network terminates at two FC branches with different losses (i.e., the third branch for viewpoint estimation in Fig. 7 is not used here), one for object class classification, and the other one for bounding box regression (see [11] for more details). We have 100 categories in our dataset, so the FC layer for classification has dimension 101 with an additional dimension for background. The FC layer for bounding box regression has dimension 4×101, i.e., for each class, it predicts the center location, width, height of the bounding box.

Table 3. Object detection evaluation in terms of mAP with the four object proposals and two CNN architectures in the Fast R-CNN framework

	SelectiveSearch [37]	EdgeBoxes [43]	MCG [6]	RPN [25]
AlexNet [16]	**56.3**	52.5	56.0	54.2
VGGNet [30]	67.3	64.5	67.0	**67.5**

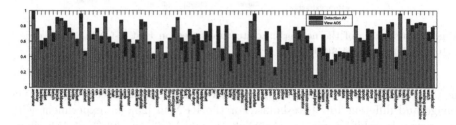

Fig. 8. Bar plot of the detection AP and viewpoint estimation AOS of the 100 categories on the test set from VGGNet with SelectiveSearch proposals

We use Average Precision (AP) to evaluate the 2D object detection performance. AP is computed as the area under the precision-recall curve for each category, where 50 % overlap threshold is used as in PASCAL VOC [8]. To evaluate the overall detection performance on the dataset, we compute mean AP (mAP) across all the categories. Table 3 presents the mAP for 2D object detection across all the 100 categories on the test set. First, we can see that VGGNet achieves significantly better mAPs compared to AlexNet. Second, among the four region proposal methods, using object proposals from SelectiveSearch and MCG achieves better detection performance than using EdgeBoxes. RPN is able to benefit from more powerful networks such as the VGGNet. Third, with VGGNet and RPN proposals, we achieve the best mAP 67.5. For reference, the best mAP on the ImageNet detection challenge 2015 (200 ImageNet categories) is 62.0 [2]. Figure 8 shows the detection AP of each category in our dataset. As we can see, some categories are relatively easy to detect such as aeroplane, motorbike and train, and some are more difficult such as cabinet, pencil and road pole. These categories either have large intra-class variability or have less discriminative features. Finally, we group all 100 categories into six super-categories: container, electronics, furniture, personal items, tools and vehicles, and analyze the detection false positives of these six groups using the diagnosing tool from [14]. Figure 9 summarizes the results. For tools and vehicles, localization error is the main source of false positives, while for the other four groups, a large portion of the detection errors is also attributed to confusion with other categories or background.

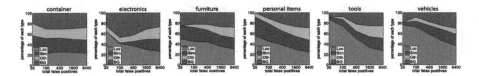

Fig. 9. Distribution of top-ranked false positive types from VGGNet with Selective Search proposals: Loc - pool localization; Sim - confusion with a similar category; Oth - confusion with a dissimilar category; BG - a false positive fires on background

4.3 Joint 2D Detection and Continuous 3D Pose Estimation

In this experiment, our goal is to jointly detect objects in 2D images and estimate their continuous 3D pose. By aligning 3D shapes with 2D objects, we provide continuous 3D pose annotations to objects in our dataset. We provide a baseline model for this task by modifying the Fast R-CNN network. As illustrated in Fig. 7, we add a viewpoint regression FC branch after the FC7 layer. So the network is trained to perform three tasks jointly: classification, bounding box regression and viewpoint regression. The FC layer for viewpoint regression has dimension 3×101, i.e., for each class, it predicts the three angles of azimuth, elevation and in-plane rotation. The smoothed L1 loss is used for viewpoint regression as for bounding box regression.

Two different metrics have been proposed for joint detection and pose estimation: Average Viewpoint Precision (AVP) in PASCAL3D+ [40] and Average Orientation Similarity (AOS) in KITTI [10]. However, they only consider the estimation error in azimuth. In order to evaluate joint detection and continuous pose estimation in three angles, i.e., azimuth, elevation and in-plane rotation, we generalize AVP and AOS, where we define the difference between the estimated pose and the ground truth pose as follows: $\Delta(R, R_{gt}) = \frac{1}{\sqrt{2}} \| \log(R^T R_{gt}) \|_F$, which is the geodesic distance between the estimated rotation matrix R and the GT rotation matrix R_{gt}. In AVP, we consider an estimation to be correct if $\Delta(R, R_{gt}) < \frac{\pi}{6}$. In AOS, the cosine similarity between poses is used: $\cos(\Delta(R, R_{gt}))$ [10].

Table 4. Joint 2D detection and 3D pose estimation evaluation in terms of AOS/AVP with the four object proposals and two CNNs in the Fast R-CNN framework

	SelectiveSearch [37]	EdgeBoxes [43]	MCG [6]	RPN [25]
	AOS / AVP			
AlexNet [16]	**48.1 / 37.3**	44.5 / 33.6	47.8 / 37.0	46.1 / 35.4
VGGNet [30]	**57.1 / 43.0**	54.2 / 39.6	56.8 / 42.9	57.0 / 42.6

Table 4 presents the joint detection and pose estimation results on the test set with four region proposal methods and two CNN architectures. Figure 8 shows

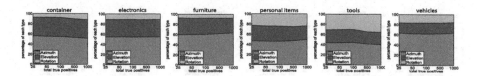

Fig. 10. Viewpoint error distribution of top-ranked true positives from VGGNet with SelectiveSearch proposals

the AOS of each category from the VGGNet with SelectiveSearch proposals. Due to the way AOS is computed, detection AP is always an upper bound of AOS. The closer AOS is to AP, the better the viewpoint estimation. By examining the gaps between AOS and AP in Fig. 8, we can figure out a few categories with poor viewpoint estimation such as comb, fork and teapot. These categories may be nearly symmetric or have large in-plane rotation angles. To understand the viewpoint error distribution in azimuth, elevation and in-plane rotation, we visualize it in Fig. 10. As we can see, azimuth error dominates for the six super-categories. For tools and personal items, such as hammer or watch, in-plane rotation error is also significant.

4.4   Image-Based 3D Shape Retrieval

In our annotation process, we propose an image-based 3D shape retrieval method by deep metric learning (Sect. 3.6). The goal is to find the most similar 3D shapes to a given 2D object. We present details of this experiment here. We learn a feature embedding for each category among the 45 categories where we have 3D shapes from ShapeNetCore. First, to generate training images, we render 100 synthetic images for each 3D shape from different viewpoints. These viewpoints are sampled from a distribution estimated with kernel density estimation using the viewpoint annotations (azimuth, elevation and in-plane rotation) in our database for that category. To mimic real images, we overlay the rendered images on randomly selected background images from the SUN database [41]. Second, we consider images rendered from the same 3D shape as in the same "class". In this way, we are able to apply existing deep metric learning methods to learn a feature embedding for the rendered images. Specifically, we experiment with the contrastive embedding [13], the triplet embedding [38] and the lifted structured embedding [31], where we fine-tune GoogLeNet [35] pre-trained on ImageNet [26] to learn the embedding. Finally, after training the network, each rendered image is represented as a feature vector (in the embedded space) computed from the last FC layer of the GoogLeNet, while a 3D shape is represented as mean of the feature vectors of its rendered images.

To evaluate the learned embedding, we conduct the following image retrieval experiment with rendered images, where we have ground truth 3D shape assignments: given a rendered image, the goal is to retrieve images rendered from the same 3D shape as the input image, which is exactly the task that the network is trained for. For each category, we use 50 % of the 3D shapes for training, and test

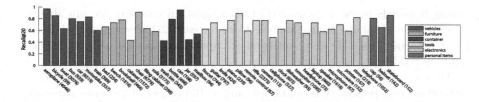

Fig. 11. Recall@20 from our user study for 42 categories that have 3D shapes from ShapeNetCore. The number of 3D shapes for each category is shown in the brackets

on the other 50 %. We compute Recall@K to evaluate the retrieval performance, which is computed as the percentage of testing images which have at least one correctly retrieved image among the top K retrieval results.

Table 5 shows the Recall@K on rendered image retrieval, where we compare the contrastive embedding, the triplet embedding and the lifted structured embedding. As we can see from the table, lifted structured embedding significantly outperforms the other two due to its ability to utilize every pairwise relationship between training examples in a batch [31]. Thus, we utilize the lifted structured embedding to retrieve 3D shapes for real images in our database. The goal is to provide the top K ranked 3D shapes for each 2D object, then ask annotators to select the most similar 3D shape among the K returned ones, since it is not feasible to ask an annotator to select the most similar shape

Table 5. Comparison between three feature embedding methods on rendered images

	Recall@1	Recall@2	Recall@4	Recall@8	Recall@16	Recall@32
Contrastive [13]	60.7±19.9	69.0±18.7	76.3±16.8	82.6±14.3	87.7±11.5	91.8±8.7
Triplet [38]	82.3±11.9	87.2±9.5	91.0±7.4	93.9±5.5	95.9±3.9	97.4±2.7
LiftedStruct [31]	**91.1±4.5**	**94.1±3.2**	**96.1±2.3**	**97.4±1.7**	**98.3±1.3**	**98.9±0.9**

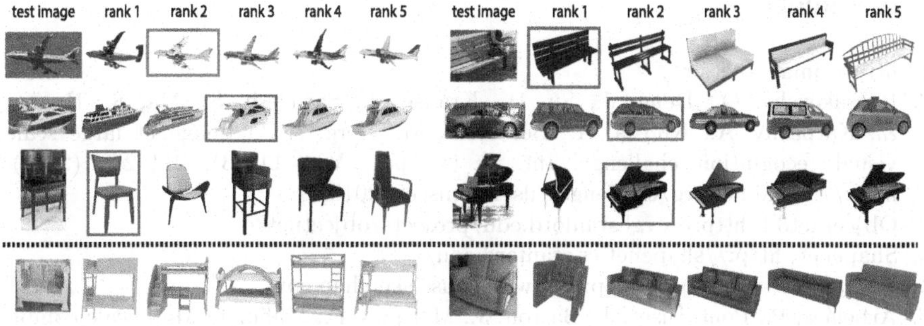

Fig. 12. Example of 3D shape retrieval. Green boxes are the selected shapes. The last row shows two examples where we cannot find a similar shape among the top 5 ones (Color figure online)

among hundreds or even thousands of 3D shapes. In this way, we are able to select a close 3D shape from ShapeNetCore for each 2D object in our dataset. Figure 12 shows some 3D shape retrieval examples using our learned lifted structured embeddings.

We have also conducted a user study to test the performance of our retrieval method on real images. We randomly sample 100 objects from each category, and ask three annotators to decide if there is a similar 3D shape among the top 20 retrieved 3D shapes for each object. Then we compute Recall@20 for each category based on the annotators' judgement. Figure 11 shows the results from the user study. The mean Recall@20 is 69.2 %. The method works well on categories with a number of 3D shapes large enough to cover the shape variations (e.g. aeroplane, chair and car). On categories with fewer 3D shapes, the task becomes more challenging, especially when the category has large intra-class variability.

5 Conclusions

In this work, we have successfully built a large scale database with 2D images and 3D shapes for 100 object categories. We provide 3D annotations to objects in our database by aligning a closest 3D shape to a 2D object. As a result, our database can be used to benchmark different object recognition tasks including 2D object detection, 3D object pose estimation and image-based 3D shape retrieval. We have provided baseline experiments on these tasks, and demonstrated the usefulness of our database.

Acknowledgments. We acknowledge the support of NSF grants IIS-1528025 and DMS-1546206, a Google Focused Research award, and grant SPO # 124316 and 1191689-1-UDAWF from the Stanford AI Lab-Toyota Center for Artificial Intelligence Research.

References

1. http://image-net.org/
2. Russakovsky, O., Deng, J., Su, H., Krause, J., Satheesh, S., Ma, S., Huang, Z., Karpathy, A., Khosla, A., Bernstein, M., Berg, A.C.: Imagenet large scale visual recognition challenge. Int. J. Comput. Vis. **115**(3), 211–252 (2015). http://image-net.org/challenges/ilsvrc+mscoco2015
3. Objectnet3d. http://cvgl.stanford.edu/projects/objectnet3d
4. Shapenet. http://shapenet.cs.stanford.edu/
5. Trimble 3D warehouse. http://3dwarehouse.sketchup.com
6. Arbeláez, P., Pont-Tuset, J., Barron, J., Marques, F., Malik, J.: Multiscale combinatorial grouping. In: CVPR, pp. 328–335 (2014)
7. Chang, A.X., Funkhouser, T., Guibas, L., Hanrahan, P., Huang, Q., Li, Z., Savarese, S., Savva, M., Song, S., Su, H., Xiao, J., Yi, L., Yu, F.: ShapeNet: an information-rich 3D model repository. Technical report [cs.GR] (2015). arXiv:1512.03012

8. Everingham, M., Van Gool, L., Williams, C.K.I., Winn, J., Zisserman, A.: The PASCAL Visual Object Classes Challenge 2012 (VOC2012) Results. http://www.pascal-network.org/challenges/VOC/voc2012/workshop/index.html
9. Fidler, S., Dickinson, S., Urtasun, R.: 3D object detection and viewpoint estimation with a deformable 3D cuboid model. In: NIPS, pp. 611–619 (2012)
10. Geiger, A., Lenz, P., Urtasun, R.: Are we ready for autonomous driving? the kitti vision benchmark suite. In: CVPR, pp. 3354–3361 (2012)
11. Girshick, R.: Fast R-CNN. In: ICCV, pp. 1440–1448 (2015)
12. Girshick, R., Donahue, J., Darrell, T., Malik, J.: Rich feature hierarchies for accurate object detection and semantic segmentation. In: CVPR, pp. 580–587 (2014)
13. Hadsell, R., Chopra, S., LeCun, Y.: Dimensionality reduction by learning an invariant mapping. In: CVPR, vol. 2, pp. 1735–1742 (2006)
14. Hoiem, D., Chodpathumwan, Y., Dai, Q.: Diagnosing error in object detectors. In: Fitzgibbon, A., Lazebnik, S., Perona, P., Sato, Y., Schmid, C. (eds.) ECCV 2012, Part III. LNCS, vol. 7574, pp. 340–353. Springer, Heidelberg (2012)
15. Kar, A., Tulsiani, S., Carreira, J., Malik, J.: Category-specific object reconstruction from a single image. In: CVPR, pp. 1966–1974 (2015)
16. Krizhevsky, A., Sutskever, I., Hinton, G.E.: Imagenet classification with deep convolutional neural networks. In: NIPS, pp. 1097–1105 (2012)
17. Lähner, Z., Rodola, E., Schmidt, F.R., Bronstein, M.M., Cremers, D.: Efficient globally optimal 2D-to-3D deformable shape matching. In: CVPR (2016)
18. Lai, K., Bo, L., Ren, X., Fox, D.: A large-scale hierarchical multi-view RGB-D object dataset. In: ICRA, pp. 1817–1824 (2011)
19. Leibe, B., Schiele, B.: Analyzing appearance and contour based methods for object categorization. In: CVPR, vol. 2, pp. II–409 (2003)
20. Lim, J.J., Pirsiavash, H., Torralba, A.: Parsing IKEA objects: fine pose estimation. In: ICCV, pp. 2992–2999 (2013)
21. Lin, T.-Y., Maire, M., Belongie, S., Hays, J., Perona, P., Ramanan, D., Dollár, P., Zitnick, C.L.: Microsoft COCO: common objects in context. In: Fleet, D., Pajdla, T., Schiele, B., Tuytelaars, T. (eds.) ECCV 2014, Part V. LNCS, vol. 8693, pp. 740–755. Springer, Heidelberg (2014)
22. Lopez-Sastre, R.J., Redondo-Cabrera, C., Gil-Jimenez, P., Maldonado-Bascon, S.: ICARO: image collection of annotated real-world objects. http://agamenon.tsc.uah.es/Personales/rlopez/data/icaro (2010)
23. Ozuysal, M., Lepetit, V., Fua, P.: Pose estimation for category specific multiview object localization. In: CVPR, pp. 778–785 (2009)
24. Pepik, B., Stark, M., Gehler, P., Schiele, B.: Teaching 3D geometry to deformable part models. In: CVPR, pp. 3362–3369. IEEE (2012)
25. Ren, S., He, K., Girshick, R., Sun, J.: Faster R-CNN: towards real-time object detection with region proposal networks. In: NIPS, pp. 91–99 (2015)
26. Russakovsky, O., Deng, J., Su, H., Krause, J., Satheesh, S., Ma, S., Huang, Z., Karpathy, A., Khosla, A., Bernstein, M., Berg, A.C., Fei-Fei, L.: ImageNet large scale visual recognition challenge. Int. J. Comput. Vis. IJCV 115(3), 1–42 (2015)
27. Russell, B.C., Torralba, A.: Building a database of 3D scenes from user annotations. In: CVPR, pp. 2711–2718 (2009)
28. Savarese, S., Fei-Fei, L.: 3D generic object categorization, localization and pose estimation. In: ICCV, pp. 1–8 (2007)
29. Silberman, N., Hoiem, D., Kohli, P., Fergus, R.: Indoor segmentation and support inference from RGBD images. In: Fitzgibbon, A., Lazebnik, S., Perona, P., Sato, Y., Schmid, C. (eds.) ECCV 2012, Part V. LNCS, vol. 7576, pp. 746–760. Springer, Heidelberg (2012)

30. Simonyan, K., Zisserman, A.: Very deep convolutional networks for large-scale image recognition. arXiv preprint (2014). arXiv:1409.1556
31. Song, H.O., Xiang, Y., Jegelka, S., Savarese, S.: Deep metric learning via lifted structured feature embedding. In: CVPR (2016)
32. Song, S., Lichtenberg, S.P., Xiao, J.: Sun RGB-D: a RGB-D scene understanding benchmark suite. In: CVPR, pp. 567–576 (2015)
33. Su, H., Huang, Q., Mitra, N.J., Li, Y., Guibas, L.J.: Estimating image depth using shape collections. ACM Trans. Graph. **33**(4), 37 (2014)
34. Su, H., Qi, C.R., Li, Y., Guibas, L.J.: Render for CNN: viewpoint estimation in images using CNNS trained with rendered 3D model views. In: ICCV, pp. 2686–2694 (2015)
35. Szegedy, C., Liu, W., Jia, Y., Sermanet, P., Reed, S., Anguelov, D., Erhan, D., Vanhoucke, V., Rabinovich, A.: Going deeper with convolutions. In: CVPR, pp. 1–9 (2015)
36. Thomas, A., Ferrari, V., Leibe, B., Tuytelaars, T., Schiele, B., Gool, L.V.: Towards multi-view object class detection. In: CVPR, pp. 1589–1596 (2006)
37. Uijlings, J.R., van de Sande, K.E., Gevers, T., Smeulders, A.W.: Selective search for object recognition. Int. J. Comput. Vis. (IJCV) **104**(2), 154–171 (2013)
38. Weinberger, K.Q., Saul, L.K.: Distance metric learning for large margin nearest neighbor classification. J. Mach. Learn. Res. **10**, 207–244 (2009)
39. Xiang, Y., Choi, W., Lin, Y., Savarese, S.: Data-driven 3D voxel patterns for object category recognition. In: CVPR, pp. 1903–1911 (2015)
40. Xiang, Y., Mottaghi, R., Savarese, S.: Beyond pascal: a benchmark for 3D object detection in the wild. In: WACV, pp. 75–82 (2014)
41. Xiao, J., Hays, J., Ehinger, K.A., Oliva, A., Torralba, A.: Sun database: large-scale scene recognition from abbey to zoo. In: CVPR, pp. 3485–3492 (2010)
42. Zia, M.Z., Stark, M., Schindler, K.: Explicit occlusion modeling for 3D object class representations. In: CVPR, pp. 3326–3333 (2013)
43. Zitnick, C.L., Dollár, P.: Edge boxes: locating object proposals from edges. In: Fleet, D., Pajdla, T., Schiele, B., Tuytelaars, T. (eds.) ECCV 2014, Part V. LNCS, vol. 8693, pp. 391–405. Springer, Heidelberg (2014)

Branching Gaussian Processes with Applications to Spatiotemporal Reconstruction of 3D Trees

Kyle Simek[1]([✉]), Ravishankar Palanivelu[2], and Kobus Barnard[3]

[1] Matterport, Inc., Sunnyvale, USA
kylesimek@gmail.com
[2] School of Plant Sciences, University of Arizona, Tucson, USA
rpalaniv@email.arizona.edu
[3] Computer Science, University of Arizona, Tucson, USA
kobus@cs.arizona.edu

Abstract. We propose a robust method for estimating dynamic 3D curvilinear branching structure from monocular images. While 3D reconstruction from images has been widely studied, estimating thin structure has received less attention. This problem becomes more challenging in the presence of camera error, scene motion, and a constraint that curves are attached in a branching structure. We propose a new general-purpose prior, a *branching Gaussian processes* (BGP), that models spatial smoothness and temporal dynamics of curves while enforcing attachment between them. We apply this prior to fit 3D trees directly to image data, using an efficient scheme for approximate inference based on expectation propagation. The BGP prior's Gaussian form allows us to approximately marginalize over 3D trees with a given model structure, enabling principled comparison between tree models with varying complexity. We test our approach on a novel multi-view dataset depicting plants with known 3D structures and topologies undergoing small nonrigid motion. Our method outperforms a state-of-the-art 3D reconstruction method designed for non-moving thin structure. We evaluate under several common measures, and we propose a new measure for reconstructions of branching multi-part 3D scenes under motion.

Keywords: Multiview stereo · Nonrigid models · Expectation propagation

1 Introduction

Curvilinear 3D tree structure is of central importance to several areas of science including the study of plants [10,34], vascular systems [8,23,28], and branching neurons [6,7]. But estimating such 3D structure from images poses unique challenges, because the 3D shapes are thin, self-occluding, and often textureless. In

Electronic supplementary material The online version of this chapter (doi:10.1007/978-3-319-46484-8_11) contains supplementary material, which is available to authorized users.

B. Leibe et al. (Eds.): ECCV 2016, Part VIII, LNCS 9912, pp. 177–193, 2016.
DOI: 10.1007/978-3-319-46484-8_11

addition, traditional reconstruction methods like visual hull or multi-view stereo require precise knowledge of camera poses and intrinsic parameters, and they assume the scene remains stationary between images. When either of these are not true, epipolar constraints are violated and 3D reconstruction fails. This can be especially problematic for multi-view 3D reconstruction of plants, because they can move a surprising amount in just a few minutes.

We propose a model-based approach to recover 3D structure in these scenarios by explicitly modeling nonrigid motion and by defining a noise model that is robust to camera errors. We introduce a new representation called a *curve tree*, which defines both the curves' geometry and their topological structure. The curve tree representation provides more than just *geometric* structure; the *logical* structure is represented as well so that distinct parts may be identified, counted, and measured, and topology of the multi-part structure may be understood. We then introduce a novel family of priors over curve trees called *branching Gaussian processes* (BGPs) that model curves as smooth Gaussian processes and enforce attachment between curves in a tree topology. We also extend the BGP to the temporal dimension to model sequences of curve trees over time. This prior aids inference by limiting the space of plausible models, and in the case of a moving scene, it is necessary to make the problem well-posed.

Using the temporal BGP prior, we pose 3D reconstruction from images as Bayesian inference. Our image-based likelihood function is non-convex and highly multimodal, making exact inference intractable. We develop an approximate inference scheme based on expectation propagation that exploits the BGP prior's Gaussian form to approximate the posterior as multivariate Gaussian. We also approximately solve the intractable Bayesian model selection problem, allowing us to compare curve trees of varying complexity in a principled way. Our method is fully trained from a single exemplar sequence and is effective at recovering 3D branching structure even in scenarios with ambiguous data and self-occlusion. When ambiguity cannot be resolved, our method provides a rich representation of uncertainty in the form of a posterior distribution. We evaluate our results using the DIADEM metric for branching structure and a new score designed to assess the logical structure of multi-part tree-structured 3D models.

2 Related Work

Gaussian processes (GP's) are an increasingly common tool for machine learning and computer vision [24], especially as smoothing priors for deformable geometry. Zhu et al. used GP's for recovery of nonrigid 3D surfaces [42], and Serradell et al. used GP priors to match graphs embedded in 2D or 3D [25]. Like us, Sugiyama et al. proposed constructing a GP over an embedded graph [29], but their covariance function is based on geodesic distance, which is not positive definite in general. Our proposed covariance function is a positive-definite alternative but still has the property that correlations are inversely monotonic with geodesic distance.

Shape estimation from images has been widely studied, but less attention has been paid to the challenges posed by thin geometry. Segmentation of thin structure in images has gained some attention in recent years [14, 20,35,39], but the problem of 3D reconstruction remains largely unexplored. Lopez et al. used space carving to recover thin branching structure as a voxel volume, but their approach relies on near-exact camera calibrations [19]. Amy Tabb achieved robustness to camera errors using a probabilistic variation of visual hull, allowing the position of thin structure to be inconsistent in some cameras and still be reconstructed [30]. Both of these approaches assume the scene is static between images, and they produce only geometry, not part labels or topology. Kahl and August propose a generative model for 3D space curves that follow a Markovian random process through space [16]. They suggest their model could be made robust to both camera errors and scene motion by modeling small perturbations to the 3D curves in each image. We achieve robustness in a similar way, but our model (a) permits a large class of Gaussian processes beyond just Markov processes, (b) introduces branching attachment between curves, (c) enforces temporal consistency between per-view perturbations, and (d) addresses the model selection problem when fitting an unknown number of curves.

Our approach seeks not just 3D shape (i.e., geometry), but 3D *structure* (e.g., topology, medial axis, distinct geometric parts). Branching topology is of particular importance since it enables measurement of morphological traits such as branch angles, branching depth, and average curvature of individual branches. Approaches exist for estimating 2D trees from images [36,37] and 3D trees from 3D data modalities like point clouds [27] and voxels (e.g., the Diadem challenge, [2,4,37,38,40,41]). Methods estimating 3D tree structure from 2D projective images are less common. Some image-based methods recover a plausible branching 3D plant model without attempting to recover the exact branching architecture [3,9,18,26,31–33]. In addition, several semi-automatic tools use human input to help reconstruct vascular systems [1], root system architectures [5,17,43], and neuron arbors [22] from images.

The motion of 3D trees has been modeled in computer graphics for generating animated synthetic trees (e.g., [9,18]). Estimating the motion of real trees is less common. Glowacki et al. recover sequences of 2D trees in a two-step process, using bottom-up methods to find a graph of tree points and integer programming to find the optimal tree-structured subgraph [13]. However, their bottom-up approach does not address self-occlusions, and they rely on the graph deformation model of Serradell et al. [25] based on Euclidean embeddings, which cannot model 2D curves that pass-by each other due to parallax.

While previous work addresses parts of our problem, we are unaware of other systems that attempt accurate estimation of 3D trees under nonrigid motion.

3   Curve Trees

We define a *curve tree* as a finite set of curves attached in a tree topology. The cth curve in a d-dimensional curve tree is defined by the *curve function* $f_c : [0, L_c] \rightarrow \mathbb{R}^d$. In the expression $f_c(t)$, the value $c \in \{1, \ldots, N\}$ is the *curve*

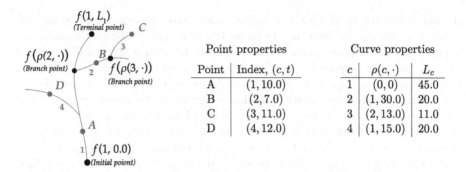

Fig. 1. Anatomy of a curve tree (best viewed in color). Curve indices are indicated in red. Initial, terminal, and branch points are noted. (Color figure online)

index, and $t \in [0, L_c]$ is the real-valued *spatial index*. The point $f_c(0)$ is the curve's *initial point*, and $f_c(L_c)$ is its *terminal point*. The Cartesian product of the curve index and spatial index is called a *point index* (c, t), and it uniquely identifies each point in a curve tree. The set of all point indices is the *index space* $\mathcal{I} = \cup_{c=1}^{N}(\{c\} \times [0, L_c]) \cup (0, 0)$, where $(0, 0)$ represents "no point," which is included for notationally convenience. The collection of curve functions are combined into a *curve-tree function* $f : \mathcal{I} \to \mathbb{R}^d$, where $f(c, t) = f_c(t)$ is the point on the cth curve with spatial index t.

If a curve's initial point lies on another curve, we say the curves are *attached*; the former curve is called a *child curve*, and the point where it attaches on the *parent curve* is called its *branch point*. Curves may have at most one parent curve, and curves with no parent are *root curves*. Attachment between curves is represented by a *branch function*. The function $\rho_C : \{0, \dots, N\} \to \{0, \dots, N\}$ maps a curve index to the index of its parent curve or zero for root curves. Similarly, $\rho_\tau : \{0, \dots, N\} \to \mathbb{R}$ maps the curve to the spatial index of its branch point on the parent curve, or zero for root curves. The *branch function* combines ρ_C and ρ_τ:

$$\rho(c, t) = \begin{cases} (\rho_C(c), \rho_\tau(c)) & \text{if } c \neq 0 \text{ and } \rho_C(c) \neq 0 \\ (0, 0) & \text{otherwise.} \end{cases} \qquad (1)$$

The input t is unused, but including it simplifies the recursive definition later. The parent/child attachment is stated formally by the *attachment constraint*:

$$f(c, 0) = f(\rho(c, t)), \qquad (2)$$

for all non-root curves $\{c : \rho(x) \neq (0, 0)\}$ and spatial indices $t \in [0, L_c]$.

A curve tree is fully defined by the number of curves N, the spatial-input upper-bounds $L = \{L_1, \dots, L_N\}$, the curve-tree function $f(c, t)$, and the branch function $\rho(c, t)$. Figure 1 illustrates these concepts.

4   Branching Gaussian Processes

A Gaussian process is a generalization of the Gaussian distribution to parameterized collections of random variables. These collections may be uncountably infinite, allowing a Gaussian process to define a probability measure over the space of continuous functions. Gaussian processes are defined by the property that any finite subset of random variables has a multivariate Gaussian distribution [24]. A Gaussian process $f : \Theta \to \mathbb{R}$ is denoted by

$$f(\theta) \sim \mathcal{GP}(\mu(\theta), k(\theta, \theta')), \tag{3}$$

where $\mu(\theta)$ is the mean function, and $k(\theta, \theta')$ is the covariance function. The choice of covariance function dictates the properties of the Gaussian process such as smoothness, periodicity, or stationarity. Without loss of generality, we assume that $\mu(\theta)$ is zero, so $k(\theta, \theta')$ fully defines the Gaussian process.

We propose a novel Gaussian process over curve trees called a *branching Gaussian process* (BGP) by defining a covariance function over the curve tree input space $\mathcal{I}$. A BGP is defined by three properties: (a) individual curves are continuous; (b) the curve tree satisfies the attachment constraint Eq. (2); and (c) each subtree is conditionally independent of the rest of the tree given the subtree's branch point. Below we define a family of branching Gaussian process kernels called a *rooted recursive kernel*, in which (a) a point's marginal variance is determined by its distance from a branch point, and (b) a child curve inherits the variance of its branch point. This is a good model for a plant, where the root point is fixed and leaf points vary more than branch points.

It is also possible to define a family of BGPs in which curves are modeled by stationary covariance functions (e.g., the squared exponential) and the marginal variance of all points are equal (see Supplementary Material).

4.1   Rooted Recursive Kernels

We define a random function $f : \mathbb{R} \to \mathbb{R}^n$ as *rooted* if and only if $f(0) = \mathbf{0}$ almost surely (i.e., it is "rooted" to the origin). A Gaussian process is rooted if and only if its covariance function has the property $k(0, t) = k(t, 0) = 0$ for any $t \in \mathbb{R}$. Two examples of rooted covariance functions are the dot product covariance function, $f(t, t') = t\,t'$, and the Weiner process covariance function, $f(t, t') = \min(t, t')$. An arbitrary covariance function $k : \mathbb{R}^2 \to \mathbb{R}$ can be converted to a rooted covariance function k' by conditioning on the point at $t = 0$:

$$k'(t, t') = k(t, t') - k(t, 0)\, k(0, 0)^{-1} k(0, t'). \tag{4}$$

Let (c, t) and (c', t') be the indices of two points in a curve tree, and without loss of generality, assume the tree depth of (c, t) is greater than or equal to (c', t'). The *rooted recursive* BGP kernel $k_r : \mathcal{I} \times \mathcal{I} \to \mathbb{R}$ is defined as

$$k_r(c, t, c', t') = \begin{cases} 0 & \text{if } c = 0 \text{ or } c' = 0 \\ \delta_{c\,c'} k_c(t, t') + k_r(\rho(c, t), c', t') & \text{otherwise} \end{cases} \tag{5}$$

where $\delta_{cc'}$ is the Kronecker delta. The *curve covariance* $k_c : \mathbb{R} \times \mathbb{R} \to \mathbb{R}$ is any rooted covariance function, and it defines smoothness properties of individual curves. The Kronecker delta ensures the first term contributes zero covariance between different curves. Inter-curve correlation comes from the second term, which is a recursion that replaces the first input with its branch index; if the resulting index is shallower than the second input, inputs are swapped so the first input is always at least as deep as the second. This recursive term contributes a constant offset equal to the variance of the nearest common ancestor point. Because k_c is rooted, it contributes no variance to initial curve points, so $k(c, 0, c, 0) = k(\rho(c), c, 0) = k(\rho(c), \rho(c))$, which implies the attachment property, $f(c, 0) = f(\rho(c, 0))$.

4.2 Temporal Branching Gaussian Processes

We may extend the curve tree model by introducing a temporal input τ to the point index, $(c, t, \tau) \in \mathcal{I} \times \mathbb{R}$. We construct a temporal BGP covariance function from the tensor product of a standard BGP covariance function and a temporal covariance function:

$$k_{\text{tBGP}}(c, t, \tau, c', t', \tau') = k_\tau(\tau, \tau') k_{\text{BGP}}(c, t, c', t'). \tag{6}$$

Here, k_τ is a covariance function over temporal inputs $\tau, \tau' \in \mathbb{R}$, and k_{BGP} is any BGP covariance function.

5   Application: Temporal 3D Tree Structure from Images

For the reconstruction task, we consider the first 18 images of an *Arabidopsis* plant on a turnable separated by 10 degrees of yaw (Fig. 2a) (the rear 18 images do not provide significant additional structural information). Images are captured at fixed time intervals, so time is represented by view-index. A camera model is estimated for each view using a crudely built calibration target, resulting in significant error (Fig. 2c). Capture takes roughly three minutes, during which time the plant moves in response to changing direction of light and temperature gradients (Fig. 2b). Our goal is to recover a 3D curve tree for each of the 18 views. This problem is underconstrained, since variation in appearance between views may be explained by either parallax, nonrigid plant motion, or both. Our temporal BGP provides a prior over motion and geometry, making the problem well-posed. We use a curve tree to represent the medial axis of a plant's stems. Stems are mostly uniform in width, so we define the plant's shape as the union of spheres with 1 mm diameter and center $f(c, t)$ for all $(c, t) \in \mathcal{I} \backslash (0, 0)$.

5.1   Prior

The motion of plants tends to arise as random perturbations around a mean shape, and we define a BGP covariance function that reflects this:

$$k(c, t, \tau, c', t', \tau') = k_{\text{BGP}}(c, t, c', t') + k_{\text{tBGP}}(c, t, \tau, c', t'\tau') + \sigma_0^2. \tag{7}$$

Fig. 2. *(a)* First three images in an 18-view sequence, with ten degrees of rotation between views. *(b)* A stationary 3D point on a turntable should trace an elliptical arc in 2D; the non-elliptical path here indicates nonrigid motion. *(c)* Turntable cameras should follow a circular path and have symmetric viewing directions. This top-down illustration shows significant camera calibration error, which complicates inference.

The first term in Eq. (7) is a branching GP covariance that represents a non-moving tree that is the center of perturbations. We implement it using the rooted-recursive covariance function from Eq. (5) with curve covariance

$$k_c(t, t') = \sigma_L^2 t t' + \sigma_s^2 \left(|t - t'| \frac{\min(t, t')^2}{2} + \frac{\min(t, t')^3}{3} \right). \qquad (8)$$

This is the sum of a dot-product kernel plus a cubic-spline covariance function. The cubic-spline process penalizes the curve's second derivative, representing a bending energy that encourages straight lines. The cubic-spline covariance can only generate curves having zero initial slope, so we add a dot-product kernel to model initial slopes.

The second term in Eq. (7) is the temporal BGP covariance from Eq. (6) and it models random perturbations. For the k_τ term in Eq. (6) we use the Ornstein Uhlenbeck covariance function,

$$k_\tau(\tau, \tau') = \exp\left(|\tau - \tau'|/\ell_\tau\right), \qquad (9)$$

which is a mean-reverting random walk that ensures random perturbations never drift too far from the mean tree structure. For the k_{BGP} term in Eq. (6) we again use a rooted recursive BGP covariance function with the same form as Eq. (8) but with different parameters $(\sigma_L')^2$ and $(\sigma_s')^2$.

The final term in Eq. (7) is a constant offset variance. Because the first two terms are rooted recursive BGP covariance functions, the tree's root point has zero marginal variance under them. Adding a constant offset variance allows trees to initiate from anywhere in $\mathbb{R}^3$, not just at the origin. We model all three (x, y, z) dimensions as i.i.d. under this prior.

Although the curve tree curves are continuous, in practice we perform inference on a discrete subset of points at indices $X = \{(c_1, t_1), \ldots, (c_M, t_M)\}$. Let $z_{ij} = f(c_j, t_j, \tau_i)$ be the jth 3D point in the curve tree at time τ_i, and let the vector $\mathbf{z}_i = (z_{i1}^\top, \ldots, z_{iM}^\top)^\top$ represent the discretely sampled curve tree at that time. Let the vector $\mathbf{Z} = \{\mathbf{z}_1, \ldots, \mathbf{z}_T\}$ represent the set of curve trees over all time indices.

Our choice of k_τ makes our model Markovian in the temporal dimension, so we can decompose the joint prior into

$$p(\boldsymbol{Z}) = p(\boldsymbol{z}_1) \prod_{i=2}^{T} p(\boldsymbol{z}_i | \boldsymbol{z}_{i-1}). \tag{10}$$

Since all factors are linear Gaussian, this represents a linear dynamical system (LDS),

$$\boldsymbol{z}_i = F_i \boldsymbol{z}_{i-1} + \epsilon_i, \tag{11}$$

with transition matrix F_i and system noise $\epsilon_i \sim \mathcal{N}(0, Q_i)$ defined as

$$F_i = \ddot{K}_{*i}^\top \ddot{K}_i^{-1}, \tag{12}$$

$$Q_i = \ddot{K}_i - \ddot{K}_{*i}^\top \ddot{K}_i^{-1} \ddot{K}_{*i}. \tag{13}$$

Here, $\ddot{K}$ denotes the Kronecker product $K \odot I_3$, and

$$(K_i)_{jk} = k(c_j, t_j, \tau_i, c_k, t_k, \tau_i), \tag{14}$$

$$(K_{*i})_{jk} = k(c_j, t_j, \tau_{i-1}, c_k, t_k, \tau_i). \tag{15}$$

The Kronecker product lifts the covariance matrix from modeling one output dimension to modeling three i.i.d. dimensions.

We train the prior using maximum marginal likelihood [24], using a gradient-free local optimizer (MATLAB's `patternsearch` function) and multiple initializations to avoid local maxima. (See Supplementary Material for trained values.)

5.2   Likelihood

The likelihood function projects the plant's 3D shape into each view, rasterizes it into a binary foreground/background image, and evaluates each pixel against the input image. We trained a random forest classifier to identify foreground (i.e., stem) pixels using a single training image [15]. The classifier generates a map D whose i^{th} pixel has value $d_i \in [0, 255]$ representing the posterior probability of the class (foreground/background) given the evidence. However, using posterior values in a likelihood function would introduce bias in favor of the more common class (i.e., background), so we next re-calibrate the classifier outputs to represent *likelihood* values, i.e., the probability of the *evidence*, given the *class*.

Let $\gamma_i^* \in \{0, 1\}$ be value of the ith binary pixel in the training foreground mask. We construct a histogram over the set $\{d_i | \gamma_i^* = 1\}$ that represents the likelihood of classifier output given a foreground label, $p(d_i | \mathbf{fg})$. We construct a background likelihood $p(d_i | \mathbf{bg})$ similarly. To avoid overfitting, we smooth the histograms with a Gaussian filter with $\sigma_{\text{lik}} = 1$. The likelihood of the image at time τ is then

$$p(D_\tau | \boldsymbol{z}_\tau) = \prod_i p(d_i | \mathbf{fg})^{\gamma_{\tau i}} p(d_i | \mathbf{bg})^{1 - \gamma_{\tau i}}. \tag{16}$$

where $\gamma_{\tau i}$ is the value of the ith binary pixel in the rasterization of z_τ into view τ. The supplementary materials describe an efficient method evaluating this likelihood. The full likelihood over all images $D = \{D_1, \ldots, D_T\}$ is the product of per-view likelihoods, $p(D|Z) = \prod_{\tau=1}^{M} p(D_\tau|z_\tau)$.

6 Inference

We begin by describing inference of a curve tree's 3D shape when its topological structure (i.e., the number of curves, point indices, and branch function) is known. Later, we present methods for bootstrapping and refining the topology using Bayesian model selection. The goal is to estimate a posterior distribution over points in the curve tree over all time frames. Closed-form inference is not possible because the likelihood function is non-convex and highly multimodal. However, the posterior distribution is likely to be highly peaked due to strong evidence from multiple views, making it well modeled by a multivariate Gaussian distribution. Thus, we seek a Gaussian approximation of the true posterior that minimizes their Kullback-Leibler divergence.

6.1   Estimating 3D Structure Given Topology

Our inference approach assumes 3D points are initially observed by a single reference image, making them well-localized in two dimensions, but their depth is uncertain; Sects. 6.2 and 6.3 describe methods for achieving such initializations. Under this assumption, inference is akin to an epipolar search in several views. Conditioned on the reference view, a point's probability density is concentrated along a 3D ridge near the reference image's backprojection line. This ridge's width is a function of camera calibration error and scene motion, and its length is loosely constrained by the prior to be near the center of the scene. We call the projection of this ridge the *epipolar region* of a point in a particular view. The prior defines strong spatiotemporal correlations between points, so ambiguous evidence in a particular image can be resolved by consulting nearby points in space and time that are unambiguous. This contextual information can shrink the ambiguous point's epipolar region, allowing some local optima to be ruled out, and making the point suitable for informing other ambiguous points.

We implement this logic using the expectation propagation algorithm (EP) where a Gaussian approximation of the posterior is iteratively updated, starting as noninformative and becoming more peaked as more evidence is considered [21]. When the likelihood in an epipolar region has multiple modes, it is approximated by a Gaussian with high variance so all modes are well supported. This effectively defers a decision on the point's location until later iterations when local context is more informative.

Let $f(\theta)$ be an arbitrary distribution and $q(\theta)$ be a Gaussian approximation. EP seeks parameters of q that minimize the Kullback-Leibler divergence:

$$KL(f\|q) = \int f(\theta) \log \frac{f(\theta)}{q(\theta)} d\theta. \tag{17}$$

Our posterior distribution has the form

$$p(\boldsymbol{Z}|D) \propto p(\boldsymbol{Z}) \prod_{i=1}^{n} L_i(\boldsymbol{Z}), \tag{18}$$

where $p(\boldsymbol{Z})$ is the temporal BGP prior in Eq. (10) and $L_i(\boldsymbol{Z}) = p(D_i|\boldsymbol{z}_i)$ are the single-view likelihood terms from Eq. (16). We seek a multivariate Gaussian approximation $q(\boldsymbol{Z}) \propto p(\boldsymbol{Z}) \prod_{i=1}^{T} \hat{L}_i(\boldsymbol{Z})$, where $\hat{L}_i(\boldsymbol{Z})$ are multivariate Gaussian approximations of $L_i(\boldsymbol{Z})$ with diagonal covariance.

Standard expectation propagation involves estimating the first two moments of the joint posterior at each iteration. In a curve-tree sequence with M points and T time frames, this would involve an intractable integral in $3TM$ dimensions. Instead, we adopt a variation of EP proposed by Gelman et al., where conditionally independent likelihood terms are updated independently in parallel in each iteration, rather than updating the entire joint posterior [11]. If we assume the likelihood of each point is independent conditioned on the 3D model, Gelman's method reduces moment-estimation to TM integrals in three dimensions. This independence assumption holds if we ignore self-occlusions which are minimal and take the limit as polyline point density approaches infinity.

Our EP implementation is shown in Algorithm 1. Here $q_{ij}(z_{ij})$ is the single-point marginal of the approximate Gaussian posterior distribution, $q(\boldsymbol{z}_i)$. We define the single-point likelihood $L_{ij}(z_{ij})$ as the likelihood of a sphere centered at z_{ij} with diameter 1 mm, evaluated under the single-view likelihood in Eq. (16). This single-point, single-view likelihood can be computed efficiently using a lookup table (see supplement). We approximate the moments of the three-dimensional marginal posterior of a point using importance sampling (again, see supplement). Gelman's algorithm requires a global update after each pass, causing the joint posterior to reflect the updated likelihood approximations. This would take $O(M^3T^3)$ time if implemented naïvely; instead, we exploit our model's LDS structure from Eq. (11) to implement the global update with a Kalman filter and smoother in $O(M^3T)$ time.

6.2   Bootstrapping

We bootstrap the inference process by using 2D image processing and backprojection to estimate an initial 3D tree whose depth is uncertain. We first construct a binary image of likely foreground pixels in the first view consisting of pixels whose foreground likelihoods are higher than their background likelihoods. The binary map is further refined by taking the median image over all views and removing any pixel whose intensity is not significantly different from the median pixel–i.e., basic background subtraction. Next, we eliminate all but the largest connected component from the foreground image. The result is a set of likely stem pixels with relatively few false positives.

We construct a 2D tree from this binary image by taking its morphological skeleton, constructing an adjacency graph of skeleton pixels, and extracting the

---

Algorithm 1. Our proposed variant of expectation propagation

---

1. Initialize $\{\hat{L}_{ij}(z_{ij})\}_{i=1}^{T}$ to improper Gaussians for $i \in \{1,\ldots,T\}$ and $j \in \{1,\ldots,|z|\}$.

2. Initialize $\{q_i(z_i)\}_{i=1}^{T}$ to the marginal BGP priors, $\{p(z_i)\}_{i=1}^{T}$.

3. For each $(i,j) \in \{1,\ldots,T\} \times \{1,\ldots,|z|\}$:

    (a) Compute the "cavity" distribution $q_{ij}^{-(i,j)}(z_{ij}) = q_{ij}(z_{ij})/\hat{L}_{ij}(z_{ij})$.

    (b) Compute the "tilted" distribution $q_{ij}^{\backslash(i,j)}(z_{ij}) = q_{ij}^{-(i,j)}(z_{ij})L_{ij}(z_{ij})$.

    (c) Update $\hat{L}_{ij}(z_{ij})$ so $q_{ij}^{-(i,j)}(z_{ij})\hat{L}_{ij}(z_{ij})$ approximates $q_{ij}^{\backslash(i,j)}(z_{ij})$:

    i. Construct a 3×3 Gaussian $q_{ij}(z_{ij})$ using the first two moments of $q_{ij}^{\backslash(i,j)}(z_{ij})$.

    ii. Set $\hat{L}_{ij}(z_{ij}) = q_{ij}(z_{ij})/q_{ij}^{-(i,j)}(z_{ij})$.

4. Use Kalman filter and smoother to re-compute the per-view marginal posteriors $\{q_1,\ldots,q_M\}$ using the new likelihood approximations $\hat{L}_{ij}$.

5. Repeat step 3 until convergence.

---

graph's Euclidean minimum spanning tree. Each point in the 2D tree is back-projected to a depth closest to the prior mean (i.e., the origin). Chains of points with degree two or less are grouped into curves; points with higher degree become branch points. Each curve's points are assigned spatial indices according to their arc-length parameterization in 3D. In this way, we derive the topological structure of a 3D curve tree: the number of curves N, curve lengths L_i, point indices X, and the branch function $\rho(c,t)$. This bootstrapping heuristic can miss some curves and mis-estimate branch points, but these errors may be fixed during the topology refinement process described in the next section.

We construct an initial likelihood approximation for the first view from the 2D tree points by

$$\hat{L}_{1j}(z_{1j}) = \mathcal{N}(z_{1j}, \Lambda_{1j}^{-1}) \text{ where} \tag{19}$$

$$\Lambda_{1j} = H'(I_2/\sigma_L^2)H \tag{20}$$

Here, z_{1j} is the jth backprojected 3D point, H is the Jacobian of the perspective projection of z_{1j} into the first view, and σ_L^2 represents the uncertainty of the detected points. We use $\sigma^2 = 1$ pixel^2, which represents error due to pixel quantization and small localization errors. The precision matrix Λ is rank deficient, reflecting a lack of evidence for the point's depth.

6.3   Topology Refinement Using Bayesian Model Selection

Trees with differing number of curves will have different dimensionality, so their posterior distributions are not comparable. This is a model selection problem, and the Bayesian solution is to integrate out the continuous parameters (i.e., the curve points) and compare the models' marginal likelihoods. The marginal likelihood does not over-fit and it includes a natural penalty for model complexity, making it an ideal model selection criterion. Computing it involves a

---

Algorithm 2. 3D Tree Structure Estimation

1. Initialize each $\hat{L}_i(z_i), q_i(z_i)$ to degenerate Gaussians for $i \in \{1, \ldots, T\}$.
2. Bootstrap: estimate $\hat{L}_1(z_1), q_1(z_1)$ using the procedure in Sect. 6.2.
3. Update $\{q_2(z_2), \ldots, q_T(z_T)\}$ with a Kalman filter pass.
4. Run three iterations of EP, keeping q_1 and $\hat{L}_1$ fixed on first pass.
5. Run pruning.
6. For each time index $i \in \{5, 9, 13, \ldots, T\}$:
   (a) Run birthing with reference image i.
   (b) Run three iterations of EP.
   (c) Run pruning.

---

high-dimensional integral that is intractable, but we estimate it using the Gaussian approximation we constructed during expectation propagation.

The marginal likelihood is $p(D|\mathcal{M})$, where $\mathcal{M}$ represents curve tree's topological parameters, i.e., the number of curves N, the point indices X, and the branch function $\rho(c, t)$. In what follows, we omit the dependence on $\mathcal{M}$.

Using the chain rule we rewrite the marginal likelihood as

$$p(\boldsymbol{D}) = p(D_1) \prod_{t=2}^{T} p(D_t|D_{1:i-1}). \tag{21}$$

Under Bayes' rule (after rearranging),

$$p(D_i|D_{1:i-1}) = p(D_i|\boldsymbol{z}_i) \left(p(\boldsymbol{z}_i|D_{1:i-1}) / p(\boldsymbol{z}_i|D_{1:i}) \right). \tag{22}$$

The first term in (22) is the true single-view likelihood, $L_i(\boldsymbol{z}_i)$. The second term is a ratio of the partial posteriors before and after considering data D_i. Gaussian approximations of these distributions are computed during Kalman filtering before and after the update step, respectively. In theory, any value of $\boldsymbol{z}_i$ can be used to evaluate Eq. (22), but our approximations are most accurate near the true posterior mode, so we use the current estimate of the mean of the approximate Gaussian posterior, $q(\boldsymbol{Z})$.

The space of tree topologies can be explored by proposing incremental changes to the current curve tree topology and keeping the model with the highest marginal likelihood. We propose two such methods: pruning and birthing.

Pruning. In the pruning step, a curve is deleted if doing so improves the marginal likelihood. Each curve is considered for pruning in random order. Pruning a parent curve causes its descendant subtrees to become independent trees. Pruning a Y-junction results in two curves attached end-to-end.

Birthing. The birthing step mimics bootstrapping, but when constructing the binary mask, we omit foreground pixels if they coincide with the projection of existing structure. The remaining pixels are skeletonized, backprojected, and converted to 3D curve trees as in bootstrapping, and the root of each new tree is attached to the nearest point on existing structure. Likelihood approximations are created for the new points in the reference view using Eq. (19). We propagate this likelihood to the other views by a pass of Kalman filtering and smoothing. A subsequent pruning step removes spurious structure added during birthing.

Algorithm 2 shows how bootstrapping, geometry estimation, and topology refinement are applied in an end-to-end system. In principle, expectation propagation should be run after each model modification before evaluating the marginal likelihood. In practice, we omit EP after the pruning step, as we observed that it caused negligible change to the model and the approximated marginal likelihood.

7 Experiments and Results

We applied our approach to recover 3D structure of plants from images. Our dataset consists of image sequences of twelve *Arabidopsis* plants as described in Sect. 5. One specimen was held out for training, the rest were used for testing. Ground truth was manually collected on every fourth image by tracing each stem with a 2D poly-Bézier curve. Curve identities were kept consistent across views, and parent/child relationships between curves were noted. Each poly-Bézier curve was sampled at one pixel intervals and each point in each image was backprojected to a depth that minimized the sum of squared distances between its 2D projection and the nearest ground truth curve point in each image. This results in a sequence of five 3D curve trees per specimen that project exactly to their 2D counterparts.

We evaluate using four measures. We compute a one-to-one matching between points with distance at most 1 cm (see supplement). We report accuracy as the RMS error of matching points and we measure completeness and spurious structure using an intersection-over-union score that compares the number of

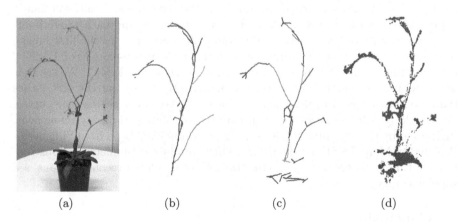

(a)   (b)   (c)   (d)

Fig. 3. Results of 3D reconstruction. *(a)* One of 18 input images. *(b)* Semi-automatic reconstruction result. Color indicates distinct parts. *(c)* Fully-automatic reconstruction result. *(d)* Voxel volume produced by [30]. (Color figure online)

matched points against the total number of points in both models. We evaluate tree topology using the DIADEM metric with a threshold of 1 cm in the x, y, and z directions [12]. However, the DIADEM metric does not distinguish "parts," so it cannot distinguish between Y- and T-junctions, and it does not recognize part-level structural errors like over-segmentations of curves or misclassified T-junctions. Further, it has no concept of time, so identity switches are not penalized.

To address these issues, we propose a *tree-structure consistency* (TSC) score that measures structural consistency in three ways: (a) the geometric consistency of matching curves, (b) matching consistency between child and parent curves, and (c) consistency of curve identity between adjacent time frames. Evaluation begins by finding a correspondence between parts that maximizes their number of matching points. Then consistency is measured with respect to the corresponding parts. The TSC score measures the number of logical errors in the structure, normalized to the range $[0,1]$, where 1 represents "no errors." For details, see the supplementary material.

Table 1. Structure estimation performance of semi- and fully-automatic reconstruction, for nine- and 18-image datatasets.

	Acc	IoU	TSC	DIADEM [12]
Semi (9)	4.7 ± 1.4	0.63 ± 0.14	0.49 ± 0.09	0.81 ± 0.09
Semi (18)	3.7 ± 1.0	0.70 ± 0.08	0.56 ± 0.06	0.84 ± 0.06
Auto (9)	7.1 ± 3.1	0.50 ± 0.11	0.41 ± 0.07	0.41 ± 0.18
Auto (18)	5.9 ± 2.2	0.59 ± 0.11	0.43 ± 0.08	0.44 ± 0.18

We ran our algorithm twice, once using all 18 images, and once using only the first nine. We also compared two variants of bootstrapping: a fully-automatic approach as described in Sect. 6.2, and a semi-automatic approach where bootstrapping is replaced with a manually traced 2D curve tree in the first image. Inference took an average of 33 min using Matlab code on a 16-core Xeon E5-2650 CPU running at 2.6 GHz. Results for all runs are shown in Table 1. We see that semiautomatic reconstruction performs significantly better on the TSC score than the fully automatic one, primarily due to the latter oversegmenting curves. This could be addressed with a "join curves" step during topology refinement. Figure 3 provides a visual comparison against Tabb's Shape-from-Silhouette-Probability-Maps (SfSPM) algorithm, which produces volumetric reconstructions of thin structure [30]. (For visualizations of all eleven reconstructions, see supplementary material.)

8   Conclusion

We have demonstrated a novel probabilistic model for branching multidimensional structure, and a Bayesian method for 3D reconstruction of moving trees from a single moving camera. Our approach obtains good results with limited training data, showing that it generalizes well and avoids overfitting. Our model selection scheme naturally penalizes complexity with no additional tunable parameters. By taking advantage of the model structure, our expectation propagation scheme locates strong modes reasonably efficiently and should outperform black-box Bayesian inference like hybrid Monte Carlo. Our proposed BGP covariance function is a general-purpose kernel and can be applied in kernel methods such as SVM, PCA, GP classification, and kernel density estimation. It is also straightforward to extend branching curves to branching surfaces; this could be used to model deformable leaves attached to the curve tree. We also contributed a new score measuring logical consistency of multi-part branching structure. Our dataset and evaluation code may be downloaded from ivilab.org.

Acknowledgments. We would like to thank Dr. Amy Tabb for sharing her Shape from Silhouette Probability Maps code. This material is based upon work supported by the National Science Foundation under Award Numbers DBI-0735191 and DBI-1265383 and the Department of Educations GAANN Fellowship through the University of Arizona's Computer Science Department.

References

1. The Vascular Modeling Toolkit. http://www.vmtk.org. Accessed 5 Mar 2015
2. Bas, E., Erdogmus, D.: Principal curves as skeletons of tubular objects. Neuroinformatics **9**(2), 181–191 (2011)
3. Chen, X., Neubert, B., Xu, Y.Q., Deussen, O., Kang, S.B.: Sketch-based tree modeling using Markov random field. In: ACM SIGGRAPH Asia 2008 Papers, pp. 109:1–109:9. ACM, New York (2008)
4. Chothani, P., Mehta, V., Stepanyants, A.: Automated tracing of neurites from light microscopy stacks of images. Neuroinformatics **9**(2–3), 263–278 (2011)
5. Clark, R.T., MacCurdy, R.B., Jung, J.K., Shaff, J.E., McCouch, S.R., Aneshansley, D.J., Kochian, L.V.: Three-dimensional root phenotyping with a novel imaging and software platform. Plant Physiol. **156**(2), 455–465 (2011)
6. Cubelos, B., Sebastián-Serrano, A., Beccari, L., Calcagnotto, M.E., Cisneros, E., Kim, S., Dopazo, A., Alvarez-Dolado, M., Redondo, J.M., Bovolenta, P., Walsh, C.A., Nieto, M.: Cux1 and Cux2 regulate dendritic branching, spine morphology, and synapses of the upper layer neurons of the cortex. Neuron **66**(4), 523–535 (2010)
7. Cuntz, H., Forstner, F., Borst, A., Häusser, M.: One rule to grow them all: a general theory of neuronal branching and its practical application. PLoS Comput. Biol. **6**(8), 1–14 (2010)
8. Den Buijs, O.J., Bajzer, Z., Ritman, L.E.: Branching morphology of the rat hepatic portal vein tree: a micro-CT study. Ann. Biomed. Eng. **34**(9), 1420–1428 (2006)
9. Diener, J., Reveret, L., Fiume, E.: Hierarchical retargetting of 2D motion fields to the animation of 3D plant models. In: ACM SIGGRAPH/Eurographics Symposium on Computer Animation, SCA 2006, Vienna, Austria (2006)
10. Evers, J.B., van der Krol, A.R., Vos, J., Struik, P.C.: Understanding shoot branching by modelling form and function. Trends Plant Sci. **16**(9), 464–467 (2011)

11. Gelman, A., Vehtari, A., Jylänki, P., Robert, C., Chopin, N., Cunningham, J.P.: Expectation propagation as a way of life, December 2014. arXiv.org
12. Gillette, T.A., Brown, K.M., Ascoli, G.A.: The DIADEM metric: comparing multiple reconstructions of the same neuron. Neuroinformatics 9(2–3), 233–245 (2011)
13. Glowacki, P., Pinheiro, M.A., Türetken, E., Sznitman, R., Lebrecht, D., Kybic, J., Holtmaat, A., Fua, P.: Reconstructing evolving tree structures in time lapse sequences. In: 2014 IEEE Conference on Computer Vision and Pattern Recognition (CVPR), pp. 3035–3042. IEEE Computer Society (2014)
14. Gu, L., Cheng, L.: Learning to boost filamentary structure segmentation. In: 2015 IEEE International Conference on Computer Vision (ICCV), pp. 639–647. IEEE (2015)
15. Hall, M., Frank, E., Holmes, G., Pfahringer, B., Reutemann, P., Witten, I.H.: The WEKA data mining software: an update. ACM SIGKDD Explor. Newsl. 11(1), 10–18 (2009)
16. Kahl, F., August, J.: Multiview reconstruction of space curves. In: 2003 IEEE International Conference on Computer Vision (ICCV), pp. 1017–1024 (2003)
17. Le Bot, J., Serra, V., Fabre, J., Draye, X., Adamowicz, S., Pagès, L.: DART: a software to analyse root system architecture and development from captured images. Plant Soil 326(1–2), 261–273 (2009)
18. Li, C., Deussen, O., Song, Y.Z., Willis, P., Hall, P.: Modeling and generating moving trees from video. In: Proceedings of the 2011 SIGGRAPH Asia Conference, pp. 127:1–127:12. ACM, New York (2011)
19. Lopez, L.D., Ding, Y., Yu, J.: Modeling complex unfoliaged trees from a sparse set of images. Comput. Graph. Forum 29, 2075–2082 (2010)
20. Marin, D., Boykov, Y., Zhong, Y.: Thin structure estimation with curvature regularization, June 2015. arXiv.org
21. Minka, T.P.: Expectation propagation for approximate Bayesian inference, January 2013. arXiv.org
22. Narro, M.L., Yang, F., Kraft, R., Wenk, C., Efrat, A., Restifo, L.L.: NeuronMetrics: software for semi-automated processing of cultured neuron images. Brain Res. 1138, 57–75 (2007)
23. Nordsletten, D.A., Blackett, S., Bentley, M.D., Ritman, E.L., Smith, N.P.: Structural morphology of renal vasculature. Am. J. Physiol. Heart Circ. Physiol. 291(1), H296–H309 (2006)
24. Rasmussen, C., Williams, C.: Gaussian Processes for Machine Learning. MIT Press, Cambridge (2006)
25. Serradell, E., Glowacki, P., Kybic, J., Moreno-Noguer, F., Fua, P.: Robust nonrigid registration of 2D and 3D graphs. In: 2012 IEEE Conference on Computer Vision and Pattern Recognition (CVPR), pp. 996–1003 (2012)
26. Shlyakhter, I., Rozenoer, M., Dorsey, J., Teller, S.: Reconstructing 3D tree models from instrumented photographs. IEEE Comput. Graph. Appl. 21(1), 53–61 (2001)
27. Song, M., Huber, D.: Automatic recovery of networks of thin structures. In: 2015 International Conference on 3D Vision (3DV), pp. 37–45. IEEE (2015)
28. Strasser, G.A., Kaminker, J.S., Tessier-Lavigne, M.: Microarray analysis of retinal endothelial tip cells identifies CXCR4 as a mediator of tip cell morphology and branching. Blood 115(24), 5102–5110 (2010)
29. Sugiyama, M., Hachiya, H., Towell, C., Vijayakumar, S.: Geodesic Gaussian kernels for value function approximation. Auton. Rob. 25(3), 287–304 (2008)

30. Tabb, A.: Shape from silhouette probability maps: reconstruction of thin objects in the presence of silhouette extraction and calibration error. In: 2013 IEEE Conference on Computer Vision and Pattern Recognition (CVPR), pp. 161–168. IEEE (2013)
31. Talton, J.O., Lou, Y., Lesser, S., Duke, J., Mech, R., Koltun, V.: Metropolis procedural modeling. ACM Trans. Graph. **30**(2), 11:1–11:14 (2011)
32. Tan, P., Fang, T., Xiao, J., Zhao, P., Quan, L.: Single image tree modeling. ACM Trans. Graph. **27**(5), 108:1–108:7 (2008)
33. Tan, P., Zeng, G., Wang, J., Kang, S.B., Quan, L.: Image-based tree modeling. ACM Trans. Graph. **26**(99), 87 (2007)
34. Trachsel, S., Kaeppler, S.M., Brown, K.M., Lynch, J.P.: Shovelomics: high throughput phenotyping of maize (Zea mays L.) root architecture in the field. Plant Soil **341**(1–2), 75–87 (2011)
35. Tu, Z., Zhu, S.C.: Parsing images into regions, curves, and curve groups. Int. J. Comput. Vis. **69**(2), 223–249 (2006)
36. Türetken, E., Benmansour, F., Andres, B., Pfister, H., Fua, P.: Reconstructing loopy curvilinear structures using integer programming. In: 2013 IEEE Conference on Computer Vision and Pattern Recognition (CVPR), pp. 1822–1829. IEEE Computer Society, June 2013
37. Türetken, E., Benmansour, F., Fua, P.: Automated reconstruction of tree structures using path classifiers and mixed integer programming. In: 2012 IEEE Conference on Computer Vision and Pattern Recognition (CVPR), pp. 566–573. IEEE (2012)
38. Türetken, E., González, G., Blum, C., Fua, P.: Automated reconstruction of dendritic and axonal trees by global optimization with geometric priors. Neuroinformatics **9**(2–3), 279–302 (2011)
39. Vicente, S., Kolmogorov, V., Rother, C.: Graph cut based image segmentation with connectivity priors. In: 2008 IEEE Conference on Computer Vision and Pattern Recognition (CVPR), pp. 1–8, June 2008
40. Wang, Y., Narayanaswamy, A., Tsai, C.L., Roysam, B.: A broadly applicable 3-D neuron tracing method based on open-curve snake. Neuroinformatics **9**(2–3), 193–217 (2011)
41. Zhao, T., Xie, J., Amat, F., Clack, N., Ahammad, P., Peng, H., Long, F., Myers, E.: Automated reconstruction of neuronal morphology based on local geometrical and global structural models. Neuroinformatics **9**(2–3), 247–261 (2011)
42. Zhu, J., Hoi, S.C., Lyu, M.R.: Nonrigid shape recovery by Gaussian process regression. In: 2009 IEEE Conference on Computer Vision and Pattern Recognition (CVPR), pp. 1319–1326 (2009)
43. Zhu, T., Fang, S., Li, Z., Liu, Y., Liao, H., Yan, X.: Quantitative analysis of 3-dimensional root architecture based on image reconstruction and its application to research on phosphorus uptake in soybean. Chin. Sci. Bull. **51**(19), 2351–2361 (2006)

Tracking Completion

Yao Sui[1]([✉]), Guanghui Wang[1,4], Yafei Tang[2], and Li Zhang[3]

[1] Department of EECS, University of Kansas, Lawrence, KS 66045, USA
suiyao@gmail.com, ghwang@ku.edu
[2] China Unicom Research Institute, Beijing 100032, China
tangyf24@chinaunicom.cn
[3] Department of EE, Tsinghua University, Beijing 100084, China
chinazhangli@tsinghua.edu.cn
[4] National Laboratory of Pattern Recognition,
Institute of Automation, CAS, Beijing, China

Abstract. A fundamental component of modern trackers is an online learned tracking model, which is typically modeled either globally or locally. The two kinds of models perform differently in terms of effectiveness and robustness under different challenging situations. This work exploits the advantages of both models. A subspace model, from a global perspective, is learned from previously obtained targets via rank-minimization to address the tracking, and a pixel-level local observation is leveraged simultaneously, from a local point of view, to augment the subspace model. A matrix completion method is employed to integrate the two models. Unlike previous tracking methods, which locate the target among all fully observed target candidates, the proposed approach first estimates an expected target via the matrix completion through partially observed target candidates, and then, identifies the target according to the estimation accuracy with respect to the target candidates. Specifically, the tracking is formulated as a problem of target appearance estimation. Extensive experiments on various challenging video sequences verify the effectiveness of the proposed approach and demonstrate that the proposed tracker outperforms other popular state-of-the-art trackers.

Keywords: Matrix completion · Object tracking · Subspace model · Local observation · Appearance estimation

1 Introduction

Visual tracking is an important topic in computer vision for its various applications, such as video analysis, robotics, and visual surveillance. In general, tracking models can be mainly classified into two categories: global and local. Global model exploits the overall information that varies in the entire target region. Local model treats the target as a series of small image patches to focus on the changes in each small region. It has been demonstrated that the global model is robust to some holistic appearance changes, like illumination variations and

© Springer International Publishing AG 2016
B. Leibe et al. (Eds.): ECCV 2016, Part VIII, LNCS 9912, pp. 194–209, 2016.
DOI: 10.1007/978-3-319-46484-8_12

pose changes [1–4]. The local model, on the other hand, is intrinsically effective to the challenges, such as partial occlusions and local deformations [5–8]. This is because only some of the local patches are influenced by the distractive objects (noise contaminated regions), while the rest are considered to be noise-free. To effectively deal with various appearance changes, a robust tracker is desired to be able to exploit the advantages of both global and local tracking models.

In this work, we propose to leverage the effectiveness of the global method in capturing the overall information, and augment it with a local model to promote the accuracy and robustness of the tracker. The proposed tracking model integrates both the global and the local methods. Two efficient while effective methods, *i.e.*, subspace learning and pixel-level local observations, are designed, and a matrix completion approach [9] is employed to integrate the two models. The fundamental idea of our approach is to estimate the appearance of the target over the global subspace model and a number of local observations. As a result, the target is accurately located by means of the similarity between the estimation and the target candidates (regions of interest in the frame). Substantially different from previous tracking methods, which test each target candidate and then determine the best one as the target, the proposed approach works in a reverse way, *i.e.*, predicts the expected target and then verifies it against each target candidate. To this end, the following two issues need to be addressed.

1.1   Subspace Method

Subspace method is a classical algorithm in visual tracking [1,10–12]. Under this paradigm, the temporally obtained targets are assumed to reside in a low-dimensional subspace. For this reason, the current target can be accurately represented by the subspace learned from the previously obtained targets. It has been demonstrated that subspace method is effective to some challenges, such as pose changes and illumination variations [13,14]. However, this method is unstable in the presence of partial occlusions. The underlying assumption of subspace method, from a stochastic perspective, is that the representation errors obey the independent and identically distributed (*i.i.d.*) Gaussian with small variances. In the case of partial occlusion, however, the representation errors actually follow the *i.i.d.* Laplace or other heavy tailed distributions, because these errors may be extremely large but sparse. Consequently, a sparse (Laplace prior) additive error term is often used to compensate the instability of subspace model [15–17].

Inspired by the previous success, we exploit the subspace structure among the previously obtained targets by using a *rank*-minimization method, instead of computing orthogonal basis vectors as used in previous methods. We stack these targets into column vectors respectively and then combine these columns into a sample matrix. Since these targets are assumed to reside in a low-dimensional subspace, this sample matrix tends to be of low-rank. Thus, we minimize the rank of this sample matrix to exploit the subspace structure. Although several tracking methods also involve low-rank matrix estimation [17,18], their subspace assumptions are quite different from ours. Zhang *et al.* [17] assume that the target candidates in each frame reside in a low-dimensional subspace and construct the subspace in the representation (transform) domain. Sui *et al.* [18] consider the obtained targets and the surrounding background regions reside in a mixture of several subspaces, and exploit these subspaces using a low-rank graph.

1.2 Integration with Local Method

Local tracking model is intrinsically robust to partial occlusions. Thus, it is reasonable to combine the subspace based tracking model with a local method to compensate the sensitivity of the subspace method in the case of occlusions. Previous local methods often transform the target region into a series of local image patches of small sizes with or without overlap. Different from those, our approach forces the local patches to shrink to the size of 1×1, leading to the *local observations*, *i.e.*, directly use a number of pixels[1]. Note that the goals of our approach and previous local methods are essentially the same: intending to sufficiently leverage the noise-free pixels (patches) and avoid the corrupted pixels (patches). In contrast to patch based methods, our approach considers the corrupted pixels as the unobserved values and intends to estimate them over the exploited target subspace. Intuitively, the pixel-level method may lose the relationship among the neighboring pixels, *i.e.*, correlations, which is well exploited in the patch-level strategy. Compared to the patches, however, the observed pixels are more flexible and much easier to be manipulated.

Matrix completion approach [9], by its nature, can be used to integrate the global target subspace model and the local observation method. The subspace model provides a prerequisite to ensure the success of the matrix completion, while the local observation method leads to a number of observed pixels to promote the accuracy of the matrix completion in the estimation of the unobserved (missing) pixels. In return, the matrix completion also implicitly maintains the subspace structure during the estimation. As demonstrated in our experiments, the estimation accuracy with respect to the target candidates, under the subspace assumption, is consistent with the similarity to the previously obtained targets, which is responsible to the target localization.

1.3   Contributions

The subspace model, from a global perspective, is learned via *rank*-minimization to address tracking, and the local observation approach, from a local point of view, is simultaneously leveraged to augment the subspace. The matrix completion is employed to integrate the two methods.

- Unlike previous methods, which emphasize on analyzing all fully observed target candidates for target localization, the proposed approach leverages each partially observed target candidate to estimate the target with the learned subspace model via the matrix completion.

---

[1] We only use *a number of* pixels from the target region; otherwise, it is, to some extent, equivalent to global method.

– The target is located according to the estimation accuracy of the matrix completion. It is shown that, under the subspace constraint, the estimation accuracy with respect to the target candidates is consistent with the similarity to the previously obtained targets. As a result, the proposed tracker performs much better than its counterparts.

2 Related Work on Tracking

Subspace learning is a conventional but effective method in visual tracking. Ross et al. [1] utilized incremental subspace learning method to represent the target and locate the target in terms of representation accuracy. Wang and Lu [11] proposed to use 2D principal component analysis method to construct a target subspace in original image domain. Sui et al. [12] proposed a group sparse subspace learning method to alleviate the influence of the distractive objects. Wang and Lu [19] employed a segmentation-like method to improve the robustness of subspace learning against occlusions. Zhang et al. [17] developed a low-rank and sparse representation to exploit the subspace structure among the candidates. Wang et al. [15] assumed the targets follow a Gaussian distribution (subspace prior) and the occlusions followed a Laplace distribution (sparsity prior).

There are extensive literatures on local tracking. Adam et al. [5] represented the target as histograms over a series local image patches. Liu et al. [6] developed a local sparse representation to describe the target. Jia et al. [7] designed an assignment pooling feature based on local sparse representation to improve the target description. Zhong et al. [20] utilized the local method to develop a collaborative target model. Kalal et al. [21] leveraged a local method to achieve a discriminative learning method for tracking. Sui and Zhang [22] constructed a locally low-rank and sparse representation to address tracking.

Many impressive tracking results are also achieved by various approaches beyond subspace and local methods. Hare et al. [4] employed the structured output support vector machine to address tracking. Gao et al. [23] analyzed the likelihood of a candidate to be the target by using Gaussian process regression. Henriques et al. [24] proposed a robust tracker via correlation filters from kernelized ridge regression point of view, achieving impressive performance.

3 *Rank*-Minimization and Matrix Completion

Recently, there has been a significant interest in $rank$-minimization. Some typical applications include matrix completion [9], robust principal component analysis [25], and low-rank representation [26]. $rank$-minimization focuses on the problem

$$\min_{\mathbf{X}} rank\left(\mathbf{X}\right), s.t. \ \mathbf{Y} = f\left(\mathbf{X}\right), \tag{1}$$

where $\mathbf{Y}$ denotes the observation matrix, $f\left(\mathbf{X}\right)$ is a restrict function with respect to the variable $\mathbf{X}$, and the $rank\left(\mathbf{X}\right)$ returns the rank of the matrix $\mathbf{X}$. The above minimization has been demonstrated to be a NP-hard problem. In practical applications, the convex conjugate $\|\cdot\|_*$, named as the *trace*-norm, is often used to approximate the $rank\,(\cdot)$ function. The *trace*-norm is defined as a sum of the singular values of the input matrix. Note that the significance of *rank*-minimization is partially attributed to its close relation to the subspace method. Specifically, Eq. (1) is equivalent to principal component analysis if the restrict function $f\,(\cdot)$ is an identical function, *i.e.*,

$$\min_{\mathbf{X}} rank\,(\mathbf{X})\,, s.t.\,\|\mathbf{Y} - \mathbf{X}\|_F^2 \leq \varepsilon, \tag{2}$$

where $\mathbf{X}$ is the reconstructed version of $\mathbf{Y}$ over the subspace, $\varepsilon > 0$ is a very small number, and $\|\cdot\|_F$ denotes the *Frobenius*-norm. In fact, the matrix variable can be decomposed into $\mathbf{X} = \mathbf{U\Sigma V}^T$ via singular value decomposition (SVD), where $\mathbf{U}$ and $\mathbf{V}$ are orthogonal matrices, and $\mathbf{\Sigma}$ is a diagonal matrix composed by the singular values of $\mathbf{X}$. It is clear that the columns of $\mathbf{U}$ form the basis vectors of the learned subspace, and the columns of $\mathbf{\Sigma V}^T$ are the subspace representations (*i.e.*, the principal components). It is also evident that minimizing the rank of $\mathbf{X}$ is equivalent to making the diagonal elements of $\mathbf{\Sigma}$ as sparse as possible. In practice, $\mathbf{X}$ is reconstructed only from a few columns of $\mathbf{U}$, which correspond to the locations of the non-zeros of $\mathbf{\Sigma}$'s diagonal elements, so that the rank of $\mathbf{X}$ is minimized, leading to a subspace reconstruction. In this case, *rank*-minimization is directly related to the subspace method.

Matrix completion [9] is one of the most popular applications of *rank*-minimization. It can accurately recover a matrix with missing entries, even if some entries are corrupted by noise. It is mathematically formulated as

$$\min_{\mathbf{X}} \|\mathbf{X}\|_* \,, s.t. \mathcal{P}_\Omega\,(\mathbf{X}) = \mathcal{P}_\Omega\,(\mathbf{Y})\,, \tag{3}$$

where $\mathbf{X}$ is the recovered matrix, $\mathbf{Y}$ is the observation matrix, of which only the entries indexed by the set Ω can be observed, and $\mathcal{P}_\Omega\,(\mathbf{X})$ is a projection function such that $[\mathcal{P}_\Omega\,(\mathbf{X})]_{ij} = \mathbf{X}_{ij}$ for $(i,j) \in \Omega$ and zero otherwise. The goal of Eq. (3) is to estimate the missing entries (outside of Ω) in terms of the observed entries (indexed by Ω) of $\mathbf{Y}$. By minimizing Eq. (3), the missing entries can be recovered. The theoretical analysis and recovering conditions can be found in [9] and the references therein. Many algorithms have been developed to solve matrix completion, such as inexact augmented Lagrange multiplier (IALM) [27], and variational Bayesian inference [28,29].

4   The Proposed Approach

4.1   Problem Statement

We describe the target region in each frame by using a motion state variable defined as

$$\mathbf{z} = \{x, y, s\}\,, \tag{4}$$

where x and y denote the 2D position of the target, and s denotes the scale coefficient. According to the motion state variable, we can crop out the corresponding region from the frame image. The cropped region is resized to a predefined value and stacked into a column vector, which is named as the *appearance observation.*

Our goal is to construct an estimator that can reliably predict an expected target appearance in each frame. Specifically, given the appearance observations $\mathbf{y}_1, \mathbf{y}_2, \ldots, \mathbf{y}_{k-1}$ of previously obtained targets in the k-th frame, we can estimate the target appearance in the current frame as

$$\hat{\mathbf{y}}_k = \varphi\left(\mathbf{y}_1, \mathbf{y}_2, \ldots, \mathbf{y}_{k-1}\right) \tag{5}$$

by using the estimator $\varphi\left(\cdot\right)$. To make the estimator as accurate as possible, some prior knowledge about the target appearance, is encouraged. Thus, the estimated appearance of the current target is reformulated as

$$\hat{\mathbf{y}}_k = \varphi\left(\mathbf{y}_1, \mathbf{y}_2, \ldots, \mathbf{y}_{k-1} | \varPhi\right) \tag{6}$$

by incorporating the prior information $\varPhi$. Then, we find a region, of which the corresponding appearance is most similar to $\hat{\mathbf{y}}_k$, as the target region in the current frame. Mathematically, given a set of the appearance observations $\mathcal{C}$ of all target candidates, the current target is located by

$$\mathbf{y}_k = \arg\min_{\mathbf{c}\in\mathcal{C}} \|\hat{\mathbf{y}}_k - \mathbf{c}\|. \tag{7}$$

From a global perspective, the previously obtained targets are considered to reside in a low-dimensional subspace due to their high similarity in appearances. From a local point of view, local observations (partial target information) can be obtained to help the estimator make a more accurate prediction. As a result, the problem is solved by integrating both the global and the local information. We exploit the global correlation to handle the previously obtained targets, and leverage the local information to deal with the target priors.

4.2   Estimator Design

As presented above, the estimator is built on the two kinds of information: the appearance observations of previously obtained targets and the prior knowledge of the target. The designed estimator will be discussed below.

Target summarization. In order to increase the computational efficiency, the tracking model employs a compact form, instead of using all appearance observations, to represent the previously obtained targets. Meanwhile, such a compact representation is also explored to maintain the subspace assumption. To this end, only a limited number of previously obtained targets, which can best describe the appearance changes of all the obtained targets, are employed as the estimation evidence of the estimator. We refer to the target template method [2] to implement the target summarization, which is called *target templates* hereafter.

Target priors. In the proposed model, the prior knowledge is extracted directly from a number of pixels in the target region, because such direct partial observations are the best and the strongest prior information for the target. There is, however, an obvious paradox, *i.e.*, we intend to estimate the target appearance, while the estimator needs to partially observe the target appearance first. For this reason, we observe a number of pixels from each target candidate, and the target candidate is employed to eliminate the paradox. Under the low-dimensional subspace assumption, the target is expected to be estimated accurately by the estimator among all target candidates. The underlying reason is straightforward: since the previously obtained targets span a low-dimensional subspace, while the current target can be well represented by this subspace.

Based on the preceding analysis, the matrix completion approach is a desirable estimator for our tracking model. On one hand, matrix completion is a reliable estimator to predict unobserved entries. On the other hand, it can implicitly maintain the subspace constraint through the *rank*-minimization.

Given an appearance observation, denoted by $\mathbf{c}$, of a target candidate in each frame[2], we use a set Ω to index the observed pixels, and consider the rest as missing values. We first generate an *observed candidate* $\mathbf{c}'$ by setting the pixels of $\mathbf{c}$ outside Ω to zeros and leaving the rest unchanged. Let a matrix $\mathbf{T} = [\mathbf{t}_1, \mathbf{t}_2, \ldots, \mathbf{t}_n]$ denote the n target templates, which are summarized from $\{\mathbf{y}_1, \ldots, \mathbf{y}_{k-1}\}$. We construct a new matrix $\mathbf{Y} = [\mathbf{T}, \mathbf{c}']$ and estimate the pixels outside Ω using matrix completion over $\mathbf{Y}$. For convenience, we use an equivalent form of Eq. (3) to address the matrix completion by introducing a slack variable $\mathbf{E}$.

$$\min_{\mathbf{X}} \|\mathbf{X}\|_*, s.t. \mathbf{Y} = \mathbf{X} + \mathbf{E}, \mathcal{P}_\Omega(\mathbf{E}) = 0. \tag{8}$$

The above minimization problem (8) can be solved by the IALM approach [27]. Let $\mathbf{X}^* = [\mathbf{T}^*, \mathbf{x}]$ denote the solution of Eq. (8), where $\mathbf{x}$ is the estimated candidate over the observed candidate $\mathbf{c}'$.

4.3   Target Localization

Within the Bayesian sequential inference framework [30,31], given all the obtained targets $\mathbf{y}_{1:k-1}$ in the k-th frame, the motion state of the k-th target, denoted by $\mathbf{z}_k$, is predicted by maximizing the posterior

$$p(\mathbf{z}_k|\mathbf{y}_{1:k-1}) = \int p(\mathbf{z}_k|\mathbf{z}_{k-1}) p(\mathbf{z}_{k-1}|\mathbf{y}_{1:k-1}) d\mathbf{z}_{k-1}, \tag{9}$$

where $p(\mathbf{z}_k|\mathbf{z}_{k-1})$ denotes the *motion model*. Then, a target candidate is generated according to its motion state $\mathbf{z}_k$. Thus, the corresponding appearance observation, denoted by $\mathbf{c}$, is obtained and the posterior is updated by

$$p(\mathbf{z}_k|\mathbf{c}, \mathbf{y}_{1:k-1}) \propto p(\mathbf{c}|\mathbf{z}_k) p(\mathbf{z}_k|\mathbf{y}_{1:k-1}), \tag{10}$$

where $p(\mathbf{c}|\mathbf{z}_k)$ denotes the *observation model*. The target on the k-th frame, denoted by $\mathbf{y}_k$, is found by

$$\mathbf{y}_k = \arg\max_{\mathbf{c} \in \mathcal{C}} p(\mathbf{z}_k|\mathbf{c}, \mathbf{y}_{1:k-1}), \tag{11}$$

---

[2] For the presentation simplicity, we use the term *candidate* to stand for the appearance observation of the target candidate hereafter.

Algorithm 1. Tracking Algorithm

Input: index set Ω and target templates $\mathbf{T}$.
Output: the target located in the k-th frame.

1 **for** *each candidate* $\mathbf{c} \in \mathcal{C}$ **do**
2   Generate the observed candidate $\mathbf{c}'$ by setting $\mathbf{c}$'s entries outside Ω to zeros and leaving the rest unchanged.
3   Construct the matrix $\mathbf{Y} = [\mathbf{T}, \mathbf{c}']$.
4   Obtain the estimated candidate $\mathbf{x}$ from Eq. (8).
5   Compute the observation model from Eq. (12).
6 **end**
7 Locate the target from Eq. (11).
8 Update the index set Ω and the target templates $\mathbf{T}$.

---

where $\mathcal{C}$ denotes the set of all the candidates that correspond to a series of regions sampled randomly in the frame according to the possibility $p(\mathbf{c}|\mathbf{z}_k)$.

The motion model in our work is defined as a Gaussian distribution $p(\mathbf{z}_k|\mathbf{z}_{k-1}) \sim \mathcal{N}(\mathbf{z}_k|\mathbf{z}_{k-1}, \mathbf{\Sigma})$, where the covariance $\mathbf{\Sigma}$ is a diagonal matrix, denoting the variances of 2D translation and scaling, respectively. We set $\mathbf{\Sigma} = diag\{3, 3, 0.005\}$ in our experiments. The observation model $p(\mathbf{c}|\mathbf{z}_k)$ reflects the likelihood of the candidate $\mathbf{c}$ to be the target. As discussed above, a good candidate can be estimated accurately by the matrix completion under our subspace assumption. The accuracy is measure by means of the estimation errors. Let us define the observation model for a candidate $\mathbf{c}$ with the motion state $\mathbf{z}_k$ as

$$p(\mathbf{c}|\mathbf{z}_k) \propto \exp\left(-\|\mathbf{c} - \mathbf{x}\|\right). \tag{12}$$

For all the candidates and their corresponding motion states, the target in the k-th frame can be located using Eq. (11). Note that under the definition of the observation model, Eq. (11) is equivalent to Eq. (7), and yields the same result in the target location. The implementation details of the tracking algorithm is outlined in Algorithm 1.

Below is a demonstration of the proposed approach. As shown in Fig. 1(a), two candidates are marked in red and blue, respectively. The representative target templates are shown in Fig. 1(b). We crop out the two target candidates from the image and resize them to the same size as the target templates, as shown in Fig. 2(a) and (e). Then, we sample a number of pixels of the two candidates at the same locations and use these pixels as the observed values, while the rest are treated as missing values, as shown in Fig. 2(b) and (f), where the missing values are set to zeros. Next, we estimate the missing values of each candidate from Eq. (8). Figure 2(c) and (g) show the two estimated candidates, respectively. Their estimation errors are shown in Fig. 2(d) and (h), respectively.

From the above results, it is evident that the good candidate (in red) is estimated much more accurately than the bad one (in blue). As shown in Fig. 2(c), the estimated good candidate is rarely influenced by the distractive object (the magazine), however, the estimated bad candidate, as shown in Fig. 2(g), is quite different from its original version shown in Fig. 2(e). Similar results can also be observed from their estimation errors. Most errors of the good candidate are small, and large errors only appear at the location of the distractive object,

(a)   (b)

Fig. 1. (a) One frame image, where a good and a bad target candidate are marked in red and blue, respectively. (b) The representative target templates. (Color figure online)

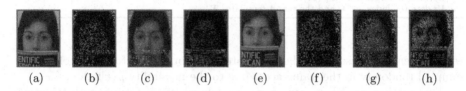

(a)   (b)   (c)   (d)   (e)   (f)   (g)   (h)

Fig. 2. (a)–(d) The good candidate, its observed pixels, estimated result, and estimation error. (e)–(h) The corresponding results as (a)–(d) with respect to the bad candidate. (Color figure online)

as shown in Fig. 2(d). In contrast, most errors of the bad candidate are large, and scatter all over the entire image, as shown in Fig. 2(h). Quantitatively, we also plot the distributions of the absolute estimation errors at the missing entries of the two candidates, as shown in Fig. 3. It can be seen that for most missing entries, the errors of the good candidates are much smaller than those of the bad ones. In addition, the residual errors of the good candidates normally converge faster than those of the bad ones because the good candidates better match the implicitly learned subspace via the *rank*-minimization. Typically, the matrix completion runs less than 30 iterations for good candidates, while about 40 iterations are required for bad candidates.

The good performance of the matrix completion in this case is attributed to two aspects: the low-dimensional subspace assumption on the previously obtained targets, and the local observations from the candidates. From a global point of view, the previously obtained targets span a low-dimensional subspace, which makes better representations of the good candidates, such that they can be estimated more accurately than the bad ones. From a local perspective, the local observations work as strong priors and promote the accuracy of the estimation.

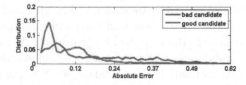

Fig. 3. Distributions of the absolute estimation errors at the missing entries of the two candidates.

Since the index set Ω is determined according to the previously obtained targets, some pixels observed from the bad candidate may be located on the distractive object, leading to a more inaccurate estimation.

4.4 Online Update

During tracking, the appearance of the target varies on successive frames. Thus, we need to update the tracker automatically to accommodate these appearance changes. In each frame, a number of pixels of the candidates are sampled so as to alleviate the influence of the distractive objects. Therefore, the set Ω is updated for every frame to exclude those unexpected pixels. Meanwhile, the target templates $\mathbf{T}$ are updated accordingly, in order to accurately reflect these appearance changes and satisfy the constraint of low-dimensional subspace.

In our work, each pixel of an obtained target is associated to a weight that reflects the possibility of this pixel to be observed in the next frame. Initially, we set all these weights equally. As analyzed in the above demonstration shown in Figs. 1, 2 and 3, the estimation errors are normally large in the regions of the distractive objects (see Fig. 2(d)). Thus, we adjust the weights in each frame to be inversely proportional to the corresponding estimation errors. To avoid that the observed pixels (they always have zero estimation errors) dominate the update, their weights are constrained during the computation. Finally, we draw the same number of entries randomly according to their weights and use these entries as the new index set Ω.

Specifically, in the k-th frame, the weight of the the j-th pixel, denoted by w_j^k, is updated by

$$
w_j^k \propto \begin{cases} \frac{1}{e_j^k}, & j \notin \Omega \\ \frac{1}{e_a + e_j^{k-1}(e_b - e_a)}, & j \in \Omega, \end{cases} \tag{13}
$$

where e_j^k denotes the estimation error of the k-th target in the j-th pixel, and e_a and e_b are determined by

$$
e_{i_1} < e_{i_2} < \cdots < e_a < e_m < e_b < \cdots < \mathbf{e}_{i_N}, \tag{14}
$$

where e_m denotes the median value of the N estimation errors, and $i_k \in \{1, 2, \ldots, N\}$. In the above equations, we divide the pixels into two categories and update their associated weights respectively. One category contains the pixels outside the index set Ω, i.e., in the case of $j \notin \Omega$ for the j-th pixel of the k-th target. Among these pixels, the pixels with large estimation errors are unexpected to be observed in the next frame, since they have high possibilities to be located on the distractive objects. Thus, we directly set their associated weights inversely proportional to their estimation error e_j^k. The other category contains the pixels indexed by Ω. Because these pixels are the observed ones in the current frame, i.e., they have zero estimation errors, they are expected to be observed in the next frame. In addition, in order to avoid that these pixels dominate the update, we deliberately decrease their possibilities to be observed to

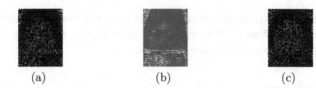

(a)   (b)   (c)

Fig. 4. Illustration of the online update of Ω between two consecutive frames. (a) The observed pixels of the current target. (b) The possibilities of the pixels to be indexed by new Ω. The cooler pixel indicates the larger value. (c) The observed pixels of the next target, which are obtained according to the possibilities in (b).

some extent. For this reason, we constraint the possibilities of these pixels within an appropriate range, or equivalently assign them certain errors within an range $[e_a, e_b]$. In practice, the median of the target estimation errors in last frame, *i.e.*, the $(k-1)$-th target, is a reasonable reference in setting e_a and e_b, such that their values are not being set too low or too high. In our experiments, e_a and e_b are set to the errors just below and above the median error, respectively.

Figure 4 illustrates the online update strategy of Ω between two consecutive frames. It can be seen from Fig. 4(b) that the pixels from the distractive object (the magazine) have higher possibilities to be excluded (*i.e.*, not indexed in Ω) in the next frame. From Fig. 4(c), it is evident that the pixels belonging to the distractive object are reduced in the local observations of the target in the next frame. In our experiments, similar to the work [32], we use ten target templates.

5   Experimental Evaluations

Our tracker is implemented in MATLAB on a PC with an Intel Core 2.8 GHz processor. The average running speed is one frame per second. The colorful pixels in each frame are converted to gray scale and normalized to $[0, 1]$. The corresponding regions of the candidates and the target templates are normalized to the size of 20×20 pixels, and 70 % pixels are observed for the candidates.

We compared our tracker with respect to 14 popular state-of-the-art trackers, including subspace methods, local methods, and other state-of-the-art methods. Their parameters were set to the values recommended by respective authors. In order to demonstrate the effectiveness of different algorithms in various challenging situations, we collect the most popular 20 video sequences for the comparisons, which demonstrate various challenges, such as heavy occlusions, illumination variations, and background clutters, as shown in Fig. 5. In each frame, the target region is manually labeled using a bounding box as ground truth. Both the source codes and the video sequences can be publicly downloaded from the respective websites of the authors.

5.1   Qualitative Evaluations

Figure 5 shows the tracking results obtained by our tracker and the 14 competing trackers on the representative frames of the 20 video sequences.

Fig. 5. Tracking results on representative frames of the 20 video sequences.

In the case of illumination changes, *e.g.*, on the video sequences *car4*, *david* and *singer1*, our tracker achieves better results, owing to the assumption of low-dimensional subspace on the previously obtained targets, which makes matrix completion work successfully. As a demonstration of the effectiveness of the subspace assumption, a very good tracking result is obtained by the proposed tracker in the case of pose changes, *e.g.*, on the video sequences *bicycle*, *polarbear*, *surfing* and *walking*. In the presence of occlusions, *e.g.*, on the video sequences *bicycle*, *caviar3*, *faceocc*, *oneleaveshop*, *thusl* and *thusy*, our tracker also achieves better or competitive tracking performance. This is attributed to: (1) the local observations and the online update strategy leverage the pixels that are not located on the distractive objects; and (2) the matrix completion leads to a high estimation accuracy.

5.2 Quantitative Evaluations

Four criteria are used to quantitatively evaluate the performance of different trackers: tracking location error (TLE), precision, overlap rates (OR), and success rate (SR). The TLE is computed from the difference between the centers of the tracking and the ground truth bounding boxes. The precision in defined as the percentage of frames where the TLE are less than a threshold δ. The OR is computed by $\frac{A_T \cap A_G}{A_T \cup A_G}$, where A_T and A_G denote the areas of the bounding boxes of the tracking result and the ground truth, respectively. The SR is defined as the percentage of frames where the OR are greater than a threshold ρ. Table 1 shows the average TLE, precision (for $\delta = 20$), OR, and SR (for $rho = 0.5$)

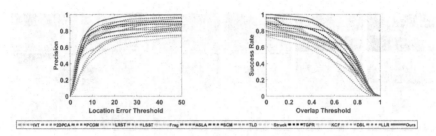

Fig. 6. Tracking performance of the proposed and the 14 competing trackers on the 20 video sequences in terms of precision (left) and success rate (right).

Table 1. Tracking performance of the proposed and the competing trackers on the 20 video sequences. The best results are shown in bold-face font.

Tracker	Ours	IVT [1]	2DPCA [11]	PCOM [19]	LRST [17]	LSST [15]	Frag [5]	ASLA [7]	SCM [20]	TLD [21]	Struck [4]	TGPR [23]	KCF [24]	DSL [33]	LLR [22]
Tracking error	5.8	46.4	23.8	48.6	25.9	28.6	34.7	30.9	29.9	30.1	20.7	23.2	22.7	15.2	9.9
Precision	0.96	0.70	0.79	0.74	0.71	0.79	0.60	0.79	0.84	0.68	0.87	0.86	0.83	0.91	0.90
Success rate	0.86	0.59	0.69	0.64	0.59	0.69	0.49	0.70	0.80	0.53	0.67	0.75	0.67	0.85	0.83
Overlap rate	0.72	0.51	0.58	0.56	0.51	0.50	0.47	0.59	0.65	0.50	0.60	0.61	0.57	0.70	0.68

of ours and the 14 competing trackers on the 20 video sequences, respectively. Figure 6 plots the precision and the success rate of our tracker and its 14 counterparts on the 20 video sequences. From the quantitative evaluations on the 20 video sequences, it is evident that the proposed tracker outperforms its 14 counterparts in terms of all four criteria.

5.3   Analysis of the Tracking Model

The impressive performance of the proposed tracker is attributed to the integration of the global subspace assumption and the local observations. This is further demonstrated below from an experimental perspective.

First, we verify the assumption that the targets reside in a low-dimensional subspace. We collect all the targets from each of the 20 experimental video sequences according to their ground truths. Then, we analyze the corresponding target subspace by using singular value decomposition. If the target subspace is of low-dimensional, the metric of *low dimension degree*, defined as the number of the non-zero singular values of the target matrix, whose sum is more than θ times the sum of all singular values, should be small for a large θ. Figure 7(a) shows the results on the 20 video sequences with respect to $\theta = 90\%$ and $\theta = 95\%$, respectively. It can be seen that most of the low dimension degrees are located within the range of $[10\%, 40\%]$, which indicates that the targets truly reside in a low-dimensional subspace.

Next, we demonstrate the effectiveness of the integration of the local observations with the global subspace assumption. We compare the tracking results of the two trackers with and without local observations on the 20 video sequences.

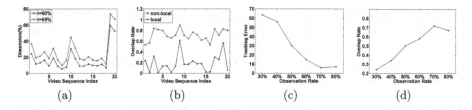

Fig. 7. Low dimension degrees (a) and overlap rates of the trackers with and without local observations (b) on the 20 experimental sequences. The order of the video sequences is identical to that showed in Fig. 5. Tracking location errors (c) and overlap rates (d) on the 20 video sequences with respect to different local observation rates.

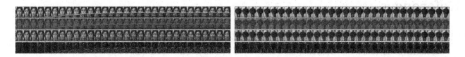

Fig. 8. Visualization of the local observation. The 1st row show the temporally obtained targets. The red pixels in the 2nd row indicate the observed pixels. The estimated targets and the residual errors are shown in the 3rd and the 4th rows, respectively. (Color figure online)

The results are shown in Fig. 7(b), from which we can see that the tracking performance is significantly improved by using the local observations. We also visualize the local observation in Fig. 8. It can be seen that, in the case of occlusion, the book tends to be observed with a small possibility, and in the case of deformation, the body of the person and the static surrounding background are encouraged to be observed, while the deformations (on shoulders and legs) are rarely observed. These experiments indicate that the local observations provide strong priors for the estimator (matrix completion), leading to more accurate estimations.

Furthermore, we show how the local observations influence the tracking results. Since the number of the observed pixels is a critical factor for the tracker, we investigate the TLEs and ORs with respect to different numbers of the observed pixels, as shown in Fig. 7(d). It is evident that our tracker yields the best performance when about 70 % pixels are observed. Observing too few pixels may lead to an inaccuracy of the matrix completion, while observing too many pixels may result in heavy influence from distractive objects. As a result, we observe 70 % pixels in our experiments for each frame.

6   Conclusion

We have formulated tracking as a problem of target appearance estimation by exploiting the advantages of both the global and local tracking models. Extensive experiments have been conducted and the results have demonstrated that: (1) our tracking model, by integrating the global and the local methods, effectively alleviates tracking failures in various challenging situations; and (2) under the subspace assumption, the matrix completion provides an accurate estimation in target appearance for the target location. Both the qualitative and the quantitative evaluations have demonstrated that the proposed tracker outperforms most popular state-of-the-art trackers.

Acknowledgments. The work is partly supported by the National Natural Science Foundation of China (NSFC) under grants 61273282, 61573351 and 61132007, and the joint fund of Civil Aviation Research by the National Natural Science Foundation of China (NSFC) and Civil Aviation Administration under grant U1533132.

References

1. Ross, D.A., Lim, J., Lin, R.S., Yang, M.H.: Incremental learning for robust visual tracking. Int. J. Comput. Vis. (IJCV) **77**(1–3), 125–141 (2007)
2. Mei, X., Ling, H.: Robust visual tracking using L1 minimization. In: IEEE International Conference on Computer Vision (ICCV), pp. 1436–1443 (2009)
3. Babenko, B., Member, S., Yang, M.H., Member, S.: Robust object tracking with online multiple instance learning. IEEE Trans. Pattern Anal. Mach. Intell. (TPAMI) **33**(8), 1619–1632 (2011)
4. Hare, S., Saffari, A., Torr, P.: Struck: structured output tracking with kernels. In: IEEE International Conference on Computer Vision (ICCV), pp. 263–270 (2011)
5. Adam, A., Rivlin, E., Shimshoni, I.: Robust fragments-based tracking using the integral histogram. In: IEEE Computer Society Conference on Computer Vision and Pattern Recognition (CVPR), vol. 1, pp. 798–805 (2006)
6. Liu, B., Huang, J., Yang, L., Kulikowsk, C.: Robust tracking using local sparse appearance model and K-selection. In: IEEE Computer Society Conference on Computer Vision and Pattern Recognition (CVPR), pp. 1313–1320, June 2011
7. Jia, X., Lu, H., Yang, M.H.: Visual tracking via adaptive structural local sparse appearance model. In: IEEE Computer Society Conference on Computer Vision and Pattern Recognition (CVPR), pp. 1822–1829 (2012)
8. Liu, T., Wnag, G., Yang, Q.: Real-time part-based visual tracking via adaptive correlation filters. In: IEEE Computer Society Conference on Computer Vision and Pattern Recognition (CVPR), pp. 4902–4912 (2015)
9. Candes, E., Plan, Y.: Matrix completion with noise. Proc. IEEE **98**(6), 925–936 (2010)
10. Kwon, J., Lee, K.: Visual tracking decomposition. In: IEEE Computer Society Conference on Computer Vision and Pattern Recognition (CVPR), pp. 1269–1276 (2010)
11. Wang, D., Lu, H.: Object tracking via 2DPCA and L1-regularization. IEEE Sig. Process. Lett. **19**(11), 711–714 (2012)
12. Sui, Y., Zhang, S., Zhang, L.: Robust visual tracking via sparsity-induced subspace learning. IEEE Trans. Image Process. (TIP) **24**(12), 4686–4700 (2015)
13. Hager, G.D., Belhumeur, P.N.: Real-time tracking of image regions with changes in geometry and illumination. In: IEEE Computer Society Conference on Computer Vision and Pattern Recognition (CVPR), pp. 403–410 (1996)
14. Belhumeur, P.N., Kriegmant, D.J.: What is the set of images of an object under all possible lighting conditions? In: IEEE Computer Society Conference on Computer Vision and Pattern Recognition (CVPR), pp. 270–277 (1996)

15. Wang, D., Lu, H., Yang, M.H.: Least soft-thresold squares tracking. In: IEEE Computer Society Conference on Computer Vision and Pattern Recognition (CVPR), pp. 2371–2378 (2013)

16. Wang, D., Lu, H., Yang, M.H.: Online object tracking with sparse prototypes. IEEE Trans. Image Process. (TIP) **22**(1), 314–325 (2013)

17. Zhang, T., Ghanem, B., Liu, S., Ahuja, N.: Low-rank sparse learning for robust visual tracking. In: Fitzgibbon, A., Lazebnik, S., Perona, P., Sato, Y., Schmid, C. (eds.) ECCV 2012, Part VI. LNCS, vol. 7577, pp. 470–484. Springer, Heidelberg (2012)

18. Sui, Y., Zhao, X., Zhang, S., Yu, X., Zhao, S., Zhang, L.: Self-expressive tracking. Pattern Recogn. (PR) **48**(9), 2872–2884 (2015)

19. Wang, D., Lu, H.: Visual tracking via probability continuous outlier model. In: IEEE Computer Society Conference on Computer Vision and Pattern Recognition (CVPR) (2014)

20. Zhong, W., Lu, H., Yang, M.H.: Robust object tracking via sparsity-based collaborative model. In: IEEE Computer Society Conference on Computer Vision and Pattern Recognition (CVPR), pp. 1838–1845 (2012)

21. Kalal, Z., Mikolajczyk, K., Matas, J.: Tracking-learning-detection. IEEE Trans. Pattern Anal. Mach. Intell. (TPAMI) **34**(7), 1409–1422 (2012)

22. Sui, Y., Zhang, L.: Robust tracking via locally structured representation. Int. J. Comput. Vis. (IJCV) **119**(2), 110–144 (2016)

23. Gao, J., Ling, H., Hu, W., Xing, J.: Transfer learning based visual tracking with gaussian processes regression. In: Fleet, D., Pajdla, T., Schiele, B., Tuytelaars, T. (eds.) ECCV 2014, Part III. LNCS, vol. 8691, pp. 188–203. Springer, Heidelberg (2014)

24. Henriques, J., Caseiro, R., Martins, P., Batista, J.: High-speed tracking with kernelized correlation filters. IEEE Trans. Pattern Anal. Mach. Intell. (TPAMI) **37**(3), 583–596 (2015)

25. Candes, E.J., Li, X., Ma, Y., Wright, J.: Robust principal component analysis? J. ACM **58**(3), 1–37 (2011)

26. Liu, G., Lin, Z., Yu, Y.: Robust subspace segmentation by low-rank representation. In: International Conference on Machine Learning (ICML) (2010)

27. Lin, Z., Chen, M., Ma, Y.: The augmented lagrange multiplier method for exact recovery of corrupted low-rank matrices, pp. 1–23. UIUC Technical report (2010)

28. Babacan, S., Luessi, M.: Low-rank matrix completion by variational sparse Bayesian learning. In: International Conference on Acoustics, Speech, and Signal Processing (ICASSP) (2011)

29. Babacan, S.D., Luessi, M., Molina, R., Katsaggelos, A.: Sparse Bayesian methods for low-rank matrix estimation. IEEE Trans. Sig. Process. (TSP) **60**, 3964–3977 (2011)

30. Isard, M.: CONDENSATION - conditional density propagation for visual tracking. Int. J. Comput. Vis. (IJCV) **29**(1), 5–28 (1998)

31. Arulampalam, M., Maskell, S., Gordon, N., Clapp, T.: A tutorial on particle filters for online nonlinear/non-Gaussian Bayesian tracking. IEEE Trans. Sig. Process. (TSP) **50**(2), 174–188 (2002)

32. Mei, X., Ling, H.: Robust visual tracking and vehicle classification via sparse representation. IEEE Trans. Pattern Anal. Mach. Intell. (TPAMI) **33**(11), 2259–2272 (2011)

33. Sui, Y., Tang, Y., Zhang, L.: Discriminative low-rank tracking. In: IEEE International Conference on Computer Vision (ICCV), pp. 3002–3010 (2015)

Inter-battery Topic Representation Learning

Cheng Zhang[1]([✉]), Hedvig Kjellström[1], and Carl Henrik Ek[2]

[1] Robotics, Perception and Learning (RPL), KTH Royal Institute of Technology,
Stockholm, Sweden
{chengz,hedvig}@kth.se

[2] Department of Computer Science, University of Bristol, Bristol, UK
carlhenrik.ek@bristol.ac.uk

Abstract. In this paper, we present the Inter-Battery Topic Model (IBTM). Our approach extends traditional topic models by learning a factorized latent variable representation. The structured representation leads to a model that marries benefits traditionally associated with a discriminative approach, such as feature selection, with those of a generative model, such as principled regularization and ability to handle missing data. The factorization is provided by representing data in terms of aligned pairs of observations as different views. This provides means for selecting a representation that separately models topics that exist in both views from the topics that are unique to a single view. This structured consolidation allows for efficient and robust inference and provides a compact and efficient representation. Learning is performed in a Bayesian fashion by maximizing a rigorous bound on the log-likelihood. Firstly, we illustrate the benefits of the model on a synthetic dataset. The model is then evaluated in both uni- and multi-modality settings on two different classification tasks with off-the-shelf convolutional neural network (CNN) features which generate state-of-the-art results with extremely compact representations.

Keywords: Factorized representation · Topic model · Multi-view model · CNN feature · Image classification

1 Introduction

The representation of an image has a large impact on the ease and efficiency with which prediction can be performed. This has generated a huge interest in directly learning representation from data [1]. Generative models for representation learning treat the desired representation as an unobserved latent variable [2–4]. Topic models, which are generally a group of generative models based on

This research has been supported by the Swedish Research Council (VR) and Stiftelsen Promobilia.

Electronic supplementary material The online version of this chapter (doi:10.1007/978-3-319-46484-8_13) contains supplementary material, which is available to authorized users.

B. Leibe et al. (Eds.): ECCV 2016, Part VIII, LNCS 9912, pp. 210–226, 2016.
DOI: 10.1007/978-3-319-46484-8_13

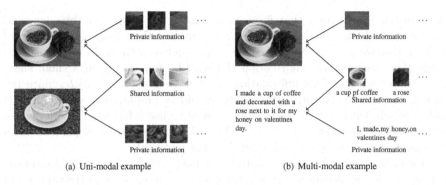

(a) Uni-modal example   (b) Multi-modal example

Fig. 1. Examples of using factorized representations in different scenarios. (a) gives an example of modeling "a cup of coffee" images. Different images with a cup of coffee all share certain patterns, such as cup handles, cup brims, etc. Moreover, each image also contains patterns that are not immediately related to the "cup of coffee" label, such as the rose or the coffee beans. These can be considered as private or instance-specific for each image. (b) gives an example of modeling the image and its caption. Different modalities describe the same content as "a cup of coffee" and "a rose". However, the wooden table pattern is not described in the caption and words such as "I made", "my honey" etc. do not correspond to the content of the image. This information can be considered as private or modality-specific.

Latent Dirichlet Allocation (LDA) [3], have successfully been applied for learning representations that are suitable for computer vision tasks [5–7]. A topic model learns a set of topics, which are distributions over words and represents each document as a distribution over topics. In computer vision applications, a topic is a distribution over visual words, while a document is usually an image or a video. Due to its generative nature, the learned representation will provide rich information about the structure of the data with high interpretability. It offers a highly compact representation and can handle incomplete data, to a high degree, in comparison to other types of representation methodologies. Topic models have been demonstrated with successful performance in many applications. Similar to other latent space probabilistic models, the topic distributions can easily be adapted with different distributions with respect to the types of the input data. In this paper, we will use a LDA model as our basic framework and apply an effective factorized representation learning scheme.

Modeling the essence of the information among all sources of information for a particular task has been shown to offer high interpretability and better performance [6,8–12]. For example, for object classification, separating the key features of the object from the intra-class variations and background information is key to the performance. The idea of factorized representation can be traced back to the early work of Tucker, 'An Inter-Battery Method of Factory Analysis' [8], hence, we name the model presented in this paper Inter-Battery Topic Model (IBTM).

Imagine a scenario in which we want to visually represent "a cup of coffee", illustrated in Fig. 1(a). Apart from a cup of coffee, such images commonly contain additional information that is not correlated to this labeling, e.g., the rose and the table in the upper image and the coffee beans in the lower image. One can think of the information that is common among all images of this class and thus correlated with the label, as the *shared* information. Images with a cup of coffee will share a set of "cup of coffee" topics between them. In addition, each image does also contain information that can be found only in a small share of the other images. This information can be thought of as *private*. Since the shared, but not the private, information should be employed in the estimation task (e.g., classification), it is highly beneficial to use a factorized model which represents the information needed for the tasks (shared topics) separately from the information that is not task related (private topics).

A similar idea can be applied in the case when two different modalities of the data are available. A common case is images as one modality and the captions of the images as another, as shown in Fig. 1(b). In this scenario, commonly not all of the content in the image has its corresponding caption words; and not every word in the caption has its corresponding image patches. However, the important aspects of the scene or object depicted in the image are also described in the caption, and vice versa, the central aspects of the caption are those that correlate with what is seen in the image. Based on this idea, an ideal multi-modal representation should factorize out information that is present in both modalities (words describing central concepts, and image patches from the corresponding image areas) and represent it separately from information that is only present in one of the modalities (words not correlated with the image, and image patches in the background). Other modality examples include video and audio data captured at the same event, or optical flow and depth measurements extracted from a video stream.

To summarize, there is a strong need of modeling information in a factorized manner such that shared information and private information are represented separately. In our model, the shared part of the representation will capture the aspects of the data that are essential for the prediction (e.g., classification) task, leading to better performance. Additionally, inspecting the factorized latent representation gives a better understanding of the structure of the data, which is helpful in the design of domain-specific modeling and data collection.

The main contribution of this paper is *a generative model, IBTM, for factorized representation learning, which efficiently factorizes essential information for an estimation task from information that is not task related* (Sect. 3). This results in a very effective latent representation that can be used for predication tasks, such as classifications. IBTM is a general framework, which is applicable to both single- and multi-modal data, and can easily be adapted to data with different noise levels. To infer the latent variables of the model, we derive an efficient variational inference algorithm for IBTMs.

We evaluate our model in different experimental scenarios (Sect. 4). Firstly, we test IBTM with a synthetic dataset to illustrate how the learning is performed. Then we apply IBTM to state-of-the-art datasets in different scenarios to illustrate how different computer vision tasks benefit from IBTM. In a multi-modal setting, modality-specific information is factorized from cross-modality information (Sects. 4.2.1.2 and 4.2.2.2). In a uni-modal setting, instance-specific information is factorized from class-specific information (Sects. 4.2.1.1 and 4.2.2.1).

2   Related Work

With respect to the scope of this paper, we will summarize the related work mainly from two aspects: Topic Modeling and Factorized Models.

Topic Modeling. Latent Dirichlet Allocation (LDA) [3] is the corner stone of topic modeling. In computer vision tasks [5–7], topic modeling assumes that each visual document is generated by selecting different themes while the themes are distributions over visual words. In correspondence with other works in representation learning, the themes can be interpreted as factors, components or dictionaries. The topic distribution for each document can be interpreted as factor weights or as a sparse and low-dimensional representation of the visual document. This has achieved promising results in different tasks and provided an intuitive understanding of the data structure. For computer vision tasks, topic modeling has been used for classification, either with supervision in the model [13–17] or by learning the topic representation in an unsupervised manner and applying standard classifiers such as softmax regression on the latent topic representation [12]. Another interesting direction using topic modeling in computer vision is the multi-modal extension of topic models; it has been applied to tasks such as image annotation [11,18–20], contextual action/object recognition [7] and video tagging [6]. Being a generative model, it represents all information found in the data. However, for a specific task, only a portion of this information might be relevant. Extracting this information is essential for a good representation of the data. Hence a model that describes key information for the current task is beneficial.

Factorized Models. The benefit of modeling the between-view variance separately from the within-view variance was first pointed out by Tucker [8]. It was rediscovered in machine learning in recent years by Ek et al. [21]. Recent research in latent structure models has also shown that modeling information in a factorized manner is advantageous for both uni-modal scenarios [10,12,22], in which only one type of data is available and multi-modal scenarios [6,9,21], in which different views correspond to different modalities. For uni-modal scenarios, a special words topic model with a background distribution (SWB) [22] is one of the first studies on factorized representation using topic model for information retrieval tasks. In addition to topics, SWB uses a words distribution for each document to represent document specific information and a global word distribution for background information. As shown in the experiments, this text-specific factorization model is less suitable for computer vision tasks than IBTM. Works that apply such a factorized scheme on multi-modal topic modeling [6,11] include the multi-modal factorized topic model [11] and Video Tags and Topics Model (VTT) [6]. The multi-modal factorized topic model which is based on correlated topic models [23] only provides an implicit link between different modalities with hierarchical Dirichlet priors since the factorization is enforced on the logistic normal prior, while VTT is only designed for the specific application.

In this paper, we present a general framework IBTM which models the topic structure in a factorized manner and can be applied to both uni- and multi-modal scenarios.

3 Model

In this section, firstly, we will shortly review LDA [3] which IBTM is based on and then present the modeling details and inference of IBTM. Finally, we will describe how the latent representation can be used for classification tasks with which we evaluate our approach.

3.1 Latent Dirichlet Allocation

LDA is a classical generative model which is able to model the latent structure of discrete data, for example, a bag of words representation of documents. Figure 2(a) shows the graphic representation of LDA [3]. In LDA, the words (visual words) w are assumed to be generated by sampling from a per document topic distribution $\theta \sim Dir(\alpha)$ and a per topic words distribution $\beta \sim Dir(\sigma)$. The Dirichlet distribution is a natural choice as it is conjugate to multinomial distribution.

3.2 Inter-battery Topic Model

We propose the IBTM which models latent variables in a factorized manner for multi-view scenarios. Firstly, we will explain how to apply IBTM to a two view scenario such that it easily can be compared to other models [7,8,18,20]. In the following, we present the more generalized IBTM, which can encode any number of views.

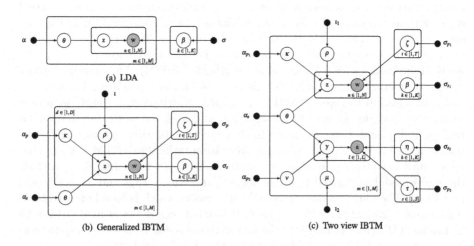

(a) LDA

(b) Generalized IBTM

(c) Two view IBTM

Fig. 2. Graphical representations

Two View IBTM. The two view version of IBTM, shown in Fig. 2(c), is an LDA-based model, in which each document contains two views and the words w and a from the two views are observed respectively. The two views can represent different types of data, such as two modalities, for example, image and caption as in Fig. 1(b); or two different descriptors for the same data, for example, SIFT and SURF features of the same image. They can also be two instances of the same class, for example, the two cups of coffee as in Fig. 1(a).

The key of IBTM is that we assume that topics are factorized. We do not force topics from two views to be matched completely since commonly each view has its view-specific information. Hence, in our model, a shared topic distribution between two views for each document is separated from a private topic distribution for each view. As in Fig. 2(c), $\theta \sim Dir(\alpha_s)$ is the *shared* per topic distribution for each document, and correspondingly $\beta \sim Dir(\sigma_{s1})$ and $\eta \sim Dir(\sigma_{s2})$ are the per shared topic words distributions for each view. $\kappa \sim Dir(\alpha_{p1})$ and $\nu \sim Dir(\alpha_{p2})$ are the *private* per document topic distributions for each view respectively, and correspondingly $\zeta \sim Dir(\sigma_{p1})$ and $\tau \sim Dir(\sigma_{p2})$ are the private per topic word distributions for each view. To determine how much information is shared and how much information is private, partition parameters $\rho \sim Beta(\iota_1)$ and $\mu \sim Beta(\iota_2)$ are used for each view. In this case, to generate topic assignments for each word in each view, z and y are sampled as[1]

$$z \sim Mult([\rho * \theta; (1 - \rho) * \kappa]), \quad y \sim Mult([\mu * \theta; (1 - \mu) * \nu]). \tag{1}$$

In the extreme cases, if $\rho = 0$ and $\mu = 0$, no information is shared between the two views and IBTM becomes two separated LDA. Otherwise, if $\rho = 1$ and $\mu = 1$, IBTM becomes a regular multi-modal topic model [7,20].

The whole IBTM is represented as:

$$p(\kappa, \theta, \nu, \rho, z, w, \mu, y, a, \zeta, \beta, \eta, \tau | \Theta)$$

$$= \left(\prod_{t=1}^{T} p(\zeta_t | \sigma_{p1}) \right) \left(\prod_{k=1}^{K} p(\beta_k | \sigma_{s1}) \right) \left(\prod_{k=1}^{K} p(\eta_k | \sigma_{s2}) \right) \left(\prod_{s=1}^{S} p(\tau_s | \sigma_{p2}) \right) \prod_{m=1}^{M} \left(p(\kappa_m | \alpha_{p1}) p(\theta_m | \alpha_s) \right.$$

$$p(\nu_m | \alpha_{p2}) p(\rho_m | \iota) p(\mu_m | \iota_2) \left(\prod_{n=1}^{N} p(z_{mn} | \kappa_m, \theta_m, \rho_m) p(w_{mn} | z_{mn}, \beta, \zeta) \right)$$

$$\left(\prod_{l=1}^{L} p(y_{ml} | \nu_m, \theta_m, \mu_m) p(a_{ml} | y_{ml}, \eta, \tau) \right) \Big)$$

where $\Theta = \{\alpha_{p1}, \alpha_s, \alpha_{p2}, \sigma_{p1}, \sigma_{p2}, \sigma_{s1}, \sigma_{s2}, \iota_1, \iota_2\}$, and as in the graphic representation of IBTM in Fig. 2(b), the total number of documents is M; the number of words for each document is N and L for the first view and the second view respectively; the number of shared topics for both views is K; the number of private topics is T and S and the vocabulary size is V and W for the first view and the second view respectively.

Mean Field Variational Inference. Exact inference on this model is intractable due to the coupling between latent variables. Variational inference and sampling

---

[1] We use $[A; B]$ to indicate matrix and vector concatenation.

based methods are the two main groups of methods to perform approximate inference. Variational inference is known for its fast convergence and theoretical attractiveness. It can also be easily adapted to online requirements when facing big data or streaming data. Hence, in this paper, we use mean field variational inference for IBTM. The fully factorized variational distribution is assumed following the mean field manner:

$$q(\kappa, \theta, \nu, \rho, z, \mu, y, \zeta, \beta, \eta, \tau) = q(\kappa)q(\theta)q(\nu)q(\rho)q(z)q(\mu)q(y)q(\zeta)q(\beta)q(\eta)q(\tau).$$

For each term above, the per document topic distributions are: $q(\kappa) = \prod_{m=1}^{M} q(\kappa_m|\delta_m)$ where $\delta_m \in \mathbb{R}^T$; $q(\theta) = \prod_{m=1}^{M} q(\theta_m|\gamma_m)$ where $\gamma_m \in \mathbb{R}^K$; $q(\nu) = \prod_{m=1}^{M} q(\nu_m|\epsilon_m)$ where $\epsilon_m \in \mathbb{R}^S$. The per word topic assignments are: $q(z) = \prod_{m=1}^{M} \prod_{n=1}^{N} q(z_{mn}|\phi_{mn})$ where $\phi_{mn} \in \mathbb{R}^{K+T}$ such that the first K topics correspond to the shared topics and the last T topics correspond to the private topics; $q(y) = \prod_{m=1}^{M} \prod_{l=1}^{L} q(y_{mn}|\chi_{mn})$ where $\chi_{mn} \in \mathbb{R}^{K+S}$ such that the first K topics correspond to the shared topics and the last S topics correspond to the private topics. The per document beta parameters are: $q(\rho) = \prod_{m=1}^{M} q(\rho_m|r_m)$ and $q(\mu) = \prod_{m=1}^{M} q(\mu_m|u_m)$. Finally, the per topic words distributions are: $q(\zeta) = \prod_{t=1}^{T} q(\zeta_t|\xi_t)$, $q(\beta) = \prod_{k=1}^{K} q(\beta_k|\lambda_k)$, $q(\eta) = \prod_{k=1}^{K} q(\eta_k|\upsilon_k)$, $q(\tau) = \prod_{s=1}^{S} q(\tau_s|o_s)$. All the variational distributions follow the same family of distributions under the model assumption.

Applying Jensen's inequality on the log likelihood of the model, we get the evidence lower bound (ELBO) $\mathscr{L}$:

$$\log p(w, a, Z|\Theta) = \log \int \frac{p(w, a, Z|\Theta)q(Z)}{q(Z)} dZ \geq \mathrm{E}_q[\log p(w, a, Z|\Theta)] - \mathrm{E}_q[\log q(Z)] = \mathscr{L}$$

where $\mathbb{Z} = \{\kappa, \theta, \nu, \rho, z, \mu, y, \zeta, \beta, \eta, \tau\}$.

By maximizing the ELBO, we get the update equations for the variational parameters. Only the ones that differ from LDA are presented here and derivation details are presented in the supplementary material. The update equations for the per document topic variational distribution are:

$$\delta_{mt} = \alpha_{p1} + \sum_{n=1}^{N} \phi_{mn(K+t)}, \quad \gamma_{mk} = \alpha_s + \sum_{n=1}^{N} \phi_{mnk} + \sum_{l=1}^{L} \chi_{mlk}, \quad \epsilon_{ms} = \alpha_{p2} + \sum_{l=1}^{L} \chi_{ml(K+s)}.$$

The update equation for the topic assignment in the first view is, when $i \leq K$:[2]

$$\phi_{mni} = \exp\left(\left(\Psi(\gamma_{mk}) - \Psi(\sum_{i=1}^{K} \gamma_{mi}) \right) + \left(\Psi(r_{m1}) - \Psi(r_{m1} \right.\right.$$
$$\left.\left. + r_{m2}) \right) + \sum_{v=1}^{V} [w_{mn} = v] \left(\Psi(\lambda_{iv}) - \Psi(\sum_{p=1}^{V} \lambda_{ip}) \right) - 1 \right);$$

and when $i > K$ (as $i = K + t$):

$$\phi_{mni} = \exp\left(\left(\left(\Psi(\delta_{m(i-K)}) - \Psi(\sum_{p=1}^{T} \delta_{mp}) \right) + \left(\Psi(r_{m2}) - \Psi(r_{m1} + r_{m2}) \right) \right)\right.$$
$$\left. + \sum_{v=1}^{V} [w_{mn} = v] \left(\Psi(\xi_{iv}) - \Psi(\sum_{p=1}^{V} \xi_{ip}) \right) - 1 \right).$$

---

[2] $\Psi(x)$ is the digamma function.

The update equations for the partition parameters are:

$$r_{m1} = \iota_{11} + \sum_{n=1}^{N} \sum_{i=1}^{K} \phi_{mni}, \quad r_{m2} = \iota_{12} + \sum_{n=1}^{N} \sum_{i=K}^{K+T} \phi_{mni}$$

The update for the second view follows equivalently.

In the implementation, all global latent variables are initialized randomly except for the shared per topic word distribution for the second modality, which is initialized uniformly. Due to the exchangeability of Dirichlet distribution which leads to rotational symmetry in the inference, initializing only one of the shared per topic word distribution randomly will increase the robustness of the model performance.

Generalized IBTM. It is straight-forward to generalize the two view IBTM to more views. The graphical representation of the generalized IBTM is shown in Fig. 2(b), where D is the total number of views. When $D = 2$, the models in Fig. 2(b) and (c) are identical. The inference procedure can be adapted easily, since the updates of both topic assignments and partition parameters for each view follow the same form. The only difference is the per document shared topic variational distribution $\gamma_{mk} = \alpha_s + \sum_{d=1}^{D} \sum_{n=1}^{N^{(d)}} \phi_{mnk}^{(d)}$, where $\phi_{mnk}^{(d)}$ is the variational distribution of the topic assignment for the d-th view.

3.3 Classification

Topic models provide a compact representation of the data. Both LDA and IBTM are unsupervised models and can be used for representation learning. The topic representation can be applied to different tasks, for example, image classification and image retrieval. Commonly, the whole topic representation will be employed for these tasks using LDA. Using IBTM, we will only rely on the shared topic space which represents the information essence. For image classification, we can simply apply a Support Vector Machine or softmax regression, taking the shared topic representation as the input. In our experimental evaluation, softmax regression is used. Although there are different types of supervised topic models [13,16] where class label is encoded as part of the model, the work in [12] shows that the performance on computer vision classification tasks using supervised model and unsupervised model with an additional classifier is similar. The minor improvement on the performance commonly comes with significant improvement of computation cost. Hence, we keep IBTM as a general framework for representation learning in an unsupervised manner.

4   Experiments

In the experiments, firstly, we will evaluate the inference scheme and demonstrate the model behavior in a controlled manner in Sect. 4.1. Then we will use two benchmark datasets to evaluate the model behavior in real world scenarios in

(a) Ground Truth ζ, β, η, τ

(b) Estimated ζ, β, η, τ

Fig. 3. (a) shows the ground truth of the four per topic word distributions in the two-view IBTM model; (b) shows the inferred distributions. Each row in the distributions represents a topic and each column presents a word. There are 5 topics in each distribution ($K = T = S = 5$), and the vocabulary size is 50 for both views ($V = W = 50$) (a) Ground Truth ζ, β, η, τ (b) Estimated ζ, β, η, τ

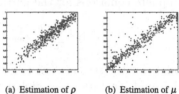

(a) Estimation of ρ (b) Estimation of μ

Fig. 4. Visualization of synthetic data experiment on inference of partition parameters ρ and μ. The x-axis is the ground truth and the y-axis is the estimation. Each dot in the plot presents the ρ and μ for a document (a) Estimation of ρ (b) Estimation of μ

Sect. 4.2. For this purpose, we use the LabelMe natural scene data for natural scene classification [18, 24, 25] and the Leeds butterfly dataset [26] for fine-grained categorization.

4.1 Inference Evaluation Using Synthetic Data

To test the inference performance, we generate a set of synthetic data using the model given different topic distributions ζ, β, η, τ and hyper-parameters for $\mu, \rho, \kappa, \theta, \nu$. We generate 500 documents and each document has 100 words for each view. Given the generated data, a correct inference algorithm will be able to recover all the latent parameters. Figure 3(a) shows the ground truth that we used for the per topic words distribution and the estimation of these latent variables using variational inference as described in Sect. 3.2. All the topics are correctly recovered. Due to the exchangeability of Dirichlet distribution, the estimation gives different order of the topics which is shown as row-wise exchanges in Fig. 3(b). Figure 4 shows the parameter recovery for the partition parameters ρ and μ which are generated from beta distribution. In the example, we use $\iota_1 = (4, 2)$ and $\iota_2 = (1, 1)$ as hyper-parameters for the beta distributions. In this setting, the first view is comparably clean; the second view is more noisy with big variations on the noise level among the data. As Fig. 4 shows, almost all the partition parameters are correctly recovered.

4.2 Performance Evaluation Using Real-World Data

In this section, model performance is evaluated on real-world data. We present two experimental groups. The first one is using the LabelMe natural scene dataset [18, 24] and the second one is using the Leeds butterfly dataset [26] for fine-grained classification. We focus on the model performance where we investigate the distribution of topics and partition parameters. This will provide us with insight into the data structure and model behavior. Thereafter, we will present the classification performance. In these experiments, the classification results are obtained by applying softmax regression on the topic representation. In all experimental settings, the hyper-parameters for the per document topic distributions are set to $\alpha_* = 0.8$, the hyper-parameters for the per topic word distributions are set to $\sigma_* = 0.6$ and the hyper-parameters for the partition variables are set to $\iota_* = (5,5)^3$. We also perform experiments with different features, including off-the-shelf CNN-features from different layers and traditional SIFT features. Here, we only present the results using off-the-shelf CNN conv5_1 features as an example. We use the pre-trained Oxford VGG 16-layer CNN [27] for feature extraction. We create sliding windows in 3 scales with a 32 pixels step size to extract features, in the same manner as [28], and use K-means clustering to create a codebook and represent each image using a bag-of-visual-words. The vocabulary size is 1024. In general, the performance is robust when higher layers are used and when the vocabulary size is sufficient. More results using different features and different parameter settings are enclosed in the supplementary material.

4.2.1   LabelMe Dataset

We use the LabelMe Dataset as in [18,25] for this group of the experiments. The LabelMe dataset contains 8 classes of 256×256 images: highway, inside city, coast, forest, tall buildings, street, open country and mountain. For each class, 200 images are randomly selected, half of which are used for training, and half of which are used for testing. This results in 800 training and 800 testing images. We perform the experiment in two different scenarios: Image and Image, where only images are available; and Image and Annotation, where different modalities are available.

4.2.1.1   Image and Image. In this experiment, we explore the scenario in which only one modality is available. We want to model essential information that captures the within class variations and explains away the instance specific variations. Both views are bag-of-CNN Conv5_1 feature representations of the image data. For each document, two training images from the same class are randomly paired. This represents the scenario as shown in the introductory Fig. 1(a). For the experimental results presented below, the numbers of topics are set to $K = 15$, $T = 15$, $S = 15$.[4]

Figure 6 shows the histograms of the partition parameters in this case. Figure 6(a) and (b) appear to be similar. This is according to intuition; since both views are images and they are randomly paired within the same classes, the statistical features are expected to be the same for both views. Most partition parameters are larger than 0.8, which means that large parts of information can be shared between images from the same class and that the CNN Conv5_1

---

[3] α_* includes α_{p_1}, α_s and α_{p_2}. σ_* includes σ_{p_1}, σ_{p_2}, σ_{s_1} and σ_{s_2}. ι_* includes ι_1 and ι_2.

[4] The performance is robust with a sufficient amount of topics, 15 or higher. More results with different numbers of topics are presented in the supplement.

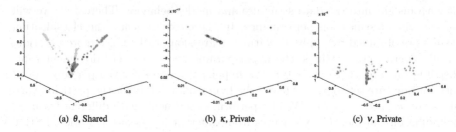

(a) θ, Shared   (b) κ, Private   (c) ν, Private

Fig. 5. Visualization of the shared topic representation (θ) and private topic representations (κ and ν) for LabelMe experiments using randomly paired images from the same class. The documents of different classes are colored differently and the plots show the first three principal components after applying PCA on the per document topic distributions for all the training data. (Color figure online)

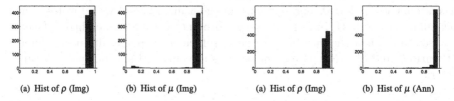

(a) Hist of ρ (Img)   (b) Hist of μ (Img)   (a) Hist of ρ (Img)   (b) Hist of μ (Ann)

Fig. 6. The histogram over partition parameters of the LabelMe image-image experiment. Img indicates that this modality uses natural images (a) Hist of ρ (Img) (b) Hist of μ (Img)

Fig. 7. The histogram over partition parameters of the LabelMe image-annotation experiment. Img indicates that this modality uses natural images. Ann indicates that this modality uses image annotations (a) Hist of ρ (Img) (b) Hist of μ (Ann)

Table 1. The performance comparison for Image and Image experiment with the LabelMe dataset. Full SVM shows the performance using SVM on the bag of Con5_1 features, while PCA 15 SVM shows the performance after applying PCA and using the top 15 principal components. LDA 15 shows the result using LDA with 15 topics and classification by softmax regression. IBTM 15 shows the result using IBTM with 15 shared topics and classification by softmax regression only on the shared topics.

DocNADE [25]	SupDocNADE [25]	Full SVM	PCA15 SVM	LDA15	SWB15 [22]	IBTM15
81.97 %	83.43 %	87 %	80.88 %	85.25 %	59.88 %	**89.75 %**

features provide a good raw representation of the images. For image pairs with more variation that does not correlate with the image class, the partition parameters will be smaller. The essential information ratio varies among images which causes the partition parameters to vary among different images.

Figure 5 visualizes the document distribution in different topic representation spaces. Figure 5(a) shows that documents from different classes are well separated in the space defined by the shared topic representation. Figure 5(b) and (c) show that documents from different classes are more mixed in the private topic spaces. Thus, the private information is used to explain instance specific features of a data point, but not class-specific features – these have been pushed into the shared space, according to the intention of the model. The variations in the private spaces are small due to the low noise ratio in the dataset. For

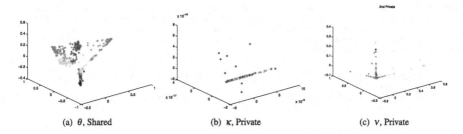

(a) θ, Shared   (b) κ, Private   (c) ν, Private

Fig. 8. Visualization of the shared topic representation (θ) and private topic representations (κ and ν) for LabelMe experiments using image features for the 1st view and annotation for the 2nd view. The documents of different classes are colored differently and the plots show the first three principal components after applying PCA on the per document topic distributions for all the training data. (Color figure online)

the classification performance where only images are available, using IBTM with classification using only the shared representation leads to a classification rate of 89.75 %. The classification results are summarized in Table 1. A standard LDA obtains better performance than PCA with the same number of dimensions. IBTM outperforms LDA with the same number of topics and can even obtain better results than using the full dimension (1024) of bag-of-Conv5_1 features together with linear SVM. While using SWB [22][5], the performance is unsatisfactory for such computer vision tasks due to the noisy properties of images. The results show that IBTM is able to learn a factorized latent representation, which separates task-relevant variation in the data from variation that is less relevant for the task at hand, here classification.

4.2.1.2 Image and Annotation. In this experiment, we explore the scenario when two different modalities are available for different views. We use the bag-of-Conv5_1 representation of images as the first view and the image annotations as the second view. The word counts for the annotations are scaled with the annotated region. For each document, 79 Conv5_1 features are extracted from the image view, and the sum over the word histogram for each view is normalized to 100. The number of topics is set to $K = 15$, $T = 15$, $S = 15$ in the experimental results presented here. Figure 7 shows the histograms of the partition parameters ρ and μ for the two views respectively. Figure 7(b) shows that the partition parameters are more concentrated around large values compared to Fig. 7(a), which indicate that most annotation information is more essential. This is consistent with the intuition of the relative noise levels in image vs annotation data.

Figure 8 shows the distribution of documents using different topic representations. As in the previous experiment, documents from different classes are well separated in the shared topic representation and are more mixed in the pri-

---

[5] We implemented SWB using Gibbs Sampling following the description in the paper [22]. The parameter settings are the same as in [22]. Linear SVM is used for classification using the topic representation from SWB. More analysis using SWB is presented in the supplementary material of this paper.

Table 2. The performance comparison for the image-annotation experiment for the LabelMe dataset. "IBTM15 1V" shows the prediction performance with only images available (1 view testing) and "IBTM15 2V" shows the prediction performance with both images and annotation available (2 view testing). For "SWB 2V", we concatenate words from images and captions for each document for both training and testing to use SWB since it is a single-view model

Full SVM	PCA 15	LDA15	SWB 2V [22]	IBTM15 1V	IBTM15 2V
87.63 %	84.88 %	85.38 %	61 %	**89.38 %**	**95 %**

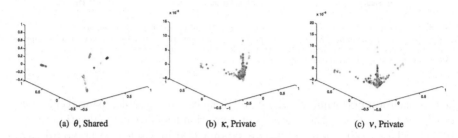

(a) θ, Shared   (b) κ, Private   (c) ν, Private

Fig. 9. Visualization of the shared topic representation (θ) and private topic representations (κ and ν) for experiments on the Leeds Butterfly dataset using randomly paired images from the same class. The documents of different classes are colored differently and the plots show the first three principal components after applying PCA on the per document topic distributions for all the training data.

vate topic representations. Table 2 summarizes the classification performance.[6] IBTM is able to outperform other methods with a performance of 89.38 % even when only images are available for testing. When both modalities are available, the performance goes up to 95 %, while ideal classification by humans for this dataset is reported to be 90 % in [24].

4.2.2   Leeds Butterfly Dataset

In this section, the Leeds butterfly dataset [26] is used to evaluate the IBTM model on a fine-grained classification task. This dataset contains 10 classes of butterfly images collected from Google image search, both the original images with cluttered background and segmentation masks for the butterflies are provided in the dataset. For each class, 55 to 100 images have been collected and there are 832 images in total. In this experiment, 30 images are randomly selected from each class for training and the remaining 532 images are used for testing. Similarly to above, we perform the experiment in two different scenarios: Image and Image, where only the natural images with cluttered backgrounds are available; and Image and Segmentation, where one modality is the natural image and the other modality is the segmented image.

4.2.2.1 Image and Image. In this experiment, we use only the natural images to evaluate the model performance in the uni-modal scenario. The experimental setting is similar to Sect. 4.2.1.1, where two images from the same class are paired

---

[6] The 0.65 % difference of Full SVM performance in Tables 1 and 2 were due to different random data partitions.

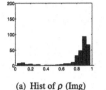 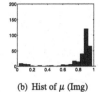

(a) Hist of ρ (Img)   (b) Hist of μ (Img)

Fig. 10. The histogram over partition parameters of the Leeds Butterfly image-image experiment. Img indicates that this modality uses natural images (a) Hist of ρ (Img) (b) Hist of μ (Img)

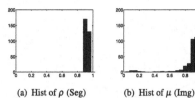

(a) Hist of ρ (Seg)   (b) Hist of μ (Img)

Fig. 11. The histogram over partition parameters of the Leeds Butterfly image-segmentation experiment. Img indicates that this modality uses natural images. Seg indicates that this modality uses segmente images (a) Hist of ρ (Seg) (b) Hist of μ (Img)

Table 3. The performance comparison with the Leeds Butterfly dataset. "II" shows the prediction performance for the paired image setting (Image-Image) for IBTM and only images for SWB. "IS" shows the prediction performance for the image and its segmentation image setting. In this setting, "1V" means that only images are available (1 view testing) and "2V" means that both images and segmentations are available (2 view testing). "IS SWB" shows the performance of using SWB with concatenated words from images and segmentations.

NLD [26][a]	Full SVM	PCA 15	II SWB15 [22]	IS SWB15 [22]	LDA15	II IBTM15	IS IBTM 1V	IS IBTM 2V
56.3 %	95.49 %	88.35 %	80.26 %	94.55 %	91.92 %	**95.86 %**	**96.05 %**	**99.06 %**

[a]Learning Models for Object Recognition from Natural Language Descriptions (NLD) trained a classification model based on text descriptors. All images are tested to use visual information to extract attributes to fit the text template for testing. The experiment setting is different from our experiments. However, we include the result from the original paper for completeness.

randomly. $K = 15$, $T = 3$ and $S = 3$ are used for the results presented here. The histograms in Fig. 10 are to the previous dataset, however, with smaller values. As natural images of butterflies have more background information that is not related to the class of the butterfly, while for the LabelMe dataset, almost the whole image has information contributing to the natural scene class.

Figure 9 visualizes the image distribution in the different topic representations, where the shared topic representation separates images from different classes better than the private ones. Table 3 summarizes the classification performance for this dataset. There "II IBTM 15" shows the result of IBTM using only natural images, which obtains the highest performance 95.86 % in this unimodality setting with only 15 topics.

4.2.2.2 Image and Segmented Image. In this experimental setting, natural images and segmented images are used as two different views for training to demonstrate the multi-modality scenario. The segmented images are used as the first view and the natural images are used as the second view. Since the model is symmetric, the order of the views has no impact on the model. Figure 11 shows the histogram of the partition parameter. It is apparent that the partition parameters of the segmented images are more concentrated around the large values. Thus, the model has learned that the segmented images contain more relevant information. This is consistent with human intuition. Figure 12 shows

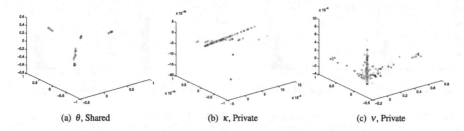

(a) θ, Shared   (b) κ, Private   (c) ν, Private

Fig. 12. Visualization of the shared topic representation (θ) and private topic representations (κ and ν) for experiments on the Leeds Butterfly dataset using images paired with their segmentation masks. The documents of different classes are colored differently and the plots show the first three principal components after applying PCA on the per document topic distributions for all the training data (a) θ, Shared (b) κ, Private (c) ν, Private (Color figure online)

the topic distribution using shared and private latent representations where the shared topic representations for different classes are naturally separated. Classification performance is summarized in Table 3. SWB performs better with this dataset than with the LabelMe dataset. The reason for this is probably that the visual words here are less noisy than in LabelMe. "IS IBTM15" denotes the performance of testing with only natural images and "IS IBTM15" shows the performance of testing with both natural images and their segmentation. We can see that IBTM performs better than other methods even if only natural images are available for testing. With the segmentation, the performance is almost ideal.

5   Conclusion

In this paper, we proposed a different variant of the topic model IBTM with a factored latent representation. It is able to model shared information and private information using different views which has been proven to be beneficial for different computer vision tasks. Experimental results show that IBTM can effectively encode the task-relevant information. Using this representation, the state-of-the-art results are achieved in different experimental scenarios.

In this paper, the focus lay on exploring the concept of factorized representations and the experiments were centered around two view scenarios. In future work, we plan to evaluate the performance of IBTM by using any number of views and in different scenarios such as cue-integration. In the end, efficient inference algorithms are the key for probabilistic graphic models in general. In this paper, we used variational inference in a batch manner. In the future, more efficient and robust inference algorithms [29, 30] can be explored.

References

1. Bengio, Y., Courville, A., Vincent, P.: Representation learning: a review and new perspectives. PAMI **35**(8), 1798–1828 (2013)
2. Tipping, M.E., Bishop, C.M.: Probabilistic principal component analysis. J. Roy. Stat. Soc. **61**(3), 611–622 (1999)

3. Blei, D.M., Ng, A.Y., Jordan, M.I.: Latent Dirichlet allocation. JMLR **3**, 993–1022 (2003)
4. Lawrence, N.D.: Gaussian process latent variable models for visualisation of high dimensional data. In: NIPS, pp. 329–336 (2004)
5. Fei-Fei, L., Perona, P.: A Bayesian hierarchical model for learning natural scene categories. In: CVPR, vol. 2, pp. 524–531. IEEE (2005)
6. Hospedales, T.M., Gong, S.G., Xiang, T.: Learning tags from unsegemented videos of multiple human actions. In: ICDM (2011)
7. Zhang, C., Song, D., Kjellstrom, H.: Contextual modeling with labeled multi-LDA. In: IROS, Tokyo, Japan (2013)
8. Tucker, L.R.: An inter-battery method of factory analysis. Psychometrika **23**(2), 111–136 (1958)
9. Damianou, A., Ek, H.C., Titsias, M., Lawrence, N.D.: Manifold relevance determination. In: ICML, pp. 145–152 (2012)
10. Zhang, C., Ek, C.H., Damianou, A., Kjellstrom, H.: Factorized topic models. In: ICLR (2013)
11. Virtanen, S., Jia, Y., Klami, A., Darrell, T.: Factorized multi-modal topic model. arXiv preprint. arXiv:1210.4920
12. Zhang, C., Kjellstrom, H.: How to supervise topic models. In: ECCV Workshop on Graphical Models in Computer Vision (2014)
13. Blei, D.M., McAuliffe, J.D.: Supervised topic models. arXiv preprint. arXiv:1003.0783 (2010)
14. Zhang, C., Ek, C.H., Gratal, X., Pokorny, F.T., Kjellström, H.: Supervised hierarchical Dirichlet processes with variational inference. In: ICCV Workshop on Inference for Probabilistic Graphical Models (2013)
15. Lacoste-Julien, S., Sha, F., Jordan, M.I.: DiscLDA: discriminative learning for dimensionality reduction and classification. In: NIPS (2008)
16. Zhu, J., Ahmed, A., Xing, E.P.: MedLDA: maximum margin supervised topic models for regression and classification. In: ICML (2009)
17. Zhu, J., Chen, N., Perkins, H., Zhang, B.: Gibbs max-margin supervised topic models with fast sampling algorithms. In: ICML (2013)
18. Wang, C., Blei, D., Fei-Fei, L.: Simultaneous image classification and annotation. In: CVPR, pp. 1903–1910. IEEE (2009)
19. Wang, Y., Mori, G.: Max-margin latent Dirichlet allocation for image classification and annotations. In: BMVC, p. 7 (2011)
20. Blei, D.M., Jordan, M.I.: Modeling annotated data. In: International Conference on Research and Development in Information Retrieval, pp. 127–134. ACM (2003)
21. Ek, C.H., Rihan, J., Torr, P.H.S., Rogez, G., Lawrence, N.D.: Ambiguity modeling in latent spaces. In: Popescu-Belis, A., Stiefelhagen, R. (eds.) MLMI 2008. LNCS, vol. 5237, pp. 62–73. Springer, Heidelberg (2008). doi:10.1007/978-3-540-85853-9_6
22. Chemudugunta, C., Smyth, P., Steyvers, M.: Modeling general and specific aspects of documents with a probabilistic topic model. NIPS **19**, 241–248 (2006)
23. Blei, D., Lafferty, J.: Correlated topic models. NIPS **18**, 147 (2006)
24. Li, L.-J., Su, H., Lim, Y., Fei-Fei, L.: Objects as attributes for scene classification. In: Kutulakos, K.N. (ed.) ECCV 2010. LNCS, vol. 6553, pp. 57–69. Springer, Heidelberg (2012). doi:10.1007/978-3-642-35749-7_5
25. Zheng, Y., Zhang, Y.J., Larochelle, H.: Topic modeling of multimodal data: an autoregressive approach. In: CVPR, pp. 1370–1377 (2014)
26. Wang, J., Markert, K., Everingham, M.: Learning models for object recognition from natural language descriptions. In: BMVC (2009)

27. Simonyan, K., Zisserman, A.: Very deep convolutional networks for large-scale image recognition. CoRR abs/1409.1556 (2014)
28. Gong, Y., Wang, L., Guo, R., Lazebnik, S.: Multi-scale orderless pooling of deep convolutional activation features. In: Fleet, D., Pajdla, T., Schiele, B., Tuytelaars, T. (eds.) ECCV 2014, Part VII. LNCS, vol. 8695, pp. 392–407. Springer, Heidelberg (2014)
29. Minka, T.P.: Divergence measures and message passing. Microsoft Research Technical report (2005)
30. Hoffman, M.D., Blei, D.M.: Structured stochastic variational inference. In: AISTATS (2015)

Online Adaptation for Joint Scene and Object Classification

Jawadul H. Bappy$^{(\boxtimes)}$, Sujoy Paul, and Amit K. Roy-Chowdhury

Department of ECE, University of California, Riverside, CA 92521, USA
{mbappy,supaul,amitrc}@ece.ucr.edu

Abstract. Recent efforts in computer vision consider joint scene and object classification by exploiting mutual relationships (often termed as context) between them to achieve higher accuracy. On the other hand, there is also a lot of interest in online adaptation of recognition models as new data becomes available. In this paper, we address the problem of how models for joint scene and object classification can be learned online. A major motivation for this approach is to exploit the hierarchical relationships between scenes and objects, represented as a graphical model, in an active learning framework. To select the samples on the graph, which need to be labeled by a human, we use an information theoretic approach that reduces the joint entropy of scene and object variables. This leads to a significant reduction in the amount of manual labeling effort for similar or better performance when compared with a model trained with the full dataset. This is demonstrated through rigorous experimentation on three datasets.

Keywords: Scene classification · Object detection · Active learning

1 Introduction

Scene classification and object detection are two challenging problems in computer vision due to high intra-class variance, illumination changes, background clutter and occlusion. Most existing methods assume that data will be labeled and available beforehand in order to train the classification models. It becomes infeasible and unrealistic to know all the labels beforehand with the huge corpus of visual data being generated on a daily basis. Moreover, adaptability of the models to the incoming data is crucial too for long-term performance guarantees. Currently, the big datasets (e.g. ImageNet [1], SUN [2]) are prepared with intensive human labeling, which is difficult to scale up as more and more new images are generated. So, we want to pose a question, '*Are all the samples equally important to manually label and learn a model from?*'. We address this question in the context of joint scene and object classification.

Electronic supplementary material The online version of this chapter (doi:10. 1007/978-3-319-46484-8_14) contains supplementary material, which is available to authorized users.

© Springer International Publishing AG 2016
B. Leibe et al. (Eds.): ECCV 2016, Part VIII, LNCS 9912, pp. 227–243, 2016.
DOI: 10.1007/978-3-319-46484-8_14

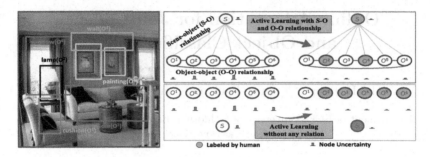

Fig. 1. This figure presents the motivation of incorporating relationship among scene and object samples within an image. Here, scene (S) and objects $(O^1, O^2, \ldots, O^6)$ are predicted by our initial classifier and detectors with some uncertainty. We formulate a graph exploiting scene-object (S-O) and object-object (O-O) relationships. As shown in the figure, even though $\{S, O^2, O^3, O^4, O^5, O^6\}$ nodes have high uncertainty, manually labeling only 3 of them is good enough to reduce the uncertainty of all the nodes if S-O and O-O relationships are considered. So, the manual labeling cost can be significantly reduced by our proposed approach.

Active learning [3] has been widely used to choose a subset of most informative samples that can achieve similar or better performance than all the data being manually labeled. In order to identify the informative samples, most active learning techniques choose the samples about which the classifier is most uncertain. Expected change in gradients [3], information gain [4], expected prediction loss [5] are some approaches used in the literature to obtain the samples for query. These approaches consider the individual samples to be independent. However, there are various tasks, such as document classification [6] and activity recognition [7], where interrelationships between samples exist. In such cases, it will be advantageous to exploit these relationships to reduce the number of samples to be manually labeled. Some active learning frameworks consider this idea and exploit different contextual relations such as link information [8], social relationships [9], spatial information [10], feature similarity [11], spatio-temporal relationships [12].

We leverage upon active learning for identifying the samples to label in the problem of joint scene and object recognition. Similar to the applications mentioned above, exploiting mutual relationships between scene and objects can yield better performance [13] than if no relationships are considered. For example, it is unlikely to find a 'cow' in a 'bedroom', but, the probability of finding 'bed' and 'lamp' in the same scene may be high. Thus gaining information about a scene can help in enhanced prediction on objects and vice versa. Previously, research in [14–17] has shown how to exploit the scene-object relationships to yield better classification performance. However, these methods require data to be manually labeled and available before learning. Although there exist some works involving active learning in scene and object classification [4,5,18], they do not exploit the scene-object(S-O) and object-object(O-O) inter-relationships. This is critical because of the hierarchical nature of the relationships between

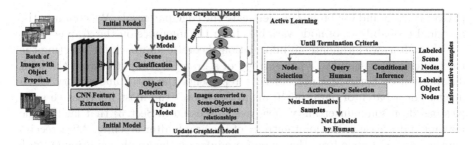

Fig. 2. This figure presents a pictorial representation of the proposed framework. At first, initial classification models and relationship model are learned from a small set of labeled images. Thereafter, as images are available in batches, scene & object classification models provide prediction scores of scene and objects. With these scores and the relationship model, the images are represented as graphs with scene and object nodes. Then, the active learning module is invoked which efficiently chooses the most informative scene or object nodes to query the human. Finally, the labels provided by the human are used to update the classification & relationship models.

objects and scenes. This relationship can be represented as a graphical model with the samples on the graph, which need to be labeled by a human, chosen using a suitable criterion. The labeling effort can be significantly reduced in this process - labeling a scene node in the graph can possibly resolve ambiguities for multiple object classes. This motivation is portrayed in Fig. 1.

Motivated by the above, we propose a novel active learning framework which exploits the S-O and O-O relationships to jointly learn scene and object classification models. Using mutual relationships between scene and objects, we can leverage upon the fact that manual labeling of one reduces the uncertainty of the other, and thus reduces labeling cost. This is achieved using an information theoretic approach that reduces the joint entropy of a graph. As presented in the figure, exploiting relationships between scene and objects can lead to lesser human labeling effort, compared to when relationships are not considered.

Framework Overview. The flow of the proposed algorithm is presented in Fig. 2. We perform two tasks simultaneously:

1. Selection of an image that contains the most informative samples (scene,objects)
2. Given an image, a sample (i.e., a node in the graph representing that image) is chosen in a way that reduces the uncertainty on other samples.

Our framework is divided into two phases. At first, we learn the initial classification models as well as the S-O and O-O relationship model with small amount of labeled data. In the second phase, with incoming unlabeled data, we first classify the unlabeled scene and object samples using the current models. Then, we represent each incoming image as a graph, where scene classification probabilities and object detection scores are utilized to represent the scene and object node potentials. S-O and O-O relations delineate the edge potentials. We compute the marginal probabilities of node variables from the inference on the graphs.

Thereafter, we formulate an information-theoretic approach for selecting the most informative samples. Joint entropy of a graph is computed from the joint distribution of scene and objects that represents the total uncertainty of an image. For a batch of data, our framework chooses the most informative samples based on some uncertainty measures (discussed in Sect. 3) that lead to the maximum decrease in the joint entropy of the graph after labeling. After receiving the label of a node from the human, we infer on the graph conditioned upon the known label. Due to this inference, the other unlabeled nodes gain information from the node labeled by human, which leads to a significant reduction in uncertainties of other nodes. The labels obtained in this process are used to update the scene and object classification models as well as the S-O and O-O relationships.

Main Contributions. Our main contributions are as follows.

- In computer vision, most of the existing active learning methods involve learning a classification model of one type of variable, e.g., scene, objects, activity, text, etc. On the other hand, the proposed active learning framework learns scene and object classification models *simultaneously*.
- In the proposed active learning framework, both scene and object classification models take advantage of the interdependence between them in order to select the most informative samples with the least manual labeling cost. To the best of our knowledge, any previous work using *active learning to classify scene and objects together* is unknown.
- Leveraging upon the inter-relationships between scene and objects, we propose a new information-theoretic sample selection strategy along with inference on a graph based on the intuition that learning a sample reduces the uncertainties of other samples. Moreover, our framework facilitates continuous and incremental learning of the classification models as well as the S-O and O-O relationship models, thus dynamically adapting to the changes in incoming data.

1.1 Related Works

Scene and Object Recognition. Many of the scene classification methods use low dimensional features such as color and texture [19], GIST [20], SIFT descriptor [21] and deep feature [22]. In object detection, current state-of-the-art methods are R-CNN [23], SPP-net [24] and fast R-CNN [25]. Another promising approach in recognition tasks has been to exploit the relationships between objects in a scene using a graphical model [13,26,27]. A Conditional Random Field (CRF) for integrating the scene and object classification for video sequences was proposed in [14]. A model for joint image segmentation, object and scene class inference was proposed in [13]. In [15], the spatial relationships between the objects within an image were exploited to compute the scene similarity score, based on which the indoor scene categories were predicted. In [16], a CRF model was constructed based on scene, object and the textual data associated with the images on the web, to label the scenes and localize objects within the image. In [28], a projection was formulated from images to a space spanned by object banks, based on which, the image was classified into different categories. In [17], a framework was developed for multiple object classification within an image, where a conditional tree model was learned based on the co-occurrences of objects.

Active Learning. Although the above mentioned works exploit the contextual relationships, they assume that all the data are labeled and available beforehand, which is not feasible and involves huge labeling cost. Active learning has been widely used to reduce the effort of manual labeling in different computer vision tasks including scene classification [4], video segmentation [29], object detection [30], activity recognition [12], tracking [31]. A generalized active learning framework for computer vision problems such as person detection, face recognition and scene classification was proposed in [32]. They used the two concepts of uncertainty and sample diversity to choose the samples for manual labeling. Some of the common techniques to measure uncertainty for selecting the informative data points are presented in [33]. Active learning has been separately used for scene or object classification [4,18,30,34], but not in their joint classification.

In [18], a framework for actively learning scene classification model was proposed, where the authors incorporated two strategies - Best vs. Second Best (BvSB) and K-centroid to select the informative subset of images. A framework based on information density measure and uncertainty measure to obtain the best subset of images for querying the human was proposed in [5]. Although their algorithm can be applied separately for both scene and object classification, they do not exploit the relationships between scene and objects. An active learning framework for object categories was proposed in [35] which considers the case where the labeler itself is uncertain about labeling an image.

In [4], the authors present an active learning framework for scene classification. In their hierarchical model, they focus on querying at the scene level, and whenever unexpected class labels are returned by the human, queries are made at the object level. Thus in their method, there exists a flow of information from the object level to the scene level. However, in our method, there is a flow of information from scene to object level and vice versa, in a collaborative manner, which paves the path for a joint scene-object classification framework.

2 Joint Scene and Object Model

In this section, we discuss how we represent an image in a graphical model with scene and object as hidden variables.

A. **Scene Classification Method.** In order to represent scenes, we extract features using Convolution Neural Networks (CNN). Given an image, we get a feature vector f from the $fc7$ layer of a CNN architecture, where $f \in \Re^{4096 \times 1}$. We train a linear multi-class Support Vector Machine (SVM) [36] to compute the probability of nth class, $p(S = s_n | f^j)$, where f^j implies the feature vector corresponding to sample j. We denote the learned model for scene classification as $\mathcal{P}_s$. Given an image, $\Phi_S \in \Re^N$ represents the classification score. N is the total number of scene categories considered in the experiment.

B. Object Detection Method. We use R-CNN presented in [23] to detect the objects in an image. In R-CNN, we extract features from deep network for each object proposal. Then, we train a binary SVM classifier for each object category to get the probability of appearance of an object. After classifying the region we form a vector that represents the confidence scores of the binary classifiers for each category. Thus, for each pth region we get Φ_{O^p} that represents the detection score vector. Finally, we use bounding box regression method [37] for better object localization. We denote the learned model for scene classification as $\mathcal{P}_o$.

C. Graphical Model Representation. In this model, two levels of nodes are used - one represents scene v_s and other set of nodes implies detected objects v_o. v_o is generally represented by $v_o = \{v_{o^1}, v_{o^2}, ..v_{o^D}\}$, where D is the number of bounding boxes appearing in an image. The link between them is depicted by edges. The joint distribution of v_s and v_o over the CRF can be written as

$$P(v_s, v_o) = \frac{1}{Z} \, \Psi_\xi(v_s, v_o) \prod_{\substack{i,j \in D \\ i \neq j}} \Psi_\xi(v_{o^i}, v_{o^j}) \prod_{w \in \{v_s, v_o\}} \Psi_v(w) \tag{1}$$

where, Z is normalizing constant. $\Psi_v(.)$ and $\Psi_\xi(.)$ denote node and edge potentials.

Node Potentials. Given an image, the scene classifier ($\mathcal{P}_s$) produces a vector that contains the probabilities of all the scene labels. From these probabilities we compute scene node potential $\Psi_v(v_s)$ as presented in Eq. 2. Similarly, given an image, the object detection scores are used to model the object node potentials $\Psi_v(v_o)$ as shown in Eq. 3.

$$\Psi_v(v_s) = \sum_{n \in N} \mathcal{I}(S_n) \beta_n^T \, \Phi_S \tag{2}$$

$$\Psi_v(v_o) = \sum_{p \in D} \sum_{m \in M} \mathcal{I}(O_m^p) \Omega_m^T \, \Phi_{O^p} \tag{3}$$

Here, Φ_S is a vector of the probability of the scene labels obtained from multi-class SVM classifier. β_n is the feature weight vector corresponding to scene label S_n and $\mathcal{I}(.)$ is the indicator function, i.e., $\mathcal{I}(S_n) = 1$ when $S = S_n$, otherwise 0. Ω_m is the weight corresponding to the detection score of the object O_m. Φ_{O^p} is the score vector of detecting all the objects in the pth bounding box. M is the number of object Classes.

Edge Potentials. We use two type of relationships, S-O and O-O. We use co-occurrence frequencies to represent edge potential. The probability of the presence of an object in a particular scene is determined by the co-occurrence statistics. For instance, in a context of *'highway'* scene, the probability of appearance of *'car'* will be higher than *'table'* or *'chair'*. In Eq. 4, $\Psi_\xi(v_s, v_o)$ represents the relationship between S and O. Similarly, $\Psi_\xi(v_{o^i}, v_{o^j})$ models the O-O relations.

$$\Psi_\xi(v_s, v_o) = \sum_{p \in D} \sum_{n \in N} \sum_{m \in M} \mathcal{I}(S_n) \mathcal{I}(O_m^p) \Phi_\xi(S_n, O_m) \tag{4}$$

$$\Psi_\xi(v_{o^i}, v_{o^j}) = \sum_{m' \in M} \sum_{m \in M} \mathcal{I}(O_{m'}^i) \mathcal{I}(O_m^j) \, \Phi_\xi(O_{m'}, O_m) \tag{5}$$

$\Phi_\xi(S_n, O_m)$ represents the co-occurrence statistics between scene and objects. Larger value implies higher probability of co-occurrence of S_n and O_m. Here, $\Phi_\xi(O^i, O^j)$ is the co-occurrence [38] between the detected objects O^i and O^j. It encodes the information about how often two objects can co-occur in a scene.

Parameter Learning. The initial model parameters of the CRF model are learned from a set of annotated images, object detectors and scene classifier. Given the ground truth object bounding boxes, we use object detectors to obtain detection scores for the corresponding bounding box region. Similarly, we get the classification score from the annotated scene label. Thus, we can easily apply maximum likelihood estimation approach to learn all the parameters $\{\beta, \Omega, \Phi_\xi(S_n, O_m), \Phi_\xi(O_{m'}, O_m)\}$ in the model.

Inference of Scene and Object Labels. To compute the marginal distributions of the node and edge, we use Loopy Belief Propagation (LBP) algorithm [39], as our graph contains cycles. LBP is not guaranteed to converge to the true marginal, but has good approximation of the marginal distributions.

3 Active Learning Framework

In the previous section, we represent an image as a graph containing v_s and v_o nodes. If we select a node from a graph, such that querying it will minimize the joint entropy of the graph maximally, then it means that the classifier will be able to gain maximum amount of information by labeling that node.

Formulation of Joint Entropy. Consider a fully connected graph $G = (V, E)$, where V and E are the set of nodes and edges respectively. It may be noted that $V = \{S, O^1, O^2, \ldots, O^D\}$. Let $\mu_i(v_i)$ and $\mu_{ij}(v_i, v_j)$ be the marginal probabilities of the node and edge of the graph. Let v_i and v_j represent the random variables for nodes $i, j \in V$. In our joint scene and object classification, $i \in \{S, O^1, O^2, \ldots, O^D\}$ as discussed in Sect. 2. The node entropy $H(v_i)$ and mutual information $I(v_i, v_j)$ between a pair of nodes are defined as,

$$H(v_i) = \mathbb{E}[-\log_2 \mu_i(v_i)] \qquad I(v_i, v_j) = \mathbb{E}[\log_2 \frac{\mu_{ij}(v_i, v_j)}{\mu_i(v_i)\mu_t(v_j)}] \tag{6}$$

Considering Q nodes in the graph, its joint entropy can be expressed as,

$$H(V) = H(v_1) + \sum_{i=2}^{Q} H(v_i|v_1, \ldots, v_{i-1})$$

$$= H(v_1) + \sum_{i=2}^{Q} \left[H(v_i) - I(v_1, \ldots, v_{i-1}; v_i) \right] \qquad (7)$$

using $I(v_1, \ldots, v_{i-1}; v_i) = H(v_i) - H(v_i|v_1, \ldots, v_{i-1})$. Again, using the chain rule, $I(v_1, \ldots, v_{i-1}; v_i) = \sum_{j=1}^{i-1} I(v_j; v_i|v_1, \ldots, v_{j-1})$, Eq. 7 becomes

$$H(V) = \sum_{i=1}^{Q} H(v_i) - \sum_{i=2}^{Q} \sum_{j=1}^{i-1} I(v_j; v_i|v_1, \ldots, v_{j-1}) \qquad (8)$$

It becomes computationally expensive to compute the conditional mutual information, as the number of node increases [40]. As we consider only pair-wise interactions between S-O and O-O, we approximate the conditional mutual information $I(v_j; v_i|v_1, \ldots, v_{j-1}) \approx I(v_j; v_i)$. Thus, the joint entropy of the graph can be approximated as,

$$H(V) \approx \sum_{i=1}^{Q} H(v_i) - \sum_{i=2}^{Q} \sum_{j=1}^{i-1} I(v_j; v_i) = \sum_{i \in V} H(v_i) - \sum_{(i,j) \in E} I(v_i; v_j) \qquad (9)$$

This expression is actually exact for a tree, but approximate for a graph having cycles. The approximation leads to the expression of joint entropy in Eq. 9, which is similar to the joint entropy expression in Bethe method [40].

Informative Node Selection. In our problem, an image is represented by a graph having several nodes with two types of hidden variables v_s and v_o. So, we require not only to find the most informative image but also need to choose the node to be manually labeled. If we manually label a node, then we assume that there is no uncertainty involved in that node. Thus, after labeling a node v_i with the label l, the node entropy becomes zero, i,e. $H(v_i = l) = 0$.

Let $H^p(V)$ be the the joint entropy of image p which can be computed using Eq. 9. We query the node such that $H^p(V)$ is maximally reduced after labeling the node and inferring the graph conditioned on the new label. Then, after labeling v_i, we find the optimal node q of image p to be queried as[1],

$$q^* = \arg \max_q \left[H^p(v_q) - \frac{1}{2} \sum_{j \in \mathcal{N}(q)} I^p(v_q, v_j) \right] \qquad (10)$$

where $\mathcal{N}(q)$ represents the neighbor nodes of q. For simplicity, let us define the uncertainty associated with node q of image p as $J_q^p = H^p(v_q) - \frac{1}{2} \sum_{j \in \mathcal{N}(q)} I^p(v_q, v_j)$ where the joint entropy for an image p is $H^p(V) = \sum_{q=1}^{n} J_q^p$

---

[1] See derivation in supplementary.

from Eqs. 9 and 10. From Eq. 10, we choose the node to query, which has the maximum uncertainty considering not only the node entropy but also the mutual information between the nodes. Next, we explain how to choose a set of nodes from a batch of images.

Simultaneous Image and Node Selection. We query the nodes of image p only if its joint entropy $H^p(V) \geq \delta$, where δ is a threshold. Since we have the information about all the node uncertainties of all images, we can perform multiple queries across multiple different images such that the learner can learn faster and more efficiently. In this paper, we consider that there is no relation between the images, thus the conditional inference on one image is independent of the other images. Thus, graphs of different images can be conditionally inferred in a parallel manner.

Let, a vector, $J^p = [J_1^p, J_2^p, \ldots, J_Q^p]^T$ contain the uncertainty associated with Q (dependent on the image) nodes for an image p. Consider another vector, $\hat{J} = [J^1 \ J^2 \ldots J^P]^T$ which is obtained after concatenating all the vectors J^p for P images, whose joint entropy is higher than threshold δ. We sort the vector $\hat{J}$ in descending order to obtain a new vector $\hat{J}_s$. Then, we perform multiple queries based on $\hat{J}_s$, which contain uncertainty of nodes from multiple images of a batch. For each image, we choose the node appearing first in $\hat{J}_s$ for labeling. We perform conditional inference with the new labels in a parallel manner over all the images. The $\hat{J}_s$ vector is again obtained using the updated uncertainties of the nodes and the process is repeated until $H^p(V) \leq \delta, \forall p$. It may be noted that P decreases or at least remains same in succeeding iterations, because nodes belonging to images attaining joint entropy less than δ are not queried and thus not included in $\hat{J}_s$. Inference reduces the uncertainty on other nodes of the same image.

As uncertainty of nodes decreases, joint entropy is also reduced. Consider a matrix S having dimension $N_n \times 2$, where N_n is the total number of nodes of all images in the batch. The first and second columns of S contain the node index of a graph (image) and the image index respectively. The order in which the elements of S are populated is the same as that of $\hat{J}_s$. We refrain from choosing more than one node per image in each iteration because labeling one node can help the other nodes attain a better decision after inference. The set of nodes $\mathcal{M}$, chosen for labeling in each iteration can be expressed as,

$$\mathcal{M}^* = \operatorname*{arg\,max}_{\substack{\mathcal{M} \\ s.t.|\mathcal{M}|=P \\ S^{i,2} \neq S^{j,2}, i,j \in \mathcal{M}}} \sum_{k \in \mathcal{M}} \left[\hat{J}_s\right]_k \tag{11}$$

where $\left[\hat{J}_s\right]_k$ denote the kth element of $\hat{J}_s$ and $S^{i,m}$ denote the ith row and m^{th} column of S, where $m \in \{1, 2\}$. All the steps of active learning are shown in Algorithm 1. The first column of S is used to identify which node of an image should be labeled. To summarize Eq. 11, the optimal set $\mathcal{M}$ can be obtained by choosing one node which has the highest entropy from each image.

Classifier Update. To classify scene and objects, we use a linear support vector machine (SVM) classifier. The probability of predicted label can be defined as

---

Algorithm 1. Online Learning for Scene and Object Sample Selection

---

INPUTS. 1. Learned scene, object and relation models after processing images in Batch$_{K-1}$: $\{\mathcal{P}_s, \mathcal{P}_o, \Phi_\xi(S_n, O_m) \ \& \ \Phi_\xi(O_{m'}, O_m)\}$
       2. Unlabeled Batch$_K$: $\mathcal{U}$
OUTPUTS. Learned Models after processing images in Batch$_K$: $\{\mathcal{P}_s, \mathcal{P}_o,$
$\Phi'_\xi(S_n, O_m) \ \& \ \Phi'_\xi(O_{m'}, O_m)\}$
Initialize: $L_s = \{\}$ (Empty set)
Step 1: Compute $H(v_i)$ and $I(v_i, v_j)$ using Eq. 6
Step 2a: Compute vector $J^p = [J_1^p, J_2^p, \ldots J_Q^p]$ containing the node uncertainties involving entropy and mutual information, for all images.
Step 2b: Obtain vector $\hat{J}$ by concatenating the vectors J^p, $\forall p$, s.t. $H^p(V) \geq \delta$
Step 2c: $\hat{J}_s \leftarrow sort(\hat{J})$ in descending order
Step 2d: Obtain a vector S storing the image id in the sequence as in $\hat{J}_s$
if $length(\hat{J}_s) \neq 0$ **then**
   | **Step 3a:** Select nodes for manual labeling to form a set $\mathcal{M}$ using Eq. 6
   | **Step 3b:** Query the nodes in $\mathcal{M}$ to the human
   | **Step 4:** $L_s = L_s \cup \mathcal{M}$ (Labels provided by human)
   | **Step 5:** Infer on the graphs conditioned on the labels provided by human
   | **Step 6:** Update $\hat{J}_s, S$ using Steps 1 & 2a–d
else
   | **Step 7:** Update models $\{\mathcal{P}_s, \mathcal{P}_o, \Phi_\xi(S_n, O_m) \ \& \ \Phi_\xi(O_{m'}, O_m)\}$ with L_s

---

$\hat{y} = w^T f(x) + b$, where $f(x)$ is the feature of scene or objects and w, b are parameters that determine the hyperplane between two classes. We use soft margins formulation presented in [36] to find the solution of w, b. The solution can be found by optimizing, $\frac{1}{2}w^2 + C\sum_1^n \epsilon_i$ subject to $y_i(w^T f(x_i) + b) \geq (1 - \epsilon_i)$ and $\epsilon_i \geq 0$ for all i samples, where ϵ_i is the slack variable.

Edge Weight Update. We update the co-occurrence statistics with new manually labeled data as presented in Eqs. 4 and 5. lets denote them by $\Phi'_\xi(S_n, O_m)$ and $\Phi'_\xi(O_{m'}, O_m)$. The updated co-occurrence matrix will be $[\Phi_\xi(S_n, O_m)]_{t+1} \leftarrow [\Phi_\xi(S_n, O_m)]_t + \Phi'_\xi(S_n, O_m)$ and $[\Phi_\xi(O_{m'}, O_m)]_{t+1} \leftarrow [\Phi_\xi(O_{m'}, O_m)]_t + \Phi'_\xi(O_{m'}, O_m)$, where the subscript $t + 1$ indicates the edge potentials after t updates.

4   Experiments

In this section, we provide experimental analysis of our active learning framework for joint scene and object recognition models on three challenging datasets. For convenience, we will use terms 'inter-relationship' and 'contextual relationship' to denote scene-object and object-object relationship.

Datasets. In our experiments, we use SUN [41], MIT-67 Indoor [42] and MSRC [43] datasets in order to analyze scene classification and object recognition performance and compare our results. These datasets are appropriate as they provide rich source of contextual information between scene and objects. In SUN dataset, we choose 125 scene classes and 80 object categories to evaluate scene classification and object detection performance, as those contain annotation for both scene and objects. MIT-67 indoor [42] dataset consists of 67 indoor scene categories with large varieties of object categories. For MSRC [43] dataset, we evaluate our results comparing with the ground truth which is available in [13].

Experimental Setup. We use a publicly available software- '*UGM Toolbox*' [44] to infer the node and edge belief in image graphs. We use pre-trained model '*VGG net*' [22] which is trained on 'places-205' dataset to extract the scene features from CNN. For object recognition, we use the model as presented in [25].

In our online learning process, we perform 5 fold-cross validation, where one fold is used as testing set and the rest are used as training set. We divide the training set into 6 batches. We assume that human-labeled samples are available in the first batch and we use it to obtain the initial S and O classification models and the S-O and O-O relations. It might be possible that we do not have all the classes for scene and objects in the first batch. So, new classes are learned incrementally as batches of data come in. Now, with current batch of data we apply our framework to choose the most informative samples to label and then, update the classification and relationship models with newly labeled data. Finally, we compute our recognition results on the test set with each updated models.

Evaluation Criterion. In order to train the object detectors, we first choose positive and negative examples. We apply standard hard negative mining [37] method to train the binary SVM. We calculate the average precision (AP) of each category by comparing with the ground truth. Precision depends on both correct labeling and localization (overlap between object detection box and ground truth box). Let the computed bounding box of an object be O_b and the ground truth box be G_b, then the overlap ratio, $OR = \frac{O_b \cap G_b}{O_b \cup G_b}$. $OR \geq 0.5$ is considered as correct localization of an object. Before presenting our results, we define all the abbreviations that will be used hereafter

⋄ **SOAL:** proposed scene-object active learning (SOAL) as discussed in Sect. 3.
⋄ **Bv2B:** Best vs Second Best active learning strategy proposed in [18].
⋄ **IL-SO:** Incremental learning (IL) approach presented in [45] is implemented for scene and object (SO) classification.
⋄ **No Rel:** No relation is considered between scene and objects.
⋄ **S-O Rel:** Only S-O relations are considered but not O-O relations.
⋄ **S-O-O Rel:** Both S-O and O-O relationships are considered.
⋄ **All+S-O:** All samples with S-O relations are considered.
⋄ **All+S-O-O:** All samples with both S-O and O-O relations are considered.
⋄ **All+No Rel:** All samples without any relation are considered.
⋄ **SO+All:** All samples in batch are considered for scene and object classification with S-O-O relationship.
⋄ **NL, AL:** NL implies no human in the loop, i.e., we do not invoke any human to learn labels. AL denotes active learning. For example, S-NL+O-AL means scene nodes are not queried but object nodes are queried.

Experimental Analysis. We perform the following set of experiments - 1. Comparison with other active learning methods, 2. Comparison of the baselines with different S-O and O-O relations, 3. Comparison against other scene and object recognition methods, and 4. Recognition performance of scene and object models while labeling either scene or object.

Comparison with Other Active Learning Methods. In Figs. 3(a–c) and 4(a–c), we compare our active learning framework with some existing active learning approaches- Bv2B [18], Random Selection, Entropy [46] and IL-SO [45]. In the case of random selection, we pick the samples with uniform distribution. For Bv2B,Entropy and IL-SO, we implement the methods to select the informative samples for scene and objects. The feature extraction stages are the same as ours. We observe that our approach outperforms other methods by a large margin in selecting the most informative samples in both scene and object recognition.

Is Contextual Information Useful in Selecting the Most Informative Samples? We conduct an experiment that implements our proposed active learning strategy by exploiting different set of relations of scene (S) and objects (O). Figures 3(d–f) and 4(d–f) show the plots for S and O respectively on three datasets. It is noticed that the highest accuracy is yielded by S-O-O Rel (proposed), followed by S-O Rel and No-Rel in scene classification as well as in object recognition. This brings out the advantage of exploiting both S-O and O-O relations in actively choosing the samples for manual labeling. Moreover, the manual labeling cost is significantly reduced when we consider more relations. It may also be noted that our proposed framework achieves similar or even better performance by only choosing a smaller subset of training data than building a model with full training set for both scene and objects. For scenes, this subset is **35 %**, **30 %** and **42 %** of whole training set on MSRC, SUN and MIT datasets respectively. Similarly, for objects, we require only **39 %**, **61 %**, **60 %** of whole training set to be manually labeled on these three datasets.

Comparison Against Other Scene and Object Classification Methods. We also compare our S and O classification performance with other state-of-the-art S and O recognition methods. For scene, we choose Holistic [13], CNN [22], DSIFT [21], MLRep [47], S^2ICA [48] and MOP-CNN [49]. Similarly, we compare against Holistic [13], R-CNN [23], DPM [37] for object detection performance. Holistic approach exploits interrelationship among S and O using graphical model. We also compare with SO-All. From Figs. 3(g–i) and 4(g–i), we can see that our proposed framework outperforms the other state-of-the-art methods.

How Does Scene and Object Sample Selection Affect Classification Score of Each Other? We perform an experiment to observe how S and O recognition performs, when we implement active sample selection of either scene or object nodes and exploit S-O and O-O relationships to improve the decisions of the other type of nodes. The results are shown in Figs. 3(j–l) and 4(j–l). Let us consider the first scenario (S-NL+O-AL) where we perform AL on the O nodes but use relationships to update the classification probabilities of the S node. We

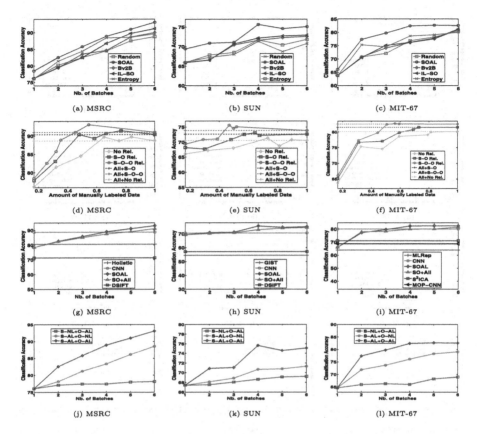

Fig. 3. In this figure, we present the scene classification performance for three datasets-MSRC [43], SUN [2] and MIT-67 Indoor [42] (left to right). Plots (a, b, c) present the comparison of SOAL (proposed) against other state-of-the-art active learning methods. Plots (d, e, f) demonstrate comparison with different contextual relations. Plots (g, h, i) demonstrate the comparison of other scene classification methods. Plots (j, k, l) show the classification performance by utilizing our active learning framework either on scene or objects and both. Please see the experimental section for details. Best viewable in color. (Color figure online)

use the first batch to learn the S and O models, but thereafter query to label only object nodes and not scene nodes.

The relationship models are updated based on the confidence of scene classifier and manual labeling of the objects obtained from a human annotator. With each update on context model, scene classification accuracy goes up even though the scene classification model is not updated. Similarly, the second scenario involves manual labeling of only S nodes but not O nodes. In this scenario, we do not consider O-O relationships. We can not rely on confidence of object classifiers to model O-O relations as it might provide wrong prediction of object labels. However, involvement of human in both scene and objects makes the sample selection even more efficient and outperforms all the scenarios

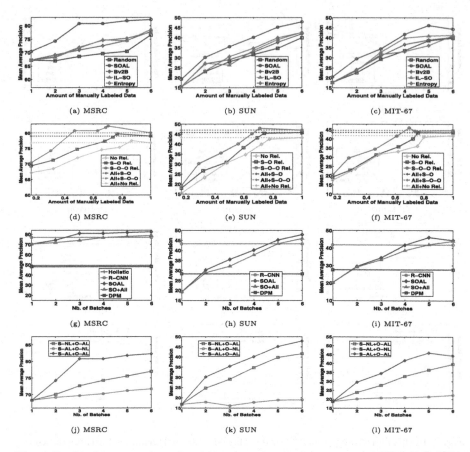

Fig. 4. In this figure, we show the object detection performances on MSRC [43], SUN [2] and MIT-67 Indoor [42] (left to right). Plots (a, b, c) present the comparison of SOAL with other state-of-the-art active learning methods. Plots (d, e, f) demonstrate comparison with different graphical relations. Plots (g, h, i) present the comparison of other object detection methods. Plots (j, k, l) show the detection performance by implementing our active learning framework either on scene or objects and both. Please see the experimental section for details. Best viewable in color. (Color figure online)

mentioned above. As shown in Figs. 3(j–l)' and 4(j–l), S-AL+O-AL achieves better performance than S-AL+O-NL by approximately 4–5 % and 4.5–5.5 % in both scene and objects on three datasets.

Some Examples of Active Learning (AL) Performance. We provide some examples of scene prediction and object detections as shown in Fig. 5. Here, scene prediction and detections are changing as models are learned over samples from each batch. Scene and object models are updated continuously with upcoming batch of data using our AL approach. With each improved model from the batch of data, classifiers become more confident in predicting scene and object labels on test image. More such examples are provided in the supplementary material.

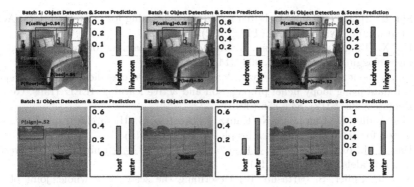

Fig. 5. Scene prediction and object detection performance on test image with updated model learned from the data of 1st, 4th and 6th batch.

5   Conclusions

In this paper, we propose a novel active learning framework for joint scene and object classification exploiting the interrelationship between them. We exploit the scene-object and object-object interdependencies in order to select the most informative samples to develop better classification models for scenes and objects. Our approach significantly reduces the human effort in labeling samples. We show in the experimental section that with only a small subset of the full training set we achieve better or similar performance compared with using full training set.

Acknowledgment. The work was partially supported by NSF grant IIS-1316934 and US Office of Naval Research contract N00014-15-C-5113 through Mayachitra, Inc.

References

1. Deng, J., Dong, W., Socher, R., Li, L.J., Li, K., Fei-Fei, L.: Imagenet: a large-scale hierarchical image database. In: CVPR (2009)
2. Xiao, J., Hays, J., Ehinger, K., Oliva, A., Torralba, A.: Sun database: large-scale scene recognition from abbey to zoo. In: CVPR (2010)
3. Settles, B.: Active learning. Synth. Lect. Artif. Intell. Mach. Learn. **6**(1), 1–114 (2012)
4. Li, X., Guo, Y.: Multi-level adaptive active learning for scene classification. In: Fleet, D., Pajdla, T., Schiele, B., Tuytelaars, T. (eds.) ECCV 2014, Part VII. LNCS, vol. 8695, pp. 234–249. Springer, Heidelberg (2014)
5. Li, X., Guo, Y.: Adaptive active learning for image classification. In: CVPR (2013)
6. Moraes, R., Valiati, J.F., Neto, W.P.G.: Document-level sentiment classification: an empirical comparison between svm and ann. Expert Syst. Appl. **40**(2), 621–633 (2013)
7. Zhang, Y., Liu, X., Chang, M.-C., Ge, W., Chen, T.: Spatio-temporal phrases for activity recognition. In: Fitzgibbon, A., Lazebnik, S., Perona, P., Sato, Y., Schmid, C. (eds.) ECCV 2012, Part III. LNCS, vol. 7574, pp. 707–721. Springer, Heidelberg (2012)

8. Shi, L., Zhao, Y., Tang, J.: Batch mode active learning for networked data. ACM Trans. Intell. Syst. Technol. (TIST) **3**(2), 33 (2012)

9. Hu, X., Tang, J., Gao, H., Liu, H.: Actnet: Active learning for networked texts in microblogging. In: SDM, pp. 306–314. SIAM (2013)

10. Li, J., Bioucas-Dias, J.M., Plaza, A.: Spectral-spatial classification of hyperspectral data using loopy belief propagation and active learning. IEEE Trans. Geosci. Remote Sens. **51**(2), 844–856 (2013)

11. Mac Aodha, O., Campbell, N., Kautz, J., Brostow, G.: Hierarchical subquery evaluation for active learning on a graph. In: CVPR (2014)

12. Hasan, M., Roy-Chowdhury, A.K.: Context aware active learning of activity recognition models. In: ICCV (2015)

13. Yao, J., Fidler, S., Urtasun, R.: Describing the scene as a whole: joint object detection, scene classification and semantic segmentation. In: CVPR (2012)

14. Wojek, C., Schiele, B.: A dynamic conditional random field model for joint labeling of object and scene classes. In: Forsyth, D., Torr, P., Zisserman, A. (eds.) ECCV 2008, Part IV. LNCS, vol. 5305, pp. 733–747. Springer, Heidelberg (2008)

15. Alberti, M., Folkesson, J., Jensfelt, P.: Relational approaches for joint object classification and scene similarity measurement in indoor environments. In: AAAI 2014 Spring Symposia: Qualitative Representations for Robots (2014)

16. Wang, B., Lin, D., Xiong, H., Zheng, Y.: Joint inference of objects and scenes with efficient learning of text-object-scene relations. IEEE Trans. Multimedia **8**(99), 1 (2016)

17. Nimmagadda, T., Anandkumar, A.: Multi-object classification and unsupervised scene understanding using deep learning features and latent tree probabilistic models. arXiv preprint arXiv:1505.00308 (2015)

18. Li, X., Guo, R., Cheng, J.: Incorporating incremental and active learning for scene classification. In: ICMLA (2012)

19. Yue, J., Li, Z., Liu, L., Fu, Z.: Content-based image retrieval using color and texture fused features. Math. Comput. Model. **54**(3), 1121–1127 (2011)

20. Li, Z., Itti, L.: Saliency and gist features for target detection in satellite images. TIP **20**(7), 2017–2029 (2011)

21. Liu, C., Yuen, J., Torralba, A.: Dense scene alignment using sift flow for object recognition. In: CVPR (2009)

22. Zhou, B., Lapedriza, A., Xiao, J., Torralba, A., Oliva, A.: Learning deep features for scene recognition using places database. In: NIPS, pp. 487–495 (2014)

23. Girshick, R., Donahue, J., Darrell, T., Malik, J.: Rich feature hierarchies for accurate object detection and semantic segmentation. In: CVPR (2014)

24. He, K., Zhang, X., Ren, S., Sun, J.: Spatial pyramid pooling in deep convolutional networks for visual recognition. In: Fleet, D., Pajdla, T., Schiele, B., Tuytelaars, T. (eds.) ECCV 2014, Part III. LNCS, vol. 8691, pp. 346–361. Springer, Heidelberg (2014)

25. Girshick, R.: Fast R-CNN. In: ICCV (2015)

26. Choi, W., Shahid, K., Savarese, S.: Learning context for collective activity recognition. In: CVPR, pp. 3273–3280 (2011)

27. Zhu, Y., Nayak, N., Roy-Chowdhury, A.: Context-aware activity modeling using hierarchical conditional random fields. PAMI **37**(7), 1360–1372 (2015)

28. Zhang, L., Zhen, X., Shao, L.: Learning object-to-class kernels for scene classification. TIP **23**(8), 3241–3253 (2014)

29. Fathi, A., Balcan, M.F., Ren, X., Rehg, J.M.: Combining self training and active learning for video segmentation. In: BMVC, vol. 29, pp. 78.1–78.11 (2011)

30. Vijayanarasimhan, S., Grauman, K.: Large-scale live active learning: training object detectors with crawled data and crowds. IJCV **108**(1–2), 97–114 (2014)
31. Vondrick, C., Ramanan, D.: Video annotation and tracking with active learning. In: NIPS (2011)
32. Elhamifar, E., Sapiro, G., Yang, A., Sasrty, S.: A convex optimization framework for active learning. In: ICCV (2013)
33. Settles, B.: Active learning literature survey, vol. 52, pp. 55–66. University of Wisconsin, Madison (2010)
34. Kapoor, A., Grauman, K., Urtasun, R., Darrell, T.: Active learning with gaussian processes for object categorization. In: ICCV (2007)
35. Kading, C., Freytag, A., Rodner, E., Bodesheim, P., Denzler, J.: Active learning and discovery of object categories in the presence of unnameable instances. In: CVPR (2015)
36. Chang, C.C., Lin, C.J.: LIBSVM: a library for support vector machines. ACM Trans. Intell. Syst. Technol. (TIST) **2**(3), 27 (2011)
37. Felzenszwalb, P.F., Girshick, R.B., McAllester, D., Ramanan, D.: Object detection with discriminatively trained part-based models. PAMI **32**(9), 1627–1645 (2010)
38. Rabinovich, A., Vedaldi, A., Galleguillos, C., Wiewiora, E., Belongie, S.: Objects in context. In: ICCV (2007)
39. Li, Y., Nevatia, R.: Key object driven multi-category object recognition, localization and tracking using spatio-temporal context. In: Forsyth, D., Torr, P., Zisserman, A. (eds.) ECCV 2008, Part IV. LNCS, vol. 5305, pp. 409–422. Springer, Heidelberg (2008)
40. Yedidia, J.S., Freeman, W.T., Weiss, Y.: Constructing free-energy approximations and generalized belief propagation algorithms. IEEE Trans. Inf. Theor. **51**(7), 2282–2312 (2005)
41. Choi, M.J., Lim, J.J., Torralba, A., Willsky, A.S.: Exploiting hierarchical context on a large database of object categories. In: CVPR (2010)
42. Quattoni, A., Torralba, A.: Recognizing indoor scenes. In: CVPR (2009)
43. Malisiewicz, T., Efros, A.A.: Improving spatial support for objects via multiple segmentations. In: BMVC (2007)
44. Schmidt, M.: UGM: a Matlab toolbox for probabilistic undirected graphical models (2010)
45. Hasan, M., Roy-Chowdhury, A.: Incremental activity modeling and recognition in streaming videos. In: CVPR (2014)
46. Druck, G., Settles, B., McCallum, A.: Active learning by labeling features. In: EMNLP (2009)
47. Doersch, C., Gupta, A., Efros, A.A.: Mid-level visual element discovery as discriminative mode seeking. In: NIPS (2013)
48. Hayat, M., Khan, S.H., Bennamoun, M., An, S.: A spatial layout and scale invariant feature representation for indoor scene classification. arXiv preprint arXiv:1506.05532 (2015)
49. Gong, Y., Wang, L., Guo, R., Lazebnik, S.: Multi-scale orderless pooling of deep convolutional activation features. In: Fleet, D., Pajdla, T., Schiele, B., Tuytelaars, T. (eds.) ECCV 2014, Part VII. LNCS, vol. 8695, pp. 392–407. Springer, Heidelberg (2014)

Real-Time Facial Segmentation and Performance Capture from RGB Input

Shunsuke Saito[1,2(✉)], Tianye Li[1,2], and Hao Li[1,2]

[1] Pinscreen, Santa Monica, USA
{shunsuke,hao}@pinscreen.com
[2] University of Southern California, Los Angeles, USA
tianyeli@usc.edu

Abstract. We introduce the concept of unconstrained real-time 3D facial performance capture through explicit semantic segmentation in the RGB input. To ensure robustness, cutting edge supervised learning approaches rely on large training datasets of face images captured in the wild. While impressive tracking quality has been demonstrated for faces that are largely visible, any occlusion due to hair, accessories, or hand-to-face gestures would result in significant visual artifacts and loss of tracking accuracy. The modeling of occlusions has been mostly avoided due to its immense space of appearance variability. To address this curse of high dimensionality, we perform tracking in unconstrained images assuming non-face regions can be fully masked out. Along with recent breakthroughs in deep learning, we demonstrate that pixel-level facial segmentation is possible in real-time by repurposing convolutional neural networks designed originally for general semantic segmentation. We develop an efficient architecture based on a two-stream deconvolution network with complementary characteristics, and introduce carefully designed training samples and data augmentation strategies for improved segmentation accuracy and robustness. We adopt a state-of-the-art regression-based facial tracking framework with segmented face images as training, and demonstrate accurate and uninterrupted facial performance capture in the presence of extreme occlusion and even side views. Furthermore, the resulting segmentation can be directly used to composite partial 3D face models on the input images and enable seamless facial manipulation tasks, such as virtual make-up or face replacement.

Keywords: Real-time facial performance capture · Face segmentation · Deep convolutional neural network · Regression

1 Introduction

Recent advances in real-time 3D facial performance capture [1–7] have not only transformed the entertainment industry with highly scalable animation and

Electronic supplementary material The online version of this chapter (doi:10.1007/978-3-319-46484-8_15) contains supplementary material, which is available to authorized users.

© Springer International Publishing AG 2016
B. Leibe et al. (Eds.): ECCV 2016, Part VIII, LNCS 9912, pp. 244–261, 2016.
DOI: 10.1007/978-3-319-46484-8_15

affordable production tools [8], but also popularized mobile social media apps with facial manipulation. Many state-of-the-art techniques have been developed to operate robustly in natural environments, but pure RGB solutions are still susceptible to occlusions (e.g., caused by hair, hand-to-face gestures, or accessories), which result in unpleasant visual artifacts or the inability to correctly initialize facial tracking.

While it is known that the shape and appearance of fully visible faces can be represented compactly through linear models [9,10], any occlusion or uncontrolled illumination could cause high non-linearities to a 3D face fitting problem. As this space of variation becomes intractable, supervised learning methods have been introduced to predict facial shapes through large training datasets of face images captured under unconstrained and noisy conditions. We observe that if such *occlusion noise* can be fully eliminated, the dimensionality of facial modeling could be drastically reduced to that of a well-posed and constrained problem. In other words, if reliable dense facial segmentation is possible, 3D facial tracking from RGB input becomes a significantly easier problem. Only recently has the deep learning community demonstrated highly effective semantic segmentations, such as the fully convolutional network (FCN) of [11] or the deconvolutional network (DeconvNet) of [12], by repurposing highly efficient classification networks [13,14] for dense predictions of general objects (e.g., humans, cars, etc.).

We present a real-time facial performance capture approach by explicitly segmenting facial regions and processing masked RGB data. We rely on the effectiveness of deep learning to achieve clean facial segmentations in order to enable robust facial tracking under severe occlusions. We propose an end-to-end segmentation network that also uses a two-stream deconvolution network with complementary characteristics, but shares the lower convolution network to enable real-time performance. A final convolutional layer recombines both outputs into a single probability map which is converted into a refined segmentation mask via graph cut algorithm [15]. Our 3D facial tracker is based on a state-of-the-art displaced dynamic expression (DDE) method [5] trained with segmented input data. Separating facial regions from occluding objects with similar colors and fine structures (e.g. hands) is extremely challenging, even for existing segmentation network. We propose a training data augmentation strategy based on perturbations, croppings, occlusion generation, hand compositings, as well as the use of negative samples containing no faces. Once our dense prediction model is trained, we replace the training database for DDE regression with masked faces obtained from our convolutional network.

We demonstrate uninterrupted tracking in the presence of highly challenging occlusions such as hands which have similar skin tones as the face and fine scale boundary details. Furthermore, our facial segmentation enables interesting compositing effects such as tracked facial models under hair and other occluding objects. These capabilities were only demonstrated recently using a robust geometric model fitting approach on depth sensor data [7].

We make the following contributions:

- We present the first real-time facial segmentation framework from pure RGB input using a convolutional neural network. We demonstrate the importance of carefully designed datasets and data augmentation strategies for handling challenging occlusions such as hands.
- We improve the efficiency and accuracy of existing segmentation networks using an architecture based on two-stream deconvolution networks and shared convolution network.
- We demonstrate superior tracking accuracy and robustness through explicitly facial segmentation and regression with masked training data, and outperform the current state-of-the-art.

2   Related Work

The fields of facial tracking and animation have undergone a long thread of major research milestones in both, the vision and graphics community, as well as influencing the industry widely over the past two decades.

In high-end film and game production, performance-driven techniques are commonly used to scale the production of realistic facial animation. An overview is discussed in Pighin and Lewis [16]. To meet the high quality bars, techniques for production typically build on sophisticated sensor equipments and controlled capture settings [17–24]. While exceptional tracking accuracy can be achieved, these methods are generally computationally expensive and the full visibility of the face needs to be ensured.

On the other extreme, 2D facial tracking methods that work in fully uncon-strained settings have been explored extensively for applications such as face recognition and emotion analytics. Even though only sparse 2D facial land-marks are detected, many techniques are designed to be robust to uncontrolled poses, challenging lighting conditions, and rely on a single-view 2D input. Early algorithms are based on parametric models [25–29], but later outperformed by more robust and real-time data-driven methods such as active appearance mod-els (AAM) [30] and constrained local models (CLM) [31]. While the landmark mean-shift approach of [32] and the supervised descent method of [33] avoid the need of user-specific training, more efficient solutions exist based on explicit shape regressions [34–36]. However, these methods are all sensitive to occlusions and only a limited number of 2D features can be detected.

Weise and colleagues [37] demonstrated the first system to produce com-pelling facial performance capture in real-time using a custom 3D depth sensor based on structured light. The intensive training procedure was later reduced significantly using an example-based algorithm developed by Li and collabo-rators [38]. With consumer depth sensors becoming mainstream (e.g., Kinect, Realsense, etc.), a whole line of real-time facial animation research have been developed with focus on deployability. The work of [1] incorporated pre-recorded motion priors to ensure stable tracking for noisy depth maps, which resulted in the popular animation software, Faceshift [8]. By optimizing the identity and expression models online, Li and coworkers [3], as well as Bouaziz and collab-orators [2] eliminated the need of user-specific calibration. For uninterrupted tracking under severe occlusions, Hsieh and colleagues [7] recently proposed an explicit facial segmentation technique, but requires a depth sensor.

While the generation of 3D facial animations from pure RGB input have been demonstrated using sparse 2D landmarks detection [39–41], a superior performance capture fidelity and robustness has only been shown recently by Cao and coworkers [4] using a 3D shape regression approach. Cao and colleagues [5] later extended the efficient two-level boosted regression technique introduced in [34] to the 3D case in order to avoid user-specific calibration. Higher fidelity facial tracking from monocular video has also been demonstrated with additional high-resolution training data [6], very large datasets of a person [42], or more expensive non-real-time computation [43,44]. While robust to unconstrained lighting environments and large head poses, these methods are sensitive to large occlusions and cannot segment facial regions.

Due to the immense variation of facial appearances in unconstrained images, it is extremely challenging to obtain clean facial segmentations at the pixel level. The hierarchical CNN-based parsing network of Luo and collaborators [45] generates masks of individual facial components such as eyes, nose, and mouth even in the presence of occlusions, but does not segment the facial region as a whole. Smith and coworkers [46] use an example-based approach for facial region and component segmentation, but the method requires sufficient visibility of the face. These two methods are computationally intensive and susceptible to wrong segmentations when occlusions have similar colors as the face. By alternating between face mask prediction and landmark localization with deformable part models, Ghiasi and Fowlkes [47] have recently demonstrated state-of-the-art facial segmentation results on the Caltech Occluded Faces in the Wild (COFW) dataset [48] at the cost of expensive computations. Without explicitly segmenting the face, occlusion handling methods have been proposed for the detection of 2D landmarks within an AAM frameworks [49], but superior results were later shown using techniques based on discriminatively trained deformable parts model [50,51]. Highly efficient landmark detection has been recently demonstrated using cascade of regressors trained with occlusion data [48,52].

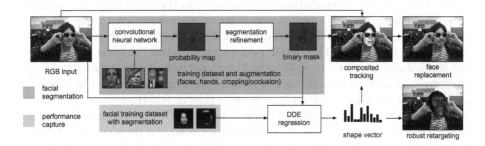

Fig. 1. Overview of our facial segmentation and performance capture pipeline. (Color figure online)

3 Overview

As illustrated in Fig. 1, our system is divided into a facial segmentation stage (blue) and a performance capture stage (green). Our pipeline takes an RGB image as input and produces a binary segmenta-

capture setting using a laptop-integrated RGB camera

tion mask in addition to a tracked 3D face model, which is parameterized by a shape vector, as output. The binary mask represents a per-pixel facial region estimated by a deep learning framework for facial segmentation. Following Cao et al.'s DDE regression technique [5], the shape vector describes the rigid head motion and the facial expression coefficients, which drive the animation of a personalized 3D tracking model. In addition, the shape of the user's identity and the focal length are solved concurrently during performance capture. While the resulting tracking model represents the shape of the subject, the shape vector can be used to retarget any digital character with compatible animation controls as input.

Our convolutional neural network first predicts a probability map on a cropped rectangular face region for which size and positions are determined based on the bounding box of the projected 3D tracking model from the previous frame. The face region of the initial frame is detected using the method of Viola and Jones [53]. The output probability map is a smaller fixed-size resolution image (128×128 pixels) and describes the likelihood for each pixel being labeled as part of the specific face region. While two output maps (one for the overall shape and one for fine-scaled details) are simultaneously produced by our two-stream deconvolution network, a single output probability map is generated through a final convolutional layer. To ensure accurate and robust facial segmentation, we train our convolutional neural network using a large dataset of segmented face images, augmented with peturbations, synthetic occlusions, croppings, and hand compositings, as well as negative samples containing no faces. We convert the resulting probability map into a binary mask using a graph cut algorithm [54] and bilinearly upsample the mask to the original input resolution.

We then use this segmentation mask as input to the facial tracker as well as for compositing partial 3D facial models during occlusions. This facial segmentation technique is also used to produce training data for the regression model of the DDE framework. Our facial performance capture pipeline is based on the state-of-the-art method of [5], which does not require any calibration step for individual users. The training process and the regression explicitly take the segmentation mask into account. Our system runs in real-time on commercially available desktop machines with sufficiently powerful GPU processors. For many mobile devices such as laptops, which are not yet ready for deep neural net computations, we can optionally offload the segmentation processing over Wi-Fi to a desktop machine with high-end GPU resources for real-time performance.

4 Facial Segmentation

Our facial segmentation pipeline computes a binary mask from the bounding box of a face in the input image. The cropped face image is first resized to a small 128 × 128 pixel resolution image, which is passed to a convolutional neural network for a dense 2-class segmentation problem. Similar to state-of-the-art segmentation networks [11,12,55], the overall network consists of two parts, (1) a lower convolution network for multi-dimensional feature extraction and (2) a higher deconvolution network for shape generation. This shape corresponds to the segmented object and is reconstructed using the features obtained from the convolution network. The output is a dense 128 × 128 probability map that assigns each pixel to either a face or non-face region. While both state-of-the-art networks, FCN [11] and DeconvNet [12] use the identical convolutional network based on VGG-16 layers [56], they approach deconvolution differently. FCN performs a simple deconvolution using a single bilinear interpolation layer, and produces coarse, but clean overall shape segmentations, because the output layer is closely connected to the convolution layers preventing the loss of spatial information. DeconvNet on the other hand, mirrors the convolution process with multiple series of unpooling, deconvolution, and rectification layers, and generates detailed segmentations at the cost of increased noise. Noh and collaborators [12] proposed to combine the outputs of both algorithms through averaging followed by a post-hoc segmentation refinement based on conditional random fields [57], but the computation is prohibitively intensive. Instead, we develop an efficient network with shared convolution layers to reduce the number of parameters and operations, but split the deconvolution part into a two-stream architecture to benefit from the advantages of both networks. The output probability map resulting from a bilinear interpolation and mirrored deconvolution network are then concatenated before a final convolutional layer merges them into a single high-fidelity output map. We then use a standard graph cut algorithm [54] to convert the probability map into a clean binary facial mask and upsample to the resolution of the original input image via bilinear interpolation.

Architecture. Our segmentation network consists of a single convolution network connected to two different deconvolution networks, DeconvNet and an 8 pixel stride FCN-8s as shown in Fig. 2. The network is based on a 16 layer VGG architecture and pre-trained on the PASCAL VOC 2012 data set with 20 object categories [13]. More specifically, VGG has 13 layers of convolutions and rectified

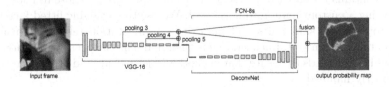

Fig. 2. ConvNet architecture with two-stream deconvolution network.

linear units (ReLU), 5 max pooling layers, two fully connected layers, and one classification layer. DeconvNet mirrors the convolutional network to generate a probability map with the same resolution as the input, by applying upsampling operations (deconvolution) and the inverse operation of pooling (unpooling). Even though deconvolution is fast, the runtime performance is blocked by the first fully connected layer which becomes the bottleneck of the segmentation pipeline. To enable real-time performance on a state-of-the-art GPU, we reduce the kernel size of the first fully connected layer from 7×7 to 4×4 pixels.

Further modifications to the FCN-8s are needed in order to connect the output of both DeconvNet and FCN deconvolution networks to the final convolutional layer. The output size of each deconvolution is controlled by zero padding, so that the size of each upsampled activation layer is aligned with the output of the previous pooling layer. While the original FCN uses the last fully connected layer as the coarsest prediction, we instead use the output of the last pooling layer, as the coarsest prediction in order to preserve spatial information like in DeconvNet. The obtained coarse prediction is then sequentially deconvoluted and fused with the output of pooling layer 4 and 3, and then a deconvolution layer upsamples the fused prediction to the input image size. Since our 2-class labeling problem is considerably less complex than multi-class ones, losing information from discarded layers would not really affect the segmentation accuracy. In the final layer, the output of both deconvolution networks are concatenated into a single matrix and we apply a 1×1 convolution to obtain a score map, followed by a softmax operation to produce the final fused probability map. In this way we can even learn blending weights between the two networks as convolution parameters, instead of a simple averaging of output maps as proposed by the separate treatment of [12]. Please refer to the supplemental materials for the detailed configuration of our proposed network.

Training. For an effective facial segmentation, our convolutional neural network needs to be trained with large image datasets containing face samples and their corresponding ground truth binary masks. The faces should span a sufficiently wide range of shapes, appearance, and illumination conditions. We therefore collect 2927 images from the LFW face database [58]

face data   hand data   cropping / occlusion   negative samples

Fig. 3. Segmentation training data. (Color figure online)

and 5094 images from the FaceWarehouse dataset [10]. While the LFW dataset already contains pre-labeled face segmentations, we segment those in FaceWarehouse using a custom semi-automatic tool. We use the available fitted face templates to estimate skin tones and perform a segmentation refinement using a graph cut algorithm [15]. Each sample is then manually inspected and corrected using additional seeds to ensure that occlusions such as hair and other accessories are properly handled.

To prevent overfitting, we augment our dataset with additional $82,770$ images using random perturbations of translation, rotation, and scale. The data consist of mostly photographs with a large variety of faces in different head poses, expressions, and under different lightings. Occlusions through hair, hands, and other objects are typically avoided. We therefore generate additional 82,770 samples based on random sized and uniformly colored rectangles on top of each face sample to increase the robustness to partial occlusions (see Fig. 3).

Skin toned objects such as hands and arms are commonly observed during hand-to-face gesticulations but are particularly challenging to segment due to similar colors as the face and fine structures such as fingers. We further augment the training dataset of our convolutional neural network with composited hands on top of the original 8021 face images. We first captured and manually segmented 1092 hand images of different skin tones, as well as under different lighting conditions and poses. We then synthesized these hand images on top of the original face images, which yields 41380 additional trainining samples using the same perturbation strategy. In total, 132,426 images were generated to train our network. Our data-augmentation strategy can effectively train the segmentation network and avoid overfitting, even though only limited amount of ground truth data is available.

We initialize the training using pre-trained weights [13] except for the first fully connected layer of the convolution network, since its kernel size is modified for our real-time purposes. Thus, the first fully connected layers and deconvolution layers are initialized with zero-mean Gaussians. The loss function is the sum of softmax functions applied to the output maps of DeconvNet, FCN, and their score maps. The weights of each softmax function is set to 0.5, 0.5, and 1.0 respectively, and the loss functions are minimized via stochastic gradient descent (SGD) with momentum for stable convergence. Notice that by only using the fused score map of DeconvNet and FCN for the loss function, only the DeconvNet model is trained and not FCN. We set 0.01, 0.9, and 0.0005 as the learning rate, momentum, and weight decay, respectively. Our training takes 9 h using 50,000 SGD iterations on our machines.

We further fine-tune the trained segmentation by adding negative samples (containing no faces) based on hand, arm, and background images to a random subset of the training data so that the amount of negative samples is equivalent to positive ones. In particular, the public datasets contain images that are both indoor and outdoors. Similar techniques for negative data augmentation has been used previously to improve the accuracy of weak supervision-based classifiers [59,60]. We use 4699 hand images that contain no faces from the Oxford hand dataset [61], and further perturb them with random translation and scalings. This fine-tuning with negative samples uses the same loss function and training parameters (momentum, weight decay, and loss weight) as with the training using positive data, but with initial learning rate of 0.001. Converges is reached after 10,000 SGD iterations with an additional 1.5 h of computation.

Segmentation Refinement. We convert the 128 × 128 pixel probability map of the convolutional neural network to a binary mask using a standard graph cut algorithm [15]. Even though our facial segmentation is reliable and accurate, a graph cut-based segmentation refinement can purge minor artifacts such as small 'uncertainty' holes at boundaries, which can still appear for challenging cases such as (extreme occlusions, motion blur, etc.). We optimize the following energy term between adjacent pixels i and j using the efficient GridCut [54] implementation:

$$\sum_i \theta_i(p_i) - \lambda \sum_{(i,j)} \theta_{i,j}. \tag{1}$$

The unary term $\theta_i(p_i)$ is determined by the facial probability map p_i, defined as $\theta_i(p_i) = -\log(p_i)$ for the sink and $\theta_i(p_i) = -\log(1.0 - p_i)$ for the source. The pairwise term $\theta_{i,j} = exp(-\frac{\|I_i - I_j\|^2}{2\sigma})$, where I is the pixel intensity, $\lambda = 10$, and $\sigma = 5$. The final binary mask is then bilinearly upsampled to the original cropped image resolution.

5   Facial Tracking

After facial segmentation, we capture the facial performance by regressing a 3D face model directly from the incoming RGB input frame. We adopt the state-of-the-art displaced dynamic expression (DDE) framework of [5] with the two-level boosted regression techniques of [34] and incorporate our facial segmentation masks into the regression and training process. More concretely, instead of computing the regression on face images with backgrounds and occlusions, where appearance can take huge variations, we only focus on segmented face regions to reduce the dimensionality of the problem. While the original DDE technique is reasonably robust for sufficiently large training datasets, we show that processing accurately segmented images significantly improves robustness and accuracy, since only facial apperance and lighting variations need to be considered. Even skin toned occlusions such as hands can be handled effectively by our method. We briefly summarize the DDE-based 3D facial regression and then describe how to explicitly incorporate facial segmentation masks.

DDE Regression. Our facial tracking is performed by regressing a facial shape displacement given the current input RGB image and an initial facial shape from the previous frame. Following the DDE model of [5], we represent a facial shape as a linear 3D blendshape model, $(\mathbf{b}_0, \mathbf{B})$, with global rigid head motion $(\mathbf{R}, \mathbf{t})$ and 2D residual displacements $\mathbf{D} = [\mathbf{d}_1 \ldots \mathbf{d}_m]^T \in \mathbb{R}^{2m}$ of $m = 73$ facial landmark positions $\mathbf{P} = [\mathbf{p}_1 \ldots \mathbf{p}_m]^T \in \mathbb{R}^{2m}$ (eye contours, mouth, etc.). We obtain $\mathbf{P}$ through perspective projection of the 3D face with 2D offsets $\mathbf{D}$:

$$\mathbf{p}_i = \Pi_f(\mathbf{R} \cdot (\mathbf{b}_0^i + \mathbf{B}^i \mathbf{x}) + \mathbf{t}) + \mathbf{d}_i, \tag{2}$$

where $\mathbf{b}_0^i$ is the 3D vertex location corresponding to the landmark $\mathbf{p}_i$ in the neutral face $\mathbf{b}_0$, $\mathbf{B} = [\mathbf{b}_1, ..., \mathbf{b}_n]$ the bases of expression blendshapes, $\mathbf{x} \in [0, 1]^n$ the $n = 46$ blendshape coefficients based on FACS [62]. Each neutral face and expression blendshape is also represented by a linear combination of 50 PCA bases of human identity shapes [9] with $[\mathbf{b}_0, \mathbf{B}] = C_r \times \mathbf{u}$, $\mathbf{u}$ the user-specific identity coefficients, and C_r the rank-3 core tensor obtained from the ZJU Face-Warehouse dataset [10]. We adopt a pinhole camera model, where the projection operator $\Pi_f : \mathbb{R}^3 \mapsto \mathbb{R}^2$ is specified by a focal length f. Thus, we can uniquely determine the 2D landmarks using the shape parameters $\mathbf{S} = \{\mathbf{R}, \mathbf{t}, \mathbf{x}, \mathbf{D}, \mathbf{u}, f\}$.

While the goal of the regression is to compute all parameters $\mathbf{S}$ given an input frame $\mathbf{I}$, we separate the optimization of the identity coefficients $\mathbf{u}$ and the focal length f from the rest, since they should be invariant over time. Therefore, the DDE regressor only updates the shape vector $\mathbf{Q} = [\mathbf{R}, \mathbf{t}, \mathbf{x}, \mathbf{D}]$ and $[\mathbf{u}, f]$ is computed only in specific key-frames and on a concurrent thread (see [5] for details). The two-level regressor structure consists of T sequential cascade regressors $\{R_t(\mathbf{I}, \mathbf{Q}_t)\}_{t=1}^{T}$ with updates $\delta\mathbf{Q}_{t+1}$ so that $\mathbf{Q}_{t+1} = \mathbf{Q}_t + \delta\mathbf{Q}_{t+1}$. Each of the weak regressors R_t classifies a set of randomly sampled feature points of $\mathbf{I}$ based on the corresponding pre-trained update vector $\delta\mathbf{Q}_{t+1}$. For each t, we sample new sets of 400 feature points via Gaussian distribution on the unit square. Notice that these points are represented as barycentric coordinates of a Delaunay triangulation of the mean of all 2D facial landmarks for improved robustness w.r.t. facial transformations. Each R_t consists of second layer of K primitive cascade regressors based on random ferns of size F (binary decision tree of depth F). Each fern regresses a weaker parameter update from a feature vector of F pixel intensity differences of feature point pairs from the 400 samples. The indices of feature point pairs are specified during training by maximizing the correlation to the ground truth regression residuals. The training process also determines the random thresholds and bin classification values of each fern.

At run-time, if a new expression or head pose is observed, we collect the resulting shape parameters $\hat{\mathbf{S}}$ as well as the landmarks $\hat{\mathbf{P}}$, and alternate the updates of the identity coefficients $\mathbf{u}$ and the focal length f by minimizing the offsets $\hat{\mathbf{D}}$ in Eq. (2) for L collected key-frames until it converges as follows:

$$\underset{\mathbf{u},f}{\operatorname{argmin}} \sum_{l=1}^{L} \sum_{i=1}^{m} \|\Pi_f(\hat{\mathbf{R}}_l \cdot (\mathbf{b}_0^i(\mathbf{u}) + \mathbf{B}^i(\mathbf{u}) \cdot \hat{\mathbf{x}}_l) + \hat{\mathbf{t}}_l) - \hat{\mathbf{p}}_{l,i}\|^2. \tag{3}$$

Training. The training process consists of constructing the ferns of the primitive regressors and specifying the F pairs of feature point indices based on a large database of facial images with corresponding ground truth facial shape parameters. We construct the ground truth parameters $\{\mathbf{S}_i^g\}_{i=1}^{M}$ from a set of images $\{\mathbf{I}_i\}_{i=1}^{M}$ and landmarks $\{\mathbf{P}_i\}_{i=1}^{M}$. Given landmarks $\mathbf{P}$, the parameters of the ground truth $\mathbf{S}^g$ are computed by minimizing the following objective function $\Theta(\mathbf{R}, \mathbf{t}, \mathbf{x}, \mathbf{u}, f)$:

input image   labeled segmentation   input image   with occlusion augmentation

Fig. 4. Regression training data

$$\Theta(\mathbf{R}, \mathbf{t}, \mathbf{x}, \mathbf{u}, f) = \sum_{i=1}^{m} \|\Pi_f(\mathbf{R} \cdot (\mathbf{b}_0^i(\mathbf{u}) + \mathbf{B}^i(\mathbf{u}) \cdot \mathbf{x}) + \mathbf{t}) - \mathbf{p}_i\|^2. \tag{4}$$

As in [5], we use $14,460$ labeled data from FaceWarehouse [10], LFW [58], and GTAV [63] and learn a mapping from an initial estimation $\mathbf{S}^*$ to the ground-truth parameters $\mathbf{S}^g$ given an input frame $\mathbf{I}$. An initial set of N shape parameters $\{\mathbf{S}_i^*\}_{i=1}^N$ are constructed by perturbing each training parameter in $\mathbf{S}$ within a predefined range. Let the suffix g denote the ground-truth value, suffix r a perturbed value.

We construct the training dataset $\{\mathbf{S}_i^* = [\mathbf{Q}_i^r, \mathbf{u}_i^g, f_i^g], \mathbf{S}_i^g = [\mathbf{Q}_i^g, \mathbf{u}_i^g, f_i^g],$ $\mathbf{I}_i\}_{i=1}^N$ and perturb the shape vectors with random rotations, translations, blend-shape coefficients as well as, identity coefficients $\mathbf{u}^r$ and the focal length f^r to improved robustness during training. Blendshapes are perturbed 15 times and the other parameters 5 times, resulting in a total of $506,100$ training data. The T cascade regressors $\{R_t(\mathbf{I}, \mathbf{Q}_t)\}_{t=1}^T$ then update $\mathbf{Q}$ so that the resulting vector $\mathbf{Q}_{t+1} = \mathbf{Q}_t + \delta\mathbf{Q}_{t+1}$ minimizes the residual to the ground truth $\mathbf{Q}^g$ among all training data N. Thus the regressor at stage t is trained as follows:

$$\delta\mathbf{Q}_{t+1} = \underset{R}{\arg\min} \sum_{i=1}^N \|\mathbf{Q}_i^g - (\mathbf{Q}_{i,t} + R_t(\mathbf{I}, \mathbf{Q}_{i,t}))\|_2^2. \tag{5}$$

Optimization. For both Eqs. 3 and 4, the blendshape and identity coefficients are solved using 3 iterations of non-linear least squares optimization with boundary constraints $\mathbf{x} \in [0,1]^n$ using an L-BFGS-B solver [64] and the rigid motions $(\mathbf{R}, \mathbf{t})$ are obtained by interleaving iterative PnP optimization steps [65].

Segmentation-based Regression. To incorporate the facial mask $\mathbf{M}$ obtained from Sect. 4 into the regressors $R_t(\mathbf{I}, \mathbf{P}_t, \mathbf{M})$, we simply mark non-face pixels in $\mathbf{I}$ for both training and inference and prevent the regressors to sample features in non-face region. To further enhance the tracking robustness under

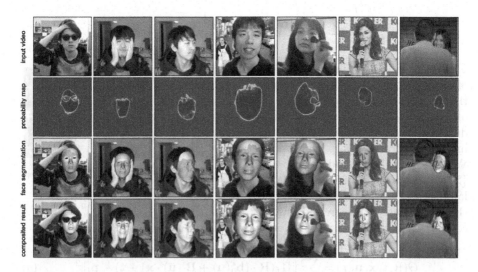

Fig. 5. Results. We visualize the input frame, the estimated probability map, the facial segmentation over the tracked template, and the composited result

arbitrary occlusions, which is equivalent to incomplete views after the segmentation process, we augment the training data by randomly cropping out parts on the segmented face images (see Fig. 4). For each of the 506, 100 training data sets, we include one additional cropped version with a rectangle centered randomly around the face region with Gaussian distribution and covering up to 80 % of the face bounding box in width and height. Figure 8 and accompanied video shows that this occlusion augmentation significantly improves the robustness under various occlusions after data augmentation.

6 Results

As shown in Fig. 5, we demonstrate successful facial segmentation and tracking on a wide range of examples with a variety of complex occlusions, including hair, hands, headwear, and props. Our convolutional network effectively predicts a dense probability map revealing face regions even when they are blocked by objects with similar skin tones such as hands. In most cases, the boundaries of the visibile face regions are correctly estimated. Even when only a small portion of the face is visibile we show that

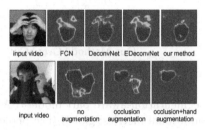

Fig. 6. Comparison of segmentation result based on different selection of neural network architectures.

reliable 3D facial fitting is possible when processing input data with clean segmentations. In contrast to most RGB-D based solutions [7], our method works seamlessly in outdoor environments and with any type of video sources.

Segmentation Evaluation and Comparison. We evaluate the accuracy of our segmentation technique on 437 color test images from the Caltech Occluded Faces in the Wild (COFW) dataset [48]. We use the commonly used intersection over union (IOU) metric between the predicted segmentations and the manually annotated ground truth masks provided by [66] in order to assess over and under-segmentations. We evaluate our proposed data augmentation strategy as well as the use of negative training samples in Fig. 6 and show that the explicit use of hand compositings significantly improves the probability map accuracy during hand occlusions. We evelute the architecture of our network in Table 1 (left) and Fig. 6 and compared our results with the state-of-the-art out of the box segmentation networks, FCN-8s [11], DeconvNet [12], and the naive ensemble of DeconvNet and FCN (EDeconvNet). Compared to FCN-8s and Deconvnet, the IOU of our method is improved by 12.7 % and 1.4 % respectively, but also contains much less noise as shown in Fig. 6. While comparable to the performance of EDeconvNet, our method achieves nearly double the performance, which enables real-time capabilities (30 fps) on the latest GPU.

We compare in Table 1 (right), our deep learning-based approach against the current state-of-the-art in facial segmentation: (1) the structured forest technique [67], (2) the regional predictive power method (RPP) [66] and (3)

Table 1. segmentation performance for different network structures (left) and state-of-the-art methods (right).

Network	Mean IOU	FPS
FCN-8s	0.739	37.99
DeconvNet	0.821	44.31
EDeconvNet	0.835	20.45
Our method	0.833	43.27

Method	Mean IOU	global	ave(face)
Structured Forest [66]	-	0.839	0.886
RPP [67]	0.724	-	-
SAPM [47]	0.835	0.886	0.871
Our method	0.833	0.882	0.929
Our Method+GraphCut	0.839	0.887	0.927

segmentation-aware part model (SAPM) [47,51]. We measure the IOU and two additional metrics: global (the percentage of all pixels that are correctly classified) and ave(face) (the average recall of face pixels), since the structured forest work [67] uses these two metrics. We demonstrate superior performance to RPP (IOU: 0.833 vs 0.724) and structured forest (global: 0.882 vs 0.839, ave(face): 0.929 vs 0.886), and comparable result to SAPM (IOU: 0.833 vs 0.835, ave(face) 0.929 vs 0.871). Our method is significantly faster than SAPM which requires up to 30 s per frame [51].

Tracking Evaluation and Comparison. In Fig. 7, we highlight the robustness of our approach on extremely challenging cases. Our method can handle difficult lighting conditions, such as shadows and flashlights, as well as side views and facial hair. We further validate our data augmentation strategy during regression training and report quantitative comparisons with the current state-of-the-art method of Cao et al. [5] in Fig. 8. Here, we produce an unoccluded face as ground truth and synthetically generated occluding box with increasing size. In our experiment, we generated three sequences of 180 frames, covering a wide range of expressions, head rotations and translations.

We observe that our explicit semantic segmentation approach is critical to ensuring high tracking accuracy. While using the masked training dataset for regression significantly improves robustness, we show that additional performance can be achieved by augmenting this data with additional synthetic occlusions. Figure 9 shows how Cao et al.'s algorithm fails in the presence of large occlusions. Our method

input video   tracked model   input video   tracked model

Fig. 7. Challenging tracking scenes.

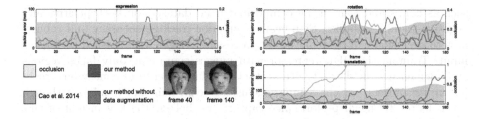

Fig. 8. Error evaluation on different tracking methods.

shows comparable occlusion-handling capabilities as the work of [7] who rely an RGB-D sensor as input. We demonstrate superior performance to a recent robust 2D landmark estimation method [48] when comparing the projected landmark positions. In particular, our method can handle larger occlusions and head rotations.

Performance. Our tracking and segmentation stages run in parallel. The full facial tracking pipeline runs at 30 fps on a quadcore i7 2.8 GHz Intel Core i7 with 16 GB RAM and the segmentation is offloaded wirelessly to a quad-core i7 3.5 GHz Intel Core i7 with 16 GB RAM with an NVIDIA GTX Titan X GPU. During tracking, our system takes 18 ms to regress the 3D face and 5 ms to optimize the identity and the focal length. For segmentation, we measure the following timings: probability map computation 23 ms, segmentation refinement 4 ms, data transmission 1 ms. run on the GPU, and the remaining implementation is multi-threaded on the CPU.

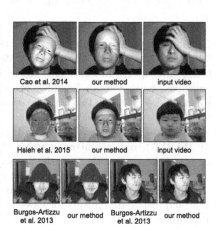

Fig. 9. Tracking comparison.

7 Conclusion

We demonstrate that real-time, accurate pixel-level facial segmentation is possible using only unconstrained RGB images with a deep learning approach. Our experiments confirm that a segmentation network with two-stream deconvolution network and shared convolution network is not only critical for extracting both the overall shape and fine-scale details effectively in real-time, but also presents the current state-of-the-art in face segmentation. We also found that a carefully designed data augmentation strategy effectively produces sufficiently large training datasets for the CNN to avoid overfitting, especially when only limited ground truth segmentations are available in public datasets. In particular, we demonstrate the first successful facial segmentations for skin-colored occlusions such as hands and arms using composited hand datasets on both positive and negative training samples. Significantly superior tracking accuracy and robustness to occlusion can be achieved by processing images with masked regions as input. Training the DDE regressor with images containing only facial regions and augmenting the dataset with synthetic occlusions ensures continuous tracking in the presence of challenging occlusions (e.g., hair and hands). Although we focus on 3D facial performance capture, we believe the key insight of this paper - reducing the dimensionality using semantic segmentation - is generally applicable to other vision problems beyond facial tracking and regression.

Limitations and Future Work. Since only limited training data is used, the resulting segmentation masks can still yield flickering boundaries. We wish to explore the use of a temporal information, as well as the modeling of domain-specific priors to better handle lighting variations. In addition to facial regions, we would also like to extend our ideas to segment other body parts to facilitate more complex compositing operations that include hands, bodies, and hair.

Acknowledgments. We would like to thank Joseph J. Lim, Qixing Huang, Duygu Ceylan, Lingyu Wei, Kyle Olszewski, Harry Shum, and Gary Bradski for the fruitful discussions and the proofreading. We also thank Rui Saito and Frances Chen for being our capture models. This research is supported in part by Adobe, Oculus & Facebook, Sony, Pelican Imaging, Panasonic, Embodee, Huawei, the Google Faculty Research Award, The Okawa Foundation Research Grant, the Office of Naval Research (ONR)/U.S. Navy, under award number N00014-15-1-2639, the Office of the Director of National Intelligence (ODNI), and Intelligence Advanced Research Projects Activity (IARPA), under contract number 2014-14071600010. The views and conclusions contained herein are those of the authors and should not be interpreted as necessarily representing the official policies or endorsements, either expressed or implied, of ODNI, IARPA, or the U.S. Government. The U.S. Government is authorized to reproduce and distribute reprints for Governmental purpose notwithstanding any copyright annotation thereon.

References

1. Weise, T., Bouaziz, S., Li, H., Pauly, M.: Realtime performance-based facial animation. ACM Trans. Graph. (TOG) **30**(4), 77 (2011). ACM
2. Bouaziz, S., Wang, Y., Pauly, M.: Online modeling for realtime facial animation. ACM Trans. Graph **32**(4), 40: 1–40: 10 (2013)
3. Li, H., Yu, J., Ye, Y., Bregler, C.: Realtime facial animation with on-the-fly correctives. ACM Trans. Graph. **32**(4), 42 (2013)
4. Cao, C., Weng, Y., Lin, S., Zhou, K.: 3D shape regression for real-time facial animation. ACM Trans. Graph. **32**(4), 41: 1–41: 10 (2013)
5. Cao, C., Hou, Q., Zhou, K.: Displaced dynamic expression regression for real-time facial tracking and animation. ACM Trans. Graph. (TOG) **33**(4), 43 (2014)
6. Cao, C., Bradley, D., Zhou, K., Beeler, T.: Real-time high-fidelity facial performance capture. ACM Trans. Graph. (TOG) **34**(4), 46 (2015)

7. Hsieh, P.L., Ma, C., Yu, J., Li, H.: Unconstrained realtime facial performance capture. In: Proceedings of the IEEE Conference on Computer Vision and Pattern Recognition, pp. 1675–1683 (2015)
8. Faceshift (2014). http://www.faceshift.com/
9. Blanz, V., Vetter, T.: A morphable model for the synthesis of 3D faces. In: SIGGRAPH 1999, pp. 187–194 (1999)
10. Cao, C., Weng, Y., Zhou, S., Tong, Y., Zhou, K.: Facewarehouse: a 3D facial expression database for visual computing. IEEE Trans. Vis. Comput. Graph. **20**(3), 413–425 (2014)
11. Long, J., Shelhamer, E., Darrell, T.: Fully convolutional networks for semantic segmentation. In: CVPR (2015, to appear)
12. Noh, H., Hong, S., Han, B.: Learning deconvolution network for semantic segmentation. In: 2015 IEEE International Conference on Computer Vision (ICCV) (2015)
13. Chatfield, K., Simonyan, K., Vedaldi, A., Zisserman, A.: Return of the devil in the details: delving deep into convolutional nets. In: British Machine Vision Conference (2014)
14. Krizhevsky, A., Sutskever, I., Hinton, G.E.: Imagenet classification with deep convolutional neural networks. In: Advances in Neural Information Processing Systems (2012)
15. Rother, C., Kolmogorov, V., Blake, A.: "grabcut": interactive foreground extraction using iterated graph cuts. In: ACM SIGGRAPH 2004 Papers, SIGGRAPH 2004, pp. 309–314. ACM, New York (2004)
16. Pighin, F., Lewis, J.P.: Performance-driven facial animation. In: ACM SIGGRAPH 2006 Courses, SIGGRAPH 2006 (2006)
17. Guenter, B., Grimm, C., Wood, D., Malvar, H., Pighin, F.: Making faces. In: SIGGRAPH 1998, pp. 55–66 (1998)
18. Zhang, L., Snavely, N., Curless, B., Seitz, S.M.: Spacetime faces: high resolution capture for modeling and animation. ACM Trans. Graph. **23**(3), 548–558 (2004)
19. Furukawa, Y., Ponce, J.: Dense 3D motion capture for human faces. In: CVPR, pp. 1674–1681 (2009)
20. Li, H., Adams, B., Guibas, L.J., Pauly, M.: Robust single-view geometry and motion reconstruction. ACM Trans. Graph. **28**(5), 175: 1–175: 10 (2009)
21. Beeler, T., Hahn, F., Bradley, D., Bickel, B., Beardsley, P., Gotsman, C., Sumner, R.W., Gross, M.: High-quality passive facial performance capture using anchor frames. ACM Trans. Graph. **30**, 75: 1–75: 10 (2011)
22. Fyffe, G., Hawkins, T., Watts, C., Ma, W.C., Debevec, P.: Comprehensive facial performance capture. In: Computer Graphics Forum, vol. 30, pp. 425–434. Wiley Online Library (2011)
23. Bhat, K.S., Goldenthal, R., Ye, Y., Mallet, R., Koperwas, M.: High fidelity facial animation capture and retargeting with contours. In: SCA 2013, pp. 7–14 (2013)
24. Fyffe, G., Jones, A., Alexander, O., Ichikari, R., Debevec, P.: Driving high-resolution facial scans with video performance capture. ACM Trans. Graph. **34**(1), 8: 1–8: 14 (2014)
25. Li, H., Roivainen, P., Forcheimer, R.: 3-D motion estimation in model-based facial image coding. TPAMI **15**(6), 545–555 (1993)
26. Bregler, C., Omohundro, S.: Surface learning with applications to lipreading. In: Advances in Neural Information Processing Systems, p. 43 (1994)
27. Black, M.J., Yacoob, Y.: Tracking and recognizing rigid and non-rigid facial motions using local parametric models of image motion. In: ICCV, pp. 374–381 (1995)

28. Essa, I., Basu, S., Darrell, T., Pentland, A.: Modeling, tracking and interactive animation of faces and heads using input from video. In: Proceedings of the Computer Animation, pp. 68–79(1996)

29. Decarlo, D., Metaxas, D.: Optical flow constraints on deformable models with applications to face tracking. Int. J. Comput. Vis. **38**(2), 99–127 (2000)

30. Cootes, T.F., Edwards, G.J., Taylor, C.J.: Active appearance models. IEEE Trans. Pattern Anal. Mach. Intell. **6**, 681–685 (2001)

31. Cristinacce, D., Cootes, T.: Automatic feature localisation with constrained local models. Pattern Recogn. **41**(10), 3054–3067 (2008)

32. Saragih, J.M., Lucey, S., Cohn, J.F.: Deformable model fitting by regularized landmark mean-shift. Int. J. Comput. Vis. **91**(2), 200–215 (2011)

33. Xiong, X., De la Torre, F.: Supervised descent method and its applications to face alignment. In: 2013 IEEE Conference on Computer Vision and Pattern Recognition (CVPR), pp. 532–539. IEEE (2013)

34. Cao, X., Wei, Y., Wen, F., Sun, J.: Face alignment by explicit shape regression. Int. J. Comput. Vis. **107**(2), 177–190 (2013)

35. Kazemi, V., Sullivan, J.: One millisecond face alignment with an ensemble of regression trees. In: 2014 IEEE Conference on Computer Vision and Pattern Recognition (CVPR), pp. 1867–1874. IEEE (2014)

36. Ren, S., Cao, X., Wei, Y., Sun, J.: Face alignment at 3000 fps via regressing local binary features. In: 2014 IEEE Conference on Computer Vision and Pattern Recognition (CVPR), pp. 1685–1692. IEEE (2014)

37. Weise, T., Li, H., Van Gool, L., Pauly, M.: Face/off: live facial puppetry. In: Proceedings of the 2009 ACM SIGGRAPH/Eurographics Symposium on Computer Animation, pp. 7–16. ACM (2009)

38. Li, H., Weise, T., Pauly, M.: Example-based facial rigging. ACM Trans. Graph. **29**(4), 32: 1–32: 6 (2010)

39. Pighin, F.H., Szeliski, R., Salesin, D.: Resynthesizing facial animation through 3D model-based tracking. In: ICCV, pp. 143–150 (1999)

40. Chuang, E., Bregler, C.: Performance driven facial animation using blendshape interpolation. Technical report. Stanford University (2002)

41. Chai, J., Xiao, J., Hodgins, J.: Vision-based control of 3D facial animation. In: SCA 2003, pp. 193–206 (2003)

42. Suwajanakorn, S., Kemelmacher-Shlizerman, I., Seitz, S.M.: Total moving face reconstruction. In: Fleet, D., Pajdla, T., Schiele, B., Tuytelaars, T. (eds.) ECCV 2014, Part IV. LNCS, vol. 8692, pp. 796–812. Springer, Heidelberg (2014)

43. Garrido, P., Valgaerts, L., Wu, C., Theobalt, C.: Reconstructing detailed dynamic face geometry from monocular video. ACM Trans. Graph. **32**(6), 158 (2013)

44. Shi, F., Wu, H.T., Tong, X., Chai, J.: Automatic acquisition of high-fidelity facial performances using monocular videos. ACM Trans. Graph. (TOG) **33**(6), 222 (2014)

45. Luo, P., Wang, X., Tang, X.: Hierarchical face parsing via deep learning. In: 2012 IEEE Conference on Computer Vision and Pattern Recognition (CVPR), pp. 2480–2487. IEEE (2012)

46. Smith, B., Zhang, L., Brandt, J., Lin, Z., Yang, J.: Exemplar-based face parsing. In: Proceedings of the IEEE Conference on Computer Vision and Pattern Recognition, pp. 3484–3491 (2013)

47. Ghiasi, G., Fowlkes, C.: Using segmentation to predict the absence of occluded parts. Proceedings of the British machine vision conference (BMVC). **22**(1–22), 12 (2015)

48. Burgos-Artizzu, X.P., Perona, P., Dollár, P.: Robust face landmark estimation under occlusion. In: 2013 IEEE International Conference on Computer Vision (ICCV), pp. 1513–1520. IEEE (2013)
49. Gross, R., Matthews, I., Baker, S.: Active appearance models with occlusion. Image Vis. Comput. **24**(6), 593–604 (2006)
50. Ramanan, D.: Face detection, pose estimation, and landmark localization in the wild. In: CVPR, pp. 2879–2886 (2012)
51. Ghiasi, G., Fowlkes, C.C.: Occlusion coherence: localizing occluded faces with a hierarchical deformable part model. In: 2014 IEEE Conference on Computer Vision and Pattern Recognition (CVPR), pp. 1899–1906. IEEE (2014)
52. Yu, X., Lin, Z., Brandt, J., Metaxas, D.N.: Consensus of regression for occlusion-robust facial feature localization. In: Fleet, D., Pajdla, T., Schiele, B., Tuytelaars, T. (eds.) ECCV 2014, Part IV. LNCS, vol. 8692, pp. 105–118. Springer, Heidelberg (2014)
53. Viola, P., Jones, M.: Robust real-time face detection. Int. J. Comput. Vis. **57**(2), 137–154 (2004)
54. GridCut. http://www.gridcut.com/
55. Chen, L.C., Papandreou, G., Kokkinos, I., Murphy, K., Yuille, A.L.: Semantic image segmentation with deep convolutional nets and fully connected CRFS. arXiv preprint arXiv:1412.7062 (2014)
56. Simonyan, K., Zisserman, A.: Very deep convolutional networks for large-scale image recognition. CoRR abs/1409.1556 (2014)
57. Krähenbühl, P., Koltun, V.: Efficient inference in fully connected CRFS with gaussian edge potentials. In: Shawe-Taylor, J., Zemel, R.S., Bartlett, P.L., Pereira, F., Weinberger, K.Q. (eds.) Advances in Neural Information Processing Systems, vol. 24, pp. 109–117. Curran Associates, Inc. (2011)
58. Huang, G.B., Ramesh, M., Berg, T., Learned-Miller, E.: Labeled faces in the wild: a database for studying face recognition in unconstrained environments. Technical report 07–49. University of Massachusetts, Amherst, October 2007
59. Siva, P., Russell, C., Xiang, T.: In defence of negative mining for annotating weakly labelled data. In: Fitzgibbon, A., Lazebnik, S., Perona, P., Sato, Y., Schmid, C. (eds.) ECCV 2012, Part III. LNCS, vol. 7574, pp. 594–608. Springer, Heidelberg (2012)
60. Song, H.O., Girshick, R., Jegelka, S., Mairal, J., Harchaoui, Z., Darrell, T.: On learning to localize objects with minimal supervision. arXiv preprint arXiv:1403.1024 (2014)
61. Mittal, A., Zisserman, A., Torr, P.H.S.: Hand detection using multiple proposals. In: British Machine Vision Conference (2011)
62. Ekman, P., Friesen, W.: Facial action coding system: a technique for the measurement of facial movement. Consulting Psychologists, San Francisco (1978)
63. Tarrés, F., Rama, A.: GTAV face database. GVAP, UPC (2012)
64. Byrd, R.H., Lu, P., Nocedal, J., Zhu, C.: A limited memory algorithm for bound constrained optimization. SIAM J. Sci. Comput. **16**(5), 1190–1208 (1995)
65. Lu, C.P., Hager, G.D., Mjolsness, E.: Fast and globally convergent pose estimation from video images. IEEE Trans. Pattern Anal. Mach. Intell. **22**(6), 610–622 (2000)
66. Jia, X., Yang, H., Lin, A., Chan, K.P., Patras, I.: Structured semi-supervised forest for facial landmarks localization with face mask reasoning. In: Proceedings British Machines Visualization Conference (BMVA) (2014)
67. Yang, H., He, X., Jia, X., Patras, I.: Robust face alignment under occlusion via regional predictive power estimation. IEEE Trans. Image Process. **24**(8), 2393–2403 (2015)

Learning Temporal Transformations from Time-Lapse Videos

Yipin Zhou[✉] and Tamara L. Berg[✉]

University of North Carolina at Chapel Hill, Chapel Hill, USA
{yipin,tlberg}@cs.unc.edu

Abstract. Based on life-long observations of physical, chemical, and biologic phenomena in the natural world, humans can often easily picture in their minds what an object will look like in the future. But, what about computers? In this paper, we learn computational models of object transformations from time-lapse videos. In particular, we explore the use of generative models to create depictions of objects at future times. These models explore several different prediction tasks: generating a future state given a single depiction of an object, generating a future state given two depictions of an object at different times, and generating future states recursively in a recurrent framework. We provide both qualitative and quantitative evaluations of the generated results, and also conduct a human evaluation to compare variations of our models.

Keywords: Generation · Temporal prediction · Time-lapse video

1 Introduction

Before they can speak or understand language, babies have a grasp of some natural phenomena. They realize that if they drop the spoon it will fall to the ground (and their parent will pick it up). As they grow older, they develop understanding of more complex notions like object constancy and time. Children acquire much of this knowledge by observing and interacting with the world.

In this paper we seek to learn computational models of how the world works through observation. Specifically, we learn models for natural transformations from video. To enable this learning, we collect time-lapse videos demonstrating four different natural state transformations: melting, blooming, baking, and rotting. Several of these transformations are applicable to a variety of objects. For example, butter, ice cream, and snow melt, bread and pizzas bake, and many different objects rot. We train models for each transformation – irrespective of the object undergoing the transformation – under the assumption that these transformations have shared underlying physical properties that can be learned.

Electronic supplementary material The online version of this chapter (doi:10. 1007/978-3-319-46484-8_16) contains supplementary material, which is available to authorized users.

© Springer International Publishing AG 2016
B. Leibe et al. (Eds.): ECCV 2016, Part VIII, LNCS 9912, pp. 262–277, 2016.
DOI: 10.1007/978-3-319-46484-8_16

To model transformations, we train deep networks to generate depictions of the future state of objects. We explore several different generation tasks for modeling natural transformations. The first task is to generate the future state depiction of an object from a single image of the object (Sect. 3.1). Here the input is a frame depicting an object at time t, and output is a generated depiction of the object at time t + k, where k is specified as a conditional label input to the network. For this task we explore two auto-encoder based architectures. The first architecture is a baseline algorithm built from a standard auto-encoder framework. The second architecture is a generative adversarial network where in addition to the baseline auto-encoder, a discriminator network is added to encourage more realistic outputs.

For our second and third future prediction tasks, we introduce different ways of encoding time in the generation process. In our two-stack model (Sect. 3.2) the input is two images of an object at time t and t + m and the model learns to generate a future image according to the implicit time gap between the input images (i.e. generate a prediction of the object at time t + 2m). These models are trained on images with varying time gaps. Finally, in our last prediction task, our goal is to recursively generate the future states of an object given a single input image of the object. For this task, we use a recurrent neural network to recursively generate future depictions (Sect. 3.3). For each of the described future generation tasks, we also explore the effectiveness of pre-training on a large set of images, followed by fine-tuning on time-lapse data for improving performance.

Future prediction has been explored in previous works for generating the next frame or next few frames of a video [1–3]. Our focus, in comparison, is to model general natural object transformations and to model future prediction at a longer time scale (minutes to days) than previous approaches.

We evaluate the generated results of each model both quantitatively and qualitatively under a variety of different training scenarios (Sect. 4). In addition, we perform human evaluations of model variations and image retrieval experiments. Finally, to help understand what these models have learned, we also visualize common motion patterns of the learned transformations. These results are discussed in Sect. 5.

The innovations introduced by our paper include: (1) A new problem of modeling natural object transformations with deep networks, (2) A new dataset of 1463 time-lapse videos depicting 4 common object transformations, (3) Exploration of deep network architectures for modeling and generating future depictions, (4) Quantitative, qualitative, and human evaluations of the generated results, and (5) Visualizations of the learned transformation patterns.

1.1 Related Work

Object state recognition: Previous works [4–6] have looked at the problem of recognizing attributes, which has significant conceptual overlap with the idea of object state recognition. For example "in full bloom" could be viewed as an attribute of flowers. Parikh and Grauman [5] train models to recognize the relative strength of attributes such as face A is "smiling more" than face B from ordered sets of images. One way to view our work is as providing methods to train relative state models in the temporal domain. Most relevant to our work, given a set of object transformation terms, such as ripe vs. unripe, [7] learns visual classification and regression models for object transformations from a collection of photos. In contrast, our work takes a deep learning approach and learns transformations from video – perhaps a more natural input format for learning temporal information.

Timelapse data analysis: Timelapse data captures changes in time and has been used for various applications. [8] hallucinates an input scene image at a different time of day by making use of a timelapse video dataset exhibiting lighting changes in an example-based color transfer technique. [9] presents an algorithm that synthesizes timelapse videos of landmarks from large internet image collections. In their follow-up work, [10] imports additional camera motion while composing videos to create transformations in time and space.

Future prediction: Future prediction has been applied to various tasks such as estimating the future trajectories of cars [11], pedestrians [12], or general objects [13] in images or videos. In the ego-centric activity domain, [14] encodes the prediction problem as a binary task of selecting which of two video clips is first in temporal ordering. Given large amounts of unlabeled video data from the internet, [15] trains a deep network to predict visual representations of future images, enabling them to anticipate both actions and objects before they appear.

Image/Frame generation: Generative models have attracted extensive attention in machine learning [16–21]. Recently many works have focused on generating novel natural or high-quality images. [22] applies deep structure networks trained on synthetic data to generate 3D chairs. [23] combines variational auto-encoders with an attention mechanism to recurrently generate different parts of a single image. Generative adversarial networks (GANs) have shown great promise for improving image generation quality [24]. GANs are composed of two parts, a generative model and a discriminative model, to be trained jointly. Some extensions have combined GAN structure with multi-scale laplacian pyramid to produce high-resolution generation results [25]. Recently [26] incorporated deep convolutional neural network structures into GANs to improve image quality. [27] proposed a network to generate the contents of an arbitrary image region according to its surroundings. Some related approaches [1–3] have trained generation models to reconstruct input video frames and/or generate the next few consecutive frames of a video. We also explore the use of DCGANs for future prediction, focusing on modeling object transformations over relatively long time scales.

2   Object-Centric Timelapse Dataset

Given the high-level goal of understanding temporal transformations of objects, we require a collection of videos showing temporal state changes. Therefore,

Table 1. Statistics of our transformation categories. Some categories contain multiple objects (e.g. ice cream, chocolate, etc. melting) while others apply only to a specific object (e.g. flowers blooming). Values indicate the total number of videos collected for each category.

Rotting: 185	Melting: 453	Baking: 242	Blooming: 583
Strawberry: 35	Ice cream: 128	Cookies: 55	Flower: 583
Watermelon: 9	Chocolate: 18	Bread: 57	
Tomato: 25	Butter: 9	Pizza: 59	
Banana: 26	Snow: 54	Cake: 48	
Apple: 23	Wax: 60	Other: 23	
Peach: 8	Ice: 184		
Other: 59			

we collect a large set of object-centric timelapse videos from the web. Time-lapse videos are ideal for our purposes since they are designed to show an entire transformation (or a portion of a transformation) within a short period of time.

2.1 Data Collection

We observe that time-lapse photography is quite popular due to the relative ease of data collection. A search on YouTube for "time lapse" results in over 11 million results. Anyone with a personal camera, GoPro, or even a cell phone can capture a simple time-lapse video and many people post and publicly share these videos on the web. We collect our object-based timelapse video dataset by directly querying keywords through the YouTube API. For this paper, we query 4 state transformation categories: Blooming, Melting, Baking and Rotting, combined with various object categories. This results in a dataset of more than 5000 videos. This dataset could be extended to a wider variety of transformations or to more complex multi-object transformations, but as a first step we focus on these 4 as our initial goal set of transformations for learning.

For ease of learning, ideally these videos should be object-centric with a static camera capturing an entire object transformation. However, many videos in the initial data collection stage do not meet these requirements. Therefore, we clean the data using Amazon Mechanical Turk (AMT) as a crowdsourcing platform. Each video is examined by 3 Turkers who are asked questions related to video quality. Videos that are not timelapse, contain severe camera motion or are not consistent with the query labels are removed. We also manually adjust parts of the videos which are playing backwards (a technique used in some time-lapse videos), contain more than one round of the specified transformation, and remove irrelevant prolog/epilog. Finally our resulting dataset contains 1463 high quality object based timelapse videos. Table 1 shows the statistics of transformation categories and their respective object counts. Figure 1 shows example frames of each transformation category.

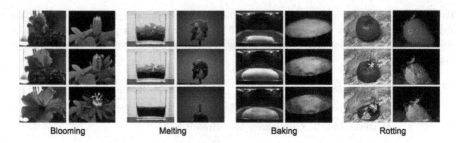

| Blooming | Melting | Baking | Rotting |

Fig. 1. Example frames from our dataset of each transformation category: Blooming, Melting, Baking, and Rotting. In each column, time increases as you move down the column, showing how an object transforms.

2.2   Transformation Degree Annotation

To learn natural transformation models of objects from videos, we need to first label the degree of transformation throughout the videos. In language, people use text labels to describe different states, for instance, fresh vs. rotted apple. However, the transformation from one state to another is really a continuous evolution. Therefore, we represent the degree of transformation with a real number, assigning the start state a value of 0 (not at all rotten) and the end state (completely rotten) a value of 1. To annotate objects from different videos we could naively assign the first frame a value of 0 and the last frame a value of 1, interpolating in between. However, we observe that some time-lapse videos may not depict entire transformations, resulting in poor alignments.

Therefore, we design a labeling task for people to assign degrees of transformation to videos. Directly estimating a real value for frames turns out to be impractical as people may have different conceptions of transformation degree. Instead our interface displays reference frames of an object category-transformation and asks Turkers to align frames from a target video to the reference frames according to degree of transformation. Specifically, for each object category-transformation pair we select 5 reference frames from a reference video showing: transformation degree values of 0, 0.25, 0.5, 0.75, and 1. Then, for the rest of the videos in that object-transformation category, we ask Turkers to select frames visually displaying the same degree of transformation as the reference frames. If the displayed video does not depict an entire transformation, Turkers may align less than 5 frames with the reference. Each target video is aligned by 3 Turkers and the median of their responses is used as annotation labels(linearly interpolating degrees between labeled target frames). This provides us with consistent degree annotations between videos.

3   Future State Generation Tasks and Approaches

Our goal is to generate depictions of the future state of objects. In this work, we explore frameworks for 3 temporal prediction tasks. In the first task (Sect. 3.1),

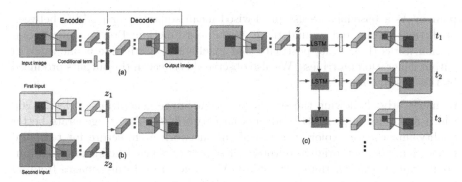

Fig. 2. Model architectures of three generation tasks: (a) Pairwise generator; (b) Two stack generator; (c) Recurrent generator.

called pairwise generation, we input an object-centric frame and the model generates an image showing the future state of this object. Here the degree of the future state transformation – how far in the future we want the depiction to show – is controlled by a conditional term in the model. In the second task (Sect. 3.2) we have two inputs to the model: two frames from the same video showing a state transformation at two points in time. The goal of this model is to generate a third image that continues the trend of the transformation depicted by the first and second input. We call this "two stack" generation. In the third task (Sect. 3.3), called "recurrent generation", the input is a single frame and the goal is to recursively generate images that exhibit future degrees of the transformation in a recurrent model framework.

3.1 Pairwise Generation

In this task, we input a frame and generate an image showing the future state. We model the task using an autoencoder style convolutional neural network. The model architecture is shown in Fig. 2(a), where the input and output size are 64×64 with 3 channels and encoding and decoding parts are symmetric. Both encoding and decoding parts consists of 4 convolution/deconvolution layers with the kernel size 5×5 and a stride of 2, meaning that at each layer the height and width of the output feature map decreases/increases by a factor of 2 with 64, 128, 256, 512/512, 256, 128, 64 channels respectively. Each conv/deconv layer, except the last layer, is followed by a batch normalization operation [28] and ReLU activation function [29]. For the last layer we use Tanh as the activation function. The size of the hidden variable z (center) is 512. We represent the conditional term encoding the degree of elapsed time between the input and output as a 4 dimensional one-hot vector, representing 4 possible degrees. This is connected with a linear layer (512) and concatenated with z to adjust the degree of the future depiction. Below we describe experiments with different loss functions and training approaches for this network.

p_mse: As a baseline, we use pixel-wised mean square error(p_MSE) between prediction output and ground truth as the loss function. Previous image generation works [1–3,27,30] postulate that pixel-wised l_2 criterion is one cause of output generation blurriness. We also observe this effect in the outputs produced by this baseline model.

p_mse + adv: Following the success of recent image generation works [24,26], which make use of generative adversarial networks (GANs) to generate better quality images, we explore the use of this network architecture for temporal generation. For their original purpose, these networks generate images from randomly sampled noise. Here, we use a GAN to generate future images from an image of an object at the current time. Specifically, we use the baseline autoencoder previously described and incorporate an adversarial loss in combination with the pixel-wise MSE. During training this means that in addition to the auto-encoder, called the generator (G), we also train a binary CNN classifier, called the discriminator (D). The discriminator takes as input, the output of the generator and is trained to classify images as real or fake (i.e. generated). These two networks are adversaries because G is trying to generate images that can fool D into thinking they are real, and D is trying to determine if the images generated by G are real. Adding D helps to train a better generator G that produces more realistic future state images. The architecture of D is the same as the encoder of G, except that the last output is a scalar and connect with sigmoid function. D also incorporates the conditional term by connecting a one-hot vector with a linear layer and reshaping to the same size as the input image then concatenating in the third dimension. The output of D is a probability, which will be large if the input is a real image and small if the input is a generated image. For this framework, the loss is formulated as a combination of the MSE and adversarial loss:

$$L_G = L_{p\_mse} + \lambda_{adv} * L_{adv} \tag{1}$$

where L_{p_mse} is the mean square error loss, where x is the input image, c is the conditional term, G(.) is the output of the generation model, and y is the ground truth future image at time = current time + c.

$$L_{p\_mse} = |y - G(x, c)|^2 \tag{2}$$

And, L_{adv} is a binary cross-entropy loss with $\alpha = 1$ that penalizes if the generated image does not look like a real image. D[.] is the scalar probability output by the discriminator.

$$L_{adv} = -\alpha \log(D[G(x, c), c]) - (1 - \alpha) \log(1 - D[G(x, c), c]) \tag{3}$$

During training, the binary cross-entropy loss is used to train D on both real and generated images. For details of jointly training adversarial structures, please refer to [24].

p_g_mse + adv: Inspired by [2], where they introduce gradient based l_1 or l_2 loss to sharpen generated images. We also evaluate a loss function that is a combination of pixel-wise MSE, gradient based MSE, and adversarial loss:

$$L_G = L_{p\_mse} + L_{g\_mse} + \lambda_{adv} * L_{adv} \tag{4}$$

where L_{g_mse} represents mean square error in the gradient domain defined as:

$$L_{g\_mse} = (g_x[y] - g_x[G(x,c)])^2 + (g_y[y] - g_y[G(x,c)])^2 \tag{5}$$

$g_x[.]$ and $g_y[.]$ are the gradient operations along the x and y axis of images. We could apply different weights to L_{p_mse} and L_{g_mse}, but in this work we simply weight them equally.

p_g_mse + adv + ft: Since we have limited training data for each transformation, we investigate the use of pre-training for improving generation quality. In this method we use the same loss function as the last method, but instead of training the adversarial network from scratch, training proceeds in two stages. The first stage is a reconstruction stage where we train the generation model using random static images for the reconstruction task. Here the goal is for the output image to match the input image as well as possible even though passing through a bottleneck during generation. In the second stage, the fine-tuning stage, we fine-tune the network for the temporal generation task using our timelapse data. By first pre-training for the reconstruction task, we expect the network to obtain a good initialization, capturing a representation that will be useful for kick-starting the temporal generation fine-tuning.

3.2 Two Stack Generation

In this scenario, we want to generate an image that shows the future state of an object given two input images showing the object in two stages of its transformation. The output should continue the transformation pattern demonstrated in the input images, i.e. if the input images depict the object at time t and t + m, then the output should depict the object at time t + 2m. We design the generation model using two stacks in the encoding part of the model as shown in Fig. 2(b). The structures of the two stacks are the same and are also identical to the encoding part of the pairwise generation model. The hidden variables z_1 and z_2 are both 512 dimensions, and are concatenated together and fed into the decoding part, which is also the same as the previous pairwise generation model. The two stacks are sequential, trained independently without shared weights.

Given the blurry results of the baseline for pairwise generation, here we only use three methods **p_mse + adv**, **p_g_mse + adv**, and **p_g_mse + adv + ft**. The structure of the discriminator is the same. For the fine-tuning method, during the reconstruction training, we make the two inputs the same static image. The optimization procedures are the same as for the pairwise generation task, but we do not have conditional term here (since time for the future generation is implicitly specified by the input images).

3.3 Recurrent Generation

In this scenario, we would like to recursively generate future images of an object given only a single image of its current temporal state. In particular, we use a recurrent neural network framework for generation where each time step generates an image of the object at a fixed degree interval in the future. This model structure is shown in Fig. 2(c). After hidden variable z, we add a LSTM [31] layer. For each time step, the LSTM layer takes both z and the output from the previous time step as inputs and sends a 512 dimension vector to the decoder. The structure of the encoder and decoder are the same as in the previous scenarios, where the decoding portions for each time slot share the same weights.

We evaluate three loss functions in this network: **p_mse + adv**, **p_g_mse + adv** and **p_g_mse + adv + ft**. The structure of the discriminator is again the same without the conditional term (as in the two-stack model). For fine-tuning, during reconstruction training, we train the model to recurrently output the same static image as the input at each time step.

4   Experiments

In this section, we discuss the training process and parameter settings for all experiments (Sect. 4.1). Then, we describe dataset pre-processing and augmentation (Sect. 4.2). Finally, we discuss quantitative and qualitative analysis of results for: pairwise generation (Sect. 4.3), two-stack generation (Sect. 4.4), and recurrent generation (Sect. 4.5).

4.1   Training and Parameter Settings

Unless otherwise specified training and parameter setting details are applied to all models. During training, we apply Adam Stochastic Optimization [32] with learning rate 0.0002 and minibatch of size 64. The models are implemented using the Tensorflow deep learning toolbox [33]. In the loss functions where we combine mean square error loss with adversarial loss (as in equation(1)), we set the weight of the adversarial loss to $\lambda_{adv} = 0.2$ for all experiments.

4.2   Dataset Preprocessing and Augmentation

Timelapse dataset: Some of the collected videos depict more than one object or the object is not located in the center of the frames. In order to help the model concentrate on learning the transformation itself rather object localization, for each video in the dataset, we obtain a cropped version of the frames centered on the main object. We randomly split the videos into training and testing sets in a ratio of 0.85:0.15. Then, we sample frame pairs (for pairwise generation) or groups of frames (for two-stack and recurrent generation) from the training and testing videos. Frames are resized to 64×64 for generation. To prevent overfitting, we also perform data augmentation on training pairs or groups by incorporating frame crops and left-right flipping.

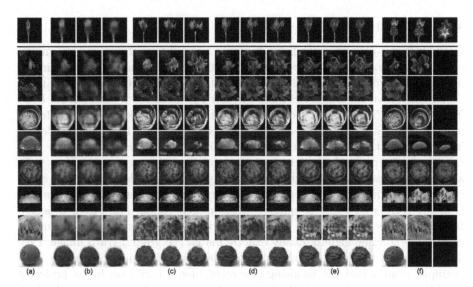

Fig. 3. Pairwise generation results for: Blooming (rows 1–3), Melting (rows 4–5), Baking (rows 6–7) and Rotting (rows 8–9). Input(a), p_mse(b), p_mse + adv(c), p_g_mse + adv(d), p_g_mse + adv + ft(e), Ground truth frames(f). Black frames in the ground truth indicate video did not depict transformation that far in the future.

Reconstruction dataset: This dataset contains static images used to pre-train our models on reconstruction tasks. Initially, we tried training only on objects depicted in the timelapse videos and observed performance improvement. However, collecting images of specific object categories is a tedious task at large-scale. Therefore, we also tried pre-training on random images (scene images or images of random objects) and found that the results were competitive. This implies that the content of the images is not as important as encouraging the networks to learn how to reconstruct arbitrary input images well. We randomly download 50101 images from ImageNet [34] as our reconstruction dataset. The advantage of this strategy is that we are able to use the same group of images for every transformation model and task.

Table 2. Quantitative Evaluation of: Pairwise generation, Two stack generation, and Recurrent tasks. For PSNR and SSIM larger is better, while for MSE lower is better.

	Pairwise			Two stack			Recurrent		
	PSNR	SSIM	MSE	PSNR	SSIM	MSE	PSNR	SSIM	MSE
p_mse + adv	17.0409	0.5576	0.0227	17.7425	0.5970	0.0185	17.2758	0.5747	0.0211
p_g_mse + adv	17.0660	0.5720	0.0224	17.9157	0.6122	0.0177	17.2951	0.5749	0.0214
p_g_mse + adv + ft	17.4784	0.6036	0.0207	18.6812	0.6566	0.0153	18.3357	0.6283	0.0166

4.3 Pairwise Generation

In the pairwise generation task, we input an image of an object and the model outputs depiction of the future state of the object, where the degree of transformation is controlled by a conditional term. The conditional term is a 4 dimensional one-hot vector which indicates whether the predicted output should be 0, 0.25, 0.5 or 0.75 degrees in the future from the input frame. We sample frame pairs from timelapse videos based on annotated degree value intervals. A 0 degree interval means that the input and output training images are identical. We consider 0 degree pairs as auxiliary pairs, useful for two reasons: (1) They help augment the training data with video frames (which display different properties from still images), and (2) The prediction quality of image reconstruction is highly correlated with the quality of future generation. Pairs from 0 degree transformations can be easily be evaluated in terms of reconstruction quality since the prediction should ideally exactly match the ground truth image. Predictions for future degree transformations are somewhat more subjective. For example, from a bud the resulting generated bloom may look like a perfectly valid flower, but may not match the exact flower shape that this particular bud grew into (an example is shown in Fig. 3 row 1).

We train pairwise generation models separately for each of the 4 transformation categories using **p_mse**, **p_mse + adv** and **p_g_mse + adv** methods, trained for 12500 iterations on timelapse data from scratch. For the **p_g_mse + adv + ft** method, the models are first trained on the reconstruction dataset for 5000 iterations with the conditional term fixed as '0 degree' and then fine-tuned on timelapse data for another 5500 iterations. We observe that the fine-tuning training converges faster than training from scratch (example results with 3 different degree conditional terms in Fig. 3). We observe that the baseline suffers from a high degree of blurriness. Incorporating other terms into the loss function improves results, as does pre-training with fine-tuning. Table 2 (cols 2–4) shows evaluations of pairwise-generation reconstruction. For evaluation, we compute the Peak Signal to Noise Ratio(PSNR), Structural Similarity Index(SSIM) and Mean Square Error (MSE) values between the output and ground truth. We can see that incorporating gradient loss slightly improves results while pre-training further improves performance. This agrees with the qualitative visual results.

4.4 Two Stack Generation

For two stack generation, the model generates an image showing the future state of an object given two input depictions at different stages of transformation. As training data, we sample frame triples from videos with neighboring frame degree intervals: 0, 0.1, 0.2, 0.3, 0.4, and 0.5. We train two stack generation models for each of the 4 transformation categories, trained for 12500 iterations for the **p_mse + adv** and **p_g_mse + adv** methods. For the **p_g_mse + adv + ft** method, the models are first pre-trained on the reconstruction dataset for 4000 iterations and then fine-tuned on timelapse data for 6500 iterations (Fig. 4 shows

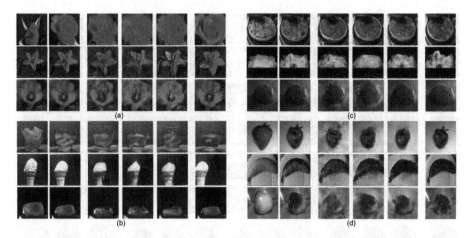

Fig. 4. Two stack generation results for Blooming (a), Melting (b), Baking (c) and Rotting (d). For each we show the two input frames (col 1–2), and results for: p_mse + adv (col 3), p_g_mse + adv (col 4), p_g_mse + adv + ft (col 5) and ground truth (col 6)

Fig. 5. Two stack generation with varying time between input images. For each example we show: the two input images (col 1–2), p_mse + adv (col 3), p_g_mse + adv (col 4), p_g_mse + adv + ft (col 5) and ground truth (col 6). The models are able to vary their outputs depending on elapsed time between inputs.

example prediction results). We observe that **p_g_mse + adv + ft** generates improved results in terms of both image quality and future state prediction accuracy. We further evaluate the reconstruction accuracy off these models in Table 2 (cols 5–7). Furthermore, in this task we expect that the models can not only predict the future state, but also learn to generate the correct time interval based on the input images. Figure 5 shows input images with different amounts of elapsed time. We can see that the models are able to vary how far in the future to generate based on the input image interval.

4.5 Recurrent Generation

For our recurrent generation task, we want to train a model to generate multiple future states of an object given a single input frame. Due to limited data we recursively generate 4 time steps. During training, we sample groups of frames from timelapse videos. Each group contains 5 frames, the first being the input, and the rests having 0, 0.1, 0.2, 0.3 degree intervals from the input. As in the previous tasks, the reconstruction outputs are used for quantitative evaluation.

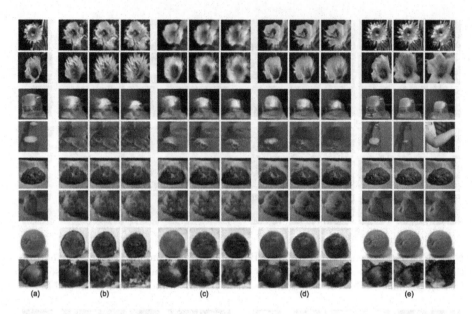

Fig. 6. Recurrent generation results for: Blooming (rows 1–2), Melting (rows 3–4), Baking (rows 5–6) and Rotting (rows 7–8). Input(a), p_mse + adv(b), p_g_mse + adv(c), p_g_mse + adv + ft(d), Ground truth frames(e).

We train the models separately for the 4 transformation categories. The models for the **p_mse + adv** and **p_g_mse + adv** methods are trained for 8500 iterations on timelapse data from scratch. For the **p_g_mse + adv + ft** method, models are pre-trained on the reconstruction dataset for 5000 iterations then fine-tuned for another 5500 iterations. Figure 6 shows prediction results (outputs of $2^{nd}, 3^{rd}$ and 4th time steps) of the three methods. Table 2 (cols 8–10) shows the reconstruction evaluation.

Table 3. Human evaluation results: BL stands for p_mse method, ADV (p_mse + adv), Grad(p_g_mse + adv) and Ft(p_g_mse + adv + ft)

	Pairwise				Two stack			Recurrent		
	BL	ADV	Grad	Ft	ADV	Grad	Ft	ADV	Grad	Ft
Blooming	0.1320	0.2300	0.2880	0.3500	0.3080	0.3240	0.3680	0.3320	0.2860	0.3820
Melting	0.1680	0.2520	0.2760	0.3040	0.3400	0.3120	0.3480	0.3180	0.3220	0.3600
Baking	0.1620	0.2600	0.2840	0.2940	0.3120	0.3200	0.3680	0.2780	0.3540	0.3680
Rotting	0.1340	0.2020	0.2580	0.4060	0.3040	0.2640	0.4320	0.2940	0.2900	0.4160
Average	0.1490	0.2360	0.2765	**0.3385**	0.3160	0.3050	**0.3790**	0.3055	0.3130	**0.3815**

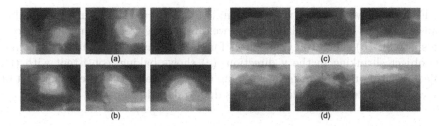

Fig. 7. Visualization results of learned transformations: x axis flows of blooming (a), y axis flows of melting (b), y axis flows of baking (c) and y axis flows of rotting (d)

5   Additional Experiments

Human Evaluations: As previously described, object future state prediction is sometimes not well defined. Many different possible futures may be considered reasonable to a human observer. Therefore, we design human experiments to judge the quality of our generated future states. For each transformation category and generation task, we randomly pick 500 test cases. Human subjects are shown one (or two for two stack generation) input image and future images generated by each method (randomly sorted to avoid biases in human selection). Subjects are asked to choose the image that most reasonably shows the future object state.

Results are shown in Table 3, where numbers indicate the fraction of cases where humans selected results from each method as the best future prediction. For pairwise generation (cols 2–5), the **p_g_mse + adv + ft** method achieves the most human preferences, while the baseline performs worst by a large margin. For both two stack generation (cols 6–8) and recurrent generation (cols 9–11), **p_mse + adv** and **p_g_mse + adv** are competitive, but again making use of pre-training plus fine-tuning obtains largest number of human preferences.

Image Retrieval: We also add a simple retrieval experiment on Pairwise generation results using pixelwise similarity. We count retrievals within reasonable distance (20 % of video length) to the ground truth as correct, achieving average accuracies on top-1/5 of **p_mse + adv**: 0.68/0.94; **p_g_mse + adv**: 0.72/0.95; and **p_g_mse + adv + ft**: 0.90/0.98.

Visualizations: Object state transformations often lead to physical changes in the shape of an object. To further understand what our models have learned, we provide some simple visualizations of motion features computed on generated images. Visualizations are computed on results of the **p_g_mse + adv + ft** recurrent model since we want to show the temporal trends of the learned transformations. For each testing case, we compute 3 optical flow maps in the x and y directions between the input image and the second, third, and fourth generated images. We cluster each using kmeans ($k = 4$). Then, for each cluster, we average the optical flow maps in the x and y directions.

Figure 7 shows the flow visualization: (a) is the x axis flow for the blooming transformation. From the visualization we observe the trend of the object growing spatially. (b) shows the y axis flows for the melting transformation, showing the object shrinking in the y direction. (c) shows baking, consistent with the object inflating up and down. For rotting (d), we observe that the upper part of the object inflates with mold or shrinks due to dehydration.

6   Conclusions

In this paper, we have collected a new dataset of timelapse videos depicting temporal object transformations. Using this dataset, we have trained effective methods to generate one or multiple future object states. We evaluate each prediction task under a number of different loss functions and show improvements using adversarial networks and pre-training. Finally, we provide human evaluations and visualizations of the learned models. Future work includes applying our methods to additional single-object transformations and to more complex transformations involving multiple objects.

References

1. Srivastava, N., Mansimov, E., Salakhudinov, R.: Unsupervised learning of video representations using LSTMs. In: ICML (2015)
2. Mathieu, M., Couprie, C., LeCun, Y.: Deep multi-scale video prediction beyond mean square error. CoRR (2015)
3. Ranzato, M., Szlam, A., Bruna, J., Mathieu, M., Collobert, R., Chopra, S.: Video (language) modeling: a baseline for generative models of natural videos. CoRR (2014)
4. Farhadi, A., Endres, I., Hoiem, D., Forsyth, D.: Describing objects by their attributes. In: CVPR (2009)
5. Parikh, D., Grauman, K.: Relative attributes. IJCV (2011)
6. Patterson, G., Hays, J.: Sun attribute database: discovering, annotating, and recognizing scene attributes. In: CVPR (2012)
7. Isola, P., Lim, J.J., Adelson, E.H.: Discovering states and transformations in image collections. In: CVPR (2015)
8. Shih, Y., Paris, S., Durand, F., Freeman, W.T.: Data-driven hallucination of different times of day from a single outdoor photo. ACM Trans. Graph. 32(6), 200:1–200:11 (2013)
9. Martin-Brualla, R., Gallup, D., Seitz, S.M.: Time-lapse mining from internet photos. ACM Trans. Graph. 34(4), 621–628 (2015)
10. Martin-Brualla, R., Gallup, D., Seitz, S.M.: 3D time-lapse reconstruction from internet photos. In: ICCV (2015)
11. Walker, J., Gupta, A., Hebert, M.: Patch to the future: unsupervised visual prediction. In: CVPR (2014)
12. Kitani, K.M., Ziebart, B.D., Bagnell, J.A., Hebert, M.: Activity forecasting. In: Fitzgibbon, A., Lazebnik, S., Perona, P., Sato, Y., Schmid, C. (eds.) ECCV 2012. LNCS, vol. 7575, pp. 201–214. Springer, Heidelberg (2012). doi:10.1007/978-3-642-33765-9_15

13. Yuen, J., Torralba, A.: A data-driven approach for event prediction. In: Daniilidis, K., Maragos, P., Paragios, N. (eds.) ECCV 2010. LNCS, vol. 6312, pp. 707–720. Springer, Heidelberg (2010). doi:10.1007/978-3-642-15552-9_51
14. Zhou, Y., Berg, T.L.: Temporal perception and prediction in ego-centric video. In: ICCV (2015)
15. Vondrick, C., Pirsiavash, H., Torralba, A.: Anticipating the future by watching unlabeled video. CoRR (2015)
16. Hinton, G.E., Sejnowski, T.J.: Learning and relearning in Boltzmann machines. In: Parallel Distributed Processing: Explorations in the Microstructure of Cognition, vol. 1 (1986)
17. Smolensky, P.: Information processing in dynamical systems: foundations of harmony theory. In: Parallel Distributed Processing: Explorations in the Microstructure of Cognition, vol. 1 (1986)
18. Lee, H., Grosse, R., Ranganath, R., Ng, A.Y.: Convolutional deep belief networks for scalable unsupervised learning of hierarchical representations. In: ICML (2009)
19. Hinton, G.E., Salakhutdinov, R.R.: Reducing the dimensionality of data with neural networks. Science **313**, 504–507 (2006)
20. Tang, Y., Salakhutdinov, R.R.: Learning stochastic feedforward neural networks. In: NIPS (2013)
21. Kingma, D.P., Welling, M.: Auto-encoding variational Bayes. ArXiv e-prints (2013)
22. Dosovitskiy, A., Springenberg, J.T., Brox, T.: Learning to generate chairs with convolutional neural networks. In: CVPR (2015)
23. Gregor, K., Danihelka, I., Graves, A., Rezende, D., Wierstra, D.: Draw: a recurrent neural network for image generation. In: ICML (2015)
24. Goodfellow, I., Pouget-Abadie, J., Mirza, M., Xu, B., Warde-Farley, D., Ozair, S., Courville, A., Bengio, Y.: Generative adversarial nets. In: NIPS (2014)
25. Denton, E.L., Chintala, S., Szlam, A., Fergus, R.: Deep generative image models using a Laplacian pyramid of adversarial networks (2015)
26. Radford, A., Metz, L., Chintala, S.: Unsupervised representation learning with deep convolutional generative adversarial networks. CoRR (2015)
27. Pathak, D., Krähenbühl, P., Donahue, J., Darrell, T., Efros, A.: Context encoders: feature learning by inpainting. arXiv preprint arXiv:1604.07379 (2016)
28. Ioffe, S., Szegedy, C.: Batch normalization: accelerating deep network training by reducing internal covariate shift. In: ICML (2015)
29. Nair, V., Hinton, G.E.: Rectified linear units improve restricted Boltzmann machines. In: ICML
30. Ridgeway, K., Snell, J., Roads, B., Zemel, R.S., Mozer, M.C.: Learning to generate images with perceptual similarity metrics. CoRR (2015)
31. Hochreiter, S., Schmidhuber, J.: Long short-term memory. Neural Comput. **9**(8), 1735–1780 (1997)
32. Kingma, D.P., Ba, J.: Adam: a method for stochastic optimization. CoRR (2014)
33. http://tensorflow.org (2015)
34. Deng, J., Dong, W., Socher, R., Li, L.J., Li, K., Fei-Fei, L.: ImageNet: a large-scale hierarchical image database. In: CVPR (2009)

Interactive Image Segmentation
Using Constrained Dominant Sets

Eyasu Zemene[(✉)] and Marcello Pelillo

Ca' Foscari University of Venice, Venice, Italy
{eyasu.zemene,pelillo}@unive.it

Abstract. We propose a new approach to interactive image segmentation based on some properties of a family of quadratic optimization problems related to dominant sets, a well-known graph-theoretic notion of a cluster which generalizes the concept of a maximal clique to edge-weighted graphs. In particular, we show that by properly controlling a regularization parameter which determines the structure and the scale of the underlying problem, we are in a position to extract groups of dominant-set clusters which are constrained to contain user-selected elements. The resulting algorithm can deal naturally with any type of input modality, including scribbles, sloppy contours, and bounding boxes, and is able to robustly handle noisy annotations on the part of the user. Experiments on standard benchmark datasets show the effectiveness of our approach as compared to state-of-the-art algorithms on a variety of natural images under several input conditions.

Keywords: Interactive segmentation · Dominant sets · Quadratic optimization

1 Introduction

User-assisted image segmentation has recently attracted considerable attention within the computer vision community, especially because of its potential applications in a variety of different problems such as image and video editing, medical image analysis, etc. [1–8]. Given an input image and some information provided by a user, usually in the form of a scribble or of a bounding box, the goal is to provide as output a foreground object in such a way as to best reflect the user's intent. By exploiting high-level, semantic knowledge on the part of the user, which is typically difficult to formalize, we are therefore able to effectively solve segmentation problems which would be otherwise too complex to be tackled using fully automatic segmentation algorithms.

Existing algorithms fall into two broad categories, depending on whether the user annotation is given in terms of a scribble or of a bounding box, and supporters of the two approaches have both good reasons to prefer one modality against

Electronic supplementary material The online version of this chapter (doi:10. 1007/978-3-319-46484-8_17) contains supplementary material, which is available to authorized users.

© Springer International Publishing AG 2016
B. Leibe et al. (Eds.): ECCV 2016, Part VIII, LNCS 9912, pp. 278–294, 2016.
DOI: 10.1007/978-3-319-46484-8_17

the other. For example, Wu et al. [3] claim that bounding boxes are the most natural and economical form in terms of the amount of user interaction, and develop a multiple instance learning algorithm that extracts an arbitrary object located inside a tight bounding box at unknown location. Yu et al. [9] also support the bounding-box approach, though their algorithm is different from others in that it does not need bounding boxes tightly enclosing the object of interest, whose production of course increases the annotation burden. They provide an algorithm, based on a Markov Random Field (MRF) energy function, that can handle input bounding box that only loosely covers the foreground object. Xian et al. [10] propose a method which avoids the limitations of existing bounding box methods - region of interest (ROI) based methods, though they need much less user interaction, their performance is sensitive to initial ROI. On the other hand, several researchers, arguing that boundary-based interactive segmentation such as intelligent scissors [8] requires the user to trace the whole boundary of the object, which is usually a time-consuming and tedious process, support scribble-based segmentation. Bai et al. [11], for example, propose a model based on ratio energy function which can be optimized using an iterated graph cut algorithm, which tolerates errors in the user input.

In general, the input modality in an interactive segmentation algorithm affects both its accuracy and its ease of use. Existing methods work typically on a single modality and they focus on how to use that input most effectively. However, as noted recently by Jain and Grauman [12], sticking to one annotation form leads to a suboptimal tradeoff between human and machine effort, and they tried to estimate how much user input is required to sufficiently segment a novel input.

In this paper, we propose a novel approach to interactive image segmentation which can deal naturally with any type of input modality and is able to robustly handle noisy annotations on the part of the user. Figure 1 shows an example of how our system works in the presence of different input annotations. Our approach is based on some properties of a parameterized family of quadratic optimization problems related to dominant-set clusters, a well-known generalization of the notion of maximal cliques to edge-weighted graph which have proven to be extremely effective in a variety of computer vision problems, including (automatic) image and video segmentation [13,14]. In particular, we show that by properly controlling a regularization parameter which determines the structure and the scale of the underlying problem, we are in a position to extract groups of dominant-set clusters which are constrained to contain user-selected elements. We provide bounds that allow us to control this process, which are based on the spectral properties of certain submatrices of the original affinity matrix.

The resulting algorithm has a number of interesting features which distinguishes it from existing approaches. Specifically: (1) it is able to deal in a flexible manner with *both* scribble-based and boundary-based input modalities (such as sloppy contours and bounding boxes); (2) in the case of noiseless scribble inputs, it asks the user to provide *only* foreground pixels; (3) it turns out to be *robust* in

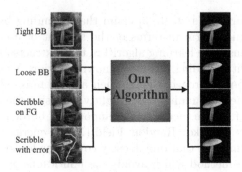

Fig. 1. Left: An input image with different user annotations. Tight bounding box (Tight BB), loose bounding box (Loose BB), a scribble made (only) on the foreground object (Scribbles on FG), scribbles with errors. **Right:** Results of the proposed algorithm.

the presence of input noise, allowing the user to draw, e.g., imperfect scribbles (including background pixels) or loose bounding boxes. Experimental results on standard benchmark datasets show the effectiveness of our approach as compared to state-of-the-art algorithms on a wide variety of natural images under several input conditions.

2   Dominant Sets and Quadratic Optimization

In this section we review the basic definitions and properties of dominant sets, as introduced in [13,14]. In the dominant set framework, the data to be clustered are represented as an undirected edge-weighted graph with no self-loops $G = (V, E, w)$, where $V = \{1, ..., n\}$ is the vertex set, $E \subseteq V \times V$ is the edge set, and $w : E \to R_+^*$ is the (positive) weight function. Vertices in G correspond to data points, edges represent neighborhood relationships, and edge-weights reflect similarity between pairs of linked vertices. As customary, we represent the graph G with the corresponding weighted adjacency (or similarity) matrix, which is the $n \times n$ nonnegative, symmetric matrix $A = (a_{ij})$ defined as $a_{ij} = w(i, j)$, if $(i, j) \in E$, and $a_{ij} = 0$ otherwise. Since in G there are no self-loops, note that all entries on the main diagonal of A are zero.

For a non-empty subset $S \subseteq V$, $i \in S$, and $j \notin S$, define

$$\phi_S(i,j) = a_{ij} - \frac{1}{|S|} \sum_{k \in S} a_{ik} \tag{1}$$

Next, to each vertex $i \in S$ we assign a weight defined (recursively) as follows:

$$w_S(i) = \begin{cases} 1, & \text{if } |S| = 1, \\ \sum_{j \in S \setminus \{i\}} \phi_{S \setminus \{i\}}(j, i) w_{S \setminus \{i\}}(j), & \text{otherwise.} \end{cases} \tag{2}$$

As explained in [13,14], a positive $w_S(i)$ indicates that adding i into its neighbors in S will increase the internal coherence of the set, whereas in the presence of a negative value we expect the overall coherence to be decreased. Finally, the total weight of S can be simply defined as

$$W(S) = \sum_{i \in S} w_S(i). \tag{3}$$

A non-empty subset of vertices $S \subseteq V$ such that $W(T) > 0$ for any non-empty $T \subseteq S$, is said to be a *dominant set* if:

1. $w_S(i) > 0$, for all $i \in S$,
2. $w_{S \cup \{i\}}(i) < 0$, for all $i \notin S$.

It is evident from the definition that a dominant set satisfies the two basic properties of a cluster: internal coherence and external incoherence. Condition 1 indicates that a dominant set is internally coherent, while condition 2 implies that this coherence will be destroyed by the addition of any vertex from outside. In other words, a dominant set is a maximally coherent data set.

Now, consider the following linearly-constrained quadratic optimization problem:

$$\begin{aligned} \text{maximize } & f(\mathbf{x}) = \mathbf{x}' A \mathbf{x} \\ \text{subject to } & \mathbf{x} \in \Delta \end{aligned} \tag{4}$$

where a prime denotes transposition and

$$\Delta = \left\{ \mathbf{x} \in R^n \ : \ \sum_{i=1}^{n} x_i = 1, \text{ and } x_i \geq 0 \text{ for all } i = 1 \dots n \right\}$$

is the standard simplex of R^n. In [13,14] a connection is established between dominant sets and the local solutions of (4). In particular, it is shown that if S is a dominant set then its "weighted characteristics vector," which is the vector of Δ defined as,

$$x_i = \begin{cases} \frac{w_S(i)}{W(s)}, & \text{if } i \in S, \\ 0, & \text{otherwise} \end{cases}$$

is a strict local solution of (4). Conversely, under mild conditions, it turns out that if $\mathbf{x}$ is a (strict) local solution of program (4) then its "support"

$$\sigma(\mathbf{x}) = \{i \in V \ : \ x_i > 0\}$$

is a dominant set. By virtue of this result, we can find a dominant set by first localizing a solution of program (4) with an appropriate continuous optimization technique, and then picking up the support set of the solution found. A generalization of these ideas to hypergraphs has recently been developed in [15].

A simple and effective optimization algorithm to extract a dominant set from a graph is given by the so-called *replicator dynamics*, developed and studied in evolutionary game theory, which are defined as follows:

$$x_i^{(t+1)} = x_i^{(t)} \frac{(A\mathbf{x}^{(t)})_i}{(\mathbf{x}^{(t)})' A(\mathbf{x}^{(t)})} \tag{5}$$

for $i = 1, \dots, n$.

3   Constrained Dominant Sets

Let $G = (V, E, w)$ be an edge-weighted graph with n vertices and let A denote as usual its (weighted) adjacency matrix. Given a subset of vertices $S \subseteq V$ and a parameter $\alpha > 0$, define the following parameterized family of quadratic programs:

$$\text{maximize } f_S^\alpha(\mathbf{x}) = \mathbf{x}'(A - \alpha \hat{I}_S)\mathbf{x}$$
$$\text{subject to } \mathbf{x} \in \Delta \tag{6}$$

where $\hat{I}_S$ is the $n \times n$ diagonal matrix whose diagonal elements are set to 1 in correspondence to the vertices contained in $V \backslash S$ and to zero otherwise, and the 0's represent null square matrices of appropriate dimensions. In other words, assuming for simplicity that S contains, say, the first k vertices of V, we have:

$$\hat{I}_S = \begin{pmatrix} 0 & 0 \\ 0 & I_{n-k} \end{pmatrix}$$

where I_{n-k} denotes the $(n-k) \times (n-k)$ principal submatrix of the $n \times n$ identity matrix I indexed by the elements of $V \backslash S$. Accordingly, the function f_S^α can also be written as follows:

$$f_S^\alpha(\mathbf{x}) = \mathbf{x}'A\mathbf{x} - \alpha \mathbf{x}_S'\mathbf{x}_S$$

$\mathbf{x}_S$ being the $(n - k)$-dimensional vector obtained from $\mathbf{x}$ by dropping all the components in S. Basically, the function f_S^α is obtained from f by inserting in the affinity matrix A the value of the parameter α in the main diagonal positions corresponding to the elements of $V \backslash S$.

Notice that this differs markedly, and indeed generalizes, the formulation proposed in [16] for obtaining a hierarchical clustering in that here, only a subset of elements in the main diagonal is allowed to take the α parameter, the other ones being set to zero. We note in fact that the original (non-regularized) dominant-set formulation (4) [14] as well as its regularized counterpart described in [16] can be considered as degenerate version of ours, corresponding to the cases $S = V$ and $S = \emptyset$, respectively. It is precisely this increased flexibility which allows us to use this idea for finding groups of "constrained" dominant-set clusters.

We now derive the Karush-Kuhn-Tucker (KKT) conditions for program (6), namely the first-order necessary conditions for local optimality (see, e.g., [17]). For a point $\mathbf{x} \in \Delta$ to be a KKT-point there should exist n nonnegative real constants $\mu_1, \ldots, \mu_n$ and an additional real number λ such that

$$[(A - \alpha \hat{I}_S)\mathbf{x}]_i - \lambda + \mu_i = 0$$

for all $i = 1 \ldots n$, and

$$\sum_{i=1}^n x_i \mu_i = 0.$$

Since both the x_i's and the μ_i's are nonnegative, the latter condition is equivalent to saying that $i \in \sigma(\mathbf{x})$ implies $\mu_i = 0$, from which we obtain:

$$[(A - \alpha \hat{I}_S)\mathbf{x}]_i \begin{cases} = \lambda, & \text{if } i \in \sigma(\mathbf{x}) \\ \leq \lambda, & \text{if } i \notin \sigma(\mathbf{x}) \end{cases}$$

for some constant λ. Noting that $\lambda = \mathbf{x}'A\mathbf{x} - \alpha\mathbf{x}'_S\mathbf{x}_S$ and recalling the definition of $\hat{I}_S$, the KKT conditions can be explicitly rewritten as:

$$\begin{cases} (A\mathbf{x})_i - \alpha x_i = \mathbf{x}'A\mathbf{x} - \alpha\mathbf{x}'_S\mathbf{x}_S, & \text{if } i \in \sigma(\mathbf{x}) \text{ and } i \notin S \\ (A\mathbf{x})_i = \mathbf{x}'A\mathbf{x} - \alpha\mathbf{x}'_S\mathbf{x}_S, & \text{if } i \in \sigma(\mathbf{x}) \text{ and } i \in S \\ (A\mathbf{x})_i \leq \mathbf{x}'A\mathbf{x} - \alpha\mathbf{x}'_S\mathbf{x}_S, & \text{if } i \notin \sigma(\mathbf{x}) \end{cases} \quad (7)$$

We are now in a position to discuss the main results which motivate the algorithm presented in this paper. Note that, in the sequel, given a subset of vertices $S \subseteq V$, the face of Δ corresponding to S is given by: $\Delta_S = \{x \in \Delta : \sigma(x) \subseteq S\}$.

Proposition 1. *Let $S \subseteq V$, with $S \neq \emptyset$. Define*

$$\gamma_S = \max_{\mathbf{x} \in \Delta_{V \setminus S}} \min_{i \in S} \frac{\mathbf{x}'A\mathbf{x} - (A\mathbf{x})_i}{\mathbf{x}'\mathbf{x}} \quad (8)$$

and let $\alpha > \gamma_S$. If $\mathbf{x}$ is a local maximizer of f_S^α in Δ, then $\sigma(\mathbf{x}) \cap S \neq \emptyset$.

Proof. Let $\mathbf{x}$ be a local maximizer of f_S^α in Δ, and suppose by contradiction that no element of $\sigma(\mathbf{x})$ belongs to S or, in other words, that $\mathbf{x} \in \Delta_{V \setminus S}$. By letting

$$i = \arg\min_{j \in S} \frac{\mathbf{x}'A\mathbf{x} - (A\mathbf{x})_j}{\mathbf{x}'\mathbf{x}}$$

and observing that $\sigma(\mathbf{x}) \subseteq V \setminus S$ implies $\mathbf{x}'\mathbf{x} = \mathbf{x}'_S\mathbf{x}_S$, we have:

$$\alpha > \gamma_S \geq \frac{\mathbf{x}'A\mathbf{x} - (A\mathbf{x})_i}{\mathbf{x}'\mathbf{x}} = \frac{\mathbf{x}'A\mathbf{x} - (A\mathbf{x})_i}{\mathbf{x}'_S\mathbf{x}_S}.$$

Hence, $(A\mathbf{x})_i > \mathbf{x}'A\mathbf{x} - \alpha\mathbf{x}'_S\mathbf{x}_S$ for $i \notin \sigma(\mathbf{x})$, but this violates the KKT conditions (7), thereby proving the proposition. $\square$

The following proposition provides an easy-to-compute upper bound for γ_S.

Proposition 2. *Let $S \subseteq V$, with $S \neq \emptyset$. Then,*

$$\gamma_S \leq \lambda_{\max}(A_{V \setminus S}) \quad (9)$$

where $\lambda_{\max}(A_{V \setminus S})$ is the largest eigenvalue of the principal submatrix of A indexed by the elements of $V \setminus S$.

Proof. Let $\mathbf{x}$ be a point in $\Delta_{V\setminus S}$ which attains the maximum γ_S as defined in (8). Using the Rayleigh-Ritz theorem [18] and the fact that $\sigma(\mathbf{x}) \subseteq V\setminus S$, we obtain:

$$\lambda_{\max}(A_{V\setminus S}) \geq \frac{\mathbf{x}'_S A_{V\setminus S}\mathbf{x}_S}{\mathbf{x}'_S \mathbf{x}_S} = \frac{\mathbf{x}'A\mathbf{x}}{\mathbf{x}'\mathbf{x}}.$$

Now, define $\gamma_S(\mathbf{x}) = \max\{(A\mathbf{x})_i \ : \ i \in S\}$. Since A is nonnegative so is $\gamma_S(\mathbf{x})$, and recalling the definition of γ_S we get:

$$\frac{\mathbf{x}'A\mathbf{x}}{\mathbf{x}'\mathbf{x}} \geq \frac{\mathbf{x}'A\mathbf{x} - \gamma_S(\mathbf{x})}{\mathbf{x}'\mathbf{x}} = \gamma_S$$

which concludes the proof.   □

The two previous propositions provide us with a simple technique to determine dominant-set clusters containing user-selected vertices. Indeed, if S is the set of vertices selected by the user, by setting

$$\alpha > \lambda_{\max}(A_{V\setminus S}) \tag{10}$$

we are guaranteed that all local solutions of (6) will have a support that necessarily contains elements of S. As customary, we can use replicator dynamics or more sophisticated algorithms to find them. Note that this does not necessarily imply that the (support of the) solution found corresponds to a dominant-set cluster of the original affinity matrix A, as adding the parameter $-\alpha$ on a portion of the main diagonal intrinsically changes the scale of the underlying problem. However, we have obtained extensive empirical evidence which supports a conjecture which turns out to be very useful for our interactive image segmentation application.

To illustrate the idea, let us consider the case where edge-weights are binary, which basically means that the input graph is unweighted. In this case, it is known that dominant sets correspond to maximal cliques [14]. Let $G = (V, E)$ be our unweighted graph and let S be a subset of its vertices. For the sake of simplicity, we distinguish three different situations of increasing generality.

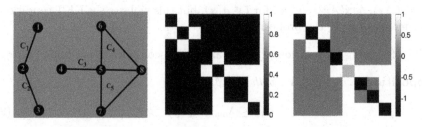

Fig. 2. An example graph (left), corresponding affinity matrix (middle), and scaled affinity matrix built considering vertex 5 as a user constraint (right). Notation C_i refers to the ith maximal clique.

Case 1. The set S is a singleton, say $S = \{u\}$. In this case, we know from Proposition 2 that all solutions $\mathbf{x}$ of f_α^S over Δ will have a support which contains u, that is $u \in \sigma(\mathbf{x})$. Indeed, we conjecture that there will be a unique local (and hence global) solution here whose support coincides with the *union* of all maximal cliques of G which contain vertex u.

Case 2. The set S is a clique, not necessarily maximal. In this case, Proposition 2 predicts that all solutions $\mathbf{x}$ of (6) will contain at least one vertex from S. Here, we claim that indeed the support of local solutions is the union of the maximal cliques that contain S.

Case 3. The set S is not a clique, but it can be decomposed as a collection of (possibly overlapping) maximal cliques $C_1, C_2, ..., C_k$ (maximal with respect to the subgraph induced by S). In this case, we claim that if $\mathbf{x}$ is a local solution, then its support can be obtained by taking the union of all maximal cliques of G containing one of the cliques C_i in S.

To make our discussion clearer, consider the graph shown in Fig. 2. In order to test whether our claims hold, we used as the set S different combinations of vertices, and enumerated all local solutions of (6) by multi-start replicator dynamics. Some results are shown below, where on the left-hand side we indicate the set S, while on the right hand-side we show the supports provided as output by the different runs of the algorithm.

$$
\begin{aligned}
&1.\ S = \{2\} &&\Rightarrow \sigma(\mathbf{x}) = \{1,2,3\}\\
&2.\ S = \{5\} &&\Rightarrow \sigma(\mathbf{x}) = \{4,5,6,7,8\}\\
&3.\ S = \{4,5\} &&\Rightarrow \sigma(\mathbf{x}) = \{4,5\}\\
&4.\ S = \{5,8\} &&\Rightarrow \sigma(\mathbf{x}) = \{5,6,7,8\}\\
&5.\ S = \{1,4\} &&\Rightarrow \sigma(\mathbf{x}_1) = \{1,2\}, \sigma(\mathbf{x}_2) = \{4,5\}\\
&6.\ S = \{2,5,8\} &&\Rightarrow \sigma(\mathbf{x}_1) = \{1,2,3\}, \sigma(\mathbf{x}_2) = \{5,6,7,8\}
\end{aligned}
$$

The previous observations can be summarized in the following general statement which does comprise all three cases. Let $S = C_1 \cup C_2 \cup ... \cup C_k$ $(k \geq 1)$ be a subset of vertices of G, consisting of a collection of cliques C_i $(i = 1 ... k)$. Suppose that condition (10) holds, and let $\mathbf{x}$ be a local solution of (6). Then, $\sigma(\mathbf{x})$ consists of the union of all maximal cliques containing some clique C_i of S.

We conjecture that the previous claim carries over to edge-weighted graphs, where the notion of a maximal clique is replaced by that of a dominant set. In the supplementary material we report the results of an extensive experimentation we have conducted on standard DIMACS graphs which provide support to our claim. This is going to play a key role in our applications of these ideas to interactive image segmentation.

4   Application to Interactive Image Segmentation

In this section we apply our model to the interactive image segmentation problem. As input modalities we consider scribbles as well as boundary-based approaches (in particular, bounding boxes) and, in both cases, we show how the system is robust under input perturbations, namely imperfect scribbles or loose bounding boxes.

In this application the vertices of the underlying graph G represent the pixels of the input image (or superpixels, as discussed below), and the edge-weights reflect the similarity between them. As for the set S, its content depends on whether we are using scribbles or bounding boxes as the user annotation modality. In particular, in the case of scribbles, S represents precisely those pixels that have been manually selected by the user. In the case of boundary-based annotation instead, it is taken to contain only the pixels comprising the box boundary, which are supposed to represent the background scene. Accordingly, the union of the extracted dominant sets, say $\mathcal{L}$ dominant sets are extracted which contain the set S, as described in the previous section and below, $\mathbf{UDS} = \mathcal{D}_1 \cup \mathcal{D}_2 ..... \cup \mathcal{D}_{\mathcal{L}}$, represents either the foreground object or the background scene depending on the input modality. For scribble-based approach the extracted set, $\mathbf{UDS}$, represent the segmentation result, while in the boundary-based approach we provide as output the complement of the extracted set, namely $\mathbf{V} \backslash \mathbf{UDS}$.

Figure 3 shows the pipeline of our system. Many segmentation tasks reduce their complexity by using superpixels (a.k.a. over-segments) as a preprocessing step [3,9,19–21]. While [3] used SLIC superpixels [9,22] used a recent superpixel algorithm [23] which considers not only the color/feature information but also boundary smoothness among the superpixels. In this work, we used the over-segments obtained from Ultrametric Contour Map (UCM) which is constructed from Oriented Watershed Transform (OWT) using globalized probability of boundary (gPb) signal as an input [24].

We then construct a graph G where the vertices represent over-segments and the similarity (edge-weight) between any two of them is obtained using a standard Gaussian kernel

$$A_{ij}^{\sigma} = \mathbb{K}_{i \neq j} exp(\|\mathbf{f}_i - \mathbf{f}_j\|^2 / 2\sigma^2)$$

where $\mathbf{f}_i$, is the feature vector of the ith over-segment, σ is the free scale parameter, and $\mathbb{K}_P = 1$ if P is true, 0 otherwise.

Given the affinity matrix A and the set S as described before, the system constructs the regularized matrix $M = A - \alpha \hat{I}_S$, with α chosen as prescribed in (10). Then, the replicator dynamics (5) are run (starting them as customary from the simplex barycenter) until they converge to some solution vector $\mathbf{x}$. We then take the support of $\mathbf{x}$, remove the corresponding vertices from the graph and restart the replicator dynamics until all the elements of S are extracted.

4.1 Experiments and Results

As mentioned above, the vertices of our graph represents over-segments and edge weights (similarities) are built from the median of the color of all pixels in RGB, HSV, and L*a*b* color spaces, and Leung-Malik (LM) Filter Bank [25]. The

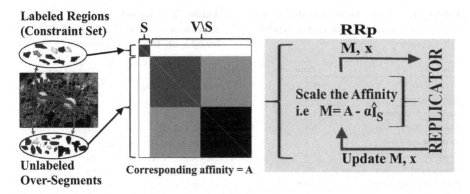

Fig. 3. Overview of our system. **Left:** Over-segmented image (output of the UCM-OWT algorithm [24]) with a user scribble (blue label). **Middle:** The corresponding affinity matrix, using each over-segments as a node, showing its two parts: S, the constraint set which contains the user labels, and $V \setminus S$, the part of the graph which takes the regularization parameter α. **Right:** RRp, starts from the barycenter and extracts the first dominant set and update $\mathbf{x}$ and $\mathbf{M}$, for the next extraction till all the dominant sets which contain the user labeled regions are extracted. (Color figure online)

number of dimensions of feature vectors for each over-segment is then 57 (three for each of the RGB, L*a*b*, and HSV color spaces, and 48 for LM Filter Bank).

In practice, the performance of graph-based algorithms that use Gaussian kernel, as we do, is sensitive to the selection of the scale parameter σ. In our experiments, we have reported three different results based on the way σ is chosen: (1) CDS_Best_Sigma, in this case the best parameter σ is selected on a per-image basis, which indeed can be thought of as the optimal result (or upper bound) of the framework. (2) CDS_Single_Sigma, the best parameter in this case is selected on a per-database basis tuning σ in some fixed range, which in our case is between 0.05 and 0.2. (3) CDS_Self_Tuning, the σ^2 in the above equation is replaced, based on [26], by $\sigma_i * \sigma_j$, where $\sigma_i = mean(KNN(f_i))$, the mean of the K_Nearest_Neighbor of the sample f_i, K is fixed in all the experiment as 7.

Datasets: We conduct four different experiments on the well-known GrabCut dataset [1] which has been used as a benchmark in many computer vision tasks [2,3,9,27–31]. The dataset contains 50 images together with manually-labeled segmentation ground truth. The same bounding boxes as those in [2] is used as a baseline bounding box. We also evaluated our scribbled-based approach using the well known Berkeley dataset which contains 100 images.

Metrics: We evaluate the approach using different metrics: error rate, fraction of misclassified pixels within the bounding box, Jaccard index which is given by, following [32], $J = \frac{|GT \cap O|}{|GT \cup O|}$, where GT is the ground truth and O is the output. The third metric is the Dice Similarity Coefficient (DSC), which measures the

Table 1. Error rates of different scribble-based approaches on the Grab-Cut dataset

Methods	Error rate
Graph Cut [7]	6.7
Lazy Snapping [5]	6.7
Geodesic Segmentation [4]	6.8
Random Walker [33]	5.4
Transduction [34]	5.4
Geodesic Graph Cut [30]	4.8
Constrained Random Walker [31]	4.1
CDS_Self Tuning (Ours)	**3.57**
CDS_Single Sigma (Ours)	**3.80**
CDS_Best Sigma (Ours)	2.72

Table 2. Jaccard index of different approaches – first 5 bounding-box-based – on Berkeley dataset

Methods	Jaccard index
MILCut-Struct [3]	84
MILCut-Graph [3]	83
MILCut [3]	78
Graph Cut [1]	77
Binary Partition Trees [35]	71
Interactive Graph Cut [7]	64
Seeded Region Growing [36]	59
Simple Interactive O.E [37]	63
CDS_Self Tuning (Ours)	**93**
CDS_Single Sigma (Ours)	**93**
CDS_Best Sigma (Ours)	95

overlap between two segmented object volume, and is computed as $DSC = \frac{2*|GT \cap O|}{|GT|+|O|}$.

Annotations: In interactive image segmentation, users provide annotations which guides the segmentation. A user usually provides information in different forms such as scribbles and bounding boxes. The input modality affects both its accuracy and ease-of-use [12]. However, existing methods fix themselves to one input modality and focus on how to use that input information effectively. This leads to a suboptimal tradeoff in user and machine effort. Jain et al. [12] estimates how much user input is required to sufficiently segment a given image. In this work, as we have proposed an interactive framework, Fig. 1, which can take any type of input modalities, we will use four different types of annotations: bounding box, loose bounding box, scribbles - only on the object of interest -, and scribbles with error as of [11].

4.1.1   Scribble Based Segmentation

Given labels on the foreground as constraint set, we built the graph and collect (iteratively) all unlabeled regions (nodes of the graph) by extracting dominant set(s) that contains the constraint set (user scribbles). We provided quantitative comparison against several recent state-of-the-art interactive image segmentation methods which uses scribbles as a form of human annotation: [7], Lazy Snapping [5], Geodesic Segmentation [4], Random Walker [33], Transduction [34], Geodesic Graph Cut [30], Constrained Random Walker [31]. Tables 1, 2 and the plots in Fig. 5 show the respective quantitative and the several qualitative segmentation results. Most of the results, reported on Table 1, are reported by previous works [2, 3, 9, 30, 31]. We can see that the proposed framework outperforms all the other approaches.

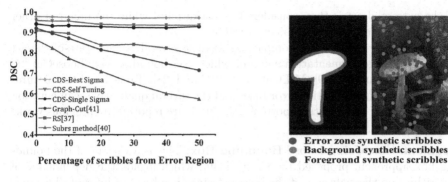

Fig. 4. **Left:** Performance of algorithms, on Grab-Cut dataset, for different percentage of synthetic scribbles from the error region. **Right:** Synthetic scribbles and error region

Error-Tolerant Scribble Based Segmentation: This is a family of scribble-based approach, proposed by Bai et al. [11], which tolerates imperfect input scribbles thereby avoiding the assumption of accurate scribbles. We have done experiments using synthetic scribbles and compared the algorithm against recently proposed methods specifically designed to segment and extract the object of interest tolerating the user input errors [11, 38–40].

Our framework is adapted to this problem as follows. We give, for the framework, the foreground scribbles as constraint set and check those scribbled regions which include background scribbled regions as their members in the extracted dominant set. Collecting all those dominant sets which are free from background scribbled regions generates the object of interest.

Experiment using synthetic scribbles. Here, a procedure similar to the one used in [11, 40] has been followed. First, 50 foreground pixels and 50 background pixels are randomly selected based on ground truth (see Fig. 4). They are then assigned as foreground or background scribbles, respectively. Then an error-zone for each image is defined as background pixels that are less than a distance D from the foreground, in which D is defined as 5 %. We randomly select 0 to 50 pixels in the error zone and assign them as foreground scribbles to simulate different degrees of user input errors. We randomly select 0, 5, 10, 20, 30, 40, 50 erroneous sample pixels from error zone to simulate the error percentage of 0 %, 10 %, 20 %, 40 %, 60 %, 80 %, 100 % in the user input. It can be observed from Fig. 4 that our approach is not affected by the increase in the percentage of scribbles from error region.

4.1.2   Segmentation Using Bounding Boxes
The goal here is to segment the object of interest out from the background based on a given bounding box. The corresponding over-segments which contain the box label are taken as constraint set which guides the segmentation. The union

of the extracted set is then considered as background while the union of other over-segments represent the object of interest.

We provide quantitative comparison against several recent state-of-the-art interactive image segmentation methods which uses bounding box: LooseCut [9], GrabCut [1], OneCut [29], MILCut [3], pPBC and [28]. Table 3 and the pictures in Fig. 5 show the respective error rates and the several qualitative segmentation results. Most of the results, reported on Table 3, are reported by previous works [2,3,9,30,31].

Segmentation Using Loose Bounding Box: This is a variant of the bounding box approach, proposed by Yu et al. [9], which avoids the dependency of algorithms on the tightness of the box enclosing the object of interest. The approach not only avoids the annotation burden but also allows the algorithm to use automatically detected bounding boxes which might not tightly encloses the foreground object. It has been shown, in [9], that the well-known GrabCut algorithm [1] fails when the looseness of the box is increased. Our framework, like [9], is able to extract the object of interest in both tight and loose boxes. Our algorithm is tested against a series of bounding boxes with increased looseness. The bounding boxes of [2] are used as boxes with 0 % looseness. A looseness L (in percentage) means an increase in the area of the box against the baseline one. The looseness is increased, unless it reaches the image perimeter where the box is cropped, by dilating the box by a number of pixels, based on the percentage of the looseness, along the 4 directions: left, right, up, and down.

For the sake of comparison, we conduct the same experiments as in [9]: 41 images out of the 50 GrabCut dataset [1] are selected as the rest 9 images contain multiple objects while the ground truth is only annotated on a single object. As other objects, which are not marked as an object of interest in the ground truth, may be covered when the looseness of the box increases, images of multiple objects are not applicable for testing the loosely bounded boxes [9]. Table 3 summarizes the results of different approaches using bounding box at different level of looseness. As can be observed from the table, our approach performs well compared to the others when the level of looseness gets increased. When the looseness $L = 0$, [3] outperforms all, but it is clear, from their definition of tight bounding box, that it is highly dependent on the tightness of the bounding box. It even shrinks the initially given bounding box by 5 % to ensure its tightness before the slices of the positive bag are collected. For looseness of $L = 120$ we have similar result with LooseCut [9] which is specifically designed for this purpose. For other values of L our algorithm outperforms all the approaches.

Complexity: In practice, over-segmenting and extracting features may be treated as a pre-processing step which can be done before the segmentation process. Given the affinity matrix, a simple and effective optimization algorithm to extract the object of interest is given by the replicator dynamics (5). Its computational complexity per step is $O(N^2)$, with N being the total number of nodes of the graph. Infection-immunization dynamics [41] is a faster alternative which has an $O(N)$ complexity for each step which allow convergence of the

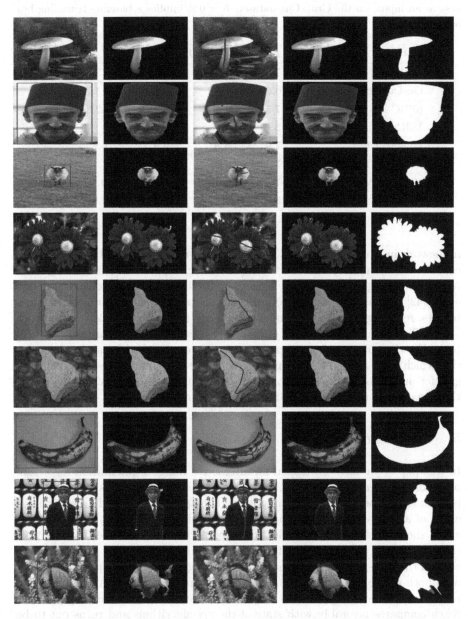

Fig. 5. Examplar results of the algorithm tested on Grab-Cut dataset. **Left:** Original image with bounding boxes of [2]. **Middle left:** Result of the bounding box approach. **Middle:** Original image and scribbles (observe that the scribles are only on the object of interest). **Middle right:** Results of the scribbled approach. **Right:** The ground truth

Table 3. Error rates of different boundin-box approaches with different level of looseness as an input, on the Grab-Cut dataset. $L = 0\%$ implies a baseline bounding box as those in [2]

Methods	$L = 0\%$	$L = 120\%$	$L = 240\%$	$L = 600\%$
GrabCut [1]	7.4	10.1	12.6	13.7
OneCut [29]	6.6	8.7	9.9	13.7
pPBC [28]	7.5	9.1	9.4	12.3
MilCut [3]	**3.6**	-	-	-
LooseCut [9]	7.9	**5.8**	6.9	6.8
CDS_Self Tuning (Ours)	7.54	6.78	**6.35**	7.17
CDS_Single Sigma (Ours)	7.48	5.9	**6.32**	**6.29**
CDS_Best Sigma (Ours)	6.0	4.4	4.2	4.9

framework in fraction of second, with a code written in Matlab and run on a core i5 6 GB of memory. As for the pre-processing step, the original *gPb-owt-ucm* segmentation algorithm was very slow to be used as a practical tools. Catanzaro et al. [42] proposed a faster alternative, which reduce the runtime from 4 min to 1.8 s, reducing the computational complexity and using parallelization which allow *gPb* contour detector and *gPb-owt-ucm* segmentation algorithm practical tools. For the purpose of our experiment we have used the Matlab implementation which takes around four minutes to converge, but in practice it is possible to give for our framework as an input, the GPU implementation [42] which allows the convergence of the whole framework in around 4 s.

5   Conclusions

In this paper, we have developed an interactive image segmentation algorithm based on the idea of finding a collection of dominant-set clusters constrained to contain the elements of a user annotation. The approach is based on some properties of a family of quadratic optimization problems related to dominant sets which show that, by properly selecting a regularization parameter that controls the structure of the underlying function, we are able to "force" all solutions to contain the user-provided elements. The resulting algorithm is capable of dealing with both scribble-based and boundary-based annotation modes. Segmentation results of extensive experiments on natural images demonstrate that the approach compares favorably with state-of-the-art algorithms and turns out to be robust in the presence of loose bounding boxes and large amount of user input errors. Future work will focus on applying the framework on video sequences and other computer vision problems such as content-based image retrieval.

Acknowledgments. This work has been partly supported by Samsung Global Research Outreach Program.

References

1. Rother, C., Kolmogorov, V., Blake, A.: "Grabcut": interactive foreground extraction using iterated graph cuts. ACM Trans. Graph. **23**(3), 309–314 (2004)
2. Lempitsky, V.S., Kohli, P., Rother, C., Sharp, T.: Image segmentation with a bounding box prior. In: ICCV, pp. 277–284 (2009)
3. Wu, J., Zhao, Y., Zhu, J., Luo, S., Tu, Z.: Milcut: a sweeping line multiple instance learning paradigm for interactive image segmentation. In: CVPR, pp. 256–263 (2014)
4. Bai, X., Sapiro, G.: Geodesic matting: a framework for fast interactive image and video segmentation and matting. Int. J. Comput. Vis. **82**(2), 113–132 (2009)
5. Li, Y., Sun, J., Tang, C., Shum, H.: Lazy snapping. ACM Trans. Graph. **23**(3), 303–308 (2004)
6. Protiere, A., Sapiro, G.: Interactive image segmentation via adaptive weighted distances. IEEE Trans. Image Process. **16**(4), 1046–1057 (2007)
7. Boykov, Y., Jolly, M.: Interactive graph cuts for optimal boundary and region segmentation of objects in N-D images. In: ICCV, pp. 105–112 (2001)
8. Mortensen, E.N., Barrett, W.A.: Interactive segmentation with intelligent scissors. Graph. Models Image Process. **60**(5), 349–384 (1998)
9. Yu, H., Zhou, Y., Qian, H., Xian, M., Lin, Y., Guo, D., Zheng, K., Abdelfatah, K., Wang, S.: Loosecut: interactive image segmentation with loosely bounded boxes. CoRR abs/1507.03060 (2015)
10. Xian, M., Zhang, Y., Cheng, H.D., Xu, F., Ding, J.: Neutro-connectedness cut. CoRR abs/1512.06285
11. Bai, J., Wu, X.: Error-tolerant scribbles based interactive image segmentation. In: CVPR, pp. 392–399 (2014)
12. Jain, S.D., Grauman, K.: Predicting sufficient annotation strength for interactive foreground segmentation. In: ICCV, pp. 1313–1320 (2013)
13. Pavan, M., Pelillo, M.: A new graph-theoretic approach to clustering and segmentation. In: CVPR, pp. 145–152 (2003)
14. Pavan, M., Pelillo, M.: Dominant sets and pairwise clustering. IEEE Trans. Pattern Anal. Mach. Intell. **29**(1), 167–172 (2007)
15. Rota Bulò, S., Pelillo, M.: A game-theoretic approach to hypergraph clustering. IEEE Trans. Pattern Anal. Mach. Intell. **35**(6), 1312–1327 (2013)
16. Pavan, M., Pelillo, M.: Dominant sets and hierarchical clustering. In: ICCV, pp. 362–369 (2003)
17. Luenberger, D.G., Ye, Y.: Linear and Nonlinear Programming. Springer, New York (2008)
18. Horn, R.A., Johnson, C.R.: Matrix Analysis. Cambridge University Press, New York (1985)
19. Hoiem, D., Efros, A.A., Hebert, M.: Geometric context from a single image. In: ICCV, pp. 654–661 (2005)
20. Wang, J., Jia, Y., Hua, X., Zhang, C., Quan, L.: Normalized tree partitioning for image segmentation. In: CVPR (2008)
21. Xiao, J., Quan, L.: Multiple view semantic segmentation for street view images. In: ICCV, pp. 686–693 (2009)
22. Achanta, R., Shaji, A., Smith, K., Lucchi, A., Fua, P., Süsstrunk, S.: SLIC superpixels compared to state-of-the-art superpixel methods. IEEE Trans. Pattern Anal. Mach. Intell. **34**(11), 2274–2282 (2012)

23. Zhou, Y., Ju, L., Wang, S.: Multiscale superpixels and supervoxels based on hierarchical edge-weighted centroidal voronoi tessellation. In: WACV, pp. 1076–1083 (2015)
24. Arbelaez, P., Maire, M., Fowlkes, C.C., Malik, J.: Contour detection and hierarchical image segmentation. IEEE Trans. Pattern Anal. Mach. Intell. **33**, 898–916 (2011)
25. Leung, T.K., Malik, J.: Representing and recognizing the visual appearance of materials using three-dimensional textons. Int. J. Comput. Vis. **43**(1), 29–44 (2001)
26. Zelnik-Manor, L., Perona, P.: Self-tuning spectral clustering. In: NIPS, pp. 1601–1608 (2004)
27. Li, H., Meng, F., Ngan, K.N.: Co-salient object detection from multiple images. IEEE Trans. Multimedia **15**(8), 1896–1909 (2013)
28. Tang, M., Ben Ayed, I., Boykov, Y.: Pseudo-bound optimization for binary energies. In: Fleet, D., Pajdla, T., Schiele, B., Tuytelaars, T. (eds.) ECCV 2014, Part V. LNCS, vol. 8693, pp. 691–707. Springer, Heidelberg (2014)
29. Tang, M., Gorelick, L., Veksler, O., Boykov, Y.: Grabcut in one cut. In: ICCV, pp. 1769–1776 (2013)
30. Price, B.L., Morse, B.S., Cohen, S.: Geodesic graph cut for interactive image segmentation. In: CVPR, pp. 3161–3168 (2010)
31. Yang, W., Cai, J., Zheng, J., Luo, J.: User-friendly interactive image segmentation through unified combinatorial user inputs. IEEE Trans. Image Process. **19**(9), 2470–2479 (2010)
32. McGuinness, K., O'Connor, N.E.: A comparative evaluation of interactive segmentation algorithms. Pattern Recogn. **43**(2), 434–444 (2010)
33. Grady, L.: Random walks for image segmentation. IEEE Trans. Pattern Anal. Mach. Intell. **28**(11), 1768–1783 (2006)
34. Duchenne, O., Audibert, J., Keriven, R., Ponce, J., Ségonne, F.: Segmentation by transduction. In: CVPR (2008)
35. Salembier, P., Garrido, L.: Binary partition tree as an efficient representation for image processing, segmentation, and information retrieval. IEEE Trans. Image Process. **9**(4), 561–576 (2000)
36. Adams, R., Bischof, L.: Seeded region growing. IEEE Trans. Pattern Anal. Mach. Intell. **16**(6), 641–647 (1994)
37. Friedland, G., Jantz, K., Rojas, R.: SIOX: simple interactive object extraction in still images. In: ISM, pp. 253–260 (2005)
38. Liu, J., Sun, J., Shum, H.: Paint selection. ACM Trans. Graph. **28**(3), 303–308 (2009)
39. Sener, O., Ugur, K., Alatan, A.A.: Error-tolerant interactive image segmentation using dynamic and iterated graph-cuts. In: IMMPD@ACM Multimedia, pp. 9–16 (2012)
40. Subr, K., Paris, S., Soler, C., Kautz, J.: Accurate binary image selection from inaccurate user input. Comput. Graph. Forum **32**(2), 41–50 (2013)
41. Rota Bulò, S., Bomze, L.M.: Infection and immunization: a new class of evolutionary game dynamics. Games Econ. Behav. **71**(1), 193–211 (2011)
42. Catanzaro, B.C., Su, B., Sundaram, N., Lee, Y., Murphy, M., Keutzer, K.: Efficient, high-quality image contour detection. In: ICCV, pp. 2381–2388 (2009)

Deep Markov Random Field for Image Modeling

Zhirong Wu$^{(\boxtimes)}$, Dahua Lin, and Xiaoou Tang

The Chinese University of Hong Kong, Sha Tin, Hong Kong
{zhirong,dhlin,xtang}@ie.cuhk.edu.hk

Abstract. Markov Random Fields (MRFs), a formulation widely used in generative image modeling, have long been plagued by the lack of expressive power. This issue is primarily due to the fact that conventional MRFs formulations tend to use *simplistic* factors to capture local patterns. In this paper, we move beyond such limitations, and propose a novel MRF model that uses fully-connected neurons to express the complex interactions among pixels. Through theoretical analysis, we reveal an inherent connection between this model and recurrent neural networks, and thereon derive an approximated feed-forward network that couples multiple RNNs along opposite directions. This formulation combines the expressive power of deep neural networks and the cyclic dependency structure of MRF in a unified model, bringing the modeling capability to a new level. The feed-forward approximation also allows it to be efficiently learned from data. Experimental results on a variety of low-level vision tasks show notable improvement over state-of-the-arts.

Keywords: Generative image model · MRF · RNN

1 Introduction

Generative image models play a crucial role in a variety of image processing and computer vision tasks, such as denoising [1], super-resolution [2], inpainting [3], and image-based rendering [4]. As repeatedly shown by previous work [5], the success of image modeling, to a large extent, hinges on whether the model can successfully capture the spatial relations among pixels.

Existing image models can be roughly categorized as *global models* and *low-level models*. Global models [6–8] usually rely on compressed representations to capture the global structures. Such models are typically used for describing objects with regular structures, *e.g.* faces. For generic images, low-level models are more popular. Thanks to their focus on local patterns instead of global appearance, low-level models tend to generalize much better, especially when there can be vast variations in the image content.

Over the past decades, *Markov Random Fields (MRFs)* have evolved into one of the most popular models for low-level vision. Specifically, the clique-based

Electronic supplementary material The online version of this chapter (doi:10. 1007/978-3-319-46484-8_18) contains supplementary material, which is available to authorized users.

© Springer International Publishing AG 2016
B. Leibe et al. (Eds.): ECCV 2016, Part VIII, LNCS 9912, pp. 295–312, 2016.
DOI: 10.1007/978-3-319-46484-8_18

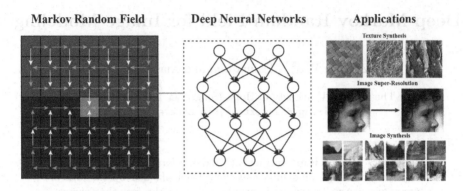

Fig. 1. We present a new class of markov random field models whose potential functions are expressed by powerful deep neural networks. We show applications of the model on texture synthesis, image super-resolution and image synthesis.

structure makes them particularly well suited for capturing local relations among pixels. Whereas MRFs as a generic mathematical framework are very flexible and provide immense expressive power, the performance of many MRF-based methods still leaves a lot to be desired when faced with challenging conditions. This occurs due to the widespread use of *simplistic* potential functions that largely restrict the expressive power of MRFs (Fig. 1).

In recent years, the rise of *Deep Neural Networks (DNN)* has profoundly reshaped the landscape of many areas in computer vision. The success of DNNs is primarily attributed to its unparalleled expressive power, particularly their strong capability of modeling complex variations. However, DNNs in computer vision are mostly formulated as end-to-end convolutional networks (CNN) for classification or regression. The modeling of local interactions among pixels, which is crucial for many low-level vision tasks, has not been sufficiently explored.

The respective strengths of MRFs and DNNs inspire us to explore a new approach to low-level image modeling, that is, to bring the expressive power of DNNs to an MRF formulation. Specifically, we propose a generative image model comprised of a grid of *hidden states*, each corresponding to a pixel. These latent states are connected to their neighbors – together they form an MRF. Unlike in classical MRF formulations, we use fully connected layers to express the relationship among these variables, thus substantially improving the model's ability to capture complex patterns.

Through theoretical analysis, we reveal an inherent connection between our MRF formulation and the RNN [9], which opens an alternative way to MRF formulation. However, they still differ fundamentally: the dependency structure of an RNN is *acyclic*, while that of an MRF is *cyclic*. Consequently, the hidden states cannot be inferred in a single *feed-forward* manner as in a RNN. This posts a significant challenge – how can one derive the back-propagation procedure without a well-defined forward function?

Our strategy to tackle this difficulty is to *unroll an iterative inference procedure into a feed-forward function*. This is motivated by the observation that while the inference is iterative, each cycle of updates is still a feed-forward procedure. Following a carefully devised scheduling policy, which we call the *Coupled Acyclic Passes (CAP)*, the inference can be unrolled into multiple RNNs operating along opposite directions that are coupled together. In this way, local information can be effectively propagated over the entire network, where each hidden state can have a complete picture of its context from all directions.

The primary contribution of this work is a new generative model that unifies MRFs and DNNs in a novel way, as well as a new learning strategy that makes it possible to learn such a model using mainstream deep learning frameworks. It is worth noting that the proposed method is generic and can be adapted to a various problems. In this work, we test it on a variety of low-level vision tasks, including texture synthesis, image super-resolution, and image synthesis.

2   Related Works

In this paper, we develop a generative image model that incorporates the expressive power of deep neural networks with an MRF. This work is related to several streams of research efforts, but moves beyond their respective limitations.

Generative image models. Generative image models generally fall into two categories: parametric models and non-parametric models. *Parametric models* typically use a compressed representation to capture an image's global appearance. In recent years, deep networks such as autoencoders [10] and adversarial networks [11,12] have achieved substantial improvement in generating images with regular structures such as faces or digits. *Non-parametric models*, including *pixel-based sampling* [13–15] and *patch-based sampling* [16–18], instead rely on a large set of exemplars to capture local patterns. Whereas these methods can produce high quality images with local patterns directly sampled from realistic images. Exhaustive search over a large exemplar set limits their scalability and often leads to computational difficulties. Our work draws inspiration from both lines of work. By using DNNs to express local interactions in an MRF, our model can capture highly complex patterns while maintaining strong scalability.

Markov random fields. For decades, MRFs have been widely used for low-level vision tasks, including texture synthesis [19], segmentation [20,21], denoising [1], and super-resolution [2]. Classical MRF models in earlier work [22] use simple hand-crafted potentials (*e.g.*, Ising models [23], Gaussian MRFs [24]) to link neighboring pixels. Later, more flexible models such as FRAME [25] and Fields of Experts [26] were proposed, which allow the potential functions to be learned from data. However, in these methods, the potential functions are usually parameterized as a set of linear filters, and therefore their expressive power remains very limited.

Recurrent neural networks. *Recurrent neural networks (RNNs)*, a special family of deep models, use a chain of nonlinear units to capture sequential relations. In computer vision, RNNs are primarily used to model sequential changes

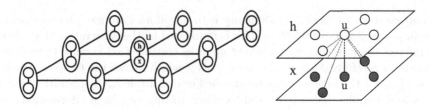

Fig. 2. Graphical model of deep MRFs. **Left**: The hidden states and the pixels together form an MRF. **Right**: Each hidden state connects to the neighboring states, the neighboring pixels, and the pixel at the same location.

in videos [27], visual attention [28,29], and hand-written digit recognition [30]. Previous work explores multi-dimensional RNNs [31] for scene labeling [32] as well as object detections [33]. The most related work is perhaps the use of 2D RNNs for generating gray-scale textures [34] or color images [35]. A key distinction of these models from ours is that 2D RNNs rely on an *acyclic graphs* to model spatial dependency, *e.g.* each pixel depends only on its left and upper neighbors – this severely limits the spatial coherence. Our model, instead, allows dependencies from all directions via iterative inference unrolling.

MRF and neural networks. Connections between both models have been discussed long ago [36]. With the rise of deep learning, recent work on image segmentation [37,38] uses mean field method to approximate a conditional random field (CRF) with CNN layers. A hybrid model of CNN and MRF has also been proposed for human pose estimation [39]. These works primarily target prediction problems (*e.g.* segmentation) and are not as effective at capturing complex pixel patterns in a purely generative way.

3   Deep Markov Random Field

The primary goal of this work is to develop a generative model for images that can express complex local relationships among pixels while being tractable for inference and learning. Formally, we consider an image, denoted by $\mathbf{x}$, as an *undirected graph* with a grid structure, as shown in Fig. 2 left. Each node u corresponds to a pixel x_u. To capture the interactions among pixels, we introduce, h_u, a hidden variable for each pixel denoting the hidden state corresponding to the pixel x_u. In the graph, each node u has a neighborhood, denoted by $\mathcal{N}_u$. Particularly, we use the *4-connected neighborhood* of a 2D grid in this work.

Joint Distribution. We consider three kinds of dependencies: (1) the dependency between a pixel x_u and its corresponding hidden state h_u, (2) the dependency between a hidden state h_u and a neighbor h_v with $v \in \mathcal{N}_u$, and (3) the dependency between a hidden state h_u and a neighboring pixel x_v. They are respectively captured by factors $\zeta(x_u, h_u)$, $\phi(h_u, h_v)$, and $\psi(h_u, x_v)$. In addition, we introduce a regularization factor $\lambda(h_u)$ for each hidden state, which gives us the leeway to encourage certain distribution over the state values. Bringing these factors together, we formulate an MRF to express the joint distribution:

$$p(\mathbf{x}, \mathbf{h}) = \frac{1}{Z} \prod_{u \in V} \zeta(x_u, h_u) \prod_{(u,v) \in E} (\phi(h_u, h_v)\psi(h_u, x_v)\psi(h_v, x_u)) \prod_{u \in V} \lambda(h_u). \quad (1)$$

Here, V and E are respectively the set of vertices and that of the edges in the image graph, Z is a normalizing constant. Figure 2 shows it structure.

Choices of Factors. Whereas the MRF provides a principled way to express the dependency structure, the expressive power of the model still largely depends on the specific forms of the factors that we choose. For example, the modeling capacity of classical MRF models are limited by their simplistic factors.

Below, we discuss the factors that we choose for the proposed model. First, the factor $\zeta(x_u, h_u)$ determines how the pixel values are generated from the hidden states. Considering the stochastic nature of natural images, we formalize this generative process as a *Gaussian mixture model (GMM)*. The rationale behind is that pixel values are on a low-dimensional space, where a GMM with a small number of components can usually provide a good approximation to an empirical distribution. Specifically, we fix the number of components to be K, and consider the concatenation of component parameters as the linear transform of the hidden state, $h_u^T \mathbf{Q} = ((\pi_u^c, \mu_u^c, \Sigma_u^c))_{c=1}^K$, where $\mathbf{Q}$ is a weight matrix of model parameters. In this way, the factor $\zeta(x_u, h_u)$ can be written as

$$\zeta(x_u, h_u) \triangleq p_{\text{GMM}}(x_u | h_u) = \sum_{c=1}^{K} \pi_u^c N(x_u | \mu_u^c, \Sigma_u^c). \quad (2)$$

To capture the rich interactions among pixels and their neighbors, we formulate the relational factors $\phi(h_u, h_v)$ and $\psi(h_u, x_v)$ with *fully connected* forms:

$$\phi(h_u, h_v) = \exp\left(h_u^T \mathbf{W} h_v\right), \quad \psi(h_u, x_v) = \exp\left(h_u^T \mathbf{R} x_v\right). \quad (3)$$

Finally, to control the value distribution of the hidden states, we further incorporate a regularization term over h_u, as

$$\lambda(h_u) = \exp\left(-\mathbf{1}^T \eta(h_u)\right) = \exp\left(-\eta(h_u^{(1)}) - \cdots - \eta(h_u^{(d)})\right). \quad (4)$$

Here, η is an element-wise nonlinear function and d is the dimension of h_u. In summary, the use of GMM in $\zeta(x_u, h_u)$ effectively accounts for the variations in pixel generation, the fully-connected factors $\phi(h_u, h_v)$ and $\psi(h_u, x_v)$ enable the modeling of complex interactions among neighbors, while the regularization term $\lambda(h_u)$ provides a way to explicitly control the distribution of hidden states. Together, they substantially increase the capacity of the MRF model.

Inference of Hidden States. With this MRF formulation, the posterior distribution of the hidden state h_u, conditioned on all other variables, is given by

$$p\left(h_u \mid x_u, x_{\mathcal{N}_u}, h_{\mathcal{N}_u}\right) \propto \zeta(x_u, h_u)\lambda(h_u) \cdot \prod_{v \in \mathcal{N}_u} \phi(h_u, h_v)\psi(h_u, x_v). \quad (5)$$

Here, h_u depends on its neighboring states, the corresponding pixel values, as well as that of its neighbors. Since the pixel x_u and its neighboring pixels $x_{\mathcal{N}_u}$ are highly correlated, to simplify our later computations, we approximate the posterior distribution as,

$$p\left(h_u \mid x_u, x_{\mathcal{N}_u}, h_{\mathcal{N}_u}\right) \simeq p\left(h_u \mid x_{\mathcal{N}_u}, h_{\mathcal{N}_u}\right) \propto \lambda(h) \prod_{v \in \mathcal{N}_u} \phi(h, h_v) \psi(h, x_v). \quad (6)$$

We performed numerical simulations for this approximation. They are indeed very close to each other, as illustrated in Fig. 3. Consequently, the MAP estimate of h_u can be *approximately* computed from its neighbors. It turns out that this optimization problem has an analytic solution given by,

$$\tilde{h}_u = \sigma\left(\sum_{v \in \mathcal{N}_u} \mathbf{W}h_v + \mathbf{R}x_v\right). \quad (7)$$

Here, σ is an element-wise function that is related to η as $\sigma^{-1}(z) = \eta'(z)$, where η' is the first-order derivative *w.r.t.* η, and σ^{-1} the inverse function of σ.

Connections to RNNs. We observe that Eq. (7) has a form that is similar to the feed-forward computations in *Recurrent Neural Networks (RNN)* [9]. In this sense, we can view the feed-forward RNN as an MAP inference process for MRF models. Particularly, given the RNN computations in the form of Eq. (7), one can formulate an MRF as in Eq. (1), where regularization function η can be derived from σ according to the relation $\sigma^{-1}(z) = \eta'(z)$, as

$$\eta(h) = \int_b^h \sigma^{-1}(z) dz + C. \quad (8)$$

Here, b is the minimum of the domain of h, which can be $-\infty$, and C is an arbitrary constant. This connection provides an alternative way to formulate an MRF model. More importantly, in this way, RNN models that have been proven to be successful can be readily transferred to an MRF formulation. Figure 3 shows the regularization functions $\eta(h)$ corresponding to popular activation functions in RNNs, such as *sigmoid* and *ReLU* [40].

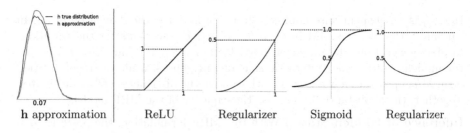

| h approximation | ReLU | Regularizer | Sigmoid | Regularizer |

Fig. 3. Left shows the numerical simulation of approximated inference for the hidden variables. **Right** shows the ReLU, sigmoid activation function and their corresponding regularizations for the hidden variables.

4   Learning via Coupled Recurrent Networks

Except for special cases [41], inference and learning on MRFs is generally intractable. Conventional estimation methods [8,42,43] either take overly long time to train or tend to yield poor estimates, especially for models with a high-dimensional parameter space. In this work, we consider an alternative approach to MRF learning, which allows us to draw on deep learning techniques [44,45] that have been proven to be highly effective [40].

Variational Learning Principle. Estimation of probabilistic models based on the *maximum likelihood* principle is often intractable when the model contains hidden variables. *Expectation-maximization* [46] is one of the most widely used ways to tackle this problem, which iteratively calculates the posterior distribution of $\mathbf{h}_i$ (in E-steps) and then optimizes $\boldsymbol{\theta}$ (in M-steps) as

$$\hat{\boldsymbol{\theta}} = \underset{\boldsymbol{\theta}}{\operatorname{argmax}} \ \frac{1}{n} \sum_{i=1}^{n} \mathrm{E}_{p(\mathbf{h}_i|\mathbf{x}_i,\boldsymbol{\theta})} \left\{ \log p(\mathbf{x}_i, \mathbf{h}_i|\boldsymbol{\theta}) \right\}. \tag{9}$$

Here, $\boldsymbol{\theta} = \{\mathbf{W}, \mathbf{Q}, \mathbf{R}\}$ is the model parameter, $\mathbf{x}_i$ is the i-th image, and $\mathbf{h}_i$ is the corresponding hidden state. As exact computation of this posterior expectation is intractable, we approximate it based on $\tilde{\mathbf{h}}_i$, the MAP estimate of $\mathbf{h}_i$, as below:

$$\hat{\boldsymbol{\theta}} = \underset{\boldsymbol{\theta}}{\operatorname{argmax}} \ \frac{1}{n} \sum_{i=1}^{n} \log p(\mathbf{x}_i|\tilde{\mathbf{h}}_i, \boldsymbol{\theta}), \ \text{with} \ \tilde{\mathbf{h}}_i \triangleq f(\mathbf{x}_i, \boldsymbol{\theta}). \tag{10}$$

This is the *learning objective* of our model. Here, f is the function that *approximately* infers the latent state $\tilde{\mathbf{h}}_i$ given an observed image $\mathbf{x}_i$. When the posterior distribution $p(\mathbf{h}_i|\mathbf{x}_i, \boldsymbol{\theta})$ is highly concentrated, which is often the case in vision tasks, this is a good approximation. For an image $\mathbf{x}$, $\log p(\mathbf{x}|\tilde{\mathbf{h}}, \boldsymbol{\theta})$ can be further expanded as a sum of terms defined on individual pixels:

$$\log p(\mathbf{x}|\tilde{\mathbf{h}}, \boldsymbol{\theta}) = \sum_{u} \log p_{\mathrm{GMM}}(x_u|\tilde{\mathbf{h}}) = \sum_{u} \log \sum_{c=1}^{K} \pi_u^c N(x_u|\tilde{\mu}_u^c, \Sigma_u^c), \tag{11}$$

where $\tilde{\mu}_u^c = \mu_u^c + \Sigma_u^c(\sum_v \mathbf{h}_v^T)\mathbf{R}$. For our problem, this learning principle can be interpreted in terms of encoding/decoding – the hidden states $\tilde{\mathbf{h}} = f(\mathbf{x}, \boldsymbol{\theta})$ can be understood as an representation that encodes the observed patterns in an image $\mathbf{x}_i$, while $\log p(\mathbf{x}|\tilde{\mathbf{h}}, \boldsymbol{\theta})$ measures how well $\tilde{\mathbf{h}}$ explains the observations.

Coupled Acyclic Passes. In the proposed model, the dependencies among neighbors are *cyclic*. Hence, the MAP estimate $\tilde{\mathbf{h}} = f(\mathbf{x}, \boldsymbol{\theta})$ cannot be computed in a single forward pass. Instead, Eq. (7) needs to be applied across the graph in multiple iterations. Our strategy is to unroll this iterative inference procedure into multiple feed-forward passes along opposite directions, such that these passes together provide a complete context to each local estimate.

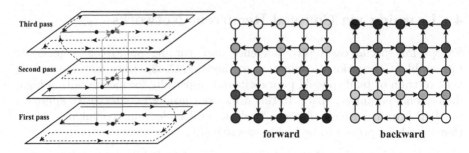

Fig. 4. Coupled acyclic passes. We decouple an undirected cyclic graph into two directed acyclic graphs with each one allowing feed-forward computation. Inference is performed by alternately traversing the two acyclic graphs, while coupling their information at each step.

Specifically, we decompose the underlying dependency graph $G = (V, E)$, which is undirected, into two *acyclic directed graphs* $G^f = (V, E^f)$ and $G^b = (V, E^b)$, as illustrated in Fig. 4, such that each undirected edge $\{u, v\} \in E$ corresponds uniquely to an edge $(u, v) \in E^f$ and an opposite edge $(v, u) \in E^b$. It can be proved that such a decomposition always exists and that for each node $u \in V$, the neighborhood $\mathcal{N}_u$ can be expressed as $\mathcal{N}_u = \mathcal{N}^f(u) \cup \mathcal{N}^b(u)$, where $\mathcal{N}^f(u)$ and $\mathcal{N}^b(u)$ are the set of parents of u respectively along G^f and G^b.

Given such a decomposition, we can derive an iterative computational procedure, where each cycle couples a *forward pass* that applies Eq. (7) along G^f and a *backward pass*[1] along G^b. After the t-th cycle, the state h_u is updated to

$$h_u^{(t)} = \sigma\left(\sum_{v \in \mathcal{N}^f(u)} \left(\mathbf{W}h_v^{(t-1)} + \mathbf{R}x_v \right) + \sum_{v \in \mathcal{N}^b(u)} \left(\mathbf{W}h_v^{(t)} + \mathbf{R}x_v \right) \right). \quad (12)$$

As states above, we have $\mathcal{N}_u = \mathcal{N}^f(u) \cup \mathcal{N}^b(u)$. Therefore, over a cycle, the updated state h_u would incorporate information from all its neighbors. Note that a given graph G can be decomposed in many different ways. In this work, we specifically choose the one that forms the *zigzag* path. The advantage over a simple raster line order is that *zigzag* path traverses all the nodes continuously, so that it conserves spatial coherence by making dependence of each node to all the previous nodes that have been visited before. The forward and backward passes resulted from such decomposition are shown in Fig. 4.

This algorithm has two important properties: First, the acyclic decomposition allows feed-forward computation as in Eq. (7) to be applied. As a result, the entire inference procedure can be viewed as a feed-forward network that couples multiple RNNs operating along different directions. Therefore, it can be learned in a way similar to other deep neural networks, using *Stochastic Gradient Descent (SGD)*. Second, the feedback mechanism embodied by the backward pass

---

[1] The word *forward* and *backward* here means the sequential order in the graph. They are not *feed-forward* and *back-propagation* in the context of deep neural networks.

facilitates the propagation of local information and thus the learning of long-range dependencies.

Discussions with 2D-RNN. Previous work has explored two-dimensional extensions of RNN [31], often referred to as *2D-RNN*. Such extensions, however, are formulated upon an acyclic graph, and can be considered as a trimmed down version of our algorithm. A major drawback of 2D-RNN is that it scans the image in a raster line order and it is not able to provide a feedback path. Therefore, the inference of each hidden state can only take into account 1/4 of the context, and there is no way to recover from a poor inference. As we will show in our experiments, this may cause undesirable effects. Whereas bidirectional RNNs [47] may partly mitigate this problem, they decouple the hidden states into multiple ones that are independent apriori, which would lead to consistency issues. Recent work [48] also finds it difficult to use in generative modeling.

Implementation Details. For inference and learning, to make the computation feasible, we just take one forward pass and one backward pass. Thus, each node is only updated twice while being able to use the information from all possible contexts. The training patch size varies from 15 to 25 depending on the specific experiment. Overall, if we unroll the full inference procedure, our model[2] is more than thousands of layers deep. We use *rmsprop* [45] for optimization and we don't use dropout for regularization, as we find it oscillates the training.

5 Experiments

In the following experiments, we test the proposed deep MRF on 3 scenarios for modeling natural images. We first study its basic properties on *texture synthesis*, and then we apply it on a prediction problem, *image super-resolution*. Finally, we integrate global CNN models with local deep MRF for *natural image synthesis*.

5.1 Texture Synthesis

The task of texture synthesis is to synthesize new texture images that possess similar patterns and statistical characteristics as a given texture sample. The study of this problem originated from graphics [13,14]. The key to successful texture reproduction, as we learned from previous work, is to effectively capture the local patterns and variations. Therefore, this task is a perfect testbed to assess a model's capability of modeling visual patterns.

Our model works in a purely generative way. Given a sample texture, we train the model on randomly extracted patches of size 25×25, which are larger than most *texels* in natural images. We set $K = 20$, initialize $\mathbf{x}$ and $\mathbf{h}$ to zeros, and train the model with back-propagation along the coupled acyclic graph. With a trained model, we can generate textures by running the RNN to derive the latent states and at the same time sampling the output pixels. As our model is stationary, it can generate texture images of arbitrary sizes.

---

[2] Code available at https://github.com/zhirongw/deep-mrf.

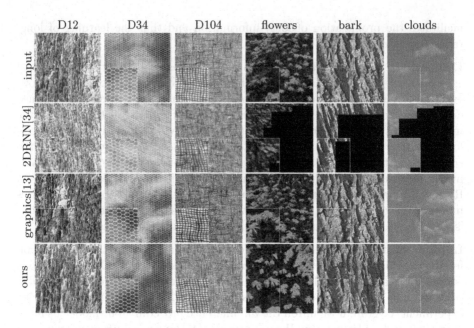

Fig. 5. Texture synthesis results.

We work on two texture datasets, Brodatz [49] for grayscale images, and VisTex [50] for color images. From the results shown in Fig. 5, our synthesis visually resembles to high resolution natural images, and the quality is close to the non-parametric approach [13]. We also compare with the 2D-RNN [34]. As we can see, the results obtained using 2D-RNN, which synthesizes based only on the left and upper regions, exhibit undesirable effects and often evolve into blacks in the bottom-right parts.

Two fundamental parameters control the behaviors of our texture model. The training patch size decides the farthest spatial relationships that could be learned from data. The number of gaussian mixtures control the dynamics of the texture landscape. We analyze our model by changing the two parameters. As shown in Fig. 6, bigger training patch size and bigger number of mixtures consistently improves the results. For non-parametric approaches, bigger patch size would dramatically bring up the computation cost. While for our model, the inference time holds the same regardless of the patch size that the model is trained on. Moreover, our parametric model is able to scale to large dataset without bringing additional computations.

5.2   Image Super-Resolution

Image super-resolution is a task to produce a high resolution image given a single low resolution one. Whereas previous MRF-based models [2,55] work reasonably,

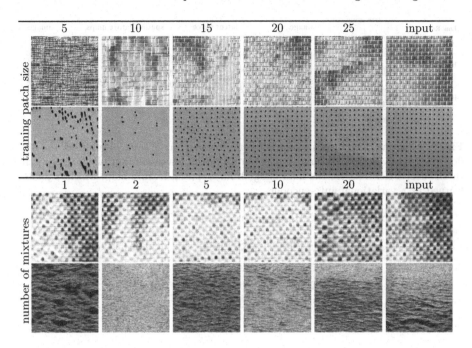

Fig. 6. Texture synthesis by varying the patch size and the number of mixtures.

the quality of their products is inferior to the state-of-the-art models based on deep learning [52,54]. With deep MRF, we wish to close the gap.

Unlike in texture synthesis, the generation of this task is driven by a low-resolution image. To incorporate this information, we introduce additional connections between the hidden states and corresponding pixels of the low-resolution image, as shown in Fig. 7. It is noteworthy that we just input *a single pixel* (instead of a *patch*) at each site, and in this way, we can test whether the model can propagate information across the spatial domain. As the task is deterministic, we use a GMM with a single component and fix its variance. In the testing stage, we output the mean of the Gaussian component at each location as the

Table 1. PSNR (dB) on Set5 dataset with upscale factor 2,3,4

Images	2× upscale				3× upscale				4× upscale			
	Bicubic	CNN	SE	Ours	Bicubic	CNN	SE	Ours	Bicubic	CNN	SE	Ours
Baby	37.07	38.30	**38.48**	38.31	33.91	35.01	**35.22**	35.15	31.78	32.98	**33.14**	32.94
Bird	36.81	40.40	**40.50**	40.36	32.58	34.91	35.58	**36.14**	30.18	31.98	**32.54**	32.49
Butterfly	27.43	32.20	31.86	**32.74**	24.04	27.58	26.86	**29.09**	22.10	25.07	24.09	**25.78**
Head	34.86	35.64	35.69	**35.70**	32.88	33.55	**33.76**	33.63	31.59	32.19	**32.52**	32.41
Women	32.14	34.94	**35.33**	34.84	28.56	30.92	31.36	**31.69**	26.46	28.21	28.92	**28.97**
Average	33.66	36.34	36.37	**36.38**	31.92	32.30	32.56	**33.14**	28.42	30.09	30.24	**30.52**

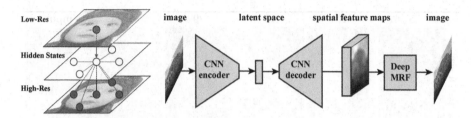

Fig. 7. Adapting deep MRFs to specific applications. Image super-resolution: the hidden state receives an additional connection from the low-resolution pixel. Image synthesis: deep MRF renders the final image from a spatial feature map, which is jointly learned by a variational auto-encoder.

Table 2. PSNR (dB) on various dataset with upscale factor 3

Dataset	Bicubic	A+ [51]	CNN [52]	SE [53]	CSCN [54]	Ours
Set5	30.39	32.59	32.30	32.56	33.10	**33.14**
Set14	27.54	29.13	29.00	29.16	**29.41**	29.38
BSD100	27.22	28.18	28.20	28.20	28.50	**28.54**

inferred high-resolution pixel. This approach is very generic – the model is not specifically tuned for the task and no pre- and post-processing steps are needed.

We train our model on a widely used super-resolution dataset [56] which contains 91 images, and test it on Set5, Set14, and BSD100 [57]. The training is on patches of size 16×16 and *rmsprop* with momentum 0.95 is used. We use PSNR for quantitative evaluation. Following previous work, we only consider the luminance channel in the *YCrCb* color space. The two chrominance channels are upsampled with bicubic interpolation.

As shown in Tables 1 and 2, our approach outperforms the CNN-based baseline [52] and compares favorably with the state-of-the-art methods dedicated to this task [53,54]. One possible explanation for the success is that our model not only learns the mapping, but also learns the image statistics for high resolution images. The training procedure which unrolls the RNN into thousands of steps that share parameters also reduces the risk of overfitting. The results also demonstrate the particular strength of our model in handling large upscaling factors and difficult images. Figure 8 shows several examples visually.

5.3   Natural Image Synthesis

Images can be roughly considered as a composition of textures with the guidance of scene and object structures. In this task, we move beyond the synthesis of homogeneous textures, and try to generate natural images with structural guidance.

While our model excels in capturing spatial dependencies, learning weak dependencies across the entire image is both computationally infeasible and

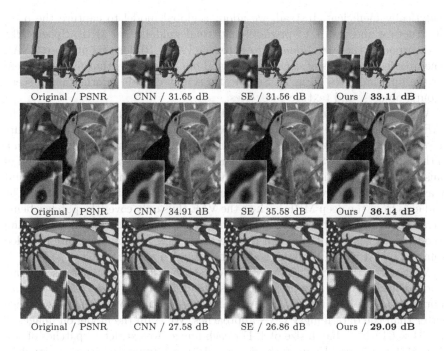

Fig. 8. Image super resolution results from Set 5 with upscaling factor 3.

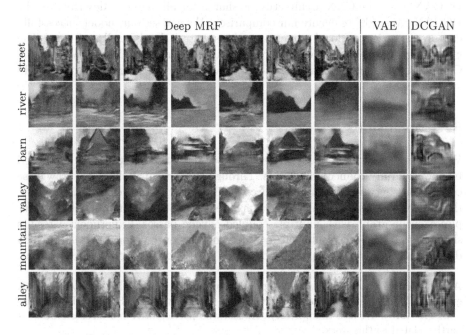

Fig. 9. Image synthesis results.

analytically inefficient. Instead, we adopt a global model to capture the overall structure and use it to provide contextual guidance to MRF. Specifically, we incorporate the *variational auto-encoder (VAE)* [10] for this purpose – VAE generates feature maps at each location and our model uses that feature to render the final image (see Fig. 7). Such features may contain information of scene layouts, objects, and texture categories.

We train the joint model end-to-end from scratch. During each iteration, the VAE first encodes the image into a latent vector, then decodes it to a feature map with the same size of the input image. We then connect this feature map to the latent states of the deep MRF. The total loss is defined as the addition of gaussian mixtures at image space and KL divergence at high-level VAE latent space. For training, we randomly extracts patches from the feature map. The gradients from the deep MRF back to the VAE thus only cover the patches being extracted. During testing, VAE randomly samples from the latent space and decodes it to generate the global feature maps. The output pixels are sampled from the GMM with 10 mixtures along the coupled acyclic graph.

We work on the MSRC [58] and SUN database [59] and select some scene categories with rich natural textures, such as *Mountains* and *Valleys*. Each category contains about a hundred images. As we will see, our approach generalizes much better than the data-hungry CNN approaches. We train the model on images of size 64×64 with a batch size of 4. For each image, we extract 16 patches of size 15×15 for training. Figure 9 shows several images generated from our models, in comparison with those obtained from the baselines, namely raw VAE [10] and DCGAN [60]. The CNN architecture is shared for all methods described in the DCGAN paper [60] to ensure fair comparison. We can see our model successfully captures a variety of local patterns, such as water, clouds, wall and trees. The global appearance also looks coherent, real and dynamic. The state-of-the-art CNN based models, which focuses too much on global structures, often yield sub-optimal local effects.

6   Conclusions

We present a new class of MRF model whose potential functions are expressed by powerful fully-connected neurons. Through theoretical analysis, we draw close connections between probabilistic deep MRFs and end-to-end RNNs. To tackle the difficulty of inference in cyclic graphs, we derive a new framework that decouples a cyclic graph with multiple coupled acyclic passes. Experimental results show state-of-the-art results on a variety of low-level vision problems, which demonstrate the strong capability of MRFs with expressive potential functions.

Acknowledgments. This work is supported by the Big Data Collaboration Research grant (CUHK Agreement No. TS1610626) and the Early Career Scheme (ECS) grant (No: 24204215). We also thank Aditya Khosla who participated in a discussion that is partly related to this work.

References

1. Portilla, J., Strela, V., Wainwright, M.J., Simoncelli, E.P.: Image denoising using scale mixtures of Gaussians in the wavelet domain. IEEE Trans. Image Process. **12**(11), 1338–1351 (2003)
2. Freeman, W.T., Pasztor, E.C., Carmichael, O.T.: Learning low-level vision. Int. J. Comput. Vis. **40**(1), 25–47 (2000)
3. Bertalmio, M., Sapiro, G., Caselles, V., Ballester, C.: Image inpainting. In: Proceedings of the 27th Annual Conference on Computer Graphics and Interactive Techniques. ACM Press/Addison-Wesley Publishing Co., pp. 417–424 (2000)
4. McMillan, L., Bishop, G.: Plenoptic modeling: an image-based rendering system. In: Proceedings of the 22nd Annual Conference on Computer Graphics and Interactive Techniques, pp. 39–46. ACM (1995)
5. Huang, J., Mumford, D.: Statistics of natural images and models. In: IEEE Computer Society Conference on Computer Vision and Pattern Recognition, vol. 1. IEEE (1999)
6. Turk, M.A., Pentland, A.P.: Face recognition using eigenfaces. In: Proceedings of IEEE Computer Society Conference on Computer Vision and Pattern Recognition, CVPR 1991, pp. 586–591. IEEE (1991)
7. Wright, J., Ma, Y., Mairal, J., Sapiro, G., Huang, T.S., Yan, S.: Sparse representation for computer vision and pattern recognition. Proc. IEEE **98**(6), 1031–1044 (2010)
8. Hinton, G.E.: Training products of experts by minimizing contrastive divergence. Neural Comput. **14**(8), 1771–1800 (2002)
9. Werbos, P.J.: Backpropagation through time: what it does and how to do it. Proc. IEEE **78**(10), 1550–1560 (1990)
10. Kingma, D.P., Welling, M.: Auto-encoding variational bayes. arXiv preprint arXiv:1312.6114 (2013)
11. Goodfellow, I., Pouget-Abadie, J., Mirza, M., Xu, B., Warde-Farley, D., Ozair, S., Courville, A., Bengio, Y.: Generative adversarial nets. In: Advances in Neural Information Processing Systems, pp. 2672–2680 (2014)
12. Denton, E.L., Chintala, S., Fergus, R., et al.: Deep generative image models using a laplacian pyramid of adversarial networks. In: Advances in Neural Information Processing Systems, pp. 1486–1494 (2015)
13. Efros, A., Leung, T.K., et al.: Texture synthesis by non-parametric sampling. In: The Proceedings of the Seventh IEEE International Conference on Computer Vision, vol. 2, pp. 1033–1038. IEEE (1999)
14. Wei, L.Y., Levoy, M.: Fast texture synthesis using tree-structured vector quantization. In: Proceedings of the 27th Annual Conference on Computer Graphics and Interactive Techniques. ACM Press/Addison-Wesley Publishing Co., pp. 479–488 (2000)
15. Hertzmann, A., Jacobs, C.E., Oliver, N., Curless, B., Salesin, D.H.: Image analogies. In: Proceedings of the 28th Annual Conference on Computer Graphics and Interactive Techniques, pp. 327–340. ACM (2001)
16. Efros, A.A., Freeman, W.T.: Image quilting for texture synthesis and transfer. In: Proceedings of the 28th Annual Conference on Computer Graphics and Interactive Techniques, pp. 341–346. ACM (2001)
17. Hays, J., Efros, A.A.: Scene completion using millions of photographs. ACM Trans. Graph. (TOG) **26**(3) (2007). Article no. 4

18. Lalonde, J.F., Hoiem, D., Efros, A.A., Rother, C., Winn, J., Criminisi, A.: Photo clip art. ACM Trans. Graph. (TOG) **26**(3) (2007). Article no. 3
19. Cross, G.R., Jain, A.K.: Markov random field texture models. IEEE Trans. Pattern Anal. Mach. Intell. **5**(1), 25–39 (1983)
20. Boykov, Y.Y., Jolly, M.P.: Interactive graph cuts for optimal boundary & region segmentation of objects in nd images. In: Proceedings of Eighth IEEE International Conference on Computer Vision, ICCV 2001, vol. 1, pp. 105–112. IEEE (2001)
21. He, X., Zemel, R.S., Carreira-Perpiñán, M.: Multiscale conditional random fields for image labeling. In: Proceedings of the 2004 IEEE Computer Society Conference on Computer Vision and Pattern Recognition, CVPR 2004, vol. 2, p. II-695. IEEE (2004)
22. Geman, S., Geman, D.: Stochastic relaxation, Gibbs distributions, and the Bayesian restoration of images. IEEE Trans. Pattern Anal. Mach. Intell. **6**(6), 721–741 (1984)
23. Ising, E.: Beitrag zur theorie des ferromagnetismus. Zeitschrift für Physik A Hadrons and Nuclei **31**(1), 253–258 (1925)
24. Rue, H., Held, L.: Gaussian Markov Random Fields: Theory and Applications. CRC Press, London (2005)
25. Zhu, S.C., Wu, Y., Mumford, D.: Filters, random fields and maximum entropy (frame): towards a unified theory for texture modeling. Int. J. Comput. Vis. **27**(2), 107–126 (1998)
26. Roth, S., Black, M.J.: Fields of experts: a framework for learning image priors. In: IEEE Computer Society Conference on Computer Vision and Pattern Recognition, CVPR 2005, vol. 2, pp. 860–867. IEEE (2005)
27. Donahue, J., Anne Hendricks, L., Guadarrama, S., Rohrbach, M., Venugopalan, S., Saenko, K., Darrell, T.: Long-term recurrent convolutional networks for visual recognition and description. In: Proceedings of the IEEE Conference on Computer Vision and Pattern Recognition, pp. 2625–2634 (2015)
28. Mnih, V., Heess, N., Graves, A., et al.: Recurrent models of visual attention. In: Advances in Neural Information Processing Systems, pp. 2204–2212 (2014)
29. Gregor, K., Danihelka, I., Graves, A., Wierstra, D.: Draw: a recurrent neural network for image generation. arXiv preprint arXiv:1502.04623 (2015)
30. Graves, A., Schmidhuber, J.: Offline handwriting recognition with multidimensional recurrent neural networks. In: Advances in Neural Information Processing Systems, pp. 545–552 (2009)
31. Graves, A., Fernandez, S., Schmidhuber, J.: Multi-dimensional recurrent neural networks. arXiv preprint arXiv:0705.2011 (2007)
32. Byeon, W., Breuel, T.M., Raue, F., Liwicki, M.: Scene labeling with LSTM recurrent neural networks. In: Proceedings of the IEEE Conference on Computer Vision and Pattern Recognition, pp. 3547–3555 (2015)
33. Bell, S., Zitnick, C.L., Bala, K., Girshick, R.: Inside-outside net: detecting objects in context with skip pooling and recurrent neural networks. arXiv preprint arXiv:1512.04143 (2015)
34. Theis, L., Bethge, M.: Generative image modeling using spatial LSTMs. In: Advances in Neural Information Processing Systems, pp. 1918–1926 (2015)
35. Oord van den, A., Kalchbrenner, N., Kavukcuoglu, K.: Pixel recurrent neural networks. arXiv preprint arXiv:1601.06759 (2016)
36. Rangarajan, A., Chellappa, R., Manjunath, B.: Markov random fields and neural networks with applications to early vision problems. Citeseer (1991)

37. Zheng, S., Jayasumana, S., Romera-Paredes, B., Vineet, V., Su, Z., Du, D., Huang, C., Torr, P.H.: Conditional random fields as recurrent neural networks. In: Proceedings of the IEEE International Conference on Computer Vision, pp. 1529–1537 (2015)
38. Chen, L.C., Papandreou, G., Kokkinos, I., Murphy, K., Yuille, A.L.: Semantic image segmentation with deep convolutional nets and fully connected CRFs. arXiv preprint arXiv:1412.7062 (2014)
39. Tompson, J.J., Jain, A., LeCun, Y., Bregler, C.: Joint training of a convolutional network and a graphical model for human pose estimation. In: Advances in Neural Information Processing Systems, pp. 1799–1807 (2014)
40. Krizhevsky, A., Sutskever, I., Hinton, G.E.: Imagenet classification with deep convolutional neural networks. In: Advances in Neural Information Processing Systems, pp. 1097–1105 (2012)
41. Pearl, J.: Probabilistic Reasoning in Intelligent Systems: Networks of Plausible Inference. Morgan Kaufmann, San Mateo (2014)
42. Li, S.Z.: Markov Random Field Modeling in Image Analysis. Springer Science & Business Media, London (2009)
43. Salakhutdinov, R.R.: Learning in Markov random fields using tempered transitions. In: Advances in Neural Information Processing Systems, pp. 1598–1606 (2009)
44. Duchi, J., Hazan, E., Singer, Y.: Adaptive subgradient methods for online learning and stochastic optimization. J. Mach. Learn. Res. **12**, 2121–2159 (2011)
45. Graves, A.: Generating sequences with recurrent neural networks. arXiv preprint arXiv:1308.0850 (2013)
46. Dempster, A., Laird, N., Rubin, D.: Maximum likelihood from incomplete data via the EM algorithm. J. Roy. Stat. Soc. **39**(1), 1–38 (1977)
47. Schuster, M., Paliwal, K.K.: Bidirectional recurrent neural networks. IEEE Trans. Signal Process. **45**(11), 2673–2681 (1997)
48. Berglund, M., Raiko, T., Honkala, M., Kärkkäinen, L., Vetek, A., Karhunen, J.: Bidirectional recurrent neural networks as generative models-reconstructing gaps in time series. arXiv preprint arXiv:1504.01575 (2015)
49. Brodatz, P.: Textures: a photographic album for artists and designers, 1966. Images downloaded in July (2009)
50. MIT Media Lab: Vision Texture Database (2002). http://vismod.media.mit.edu
51. Timofte, R., De Smet, V., Van Gool, L.: A+: adjusted anchored neighborhood regression for fast super-resolution. In: Cremers, D., Reid, I., Saito, H., Yang, M.-H. (eds.) ACCV 2014. LNCS, vol. 9006, pp. 111–126. Springer, Heidelberg (2015)
52. Dong, C., Loy, C.C., He, K., Tang, X.: Learning a deep convolutional network for image super-resolution. In: Fleet, D., Pajdla, T., Schiele, B., Tuytelaars, T. (eds.) ECCV 2014, Part IV. LNCS, vol. 8692, pp. 184–199. Springer, Heidelberg (2014)
53. Huang, J.B., Singh, A., Ahuja, N.: Single image super-resolution from transformed self-exemplars. In: 2015 IEEE Conference on Computer Vision and Pattern Recognition (CVPR), pp. 5197–5206. IEEE (2015)
54. Wang, Z., Liu, D., Yang, J., Han, W., Huang, T.: Deep networks for image super-resolution with sparse prior. In: Proceedings of the IEEE International Conference on Computer Vision, pp. 370–378 (2015)
55. Freeman, W., Liu, C.: Markov random fields for super-resolution and texture synthesis. In: Advances in Markov Random Fields for Vision and Image Processing, vol. 1 (2011)
56. Bevilacqua, M., Roumy, A., Guillemot, C., Alberi-Morel, M.L.: Low-complexity single-image super-resolution based on nonnegative neighbor embedding, BMVA press (2012)

57. Martin, D., Fowlkes, C., Tal, D., Malik, J.: A database of human segmented natural images and its application to evaluating segmentation algorithms and measuring ecological statistics. In: Proceedings of 8th International Conference on Computer Vision, vol. 2, pp. 416–423, July 2001
58. Shotton, J., Winn, J., Rother, C., Criminisi, A.: Textonboost for image understanding: multi-class object recognition and segmentation by jointly modeling texture, layout, and context. Int. J. Comput. Vis. **81**(1), 2–23 (2009)
59. Xiao, J., Hays, J., Ehinger, K.A., Oliva, A., Torralba, A.: Sun database: large-scale scene recognition from abbey to zoo. In: 2010 IEEE Conference on Computer Vision and Pattern Recognition (CVPR), pp. 3485–3492. IEEE (2010)
60. Radford, A., Metz, L., Chintala, S.: Unsupervised representation learning with deep convolutional generative adversarial networks. arXiv preprint arXiv:1511.06434 (2015)

A Symmetry Prior for Convex Variational 3D Reconstruction

Pablo Speciale[1]([⊠]), Martin R. Oswald[1], Andrea Cohen[1], and Marc Pollefeys[1,2]

[1] ETH Zürich, Zurich, Switzerland
pablo.speciale@inf.ethz.ch
[2] Microsoft, Redmond, USA

Abstract. We propose a novel prior for variational 3D reconstruction that favors symmetric solutions when dealing with noisy or incomplete data. We detect symmetries from incomplete data while explicitly handling unexplored areas to allow for plausible scene completions. The set of detected symmetries is then enforced on their respective support domain within a variational reconstruction framework. This formulation also handles multiple symmetries sharing the same support. The proposed approach is able to denoise and complete surface geometry and even hallucinate large scene parts. We demonstrate in several experiments the benefit of harnessing symmetries when regularizing a surface.

Keywords: Symmetry prior · 3D reconstruction · Variational methods · Convex optimization

1 Introduction

One of the long-time goals of computer vision algorithms is to imitate the numerous powerful abilities of the human visual system to achieve better scene understanding. Many methods have actually been inspired by the physiology of the visual cortex of mammalian brains. One of the strongest cues that humans use in order to infer the underlying geometry of a scene despite having access to only a partial view is symmetry, as shown in [20]. Moreover, symmetry is a very strong and useful concept because it applies to many natural and man-made environments. Following this inspiration, we propose a method which leverages symmetry information directly within a 3D reconstruction procedure in order to complete or denoise symmetric surface regions which have been partially occluded or where the input information has low quality. In contrast to the majority of 3D reconstruction methods which fit minimal surfaces in order to fill unobserved surface parts, our method favors solutions which align with symmetries and adhere to required smoothness properties at the same time. Similarly to how humans extrapolate occluded areas and 3D information from just a few view points, our method can hallucinate entire scene parts in unobserved areas, fill small holes, or denoise observed surface geometry once a symmetry has been detected. An example of our approach is shown in Fig. 1.

Equal contribution from P. Speciale and M.R. Oswald.

© Springer International Publishing AG 2016
B. Leibe et al. (Eds.): ECCV 2016, Part VIII, LNCS 9912, pp. 313–328, 2016.
DOI: 10.1007/978-3-319-46484-8_19

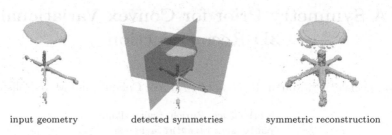

input geometry   detected symmetries   symmetric reconstruction

Fig. 1. Example application of our approach. A model of a stool was scanned by a depth camera and the result is incomplete due to occlusions. With only two detected symmetries we can complete the 5-way symmetry of the model.

1.1 Contributions

We propose to use symmetry information as a prior in 3D reconstruction in order to favor symmetric solutions when dealing with noisy and incomplete data. For this purpose, we extend standard symmetry detection algorithms to be able to exploit partially unexplored domains. Our framework naturally unifies the applications of symmetry-based surface denoising, completion and the hallucination of unexplored surface areas. To the best of our knowledge, we present the first method that handles multiple symmetries with a shared support region, since the proposed algorithm computes an approximation to a non-trivial projection to equally satisfy a set of symmetries. Finally, our method extends the toolbox of priors for many existing variational 3D reconstruction methods and we show that a symmetry prior can achieve quality improvements with a moderate runtime overhead.

1.2 Related Work

The works by Liu *et al.* [13] and Mitra *et al.* [16] give a broad overview of symmetry detection methods, although most of the work they discuss focuses on symmetry extraction for computer graphics applications. Therefore, their applicability is mostly shown on perfect synthetic data. In this section, we focus on works that detect and exploit symmetries from real data for vision applications.

Köser *et al.* [11] detect planar reflective symmetries in a single 2D image. They demonstrate that the arising stereo problem can be solved with standard stereo matching when the distance of the camera to the symmetry plane corresponds to a reasonable baseline.

Kazhdan *et al.* [7] define a reflective symmetry descriptor for 3D models by continuously measuring symmetry scores for all planes through the models' center of mass. We briefly repeat some of their theoretic results as we are going to use them in Sect. 2. Let $\gamma \in \Gamma$ be a symmetric transformation and u be a symmetric object, then u is symmetric with respect to γ if it is invariant under the symmetric transformation, that is, $\gamma(u) = u$. Using the group properties of the symmetry transform, Kazhdan *et al.* define the following symmetry distance

$$\mathrm{SD}(u, \gamma) = \min_{v:\gamma(v)=v} \|u - v\| = \|u - \varPi_\gamma(u)\| = \left\| \frac{u - \gamma(u)}{2} \right\|, \tag{1}$$

in which $\varPi_\gamma(u) = \frac{1}{2}(u + \gamma(u))$ is the orthogonal projection of object u onto the set of objects which are symmetric with respect to the symmetry γ.

Based on these results, Podolak et al. [23] focused on planar reflective symmetries and generalized the descriptor to detect also non-object-centered symmetries. They further define geometric properties which can be used for model alignment or classification. Both [4,22] detect symmetries in meshes and propose a symmetric remeshing of objects for quality improvements of the mesh and for more consistent mesh approximations during simplification operations. Similarly, Mitra et al. [15] use approximate symmetry information of objects to allow their transformation into perfectly symmetric objects.

Cohen et al. [2] detect symmetries in sparse point clouds by using appearance-based 3D-3D point matching in a RANSAC-based procedure. They then exploit these symmetries to remove drift from point-clouds. Although their work is done on sparse point clouds, we present a similar approach for voxel grids in Sect. 2.

Symmetries have also been used for many applications, e.g. shape matching and feature point matching [6], object part segmentation, and canonical coordinate frame selection [23]. Our goal is to apply these concepts into the domain of dense 3D reconstruction. Nevertheless, our work is not the first one leveraging symmetry information in this domain. One of the earliest attempts to incorporate symmetry priors into surface reconstruction methods was by Terzopoulos et al. [25] who use a deformable spine model to create a generalized cylinder shape from a single image.

Application-wise, the work by Thrun and Wegbreit [26] is closely related to ours. They detect an entire hierarchy of different symmetry types in point cloud data and subsequently demonstrate the completion of unexplored surface parts. As opposed to our approach, they do not simultaneously denoise the input data and they do not compute a water-tight surface.

In contrast, we propose to integrate knowledge about symmetries directly into the surface reconstruction process in order to better reason about noisy or incomplete input data which can come from image-based matching algorithms or 3D depth sensors. Furthermore, our approach can handle any number of symmetries and their support domains can arbitrarily overlap. To the best of our knowledge no other method deals with several symmetries that share the same domain in a way that the "symmetrized" result obeys the group structure of several symmetries at once.

We build our symmetry prior into the variational volumetric 3D reconstruction framework which has been used in various settings, e.g. depth map fusion [29], 3D reconstruction [9,27], multi-label semantic reconstruction [5], and spatio-temporal reconstruction [17], with anisotropic regularization [5,10,18] or connectivity constraints [19]. The proposed method extends these lines of works by a symmetry prior which can be easily combined with any of these works.

Moreover, since the 3D reconstruction is formulated as a 3D segmentation problem, the proposed prior is also directly applicable to a large set of segmentation methods like [24, 28].

2   Symmetry Detection

In order to exploit symmetry priors for reconstruction, we first need to detect the symmetries that best fit the data. In this paper, we focus on detecting planar symmetries. As input we use integrated depth information, which is represented by a truncated signed distance function (TSDF) on a volume $V \subset \mathbb{R}$ [3]. The TSDF assigns a positive value for voxels corresponding to free space and a negative value for occupied voxels (which are placed behind the observed depth values). A zero value in this function denotes an unobserved (or occluded) voxel. A surface is then implicitly defined as the transition between positive and negative values. Since we are only interested in voxels lying on the surface of the object, we only look at the voxels for which the gradient is very strong.

Furthermore, since planar surfaces are symmetric with respect to all planes perpendicular to them, which is not very informative for the global scene or even for a small object, we decide to look only at those voxels that exhibit a certain degree of curvature. Thus, the goal is to find the symmetry planes that best reflect these high-gradient and high-curvature voxels into positions that also have a large gradient and curvature or that are otherwise unknown or occluded. Note that [8] detect partial symmetries in volumetric data via sparse matching of extracted line features, which is a more sophisticated way of using the gradient on the data. While trying to find the symmetries of a scene, we define the symmetry support $V_\gamma \subseteq V \subset \mathbb{R}^3$ as a hole-free, connected subset of the reconstruction domain V that fits the detected symmetry, that is, we try to include all occupied and free space which complies with the symmetry γ. Unobserved regions will be included an treated in a way such that they perfectly fulfill the symmetry to allow for hole filling and hallucination.

2.1   RANSAC

We apply a RANSAC-based approach by taking as input the list of high-gradient and high-curvature voxels, which we will refer to as surface voxels, and the list of unknown voxels. First, we randomly sample two surface voxels, which define a unique symmetry plane that reflect one of these voxels into the other. Next, we look through all of the surface voxels and reflect them over this plane to look for inliers to this particular symmetry. If the reflection of a surface voxel falls into the position of another surface voxel, then they are both considered as inliers to this symmetry plane. However, if it falls into an unknown voxel position, then we also consider it as an inlier since this could be a potential occluded part of a symmetric object. We randomly sample planes from two surface voxels as many times as stated by the RANSAC termination formula.

The plane with the most inliers is chosen as the best global symmetry plane γ for this surface, and its inliers define the support V_γ. Since we are interested in potentially finding many symmetries for the same scene, RANSAC could be applied sequentially by removing the inliers for the best symmetry and then subsequently re-detecting the next best symmetry among the remaining surface voxels. However, since there could be many symmetries with the same support, we modify RANSAC and keep track of the set of best N solutions (where N has to be determined a-priori). This way, we extract the N symmetries that best fit the entire surface. We will refer to this set of symmetries as Γ.

Local Symmetry Detection. A scene can be composed of several objects with different sizes and symmetries. However, due to the size variability, applying RANSAC on the whole volume as described before would miss most of the symmetries for small objects and also cluster different objects with similar symmetry planes into one approximate, noisy, symmetry plane. Therefore, we apply the described RANSAC approach for sliding boxes of different sizes over the entire volume. This allows the segmentation of objects as the support for the different symmetries found. The symmetry planes with the bigger inlier ratios and their support are chosen as candidates for local object symmetries. For multiple detections of the same object (parts) at different scales we gave preference to larger support domains and rejected detections whose support is a subset of another.

2.2 Hough Transform

Alternatively to RANSAC, we also implement a method based on [23], which resembles the Hough transform approach, in order to have additional insights in the space of planar symmetries belonging to an object. As cost for the hough space voting, we use the Planar-Reflective Symmetry Transform (PRST), which is defined according to [23] as follows

$$\text{PRST}(u, \gamma) = 1 - \frac{\text{SD}^2(u, \gamma)}{\|u\|^2} = \frac{1 + u \cdot \gamma(u)}{2}. \tag{2}$$

We parametrize planes in 3D by the spherical coordinates of their normals $\theta \in [0, \pi]$, $\phi \in [0, \pi]$ and the distance to the origin $d \in [d_{min}, d_{max}]$. After finding the peaks in the Hough Space using a non-maximal suppression scheme, we can obtain planar symmetries with high PRST values, as illustrated in Fig. 2.

If we consider the special case when u values are binaries, representing an occupancy grid, the Eq. (2) becomes the number of inliers of the γ symmetric plane, a metric also used in the RANSAC method described previously. Therefore, the methods are essentially very similar and the decision between one or the other depends only on technical considerations. For example, the runtime of Hough Transform is fixed, which is the number of iterations used in the plane sampling; on the other hand, the number of iterations ran by RANSAC depends on the current inlier threshold and, therefore, could possibly finish sooner. Another advantage of RANSAC is its low memory footprint

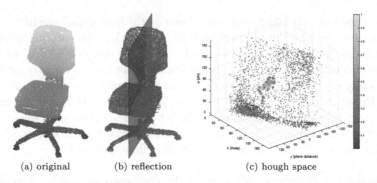

(a) original   (b) reflection   (c) hough space

Fig. 2. Hough transform example: (a) Shows a 3D scan of a real chair. (b) Illustrates the planar symmetry reflection (red) of the high-gradient voxels (blue). Finally, (c) is the Hough space obtained by *importance sampling* in a Monte Carlo framework, as described in [23]. (Color figure online)

and the fact that it doesn't require a non-maximal suppression step. However, knowing the Hough space can be a handy tool to visually understand the type of symmetries obtained in the process.

One should notice that there are more sophisticated methods in the literature to better extract symmetries, for instance [15,26]. However, the main contribution of the paper is the use of these detected symmetries in a variational optimization framework, described in the following section.

3   Surface Reconstruction with a Symmetry Prior

Given the set of detected symmetries Γ as described in Sect. 2, the goal is to find the 3D reconstruction of a surface which fulfills three simultaneous conditions: it should interpolate the given depth data, align with the given symmetries, and adhere to the defined degree of smoothness. We represent the surface by the implicit binary labeling function $u : V \subset \mathbb{R}^3 \to \{0,1\}$. The depth information is fused into the data cost $f : V \to \mathbb{R}$ which encodes the depth measurements volumetrically as a truncated signed distance function similar as in [29]. Similarly to this work, we integrate the data cost on the entire ray from the measured depth towards the camera. This has the advantage of being able to directly identify unexplored areas within the data cost, since unseen voxels will keep their initial value $f = 0$. In this way, a zero value in the computed TSFD shows no preference towards occupied or free-space, thus implying an unobserved voxel. On the other hand, this approach has the disadvantage that outliers in the depth map carve incorrect holes into the aggregated cost. Using the symmetry distance from Eq. (1), the surface can then be found as the minimizer of the following energy

$$E(u) = \int_V \left(|Du| + \lambda f u \right) dx + \mu \sum_{\gamma \in \Gamma} \omega_\gamma \cdot \mathrm{SD}_{V_\gamma}^2 (u, \gamma) , \qquad (3)$$

in which $\lambda, \mu \in \mathbb{R}_{\geq 0}$ respectively weigh the contributions of each term to control the amount of surface smoothness and symmetry. The first term is the Total Variation regularizer in which D is the derivative in a distributional sense. The last term of Eq. (3) minimizes the distance of all symmetries given by Γ for which we use a slightly modified distance measure (Eq. (1)) in such a way that the distance is only evaluated for points within the corresponding support domain V_γ. Furthermore, the weights ω_γ can be used to change the impact among individual symmetries.

Symmetry Projection. For a given set of m symmetries $\Gamma = \{\gamma_1, \gamma_2, \ldots, \gamma_m\}$, minimizing energy (3) approximates the joint projection onto a set of symmetries

$$\Pi_\Gamma(u) = \Pi_{\gamma_1, \gamma_2, \ldots, \gamma_m}(u) = \min_{v: \forall \gamma_i \in \Gamma : \gamma_i(v) = v} \|u - v\| , \qquad (4)$$

and if the regularization is turned off, i.e. for $\lambda, \mu \to \infty$ and uniform weights ω_γ this projection corresponds to the minimizer of (3), i.e. $\Pi_\Gamma(u) = \arg\min_u E(u)$. This relation can be seen by replacing the and-condition over the symmetries in Eq. (4) by the sum of the costs which leads to a similar expression as in Eq. (3).

Remark. As shown in [7] and stated in Eq. (1), the projection $\Pi_\gamma(u)$ of function u onto a single symmetry has a simple analytic solution: being the average of u and $\gamma(u)$. This is not the case for the projection onto a set of symmetries. Figure 3 illustrates that even the projection $\Pi_{\gamma_1, \gamma_2}(u)$ onto only two symmetries is not a simple combination of the individual projections $\Pi_{\gamma_1}(u), \Pi_{\gamma_2}(u)$. Since our method minimizes the symmetry distance to an arbitrary set of symmetries, the minimizer of energy (3) for an infinite symmetry term weight ($\mu \to \infty$) approaches the joint projection Π_Γ onto all symmetries in Γ which inherently generates a complex symmetry group as a combination of the input symmetries.

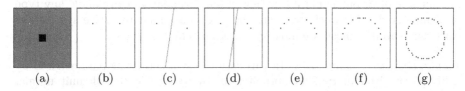

(a)   (b)   (c)   (d)   (e)   (f)   (g)

Fig. 3. A toy example illustrating the projection onto multiple symmetries. (a) Shows data cost f which enforces a single point (white corresponds to $f < 0$) as being occupied, and a small region to be free-space (black $\cong f > 0$) in order to avoid a constant solution. The rest of the image has no data cost (gray $\cong f = 0$). (b) A planar-reflective symmetry γ_1 and corresponding projection $\Pi_{\gamma_1}(u)$. (c) γ_2, $\Pi_{\gamma_2}(u)$. (d) Overlaid solution of $\Pi_{\gamma_1}(u), \Pi_{\gamma_2}(u)$ - this image corresponds to a solution of Eq. (3) with a low weight μ for the symmetry term. (d)–(g) In our setup we can continuously steer the amount of enforced symmetry by increasing μ until the image eventually fully adheres to the group structure of both symmetries.

4 Numerical Optimization

In order to minimize Eq. (3) we discretize the volume domain V on a regular voxel grid. In a discrete setting u is a stacked vector of all voxels in the volume domain. The symmetry dependencies between different points can be represented as a linear transformation, that is, the symmetry distance in Eq. (3) can be rewritten as $SD^2(u, \gamma) = \|A_\gamma u - b\|^2$. As a result, all three terms of the functional are convex and we can efficiently minimize energy (3) with the preconditioned first-order primal-dual algorithm [21]. In our setting the algorithm alternatingly iterates the following projected gradient ascent, gradient decent and linear extrapolation steps.

$$p^{n+1} = \Pi_{\|p\|\leq 1}\left[p^n + \sigma D\bar{u}^n\right]$$
$$u^{n+1} = \Pi_{[0,1]}\left[u^n + \tau\left(\operatorname{div} p^{n+1} - \lambda f - \mu \sum_{\gamma \in \Gamma} \omega_\gamma A_\gamma^T(A_\gamma u^n - b)\right)\right] \quad (5)$$
$$\bar{u}^{n+1} = 2u^{n+1} - u^n$$

with $\Pi_{\|p\|\leq 1}[p] = p/\max(1, \|p\|)$ being the projection onto the unit ball and $\Pi_{[0,1]}(x) = \max(0, \min(1, x))$ being a simple clamping. The derivative and divergence operators are discretized by forward and backward differences, respectively.

The primal-dual surface optimization lends itself to a parallel implementation for which we used the CUDA framework. Without further processing, we finally extract a mesh as the 0.5 iso-surface from the implicit surface representation u using the Marching cubes [14] algorithm.

Although the most common types of symmetries, like planar reflective symmetries, rotational, and translational symmetries are represented by linear transformations, the convexity of the energy is also not violated if the symmetry transformation is non-linear. This is because the transformation affects only the argument x of u, but not u itself. Hence, our formulation can handle any type of symmetry. In this work, we focus, however, on planar reflective symmetries since these are the most common ones in many environments.

Planar Reflective Symmetries. In this case the symmetry γ is parametrized by a 3D plane given in Hessian normal form by $nx - d = 0$ with unit normal $n \in \mathbb{R}^3$ and the distance from the origin $d \in \mathbb{R}$. The linear transformation inside the symmetry term in Eq. (5) is then given by $b = 0$, $A_\gamma = (\mathbb{I} - M_\gamma)$, with $\mathbb{I}$ being the identity matrix. The binary matrix $M_\gamma \in \{0, 1\}^{|V| \times |V|}$ (with $|V|$ being the number of voxels in the discretized volume domain) encodes all pairwise dependencies between voxels being linked by the symmetry γ and is defined as

$$(M_\gamma)_{ij} = \begin{cases} 1 & \text{if } m(j) = m(i) - 2n(m(i)^T n - d) \\ 0 & \text{otherwise.} \end{cases} \quad (6)$$

Here function $m : \mathbb{Z} \to \mathbb{Z}^3$ converts between the stacked 1D voxel index and the corresponding 3D voxel index. Further, pairwise dependencies (non-zero entries in matrix M_γ) are only added for voxels inside the corresponding symmetry support domain V_γ. In sum, for the case of planar reflective symmetries the relations in Eq. (6) essentially add pairwise interactions according to the symmetry for all points in the symmetry support domain V_γ.

5 Experiments

Although our approach inherently combines surface denoising, completion and hallucination, we try to isolate and evaluate these properties separately in the following experiments.

5.1 Surface Denoising and Completion

In order to evaluate the denoising properties of our approach, we artificially degraded the 3D reconstruction of a building by dropping every second depth map from the original reconstruction. These depth maps were created by a plane sweep stereo matching approach from a sequential set of 118 images taken from all sides of the building. To improve the degraded model, we used the symmetry prior with the best scoring vertical symmetries in the scene, see Fig. 4.

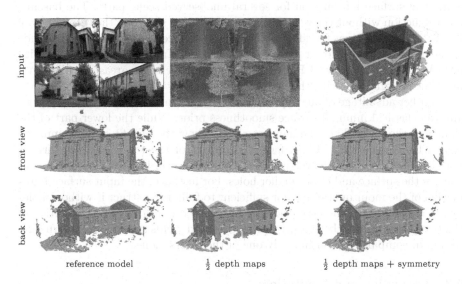

Fig. 4. Reconstruction of the building "g-hall" with large occlusions in the input data due to vegetation. The top row shows example input images, corresponding depth maps and the two best scoring planar symmetries. For comparison purposes, we degraded the original reconstruction (left column) by taking out half of the depth maps (center column) in order to introduce noise and missing data. Applying a symmetry prior to the degraded model completes many occluded areas on the backside, reduces the noise and enhances details like the window frames.

5.2   Surface Hallucination

In Fig. 5 we demonstrate the ability of our method to hallucinate large parts of a scene in unexplored areas. To this end, we took the Capitol data set from [1] consisting of a large building captured with 359 images. For the experiment, we selected one of the connected components with 129 images of the data set, representing half of the building as shown in the center column of Fig. 5. Using the two best scoring planar reflective symmetries, we were able to hallucinate the other half of the building and compared the result to the full stitched model presented as a result in [1]. An overlay of the two reconstructions reveals that the center part of this building is actually not exactly symmetric. Naturally, surrounding objects like the stairs do not fit to the reflected surface, but it is also visible that large parts of the walls and details like the windows align well.

5.3   Local Symmetries

Figure 6 shows an experiment with multiple local symmetries of objects in a desk scene. The local symmetries were detected using the RANSAC approach with sliding search boxes as described in Sect. 2.1. The first row in Fig. 6 depicts the input data which was scanned with a structured light RGB-D sensor and is missing surface information for several unobserved scene parts. The baseline reconstruction without the symmetry term ($\mu = 0$) is shown in the second row of Fig. 6. Some of its areas are filled with minimal surfaces as visible in the backside of the monitor and the lower part of the office chair. In contrast, the results with our approach (third row of Fig. 6) demonstrate that these areas are filled in a more meaningful way with the help of the symmetry information.

Another advantage of our approach is the combination of the symmetry prior and the classical minimal surface smoothness prior. While the lower part of the chair and the backside of the monitor clearly show the benefit of the symmetry term while regularizing the surface, the impact of the total variation term is not clear in these cases. Nevertheless, its impact is still important as it helps to denoise the surface and close smaller holes. For instance, the input surface information of the monitor stand is not sufficient to fully reconstruct it without holes by solely using the symmetry prior. As highlighted in Fig. 8, the combination of the two priors unifies their desired properties and yields superior reconstruction results in comparison to using only one of the priors alone.

5.4   Discussion and Limitations

While the proposed symmetry detection is rather robust to noise, the subsequent surface optimization with the proposed symmetry prior is sensitive even to very small changes of the symmetry parameters: (1) The accuracy of the symmetry support (up to surface noise) is essential, because otherwise inconsistent scene parts are forced to take consistent occupancy labels and the resulting label depends on the data support, the smoothness parameter and the number of pairwise inconsistencies within the group structure of the favored symmetry.

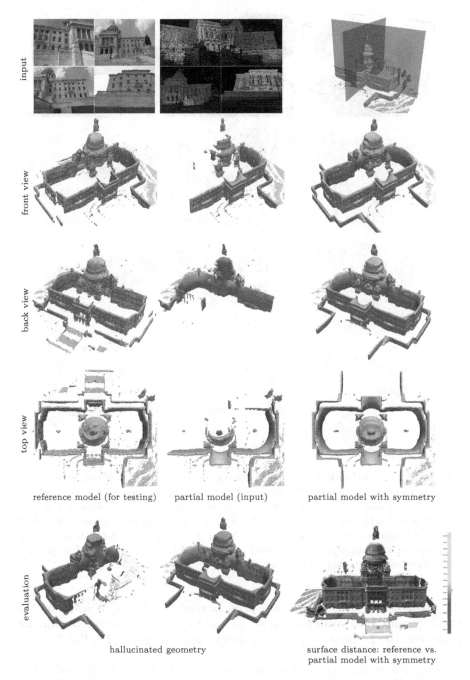

Fig. 5. This experiment shows a symmetric reconstruction of the capitol building in Providence (Rhode Island, USA) with a large unexplored area. We created a partial model by leaving out depth maps and then detected symmetries and hallucinated the rest of the building into the unexplored area.

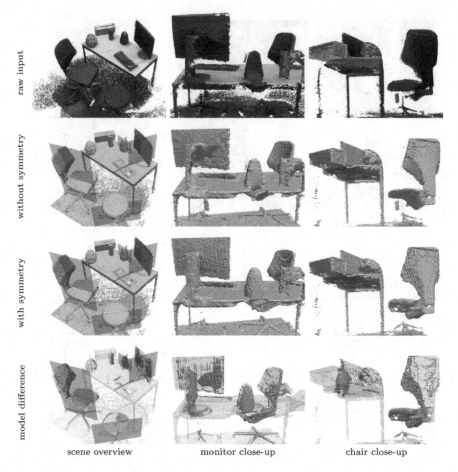

raw input

without symmetry

with symmetry

model difference

scene overview   monitor close-up   chair close-up

Fig. 6. Experiment with a desk scene containing multiple local planar symmetries shown as teal-colored planes in the first column. Several scene parts such as the backside of the monitor and the lower part of the chair were occluded during data acquisition. The figure shows the reconstruction results of the baseline approach (second row) which fills-in a minimal surface into the unknown regions in comparison to reconstruction with the proposed symmetry prior (third row) which completes these regions while obeying to the previously detected symmetries.

(2) The accuracy of the symmetry plane normal has strong influence on the result, because even small angular errors lead to large reconstruction errors for points that are far away from the symmetry plane as explained in Fig. 7.

Parameter Settings. We experimented with several settings for the individual symmetry weights ω_γ, like e.g. the support size, inlier ratios, or number of inliers, following the idea that symmetries with a stronger data support should also be enforced in a stronger way. However, we found that uniform weights ($\forall \gamma : \omega_\gamma = 1$) gave the best results and used them in all of our experiments.

raw input + symmetry plane   with symmetry ($\mu = 200$)

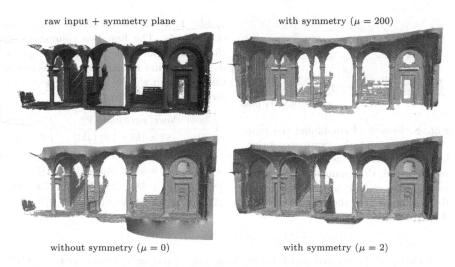

without symmetry ($\mu = 0$)   with symmetry ($\mu = 2$)

Fig. 7. Partial scan of a symmetric hallway. The figure shows different values of symmetry term weights μ in comparison. Even the very small angular error in the symmetry plane leads to inconsistencies in surface areas like the floor and walls and makes them disappear if the symmetry is enforced strongly ($\mu = 200$). Our approach allows for a compromise by only putting a low symmetry weight ($\mu = 2$), which leads to a not fully symmetric scene, but allows to recover the floor and all the walls in this dataset.

The other model parameters (volume resolution, data term weight λ, and symmetry term weight μ) are summarized in Table 1. The choice of these parameters is intuitive and careful tuning was not necessary. In order to weigh the amount of smoothness, data fidelity and symmetry against each other, we found as a rule of thumb that the data term weight and the symmetry term weight should be changed in a similar manner in order to keep a similar amount of smoothness, e.g. when enforcing more symmetry, the data term weight should be raised as well to maintain the amount of data fidelity. Conversely, for less smoothness the data term weight is raised and the symmetry term weight needs to be raised as well in order to maintain a comparable impact of the symmetry term. For more sophisticated symmetries like the stool or the toy example in Fig. 3, large symmetry term weights are required to enforce the full group structure.

For the detection of the global symmetries, we achieved better results and shorter runtimes on the larger data sets with the Hough transform, while for the local symmetry detection, the RANSAC approach gave better symmetry proposals. As mentioned in Sect. 2, we use a sliding box approach (3D convolution) with different box sizes to better detect all the objects in the scene. We chose sliding boxes of sizes 20 %, 30 %, 40 %, and 60 % of the total volume size and moved them by quarter box length quantities. For the symmetry support regions V_γ, we simply took the tight bounding box of the inlier points of the symmetry, but a better symmetry-based segmentation could also be used [26].

without symmetry   with symmetry prior

Fig. 8. Benefit of combining the minimal surface and the symmetry prior: less than half of the monitor stand was observed, the symmetry prior alone would leave a hole in the stand, but the combination of the priors yields the desired result.

Table 1. Overview of parameters for all experiments. The first two columns show the voxel resolution next to the corresponding dataset and the last two columns show the data term weight λ and the symmetry term weight μ (see Eq. (3)).

Dataset	Voxel resolution $|V|$	λ	μ
Stool	$191 \times 158 \times 135$ (4M)	10^8	10^7
Capitol	$700 \times 560 \times 560$ (220M)	1.5	6
g-hall	$512 \times 512 \times 213$ (56M)	0.75	6
Desk	$311 \times 289 \times 239$ (21M)	1500	300
Hallway	$730 \times 436 \times 301$ (96M)	200	200

Computation Time. All results have been computed on a Linux-based i7 CPU with a GeForce GTX 780 graphics card. While the symmetry detection is performed by unoptimized CPU code, the surface optimization with a symmetry prior has been implemented on the GPU. The computation times for the symmetry detection vary depending on the dataset and are within seconds for simple scenes like the stool and up to 2 h for the sliding box approach on the desk dataset. The computation time for the surface optimization with and without symmetry constraints with 80M voxels were 2:20 min and 1:03 min, respectively. This highly depends on the grid resolution, e.g., the reconstruction of the stool in Fig. 1 with 4M voxels took only 5 s with- and 2 s without symmetry constraints.

6   Conclusion

In this paper we proposed a novel symmetry prior for variational 3D reconstruction. Our method is able to enforce several symmetries with the same support area, allowing for symmetry interactions that proved to be very useful for several applications such as surface denoising and completion, as well as surface hallucination in the case of highly incomplete data. We also discussed two planar symmetry detection approaches and how to handle and exploit unobserved areas in order to more robustly detect such symmetries. We showed the results of our method in several datasets, ranging from noisy and slightly incomplete reconstructions, to models with almost half of its surface missing. We also showed results on scenes with several local symmetries with different support sizes. In future work, we would like to explore better symmetry detection methods, as well as experiment with different kinds of symmetries, such as rotational, translational or curved symmetries (e.g. as in [12]).

Acknowledgments. This work was supported by the Horizon 2020 research and innovation programme under grant agreement No. 637221, and by the CTI Switzerland grant No. 17136.1 Geometric and Semantic Structuring of 3D point clouds.

References

1. Cohen, A., Sattler, T., Pollefeys, M.: Merging the unmatchable: stitching visually disconnected SFM models. In: ICCV, December 2015
2. Cohen, A., Zach, C., Sinha, S., Pollefeys, M.: Discovering and exploiting 3D symmetries in structure from motion. In: CVPR, June 2012
3. Curless, B., Levoy, M.: A volumetric method for building complex models from range images. In: SIGGRAPH (1996)
4. Golovinskiy, A., Podolak, J., Funkhouser, T.: Symmetry-aware mesh processing. In: Hancock, E.R., Martin, R.R., Sabin, M.A. (eds.) Mathematics of Surfaces XIII. LNCS, vol. 5654, pp. 170–188. Springer, Heidelberg (2009)
5. Häne, C., Zach, C., Cohen, A., Angst, R., Pollefeys, M.: Joint 3D scene reconstruction and class segmentation. In: CVPR, pp. 97–104 (2013)
6. Hauagge, D.C., Snavely, N.: Image matching using local symmetry features. In: CVPR, pp. 206–213 (2012)
7. Kazhdan, M.M., Chazelle, B., Dobkin, D.P., Funkhouser, T.A., Rusinkiewicz, S.: A reflective symmetry descriptor for 3D models. Algorithmica 38(1), 201–225 (2003)
8. Kerber, J., Wand, M., Krüger, J.H., Seidel, H.: Partial symmetry detection in volume data. In: Proceedings of the Vision, Modeling, and Visualization Workshop, Berlin, Germany, 4–6 October 2011, pp. 41–48 (2011)
9. Kolev, K., Klodt, M., Brox, T., Cremers, D.: Continuous global optimization in multiview 3D reconstruction. IJCV 84(1), 80–96 (2009)
10. Kolev, K., Pock, T., Cremers, D.: Anisotropic minimal surfaces integrating photoconsistency and normal information for multiview stereo. In: ECCV, Heraklion, Greece, September 2010
11. Köser, K., Zach, C., Pollefeys, M.: Dense 3D reconstruction of symmetric scenes from a single image. In: Mester, R., Felsberg, M. (eds.) DAGM 2011. LNCS, vol. 6835, pp. 266–275. Springer, Heidelberg (2011)
12. Liu, J., Liu, Y.: Curved reflection symmetry detection with self-validation. In: Kimmel, R., Klette, R., Sugimoto, A. (eds.) ACCV 2010, Part IV. LNCS, vol. 6495, pp. 102–114. Springer, Heidelberg (2011)
13. Liu, Y., Hel-Or, H., Kaplan, C.S., Gool, L.V.: Computational symmetry in computer vision and computer graphics. Found. Trends Comput. Graph. Vis. 5(12), 1–195 (2010)
14. Lorensen, W.E., Cline, H.E.: Marching cubes: a high resolution 3D surface construction algorithm. SIGGRAPH Comput. Graph. 21, 163–169 (1987)
15. Mitra, N.J., Guibas, L.J., Pauly, M.: Symmetrization. ACM Trans. Graph. 26(3), 63 (2007)
16. Mitra, N.J., Pauly, M., Wand, M., Ceylan, D.: Symmetry in 3D geometry: extraction and applications. Comput. Graph. Forum 32(6), 1–23 (2013)
17. Oswald, M.R., Cremers, D.: A convex relaxation approach to space time multi-view 3D reconstruction. In: ICCV - Workshop on Dynamic Shape Capture and Analysis (4DMOD) (2013)
18. Oswald, M.R., Cremers, D.: Surface normal integration for convex space-time multi-view reconstruction. In: Proceedings of the British Machine and Vision Conference (BMVC) (2014)
19. Oswald, M.R., Stühmer, J., Cremers, D.: Generalized connectivity constraints for spatio-temporal 3D reconstruction. In: Fleet, D., Pajdla, T., Schiele, B., Tuytelaars, T. (eds.) ECCV 2014, Part IV. LNCS, vol. 8692, pp. 32–46. Springer, Heidelberg (2014)

20. Pizlo, Z., Sawada, T., Li, Y., Kropatsch, W.G., Steinman, R.M.: New approach to the perception of 3D shape based on veridicality, complexity, symmetry and volume. Vision. Res. **50**, 1–11 (2010)
21. Pock, T., Chambolle, A.: Diagonal preconditioning for first order primal-dual algorithms in convex optimization. In: ICCV, Washington, DC, USA, pp. 1762–1769 (2011)
22. Podolak, J., Golovinskiy, A., Rusinkiewicz, S.: Symmetry-enhanced remeshing of surfaces. In: Proceedings of the Fifth Eurographics Symposium on Geometry Processing, Barcelona, Spain, 4–6 July 2007, pp. 235–242 (2007)
23. Podolak, J., Shilane, P., Golovinskiy, A., Rusinkiewicz, S., Funkhouser, T.A.: A planar-reflective symmetry transform for 3D shapes. ACM Trans. Graph. **25**(3), 549–559 (2006)
24. Reinbacher, C., Pock, T., Bauer, C., Bischof, H.: Variational segmentation of elongated volumetric structures. In: CVPR (2010)
25. Terzopoulos, D., Witkin, A., Kass, M.: Symmetry-seeking models and 3D object reconstruction. IJCV **1**, 211–221 (1987)
26. Thrun, S., Wegbreit, B.: Shape from symmetry. In: ICCV, Bejing, China. IEEE (2005)
27. Ummenhofer, B., Brox, T.: Dense 3D reconstruction with a hand-held camera. In: Pinz, A., Pock, T., Bischof, H., Leberl, F. (eds.) DAGM and OAGM 2012. LNCS, vol. 7476, pp. 103–112. Springer, Heidelberg (2012)
28. Unger, M., Pock, T., Cremers, D., Bischof, H.: TVSeg - interactive total variation based image segmentation. In: Proceedings of the British Machine and Vision Conference (BMVC), Leeds, UK, September 2008
29. Zach, C., Pock, T., Bischof, H.: A globally optimal algorithm for robust TV-l1 range image integration. In: ICCV, pp. 1–8 (2007)

SPLeaP: Soft Pooling of Learned Parts for Image Classification

Praveen Kulkarni[1,2(✉)], Frédéric Jurie[2], Joaquin Zepeda[1],
Patrick Pérez[1], and Louis Chevallier[1]

[1] Technicolor, Cesson-Sévigné, France
{praveen.kulkarni,joaquin.zepeda,patrick.pérez,
louis.chevallier}@technicolor.com
[2] Normandie Univ, UNICAEN, ENSICAEN, CNRS, Caen, France
{praveen.kulkarni,frédéric.jurie}@unicaen.fr

Abstract. The aggregation of image statistics – the so-called pooling step of image classification algorithms – as well as the construction of part-based models, are two distinct and well-studied topics in the literature. The former aims at leveraging a whole set of local descriptors that an image can contain (through spatial pyramids or Fisher vectors for instance) while the latter argues that only a few of the regions an image contains are actually useful for its classification. This paper bridges the two worlds by proposing a new pooling framework based on the discovery of useful parts involved in the pooling of local representations. The key contribution lies in a model integrating a boosted non-linear part classifier as well as a parametric soft-max pooling component, both trained jointly with the image classifier. The experimental validation shows that the proposed model not only consistently surpasses standard pooling approaches but also improves over state-of-the-art part-based models, on several different and challenging classification tasks.

1 Introduction

This paper addresses the problem of image classification with Part-Based Models (PBMs). Decomposing images into salient parts and aggregating them to form discriminative representations is a central topic in the computer vision literature. It is raising several important questions such as: How to find discriminative features? How to detect them? How to organize them into a coherent model? How to model the variation in the appearance and spatial organization? Even if works such as the pictorial structure [1], the constellation model [2], object fragments [3], the Deformable Part Model [4] or the Discriminative Modes Seeking approach of [5] brought interesting contributions, as well as those in [6–8], the automatic discovery and usage of discriminative parts for image classification remains a difficult and open question.

Recent PBMs for image classification *e.g.*, [5–9] rely on five key components: (i) The generation of a large pool of candidate regions per image from (annotated) training data; (ii) The mining of the most discriminative and representative regions from the pool of candidate parts; (iii) The learning of part classifiers

© Springer International Publishing AG 2016
B. Leibe et al. (Eds.): ECCV 2016, Part VIII, LNCS 9912, pp. 329–345, 2016.
DOI: 10.1007/978-3-319-46484-8_20

using the mined parts; (iv) The definition of a part-based image model aggregating (independently) the learnt parts across a pool of candidate parts per image; (v) The learning of final image classifiers over part-based representations of training images.

One key challenge in the 2nd and 3rd components of PBMs lies in the selection of discriminative regions and the learning of interdependent part classifiers. For instance, one cannot learn the part classifiers before knowing discriminative regions and vice-versa. Extensive work has been done to alleviate the problem of identifying discriminative regions in a huge pool of candidate regions, *e.g.*, [5,7,8].

Once the discriminative regions are discovered and subsequently part classifiers are trained, the 4th component in a PBM – *i.e.*, the construction of the image model based on the per image part presence – is basically obtained by average or sum pooling of part classifier responses across the pool of candidate regions in the image. The final classifiers are then learnt on top of this part-based image representation. Although the aforementioned methods address one of the key components of PBMs, *i.e.*, mining discriminative regions by using some heuristics to improve final classification, they fail to leverage the advantage of jointly learning all the components together.

The joint learning approach of all components of PBMs is indeed particularly appealing since the discriminative regions are explicitly optimized for the targeted task. But intertwining all components makes the problem highly non-convex and initialization critical. The recent works of Lobel *et al.* [10] and Parizi *et al.* [9] showed that the joint learning of a PBM is possible. However, these approaches suffer from several limitations. First, their intermediate part classifiers are simple linear classifiers and the expression power of these part classifiers is limited in capturing complex patterns in regions. Furthermore, they pool the part classifier responses over candidate regions per image using max pooling which is suboptimal [11]. Finally, as the objective function is non-convex they rely on a strong initialization of the parts.

In the present work, we propose a novel framework, coined "Soft Pooling of Learned Parts" (SPLeaP), to jointly optimize all the five components of the proposed PBM. A first contribution is that we describe each part classifier as a linear combination of weak non-linear classifiers, learned greedily and resulting in a strong classifier which is non-linear. This greedy approach is inspired by [12,13] wherein they use gradient descent for choosing linear combinations of weak classifiers. The complexity of the part detector is increased along with the construction of the image model. This classifier is eventually able to better capture the complex patterns in regions. A second contribution is that we softly aggregate the computed part classifier responses over all the candidate regions per image. We introduce a parameter, referred as the "pooling parameter", for each part classifier independently inside the optimization process. The value of this pooling parameter determines the softness level of the aggregation done over all candidate regions, with higher softness levels approaching sum pooling and lower softness levels resembling max pooling. This permits to leverage different pooling regimes for different part classifiers. It also offers an interesting way to relax the assignment between regions and parts and lessens the need for strong initialization of the parts. The outputs of all part classifiers are fed to the final classifiers driven by the classifier loss objective.

The proposed PBM can be applied to various visual recognition problems, such as the classification of objects, scenes or actions in still images. In addition, our approach is agnostic to the low-level description of image regions and can easily benefit from the powerful features delivered by modern Convolutional Neural Nets (CNNs). By relying on such representations, and outperforming [14,15], the proposed approach can also be seen as a low-cost adaptation mechanism: pre-trained CNNs features are fed to a mid-to-high level model that is trained for a new target task. To validate this adaptation scheme we use the pre-trained CNNs of [15]. Note that this network is not fine-tuned on target datasets.

We validated our method on three challenging datasets: Pascal-VOC-2007 (object), MIT-Indoor-67 (scenes) and Willow (actions). We improve over state-of-the-art PBMs on the three of them.

The rest of the paper is organized as follows. The next section presents a review of the related works, followed by the presentation of the method in Sect. 3. Section 4 describes the algorithm proposed to jointly optimize the parameters, while Sect. 5 contains the experimental validation of our work.

2 Related Works

Most of the recent advances on image classification are concentrated on the development of novel Convolutional Neural Networks (CNNs), motivated by the excellent performance obtained by Krizhevsky *et al.* [16]. As CNNs require huge amount of training data (*e.g.*, ImageNet) and are expensive to train, some authors such as Razavian *et al.* [17] showed that the descriptors produced by CNNs *pre-trained* on a large dataset are generic enough to outperform many classification tasks on diverse small datasets, with reduced training cost. Oquaba *et al.* [14] and Chatfield *et al.* [15] were the first to leverage the benefit of fine-tuning the pre-trained CNNs to new datasets such as Pascal-VOC-2007 [18]. Oquab *et al.* [14] reused the weights of initial layers of CNN pre-trained on ImageNetand added two new adaptation layers. They trained these two new layers using multi-scale overlapping regions from Pascal-VOC-2007 training images, using the provided bounding box annotations. Chatfield *et al.* [15], on the other hand, fine-tuned the whole network to new datasets, which involved intensive computations due to the large number of network parameters to be estimated. They reported state-of-art performance on Pascal-VOC-2007 till date by fine-tuning pre-trained CNN architecture.

In line with many other authors, [15,17] utilized the penultimate layer of CNNs to obtain global descriptors of images. However, it has been observed that computing and aggregating local descriptors on multiple regions described by pre-trained CNNs provides an even better image representation and improves classification performance. Methods such as Gong *et al.* [19], Kulkarni *et al.* [20] and Cimpoi *et al.* [21] relied on such aggregation using standard pooling techniques, *e.g.*, VLAD, Bag-of-Words and Fisher vectors respectively.

On the other hand, Part-Based Models (PBMs) proposed in the recent literature, *e.g.*, [5–8], can be seen as more powerful aggregators compared to [19,20,22]. PBMs attempt to select few relevant patterns or discriminative regions and focus on them in the aggregation, making the image representation more robust to occlusions or to frequent non-discriminative background regions.

PBMs differ in the way they discover discriminative parts and combine them into a unique description of the image. The Deformable Part Model proposed by Felzenszwalb *et al.* [4] solves the aforementioned problems by selecting discriminative regions that have significant overlap with the bounding box location. The association between regions and part is done through the estimation of latent variables, *i.e.*, the positions of the regions w.r.t. the position of the root part of the model. Differently, Singh *et al.* [6] aimed at discovering a set of relevant patches by considering the representative and frequent enough patches which are, in addition, discriminative w.r.t. the rest of the visual world. The problem is formulated as an unsupervised discriminative clustering problem on a huge dataset of image patches, optimized by an iterative procedure alternating between clustering and training discriminative classifiers. More recently, Juneja *et al.* [7] also aimed at discovering distinctive parts for an object or scene class by first identifying the likely discriminative regions by low-level segmentation cues, and then, in a second time, learning part classifiers on top of these regions. The two steps are alternated iteratively until a convergence criterion based on Entropy-Rank is satisfied. Doersch *et al.* [5] used density based mean-shift algorithms to discover discriminative regions. Starting from a weakly-labeled image collection, coherent patch clusters that are maximally discriminative with respect to the labels are produced, requiring a single pass through the data.

Contrasting with previous approaches, Li *et al.* [23] were among the first to rely on CNN activations as region descriptors. Their approach discovers the discriminative regions using association rule mining techniques, well-known in the data mining community. Sicre *et al.* [24] also build on CNN-encoded regions, introducing an algorithm that models image categories as collections of automatically discovered distinctive parts. Parts are matched across images while learning their visual model and are finally pooled to provide images signatures.

One common characteristic of the aforementioned approaches is that they discover the discriminative parts first and then combine them into a model of the classes to recognize. There is therefore no guaranty that the so-learned parts are optimal for the classification task. Lobel *et al.* [10] showed that the joint learning of part and category models was possible. More recently, Parizi *et al.* [9] build on the same idea, using max pooling and l_1/l_2 regularization.

Variour authors have likewise studied learned soft-pooling mechanisms. Gulcehre *et al.* [25] investigate the effect of using generalized soft pooling as a nonlinear activation unit, bearing some similarity with the maxout non-linear unit of [26]. In contrast, our method uses a generalized soft pooling strategy as a down sampling layer. Our method is close to that of Lee *et al.* [27], who use linear interpolation of max and average pooling. Our approach, on the other hand, uses a non-linear interpolation of these two extrema.

3 Proposed Approach

Our goal is to represent each category involved in the visual recognition problem of interest as a collection of discriminative regions. These regions are automatically identified using learned part classifiers, that will operate on a pool of proposed fragments. A "part" classifier is meant to capture specific visual patterns. As such it does not necessarily capture a strong, human understandable semantic: it might respond highly on more than one region of the given image or, conversely, embrace at once several identifiable parts of the object. On images from "horse" class for instance, one part classifier might focus on the head of the animal when another one turns out to capture a large portion of the horse body.

Formally, we consider an image as a bag of R regions, each one equipped with a descriptor $\mathbf{x}_r \in \mathbb{R}^D$. The image is thus represented at first by the descriptor collection $\mathcal{X} = \{\mathbf{x}_r\}_{r=1}^R$. The number of regions will be image-dependent in general even if we assume it is not for notational convenience.

Based on training images spanning C images categories, P "part" classifiers will be learned, each as a weighted sum of K base classifiers applied to a region's descriptor (K chosen by cross-validation). The score of the p-th part classifier for a given descriptor $\mathbf{x}$ is defined as:

$$H_p(\mathbf{x}; \boldsymbol{\theta}_p) = \sum_{k=1}^K a_k^p \sigma(\mathbf{x}^\top \mathbf{u}_k^p + b_k^p), \qquad (1)$$

where σ is the sigmoid function, a_k^p is the weight of the k-th base classifier, $\mathbf{u}_k^p \in \mathbb{R}^D$ and $b_k^p \in \mathbb{R}$ are its parameters and $\boldsymbol{\theta}_p = \text{vec}(a_{1:K}^p, \mathbf{u}_{1:K}^p, b_{1:K}^p) \in \mathbb{R}^{K(D+2)}$ is the vector of all the parameters that define the part classifier. This score is aggregated over the pool of R regions a follows:

$$f_p(\mathcal{X}) = \sum_{r=1}^R \pi_r^p H_p(\mathbf{x}_r; \boldsymbol{\theta}_p), \qquad (2)$$

where normalized weights are defined as

$$\pi_r^p \propto \exp\left(\beta_p H_p(\mathbf{x}_r; \boldsymbol{\theta}_p)\right), \quad \sum_{r=1}^R \pi_r^p = 1, \qquad (3)$$

with β_p a part-dependent "pooling" parameter. For large values of this parameter the scores are max-pooled, while they are averaged for very small values.

Given a set of part classifiers with parameter $\Theta = [\boldsymbol{\theta}_1| \cdots |\boldsymbol{\theta}_P]$ and associated pooling parameters $\boldsymbol{\beta} = [\beta_p]_{p=1}^P$, the bag of R region descriptors $\mathcal{X} = \{\mathbf{x}_r\}_r$ attached to an input image is turned into a part-based description:

$$\mathbf{f}(\mathcal{X}; \Theta, \boldsymbol{\beta}) = [f_p(\mathcal{X})]_{p=1}^P. \tag{4}$$

The multiclass classification problem at hand is cast on this representation. Resorting to logistic regression, we aim at learning P-dimensional vectors, $\mathbf{w}_c = [w_1^c \cdots w_P^c]^\top \in \mathbb{R}^P$, one per class, so that the class label $y \in \{1 \cdots C\}$ of an input image $\mathcal{X}$ is predicted according to distribution

$$\Pr(y = c|\mathcal{X}; \Theta, \boldsymbol{\beta}, W) = \frac{\exp\left(\mathbf{w}_c^\top \mathbf{f}(\mathcal{X}; \Theta, \beta)\right)}{\sum_{d=1}^C \exp\left(\mathbf{w}_d^\top \mathbf{f}(\mathcal{X}; \Theta, \beta)\right)}, \tag{5}$$

where $W = [\mathbf{w}_1| \cdots |\mathbf{w}_C]$. For simplicity in notation, we have omitted the bias term associated with each class. In practice, we append each of them to the corresponding vectors $\mathbf{w}_c$s and entry one is appended to descriptor $\mathbf{f}(\mathcal{X}; \Theta, \beta)$.

Discriminative learning is conducted on annotated training dataset $\mathcal{T} = \{(\mathcal{X}_n, y_n)\}_{n=1}^N$, with $\mathcal{X}_n = \{\mathbf{x}_r^n\}_{r=1}^R$ and $y_n \in \{1, \ldots, C\}$. Part-level and category-level classifiers are jointly learned by minimizing a regularized multiclass cross entropy loss:

$$\min_{\Theta, \boldsymbol{\beta}, W} - \sum_{n=1}^N \sum_{c=1}^C [y_n = c] \ln \Pr(c|\mathcal{X}_n; \Theta, \beta, W) + \mu\|\Theta\|_F^2 + \delta\|W\|_F^2, \tag{6}$$

where $[.]$ is Iverson bracket. The two regularization weights μ and δ, the number P of part classifiers and the number K of base learners in each part are set by cross-validation. Learning is done by block-wise stochastic gradient descent, as explained next into more details.

The multi-class loss in (6) being based on softmax (5), it requires that each image in the training set is assigned to a single class. If this is not the case, one can use instead a one-vs.-all binary classification approach, which can be easily combined as well with the proposed PBM.

4   Optimization Specific Details

In this section we provide details on how the joint optimization problem (6) is addressed. It aims at learning the final category-level classifiers (defined W), the part classifiers (defined by Θ) and the part-dependent pooling coefficients in β. By conducting jointly these learnings, part classifiers are optimized for the target recognition task. Additionally, learning part-specific parameter β_p enables to accommodate better the specifics of each part by adapting the softness of its region pooling.

Algorithm 1 summarizes the different steps of the optimization. In Algorithm 1, we denote $\boldsymbol{\theta}_{(k)}$ the vector of parameters associated to k-th base classifiers in matrix Θ, that is $\boldsymbol{\theta}_{(k)} = \text{vec}(a_k^{1:P}, \mathbf{u}_k^{1:P}, b_k^{1:P})$ and $\mathcal{L}_n = \log \Pr(y_n | \mathcal{X}_n; \Theta, \beta, W)$ the log-likelihood of n-th training pair $(\mathcal{X}_n, y_n)$.

We perform E epochs of block-coordinate stochastic gradient descent. If part-related parameters Θ and β were known and fixed, the optimization of image classifiers W alone in the proposed algorithm would amount to the classic learning of logistic regressors on image descriptors $\mathbf{f}(\mathcal{X})$ defined in (4). The interleaved learning of the P part-classifiers defined by Θ is more involved. It relies on a stage-wise strategy whereby base classifiers are progressively incorporated. More precisely, we start with a single weak classifier per part, randomly initialized and optimized over the first S epochs. Past this first stage with training a single weak classifier, each part-classifier is then allowed an additional weak classifier per epoch. With initialization to zero of the parameters of this new learner, non-zero gradients for these parameters is produced by training samples that were previously misclassified. Note that at each epoch, only the last weak classifier is updated for each part while previous ones are kept fixed.

We set all algorithm's parameters (number P of parts, number K of weak classifiers per part, number S of epochs with part classifiers based only on a single weak learner, learning rates γ_W, γ_θ and γ_β) through careful cross-validation.

Algorithm 1. SPLeaP Training: joint part-category classifier learning

---

1: **procedure** LEARN($\mathcal{J}$)
2:     parameters: P, K, μ, δ, S, γ_W, γ_θ, γ_β
3:     $W \leftarrow 0$
4:     $\boldsymbol{\theta}_{(1)} \leftarrow \text{rand}()$
5:     $\boldsymbol{\theta}_{(2:K)} \leftarrow 0$
6:     $\beta \leftarrow \text{rand}()$
7:     $k \leftarrow 1$
8:     **for** $e = 1$ to $E = K + S - 1$ **do**
9:         $\mathcal{J} \leftarrow RandomShuffle(\mathcal{J})$
10:         **for** $n = 1$ to N **do**
11:             $W \leftarrow (1 - \gamma_W)W + \gamma_W \sum_{(\mathcal{X}_n, y_n) \in \mathcal{J}} \nabla_W \mathcal{L}_n$
12:             $\boldsymbol{\theta}_{(k)} \leftarrow (1 - \gamma_\theta)\boldsymbol{\theta}_{(k)} + \gamma_\theta \sum_{(\mathcal{X}_n, y_n) \in \mathcal{J}} \nabla_{\boldsymbol{\theta}_{(k)}} \mathcal{L}_n$
13:             $\beta \leftarrow \beta + \gamma_\beta \sum_{(\mathcal{X}_n, y_n) \in \mathcal{J}} \nabla_\beta \mathcal{L}_n$
14:         **end for**
15:         **if** $e > S$ **then**
16:             $k \leftarrow k + 1$
17:         **end if**
18:     **end for**
19:     Return W, Θ, β
20: **end procedure**

---

5   Results

5.1   Experimental Settings

Datasets. We evaluate our proposed method using three well-known datasets described below:

Pascal-VOC-2007. The `Pascal-VOC-2007` dataset [18] is an image classification dataset consisting of 9963 images of 20 different visual object classes divided into 5011 training images (of which 2510 are validation images) and 4952 testing images. The images contain natural scenes and the visual object classes span a wide range, including animals (*e.g.*, dog, cat), vehicles (*e.g.*, aeroplane, car) and other manufactured objects (*e.g.*, tv monitor, chair).

MIT Indoor 67. As opposed to objects, scenes are non-localized visual concepts and might even be characterized by the presence or absence of several objects. The `MIT-Indoor-67`[28] dataset is a scene recognition dataset consisting of 67 indoor scenes (*e.g.*, nursery, movie theater, casino or meeting room) each represented by 80 training images and 20 test images. We use 20 randomly chosen training images from each class as a validation set.

Willow Dataset. Recognizing human action in photos is a challenging task due the absence of temporal information. Dedicated to this task, the `Willow` dataset [29] consists of 7 action categories such as "play instrument", "walk" or "ride horse" spread across 490 training images (of which 210 are validation images) and 421 test images.

Region Proposal Schemes. We explored three different strategies to extract the pool of region proposals from each image:

Selective Search (SS). We use the selective search region proposal scheme of [30] to extract between 100 and 5000 region proposals per image, with an average of 800, using Matlab code provided by [31].

Augmentation (aug). Following the data augmentation technique of [15], we derive ten images from each input image by taking one center crop and four corner crops from the original image and further mirroring each crop vertically. The ten resulting modified image crops are used as region proposals.

Selective search+augmentation (SS+aug). We also explore merging the outputs of the two previous strategies into a single pool of region proposals.

Region Feature Extraction. From each of the candidate regions obtained using one of the above described region proposal methods, we extract one feature vector consisting of the activation coefficients of the previous-to-last layer of several state-of-the-art CNN architectures. The CNN architectures we consider, available in CAFFE [32], are (*i*) the 128-dimensional feature extracted from the 13-layer architecture of [15] (VGG-128), (*ii*) the 16-layer architecture of [33] producing 4096 dimensional features (VD-16) and (*iii*) the architecture of [34] corresponding to Krizhevsky's architecture [16] pre-trained using `ImageNet` (978 categories) and the `Places` database (HybridCNN).

Cross-Validation of Hyper-parameters. We use Stochastic Gradient Descent (SGD) to train our model. The performance of the model depends on the value of the various hyper-parameters: the number of parts P and of weak learners in each part classifier K, the regularization weights μ and δ in (6), the number of epochs E and the various learning rates (see Algorithm 1). For the Pascal-VOC-2007 and Willow datasets, we use piecewise-constant learning rates decreased every ten epochs empirically, similarly to the appraoch of [15]. For the MIT-Indoor-67dataset, we use learning rates of the form $\gamma(i) = \frac{\gamma_0}{1.0+\lambda i}$, where γ_0 and λ are hyper parameters that are cross-validated.

We select the values of these hyper-parameters using cross-validation. After the cross-validation phase, the hyper-parameters are set accordingly and the training and validation data are merged to re-train our model.

5.2   Experimental Validation of the Contributions

We now establish experimentally the benefits of our main contributions: weakly supervised parts learning, soft-max pooling with learned, per-part softness coefficients, and part detectors based on weak learners. To this end, we use the Pascal-VOC-2007 dataset along with the mean Average Precision (mAP) performance measure specified by the dataset's authors, using VGG-128 features to represent all region proposals.

Comparison with Unsupervised Aggregation. In Table 1, we first verify that the improvements of our method are not due to simply the region proposal strategies we employ. We hence compare our supervised SPLeaPmethod to three analogous baseline features not employing supervised learning. The first baseline, denoted *VGG-128-G*, uses the global feature vector extracted from the whole image. The second baseline, denoted *VGG-128-sum*, aggregates VGG-128 features extracted from each candidate region using average pooling, similarly to an approach used in [35]. Both of these baselines result in 128-dimensional feature vectors. In a third baseline, denoted *VGG-128-K-means*, we perform K-means on all candidate regions from all images in the database to obtain $P = 40$ centroids. Computing an image feature then consists of selecting the image's $P \ll R$ candidate region whose features are closest to the P centroids and concatenating them into a single vector of size $128P$.

For each of the aforementioned feature construction methods, the resulting image feature vectors are ℓ_2-normalized and then used to learn linear SVMs using a one-vs.-rest strategy.

The results in Table 1 establish that large performance gains (more than 8 mAP points) are obtained by proposed SPLeaPmethod relative to the different baseline aggregation strategies, and hence the gain does not follow simply from using our region proposal strategies. Interestingly, contrary to the baseline strategies, our method succeeds in exploiting the merged *SS+aug* region proposal strategy (0.47 mAP improvement relative to *SS*).

Table 1. Comparison against unsupervised aggregation baselines

VGG-128-G	VGG-128-sum			VGG-128-K-means		SPLeaP	
	SS	aug	SS+aug	SS	SS+aug	SS	SS+aug
75.32	77.31	78.21	77.36	76.28	76.8	84.21	**84.68**

Table 2. Importance of per-part softness coefficients

Average pooling	Max pooling	Cross-valid. $\beta_p = \beta$	Learned β_p
80.77	83.23	84.31	**84.68**

Importance of Per-Part Softness Coefficient. In Table 2, we evaluate our proposed soft-max pooling strategy in (3) that employs a learned, per-part softness coefficient β_p. We compare per-part softness coefficients to three alternatives: *(i)* average pooling, wherein $\forall p, \beta_p = 0$; *(ii)* max pooling, which is equivalent to $\forall p, \beta_p \rightarrow \infty$; and *(iii)* a cross-validated softness coefficient that is constant for all parts, $\forall p, \beta_p = \beta$. In all three of these alternatives, we run the complete SPLeaPoptimization process discussed in Sect. 4. As illustrated in the table, using our proposed learned, per-part softness coefficient yields the best performance, with an improvement of close to 4 mAP points over average pooling, 1.5 mAP points over max pooling, and 0.4 mAP points over a cross-validated but constant softness coefficient. Note that allowing the algorithm to choose β_p during the optimization process eliminates the need for a costly cross validation of the β_p.

Effect of Number of Weak Learners K. In Fig. 1 we evaluate the effect of the number K of weak learners per part by plotting mAP as a function of the number of training epochs. Note that, for a fixed number of learning iterations, adding more weak learners results in higher performance. We have tried the effect of other design choices such as averaging K weak learners in contrast to greedily adding the weak learners. We obtain slight improvement *i.e.* we obtain 84.78 mAP for $K = 3$. We also compared adding weak learners to dropout, which is known to behave as averaging multiple thinned networks, and obtained a reduction in mAP of 0.5 % (83.98 mAP with 50 % dropout).

5.3 Parameters/Design Related Choices

Per-Category Parts and Number P of Parts. When learning SPLeaPfor the MIT-Indoor-67dataset, we learn P part classifiers that are common to all 67 categories using the multi-class objective described in Sect. 3. For Willow and Pascal-VOC-2007, on the other hand, we learn P different part classifiers for each category, using a one-vs.-rest strategy to learn each SPLeaPmodel independently for each class.

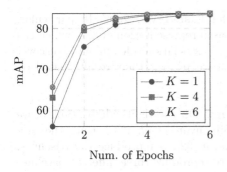
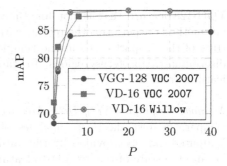

Fig. 1. Plot of test mAP versus number of training epochs.

Fig. 2. Plot of test mAP versus the number of parts P.

In Fig. 2 we evaluate mAP on `Pascal-VOC-2007` as a function of the number of parts P. We show that even with a small number of parts $P = 6$ per class, we obtain a very good mAP of 83.94.

5.4 Comparisons with State-of-the-art

Pascal-VOC-2007. In Table 3 we compare SPLeaPto various existing state-of-the-art methods on the `Pascal-VOC-2007` dataset.

Methods Employing Krizhevsky-Type Architectures. On the left side of Table 3, we compare against Krizhevsky's original 13-layer architecture [16] and variants thereof such as VGG-128 [15]. In particular, the architectures of [14,15] were first learned on `ImageNet` and subsequently fine-tuned specifically for `Pascal-VOC-2007`.

Note that, when using architectures derived from [16], including architectures fine-tuned specifically for `Pascal-VOC-2007`, our method outperforms all of these baselines by at least 3 absolute mAP points, despite using the 128-dimensional

Table 3. Comparison of results on `Pascal-VOC-2007` dataset ($P = 40$ parts per class, $K = 1$) using CNN features extracted from *(left)* Krizhevsky-like [16] and *(right)* very deep architectures [33]

Methods	*mAP*	Methods	*mAP*
VGG-G	75.35		
Oquab *et al.* [14]	77.31	VD-16-G [33]	81.73
Li *et al.* [23]	77.90	VD-16 (*dense_evaluation*)	84.67
Cimpoi *et al.* [21]	79.50	VD-16-sum (*SS+ext. aug*)	82.58
CNN-S fine tuned [15]	82.42	Cimpoi *et al.* [21]	85.10
SPP [36]	82.44		
SPLeaP-VGG-128 (*SS+ext. aug*)	**84.68**	SPLeaP-VD-16 (*SS+ext. aug*)	**88.01**

VGG-128 feature that is not fine-tuned for Pascal-VOC-2007. In particular, our method outperforms the recent, part-based representation of [23], which is a state-of-the-art part-based method employing association rule mining to discover discriminative patterns/regions. In Table 3 we present their results based on features from [16].

Methods Employing Very Deep Architectures. On the right side of Table 3, we compare against the deep pipelines of Simonyan *et al.* [33], using the pre-computed models provided by the authors in [32] to reproduce the baselines. We use the state-of-the-art VD-16 feature to reproduce three different baselines using our own implementations.

The first one (VD-16-G) uses a global VD-16 feature by feeding the entire image to the CNN architecture.

The second one, VD-16 *dense_evaluation*, follows [33] in employing their CNN architecture as a fully convolutional architecture by treating the weights of the last two fully connected layers as 7×7 and 1×1 convolutional kernels, respectively. This enables them to process images of arbitrary size. The approach further employs scaling, cropping and flipping to effectively produce a pool of close to 500 region proposals that are subsequently average-pooled. The resulting descriptor is ℓ_2 normalized and used to compute linear SVMs, and achieves state-of-the-art results on Pascal-VOC-2007.[1]

For completeness, we further explore a third baseline that employs the extended augmentation (*ext. aug.*) strategy employed by [37], which effectively produces 144 crops per image, as opposed to the 10 crops of the *aug* strategy discussed above. We further extend this region proposals by the selective search region proposals and employ sum pooling.

The results, summarized in Table 3, show that proposed SPLeaPsystem outperforms all three baselines, and further outperforms a very recent baseline [21] relying on a hybrid bag-of-words/CNN scheme.

Willow Action Dataset. Our best results on Willow (Table 4 left) likewise outperforms VD-16-G by 3.35 mAP points and VD-16 *dense_evaluation* (Table 4 left) by 2.8 mAP points. For completeness, we have included several, previously-published results. To our knowledge, our approach outperforms the highest published results on this dataset.

MIT-Indoor-67. In Table 4, we present results on the MIT-Indoor-67dataset. For this dataset, we represent candidate regions using the Hybrid CNN model of [34], which is learned on a training set obtained by merging ImageNet and the Places database [34] and is better suited for scene recognition. Given the large size (4096) of these features, we reduce them to size 160 using PCA, similarly to the approach of [9]. Note that our method outperforms all other methods in

---

[1] Our own implementation of this method achieves results below those reported in [33].

Table 4. Comparison of results on the `Willow` dataset ($P = 7$ parts per-class, $K = 1$) *(left)* and the `MIT-Indoor-67`dataset ($P = 500$ parts, common to all classes, $K = 2$) *(right)*

Methods	mAP	Methods	mAP
Khan *et al.* [38]	70.10	Orderless [19]	68.80
Sharma *et al.* [39]	65.90	MLPM [23]	69.69
Sharma *et al.* [40]	67.60	HybridCNN-G [34]	72.54
Sicre *et al.* [24]	81.90	HybridCNN-sum [34]	70.36
VD-16-G	85.12	Parizi *et al.* [9]	73.30
VD-16 (dense_evaluation)	85.67	SPLeaP-PCA160 (*SS*)	**73.45**
SPLeaP (*SS+aug*)	**88.47**		

Table 4. Unlike our reported results, those of [9] use a spatial pyramid with two scales and five cells (1×1, 2×2), as well as a different number of parts and PCA-reduction factor, resulting in features that are 3.73 times bigger than ours.

6 Qualitative Analysis

We now present qualitative results to illustrate the response of our learned part classifiers on `Pascal-VOC-2007` test examples.

In Fig. 3 we demonstrate the selectivity of our part detectors by presenting image triplets consisting, in order, of *(i)* the image with candidate region bounding boxes superposed, *(ii)* the original image, and *(iii)* heatmaps for the part responses of each candidate region. Note in particular the selectivity of our part detectors: in all examples, the actual object occupies but a small fraction of the image area.

Fig. 3. Heatmaps for images `Pascal-VOC-2007` of classes *(clockwise from top-left)* "potted plant", "bird", "bottle" and "TV monitor".

Fig. 4. Discriminative parts for the four `Pascal-VOC-2007` classes *(clockwise from top-left)* "horse", "motorbike", "dining table", and "potted plant".

In Fig. 4, we illustrate the highest ranking candidate regions from all images for the part classifiers associated to the largest entries in the corresponding weight vector $\mathbf{w}_c$, with each row of each group of images corresponding to a different part classifier. Note that the part classifiers all become specialized to different object parts or poses.

7   Conclusions

We introduce SPLeapP, a novel part-based model for image classification. Based on non-linear part classifiers combined with part-dependent soft pooling – both being trained jointly with the image classifier – this new image model consistently surpasses standard pooling approaches and part-based models on several challenging classification tasks. In addition, we have experimentally observed that the proposed method does not need any particular initialization of the parts, contrarily to most of the recent part-based models which require a first step for selecting a few regions candidates from the training images before they actually start learning the parts.

References

1. Fischler, M.A., Elschlager, R.A.: The representation and matching of pictorial structures. IEEE Trans. Comput. **22**(1), 67–92 (1973)

2. Weber, M., Welling, M., Perona, P.: Towards automatic discovery of object categories. In: IEEE International Conference on Computer Vision and Pattern Recognition (2000)
3. Ullman, S., Sali, E., Vidal-Naquet, M.: A fragment-based approach to object representation and classification. In: Arcelli, C., Cordella, L.P., Sanniti di Baja, G. (eds.) IWVF 2001. LNCS, vol. 2059, pp. 85–100. Springer, Heidelberg (2001). doi:10.1007/3-540-45129-3_7
4. Felzenszwalb, P.F., Girshick, R.B., McAllester, D., Ramanan, D.: Object detection with discriminatively trained part-based models. IEEE Trans. Pattern Anal. Mach. Intell. **32**(9), 1627–1645 (2010)
5. Doersch, C., Gupta, A., Efros, A.A.: Mid-level visual element discovery as discriminative mode seeking. In: Proceedings on Neural Information Processing Systems (2013)
6. Singh, S., Gupta, A., Efros, A.: Unsupervised discovery of mid-level discriminative patches. In: European Conference on Computer Vision, pp. 73–86 (2012)
7. Juneja, M., Vedaldi, A., Jawahar, C., Zisserman, A.: Blocks that shout: distinctive parts for scene classification. In: IEEE International Conference on Computer Vision and Pattern Recognition (2013)
8. Doersch, C., Singh, S., Gupta, A., Sivic, J., Efros, A.: What makes Paris look like paris? ACM Trans. Graph. **31**(4) (2012)
9. Parizi, S.N., Vedaldi, A., Zisserman, A., Felzenszwalb, P.: Automatic discovery and optimization of parts for image classification. In: International Conference on Learning Representations (2015)
10. Lobel, H., Vidal, R., Soto, A.: Hierarchical joint max-margin learning of mid and top level representations for visual recognition. In: IEEE International Conference on Computer Vision (2013)
11. Hoai, M., Zisserman, A.: Improving human action recognition using score distribution and ranking. In: Asian Conference on Computer Vision (2014)
12. Mason, L., Baxter, J., Bartlett, P., Frean, M.: Boosting algorithms as gradient descent in function space. In: NIPS (1999)
13. Friedman, J., Hastie, T., Tibshirani, R., et al.: Additive logistic regression: a statistical view of boosting (with discussion and a rejoinder by the authors). Ann. Stat. **28**(2), 337–407 (2000)
14. Oquab, M., Bottou, L., Laptev, I., Sivic, J.: Learning and transferring mid-level image representations using convolutional neural networks. In: IEEE International Conference on Computer Vision and Pattern Recognition (2014)
15. Chatfield, K., Simonyan, K., Vedaldi, A., Zisserman, A.: Return of the devil in the details: delving deep into convolutional nets. In: British Machine Vision Conference (2014)
16. Krizhevsky, A., Sutskever, I., Hinton, G.E.: ImageNet classification with deep convolutional neural networks. In: Proceedings on Neural Information Processing Systems (2012)
17. Razavian, A.S., Azizpour, H., Sullivan, J., Carlsson, S.: CNN features off-the-shelf: an astounding baseline for recognition. In: Computer Vision and Pattern Recognition Workshops (2014)
18. Everingham, M., Eslami, S.M.A., Van Gool, L., Williams, C.K.I., Winn, J., Zisserman, A.: The pascal visual object classes challenge: a retrospective. Int. J. Comput. Vis. **111**(1), 98–136 (2015)
19. Gong, Y., Wang, L., Guo, R., Lazebnik, S.: Multi-scale orderless pooling of deep convolutional activation features. In: European Conference on Computer Vision (2014)

20. Kulkarni, P., Zepeda, J., Jurie, F., Perez, P., Chevallier, L.: Hybrid multi-layer deep cnn/aggregator feature for image classification. In: IEEE International Conference on Acoustics, Speech, and Signal Processing (2015)
21. Cimpoi, M., Maji, S., Vedaldi, A.: Deep filter banks for texture recognition and segmentation. In: IEEE International Conference on Computer Vision and Pattern Recognition (2015)
22. Jégou, H., Douze, M., Schmid, C., Pérez, P.: Aggregating local descriptors into a compact image representation. In: IEEE International Conference on Computer Vision and Pattern Recognition (2010)
23. Li, Y., Liu, L., Shen, C., van den Hengel, A.: Mid-level deep pattern mining. In: IEEE International Conference on Computer Vision and Pattern Recognition (2015)
24. Sicre, R., Jurie, F.: Discovering and aligning discriminative mid-level features for image classification. In: International Conference on Pattern Recognition (2014)
25. Gulcehre, C., Cho, K., Pascanu, R., Bengio, Y.: Learned-norm pooling for deep feedforward and recurrent neural networks. In: Calders, T., Esposito, F., Hüllermeier, E., Meo, R. (eds.) ECML PKDD 2014. LNCS (LNAI), vol. 8724, pp. 530–546. Springer, Heidelberg (2014). doi:10.1007/978-3-662-44848-9_34
26. Goodfellow, I.J., Warde-Farley, D., Mirza, M., Courville, A.C., Bengio, Y.: Maxout networks. ICML 28(3), 1319–1327 (2013)
27. Lee, C.Y., Gallagher, P.W., Tu, Z.: Generalizing pooling functions in convolutional neural networks: mixed, gated, and tree. In: International Conference on Artificial Intelligence and Statistics (2016)
28. Quattoni, A., Torralba, A.: Recognizing indoor scenes. In: IEEE International Conference on Computer Vision and Pattern Recognition (2009)
29. Delaitre, V., Laptev, I., Sivic, J.: Recognizing human actions in still images: a study of bag-of-features and part-based representations. In: British Machine Vision Conference (2010)
30. van de Sande, K.E.A., Uijlings, J.R.R., Gevers, T., Smeulders, A.W.M.: Segmentation as selective search for object recognition. In: IEEE International Conference on Computer Vision (2011)
31. Chavali, N., Agrawal, H., Mahendru, A., Batra, D.: Object-proposal evaluation protocol is 'gameable'. arXiv:1505.05836 (2015)
32. Jia, Y., Shelhamer, E., Donahue, J., Karayev, S., Long, J., Girshick, R., Guadarrama, S., Darrell, T.: Caffe: convolutional architecture for fast feature embedding. In: Proceedings of the 22nd ACM International Conference on Multimedia (2014)
33. Simonyan, K., Zisserman, A.: Very deep convolutional networks for large-scale image recognition. arXiv preprint arXiv:1409.1556 (2014)
34. Zhou, B., Lapedriza, A., Xiao, J., Torralba, A., Oliva, A.: Learning deep features for scene recognition using places database. In: Proceedings on Neural Information Processing Systems (2014)
35. Kulkarni, P., Zepeda, J., Jurie, F., Perez, P., Chevallier, L.: Max-margin, single-layer adaptation of transferred image features. In: BigVision Workshop, Computer Vision and Pattern Recognition (2015)
36. He, K., Zhang, X., Ren, S., Sun, J.: Spatial pyramid pooling in deep convolutional networks for visual recognition. IEEE Trans. Pattern Anal. Mach. Intell. 37(9), 1904–1916 (2015)
37. Szegedy, C., Liu, W., Jia, Y., Sermanet, P., Reed, S., Anguelov, D., Erhan, D., Vanhoucke, V., Rabinovich, A.: Going deeper with convolutions. In: IEEE International Conference on Computer Vision and Pattern Recognition (2015)

38. Khan, F.S., Anwer, R.M., van de Weijer, J., Bagdanov, A.D., Lopez, A.M., Felsberg, M.: Coloring action recognition in still images. Int. J. Comput. Vis. **105**(3), 205–221 (2013)
39. Sharma, G., Jurie, F., Schmid, C.: Discriminative spatial saliency for image classification. In: IEEE International Conference on Computer Vision and Pattern Recognition (2012)
40. Sharma, G., Jurie, F., Schmid, C.: Expanded parts model for human attribute and action recognition in still images. In: IEEE International Conference on Computer Vision and Pattern Recognition (2013)

Spatial Attention Deep Net with Partial PSO for Hierarchical Hybrid Hand Pose Estimation

Qi Ye, Shanxin Yuan$^{(\boxtimes)}$, and Tae-Kyun Kim

Department of Electrical and Electronic Engineering,
Imperial College London, London, UK
{q.ye14,s.yuan14,tk.kim}@imperial.ac.uk

Abstract. Discriminative methods often generate hand poses kinematically implausible, then generative methods are used to correct (or verify) these results in a hybrid method. Estimating 3D hand pose in a hierarchy, where the high-dimensional output space is decomposed into smaller ones, has been shown effective. Existing hierarchical methods mainly focus on the decomposition of the output space while the input space remains almost the same along the hierarchy. In this paper, a hybrid hand pose estimation method is proposed by applying the kinematic hierarchy strategy to the input space (as well as the output space) of the discriminative method by a spatial attention mechanism and to the optimization of the generative method by hierarchical Particle Swarm Optimization (PSO). The spatial attention mechanism integrates cascaded and hierarchical regression into a CNN framework by transforming both the input (and feature space) and the output space, which greatly reduces the viewpoint and articulation variations. Between the levels in the hierarchy, the hierarchical PSO forces the kinematic constraints to the results of the CNNs. The experimental results show that our method significantly outperforms four state-of-the-art methods and three baselines on three public benchmarks.

Keywords: Hierarchical hand pose estimation · Particle Swarm Optimization · Convolutional neural network · Iterative refinement · Spatial attention · Hybrid method · Kinematic constraints

1 Introduction

The problem of 3D hand pose estimation can be formulated as the configuration of the variables representing a hand model given depth images. The problem is challenging with complicated variations caused by high Degree of Freedom (DoF)

Q. Ye and S. Yuan are equally contributed.

Electronic supplementary material The online version of this chapter (doi:10. 1007/978-3-319-46484-8_21) contains supplementary material, which is available to authorized users.

© Springer International Publishing AG 2016
B. Leibe et al. (Eds.): ECCV 2016, Part VIII, LNCS 9912, pp. 346–361, 2016.
DOI: 10.1007/978-3-319-46484-8_21

articulations, multiple viewpoints, self-similar parts, severe self-occlusions, different shapes and sizes. With these variations, configurations of the hand variables given a depth image lie in a high-dimensional space.

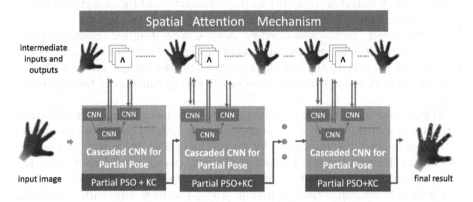

Fig. 1. Structure of the proposed method. The Spatial Attention Mechanism integrates the cascaded and hierarchical hand pose estimation into one framework. The hand pose is estimated layer by layer in the order of the articulation complexity, with the spatial attention module to transform the input/feature and output space. Within each layer, the partial pose is iteratively refined both in viewpoint and location with the spatial attention module, which leads both the feature and output space to a canonical one. After the refinement, the partial PSO is applied to select estimations within the hand kinematic constraints (short as KC in the figure) among the results of the cascaded estimation. Λ denotes the CNN feature maps.

Many prior works have achieved good performance by different methods [1–16]. Among the discriminative methods that learn the mapping from the depth images to the hand pose configurations, Sun *et al.* [17] refine the hand pose by two levels of a hierarchy (palm, and fingers) in a cascaded manner by viewpoint-invariant pixel difference features in random forest. Oberweger *et al.* [18] apply the cascaded method to CNN for iteratively refining partial poses, initialized by the full hand pose estimation.

The discriminative and generative methods are combined in a hierarchy in the Hierarchical Sampling Optimization (HSO) [19]. In each layer, random forests are first used to regress partial poses and a partial joint energy function is introduced to evaluate the results and select the best one to the next layer. The hierarchical optimization with refinement that estimates the hand pose in the order of articulation complexity of the hand is a promising framework as the searching space is decomposed into smaller parts and the refinement leads to more accurate results.

However, the method in [17] and the discriminative part of HSO [19] only focus on breaking down the complexity in the output space hierarchically, i.e., decomposing the hand variables; in other words, the hierarchical strategy is carried out in the output space while the input space or the feature space stays the same along the hierarchy. For the cascaded refinement [17,18], the input or feature space is only partially updated with results from previous stages, either by cropping or rotating, and the features [17] are computed on the original whole images in each iteration. In addition, the optimization of the energy function is performed in a brute force way in [19].

In this paper, we propose a hybrid method with iterative (cascade) refinement for hand pose estimation, illustrated in Fig. 1, which not only applies the hierarchical strategy to the output space but also the feature space of the discriminative part and the optimization of the energy function of the generative part.

For the discriminative part, a spatial attention mechanism is introduced to integrate cascaded (with multiple stages) and hierarchical (with multiple layers) regression into a CNN framework by transforming both the input (and feature space) and the output space. In the transformed space, the viewpoint and articulation variations of the feature space and the output space is largely reduced, which greatly simplifies the estimation. Along the hierarchy, with the spatial attention mechanism, the features for the initial stage of each layer are spatially transformed from input images based on the estimation results of the last stage of the previous layer. Within each layer, the features are iteratively updated by the spatial attention mechanism. By this dynamic spatial attention mechanism, not only the most relevant features for the hand variable estimation are selected but also the features are transformed to a canonical, expected viewpoint gradually, which simplifies the estimations in the following stages and layers. As such, discriminative features are extracted for each partial pose estimation in each iteration. In this way, we learn a deep net with spatial transformation tailored towards our hand pose estimation problem.

In the generative part, the optimization organized in the hierarchy prevents error accumulation from previous layers. Between the levels of the hierarchy, partial PSO with a new energy function is incorporated to enforce hand kinematic constraints. It generates samples under the Gaussian distribution centered on the results of the discriminative method, and selects estimations within the hand kinematic constraints. The search space of the generative method is largely reduced by estimating partial poses.

To evaluate our method, extensive experiments have been conducted on three public benchmarks. The experimental results show that our method significantly outperforms state-of-the-art methods on these datasets.

2   Related Work

Feature Selection with Attention. Learning or selecting transformation-invariant representations or features by neural networks has been studied in many prior works and among them, attention mechanism has gained much attention in object recognition and localization recently. Girshick *et al.* [20] produce region proposals as representations for CNN to focus its localization capacity on these regions instead of a whole image. DRAW [21] integrates a spatial attention mechanism mimicking that of human eye into a generative model to generate image samples in different transformations. Sermanet*et al.* [22] use an attention model to direct a high resolution input to the most discriminative regions to do fine-grained categorization. An end-to-end spatial transformation neural network is proposed in [23].

The attention mechanism is tailored to our highly articulated problem by breaking down to the viewpoint and articulation complexity in a hierarchy and refining estimation results in a cascade. The hierarchical structure with cascade refinement enables us to use a spatial transformation to not only select most relevant features as in prior works aforementioned and also transform the feature and the output space into a new one which leads to our expected, canonical space.

Cascaded and Hierarchical Estimation. The cascaded regression strategy has shown good performances in the face analyses [24,25], human body estimation [26,27] and hand pose estimation [17,18] and in most of these works, the features are hand-crafted, such as pixel difference features [17,26], landmark distance features [24], SIFT [28]. Oberweger *et al.* [18] use CNN to learn features automatically but with only partial spatial transformations by cropping input images and in another work [4], they use the images generated by CNN as the feedback to refine the estimation. Sun *et al.* [17] refine the hand pose using pixel difference features updated for viewpoints of whole images in each iteration. The features in both works are partially transformed either by cropping patches from the input images or rotating features calculated from the whole image. On the other hand, a hierarchical strategy that estimates hand poses in the order of hand articulation complexity achieves good performance [17,19]. HSO [19] estimates partial poses separately in the kinematic hierarchy while the input space remains unchanged. Sun *et al.* [17] estimate partial poses holistically in two layers of a hierarchy by calculating rotation invariant pixel difference features from the whole image.

Our proposed method fully transforms the feature space and the output space together in both cascaded and hierarchical manner. For each iteration of the cascade, no new features are learned as features are obtained by a spatial transformation applied to the feature maps of an initial stage. For the hierarchy, only a small region which has been transformed to a canonical view is fed into CNN. In this way, the hierarchical and cascaded strategy is not only applied to the output space as in prior work but also the transformed input and feature space.

Hybrid Methods. A standard way of combining the discriminative methods and the generative methods is first providing candidate results by the discriminative methods, then using them as the initial state of the generative methods to optimize full hand poses [3,16,29,30], and it has demonstrated good performances. As discussed in the above, searching the full hand pose space has a high complexity. We adopt a partial pose optimization to reduce the complexity of each estimation, which is integrated into our hierarchical structure. HSO [19] also has partial pose evaluations between the levels of a hierarchy but the evaluations are carried out in a brute-force way, while we propose a new kinematic energy function which is optimized by the partial PSO.

3   Method Overview

Hand pose estimation is to estimate the 3-D locations of the hand's 21 key joints S given depth image I, which is normalized by the size of the depth image. The ground truth of S is denoted as S^*. In our approach we divide the 21 joints into four layers $\{S_l\}_{l=0}^{3}$ where the value of l is also the order of our hierarchical estimation, see Fig. 2. For each layer l, j is used to denote a single joint on one finger, in the order from thumb to pinky with the number starting from 1 to 5 (for the wrist joint in the first layer, j is 0). With all the definitions, the hand variables to be estimated are expressed as $\{\{S_{lj}\}_{j=0}^{5}\}_{l=0} \cup \{\{S_{lj}\}_{j=1}^{5}\}_{l=1}^{3}$.

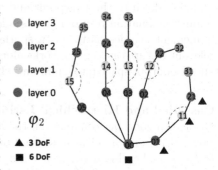

Fig. 2. Hand model. 21 joints are divided into four layers, each joint overlaid with index number. φ_2 is the bone rotations for five joints in Layer 2.

Our method estimates (and trains) 4 layers sequentially with the spatial attention mechanism(see Sect. 4.1) linking the layers by transforming the input (and feature) and output space interactively and partial PSO enforcing kinematic constraints to the CNN prediction, which is shown in Fig. 1. In each layer l, the estimation is refined iteratively by learning the residual of the ground truth S_{lj}^* to the results S_{lj}^{k-1} of the previous stage, where k denotes the kth cascaded stage (for details, see Sect. 4.2). The spatial transformation modules are applied to the feature maps from the initial stage of the cascade and the outputs of stage $k-1$ to get aligned attention features and output space for the learning of residual of stage k.

The result $S_{lj}^{K_l}$ of the final stage K_l is fed into the post-optimization process using PSO for initialization. The partial PSO (see Sect. 5) is introduced to enforce kinematic constraints to the results from the cascaded estimation and refine the partial pose. Along with PSO, we adopt the hand bone model (Fig. 2), which has 51 DoFs: layer 0 has 6 DoFs, denoting the global orientation (represented by a 4-D unit quaternion) and global location (3 DoFs); each of layer 1, 2, 3, has 15 DoFs, denoting the five bone rotations. Our hand model fixes the six joints on the palm and keeps the bone lengths of the fingers.

The optimal of the PSO is passed to layer $l + 1$. Before the estimation of the next layer, the spatial attention mechanism is applied on input images and estimation results of current layer (and the ground truth for next layer during training).

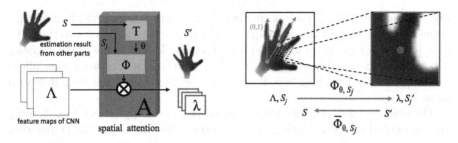

Fig. 3. Spatial attention mechanism. Left: the spatial attention module is split into the calculation of rotation T and the spatial transformation Φ. Right: the mapping between input feature maps and output features maps. For clarity, we use hand images to represent the feature maps. Both the feature maps, estimation results (and ground truth in training) are transformed to a new space by Φ_{θ, S_j}. The locations can be transformed back by the inverse function $\bar{\Phi}_{\theta, S_j}$.

4   Partial Pose Estimation by Spatial Attention Deep Net

4.1   Spatial Attention Mechanism for Hand Space

Before the elaboration of the hand pose estimation, the mechanism of spatial attention is explained. For notational simplicity, we skip the layer index l and the stage index k as the mechanism is applied to all layers and all stages similarly. The inputs of the spatial attention module are the estimation result of S_j , where j denotes j_{th} joint in the layer, and the features maps of CNN (and input images), denoted by $\Lambda \in \mathbb{R}^{W \times H}$.

The spatial module A, illustrated in the left figure of Fig. 3, can be split into two parts: the calculation of rotation T and the pixel mapping Φ. The global in-plane rotation θ (see the right figure of Fig. 3) is the angle between the vector of the wrist joint (joint 00 in Fig. 2) to the root joint of middle finger (joint 03 in Fig. 2) in Layer 0 and the vector $(0, 1)$ representing the upright hand pose and can be expressed as $\theta = T(S_3, S_0)$. For the other layers l ($l > 0$), the rotation is obtained from Layer 0.

For the pixel mapping, displayed in the right figure of Fig. 3, in which *pixel* here means an element of the feature maps (and input images), we use (x^i, y^i) to denote a pixel on the input feature map Λ and (x^o, y^o) on the output feature maps $\lambda \in \mathbb{R}^{W' \times H'}$. For the deep features for joint j, the translation parameter is the xy coordinates of S_j on the feature map (Λ) coordinate system, i.e. (t_x, t_y). The mapping between (x^i, y^i) and (x^o, y^o) is

$$\begin{bmatrix} x^i \\ y^i \\ 1 \end{bmatrix} = \begin{bmatrix} b \cdot \cos(\theta) & b \cdot \sin(\theta) & t_x \\ -b \cdot \sin(\theta) & b \cdot \cos(\theta) & t_y \end{bmatrix} \begin{bmatrix} x^o \\ y^o \\ 1 \end{bmatrix} \tag{1}$$

$$(\lambda, S') = \Phi_{\theta, S_j}(\Lambda, S) \tag{2}$$

where (x^i, y^i) and (x^o, y^o) are normalized by its corresponding width and height of the input and output feature maps. b is the ratio of the width of λ to the width of Λ (or the height as we keep the aspect ratio). If b is 1, the transformation is rotation and translation. When b is less than 1, the transformation allows cropping and the cropping size is the same as the size of the output feature maps λ.

Once we get the transformation parameters, the mapping between λ and Λ are established by interpolating the pixel values. We also apply the transformation to the estimation results S (and the ground truth S^* in training) by Eq. 1, only on their xy coordinates, the value of the z coordinate remains unchanged. All the inputs are in a new coordinate system, or a new space. We use Φ_{θ, S_j} in Eq. 2 to wrap the mapping function in Eq. 1 for all the pixels on the feature maps Λ and also symbolize the transformation for S. $\bar{\Phi}_{\theta, S_j}$, denoting the inverse function of Φ_{θ, S_j}, acquired by replacing θ by $-\theta$, (t_x, t_y) by $-(t_x, t_y)$ and b by $1/b$ in Eq. 1, transforms the output space of CNNs to the original one.

4.2   Cascaded Regression Within Each Hierarchical Layer

Within each layer of the hierarchy, the joint locations $\{S_j\}$ are estimated in a cascaded manner, shown in Fig. 4. We leave out the layer subscript l as the cascaded regression is applied to all layers. At first, an initial CNN model ($\{f_j^0\}$) regresses the joint location $\{S_j\}$. It not only provides an initial state $\{S_j^0\}$ for the following iterative refinements but also deep feature maps Λ for other regressors. In the following stages, the joint locations are refined iteratively. Between the refinement stages, the spatial attention modules A transform the deep feature maps Λ to a new space based on the estimation result $\{S_j^{k-1}\}$ from the previous stage to achieve viewpoint-invariant and discriminative features for the following regressors.

For a certain joint j in stage k, the features λ_j^k is mapped from Λ by $\Phi_{\theta^{k-1}, S_j^{k-1}}$, where the S_j^{k-1} is the result of the previous stage and θ^{k-1} is calculated by $T(S_0^{k-1}, S_3^{k-1})$ (the updating of θ happens only in Layer 0, and for

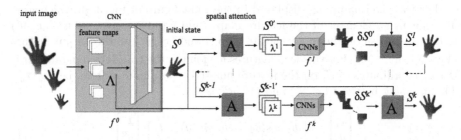

Fig. 4. Cascaded partial pose estimation with spatial attention modules for Layer 0. The feature maps Λ from the initial stage is transformed by spatial attention modules A with estimation result S^{k-1} form previous stage before feeding into the current stage k.

other layers the value of θ is fixed after Layer 0). At the same time, the estimation result S_j^{k-1} and the ground truth S_j^* are both transformed by the module, resulting $S_j^{k-1'}$ and $S_j^{*'}$. Therefore, all the inputs for the regressor f_j^k in stage k that estimates the residual $S_j^{*'} - S_j^{k-1'}$ of joint j are in a new space. After training or testing, the output of the regressor is then transformed back by $\bar{\Phi}_{\theta,S_j}$. For the joint j, the process is repeated until a satisfactory result is achieved (seen Sect. 6 for the choice of cascaded stages)and we use K_l to denote the final stage for Layer l. For other joints, the refinement is carried out in parallel with the same process.

The above refinements for a single joint can be mathematically expressed as

$$(\lambda_j^k, S_j^{k-1'}) = \Phi_{\theta^{k-1}, S_j^{k-1}}(\Lambda, S_j^{k-1}) \tag{3}$$

$$S_j^k = \bar{\Phi}_{\theta^{k-1}, S_j^{k-1}}(f_j^k(\lambda_j^k) + S_j^{k-1'}) \tag{4}$$

where Eq. 3 is the spatial attention mechanism which transforms all the inputs of stage k to a new space and Eq. 4 estimates the residual $\delta S_j^{k'}$ by $f_j^k(\lambda_j^k)$, updates the estimation by adding the residual estimated $\delta S_j^{k'}$ to the result from the previous stage $S_j^{k-1'}$, and transforms the added result back to the original space.

4.3   Hierarchical Regression

For the regression in layer 0, all the joints in the initial stage are learned together in order to keep the kinematic constraints among them as the values of these joints are highly correlated. The input of the initializor f_0^0 is multi-resolution images I, the original image and the images downsampled from the original one by the factor of 2 and 4, the output is the joint locations. The input and feature space of the regressors for different joints in the cascaded stages are updated separately by the spatial function $\Phi_{\theta^{k-1}, S_{0j}^{k-1}}$. The output of the regressor in the stage k refines the estimation result S_{0j}^{k-1} in the previous stage $k-1$ in a new space and are transformed back by $\bar{\Phi}_{\theta^{k-1}, S_{0j}^{k-1}}$. The cascaded regression stop in stage K_0. The whole refinement stages are the same as in Sect. 4.2.

For the hierarchical estimation in layer $l(l > 0)$, the inputs are multi-resolution input images I, the estimation result $\{S_{l-1,j}^{K_{l-1}}\}$ from the previous layer $l-1$ and the viewpoint estimation θ^{K_0} from layer 0. For notational simplicity, we denote θ^{K_0} as θ and skip the joint index j. θ is fixed for all layers $(l > 0)$ and the same process is applied to all the joints separately.

The input space for the initializor f_l^0 of layer l is transformed from multi-resolution images I by the spatial attention module. The mapping is

$$(I', S_{l-1}^{K_{l-1}}, S_l^{*'}) = \Phi_{\theta, S_{l-1}^{K_{l-1}}}(I, S_{l-1}^{K_{l-1}}, S_l^*) \tag{5}$$

so the input for the initializor f_l^0 is patches I' cropped from multi-resolution input images I centred at $S_{l-1}^{K_{l-1}}$ and its corresponding coordinates in the downsampled images, and rotated by θ. The offset labels for training f_l^0 is $\Delta S_l^{*'} = S_l^{*'} - S_{l-1}^{K_{l-1}'}$, which is equivalent to the sum of the ground truth offset $S_l^{*'} - S_{l-1}^{*'}$ and the remaining residual of the previous layer $S_{l-1}^{*'} - S_{l-1}^{K_{l-1}'}$. This implies the initializor f_l^0 not only predicts the joint offsets of the current layer to the previous layer but also corrects the residual errors of the previous layer.

The initializor f_l^0 provides the initial offset state $\Delta S_l^{0'}$ and feature maps Λ for the refinement stages. For the refinement stages, the procedure is the same as discussed in Sect. 4.2. The only difference from Sect. 4.2 is that the viewpoint is static, whose value is the result of the final cascaded stage in Layer 0, and feature maps Λ has already been transformed by rotation in the initial stage; thus for the stage k, the feature space is transformed and updated by the function $\Phi_{S_l^{k-1}}$ (no rotation transformation) and the output space is transformed with $\Phi_{\theta, S_l^{k-1}}$ (rotation and translation transformation).

The parameter b in the spatial attention module needs to be set. For the initial stage (except the initial stage of layer 0), it is set according to the offset range. All the ground truth S_l^* and the estimation result $S_{l-1}^{K_{l-1}}$ of layer $l-1$ is first transformed by $\Phi_{\theta, S_{l-1}^{K_{l-1}}}$ with $b = 1$ to get means along the xy coordinates of the absolute value of the offsets for all the training data in the new space. b is set to be two times of the larger offset mean divided by original image width W. For the refinement stages, they are set according to the residual range of the estimation results in the initial stage. All the ground truth and the estimation results of the initial stage are first transformed by Φ_{θ^0, S_j^0} (for layer $l(l > 0)$, θ^0 is the final estimation result θ^{K_0} of layer 0) with $b = 1$ to get means along the xy coordinates of the absolute value of the residuals for all the training data in the new space. As the feature maps are filtered by kernels, max-pooled, and have different resolutions but the ground truth are normalized according to original image size, S_j^0 and the mean of residual should also be changed with the kernel size, the pool size and the downsampling ratio to set the value of b.

5 Partial PSO with Kinematic Constraints for Final Refinement

For each layer, based on our discriminative part's prediction, we do final refinement by explicitly introducing partial kinematic constraints with Particle Swarm Optimization. Particle Swarm Optimization (PSO) is a stochastic optimization algorithm introduce by Kennedy and Eberhart [31] in 1995, originated in the social behaviors' studies of synchronous bird flocking and fish schooling. The original PSO algorithm has been modified by several researchers to improve its convergence properties and search capabilities. We adopt the variant of PSO with an inertia weight parameter [32].

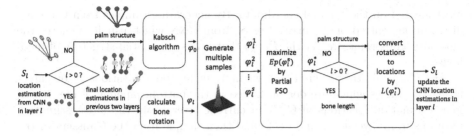

Fig. 5. Pose refinement with partial PSO enforcing kinematic constraint. Given palm spatial structure and layer 0's location estimation by CNN, we first inference the φ_0 using Kabsch algorithm [33], and then find φ_0^* maximizing the energy function by partial PSO. The rotation φ_0^* is converted to locations using the palm structure to update the CNN estimation result. For other partial pose $\varphi_l (l > 0)$, the optimization is the same with layer 0 while the inference for the initialization of the optimization is calculating the bone rotation and the conversion back to locations uses the bone length.

Our whole hand pose for PSO is defined as $\{\varphi_0, \varphi_1, \varphi_2, \varphi_3\}$, where $\varphi_0 \in \mathbb{R}^7$ and $\varphi_l(l = 1, 2, 3) \in \mathbb{R}^{15}$ are our partial poses. $\varphi_0 = \{q, x, y, z\}$, where q is a 4-D unit quaternion [1,3] representing the global rotation, $[x, y, z]$ is the global location of the whole hand. φ_l denotes five 3D Euler angles in layer l, each angle representing a bone rotation which is the angle between the bone connecting the joint in layer l and the corresponding joint in layer $l - 1$ and the other bone connecting the joint in layer $l - 1$ and the corresponding joint in layer $l - 2$ (when $l - 2 < 0$, the corresponding joint in layer $l - 2$ is wrist). Figure 2 demonstrates φ_2, five angles in layer $l = 2$.

Energy Function. For each layer, PSO is used to estimate the final partial pose base on the inferred partial pose. We designed a new energy function that applied to partial pose and explicitly taking into account the kinematic constraints. Our energy function Ep for each layer is as follows:

$$Ep(\varphi_l^s) = P(\varphi_l^s)Q(\varphi_l^s), \tag{6}$$

where the first item, $P(\varphi_l^s) \propto N(\varphi_l^s; \varphi_l, \Sigma)$, is the prior probability of the s_{th} Gaussian sample from mean φ_l, Σ is a diagonal covariance matrix that is manually set to ensure that each parameter varies in valid ranges. $s = 1, 2, ..., N$ is the index of samples for each layer, we set $N = 100$ in our experiments. $P(\varphi_0^s)$ encodes the spatial structure of the six joints on the palm and $P(\varphi_l^s)(l = 1, 2, 3)$ keeps the bone length information.

To acquire the prior probability $P(\varphi_0^s)$, we first choose Kabsch algorithm [33] to find the optimal affine transformation matrix (global translation and rotation, i.e. φ_0) from our hand model for the six joints on the palm to the CNN results, as shown in the top pipeline of Fig. 5. The hand model for the palm joints can be seen as the palm joint locations of an upfront reference hand pose with wrist located on the original coordinate. By generating samples from Gaussian distribution centred on φ_0 instead of S_0 from CNN which usually violates the kinematic constraint, we get the $P(\varphi_0^s)$ that keeps the spatial structure of palm joints.

For $P(\varphi_l^s)$ of other layers $l > 0$, we first get five bone rotations φ_l by calculating the angles which are demonstrated in the bottom pipeline of Fig. 5 with joint estimation locations of CNN in current layer l and the joint estimation locations from layer $l-1$ and $l-2$, and then sample from the Gaussian distribution centred on φ_l. When converting rotations to locations for evaluations of the second term, we enforce the constraint of the bone length.

The second item, $Q(\varphi_l^s) \propto \sum_{S_{lj}^s \in L(\varphi_l)}[B(S_{lj}^s) + D(S_{lj}^s)]$, denotes the likelihood of all joint $\{S_{lj}^s\}$ belongs to the hand, where $L(\varphi_l^s)$ converts rotations φ_l^s into locations $\{S_{lj}^s\}$. Similar to Tang et al. [19] silver function, the term $B(S_{lj}^s)$ forces each joint joint S_{lj}^s to lie inside the hand silhouette. The term $D(S_{lj}^s)$ makes sure joint S_{lj}^s lies inside the depth range of a major point cloud.

6 Experiment

The evaluation of our proposed method is conducted on three publicly datasets. **ICVL** [19] dataset is a real sequence captured by Intel RealSense with the range of view about 120 degrees consisting 1596 test frames and 16008 training frames. 16 bone centre locations are provided for each hand pose. **NYU** [30] dataset is a real sequence acquired by PrimeSense containing 8252 test-set and 72757 training-set frames with a full range of views. 36 joint locations are provided for each hand pose. **MSRC** [3] dataset is a challenging dataset that covers a full range of views and complex articulations with 100000 synthetic images in the training-set and 2000 synthetic images in the test set. 22 joint locations are provided for each hand pose. As the annotations of these datasets do not conform to each other, we use the annotation version in [19] that labels locations of the joints as demonstrated in Fig. 2.

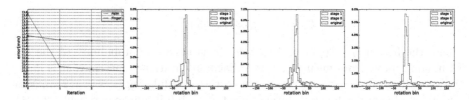

Fig. 6. First: Errors for a joint on the palm S_{00} and a joint on the middle finger S_{13} for 4 stages. Second, third and forth: In-plane viewpoint distribution of testing set for different stages on ICVL, NYU, MSRC respectively. The blue, green and red line corresponds to the in-plane rotation distribution of original ground truth, ground truth rotated after initial stage and the first stage. The rotation estimation error after the initial stage and the first stage is 5.9 and 4.4 for ICVL, 8.0 and 6.1 for NYU, 10.9 and 9.2 for MSRC in the unit of degree. (Color figure online)

We compare the results of different methods by the proportion of joints within a certain maximum error of the distance of the predicted results to the ground truth [3]. We set the number of iterations K on the observation of the error saturates after a certain stage in the cascaded stages, shown in the first figure of Fig. 6. We set K_0 for Layer 0 to 1 and $K_l, l > 0$ to 0, which gives us a good balance between the accuracy and the memory consumption. All the experiments are run with Intel i7, 24 GB RAM and NVIDIA GeForce GTX 750 Ti. The structures for our CNN models are implemented by Theano [34] and the details are provided in the supplementary material. For our partial PSO, we generates 100 samples for each layer, and iterate 5 generations.

6.1 Self-comparison

To evaluate our proposed method (Hybr_Hier_SA) and the discriminative part Hier_SA, we implement three baselines. The first baseline (Holi) estimates the whole hand pose with a single CNN. The second baseline (Holi_Derot) consists of two steps: one step predicting the in-plane rotation of the hand pose by a CNN and rotating the hand pose to upright view; the other step estimating the whole hand pose by another CNN. The third one (Holi_SA) is a holistic cascaded regression network without hierarchy, which initializes the whole hand pose with a CNN and refines the hand pose joint by joint via spatial attention mechanism by a set of CNNs. For fair comparison, we set the size of the parameters of the methods to be roughly the same: the parameters are stored in 32 bit float and the size of parameters is 130 MB.

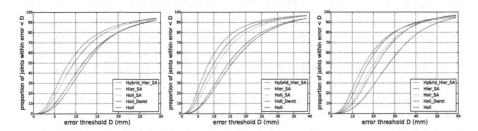

Fig. 7. Comparison of different methods on three datasets. Left:ICVL; Middle: NYU; Right: MSRC.

On all the datasets, Hier_SA outperforms the baselines significantly, see Fig. 7. The improvement margin is related to the range of viewpoints and the complexity of articulations. The in-plane rotation distributions of original data, the ones after the initial stage and the first stage are shown in Fig. 6. As MSRC dataset covers a full range of viewpoints and articulations, the improvement on this dataset from the baseline Holi is the largest. For example, the percentages of frames under 20 mm on ICVL, NYU and MSRC are improved by Hier_SA with margins of 5 %, 18 % and 30 % respectively, compared to that of Holi.

The curves of Hier_SA and Holi_SA on three datasets illustrate the efficacy of hierarchical strategy in conquering the articulations, while the curves of Holi_SA, Holi and Holi_Derot show that spatial attention mechanism is effect in reducing the viewpoint and articulation complexity. By refining viewpoints with stages and spatially transforming the feature space to focus on the most relevant area for a certain joint estimation, Holi_SA achieves better results than Holi and Holi_Derot. Note that the curve of Holi_Derot is under that of Holi on ICVL dataset, which implies that the error of estimating the rotation by a separate network may deteriorate the later estimation when the variations of the viewpoint in training set is small.

Hybr_Hier_SA further improves the result of Hier_SA by a large margin consistently on all the datasets, which verifies that the kinematic constraints by the partial PSO is effective.

6.2 Comparison with Prior Works

We compare our work with 4 state-of-the-arts methods: Hierarchical Sampling Optimization (HSO) [19], Sharp et al. [3], HandsDeep [18], FeedLoop [4] on three datasets, see Fig. 8. The former two are hybrid methods and the latter two are refinement method based on CNN. The results are obtained either from the authors for HSO [19] or from the reported accuracies [3,4,18]. The examples of the estimation results of HandsDeep, FeedLoop, HSO and our method are shown in Fig. 9.

On ICVL dataset, we compare HSO with parameters set as $N = 100, M = 150$. Our method is better by 26 % of joints within $D = 10$ mm. On NYU dataset, we compare our method with HandsDeep and FeedLoop which are all based on CNN. As the hand model of these methods are different, we evaluate the result by comparing the error of the subset of 11 joint locations (removing the palm joints except the root joint of thumb). Our estimation result is better than HandsDeep by a large margin, for example, an improvement of 10 % within $D = 30$ mm, and achieves roughly the same accuracy with FeedLoop.

We finally test our method with HSO and Sharp et al. on MSRC dataset. The dataset is more challenging than the above two as it covers a wider range of viewpoints and articulations. The curves demonstrate the superiority of our

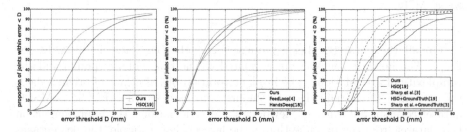

Fig. 8. Comparison of prior work on three datasets. Left:ICVL; Middle: NYU; Right: MSRC.

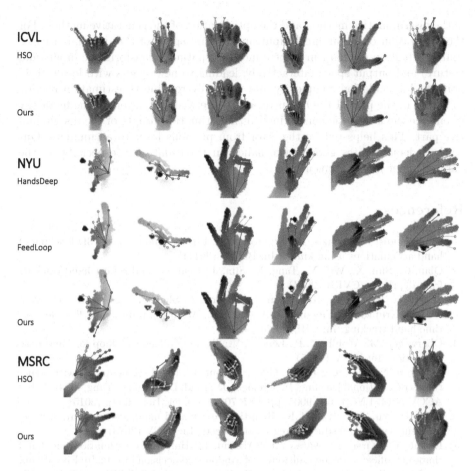

Fig. 9. Examples comparing to prior work on three datasets. The first two rows, the middle three rows, and the last two rows are examples from ICVL dataset, NYU dataset and MSRC dataset, respectively. Compared to other methods, our method has a good performance in discriminating the fingers and a better precision. For many challenging viewpoints, our method still has a good estimation.

method under large variations. For example, the proportion of joints (when $D = 30\,\mathrm{mm}$) of our method is 35 % and 50 % more than those of HSO and Sharp *et al.* respectively. Note that our estimation is even better than the results of HSO and Sharp *et al.* using ground truth rotation [19].

7 Conclusion

To apply the hierarchy strategy to the input and feature space and enforce the hand kinematic constraints to the hand pose estimation, we present a hybrid method by applying the kinematic hierarchy to both the input and feature space of the discriminative method and the optimization of the generative method. For the integration of hierarchical input and feature space of the discriminative, a spatial attention mechanism is introduced to spatially transform the input (and feature) and output space interactively, leading to new spaces with lesser viewpoint and articulation complexity and gradually refining th estimation results. In addition, the partial PSO is incorporated between the layers of the hierarchy to enforce the kinematic constraints to the estimation results of the discriminative part. This helps reduce the error from previous layer to accumulate. Our method demonstrates good performance on three datasets, especially on the dataset under large variations.

References

1. Oikonomidis, I., Kyriazis, N., Argyros, A.A.: Efficient model-based 3D tracking of hand articulations using kinect. In: BMVC (2011)
2. Qian, C., Sun, X., Wei, Y., Tang, X., Sun, J.: Realtime and robust hand tracking from depth. In: CVPR (2014)
3. Sharp, T., Keskin, C., Robertson, D., Taylor, J., Shotton, J., Leichter, D., Wei, A.V.Y., Krupka, D., Fitzgibbon, A., Izadi, S.: Accurate, robust, and flexible real-time hand tracking. In: CHI (2015)
4. Oberweger, M., Wohlhart, P., Lepetit, V.: Training a feedback loop for hand pose estimation. In: ICCV (2015)
5. Neverova, N., Wolf, C., Taylor, G.W., Nebout, F.: Hand segmentation with structured convolutional learning. In: Cremers, D., Reid, I., Saito, H., Yang, M.-H. (eds.) ACCV 2014. LNCS, vol. 9005, pp. 687–702. Springer, Heidelberg (2015)
6. Tang, D., Yu, T.H., Kim, T.K.: Real-time articulated hand pose estimation using semi-supervised transductive regression forests. In: ICCV (2013)
7. Keskin, C., Kıraç, F., Kara, Y.E., Akarun, L.: Hand pose estimation and hand shape classification using multi-layered randomized decision forests. In: Fitzgibbon, A., Lazebnik, S., Perona, P., Sato, Y., Schmid, C. (eds.) ECCV 2012, Part VI. LNCS, vol. 7577, pp. 852–863. Springer, Heidelberg (2012)
8. Ionescu, C., Carreira, J., Sminchisescu, C.: Iterated second-order label sensitive pooling for 3D human pose estimation. In: CVPR (2014)
9. Liang, H., Yuan, J., Thalmann, D.: Parsing the hand in depth images. TMM $16(5)$, 1241–1253 (2014)
10. Rogez, G., Supancic III., J.S., Khademi, M., Montiel, J.M.M., Ramanan, D.: 3D hand pose detection in egocentric RGB-D images. In: ECCV Workshop (2014)
11. Stenger, B., Thayananthan, A., Torr, P.H., Cipolla, R.: Model-based hand tracking using a hierarchical bayesian filter. TPAMI $28(9)$, 1372–1384 (2006)
12. Ballan, L., Taneja, A., Gall, J., Van Gool, L., Pollefeys, M.: Motion capture of hands in action using discriminative salient points. In: Fitzgibbon, A., Lazebnik, S., Perona, P., Sato, Y., Schmid, C. (eds.) ECCV 2012, Part VI. LNCS, vol. 7577, pp. 640–653. Springer, Heidelberg (2012)
13. Intel: Perceptual computing SDK (2013)
14. Supancic III., J.S., Rogez, G., Yang, Y., Shotton, J., Ramanan, D.: Depth-based hand pose estimation: methods, data, and challenges. arXiv preprint arXiv:1504.06378 (2015)

15. Taylor, J., Stebbing, R., Ramakrishna, V., Keskin, C., Shotton, J., Izadi, S., Hertzmann, A., Fitzgibbon, A.: User-specific hand modeling from monocular depth sequences. In: CVPR (2014)
16. Krejov, P., Gilbert, A., Bowden, R.: Combining discriminative and model based approaches for hand pose estimation. In: FG (2015)
17. Sun, X., Wei, Y., Liang, S., Tang, X., Sun, J.: Cascaded hand pose regression. In: CVPR (2015)
18. Oberweger, M., Wohlhart, P., Lepetit, V.: Hands deep in deep learning for hand pose estimation. arXiv preprint arXiv:1502.06807 (2015)
19. Tang, D., Taylor, J., Kohli, P., Keskin, C., Kim, T.K., Shotton, J.: Opening the black box: hierarchical sampling optimization for estimating human hand pose. In: ICCV (2015)
20. Girshick, R., Donahue, J., Darrell, T., Malik, J.: Rich feature hierarchies for accurate object detection and semantic segmentation. In: CVPR (2014)
21. Gregor, K., Danihelka, I., Graves, A., Wierstra, D.: Draw: a recurrent neural network for image generation. arXiv preprint arXiv:1502.04623 (2015)
22. Sermanet, P., Frome, A., Real, E.: Attention for fine-grained categorization. arXiv preprint arXiv:1412.7054 (2014)
23. Jaderberg, M., Simonyan, K., Zisserman, A., et al.: Spatial transformer networks. In: NIPS (2015)
24. Zhao, X., Kim, T.K., Luo, W.: Unified face analysis by iterative multi-output random forests. In: CVPR (2014)
25. Zhu, S., Li, C., Change Loy, C., Tang, X.: Face alignment by coarse-to-fine shape searching. In: CVPR (2015)
26. Dollár, P., Welinder, P., Perona, P.: Cascaded pose regression. In: CVPR (2010)
27. Toshev, A., Szegedy, C.: Deeppose: human pose estimation via deep neural networks. In: CVPR (2014)
28. Xiong, X., Torre, F.: Supervised descent method and its applications to face alignment. In: CVPR (2013)
29. Sridhar, S., Mueller, F., Oulasvirta, A., Theobalt, C.: Fast and robust hand tracking using detection-guided optimization. In: CVPR (2014)
30. Tompson, J., Stein, M., Lecun, Y., Perlin, K.: Real-time continuous pose recovery of human hands using convolutional networks. TOG 33(5), 169 (2014)
31. Kennedy, J., Eberhart, R.: Particle swarm optimization. In: International Conference on Neural Networks (1995)
32. Shi, Y., Eberhart, R.: A modified particle swarm optimizer. In: Proceedings of IEEE International Conference on Evolutionary Computation (1998)
33. Kabsch, W.: A solution for the best rotation to relate two sets of vectors. Acta Crystallographica Section A: Crystal Physics, Diffraction, Theoretical and General Crystallography (1976)
34. Theano Development Team: Theano: A Python framework for fast computation of mathematical expressions. arXiv.1605.02688, May 2016

VolumeDeform: Real-Time Volumetric Non-rigid Reconstruction

Matthias Innmann[1(✉)], Michael Zollhöfer[2], Matthias Nießner[3],
Christian Theobalt[2], and Marc Stamminger[1]

[1] University of Erlangen-Nuremberg, Erlangen, Germany
matthias.innmann@fau.de
[2] Max-Planck-Institute for Informatics, Saarbrücken, Germany
[3] Stanford University, Stanford, USA

Abstract. We present a novel approach for the reconstruction of dynamic geometric shapes using a single hand-held consumer-grade RGB-D sensor at real-time rates. Our method builds up the scene model from scratch during the scanning process, thus it does not require a pre-defined shape template to start with. Geometry and motion are parameterized in a unified manner by a volumetric representation that encodes a distance field of the surface geometry as well as the non-rigid space deformation. Motion tracking is based on a set of extracted sparse color features in combination with a dense depth constraint. This enables accurate tracking and drastically reduces drift inherent to standard model-to-depth alignment. We cast finding the optimal deformation of space as a non-linear regularized variational optimization problem by enforcing local smoothness and proximity to the input constraints. The problem is tackled in real-time at the camera's capture rate using a data-parallel flip-flop optimization strategy. Our results demonstrate robust tracking even for fast motion and scenes that lack geometric features.

1 Introduction

Nowadays, RGB-D cameras, such as the Microsoft Kinect, Asus Xtion Pro, or Intel RealSense, have become an affordable commodity accessible to everyday users. With the introduction of these sensors, research has started to develop efficient algorithms for dense static 3D reconstruction. KinectFusion [1,2] has shown that despite their low camera resolution and adverse noise characteristics, high-quality reconstructions can be achieved, even in real time. Follow-up work extended the underlying data structures and depth fusion algorithms in order to provide better scalability for handling larger scenes [3–6] and a higher reconstruction quality [7,8].

Video: https://youtu.be/lk_yX-O_Y5c.

Electronic supplementary material The online version of this chapter (doi:10.1007/978-3-319-46484-8_22) contains supplementary material, which is available to authorized users.

© Springer International Publishing AG 2016
B. Leibe et al. (Eds.): ECCV 2016, Part VIII, LNCS 9912, pp. 362–379, 2016.
DOI: 10.1007/978-3-319-46484-8_22

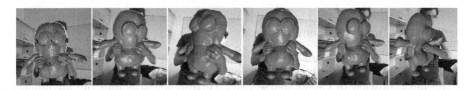

Fig. 1. Real-time non-rigid reconstruction result overlayed on top of RGB input

While these approaches achieve impressive results on static environments, they do not reconstruct dynamic scene elements such as non-rigidly moving objects. However, the reconstruction of deformable objects is central to a wide range of applications, and also the focus of this work. In the past, a variety of methods for dense deformable geometry tracking from multi-view camera systems [9] or a single RGB-D camera, even in real-time [10], were proposed. Unfortunately, all these methods require a complete static shape template of the tracked scene to start with; they then deform the template over time.

Object type specific templates limit applicability in general scenes, and are often hard to construct in practice. Therefore, template-free methods that jointly build up the shape model along with tracking its non-rigid deformations – from partial scans only – have been investigated [11–16], but none of them achieves real-time performance.

Recently, a first method has been proposed that tackles the hard joint model reconstruction and tracking problem at real-time rates: *DynamicFusion* [17] reconstructs an implicit surface representation – similar to *KinectFusion* – of the tracked object, while jointly optimizing for the scene's rigid and non-rigid motion based on a coarse warping field. Although the obtained results are impressive given the tight real-time constraint, we believe that this is not the end of the line. For instance, their depth-only model-to-frame tracking strategy cannot track tangential motion, since all color information is omitted. Without utilizing global features as anchor points, model-to-frame tracking is also prone to drift and error accumulation. In our work, we thus propose the use of sparse RGB feature matching to improve tracking robustness and to handle scenes with little geometric variation. In addition, we propose an alternative representation for the deformation warp field.

In our new algorithm, we perform non-rigid surface tracking to capture shape and deformations on a fine level of discretization instead of a coarse deformation graph. This is realized by combining as-rigid-as-possible (ARAP) volume regularization of the space embedding the surface [18] with automatically generated volumetric control lattices to abstract geometric complexity. The regular structure of the lattice allows us to define an efficient multi-resolution approach for solving the underlying non-linear optimization problem. Finally, we incorporate globally-consistent sparse SIFT feature correspondences over the complete history of observed input frames to aid the alignment process. This minimizes the risk of drift, and enables stable tracking for fast motions.

Our real-time, non-rigid volumetric reconstruction approach is grounded on the following three main contributions:

- a dense unified volumetric representation that encodes both the scene's geometry and its motion at the same resolution,
- the incorporation of global sparse SIFT correspondences into the alignment process (e.g., allowing for robust loop closures),
- and a data-parallel optimization strategy that tackles the non-rigid alignment problem at real-time rates.

2   Related Work

Online Static Reconstruction: Methods for offline static 3D shape reconstruction from partial RGB-D scans differ in the employed scene representation, such as point-based representations [19–21] or meshes [22]. In the context of commodity range sensors, implicit surface representations became popular [23–26] since they are able to efficiently regularize out noise from low-quality input data. Along with an appropriate surface representation, methods were developed that are able to reconstruct small scenes in real time [27,28]. One prominent example for *online* static 3D scene reconstruction with a hand-held commodity sensor is *KinectFusion* [1,2]. A dense reconstruction is obtained based on a truncated signed distance field (TSDF) [23] that is updated at framerate, and model-to-frame tracking is performed using fast variants of the Iterative Closest Point (ICP) algorithm [29]. Recently, the scene representation has been extended to scale to larger reconstruction volumes [3–6,8,30].

Non-rigid Deformation Tracking: One way to handle dynamics is by tracking non-rigid surface deformations over time. For instance, objects of certain types can be non-rigidly tracked using controlled multi-RGB [31] or multi-depth [32,33] camera input. Template-based methods for offline deformable shape tracking or performance capture of detailed deforming meshes [34–41] were also proposed. Non-rigid structure-from-motion methods can capture dense deforming geometry from monocular RGB video [42]; however, results are very coarse and reconstruction is far from real-time. The necessity to compensate for non-rigid distortions in shape reconstruction from partial RGB-D scans may also arise when static reconstruction is the goal. For instance, it is hard for humans to attain the exact same pose in multiple partial body scans. Human scanning methods address this by a non-rigid compensation of posture differences [11,43,44], or use template-based pose alignment to fuse information from scans in various poses [15,45]. Real-time deformable tracking of simple motions of a wide range of objects has been demonstrated [10], but it requires a Kinect-Fusion reconstruction of a static template before acquisition. Hence, template-free methods that simultaneously track the non-rigidly deforming geometry of a moving scene and build up a shape template over time were investigated. This hard joint reconstruction and tracking problem has mostly been looked at in an offline context [11–16,46,47]. In addition to runtime, drift and oversmoothing of the shape model are a significant problem that arises with longer input sequences. The recently proposed *DynamicFusion* approach [17] is the first to jointly reconstruct and track a non-rigidly deforming shape from RGB-D input in real-time (although the color channel is not used). It reconstructs an implicit surface representation - similar to the *KinectFusion* approach - while jointly optimizing for the scene's rigid and non-rigid motion based on a coarse warping field parameterized by a sparse deformation graph [48]. Our approach tackles the same setting, but uses a dense volumetric representation to embed both the reconstructed model and the deformation warp field. While *DynamicFusion* only uses geometric correspondences, we additionally employ sparse photometric feature correspondences over the complete history of frames. These features serve as global anchor points and mitigate drift, which typically appears in model-to-frame tracking methods.

3   Method Overview

Input to our method is a 30 Hz stream captured by a commodity RGB-D sensor. At each time step t, a color map $\mathcal{C}_t$ and a depth map $\mathcal{D}_t$ are recorded, both at a resolution of 640 × 480 pixels. Color and depth are assumed to be spatially and temporally aligned. For reconstruction and non-rigid tracking of the observed scene, we use a unified volumetric representation (Sect. 4) that models both the scene's geometry as well as its deformation. The scene is fused into a truncated signed distance field (TSDF) [23], which stores the scene's geometry and color in its initial, *undeformed* shape. A deformation field is stored at the same resolution as the TSDF in order to define a rigid transformation per voxel. In each frame, we continuously update the deformation field and fuse new RGB-D images into the undeformed shape. An overview of the steps performed each frame is shown in Fig. 2. We first generate a polygonal mesh of the shape $\mathbf{P}$, which is the current isosurface of D with the current deformation field applied. Next, we search for suitable correspondences between $\mathbf{P}$ and the input depth and color map (Sect. 5), based on sparse color feature matching as well as a dense depth-based correspondence search. Based on the correspondences, we adapt the space deformation (Sect. 6) such that the scene's geometry and color best match the observed input depth and detected features. The update of the deformation field is repeated in an Iterative Closest Point (ICP) fashion. Finally, we fuse the per-frame captured depth and color data into the TSDF (Sect. 8). The underlying high-dimensional non-linear optimization problem is solved in every step using a data-parallel flip-flop iteration strategy (Sect. 7). We demonstrate online non-rigid reconstruction results at framerate and compare to template-free and template-based state-of-the-art reconstruction and tracking approaches (Sect. 9). Finally, we discuss limitations (Sect. 10) and future directions (Sect. 11).

4   Scene Representation

We reconstruct non-rigid scenes incrementally by joint motion tracking and surface reconstruction. The two fundamental building blocks are a truncated signed

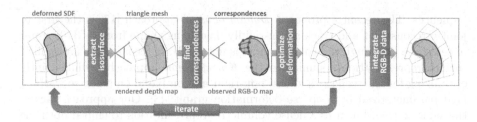

Fig. 2. Method overview: first, a deformed 3D mesh is extracted from the signed distance field using Marching Cubes. The mesh is rendered to obtain a depth map, which is used to generate dense depth correspondences. Next, we match SIFT features of the current frame with those of all previous frames. Based on all correspondences, we optimize the deformation field such that the resulting model explains the current depth and color observation. Finally, we integrate the RGB-D data of the current frame

distance (TSDF) function [23] for reconstruction of the shape in its initial, *undeformed* pose and a space deformation field to track the deformations. We discretize both in a unified manner on a shared regular volumetric grid $\mathcal{G}$. The grid is composed of a set of grid points enumerated by a three-dimensional index i. Each grid point stores six attributes. The first three attributes represent the scene in its undeformed pose by a truncated signed distance $D_i \in \mathbb{R}$, a color $\mathbf{C}_i \in [0, 255]^3$, and a confidence weight $W_i \in \mathbb{R}$. The zero level set of D is the undeformed shape $\hat{\mathbf{P}} = D^{-1}(0)$, which we call *canonical pose* in the following. New depth data is continuously integrated into this canonical frame, where the confidence weights are used to update D based on a weighted floating average (see Sect. 8). The grid points also maintain information about the current space deformation. For the ith gridpoint, we store its position after deformation $\mathbf{t}_i$, as well as its current local rotation $\mathbf{R}_i$, stored as three Euler angles. On top of the deformation field, we model the global motion of the scene by a global rotation $\mathbf{R}$ and translation $\mathbf{t}$. Initially, all per grid point data is set to zero, except for the positions $\mathbf{t}_i$, which are initialized to represent a regular grid. In contrast to the *DynamicFusion* approach [17], this grid-based deformation representation operates on a finer scale. Attribute values inbetween grid points are obtained via trilinear interpolation. A point $\mathbf{x}$ is deformed via the space deformation $\mathcal{S}(\mathbf{x}) = \mathbf{R} \cdot \left[\sum_{i=1}^{|\mathcal{G}|} \alpha_i(\mathbf{x}) \cdot \mathbf{t}_i \right] + \mathbf{t}$. Here, $|\mathcal{G}|$ is the total number of grid points and the $\alpha_i(\mathbf{x})$ are the trilinear interpolation weights of $\mathbf{x}$. We denote as $\mathbf{P}$ the current deformed surface; i.e., $\mathbf{P} = \mathcal{S}(\hat{\mathbf{P}})$.

Since the deformation field stores deformation only in forward direction, an isosurface extraction via raycasting [1,2] is not easily applicable. Thus, we use a data-parallel implementation of marching cubes [49] to obtain a polygonal representation of $\hat{\mathbf{P}}$, and then apply the deformation to the vertices. We first find all grid cells that contain a zero crossing based on a data-parallel prefix sum. One thread per valid grid cell is used to extract the final list of triangles. The resulting vertices are immediately deformed according to the current deformation field, resulting in a polygonal approximation of $\mathbf{P}$. This deformed mesh is the basis for the following correspondence association and visualization steps.

5   Correspondence Association

To update the deformation field, two distinct and complementary types of correspondences between the current deformed shape $\mathbf{P}$ and the new color and depth input are searched: for depth-image alignment, we perform a fast data-parallel projective lookup to obtain dense depth correspondences (see Sect. 5.1). Since in many situations depth features are not sufficient for robust tracking, we also use color information, and extract a sparse set of robust color feature correspondences (see Sect. 5.2). These also serve as global anchor points, since their descriptors are not modified over time.

5.1   Projective Depth Correspondences

Like most state-of-the-art online reconstruction approaches [1,2,17], we establish depth correspondences via a fast projective association step. Unlike them, we first extract a mesh-based representation of the isosurface $\mathbf{P}$ as described above, and then rasterize this mesh. The resulting depth buffer contains sample points $\mathbf{p}_c$ of the current isosurface. To determine a candidate for a correspondence, we project each $\mathbf{p}_c$ into the current depth map $\mathcal{D}_t$ and read the sample $\mathbf{p}_c^a$ at the target position. We generate a correspondence between $\mathbf{p}_c$ and $\mathbf{p}_c^a$, if the two points are considered sufficiently similar and appropriate for optimization. To measure similarity, we compute their world space distance $\|\mathbf{p}_c - \mathbf{p}_c^a\|_2$, and measure their normals' similarity using their dot product $\mathbf{n}_c \circ \mathbf{n}_c^a$. To make optimization more stable, we prune points close to silhouettes by looking at $\mathbf{n}_c \circ \mathbf{v}$, where $\mathbf{v}$ is the camera's view direction.

More precisely, we use three thresholds ϵ_d (distance), ϵ_n (normal deviation), and ϵ_v (view direction), and define a family of kernels $\Phi_r(x) = 1 - \frac{x}{\epsilon_r}$. If $\Phi_d(\|\mathbf{p}_c - \mathbf{p}_c^a\|_2) < 0$, $\Phi_n(1 - \mathbf{n}_c \circ \mathbf{n}_c^a) < 0$ or $\Phi_v(1 - \mathbf{n}_c \circ \mathbf{v}) < 0$, the correspondence is pruned by setting the confidence weight associated with the correspondence to zero $w_c = 0$. For valid correspondences, the confidence is $w_c = \left(\frac{\Phi_d(\|\mathbf{p}_c - \mathbf{p}_c^a\|_2) + \Phi_n(1 - \mathbf{n}_c \circ \mathbf{n}_c^a) + \Phi_v(1 - \mathbf{n}_c \circ \mathbf{v})}{3} \right)^2$.

5.2   Robust Sparse Color Correspondences

We use a combination of dense and sparse correspondences to improve stability and reduce drift. To this end, we compute SIFT [50,51] matches to all previous input frames on the GPU. Feature points are lifted to 3D and stored in the canonical pose by applying $\mathcal{S}^{-1}$ after detection. When a new frame is captured, we use the deformation field to map all feature points to the previous frame. We assume a rigid transform for the matching between the previous and the current frame. The rest of the pipeline is split into four main components: keypoint detection, feature extraction, correspondence association, and correspondence pruning.

Keypoint Detection: We detect keypoint locations as scale space maxima in a DoG pyramid of the grayscale image using a data-parallel feature detection approach. We use 4 octaves, each with 3 levels. Only extrema with a valid associated depth are used, since we later lift the keypoints to 3D. All keypoints on the same scale are stored in an array. Memory is managed via atomic counters. We use at most 150 keypoints per image. For rotational invariance, we associate each keypoint with up to 2 dominant gradient orientations.

Feature Extraction: We compute a 128-dimensional SIFT descriptor for each valid keypoint. Each keypoint is thus composed of its 3D position, scale, orientation, and SIFT descriptor. Our GPU implementation extracts keypoints and descriptors in about 6 ms at an image resolution of 640×480.

Correspondence Association: Extracted features are matched with features from all previous frames using a data-parallel approach (all extracted features are stored for matching in subsequent frames). We exhaustively compute all pairwise feature distances from the current to all previous frames and vice versa. The best matching features in both directions are determined by minimum reductions in shared memory. We use at most 128 correspondences between two frames.

Correspondence Pruning: Correspondences are sorted based on feature distance using shared memory bubble sort. We keep the 64 best correspondences per image pair. Correspondences with keypoints not close enough in feature space, screen space, or 3D space are pruned.

6   Deformation Energy

To reconstruct non-rigid surfaces in real time, we have to update the space deformation $\mathcal{S}$ at sensor rate. We estimate the corresponding global pose parameters using dense projective ICP [29].

For simplicity of notation, we stack all unknowns of local deformations in a single vector:

$$\mathbf{X} = (\ \underbrace{\cdots, \mathbf{t}_i^T, \cdots}_{3|\mathcal{G}|\ coordinates}\ |\ \underbrace{\cdots, \mathbf{R}_i^T, \cdots}_{3|\mathcal{G}|\ angles}\ )^T.$$

To achieve real-time performance, even for high-resolution grids, we cast finding the best parameters as a non-linear variational optimization problem. Based on these definitions, we define the following highly non-linear registration objective:

$$E_{total}(\mathbf{X}) = \underbrace{w_s E_{sparse}(\mathbf{X}) + w_d E_{dense}(\mathbf{X})}_{data\ term} + \underbrace{w_r E_{reg}(\mathbf{X})}_{prior\ term}. \tag{1}$$

The objective is composed of two data terms that enforce proximity to the current input, and a prior for regularization. The prior E_{reg} regularizes the problem by favoring smooth and locally rigid deformations. The data terms are a sparse feature-based alignment objective E_{sparse} and a dense depth-based correspondence measure E_{dense}. The weights w_s, w_d, and w_r control the relative influence of the different objectives and remain constant for all shown experiments. In the following, we explain the different terms of our energy in more detail.

Point-to-Plane Alignment: We enforce dense alignment of the current surface **P** with the captured depth data based on a point-to-plane distance metric. The point-to-plane metric can be considered a first order approximation of the real surface geometry. This allows for sliding, which is especially useful given translational object or camera motion. To this end, we first extract a triangulation using marching cubes and rasterize the resulting mesh to obtain sample point $\mathcal{S}(\hat{\mathbf{p}}_c)$ on the isosurface. Target positions $\mathbf{p}_c^a$ are computed based on our projective correspondence association strategy presented in the previous section. The objective is based on the extracted C correspondences:

$$E_{dense}(\mathbf{X}) = \sum_{c=1}^{C} w_c \cdot \left[\left(\mathcal{S}(\hat{\mathbf{p}}_c) - \mathbf{p}_c^a \right)^T \cdot \mathbf{n}_c^a \right]^2. \tag{2}$$

Here, $\mathbf{n}_c^a$ is the normal vector at $\mathbf{p}_c^a$ and w_c denotes the confidence of the correspondence, see previous section.

Sparse Feature Alignment: In addition to the dense depth correspondence association, we use the set of S sparse color-based SIFT matches (see Sect. 5) as constraints in the optimization. Let $\hat{\mathbf{f}}_s$ be the position of the sth SIFT feature match in the canonical frame and $\mathbf{f}_s$ its current world space position. Sparse feature alignment is enforced by:

$$E_{sparse}(\mathbf{X}) = \sum_{s=1}^{S} \|\mathcal{S}(\hat{\mathbf{f}}_s) - \mathbf{f}_s\|_2^2. \tag{3}$$

This term adds robustness against temporal drift and allows to track fast motions.

Prior Term: Since we operate on a fine volumetric grid, rather than a coarse deformation graph, we need an efficient regularization strategy to make the highly underconstrained non-rigid tracking problems well posed. To this end, we impose the as-rigid-as-possible (ARAP) [18] prior on the grid:

$$E_{reg}(\mathbf{X}) = \sum_{i \in \mathcal{M}} \sum_{j \in \mathcal{N}_i} \left\| (\mathbf{t}_i - \mathbf{t}_j) - \mathbf{R}_i(\hat{\mathbf{t}}_i - \hat{\mathbf{t}}_j) \right\|_2^2. \tag{4}$$

Here, $\mathcal{N}_i$ is the one-ring neighborhood of the ith grid point and $\mathcal{M}$ is the set of all grid points used during optimization. In our approach, $\mathcal{M}$ is the isosurface plus its one-ring. This prior is highly non-linear due to the rotations $\mathbf{R}_i$. It measures the residual non-rigid component of the deformation, which we seek to minimize.

7   Parallel Energy Optimization

Finding the optimum $\mathbf{X}^*$ of the tracking energy E_{total} is a high-dimensional non-linear least squares problem in the unknown parameters. In fact, we only optimize the values in a one-ring neighborhood $\mathcal{M}$ around the isosurface. The objective thus has a total of $6N$ unknowns (3 for position and 3 for rotation), with $N = |\mathcal{M}|$. For the minimization of this high-dimensional non-linear objective at real-time rates, we propose a novel hierarchical data-parallel optimization strategy. First, we describe our approach for a single hierarchy level.

7.1 Per-Level Optimization Strategy

Fortunately, the non-linear optimization objective E_{total} can be split into two independent subproblems [18] by employing an iterative flip-flop optimization strategy: first, the rotations $\mathbf{R}_i$ are fixed and we optimize for the best positions $\mathbf{t}_i$. Second, the positions $\mathbf{t}_i$ are considered constant and the rotations $\mathbf{R}_i$ are updated. These two step are iterated until convergence. The two resulting subproblems can both be solved in a highly efficient data-parallel manner, as discussed in the following.

Data-Parallel Rotation Update: Solving for the best rotations is still a non-linear optimization problem. Fortunately, this subproblem is equivalent to the shape matching problem [52] and has a closed-form solution. We obtain the best fitting rotation based on Procrustes analysis [53,54] with respect to the canonical pose. Since the per grid point rotations are independent, we solve for all optimal rotations in parallel. To this end, we run one thread per gridpoint, compute the corresponding cross-covariance matrix and compute the best rotation based on SVD. With our data-parallel implementation, we can compute the best rotations for 400 K voxels in 1.9 ms.

Data-Parallel Position Update: The tracking objective E_{total} is a quadratic optimization problem in the optimal positions $\mathbf{t}_i$. We find the optimal positions by setting the corresponding partial derivatives $\frac{\partial E_{total}(\mathbf{X})}{\partial \mathbf{t}_i} = \mathbf{0}$ to zero, which yields $(\mathbf{L} + \mathbf{B}^T\mathbf{B}) \cdot \mathbf{t} = \mathbf{b}$. Here, $\mathbf{L}$ is the Laplacian matrix, $\mathbf{B}$ encodes the point-point and point-plane constraints (including the tri-linear interpolation of positions). The right-hand side $\mathbf{b}$ encodes the fixed rotations and the target points of the constraints. We solve the linear system of equations using a data-parallel preconditioned conjugate gradient (PCG) solver, similar to [10,55–58], which we run on the GPU. Since the matrix $\mathbf{L}$ is sparse, we compute it on-the-fly in each iteration step. In contrast, $\mathbf{B}^T\mathbf{B}$ has many non-zero entries, due to the involved tri-linear interpolation. In addition, each entry is computationally expensive to compute, since we have to sum per-voxel over all contained constraints. This is a problem, especially on the coarser levels of the hierarchy, since each voxel may contain several thousand correspondences. To alleviate this problem, we pre-compute and cache $\mathbf{B}^T\mathbf{B}$, before the PCG iteration commences. In every PCG step, we read the cached values which remain constant across iterations.

7.2 Hierarchical Optimization Strategy

This efficient flip-flop solver has nice convergence properties on coarse resolution grids, since updates are propagated globally within only a few steps. On finer resolutions, which are important for accurate tracking, spatial propagation of updates would require too many iterations. This is a well known drawback of iterative approaches, which are known to deal well with high-frequency errors, while low-frequency components are only slowly resolved. To alleviate this problem, we opt for a *nested* coarse-to-fine optimization strategy. This provides a good trade-off between global convergence and runtime efficiency. We solve in a coarse-to-fine fashion and prolongate the solutions to the next finer level to jump-start the optimization. When downsampling constraints, we gather all constraints of a parent voxel from its 8 children on the next finer level. We keep all constraints on coarser levels and express them as a tri-linear combination of the coarse grid points.

8 Fusion

The depth data $\mathcal{D}_t$ of each recorded RGB-D frame is incrementally fused into the canonical TSDF following the non-rigid fusion technique introduced in DynamicFusion [17]. Non-rigid fusion is a generalization of the projective truncated signed distance function integration approach introduced by [23]. [17] define the warp field through the entire canonical frame. In contrast, we only integrate into voxels of $\mathcal{M}$ (one-ring of the current isosurface) that have been included in the optimization for at least $K_{min} = 3$ optimization steps. This ensures that data is only fused into regions with well-defined space deformations; otherwise, surface geometry may be duplicated. During runtime, the isosurface is expanding to account for previously unseen geometry. This expansion also adds new points to the grid to account for voxels that become for the first time part of $\mathcal{M}$. The position and rotation attributes of these grid points do not match the current space deformation, since they have not yet been included in the optimization. Therefore, we initialize the position $\mathbf{t}_i$ and rotation $\mathbf{R}_i$ of each new grid point by extrapolating the current deformation field. This jump-starts the optimization for the added variables.

9 Results

We demonstrate a variety of non-rigid reconstruction results in Figs. 1 and 3. For a list of parameter values and additional results, we refer to the supplemental material and the accompanying video. Runtime performance and convergence analysis of our solver is also provided in the supplemental document.

In all examples, we capture an RGB-D stream using an Asus Xtion PRO, a KinectV1-style range sensor. We would like to point out that all reconstructions are obtained in real-time using a commodity desktop PC (timings are provided in the supplemental material). In addition, our method does not require any pre-computation, and we do not rely on a pre-scanned template model – all reconstructions are built from scratch.

Importance of Sparse Color Correspondences: A core aspect of our method is the use of sparse RGB features as global anchor points for robust

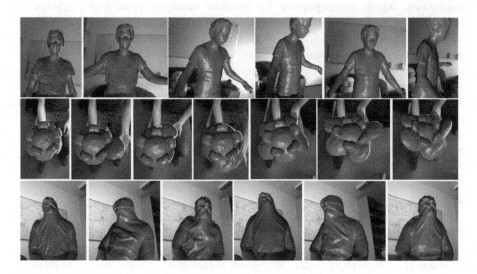

Fig. 3. A variety of non-rigid scenes reconstructed with our approach at real-time rates: UPPER BODY, SUNFLOWER, and HOODIE (top to bottom)

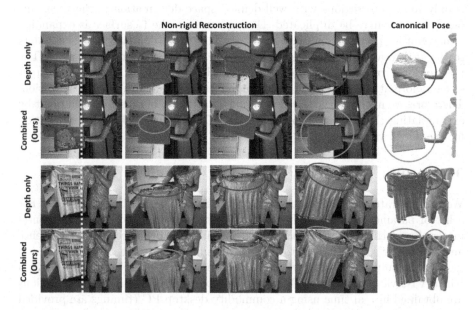

Fig. 4. Comparison of reconstructions with and without our sparse color alignment objective. Whereas depth-only reconstruction fails for tangential motion and objects with few geometric features, we achieve robust reconstructions using color features (Color figure online)

tracking. Figure 4 illustrates the improvement achieved by including the SIFT feature alignment objective. If the input lacks geometric features, dense depth-based alignment is ill-posed and results in drift, especially for tangential motion. By including color features, we are able to successfully track and reconstruct these cases.

Comparison to Template-Based Approaches: In Fig. 5, we compare against the template-tracking method of Li et al. [39], which runs offline. Since their method uses a high-quality pre-scanned template model obtained from a static reconstruction, we can quantitatively evaluate the reconstruction generated from the dynamic sequence. To this end, we compute the geometric distance of our final reconstruction (canonical pose) to the template mesh of the first frame; see Fig. 5, right. The average error in non-occluded regions is 1mm; occluded regions cannot be reconstructed.

We further compare our approach to the real-time template-tracking method by Zollhöfer et al. [10]; see Fig. 6. Even though our 3D model is obtained on-the-fly, the reconstruction quality is similar, or even higher.

Comparison to Template-Free Approaches: Currently, *DynamicFusion* [17] is the only non-rigid reconstruction method that runs online and does not require a pre-scanned template. In Fig. 7, we compare our approach against DynamicFusion on two scenes used in their publication. Overall, we obtain at least comparable or even higher quality reconstructions. In particular,

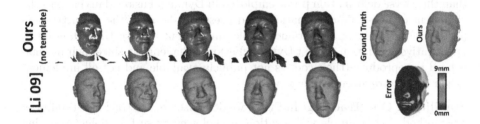

Fig. 5. Comparison to the template-based approach of Li et al. [39]: we obtain similar quality reconstructions without requiring an initial template model. On the right, we quantitatively evaluate the reconstruction quality: we compute the geometric distance of our final reconstruction (canonical pose) to the template mesh of the first frame, which is obtained from a high-quality, static pre-scanned reconstruction

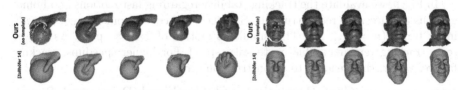

Fig. 6. Comparison to the template-based approach of Zollhöfer et al. [10]: although our reconstruction is from scratch and does not require an initial template model, we obtain reconstructions of similar quality

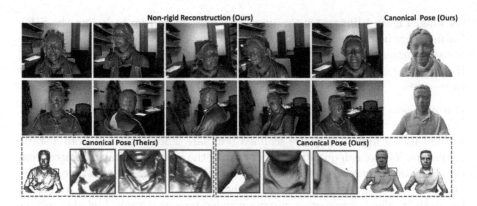

Fig. 7. Comparison to *DynamicFusion* [17]: we obtain at least comparable or even higher quality reconstructions. In particular, our canonical pose is of higher quality, since our warp field has a higher resolution than a coarse deformation proxy. In addition, our sparse feature alignment objective mitigates drift and enables more robust tracking

our canonical pose is of higher quality – we attribute this to the key differences in our method: first, our sparse RGB feature term mitigates drift and makes tracking much more robust (for the comparison /w and w/o SIFT feature matching, see Fig. 4). Second, our deformation field is at a higher resolution level than the coarse deformation proxy employed in DynamicFusion. This enables the alignment of fine-scale deformations and preserves detail in the reconstruction (otherwise newly-integrated frames would smooth out detail). Unfortunately, a quantitative evaluation against DynamicFusion is challenging, since their method is hard to reproduce (their code is not publicly available and not all implementation details are given in the paper).

Stability of Our Tracking: In Fig. 8, we demonstrate the tracking stability of our method with a simple visualization: we color every surface point according to its position in the canonical grid. In the case of successful non-rigid tracking, surface color remains constant; in case of tracking failure or drift, the surface would change its color over time. As we can see, our method is able to track surface points faithfully throughout the entire sequence, and all points remain stable at their undeformed positions; i.e., no drift occurs.

In Fig. 9, we evaluate the tracking stability regarding fast motions and homogeneous textures. We reconstruct the SUNFLOWER scene by only using every n^{th} input frame ($n = 2, \ldots, 6$). This simulates motion of $2\times$–$6\times$ speed. As can be seen, tracking remains stable up to $\approx 3\times$ speed. For higher speedups, tracking failures occur, thus leading to reconstruction errors.

Importance of Grid Resolution and Combined Dense and Sparse Tracking: We evaluate the importance of the fine warp-field resolution as well as the relevance of our sparse color feature term in terms of obtained deformation quality; see Fig. 10. For a low-resolution deformation grid, the warp field

Fig. 8. Evaluation of tracking stability: surface points are colored according to the position in the canonical pose. Our non-rigid tracking maps each surface point close to its undeformed position. In case of tracking failures or drift, the surface would change its color over time (Color figure online)

Fig. 9. Temporal Coherence: we skip every n^{th} frame of the SUNFLOWER sequence. Tracking remains stable up to a 3× speedup. Beyond this, tracking quality degrades

is not flexible enough and fine-scale deformations cannot be handled. If we use only depth data, tracking is considerably less accurate leading to local drift and may even fail completely if no geometric features are present. Only for high-resolution deformation grids and our combined tracker, drift is reduced and the texture can be reconstructed at a good quality. Note that our grids have a significantly higher number of degrees of freedom than the coarse deformation graph employed by DynamicFusion [17]; in their examples, they use only about 400 deformation nodes. We can only speculate, but based on their low-resolution warp field, DynamicFusion cannot reconstruct RGB textures.

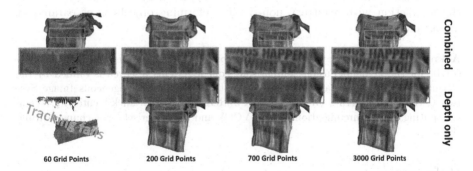

Fig. 10. Impact of grid resolution and color features: low-resolution warp fields (left) cannot capture fine-scale deformations leading to drift and blur. Depth-only tracking (bottom) also results in drift and blur. In contrast, our combined approach together with a high-resolution grid (top right) mitigates drift and leads to sharp textures

10   Limitations

While we are able to demonstrate compelling results and our method works well on a variety of examples, there are still limitations. First of all, robust tracking is fundamentally hard in the case of non-rigid deforming surfaces. Although global SIFT matching helps to improve robustness and minimizes alignment errors, drift is not completely eliminated. Ideally, we would like to solve a non-rigid, global bundle adjustment problem, which unfortunately exceeds the real-time computational budget.

High levels of deformation, such as fully bending a human arm, may cause problems, as our regularizer distributes deformations smoothly over the grid. We believe that adaptive strategies will be a key in addressing this issue; e.g., locally adjusting the rigidity.

Another limitation is the relatively small spatial extent that can be modeled with a uniform grid. We believe a next step on this end would be the combination of our method with a sparse surface reconstruction approach; e.g., [5,6]. Nonetheless, we believe that our method helps to further improve the field of non-rigid 3D surface reconstruction, which is both a fundamentally hard and important problem.

11   Conclusion

We present a novel approach to jointly reconstruct the geometric shape as well as motion of an arbitrary non-rigidly deforming scene at real-time rates. The foundation is a novel unified volumetric representation that encodes both, geometry and motion. Motion tracking uses sparse color as well as dense depth constraints and is based on a fast GPU-based variational optimization strategy. Our results demonstrate non-rigid reconstruction results, even for scenes that lack geometric features. We hope that our method is another stepping stone for future work, and we believe that it paves the way for new applications in VR and AR, where the interaction with arbitrary non-rigidly deforming objects is of paramount importance.

Acknowledgments. We thank Angela Dai for the video voice over and Richard Newcombe for the DynamicFusion comparison sequences. This research is funded by the German Research Foundation (DFG) – grant GRK-1773 Heterogeneous Image System –, the ERC Starting Grant 335545 CapReal, the Max Planck Center for Visual Computing and Communications (MPC-VCC), and the Bayerische Forschungsstiftung (For3D).

References

1. Newcombe, R.A., Izadi, S., Hilliges, O., Molyneaux, D., Kim, D., Davison, A.J., Kohli, P., Shotton, J., Hodges, S., Fitzgibbon, A.: KinectFusion: real-time dense surface mapping and tracking. In: Proceedings of ISMAR, pp. 127–136 (2011)

2. Izadi, S., Kim, D., Hilliges, O., Molyneaux, D., Newcombe, R., Kohli, P., Shotton, J., Hodges, S., Freeman, D., Davison, A., Fitzgibbon, A.: KinectFusion: real-time 3D reconstruction and interaction using a moving depth camera. In: Proceedings of UIST, pp. 559–568 (2011)
3. Roth, H., Vona, M.: Moving volume KinectFusion. In: Proceedings of BMVC (2012)
4. Zeng, M., Zhao, F., Zheng, J., Liu, X.: Octree-based fusion for realtime 3D reconstruction. Graph. Models **75**, 126–136 (2012)
5. Chen, J., Bautembach, D., Izadi, S.: Scalable real-time volumetric surface reconstruction. ACM Trans. Graph. (TOG) **32**(4), 113 (2013)
6. Nießner, M., Zollhöfer, M., Izadi, S., Stamminger, M.: Real-time 3D reconstruction at scale using voxel hashing. ACM Trans. Graph. (TOG) **32**, 169 (2013)
7. Whelan, T., Johannsson, H., Kaess, M., Leonard, J., McDonald, J.: Robust tracking for real-time dense RGB-D mapping with kintinuous. Technical report Query date: 2012-10-25(2012)
8. Steinbruecker, F., Sturm, J., Cremers, D.: Volumetric 3D mapping in real-time on a CPU. In: Proceedings of ICRA, Hongkong, China (2014)
9. Theobalt, C., de Aguiar, E., Stoll, C., Seidel, H.P., Thrun, S.: Performance capture from multi-view video. In: Ronfard, R., Taubin, G. (eds.) Image and Geometry Processing for 3-D Cinematography, pp. 127–149. Springer, Heidelberg (2010)
10. Zollhöfer, M., Nießner, M., Izadi, S., Rehmann, C., Zach, C., Fisher, M., Wu, C., Fitzgibbon, A., Loop, C., Theobalt, C., Stamminger, M.: Real-time non-rigid reconstruction using an rgb-d camera. ACM Trans. Graph. (TOG) **33**(4), 1–12 (2014)
11. Zeng, M., Zheng, J., Cheng, X., Liu, X.: Templateless quasi-rigid shape modeling with implicit loop-closure. In: Proceedings of CVPR, pp. 145–152. IEEE (2013)
12. Mitra, N.J., Flöry, S., Ovsjanikov, M., Gelfand, N., Guibas, L.J., Pottmann, H.: Dynamic geometry registration. In: Proceedings of SGP, pp. 173–182 (2007)
13. Tevs, A., Berner, A., Wand, M., Ihrke, I., Bokeloh, M., Kerber, J., Seidel, H.P.: Animation cartographyintrinsic reconstruction of shape and motion. ACM TOG **31**(2), 12 (2012)
14. Bojsen-Hansen, M., Li, H., Wojtan, C.: Tracking surfaces with evolving topology. ACM TOG **31**(4), 53 (2012)
15. Dou, M., Fuchs, H., Frahm, J.M.: Scanning and tracking dynamic objects with commodity depth cameras. In: Proceedings of ISMAR, pp. 99–106. IEEE (2013)
16. Dou, M., Taylor, J., Fuchs, H., Fitzgibbon, A., Izadi, S.: 3D scanning deformable objects with a single RGBD sensor. In: Proceedings of CVPR, June 2015
17. Newcombe, R.A., Fox, D., Seitz, S.M.: DynamicFusion: reconstruction and tracking of non-rigid scenes in real-time. In: The IEEE Conference on Computer Vision and Pattern Recognition (CVPR), June 2015
18. Sorkine, O., Alexa, M.: As-rigid-as-possible surface modeling. In: Proceedings of SGP, Citeseer, pp. 109–116 (2007)
19. Henry, P., Krainin, M., Herbst, E., Ren, X., Fox, D.: RGB-D mapping: using kinect-style depth cameras for dense 3D modeling of indoor environments. Int. J. Robot. Res. **31**, 647–663 (2012)
20. Stückler, J., Behnke, S.: Integrating depth and color cues for dense multi-resolution scene mapping using RGB-D cameras. In: Proceedings of IEEE MFI (2012)
21. Keller, M., Lefloch, D., Lambers, M., Izadi, S., Weyrich, T., Kolb, A.: Real-time 3D reconstruction in dynamic scenes using point-based fusion. In: Proceedings of 3DV, pp. 1–8. IEEE (2013)
22. Turk, G., Levoy, M.: Zippered polygon meshes from range images. In: Proceedings of SIGGRAPH, pp. 311–318 (1994)

23. Curless, B., Levoy, M.: A volumetric method for building complex models from range images. In: Proceedings of SIGGRAPH, pp. 303–312. ACM (1996)
24. Kazhdan, M., Bolitho, M., Hoppe, H.: Poisson surface reconstruction. In: Proceedings of SGP (2006)
25. Zhou, Q.Y., Koltun, V.: Dense scene reconstruction with points of interest. ACM TOG **32**(4), 112 (2013)
26. Fuhrmann, S., Goesele, M.: Floating scale surface reconstruction. In: Proceedings of ACM SIGGRAPH (2014)
27. Rusinkiewicz, S., Hall-Holt, O., Levoy, M.: Real-time 3D model acquisition. ACM TOG **21**(3), 438–446 (2002)
28. Weise, T., Wismer, T., Leibe, B., Gool, L.V.: In-hand scanning with online loop closure. In: Proceedings of 3DIM, October 2009
29. Rusinkiewicz, S., Levoy, M.: Efficient variants of the ICP algorithm. In: Proceedings of 3DIM, pp. 145–152 (2001)
30. Steinbruecker, F., Kerl, C., Sturm, J., Cremers, D.: Large-scale multi-resolution surface reconstruction from RGB-D sequences. In: ICCV, Sydney, Australia (2013)
31. Starck, J., Hilton, A.: Surface capture for performance-based animation. CGAA **27**(3), 21–31 (2007)
32. Ye, G., Liu, Y., Hasler, N., Ji, X., Dai, Q., Theobalt, C.: Performance capture of interacting characters with handheld kinects. In: Fitzgibbon, A., Lazebnik, S., Perona, P., Sato, Y., Schmid, C. (eds.) ECCV 2012, Part II. LNCS, vol. 7573, pp. 828–841. Springer, Heidelberg (2012)
33. Collet, A., Chuang, M., Sweeney, P., Gillett, D., Evseev, D., Calabrese, D., Hoppe, H., Sullivan, S.: High-quality streamable free-viewpoint video. ACM Trans. Graph. (SIGGRAPH) **34**, 4 (2015)
34. de Aguiar, E., Stoll, C., Theobalt, C., Ahmed, N., Seidel, H.P., Thrun, S.: Performance capture from sparse multi-view video. ACM TOG (Proc. SIGGRAPH) **27**, 1–10 (2008)
35. Allain, B., Franco, J.S., Boyer, E.: An efficient volumetric framework for shape tracking. In: CVPR 2015-IEEE International Conference on Computer Vision and Pattern Recognition (2015)
36. Guo, K., Xu, F., Wang, Y., Liu, Y., Dai, Q.: Robust non-rigid motion tracking and surface reconstruction using l0 regularization. In: Proceedings of ICCV (2015)
37. Hernández, C., Vogiatzis, G., Brostow, G.J., Stenger, B., Cipolla, R.: Non-rigid photometric stereo with colored lights. In: Proceedings of ICCV, pp. 1–8. IEEE (2007)
38. Li, H., Sumner, R.W., Pauly, M.: Global correspondence optimization for non-rigid registration of depth scans. In: Computer Graphics Forum, vol. 27, pp. 1421–1430. Wiley Online Library (2008)
39. Li, H., Adams, B., Guibas, L.J., Pauly, M.: Robust single-view geometry and motion reconstruction. ACM TOG **28**(5), 175 (2009)
40. Li, H., Luo, L., Vlasic, D., Peers, P., Popović, J., Pauly, M., Rusinkiewicz, S.: Temporally coherent completion of dynamic shapes. ACM Trans. Graph. (TOG) **31**(1), 2 (2012)
41. Gall, J., Rosenhahn, B., Seidel, H.P.: Drift-free tracking of rigid and articulated objects. In: IEEE Conference on Computer Vision and Pattern Recognition, 2008, CVPR 2008, pp. 1–8, June 2008
42. Garg, R., Roussos, A., Agapito, L.: Dense variational reconstruction of non-rigid surfaces from monocular video. In: Proceedings of the IEEE Conference on Computer Vision and Pattern Recognition, pp. 1272–1279 (2013)

43. Li, H., Vouga, E., Gudym, A., Luo, L., Barron, J.T., Gusev, G.: 3D self-portraits. ACM TOG **32**(6), 187 (2013)
44. Tong, J., Zhou, J., Liu, L., Pan, Z., Yan, H.: Scanning 3D full human bodies using Kinects. TVCG **18**(4), 643–650 (2012)
45. Malleson, C., Klaudiny, M., Hilton, A., Guillemaut, J.Y.: Single-view RGBD-based reconstruction of dynamic human geometry. In: 2013 IEEE International Conference on Computer Vision Workshops (ICCVW), pp. 307–314, December 2013
46. Malleson, C., Klaudiny, M., Guillemaut, J.Y., Hilton, A.: Structured representation of non-rigid surfaces from single view 3D point tracks. In: 2014 2nd International Conference on 3D Vision, vol. 1, pp. 625–632, December 2014
47. Wang, R., Wei, L., Vouga, E., Huang, Q., Ceylan, D., Medioni, G., Li, H.: Capturing dynamic textured surfaces of moving targets. In: Proceedings of the European Conference on Computer Vision (ECCV) (2016)
48. Sumner, R.W., Schmid, J., Pauly, M.: Embedded deformation for shape manipulation. ACM TOG **26**(3), 80 (2007)
49. Lorensen, W., Cline, H.: Marching cubes: a high resolution 3D surface construction algorithm. Proc. SIGGRAPH **21**(4), 163–169 (1987)
50. Lowe, D.G.: Object recognition from local scale-invariant features. In: ICCV 1999 (1999)
51. Lowe, D.G.: Distinctive image features from scale-invariant keypoints. IJCV **60**, 91–110 (2004)
52. Horn, B.K.P.: Closed-form solution of absolute orientation using unit quaternions. J. Opt. Soc. Am. A **4**(4), 629–642 (1987)
53. Gower, J.C.: Generalized procrustes analysis. Psychometrika **40**(1), 31–51 (1975)
54. Umeyama, S.: Least-squares estimation of transformation parameters between two point patterns. IEEE Trans. Pattern Anal. Mach. Intell. **13**(4), 376–380 (1991)
55. Weber, D., Bender, J., Schnoes, M., Stork, A., Fellner, D.: Efficient GPU data structures and methods to solve sparse linear systems in dynamics applications. CGF **32**(1), 16–26 (2013)
56. Wu, C., Zollhöfer, M., Nießner, M., Stamminger, M., Izadi, S., Theobalt, C.: Real-time shading-based refinement for consumer depth cameras. ACM Trans. Graph. (TOG) **33**(6) (2014). doi:10.1145/2661229.2661232
57. Zollhöfer, M., Dai, A., Innmann, M., Wu, C., Stamminger, M., Theobalt, C., Nießner, M.: Shading-based refinement on volumetric signed distance functions. ACM Trans. Graph. (TOG) **34** (2015). doi:10.1145/2766887
58. DeVito, Z., Mara, M., Zollöfer, M., Bernstein, G., Theobalt, C., Hanrahan, P., Fisher, M., Nießner, M.: Opt: a domain specific language for non-linear least squares optimization in graphics and imaging. arXiv preprint arXiv:1604.06525 (2016)

πMatch: Monocular vSLAM and Piecewise Planar Reconstruction Using Fast Plane Correspondences

Carolina Raposo[✉] and João P. Barreto

Institute of Systems and Robotics, University of Coimbra, Coimbra, Portugal
{carolinaraposo,jpbar}@isr.uc.pt

Abstract. This paper proposes πMatch, a monocular SLAM pipeline that, in contrast to current state-of-the-art feature-based methods, provides a dense Piecewise Planar Reconstruction (PPR) of the scene. It builds on recent advances in planar segmentation from affine correspondences (ACs) for generating motion hypotheses that are fed to a PEaRL framework which merges close motions and decides about multiple motion situations. Among the selected motions, the camera motion is identified and refined, allowing the subsequent refinement of the initial plane estimates. The high accuracy of this two-view approach allows a good scale estimation and a small drift in scale is observed, when compared to prior monocular methods. The final discrete optimization step provides an improved PPR of the scene. Experiments on the KITTI dataset show the accuracy of πMatch and that it robustly handles situations of multiple motions and pure rotation of the camera. A Matlab implementation of the pipeline runs in about 0.7 s per frame.

Keywords: Monocular visual SLAM · Piecewise planar reconstruction

1 Introduction

Monocular Visual Simultaneous Localization and Mapping (vSLAM) is the process of estimating the camera position and orientation while building 3D maps of the environment, from a single camera. Although there has been intensive research on this topic, current methods still face several challenges and difficulties, including (i) presence of outliers, (ii) dynamic foregrounds and pure rotation of the camera, (iii) large baselines, (iv) scale drift, (v) density of 3D reconstruction, and (vi) computational efficiency. Nowadays, existing methods for monocular vSLAM follow two distinct approaches: feature extraction and direct image alignment. Each paradigm is effective in solving some of these challenges but, to the best of our knowledge, there is no monocular vSLAM algorithm that is able to tackle all these issues. While feature-based methods work on top of extracted features and are usually robust to outliers by applying RANSAC-based schemes [11], direct methods perform whole image alignment

© Springer International Publishing AG 2016
B. Leibe et al. (Eds.): ECCV 2016, Part VIII, LNCS 9912, pp. 380–395, 2016.
DOI: 10.1007/978-3-319-46484-8_23

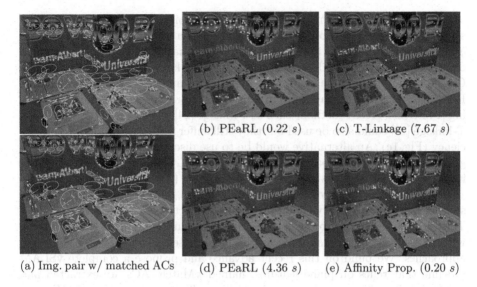

(b) PEaRL (0.22 s)   (c) T-Linkage (7.67 s)

(a) Img. pair w/ matched ACs   (d) PEaRL (4.36 s)   (e) Affinity Prop. (0.20 s)

Fig. 1. Plane segmentation problem solved using different methods: (b) PEaRL [14] with 300 homography hypotheses, (c) T-linkage [18] with 300 hypotheses,(d) PEaRL with 5000 hypotheses, and (e) affinity propagation [7]. The computational times of PEaRL and T-linkage hamper real-time performance. On the contrary, affinity propagation is fast and is able to detect all the planes present in the image. Red points correspond to outliers. (Color figure online)

and cannot handle outliers [2, 4, 19]. Moreover, the former work with wide baselines and provide sparse reconstructions, as opposed to the latter that require small baselines, which is typically accomplished by high frame rates that tend to limit image resolution, and provide dense scene models. All feature-based methods [3, 15] perform tracking and mapping as separate tasks. This greatly reduces the complexity of the problem, allowing them to work in real-time. On the other hand, direct methods such as [19, 20] compute dense depth maps using variational approaches which are computationally expensive and require powerful GPUs to achieve real-time performance. Only recently, direct methods that estimate semi-dense depth maps have been proposed [2, 4, 5], allowing real-time operation on a CPU. Most feature-based monocular methods assume there is significant camera translation and that the scene is mainly rigid for applying epipolar geometry. However, there might be situations where this does not hold and a scheme to robustly estimate the camera motion is desirable. Both direct and non-direct methods perform poorly in the presence multiple motions and tend to drift in scale. While there is no explicit solution for the first problem in the state-of-the-art, the last issue is typically solved using prior information such as the height of the camera [11, 23] or the existence of loop closures for performing global optimization [4].

The advantages of using planes as opposed to point features has been demonstrated by recent work on Structure-from-Motion (SfM) with a stereo camera [21]. Performing PPR in monocular sequences has never been much explored due to the difficulties in detecting planes without knowing the camera motion. One possibility would be to use an hypothesize-and-test framework, such as RANSAC, to fit homographies, but this lacks robustness and is time consuming [14]. Other greedy methods such as J-linkage [24] or its continuous relaxation T-linkage [18] could also be used but they still suffer from low computational efficiency (Fig. 1c). An alternative would be to use discrete optimization to replace greedy methods by a global scheme such as PEaRL [14] but, although there are improvements, the results are still not satisfactory (Figs. 1b and d).

Recent work using affine correspondences (ACs) [22] has shown that it is possible to establish necessary conditions for two ACs to belong to the same plane. The authors define an error metric that allows to quickly segment ACs in planes, without the need to generate homography hypotheses as in hypothesize-and-test approaches. We build on this recent advance and propose a complete vSLAM pipeline that relies on plane features, named πMatch. ACs are extracted and quickly clustered into coplanar regions using affinity propagation [7] (Fig. 1e) based on the new metric. For each plane cluster, a fast, robust scheme estimates the corresponding homography, which is decomposed into two solutions for rotation R and translation t (Sect. 2.1). The obtained motion hypotheses are used as input to a PEaRL formulation that merges close motions and decides about multiple motion situations (e.g. dynamic foreground, pure rotation of camera, etc.) (Sect. 2.2). Given the refined camera motion, the initial plane hypotheses are also merged and refined in a PEaRL framework, and, as an option, used as input to a standard Markov Random Field (MRF) formulation [1,8] for dense pixel labeling and subsequent PPR (Sect. 2.3). This two-view pipeline is applied to each image pair, providing camera motion estimations up to scale. As a final step, we use a fast scheme for scale estimation based on the minimization of the reprojection error that benefits from the high accuracy in the estimation of R and t. This is followed by a discrete optimization step for improving the final PPR of the scene (Sect. 4). πMatch makes considerable advances in handling the aforementioned difficulties, being advantageous with respect to the state-of-the-art methods (Table 1).

2   Two-View SfM and PPR Using πMatch

We propose πMatch, a Structure-from-Motion framework that is able to automatically recover the camera motion and a PPR of the scene from a monocular sequence. For each image pair, ACs are extracted and used for computing the error metric of compatibility between two ACs and an homography proposed in [22]. These measures of similarity between pairs of ACs are used for segmenting planes by affinity propagation (AP) [7]. A robust MSAC scheme [25] is then applied to each cluster for filtering out outliers. This step provides a plane segmentation and a set of motion hypotheses, from which the ones present in the

Table 1. Advantages of the proposed method πMatch over existing feature-based and direct methods.

	Feature-based	Direct	πMatch
Robust to outliers	+	−	+
Dynamic foreground/pure rotation	−	−	+
Wide baselines	+	−	+
Scale drift problem	*Camera height*	*Loop closure*	*No priors*
Model density	−	+	+
Computational efficiency	*Real-time*	*Parallelizable*	*Near real-time*

image pair are selected in a PEaRL [14] framework. The dominant one, which is assumed to be the camera motion, is identified and refined. Another PEaRL step is applied for plane merging and refinement, and a final standard MRF [1,8] can be used for dense pixel-labeling. Figure 2 shows the sequence of steps of the proposed pipeline. The next subsections detail each building block using the image pair of Fig. 1 as an illustrative example.

2.1 Generation of Motion Hypotheses

An AC consists in a point correspondence $(\mathbf{x}, \mathbf{y})$ across views and a non-singular 2×2 matrix A that maps image points surrounding $\mathbf{x}$ into image points in the neighbourhood of $\mathbf{y}$, with

$$\mathbf{x} = \begin{bmatrix} x_1 \ x_2 \end{bmatrix}^\mathsf{T}, \mathbf{y} = \begin{bmatrix} y_1 \ y_2 \end{bmatrix}^\mathsf{T}, \mathsf{A} = \begin{bmatrix} a_1 \ a_3 \\ a_2 \ a_4 \end{bmatrix}. \tag{1}$$

Recent research on ACs [22] has shown that 2 ACs, $(\mathbf{x}, \mathbf{y}, \mathsf{A})$ and $(\mathbf{z}, \mathbf{w}, \mathsf{B})$, must satisfy 4 conditions in order to be compatible with the same homography:

$$\begin{aligned}
(\mathbf{w} - \mathbf{y})^\mathsf{T} \mathsf{PA}(\mathbf{z} - \mathbf{x}) &= 0 \\
(\mathbf{w} - \mathbf{y})^\mathsf{T} \mathsf{PB}(\mathbf{z} - \mathbf{x}) &= 0 \\
\begin{bmatrix} s + a_2 b_3 - a_3 b_2 & -(a_1 b_3 - a_3 b_1) \\ a_2 b_4 - a_4 b_2 & s - (a_1 b_4 - a_4 b_1) \end{bmatrix} (\mathbf{w} - \mathbf{y}) &= 0, \text{ with.}
\end{aligned} \tag{2}$$

$$s = \frac{[-a_2 + b_2 \ \ a_1 - b_1](\mathbf{w} - \mathbf{y}) - (a_1 b_2 - a_2 b_1)(x_1 - z_1)}{(x_2 - z_2)} \text{ and } \mathsf{P} = \begin{bmatrix} 0 & 1 \\ -1 & 0 \end{bmatrix}$$

The authors devised an error metric from this result, which was validated in a plane segmentation experiment. Following this idea, for each pair of ACs, we compute an error metric by taking the average of the errors obtained for each condition, which are the values of the expression on the left-hand side of each equation in the system of Eq. 2. For C ACs, this results in a $C \times C$ matrix of similarities between pairs of ACs, which is fed to an AP method [7] for clustering the ACs into scene planes. Since all data points are assigned to a cluster, the obtained segmentation contains outliers. Moreover, there are cases in which AP

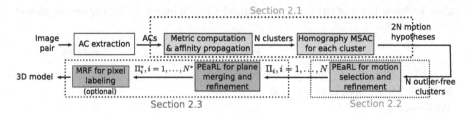

Fig. 2. Pipeline of the proposed method πMatch for two-view SfM and PPR. ACs are used for segmenting the scene into planes and providing motion hypotheses. The existing motions are selected in a PEaRL framework, and the dominant one is identified and refined. Plane hypotheses are generated from the clustering result and the refined motion, and PEaRL is again used for plane segmentation and refinement. A standard MRF scheme can be used for dense pixel-labeling.

tends to oversegment, providing several clusters that correspond to the same scene plane. This is shown in Fig. 3a, where the ground plane is segmented into 3 different clusters and there are data points incorrectly labeled.

In order to filter out outliers, each cluster is used as input to a MSAC framework for homography estimation. We consider the minimal set of 2 ACs for generating homography hypotheses as proposed in [22], which provides a speed-up of approximately 3× when compared using a 4-point minimal set of point correspondences. Also, since each MSAC is performed for each cluster independently, they can run in parallel, significantly speeding up the process.

The output of this MSAC step is a set of homographies and corresponding outlier-free clusters (Fig. 3b). Decomposing each homography yields two solutions for the camera rotation R, translation $\mathbf{t}$, and plane $\mathbf{n}$, up to scale [17].

2.2 PEaRL for Motion Selection

Cases in which the camera motion is a pure rotation must be correctly identified since nor the scene planes neither the scale of translation can be recovered, and schemes must be devised to overcome this problem (Sect. 4). The previous step of the pipeline outputs N outlier-free clusters and $2N$ motion hypotheses. Firstly, the motions that correspond to pure rotations are identified. This is done by considering the corresponding homography H and computing the distance between the identity matrix I and the matrix HH^T. We opted to use metric Φ_4 proposed in [13] for computing this distance as it is the most computationally efficient. Homographies for which this distance lies below a pre-defined threshold are decomposed and only the rotation component is considered by setting $\mathbf{t} = \mathbf{0}$.

There may be more than one motion present in the image due to moving objects in the foreground. In case these objects are planar, they will be identified by the plane segmentation step of the pipeline. Thus, a scheme to decide which planes correspond to rigid structures is required. We propose to solve this problem by selecting the motions present in the image in a PEaRL framework, and afterwards identifying the camera motion. The motion selection task can be

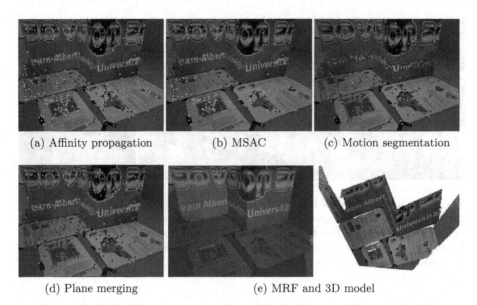

(a) Affinity propagation   (b) MSAC   (c) Motion segmentation

(d) Plane merging   (e) MRF and 3D model

Fig. 3. Results for the image pair in Fig. 1a after each step of the pipeline. (a) AP tends to oversegment and does not identify outliers. (b) A robust scheme is required for filtering each cluster. (c) The best motion hypothesis is selected and (d) plane segmentation is performed, where the original plane hypotheses are merged. (e) πMatch provides an accurate 3D model of the scene from only two views. Colors across images identify planes. Outliers are shown in red. (Color figure online)

cast as a labeling problem where the nodes of the graph are the point correspondences $\mathbf{p}$, to which a label $l_{\mathbf{p}}$ must be assigned. The label set $\mathcal{L} = \{\{\mathcal{R}_0, \mathcal{T}_0\}, l_\emptyset\}$ consists of the set of motion hypotheses $\{\mathcal{R}_0, \mathcal{T}_0\}$ and the discard label $l_\emptyset$. This labeling problem is solved by minimizing an energy function E defined by

$$E(\mathbf{l}) = \underbrace{\sum_{\mathbf{p}} D_{\mathbf{p}}(l_{\mathbf{p}})}_{\text{Data term}} + \lambda_S \underbrace{\sum_{(\mathbf{p},\mathbf{q}) \in \mathcal{N}} w_{\mathbf{pq}} \delta(l_{\mathbf{p}} \neq l_{\mathbf{q}})}_{\text{Smoothness term}} + \underbrace{\lambda_L |\mathcal{L}_{\mathbf{l}}|}_{\text{Label term}} , \qquad (3)$$

where λ_S and λ_L are weighting constants, $\mathbf{l}$ is the labeling being analysed, $\mathcal{N}$ is the neighbourhood of $\mathbf{p}$, weights $w_{\mathbf{pq}}$ set penalties for each pair of neighbouring data points $\mathbf{p}, \mathbf{q}$, and δ is 1 whenever the condition inside the parentheses is satisfied and 0 otherwise. The data term $D_{\mathbf{p}}$ is defined as the symmetric transfer error (STE) [12] if the label corresponds to a pure rotation and the Sampson distance [12] otherwise. Two nodes $\mathbf{p}$ and $\mathbf{q}$ are neighbours if they belong to the same cluster from the set of clusters provided by the MSAC step (Sect. 2.1). We set $w_{\mathbf{pq}} = 1$, meaning that an equal penalty is set to all neighbours. This definition of neighbourhood forces points belonging to the same scene plane to be assigned the same motion label. Finally, the label term forces the algorithm to use as few motion hypotheses as possible. Due to the small size of the label set

Fig. 4. Image pairs with the extracted ACs for 4 different scenarios: 1 - normal motion, 2 - dominant dynamic foreground, 3 - static camera/pure rotation, and 4 - four motions besides the camera motion. Examples 1 to 3 are from the KITTI dataset [9,10] and Example 4 is from the Hopkins dataset [26]. πMatch is applied to each scenario and the results are shown in Figs. 5 and 6.

(typically 8–14 motion hypotheses), this discrete optimization step is very fast. Figure 3c shows that the algorithm selected only one motion and some points were assigned the discard label $l_\emptyset$. If more than one motion is chosen, the one to which more clusters are associated is selected as the camera motion. In case this is satisfied by more than one hypothesis, the one to which more points were assigned is considered. The camera motion is finally refined with the selected inliers in a standard bundle adjustment with point correspondences.

2.3 Plane Refinement and PPR

Having the refined camera motion, the final step of the two-view pipeline is to merge and refine the initial plane hypotheses obtained from the AP step. This can only be done if the camera motion is not a pure rotation. Otherwise, the algorithm stops. For each cluster associated to the camera motion, a plane hypothesis is generated by reconstructing its points and finding the 3D plane that best fits the point cloud by linear least squares. From the set of plane hypotheses $\mathcal{P}_0$, the objective is to find the minimum number of planes that best describes the scene. Similarly to Sect. 2.2, this task can be cast as a labeling problem where the goal is to assign each point $\mathbf{p}$ to a label from the label set $\mathcal{P} = \{\mathcal{P}_0, l_\emptyset\}$. Again, this is solved by minimizing an energy function E defined as in Eq. 3, where the data cost is the STE obtained for the homographies computed using the refined camera motion and the plane hypotheses. In this case, our set of neighbours $(\mathbf{p}, \mathbf{q}) \in \mathcal{N}$ is determined by a Delaunay triangulation of points to account for possible small errors in the initial plane segmentation. The weights $w_{\mathbf{pq}}$ are defined as the inverse distance between points $\mathbf{p}$ and $\mathbf{q}$ because closer points are more likely to belong to the same plane. Figure 3d shows that the three initial plane hypotheses belonging to the ground plane were correctly merged into one plane, allowing its proper estimation. Also, some incorrectly labeled points in the

MSAC stage (Fig. 3b) were now assigned the correct label. Each selected plane is then refined in an optimization scheme that minimizes the STE. Since each plane is refined independently, this procedure can be performed in parallel, providing a significant speed-up. As a final step, a dense pixel labeling can be obtained using a standard MRF formulation [1,8]. Figure 3e shows that the proposed method is able to provide an accurate and visually pleasing dense PPR from only two views.

3   Two-View Experimental Results

In this section, we apply the proposed two-view pipeline to 4 different example scenarios (Fig. 4) and show the obtained results after each step. The first three examples were selected from the KITTI dataset [9,10] and illustrate cases of normal motion, dominant dynamic foreground caused by a large vehicle moving, and static camera. The last example is the situation of a moving camera observing multiple planar motions, and was selected from the Hopkins dataset [26].

In all experiments, affine covariant features were extracted with the Difference of Gaussians operator using the VLFeat library [27]. We limit the number of extracted ACs to approximately 500 for computational efficiency. We used the publicly available implementations of AP [6] and graph cut optimization [28] for the PEaRL steps. The estimations of the relative rotation R and translation t up to scale are compared with the ground truth R_{GT} and t_{GT}. The error in rotation (e_R) is quantified by the angular magnitude of the residual rotation $R^T R_{GT}$ and the error in translation e_t is defined as the angle between vectors t and t_{GT}. In all experiments, red points correspond to outliers.

Figure 5 shows the outcome of each step of the pipeline for the KITTI image pairs. The first example corresponds to the most common scenario of a moving camera and static scene. AP initially segmented the scene into 7 clusters which were then merged into 6 clusters corresponding to different scene planes. Not only the larger planes corresponding to the ground and building façade were recovered, but also the smaller orange plane was accurately estimated, as shown in the 3D model of Fig. 5b. Moreover, the camera motion was accurately estimated: $e_R = 10e - 3°, e_t = 1.2°$.

Example 2 illustrates the case of dominant dynamic foreground, where AP detects 5 different clusters, 2 of which correspond to the moving vehicle. The PEaRL step described in Sect. 2.2 correctly detects two motions in the image, where the one to which more clusters are associated is selected as the camera motion. After refinement with the inliers (magenta points in the third row) the rotation and translation errors are $e_R = 14e - 3°$ and $e_t = 0.98°$, respectively. 3 planes are then segmented in the image, with the remaining points being labeled as outliers. A final 3D model of the scene is shown in Fig. 5b, where it can be seen that even the faraway plane corresponding to building façade is accurately estimated. VISO2-Mono uses a scheme for detecting if the camera motion is too small, providing the identity matrix as the result for the camera motion in those cases. For this image pair, although the true translation has a norm of

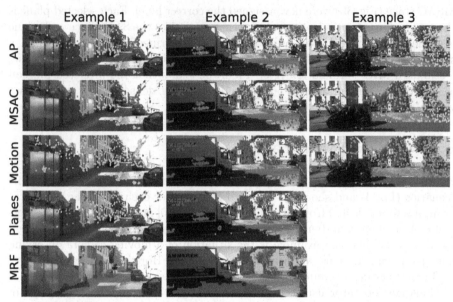

(a) Results for each step of the pipeline. Red points correspond to outliers.

(b) Final 3D model

Fig. 5. (a) Results obtained after each step of the proposed pipeline for the first 3 scenarios in Fig. 4. Since scenario 3 corresponds to a static camera, the planes cannot be estimated and thus the last two steps are not performed. (b) PPR obtained for scenarios 1 and 2. (Color figure online)

Fig. 6. Results obtained for the scenario of presence of multiple motions in Fig. 4. The dominant motion is selected as the one which has the largest number of associated clusters, which, in this case, does not correspond to the camera motion. This leads to the segmentation of only one plane in the last step of the pipeline, and all remaining correspondences being assigned as outliers (red). (Color figure online)

Table 2. Computational times on a Intel Core i7 3.4 GHz

AC extraction & matching	Metric computation & affinity propagation	Homography MSAC	Motion seg-mentation	Plane merging	Total
0.21 s	0.20 s	0.08 s	0.07 s	0.09 s	0.65 s

$||\mathbf{t}_{GT}|| = 46.4$ cm, VISO2-Mono identified this case as small motion and did not provide an estimation. By increasing the threshold, we forced VISO2-Mono to estimate the camera motion and observed that it selected many points on the moving vehicle as inliers, providing a poor estimation of the camera motion: $e_\mathsf{R} = 1.99°$, $e_\mathsf{t} = 77.9°$ and $||\mathbf{t}|| = 11.1$ m.

The third example corresponds to the case of static camera. In fact, there is a residual rotation which allows the scene to be correctly segmented into planes and the camera rotation to be accurately estimated ($e_\mathsf{R} = 40e - 4°$). However, since the translation component is negligible, it is not possible to estimate the scene planes. By forcing VISO2-Mono to provide an estimation for the camera motion, poor results were obtained: $e_\mathsf{R} = 0.03°$, $e_\mathsf{t} = 26.0°$ and $||\mathbf{t}|| = 69.3$ cm.

Figure 6 shows example 4 that consists in a moving camera observing 4 different planar motions. It can be seen that 7 clusters were initially segmented, and 5 different motions were correctly detected by the PEaRL framework described in Sect. 2.2. Since the larger plane was initially segmented into two clusters, its motion is incorrectly identified as the camera motion and only this plane is segmented in the final step. In this case, the rigid structure has little image support, so a more sophisticated scheme for identifying the camera motion is required. A possibility would be to used temporal consistency as proposed in [16].

Table 2 shows the computational times of each step of the proposed pipeline. Except for the C++ implementation of the graph cut optimization [28], the rest of the algorithm is implemented in Matlab. We believe that a C++ implementation of the whole algorithm would allow it to reach a frame rate of 5–10 fps.

4   vSLAM Pipeline

In this section we describe our proposed method πMatch that takes as input a sequence of images and outputs the camera motions and a PPR of the scene. We presented in Sect. 2 a two-view pipeline that takes as input a pair of images and outputs the camera motion, with the translation estimated up to scale, along with the PPR of the scene. In order to be able to work with image sequences, the relative scale of translation between motions must be estimated.

For every two consecutive motions $(\mathsf{R}_i, \mathbf{t}_i)$ and $(\mathsf{R}_{i+1}, \mathbf{t}_{i+1})$, where $(\mathsf{R}_i, \mathbf{t}_i)$ is the motion between frames i and $i+1$, the scale of translation s_i^{i+1} is estimated by fixing the norm of $\mathbf{t}_i$ and computing the new translation vector $s_i^{i+1}\mathbf{t}_{i+1}$. We consider point tracks between frames i and $i+2$ and start by reconstructing the 3D points in frames i and $i+1$ using motions $(\mathsf{R}_i, \mathbf{t}_i)$ and $(\mathsf{R}_{i+1}, \mathbf{t}_{i+1})$, respectively. We consider as inliers the 3D points whose reprojection error lies

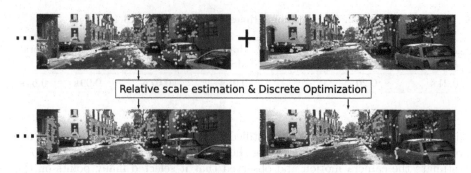

Fig. 7. The two-view pipeline described in Sect. 2 is a applied to each new image pair and its scale is estimated. This allows to select the best planes across multiple views in a PEaRL framework. An important advantage is the backpropagation of planes: the fronto-parallel plane corresponding to the building façade (cyan in the output images) is correctly detected in the incoming image and backpropagated to previous images. Colors identify planes in the output images. Red identifies outlier points. (Color figure online)

below a pre-defined threshold. We observed that the accurate estimation of the rotation and direction of translation allows a good selection of inliers. The two sets of reconstructed 3D points $\mathbf{X}_i$ and $\mathbf{X}_{i+1}$ correspond to the same scene points represented in different reference frames. Thus, using motion $(\mathsf{R}_i, \mathbf{t}_i)$, $\mathbf{X}_i$ can be represented in reference frame $i + 1$, and scale s_i^{i+1} is initialized by taking the median of the element-wise ratio $\frac{\mathbf{X}_i'}{\mathbf{X}_{i+1}}$, where $\mathbf{X}_i' = \mathsf{R}_i\mathbf{X}_i + \mathbf{t}_i$. Scale s_i^{i+1} is then refined by minimizing the maximum reprojection error of the 3D points $\mathbf{X}_i'$ in frames $i + 1$ and $i + 2$, computed using motion $(\mathsf{R}_{i+1}, s_i^{i+1}\mathbf{t}_{i+1})$:

$$s_i^{i+1*} = \min_{s_i^{i+1}} \sum_k \left(\max(d_k^{i+1}, d_k^{i+2})\right)^2, \tag{4}$$

where d_k^i is the reprojection error of point k in frame i. Due to the good selection of inliers, this procedure provides accurate results. Also, since we only optimize one parameter, the computational time of this refinement step is very low (approximately 18 ms in our experiments). For images in which the camera motion is a pure rotation, the scale is not estimated. When the camera resumes the movement, the scale is determined using the new motion and the previous one which was not a pure rotation. This scheme allows the relative scale information to be kept through the whole sequence.

The last step of the pipeline concerns the refinement of the piecewise planar structure by selecting the best planes across multiple frames. This is an adaptation of the discrete optimization step proposed in [21] for stereo sequences, where the authors propose to refine the camera motion and the PPR in a PEaRL framework by considering multiple stereo pairs simultaneously. In this case, for the sake of computational efficiency and since both the camera motion and the planes have already been refined, we propose to include a final discrete optimization step in a sliding window approach for improving the overall PPR. As explained in [21], optimizing over multiple frames allows the backpropagation of planes, significantly improving the accuracy and visual perception of the 3D model. Figure 7 depicts this advantage, where it can be seen that the fronto-parallel plane of the building façade is detected in the new image and backpropagated to the previous one, providing a much more realistic 3D model.

We formulate this discrete optimization as a labeling problem where the goal is to minimize an objective function E defined as

$$E(1) = \underbrace{\sum_i \sum_{\mathbf{p}^i} D_{\mathbf{p}^i}(l_{\mathbf{p}^i})}_{\text{Data term}} + \underbrace{\lambda_{S'} \sum_i \sum_{(\mathbf{p}^i, \mathbf{q}^i) \in \mathcal{N}'} w_{\mathbf{p}^i \mathbf{q}^i} \delta(l_{\mathbf{p}^i} \neq l_{\mathbf{q}^i})}_{\text{Smoothness term}} + \underbrace{\lambda_{L'} |\mathcal{L}_1|}_{\text{Label term}} , \quad (5)$$

where the label set is the union of the planes detected in each image pair i separately ($\mathcal{L} = \{\bigcup_i \Pi^i, l_\emptyset\}$), the nodes $\mathbf{p}^i$ are the point correspondences in all images i and $\lambda_{S'}$ and $\lambda_{L'}$ are weighting constants. We use the refined motions $R_i, \mathbf{t}_i, s_i^{i+1}$ to represent the planes in the label set in all reference frames i and compute the STE for defining the data cost $D_{\mathbf{p}^i}$. The neighbourhood $\mathcal{N}'$ is defined by Delaunay triangulation of the points in each image i. We also define as neighbours the points $\mathbf{p}^i$ and $\mathbf{q}^i$ that correspond to the same point track, and set the weight $w_{\mathbf{p}^i \mathbf{q}^i}$ to a large value in this case. This forces points belonging to the same track to be assigned the same label across frames. The remaining weights $w_{\mathbf{p}^i \mathbf{q}^i}$ are the inversely proportional to the distance between $\mathbf{p}^i$ and $\mathbf{q}^i$. In our experiments, for a sliding window of 5 frames (4 camera motions) this optimization took around 50 ms.

5   Large-Scale Experiments

This section reports experiments on 4 sequences of the KITTI dataset [9,10] performed with the monocular method VISO2-Mono [11], the stereo method VISO2-Stereo [11], and our proposed method πMatch. Figure 8 shows the results obtained for the 3 methods, with the errors being quantified using the error metric described in Sect. 3 and the metric proposed in [11].

The first observation is that, when compared to the other monocular method VISO2-Mono, our method is far more superior in the estimation of rotation and translation. Regarding the scale estimation, while VISO2-Mono uses information about the height of the camera, πMatch does not make any prior assumptions and still significantly outperforms this method. Moreover, another important observation is that for the 3 shortest sequences, πMatch also manages to outperform the stereo method VISO2-Stereo, begin particularly more accurate in the estimation of the rotation. This demonstrates the effectiveness of our proposed motion hypotheses generation and selection scheme.

Regarding the 1100-frame sequence, the trajectory makes it evident that VISO2-Stereo outperforms our method. However, from the boxplots showing the individual rotation e_R and translation e_t errors, it can be seen that πMatch

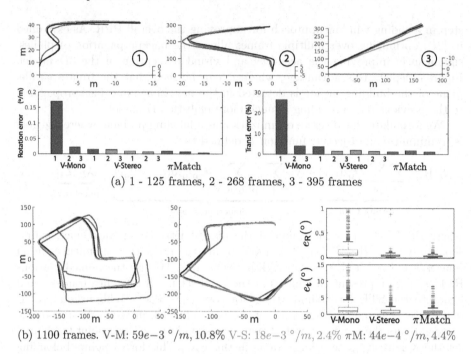

(a) 1 - 125 frames, 2 - 268 frames, 3 - 395 frames

(b) 1100 frames. V-M: $59e-3\,°/m, 10.8\%$ V-S: $18e-3\,°/m, 2.4\%$ πM: $44e-4\,°/m, 4.4\%$

Fig. 8. Results obtained on 4 sequences of the KITTI dataset [9,10] using the monocular method VISO2-Mono [11], the stereo method VISO2-Stereo [11], and our proposed monocular method πMatch. The bar plots and caption (b) show the average rotation and translation errors computed using the metric proposed in [10]. The boxplots show the distribution of rotation (e_R) and translation (e_t) errors computed for each image pair.

provides more accurate estimations, leading to the conclusion that the reason for the overall inferior performance of our method is some inaccuracy in the scale estimation. We observed that the estimation of the scale is frequently very accurate, and only fails in few cases. Due to the propagation of error, one poorly estimated scale will influence all subsequent ones, which does not happen in stereo methods. In order to illustrate this fact, we show in Fig. 8b the trajectories for the same sequence after removing the first 300 frames, where it can be seen that the πMatch outperforms VISO2-Stereo. For this sub-trajectory, VISO2-Stereo provided an error of $23e - 3°/m$ in rotation and 2.55% in translation while our method was more accurate: $50e - 4°/m$ in rotation and 1.96% in translation.

In Fig. 9, the PPR obtained for the 268-frame sequence demonstrates not only the accuracy of our method but also the importance of the last discrete optimization step, where the best planes across multiple frames (5 in this case) are selected. Since we are simply concatenating the individual PPRs for each image pair, the final 3D model would be visually significantly worse if this optimization stage had not been used. This experiment shows that πMatch performs

Fig. 9. PPR of the 268-frame sequence in Fig. 8a. A proper alignment of the individual PPRs of each image pair is observed, confirming the good quality of the scale estimation step. Some areas are shown in greater detail.

accurate vSLAM and dense PPR from monocular sequences, significantly outperforming the monocular method VISO2-Mono, and also being superior in the estimation of rotation to the state-of-the-art stereo system VISO2-Stereo.

6 Conclusions

We describe the first feature-based pipeline for vSLAM and dense PPR from a monocular sequence. It works by extracting ACs and employing a recently proposed error metric [22] for detecting scene planes. These planes are used for generating motion hypotheses that allow not only the accurate estimation of the camera motion, but also of other motions present in the image, in a PEaRL framework. The refined camera motion and initial plane hypotheses are used in another PEaRL scheme, yielding good PPRs of the scene from two views. The extension to longer sequences is done by estimating the scale between every two consecutive image pairs, and a final discrete optimization step allows the exchange of planes between frames, providing improved PPR results. The final experiment shows that scale drift may occur due to a few poor estimations of the scale of translation. As future work, we intend to devise a method to overcome this problem by making use of the detected planes. The idea is that since planes are more constant over time than points, using plane correspondences across frames could significantly reduce the scale drift. The total execution time of πMatch mainly implemented in Matlab is approximately 0.72 s. We will implement a C++ version of the pipeline, which we expect to run in about 5–10 fps.

Acknowledgments. Carolina Raposo acknowledges the Portuguese Science Foundation (FCT) for funding her PhD under grant SFRH/BD/88446/2012. The authors also thank FCT and COMPETE2020 program for generous funding through project VisArthro with reference PTDC/EEI-AUT/3024/2014.

References

1. Antunes, M., Barreto, J.P., Nunes, U.: Piecewise-planar reconstruction using two views. Image Vis. Comput. **46**, 47–63 (2016). http://www.sciencedirect.com/science/article/pii/S0262885615001390
2. Concha, A., Civera, J.: DPPTAM: dense piecewise planar tracking and mapping from a monocular sequence. In: 2015 IEEE/RSJ International Conference on Intelligent Robots and Systems (IROS), pp. 5686–5693, September 2015
3. Davison, A., Reid, I., Molton, N., Stasse, O.: MonoSLAM: real-time single camera SLAM. IEEE Trans. Pattern Anal. Mach. Intell. **29**(6), 1052–1067 (2007)
4. Engel, J., Schöps, T., Cremers, D.: LSD-SLAM: large-scale direct monocular SLAM. In: Fleet, D., Pajdla, T., Schiele, B., Tuytelaars, T. (eds.) ECCV 2014. LNCS, vol. 8690, pp. 834–849. Springer, Heidelberg (2014). doi:10.1007/978-3-319-10605-2_54
5. Engel, J., Sturm, J., Cremers, D.: Semi-dense visual odometry for a monocular camera. In: 2013 IEEE International Conference on Computer Vision (ICCV), pp. 1449–1456, December 2013
6. Frey, B.J.: Affinity propagation. http://www.psi.toronto.edu/index.php?q=affinity%20propagation
7. Frey, B.J., Dueck, D.: Clustering by passing messages between data points. Science **315**, 972–976 (2007). www.psi.toronto.edu/affinitypropagation
8. Gallup, D., Frahm, J.M., Pollefeys, M.: Piecewise planar and non-planar stereo for urban scene reconstruction. In: 2010 IEEE Conference on Computer Vision and Pattern Recognition (CVPR), pp. 1418–1425, June 2010
9. Geiger, A., Lenz, P., Stiller, C., Urtasun, R.: Vision meets robotics: the kitti dataset. Int. J. Robot. Res. (IJRR) **32**, 389–395 (2013)
10. Geiger, A., Lenz, P., Urtasun, R.: Are we ready for autonomous driving? The kitti vision benchmark suite. In: Conference on Computer Vision and Pattern Recognition (CVPR) (2012)
11. Geiger, A., Ziegler, J., Stiller, C.: StereoScan: dense 3D reconstruction in real-time. In: Intelligent Vehicles Symposium (IV) (2011)
12. Hartley, R.I., Zisserman, A.: Multiple View Geometry in Computer Vision, 2nd edn. Cambridge University Press, Cambridge (2004). ISBN: 0521540518
13. Huynh, D.Q.: Metrics for 3D rotations: comparison and analysis. J. Math. Imaging Vis. **35**(2), 155–164 (2009). http://dx.doi.org/10.1007/s10851-009-0161-2
14. Isack, H., Boykov, Y.: Energy-based geometric multi-model fitting. Int. J. Comput. Vis. **97**(2), 123–147 (2012). http://dx.doi.org/10.1007/s11263-011-0474-7
15. Klein, G., Murray, D.: Parallel tracking and mapping for small AR workspaces. In: Proceedings of Sixth IEEE and ACM International Symposium on Mixed and Augmented Reality (ISMAR 2007), Nara, Japan, November 2007
16. Lourenço, M., Stoyanov, D., Barreto, J.P.: Visual odometry in stereo endoscopy by using PEaRL to handle partial scene deformation. In: Linte, C.A. (ed.) AE-CAI 2014. LNCS, vol. 8678, pp. 33–40. Springer, Heidelberg (2014). http://dx.doi.org/10.1007/978-3-319-10437-9_4
17. Ma, Y., Soatto, S., Kosecka, J., Sastry, S.S.: An Invitation to 3-D Vision: From Images to Geometric Models. Springer, New York (2003)
18. Magri, L., Fusiello, A.: T-linkage: a continuous relaxation of J-linkage for multimodel fitting. In: IEEE Conference on Computer Vision and Pattern Recognition (2014), pp. 3954–3961 (2014)

19. Newcombe, R.A., Lovegrove, S.J., Davison, A.J.: DTAM: dense tracking and mapping in real-time. In: Proceedings of the 2011 International Conference on Computer Vision, ICCV 2011, pp. 2320–2327. IEEE Computer Society, Washington, DC (2011). http://dx.doi.org/10.1109/ICCV.2011.6126513

20. Pizzoli, M., Forster, C., Scaramuzza, D.: REMODE: probabilistic, monocular dense reconstruction in real time. In: 2014 IEEE International Conference on Robotics and Automation (ICRA), pp. 2609–2616, May 2014

21. Raposo, C., Antunes, M., Barreto, J.P.: Piecewise-planar StereoScan:Structure and motion from plane primitives. In: Fleet, D., Pajdla, T., Schiele, B., Tuytelaars, T. (eds.) ECCV 2014, Part II. LNCS, vol. 8690, pp. 48–63. Springer, Heidelberg (2014). http://dx.doi.org/10.1007/978-3-319-10605-2_4

22. Raposo, C., Barreto, J.P.: Theory and pratice of structure-from-motion using affine correspondences. In: Conference on Computer Vision and Pattern Recognition (CVPR) (2016). http://arthronav.isr.uc.pt/~carolina/files/CVPRsubm.pdf

23. Song, S., Chandraker, M.: Robust scale estimation in real-time monocular SFM for autonomous driving. In: 2014 IEEE Conference on Computer Vision and Pattern Recognition (CVPR), pp. 1566–1573, June 2014

24. Toldo, R., Fusiello, A.: Robust multiple structures estimation with J-linkage. In: Forsyth, D., Torr, P., Zisserman, A. (eds.) ECCV 2008, Part I. LNCS, vol. 5302, pp. 537–547. Springer, Heidelberg (2008). http://dx.doi.org/10.1007/978-3-540-88682-2_41

25. Torr, P.H.S., Zisserman, A.: Mlesac: A new robust estimator with application to estimating image geometry. Comput. Vis. Image Underst. 78, 138–156 (2000)

26. Tron, R., Vidal, R.: A benchmark for the comparison of 3-D motion segmentation algorithms. In: IEEE Conference on Computer Vision and Pattern Recognition, 2007, CVPR 2007, 1–8 June 2007

27. Vedaldi, A., Fulkerson, B.: VLFeat: an open and portable library of computer vision algorithms (2008). http://www.vlfeat.org/

28. Veksler, O., Delong, A.: Multi-label optimization. http://vision.csd.uwo.ca/code/

Peripheral Expansion of Depth Information via Layout Estimation with Fisheye Camera

Alejandro Perez-Yus$^{(\boxtimes)}$, Gonzalo Lopez-Nicolas, and Jose J. Guerrero

Instituto de Investigación en Ingeniería de Aragón (I3A),
Universidad de Zaragoza, Zaragoza, Spain
{alperez,gonlopez,josechu.guerrero}@unizar.es

Abstract. Consumer RGB-D cameras have become very useful in the last years, but their field of view is too narrow for certain applications. We propose a new hybrid camera system composed by a conventional RGB-D and a fisheye camera to extend the field of view over 180°. With this system we have a region of the hemispherical image with depth certainty, and color data in the periphery that is used to extend the structural information of the scene. We have developed a new method to generate scaled layout hypotheses from relevant corners, combining the extraction of lines in the fisheye image and the depth information. Experiments with real images from different scenarios validate our layout recovery method and the advantages of this camera system, which is also able to overcome severe occlusions. As a result, we obtain a scaled 3D model expanding the original depth information with the wide scene reconstruction. Our proposal expands successfully the depth map more than eleven times in a single shot.

Keywords: 3D layout estimation · RGB-D · Omnidirectional cameras · Multi-camera systems

1 Introduction

Recent low cost RGB-D cameras have caused a great impact in the fields of computer vision and robotics. These devices usually have a field of view (FoV) too narrow for certain applications, and it is necessary to move the camera in order to capture different views of the scene. However, that is often not easy to achieve or requires to use SLAM algorithms or additional sensors to maintain the system well localized. Recently, some alternatives to extend the FoV of depth cameras using additional elements have been proposed: [1] uses two planar mirrors as a catadioptric extension of the RGB-D device and [2] a consumer set of wide angle lens. Fernandez-Moral et al. [3] proposed a method to calibrate an

Electronic supplementary material The online version of this chapter (doi:10. 1007/978-3-319-46484-8_24) contains supplementary material, which is available to authorized users.

B. Leibe et al. (Eds.): ECCV 2016, Part VIII, LNCS 9912, pp. 396–412, 2016.
DOI: 10.1007/978-3-319-46484-8_24

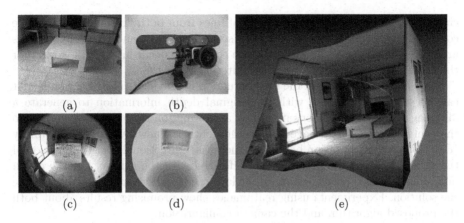

Fig. 1. (a) Image scene as view from a conventional RGB-D camera. (b) Proposed camera system. (c) Depth map projected to the fisheye camera. (d) Expansion of the depth map through spatial layout estimation. (e) From the wide field of view depth map of the scene, we compute a 3D model in a single shot.

omnidirectional RGB-D multi-camera rig. While these approaches are interesting, they are either complex to build and calibrate [1,3], or do not provide good enough depth maps [2].

Here, we propose a new hybrid camera system composed by a depth and a fisheye camera. The FoV of the fisheye is over 180°, in contrast with the usual FoV of 43° × 57° of consumer depth cameras (Fig. 1a). Once the cameras are calibrated, the system (Fig. 1b) is capable of viewing over a hemisphere of color information where the central part of the image has also depth data (about 8.7 % of the total number of pixels, as shown in Fig. 1c). One can think of this configuration inspired in the vision of the human eye, where the central part provides richer information (foveal vision) than the periphery, and the field of view is slightly over 180°. To our knowledge, this is the first time this configuration has been used, although the interest in such sensor pairing is clear in the recent Google's Tango[1]. Notice that, although our work uses a fisheye camera, the approach could be extended to other kinds of omnidirectional systems.

The main contribution of this work is the proposal of a method to extend 3D information from a conventional depth camera to over 180° of field of view in one single shot. The depth camera provides a region of the image with 3D scaled data, from which some basic information about the scene can be recovered. To extend the depth information we propose a spatial layout estimation algorithm based on line segments from the fisheye image, which provides scaled solutions rooted on the seed depth information (Fig. 1d). The line segments from the fisheye image are classified according to the Manhattan directions and projected to a scaled 2D map where the layout hypotheses are built based on physically coherent wall distributions. The algorithm is able to work even under high clutter

---

[1] https://get.google.com/tango/.

circumstances due to the combination of lines from both floor and ceiling. The corners of the map are evaluated by our scoring function, and layout hypotheses are proposed by the probability of these corners to occur in the real world. For the evaluation stage we propose three alternative methods.

As a result, a final 3D scene reconstruction is provided. The 3D room layout can be seamlessly merged with the original depth information to generate a 3D image with the periphery providing an estimation of the spatial context to the central part of the image, where the depth is known with good certainty (Fig. 1e). The collaboration between cameras is bidirectional, as the extension of the scene layout to the periphery is performed with the fisheye, but the depth information is used both to enhance the layout estimation algorithm and to scale the solution. Experiments using real images show promising results about both the proposed algorithm and the camera configuration.

2   Related Work

Probably the first attempt to recover 3D reconstructions of indoor environments with single images was [4], which uses a Bayesian network model to find the floor-wall boundary. In contrast, Lee et al. [5] use line segments to generate layout hypotheses evaluating their fitness to an orientation map. Using lines has the advantage of producing results without relying on scene-specific properties such as colors and image gradients. However, while some lines can actually include structural information of the environment (e.g. intersections wall-wall or wall-floor), usually most of them belong to clutter or are useless and misleading.

To help with this problem, some assumptions are made, and consequently some set of rules are proposed based on physical coherence. Usually the main assumptions are that all structures in indoor environments are composed by planar surfaces and that these surfaces are oriented according to three orthogonal directions (known as Manhattan World assumption [6]). This assumption holds for most indoor environments, and it is widely used in the literature [7,8]. Other works try to simplify the problem by making assumptions about the structure, e.g. assuming that the room is a 3D box [9–12]. In [13–17] they used this kind of reasoning to simultaneously perform object detection. Other approaches make use of video sequences instead of single images [18,19].

These methods have in common that all of them use images from conventional cameras. As opposed to that, some recent works use omnidirectional cameras such as catadioptric systems or fisheye cameras. Having greater field of view has many advantages for this task:

- Cameras are able to capture more portion of the room at the same time, which provides complete room reconstructions.
- Line segments appear entirely, so the reasoning is based on more evidence.
- Larger field of view (FoV) provides better view of the ceiling, which may help in cluttered scenes assuming structural floor-ceiling symmetry.

Some related works taking advantage of omnidirectional cameras are [20–23]. In [20], they use a fisheye camera to perform layout retrieval, essentially extending the work from [5]. Lopez-Nicolas et al. in [21] perform the layout recovery using a catadioptric system mounted in a helmet. Jia and Li [22] use 360° panorama full-view images, which allows them to recover the layout of the whole scene at once. Similarly, [23] uses the same type of images to perform layout retrieval along with a whole-room context model in 3D including bounding boxes of the main objects inside the room.

One common feature of all these approaches mentioned above is that the recovered 3D layout is obtained up to a scale. Our proposal combines the advantages of omnidirectional cameras (recover wider information) and depth cameras (provide 3D certainty and scale) with an easy to reproduce camera system.

3 Depth and Fisheye Images Processing

Before addressing the layout recovery, in this section we present the essential computer vision procedures in our approach, including calibration of the system (Sect. 3.1), line extraction (Sect. 3.2), estimation of Vanishing Points (Sect. 3.3) and classification of lines and points (Sect. 3.4).

3.1 System Calibration

To map world points $\mathbf{X}$ from the depth camera reference frame D to the fisheye camera reference frame F, it is necessary to calibrate the extrinsic parameters $(\mathbf{R}, \mathbf{t})$ and the intrinsic parameters of both cameras. The extrinsic calibration of range sensors to cameras is not a new issue, but most related works require manual selection of correspondences or do not support omnidirectional cameras [24–26]. To obtain the intrinsic parameters of the fisheye camera, we need a specific method with an appropriate camera model [27]. We adapted the proposal from [28], substituting the color camera model to the one from [29]. The intrinsic parameters of the depth camera are also computed as defined in [28] to improve the default parameters of the system. The depth images as captured by the sensor are transformed to point clouds using these parameters, and then they are rotated and translated to the fisheye camera reference frame, following $\mathbf{X}_F = \mathbf{R} \cdot \mathbf{X}_D + \mathbf{t}$. From now on, every computation is done in that frame. A more detailed analysis of our calibration procedure is presented in [30].

3.2 Line Extraction in the Fisheye Image

For the line extraction in the fisheye camera we choose the work from [31], which includes a method for self-calibration and line extraction for central catadioptric and dioptric systems with revolution symmetry. It uses the sphere camera model [32] to describe the point projection in dioptric systems (Fig. 2a). Every 3D world point $\mathbf{X}_i$ is first projected in a point $\mathbf{x}_i$ onto a unitary sphere around the viewpoint of the system. In the case of our equiangular fisheye lens this point is

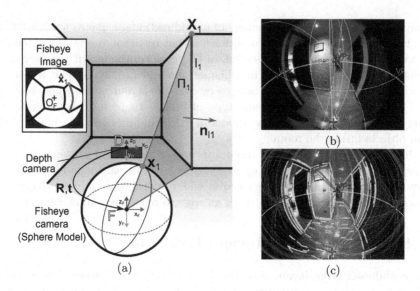

(a)   (b)   (c)

Fig. 2. (a) Scheme of the system in a 3D world scene and the correspondent fisheye image. (b) Depth planes classified according to the Manhattan directions (red in $\mathbf{m}_x$, green in $\mathbf{m}_y$, blue in $\mathbf{m}_z$), initial extracted vanishing points, horizon line (white dotted line), and 3D intersections in yellow lines. (c) Line-images classified with their contours in white and the vanishing points after the second optimization. (Color figure online)

projected to $\hat{\mathbf{x}}_i$ in the image plane by using the projection function $\hat{r} = f\phi$, where $\hat{\mathbf{x}} = (\hat{r}, \hat{\theta})$ is expressed in polar coordinates with respect to the image center, ϕ is the elevation angle in the sphere and f is the main calibration parameter.

Unlike conventional cameras, 3D lines in space do not appear as straight lines in the omnidirectional images, but they are projected to curves called line-images. In the schematic scene from Fig. 2a we can see highlighted a vertical line on the sphere model and its projection in the fisheye image. The shape of these line-images changes with the type of omnidirectional camera and its specific camera configuration. We have used the implementation from [31] to extract the main calibration parameter f and optical center from the images.

The projection of a line l_i in the 3D space can be represented by the normal of the plane $\mathbf{\Pi}_i$ defined by the line itself and the viewpoint of the system, with normal $\mathbf{n}_{l_i} = (n_x, n_y, n_z)^\top$. The points $\mathbf{X}$ lying on a 3D line l are projected to points $\mathbf{x}$ satisfying the condition $\mathbf{n_l}^\top \mathbf{x} = 0$. From [31], the constraint for points on the line projection in image coordinates for equiangular dioptric systems with symmetry of revolution is:

$$n_x \hat{x} + n_y \hat{y} + n_z \hat{r} \cot(\hat{r}/f) = 0 \tag{1}$$

where $\hat{x}$ and $\hat{y}$ are the image coordinates centered in the principal point, $\hat{\mathbf{x}} = (\hat{x}, \hat{y})$. The line-images are non-polynomial and do not have conic shape. To extract them is necessary to solve a minimization problem [31].

3.3   Extraction of the Vanishing Points

In this work we assume the scenes satisfy the Manhattan World assumption, i.e. the world is organized according to three orthogonal directions $(\mathbf{m}_x, \mathbf{m}_y, \mathbf{m}_z)$. Parallel lines in the 3D world intersect in one single point in perspective images, called Vanishing Point (VP). In omnidirectional images, line projections result in curved line-images, and parallel lines intersect in two VPs. We estimate the VPs to classify lines and planar surfaces from the depth information according to the three Manhattan directions.

There are previous approaches to obtain the VPs from omnidirectional images [33]. However, we propose a method to extract the VPs taking advantage of both cameras with a two step optimization problem. Depth information is more robust, but less accurate than RGB information. Using fisheye images typically obtain a more accurate VP solution, but the problem may be unable to converge if the initial solution is not good enough. Besides that, a joint optimization is problematic as it needs to weight both terms appropriately. Experiments showed that our two-stage optimization procedure performs well with no extra cost.

The initial solution of the Manhattan direction is set as a trivial three orthogonal vector base ($I = \{\mathbf{e}_1, \mathbf{e}_2, \mathbf{e}_3\}$). The variables to optimize are the roll-pitch-yaw angles (α, β and γ) that form the rotation matrix $R_{\alpha,\beta,\gamma}$ that after the optimization process should orient the vector base according to the Manhattan directions, $[\mathbf{m}_x, \mathbf{m}_y, \mathbf{m}_z] = R_{\alpha,\beta,\gamma} \cdot I = R_{\alpha,\beta,\gamma}$. The two stages are:

1. The vector base is rotated until the angle between the normals of as many points from the point cloud as possible and one of the three vectors from the base is minimized. The normals $\mathbf{n}_{\mathbf{X}_i}$ of every point $\mathbf{X}_i$ can be estimated using the method from [34]. To reduce computation time, the cloud can be previously downsampled (e.g. with a voxel grid filter).
2. The vector base is rotated until the angle between the normals of as many lines as possible and one of the three vectors from the base is as close of being orthogonal as possible, using the initial solution provided by stage 1. This is based in that, by definition, the normal $\mathbf{n}_l$ of every line l_i is orthogonal to the direction of the line in the 3D world, and therefore, if a line follows the Manhattan direction $\mathbf{m}_j$, then $\mathbf{n}_{l_i}^\top \cdot \mathbf{m}_j = 0$.

The columns of the final rotation matrix $R_{\alpha,\beta,\gamma}$ are the three Manhattan directions. Our convention is to denote $\mathbf{m}_y$ the column whose vector is closest to the gravity vector given an intuition of how the camera is posed (pointing to the front, slightly downwards). We choose $\mathbf{m}_z$ to be the column pointing to the front and leaving $\mathbf{m}_x$ orthogonal to the previous two. The VPs are the points in the image that result of projecting rays following the Manhattan directions according to the sphere model.

3.4   Classification of Lines and Points

The points from the point cloud $\mathbf{X}$ are classified depending on the orientation of their normals $\mathbf{n}_{\mathbf{X}}$ in the three orthogonal classes. A 3D clustering is then performed for each class to recover the planes P in the image (Fig. 2b). For those with normal $\mathbf{n}_P = \mathbf{m}_y$, the lowest one is chosen as *floor plane* (P_{floor}). Those lines l_i whose minimum angular distance to their closest Manhattan direction $\mathbf{m}_j$ is below a threshold are classified as lines in that direction L_j, where $j = x, y, z$ (Fig. 2c). The *horizon line* is the line-image l_H corresponding to the normal $\mathbf{n}_{l_H} = \mathbf{m}_y$ (drawn in dotted white line in Fig. 2c). Lines oriented in $\mathbf{m}_x$ and $\mathbf{m}_z$ are classified as *upper lines* ($\overline{L}$) when they are above horizon, and *lower lines* ($\underline{L}$) when they are below. Lines oriented in $\mathbf{m}_y$ (L_y) are classified as *long lines* when they have contour points above and below the horizon.

Some lines correspond to intersections of 3D planes extracted from the depth image. In order to detect such correspondences, we compute the 3D intersection lines of wall planes with the floor plane and between walls. When there are two consecutive wall planes of the same orientation, the line of the border is computed instead. An example is shown in Fig. 2b, where the 3D lines have been drawn in yellow. These 3D intersection lines can be projected to the fisheye image and have its line normal computed. To perform the association, we evaluate the angular distance between their normals, and choose the closest if the angular distance is below a small threshold. Those lines supported by 3D evidence have more relevance when generating layout hypotheses.

4 Layout Estimation

To extend the depth information to the periphery, we look for features in the fisheye image that allow us to draw coherent layout hypotheses. We choose *corners*, i.e. points of intersection of three alternatively oriented planes in the 3D world, manifested in the image as intersections of line-images. The intersections between lines in a general case with a highly populated scene can be endless, so we consider only those segments close to each other as more likely to actually intersect. To determine the proximity between segments, instead of using pixel distances, we reason in the 3D world with metric distances. Pixel distance is misleading, as it is affected by how far the points are from the camera, the perspective and the heavy distortion of the fisheye camera. Note that it is also difficult to deal with distances in the 3D world when there is no scale information available. With our system we can integrate scale information in the process.

We assume that, from previous steps, we have the 3D location of at least one structural plane from the depth data. Without loss of generality, we use the floor plane, which is the most probable plane to be in every scene. We use that plane to project all the lower lines and place them in a scaled 2D floor plan of the scene, we call *XZ-plane*. Similarly, the upper lines are projected to the *ceiling plane* (P_{ceil}), as explained in Sect. 4.1. Both floor and ceiling are going to be considered unique and symmetric. Together with the Manhattan World assumption, the 3D layouts we estimate from the images are a sequence of vertical walls alternatively oriented in $\mathbf{m}_x$ and $\mathbf{m}_z$, closed by the floor and ceiling planes. One of the main advantages of using a 2D projection is that the layout hypotheses can be generated using corners from floor or ceiling indistinctly, potentially overcoming hidden corners.

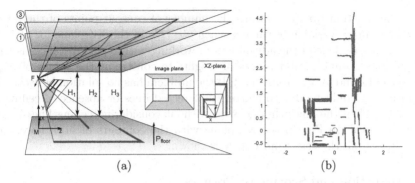

(a)   (b)

Fig. 3. (a) Projection of the lower line segments in the image to the P_{floor} and the upper segments to three virtual ceiling planes at different H_{ceil}. The chosen H_{ceil} is the one with most overlapping in the XZ-plane (H_2 in the example). (b) Real example of contour projection of lower lines (blue) and upper lines (red) to the XZ-plane. The small circle represents the position of the camera system. (Color figure online)

In Sect. 4.2 we describe how the corners are detected and scored. The generation of layout hypotheses is explained in Sect. 4.3, to finally deal with the evaluation process in Sect. 4.4.

4.1 Extraction of the Ceiling Plane for Horizontal Line Scaling

We can get the ray emanating from the optical center to every contour point of every lower line in X and Z and intersect it with the P_{floor} in 3D (Fig. 3a). With the floor plane equation and the Manhattan directions, we can transform these points from the camera reference frame F to a new reference axis M, with the Manhattan directions and origin at the floor level. If we plot the transformed points in the axis XZ, we can get a 2D scaled floor plan of the contours with scale (the *XZ-plane* in Fig. 3a).

As for the upper lines, the rays traced from the optical center to the contour points must be intersected with the P_{ceil} instead. As we assume structural symmetry, we know that the normal of the ceiling plane will be the same as the floor normal, but the distance to the origin is still unknown. To estimate H_{ceil} we use the fact that, in the XZ-plane view, wall-floor (l_j) and wall-ceiling ($\overline{l_i}$) intersections must be coincident. We can generate a P_{ceil} at an arbitrary height, compute the 3D intersections of the projection rays and evaluate how well the contours from upper segments $\overline{C}_i$ coincide with contours from lower segments $\underline{C}_j$ in the XZ-plane. In Fig. 3a there is a visual example with three different H_{ceil}. H_1 is too small and H_3 too big, so the segments of the floor do not match the segments of the ceiling in the XZ-plane. H_2 is the best one as contours from both planes match perfectly. Mathematically, we propose the following optimization problem:

$$\underset{H_{ceil}}{\arg\max} \sum_{i=1}^{N_{\overline{L}}} card(\overline{C}_i) \cdot \delta \qquad (2)$$

where the function $card(C_i)$ means the number of contour points of the line l_i and δ is a binary variable of value 1 when $\overline{C}_i \cap \underline{C}_j$ in the XZ-plane for at least one $\underline{l}_j$ in the set. One of the advantages of working with scaled distances is that we can set reasonable valid ranges of heights to constraint the values of H_{ceil} (e.g. 2–3 m for indoor environments). If the problem has no solution between the valid range it could be due to clutter, undetected lines or absence of ceiling in the image. Then the algorithm goes on without considering ceiling lines in the layout retrieval. In Fig. 3b the XZ-plane with the contours of both lower and upper lines from the case from Fig. 2c is shown.

4.2   Detection and Scoring of Corners

Line segments are the main piece of information we use to create layout hypotheses. However, we do not know whether they come from actual wall-ceiling or wall-wall intersections, or from other elements of the scene. In the literature there are many approaches to tackle this problem. For instance, [5] defines a corner when a minimal set of three or four line segments in certain orientations are detected. This requires having clear environments where most line segments can be perfectly detected. However, in the real world, occlusions or bad lighting conditions may cause some contours to remain undetected. In a Manhattan World, two line segments are enough to define a corner. Other works such as [21,22] tend to give more emphasis to vertical lines and the extension of their segments in their corner definition, which may be problematic for the same reason as before.

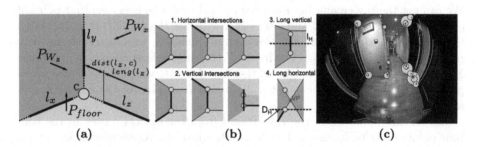

Fig. 4. (a) Graphical definition of a corner c, its line segments (l_x, l_y, l_z) and the *dist* and *leng* functions used in our scoring method. (b) Different types of corners we consider. (c) Example of a subset of the 100 most scored corners plotted as a yellow circles of diameter proportional to their score projected to the image in floor and ceiling. (Color figure online)

We propose to use more relaxed requirements to define corners, using just one or two line segments, and then use a scoring function to select the most salient ones and favor their appearance in the layout hypotheses generation. A corner c is then defined by a set of N_l line segments, and its score depends on the number of lines and their score value, which is defined by:

$$S_{l_i} = (leng(l_i) - dist(l_i, c)) \cdot \lambda \tag{3}$$

where *leng* measures the length of the line segment in meters, *dist* measures the distance of the closest point of the segment to the actual intersection point c in meters and λ is a multiplier of value 2 when the line is associated to a 3D line obtained from the depth camera and 1 when it is not (Fig. 4a). The score of a corner is the sum of line scores multiplied by the N_l to increase the score of corners supported by more lines:

$$S_{c_j} = N_{l_j} \cdot \sum_{i=1}^{N_{l_j}} S_{l_i} \tag{4}$$

We consider four different cases of corners to be retrieved depending on the classification of the lines involved according to our criterion (Fig. 4b):

1. **Horizontal intersections** $(l_x - l_z)$: If there is a l_y passing through the intersection point c, the contour points of l_y are scaled by assuming they share the same wall as l_x (i.e. 3D plane P_{W_x}) or l_z (P_{W_z}). If the scaled 3D contours of l_y have heights between 0 and H_{ceil} the vertical is included to improve the score of the corner.
2. **Vertical intersections** $(l_x - l_y$ or $l_y - l_z)$: As with the previous case, the segment l_y is scaled to verify plausability. The case of occluding walls is also considered in this type of intersection.
3. **Long vertical lines** (l_y): Only the ones crossing the horizon are considered as they are more likely to be wall to wall intersections instead of clutter. The projection of their topmost contour point to the P_{ceil} and the bottommost one to the P_{floor} are considered as two separate corners.
4. **Long horizontal lines** $(l_x$ or $l_z)$: Sometimes there is no visible or detected corner at the farther end of a corridor or a big room. We consider the possibility of long horizontal lines to intersect with the horizon. To keep layouts of reasonable size we restrict the distance to a maximum of D_H (in particular we set $D_H = 10$ m). The line score for this case is modified:

$$S_{l_i} = length(l_i) \cdot \lambda \cdot max(D_H - dist(l_i, c), 0) \tag{5}$$

After the extraction of corners we keep those with $S_c > 0$. To avoid redundant corners we merge those which are horizontally close to each other, summing the score of all corners involved to increase the likelihood of the resulting corner to appear in the hypotheses generation process. For this merging it is necessary to watch that the direction of the contours is compatible to the physical coherence (e.g. a corner supported by line segments directed towards $\mathbf{m}_x$ and $\mathbf{m}_z$ cannot be merged with another corner whose line segments are directed towards $-\mathbf{m}_x$ and $-\mathbf{m}_z$). In Fig. 4c there is an example of the 100 most scored corners after the merging.

4.3   Layout Hypotheses Generation

Our algorithm for layout hypotheses generation starts by picking up a set of corners from the set and sorting them clockwise in the XZ-plane. We proportionally increase the probability of choosing corners rewarding those with higher score. In order, we generate 2D corner distributions where every wall in direction $\mathbf{m}_x$ is followed by a wall in $\mathbf{m}_z$. We look for closed layout hypotheses. As the fisheye can only view a hemisphere, if there is no corners from behind the camera, the layout would be generated so it ends at the rear VPz (or by our design at D_H). We extract the layout only of the room where the camera is, so all hypotheses which are closed leaving out the camera position are discarded. As we have the contour points that define the lines of the corners, the hypothetic walls must not contradict their location in the map, otherwise the hypothesis is discarded as well. One of the keypoints of our method is that, taking advantage of the Manhattan assumption, we can integrate in the layout undetected corners and form a closed solution: when consecutive corners do not generate walls in Manhattan directions, intermediate virtual corners are created in order to generate two Manhattan-oriented walls. A more detailed description of the generation of layout hypotheses with special cases can be found in the supplementary material.

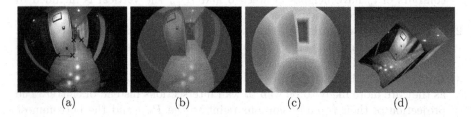

(a)   (b)   (c)   (d)

Fig. 5. (a) Sample hypothesis with the selected corners and the corresponding contours drawn. (b) Overlay of the planes generated by the layout colored depending on their orientation. (c) Extended depth map of the scene. (d) Colored point cloud of the layout obtained from the depth map. (Color figure online)

In Fig. 5 there is an example of a layout hypothesis with the contours and corners drawn in (a) and the resulting wall distribution colored in (b). As the XZ-plane is scaled and the H_{ceil} has been estimated we can generate a 3D depth map of the scene (Fig. 5c). We compare the result with the depth map provided by the depth camera, and use that to discard contradictory hypotheses (i.e. there cannot be walls in front of the given depth map). Finally, the depth map can be used to recover the 3D point cloud of the complete layout (Fig. 5d).

4.4   Evaluation of the Hypotheses

We have described a method to find the relevant corners in the image and to generate layout hypotheses. Next, we propose three methods to select the best hypothesis:

- **Sum of Scores (SS):** We define the score of an hypothesis as the sum of scores of the corners that have been used to generate it. The additional corners defined to generate Manhattan layouts have a score of zero.

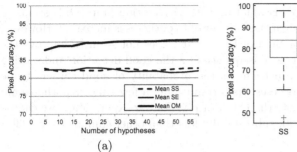
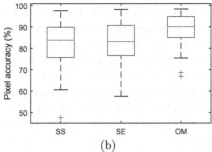

(a)

(b)

Fig. 6. (a) Pixel accuracy over the number of hypotheses generated. (b) Boxplot of the results using the three evaluation methods with the set of 70 images.

- **Sum of Edges (SE):** The polygon defined by the corners of the hypotheses as vertices can be drawn on the XZ-plane in order to choose the hypotheses which overlaps the most with the observed contours.
- **Orientation Map (OM):** It requires to build a reference image called *orientation map* [5], which is an image whose pixels encode the believed orientation given the line segments for perspective cameras. To build that image we create a set of overlapping perspective images from the fisheye image, apply the orientation map algorithm from [5] in each one of them and finally stitch them back together to form an omnidirectional orientation map. The evaluation consists in selecting that layout hypotheses which have better fitness between pixels with the same orientation.

In general, the fastest method is to score the hypotheses, which does not require any extra computation. Using the orientation map usually provides the best results, but it requires the previous computation of the map itself, which can be time consuming.

5   Experiments

In this work, we use a novel camera system with fisheye and depth image. Many datasets for indoor layout retrieval are usually based on conventional images, but not so many on omni-images, and none combining them with depth. For the experimental evaluation we have collected a set of 70 captures of indoor scenarios ourselves, including 23 from corridors/entrances, 15 from four different bedrooms, 4 from a bathroom, 12 from two living rooms, 4 from a kitchen and 12 from two small cluttered rooms. In order to perform a quantitative evaluation we have manually labelled these images to provide a per pixel tag between the three main classes (walls in X or Z and floor/ceiling). The measure employed is the percentage of pixels correctly tagged over the totality of pixels from the ground truth, which we call *pixel accuracy* (PA).

To choose the best fixed number of geometrically valid hypotheses to draw, we have tried with different quantities and observed the pixel accuracy for the three evaluation methods (Fig. 6a). Evaluating with Orientation Map (OM) seems to slightly improve the score when the number of hypotheses is increased. However, using Sum of Scores (SS) or Sum of Edges (SE) does not seem to improve the pixel accuracy at all. This is a consequence of a the good detection and scoring of corners in our method, which affects the probability of good corners to be selected when drawing hypotheses. As a result, only a few valid hypotheses are necessary to get one with more than 80 % of PA. For our experiments, we choose a number of hypotheses of 20, substantially less than other similar works [23].

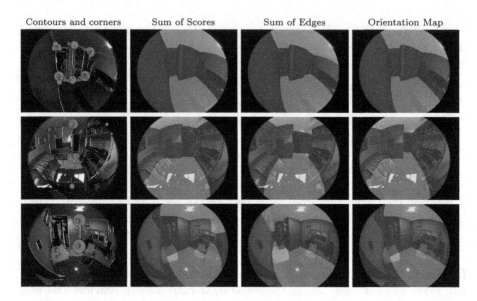

| Contours and corners | Sum of Scores | Sum of Edges | Orientation Map |

Fig. 7. Three examples of results from images from our set with best layout proposal for each method. More examples in the supplementary material.

In Fig. 6b there is a boxplot showing the distribution of pixel accuracy in the 70 images with the three evaluation methods. We can see how the SS and SE evaluation methods are able to tag correctly about 83 % of the pixels in the image (83.8 % and 83.2 % respectively). Using the orientation map reaches the 90 % and has less variance. However, the need for the previous computation of the orientation map makes this approach the least suitable for real-time applications: In our current implementation it takes around 23 s just to generate the map. The rest of the computations, including depth and fisheye preprocessing, corner extraction, generation of hypotheses and evaluation in our current implementation take an average sum of 33 s. Some examples of scenes from our set and their best results are shown in Fig. 7.

There is no fair comparison to be made with other works, because no other related work known to the authors use similar type of image combination. However, we explore the benefits of using such camera system compared to merely

Table 1. Mean pixel accuracy of the system with and without depth information (%).

Method	With depth	No depth
SS	82.7	71.7
SE	82.5	72.2
OM	89.2	80.2

Table 2. Mean pixel accuracy depending on the type of scene tested (%).

Room	SS	SE	OM
Corridor	86.5	84.3	90.3
Bedroom	78.6	79.6	87.7
Bathroom	75.0	69.6	84.9
Living room	85.1	87.5	91.2
Kitchen	83.2	76.9	85.3
Other	81.6	84.5	90.3

using a fisheye camera. We repeated the experiments aforementioned removing all depth information throughout the system in order to numerically observe how the results are affected. The first thing to notice is that the scale of the system is now arbitrary. Also, the absence of depth affects the computation of the VPs, the scoring of lines, the retrieval of the H_{ceil} and the elimination of contradictory hypotheses. A comparison of mean results with and without depth information is shown in Table 1, where it can be observed how the mean pixel accuracy decreases about 10 %.

A breakdown of the results depending on the type of room is provided in Table 2. In general we have experienced better performance in uncluttered environments (corridors), where structural lines can be easily seen. Compared to conventional perspective images, using omnidirectional cameras are better suited to overcome highly cluttered scenes, as the probability of encounter important lines either from the wall-floor or wall-ceiling intersections is higher. Sometimes, the problem does not come from the lines being occluded, but on the difficulty of them being detected. When the walls and the ceiling have similar color or the lightning conditions are poor, the line extraction algorithm might fail to detect important lines. This is a common problem to all similar methods in the literature. However, the depth information remains invariant to such problems in indoor environments, so the hybrid camera system we propose for this task always has some safe zone where we know for certain the shape of what is in front of the camera, even when the scene visual conditions are far from perfect. In normal conditions, with our camera configuration we are able to estimate the omnidirectional scaled layouts in one single shot, where the information from the depth camera can be integrated seamlessly and be used to detect objects inside the room or generate complete 3D models as the one shown in Fig. 1e.

Additional experiments detailing failure cases, as well as a summary video, can be found in the supplementary material.

6   Conclusion

In this work we have developed a new method to extend the 3D information of a depth camera to a field of view of over 180°. To do that, we propose a novel spatial layout retrieval algorithm, whose main novelty is combining a fisheye and a depth camera. The large field of view helps to use information from both the ceiling and the floor, which is helpful when there is clutter in the scene. To take advantage of that, we look for relevant corners by using the line segments extracted from the fisheye image and the depth information to assign probability of being actual corners in the scene. A heuristic procedure is then used to generate layout hypotheses from these corners, which are then put through an evaluation procedure for which we propose three methods. Experimental evaluation with real images of indoor environments shows great results in terms of accuracy, improving the state of the art in functionality: our method has less layout shape restrictions, needs less hypotheses and provide 3D models of the scene with scale in a single shot.

Acknowledgments. This work was supported by Projects DPI2014-61792-EXP and DPI2015-65962-R (MINECO/FEDER, UE) and grant BES-2013-065834 (MINECO).

References

1. Endres, F., Sprunk, C., Kummerle, R., Burgard, W.: A catadioptric extension for RGB-D cameras. In: IEEE/RSJ International Conference on Intelligent Robots and Systems (IROS), pp. 466–471(2014)
2. Tomari, R., Kobayashi, Y., Kuno, Y.: Wide field of view kinect undistortion for social navigation implementation. In: Bebis, G., et al. (eds.) ISVC 2012. LNCS, vol. 7432, pp. 526–535. Springer, Heidelberg (2012). doi:10.1007/978-3-642-33191-6_52
3. Fernandez-Moral, E., González-Jiménez, J., Rives, P., Arévalo, V.: Extrinsic calibration of a set of range cameras in 5 seconds without pattern. In: IEEE/RSJ International Conference on Intelligent Robots and Systems (IROS), pp. 429–435 (2014)
4. Delage, E., Lee, H., Ng, A.Y.: A dynamic bayesian network model for autonomous 3D reconstruction from a single indoor image. In: IEEE Conference on Computer Vision and Pattern Recognition (CVPR), vol. 2, pp. 2418–2428 (2006)
5. Lee, D.C., Hebert, M., Kanade, T.: Geometric reasoning for single image structure recovery. In: IEEE Conference on Computer Vision and Pattern Recognition (CVPR), pp. 2136–2143 (2009)
6. Coughlan, J.M., Yuille, A.L.: Manhattan world: Compass direction from a single image by bayesian inference. In: IEEE International Conference on Computer Vision (ICCV), vol. 2, pp. 941–947 (1999)
7. Del Pero, L., Bowdish, J., Fried, D., Kermgard, B., Hartley, E., Barnard, K.: Bayesian geometric modeling of indoor scenes. In: IEEE Conference on Computer Vision and Pattern Recognition (CVPR), pp. 2719–2726 (2012)
8. Chang, H.C., Huang, S.H., Lai, S.H.: Using line consistency to estimate 3D indoor Manhattan scene layout from a single image. In: IEEE International Conference on Image Processing (ICIP), pp. 4723–4727 (2015)
9. Hedau, V., Hoiem, D., Forsyth, D.: Recovering the spatial layout of cluttered rooms. In: IEEE International Conference on Computer Vision (ICCV), pp. 1849–1856 (2009)
10. Schwing, A.G., Hazan, T., Pollefeys, M., Urtasun, R.: Efficient structured prediction for 3D indoor scene understanding. In: IEEE Conference on Computer Vision and Pattern Recognition (CVPR), pp. 2815–2822 (2012)

11. Ramalingam, S., Pillai, J., Jain, A., Taguchi, Y.: Manhattan junction catalogue for spatial reasoning of indoor scenes. In: IEEE Conference on Computer Vision and Pattern Recognition (CVPR), pp. 3065–3072 (2013)
12. Mallya, A., Lazebnik, S.: Learning informative edge maps for indoor scene layout prediction. In: IEEE International Conference on Computer Vision (ICCV), pp. 936–944 (2015)
13. Hedau, V., Hoiem, D., Forsyth, D.: Thinking inside the box: using appearance models and context based on room geometry. In: Daniilidis, K., Maragos, P., Paragios, N. (eds.) ECCV 2010, Part VI. LNCS, vol. 6316, pp. 224–237. Springer, Heidelberg (2010)
14. Gupta, A., Hebert, M., Kanade, T., Blei, D.M.: Estimating spatial layout of rooms using volumetric reasoning about objects and surfaces. In: Advances in Neural Information Processing Systems, vol. 23, pp. 1288–1296. Curran Associates, Inc. (2010)
15. Del Pero, L., Guan, J., Brau, E., Schlecht, J., Barnard, K.: Sampling bedrooms. In: IEEE Conference on Computer Vision and Pattern Recognition (CVPR), pp. 2009–2016 (2011)
16. Choi, W., Chao, Y.W., Pantofaru, C., Savarese, S.: Understanding indoor scenes using 3D geometric phrases. In: IEEE Conference on Computer Vision and Pattern Recognition (CVPR), pp. 33–40 (2013)
17. Schwing, A.G., Fidler, S., Pollefeys, M., Urtasun, R.: Box in the box: Joint 3D layout and object reasoning from single images. In: IEEE International Conference on Computer Vision (ICCV) (2013)
18. Flint, A., Murray, D., Reid, I.: Manhattan scene understanding using monocular, stereo, and 3D features. In: IEEE International Conference on Computer Vision (ICCV), pp. 2228–2235 (2011)
19. Furlan, A., Miller, S.D., Sorrenti, D.G., Li, F.F., Savarese, S.: Free your camera: 3D indoor scene understanding from arbitrary camera motion. In: British Machine Vision Conference (BMVC) (2013)
20. Jia, H., Li, S.: Estimating the structure of rooms from a single fisheye image. In: IAPR Asian Conference on Pattern Recognition (ACPR), pp. 818–822 (2013)
21. López-Nicolás, G., Omedes, J., Guerrero, J.J.: Spatial layout recovery from a single omnidirectional image and its matching-free sequential propagation. Robot. Auton. Syst. **62**(9), 1271–1281 (2014)
22. Jia, H., Li, S.: Estimating structure of indoor scene from a single full-view image. In: IEEE International Conference on Robotics and Automation (ICRA), pp. 4851–4858 (2015)
23. Zhang, Y., Song, S., Tan, P., Xiao, J.: PanoContext: a whole-room 3D context model for Panoramic scene understanding. In: Fleet, D., Pajdla, T., Schiele, B., Tuytelaars, T. (eds.) ECCV 2014, Part VI. LNCS, vol. 8694, pp. 668–686. Springer, Heidelberg (2014)
24. Zhang, Q., Pless, R.: Extrinsic calibration of a camera and laser range finder (improves camera calibration). In: IEEE/RSJ International Conference on Intelligent Robots and Systems (IROS), pp. 2301–2306 (2004)
25. Scaramuzza, D., Harati, A., Siegwart, R.: Extrinsic self calibration of a camera and a 3D laser range finder from natural scenes. In: IEEE/RSJ International Conference on Intelligent Robots and Systems (IROS), pp. 4164–4169 (2007)
26. Geiger, A., Moosmann, F., Car, O., Schuster, B.: Automatic camera and range sensor calibration using a single shot. In: IEEE International Conference on Robotics and Automation (ICRA), pp. 3936–3943 (2012)

27. Puig, L., Bermudez-Cameo, J., Sturm, P., Guerrero, J.J.: Calibration of omnidirectional cameras in practice: a comparison of methods. Comput. Vis. Image Underst. **116**(1), 120–137 (2012)
28. Herrera C, D., Kannala, J., Heikkilä, J.: Joint depth and color camera calibration with distortion correction. IEEE Trans. Pattern Anal. Mach. Intell. **34**(10), 2058–2064 (2012)
29. Scaramuzza, D., Martinelli, A., Siegwart, R.: A toolbox for easily calibrating omnidirectional cameras. In: IEEE/RSJ International Conference on Intelligent Robots and Systems (IROS), pp. 5695–5701 (2006)
30. Perez-Yus, A., Lopez-Nicolas, G., Guerrero, J.J.: A novel hybrid camera system with depth and fisheye cameras. In: IAPR International Conference on Pattern Recognition (ICPR) (2016)
31. Bermudez-Cameo, J., Lopez-Nicolas, G., Guerrero, J.J.: Automatic line extraction in uncalibrated omnidirectional cameras with revolution symmetry. Int. J. Comput. Vis. **114**(1), 16–37 (2015)
32. Geyer, C., Daniilidis, K.: A unifying theory for central panoramic systems and practical implications. In: Vernon, D. (ed.) ECCV 2000. LNCS, vol. 1843, pp. 445–461. Springer, Heidelberg (2000)
33. Bazin, J.C., Kweon, I., Demonceaux, C., Vasseur, P.: A robust top-down approach for rotation estimation and vanishing points extraction by catadioptric vision in urban environment. In: IEEE/RSJ International Conference on Intelligent Robots and Systems (IROS), pp. 346–353 (2008)
34. Rusu, R.B., Cousins, S.: 3D is here: point cloud library (PCL). In: IEEE International Conference on Robotics and Automation (ICRA) (2011)

Built-in Foreground/Background Prior
for Weakly-Supervised Semantic Segmentation

Fatemehsadat Saleh[1,2]($\boxtimes$), Mohammad Sadegh Ali Akbarian[1,2],
Mathieu Salzmann[1,3], Lars Petersson[1,2], Stephen Gould[1],
and Jose M. Alvarez[1,2]

[1] The Australian National University (ANU), Canberra, Australia
stephen.gould@anu.edu.au
[2] CSIRO, Canberra, Australia
{fatemehsadat.saleh,mohammadsadegh.aliakbarian,lars.petersson,
jose.alvarezlopez}@data61.csiro.au
[3] CVLab, EPFL, Lausanne, Switzerland
mathieu.salzmann@epfl.ch

Abstract. Pixel-level annotations are expensive and time consuming to obtain. Hence, weak supervision using only image tags could have a significant impact in semantic segmentation. Recently, CNN-based methods have proposed to fine-tune pre-trained networks using image tags. Without additional information, this leads to poor localization accuracy. This problem, however, was alleviated by making use of objectness priors to generate foreground/background masks. Unfortunately these priors either require training pixel-level annotations/bounding boxes, or still yield inaccurate object boundaries. Here, we propose a novel method to extract markedly more accurate masks from the pre-trained network itself, forgoing external objectness modules. This is accomplished using the activations of the higher-level convolutional layers, smoothed by a dense CRF. We demonstrate that our method, based on these masks and a weakly-supervised loss, outperforms the state-of-the-art tag-based weakly-supervised semantic segmentation techniques. Furthermore, we introduce a new form of inexpensive weak supervision yielding an additional accuracy boost.

Keywords: Semantic segmentation · Weak annotation · Convolutional neural networks · Weakly-supervised segmentation

1 Introduction

Semantic scene segmentation, i.e., assigning a class label to every pixel in an input image, has received growing attention in the computer vision community, with accuracy greatly increasing over the years [1–6]. In particular,

Electronic supplementary material The online version of this chapter (doi:10.1007/978-3-319-46484-8_25) contains supplementary material, which is available to authorized users.

© Springer International Publishing AG 2016
B. Leibe et al. (Eds.): ECCV 2016, Part VIII, LNCS 9912, pp. 413–432, 2016.
DOI: 10.1007/978-3-319-46484-8_25

fully-supervised approaches based on Convolutional Neural Networks (CNNs) have recently achieved impressive results [1–4, 7]. Unfortunately, these methods require large amounts of training images with pixel-level annotations, which are expensive and time-consuming to obtain. Weakly-supervised techniques have therefore emerged as a solution to address this limitation [8–15]. These techniques rely on a weaker form of training annotations, such as, from weaker to stronger levels of supervision, image tags [12, 14, 16, 17], information about object sizes [17], labeled points or squiggles [12] and labeled bounding boxes [13, 18]. In the current Deep Learning era, existing weakly-supervised methods typically start from a network pre-trained on an object recognition dataset (e.g., ImageNet [19]) and fine-tune it using segmentation losses defined according to the weak annotations at hand [12–14, 16, 17].

In this paper, we are particularly interested in exploiting one of the weakest levels of supervision, i.e., image tags, which is a rather inexpensive attribute to annotate and thus more common in practice (e.g., Flickr [20]). Image tags simply determine which classes are present in the image without specifying any other information, such as the location of the objects. In this extreme setting, a naive weakly-supervised segmentation algorithm will typically yield poor localization accuracy. Therefore, recent works [12, 16, 21] have proposed to make use of objectness priors [22–25], which provide each pixel with a probability of being an object. In particular, these methods have exploited existing objectness algorithms, such as [22–24], with the drawback of introducing external sources of potential error. Furthermore, [22] typically only yields a rough foreground/background estimate, and [23, 24] rely on additional training data with pixel-level annotations.

Here, by contrast, we introduce a Deep Learning approach to weakly-supervised semantic segmentation where the localization information is directly extracted from the network itself. Our approach relies on the following intuition: One can expect that a network trained for the task of object recognition extracts features that focus on the objects themselves, and thus has hidden layers with units firing up on foreground objects, but not on background regions. A similar intuition was also recently explored for other tasks, such as object localization [26] and detection [27]. Starting from a fully-convolutional network pre-trained on ImageNet, we therefore propose to extract a foreground/background mask by directly exploiting the unit activations of some of the hidden layers in the network.

In particular, we focus on the fourth and fifth convolution layers of the VGG-16 pre-trained network [28], which provide higher-level information than the first three layers, such as highlighting complete objects or object parts. We then make use of a fully-connected Conditional Random Field (CRF) to smooth out this information and generate a foreground/background mask. We finally incorporate the resulting masks in our network via a weakly-supervised loss. The resulting masks can also be thought of as a form of objectness measure. While several CNN-based approaches have proposed to learn objectness, or saliency measures from annotations [29–31], to the best of our knowledge, our approach is the first extract this information directly from the hidden layer activations of a

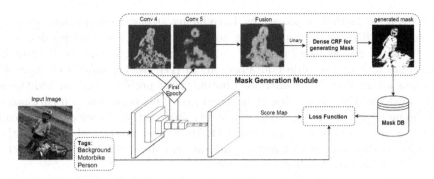

Fig. 1. Our weakly-supervised network with built-in foreground/background prior.

segmentation network, and employ the resulting masks as localization cues for weakly-supervised semantic segmentation. Ultimately, our model, illustrated by Fig. 1, can therefore be thought of as a weakly-supervised segmentation network with built-in foreground/background prior.

We demonstrate the benefits of our approach on two datasets (Pascal VOC 2012 [32] and a subset of Flickr (MIRFLICKR-1M) [20]). Our experiments show that our approach outperforms the state-of-the-art methods that use image tags only, and even some methods that leverage additional supervision, such as object size information [17] and point supervision [12]. Furthermore, we extend our framework to incorporate some additional, yet cheap, supervision, taking the form of asking the user to select the best foreground/background mask among several automatically generated candidates. Our experiments reveal that this additional supervision only costs the user roughly 2–3 seconds per image and yields another significant accuracy boost over our tags-only results.

2   Related Work

Weakly-supervised semantic segmentation has attracted a lot of attention, because it alleviates the painstaking process of manually generating pixel-level training annotations. Over the years, great progress has been made [9–14,16–18,33]. In particular, recently, Convolutional Neural Networks have been applied to the task of weakly-supervised segmentation with great success. In this section, we discuss these CNN-based approaches, which are the ones most related to our work.

The work of [14] constitutes the first method to consider fine-tuning a pre-trained CNN using image-level tags only within a weakly-supervised segmentation context. This approach relies on a simple Multiple Instance Learning (MIL) loss to account for image tags during training. While this loss improves segmentation accuracy over a naive baseline, this accuracy remains relatively low, due to the fact that no other prior than image tags is employed. By contrast, [13] incorporates an additional prior in the MIL framework in the form of an adaptive foreground/background bias. This bias significantly increases accuracy, which [13] shows can be further improved by introducing stronger supervision, such as labeled bounding boxes. Importantly, however, this bias is data-dependent and not trivial to re-compute for a new dataset. Furthermore, the results remain inaccurate in terms of object localization. In [17], weakly-supervised segmentation is formulated as a constrained optimization problem, and an additional prior modeling the size of objects is introduced. This prior relies on thresholds determining the percentage of the image area that certain classes of objects can occupy, which again is problem-dependent. More importantly, and as in [13], the resulting method does not exploit any information about the location of objects, and thus yields poor localization accuracy.

To overcome this weakness, some approaches [12,16,21] have proposed to exploit the notion of objectness. In particular, [16] makes use of a post-processing step that smoothes their initial segmentation results using the object proposals obtained by BING [23] or MCG [24]. While it improves localization, being a post-processing step, this procedure is unable to recover from some mistakes made by the initial segmentation. By contrast, [12,21] directly incorporate an objectness score [22,24] in their loss function. While accounting for objectness when training the network indeed improves segmentation accuracy, the whole framework depends on the success of the external objectness module, which, in practice, only produces a coarse heat map and does not accurately determine the location and shape of the objects (as evidenced by our results in supplementary materials).

Note that BING and MCG have been trained from PASCAL *train* images with full pixel-level annotations or bounding boxes, and thus [16,21] inherently makes use of stronger supervision than our approach. Here, instead of relying on an external objectness method, we leverage the intuition that, within its hidden layers, a network pre-trained for object recognition should already have learned to focus on the object themselves. This lets us develop a foreground/background mask directly from the information built into the network, which we empirically show provides a more accurate object localization prior. A relevant idea is also presented in an arxiv paper [34] which is further evidencing the popularity and importance of this research trend.

3   Our Approach

In this section, we introduce our approach to weakly-supervised semantic segmentation. After briefly discussing the CNN architecture that we use, we present our approach to extracting a foreground/background mask directly from the network itself. We then introduce our weakly-supervised learning algorithm that leverages this foreground/background information, and finally discuss our novel way to introduce additional weak supervision in the process.

3.1   Network Architecture

As most recent weakly-supervised semantic segmentation algorithms [12–14,16, 17], and as shown in Fig. 2, our architecture is based on the VGG-16-layer

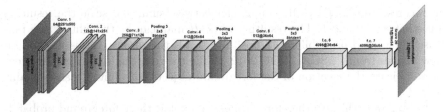

Fig. 2. Network architecture: fully convolutional neural network, derived from the VGG-16 network. We employ a receptive field of 128 pixels and a stride of 8.

network [28], whose weights were trained on ImageNet for the task of object recognition. Following the fully-convolutional approach [1], all fully-connected layers are converted to convolutional layers, and the final classifier replaced with a 1×1 convolution layer with N channels, where N represents the number of classes of the problem. As a modification to this fully convolutional network which has a stride of 32, inspired from [3], we use a stride of 8 and also a smaller receptive field (128 pixels), which has proven to be effective in practice in weakly-supervised semantic segmentation [13]. At the end of the network, we add a deconvolution layer to up-sample the output of the network to the size of the input image. In short, the network takes an image of size $W \times H$ as input and generates an $N \times W \times H$ output encoding a score for each pixel and for each class.

3.2 Built-in Foreground/Background Model

We now introduce our approach to extracting a foreground/background mask directly from our network. In Sect. 3.3, we show how this mask can be employed for weakly-supervised semantic segmentation.

Intuitively, we expect that a network trained for an object recognition task has learned to focus on the objects themselves, and their parts, rather than on background regions. In other words, it should produce high activation values on objects and their parts. To evaluate this, we studied the activation of the different hidden layers of our initial network pre-trained on ImageNet. To this end, we forward each image through the network and visualize each activation by computing the mean over the channels after resizing the activation map to the input image size. Perhaps unsurprisingly, this lead to the following observations, illustrated in Fig. 3. The first two convolutional layers of the VGG network extract image edges. As we move deeper in the network, the convolutional layers extract higher-level features. In particular, the third convolutional layer fires up on prototypical object shapes. The fourth layer indicates the location of complete objects, and the fifth one fires up on the most discriminative object parts [35].

Based on these observations, we propose to make use of the fourth and fifth layers to produce an initial foreground/background mask estimate. To this end, we first convert these two layers from 3D tensors ($512 \times W \times H$) to 2D matrices ($W \times H$) via an average pooling operation over the 512 channels. We then fuse the two resulting matrices by simple elementwise sum, and scale the resulting values between 0 and 1. The resulting $W \times H$ map can be thought of as a pixelwise foreground probability. Figure 3 illustrates the results of this method on a few images from PASCAL VOC 2012. While the resulting scores indeed accurately indicate the location of the foreground objects, this initial mask remains noisy.

To overcome this, we therefore propose to exploit these foreground probabilities as unary potentials in a fully-connected CRF. Let $\mathbf{x} = \{x_i\}_{i=1}^{W \cdot H}$ be the set of random variables, where x_i encodes the label of pixel i, i.e., either foreground or background. We encode the joint distribution over all pixels with a Gibbs energy of the form

$$E(\mathbf{x} = \mathbf{X}) = -\sum_i \log P_f(x_i = X_i) + \sum_i \sum_{j>i} \theta_{ij}(x_i = X_i, x_j = X_j), \quad (1)$$

where $P_f(x_i = X_i)$ is the probability of pixel i taking label assignment X_i, obtained directly from the foreground probability of our initial fusion strategy. Following [36], we define the pairwise term θ_{ij} as a contrast-sensitive Potts model using two Gaussian kernels encoding color similarity and spatial smoothness. This form lets us make use of the filtering-based mean-field strategy of [36] to perform inference efficiently. Some resulting masks are shown in the last column of Fig. 3.

Note that our foreground/background masks can be thought of as a form of objectness measure. While objectness has been used previously for weakly-supervised semantic segmentation (MCG and BING in [16], and the generic objectness [22] in [12]), the benefits of our approach are twofold. First, we extract this information directly from the same network that will be used for semantic segmentation, which prevents us from having to rely on an external method. Second, as opposed to BING and MCG, we require neither object bounding boxes, nor object segments to train our method. While [22] predicts objectness after training on a set of images, as shown in our experiments in the supplementary materials, our method yields much more accurate object localization than this technique. To further evidence the benefits of our approach, in supplementary material, we evaluate the masks obtained using the probabilities of [22,24] as unary potentials in the same dense CRF.

3.3   Weakly-Supervised Learning

We now introduce our learning algorithm for weakly-supervised semantic segmentation. We first introduce a simple loss based on image tags only, and then show how we can incorporate our foreground/background masks in our framework.

Intuitively, given image tags, one would like to encourage the image pixels to be labeled as one of the classes that are observed in the image, while preventing them to be assigned to unobserved classes. Note that this assumes that the tags cover all the classes depicted in the image. This assumption, however,

Image   1st Conv. 2nd Conv. 3rd Conv. 4th Conv. 5th Conv.   Fusion   Our mask   G.T

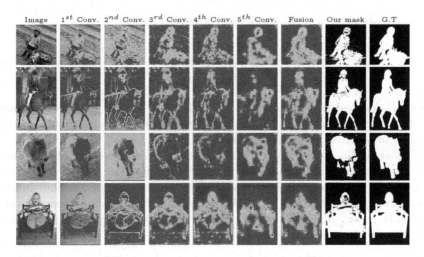

Fig. 3. Built-in foreground/background mask. From left to right, there is the image, the activations of 1st, 2nd, 3rd ,4th, and 5th Conv. layers, the results of our fusion strategy, and the final mask after CRF smoothing followed by G.T. Note that "Fusion" constitutes the unary potential of the dense CRF used to obtain "Our mask".

is commonly employed in weakly-supervised semantic segmentation [12,14,16]. Formally, given an input image I, let $\mathcal{L}$ be the set of classes that are present in the image (including background) and $\bar{\mathcal{L}}$ the set of classes that are absent. Furthermore, let us denote by $s_{i,j}^k(\theta)$ the score produced by our network with parameters θ for the pixel at location (i,j) and for class k, $0 \leq k < N$. Note that, in general, we will omit the explicit dependency of the variables on the network parameters. Finally, let $S_{i,j}^k$ be the probability of class k obtained after a softmax layer, i.e.,

$$S_{i,j}^k = \frac{\exp(s_{i,j}^k)}{\sum_{c=1}^N \exp(s_{i,j}^c)}. \tag{2}$$

Encoding the above-mentioned intuition can then simply be achieved by designing a loss of the form

$$L_{weak} = -\frac{1}{|\mathcal{L}|} \sum_{k \in \mathcal{L}} \log S^k - \frac{1}{|\bar{\mathcal{L}}|} \sum_{k \in \bar{\mathcal{L}}} \log(1 - S^k), \tag{3}$$

where S^k represents a candidate score for each class in the image. In short, the first term in Eq. 3 expresses the fact that the present classes should be in the image, while the second term penalizes the pixels that have high probabilities for the absent classes. In practice, instead of computing S^k as the maximum probability (as previously used in [12,14]) for class k over all pixels in the image, we make use of the convex Log-Sum-Exp (LSE) approximation of the maximum (as previously used in [16]), which can be written as

$$\tilde{S}^k = \frac{1}{r}\log\left[\frac{1}{|I|}\sum_{i,j\in I}\exp(rS_{i,j}^k)\right], \tag{4}$$

where $|I|$ denotes the total number of pixels in the image and r is a parameter allowing this function to behave in a range between the maximum and the average. In practice, following [16], we set r to 5.

The loss in Eq. 3 does not rely on any notion of foreground and background. As a consequence, minimizing it will typically yield poor object localization accuracy. To overcome this issue, we propose to make use of our built-in foreground/background mask introduced in Sect. 3.2. Let $M_{i,j}$ denote the mask value at pixel (i,j), i.e., $M_{i,j} = 1$ if pixel (i,j) belongs to the foreground and 0 otherwise. We can then re-write our loss as

$$L_{mask} = -\frac{1}{|\mathcal{L}|-1}\sum_{k\in\mathcal{L},k\neq 0}\log(S_f^k) - \log(S^0) - \frac{1}{|\bar{\mathcal{L}}|.|I|}\sum_{i,j\in I,\,k\in\bar{\mathcal{L}}}\log(1-S_{i,j}^k), \tag{5}$$

where

$$S_f^k = \frac{1}{r}\log\left[\frac{1}{|M|}\sum_{i,j|M_{i,j}=1}\exp(rS_{i,j}^k)\right], \tag{6}$$

and

$$S^0 = \frac{1}{r}\log\left[\frac{1}{|\bar{M}|}\sum_{i,j|M_{i,j}=0}\exp(rS_{i,j}^0)\right]. \tag{7}$$

where $|M|$ and $|\bar{M}|$ denote the number of foreground and background pixels, respectively, and S_f^k computes an approximate maximum probability for the present class k over all pixels in the foreground mask. Similarly, S^0 denotes an approximate maximum probability for the background class over all pixels outside the foreground mask. In short, the loss of Eq. 5 favors present classes to appear in the foreground mask, while pixels predicted as background should be assigned to the background class and no pixels should take on an absent label.

To learn the parameters of our network, we follow a standard back-propagation strategy to search for the parameters θ that minimize the loss in Eq. 10. In particular, the network is fine-tuned using stochastic gradient descent (SGD) with momentum μ to update the weights by a linear combination of the negative gradient and the previous weight update. At inference time, given the test image, the network performs a dense prediction. We optionally apply a fully connected CRF to smooth the segmentation using the default parameters of [3].

Remark. Although our loss function performs well, an alternative to this loss function can be expressed as

$$L_{weak} = -\frac{1}{|I|}\sum_{i,j\in I}\log(S_{i,j}) - \frac{1}{|I|}\sum_{i,j\in I,\,k\in\bar{\mathcal{L}}}\log(1-S_{i,j}^k), \tag{8}$$

where $S_{i,j}$ represents the approximation of the maximum by using the LSE over the observed classes for each pixel as

$$S_{i,j} = \frac{1}{r} \log \left[\frac{1}{|\mathcal{L}|} \sum_{k \in \mathcal{L}} \exp(rS_{i,j}^k) \right]. \tag{9}$$

Such a formulation can also be extended to incorporate our mask, which yields

$$L_{mask} = -\frac{1}{|M|} \sum_{i,j|M_{i,j}=1} \log(S_{i,j}^f) - \frac{1}{|\bar{M}|} \sum_{i,j|M_{i,j}=0} \log(S_{i,j}^0) - \frac{1}{|I|} \sum_{i,j \in I,\ k \in \bar{\mathcal{L}}} \log(1 - S_{i,j}^k), \tag{10}$$

where $S_{i,j}^0$ denotes the probability for the background class and

$$S_{i,j}^f = \frac{1}{r} \log \left[\frac{1}{|\mathcal{L}|-1} \sum_{k \in \mathcal{L},\ k \neq 0} \exp(rS_{i,j}^k) \right] \tag{11}$$

computes an approximate maximum probability over the observed foreground classes.

We found that, while the two approaches starting from the losses in Eqs. 3 and 8 differ from each other, incorporating our masks in both of them using Eqs. 5 and 10 improves the segmentation quality considerably. Empirically, however, we found that this second formulation was slightly less effective than the one in Eq. 5. This will be further discussed in the experiments.

3.4   A Novel Weak Supervision: The *CheckMask* Procedure

The masks obtained with the approach introduced in Sect. 3.2 are not always perfect. This is due to the fact that the information obtained by fusing the activations of the fourth and fifth layers is noisy, and thus the solution found by inference in the CRF is not always the desired one. As a matter of fact, many other solutions also have a low energy (Eq. 1). Rather than relying on a single mask prediction, we propose to generate multiple such predictions, and provide them to a user who decides which one is the best one.

The problem of generating several predictions in a given CRF is known as the M-best problem. Here, in particular, we are interested in generating solutions that all have low energy, but are diverse, and thus follow the approach of [37]. In essence, this approach iteratively generates solutions, and, at each iteration, modifies the energy of Eq. 1 to encourage the next solution to be different from the ones generated previously. In practice, we make use of the Hamming distance as a diversity measure. This diversity measure can be encoded as an additional unary potential in Eq. 1, and thus comes at virtually no additional cost in the inference procedure. For more details about the diverse M-best strategy, we refer the reader to [37].

Ultimately, we generate several masks with this procedure, and ask the user to click on the one that best matches the input image. Such a selection can

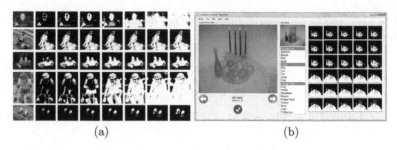

(a)   (b)

Fig. 4. (a) Mask candidates generated with our approach. From left to right, we show the input image, the 1st, 5th, 10th, 15th, 20th, 25th and 30th solutions. (b) Our new level of supervision: The annotator selects a mask which he/she thinks contains all foreground object(s) and the minimum amount of background.

be achieved very quickly. In practice, we found that a user takes roughly 2–3 seconds per image to select the best mask. As a consequence, this new source of weak supervision remains very cheap, while, as evidenced by our experiments, allows us to achieve a significant improvement over our tags-only formulation (Fig. 4).

4   Experiments

In this section, we first describe the datasets used for our experiments, and give some details about our learning and inference procedures. We then compare our approach to the state-of-the-art methods that use the same level of supervision as us. We provide an evaluation of our foreground/background masks in supplementary material.

4.1   Datasets

In our experiments, we first made use of the standard Pascal VOC 2012 dataset [32], which serves as a benchmark in most weakly-supervised semantic segmentation papers [12–14,16,17]. Similar to the dataset used in [12,13,17], this dataset contains $N = 21$ classes, and 10,582 training images (the VOC 2012 training set and the additional data annotated by [38]), 1,449 validation images and 1,456 test images. The image tags were obtained from the pixel-level annotations by simply listing the classes observed in each image. As in [12,13,16,17], we report results on both the validation and the test set.

To further demonstrate the generality of our approach, we applied our method to a dataset that truly contains only image tags. To this end, we created a new training dataset from a subset of the MIRFLICKR-1M dataset [20]. In order to facilitate comparison, this subset was built using images containing the same classes as Pascal VOC 2012. In total it contains 7238 images, which were used for training purposes only. This new Flickr-based dataset does not provide any ground-truth pixel level annotations and, hence, the Pascal VOC validation set was used as test data. This training data will be made publicly available upon acceptance of the paper.

For both datasets, we report the mean intersection over union (mIOU), averaged over the 21 classes.

4.2 Implementation Details

Our network architecture is detailed in Sect. 3.1. The parameters of this network were found by using stochastic gradient descent with a fixed learning rate of 10^{-4} for the first 40k iterations, 10^{-5} for the next 20k iterations, a momentum of 0.9, a weight decay of 0.0005, and mini-batches of size 1. Similar to recent weakly-supervised segmentation methods [12–14,16,17], the network weights were initialized with those of a network pre-trained for a 1000-way classification task on the ILSVRC 2012 dataset [19]. Hence, for the last convolutional layer, we used the weights corresponding to the 20 classes shared by Pascal VOC and ILSVRC. For the background class, we initialized the weights with zero-mean Gaussian noise with a standard deviation of 0.1. At inference time, given only the test image, the network generates a dense prediction as a complete semantic segmentation map. We used C++ and Python (Caffe framework [39]) for our implementation. As other methods [13,17], we further optionally apply a dense CRF to refine this initial segmentation. To this end, we used the same CRF parameter values as these other approaches, i.e., the same as in [3].

4.3 Semantic Segmentation Results

We now compare our approach with state-of-the-art baselines. We first present the results obtained with image tags only, and then those with additional weak supervision. For the sake of completeness, in addition to the state-of-the-art baselines, we also report the results of our approach without using our foreground/background masks, i.e., by using Eq. 3 as training loss. We also provide the segmentation results achieved by training a model using the losses introduced in Eqs. 8 and 10. In the following, we will refer to our baseline as *Ours (baseline)*, to our approach with tags only as *Ours (tags)* and to our approach with additional weak supervision as *Ours (CheckMask)*. We indicate the additional use of a dense CRF to further refine our results with *+CRF* after the method's name.

Pascal VOC with Image Tags. In Table 1, we compare our approach with our mask-free baseline and state-of-the-art methods on the task of semantic segmentation given only image tags during training. Note that our approach outperforms all the baselines by a large margin, whether we use CRF smoothing or not. Importantly, we outperform the methods based on an objectness prior [12,16], which clearly shows the benefits of using our built-in foreground/background masks instead of external objectness algorithms. The importance of our mask is further evidenced by the fact that we outperform our mask-free baseline by 13.8 mIOU points. Note that the best-performing baseline (MIL w/ILP) [16] uses a large amount of additional images (roughly 700K) from the ILSVRC2013 dataset to boost the accuracy of the basic MIL method. Note that we still outperform this baseline, even without using any such additional data.

Pascal VOC with Additional Weak Supervision. We then evaluate our approach on Pascal VOC with our additional CheckMask weak supervision procedure. While no other approaches have used this same kind of weak supervision, we report the results of methods that have used additional weak supervision of a similar cost to compute. In particular, these includes the point supervision of [12], the random crops of [13], the size information of [17] and the MCG segments of [16,21]. The results of this comparison are provided in Table 2. Note that our CheckMask procedure yields an improvement of 4.2 mIOU point (and 4.9 mIOU point when a CRF is applied) over our tag-only approach. More importantly, our approach outperforms the baselines by a large margin. Note that other approaches have proposed to rely on labeled bounding boxes, which require a user to provide a bounding box for each individual foreground object in an image and to associate a label to each such bounding box. While this procedure is clearly more costly than ours, we achieve similar accuracy to these baselines (52.5 % for [13] when using labeled bounding boxes and 54.1 % for [13] when using labeled bounding boxes in an EM process vs. 51.49 % for our approach). We believe that this further evidences the benefits of our approach. We also report the results on the test set of Pascal VOC 2012 and compare our method with other baselines (see Table 3).

Flickr (MIRFLICKR-1M) with Image Tags and Additional Weak Supervision. We now evaluate our method by training it using our new dataset containing a subset of the MIRFLICKR-1M images [20]. Since no other results have been reported on this dataset, we also computed the results of CCNN [17] whose code is publicly available, and which has shown to yield good accuracy in the previous experiments. In Table 4, we compare the results of our approach with this baseline when trained using tags only, and, as mentioned before, tested on the Pascal VOC 2012 validation dataset, since no ground-truth pixel level annotations are available in Flickr. Note that our approach significantly outperforms both our mask-free baseline and the CCNN by a large margin. It is worth mentioning that this dataset contains three rare classes, Chair, Dining Table, and the Sofa which have 1.1 %, 0.5 %, and 1.3 % of the whole dataset respectively. Although these classes have a negligible contribution in constructing this dataset, our approach performs well in comparison to CCNN in segmenting these classes (17.0 % vs. 10.7 %, 31.2 % vs. 0 %, and 16.8 % vs. 0 % in these classes respectively).

We then further used our CheckMask procedure to evaluate how much can be gained by some cheap additional weak supervision. Note that, here, we were unable to report the result of the CCNN with additional supervision, since, in practice, we did not have access to per-image object size information. Our results

Table 1. Per class IOU on the PASCAL VOC 2012 validation set for methods trained using image tags.

Method	bg	aero	bike	bird	boat	bottle	bus	car	cat	chair	cow	table	dog	horse	mbike	person	plant	sheep	sofa	train	tv	mIOU
Ours (baseline), Eq. 8	65.4	19.1	14.1	19.5	18.8	25.5	36.9	34.6	43.0	9.0	11.9	14.6	33.7	21.1	33.0	35.3	25.2	15.2	10.3	30.2	29.8	26.0
Ours (baseline)	59.2	25.2	14.6	21.9	19.0	28.6	49.5	41.9	42.7	10.1	32.9	25.6	36.8	29.8	34.5	32.5	24.6	31.2	21.6	39.3	29.0	31.0
MIL(Tag) [16]	37.0	10.4	12.4	10.8	5.3	5.7	25.2	21.1	25.15	4.8	21.5	8.6	29.1	25.1	23.6	25.5	12.0	28.4	8.9	22.0	11.6	17.8
MIL(Tag) w/ILP [16]	73.2	25.4	18.2	22.7	21.5	28.6	39.5	44.7	46.6	11.9	40.4	11.8	45.6	40.1	35.5	35.2	20.8	41.7	17.0	34.7	30.4	32.6
MIL(Tag) w/ILP+sspxl [16]	77.2	37.3	18.4	25.4	28.2	31.9	41.6	48.1	50.7	12.7	45.7	14.6	50.9	44.1	39.2	37.9	28.3	44.0	19.6	37.6	35.0	36.6
What's the point(Tag) W/Obj [12]	78.8	41.6	19.8	38.7	33.0	17.2	33.8	38.8	45.0	10.4	35.2	12.6	42.3	34.3	33.2	22.7	18.6	40.1	14.9	37.7	28.1	32.2
EM-Fixed(Tag)+CRF [13]	-	-	-	-	-	-	-	-	-	-	-	-	-	-	-	-	-	-	-	-	-	20.8
EM-Adapt(Tag)+CRF [13]	-	-	-	-	-	-	-	-	-	-	-	-	-	-	-	-	-	-	-	-	-	38.2
CCNN(Tag) [17]	66.3	24.6	17.2	24.3	19.5	34.4	45.6	44.3	44.7	14.4	33.8	21.4	40.8	31.6	42.8	39.1	28.8	33.2	21.5	37.4	34.4	33.3
CCNN(Tag)+CRF [17]	68.5	25.5	18.0	25.4	20.2	36.3	46.8	47.1	48.0	15.8	37.9	21.0	44.5	34.5	46.2	40.7	30.4	36.3	22.2	38.8	36.9	35.3
Ours (Tags), Eq. 10	79.7	56.4	19.2	54.0	40.9	44.7	62.9	49.9	56.2	12.2	44.5	33.7	55.0	44.1	52.2	46.2	32.3	50.0	26.7	52.9	26.5	44.8
Ours (Tags)+CRF, Eq. 10	81.0	57.6	19.7	45.8	41.5	46.4	62.5	53.2	59.3	14.0	44.4	38.0	55.4	46.5	54.2	49.3	34.2	50.7	27.1	55.3	25.9	45.8
Ours (Tags)	79.7	56.2	19.1	53.8	41.3	44.6	62.8	50.1	56.1	12.1	44.8	33.9	54.9	44.3	52.3	46.1	33.1	49.5	26.9	52.7	26.7	44.8
Ours (Tags)+CRF	79.2	60.1	20.4	50.7	41.2	46.3	62.6	49.2	62.3	13.3	49.7	38.1	58.4	49.0	57.0	48.2	27.8	55.1	29.6	54.6	26.6	46.6

Table 2. Per class IOU on the PASCAL VOC 2012 validation set using additional supervision during training.

Method: Additional Supervision	bg	aero	bike	bird	boat	bottle	bus	car	cat	chair	cow	table	dog	horse	mbike	person	plant	sheep	sofa	train	tv	mIOU
[16]: MIL(Tag) w/ILP+bbox	78.6	46.9	18.6	27.9	30.7	38.4	44.0	49.6	49.8	11.6	44.7	14.6	50.4	44.7	40.8	38.5	26.0	45.0	20.5	36.9	34.8	37.8
[16]: MIL(Tag) w/ILP+seg	79.6	50.2	21.6	40.6	34.9	40.5	45.9	51.5	60.6	12.6	51.2	11.6	56.8	52.9	44.8	42.7	31.2	55.4	21.5	38.8	36.9	42.0
[21]: SN-B+MCG seg	80.7	54.6	10.7	55.6	37.5	51.8	46.3	42.6	48.0	16.0	46.3	10.0	54.6	45.9	47.5	34.4	24.5	53.7	23.0	47.8	48.6	41.9
[34]: STC+Additional train data	84.5	68.0	19.5	60.5	42.5	44.8	68.4	64.0	64.8	14.5	52.0	22.8	58.0	55.3	57.8	60.5	40.6	56.7	23.0	57.1	31.2	49.8
[12]: Objectness	78.8	41.6	19.8	38.7	33.0	17.2	33.8	38.8	45.0	10.4	35.2	12.6	42.3	34.3	33.2	22.7	18.6	40.1	14.9	37.7	28.1	32.2
[12]: 1Point	56.2	24.5	16.1	21.5	20.0	30.8	53.0	34.2	53.0	7.9	41.4	41.6	42.7	40.1	42.0	45.9	24.0	37.5	28.5	45.6	29.8	35.1
[12]: Objectness+1Point	77.9	48.6	22.6	36.6	36.9	37.4	57.4	50.4	50.9	13.7	40.0	40.9	49.5	38.1	51.1	46.9	31.2	48.2	27.8	48.9	44.9	42.7
[12]: Objectness+AllPoints	78.5	48.5	21.3	39.5	37.9	37.7	49.5	45.3	52.5	17.0	42.7	39.9	46.8	44.0	51.0	50.6	22.0	46.6	28.9	52.3	44.3	42.7
[12]: Objectness+1Point(GT)	79.6	49.4	22.9	38.6	40.9	45.8	60.4	60.9	55.5	17.7	37.8	41.0	54.1	41.7	54.9	56.9	32.2	51.1	26.4	54.5	45.3	46.1
[17]: Random Crops	-	-	-	-	-	-	-	-	-	-	-	-	-	-	-	-	-	-	-	-	-	34.4
[17]: Random Crops+CRF	-	-	-	-	-	-	-	-	-	-	-	-	-	-	-	-	-	-	-	-	-	36.4
[17]: Size Info	-	-	-	-	-	-	-	-	-	-	-	-	-	-	-	-	-	-	-	-	-	40.5
[17]: Size Info.+CRF	-	-	-	-	-	-	-	-	-	-	-	-	-	-	-	-	-	-	-	-	-	42.4
Ours (CheckMask), Eq. 10	85.2	65.2	21.4	49.7	50.2	48.5	67.3	63.2	58.5	16.1	43.3	36.1	56.1	45.4	53.7	52.3	36.5	47.1	27.0	61.9	37.2	48.7
Ours (CheckMask)+CRF, Eq. 10	86.3	70.4	22.1	48.9	53.4	49.8	71.0	66.0	61.5	17.7	46.4	38.3	59.9	49.1	57.4	55.8	38.5	50.6	28.4	64.3	36.0	51.0
Ours (CheckMask)	85.2	65.2	21.1	52.1	49.9	48.6	67.3	63.6	59.7	15.5	43.2	36.6	56.9	45.9	53.7	52.6	37.0	48.2	27.6	61.7	36.9	49.0
Ours (CheckMask)+CRF	86.4	70.1	21.7	53.1	52.5	50.7	70.9	66.6	63.2	16.9	45.8	39.1	61.1	50.0	56.8	56.2	40.0	51.9	29.3	63.1	05.9	51.5

Table 3. Per class IOU on the PASCAL VOC 2012 test set.

Method	bg	aero	bike	bird	boat	bottle	bus	car	cat	chair	cow	table	dog	horse	mbike	person	plant	sheep	sofa	train	tv	mIOU
CCNN (tags) [17]	-	24.2	19.9	26.3	18.6	38.1	51.7	42.9	48.2	15.6	37.2	18.3	43.0	38.2	52.2	40.0	33.8	36.0	21.6	33.4	38.3	35.6
CCNN (tags)+size [17]	-	36.7	23.6	47.1	30.2	40.6	59.5	54.3	51.9	15.9	43.3	34.8	48.2	42.5	59.2	43.1	35.5	45.2	31.4	46.2	42.2	43.3
CCNN (tags)+size+CRF [17]	42.3	24.5		56.0	30.6	39.0	58.8	52.7	54.8	14.6	48.4	34.2	52.7	46.9	61.1	44.8	37.4	48.8	30.6	47.7	41.7	45.1
MIL-FCN [16]	-	-	-	-	-	-	-	-	-	-	-	-	-	-	-	-	-	-	-	-	-	25.7
MIL-sppxl [16]	74.7	38.8	19.8	27.5	21.7	32.8	40.0	50.1	47.1	7.2	44.8	15.8	49.4	47.3	36.6	36.4	24.3	44.5	21.0	31.5	41.3	35.8
MIL-obj [16]	76.2	42.8	20.9	29.6	25.9	38.5	40.6	51.7	49.0	9.1	43.5	16.2	50.1	46.0	35.8	38.0	22.1	44.5	22.4	30.8	43.0	37.0
MIL-seg [16]	78.7	48.0	21.2	31.1	28.4	35.1	51.4	55.5	52.8	7.8	56.2	19.9	53.8	50.3	40.0	38.6	27.8	51.8	24.7	33.3	46.3	40.6
WhatsThePnt+Obj+1Point [12]	80.6	50.2	23.9	38.4	33.1	38.5	52.0	50.9	55.4	18.3	38.2	37.7	51.0	46.1	54.7	43.2	35.4	45.1	33.0	49.6	40.0	43.6
EM-Adapt+CRF [13]	76.3	37.1	21.9	41.6	26.1	38.5	50.8	44.9	48.9	16.7	40.8	29.4	47.1	45.8	54.8	28.2	30.0	44.0	29.2	34.3	46.0	39.6
SN-B+MCG seg [21]	82.1	53.6	12.4	53.5	29.5	41.6	46.9	46.3	50.3	16.8	48.7	17.2	60.6	51.8	61.7	36.4	25.2	58.3	19.3	48.5	45.5	43.2
Ours (Tags)	80.6	54.7	22.0	63.2	34.0	44.3	64.5	49.4	53.0	12.5	45.6	38.8	53.9	45.0	61.6	42.5	40.3	51.3	31.0	42.5	32.0	45.8
Ours (Tags)+CRF	80.3	57.5	24.1	66.9	31.7	43.0	67.5	48.6	56.7	12.6	50.9	42.6	59.4	52.9	65.0	44.8	41.3	51.1	33.7	44.4	33.2	48.0
Ours (CheckMask)	86.1	61.8	24.9	60.8	42.8	49.7	68.6	61.7	56.3	15.5	44.2	41.0	56.1	47.2	64.1	50.2	40.9	48.1	33.1	55.6	41.4	50.0
Ours (CheckMask)+CRF	87.4	65.7	26.0	64.2	43.7	53.2	72.6	63.6	59.5	17.1	48.0	43.7	61.2	52.0	69.3	54.8	43.0	50.3	34.6	59.2	42.0	52.9

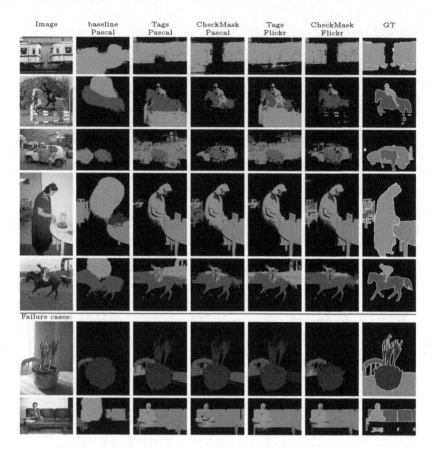

Fig. 5. Qualitative results: from left to right, there is image, the results of the model trained on Pascal VOC (column 2, 3, and 4), the results of the model trained on Flickr (column 5 and 6), and the groundtruth. The last two row shows the failure cases.

in Table 4 evidence the benefits of our CheckMask procedure over our tag-only approach (See also Fig. 5 for qualitative results). Note that selecting the best mask for all 7238 training images took roughly 5 h, which corresponds to 2.5 sec per image. This shows that our additional level of weak supervision remains very cheap to compute.

5   Conclusion

We have introduced a Deep Learning approach to weakly-supervised semantic segmentation that leverages foreground/background masks directly extracted from our network pre-trained for the task of object recognition. Our experiments have shown that our approach outperforms the state-of-the-art methods when trained on image tags only. Furthermore, we have introduced a new level of weak supervision, consisting of selecting one mask among a set of candidates.

Table 4. Per class IOU on the PASCAL VOC 2012 validation set for models trained with a subset of the MIRFLICKR-1M dataset.

Method	bg	aero	bike	bird	boat	bottle	bus	car	cat	chair	cow	table	dog	horse	mbike	person	plant	sheep	sofa	train	tv	mIOU
CCNN (tags) [17]	70.8	28.6	16.3	26.8	24.3	33.8	42.4	46.4	41.0	11.7	19.7	0	39.6	31.0	44.2	42.3	24.3	34.0	0	37.8	25.4	30.5
CCNN (tags)+CRF [17]	75.4	32.8	13.1	32.1	27.3	32.9	41.3	45.6	43.3	10.7	16.5	0	44.8	37.3	47.2	46.2	27.1	36.8	0	38.8	26.9	32.2
Ours (baseline)	69.8	28.2	17.2	25.9	20.6	29.2	39.2	45.4	39.2	10.9	16.9	15.0	39.2	30.3	40.8	36.9	25.8	28.6	21.2	34.2	28.6	30.6
Ours (Tags)	75.2	52.8	15.3	46.4	33.1	44.3	51.4	46.1	47.9	15.1	23.1	27.0	53.8	34.5	47.1	40.7	20.3	43.3	18.2	45.6	19.3	38.1
Ours (Tags)+CRF	76.9	57.1	15.6	40.1	35.6	41.0	54.8	49.1	48.8	17.0	21.1	31.2	54.4	35.7	51.6	42.8	21.2	42.7	16.8	47.4	18.2	39.0
Ours (CheckMask)	82.6	63.4	20.5	53.6	43.2	46.4	58.5	57.8	52.8	14.0	27.7	26.9	55.7	41.7	54.2	47.7	25.8	48.6	21.5	54.2	25.6	43.9
Ours (CheckMask)+CRF	83.8	68.2	17.2	57.7	46.4	48.7	62.1	59.4	56.2	14.7	29.3	28.8	59.3	45.6	57.5	50.6	27.4	53.4	23.2	56.5	26.4	46.3

This procedure can be achieve very easily, taking only roughly 2–3 seconds per image, and yields a further significant boost in accuracy. In the future, we intend to study if jointly training the foreground/background mask extraction procedure and the weakly-supervised segmentation network can further improve our results.

References

1. Long, J., Shelhamer, E., Darrell, T.: Fully convolutional networks for semantic segmentation. In: The IEEE Conference on Computer Vision and Pattern Recognition (CVPR), June 2015
2. Noh, H., Hong, S., Han, B.: Learning deconvolution network for semantic segmentation. In: Proceedings of the IEEE International Conference on Computer Vision, pp. 1520–1528 (2015)
3. Chen, L., Papandreou, G., Kokkinos, I., Murphy, K., Yuille, A.L.: Semantic image segmentation with deep convolutional nets and fully connected crfs. CoRR abs/1412.7062 (2014)
4. Zheng, S., Jayasumana, S., Romera-Paredes, B., Vineet, V., Su, Z., Du, D., Huang, C., Torr, P.H.: Conditional random fields as recurrent neural networks. In: Proceedings of the IEEE International Conference on Computer Vision, pp. 1529–1537 (2015)
5. Mostajabi, M., Yadollahpour, P., Shakhnarovich, G.: Feedforward semantic segmentation with zoom-out features. In: Proceedings of the IEEE Conference on Computer Vision and Pattern Recognition, pp. 3376–3385 (2015)
6. Sharma, A., Tuzel, O., Jacobs, D.W.: Deep hierarchical parsing for semantic segmentation. In: Proceedings of the IEEE Conference on Computer Vision and Pattern Recognition, pp. 530–538 (2015)
7. Farabet, C., Couprie, C., Najman, L., LeCun, Y.: Learning hierarchical features for scene labeling. IEEE Trans. Pattern Anal. Mach. Intell. **35**(8), 1915–1929 (2013)
8. Pourian, N., Karthikeyan, S., Manjunath, B.: Weakly supervised graph based semantic segmentation by learning communities of image-parts. In: Proceedings of the IEEE International Conference on Computer Vision, pp. 1359–1367 (2015)
9. Xu, J., Schwing, A., Urtasun, R.: Tell me what you see and i will show you where it is. In: Proceedings of the IEEE Conference on Computer Vision and Pattern Recognition, pp. 3190–3197 (2014)
10. Vezhnevets, A., Ferrari, V., Buhmann, J.M.: Weakly supervised semantic segmentation with a multi-image model. In: 2011 IEEE International Conference on Computer Vision (ICCV), pp. 643–650. IEEE (2011)
11. Xu, J., Schwing, A.G., Urtasun, R.: Learning to segment under various forms of weak supervision. In: Proceedings of the IEEE Conference on Computer Vision and Pattern Recognition, pp. 3781–3790 (2015)
12. Bearman, A., Russakovsky, O., Ferrari, V., Fei-Fei, L.: What's the point: semantic segmentation with point supervision. ArXiv e-prints (2015)
13. Papandreou, G., Chen, L.C., Murphy, K.P., Yuille, A.L.: Weakly- and semi-supervised learning of a deep convolutional network for semantic image segmentation. In: The IEEE International Conference on Computer Vision (ICCV), December 2015
14. Pathak, D., Shelhamer, E., Long, J., Darrell, T.: Fully convolutional multi-class multiple instance learning. In: ICLR Workshop (2015)

15. Qi, X., Shi, J., Liu, S., Liao, R., Jia, J.: Semantic segmentation with object clique potential. In: Proceedings of the IEEE International Conference on Computer Vision, pp. 2587–2595 (2015)
16. Pinheiro, P.O., Collobert, R.: From image-level to pixel-level labeling with convolutional networks. In: The IEEE Conference on Computer Vision and Pattern Recognition (CVPR), June 2015
17. Pathak, D., Krahenbuhl, P., Darrell, T.: Constrained convolutional neural networks for weakly supervised segmentation. In: The IEEE International Conference on Computer Vision (ICCV), December 2015
18. Dai, J., He, K., Sun, J.: Boxsup: exploiting bounding boxes to supervise convolutional networks for semantic segmentation. In: Proceedings of the IEEE International Conference on Computer Vision, pp. 1635–1643 (2015)
19. Russakovsky, O., Deng, J., Su, H., Krause, J., Satheesh, S., Ma, S., Huang, Z., Karpathy, A., Khosla, A., Bernstein, M., Berg, A.C., Fei-Fei, L.: ImageNet large scale visual recognition challenge. Int. J. Comput. Vis. (IJCV) **115**(3), 211–252 (2015)
20. Huiskes, M.J., Thomee, B., Lew, M.S.: New trends and ideas in visual concept detection: the MIR flickr retrieval evaluation initiative. In: Proceedings of the 2010 ACM International Conference on Multimedia Information Retrieval, MIR 2010, pp. 527–536. ACM, New York (2010)
21. Wei, Y., Liang, X., Chen, Y., Jie, Z., Xiao, Y., Zhao, Y., Yan, S.: Learning to segment with image-level annotations. Pattern Recognit. **59**, 234–244 (2016)
22. Alexe, B., Deselaers, T., Ferrari, V.: Measuring the objectness of image windows. IEEE Trans. Pattern Anal. Mach. Intell. **34**(11), 2189–2202 (2012)
23. Cheng, M.M., Zhang, Z., Lin, W.Y., Torr, P.: Bing: binarized normed gradients for objectness estimation at 300fps. In: The IEEE Conference on Computer Vision and Pattern Recognition (CVPR), June 2014
24. Arbeláez, P., Pont-Tuset, J., Barron, J., Marques, F., Malik, J.: Multiscale combinatorial grouping. In: Proceedings of the IEEE Conference on Computer Vision and Pattern Recognition, pp. 328–335 (2014)
25. Carreira, J., Sminchisescu, C.: Constrained parametric min-cuts for automatic object segmentation. In: 2010 IEEE Conference on Computer Vision and Pattern Recognition (CVPR), pp. 3241–3248. IEEE (2010)
26. Oquab, M., Bottou, L., Laptev, I., Sivic, J.: Is object localization for free?-Weakly-supervised learning with convolutional neural networks. In: Proceedings of the IEEE Conference on Computer Vision and Pattern Recognition, pp. 685–694 (2015)
27. Zhou, B., Khosla, A., Lapedriza, A., Oliva, A., Torralba, A.: Object detectors emerge in deep scene CNNs. arXiv preprint arXiv:1412.6856 (2014)
28. Simonyan, K., Zisserman, A.: Very deep convolutional networks for large-scale image recognition. CoRR abs/1409.1556 (2014)
29. Ghodrati, A., Diba, A., Pedersoli, M., Tuytelaars, T., Van Gool, L.: Deepproposal: Hunting objects by cascading deep convolutional layers. In: Proceedings of the IEEE International Conference on Computer Vision, pp. 2578–2586 (2015)
30. Kuo, W., Hariharan, B., Malik, J.: Deepbox: Learning objectness with convolutional networks. In: Proceedings of the IEEE International Conference on Computer Vision, pp. 2479–2487 (2015)
31. Zou, W., Komodakis, N.: Harf: hierarchy-associated rich features for salient object detection. In: The IEEE International Conference on Computer Vision (ICCV), December 2015

32. Everingham, M., Eslami, S.M.A., Van Gool, L., Williams, C.K.I., Winn, J., Zisserman, A.: The pascal visual object classes challenge: a retrospective. Int. J. Comput. Vis. **111**(1), 98–136 (2015)

33. Vezhnevets, A., Ferrari, V., Buhmann, J.M.: Weakly supervised structured output learning for semantic segmentation. In: 2012 IEEE Conference on Computer Vision and Pattern Recognition (CVPR), pp. 845–852. IEEE (2012)

34. Wei, Y., Liang, X., Chen, Y., Shen, X., Cheng, M.M., Zhao, Y., Yan, S.: STC: a simple to complex framework for weakly-supervised semantic segmentation. arXiv preprint arXiv:1509.03150 (2015)

35. Bertasius, G., Shi, J., Torresani, L.: Deepedge: a multi-scale bifurcated deep network for top-down contour detection. CoRR abs/1412.1123 (2014)

36. Koltun, V.: Efficient inference in fully connected CRFs with Gaussian edge potentials. In: Advances in Neural Information Processing Systems (2011)

37. Batra, D., Yadollahpour, P., Guzman-Rivera, A., Shakhnarovich, G.: Diverse M-best solutions in Markov random fields. In: Fitzgibbon, A., Lazebnik, S., Perona, P., Sato, Y., Schmid, C. (eds.) ECCV 2012, Part V. LNCS, vol. 7576, pp. 1–16. Springer, Heidelberg (2012)

38. Hariharan, B., Arbeláez, P., Bourdev, L., Maji, S., Malik, J.: Semantic contours from inverse detectors. In: 2011 IEEE International Conference on Computer Vision (ICCV), pp. 991–998. IEEE (2011)

39. Jia, Y., Shelhamer, E., Donahue, J., Karayev, S., Long, J., Girshick, R., Guadarrama, S., Darrell, T.: Caffe: convolutional architecture for fast feature embedding. In: Proceedings of the ACM International Conference on Multimedia, pp. 675–678. ACM (2014)

It's Moving! A Probabilistic Model for Causal Motion Segmentation in Moving Camera Videos

Pia Bideau$^{(\boxtimes)}$ and Erik Learned-Miller

College of Information and Computer Sciences,
University of Massachusetts, Amherst, USA
{pbideau,elm}@cs.umass.edu

Abstract. The human ability to detect and segment moving objects works in the presence of multiple objects, complex background geometry, motion of the observer, and even camouflage. In addition to all of this, the ability to detect motion is nearly instantaneous. While there has been much recent progress in motion segmentation, it still appears we are far from human capabilities. In this work, we derive from first principles a likelihood function for assessing the probability of an optical flow vector given the 2D motion direction of an object. This likelihood uses a novel combination of the angle and magnitude of the optical flow to maximize the information about how objects are moving differently. Using this new likelihood and several innovations in initialization, we develop a motion segmentation algorithm that beats current state-of-the-art methods by a large margin. We compare to five state-of-the-art methods on two established benchmarks, and a third new data set of camouflaged animals, which we introduce to push motion segmentation to the next level.

Keywords: Motion segmentation · Video segmentation · Optical flow · Moving camera · Background subtraction

1 Introduction

"Motion is a powerful cue for image and scene segmentation in the human visual system. This is evidenced by the ease with which we see otherwise perfectly camouflaged creatures as soon as they move." –Philip Torr [1]

How can we match the ease and speed with which humans and other animals detect motion? This remarkable capability works in the presence of complex background geometry, camouflage, and motion of the observer. Figure 1 shows a frame from a video of a "walking stick" insect. Despite the motion of the camera, the rarity of the object, and the high complexity of the background geometry, the insect is immediately visible as soon as it starts moving.

Electronic supplementary material The online version of this chapter (doi:10.1007/978-3-319-46484-8_26) contains supplementary material, which is available to authorized users.

© Springer International Publishing AG 2016
B. Leibe et al. (Eds.): ECCV 2016, Part VIII, LNCS 9912, pp. 433–449, 2016.
DOI: 10.1007/978-3-319-46484-8_26

Fig. 1. Where is the camouflaged insect? Before looking at Fig. 2, which shows the ground truth localization of this insect, try identifying the insect. While it is virtually impossible to see without motion, it immediately "pops out" to human observers as it moves in the video.

To develop such a motion segmentation system, we re-examined classical methods based upon perspective projection, and developed a new probabilistic model which accurately captures the information about 3D motion in each observed optical flow vector v. First, we estimate the portion of the optical flow due to rotation, and subtract it from v to produce v_t, the translational portion of the optical flow. Next, we derive a new *conditional flow angle likelihood* $\mathcal{L} = p(\theta_{v_t} \mid M, \|v_t\|)$, the probability of observing a particular flow angle θ_{v_t} given a model M of the angle part of a particular object's (or the background's) motion field and the flow magnitude $\|v_t\|$.

M, which we call an *angle field*, describes the motion *directions* of an object in the image plane. It is a function of the object's relative motion (U, V, W) and the camera's focal length f, but can be computed more directly from a set of *motion field parameters* $(U', V', W) = (fU, fV, W)_2$, where the "2" subscript indicates L_2 normalization.

Our new angle likelihood helps us to address a fundamental difficulty of motion segmentation: the ambiguity of 3D motion given a set of noisy flow vectors. While we cannot eliminate this problem, the angle likelihood allows us to weigh the evidence for each image motion properly based on the optical flow. In particular, when the underlying image motion is very small, moderate errors in the optical flow can completely change the apparent motion direction (i.e., the angle of the optical flow vector). When the underlying image motion is large, typical errors in the optical flow will not have a large effect on apparent motion direction. This leads to the critical observation that small optical flow vectors are less informative about motion than large ones. Our derivation of the angle likelihood (Sect. 3) quantifies this notion and makes it precise in the context of a Bayesian model of motion segmentation.

We evaluate our method on three diverse data sets, achieving state-of-the-art performance on all three. The first is the widely used Berkeley Motion Segmentation (BMS-26) database [2,3], featuring videos of cars, pedestrians, and other common scenes. The second is the Complex Background Data Set [4], designed to test algorithms' abilities to handle scenes with highly variable depth. Third, we introduce a new and even more challenging benchmark for motion segmentation algorithms: the *Camouflaged Animal Data Set*. The nine (moving

Fig. 2. Answer: the insect from Fig. 1 in shown in red. The insect is trivial to see in the original video, though extremely difficult to identify in a still image. In addition to superior results on standard databases, our method is also one of the few that can detect objects in such complex scenes. (Color figure online)

camera) videos in this benchmark exhibit camouflaged animals that are difficult to see in a single frame, but can be detected based upon their motion across frames.

2 Related Work

A large number of motion segmentation approaches have been proposed, including [2,4–25]. We focus our review on recent methods.

Many methods for motion segmentation work by tracking points or regions through multiple frames to form motion trajectories, and grouping these trajectories into coherent moving objects [2,17,18,20,26]. Elhamifar and Vidal [26] track points through multiple images and show that rigid objects are represented by low-dimensional subspaces in the space of tracks. They use sparse subspace clustering to identify separate objects. Brox and Malik [2] define a pairwise metric on multi-frame trajectories so that they may be clustered to perform motion segmentation. Fragkiadaki et al. [20] detect discontinuities of the embedding density between spatially neighboring trajectories. These discontinuities are used to infer object boundaries and perform segmentation. Papazoglou and Ferrari [17] develop a method that looks both forward and backward in time, using flow angle and flow magnitude discontinuities, appearance modeling, and superpixel mapping across images to connect independently moving objects across frames. Keuper et al. [18] also track points across multiple frames and use minimum cost multicuts to group the trajectories.

These trajectory-based methods are *non-causal*. To segment earlier frames, the knowledge of future frames is necessary. We propose a causal method, relying only on the flow between two frames and information passed forward from previous frames. Despite this, we outperform trajectory-based methods, which in general tend to a depth dependent motion segmentation (see Experiments).

Another set of methods analyze optical flow between a pair of frames, grouping pixels into regions whose flow is consistent with various motion models. Torr [1] develops a sophisticated probabilistic model of optical flow, building a mixture model that explains an arbitrary number of rigid components within the scene. Interestingly, he assigns different types of motion models to each object based on model fitting criteria. His approach is fundamentally based on projective geometry rather based directly on perspective projection equations, as in our approach. Horn has identified drawbacks of using projective geometry in such estimation problems and has argued that methods based directly on perspective projection are less prone to overfitting in the presence of noise [27]. Zamalieva et al. [16] present a combination of methods that rely on homographies and fundamental matrix estimation. The two methods have complementary strengths, and the authors attempt to select among the best dynamically. An advantage of our method is that we do not depend upon the geometry of the scene to be well-approximated by a group of homographies, which enables us to address videos with very complex background geometries. Narayana et al. [4] remark that for translational only motions, the angle field of the optical flow will consist of one of a set of canonical angle fields, one for each possible motion direction, regardless of the focal length. They use these canonical angle fields as a basis with which to segment a motion image. However, they do not handle camera rotation, which is a significant limitation.

Another set of methods using occlusion events in video to reason about depth ordering and independent object motion [19,28]. Ogale et al. [28] use occlusion cues to further disambiguate non-separable solutions to the motion segmentation problem. Taylor et al. [19] introduce a causal framework for integrating occlusion cues by exploiting temporary consistency priors to partition videos into depth layers.

3   Methods

The *motion field* of a scene is a 2D representation of 3D motion. Motion vectors, describing the displacement in 3D, are projected onto the image plane forming a 2D motion field. This field is created by the movement of the camera relative to a stationary environment and the additional motion of independently moving objects. We use the optical flow, or estimated motion field, to segment each video image into static environment and independently moving objects.

The observed flow field consists of the flow vectors v at each pixel in the image. Let m be the flow vectors describing the motion field caused only by a rotating and translating camera in its stationary 3D environment – m does not include motion of other independently moving objects. The flow vectors m can be decomposed in a *translational component* m_t and a *rotational component* m_r. Let the direction or angle of a flow vector of a translational camera motion at a particular pixel (x, y) be θ_{m_t}.

When the camera is only translating, there are strong constraints on the optical flow field – the *direction* θ_{m_t} of the motion at each pixel is determined by the camera translation (U, V, W), the image location of the pixel (x, y), and the camera's focal length f, and has no dependence on scene depth [29].

$$\theta_{m_t} = \arctan(W \cdot y - V \cdot f, W \cdot x - U \cdot f) \tag{1}$$
$$= \arctan(W \cdot y - V', W \cdot x - U') \tag{2}$$

The collection of θ_{m_t} forms a translational angle field M representing the camera's translation direction on the 2D image plane.

Simultaneous camera rotation and translation, however, couple the scene depth and the optical flow, making it much harder to assign pixels to the right angle field M described by the estimated translation parameters (U', V', W).

To address this, we wish to subtract off the flow vectors m_r describing the rotational camera motion field from the observed flow vectors v to produce a flow v_t comprising camera translation only. The subsequent assignment of flow vectors to particular angle fields is thus greatly simplified. However estimating camera rotation in the presence of multiple motions is challenging. We organize the Methods section as follows:

In Sect. 3.1, we describe how all frames after the first frame are segmented, using the segmentation from the previous frame and our novel angle likelihood. After reviewing Bruss and Horn's motion estimation technique [30] in Sect. 3.2, Sect. 3.3 describes how our method is initialized in the first frame, including a novel process for estimating camera motion in the presence of multiple motions.

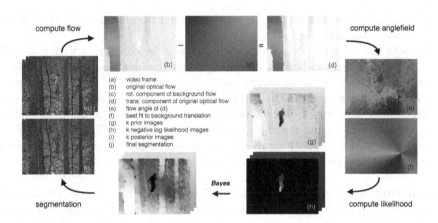

Fig. 3. Our segmentation procedure. Given the optical flow (b) the camera rotation is estimated. Then, the flow m_r due to camera rotation defined by the motion parameters (A, B, C) (c) is subtracted from the optical flow v to produce a translational flow v_t. The flow angles θ_{v_t} of v_t are shown in (e). The best fitting translation parameters (U', V', W) to the static environment of v_t yield an estimated angle field M (f), which clearly shows the forward motion of the camera (rainbow focus of expansion pattern) not visible in the original angle field. The motion component priors (g) and negative log likelihoods (h) yield the posteriors (i) and the final segmentation (j).

3.1 A Probabilistic Model for Motion Segmentation

Given a prior motion segmentation of frame $t - 1$ into k different motion components and an optical flow from frames t and $t + 1$, segmenting frame t requires several ingredients: **(a)** the *prior* probabilities $p(M_j)$ for each pixel that it is assigned to a particular angle field M_j, **(b)** the estimate of the translational angle field M_j, $1 \leq j \leq k$ to be able to model the motion for each of the k motion components from the previous frame, **(c)** for each pixel position, a *likelihood* $\mathcal{L}_j = p(v_t \mid M_j)$, the probability of observing a flow vector v_t under an estimated angle field M_j, and **(d)** the prior probability $p(M_{k+1})$ and angle likelihoods $\mathcal{L}_{k+1}$ given an angle field M_{k+1} to model a *new motion*. Given these priors and likelihoods, we use Bayes' rule to obtain a *posterior* probability for each translational angle field at each pixel location. We have

$$p(M_j \mid v_t) \propto p(v_t \mid M_j) \cdot p(M_j) \tag{3}$$

We directly use this posterior for segmentation. We now describe how the above quantities are computed.

Propagating the posterior for a new prior. We start from the optical flow of Sun et al. [31] (Fig. 3b). We then create a prior at each pixel for each angle field M_j in the new frame (Fig. 3g) by propagating the posterior from the previous frame (Fig. 3i) in three steps.

1. Use the previous frame's flow to map posteriors from frame $t-1$ (Fig. 3i) to new positions in frame t.
2. Smooth the mapped posterior in the new frame by convolving with a spatial Gaussian, as done in [4,32]. This implements the idea that object locations in future frames are likely to be close to their locations in previous frames.
3. Renormalize the smoothed posterior from the previous frame to form a proper probability distribution at each pixel location, which acts as the prior on the k motion components for the new frame (Fig. 3g). Finally, we set aside a probability of $1/(k+1)$ for the prior of a new motion component, while rescaling the priors for the pre-existing motions to sum to $k/(k+1)$.

Estimating and removing rotational flow. We use the prior for the motion component of the static environment to weight pixels for estimating the current frame's flow due to the camera motion. We estimate the camera translation parameters (U', V', W) and rotation parameters (A, B, C) using a modified version of the Bruss and Horn algorithm [30] (Sect. 3.2). As described above, we then render the flow angle independent of the unknown scene depth by subtracting the estimated rotational flow (Fig. 3c) from the original flow (Fig. 3b) to produce an estimate of the flow without influences of camera rotation (Fig. 3d). For each flow vector we compute:

$$\hat{v}_t = v - \hat{m}_r(\hat{A}, \hat{B}, \hat{C}) \tag{4}$$

$$\theta_{v_t} = \angle(\hat{v}_t, n) \tag{5}$$

where n is a unit vector $[1, 0]^T$.

For each additional motion component j besides the static environment, we estimate 3D translation parameters (U', V', W) using the segment priors to select pixels, weighted according to the prior, such that the motion perceived from video frame t to $t+1$ is described by j independent angle fields M_j.

The flow angle likelihood. Once we have obtained a translational flow field by removing the rotational flow, we use each flow vector v_t to decide which motion component it belongs to. Most of the information about the 3D motion direction is contained in the flow angle, not the flow magnitude. This is because for a given translational 3D motion direction (relative to the camera), the flow angle is completely determined by that motion and the location in the image, whereas the flow magnitude is a function of the object's depth, which is unknown. However, as discussed above, the *amount of information* in the flow angle depends upon the flow magnitude–flow vectors with greater magnitude are much more reliable indicators of true motion direction. This is why it is critical to formulate the angle likelihood conditioned on the flow magnitude.

Other authors have used flow angles in motion segmentation. For example, Papazoglou and Ferrari [17] use both a gradient of the optical flow and a separate function of the flow angle to define motion boundaries. Narayana et al. [4] use *only* the optical flow angle to evaluate motions. But our derivation gives a principled and effective method of using the flow angle and magnitude together to mine accurate information from the optical flow. In particular, we show that while (under certain mild assumptions) the translational magnitudes alone have no information about which motion is most likely, the magnitudes play an important role in specifying the *informativeness* of the flow angles. In our experiments section, we demonstrate that failing to condition on flow magnitudes in this way results in greatly reduced performance over our derived model.

We now derive the key element of our method, the *conditional flow angle likelihood* $p(\theta_{v_t} \mid M_j, \|v_t\|)$, the probability of observing a flow direction θ_{v_t} given that a pixel was part of a motion component undergoing the 2D motion direction M_j, and that the flow magnitude was $\|v_t\|$. We make the following modeling assumptions:

1. We assume the observed translational flow $v_t = (\|v_t\|, \theta_{v_t})$ at a pixel is a noisy observation of the translational motion field $m_t = (\|m_t\|, \theta_{m_t})$:

$$v_t = m_t + \eta, \tag{6}$$

   where η is independent 2D Gaussian noise with zero mean and circular but unknown covariance.
2. We assume the translational motion field magnitude $\|m_t\|$ is statistically independent of the translation angle field M created by the estimated 3D translation parameters (U', V', W). It follows that $\|m_t\| = \|m_t\| + \eta$ is also independent of M, and hence $p(\|v_t\| \mid M) = p(\|v_t\|)$.

With these assumptions, we have

$$p(v_t \mid M_j) \overset{(1)}{=} p(\|v_t\|, \theta_{v_t} \mid M_j) \tag{7}$$

$$= p(\theta_{v_t} \mid \|v_t\|, M_j) \cdot p(\|v_t\| \mid M_j) \tag{8}$$

$$\overset{(2)}{=} p(\theta_{v_t} \mid \|v_t\|, M_j) \cdot p(\|v_t\|) \tag{9}$$

$$\propto p(\theta_{v_t} \mid \|v_t\|, M_j), \tag{10}$$

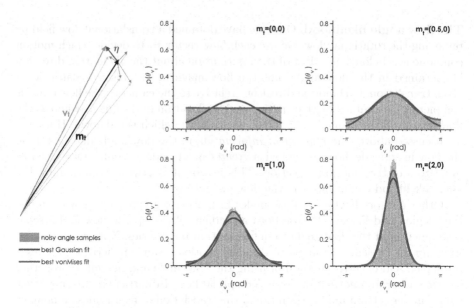

Fig. 4. The von Mises distribution. When a motion field vector m_t is perturbed by added Gaussian noise η (figure top left), the resulting distribution over optical flow angles θ_{v_t} is well-modeled by a *von Mises* distribution. The figure shows how small motion field vectors result in a broad distribution of angles after noise is added, while larger magnitude motion field vectors result in a narrower distribution of angles. The red curve shows the best von Mises fit to these sample distributions and the blue curve shows the lower quality of the best Gaussian fit. (Color figure online)

where the numbers over each equality give the assumption that is invoked. Equation (10) follows since $p(\|v_t\|)$ is constant across all estimated angle fields.

We model $p(\theta_{v_t} \mid \|v_t\|, M)$ using a *von Mises* distribution $\mathcal{V}(\mu, \kappa)$ with parameters μ, the preferred direction, and concentration parameter κ. We set $\mu = \theta_{m_t}$, since θ_{m_t} is the most likely direction assuming a noisy observation of a translational motion θ_{v_t}. To set κ, we observe that when the ground truth flow magnitude $\|m_t\|$ is small, the distribution of observed angles θ_{v_t} will be near uniform (see Fig. 4, $m_t = (0,0)$), whereas when $\|m_t\|$ is large, the observed angle θ_{v_t} is likely to be close to the flow angle θ_{m_t} (Fig. 4, $m_t = (2,0)$). We can achieve this basic relationship by setting $\kappa = a(\|m_t\|)^b$, where a and b are parameters that give added flexibility to the model. Since we don't have direct access to $\|m_t\|$, we use $\|v_t\|$ as a surrogate, yielding

$$p(\theta_{v_t} \mid \|v_t\|, M_j) \propto \mathcal{V}(\theta_{v_t}; \mu = \theta_{m_t}, \kappa = a\|v_t\|^b). \tag{11}$$

Note that this likelihood treats zero-length translation vectors as uninformative–it assigns them the same likelihood under all motions. This makes sense, since the direction of a zero-length optical flow vector is essentially random. Similarly, the longer the optical flow vector, the more reliable and informative it becomes.

Likelihood of a new motion. Lastly, with no prior information about new motions, we set $p(\theta_{v_t} \mid \|v_t\|, M_j) = \frac{1}{2\pi}$, a uniform distribution.

Once we have priors and likelihoods, we compute the posteriors (Eq. 3) and label each pixel as

$$L = \arg\max_j p(M_j \mid v_t). \tag{12}$$

3.2 Bruss and Horn's Motion Estimation

To estimate the translation parameters (U', V', W) of the camera relative to the static environment, we use the method of Bruss and Horn [30] and apply it to pixels selected by the prior of M_j. The observed optical flow vector v_i at pixel i can be decomposed as $v_i = p_i + e_i$, where v_i is the component of v_i in the predicted direction θ_{m_t} and e_i is the component orthogonal to v_i. The authors find the motion parameters that minimizes the sum of these "error" components e_i. The optimization for translation-only is

$$\arg\min_{U',V',W} \sum_i \|e_i(v_i, U', V', W)\|, \tag{13}$$

where $(U', V', W) = (Uf, Vf, W)$ are the three translation parameters. Since we do not know the focal length it's not possible to compute the correct 3D translation, but we are able to estimate the parameters (U', V', W), which shows the same angular characteristics in 2D as the true 3D translation (U, V, W). Bruss and Horn give a closed form solution to this problem for the translation-only case.

Recovering camera rotation. Bruss and Horn also outline how to solve for rotation, but give limited details. We implement our own estimation of rotations (A, B, C) and translation as a nested optimization:

$$\hat{M} = \arg\min_{A,B,C,U',V',W} \left[\min_{U,V,W} \sum_i \|e_i(v_i, A, B, C, U', V', W)\| \right]. \tag{14}$$

Given (A, B, C) one can compute the flow vectors m_r describing the rotational motion field of the observed flow, one can subtract off the rotation since it does not depend on scene geometry: $\hat{v}_t = v - \hat{m}_r(\hat{A}, \hat{B}, \hat{C})$. Subtracting the rotation (A, B, C) from the observed flow reduces the optimization to the translation only case. We solve the optimization over the rotation parameters A, B, C by using Matlab's standard gradient descent optimization, while calling the Bruss and Horn closed form solution for the translation variables given the rotational variables as part of the internal function evaluation. Local minima are a concern, but since we are estimating camera motion between two video frames, the rotation is almost always small and close to the optimization's starting point.

3.3 Initialization: Segmenting the First Frame

The goals of the initialization are (a) estimating translation parameters (U', V', W) and the rotation (A, B, C) of the motion of static environment due to camera motion, (b) the estimated set of parameters (U', V', W) form an angle field M corresponging to the observed flow (c) finding pixels whose flow is consistent with M, and (d) assigning inconsistent groups of contiguous pixels to additional angle fields. Bruss and Horn's method was not developed to handle scenes with multiple different motions, and so large or fast-moving objects can result in poor motion estimates (Fig. 7).

Input: video with n frames
Output: binary motion segmentation

1   **for** $t \leftarrow 1$ *to* $n - 1$ **do**
2   compute optical flow from frame t to frame $t + 1$
3   **if** *first frame* **then**
4   **foreach** *RANSAC iteration* **do**
5   find best set of translation parameters (U', V', W) for 10 random patched (3 in corners)
6   retain best angle field for the static environment M_k
7   **end**
8       $p(M) \leftarrow$ segment MBH error image into k comp. using Otsu's method
9   **else**
10       $p(M) \leftarrow$ propagate posterior $p(M \mid v_t)$
11   find (U', V', W) and rotation (A, B, C) of static environment using gradient descent
12   **foreach** *flow vector v* **do**
13         $v_t = v - m_r(A, B, C)$
14   **end**
15   **end**
16   **for** $j \leftarrow 1$ *to* k **do**
17   compute angle field M_j of motion component j
18   **foreach** *flow vector v_t* **do**
19         $p(\theta_{v_t} \mid M_j, \|v_t\|) \leftarrow \mathcal{V}(\theta_{v_t}; \mu = \theta^j_{m_t}, \kappa = a\|v_t\|^b)$
20   **end**
21   **end**
22   **foreach** *flow vector v_t* **do**
23       $p(M_{k+1}) \leftarrow \frac{1}{k+1}$
24       $p(\theta_{v_t} \mid M_{k+1}, \|v_t\|) \leftarrow \frac{1}{2\pi}$
25   normalize $p(M_j)$ that they sum up to $1 - p(M_{k+1})$
26       $p(M \mid v_t) \leftarrow p(\theta_{v_t} \mid M, \|v_t\|) \cdot p(M)$
27   **end**
28   given the posteriors $p(M \mid v_t)$ assign every pixel one of two labels: static environment or moving objects
29 **end**

Algorithm 1: A causal motion segmentation algorithm

Constrained RANSAC. To address this problem we use a modified version of RANSAC [33] to robustly estimate motion of static environment (Fig. 5). We use 10 random SLIC superpixels [34][1] to estimate camera motion (Sect. 3.2). We modify the standard RANSAC procedure to force the algorithm to choose three of the 10 patches from the image corners, because image corners are prone to errors due to a misestimated camera rotation. Since the Bruss and Horn error function (Eq. 14) does not penalize motions in a direction opposite of the predicted motion, we modify it to penalize these motions appropriately (details in Supp. Mat.). 5000 RANSAC trials are run, and the camera motion resulting in the fewest outlier pixels according to the *modified Bruss-Horn* (MBH) error is retained, using a threshold of 0.1.

Otsu's Method. While using the RANSAC threshold on the MBH image produces a good set of pixels to estimate the motion of the static environment due to camera motion, the method often excludes some pixels that should be included in the motion component of static environment. We use Otsu's method [35] to separate the MBH image into a region of low error (static environment) and high error: (1) Use Otsu's threshold to divide the errors, minimizing the intraclass variance. Use this threshold to do a binary segmentation of the image. (2) Find the connected component C with highest average error. Remove these pixels ($I \leftarrow I \backslash C$), and assign them to an additional angle field M. These steps are repeated until Otsu's *effectiveness* parameter is below 0.6.

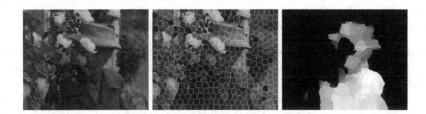

Fig. 5. RANSAC procedure. The result of our RANSAC procedure is to find image patches of the static environment. Notice that none of the patches are on the person moving in the foreground. Also notice that we force the algorithm to pick patches in three of the four image corners (a "corner" is 4 % of the image). The right figure shows the negative log likelihood of the static environment.

4   Experiments

Several motion segmentation benchmarks exist, but often a clear definition of what people intend to segment in ground truth is missing. The resulting inconsistent segmentations complicate the comparison of methods. We define motion segmentation as follows.

---

[1] We use the http://www.vlfeat.org/api/slic.html code with regionSize = 20 and regularizer = 0.5.

(I) Every pixel is given one of **two labels**: static environment or moving objects.

(II) If only part of an object is moving (like a moving person with a stationary foot), the **entire object** should be segmented.

(III) **All freely moving objects** (not just one) should be segmented, but nothing else. We do not considered tethered objects such as trees to be freely moving.

(IV) Stationary objects are not segmented, even when they moved before or will move in the future. We consider segmentation of previously moving objects to be *tracking*. Our focus is on segmentation by motion analysis.

Experiments were run on two previous data sets and our new camouflaged animals videos. The first was the Berkeley Motion Segmentation (BMS-26) database [2,3] (Fig. 8, rows 5,6). Some BMS videos have an inconsistent definition of ground truth from both our definition and from the other videos in the benchmark. An example is *Marple10* whose ground truth segments a wall in the foreground as a moving object (see Fig. 6). While it is interesting to use camera motion to segment static objects (as in [36]), we are addressing the segmentation of objects that are moving differently than the static environment, and so we excluded ten such videos from our experiments (see Supp. Mat.). The second database used is the Complex Background Data Set [4], which includes significant depth variation and also significant amounts of camera rotation (Fig. 8, rows 3, 4). We also introduce the Camouflaged Animals Data Set (Fig. 8, rows 1, 2) which will be released at camera-ready time. These videos were ground-truthed every 5th frame. See Supp. Mat. for more.

Setting von Mises parameters. There are two parameters a and b that affect the von Mises concentration $\kappa = a\|\boldsymbol{m}_t\|^b$. To set these parameters for each video, we train on the remaining videos in a leave-one-out paradigm, maximizing over the values $0.5, 1.0, 2.0, 4.0$ for multiplier parameter a and the values $0, 0.5, 1, 2$ for the exponent parameter b. Cross validation resulted in the selection of the parameter pair $(a = 4.0, b = 1.0)$ for most videos, and we adopted these as our final values.

Fig. 6. Bad ground truth. Some BMS-26 videos contain significant ground truth errors, such as this segmentation of the foreground wall, which is clearly not a moving object.

Table 1. Comparison to state-of-the-art. Matthew's correlation coefficient and F-measure for each method and data set. The "Total avg." numbers average across all valid videos.

		Keuper [18]	Papaz. [17]	Frag. [20]	Zama. [16]	Naray. [4]	Ours
Camouflage	MCC	**0.4305**	0.3517	0.1633	0.3354	-	0.5344
	F	**0.4379**	0.3297	0.1602	0.3007	-	0.5276
BMS-26	MCC	0.6851	0.6112	**0.7187**	0.6349	-	0.7576
	F	**0.7306**	0.6412	0.7276	0.6595	0.6246	0.7823
Complex	MCC	0.4752	**0.6359**	0.3257	0.3661	-	0.7491
	F	0.4559	**0.6220**	0.3300	0.3297	0.3751	0.7408
Total avg.	MCC	**0.5737**	0.5375	0.4866	0.5003	-	0.6918
	F	**0.5970**	0.5446	0.4911	0.4969	-	0.6990

Results. In Table 1, we compare our model to five different state-of-the-art methods [4,16–18,20]. We compared against methods for which either code was available or that had results on either of the two public databases that we used. However, we excluded some methods (such as [19]), as their published results were less accurate than [18], to whom we compared.

Some authors have scored algorithms using the number of correctly labeled pixels. However, when the moving object is small, a method can achieve a very high score simply by segmenting the entire video with the label static environment. The F-measure is also not symmetric with respect to a binary segmentation, and is not well-defined when a frame contains no moving pixels. Matthew's Correlation Co-efficient (MCC) handles both of these issues, and is recommended for scoring such binary classification problems when there is a large imbalance between the number of pixels in each category [37]. However, in order to enable comparison with [4], and to allow easier comparison to other methods, we also included F-measures. Table 1 shows the highest average accuracy per data set in green and the second best in **blue**, for both the F-measure and MCC. We were not able to obtain code for Narayana et al. [4], but reproduced F-measures directly from their paper. The method of [20] failed on several videos (only in the BMS data set), possibly due to the length of these videos. In these cases, we assigned scores for those videos by assigning all pixels to static environment.

Our method outperforms all other methods by a large margin, on all three data sets, using both measures of comparison.

5 Analysis and Conclusions

Conditioning our angle likelihood on the flow magnitude is an important factor in our method. Table 2 shows the detrimental effect of using a constant von Mises concentration κ instead of one that depends upon $\|m_t\|$. In this experiment, we set the parameter b which governs the dependence of κ on $\|m_t\|$ to 0, and set the value of κ to maximize performance. Even with the optimum constant κ, the drop in performance was 7 %, 5 %, and 22 % across three data sets.

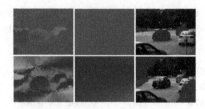

Fig. 7. RANSAC vs. no RANSAC. Top row: robust initialization with RANSAC. Bottom row: using Bruss and Horn's method directly on the entire image. Left to right: flow angles of observed translational flow, angle field M of static environment and segmentation.

Table 2. Effect of RANSAC and variable κ.

	Final	Constant κ	No RANSAC
BMS-26	0.7576	0.6843	0.6450
Complex	0.7491	0.7000	0.5757
Camouflage	0.5344	0.3128	0.5176

We also show the consistent gains stemming from our constrained RANSAC initialization procedure. In this experiment, we segmented the first frame of video without rejecting any pixels as outliers. In some videos, this had little effect, but sometimes the effect was large, as shown in Fig. 7 – here the estimated M is the best fit for the car instead of static environment.

The method by Keuper et al. [18] performs fairly well, but often makes errors in segmenting rigid parts of the foreground near the observer. This can be seen in the third and fourth rows of Fig. 8, which shows sample results from the Complex Background Data Set. In particular, note that Keuper et al.'s method segments the tree in the near foreground in the third row and the wall in the near foreground in the fourth row. The method of Fragkiadaki et al., also based on trajectories, has similar behavior. These methods in general seem to have difficulty with high variability in depth.

Another reason for our good results may be that we are directly using the perspective projection equations to analyze motion, as has been advocated by Horn [27], rather than approximations based on projective geometry. Code is available: http://vis-www.cs.umass.edu/motionSegmentation/.

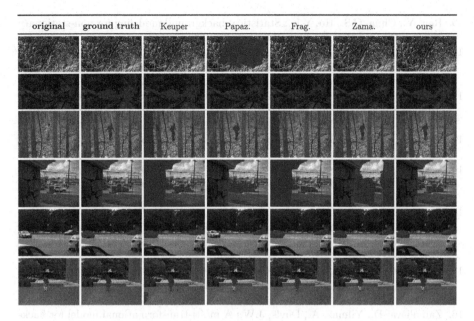

Fig. 8. Sample results Left to right: original image, ground truth, [16–18,20] and our binary segmentations. Rows 1–2: sample results on the Animal Camouflage Data Set (chameleon and stickinsect). Rows 3–4: sample results on Complex Background (traffic and forest). Rows 5–6: sample results on BMS-26 (cars5 and people1).

References

1. Torr, P.H.: Geometric motion segmentation and model selection. Philos. Trans. Royal Soc. Lond. Math. Phys. Eng. Sci. **356**(1740), 1321–1340 (1998)
2. Brox, T., Malik, J.: Object segmentation by long term analysis of point trajectories. In: Daniilidis, K., Maragos, P., Paragios, N. (eds.) ECCV 2010, Part V. LNCS, vol. 6315, pp. 282–295. Springer, Heidelberg (2010)
3. Tron, R., Vidal, R.: A benchmark for the comparison of 3-D motion segmentation algorithms. In: CVPR (2007)
4. Narayana, M., Hanson, A., Learned-Miller, E.: Coherent motion segmentation in moving camera videos using optical flow orientations. In: 2013 IEEE International Conference on Computer Vision (ICCV), pp. 1577–1584. IEEE (2013)
5. Grundmann, M., Kwatra, V., Han, M., Essa, I.: Efficient hierarchical graph-based video segmentation. In: 2010 IEEE Conference on Computer Vision and Pattern Recognition (CVPR), pp. 2141–2148. IEEE (2010)
6. Lezama, J., Alahari, K., Sivic, J., Laptev, I.: Track to the future: spatio-temporal video segmentation with long-range motion cues. In: Proceedings of the IEEE Conference on Computer Vision and Pattern Recognition (2011)
7. Kumar, M.P., Torr, P.H., Zisserman, A.: Learning layered motion segmentations of video. Int. J. Comput. Vis. **76**(3), 301–319 (2008)
8. Irani, M., Rousso, B., Peleg, S.: Computing occluding and transparent motions. Int. J. Comput. Vis. **12**, 5–16 (1994)

9. Ren, Y., Chua, C.S., Ho, Y.K.: Statistical background modeling for non-stationary camera. Pattern Recogn. Lett. **24**, 183–196 (2003)
10. Sheikh, Y., Javed, O., Kanade, T.: Background subtraction for freely moving cameras. In: IEEE 12th International Conference on Computer Vision, ICCV 2009, Kyoto, Japan, September 27–October 4 2009, pp. 1219–1225. IEEE (2009)
11. Elqursh, A., Elgammal, A.: Online moving camera background subtraction. In: Fitzgibbon, A., Lazebnik, S., Perona, P., Sato, Y., Schmid, C. (eds.) ECCV 2012, Part VI. LNCS, vol. 7577, pp. 228–241. Springer, Heidelberg (2012)
12. Ochs, P., Brox, T.: Higher order motion models and spectral clustering. In: CVPR (2012)
13. Kwak, S., Lim, T., Nam, W., Han, B., Han, J.H.: Generalized background subtraction based on hybrid inference by belief propagation and Bayesian filtering. In: ICCV (2011)
14. Rahmati, H., Dragon, R., Aamo, O.M., Gool, L., Adde, L.: Motion segmentation with weak labeling priors. In: Jiang, X., Hornegger, J., Koch, R. (eds.) GCPR 2014. LNCS, vol. 8753, pp. 159–171. Springer, Heidelberg (2014). doi:10.1007/978-3-319-11752-2_13
15. Jain, S.D., Grauman, K.: Supervoxel-consistent foreground propagation in video. In: Fleet, D., Pajdla, T., Schiele, B., Tuytelaars, T. (eds.) ECCV 2014, Part IV. LNCS, vol. 8692, pp. 656–671. Springer, Heidelberg (2014)
16. Zamalieva, D., Yilmaz, A., Davis, J.W.: A multi-transformational model for background subtraction with moving cameras. In: Fleet, D., Pajdla, T., Schiele, B., Tuytelaars, T. (eds.) ECCV 2014, Part I. LNCS, vol. 8689, pp. 803–817. Springer, Heidelberg (2014)
17. Papazoglou, A., Ferrari, V.: Fast object segmentation in unconstrained video. In: 2013 IEEE International Conference on Computer Vision (ICCV), pp. 1777–1784. IEEE (2013)
18. Keuper, M., Andres, B., Brox, T.: Motion trajectory segmentation via minimum cost multicuts. In: Proceedings of the IEEE International Conference on Computer Vision, pp. 3271–3279 (2015)
19. Taylor, B., Karasev, V., Soatto, S.: Causal video object segmentation from persistence of occlusions. In: Proceedings of the IEEE Conference on Computer Vision and Pattern Recognition, pp. 4268–4276 (2015)
20. Fragkiadaki, K., Zhang, G., Shi, J.: Video segmentation by tracing discontinuities in a trajectory embedding. In: 2012 IEEE Conference on Computer Vision and Pattern Recognition (CVPR), pp. 1846–1853. IEEE (2012)
21. Sawhney, H.S., Guo, Y., Asmuth, J., Kumar, R.: Independent motion detection in 3D scenes. In: The Proceedings of the Seventh IEEE International Conference on Computer Vision, vol. 1, pp. 612–619. IEEE (1999)
22. Dey, S., Reilly, V., Saleemi, I., Shah, M.: Detection of independently moving objects in non-planar scenes via multi-frame monocular epipolar constraint. In: Fitzgibbon, A., Lazebnik, S., Perona, P., Sato, Y., Schmid, C. (eds.) ECCV 2012, Part V. LNCS, vol. 7576, pp. 860–873. Springer, Heidelberg (2012)
23. Namdev, R.K., Kundu, A., Krishna, K.M., Jawahar, C.V.: Motion segmentation of multiple objects from a freely moving monocular camera. In: International Conference on Robotics and Automation (2012)
24. Csurka, G., Bouthemy, P.: Direct identification of moving objects and background from 2D motion models. In: The Proceedings of the Seventh IEEE International Conference on Computer Vision, vol. 1, pp. 566–571. IEEE (1999)

25. Sharma, R., Aloimonos, Y.: Early detection of independent motion from active control of normal image flow patterns. IEEE Trans. Syst. Man Cybernet. B (Cybernetics) **26**(1), 42–52 (1996)
26. Elhamifar, E., Vidal, R.: Sparse subspace clustering. In: IEEE Conference on Computer Vision and Pattern Recognition, CVPR 2009, pp. 2790–2797. IEEE (2009)
27. Horn, B.K.: Projective geometry considered harmful (1999)
28. Ogale, A.S., Fermüller, C., Aloimonos, Y.: Motion segmentation using occlusions. IEEE Trans. Pattern Anal. Mach. Intell. **27**(6), 988–992 (2005)
29. Horn, B.: Robot Vision. MIT Press, Cambridge (1986)
30. Bruss, A.R., Horn, B.K.: Passive navigation. Comput. Vis. Graph. Image Process. **21**(1), 3–20 (1983)
31. Sun, D., Roth, S., Black, M.J.: Secrets of optical flow estimation and their principles. In: 2010 IEEE Conference on Computer Vision and Pattern Recognition (CVPR), pp. 2432–2439. IEEE (2010)
32. Narayana, M., Hanson, A., Learned-Miller, E.G.: Background subtraction: separating the modeling and the inference. Mach. Vis. Appl. **25**(5), 1163–1174 (2014)
33. Fischler, M.A., Bolles, R.C.: Random sample consensus: a paradigm for model fitting with applications to image analysis and automated cartography. Commun. ACM **24**(6), 381–395 (1981)
34. Achanta, R., Shaji, A., Smith, K., Lucchi, A., Fua, P., Susstrunk, S.: SLIC superpixels compared to state-of-the-art superpixel methods. IEEE Trans. Pattern Anal. Mach. Intell. **34**(11), 2274–2282 (2012)
35. Otsu, N.: A threshold selection method from gray-level histograms. IEEE Trans. Syst. Man, Cybernet. **9**, 62–66 (1979)
36. Wang, J.Y., Adelson, E.H.: Representing moving images with layers. IEEE Trans. Image Process **3**(5), 625–638 (1994)
37. Powers, D.M.: Evaluation: from precision, recall and f-measure to ROC, informedness, markedness and correlation. Technical report SIE-07-001. Flinders University, Adelaide (2007)

Kernelized Subspace Ranking
for Saliency Detection

Tiantian Wang, Lihe Zhang[✉], Huchuan Lu, Chong Sun, and Jinqing Qi

School of Information and Communication Engineering,
Dalian University of Technology, Dalian, China
tiantianwang.ice@gmail.com, {zhanglihe,lhchuan,Jinqing}@dlut.edu.cn,
waynecool@mail.dlut.edu.cn

Abstract. In this paper, we propose a novel saliency method that takes advantage of object-level proposals and region-based convolutional neural network (R-CNN) features. We follow the learning-to-rank methodology, and solve a ranking problem satisfying the constraint that positive samples have higher scores than negative ones. As the dimensionality of the deep features is high and the amount of training data is low, ranking in the primal space is suboptimal. A new kernelized subspace ranking model is proposed by jointly learning a Rank-SVM classifier and a subspace projection. The projection aims to measure the pairwise distances in a low-dimensional space. For an image, the ranking score of each proposal is assigned by the learnt ranker. The final saliency map is generated by a weighted fusion of the top-ranked candidates. Experimental results show that the proposed algorithm performs favorably against the state-of-the-art methods on four benchmark datasets.

Keywords: Saliency detection · Subspace ranking · Feature projection

1 Introduction

The task of saliency detection is to identify the most attractive and informative regions in images and videos. It has gained much popularity in recent years, owing to its series of important applications in computer vision, such as adaptive compression, context-aware image editing and image resizing. An effective saliency model can save lots of unnecessary human labour in vision tasks. Although much progress in saliency detection has been made in recent years, it remains a challenging problem.

The early works [19,21] exploit the low-level image properties of pixels, such as intensity, color, orientation, texture and motion, to compute saliency. Numerous region-wise saliency methods [10,13,43] are proposed subsequently, which investigate the mid-level structure properties of image regions and incorporate the contextual information to measure the saliency for each region. The aforementioned works, either in the pixel-wise or region-wise fashion, have to fully consider the relationship between image elements from overall and local perspectives to guarantee the semantic completeness of salient objects. In this work, we

© Springer International Publishing AG 2016
B. Leibe et al. (Eds.): ECCV 2016, Part VIII, LNCS 9912, pp. 450–466, 2016.
DOI: 10.1007/978-3-319-46484-8_27

explore the category-independent object characteristics of region proposals, and propose a principled framework to weight and combine these region candidates, thereby highlighting the salient instances.

Object proposals technique has been widely applied to many vision fields. It generally produces either bounding box proposals [2,8] which inevitably aggregate visual information from objects and background clutter, or region proposals [4,11,32] that shape an informative and well-defined contour. This technique, striving to find instances of all categories, usually produces thousands of object candidates which significantly reduce the search space of salient object detection. Furthermore, good proposals encapsulate the visual information of objects and have informative boundary shape cues, which provide the necessary object-level prior knowledge for saliency detection. However, a very large proportion of proposals contain very few object regions, even may contain only the backgrounds. Owing to the diversity of object categories and backgrounds as well as the varied shape and size of proposals, it is extremely difficult to select the proposals most similar to the ground truth. Therefore, the proposal-based salient object detection remains a very challenging task. Recent works [22,25,36] simply integrate the bounding box proposals weighted by their objectness scores [2] as a feature map to help saliency detection. Since the computed score in [2] is inaccurate, the feature map only coarsely indicates the location of the objects in the image. In this work, we aim to sort out some good region proposals that contain a part of the objects even a complete object instance, and employ them to detect salient objects. Figure 1 shows some examples of object proposal. Actually, background proposals (i.e., contain much more background pixels than foreground ones) are in majority in the proposal pool compared with foreground proposals.

Recent progress on metric learning models [20,44,47] reveals the effectiveness of an optimal distance metric, which can significantly narrow the distances between similar samples and simultaneously expand the gaps of dissimilar samples. Besides, the performance of ranking models highly depends on the pairwise similarity/dissimilarity constraints. Therefore, we combine the two learning mechanisms together to propose a novel ranking model for proposal selection. The core idea of the proposed model is to learn a category-independent ranker upon distance metric learning of object proposals with a joint learning approach, thereby obtaining the optimal orderings of object proposals and linearly combining the top-ranked candidates weighted by their ranking scores. By using the projection obtained in distance learning, data points (i.e. object proposals) are mapped into a low-dimensional subspace, and further ranked on the data manifold constructed by the learnt distances. Thus the positive and negative pairs of data can be more easily separated. Different from superpixels that contain the low-level and mid-level image information, object proposals carry more higher-level and object-level cues. Therefore, the hand-crafted features used to represent the superpixels are not suitable for the proposals. To overcome this problem, we adopt the region-based convolutional neural network (R-CNN) features, which depict both the low-level and high-level image cues and demonstrate very powerful representation capability, as witnessed in recent works [12,33].

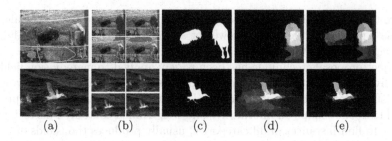

<table>
<tr><td>(a)</td><td>(b)</td><td>(c)</td><td>(d)</td><td>(e)</td></tr>
</table>

Fig. 1. Several examples of object proposals. From left to right: (a) input, (b) foreground proposals (blue color) and background proposals (red color). (c) ground truth. (d) saliency map generated by ranking in the primal space. (e) saliency map generated by ranking in the kernelized subspace. (Color figure online)

The contributions of this work are listed as follows:

- We jointly learn a ranker and a distance metric with a kernel approach to formulate salient object detection as a subspace ranking issue.
- We propose a object-wise saliency model, which purely exploits object candidates represented with R-CNN features to achieve saliency detection. The deep features can capture the high-level saliency cues of object candidates.
- It is demonstrated that the proposed algorithm performs favorably against the state-of-the-art saliency detection methods on MSRA-5000, ECSSD, PASCAL-S and SOD benchmark datasets.

2   Related Work

Numerous saliency models and algorithms have emerged recently, which can be roughly classified into unsupervised, semi-supervised and supervised schemes. We refer the readers to a comprehensive review on this topic in [3,50].

Unsupervised approaches usually heuristically characterize visual rarity or distinctness to define image saliency. The most common way to quantify rarity is to calculate the difference between various visual elements. Itti *et al.* [21] integrate the center-surround contrasts on multiple feature channels and scales to estimate visual saliency. Achanta *et al.* [1] compute the different between Gaussian blurred features and mean image features to define rarity. Some methods combine appearance difference and spatial coherence to calculate the global contrast with different image abstraction representations [9,10,48]. While Goferman *et al.* [13] and Wang *et al.* [53] investigate image saliency from both local and global perspectives. Wei *et al.* [55] compute the shortest distance of each patch to image boundary as saliency measure. In addition, much effort has been made to design discriminative features [37,43,53], domain models [16,19], distance metrics [31], speed strategy [59].

Generally, semi-supervised approaches achieve saliency detection by label propagation from the labeled elements to the unlabeled ones based on their pairwise affinities. Harel *et al.* [17] formulate saliency labeling as a random walk problem, construct an ergodic Markov chain and use the equilibrium distribution to define image saliency. Wang *et al.* [54] and Gopalakrishnan *et al.* [15] respectively introduce the entropy rate and the hitting time based on ergodic Markov chains. Different from the aforementioned methods, Jiang *et al.* [23] construct an absorbing Markov chain and use the absorbed time to measure the saliency. While Yang *et al.* [58] cast saliency detection into a manifold ranking problem, which is also a propagation-based method. Recently, Li *et al.* [34] combine random walks and manifold ranking to propose the regularized random walks ranking with a newly defined constraint to consider local image data and prior estimation. Li and Yu [35] use quadratic energy models to refine the initial saliency results generated by deep convolutional neural networks. There are some similar methods [5,14,26,41,49,57,63]. They use a semi-supervised learning mechanism to assign saliency labels based on various initial labeling.

Supervised learning is also applied in saliency detection. Jiang *et al.* [27] learn the prior knowledge in a supervised manner. Some methods learn to combine multiple saliency features using the conditional random field models [39,42] and the regression model [61]. Lu *et al.* [40] use the large-margin formulation to learn the optimal set of salient seeds for saliency propagation. While some other methods train the support vector machines [28,29] and the regressor [24] to distinguish salient regions from the backgrounds. Li *et al.* [36] learn a generic distance metric to depict the global distribution of the whole training set. The aforementioned methods require a large number of annotated images to train the parameter models. Recently, Tong *et al.* [51] uses the pseudo labels rather than human annotated ones to train saliency models. They integrates three priors to determine the pseudo positive and pseudo negative samples. In this work, we jointly learn a ranker and a feature projection in a supervised manner to select region proposals on top of the R-CNN features. The proposed model makes full use of the object-level information to improve salient object detection.

3   Kernelized Subspace Ranking

The proposed approach can be divided into three main stages: (i) segment an image into object proposals and extract the deep features. (ii) Learn to rank in the kernelized subspace by jointly optimizing the Rank-SVM and distance metric objectives. (iii) Compute saliency map by a weighted fusion of the top-ranked proposals. The overview of the proposed algorithm is shown in Fig. 2.

3.1   Object Proposal

We employ the geodesic object proposal algorithm [32] to generate region proposals and take region proposals as basic processing units. Region proposals can model the appearance of objects and shapes with a well-defined closed boundary. For each proposal, we extract the CNN features using the pre-trained model provided in [18]. Compared with the hand-crafted features, the CNN feature

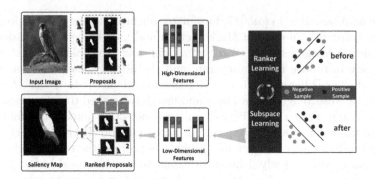

Fig. 2. The overview of the proposed algorithm

can capture richer structure information including low-level visual information (extracted in the earlier layers) and higher-level semantic information (extracted in the latter layers). Features in different layers serve as complementary ones, because the low-level features helps to handle the relative simple scenes and the higher-level features more easily detects the complex semantic objects.

3.2 Problem Formulation

Ranking in primal space. Most candidate objects generated by existing algorithms cannot exactly detect the contours and shapes of salient objects. In order to separate foreground proposals from background ones and obtain accurate saliency result, we cast saliency detection as a ranking problem. We wish to sort out the object proposals with high segmentation precision and recall to detect salient objects via a weighted fusion of them.

We investigate a primal-based Rank-SVM (PRSVM) proposed by Chapelle and Keerthi [6] as it makes the training for large amounts of imbalanced positive and negative samples available. Assume there exists a set of candidate objects $\mathbf{X} = [\mathbf{x}_1, \mathbf{x}_2, \ldots, \mathbf{x}_n]$ with relevance ranks $\mathbf{x}_n \succ \cdots \succ \mathbf{x}_i \succ \mathbf{x}_j \succ \cdots \succ \mathbf{x}_1$, where $\succ$ denotes the order and $\mathbf{x}_k \in \mathbb{R}^d$ is the feature vector of the k-th instance. In a Rank-SVM problem, we wish that instances ranking ahead have higher scores than the behind ones, which can be described in the following formula:

$$\min_{\mathbf{w}, \varepsilon} \frac{1}{2} ||\mathbf{w}||^2 + \lambda \sum_{(i,j) \in \mathcal{P}} \varepsilon_{ij} \tag{1}$$
$$s.t. \mathbf{w}^T (\mathbf{x}_i - \mathbf{x}_j) \geq 1 - \varepsilon_{ij}, \varepsilon_{ij} \geq 0,$$

where $\mathbf{w}$ corresponds to a weight vector which indicates the importance of each feature. The parameter λ is a trade-off for the regularization and loss term and ε_{ij} is the slack variable. $\mathcal{P}$ represents the preference pairs that satisfies $\mathcal{P} = \{(i,j)|y_i > y_j\}$, and $y_i \in \{-1, +1\}$ is the label of the i-th training instance. Note that, for computation efficiency, our preference pairs are only defined on the between-class instances (i.e., positive and negative instances).

The above function can be rewritten as an unconstrained optimization problem by exploiting the hinge loss function using the L2-loss:

$$\min_{\mathbf{w}} \frac{1}{2}||\mathbf{w}||^2 + \lambda \sum_{(i,j)\in\mathcal{P}} \max(0, 1 - \mathbf{w}^T(\mathbf{x}_i - \mathbf{x}_j))^2. \tag{2}$$

To determine positive and negative instances, we mainly consider the confidence measure, which is an overall performance measurement weighted by the accuracy score A and coverage score C as mentioned in [52]. A_i and C_i can be computed as $A_i = \frac{|O_i \cap G|}{|O_i|}, C_i = \frac{|O_i \cap G|}{|G|}$. O_i, G respectively represent the i-th proposal and the corresponding ground truth with binary annotation. The notation $|\cdot|$ denotes the number of matrix elements equal to 1.

The accuracy score A_i measures the percentage of the i-th proposal pixels correctly assigned to the salient object, while the coverage score C_i is defined as the ratio of the corresponding ground truth area overlapped with the i-th proposal.

The confidence score is given by $conf_i = \frac{(1+\xi) \times A_i \times C_i}{\xi A_i + C_i}$, where ξ is used to balance the weight between accuracy score and coverage score. The instances with confidence score higher than 0.9 are regarded as positive samples, and instances with confidence score lower than 0.6 are treated as negative ones. In this paper, we use all possible positive samples but only a fraction of the negative ones.

Kernelized subspace ranking. Although R-CNN features have many good properties as described above, they usually have much redundant information in very high-dimensional space. This may reduce the reliability of the ranking problem. To address this issue, we learn a feature projection matrix to project high-dimensional features into a low-dimensional subspace with a kernel approach.

Several methods are proposed in literature aiming at learning a linear projection matrix that maps data points into a low-dimensional subspace. Mignon and Jurie [45] firstly propose pairwise constrained component analysis (PCCA) for learning this transformation matrix with similarity and dissimilarity constraints. Xiong et al. [56] further improve it by incorporating a regularization model.

In this work, we simultaneously consider the ranker and subspace learning in a unified formula:

$$\min_{\mathbf{w},\mathbf{L}} E = \frac{1}{2}||\mathbf{w}||^2 + \lambda \sum_{(i,j)\in\mathcal{P}} \max(0, 1 - \mathbf{w}^T\mathbf{L}(\psi(\mathbf{x}_i) - \psi(\mathbf{x}_j)))^2$$
$$+ \sum_{n=1}^{p} \ell_\delta(y_n(||\mathbf{L}(\psi(\mathbf{x}_{i_n}) - \psi(\mathbf{x}_{j_n}))||^2 - 1)) + \mu||\mathbf{L}||_F^2, \tag{3}$$

where $\ell_\delta(x) = \frac{1}{\delta}\log(1+e^{\delta x})$ is the generalized logistic loss function as mentioned in [60]. $||\cdot||$ represents the Euclidean distance and $||\cdot||_F$ is the Frobenius norm of matrix. $\psi(\mathbf{x}_i)$ is the feature of instance $\mathbf{x}_i$ through kernel projection. p is the number of constraints for the instance pairs $\mathbf{x}_{i_n}$ and $\mathbf{x}_{j_n}$, where (i_n, j_n) indicates the indices of two instances for the n-th constraint. $y_n \in \{-1, +1\}$ indicates whether the instances belong to the same class or not. $\mathbf{L} \in \mathbb{R}^{l \times d}(l < d)$ is the learnt projection matrix and μ is the regularization parameter. The first two terms are the Rank-SVM formula defined in the subspace, which encourage that foreground proposals should have higher ranking scores than background proposals. The third term acts as a loss function encouraging that the intra-class instances have smaller distances than the inter-class instances, while the fourth term is the regularization term for the projection matrix $\mathbf{L}$.

To further handle the problem where some instances are linearly inseparable, we apply a feature projection matrix $\mathbf{P} \in \mathbb{R}^{l \times N}$ to project primal features into a kernel subspace, where N is the number of training instances. Specially, we let $\mathbf{L} = \mathbf{P}\psi^T(\mathbf{X})$. Then $\mathbf{L}\psi(\mathbf{x}_i) = \mathbf{P}\psi^T(\mathbf{X})\psi(\mathbf{x}_i) = \mathbf{P}\mathbf{k}_i$, where $\mathbf{k}_i = \psi^T(\mathbf{X})\psi(\mathbf{x}_i)$ is the i-column of the kernel matrix $\mathbf{K} = \psi^T(\mathbf{X}) \times \psi(\mathbf{X})$. Equation 3 can be rewritten as

$$
\min_{\mathbf{w},\mathbf{P}} E = \frac{1}{2}||\mathbf{w}||^2 + \lambda \sum_{(i,j)\in\mathcal{P}} \max(0, 1 - \mathbf{w}^T\mathbf{P}(\mathbf{k}_i - \mathbf{k}_j))^2
$$
$$
+ \sum_{n=1}^{p} l_\delta(y_n(||\mathbf{P}(\mathbf{k}_{i_n} - \mathbf{k}_{j_n})||^2 - 1)) + \mu Tr(\mathbf{P}\mathbf{K}\mathbf{P}^T),
\tag{4}
$$

where $Tr(\cdot)$ denotes the trace of a matrix. As shown in Fig. 3, the object proposals are sorted using our ranker in descending order. The decimals in yellow font denote the corresponding confidence scores computed by using ground truth. The figure shows that the overall confidence scores of the top-ranked proposals in kernelized subspace are higher than that of the top-ranked proposals in primal space.

The recently proposed methods HARF [64], MCDL [62] and LEGS [52] employ deep features directly or indirectly. Our method is significantly different from these methods in the following aspects: (i) HARF casts saliency detection as a regression problem and works in region-wise manner. This method segments an image into multi-level regions, then compute regional deep features and hand-crafted features and feed them to a regressor for saliency prediction. Our method treats saliency detection as a subspace ranking problem and works in object-wise manner. Object proposals carry rich higher-level and object-level structural information, which guarantees the semantic completeness of salient objects. (ii) Both MCDL and LEGS treat saliency detection as a binary classification problem. They train existing deep neural networks to predict the probabilities of pixels (or superpixels) as their saliency values, respectively. We extract deep features and propose a joint subspace ranking framework, and obtain saliency map by weighted combination of the top-ranked proposals.

3.3   Joint Ranker and Subspace Learning

In this section, we aim to learn the Rank-SVM model coefficient $\mathbf{w}$ and projection matrix $\mathbf{P}$ jointly by optimizing Eq. 4. The proposed optimization problem can be efficiently solved using the alternating optimization method.

Fig. 3. Ranking results in different feature spaces. Top: results ranked in the primal space. Bottom: results ranked in the kernelized subspace. The decimals in yellow font denote the corresponding confidence scores. (Color figure online)

Update the ranking coefficient w. Given the estimated projection matrix **P**, Eq. 4 becomes a Rank-SVM problem, and we use the Truncated Newton optimization similar to [6] to solve it efficiently. The gradient of the objective (4) with respect to **w** is,

$$\mathbf{g} := \mathbf{w} + 2\lambda \sum_{(i,j) \in \mathcal{SV}} (\mathbf{w}^T \mathbf{P}(\mathbf{k}_i - \mathbf{k}_j) - 1) \cdot \mathbf{P}(\mathbf{k}_i - \mathbf{k}_j), \tag{5}$$

and the Hessian matrix is,

$$\mathbf{H} := \mathbf{I} + 2\lambda \sum_{(i,j) \in \mathcal{SV}} (\mathbf{P}(\mathbf{k}_i - \mathbf{k}_j))(\mathbf{P}(\mathbf{k}_i - \mathbf{k}_j))^T, \tag{6}$$

where $\mathcal{SV}$ is the set of "support vector pairs" with $\mathcal{SV} = \{(i,j)|(i,j) \in \mathcal{P}, \mathbf{w}^T \mathbf{P}(\mathbf{k}_i - \mathbf{k}_j) < 1\}$. **I** is the identify matrix. The ranking coefficient **w** is iteratively computed by

$$\mathbf{w}_{t+1} = \mathbf{w}_t - \eta \cdot \mathbf{H}^{-1} \mathbf{g}, \tag{7}$$

where η is found by line search.

Update the projection matrix P. Given the ranking coefficient **w**, Eq. 4 becomes a metric learning problem with kernel trick. We handle the problem directly using gradient descent algorithm. The derivative of the Eq. 4 with respect to **P** is

$$\frac{\partial E}{\partial \mathbf{P}} = 2\mathbf{P} \sum_{n=1}^{p} y_n \sigma_\delta(y_n(\|\mathbf{P}(\mathbf{k}_{i_n} - \mathbf{k}_{j_n})\|^2 - 1))\mathbf{K}\mathbf{T}_n\mathbf{K} + 2\mu PK$$
$$+ 2\lambda \sum_{(i,j) \in \mathcal{SV}} (\mathbf{w}^T \mathbf{P}(\mathbf{k}_i - \mathbf{k}_j) - 1)\mathbf{w}(\mathbf{k}_i - \mathbf{k}_j)^T, \tag{8}$$

where $\mathbf{T}_n = (\mathbf{e}_{i_n} - \mathbf{e}_{j_n})(\mathbf{e}_{i_n} - \mathbf{e}_{j_n})^T$. $\sigma_\delta(x)$ denotes the value of $(1 + e^{-\delta x})^{-1}$ and $\mathbf{e}_k$ is the k-th vector of the cannonical basis, with 1 located in the k-th element and 0 in others.

By multiplying the first two terms of the above computed gradient matrix with preconditioner $\mathbf{K}^{-1}$, the kernel projection matrix **P** is computed by iteratively solving the following problem

$$\mathbf{P}_{t+1} = \mathbf{P}_t - 2\alpha \left(\mathbf{P} \sum_{n=1}^{p} \mathbf{A}_n^t \mathbf{K} \mathbf{T}_n + \mu \mathbf{P} + \lambda \sum_{(i,j) \in \mathcal{SV}} \mathbf{Q}_{ij}^t \right), \tag{9}$$

where $\mathbf{Q}_{ij}^t = (\mathbf{w}^T \mathbf{P}(\mathbf{k}_i - \mathbf{k}_j) - 1)\mathbf{w}(\mathbf{k}_i - \mathbf{k}_j)^T$, $\mathbf{A}_n^t = y_n \sigma_\delta(y_n(\|\mathbf{P}(\mathbf{k}_{i_n} - \mathbf{k}_{j_n})\|^2 - 1))$ at the t-th iteration. And α represents the learning rate.

The proposed joint learning algorithm is summarized in Algorithm 1.

Algorithm1: Kernelized Subspace Ranking

Input: K (kernel matrix); λ (trade-off parameter); y_n (label of instance pairs); $\mathcal{P}$ (preference pairs); μ (regularization parameter); (i_n, j_n) (indices of instance pairs for the n-th constraint, $n = 1, \cdots, p$)
Output: ranking coefficient **w** and projection matrix **P**.
1: **repeat**
2:     • Update the ranking weight **w** with fixed **P**,
3:         **repeat**
4:             Evaluate the ranking gradient **g** by Equation 5;
5:             Compute the ranking Hessian matrix **H** by Equation 6;
6:             Update the ranking weight **w by** Equation 7;
7:                 $\mathbf{w}_{t+1} = \mathbf{w}_t - \eta \cdot \mathbf{H}^{-1}\mathbf{g}$ (η found by line search);
8:         **until** Convergence
8:     • Update the projection matrix **P** with fixed **w**,
9:         **repeat**
10:            Solve the derivative $\frac{\partial E}{\partial \mathbf{P}}$ by Equation 8;
11:            Update the projection matrix **P** by Equation 9;
12:                $\mathbf{P}_{t+1} = \mathbf{P}_t - 2\alpha(\mathbf{P} \sum_{n=1}^{p} \mathbf{A}_n^t \mathbf{K} \mathbf{T}_n + \mu \mathbf{P} + \lambda \sum_{(i,j) \in \mathcal{SV}} \mathbf{Q}_{ij}^t)$;
13:        **until** Convergence
14: **until** iteration stopping criterion is reached

3.4   Saliency Map

Given the Rank-SVM coefficient **w** and projection matrix **P**, we compute the ranking score of the i-th proposal as $s_i = \mathbf{w}^T \mathbf{P} \mathbf{k}_i$. We consider the top-ranked object candidates to contain salient objects with high precision and recall. As the proposals may cover each other, in order to highlight salient regions, we combine the top-ranked proposals weighted by their ranking scores to compute the saliency score for each pixel:

$$S(x) = \sum_{i=1}^{K} \exp(2 \times s_i) \times m_i(x), \tag{10}$$

where $m_i(x)$ is 1 if pixel x is included in the i-th proposal, and 0 otherwise. After the saliency scores of all pixels are computed, the final saliency map is obtained by a min-max normalization.

4   Experiments

We extensively evaluate the proposed algorithm on four representative benchmark datasets, and compare it with thirteen state-of-the-art saliency methods,
including the BL [51], AMC [23], DRFI [24], DSR [37], GC [7], HDCT [30],
HS [57], LEGS [52], MR [58], PCA [43], RR [34], UFO [25] and wCtr [63]. We
get the saliency results of these competitors either by running the source codes
or directly using the saliency maps provided by the authors. Subsequently, we
detail the datasets, parameter settings, quantitative and qualitative comparison.

Datasets: We use the MSRA-5000, ECSSD, PASCAL-S and SOD datasets. The
MSRA-5000 dataset contains 5,000 images with a large variety of image contents, which is constructed by Liu et al. [39]. They exclude very large salient
objects and label the ground truth with a bounding box. Afterwards, Jiang
et al. [24] provide more accurate pixel-wise annotations for saliency evaluation.
The ECSSD dataset [57] contains 1,000 images with structurally complex foregrounds and cluttered backgrounds. The PASCAL-S dataset [38] contains 850
natural images surrounded by cluttered backgrounds, which ascends from the
validation set of the PASCAL VOC 2012 segmentation challenge. This dataset
is one of the most challenging saliency datasets without various design biases
(e.g., center bias and color contrast bias). The SOD dataset [46] contains 300
images from the challenging Berkeley segmentation dataset. Some of the images
include multiple salient objects with various sizes.

Parameter Settings: The confidence score parameter ξ is 0.3 in the implementation to emphasize the impact of the accuracy score on the final confidence. The
trade-off parameters λ and μ in Eq. 3 are set to be 10^{-4} and 0.01, respectively.
The learning rate α in Eq. 9 is fixed to be 0.01, similar to [56]. In addition, we use
the Gaussian RBF kernel $k(\mathbf{x}, \mathbf{x}') = \exp(-\|\mathbf{x} - \mathbf{x}'\|/\sigma^2)$. The kernel parameter σ
is equal to the first quantile of all distances [56]. We fuse the top-16 candidates
to compute the final saliency map.

The proposal algorithm [32] roughly produces 1,000 candidate segments for
each image. There are many too small or too large candidates which make little
contribution to saliency detection. Therefore, we compute the percentage of the
area of the proposals with respect to the whole image and remove the oversized
proposals ($>70\%$) and undersized ones ($<2\%$). Besides, we remove the proposals
which touch four boundaries of an image. We randomly sample 2,000 images
from the MSRA-5000 dataset to train our model and treat the rest images as
the testing dataset. Rather than training a model for each dataset, we use the
model trained from the MSRA-5000 dataset and test it over others. Because we
actually learn a category-independent ranker to rank the proposals according to
their objectness without using any knowledge about object categories.

Quantitative Comparison: We use the precision-recall curve, F-measure and
Area Under Curve (AUC) to quantitatively evaluate the experimental results.
The precision value corresponds to the ratio of salient pixels correctly assigned
to all pixels of the extracted regions, while the recall value is defined as the

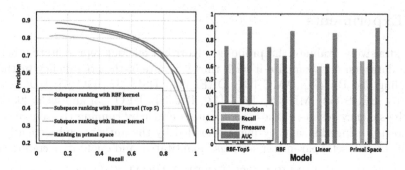

Fig. 4. Performance comparison on the PASCAL-S dataset by the proposed algorithm with different design options.

percentage of detected salient pixels with respect to the ground-truth data. Given a saliency map with intensity values normalized to the range of 0 and 255, a number of binary maps are produced by using every possible fixed threshold in [0; 255]. We compute the precision/recall pairs of all the binary maps to plot the precision-recall curve. Meanwhile, we obtain true positive and false positive rates to plot the ROC curve and AUC score. Similar to existing methods, we also compute the precision, recall and F-measure with an adaptive threshold, defined as twice the mean saliency of an input image [1]. The F-measure is the overall performance indicator computed by the weighted harmonic of precision and recall as follows: $F_\gamma = \frac{(1+\gamma^2) \times Precision \times Recall}{\gamma^2 Precision + Recall}$, where γ^2 is set to be 0.3 to weigh more on precision as suggested in [1]. Figure 6 shows the precision-recall curves and F-measure of different methods on all four datasets. Because the DRFI [24] and LEGS [52] methods also randomly select the images from the MSRA-5000 dataset to train their models, where the former learns a random forest regressor and the latter trains a convolutional neural network, and both of them only provide the pre-training models, we don't give the experimental results of the two methods on the MSRA-5000 dataset for a fair comparison. As shown in Fig. 6, we can see that the precision-recall curve of the proposed algorithm significantly performs better than other methods on the SOD dataset and slightly better than the second best method (LEGS [52]) on the ECSSD and PASCAL-S datasets. In terms of F-measure score, the proposed algorithm outperforms other methods on the SOD and MSRA-5000 datasets, and is the second best on the PASCAL-S and ECSSD datasets, slightly worse than the LEGS [52], as shown in Table 1. Table 2 shows the AUC values of all evaluated methods. The proposed algorithm consistently performs better than these competitors on the SOD, MSRA-5000 and PASCAL-S datasets and slightly poorly compared to the DRFI [24] on the ECSSD dataset.

In addition, we evaluate the performance of subspace ranking with different kernels and primal space ranking (i.e., without feature projection matrix **P**) on the PASCAL-S dataset. We utilize the performance of directly averaging the top 5 proposals ranked in the kernelized subspace. The results are shown in Fig. 4, we can see that the performance is significantly improved by using the

Table 1. Quantitative comparisons in terms of F-measure score. The best and second best results are shown in red color and blue color respectively.

Datasets	AMC	BL	DSR	GC	HDCT	HS	MR
MSRA	0.7575	0.7328	0.7440	0.6575	0.7364	0.7115	0.7510
SOD	0.5888	0.5723	0.5968	0.4642	0.6108	0.5210	0.5697
PASCAL	0.5987	0.5668	0.5513	0.4861	0.5824	0.5278	0.5881
ECSSD	0.7002	0.6825	0.6636	0.5726	0.6897	0.6363	0.6932
	PCA	RR	UFO	wCtr	DRFI	LEGS	Ours
MSRA	0.6723	0.7575	0.7265	0.7437	-	-	0.7763
SOD	0.5370	0.5665	0.5480	0.5978	0.6031	0.6492	0.6622
PASCAL	0.5298	0.5873	0.5502	0.5972	0.6159	0.6951	0.6760
ECSSD	0.5796	0.6577	0.6442	0.6774	0.7337	0.7852	0.7705

Table 2. Quantitative comparison in terms of AUC score. The best and second best results are shown in red color and blue color respectively

Datasets	AMC	BL	DSR	GC	HDCT	HS	MR
MSRA	0.9292	0.9360	0.9247	0.8398	0.9318	0.9043	0.9044
SOD	0.8391	0.8503	0.8210	0.7046	0.8504	0.8145	0.7899
PASCAL	0.8616	0.8633	0.8079	0.7321	0.8582	0.8330	0.8205
ECSSD	0.9067	0.9147	0.8604	0.7848	0.9039	0.8821	0.8820
	PCA	RR	UFO	wCtr	DRFI	LEGS	Ours
MSRA	0.9248	0.9089	0.8950	0.9169	-	-	0.9376
SOD	0.8212	0.7888	0.7840	0.8014	0.8464	0.8117	0.8510
PASCAL	0.8371	0.8251	0.8088	0.8433	0.8913	0.8857	0.8970
ECSSD	0.8737	0.8283	0.8587	0.8779	0.9391	0.9239	0.9257

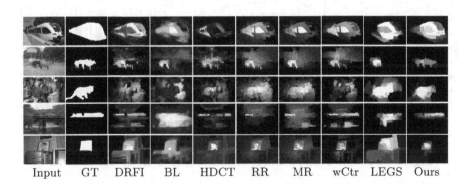

Input   GT   DRFI   BL   HDCT   RR   MR   wCtr   LEGS   Ours

Fig. 5. Visual comparison with seven state-of-the-art methods.

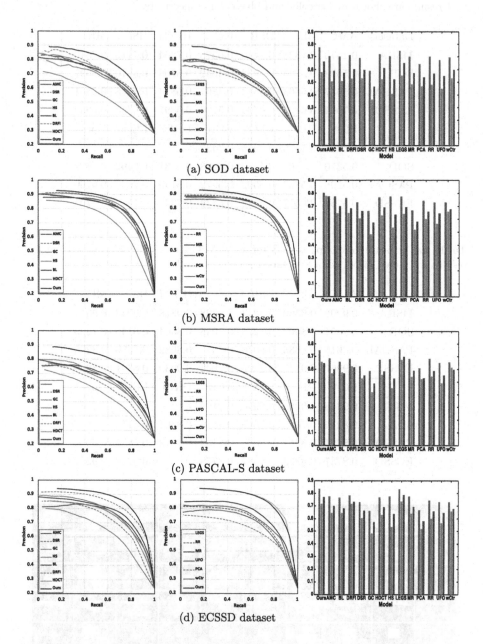

Fig. 6. Quantitative comparison of different methods on all four datasets.

Gaussian-RBF kernel projection, compared to the linear kernel projection and primal space ranking. Moreover, the weighted fusion by the ranking scores performs better than non-weighted fusion.

Qualitative Comparison: Figure 5 shows a few saliency maps generated by the evaluated methods. We note that the proposed algorithm uniformly highlights the salient regions with well-defined contours. Owing to the contribution of the subspace ranking and kernel projection, the proposed method can detect salient objects accurately when the backgrounds are cluttered or the objects and backgrounds have similar appearance. More results can be found in the supplementary material[1].

5   Conclusions

In this paper, we explore a novel and effective ranking based approach for saliency detection by jointly learning a SVM ranker and a distance metric in a unified framework. The learnt metric uses kernel projection matrix to map the high-dimensional R-CNN features into a low-dimensional subspace, thereby removing the redundancy of feature channels and prompting sample pairs more separable. Different from existing methods that concentrate on the pixel or superpixel level to detect salient objects, we present a proposal-based saliency approach, which exploits the object-level saliency cues of proposals to increase the completeness of detected results and avoid fitting to locally salient parts. Specifically, we rank the object candidates and compute the saliency map by a weighted fusion of the top-ranked candidates according to their ranking scores. We conduct extensive experiments on four benchmark datasets and demonstrate favorable performance against thirteen state-of-the-art methods.

Acknowledgments. The work was supported by the National Natural Science Foundation of China under Grant #61371157, Grant #61472060 and Grant #61528101.

References

1. Achanta, R., Hemami, S., Estrada, F., Susstrunk., S.: Frequency-tuned salient region detection. In: CVPR, pp. 1597–1604 (2009)
2. Alexe, B., Deselaers, T., Ferrari, V.: Measuring the objectness of image windows. IEEE TPAMI **34**(11), 2189–2202 (2012)
3. Borji, A., Itti, L.: State-of-the-art in visual attention modeling. IEEE Trans. Pattern Anal. Mach. Intell. **35**(1), 185–207 (2013)
4. Carreira, J., Sminchisescu, C.: CPMC: automatic object segmentation using constrained parametric min-cuts. IEEE TPAMI **34**(7), 1312–1328 (2012)
5. Chang, K.Y., Liu, T.L., Chen, H.T., Lai., S.H.: Fusing generic objectness and visual saliency for salient object detection. In: ICCV, pp. 914–921 (2011)
6. Chapelle, O., Keerthi, S.S.: Efficient algorithms for ranking with SVMs. Inf. Retrieval **13**(3), 201–215 (2010)

---

[1] http://ice.dlut.edu.cn/lu/index.html.

7. Cheng, M.M., Warrell, J., Lin, W.Y., Zheng, S., Vineet, V., Crook, N.: Efficient salient region detection with soft image abstraction. In: Proceedings of the IEEE International Conference on Computer Vision, pp. 1529–1536 (2013)
8. Cheng, M.M., Zhang, Z., Lin, W.Y., Torr, P.: Bing: binarized normed gradients for objectness estimation at 300 fps. In: CVPR (2014)
9. Cheng, M., Warrell, J., Lin, W., Zheng, S., Vineet, V., Crook., N.: Efficient salient region detection with soft image abstraction. In: ICCV, pp. 1529–1536 (2013)
10. Cheng, M., Zhang, G., Mitra, N., Huang, X., Hu., S.: Global contrast based salient region detection. In: CVPR, pp. 409–416 (2011)
11. Endres, I., Hoiem, D.: Category independent object proposals. In: Daniilidis, K., Maragos, P., Paragios, N. (eds.) ECCV 2010, Part V. LNCS, vol. 6315, pp. 575–588. Springer, Heidelberg (2010)
12. Girshick, R., Donahue, J., Darrell, T., Malik, J.: Heterogeneous metric learning with joint graph regularization for cross-media retrieval. In: CVPR (2014)
13. Goferman, S., Zelnik-Manor, L., Tal, A.: Context-aware saliency detection. In: CVPR, pp. 2376–2383 (2010)
14. Gong, C., Tao, D., Liu, W., Maybank, S.J., Fang, M., Fu, K., Yang, J.: Saliency propagation from simple to difficult. In: Proceedings of the IEEE Conference on Computer Vision and Pattern Recognition, pp. 2531–2539 (2015)
15. Gopalakrishnan, V., Hu, Y., Rajan, D.: Random walks on graphs for salient object detection in images. IEEE TIP 19(12), 3232–3242 (2010)
16. Guo, C., Ma, Q., Zhang., L.: Spatio-temporal saliency detection using phase spectrum of quaternion fourier transform. In: CVPR (2008)
17. Harel, J., Koch, C., Perona, P.: Graph-based visual saliency. In: NIPS, pp. 545–552 (2006)
18. Hariharan, B., Arbeláez, P., Girshick, R., Malik, J.: Simultaneous detection and segmentation. In: Fleet, D., Pajdla, T., Schiele, B., Tuytelaars, T. (eds.) ECCV 2014, Part VII. LNCS, vol. 8695, pp. 297–312. Springer, Heidelberg (2014)
19. Hou, X., Zhang., L.: Saliency detection: a spectral residual approach. In: CVPR, pp. 1–8 (2007)
20. Huang, Z., Wang, R., Shan, S., Chen, X.: Learning Euclidean-to-Riemannian metric for point-to-set classification. In: CVPR, pp. 1677–1684 (2014)
21. Itti, L., Koch, C., Niebur, E.: A model of saliency-based visual attention for rapid scene analysis. IEEE TPAMI 20(11), 1254–1259 (1998)
22. Jia, Y., Han., M.: Category-independent object-level saliency detection. In: ICCV, pp. 1761–1768 (2013)
23. Jiang, B., Zhang, L., Lu, H., Yang, C., Yang, M.H.: Saliency detection via absorbing markov chain. In: ICCV, pp. 1665–1672 (2013)
24. Jiang, H., Wang, J., Yuan, Z., Wu, Y., Zheng, N., Li, S.: Salient object detection: a discriminative regional feature integration approach. In: CVPR (2013)
25. Jiang, P., Ling, H., Yu, J., Peng, J.: Salient region detection by UFO: Uniqueness, Focusness and Objectness. In: ICCV, pp. 1976–1983 (2013)
26. Jiang, P., Vasconcelos, N., Peng, J.: Generic promotion of diffusion-based salient object detection. In: Proceedings of the IEEE International Conference on Computer Vision, pp. 217–225 (2015)
27. Jiang, Z., Davis, L.: Submodular salient region detection. In: CVPR, pp. 2043–2050 (2013)
28. Judd, T., Ehinger, K., Durand, F., Torralba., A.: Learning to predict where humans look. In: ICCV, pp. 2106–2113 (2009)
29. Kienzle, W., Wichmann, F.A., Schölkopf, B., Franz, M.O.: A nonparametric approach to bottom-up visual saliency. In: NIPS, pp. 417–424 (2007)

30. Kim, J., Han, D., Tai, Y.W., Kim, J.: Salient region detection via high-dimensional color transform. In: CVPR, pp. 883–890 (2014)

31. Klein, D., Frintrop., S.: Center-surround divergence of feature statistics for salient object detection. In: ICCV, pp. 2214–2219 (2011)

32. Krähenbühl, P., Koltun, V.: Geodesic object proposals. In: Fleet, D., Pajdla, T., Schiele, B., Tuytelaars, T. (eds.) ECCV 2014, Part V. LNCS, vol. 8693, pp. 725–739. Springer, Heidelberg (2014)

33. Krizhevsky, A., Sutskever, I., Hinton, G.: Imagenet classification with deep convolutional neural networks. In: NIPS (2012)

34. Li, C., Yuan, Y., Cai, W., Xia, Y., Feng, D.D.: Robust saliency detection via regularized random walks ranking. In: CVPR, pp. 2710–2717 (2015)

35. Li, G., Yu, Y.: Visual saliency based on multiscale deep features. In: CVPR (2015)

36. Li, S., Lu, H., Lin, Z., Shen, X., Price, B.: Adaptive metric learning for saliency detection. IEEE TIP **24**(11), 3321–3331 (2015)

37. Li, X., Lu, H., Zhang, L., Ruan, X., Yang, M.H.: Saliency detection via dense and sparse reconstruction. In: ICCV, pp. 2976–2983 (2013)

38. Li, Y., Hou, X., Koch, C., Rehg, J.M., Yuille, A.L.: The secrets of salient object segmentation. In: CVPR, pp. 280–287 (2014)

39. Liu, T., Yuan, Z., Sun, J., Wang, J., Zheng, N., Tang, X., Shum, H.: Learning to detect a salient object. IEEE Trans. Pattern Anal. Mach. Intell. **33**(2), 353–367 (2011)

40. Lu, S., Mahadevan, V., Vasconcelos, N.: Learning optimal seeds for diffusion-based salient object detection. In: CVPR, pp. 2790–2797 (2014)

41. Lu, Y., Zhang, W., Lu, H., Xue, X.: Salient object detection using concavity context. In: ICCV, pp. 233–240 (2011)

42. Mai, L., Niu, Y., Liu, F.: Saliency aggregation: a data-driven approach. In: CVPR, pp. 1131–1138 (2013)

43. Margolin, R., Tal, A., Zelnik-Manor, L.: What makes a patch distinct? In: CVPR, pp. 1139–1146 (2013)

44. Mcfee, B., Lanckriet, G., Jebara, T.: Learning multi-modal similarity. JMLR **12**(2), 491–523 (2011)

45. Mignon, A., Jurie, F.: PCCA: a new approach for distance learning from sparse pairwise constraints. In: 2012 IEEE Conference on Computer Vision and Pattern Recognition (CVPR), pp. 2666–2672 (2012)

46. Movahedi, V., Elder, J.: Design and perceptual validation of performance measures for salient object segmentation. In: CVPR Workshop, pp. 49–56 (2010)

47. Peng, Y., Xiao, J.: Heterogeneous metric learning with joint graph regularization for cross-media retrieval. In: AAAI, pp. 1198–1204 (2013)

48. Perazzi, F., Krahenbuhl, P., Pritch, Y., Hornung., A.: Saliency filters: contrast based filtering for salient region detection. In: CVPR, pp. 733–740 (2012)

49. Qin, Y., Lu, H., Xu, Y., Wang, H.: Saliency detection via cellular automata. In: Proceedings of the IEEE Conference on Computer Vision and Pattern Recognition, pp. 110–119 (2015)

50. Toet, A.: Computational versus psychophysical bottom-up image saliency: a comparative evaluation study. IEEE TPAMI **33**(11), 2131–2146 (2011)

51. Tong, N., Lu, H., Ruan, X., Yang, M.H.: Salient object detection via bootstrap learning. In: CVPR, pp. 1884–1892 (2015)

52. Wang, L., Lu, H., Ruan, X., Yang, M.H.: Deep networks for saliency detection via local estimation and global search. In: Proceedings of the IEEE Conference on Computer Vision and Pattern Recognition, pp. 3183–3192 (2015)

53. Wang, M., Konrad, J., Ishwar, P., Jing, K., Rowley, H.: Image saliency: from intrinsic to extrinsic context. In: CVPR, pp. 417–424 (2011)
54. Wang, W., Wang, Y., Huang, Q., Gao., W.: Measuring visual saliency by site entropy rate. In: CVPR, pp. 2368–2375 (2010)
55. Wei, Y., Wen, F., Zhu, W., Sun, J.: Geodesic saliency using background priors. In: Fitzgibbon, A., Lazebnik, S., Perona, P., Sato, Y., Schmid, C. (eds.) ECCV 2012, Part III. LNCS, vol. 7574, pp. 29–42. Springer, Heidelberg (2012)
56. Xiong, F., Gou, M., Camps, O., Sznaier, M.: Person re-identification using kernel-based metric learning methods. In: Fleet, D., Pajdla, T., Schiele, B., Tuytelaars, T. (eds.) ECCV 2014, Part VII. LNCS, vol. 8695, pp. 1–16. Springer, Heidelberg (2014)
57. Yan, Q., Xu, L., Shi, J., Jia, J.: Hierarchical saliency detection. In: CVPR, pp. 1155–1162 (2013)
58. Yang, C., Zhang, L., Lu, H., Ruan, X., Yang, M.H.: Saliency detection via graph-based manifold ranking. In: CVPR, pp. 3166–3173 (2013)
59. Zhang, J., Sclaroff, S., Lin, Z., Shen, X., Price, B., Mech, R.: Minimum barrier salient object detection at 80 fps. In: Proceedings of the IEEE International Conference on Computer Vision, pp. 1404–1412 (2015)
60. Zhang, T., Oles, F.J.: Text categorization based on regularized linear classification methods. Inf. Retrieval 4(1), 5–31 (2001)
61. Zhao, Q., Koch, C.: Learning a saliency map using fixated locations in natural scenes. JoV 11(3), 1–15 (2011)
62. Zhao, R., Ouyang, W., Li, H., Wang, X.: Saliency detection by multi-context deep learning. In: Proceedings of the IEEE Conference on Computer Vision and Pattern Recognition, pp. 1265–1274 (2015)
63. Zhu, W., Liang, S., Wei, Y., Sun, J.: Saliency optimization from robust background detection. In: CVPR, pp. 2814–2821 (2014)
64. Zou, W., Komodakis, N.: HARF: hierarchy-associated rich features for salient object detection. In: Proceedings of the IEEE International Conference on Computer Vision, pp. 406–414 (2015)

Depth-Aware Motion Magnification

Julian F.P. Kooij[1,2(✉)] and Jan C. van Gemert[1]

[1] Delft University of Technology, Delft, The Netherlands
{J.F.P.Kooij,J.C.vanGemert}@tudelft.nl
[2] Leiden University Medical Center, Leiden, The Netherlands

Abstract. This paper adds depth to motion magnification. With the rise of cheap RGB+D cameras depth information is readily available. We make use of depth to make motion magnification robust to occlusion and large motions. Current approaches require a manual drawn pixel mask over all frames in the area of interest which is cumbersome and error-prone. By including depth, we avoid manual annotation and magnify motions at similar depth levels while ignoring occlusions at distant depth pixels. To achieve this, we propose an extension to the bilateral filter for non-Gaussian filters which allows us to treat pixels at very different depth layers as missing values. As our experiments will show, these missing values should be ignored, and not inferred with inpainting. We show results for a medical application (tremors) where we improve current baselines for motion magnification and motion measurements.

Keywords: Motion magnification · Bilateral filter · RGB+D

1 Introduction

Magnifying tiny motions in video [3,4] opened up a wealth of applications. Examples include: reconstructing speech exclusively from small visual vibrations [5], detecting a heart-beat either from blood flow [4] or from tiny head motions [6], magnifying muscle tremors [7], segmenting blood vessels [8] or estimating material properties by the way it moves [9]. In this paper we propose to only magnify motion at selected depth ranges, which makes motion magnification robust to occlusions and large motions at other depths. Robustness is especially important to open up new applications in the medical domain such as tremor assessment [10–12], where the interaction between doctor and patient should not be disturbed, and prerequisites for video processing should not limit the poses and exercises dictated by the medical protocol.

Currently though, magnifying tiny motions requires that there are no occlusions or large motions [1,3,4]. A recent solution proposes to manually indicate the large motions by drawing a binary pixel mask on the frames of interest [2].

Electronic supplementary material The online version of this chapter (doi:10. 1007/978-3-319-46484-8_28) contains supplementary material, which is available to authorized users.

© Springer International Publishing AG 2016
B. Leibe et al. (Eds.): ECCV 2016, Part VIII, LNCS 9912, pp. 467–482, 2016.
DOI: 10.1007/978-3-319-46484-8_28

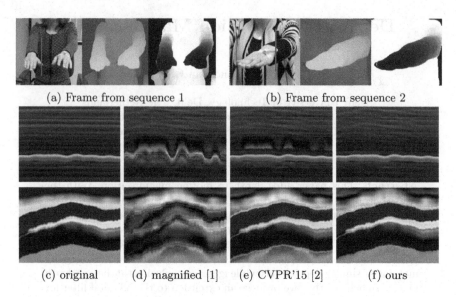

(a) Frame from sequence 1   (b) Frame from sequence 2

(c) original   (d) magnified [1]   (e) CVPR'15 [2]   (f) ours

Fig. 1. Comparison of our and baseline magnification approaches when magnifying small motions in the background (here, body) behind moving occluders (here, trembling hands). (a), (b) For two sequences, the input image, depth map, and depth-dependent magnification matte of one frame (black/white is zero/full magnification). (c)–(f) Space-time slices for the red lines in input images. Our approach suppresses unwanted magnification artifacts from the foreground in the magnified background. *See supplementary material for videos.* (Color figure online)

While a mask indicates which pixels should be used, it does not solve how to ignore the motion filter responses on the edge of the mask. Motion filters have a certain spatial extent and they 'leak' across the mask border. Moreover, manually drawing such a mask on a moving target is challenging and time-consuming. We instead exploit depth to automatically define the mask. Furthermore, we prevent the 'leaking' by ignoring motion responses from very different depths whereas filter responses from close-by depth layers are weighted.

Several techniques are available for weighting filter responses [13–16]. These techniques allow weighted Gaussian smoothing or interpolation, for example, on intensity differences resulting in edge-preserving smoothing. However, high-quality motion magnification [1] depends on the complex steerable pyramid [17,18] which consists of non-Gaussian filters for which standard weighting of filter responses [13,14,16] cannot be used. To illustrate, consider a Gaussian derivative filter. Since it integrates to zero, it will give no response on a constant valued input image. Intuitively, the response should not change if some parts of the input are ignored, but reducing some filter weights to zero would now actually yield non-zero output. In other words, the Gaussian derivative cannot be treated as a weighted input aggregate. In this paper we therefore develop filter weighting of non-Gaussian filters, which can ignore input by treating it as missing values.

When images have missing values, there are several advanced inpainting techniques [19–23] available to estimate what is lost. It is not clear, however, how inpainting can be used to infer missing values between multiple depth layers. We propose a different goal. We do not want to recover what is lost: we want to ignore what is there.

In the following sections we first discuss related work, then how to ignore filter responses from different depth layers, and how this allows depth-aware motion magnification. We experimentally compare against inpainting and show example applications in the medical domain on hand tremors.

2 Related Work

Motion can be magnified by explicitly tracking feature points with optical flow [24]. The motion is magnified by re-scaling the moving points and adding them back to the video. Optical flow is estimated locally between pairs of frames which is noisy. This noise affects the motion magnification since local motion is represented by a single unique feature point. In contrast to feature point tracking, Eulerian video magnification [4] estimates motion frequency over longer time periods which is more stable. Thus, the method is well-suited for amplifying tiny imperceptible motions. Impressive improvements [1] on the stability of linear motion magnification [4] are made by relying on complex steerable pyramid filters [17,18]. A significant speedup without perceptual decrease in quality can be obtained by approximating the complex pyramid with the Riesz pyramid [25]. While extremely successful for clean video sequences, all these methods assume that there are no occlusions or large motions present. Our method is specifically designed to deal with such cases.

With some help by the user, occlusion or large motions can be manually indicated. Examples of user input on video processing include de-animation [26], blending between face performances [27], video segmentation [28], and video stabilization [29]. For motion magnification a manual drawn mask can specify which pixels to magnify and which pixels to ignore [2]. In this paper we extend this line of reasoning, replacing the manual drawn mask by a weighted mask obtained from depth to ignore filter responses outside a target depth range.

Incorporating weighted responses in a filter is done with the bilateral filter [16]. It applies Gaussian blurring to an image, but locally adapts the Gaussian weights to suppress contributions of neighbourhood pixels with very different intensity levels. The fast bilateral filter [15] offers a significant speedup by approximation. This is achieved by transforming the 2D input image into a 3D sparse matrix, where the 3rd z-dimension is given by a pixel's intensity level. The speedup comes from allowing standard 3D convolutions to obtain intensity-weighted responses. In this paper we begin with the fast bilateral filter [15] due to its speed. However, where the bilateral filter only allows weighted Gaussian smoothing or interpolation we require non-Gaussian filters: the complex steerable pyramid [17,18] as used in high-quality motion magnification [1]. Instead of weighting values, we adapt the bilateral filter so it can handle missing values.

Inferring missing values in images by inpainting typically exploits texture synthesis and pixel consistency [19,30]. Strong step edges can be retained [21] and image statistics through patch-exemplars can give a good prior on what values to infer [23]. Inpainting can be done efficiently [20], making it in principle suitable for video processing. While inpainting could be used to fill in missing values for very different depth layers, it is not clear how to use inpainting to combine closer depth layers. In contrast to inpainting we do not wish to infer what should be present at all depth layers. Our goal is to remove all filter influences from pixels at different depth layers.

3   Approach

This section starts with the bilateral filter formulation [16], followed by our non-Gaussian extension. We then apply the developed technique to complex steerable pyramids and use these for occlusion-aware Eulerian motion magnification [1,2,24] and measurement [31]. We note that other image processing tasks could also benefit from the non-Gaussian bilateral filter (see supplementary material for examples), and for instance use intensity, optical flow, or color instead of depth to filter micro-textures, stationaries, surfaces.

3.1   Bilateral Filter

The bilateral filter [16] can be used for depth-aware smoothing. Given input image I and corresponding depth image E, the bilateral filter computes output image O. By defining $y \in N(x)$ as the local a neighbourhood of 2D image locations $x = (u, v)$, and using $O(x)$ as a shorthand for $O(u, v)$, the bilateral filter can be written as a weighted average

$$O(x) = \frac{1}{W(x)} \sum_{y \in N(x)} w(|x - y|, E(x) - E(y))\, I(y) \qquad (1)$$

$$w(d_s, d_E) = G(d_s; \sigma_s) \times G(d_E; \sigma_r) \qquad (2)$$

where $W(x) = \sum_{y \in N(x)} w(|x-y|, E(x)-E(y))$ is the weight normalization term at x, and $G(x; \sigma) = \exp\left(-\frac{x}{2\sigma^2}\right)$ is the Gaussian kernel. The positive weights $w(d_I, d_E)$ approach zero as the spatial distance d_s or the depth distance d_E increases. There are two smoothing parameters, the spatial standard deviation σ_s, which controls the amount of spatial blurring as is in a normal Gaussian image filter, and the depth standard deviation σ_r, which controls how strong pixels on different depth layers are weighted.

3.2   Bilateral Filter for Non-Gaussian Kernels

Consider some non-Gaussian kernel F with negative values, for instance F is an oriented band-pass filter used in a steerable pyramid [18], or a Gaussian derivative. As with the Gaussian bilateral filter, we would like to apply F to an input image I, but obtain filter responses representative of the local spatial neighbourhood with nearby depth values. While the bilateral filter with Gaussian kernel can be seen as a weighted average, we cannot simply replace the kernel by F. For instance, the integral of a Gaussian derivative kernel is zero, and would yield a division by zero in normalization. Also, one cannot ignore part of the input by reducing corresponding weights to zero, since this introduces unwanted edge responses as if the input itself partly has zero values; our experiments in Sect. 4.1 will illustrate this point.

Instead, we propose to reduce the influence of regions in distant depth layers by smoothly incorporating the spatial image structure at the local depth layer. Using $\xi = E(z)$ to denote the depth at the output location z, the non-Gaussian bilateral filter with output Q is written as

$$Q(z) = \sum_{x \in N(z)} F(|x - z|)O^+(x, E(z)) \tag{3}$$

$$O^+(x, \xi) = \frac{1}{W^+(x, \xi)} \sum_{y \in N(z)} w(|x - y|, \xi - E(y))I(y) \tag{4}$$

with $w(d_s, d_E)$ again some weight function (which we will define in a moment), and $W^+(x, \xi) = \sum_{y \in N(z)} w(|x - y|, \xi - E(y))$. Here the $+$ suffix indicates that a function operates on 3D space by extending the spatial domain with additional depth information from E. Throughout this paper we shall use the $+$ suffix notation more frequently, and refer to it as an *extended* representation. Note that $Q(x)$ is not just a convolution with F after applying a bilateral filter, since $O^+(x, \xi)$ is not only a function of x. But, our formulation does have the regular bilateral filter, Eq. (1), as special case when $F(x) = 1$ iff $x = 0$ and 0 otherwise.

We reformulate our filter to a 3D representation similar to the fast bilateral filter [15]. This has two benefits: One, as with the standard bilateral filter, explicit evaluation of Eq. (3) is inefficient, since filter coefficients need to be reweighted at each spatial location. The 3D representation instead offers a trade off between quality and speed [15]. Two, this 3D representation explicitly keeps filter responses at different depths separated, which will be exploited in our applications to perform depth-aware temporal filtering.

First, an extra dimension r is introduced, representing possible depth values for $E(y)$ in the domain of all depth values R. We rewrite Eq. (4) as

$$W^+(x, \xi)O^+(x, \xi) = \sum_{r \in R} \sum_{y \in N} w(|x - y|, \xi - r)\delta(r, E(y)) I(y) \tag{5}$$

where $\delta(r, E(y)) = 1$ iff $r = E(y)$ and 0 otherwise. Next, the term $\delta(r, E(y))$ and the 2D input image are used to define equivalent extended representations (indicated by the $+$ suffix) I^+ for input, and V^+ to weight the input,

$$V^+(y, r) = \delta(r, E(y)) \tag{6}$$

$$I^+(y, r) = I(y) \tag{7}$$

$$\delta(r, E(y))I(y) = V^+(y, r)I^+(y, r). \tag{8}$$

We see that $I^+(y,r)$ indeed has 3D coordinates $(y,r) = (u_y, v_y, r)$, and similarly, $V^+(y,r)$ constitutes a 3D binary mask indicating which part of the space contains valid input. We write out the terms of (5) as

$$W^+(x,\xi)O^+(x,\xi) = \sum_{r \in R} \sum_{y \in N(z)} w(|x - y|, \xi - r)\, V^+(y,r)I^+(y,r), \quad (9)$$

$$W^+(x,\xi) = \sum_{r \in R} \sum_{y \in N(z)} w(|x - y|, \xi - r)\, V^+(y,r). \quad (10)$$

Now we can recognize the nested summation as a 3D convolution over the extended representations using the weight function w as a 3D kernel, which is the first step in our non-Gaussian filtering method,

$$W^+O^+ = w \otimes V^+I^+ \qquad \text{step 1:} \quad \text{3D Gauss convolution} \qquad (11)$$

$$W^+ = w \otimes V^+. \qquad (12)$$

If we would use the bilateral filter weight function (2), the 3D convolution will expand the local 3D neighbourhood of a target image location into regions with different depth values. Thereby, increasing depth distances result in less contribution in the convolved result. However, this kernel also blurs the original image values, inadvertently removing details from the input before the filter F is applied in Eq. (3), even at regions with uniform depth that should not be affected.

Therefore, we consider a weighting function

$$w(d_I, d_E) = \begin{cases} \alpha & \text{iff } d_I = 0 \text{ and } d_E = 0, \\ G(d_I; \sigma_s) \times G(d_E; \sigma_r) & \text{otherwise,} \end{cases} \quad (13)$$

such that as $\alpha \to \infty$, the weight of the local image value $I^+(y,r)$ dominates all other weights in (9) and (10) when $y = x, r = \xi$, and when $V^+(y,r) = 1$. In other words, the 3D convolution will not blur the actual input values, and not affect the filter response F in uniform depth regions. But the Gaussian weighting is still used in include valid input from the neighbourhood when $V^+(y,r) = 0$, i.e. at regions with missing values in the extended representation. In practice we do not explicitly evaluate (13), but instead produce the result of $\alpha \to \infty$ by applying the normal kernel first to a temporary result Θ^+, and then placing back the original values to obtain the intended result. The remaining steps to apply our filter method are therefore,

$$\Theta^+ = W^+O^+/W^+ \qquad \text{step 2:} \quad \text{element-wise division} \qquad (14)$$

$$O^+ = V^+I^+ + (1 - V^+)\Theta^+ \qquad \text{step 3:} \quad \text{restore valid original data} \qquad (15)$$

$$Q^+ = F \otimes O^+ \qquad \text{step 4:} \quad \text{apply } F \text{ at all depth layers} \qquad (16)$$

$$Q(x) = Q^+(x, E(x)) \qquad \text{step 5:} \quad \text{back-project to 2D} \qquad (17)$$

The final step, (17), back-projects the extended space to the original 2D image space, which completes the evaluation of Eq. (3). Following [15], discretizing the depth dimensions r into D depth layers results in a fast approximation, and convolutions on the depth layers can be processed in parallel. Additionally, we downsample the image instead of expanding the spatial Gaussian kernel [15].

3.3   Depth-Aware Video Magnification

For phase-based motion magnification [1], the non-Gaussian complex steerable pyramid is used. The principle behind this approach is that small temporal changes in the spatial offset of edges translates to small temporal changes in the phases of the complex filter responses in the pyramid. Likewise, augmenting temporal phase variations results in magnifying periodic movements in the video. With a magnification factor M, phases ϕ_t of the pyramid components p_t at time t are augmented with respect to the temporally low-pass filtered phases $\bar{\phi}$ to obtain magnified pyramid phase $\hat{\phi}_t = (1 + M) \cdot (\phi_t - \bar{\phi}) + \bar{\phi}$.

To exploit the depth information in the complex steerable pyramid, we apply the non-Gaussian bilateral filtering from Sect. 3.2. Figure 2 illustrates the steps to construct a bilateral steerable pyramid from an input grey scale and depth image pair (I, E). First, an extended representation is created following Eq. (11)–(15). This representation is then used in the pyramid construction by applying the low-pass and complex band-pass filters of [18] to each of the depth layers, i.e. Eq. (16). The result is an extended complex steerable pyramid. The bottom row of Fig. 2 illustrates that when the extended pyramid is back-projected using the depth map E (Eq. (17)), the resulting pyramid coefficients are *depth-aware*: filter responses of fore- and background edges are separated as seen by the discontinuities. In the standard pyramid, strong filter responses from the foreground (depicting two hands) 'leak' into the background, especially at higher pyramid levels where the filters have larger spatial extent.

Figure 3, depicts our proposed magnification pipeline. The phase augmentation principle is applied to components in all depth layers of the extended pyramid. However, we adapt the factor per layer with a depth-dependent function, resulting in a spatially varying magnification matte $M(x) = M_{\max} \times \exp\left(-(E(x) - \mu_d)/(2\sigma_d^2)\right)$, parametrized by $(\mu_d, \sigma_d, M_{\max})$. In the last processing step, the magnified pyramids are back-projected to 2D frames, and the matte is used to smoothly blend the magnified results of the discrete depth layers.

The recently proposed method by [2] also considers magnification of subtle motions that occur in videos with large movements, utilizing an opacity matte to blend selected regions of a magnified frame into the original unmagnified frame. For our comparison, we adapted their method to our setting which entails that (a) instead of using a tool to manually select a binary foreground region, the opacity matte M is used, (b) we do not perform initial video stabilization as the camera viewpoint is already static, (c) the motion of matte M itself is not magnified as we do not wish to magnify the motion of the occluding object, but rather that of the occluded region. Figure 3 also shows the difference between both approaches. The baseline introduces the depth information at the last step only. Our approach uses depth from the start to obtain and operate on a depth-aware representation. Section 4.2 shall empirically compare both approaches.

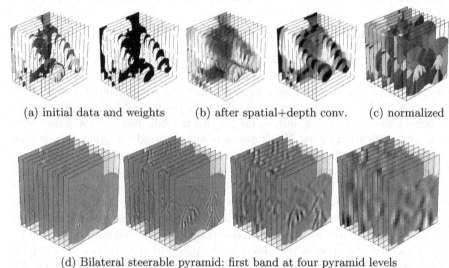

(a) initial data and weights   (b) after spatial+depth conv.   (c) normalized

(d) Bilateral steerable pyramid: first band at four pyramid levels

(e) Bilateral pyramid (back-projected)   (f) Standard steerable pyramid

Fig. 2. Constructing a bilateral steerable pyramid on the frame from Fig. 1a with the steps in Sect. 3.2. (a) the input image and depth map are used to construct a 3D image representation image I^+ and input weight map V^+ by discretizing the depth into multiple layers. (b) *step 1:* Both representations are filtered in 3D (2D and the image coordinates + 1D depth coordinate). (c) *step 2, 3:* The filtered 3D image is normalized using the filtered weights, and valid input is restored. (d) *step 4:* the steerable pyramid is constructed on each discrete depth layer. Here, the result is shown at various levels in the pyramid of a single orientation band. (e) *step 5:* The 3D representation can be back-projected to a normal pyramid using depth map, resulting in an edge-aware steerable pyramid. Note how the responses of edges in the nearby hand remain within the foreground region, resulting in hard edges (e.g. see red arrows). (f) In contrast, a normal steerable pyramid induces soft object edges which 'leak' from the foreground into the surrounding background, especially at the higher pyramid levels (e.g. see red arrows). (Color figure online)

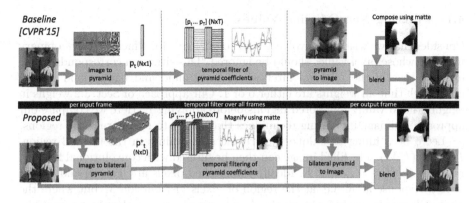

Fig. 3. Video magnification pipelines. (Top) baseline approach from [2], which composes a magnified and unmagnified version of each frame. The composition is based on an opacity matte, based on the depth map. (Bottom) our approach instead uses the depth map directly in the pyramid construction/deconstruction.

3.4   Motion Measurements with a Bilateral Pyramid

In addition to magnification, another use for complex steerable filters is to measure subtle periodic motions in the video. In [31], an image is first down scaled and filtered with $B = 2$ bands for the u and v direction, i.e. $b \in \{0°, 90°\}$. Changes in phase can be translated to a local motion estimate $(\Delta u, \Delta v)$, as

$$\Delta u_t(u,v) = -\frac{\partial u}{\phi_t^{0°}(u,v)} \frac{\phi_t^{0°}(u,v)}{\partial t} \quad \Delta v_t(u,v) = -\frac{\partial v}{\phi_t^{90°}(u,v)} \frac{\phi_t^{90°}(u,v)}{\partial t}. \quad (18)$$

In each equation, the first r.h.s. term is the inverse of a spatial derivative, and the second term is a temporal derivative.

For a depth-aware version, we can use the bands of our bilateral complex pyramid, using $B = 2$ bands, and select a particular layer l for scale. To ensure that the spatial and temporal derivatives are depth-aware, we compute Eq. (18) in the extended space $\phi_t^{l,b+}(u,v,r)$ and obtain $\Delta u_t^+(u,v,r), \Delta v_t^+(u,v,r)$. Only afterwards are these back-projected to 2D motion maps Δu_t and Δv_t.

4   Experiments

We first evaluate against inpainting techniques. Then, we introduce a novel RGB+Depth dataset targeting tremor analysis, which is an important medical application [10,12]. On this dataset we compare our depth-aware motion magnification against the state-of-the-art [2], and we show the effect of bilateral filtering on motion measurements in fore- and background.

4.1   Filtering Near Missing Values

Consider that we wish to convolve filter F on image I for which we have a binary mask M whose pixel values should be ignored. This situation corresponds to the extreme case of the bilateral filter where foreground and background are far apart such that all weights are either 0 or 1. Our approach of Sect. 3.2 weighs in neighborhood values in ignored regions before applying F. Here we compare our approach to image inpainting techniques that intent to reconstruct the regions.

Let g be a filling technique that replaces the values in the masked region, $I_{g,M} = g(I, M)$. The filled image can then be filtered with convolutional filter F, resulting in $I_{g,M}^F = I_{g,M} \otimes F$. Ideally the masked pixels are ignored and do not have a response at $\mathcal{R}$, i.e. at the region of pixels just outside M but where the filter still covers masked out pixels. As error measure, we therefore report the L1 norm over the pixels in $\mathcal{R}$. Let $\mathbb{L}_1(g, I, M, F)$ be the norm for a particular technique g on image I and mask M after applying filter F, then error(g) is the total norm over all tested images, masks and filters, i.e.

$$\mathbb{L}_1(g, I, M, F) = \sum_{x \in \mathcal{R}} |I_{g,M}^F(x)| \quad \text{error}(g) = \sum_I \sum_M \mathbb{L}_1(g, I, M, F). \quad (19)$$

We evaluate on a public inpainting dataset [22], which contains 17 images of 640×480 pixels (all images are converted to grayscale), 4 image masks, and also provides on each image-mask pair state-of-the-art inpainting results for *Bugeau* [19], *Herling* [20], *Total Variation (TV)* [21] and *Xu* [23]. We also compare against replacing the missing region with *zeros*, or the *actual* pixel values (an ideal inpainting algorithm). First, we use the 7 filters used in the construction of the bilateral pyramid, and tested varying the spatial parameters σ_s, but found that $\sigma_s = 1$ performed best on the steerable pyramids features. The results in Fig. 4a show that our proposed approach results in lower errors than the other inpainting techniques. As expected, the naive approach of replacing the masked region with zeros results in strong responses near the mask border, as shown by the error plots. One of the better results is obtained with TV [21], which in fact produces quite bland areas. Indeed, even using an ideal inpainting algorithm (i.e. *actual*) would introduce more unwarranted filter responses.

To test if these results generalize, we also use 64 filters from the trained VGG convolutional neural network [32] (normalized by subtracting DC components divided by norm). Figure 4b shows that similar results were obtained.

4.2   Depth-Aware Motion Magnification and Measurements

The next section describes our novel tremor dataset, and then the experiments on motion magnification and motion measurement.[1] Please see the accompanying videos in the supplementary material.

---

[1] The bilateral pyramid, depth-aware magnification code and dataset (RGB, Depth, skeleton) can be found at https://github.com/jkooij/depthaware-momag.

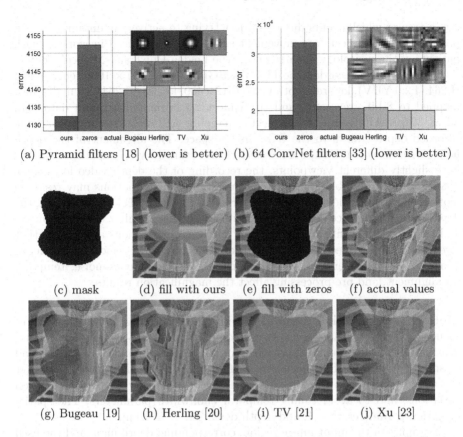

(a) Pyramid filters [18] (lower is better)   (b) 64 ConvNet filters [33] (lower is better)

(c) mask   (d) fill with ours   (e) fill with zeros   (f) actual values

(g) Bugeau [19]   (h) Herling [20]   (i) TV [21]   (j) Xu [23]

Fig. 4. (a)–(b) Errors for steerable pyramid and ConvNet features when filtering around a masked region. Insets show visualizations of (some of) these filters (c) one of the masks, black indicates missing values. (d)–(j) Output examples of filling methods (includes inpainting results by [22]). Red shows the evaluation region $\mathcal{R}$ of Eq. (19) where the filters will be affected by missing values. (Color figure online)

RGB+D Tremor Dataset. Tremors are manifestations of periodic movements in the body, and assessing their properties (frequency, amplitude) is critical for health monitoring [11,12]. Since in practice only few accelerometers can be placed on the body they are typically placed where the amplitude of the tremor is most clearly visible, e.g. on the hand and arm. Video based measuring and magnification could help discover more subtle occurrences, visualize where tremors originate or how they move trough the body, and even make objective tremor assessment possible without expensive hospital equipment.

We therefore collected a novel dataset with the Microsoft Kinect 2 to study visual tremor assessment using (1) visualization, and (2) by measuring frequency. The dataset contains 4 RGB+Depth sequences of subjects with a simulated tremor in the hand, observed with their arms extended for several seconds. This is a common task in tremor assessment, intended to induce a *postural tremor* (i.e. a tremor which occurs due to subject trying to actively maintain a certain pose) [11]. The subjects are movement scientists, experienced in working with patients of the neurology department at the Leiden University Medical Center.

Using [33], we recorded the high-res RGB video (1920 × 1090, encoded in H.264, 4:2:0 YUV), low-res depth video (512 × 450, lossless H.264, 0–4 m distance mapped to 8-bit greyscale), and the Kinect 2's estimated skeleton data [34], all at 30 fps. Afterwards, the Kinect's mapping API was used to project the recorded depth frames to the RGB image space. The alignment of the depth image with the colour images is not perfect, however: the video and depth camera have slightly different viewpoints, the recording of the depth video loses some quality due to the 8-bit greyscale conversion, and quick motions may result in motion blur in the video that is not observed in the depth. For these reasons, the depth data is pre-processed by first running a 2D median filter to remove noise, and then a 2D max filter. This extends the occluding regions and ensure that foreground in the video is also fully enclosed in the nearby regions of the depth image. The supplementary material demonstrates how depth noise, temporal misalignment, and pre-processing affect the magnification results.

Motion Magnification Behind Moving Occluder. On the first three sequences, each 91 frames (= 3 s), we compare our depth-aware video magnification to the the baseline approach from [2], as described in Sect. 3.3. Instead of specifying specific frequencies to magnify [1], we use the mean phase over the whole sequence as the low-pass $\bar{\phi}$ in order to magnify all periodic motion variations, and to avoid tuning temporal bandwidth parameters. The spatial deviation parameter $\sigma_s = 1$, and depth deviation $\sigma_r = 0.1$ m.

Examples of the input image region, corresponding depth map, and the used magnification matte (which in all cases has been set to magnify the body's depth range) can be seen in Fig. 1a and b. The results of the various magnification methods are visualized as space-time slices of Fig. 1. Figure 5 shows additional single frame comparisons. On the third sequence the clothing is very dark. Here the intensity channel has been enhanced to more clearly show the details in the body. The figure illustrates that compositing the magnified and original image, as in the baseline [2], results in notable artifacts in both textured on non-textured backgrounds. We conclude that the approach in [2], which is designed to magnify foreground under heavy camera motion, does not properly magnify background behind non-static occluders. Our approach instead suppresses the artifacts.

Motion Frequency for Overlapping Body Regions. We applied the bilateral motion measurement on the 4th and longer sequence (∼ 17 s.) to determine the vertical motion in the hand (foreground) and chest region (background) surrounding the hand. In each frame, the measured motion is averaged over a body part mask automatically extracted using the Kinect 2's built-in skeleton estimate, resulting in a single temporal signal for each body region. The time aligned groundtruth data of an accelerometer on the chest demonstrates that this sequence contains two breathing cycles of about 8.5 s., see Fig. 6a. When we

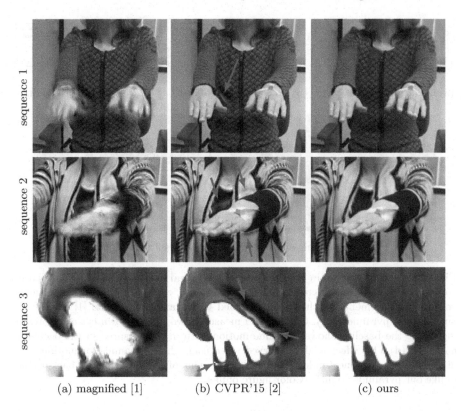

sequence 1

sequence 2

sequence 3

(a) magnified [1]   (b) CVPR'15 [2]   (c) ours

Fig. 5. Frames from motion magnification results on three sequences (top-to-bottom $M_{max} = 10, 3, 5$). The method of [2] blends the standard magnification result [1] with the original frame using an opacity matte, but this does not prevent unwanted artifacts of the foreground occurring the magnified background (see red arrows), even though the (unmagnified) foreground is corrected. Our approach using the bilateral filtered pyramid does avoids such artifacts. (Color figure online)

apply a low-pass filter to only keep frequencies in the 0–0.2 Hz range, we observe that without the bilateral filter the measurements in the chest are virtually the same as those in the hand, see dashed blue lines Figs. 6b and c. With bilateral filtering we obtain the same motion measurements in the foreground, but discover two periodic cycles in the background (see red lines).

The corresponding video magnification results in Fig. 6d again demonstrate that the moving foreground 'leaked' into the background. Our bilateral pyramid yields more robust phase-based measurements in such situations.

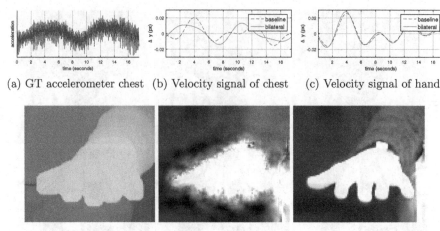

(a) GT accelerometer chest   (b) Velocity signal of chest   (c) Velocity signal of hand

(d) Depth, baseline, and our magnification results on sequence 4

Fig. 6. Measuring motion in chest behind moving hand on sequence 4. (a) Accelerometer on chest shows that there are 2 respiration cycles, each taking 9 s. (b) Low-passed velocity measurements on the chest, obtained with standard pyramid [1] (blue), and our bilateral pyramid (red). Our method measures two full up-down cycles of breathing, while the baseline shows the same motion pattern as measured in the occluding hand (c). (d) This effect is also observed when using these pyramids for motion magnification: the baseline (middle) contains movement of the hand in the background, unlike our pyramids (right). (Color figure online)

5   Conclusions

Our work exploits depth to make motion magnification robust against moving occluders. To construct depth-aware steerable pyramids, the bilateral filter was adapted to non-Gaussian kernels, such that filter responses can ignore local image values at distant depth layers. We proposed a simple and efficient filling technique that is less prone to introducing additional filter responses than state-of-the-art image inpainting techniques. Depth-aware motion magnification was demonstrated on a novel RGB+D dataset recorded with Microsoft Kinect 2 for tremor assessment, an important application in the medical domain. On this dataset with small motions in the background behind large motions in the foreground, we show improved qualitative motion magnification results with less visual artifacts compared to a state-of-the-art magnification baseline, which only exploits depth information as a final processing step. The bilateral pyramid also resulted in improved phase-based motion measurements.

Future work includes extending the dataset with more subjects, extract more measures used in medical practice, and investigate application to computationally efficient Riesz pyramids [25]. Our aim is to develop the explored methods into cheap and objective techniques to discover, monitor and classify tremors and other movement disorders (e.g. dystonia's) all over the body. Other uses of the non-Gaussian bilateral filter are also considered.

Acknowledgments. This work is part of the research programme Technology in Motion (TIM [628.004.001]), financed by the Netherlands Organisation for Scientific Research (NWO).

References

1. Wadhwa, N., Rubinstein, M., Durand, F., Freeman, W.T.: Phase-based video motion processing. ACM Trans. Graph. **32**(4), 80:1–80:9 (2013). (Proceedings SIG-GRAPH)
2. Elgharib, M.A., Hefeeda, M., Durand, F., Freeman, W.T.: Video magnification in presence of large motions. In: 2015 IEEE Conference on Computer Vision and Pattern Recognition (CVPR), pp. 4119–4127. IEEE (2015)
3. Rubinstein, M., Wadhwa, N., Durand, F., Freeman, W.T.: Revealing invisible changes in the world. Science **339**(6119), 519–519 (2013)
4. Wu, H.Y., Rubinstein, M., Shih, E., Guttag, J., Durand, F., Freeman, W.T.: Eulerian video magnification for revealing subtle changes in the world. ACM Trans. Graph. **31**(4), 65:1–65:8 (2012). (Proceedings SIGGRAPH)
5. Davis, A., Rubinstein, M., Wadhwa, N., Mysore, G., Durand, F., Freeman, W.T.: The visual microphone: passive recovery of sound from video. ACM Trans. Graph. **33**(4), 79:1–79:10 (2014). (Proceedings of SIGGRAPH)
6. Balakrishnan, G., Durand, F., Guttag, J.: Detecting pulse from head motions in video. In: Proceedings of the IEEE Conference on Computer Vision and Pattern Recognition, pp. 3430–3437 (2013)
7. Aziz, N.A., Tannemaat, M.R.: A microscope for subtle movements in clinical neurology. Neurology **85**(10), 920–920 (2015)
8. Amir-Khalili, A., Peyrat, J.-M., Abinahed, J., Al-Alao, O., Al-Ansari, A., Hamarneh, G., Abugharbieh, R.: Auto localization and segmentation of occluded vessels in robot-assisted partial nephrectomy. In: Golland, P., Hata, N., Barillot, C., Hornegger, J., Howe, R. (eds.) MICCAI 2014, Part I. LNCS, vol. 8673, pp. 407–414. Springer, Heidelberg (2014)
9. Davis, A., Bouman, K.L., Chen, J.G., Rubinstein, M., Durand, F., Freeman, W.T.: Visual vibrometry: estimating material properties from small motions in video. In: 2015 IEEE Conference on Computer Vision and Pattern Recognition (CVPR), pp. 5335–5343. IEEE (2015)
10. Bain, P.G.: Parkinsonism & related disorders. Tremor **13**, S369–S374 (2007)
11. Deuschl, G., Bain, P., Brin, M.: Consensus statement of the movement disorder society on tremor. Mov. Disord. **13**(S3), 2–23 (1998)
12. Schwingenschuh, P., Katschnig, P., Seiler, S., Saifee, T.A., Aguirregomozcorta, M., Cordivari, C., Schmidt, R., Rothwell, J.C., Bhatia, K.P., Edwards, M.J.: Moving toward laboratory-supported criteria for psychogenic tremor. Mov. Disord. **26**(14), 2509–2515 (2011)
13. Fattal, R.: Edge-avoiding wavelets and their applications. ACM Trans. Graph. **28**(3), 22:1–22:10 (2009). (Proceedings SIGGRAPH)
14. He, K., Sun, J., Tang, X.: Guided image filtering. IEEE Trans. Pattern Anal. Mach. Intell. **35**(6), 1397–1409 (2013)
15. Paris, S., Durand, F.: A fast approximation of the bilateral filter using a signal processing approach. Int. J. Comput. Vis. **81**(1), 24–52 (2009)
16. Tomasi, C., Manduchi, R.: Bilateral filtering for gray and color images. In: Sixth International Conference on Computer Vision, pp. 839–846. IEEE (1998)

17. Freeman, W.T., Adelson, E.H.: The design and use of steerable filters. IEEE Trans. Pattern Anal. Mach. Intell. **9**, 891–906 (1991)
18. Simoncelli, E.P., Freeman, W.T.: The steerable pyramid: a flexible architecture for multi-scale derivative computation. In: ICIP, p. 3444. IEEE (1995)
19. Bugeau, A., Bertalmío, M., Caselles, V., Sapiro, G.: A comprehensive framework for image inpainting. IEEE Trans. Image Process. **19**(10), 2634–2645 (2010)
20. Herling, J., Broll, W.: Pixmix: A real-time approach to high-quality diminished reality. In: 2012 IEEE International Symposium on Mixed and Augmented Reality (ISMAR), pp. 141–150. IEEE (2012)
21. Getreuer, P.: Total variation inpainting using split bregman. Image Process. Line **2**, 147–157 (2012)
22. Tiefenbacher, P., Bogischef, V., Merget, D., Rigoll, G.: Subjective and objective evaluation of image inpainting quality. In: 2015 IEEE International Conference on Image Processing (ICIP), pp. 447–451. IEEE (2015)
23. Xu, Z., Sun, J.: Image inpainting by patch propagation using patch sparsity. IEEE Trans. Image Process. **19**(5), 1153–1165 (2010)
24. Liu, C., Torralba, A., Freeman, W.T., Durand, F., Adelson, E.H.: Motion magnification. ACM Trans. Graph. (Proceedings SIGGRAPH) **24**(3), 519–526 (2005)
25. Wadhwa, N., Rubinstein, M., Durand, F., Freeman, W.T.: Riesz pyramids for fast phase-based video magnification. In: 2014 IEEE International Conference on Computational Photography (ICCP), pp. 1–10. IEEE (2014)
26. Bai, J., Agarwala, A., Agrawala, M., Ramamoorthi, R.: Selectively de-animating video. ACM Trans. Graph. **31**(4), 66:1–66:10 (2012). (Proceedings SIGGRAPH)
27. Malleson, C., Bazin, J.C., Wang, O., Bradley, D., Beeler, T., Hilton, A., Sorkine-Hornung, A.: Facedirector: continuous control of facial performance in video. In: Proceedings of the IEEE International Conference on Computer Vision, pp. 3979–3987 (2015)
28. Shankar Nagaraja, N., Schmidt, F.R., Brox, T.: Video segmentation with just a few strokes. In: Proceedings of the IEEE International Conference on Computer Vision, pp. 3235–3243 (2015)
29. Bai, J., Agarwala, A., Agrawala, M., Ramamoorthi, R.: User-assisted video stabilization. Comput. Graph. Forum **33**(4), 61–70 (2014)
30. Efros, A.A., Leung, T.K.: Texture synthesis by non-parametric sampling. In: The Proceedings of the Seventh IEEE International Conference on Computer Vision, vol. 2, pp. 1033–1038. IEEE (1999)
31. Chen, J.G., Wadhwa, N., Cha, Y.J., Durand, F., Freeman, W.T., Buyukozturk, O.: Modal identification of simple structures with high-speed video using motion magnification. J. Sound Vibr. **345**, 58–71 (2015)
32. Simonyan, K., Zisserman, A.: Very deep convolutional networks for large-scale image recognition (2014). arXiv preprint arXiv:1409.1556
33. Kooij, J.F.P.: SenseCap: synchronized data collection with Microsoft Kinect2 and LeapMotion. In: Proceedings of the 22nd ACM International Conference on Multimedia. ACM (2016, to appear)
34. Shotton, J., Sharp, T., Kipman, A., Fitzgibbon, A., Finocchio, M., Blake, A., Cook, M., Moore, R.: Real-time human pose recognition in parts from single depth images. Commun. ACM **56**(1), 116–124 (2013)

Stacked Hourglass Networks for Human Pose Estimation

Alejandro Newell[(⊠)], Kaiyu Yang, and Jia Deng

University of Michigan, Ann Arbor, USA
{alnewell,yangky,jiadeng}@umich.edu

Abstract. This work introduces a novel convolutional network architecture for the task of human pose estimation. Features are processed across all scales and consolidated to best capture the various spatial relationships associated with the body. We show how repeated bottom-up, top-down processing used in conjunction with intermediate supervision is critical to improving the performance of the network. We refer to the architecture as a "stacked hourglass" network based on the successive steps of pooling and upsampling that are done to produce a final set of predictions. State-of-the-art results are achieved on the FLIC and MPII benchmarks outcompeting all recent methods.

Keyword: Human pose estimation

1 Introduction

A key step toward understanding people in images and video is accurate pose estimation. Given a single RGB image, we wish to determine the precise pixel location of important keypoints of the body. Achieving an understanding of a person's posture and limb articulation is useful for higher level tasks like action recognition, and also serves as a fundamental tool in fields such as human-computer interaction and animation (Fig. 1).

As a well established problem in vision, pose estimation has plagued researchers with a variety of formidable challenges over the years. A good pose estimation system must be robust to occlusion and severe deformation, successful on rare and novel poses, and invariant to changes in appearance due to factors like clothing and lighting. Early work tackles such difficulties using robust image features and sophisticated structured prediction [1–9]: the former is used to produce local interpretations, whereas the latter is used to infer a globally consistent pose.

This conventional pipeline, however, has been greatly reshaped by convolutional neural networks (ConvNets) [10–14], a main driver behind an explosive rise in performance across many computer vision tasks. Recent pose estimation systems [15–20] have universally adopted ConvNets as their main building block, largely replacing hand-crafted features and graphical models; this strategy has yielded drastic improvements on standard benchmarks [1,21,22].

© Springer International Publishing AG 2016
B. Leibe et al. (Eds.): ECCV 2016, Part VIII, LNCS 9912, pp. 483–499, 2016.
DOI: 10.1007/978-3-319-46484-8_29

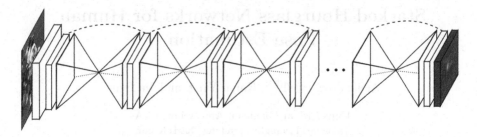

Fig. 1. Our network for pose estimation consists of multiple stacked hourglass modules which allow for repeated bottom-up, top-down inference.

We continue along this trajectory and introduce a novel "stacked hourglass" network design for predicting human pose. The network captures and consolidates information across all scales of the image. We refer to the design as an hourglass based on our visualization of the steps of pooling and subsequent upsampling used to get the final output of the network. Like many convolutional approaches that produce pixel-wise outputs, the hourglass network pools down to a very low resolution, then upsamples and combines features across multiple resolutions [15,23]. On the other hand, the hourglass differs from prior designs primarily in its more symmetric topology.

We expand on a single hourglass by consecutively placing multiple hourglass modules together end-to-end. This allows for repeated bottom-up, top-down inference across scales. In conjunction with the use of intermediate supervision, repeated bidirectional inference is critical to the network's final performance. The final network architecture achieves a significant improvement on the state-of-the-art for two standard pose estimation benchmarks (FLIC [1] and MPII Human Pose [21]). On MPII there is over a 2 % average accuracy improvement across all joints, with as much as a 4–5 % improvement on more difficult joints like the knees and ankles[1].

2   Related Work

With the introduction of "DeepPose" by Toshev et al. [24], research on human pose estimation began the shift from classic approaches [1–9] to deep networks. Toshev et al. use their network to directly regress the x, y coordinates of joints. The work by Tompson et al. [15] instead generates heatmaps by running an image through multiple resolution banks in parallel to simultaneously capture features at a variety of scales. Our network design largely builds off of their work, exploring how to capture information across scales and adapting their method for combining features across different resolutions.

A critical feature of the method proposed by Tompson et al. [15] is the joint use of a ConvNet and a graphical model. Their graphical model learns typical

---

[1] Code is available at http://www-personal.umich.edu/~alnewell/pose.

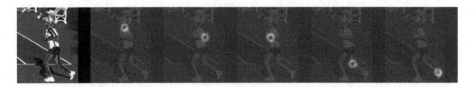

Fig. 2. Example output produced by our network. On the left we see the final pose estimate provided by the max activations across each heatmap. On the right we show sample heatmaps. (From left to right: neck, left elbow, left wrist, right knee, right ankle)

spatial relationships between joints. Others have recently tackled this in similar ways [17,20,25] with variations on how to approach unary score generation and pairwise comparison of adjacent joints. Chen et al. [25] cluster detections into typical orientations so that when their classifier makes predictions additional information is available indicating the likely location of a neighboring joint. We achieve superior performance without the use of a graphical model or any explicit modeling of the human body (Fig. 2).

There are several examples of methods making successive predictions for pose estimation. Carreira et al. [19] use what they refer to as Iterative Error Feedback. A set of predictions is included with the input, and each pass through the network further refines these predictions. Their method requires multi-stage training and the weights are shared across each iteration. Wei et al. [18] build on the work of multi-stage pose machines [26] but now with the use of ConvNets for feature extraction. Given our use of intermediate supervision, our work is similar in spirit to these methods, but our building block (the hourglass module) is different. Hu and Ramanan [27] have an architecture more similar to ours that can also be used for multiple stages of predictions, but their model ties weights in the bottom-up and top-down portions of computation as well as across iterations.

Tompson et al. build on their work in [15] with a cascade to refine predictions. This serves to increase efficency and reduce memory usage of their method while improving localization performance in the high precision range [16]. One consideration is that for many failure cases a refinement of position within a local window would not offer much improvement since error cases often consist of either occluded or misattributed limbs. For both situations, any further evaluation at a local scale will not improve the prediction.

There are variations to the pose estimation problem which include the use of additional features such as depth or motion cues. [28–30] Also, there is the more challenging task of simultaneous annotation of multiple people [17,31]. In addition, there is work like that of Oliveira et al. [32] that performs human part segmentation based on fully convolutional networks [23]. Our work focuses solely on the task of keypoint localization of a single person's pose from an RGB image.

Our hourglass module before stacking is closely connected to fully convolutional networks [23] and other designs that process spatial information at multiple scales for dense prediction [15,33–41]. Xie et al. [33] give a summary of

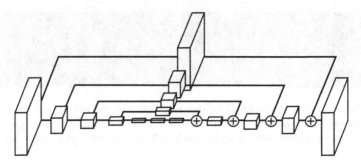

Fig. 3. An illustration of a single "hourglass" module. Each box in the figure corresponds to a residual module as seen in Fig. 4. The number of features is consistent across the whole hourglass.

typical architectures. Our hourglass module differs from these designs mainly in its more symmetric distribution of capacity between bottom-up processing (from high resolutions to low resolutions) and top-down processing (from low resolutions to high resolutions). For example, fully convolutional networks [23] and holistically-nested architectures [33] are both heavy in bottom-up processing but light in their top-down processing, which consists only of a (weighted) merging of predictions across multiple scales. Fully convolutional networks are also trained in multiple stages.

The hourglass module before stacking is also related to conv-deconv and encoder-decoder architectures [42–45]. Noh et al. [42] use the conv-deconv architecture to do semantic segmentation, Rematas et al. [44] use it to predict reflectance maps of objects. Zhao et al. [43] develop a unified framework for supervised, unsupervised and semi-supervised learning by adding a reconstruction loss. Yang et al. [46] employ an encoder-decoder architecture without skip connections for image generation. Rasmus et al. [47] propose a denoising auto-encoder with special, "modulated" skip connections for unsupervised/semi-supervised feature learning. The symmetric topology of these networks is similar, but the nature of the operations is quite different in that we do not use unpooling or deconv layers. Instead, we rely on simple nearest neighbor upsampling and skip connections for top-down processing. Another major difference of our work is that we perform repeated bottom-up, top-down inference by stacking multiple hourglasses.

3   Network Architecture

3.1   Hourglass Design

The design of the hourglass is motivated by the need to capture information at every scale. While local evidence is essential for identifying features like faces and hands, a final pose estimate requires a coherent understanding of the full body. The person's orientation, the arrangement of their limbs, and the relationships of adjacent joints are among the many cues that are best recognized at different scales in the image. The hourglass is a simple, minimal design that has the capacity to capture all of these features and bring them together to output pixel-wise predictions.

The network must have some mechanism to effectively process and consolidate features across scales. Some approaches tackle this with the use of separate pipelines that process the image independently at multiple resolutions and combine features later on in the network [15, 18]. Instead, we choose to use a single pipeline with skip layers to preserve spatial information at each resolution. The network reaches its lowest resolution at 4×4 pixels allowing smaller spatial filters to be applied that compare features across the entire space of the image.

The hourglass is set up as follows: Convolutional and max pooling layers are used to process features down to a very low resolution. At each max pooling step, the network branches off and applies more convolutions at the original pre-pooled resolution. After reaching the lowest resolution, the network begins the top-down sequence of upsampling and combination of features across scales. To bring together information across two adjacent resolutions, we follow the process described by Tompson et al. [15] and do nearest neighbor upsampling of the lower resolution followed by an elementwise addition of the two sets of features. The topology of the hourglass is symmetric, so for every layer present on the way down there is a corresponding layer going up.

After reaching the output resolution of the network, two consecutive rounds of 1×1 convolutions are applied to produce the final network predictions. The output of the network is a set of heatmaps where for a given heatmap the network predicts the probability of a joint's presence at each and every pixel. The full module (excluding the final 1×1 layers) is illustrated in Fig. 3.

3.2 Layer Implementation

While maintaining the overall hourglass shape, there is still some flexibility in the specific implementation of layers. Different choices can have a moderate impact on the final performance and training of the network. We explore several options for layer design in our network. Recent work has shown the value of reduction steps with 1×1 convolutions, as well as the benefits of using consecutive smaller filters to capture a larger spatial context. [12, 14] For example, one can replace a 5×5 filter with two separate 3×3 filters. We tested our overall network design, swapping in different layer modules based off of these insights. We experienced an increase in network performance after switching from standard convolutional layers with large filters and no reduction steps to newer methods like the residual learning modules presented by He et al. [14] and "Inception"-based designs [12]. After the initial performance improvement with these types of designs, various additional explorations and modifications to the layers did little to further boost performance or training time.

Our final design makes extensive use of residual modules. Filters greater than 3×3 are never used, and the bottlenecking restricts the total number of parameters at each layer curtailing total memory usage. The module used in

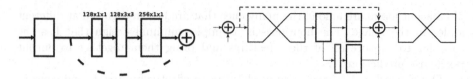

Fig. 4. Left: Residual Module [14] that we use throughout our network. **Right:** Illustration of the intermediate supervision process. The network splits and produces a set of heatmaps (outlined in blue) where a loss can be applied. A 1 × 1 convolution remaps the heatmaps to match the number of channels of the intermediate features. These are added together along with the features from the preceding hourglass. (Color figure online)

our network is shown in Fig. 4. To put this into the context of the full network design, each box in Fig. 3 represents a single residual module.

Operating at the full input resolution of 256 × 256 requires a significant amount of GPU memory, so the highest resolution of the hourglass (and thus the final output resolution) is 64 × 64. This does not affect the network's ability to produce precise joint predictions. The full network starts with a 7 × 7 convolutional layer with stride 2, followed by a residual module and a round of max pooling to bring the resolution down from 256 to 64. Two subsequent residual modules precede the hourglass shown in Fig. 3. Across the entire hourglass all residual modules output 256 features.

3.3   Stacked Hourglass with Intermediate Supervision

We take our network architecture further by stacking multiple hourglasses end-to-end, feeding the output of one as input into the next. This provides the network with a mechanism for repeated bottom-up, top-down inference allowing for reevaluation of initial estimates and features across the whole image. The key to this approach is the prediction of intermediate heatmaps upon which we can apply a loss. Predictions are generated after passing through each hourglass where the network has had an opportunity to process features at both local and global contexts. Subsequent hourglass modules allow these high level features to be processed again to further evaluate and reassess higher order spatial relationships. This is similar to other pose estimations methods that have demonstrated strong performance with multiple iterative stages and intermediate supervision [18,19,30].

Consider the limits of applying intermediate supervision with only the use of a single hourglass module. What would be an appropriate place in the pipeline to generate an initial set of predictions? Most higher order features are present only at lower resolutions except at the very end when upsampling occurs. If supervision is provided after the network does upsampling then there is no way for these features to be reevaluated relative to each other in a larger global context. If we want the network to best refine predictions, these predictions cannot be exclusively evaluated at a local scale. The relationship to other joint predictions as well as the general context and understanding of the full image is crucial. Applying supervision earlier in the pipeline before pooling is a possibility, but at this point the features at a given pixel are the result of processing a relatively local receptive field and are thus ignorant of critical global cues.

Repeated bottom-up, top-down inference with stacked hourglasses alleviates these concerns. Local and global cues are integrated within each hourglass module, and asking the network to produce early predictions requires it to have a high-level understanding of the image while only partway through the full network. Subsequent stages of bottom-up, top-down processing allow for a deeper reconsideration of these features.

This approach for going back and forth between scales is particularly important because preserving the spatial location of features is essential to do the final localization step. The precise position of a joint is an indispensable cue for other decisions being made by the network. With a structured problem like pose estimation, the output is an interplay of many different features that should come together to form a coherent understanding of the scene. Contradicting evidence and anatomic impossiblity are big giveaways that somewhere along the line a mistake was made, and by going back and forth the network can maintain precise local information while considering and then reconsidering the overall coherence of the features.

We reintegrate intermediate predictions back into the feature space by mapping them to a larger number of channels with an additional 1×1 convolution. These are added back to the intermediate features from the hourglass along with the features output from the previous hourglass stage (visualized in Fig. 4). The resulting output serves directly as the input for the following hourglass module which generates another set of predictions. In the final network design, eight hourglasses are used. It is important to note that weights are not shared across hourglass modules, and a loss is applied to the predictions of all hourglasses using the same ground truth. The details for the loss and ground truth are described below.

3.4 Training Details

We evaluate our network on two benchmark datasets, FLIC [1] and MPII Human Pose [21]. FLIC is composed of 5003 images (3987 training, 1016 testing) taken from films. The images are annotated on the upper body with most figures facing the camera straight on. MPII Human Pose consists of around 25k images with annotations for multiple people providing 40k annotated samples (28k training, 11k testing). The test annotations are not provided so in all of our experiments we train on a subset of training images while evaluating on a heldout validation set of around 3000 samples. MPII consists of images taken from a wide range of human activities with a challenging array of widely articulated full-body poses.

There are often multiple people visible in a given input image, but without a graphical model or other postprocessing step the image must convey all necessary information for the network to determine which person deserves the annotation. We deal with this by training the network to exclusively annotate the person in

Fig. 5. Example output on MPII's test set.

the direct center. This is done in FLIC by centering along the x-axis according to the torsobox annotation - no vertical adjustment or scale normalization is done. For MPII, it is standard to utilize the scale and center annotations provided with all images. For each sample, these values are used to crop the image around the target person. All input images are then resized to 256×256 pixels. We do data augmentation that includes rotation ($\pm 30°$), and scaling (.75–1.25). We avoid translation augmentation of the image since location of the target person is the critical cue determining who should be annotated by the network.

The network is trained using Torch7 [48] and for optimization we use rmsprop [49] with a learning rate of 2.5e−4. Training takes about 3 days on a 12 GB NVIDIA TitanX GPU. We drop the learning rate once by a factor of 5 after validation accuracy plateaus. Batch normalization [13] is also used to improve training. A single forward pass of the network takes 75 ms. For generating final test predictions we run both the original input and a flipped version of the image through the network and average the heatmaps together (accounting for a 1 % average improvement on validation). The final prediction of the network is the max activating location of the heatmap for a given joint.

The same technique as Tompson et al. [15] is used for supervision. A Mean-Squared Error (MSE) loss is applied comparing the predicted heatmap to a ground-truth heatmap consisting of a 2D gaussian (with standard deviation of 1 px) centered on the joint location. To improve performance at high precision thresholds the prediction is offset by a quarter of a pixel in the direction of its next highest neighbor before transforming back to the original coordinate space of the image. In MPII Human Pose, some joints do not have a corresponding

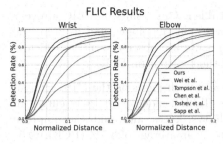

Fig. 6. PCK comparison on FLIC

Table 1. FLIC results (PCK@0.2)

	Elbow	Wrist
Sapp et al. [1]	76.5	59.1
Toshev et al. [24]	92.3	82.0
Tompson et al. [16]	93.1	89.0
Chen et al. [25]	95.3	92.4
Wei et al. [18]	97.6	95.0
Our model	**99.0**	**97.0**

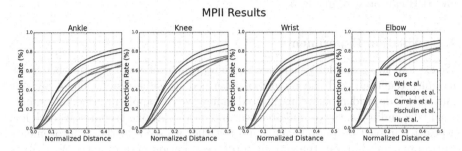

Fig. 7. PCKh comparison on MPII

Table 2. Results on MPII Human Pose (PCKh@0.5)

	Head	Shoulder	Elbow	Wrist	Hip	Knee	Ankle	Total
Tompson et al. [16], CVPR 2015	96.1	91.9	83.9	77.8	80.9	72.3	64.8	82.0
Carreira et al. [19], CVPR 2016	95.7	91.7	81.7	72.4	82.8	73.2	66.4	81.3
Pishchulin et al. [17], CVPR 2016	94.1	90.2	83.4	77.3	82.6	75.7	68.6	82.4
Hu et al. [27], CVPR 2016	95.0	91.6	83.0	76.6	81.9	74.5	69.5	82.4
Wei et al. [18], CVPR 2016	97.8	95.0	88.7	84.0	88.4	82.8	79.4	88.5
Our model	**98.2**	**96.3**	**91.2**	**87.1**	**90.1**	**87.4**	**83.6**	**90.9**

ground truth annotation. In these cases the joint is either truncated or severely occluded, so for supervision a ground truth heatmap of all zeros is provided.

4   Results

4.1   Evaluation

Evaluation is done using the standard Percentage of Correct Keypoints (PCK) metric which reports the percentage of detections that fall within a normalized distance of the ground truth. For FLIC, distance is normalized by torso size, and for MPII, by a fraction of the head size (referred to as PCKh).

FLIC: Results can be seen in Fig. 6 and Table 1. Our results on FLIC are very competitive reaching 99% PCK@0.2 accuracy on the elbow, and 97% on the wrist. It is important to note that these results are observer-centric, which is consistent with how others have evaluated their output on FLIC.

MPII: We achieve state-of-the-art results across all joints on the MPII Human Pose dataset. All numbers can be seen in Table 2 along with PCK curves in Fig. 7. On difficult joints like the wrist, elbows, knees, and ankles we improve upon the most recent state-of-the-art results by an average of 3.5% (PCKh@0.5) with an average error rate of 12.8% down from 16.3%. The final elbow accuracy is 91.2% and wrist accuracy is 87.1%. Example predictions made by the network on MPII can be seen in Fig. 5.

4.2 Ablation Experiments

We explore two main design choices in this work: the effect of stacking hourglass modules together, and the impact of intermediate supervision. These are not mutually independent as we are limited in how we can apply intermediate supervision depending on the overall architectural design. Applied separately, each has a positive impact on performance, and together we see a further improvements to training speed and in the end, final pose estimation performance. We look at the rate of training of a few different network designs. The results of which can be seen in Fig. 8 which shows average accuracy on the validation set as training progresses. The accuracy metric considers all joints excluding those associated with the head and torso to allow for easier differentiation across experiments.

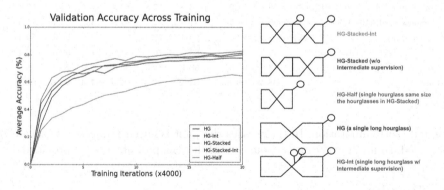

Fig. 8. Comparison of validation accuracy as training progresses. The accuracy is averaged across the wrists, elbows, knees, and ankles. The different network designs are illustrated on the right, the circle is used to indicate where a loss is applied

First, to explore the effect of the stacked hourglass design we must demonstrate that the change in performance is a function of the architecture shape and not attributed to an increase in capacity with a larger, deeper network. To make this comparison, we work from a baseline network consisting of eight hourglass modules stacked together. Each hourglass has a single residual module at each resolution as in Fig. 3. We can shuffle these layers around for various network arrangements. A decrease in the number of hourglasses would result in an increase in the capacity of each hourglass. For example, a corresponding network could stack four hourglasses and have two consecutive residual modules at each resolution (or two hourglasses and four residual modules). This is illustrated in Fig. 9. All networks share the same number of parameters and layers, though a slight difference is introduced when more intermediate supervision is applied.

To see the effect of these choices we first compare a two-stacked network with four residual modules at each stage in the hourglass, and a single hourglass but with eight residual modules instead. In Fig. 8 these are referred to as HG-Stacked and HG respectively. A modest improvement in training can be seen when using the stacked design despite having approximately the same number of layers and parameters. Next, we consider the impact of intermediate supervision. For the two-stack network we follow the procedure described in the paper to apply supervision. Applying this same idea with a single hourglass is nontrivial since higher order global features are present only at lower resolutions, and the features across scales are not combined until late in the pipeline. We explore applying supervision at various points in the network, for example either before or after pooling and at various resolutions. The best performing method is shown as HG-Int in Fig. 8 with intermediate supervision applied after upsampling at the next two highest resolutions before the final output resolution. This supervision does offer an improvement to performance, but not enough to surpass the improvement when stacking is included (HG-Stacked-Int).

In Fig. 9 we compare the validation accuracy of 2-, 4-, and 8-stack models that share approximately the same number of parameters, and include the accuracy of their intermediate predictions. There is a modest improvement in final performance for each successive increase in stacking from 87.4 % to 87.8 % to 88.1 %. The effect is more notable at intermediate stages. For example, halfway

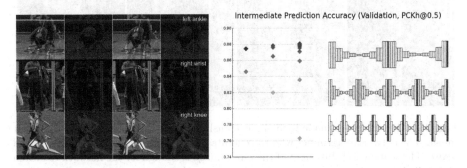

Fig. 9. Left: Example validation images illustrating the change in predictions from an intermediate stage (second hourglass) (left) to final predictions (eighth hourglass) (right). **Right:** Validation accuracy at intermediate stages of the network compared across different stacking arrangements.

through each network the corresponding accuracies of the intermediate predictions are: 84.6 %, 86.5 %, and 87.1 %. Note that the accuracy halfway through the 8-stack network is just short of the final accuracy of the 2-stack network.

It is interesting to observe the mistakes made early and corrected later on by the network. A few examples are visualized in Fig. 9. Common mistakes show up like a mix up of other people's joints, or misattribution of left and right. For the running figure, it is apparent from the final heatmap that the decision between left and right is still a bit ambiguous for the network. Given the appearance of the image, the confusion is justified. One case worth noting is the middle example where the network initially activates on the visible wrists in the image. Upon further processing the heatmap does not activate at all on the original locations, instead choosing a reasonable position for the occluded wrist.

5 Further Analysis

5.1 Multiple People

The issue of coherence becomes especially important when there are multiple people in an image. The network has to decide who to annotate, but there are limited options for communicating who exactly deserves the annotation. For the purposes of this work, the only signal provided is the centering and scaling of the target person trusting that the input will be clear enough to parse. Unfortunately, this occasionally leads to ambiguous situations when people are very close together or even overlapping as seen in Fig. 10. Since we are training a system to generate pose predictions for a single person, the ideal output in an ambiguous situation would demonstrate a commitment to the joints of just one figure. Even if the predictions are lower quality, this would show a deeper understanding of the task at hand. Estimating a location for the wrist with a disregard for whom the wrist may belong is not desired behavior from a pose estimation system.

Fig. 10. The difference made by a slight translation and change of scale of the input image. The network determines who to generate an annotation for based on the central figure. The scaling and shift right of the input image is enough for the network to switch its predictions.

The results in Fig. 10 are from an MPII test image. The network must produce predictions for both the boy and girl, and to do so, their respective center and scale annotations are provided. Using those values to crop input images for the network result in the first and third images of the figure. The center annotations for the two dancers are off by just 26 pixels in a 720×1280 image. Qualitatively, the most perceptible difference between the two input images is the change in scale. This difference is sufficient for the network to change its estimate entirely and predict the annotations for the correct figure.

A more comprehensive management of annotations for multiple people is out of the scope of this work. Many of the system's failure cases are a result of confusing the joints of multiple people, but it is promising that in many examples with severe overlap of figures the network will appropriately pick out a single figure to annotate.

5.2   Occlusion

Occlusion performance can be difficult to assess as it often falls into two distinct categories. The first consists of cases where a joint is not visible but its position is apparent given the context of the image. MPII generally provides ground truth locations for these joints, and an additional annotation indicates their lack of visibility. The second situation, on the other hand, occurs when there is absolutely no information about where a particular joint might be. For example, images where only the upper half of the person's body is visible. In MPII these joints will not have a ground truth annotation associated with them.

Our system makes no use of the additional visibility annotations, but we can still take a look at the impact of visibility on performance. About 75 % of the elbows and wrists with annotations are labeled visible in our held-out validation set. In Fig. 11, we compare performance averaged across the whole validation set with performance on the three-quarters of joints that are visible and performance on the remaining quarter that are not. While only considering visible joints, wrist accuracy goes up to 93.6 % from 85.5 % (validation performance is slightly worse than test set performance of 87.1 %). On the other hand, performance on exclusively occluded joints is 61.1 %. For the elbow, accuracy goes from a baseline of 90.5 % to 95.1 % for visible joints and down to 74.0 % for occluded joints. Occlusion is clearly a significant challenge, but the network still makes strong estimates in most cases. In many examples, the network prediction and ground-truth annotation may not agree while both residing in valid locations, and the ambiguity of the image means there is no way to determine which one is truly correct.

We also consider the more extreme case where a joint may be severely occluded or truncated and therefore have no annotation at all. The PCK metric used when evaluating pose estimation systems does not reflect how well these situations are recognized by the network. If there is no ground truth annotation provided for a joint it is impossible to assess the quality of the prediction made by the system, so it is not counted towards the final reported PCK value. Because of this, there is no harm in generating predictions for all joints even though the predictions for completely occluded or truncated joints will make no sense. For use in a real system, a degree of metaknowledge is essential, and

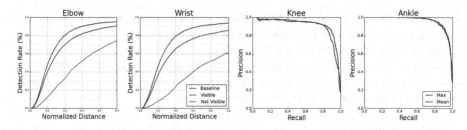

Fig. 11. Left: PCKh curves on validation comparing performance when exclusively considering joints that are visible (or not). **Right:** Precision recall curves showing the accuracy of predicting whether an annotation is present for a joint when thresholding on either the mean or max activation of a heatmap.

the understanding that no good prediction can be made on a particular joint is very important. We observe that our network gives consistent and accurate predictions of whether or not a ground truth annotation is available for a joint.

We consider the ankle and knee for this analysis since these are occluded most often. Lower limbs are frequently cropped from images, and if we were to always visualize all joint predictions of our network, example pose figures would look unacceptable given the nonsensical lower body predictions made in these situations. For a simple way to filter out these cases we examine how well one can determine the presence of an annotation for a joint given the corresponding heatmap activation. We consider thresholding on either the maximum value of the heatmap or its mean. The corresponding precision-recall curves can be seen in Fig. 11. We find that based solely off of the mean activation of a heatmap it is possible to correctly assess the presence of an annotation for the knee with an AUC of 92.1 % and an annotation for the ankle with an AUC of 96.0 %. This was done on a validation set of 2958 samples of which 16.1 % of possible knees and 28.4 % of possible ankles do not have a ground truth annotation. This is a promising result demonstrating that the heatmap serves as a useful signal indicating cases of truncation and severe occlusion in images.

6   Conclusion

We demonstrate the effectiveness of a stacked hourglass network for producing human pose estimates. The network handles a diverse and challenging set of poses with a simple mechanism for reevaluation and assessment of initial predictions. Intermediate supervision is critical for training the network, working best in the context of stacked hourglass modules. There still exist difficult cases not handled perfectly by the network, but overall our system shows robust performance to a variety of challenges including heavy occlusion and multiple people in close proximity.

References

1. Sapp, B., Taskar, B.: Modec: multimodal decomposable models for human pose estimation. In: 2013 IEEE Conference on Computer Vision and Pattern Recognition (CVPR), pp. 3674–3681. IEEE (2013)
2. Felzenszwalb, P., McAllester, D., Ramanan, D.: A discriminatively trained, multiscale, deformable part model. In: IEEE Conference on Computer Vision and Pattern Recognition, CVPR 2008. IEEE, pp. 1–8 (2008)
3. Pishchulin, L., Andriluka, M., Gehler, P., Schiele, B.: Strong appearance and expressive spatial models for human pose estimation. In: 2013 IEEE International Conference on Computer Vision (ICCV), pp. 3487–3494. IEEE (2013)
4. Bourdev, L., Malik, J.: Poselets: body part detectors trained using 3d human pose annotations. In: IEEE 12th International Conference on Computer Vision, 2009, pp. 1365–1372. IEEE (2009)
5. Johnson, S., Everingham, M.: Learning effective human pose estimation from inaccurate annotation. In: 2011 IEEE Conference on Computer Vision and Pattern Recognition (CVPR), pp. 1465–1472. IEEE (2011)
6. Ramanan, D.: Learning to parse images of articulated objects. In: Advances in Neural Information Processing Systems, p. 134 (2006)
7. Yang, Y., Ramanan, D.: Articulated human detection with flexible mixtures of parts. IEEE Trans. Pattern Anal. Mach. Intell. 35(12), 2878–2890 (2013)
8. Ferrari, V., Marin-Jimenez, M., Zisserman, A.: Progressive search space reduction for human pose estimation. In: IEEE Conference on Computer Vision and Pattern Recognition, CVPR 2008, pp. 1–8. IEEE (2008)
9. Ladicky, L., Torr, P.H., Zisserman, A.: Human pose estimation using a joint pixelwise and part-wise formulation. In: 2013 IEEE Conference on Computer Vision and Pattern Recognition (CVPR), pp. 3578–3585. IEEE (2013)
10. LeCun, Y., Bottou, L., Bengio, Y., Haffner, P.: Gradient-based learning applied to document recognition. Proc. IEEE 86(11), 2278–2324 (1998)
11. Krizhevsky, A., Sutskever, I., Hinton, G.E.: Imagenet classification with deep convolutional neural networks. In: Advances in Neural Information Processing Systems, pp. 1097–1105 (2012)
12. Szegedy, C., Liu, W., Jia, Y., Sermanet, P., Reed, S., Anguelov, D., Erhan, D., Vanhoucke, V., Rabinovich, A.: Going deeper with convolutions. In: Proceedings of the IEEE Conference on Computer Vision and Pattern Recognition, pp. 1–9 (2015)
13. Ioffe, S., Szegedy, C.: Batch normalization: accelerating deep network training by reducing internal covariate shift. In: Proceedings of the 32nd International Conference on Machine Learning (2015)
14. He, K., Zhang, X., Ren, S., Sun, J.: Deep residual learning for image recognition. In: IEEE Conference on Computer Vision and Pattern Recognition, CVPR 2015 (2015)
15. Tompson, J.J., Jain, A., LeCun, Y., Bregler, C.: Joint training of a convolutional network and a graphical model for human pose estimation. In: Advances in Neural Information Processing Systems, pp. 1799–1807 (2014)
16. Tompson, J., Goroshin, R., Jain, A., LeCun, Y., Bregler, C.: Efficient object localization using convolutional networks. In: Proceedings of the IEEE Conference on Computer Vision and Pattern Recognition, pp. 648–656 (2015)

17. Pishchulin, L., Insafutdinov, E., Tang, S., Andres, B., Andriluka, M., Gehler, P., Schiele, B.: Deepcut: joint subset partition and labeling for multi person pose estimation. In: 2016 IEEE Conference on Computer Vision and Pattern Recognition (CVPR) (2015)

18. Wei, S.E., Ramakrishna, V., Kanade, T., Sheikh, Y.: Convolutional pose machines. In: 2016 IEEE Conference on Computer Vision and Pattern Recognition (CVPR) (2016)

19. Carreira, J., Agrawal, P., Fragkiadaki, K., Malik, J.: Human pose estimation with iterative error feedback. In: 2016 IEEE Conference on Computer Vision and Pattern Recognition (CVPR) (2016)

20. Fan, X., Zheng, K., Lin, Y., Wang, S.: Combining local appearance and holistic view: dual-source deep neural networks for human pose estimation. In: 2015 IEEE Conference on Computer Vision and Pattern Recognition (CVPR), pp. 1347–1355. IEEE (2015)

21. Andriluka, M., Pishchulin, L., Gehler, P., Schiele, B.: 2d human pose estimation: new benchmark and state of the art analysis. In: 2014 IEEE Conference on Computer Vision and Pattern Recognition (CVPR), pp. 3686–3693. IEEE (2014)

22. Johnson, S., Everingham, M.: Clustered pose and nonlinear appearance models for human pose estimation. In: Proceedings of the British Machine Vision Conference (2010). doi:10.5244/C.24.12

23. Long, J., Shelhamer, E., Darrell, T.: Fully convolutional networks for semantic segmentation. In: Proceedings of the IEEE Conference on Computer Vision and Pattern Recognition, pp. 3431–3440 (2015)

24. Toshev, A., Szegedy, C.: Deeppose: human pose estimation via deep neural networks. In: 2014 IEEE Conference on Computer Vision and Pattern Recognition (CVPR), pp. 1653–1660. IEEE (2014)

25. Chen, X., Yuille, A.: Articulated pose estimation by a graphical model with image dependent pairwise relations. In: Advances in Neural Information Processing Systems (NIPS) (2014)

26. Ramakrishna, V., Munoz, D., Hebert, M., Andrew Bagnell, J., Sheikh, Y.: Pose machines: articulated pose estimation via inference machines. In: Fleet, D., Pajdla, T., Schiele, B., Tuytelaars, T. (eds.) ECCV 2014, Part II. LNCS, vol. 8690, pp. 33–47. Springer, Heidelberg (2014). doi:10.1007/978-3-319-10605-2_3

27. Hu, P., Ramanan, D.: Bottom-up and top-down reasoning with hierarchical rectified gaussians. In: 2016 IEEE Conference on Computer Vision and Pattern Recognition (CVPR). IEEE (2016)

28. Jain, A., Tompson, J., LeCun, Y., Bregler, C.: MoDeep: a deep learning framework using motion features for human pose estimation. In: Cremers, D., Reid, I., Saito, H., Yang, M.-H. (eds.) ACCV 2014. LNCS, vol. 9004, pp. 302–315. Springer, Heidelberg (2015). doi:10.1007/978-3-319-16808-1_21

29. Shotton, J., Sharp, T., Kipman, A., Fitzgibbon, A., Finocchio, M., Blake, A., Cook, M., Moore, R.: Real-time human pose recognition in parts from single depth images. Commun. ACM 56(1), 116–124 (2013)

30. Pfister, T., Charles, J., Zisserman, A.: Flowing convnets for human pose estimation in videos. In: Proceedings of the IEEE International Conference on Computer Vision, pp. 1913–1921 (2015)

31. Chen, X., Yuille, A.L.: Parsing occluded people by flexible compositions. In: Proceedings of the IEEE Conference on Computer Vision and Pattern Recognition, pp. 3945–3954 (2015)

32. Oliveira, G.L., Valada, A., Bollen, C., Burgard, W., Brox, T.: Deep learning for human part discovery in images. In: IEEE International Conference on Robotics and Automation (ICRA) (2016)
33. Xie, S., Tu, Z.: Holistically-nested edge detection. In: Proceedings of the IEEE International Conference on Computer Vision, pp. 1395–1403 (2015)
34. Eigen, D., Puhrsch, C., Fergus, R.: Depth map prediction from a single image using a multi-scale deep network. In: Advances in Neural Information Processing Systems, pp. 2366–2374 (2014)
35. Farabet, C., Couprie, C., Najman, L., LeCun, Y.: Learning hierarchical features for scene labeling. IEEE Trans. Pattern Anal. Mach. Intell. **35**(8), 1915–1929 (2013)
36. Pinheiro, P., Collobert, R.: Recurrent convolutional neural networks for scene labeling. In: Proceedings of the 31st International Conference on Machine Learning (ICML 2014), pp. 82–90 (2014)
37. Eigen, D., Fergus, R.: Predicting depth, surface normals and semantic labels with a common multi-scale convolutional architecture. In: Proceedings of the IEEE International Conference on Computer Vision, pp. 2650–2658 (2015)
38. Mathieu, M., Couprie, C., LeCun, Y.: Deep multi-scale video prediction beyond mean square error. In: International Conference on Learning Representations (ICLR) (2016)
39. Couprie, C., Farabet, C., Najman, L., LeCun, Y.: Indoor semantic segmentation using depth information. In: International Conference on Learning Representations (ICLR) (2013)
40. Bertasius, G., Shi, J., Torresani, L.: Deepedge: a multi-scale bifurcated deep network for top-down contour detection. In: Proceedings of the IEEE Conference on Computer Vision and Pattern Recognition, pp. 4380–4389 (2015)
41. Hariharan, B., Arbeláez, P., Girshick, R., Malik, J.: Hypercolumns for object segmentation and fine-grained localization. In: Proceedings of the IEEE Conference on Computer Vision and Pattern Recognition, pp. 447–456 (2015)
42. Noh, H., Hong, S., Han, B.: Learning deconvolution network for semantic segmentation. In: Proceedings of the IEEE International Conference on Computer Vision, pp. 1520–1528 (2015)
43. Zhao, J., Mathieu, M., Goroshin, R., Lecun, Y.: Stacked what-where auto-encoders. arXiv preprint arXiv:1506.02351 (2015)
44. Rematas, K., Ritschel, T., Fritz, M., Gavves, E., Tuytelaars, T.: Deep reflectance maps. In: IEEE Conference on Computer Vision and Pattern Recognition, CVPR 2015 (2015)
45. Badrinarayanan, V., Kendall, A., Cipolla, R.: Segnet: a deep convolutional encoder-decoder architecture for image segmentation. arXiv preprint arXiv:1511.00561 (2015)
46. Yang, J., Reed, S.E., Yang, M.H., Lee, H.: Weakly-supervised disentangling with recurrent transformations for 3d view synthesis. In: Cortes, C., Lawrence, N.D., Lee, D.D., Sugiyama, M., Garnett, R. (eds.) Advances in Neural Information Processing Systems, vol. 28, pp. 1099–1107. Curran Associates, Inc. (2015)
47. Rasmus, A., Berglund, M., Honkala, M., Valpola, H., Raiko, T.: Semi-supervised learning with ladder networks. In: Advances in Neural Information Processing Systems, pp. 3546–3554 (2015)
48. Collobert, R., Kavukcuoglu, K., Farabet, C.: Torch7: a matlab-like environment for machine learning. In: BigLearn, NIPS Workshop (2011)
49. Tieleman, T., Hinton, G.: Lecture 6.5-rmsprop: divide the gradient by a running average of its recent magnitude. In: COURSERA: Neural Networks for Machine Learning (2012)

Real-Time Large-Scale Dense 3D Reconstruction with Loop Closure

Olaf Kähler, Victor A. Prisacariu$^{(\boxtimes)}$, and David W. Murray

Department of Engineering Science, University of Oxford, Oxford, UK
{olaf,victor,dwm}@robots.ox.ac.uk

Abstract. In the highly active research field of dense 3D reconstruction and modelling, loop closure is still a largely unsolved problem. While a number of previous works show how to accumulate keyframes, globally optimize their pose on closure, and compute a dense 3D model as a post-processing step, in this paper we propose an online framework which delivers a consistent 3D model to the user in real time. This is achieved by splitting the scene into submaps, and adjusting the poses of the submaps as and when required. We present a novel technique for accumulating relative pose constraints between the submaps at very little computational cost, and demonstrate how to maintain a lightweight, scalable global optimization of submap poses. In contrast to previous works, the number of submaps grows with the observed 3D scene surface, rather than with time. In addition to loop closure, the paper incorporates relocalization and provides a novel way of assessing tracking quality.

1 Introduction

The prompt delivery of highly detailed dense reconstructions of the 3D environment is currently one of the major frontiers in computer vision [1–6]. While off-line dense reconstruction and real-time sparse reconstruction are quite mature (e.g. [7–10]) it is only recently that real-time dense modelling and reconstruction have become feasible. There are two obvious enablers and catalysts. The first is the release of affordable RGB-D sensors such as the Kinect, and the second is the opening up of graphics processing units for general purpose computing.

As the area develops, one can discern the research focus shifting from basic processing to obtain *any* reconstruction to more refined aspects of 3D representation and modelling. Earlier works such as [2,11,12] have firmly established volumetric representations as a powerful approach. Their memory requirements have been reduced by an order of magnitude more recently [13–17], rendering them attractive for large-scale mapping. While the competing surfel based representations (e.g. [18]) never had this issue, two common problems arising in all large scale mapping tasks are those of tracking drift and loop closure.

Electronic supplementary material The online version of this chapter (doi:10.1007/978-3-319-46484-8_30) contains supplementary material, which is available to authorized users.

© Springer International Publishing AG 2016
B. Leibe et al. (Eds.): ECCV 2016, Part VIII, LNCS 9912, pp. 500–516, 2016.
DOI: 10.1007/978-3-319-46484-8_30

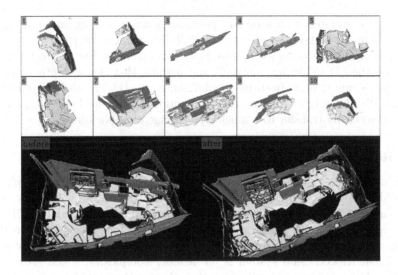

Fig. 1. Example reconstruction. The last row shows the results before and after loop closure, with images 1–10 showing constituent submaps.

Among the current methods addressing loop closure for dense 3D reconstruction, a first group [19–22] selects a subset of keyframes and gathers constraints between them to solve the alignment problem, and only then considers dense reconstruction as a post-processing step. For this group, dense reconstruction typically has to be repeated from scratch whenever there are changes to the graph of keyframes. Rather than using keyframes, a second approach to loop closure is to accumulate constraints continuously and integrate them into the 3D model by deforming the reconstruction [18,23]. However, the relatively high computational complexity of repeatedly deforming the entire dense model leads to poor scalability. A third line of works employs submaps [24–26] to enable loop closure. The idea is to accumulate the information from every single camera image into various overlapping submaps, and to adjust the position and orientation of these submaps as relative constraints between them become available.

In the present work we pick up this idea of submaps, but extend it significantly. First, by gathering the relative constraints in a much more efficient manner, we develop an online system running in real time rather than minutes [25] or hours [26]. Second, we propose a novel way of delineating the submaps from each other, leading to memory growth that scales with the size of the represented 3D scene surface rather than with the sequence length [25,26] or trajectory length [24]. Third, we present a method of fusing the individual submaps into a global model online and on the fly. As enabling tools for the overall pipeline, we also introduce a novel way of assessing the camera tracking quality in dense image alignment and introduce camera relocalisation to the whole pipeline. All of these combine to yield a system which allows interruption of the map building process and resumption later at an arbitrary position, hence extending and growing the map on demand without requiring a carefully pre-planned trajectory.

A reconstruction obtained by our system is shown in Fig. 1. We focus this paper on the 3D modelling methods and assume that dense depth maps are available as input, be it from monocular sequences [11,12], stereo, or RGB-D sensors. We also rely on volumetric representations, but we believe that many of the ideas easily transfer to a much wider range of applications.

1.1 Related Work

The KinectFusion system [2] has spurred a range of further research into efficient dense 3D mapping. Central to most of these efforts is a 3D volumetric scene representation using a truncated signed distance function (T-SDF) [27]. The same representation has been exploited in systems relying exclusively on RGB cameras without depth sensing [11,12]. However, a fundamental limitation of the original KinectFusion system is its memory complexity, which grows with the size of the represented volume rather than with that of the represented surface, rendering large scale reconstruction and loop closure infeasible. This has been overcome in later works by storing only sparse blocks of the T-SDF around the actual surface and addressing the blocks via tree structures [13–15] and hash functions [16,17]. Our work in particular relies on the highly efficient implementation of voxel block hashing given in [17].

However, such large scale reconstruction quickly shows the drawbacks of the separate handling of tracking and reconstruction in dense methods: tracking drift becomes significant before loop closure. Drift can be reduced by additional sensing such as IMU measurements [28,29]. Nevertheless, drift can not be completely avoided and a more substantial change to the representation is required to ensure earlier tracking errors can be tolerated or even corrected by later measurements.

One approach to this issue is to reduce the recorded image sequence to a number of carefully selected keyframes, which are stored along with their 3D poses. Upon loop closure, the accumulated error is distributed by applying pose graph optimisation [30]. In some implementations (e.g. [20]), information from those frames not selected as keyframes is lost to the 3D modelling process, but other methods try to accumulate the non-keyframe information by improving or filtering the keyframe measurements [19,21,22]. In both cases, the keyframes only store 2.5D information, which is precisely what makes these approaches memory efficient and feasible at large scale. To provide the user with feedback, or potentially a robot with a global map for path planning, the local 2.5D maps have to be merged to a globally consistent 3D map. In the above works this step is not detailed, but the underlying assumption is that this can be achieved by fusing the individual keyframes after their final poses have been computed.

Quite the opposite is done in the map-centric representation used in Kintinuous 2.0 [31], ElasticFusion [18] and an earlier work along the same lines [23]. In these systems, the 3D world is deformed globally whenever loop closure requires such changes. However, another problem of dense mapping becomes obvious with this strategy: the deformation has to be applied to the whole 3D model over and over again and, given the sheer amount of data provided by large scale dense reconstructions, the computational cost becomes significant.

In the works of [24–26] another alternative is picked up, that of local submaps. Submaps date back to much earlier work in SLAM (e.g. [32–34]), but have only recently been considered in the context of dense 3D modelling. In contrast to a single global map, such as that used in KinectFusion, the local submaps can be shuffled around to accommodate loop closure errors. Unlike in the keyframe based methods mentioned earlier, submaps provide a convenient way of accumulating measurements from all intermediate frames, and furthermore they allow "banking" of the computational effort required to fuse this information. In contrast to the global deformations performed by ElasticFusion, the piecewise rigid transformations scale much more readily to large 3D models.

However, some fundamental questions have to be addressed to realize submapping approaches. First, the map has to be split into submaps, and while in [24] a classical threshold on camera motion is used, both lines of research in [25,26] split the image sequence by time, coincidentally choosing to spawn a new submap every 50 frames. While these subdivision schemes are easy to implement, they will scale poorly in case of real world exploratory trajectories. In our work we therefore propose a novel way of delineating submaps based on the part of the global 3D map that is observed in the images, and spawn new submaps only when the camera *view* moves on to explore new parts of the 3D scene.

Second, relative constraints between the submaps have to be evaluated, and all of [24–26] achieve this using a relatively costly alignment of the 3D content. For example, [25] uses a global optimisation operating on full 3D volumes. As such, when a new subvolume is added to the optimisation, the zero-level set and 3D normals need to be extracted, correspondences between volumes need to be found, and a large ICP optimisation has to be run. In contrast, by tracking the camera relative to multiple submaps simultaneously and by exploiting that the resulting trajectory should be unique, we gain the relative constraints "for free" as a side product of normal pose estimation and tracking operations. The computational overhead is therefore reduced to (i) one extra per-frame alignment between a depth map and a local scene, taking a few extra ms each frame, and (ii) a much simplified global optimisation to estimate submap locations working only on 3D poses, without needing any further surface alignments. Overall, the previous works based on submaps aim at offline operation, whereas we very much aim at a real-time system that provides the user with immediate feedback, similar to that which ElasticFusion [18] achieves at smaller scale.

1.2 Outline

The rest of the paper is ordered as follows. We revise the background and basic technologies underlying our system in Sect. 2. The detail of our core contributions is provided in Sect. 3, and an evaluation follows in Sect. 4. We summarise and draw conclusions in Sect. 5.

2   Basic System

Our system is built on the principles behind KinectFusion [2] and voxel block hashing [16]. More specifically, we use the highly efficient implementation of both provided by InfiniTAM [17], the source code of which is provided online. Our contribution as presented in Sect. 3 can readily transfer to alternative systems.

In Sect. 2.1 we revise the camera tracking and integration of depth images from [17]. As a first contribution, we present a method of evaluating tracking quality in Sect. 2.2, which is key for our further work. We also discuss a novel method for splitting a large scene into submaps. Since this is closely related to the representation in our base system, we present this in Sect. 2.3.

2.1   Integration of Depth Maps

We represent the scene in our map as a truncated signed distance function (T-SDF) denoted as $F(\mathbf{X})$. For each 3D point $\mathbf{X}$ within a truncation band $[-\mu \ldots \mu]$, the function F returns a tuple $(d, w, \mathbf{c})$, where d denotes the distance of the point $\mathbf{X}$ to the nearest surface, w the number of accumulated observations and (optionally) $\mathbf{c}$ an estimate of the colour. Outside the truncation band, $w = 0$ and d and $\mathbf{c}$ are undefined. The function F is stored volumetrically, sampled on a voxel grid with fixed resolution s, and typically $s = 5\,\mathrm{mm}$ or $10\,\mathrm{mm}$. For voxel block hashing [16,17], the volume is divided into small blocks of $8 \times 8 \times 8$ voxels each, which are allocated sparsely to cover the truncation band $\pm\mu$ around the surface. To find the corresponding block for a point $\mathbf{X}$, a hash function is applied, providing an almost constant time lookup of the tuples $(d, w, \mathbf{c})$.

Each incoming image is processed in three steps: tracking, integration and raycasting. In the tracking step, we estimate the camera pose relative to the model, in the integration step we fuse the depth image into the T-SDF, and lastly we extract the surface from the implicit representation using raycasting.

Our tracking step is based on the Iterative Closest Points algorithm with projective data association [2]. Using the pre-calibrated intrinsic camera parameters $\mathbf{K}$ we first compute a 2D map of 3D points from each depth image D_t:

$$\mathcal{P}(\mathbf{x}) = D_t(\mathbf{x})\mathbf{K}^{-1}\begin{pmatrix}\mathbf{x}\\1\end{pmatrix}, \tag{1}$$

At each time t, we now want to estimate the camera pose $\mathbf{T}_t = (\mathbf{R}_t, \mathbf{t}_t)$ for the depth image, consisting of rotation $\mathbf{R}_t$ and translation $\mathbf{t}_t$. As additional input we require a 2D map of 3D points $\mathcal{V}_{t-1}(\mathbf{x})$ and surface normals $\mathcal{N}_{t-1}(\mathbf{x})$ as extracted from the T-SDF for a known pose $\mathbf{T}_{t-1}$. We compute $\mathbf{T}_t$ minimising:

$$\epsilon_{\mathrm{ICP}}(\mathbf{T}_t) = \sum_{\mathbf{x}} \rho\left(\left(\mathbf{T}_t^{-1}\mathcal{P}(\mathbf{x}) - \mathcal{V}_{t-1}(\bar{\mathcal{P}}(\mathbf{x}))\right)^T \mathcal{N}_{t-1}(\bar{\mathcal{P}}(\mathbf{x}))\right), \tag{2}$$

where ρ is a robust error norm and $\bar{\mathcal{P}}(\mathbf{x}) = \pi(\mathbf{K}\mathbf{T}_{t-1}\mathbf{T}_t^{-1}\mathcal{P}(\mathbf{x}))$ is the reprojection of $\mathcal{P}(\mathbf{x})$ into the frame of the provided reference maps $\mathcal{V}$ and $\mathcal{N}$. Using the well known local frame representation of rotations, this function is linearized and minimised using the Levenberg-Marquardt optimisation algorithm.

To integrate D_t into the T-SDF we follow [17]. For the set of points $\{\mathbf{T}_t^{-1}\mathcal{P}(\mathbf{x})\}$ and the truncation band $\pm\mu$ around them, we allocate the corresponding voxel blocks in the hash table and declare them part of the visible set $\mathbb{V}$. Then we project all voxels $\mathbf{X}$ in the currently visible voxel blocks into the depth and, optionally, colour images. The tuples $(d, w, \mathbf{c})$ are updated as:

$$d \leftarrow \frac{wd + d^*}{w + 1}, \qquad \mathbf{c} \leftarrow \frac{w\mathbf{c} + \mathbf{c}^*}{w + 1}, \qquad w \leftarrow w + 1, \tag{3}$$

with $d^* = D_t(\pi(\mathbf{KT}_t\mathbf{X})) - [\mathbf{T}_t\mathbf{X}]_{(z)}$ clamped to $[-\mu \dots \mu]$ and, if a colour image C_t is available and desired, $\mathbf{c}^* = C_t(\pi(\mathbf{KT}_t\mathbf{X}))$.

Finally the vertex and normal maps of the surface $\mathcal{V}$ and $\mathcal{N}$ are obtained from the T-SDF by raycasting. After forward projecting bounding boxes for all visible voxel blocks to obtain a valid search range, a ray is cast for each pixel $\mathbf{x}$ in $\mathcal{V}$ to find the zero level set of the T-SDF [17]. Iteratively reading the d values from F, steps are taken until the zero crossing $d = 0$ is found and $\mathcal{V}$ is set to the corresponding 3D point. The field of normals $\mathcal{N}$ is then obtained by computing the cross product between neighbouring pixels in $\mathcal{V}$.

2.2   Evaluation of Tracking Accuracy

Camera tracking can fail, and sometimes does. Many current systems, in particular [17], do not explicitly manage this problem. Detecting tracking failure is essential both for building a robust mapping system, and, as shown later in our paper, in our approach to building constraints between submaps.

The elementary approach for detecting tracking failure is manually to set thresholds on metrics extracted from the tracking process. These could require, for example, that the residual should not be larger than a threshold. In this work we instead train a classifier to separate tracking failure cases and success. For each optimization of ϵ_{ICP}, we measure the percentage of inlier pixels, the determinant of the Hessian and the final residual. We next expand these three values into a 20-dimensional descriptor using a χ^2 kernel map [35]. Lastly, we use an SVM classifier to separate between tracking success and failure. We obtain the required classification parameters by training on the '7 scenes' dataset of [36].

This dataset contains a set of 7 scenes and for each scene, several image sequences are captured and split into a training and a test set. We use the training set to build 3D reconstructions as in Sect. 2.1 and start tracking attempts for the test set using relocalisation [36]. If the pose is correctly estimated with less than 2 mm translational error and less than 2° rotational error from the ground truth, we consider tracking successful. Splitting the resulting 167220 tracking results along with their 3-dimensional feature vectors into half for training and half for test, we obtain a tracking failure detection accuracy of 95 %. Without the kernel expansion accuracy drops to 92.4 %, with virtually no gain in processing speed. In addition to successful and failed tracking, the distance from the support vector becomes an indicator for poor and good tracking accuracy.

2.3   Construction of Submaps

One of the key features of our proposed method is the use of submaps. In the works of [25,26], submaps are created entirely based on a temporal criterion: every k frames a new subvolume is created, and coincidentally the default is $k = 50$ in both works. This means the number of submaps grows linearly with time, not with the explored area, and the submap characteristics change depending on the speed of camera motion. Alternative approaches (e.g. [24]) use thresholds on camera motion to start submaps. Instead we propose a novel criterion: we evaluate the visibility of parts of the scene, and start a new submap once the camera viewport moves away from the central part of the previous submap.

Voxel block hashing lends itself ideally towards such a method. As revised in Sect. 2.1, we allocate new parts of the scene in blocks of $8 \times 8 \times 8$ voxels. Furthermore we maintain a list of visible blocks $\mathbb{V}$. Since blocks allocated early on are more likely to reside near the *core* of a submap, we evaluate the fraction r_{vis} of visible blocks within $\mathbb{V}$ with a smaller creation index than a threshold B. If the fraction drops below a threshold $r_{\text{vis}} < \theta$, the camera viewport has moved on and we can consider starting a new submap. The parameters B and θ therefore jointly determine the typical size of submaps.

3   Large Scale Reconstruction

We have defined the preliminaries of our 3D mapping pipeline, along with criteria for assessing the tracking quality and for determining whether to start a new submap. In the following, we clarify (i) how we relate multiple submaps to each other (Sect. 3.1), (ii) how we incorporate loop closures (Sects. 3.2, 3.3 and 3.4) and (iii) how we visualize our collection of submaps (Sect. 3.5).

3.1   Constraints Between Submaps

As in previous works [24–26], a fundamental idea is that local submaps can overlap each other. However, unlike these previous works, we process multiple submaps concurrently, which is still easily possible in real time thanks to the extremely efficient implementation of voxel block hashing in [17].

Whenever we hypothesize a new overlap of submaps, we run an additional independent instance of the map building process. Tracking continues in as many submaps as possible, noting that the camera trajectories should be identical in a global reference frame. This gives us constraints between the submaps. The transformation $\mathbf{T}_{t,i,j}$ from submap i to submap j, as observed at time t is:

$$\mathbf{T}_{t,i,j} = \mathbf{T}_{t,j}^{-1}\mathbf{T}_{t,i}, \tag{4}$$

where $\mathbf{T}_{t,i}$ and $\mathbf{T}_{t,j}$ are the poses tracked in submaps i and j respectively.

Of course, we get the highest quality valid constraints $\mathbf{T}_{t,i,j}$ when tracking is successful. To enforce consistency, multiple such constraints are furthermore aggregated to an robust overall estimate $\mathbf{T}_{i,j}$. We consider $\mathbf{v}(\mathbf{T})$ to be a compact 6-vector representing the transformation $\mathbf{T}$ and compute

$$\mathbf{v}(\hat{\mathbf{T}}_{i,j}) = \sum_t w_t \mathbf{v}(\mathbf{T}_{t,i,j}) + w\mathbf{v}(\mathbf{T}_{i,j}) \sum_t w_t + w, \qquad (5)$$

with $w_t = \frac{\sqrt{2b\hat{r} - b^2}}{\hat{r}}$ and $\hat{r} = \max(\|\mathbf{v}(\mathbf{T}_{t,i,j}) - \mathbf{v}(\hat{\mathbf{T}}_{i,j})\|, b)$ resulting from the robust Huber error norm with outlier threshold b, and w the number of previous observations that went into the estimation of $\mathbf{T}_{i,j}$, if any. Using iteratively reweighted least squares, we compute not only an estimate $\hat{\mathbf{T}}_{i,j}$, but also the inliers amongst the set of new constraints $\mathbf{T}_{t,i,j}$. As we will detail in the following sections, we can stop tracking a submap and discard the newly computed $\mathbf{T}_{t,i,j}$ if they are not self-consistent or if they are not consistent with our previous estimate $\mathbf{T}_{i,j}$.

In contrast to the ideas presented in previous works [24–26], the constraints between submaps in our system are essentially computed for free, as the tracking has to be performed anyway and the aggregation is lightweight. This greatly reduces the overall computational cost.

3.2 Loop Closure Detection and Relocalisation

In order to manage loop closures, we have to detect whenever the camera is revisiting a previously observed part of the scene. We use the keyframe based relocalisation system of Glocker et al. [36] for this, due to its simplicity and efficiency. While the tracking and mapping of the volumetric base system is running almost entirely on the GPU, this relocalisation module can easily run in parallel on a single CPU core without a noticeable impact on performance.

Each incoming depth image D_t is subsampled to a resolution of 40×30 pixels and filtered with a Gaussian with $\sigma = 2.5$, resulting in $\tilde{D}_t$. We then use a fern conservatory to compute a simplified encoding for the image. In our implementation, the conservatory consists of $n_F = 500$ ferns and each computes $n_B = 4$ binary decisions. Each binary decision is thresholding an individual pixel in $\tilde{D}_t$ according to $\tilde{D}_t(\mathbf{x}_i) < \vartheta_i$, where $\mathbf{x}_i$ and ϑ_i are chosen randomly at initialisation. The concatenation of binary codes $f_i = \{0, 1\}$ of one fern results in a code block $b_j = (f_1, \ldots, f_{n_B})$. Using the operator $\neq$ to return a binary value $\{0, 1\}$, [36] describes an efficient way of computing the dissimilarity

$$\text{BlockHD}(\tilde{D}_{t_1}, \tilde{D}_{t_2}) = \frac{1}{n_F} \sum_j \left(b_j(\tilde{D}_{t_1}) \neq b_j(\tilde{D}_{t_2}) \right) \qquad (6)$$

between multiple codes simultaneously. A list of codes for the keyframes is maintained, and if the minimum dissimilarity score of $\tilde{D}_t$ to all existing keyframes is above a threshold, the image is considered for addition as a new keyframe.

As explained in the following, we use this process both for detecting loop closures and for relocalisation.

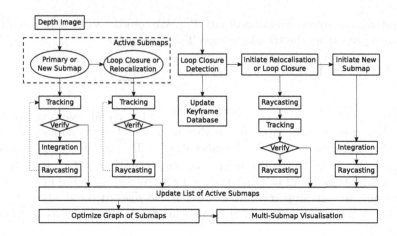

Fig. 2. Overview of the control logic. See Sect. 3.3 for detailed explanation.

3.3   Control Logic and Validation of Loop Closure

The loop closure detection process returns only keyframe IDs. While these can readily be linked to tuples of poses and submap indices, a more sophisticated treatment is clearly required to verify the proposals. This is done by our control logic, an outline of which is given in Fig. 2.

We maintain a list of *active submaps* at all times. While tracking and raycasting are usually performed in all active submaps, new depth information usually only gets integrated into one selected *primary submap*. At the beginning of the processing, this is just the first and only submap in our list. We evaluate each tracking result as outlined in Sect. 2.2 and if tracking is poor, we do not integrate depth information at all but still continue tracking. If tracking is lost in any submap, it becomes inactive.

Once the camera has moved away from the core of the primary submap according to the criterion defined in Sect. 2.3, we initiate a *new submap*. Since this new submap is initially empty, we also have to integrate depth information there in order to start the raycasting and tracking process. We accumulate constraints between the primary and the new submap as outlined in Sect. 3.1 and, once we have a stable estimate of the relative pose with a number N_{stable} inlier frames, we declare the new submap as readily initialised.

In parallel, we run the Loop Closure Detection system outlined in Sect. 3.2. If we have a stable tracking result from the primary scene, and if the internal criteria of the loop closure detection system suggest adding a new keyframe, we update the database of keyframes. Furthermore, if the Loop Closure Detection system suggests that we have seen a similar depth image before while tracking in a submap, that is not currently active, we initiate a new *loop closure attempt*. This means we declare the newly detected other submap as an active submap and start raycasting and tracking in it. Since we attempt to track subsequent frames in both (i) the current primary submap and (ii) the submap where we attempt to close the loop, we can again establish constraints between the two. We still have to verify the loop closure, and for this we attempt to robustly estimate a relative pose between the two submaps as before, but this time honouring the aggregagte of the previously acquired pose constraints. Once we get N_{stable} inlier frames, we declare the loop closure successful. If this is not the case after $N_{attempts}$ frames, we dismiss the attempted loop closure as erroneous.

Obviously, if tracking of all active scenes is lost, we can not establish relative pose constraints, but instead attempt relocalization. In this case, we declare the relocalisation successful if N_{stable} tracking attempts have been declared successful by our tracking quality criterion from Sect. 2.2, and we declare it failed if it is not successful for $N_{attempts}$ frames.

At the end of the processing pipeline, we maintain the list of *active submaps*, removing submaps that can no longer be tracked and loop closure or relocalisation attempts that have failed. If there are multiple candidates, we also pick a new *primary scene* by checking our submap visibility constraint from Sect. 2.3 and selecting the submap with the largest portion currently visible. If any new scenes or loop closure attempts have been successfully validated, we also trigger a new process for optimising the graph of submaps, which we explain in the following Sect. 3.4. The results from this optimization are not used by the core pipeline outlined above in any way, but are crucially important for visualizing or evaluating the global map, as we shall discuss in Sect. 3.5.

3.4 Submap Graph Optimisation

From the above pipeline we obtain a number of constraints between pairs of submaps which can be used to estimate the pose of each submap in global coordinates. If there are no loop closures it is trivial to compute the exact submap poses, but more generally a pose graph optimization problem [30] arises.

Denote by $\hat{\mathbf{q}}(\mathbf{T})$ the three imaginary components of the quaternion representing the rotational part of an Euclidean transformation $\mathbf{T}$. Further let $\mathbf{t}(\mathbf{T})$ be the vector of the translational components and $\mathbf{v}(\mathbf{T}) = (\hat{\mathbf{q}}(\mathbf{T}), \mathbf{t}(\mathbf{T}))^{\top}$ the concatenation of the two. If $\mathbf{P}_i$ denotes the pose of a submap i and $\mathbf{T}_{i,j}$ the relative constraint between them as described in Sect. 3.1, then the error function we want to minimize is:

$$\epsilon_{graph} = \sum_{\{i,j\} \in \mathbb{T}} \|\mathbf{v}(\mathbf{P}_i \mathbf{P}_j^{-1} \mathbf{T}_{i,j})\|_2, \qquad (7)$$

where $\mathbb{T}$ denotes the set of all pairwise constraints $\mathbf{T}_{i,j}$ that have been gathered so far. This function can be optimised with standard non-linear methods (in our case Levenberg-Marquardt), and as in [30] we use the quaternion representation for the ease of computing derivatives $\nabla \hat{\mathbf{q}}$. It is also noteworthy that the Hessian $\nabla^2 \epsilon_{graph}$ or its approximation is sparse. While for a small number of up to 100 submaps there is no noticeable difference, the use of sparse and super-nodal matrix factorisation methods [37] is advisable. In practice this optimisation is only triggered occasionally and its low computational complexity allows it to easily run in a background thread on the CPU.

3.5 Global Model Visualisation

The results of the Submap Graph Optimisation and of the online updates of the local submaps are crucially important for the live, real time visualisation of the global map. This provides users with immediate feedback and allows them to perform future path planning according to their desired exploration goals.

The representation of local submaps as T-SDFs has the major advantage, that the individual submaps can be fused on the fly while rendering the global map. To this effect, we define a new, combined T-SDF $\hat{F}$ as

$$\hat{F}(\mathbf{X}) = \sum_i F_w(\mathbf{P}_i \mathbf{X}) F(\mathbf{P}_i \mathbf{X}), \tag{8}$$

where $\mathbf{P}_i$ denotes the pose of submap i as estimated using Eq. (7) and where we use the notation F_w to denote taking the w entry out of a T-SDF F. We can simply substitute $\hat{F}$ in the raycasting step as outlined in Sect. 2.1 and extract the 3D surface, normals and (optionally) colours as before. Note that, while the computational complexity naturally increases when many submaps are visible at the same time, we can still easily display a number of them simultaneously while still estimating the global map in the background using standard, consumer grade hardware. This can be further optimised by limiting the number of submaps displayed simultaneously and pre-selecting a list of suitable submaps.

4 Evaluation

We illustrate the results achieved with our system in Figs. 1 and 3. Along with the video attachment in the supplementary material, these provide a qualitative impression of our method. In the following we will also evaluate our system quantitatively (Sect. 4.1) and investigate its memory requirements (Sect. 4.2) and runtime (Sect. 4.3).

4.1 Quantitative Results

While many previous works evaluate the accuracy of the camera trajectory as a proxy for the overall reconstruction and mapping process, this is not an option for us. Our method is map-centric, and we do not estimate a unique and globally consistent camera trajectory. In fact, we explicitly track the camera multiple times simultaneously relative to different local submaps. Our evaluation therefore focusses on the accuracy of the 3D maps that we generate.

We use the dataset from [39], and in particular the synthetically rendered living-room sequences that come with a ground truth 3D model. We run our proposed system on the image sequences provided, then extract a surface mesh from the combined SDF $\hat{F}$ using Marching Cubes, and register the resulting reconstruction with the original 3D model. The observed average errors are reported in Table 1. Note in particular that the sequence lr-kt3 does trigger a loop closure event and therefore tests our whole pipeline.

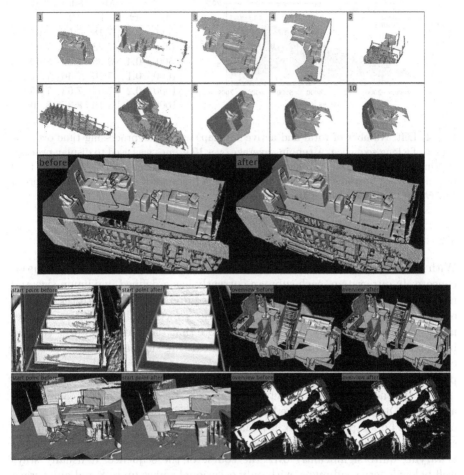

Fig. 3. Example reconstructions. We show the reconstruction result before and after loop closure, along with (top) images 1–10 showing constituent submaps and (bottom) the point of closure. The data for the top sequence is from [38].

Table 1. Left: Surface reconstruction error as evaluated on the ICL-NUIM dataset [39]. Right: Top and bottom views of the reconstruction obtained for sequence lr-kt3.

sequence	lr-kt0	lr-kt1	lr-kt2	lr-kt3
DVO SLAM	0.032	0.061	0.119	0.053
RGB-D SLAM	0.044	0.032	0.031	0.167
MRSMap	0.061	0.140	0.098	0.248
Kintinouous	0.011	0.008	0.009	0.150
ElasticFusion	**0.007**	**0.007**	0.008	0.028
Our system	0.013	0.011	**0.001**	**0.014**

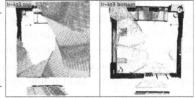

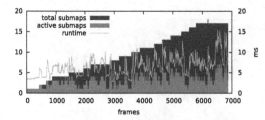

B	Θ	Max Reloc Seeds		
		1	2	3
500	0.1	7.18	7.51	7.61
500	0.2	7.33	7.70	7.99
500	0.4	8.06	8.39	8.40
1000	0.1	7.16	7.46	7.62
1000	0.2	7.57	7.63	7.85
1000	0.4	8.10	8.37	8.40

Fig. 4. Left: Number of total and active submaps as well as processing time over the course of a long sequence. A running average over 10 frames was used to display processing times. Right: Overall average processing time (in milliseconds) for the sequence used to generate the bottom-most result in Fig. 3, as a function of scene size (parameters B and Θ) and the maximum allowed number of relocalisation seeds.

4.2 Memory Requirements

With large-scale 3D reconstruction in mind, scalability is obviously a major concern. In our system, each submap currently has a defined maximum size and memory footprint, and the overall memory requirements scale with the number of allocated submaps. In Fig. 4 we illustrate the growth of these memory requirements over the course of a long sequence. Note that the plateau towards the end indicates that the system is tracking within existing submaps because of a loop closure. The steps in between indicate rapid or not so rapid exploration of new parts of the scene.

We also note that not all submaps have to be kept in active memory at all times. Only a subset is used for tracking and updating the map, and the others can be swapped out, to host memory or even to disk. Figure 4(left) also shows the number of active submaps at any given time, and, while this number is varying quite significantly over the course of the sequence, it usually stays well below 5 active submaps, with only occasional spikes up to 8 and an average of 2.7. With well implemented swapping methods, this behaviour allows almost constant active memory requirements regardless of the sequence length.

Using the block based representation of our base system [17], our submaps consist on average of about 14636 allocated voxel blocks, the largest one of 29428 blocks for this sequence. This is at a voxel grid resolution of $s = 5\,\mathrm{mm}$: at coarser resolutions the memory requirements of submaps shrink accordingly. In our current system we therefore limit the maximum number of blocks per submap to 65536. With each block representing $8 \times 8 \times 8$ voxels, and each voxel requiring 3 bytes of memory, along with an overhead of about 1 MB for the hash table data, each submap therefore requires about 100 MB of memory. Colour information, if desired, requires another 3 bytes per voxel, hence doubling the memory requirements of each submap. Still, even lower grade consumer graphics hardware will easily hold a few such submaps in memory.

4.3 Runtime

One of the key contributions of this work is an online system running in real time. To verify this claim, we measure the overall processing time for each frame on a test system with a Intel Core i7-5960X CPU and a Nvidia Titan X GPU. Our measurements take into account the tracking, integration and raycasting in each submap (Sect. 2.1), as well as all loop closure detection (Sect. 3.2), verification and other maintainance (Sect. 3.3), and they are the joint CPU and GPU times.

The resulting numbers are included in Fig. 4(left) for the sequence shown in Fig. 1. Obviously there is a high correlation between the number of active submaps and the processing time, and as [17] explains, the majority of the runtime is spent in raycasting and tracking, which are the key steps to our approach. Since the number of active submaps is independent of sequence length and overall scene size, the processing time also does not grow, but remains fairly constant. Even at peak times the processing requires just about 15.4 ms, and the average over the whole sequence is 6.6 ms, corresponding to about 150 frames processed per second. Figure 4(right) shows the average processing time for the sequence used to generate the bottom-most result in Fig. 3, w.r.t. scene size (parameters B and Θ) and the maximum allowed number of relocalisation seeds. The processing time required for the same sequence without using the loop closure algorithm was 5.4 ms, meaning that the loop closure operations adds as little as *1.8* ms over the original processing. This overhead is proportional to the number of scenes, as shown also by Fig. 4(left), but the increase is minor.

5 Conclusions

In this paper we have described an end-to-end processing pipeline which delivers large scale, dense, and 3D maps to the user from depth imagery at frame rate and with a average latency per frame of less than 7 ms. Loops are closed on the fly. The underlying representation and processing shares much with earlier works — a volumetric representation utilizing a truncated signed distance function is combined with a very carefully coded voxel block hashing scheme to mitigate memory growth. But key to overall performance, and performance through loop closure, is the use of submapping, a technique common in sparse reconstruction but less so in dense approaches.

We propose a novel criterion for dense submap initiation, involving detection of when the camera moves away from its current quasi-local viewing volume, which suppresses the over-frequent creation of submaps using earlier methods. Conveniently, our method is well-suited to voxel block hashing. We introduce a method of submap alignment which demands concordance of camera trajectories rather than full structural agreement in overlapping regions, a simplification which greatly reduces computation load, indeed to the point where alignment is essentially cost-free. Last, we describe a process for loop closure detection based on an earlier method of sensor relocalization.

The system is fully implemented on a single high-end GPU and host CPU. Further to the swapping described in previous works [16,17], very large scale

514   O. Kähler et al.

global maps can easily be swapped out from active GPU memory to main memory or even to disk. Future experimentation is aimed at characterizing performance during swapping in ever longer runs.

Acknowledgments. This work is partially supported by Huawei Technologies Co. Ltd. any by grant EP/J014990 from the UK's Engineering and Physical Science Research Council.

References

1. Newcombe, R.A., Davison, A.J.: Live dense reconstruction with a single moving camera. In: Proceedings 23rd IEEE Conference on Computer Vision and Pattern Recognition, pp. 1498–1505 (2010)
2. Newcombe, R.A., Izadi, S., Hilliges, O., Molyneaux, D., Kim, D., Davison, A.J., Kohli, P., Shotton, J., Hodges, S., Fitzgibbon, A.: KinectFusion: real-time dense surface mapping and tracking. In: International Symposium on Mixed and Augmented Reality, pp. 127–136 (2011)
3. Whelan, T., Johannsson, H., Kaess, M., Leonard, J.J., McDonald, J.: Robust real-time visual odometry for dense RGB-D mapping. In: Proceedings of 2013 IEEE International Conference on Robotics and Automation, pp. 5724–5731 (2013)
4. Bylow, E., Sturm, J., Kerl, C., Kahl, F., Cremers, D.: Real-time camera tracking and 3D reconstruction using signed distance functions. In: Proceedings Robotics: Science and Systems Conference (2013)
5. Engel, J., Schöps, T., Cremers, D.: LSD-SLAM: large-scale direct monocular SLAM. In: Proceedings of 13th European Conference on Computer Vision, pp. 834–849 (2014)
6. Newcombe, R.A., Fox, D., Seitz, S.M.: Dynamic fusion: reconstruction and tracking of non-rigid scenes in real time. In: Proceedings of 28th IEEE Conference on Computer Vision and Pattern Recognition (2015)
7. Pollefeys, M., van Gool, L., Vergauwen, M., Verbiest, F., Cornelis, K., Tops, J., Koch, R.: Visual modeling with a hand-held camera. Int. J. Comput. Vis. **59**(3), 207–232 (2004)
8. Seitz, S.M., Curless, B., Diebel, J., Scharstein, D., Szeliski, R.: A comparison and evaluation of multi-view stereo reconstruction algorithms. In: Proceedings of 19th IEEE Conference on Computer Vision and Pattern Recognition, pp. 519–528 (2006)
9. Davison, A.J., Reid, I.D., Molton, N.D., Stasse, O.: MonoSLAM: real-time single camera SLAM. IEEE Trans. Pattern Anal. Mach. Intell. **26**(6), 1052–1067 (2007)
10. Klein, G., Murray, D.W.: Parallel tracking and mapping for small AR workspaces. In: Proceedings of 6th IEEE/ACM International Symposium on Mixed and Augmented Reality, pp. 225–234 (2007)
11. Newcombe, R.A., Lovegrove, S.J., Davison, A.J.: DTAM: dense tracking and mapping in real-time. In: International Conference on Computer Vision (ICCV), pp. 2320–2327 (2011)
12. Pradeep, V., Rhemann, C., Izadi, S., Zach, C., Bleyer, M., Bathiche, S.: MonoFusion: real-time 3D reconstruction of small scenes with a single web camera. In: International Symposium on Mixed and Augmented Reality, pp. 83–88 (2013)
13. Steinbruecker, F., Sturm, J., Cremers, D.: Volumetric 3D mapping in real-time on a CPU. In: International Conference on Robotics and Automation (ICRA), pp. 2021–2028 (2014)

14. Chen, J., Bautembach, D., Izadi, S.: Scalable real-time volumetric surface reconstruction. ACM Trans. Graph. **32**(4), 113:1–113:16 (2013)
15. Zeng, M., Zhao, F., Zheng, J., Liu, X.: Octree-based fusion for realtime 3D reconstruction. Graph. Models **75**(3), 126–136 (2013)
16. Nießner, M., Zollhöfer, M., Izadi, S., Stamminger, M.: Real-time 3D reconstruction at scale using voxel hashing. ACM Trans. Graph. **32**(6), 169:1–169:11 (2013)
17. Kähler, O., Prisacariu, V.A., Ren, C.Y., Sun, X., Torr, P.H., Murray, D.W.: Very high frame rate volumetric integration of depth images on mobile devices. IEEE Trans. Vis. Comput. Graph. (Proceedings International Symposium on Mixed and Augmented Reality 2015) **21**(11), 1241–1250 (2015)
18. Whelan, T., Leutenegger, S., Moreno, R.S., Glocker, B., Davison, A.: Elasticfusion: dense SLAM without a pose graph. In: Proceedings of Robotics: Science and Systems (2015)
19. Endres, F., Hess, J., Sturm, J., Cremers, D., Burgard, W.: 3-D mapping with an RGB-D camera. IEEE Trans. Robot. **30**(1), 177–187 (2014)
20. Kerl, C., Sturm, J., Cremers, D.: Dense visual SLAM for RGB-D cameras. In: Intelligent Robots and Systems (IROS), pp. 2100–2106 (2013)
21. Meilland, M., Comport, A.I.: On unifying key-frame and voxel-based dense visual SLAM at large scales. In: Intelligent Robots and Systems (IROS), pp. 3677–3683 (2013)
22. Engel, J., Schöps, T., Cremers, D.: LSD-SLAM: large-scale direct monocular SLAM. In: Fleet, D., Pajdla, T., Schiele, B., Tuytelaars, T. (eds.) ECCV 2014, Part II. LNCS, vol. 8690, pp. 834–849. Springer, Heidelberg (2014)
23. Weise, T., Wismer, T., Leibe, B., Gool, L.V.: Online loop closure for real-time interactive 3D scanning. Comput. Vis. Image Underst. **115**(5), 635–648 (2011). Special issue on 3D Imaging and Modelling
24. Stuckler, J., Behnke, S.: Multi-resolution surfel maps for efficient dense 3D modeling and tracking. J. Vis. Commun. Image Representation **25**(1), 137–147 (2014). Visual Understanding and Applications with RGB-D Cameras
25. Fioraio, N., Taylor, J., Fitzgibbon, A., Stefano, L.D., Izadi, S.: Large-scale and drift-free surface reconstruction using online subvolume registration. In: Computer Vision and Pattern Recognition (CVPR), pp. 4475–4483 (2015)
26. Choi, S., Zhou, Q.Y., Koltun, V.: Robust reconstruction of indoor scenes. In: Computer Vision and Pattern Recognition (CVPR), pp. 5556–5565 (2015)
27. Curless, B., Levoy, M.: A volumetric method for building complex models from range images. In: Conference on Computer Graphics and Interactive Techniques (SIGGRAPH), pp. 303–312 (1996)
28. Klingensmith, M., Dryanovski, I., Srinivasa, S., Xiao, J.: Chisel: Real time large scale 3D reconstruction onboard a mobile device using spatially hashed signed distance fields. In: Proceedings of Robotics: Science and Systems (2015)
29. Schops, T., Sattler, T., Hane, C., Pollefeys, M.: 3D modeling on the go: interactive 3D reconstruction of large-scale scenes on mobile devices. In: International Conference on 3D Vision (3DV), pp. 291–299 (2015)
30. Kümmerle, R., Grisetti, G., Strasdat, H., Konolige, K., Burgard, W.: g2o: a general framework for graph optimization. In: International Conference on Robotics and Automation (ICRA), pp. 3607–3613 (2011)
31. Whelan, T., Kaess, M., Johannsson, H., Fallon, M., Leonard, J.J., McDonald, J.: Real-time large-scale dense RGB-D SLAM with volumetric fusion. Int. J. Robot. Res. **34**(4–5), 598626 (2015)

32. Eade, E., Drummond, T.: Unified loop closing and recovery for real time monocular SLAM. In: Proceedings of the British Machine Vision Conference, pp. 6.1–6.10 (2008)
33. Williams, B., Cummins, M., Neira, J., Newman, P., Reid, I., Tardos, J.: An image-to-map loop closing method for monocular SLAM. In: Proceedings of International Conference on Intelligent Robots and and Systems, pp. 2053–2059 (2008)
34. Estrada, C., Neira, J., Tardos, J.D.: Hierarchical SLAM: real-time accurate mapping of large environments. IEEE Trans. Robot. **21**(4), 588–596 (2005)
35. Vedaldi, A., Zisserman, A.: Efficient additive kernels via explicit feature maps. Pattern Anal. Mach. Intell. **34**(3), 480–492 (2011)
36. Glocker, B., Izadi, S., Shotton, J., Criminisi, A.: Real-time RGB-D camera relocalization. In: International Symposium on Mixed and Augmented Reality (ISMAR), pp. 173–179 (2013)
37. Davis, T.A.: Direct Methods for Sparse Linear Systems. SIAM Series on Fundamentals of Algorithms. PWS Publishing, New York (2006)
38. Zhou, Q.Y., Koltun, V.: Dense scene reconstruction with points of interest. ACM Trans. Graph. **32**(4), 112:1–112:8 (2013)
39. Handa, A., Whelan, T., McDonald, J., Davison, A.: A benchmark for RGB-D visual odometry, 3D reconstruction and SLAM. In: International Conference on Robotics and Automation, pp. 1524–1531 (2014)

Pixel-Level Domain Transfer

Donggeun Yoo[1(✉)], Namil Kim[1], Sunggyun Park[1], Anthony S. Paek[2],
and In So Kweon[1]

[1] KAIST, Daejeon, South Korea
{dgyoo,nikim}@rcv.kaist.ac.kr, {sunggyun,iskweon}@kaist.ac.kr
[2] Lunit Inc., Seoul, South Korea
apaek@lunit.io

Abstract. We present an image-conditional image generation model.
The model transfers an input domain to a target domain in semantic
level, and generates the target image in pixel level. To generate realistic
target images, we employ the real/fake-discriminator as in Generative
Adversarial Nets [6], but also introduce a novel domain-discriminator to
make the generated image relevant to the input image. We verify our
model through a challenging task of generating a piece of clothing from
an input image of a dressed person. We present a high quality clothing
dataset containing the two domains, and succeed in demonstrating decent
results.

Keywords: Domain transfer · Generative Adversarial Nets

1 Introduction

Every morning, we agonize in front of the closet over what to wear, how to
dress up, and imagine ourselves with different clothes on. To generate mental
images [4] of ourselves wearing clothes on a hanger is an effortless work for our
brain. In our daily lives, we ceaselessly perceive visual scene or objects, and often
transfer them to different forms by the mental imagery. Our focus of this paper
lies on the problem; to enable a machine to transfer a visual input into different
forms and to visualize the various forms by generating a pixel-level image.

Image generation has been attempted by a long line of works [9,21,24] but
generating realistic images has been challenging since an image itself is high
dimensional and has complex relations between pixels. However, several recent
works have succeeded in generating realistic images [6,8,22,23], with the drastic
advances of deep learning. Although these works are similar to ours in terms of
image generation, ours is distinct in terms of *image-conditioned image generation*. We take an image as a conditioned input lying in a domain, and re-draw a
target image lying on another.

Electronic supplementary material The online version of this chapter (doi:10.
1007/978-3-319-46484-8_31) contains supplementary material, which is available to
authorized users.

© Springer International Publishing AG 2016
B. Leibe et al. (Eds.): ECCV 2016, Part VIII, LNCS 9912, pp. 517–532, 2016.
DOI: 10.1007/978-3-319-46484-8_31

A source image.   Possible target images.

Fig. 1. A real example showing non-deterministic property of target image in the pixel-level domain transfer problem.

In this work, we define two domains; a source domain and a target domain. The two domains are connected by a semantic meaning. For instance, if we define an image of a dressed person as a source domain, a piece of the person's clothing is defined as the target domain. Transferring an image domain into a different image domain has been proposed in computer vision [1,7,10,12,16,20], but all these adaptations take place in the feature space, i.e. the model parameters are adapted. However, our method directly produces target images.

We transfer a knowledge in a source domain to a pixel-level target image while overcoming the semantic gap between the two domains. Transferred image should look realistic yet preserving the semantic meaning. To do so, we present a pixel-level domain converter composed of an encoder for semantic embedding of a source and a decoder to produce a target image. However, training the converter is not straightforward because the target is not deterministic [25]. Given a source image, the number of possible targets is unlimited as the examples in Fig. 1 show. To challenge this problem, we introduce two strategies as follows.

To train our converter, we first place a separate network named *domain discriminator* on top of the converter. The domain discriminator takes a pair of a source image and a target image, and is trained to make a binary decision whether the input pair is associated or not. The domain discriminator then supervises the converter to produce associated images. Both of the networks are jointly optimized by the adversarial training method, which Goodfellow *et al.* [6] propose for generating realistic images. Such binary supervision solves the problem of non-deterministic property of the target domain and enables us to train the semantic relation between the domains. Secondly, in addition to the domain discriminator, we also employ the discriminator of [6], which is supervised by the labels of "real" or "fake", to produce realistic images.

Our framework deals with the three networks that play distinct roles. Labels are given to the two discriminators, and they supervise the converter to produce images that are realistic yet keeping the semantic meaning. Those two discriminators become unnecessary after the training stage and the converter is our ultimate goal. We verify our method by quite challenging settings; the source domain is a natural human image and the target domain is a product image of the person's top. To do so, we have made a large dataset named LookBook, which contains in total of 84k images, where 75k human images are associated with 10k top product images. With this dataset, our model succeeds in generating decent target images, and the evaluation result verifies the effectiveness of our *domain discriminator* to train the converter.

1.1 Contributions

In summary, our contributions are,

1. Proposing the first framework for semantically transferring a source domain to a target domain in pixel-level.
2. Proposing a novel discriminator that enables us to train the semantic relation between the domains.
3. Building a large clothing dataset containing two domains, which is expected to contribute to a wide range of domain adaptation researches.

2   Related Work

Our work is highly related with the image-generative models since our final result from an input image is also an image. The image-generative models can be grouped into two families; generative parametric approaches [9,21,24] and adversarial approaches [2,6,15,17]. The generative parametric approaches often have troubles in training complexities, which results in a low rate of success in generating realistic natural images. The adversarial approaches originate from Generative Adversarial Nets (GAN) proposed by Goodfellow *et al.* [6]. GAN framework introduces a generator (i.e. a decoder), which generates images, and a discriminator, which distinguishes between generated samples and real images. The two networks are optimized to go against each other; the discriminator is trained to distinguish between real and fake samples while the generator is trained to confuse the discriminator. Mirza and Osindero [15] extend GAN to a class conditional version, and Denton *et al.* [2] improve the image resolution in a coarse-to-fine fashion. However, GAN is known to be unstable due to the adversarial training, often resulting in incomprehensible or noisy images. Quite recently, Radford *et al.* [17] have proposed architectures named Deep Convolutional GANs, which is relatively more stable to be trained, and have succeeded in generating high quality images. As approaches focusing on different network architectures, a recurrent network based model [8] and a deconvolutional network based model [3] have also been proposed.

The recent improvements of GAN framework and its successful results motivate us to adopt the networks. We replace the generator with our converter which is an image-conditioned model, while [15] is class-conditional and [25] is attribute-conditional. The generator of Mathieu *et al.* [14] is similar to ours in that it is conditioned with video frames to produce next frames. They add a mean square loss to the generator to strongly relate the input frames to the next frames. However, we cannot use such loss due to the non-deterministic property of the target domain. We therefore introduce a novel discriminator named domain discriminator.

Our work is also related with the transfer learning, also called as the domain adaptation. This aims to transfer the model parameter trained on a source domain to a different domain. For visual recognition, many methods to adapt domains [7,12,20] have been proposed. Especially for the recent use of the deep convolutional neural network [13], it has been common to pre-train a large network [11] over ImageNet [19] and transfer the parameters to a target domain [16,18,26]. Similar to our clothing domains, Chen et al. [1] and Huang et al. [10] address a gap between fashion shopping mall images and unconstrained human images for the clothing attribute recognition [1] and the product retrieval [10]. Ganin and Lempitsky [5] also learns domain-invariant features by the adversarial training method. However, all these methods are different from ours in respect of cross-domain *image generation*. The adaptation of these works takes place in the feature space, while we directly produce target images from the source images.

3   Review of Generative Adversarial Nets

Generative Adversarial Nets (GAN) [6] is a generalized framework for generative models which [2,14,17] and we utilize for visual data. In this section, we briefly review GAN in the context of image data. GAN is formed by an adversarial setting of two networks; a generator and a discriminator. The eventual goal of the generator is to map a small dimensional space Z to a pixel-level image space, i.e., to enable the generator to produce a realistic image from an input random vector $z \in Z$.

To train such a generator, a discriminator is introduced. The discriminator takes either a real image or a fake image drawn by the generator, and distinguishes whether its input is real or fake. The training procedure can be intuitively described as follows. Given an initialized generator G^0, an initial discriminator D_R^0 is firstly trained with real training images $\{I^i\}$ and fake images $\{\hat{I}^j = G^0(z^j)\}$ drawn by the generator. After that, we freeze the updated discriminator D_R^1 and train the generator G^0 to produce better images, which would lead the discriminator D_R^1 to misjudge as real images. These two procedures are repeated until they converge. The objective function can be represented as a minimax objective as,

$$\min_{\Theta^G} \max_{\Theta_R^D} \mathbb{E}_{I \sim p_{\text{data}}(\mathbf{I})}[\log(D_R(I))] + \mathbb{E}_{z \sim p_{\text{noise}}(\mathbf{z})}[\log(1 - D_R(\hat{I}))], \quad (1)$$

where Θ^G and Θ_R^D indicate the model parameters of the generator and the discriminator respectively. Here, the discriminator produces a scalar probability that is high when the input I is real but otherwise low. The discriminator loss function $\mathcal{L}_R^D$ is defined as the binary cross entropy,

$$\mathcal{L}_R^D(I) = -t \cdot \log[D_R(I)] + (t-1) \cdot \log[1 - D_R(I)],$$

$$\text{s.t.}\ \ t = \begin{cases} 1 & \text{if } I \in \{I^i\} \\ 0 & \text{if } I \in \{\hat{I}^j\}. \end{cases} \quad (2)$$

One interesting fact in the GAN framework is that the model is trained under the lowest level of supervision; real or fake. Without strong and fine supervisions (e.g. mean square error between images), this framework succeeds in generating realistic images. This motivates us to raise the following question. Under such a low-level supervision, would it be possible to train a connection between distinct image domains? If so, could we transform an image lying in a domain to a realistic image lying on another? Through this study, we have succeeded in doing so, and the method is to be presented in Sect. 4.

4   Pixel-Level Domain Transfer

In this section, we introduce the pixel-level domain transfer problem. Let us define a source image domain $S \subset \mathbb{R}^{W \times H \times 3}$ and a target image domain $T \subset \mathbb{R}^{W \times H \times 3}$. Given a transfer function named a converter C, our task is to transfer a source image $I_S \in S$ to a target image $\hat{I}_T \in T$ such as

$$\hat{I}_T = C(I_S | \Theta^C), \tag{3}$$

where Θ^C is the model parameter of the converter. Note that the inference $\hat{I}_T$ is not a feature vector but itself a target image of $W \times H \times 3$ size. To do so, we employ a convolutional network model for the converter C, and adopt a supervised learning to optimize the model parameter Θ^C. In the training data, each source image I_S should be associated with a ground-truth target image I_T.

4.1   Converter Network

Our target output is a *pixel-level* image. Furthermore, the two domains are connected by a *semantic* meaning. Pixel-level generation itself is challenging but the semantic transfer makes the problem even more difficult. A converter should selectively summarize the semantic attributes from a source image and then produce a transformed pixel-level image.

The top network in Fig. 2 shows the architecture of the converter we propose. The converter is a unified network that is end-to-end trainable but we can divide it into the two parts; an encoder and a decoder. The encoder part is composed of five convolutional layers to abstract the source into a semantic 64-dimensional code. This abstraction procedure is significant since our source domain (e.g. natural fashion image) and target domain (e.g. product image) are paired in a semantic content (e.g. the product). The 64-dimensional code should capture the semantic attributes (e.g. category, color, etc.) of a source to be well decoded into a target. The code is then fed by the decoder, which constructs a relevant target through the five decoding layers. Each decoding layer conducts the fractional-strided convolutions, where the convolution operates in the opposite direction. The reader is referred to Table 1 for more details about the architectures of the encoder and the decoder.

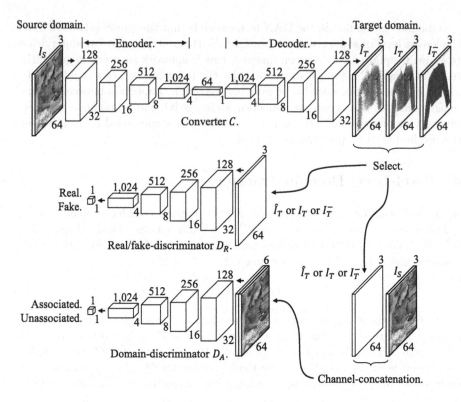

Fig. 2. Whole architecture for pixel-level domain transfer.

Table 1. Details of each network. In (a), each entry in {·} corresponds to each network. L-ReLU is leaky-ReLU. In (b), F denotes fractional-stride. The activation from the first layer is reshaped into $4 \times 4 \times 1{,}024$ size before being fed to the second layer.

Layer	Number of filters	Filter size (w×h×ch)	Stride	Pad	Batch norm.	Activation function
Conv. 1	128	5×5×{3, 3, 6}	2	2	×	L-ReLU
Conv. 2	256	5×5×128	2	2	○	L-ReLU
Conv. 3	512	5×5×256	2	2	○	L-ReLU
Conv. 4	1,024	5×5×512	2	2	○	L-ReLU
Conv. 5	{64, 1, 1}	1×1×1,024	1	0	{○, ×, ×}	{L-ReLU, sigmoid, sigmoid}

(a) Details of the {encoder, real/fake discriminator, domain discriminator}.

Layer	Number of filters	Filter size (w×h×ch)	Stride	Pad	Batch norm.	Activation function
Conv. 1	4×4×1,024	1×1×64	1	0	○	ReLU
F-Conv. 2	1,024	5×5×512	1/2	-	○	ReLU
F-Conv. 3	512	5×5×256	1/2	-	○	ReLU
F-Conv. 4	256	5×5×128	1/2	-	○	ReLU
F-Conv. 5	128	5×5×3	1/2	-	×	tanh

(b) Details of the decoder.

4.2 Discriminator Networks

Given the converter, a simple choice of a loss function to train it is the mean-square error (MSE) such as $||\hat{I}_T - I_T||_2^2$. However, MSE may not be a proper choice due to critical mismatches between MSE and our problem. Firstly, MSE is not suitable for pixel-level supervision for natural images. It has been well known that MSE is prone to produce blurry images because it inherently assumes that the pixels are drawn from Gaussian distribution [14]. Pixels in natural images are actually drawn from complex multi-modal distributions. Besides its intrinsic limitation, it causes another critical problem especially for the pixel-level domain transfer as follows.

Given a source image, the target is actually not unique in our problem. Our target domain is the lowest pixel-level image space, not the high-level semantic feature space. Thus, the number of possible targets from a source is infinite. Figure 1 is a typical example showing that the target is not unique. The clothing in the target domain is captured in various shapes, and all of the targets are true. Besides the shapes, the target image can be captured from various viewpoints, which results in geometric transformations. However, minimizing MSE always forces the converter to fit into one of them. Image-to-image training with MSE never allows a small geometric miss-alignment as well as various shapes. Thus, training the converter with MSE is not a proper use for this problem. It would be better to introduce a new loss function which is tolerant to the diversity of the pixel-level target domain.

In this paper, on top of the converter, we place a discriminator network which plays a role as a loss function. As in [2,6,17], the discriminator network guides the converter to produce realistic target under the supervision of real/fake. However, this is not the only role that our discriminator plays. If we simply use the original discriminator replacing MSE, a produced target could look realistic but its contents may not be relevant to the source. This is because there is no pairwise supervision such as MSE. Only real/fake supervision exists.

Given arbitrary image triplets $(I_S^+, I_S^\oplus, I_S^-)$ in the source domain S, where I_S^+ and $I_S^\oplus$ are about the same object while I_S^- is not, a converter transfers them into the images $(\hat{I}_T^+, \hat{I}_T^\oplus, \hat{I}_T^-)$ in the target domain T. Let us assume that these transferred images look realistic due to the real/fake discriminator. Beyond the realistic results, the best converter C should satisfy the following condition,

$$s\left(\hat{I}_T^+, \hat{I}_T^\oplus\right) > s\left(\hat{I}_T^+, \hat{I}_T^-\right) \quad \text{and} \quad s\left(\hat{I}_T^+, \hat{I}_T^\oplus\right) > s\left(\hat{I}_T^\oplus, \hat{I}_T^-\right), \tag{4}$$

where $s(\cdot)$ is a semantic similarity function. This condition means that an estimated target should be semantically associated with the source. One supervision candidate to let the converter C meet the condition is the combined use of MSE with the real/fake loss. However, again, it is not the best option for our problem because the ground-truth I_T is not unique. Thus, we propose a novel discriminator, named domain discriminator, to take the pairwise supervision into consideration.

The domain discriminator D_A is the lowest network illustrated in Fig. 2. To enable pairwise supervision while being tolerant to the target diversity, we significantly loosen the level of supervision compared to MSE. The network D_A takes a pair of source and target as input, and produces a scalar probability of whether the input pair is associated or not. Let us assume that we have a source I_S, its ground truth target I_T and an irrelevant target I_T^-. We also have an inference $\hat{I}_T$ from the converter C. We then define the loss $\mathcal{L}_A^D$ of the domain discriminator D_A as,

$$\mathcal{L}_A^D(I_S, I) = -t \cdot \log[D_A(I_S, I)] + (t-1) \cdot \log[1 - D_A(I_S, I)],$$

$$\text{s.t. } t = \begin{cases} 1 & \text{if } I = I_T \\ 0 & \text{if } I = \hat{I}_T \\ 0 & \text{if } I = I_T^-. \end{cases} \quad (5)$$

The source I_S is always fed by the network as one of the input pair while the other I is chosen among $(I_T^-, \hat{I}_T, I_T)$ with equal probability. Only when the source I_S and its ground-truth I_T is paired as input, the domain discriminator is trained to produce high probability whereas it minimizes the probability in other cases. Here, let us pay more attention to the input case of $(I_S, \hat{I}_T)$.

The produced target $\hat{I}_T$ comes from the source but we regard it as an unassociated pair $(t = 0)$ when we train the domain discriminator. Our intention of doing so is for *adversarial training* of the converter and the domain discriminator. The domain discriminator loss is minimized for training the domain discriminator while it is maximized for training the converter. The better the domain discriminator distinguishes a ground-truth I_T and an inference $\hat{I}_T$, the better the converter transfers the source into a relevant target.

In summary, we employ both of the real/fake discriminator and the domain discriminator for adversarial training. These two networks play a role as a loss to optimize the converter, but have different objectives. The real/fake discriminator penalizes an unrealistic target while the domain discriminator penalizes a target being irrelevant to a source. The architecture of the real/fake discriminator is identical to that of [17] as illustrated in Fig. 2. The domain discriminator also has the same architecture except for the input filter size since our input pair is stacked across the channel axis. Several architecture families have been proposed to feed a pair of images to compare them but a simple stack across the channel axis has shown the best performance as studied in [27]. The reader is referred to Table 1 for more details about the discriminator architectures.

4.3 Adversarial Training

In this section, we present the method for training the converter C, the real/fake discriminator D_R and the domain discriminator D_A. Because we have the two discriminators, the two loss functions have been defined. The real/fake discriminator loss $\mathcal{L}_R^D$ is Eq. (2), and the domain discriminator loss $\mathcal{L}_A^D$ is Eq. (5). With the two loss functions, we follow the adversarial training procedure of [6].

Given a paired image set for training, let us assume that we get a source batch $\{I_S^i\}$ and a target batch $\{I^i\}$ where a target sample I^i is stochastically chosen from $(I_T^i, I_T^{i-}, \hat{I}_T^i)$ with an equal probability. At first, we train the discriminators.

Algorithm 1. Adversarial training for the pixel-level domain transfer.

Set the learning rate η and the batch size B.
Initialize each network parameters $\Theta^C, \Theta_R^D, \Theta_A^D$,
Data: Paired image set $\{I_S^n, I_T^n\}_{n=1}^N$.
while *not converged* **do**

    Get a source batch $\{I_S^i\}_{i=1}^B$ and a target batch $\{I^i\}_{i=1}^B$,
       where I^i is a target sample randomly chosen from $(I_T^i, I_T^{i-}, \hat{I}_T^i)$.
    Update the real/fake discriminator D_R:
$$\Theta_R^D \leftarrow \Theta_R^D - \eta \cdot \frac{1}{B}\sum_{i=1}^B \frac{\partial \mathcal{L}_R^D(I^i)}{\partial \Theta_R^D}$$
    Update the domain discriminator D_A:
$$\Theta_A^D \leftarrow \Theta_A^D - \eta \cdot \frac{1}{B}\sum_{i=1}^B \frac{\partial \mathcal{L}_A^D(I_S^i, I^i)}{\partial \Theta_A^D}$$
    Update the converter C:
$$\Theta^C \leftarrow \Theta^C - \eta \cdot \frac{1}{B}\sum_{i=1}^B \frac{\partial \mathcal{L}^C(I_S^i, I^i)}{\partial \Theta^C}$$

end

We train the real/fake discriminator D_R with the target batch to reduce the loss of Eq. (2). The domain discriminator D_A is trained with both of source and target batches to reduce the loss of Eq. (5). After that, we freeze the updated discriminator parameters $\{\hat{\Theta}_R^D, \hat{\Theta}_A^D\}$, and optimize the converter parameters Θ^C to *increase* the losses of both discriminators. The loss function of the converter can be represented as,

$$\mathcal{L}^C(I_S, I) = -\frac{1}{2}\mathcal{L}_R^D(I) - \frac{1}{2}\mathcal{L}_A^D(I_S, I), \quad \text{s.t.} \quad I = \text{sel}\left(\{I_T, \hat{I}_T, I_T^-\}\right), \quad (6)$$

where $\text{sel}(\cdot)$ is a random selection function with equal probability. The reader is referred to Algorithm 1 for more details of the training procedures.

5 Evaluation

In this section, we verify our pixel-level domain transfer by a challenging task; a natural human image belongs to the source domain, and a product image of that person's top belongs to the target domain. We first give a description on the dataset in Sect. 5.1. We then provide details on the experimental setting in Sect. 5.2, and we demonstrate and discuss the results in Sects. 5.3–5.5.

5.1 LookBook Dataset

We make a dataset named LookBook that covers two fashion domains. Images of one domain contain fashion models, and those of the other domain contain top products with a clean background. Real examples are shown in Fig. 3. We manually associate each product image with corresponding images of a fashion model fitting the product, so each pair is accurately connected with the same product.

Fig. 3. Example images of LookBook. A product image is associated with multiple fashion model images.

LookBook contains 84,748 images where 9,732 top product images are associated with 75,016 fashion model images. It means that a product has around 8 fashion model images in average. We collect the images from five on-line fashion shopping malls[1] where a product image and its fashion model images are provided. Although we utilize LookBook for the pixel-level domain transfer, we believe that it can contribute to a wide range of domain adaptation researches.

Chen *et al.* [1] also has presented a similar fashion dataset dealing with two domains. However, it is not suitable for our task since the domains are differently defined in details. They separate the domain into user taken images and on-line shopping mall images so that both domains include humans.

5.2 Experiment Details

Before training, we rescale all images in LookBook to have 64 pixels at a longer side while keeping the aspect ratio, and fill the margins of both ends with 255s. Pixels are normalized to a range of $[-1, 1]$ according to the tanh activation layer of the converter. We then randomly select 5 % images to define a validation set, and also 5 % images for a test set. Since LookBook has 9,732 products, each of the validation set and the test set is composed of 487 product images and their fashion model images. The remaining images compose a training set.

The filters of the three networks are randomly initialized from a zero mean Gaussian distribution with a standard deviation of 0.02. The leak slope of the LeakyReLU in Table 1-(a) is 0.2. All models were trained with Stochastic Gradient Descent with mini-batch of 128 size. We also follow the learning rate of 0.0002 and the momentum of 0.5 suggested by [17]. After 25 epochs, we lessen the learning rate to 0.00002 for 5 more epochs.

Table 2 shows the notations and the descriptions of the 4 baselines and our method. The training details of all the baselines are identical to those of ours.

5.3 Qualitative Evaluation

First, we show qualitative results in Fig. 5, where the examples are chosen from the test set. Our results look more relevant to the source image and more realistic compared to those of baselines. Boundaries of products are sharp, and small

---

[1] {bongjashop, jogunshop, stylenanda}.com, {smallman, wonderplace}.co.kr.

Table 2. Notations and descriptions of baselines and our method.

Notations	Descriptions
C+RF	A converter trained only with the real/fake discriminator
C+MSE	A converter trained only with the mean square loss
C+RF+DD−Neg	A converter trained with both of the discriminators. Negative pairs are not used
	Only positive pairs are used
Retrieval by DD-score	Retrieving the nearest product image in the training set
	The queries are the human images in the test set
	The retrieval scores come from the domain discriminator
C+RF+DD (Ours)	A converter trained with both of the discriminators

Table 3. Quantitative evaluations. All the values are normalized to a range of $[0, 1]$.

User study score				Pixel-level (dis)similarity		
Methods	Real	Att	Cat	Methods	RMSE	C-SSIM
C+RF	0.40	0.21	0.06	C+RF	0.39	0.18
C+MSE	0.28	0.60	0.60	C+MSE	**0.26**	0.20
C+RF+DD (Ours)	**0.82**	**0.67**	**0.77**	C+RF+DD−Neg	0.32	0.18
				Retrieval by DD-score	0.44	0.19
				C+RF+DD (Ours)	0.32	**0.21**

details such as stripes, patterns are well described in general. The results of "C+RF" look realistic but irrelevant to the source image, and those of "C+MSE" are quite blurry.

Figure 4 verifies how well the encoder of the converter encodes clothing attributes under the various conditions of source images. The source images significantly vary in terms of backgrounds, viewpoints, human poses and self-occlusions. Despite these variations, our converter generates less varying targets while reflecting the clothing attributes and categories of the source images. These results imply that the encoder robustly summarizes the source information in a semantic level.

5.4   Quantitative Evaluation by User Study

Since the target domain is not deterministic, it is difficult to quantitatively analyze the performance. Thus, we conduct a user study on our generation results as a primary evaluation. We compare our method with the top two baselines in Table 2. For this study, we created a sub-test set composed of 100 source images randomly chosen from the test set. For each source image, we showed users three target images generated by the two baselines and our method. Users were asked to rate them three times in accordance with three different evaluation criteria as follows. A total of 25 users participated in this study.

1. How realistic is each result? Give a score from 0 to 2.
2. How well does each result capture the attributes (color, texture, logos, etc.) of the source image? Give a score from 0 to 2.
3. Is the category of each result identical to that of the source image? Give a binary score of 0 or 1.

The left part of Table 3 shows the user study results. In the "Realistic" criteria, it is not surprising that "C+MSE" shows the worst performance due to the intrinsic limitation of the mean square loss for image generation. Its assumption of Gaussian distribution results in blurry images as shown in Fig. 5. However, the strong pairwise supervision of the mean square loss relatively succeeds in representing the category and attributes of a product.

When the converter is supervised with the real/fake discriminator only, the generated images are more realistic than those of "C+MSE". However, it fails to produce targets relevant to inputs and yields low attribute and category scores.

The user study results demonstrate the effectiveness of the proposed method. For all valuation criteria, our method outperforms the baselines. Especially, the ability to capture attributes and categories is better than that of "C+MSE". This result verifies the effectiveness of our domain discriminator.

Another interesting observation is that our score of "Realistic" criteria is higher than that of "C+RF". Both of the methods include the real/fake discriminator but demonstrate distinct results. The difference may be caused by the domain discriminator which is added to the adversarial training in our method.

Fig. 4. Generation results under varying input conditions. The odd rows are inputs, and the even rows are generation results. Each image is in $64 \times 64 \times 3$ dimensions.

Source RF MSE Ours   Source RF MSE Ours   Source RF MSE Ours

Fig. 5. Qualitative comparisons. Each image from the left to the right respectively corresponds to a source image, a "C+RF" result, a "C+MSE" result and our result. Each image is in $64 \times 64 \times 3$ dimensions.

530 D. Yoo et al.

When we train the domain discriminator, we regard all produced targets as "unassociated". This setting makes the converter better transfer a source image into a more *realistic* and relevant target image.

5.5 Quantitative Evaluation by Pixel-Level (Dis)similarity

For each method, we measure a pixel-level dissimilarity by Root Mean Square Error (RMSE) between a generated image and a target image over the test set. We also measure a pixel-level similarity by Structural Similarity (SSIM), since SSIM is known to be more consistent with human perception than RMSE. We use a color version of SSIM by averaging SSIMs for each channel.

The right part of Table 3 shows the results. As we can expect, "C+MSE" shows the lowest RMSE value because the converter is trained by minimizing the mean square loss. However, in case of SSIM, our method outperforms all the baselines.

To verify the effectiveness of the "associated/unassociated" supervision when we train the domain discriminator, we compare ours with "C+RF+DD−Neg". In Table 3, our method outperforms this method. Without the irrelevant input pairs, the generation results could look realistic, but relatively fail to describe the attributes of items. This is why we added the irrelevant input pairs into supervision to encourage our model to capture discriminative attributes.

To verify the generalization capability of our model, we also compare ours with "Retrieval by DD-score". If our model fails in generalization (i.e. just memorizes and copies training items which are similar to query), our generation results could not be better than the retrieved items which are real. However, our method outperforms the retrieval method. It verifies the capability of our model to draw unseen items.

6 Conclusion

We have presented pixel-level domain transfer based on Generative Adversarial Nets framework. The proposed domain discriminator enables us to train the semantic relation between the domains, and the converter has succeeded in generating decent target images. Also, we have presented a large dataset that could contribute to domain adaptation researches. Since our framework is not constrained to specific problems, we expect to extend it to other types of pixel-level domain transfer problems from low-level image processing to high-level synthesis.

Acknowledgments. This work was supported by the National Research Foundation of Korea (NRF) grant funded by the Korea government (MSIP) (No. 2010-0028680) and KEPCO chair professor funding.

References

1. Chen, Q., Huang, J., Feris, R., Brown, L.M., Dong, J., Yan, S.: Deep domain adaptation for describing people based on fine-grained clothing attributes. In: Proceedings of the IEEE Conference on Computer Vision and Pattern Recognition, pp. 5315–5324 (2015)
2. Denton, E.L., Chintala, S., Fergus, R., et al.: Deep generative image models using a Laplacian pyramid of adversarial networks. In: Advances in Neural Information Processing Systems, pp. 1486–1494 (2015)
3. Dosovitskiy, A., Tobias Springenberg, J., Brox, T.: Learning to generate chairs with convolutional neural networks. In: Proceedings of the IEEE Conference on Computer Vision and Pattern Recognition, pp. 1538–1546 (2015)
4. Eysenck, M.W.: Fundamentals of Cognition. Psychology Press, Hove (2006)
5. Ganin, Y., Lempitsky, V.: Unsupervised domain adaptation by backpropagation. In: Proceedings of the 32nd International Conference on Machine Learning (2015)
6. Goodfellow, I., Pouget-Abadie, J., Mirza, M., Xu, B., Warde-Farley, D., Ozair, S., Courville, A., Bengio, Y.: Generative adversarial nets. In: Advances in Neural Information Processing Systems, pp. 2672–2680 (2014)
7. Gopalan, R., Li, R., Chellappa, R.: Domain adaptation for object recognition: an unsupervised approach. In: 2011 IEEE International Conference on Computer Vision (ICCV), pp. 999–1006. IEEE (2011)
8. Gregor, K., Danihelka, I., Graves, A., Rezende, D., Wierstra, D.: Draw: a recurrent neural network for image generation. In: Proceedings of The 32nd International Conference on Machine Learning, pp. 1462–1471 (2015)
9. Hinton, G.E., Salakhutdinov, R.R.: Reducing the dimensionality of data with neural networks. Science 313(5786), 504–507 (2006)
10. Huang, J., Feris, R.S., Chen, Q., Yan, S.: Cross-domain image retrieval with a dual attribute-aware ranking network. In: Proceedings of the IEEE International Conference on Computer Vision, pp. 1062–1070 (2015)
11. Krizhevsky, A., Sutskever, I., Hinton, G.E.: Imagenet classification with deep convolutional neural networks. In: Advances in Neural Information Processing Systems, pp. 1097–1105 (2012)
12. Kulis, B., Saenko, K., Darrell, T.: What you saw is not what you get: domain adaptation using asymmetric kernel transforms. In: 2011 IEEE Conference on Computer Vision and Pattern Recognition (CVPR), pp. 1785–1792. IEEE (2011)
13. LeCun, Y., Boser, B., Denker, J.S., Henderson, D., Howard, R.E., Hubbard, W., Jackel, L.D.: Backpropagation applied to handwritten zip code recognition. Neural Comput. 1(4), 541–551 (1989)
14. Mathieu, M., Couprie, C., LeCun, Y.: Deep multi-scale video prediction beyond mean square error. arXiv preprint arXiv:1511.05440 (2015)
15. Mirza, M., Osindero, S.: Conditional generative adversarial nets. arXiv preprint arXiv:1411.1784 (2014)
16. Oquab, M., Bottou, L., Laptev, I., Sivic, J.: Learning and transferring mid-level image representations using convolutional neural networks. In: Proceedings of the IEEE Conference on Computer Vision and Pattern Recognition, pp. 1717–1724 (2014)
17. Radford, A., Metz, L., Chintala, S.: Unsupervised representation learning with deep convolutional generative adversarial networks. arXiv preprint arXiv:1511.06434 (2015)

18. Razavian, A., Azizpour, H., Sullivan, J., Carlsson, S.: CNN features off-the-shelf: an astounding baseline for recognition. In: Proceedings of the IEEE Conference on Computer Vision and Pattern Recognition Workshops, pp. 806–813 (2014)
19. Russakovsky, O., Deng, J., Su, H., Krause, J., Satheesh, S., Ma, S., Huang, Z., Karpathy, A., Khosla, A., Bernstein, M., et al.: Imagenet large scale visual recognition challenge. Int. J. Comput. Vis. 115(3), 211–252 (2015)
20. Saenko, K., Kulis, B., Fritz, M., Darrell, T.: Adapting visual category models to new domains. In: Daniilidis, K., Maragos, P., Paragios, N. (eds.) ECCV 2010, Part IV. LNCS, vol. 6314, pp. 213–226. Springer, Heidelberg (2010). doi:10.1007/978-3-642-15561-1_16
21. Salakhutdinov, R., Hinton, G.E.: Deep Boltzmann machines. In: International Conference on Artificial Intelligence and Statistics, pp. 448–455 (2009)
22. Sohl-Dickstein, J., Weiss, E., Maheswaranathan, N., Ganguli, S.: Deep unsupervised learning using nonequilibrium thermodynamics. In: Proceedings of the 32nd International Conference on Machine Learning, pp. 2256–2265 (2015)
23. Theis, L., Bethge, M.: Generative image modeling using spatial LSTMs. In: Advances in Neural Information Processing Systems, pp. 1918–1926 (2015)
24. Vincent, P., Larochelle, H., Bengio, Y., Manzagol, P.A.: Extracting and composing robust features with denoising autoencoders. In: Proceedings of the 25th international conference on Machine learning, pp. 1096–1103. ACM (2008)
25. Yan, X., Yang, J., Sohn, K., Lee, H.: Attribute2image: conditional image generation from visual attributes. arXiv preprint (2015). arXiv:1512.00570
26. Yoo, D., Park, S., Lee, J.Y., Kweon, I.: Multi-scale pyramid pooling for deep convolutional representation. In: Proceedings of the IEEE Conference on Computer Vision and Pattern Recognition Workshops, pp. 71–80 (2015)
27. Zagoruyko, S., Komodakis, N.: Learning to compare image patches via convolutional neural networks. In: Proceedings of the IEEE Conference on Computer Vision and Pattern Recognition, pp. 4353–4361 (2015)

Accelerating Convolutional Neural Networks with Dominant Convolutional Kernel and Knowledge Pre-regression

Zhenyang Wang, Zhidong Deng$^{(\boxtimes)}$, and Shiyao Wang

State Key Laboratory of Intelligent Technology and Systems,
Tsinghua National Laboratory for Information Science and Technology,
Department of Computer Science, Tsinghua University, Beijing 100084, China
crazycry2010@gmail.com, michael@tsinghua.edu.cn,
sy-wang14@mails.tsinghua.edu.cn

Abstract. Aiming at accelerating the test time of deep convolutional neural networks (CNNs), we propose a model compression method that contains a novel dominant kernel (DK) and a new training method called knowledge pre-regression (KP). In the combined model DK^{2}PNet, DK is presented to significantly accomplish a low-rank decomposition of convolutional kernels, while KP is employed to transfer knowledge of intermediate hidden layers from a larger teacher network to its compressed student network on the basis of a cross entropy loss function instead of previous Euclidean distance. Compared to the latest results, the experimental results achieved on CIFAR-10, CIFAR-100, MNIST, and SVHN benchmarks show that our DK^{2}PNet method has the best performance in the light of being close to the state of the art accuracy and requiring dramatically fewer number of model parameters.

Keywords: Dominant convolutional kernel · Knowledge pre-regression · Model compression · Knowledge distilling

1 Introduction

In recent years, deep convolutional neural network (CNN) has made impressive success in several computer vision tasks such as image classification [1], object detection and localization [2,3]. On many benchmark challenges [1,4–6], records have been being consecutively broken with CNNs since 2012 [1] on. Surprising performance, however, usually comes with a heavy computational burden due to the use of deeper and/or wider architectures. Complicated models with numerous parameters may lead to an unacceptable test or inference time consuming for a variety of real applications. To resolve such challenging problem, there was an early interest in hardware-specific optimization [1,7–10]. But it is very likely to be unable to meet increasingly demands for model acceleration in an era of mobile Internet. The reason is that huge amounts of portable devices such as

© Springer International Publishing AG 2016
B. Leibe et al. (Eds.): ECCV 2016, Part VIII, LNCS 9912, pp. 533–548, 2016.
DOI: 10.1007/978-3-319-46484-8_32

smart phones and tablets are often equipped with low-end CPUs and GPUs as well as limited memory.

To speed up cumbersome CNNs, one is to directly compress existing large models or ensembles into small and fast-to-execute models [11–15]. Another is to employ deep and wide top-performing teacher networks to train shallow and/or thin student networks [16–19]. Based on low rank expansions, convolutional operator is decomposed into two procedures: feature extraction and feature combination (Sect. 3.1). Initially inspired from low rank approximation of responses proposed by Zhang et al. [15], this paper proposes a novel dominant convolutional kernel (DK) for greatly compressing filter banks. To deal with performance degradation problems caused by model compression, we present a new knowledge pre-regression (KP) training method for compressed CNN architectures, which expands the FitNet training method [19] to make it much easier to converge and implement. Such KP-based training method fills the intermediate representation gap between original teacher network and compressed student.

In this paper, our CNN models with DK, together with KP-based training method, are referred to as DK^{2}PNet. It can be viewed as combination of two model acceleration methods mentioned above. For compact DK^{2}PNet, we conduct extensive experiments on different benchmark datasets, including CIFAR-10 [4], CIFAR-100 [4], MNIST [5], and SVHN [6]. When compared to several recently published CNN models, our experimental results show that the proposed DK^{2}PNet method has the best performance that is close to state of the art test errors, while using remarkable less number of parameters.

2   Related Work

In general, there are three types of model acceleration methods for CNN architecture, i.e. model compression approach, knowledge distillation based training method, and hardware-specific acceleration.

Model compression approaches are exploited to directly compress parameters of large CNN models layer by layer. They generally include two components: decomposition that are adopted to reduce computational cost, and optimization for such decomposition. Among optimization schemes, the most widely used method includes filter reconstruction, which rebuilds the filter weights, and data reconstruction , through which each layer's responses are remodeled [15]. Actually, decomposition method attracts more attention, among which low rank decomposition methods become increasingly hotspot of research. LeCun et al. [20] use optimal brain damage interactively to reduce the number of parameters in neural network by a factor of four. Denil et al. [11] demonstrate that there are usually heavy over-parameterization problems for deep networks. Thus a small subset of parameters should be employed to accurately predict remaining ones. Jaderberg et al. [12] further adopt low rank decomposition to speed up processing of convolutional layers. They present two rank-1 filter decomposition schemes to attain approximations for scene text character recognition. Similar work is concurrently investigated by Denton et al. [13], who extend low rank tensor approximation methods to a remarkable larger model. But they only illustrate effectiveness of their methods on the first two convolutional layers. Lebedev et al. [14] decompose low rank convolutional product of 4D convolutional kernel tensor into a sum of four small number of rank-1 tensors. Instead of approximating linear filters or linear responses, Zhang et al. [15] minimize the reconstruction error of nonlinear responses and exploit channel level decomposition to reduce complexity. Chen et al. [21] further propose HashedNets to exploit inherent redundancy in neural networks.

The second approaches for accelerating test time computation are knowledge distilling based training methods, which aim to teach small student network with large teacher network. Knowledge distilling is proposed by Hinton et al. [16] so as to speed up inference time. They are viewed as a different kind of training method, where knowledge is compressed and transferred from cumbersome model into compact one. In fact, similar ideas could date back to [17], where large complex ensembles are compressed into single fast model without any significant loss of accuracy. Similar to knowledge distillation, a learning method with teacher-student architecture is presented by Ba and Caruana [18], which demonstrates that shallow network can also learn complicated nonlinear mappings from deep network and then achieve accuracy similar to deep network. Following such work, a deep and thin network FitNet [19] is trained . In addition, knowledge is transferred from intermediate hidden layers of teacher network (hint) to that of student network (guided) in hint/guided-based training.

In addition to the above-mentioned two methods, hardware-specific optimization can also reduce test time complexity. Vanhoucke et al. [7] make efforts to lower computational cost on x86 CPUs, where data layout, computation batching, and fixed-point SIMD operations can be utilized to effectively optimize large matrix computations. Farabet et al. [8] design a large scale FPGA-based architecture for convolutional networks. A new way to parallelize training of CNNs across multiple GPUs is presented in [9]. As major open source frameworks, both cuda-convnet [1] and caffe [10] provide effective GPU acceleration for CNN computation. Besides that, based on FFT, Mathieu et al. [22] transform convolutional operation to the Fourier domain, where feedforward convolutional operation with speed-up of approximately 2 times is done.

3   Method

3.1   CNN Architecture with Dominant Convolutional Kernels

Convolutional layer, which has a set of learnable parameters, plays a critical role in CNNs. In fact, most of parameters and computational burden lie in such convolutional layers. To compress regular CNN architecture, convolutional layer is the most profitable target. In this paper, we propose a new dominant convolutional kernel method to accomplish compression of convolutional layers.

Suppose that c_i and c_o indicate the number of input and output channels, respectively, and k_h and k_w the height and width of convolutional kernel, respectively. For regular convolution (Fig. 1(a)), we have convolutional kernels of $c_i \times c_o$

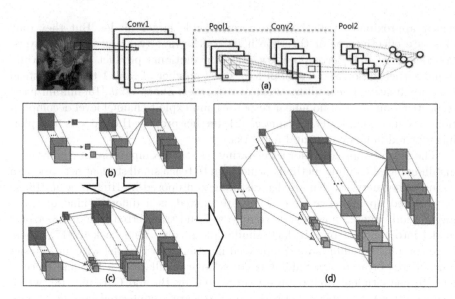

Fig. 1. Dominant Convolutional Kernel (DK). (a) Regular convolutional kernel; (b) DK of 1×1; (c) DK of 1×2; (d) DK of $1 \times n$.

in total. In fact, convolutional operations on input feature maps are regarded as feature extraction, while the summation of corresponding temporarily convolved feature maps could be considered as feature combination.

As for our dominant convolutional kernels shown in Figs. 1(b) and 3(d), feature is extracted only for single incoming feature map, while feature combination is done across temporarily convolved maps through 1×1 weights. Specifically, instead of convolving input feature maps with $c_i \times c_o$ convolutional kernels in regular convolutional layer, we merely employ c_i convolutional kernels, called dominant kernel (DK) in this paper. Apparently, there is 1-to-1 correspondence between inputs and temporarily convolved feature maps. This can be extended to the 1-to-n case, where $1 \le n \le k_h \times k_w$ as shown in Fig. 1(c) and (d). As a result, we have a total of parameters of $n \times c_i \times k_h \times k_w$ in such feature extraction phase. During feature combination, each output channel is a weighted sum of all the temporarily convolved maps. Note that weight vectors of $n \times c_i$ are exploited for combination of different maps. Thus there are totally $n \times c_i \times c_o$ parameters in such combination procedure. As n reaches up to the maximum of $k_h \times k_w$, our dominant convolutional layer may have capabilities of approximation similar as regular convolutional layer. It is because linear independence vectors of $k_h \times k_w$ determine a set of basis vectors for $k_h \times k_w$-dimensional feature spaces.

Our dominant convolutional layer uses parameters of $n \times c_i \times k_h \times k_w + n \times c_i \times c_o$ in total, which is only as many as $n/c_o + n/(k_h \times k_w)$ times of regular convolutional layer. For example, let us consider a commonly used convolutional configuration with a receptive field of 3×3 and 96×96 convolutional kernels. In this case, a dominant convolutional layer merely contains 12 % (1-to-1) and 24 %

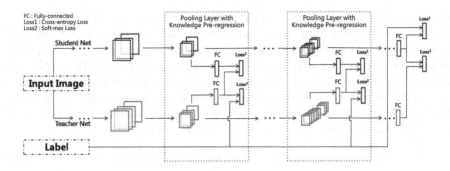

Fig. 2. Knowledge Pre-regression training method.

(1-to-2) of the parameters. Owing to the fact that computational compl exity is proportional to the number of parameters in a convolutional layer, time consuming is dramatically reduced. Moreover, the hyper-parameter n can be exploited to balance approximation capability and computational cost of a dominant convolutional layer.

3.2 Knowledge Pre-regression Training Method

Knowledge distillation lately proposed by Hinton *et al.* [16] aims to transfer knowledge from teacher network to student network. Knowledge of teacher network is usually stored in a form of parameters. Convolutional kernel parameters seem like too abstract, which makes it even hard to carry out knowledge transfer. In general, knowledge is defined as nonlinear mappings that map an input image to a target probability distribution (*i.e.* the output of softmax layer). Furthermore, such probability distribution of teacher network is transferred to student network. Romero *et al.* [19] extend such idea to transfer knowledge of intermediate hidden layers of teacher network to student network. Following this, we propose a knowledge pre-regression (KP) method to perform such knowledge transfer between teacher and student networks. In addition, we take advantage of the cross entropy loss function as our objective function, rather than Euclidean distance utilized in [19]. Actually, it is demonstrated to be more stable and robust.

Second, we choose the hint and guided layer pairs [19] for teacher network and student network, respectively. Considering that student network is often much simpler than its teacher network, a layer-by-layer pre-regression may lower recognition capabilities of student network. Based on our empirical data, the selection of pooling layers as hint/guided layers, which are further employed for performing knowledge pre-regression, is verified to be effective enough.

The hint/guided layer pairs, however, usually have different dimensions. Romero *et al.* [19] deal with this problem by introducing a convolutional regressor to match their dimensions, where Euclidean loss is utilized to optimize them. Although this method is simple, it is hard to converge. In this paper, we propose a KP-based training method to tackle such problem, as shown in Fig. 2. An auxiliary regressor with a fully-connected layer R_t and the ground truth label l is introduced to the hint layer to generate a target probability distribution b_t. The probability distribution is then transferred to the guided layer. Meanwhile, we add another auxiliary regressor with a fully-connected layer R_s for the guided layer of student network. Furthermore, we adopt the cross entropy loss function to connect the hint and the guided layers. The loss function in our KP-based training method can be written as Eqs. (1), (2), and (3),

$$\mathcal{L}_{KB}(W_s, R_t, R_s) = \lambda\mathcal{H}(b_t^\tau, b_s^\tau) + \mathcal{S}(l, b_t) \qquad (1)$$

$$b_t^\tau = softmax\left(\frac{h(x; W_t, R_t)}{\tau}\right) \qquad (2)$$

$$b_s^\tau = softmax\left(\frac{g(x; W_s, R_s)}{\tau}\right) \qquad (3)$$

where $\mathcal{S}$ and $\mathcal{H}$ represent the loss function of softmax and cross entropy, respectively, h and g are two functions that map an input image x to the hint and the guided layers, respectively, W_t and W_s stand for parameters in teacher network and student network, respectively, a temperature parameter τ [16] is utilized to soften the probability distribution over classes, and λ is a hyper-parameter used to balance these two loss functions.

We train our student network by minimizing the loss function below,

$$\mathcal{L}(W_s) = \lambda\mathcal{H}(p_t^\tau, p_s^\tau) + \mathcal{S}(l, p_s) + \sum_{i=1\cdots l} \lambda_i\mathcal{H}(b_t^{\tau^{(i)}}, b_s^{\tau^{(i)}}) + \mathcal{S}(l, b_t^{(i)}) \qquad (4)$$

where p_t and p_s are the output probability of the teacher and student networks, respectively, and l indicates the hint/guided layers that we select. In our experiments, only the first two pooling layers are chosen as our hint/guided layers, which are further used for knowledge pre-regression.

3.3   Discussion

As described above, we present a model compression method using dominant convolutional layers, which can greatly decrease the number of parameters and computational burden as well. Although our method is also based on a low rank decomposition method, it is different from Jaderberg et al.'s [12] and Zhang et al.'s[15] methods, as shown in Fig. 3. Jaderberg et al. (Fig. 3(b)) approximate regular convolution as a composition of two linear mappings with intermediate maps. Each of two mappings convolves its input with a receptive field of $1 \times d$ or $d \times 1$. Zhang et al. (Fig. 3(c)) also adopt a two-step decomposition with intermediate maps. The decomposition is only conducted on the channel. Our dominant convolutional kernel (Fig. 3(d)) seems very similar to Zhang et al.'s method.

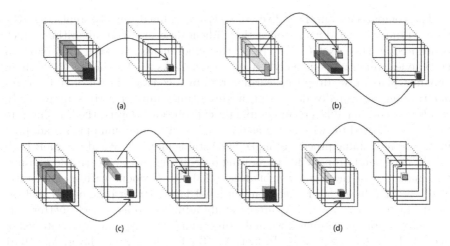

Fig. 3. Comparison to existing model compression methods. (a) Regular convolution operation; (b) Jaderberg *et al.*'s [12]; (c) Zhang *et al.*'s [15]; (d) The proposed DK decomposition.

But the difference is on the first decomposition step, instead of using a regular convolution, we use single or multiple dominant convolutional kernels to separately convolve each incoming feature map in order to further reduce computational complexity.

In order to improve performance of compressed model, we introduce a KP-based training method. We follow the work of Hinton *et al.* [16] and Romero *et al.* [19] and extend such work to intermediate layers and make it easy to converge through reconstructing objective function. As shown in Fig. 2, this architecture looks like two DSN models [23], although they have different meanings. DSN pays attention to improving classification performance of single model by introducing so-called companion objective to individual hidden layers, while our KP-based method focuses on knowledge transfer. Knowledge pre-regression enables our student model to have possibility of retaining a good balance between recognition and generalization capabilities.

4   Experimental Results

4.1   Overall Settings

We conduct our experiments based on the framework of caffe [10], running on two GPUs with data parallelism. We test the DK^{2}PNet models on several different benchmark datasets, including CIFAR-10 [4], CIFAR-100 [4], MNIST [5], and SVHN [6]. As an exceptional case, we complete more experiments on CIFAR-10 so as to specifically demonstrate effectiveness and efficiency of the proposed method.

For comparison, our DK^{2}PNet models are trained only by replacing KP-based training method with stochastic gradient descent (SGD) algorithm, which is denoted as DK^{2}PNet (SGD). In all the experiments, we set a mini-batch of 96. The learning rate is initially assigned to 0.01. As the loss begins to reach an apparent plateau, we drop this learning rate by a constant factor of 10 throughout training, repeatedly decreasing it three times until it arrives to 1e−5. In regular convolutional layers and dominant convolutional layers, the learning rate for bias is selected to twice as big as for weights. A momentum of 0.9 is adopted in the entire training process to make SGD stable and fast. We also exploit both weight decay and dropout for preventing over-fitting. All the learnable parameters make use of the same weight decay of 0.004. Dropout with a small ratio of 0.1 is introduced after each convolutional layer. Hyper-parameters such as weight factors of λ, λ_1 and λ_2 are carefully adjusted so as to yield better performance. In our experiment, we make fine-tuning of λ, λ_1, and λ_2 in interval of [0.0001, 1], where $\lambda \geq \lambda_1 \geq \lambda_2$. In fact, $\lambda = 0.1$ for the softmax layer, $\lambda_1 = 0.01$ for the second pooling layer, and $\lambda_2 = 0.001$ for the first pooling layer are a set of workable parameters. For all the datasets, image samples are preprocessed with removing the pre-pixel mean over their entire training dataset.

4.2 Setup of DK^{2}PNet Architecture

We design a couple of DK^{2}PNets with similar architecture but different parameters. Assume that there are K incoming feature maps for all the convolutional layers, whatever they are either regular or dominant. We adopt the same notation as [24] for convenience, *i.e.* DK^{2}PNet-K or CNN-K, which stands for the teacher network in our experiments, means that there are K feature maps in each layer.

The CNN-K is composed of 11 layers, including ten convolutional layers and one fully-connected layer. Three pooling layers succeed the 2nd, the 6th, and the 10th convolutional layers, respectively. Finally, a softmax layer is utilized to produce the final classification.

As the student network, DK^{2}PNet-K is structurally similar as its teacher network CNN-K. By substituting the second convolutional layer to the last one of CNN-K with dominant convolutional layers, it gives rise to our DK^{2}PNet-K. Note that the first convolutional layer in DK^{2}PNet-K is just a regular convolutional layer as warm-up.

In all regular and dominant convolutional layers, a reception field of 3×3 with stride and padding of 1 is employed for preserving spatial resolution. For the first two average pooling layers, we use a pooling area of 2×2 with stride of 2. A global average pooling is exploited as the last pooling layer. Additionally, all convolutional layers are combined with regularization of batch normalization [25], ReLU non-linearity, and dropout with a small drop ratio of 0.1. As a result, the DK2PNet-K (1-to-1) has a total of $(9K^2 + 108K)$ parameters, while regular teacher CNN-K has $(81K^2 + 27K)$ parameters.

4.3   CIFAR-10

CIFAR-10 [4] is a labeled subset of 80 million tiny image dataset. It contains 60,000 color images with size of 32×32. These images are categorized into 10 classes with 6,000 images per class. Such dataset is divided into five training batches and one test batch. Consequently, there are 50,000 training image samples and 10,000 test ones.

Table 1. Approximation capabilities of dominant convolutional kernel.

Model	CNN-96	DK^{2}PNet-96								
		1-to-1	1-to-2	1-to-3	1-to-4	1-to-5	1-to-6	1-to-7	1-to-8	1-to-9
#param	0.75 M	0.09 M	0.18 M	0.28 M	0.37 M	0.46 M	0.55 M	0.64 M	0.73 M	0.82M
Error (%)	**7.82**	9.59	8.98	8.55	8.26	**7.98**	8.25	8.56	8.21	8.03

To gain insight into approximation capabilities of DK^{2}PNet, nine DK^{2}PNet-96 models with different compression ratio are trained for comparison. As shown in Table 1, the teacher network CNN-96 is the base line model, while the student network DK^{2}PNet-96 is the compressed model produced by replacing the second to the last convolutional layers with the dominant convolutional layers. All these 10 models are embedded with BN and Dropout, and trained with SGD algorithm for the sake of comparison. The experimental results obtained are rather encouraging, the DK^{2}PNet-96 (1-to-1) with 0. 09 million parameters can achieve a test error of 9.59 %. Although it is not the best model on CIFAR-10, it is most likely to be the smallest model with test error of less than 10 %. By decreasing the compression ratio, we are able to improve performance of DK^{2}PNet-96, and the best compression performance is achieved by the DK^{2}PNet-96 (1-to-5). Unexpectedly, the DK^{2}PNet-96 (1-to-9), which has a slightly larger number of parameters compared to its teacher, cannot perform as good as its teacher. Such performance degradation is probably attributed to the training difficulty caused by the increase in depths and free parameters.

Furthermore, we complete comparative study to verify effectiveness of our knowledge pre-regression (KP) training method given in Sect. 3.2. From Table 2, the four DK^{2}PNets are trained with KP-based method and SGD algorithm, respectively. For the KP-based training method, we choose two teacher networks with different recognition performance to teach our DK^{2}PNet. Compared to SGD algorithm, KP-based training method is able to improve performance of all the four models. There is only a slight improvement for DK^{2}PNet-96 (1-to-1). The reason is that it seems like too small to optimize. Using KP-based training method, performance of DK^{2}PNet-128 (1-to-2) with more parameters is made better from a test error rate of 8.31 % to that of 7. 90 %. Even given that a teacher network achieves relatively poor performance, the use of it to train student networks also helps improve accuracy. By contrast, a good teacher could be more valuable.

Table 2. Comparison of our KP training method with SGD algorithm.

Model	#parameter	Test error (%)
SGD training		
DK^{2}PNet-96 (1-to-1, BN)	0.09 M	9.59
DK^{2}PNet-96 (1-to-2, BN)	0.18 M	8.98
DK^{2}PNet-128 (1-to-2, BN)	0.32 M	8.31
DK^{2}PNet-160 (1-to-2, BN)	0.49 M	7.91
KB-based training		
Good teacher	0.75 M	7.82
DK^{2}PNet-96 (1-to-1, BN)	0.09 M	9.52
DK^{2}PNet-96 (1-to-2, BN)	0.18 M	8.73
DK^{2}PNet-128 (1-to-2, BN)	0.32 M	7.90
DK^{2}PNet-160 (1-to-2, BN)	0.49 M	7.60
Poor teacher	0.75 M	12.18
DK^{2}PNet-96 (1-to-1, BN)	0.09 M	9.57
DK^{2}PNet-96 (1-to-2, BN)	0.18 M	8.78
DK^{2}PNet-128 (1-to-2, BN)	0.32 M	7.96
DK^{2}PNet-160 (1-to-2, BN)	0.49 M	7.70

Table 3. Comparison between different normalizations on CIFAR-10.

Model	#parameter	Test error (%)
CNN-96 (LRN)	0.75 M	12.18
DK^{2}PNet-96 (1-to-1, LRN)	0.09 M	26.88
DK^{2}PNet-96 (1-to-2, LRN)	0.18 M	26.52
DK^{2}PNet-128 (1-to-2, LRN)	0.32 M	25.01
CNN-96 (BN)	0.75 M	7.82
DK^{2}PNet-96 (1-to-1, BN)	0.09 M	9.59
DK^{2}PNet-96 (1-to-2, BN)	0.18 M	8.98
DK^{2}PNet-128 (1-to-2, BN)	0.32 M	8.31

Excellent performance of DK^{2}PNet should be partially attributed to regularization of batch normalization (BN) [25]. Comparative study of this issue is conducted on regular CNN and DK^{2}PNet. We train the following two sets of models: one is included with BN layers and another with LRN layers, instead of. The experimental results obtained are provided in Table 3. Apparently, the networks with LRN layers have very poor performance. This illustrates that normalization is able to significantly enhance approximation capabilities of CNN models, which gives us more confidence to take advantage of our KP-based training method presented in Sect. 3.2. In fact, the KP-based training method can also be seen as a kind of regularization.

Finally, we compare our methods with the state of the art models without any data augmentation. First, the teacher network CNN-96 with 0.75 million parameters is trained as our base line model. Second, we compress CNN-96 to give rise to the small model of DK^{2}PNet-96 (1-to-2) with 0.18 million parameters and then achieve a test error of 8.73 %. We expand this model with more hidden units. The generated DK^{2}PNet-160 (1-to-2) with 0.49 million parameters has a test error of 7.60 % and outperforms its teacher network, which becomes the best record on such dataset if any data augmentation is not adopted (Table 4).

To keep consistent with previous work, we also test our models with data augmentation of translation and horizontal flipping on CIFAR-10. We randomly crop a portion of 24×24 pixels from original images and flip them horizontal randomly. In the test phase, five 24×24 crops from four corners and one center with their horizontal flipping crops are employed for testing. The final test results are found by an average of all the outputs of ten crops. With SGD training, the DK^{2}PNet-96 (1-to-1, SGD) with 0.09 million parameters yields a test error of 8.78 %, while a test error of 6.44 % of the DK^{2}PNet-256 (1-to-1, SGD) almost approaches the state of the art result of 6. 05 % provided in [29]. But our DK^{2}PNet-256 (1-to-1) model merely exploits 34 % of the parameters in comparison with [29].

4.4 CIFAR-100

Like CIFAR-10, CIFAR-100 [4] has the same training and test sizes but contains 100 classes. Using the same procedure as CIFAR-10, we train a couple of DK^{2}PNet models on such dataset and compare them with the state of the art models (as listed in Table 5). It is easy to see that the DK^{2}PNet-160 (1-to-2) achieves a test error of 31.39 % without any data augmentation. Note that it contains only 0.49 million parameters, which is less than its teacher network CNN-96, and reaches roughly 26 % of the state of the art lightweight model [24].

4.5 MNIST

MNIST [5] is a handwritten digits dataset with digits from 0 to 9. Each image sample in MNIST has been centered and size-normalized to 28×28 grayscale image. It contains 60,000 training images and 10,000 test images. We exploit the small DK^{2}PNet-96 (1-to-2) model with 0.18 million parameters for such relatively simple benchmark problem. It is readily observed from Table 6 that we achieve a test error rate of 0.31 % that is very close to [29], while requiring the least number of parameters, which is reduced by 0.15 million *w.r.t.* its teacher network CNN-64 and by 1.67 million compared to Tree+Max+Avg [29].

4.6 SVHN

SVHN [6] is a real image dataset, which is collected from house numbers in Google street view images. It includes 73,257 training images, 26,032 test images,

Table 4. Comparison with existing models on CIFAR-10.

Model	#parameter	Test error (%)
Without data augmentation		
Maxout [26]	>5 M	11.68
NIN [27]	0.97 M	10.41
DSN [23]	0.97 M	9.69
RCNN [24]	1.86 M	8.69
ALL-CNN [28]	1.4 M	9.08
Tree+Max-Avg [29]	1.85M	**7.62**
Teacher (CNN-96)	0.75 M	7.82
DK^{2}PNet-96 (1-to-2)	0.18 M	8.73
DK^{2}PNet-128 (1-to-2)	0.32 M	7.90
DK^{2}PNet-160 (1-to-2)	0.49 M	**7.60**
With data augmentation		
Maxout [26]	>5 M	9.38
DropConnect [30]	-	9.32
NIN [27]	0.97 M	8.81
DSN [23]	0.97 M	8.22
RCNN [24]	1.86 M	7.09
Highway Network [31]	2.3 M	7.54 (7.72 ± 0.16)
ALL-CNN [28]	1.4 M	7.25
ResNet [32]	1.7M	6.43 (6.61 ± 0.16)
Fitnet4-LSUV [33]	2.5M	6.06
Tree+Max-Avg [29]	1.85M	**6.05**
Tuned CNN [34]	1.29M	6.37
DK^{2}PNet-96 (1-to-1, SGD)	0.09 M	8.78
DK^{2}PNet-96 (1-to-2, SGD)	0.18 M	7.68
DK^{2}PNet-128 (1-to-2, SGD)	0.32 M	7.06
DK^{2}PNet-160 (1-to-2, SGD)	0.49 M	7.06
DK^{2}PNet-256 (1-to-1, SGD)	0.62 M	**6.44**

and an extra 531,131 additional samples of less difficulty for training. Among two formats for such dataset, we adopt the second format. When multiple digits simultaneously appear in single image, we only need to recognize the centering one. The experimental results show that our DK^{2}PNet-160 (1-to-2) with 0.49 million parameters yields a test error of 1.83 %, as listed in Table 7. Note that the number of parameters of DK^{2}PNet-160 (1-to-2) is significantly decreased compared to RCNN [24] and Tree+Max+Avg [29].

Table 5. Comparison with existing models on CIFAR-100.

Model	#parameter	Test error (%)
Without data augmentation		
Maxout [26]	>5 M	38.57
Tree based priors [35]	-	36.85
NIN [27]	0.98 M	35.68
DSN [23]	0.98 M	34.57
RCNN [24]	1.86 M	**31.75**
ALL-CNN [28]	1.3 M	33.71
Highway Network [31]	2.3 M	32.24
Tree+Max-Avg [29]	1.76 M	32.37
ELU-Network [36]	39.32 M	**24.28**
Teacher (CNN-96)	0.75 M	33.63
DK^{2}PNet-96 (1-to-2)	0.18 M	35.24
DK^{2}PNet-128 (1-to-2)	0.32 M	34.48
DK^{2}PNet-160 (1-to-2)	0.49 M	**31.39**
With data augmentation		
Fitnet4-LSUV [33]	2.5 M	27.66
Tuned CNN [34]	1.29 M	27.40

Table 6. Comparison with existing models on MNIST.

Model	#parameter	Test error (%)
Without data augmentation		
Maxout [26]	0.42 M	0.45
NIN [27]	0.35 M	0.47
DSN [23]	0.35 M	0.39
RCNN [24]	0.67 M	0.31
Tree+Max-Avg [29]	1.85 M	0.31
FitNet-LSUV-SVM [33]	0.03 M	0.38
Tree+Max+Avg [29]	1.85 M	**0.29**
Teacher (CNN-64)	0.33 M	0.33
DK^{2}PNet-64 (1-to-2)	0.09 M	0.38
DK^{2}PNet-96 (1-to-1)	0.09 M	0.36
DK^{2}PNet-96 (1-to-2)	0.18 M	**0.31**
With data augmentation		
Dropconnect [30]	-	0.21
MCDNN[37]	-	0.23

Table 7. Comparison with existing models on SVHN.

Model	#parameter	Test error (%)
The state of the art models		
Maxout [26]	>5 M	2.47
NIN [27]	1.98 M	2.35
DSN [23]	1.98 M	1.92
RCNN [24]	2.67 M	**1.77**
Tree+Max+Avg [29]	4.00M	**1.69**
Teacher (CNN-96)	0.75 M	1.82
DK^{2}PNet-96 (1-to-2)	0.18 M	2.04
DK^{2}PNet-128 (1-to-2)	0.32 M	1.95
DK^{2}PNet-160 (1-to-2)	0.49 M	**1.83**

5   Conclusion

In this paper, we propose a model acceleration method using dominant convolutional kernel and knowledge pre-regression. First, by replacing regular convolutional layers with dominant convolutional layers, CNN architecture can be simplified significantly, resulting in efficient model acceleration. To tackle performance degradation problems caused by compression, a new knowledge pre-regression training method is further presented to transfer knowledge of intermediate hidden layers from original teacher network to its compressed student network. It makes student network quickly learn and generalize well. Finally, our experimental results show that the proposed DK^{2}PNet provides near state of the art test errors, while requiring notably fewer parameters than regular CNN models. For example, without any data augmentation, the DK^{2}PNet-160 yields the best performance of 7.60 % on CIFAR-10 using almost 3.8 times less parameters, when compared to existing state of the art results of 7.62 % [29]. On CIFAR-100, while the DK^{2}PNet-160 achieves better performance with a test error of 31.39 % that is close to [36], it only requires roughly 80.2 times fewer parameters. On MNIST without any data augmentation, the DK^{2}PNet-96 with 0.18 million parameters, which is the least number of parameters adopted, obtains a test error of 0.31 %. Our DK^{2}PNet-160 receives near state of the art result of 1.83 % on SVHN benchmark with roughly 12 % of the parameters in comparison with [29], dramatically reducing the number of parameters by a factor of 8.

Acknowledgements. This work was supported in part by the National Science Foundation of China (NSFC) under Grant Nos. 91420106, 90820305, and 60775040, and by the National High-Tech R&D Program of China under Grant No. 2012AA041402.

References

1. Krizhevsky, A., Sutskever, I., Hinton, G.E.: Imagenet classification with deep convolutional neural networks. In: Advances in neural information processing systems, pp. 1097–1105 (2012)
2. Girshick, R., Donahue, J., Darrell, T., Malik, J.: Rich feature hierarchies for accurate object detection and semantic segmentation. In: Proceedings of the IEEE Conference on Computer Vision and Pattern Recognition, pp. 580–587 (2014)
3. Sermanet, P., Eigen, D., Zhang, X., Mathieu, M., Fergus, R., LeCun, Y.: Overfeat: integrated recognition, localization and detection using convolutional networks. arXiv preprint arXiv:1312.6229 (2013)
4. Krizhevsky, A.: Learning multiple layers of features from tiny images. Master's thesis, Department of Computer Science, University of Toronto (2009)
5. LeCun, Y., Bottou, L., Bengio, Y., Haffner, P.: Gradient-based learning applied to document recognition. Proc. IEEE **86**(11), 2278–2324 (1998)
6. Netzer, Y., Wang, T., Coates, A., Bissacco, A., Wu, B., Ng, A.Y.: Reading digits in natural images with unsupervised feature learning. In: NIPS Workshop on Deep Learning and Unsupervised Feature Learning, Granada, Spain, vol. 2011, p. 4 (2011)
7. Vanhoucke, V., Senior, A., Mao, M.Z.: Improving the speed of neural networks on CPUs. In: Proceedings of Deep Learning and Unsupervised Feature Learning NIPS Workshop, vol. 1 (2011)
8. Farabet, C., LeCun, Y., Kavukcuoglu, K., Culurciello, E., Martini, B., Akselrod, P., Talay, S.: Large-scale FPGA-based convolutional networks. In: Scaling up Machine Learning: Parallel and Distributed Approaches, pp. 399–419 (2011)
9. Krizhevsky, A.: One weird trick for parallelizing convolutional neural networks. arXiv preprint arXiv:1404.5997 (2014)
10. Jia, Y., Shelhamer, E., Donahue, J., Karayev, S., Long, J., Girshick, R., Guadarrama, S., Darrell, T.: Caffe: convolutional architecture for fast feature embedding. In: Proceedings of the ACM International Conference on Multimedia, pp. 675–678. ACM (2014)
11. Denil, M., Shakibi, B., Dinh, L., de Freitas, N., et al.: Predicting parameters in deep learning. In: Advances in Neural Information Processing Systems, pp. 2148–2156 (2013)
12. Jaderberg, M., Vedaldi, A., Zisserman, A.: Speeding up convolutional neural networks with low rank expansions. In: Proceedings of the British Machine Vision Conference. BMVA Press (2014)
13. Denton, E.L., Zaremba, W., Bruna, J., LeCun, Y., Fergus, R.: Exploiting linear structure within convolutional networks for efficient evaluation. In: Advances in Neural Information Processing Systems, pp. 1269–1277(2014)
14. Lebedev, V., Ganin, Y., Rakhuba, M., Oseledets, I., Lempitsky, V.: Speeding-up convolutional neural networks using fine-tuned cp-decomposition. arXiv preprint arXiv:1412.6553 (2014)
15. Zhang, X., Zou, J., Ming, X., He, K., Sun, J.: Efficient and accurate approximations of nonlinear convolutional networks. In: Proceedings of the IEEE Conference on Computer Vision and Pattern Recognition, pp. 1984–1992 (2015)
16. Hinton, G., Vinyals, O., Dean, J.: Distilling the knowledge in a neural network. arXiv preprint arXiv:1503.02531 (2015)
17. Buciluă, C., Caruana, R., Niculescu-Mizil, A.: Model compression. In: Proceedings of the 12th ACM SIGKDD International Conference on Knowledge Discovery and Data Mining, pp. 535–541. ACM (2006)

18. Ba, J., Caruana, R.: Do deep nets really need to be deep? In: Advances in neural information processing systems, pp. 2654–2662 (2014)
19. Romero, A., Ballas, N., Kahou, S.E., Chassang, A., Gatta, C., Bengio, Y.: Fitnets: hints for thin deep nets. arXiv preprint arXiv:1412.6550 (2014)
20. LeCun, Y., Denker, J.S., Solla, S.A., Howard, R.E., Jackel, L.D.: Optimal brain damage. In: NIPS, pp. 598–605(1989)
21. Chen, W., Wilson, J., Tyree, S., Weinberger, K., Chen, Y.: Compressing neural networks with the hashing trick. In: ICML, pp. 2285–2294 (2015)
22. Mathieu, M., Henaff, M., LeCun, Y.: Fast training of convolutional networks through FFTs. arXiv preprint arXiv:1312.5851 (2013)
23. Lee, C.Y., Xie, S., Gallagher, P., Zhang, Z., Tu, Z.: Deeply-supervised nets. In: Proceedings of the Eighteenth International Conference on Artificial Intelligence and Statistics, pp. 562–570 (2015)
24. Liang, M., Hu, X.: Recurrent convolutional neural network for object recognition. In: Proceedings of the IEEE Conference on Computer Vision and Pattern Recognition, pp. 3367–3375 (2015)
25. Ioffe, S., Szegedy, C.: Batch normalization: accelerating deep network training by reducing internal covariate shift. In: Proceedings of the 32nd International Conference on Machine Learning, pp. 448–456 (2015)
26. Goodfellow, I., Warde-farley, D., Mirza, M., Courville, A., Bengio, Y.: Maxout networks. In: Proceedings of the 30th International Conference on Machine Learning (ICML 2013), pp. 1319–1327 (2013)
27. Lin, M., Chen, Q., Yan, S.: Network in network. arXiv preprint arXiv:1312.4400 (2013)
28. Springenberg, J.T., Dosovitskiy, A., Brox, T., Riedmiller, M.: Striving for simplicity: the all convolutional net. arXiv preprint arXiv:1412.6806 (2014)
29. Lee, C.Y., Gallagher, P.W., Tu, Z.: Generalizing pooling functions in convolutional neural networks: Mixed, gated, and tree. arXiv preprint arXiv:1509.08985 (2015)
30. Wan, L., Zeiler, M., Zhang, S., Cun, Y.L., Fergus, R.: Regularization of neural networks using dropconnect. In: Proceedings of the 30th International Conference on Machine Learning (ICML 2013), pp. 1058–1066 (2013)
31. Srivastava, R.K., Greff, K., Schmidhuber, J.: Training very deep networks. In: Advances in Neural Information Processing Systems, pp. 2368–2376 (2015)
32. He, K., Zhang, X., Ren, S., Sun, J.: Deep residual learning for image recognition. arXiv preprint arXiv:1512.03385 (2015)
33. Mishkin, D., Matas, J.: All you need is a good init. arXiv preprint arXiv:1511.06422 (2015)
34. Snoek, J., Rippel, O., Swersky, K., Kiros, R., Satish, N., Sundaram, N., Patwary, M., Prabhat, M., Adams, R.: Scalable bayesian optimization using deep neural networks. In: Proceedings of the 32nd International Conference on Machine Learning (ICML 2015), pp. 2171–2180 (2015)
35. Srivastava, N., Salakhutdinov, R.R.: Discriminative transfer learning with tree-based priors. In: Advances in Neural Information Processing Systems, pp. 2094–2102 (2013)
36. Clevert, D.A., Unterthiner, T., Hochreiter, S.: Fast and accurate deep network learning by exponential linear units (ELUs). arXiv preprint arXiv:1511.07289 (2015)
37. Ciresan, D., Meier, U., Schmidhuber, J.: Multi-column deep neural networks for image classification. In: 2012 IEEE Conference on Computer Vision and Pattern Recognition (CVPR), pp. 3642–3649. IEEE (2012)

Learning Social Etiquette: Human Trajectory Understanding In Crowded Scenes

Alexandre Robicquet$^{(\boxtimes)}$, Amir Sadeghian,
Alexandre Alahi, and Silvio Savarese

CVGL, Stanford University, Stanford, USA
{arobicqu,amirabs,alahi,ssilvio}@stanford.edu

Abstract. Humans navigate crowded spaces such as a university campus by following common sense rules based on social etiquette. In this paper, we argue that in order to enable the design of new target tracking or trajectory forecasting methods that can take full advantage of these rules, we need to have access to better data in the first place. To that end, we contribute a new large-scale dataset that collects videos of various types of targets (not just pedestrians, but also bikers, skateboarders, cars, buses, golf carts) that navigate in a real world outdoor environment such as a university campus. Moreover, we introduce a new characterization that describes the *"social sensitivity"* at which two targets interact. We use this characterization to define *"navigation styles"* and improve both forecasting models and state-of-the-art multi-target tracking–whereby the learnt forecasting models help the data association step.

Keywords: Trajectory forecasting · Multi-target tracking · Social Forces · UAV

1 Introduction

When pedestrians or bicyclists navigate their way through crowded spaces such as a university campus, a shopping mall or the sidewalks of a busy street, they follow common sense conventions based on social etiquette. For instance, they would yield the right-of-way at an intersection as a bike approaches very quickly from the side, avoid walking on flowers, and respect personal distance. By constantly observing the environment and navigating through it, humans have learnt the way other humans typically interact with the physical space as well as with the targets that populate such spaces *e.g.*, humans, bikes, skaters, electric carts, cars, toddlers, etc. They use these learned principles to operate in very complex scenes with extraordinary proficiency.

Researchers have demonstrated that it is indeed possible to model the interaction between humans and their surroundings to improve or solve numerous computer vision tasks: for instance, to make pedestrian tracking more robust and accurate [1–5], to enable the understanding of activities performed by groups of

© Springer International Publishing AG 2016
B. Leibe et al. (Eds.): ECCV 2016, Part VIII, LNCS 9912, pp. 549–565, 2016.
DOI: 10.1007/978-3-319-46484-8_33

individuals [6–9], to enable accurate prediction of target trajectories in future instants [10–13]. Most of the time, however, these approaches operate under restrictive assumptions whereby the type and number of interactions are limited or the testing environment is often contrived or artificial.

Fig. 1. We aim to understand human social navigation in a multi-class setting where pedestrians, bicyclists, skateboarders and carts (to name a few) share the same space. To that end, we have collected a new dataset with a quadcopter flying over more than 100 different crowded campus scenes.

In this paper, we argue that in order to learn and use models that allow mimicking, for instance, the remarkable human capability to navigate in complex and crowded scenes, the research community needs to have access to better data in the first place. To that end, we contribute a new large scale dataset that collects videos of various types of targets (not just pedestrians, but also bikes, skateboarders, cars, buses, golf carts) that navigate in a real world outdoor environment such as a university campus. Our dataset comprises of more than 100 different top-view scenes for a total of 20,000 targets engaged in various types of interactions. Target trajectories along with their target IDs are annotated which makes this an ideal testbed for learning and evaluating models for multi-target tracking, activity understanding and trajectory prediction at scale (see Figs. 1 and 2).

Among all the problems discussed above, in this paper we are interested in evaluating techniques related to two classes of problems: (i) target trajectory forecasting - whereby the ability to comply to social etiquettes and common sense behavior is critical, (ii) Multi-Target Tracking (MTT) - whereby the learnt forecasting model is used to enhance tracking results. In particular, we believe that our new dataset creates the opportunity to generalize state-of-the-art methods for understanding human trajectory, and evaluate them on a more effective playground. For instance, two leading families of methods for target trajectory forecasting (Social Forces [1,2,14,15] and Gaussian Processes [12,16,17]) have shown promising results on existing datasets [11,18]; however, they have never been tested at scale and in real-world scenarios where multiple classes of targets are present (i.e., not just pedestrian but also cars, bikes, etc.) as part of a complex ecosystem of interacting targets.

In addition to evaluating state-of-the-art forecasting and tracking methods, in this paper we also introduce a novel characterization that describes the *"social sensitivity"* at which two targets interact. It captures both the preferred distance a target wants to preserve with respect to its surrounding as well as when (s)he decides to avoid other targets. Low values for the social sensitivity feature means that a target motion is not affected by other targets that are potentially interacting with it. High values for the social sensitivity feature means that the target navigation is highly dependent on the position of other targets. This characterization allows to define the *"navigation style"* targets follow in interacting with their surrounding. We obtain different classes of navigation styles by clustering trajectory samples in the *social sensitivity space* (see Fig. 3 for examples). This allows to increase the flexibility in characterizing various modalities of interactions - for instance, some pedestrians may look more aggressive while walking because they are in rush whereas others might show a milder behavior because they are just enjoying their walk. Navigation style classes are used to select the appropriate forecasting model to best predict targets' trajectories as well as improve multi-target tracking. We believe that the ability to model social sensitivity is a key step toward learning common sense conventions based on social etiquette for enhancing forecasting and tracking tasks.

We present an extensive experimental evaluation that compares various state-of-the-art methods on the newly proposed dataset, and demonstrates that our social sensitivity feature and the use of navigation style enable better prediction and tracking results than previous methods that assume that all the targets belong to the same class (*i.e.*, follow the same navigation style).

2   Previous Work

A large variety of methods has been proposed in the literature to describe, model and predict human behaviors in a crowded space. Here we summarize the most relevant methods for human trajectory forecasting and multi-target tracking.

Human trajectory forecasting. An exhaustive study of crowd analysis is introduced by Treuille *et al.* [19]. Antonini *et al.* use the Discrete Choice Model to synthesize human trajectories in crowded scenes [20,21]. Other methods [12,17,22] use Gaussian Processes to forecast human trajectories. They avoid the problems associated with discretization and their generated motion paths are smooth. Unfortunately, they often assume that the location of the destination is known. More recently, a set of methods use Inverse Reinforcement Learning [10,23,24] whereby a reward (or cost) function is learnt that best explains the final decisions [25]. While these techniques have shown to work extremely well in several applications [25–27], they assume that all feature values are known and static during each demonstrated planning cycle. They have been used to mainly model human and static space interaction as opposed to the dynamic content.

The most popular method for multi-target trajectory forecasting remains the *Social forces* (SF) model by D. Hellbing and P. Molnar [15]. Targets react to energy potentials caused by the interactions with other targets and static obstacles through forces (repulsion or attraction). The SF model has been extensively used in robotics [28], and in the context of target tracking [1,2,29–33]. All these previous work use a single set of parameters to model multiple targets. We argue and show in the remainder of this paper that a single set of parameters is too limited to model all the navigation styles in complex crowded scenes when multiple classes of targets are present (pedestrians, bikers, skateboarders,...).

Multi-Target Tracking. Over the past decade, Multi-Target Tracking (MTT) algorithms have made great progress in solving the data association problem as a graph theoretic problem [30,34–38]. Several methods have incorporated the Social Forces (SF) model to improve the motion prior [1–5]. Recently, Xiang *et al.* [39] demonstrate the power of a strong appearance model over all these previous work. They reached state-of-the-art performance over the publicly available MTT challenge [40]. In this work, we use their method and demonstrates the impact of our "social sensitivity" feature in crowded multi-class complex scenes.

Fig. 2. Some examples of the scenes captured in our dataset. We have annotated all the targets (with bounding boxes) as well as the static scene semantics. The color codes associated to target bounding boxes represents different track IDs.

In the next sections, we first present our collected dataset. Then, we introduce our social sensitivity feature. In Sect. 5, we share details behind our forecasting and tracking model. Finally, we conclude with a detailed evaluation of our forecasting task, and its impact on the Multi-Target Tracking task.

3   Campus Dataset

We aim to learn the remarkable human capability to navigate in complex and crowded scenes. Existing datasets mainly capture the behavior of humans in spaces occupied by a single class of target, *e.g.*, pedestrian-only scenes [11,18,31]. However, in practice, pedestrians share the spaces with other classes of targets such as bicyclists, or skateboarders to name a few. For instance, on university campuses, a large variety of these targets interacts at peak hours. We want to study social navigation in these complex and crowded scenes occupied by several classes of targets. Datasets such as [41,42] do contain multiple classes of objects but are either limited in the number of scenes (just one for [41]), or in the number of classes of moving targets (just pedestrians in [42]).

To the best of our knowledge, we have collected the first large-scale dataset that has images and videos of various classes of targets that are moving and interacting in a real-world university campus. The dataset comprises more than 19K targets consisting of 11.2K pedestrians, 6.4K bicyclists, 1.3K cars, 0.3K skateboarders, 0.2K golf carts, and 0.1K buses. Although only videos of campus scenes are collected, the data is general enough to capture all type of interactions:

- target-target interactions, *e.g.*, a bicyclist avoiding a pedestrian,
- target-space interactions, *e.g.*, a skateboarder turning around a roundabout.

Target-target interactions We say that two targets interact when their collision energy (described by Eq. 1) is non-zero, *e.g.*, a pedestrian avoiding a skateboarder. These interactions involve multiple physical classes of targets (pedestrians, bicyclists, or skateboarders to name a few), resulting into 185 K annotated target-target interactions. We intentionally collected data at peak hours (between class breaks in our case) to observe high density crowds. For instance, during a period of 20 s, we observe in average from 20 to 60 targets in a scene (of approximately 900 m^2).

Target-space interactions. We say that a target interacts with the space when its trajectory deviates from a linear one in the absence of other targets in its surrounding, *e.g.*, a skateboarder turning around a roundabout. To further analyze these interactions, we also labeled the scene semantics of more than 100 static scenes with the following labels: road, roundabout, sidewalk, grass, building, and bike rack (see Fig. 2). We have approximately 40k "target-space" interactions.

In our model, the whole target space interaction is implicitly considered in the Social Force model. We only take dynamic obstacles into account. However, in most common scenes, people will also try to avoid static obstacles. Similar to [18] we model such obstacles as agents with zero velocity.

Tables 1 presents more details on our collected dataset. The scenes are grouped into 6 areas based on their physical proximity on campus. Each scene is captured with a 4k camera mounted on a quadcopter platform (a 3DR solo) hovering above various intersections on a University campus at an altitude of approximately eighty meters. The videos have a resolution of 1400 × 1904 and have been processed (*i.e.* undistorted and stabilized). Targets are annotated with their class label and their trajectory in time and space is identified.

4   Modeling Social Sensitivity

We claim that modeling human trajectory with a single navigation style is not suitable for capturing the variety of social behaviors that targets exhibit when interacting in complex scenes. We believe that conditioning such models on *navigation style* (*i.e.*, the way targets avoid each other) is a better idea and propose

Table 1. Our campus dataset characteristics. We group the scenes and refer to them using fictional places from the "Lord of the Rings". Bi = bicyclist, Ped = pedestrian, Skate = skateboarders

Dataset	Frames	Targets	Interactions	Bi	Ped	Skate	Carts	Car	Bus
ISENGARD	134079	2044	6472	1004	926	57	19	23	15
HOBBITON	138513	3821	14084	163	2493	24	18	1065	58
EDORAS	47864	1186	4684	224	956	2	2	2	0
MORDOR	139364	4542	68459	2594	1492	111	154	165	26
FANGORN	249967	3126	45520	1017	1991	50	30	27	11
VALLEY	219712	4845	46062	1362	3358	89	21	10	5
TOTAL	929499	19564	185281	6364	11216	333	244	1292	115

a characterization (feature) which we call *social sensitivity*. Given this characterization, we hence assign a navigation style to each target to better forecast its trajectory and improve tracking.

Social Sensitivity feature. Inspired by the Social Forces model (SF) [1], we model targets' interactions with an energy potential E_{ss}. A high potential means that the target is highly sensitive to others. We define E_{ss} as follows:

At each time step t, the target i is defined by a state variable $s_i^{(t)} = \{\mathbf{p}_i^{(t)}, \mathbf{v}_i^{(t)}\}$, where $\mathbf{p}_i^{(t)}$ is the position, and $\mathbf{v}_i^{(t)}$ the velocity. The energy potential encoding the social sensitivity is computed as follows:

$$E_{ss}(\mathbf{v_i^{(t)}}; s_i, \mathbf{s}_{-i} | \sigma_d, \sigma_w, \beta) = \sum_{j \neq i} w(s_i, s_j) \exp\left(-\frac{d^2(\mathbf{v}, s_i, s_j)}{2\sigma_d^2}\right), \qquad (1)$$

with $w(s_i, s_j)$ defined as:

$$w(s_i, s_j) = \exp\left(-\frac{|\Delta\mathbf{p}_{ij}|}{2\sigma_\omega}\right) \cdot \left(\frac{1}{2}\left(1 - \frac{\Delta\mathbf{p}_{ij}}{|\Delta\mathbf{p}_{ij}|}\frac{\mathbf{v}_i}{|\mathbf{v}_i|},\right)\right)^\beta, \qquad (2)$$

and

$$d^2(\mathbf{v}, s_i, s_j) = \left|\Delta\mathbf{p}_{ij} - \frac{\Delta\mathbf{p}_{ij}(\mathbf{v} - \mathbf{v}_j)}{|\mathbf{v} - \mathbf{v}_j|^2}(\mathbf{v} - \mathbf{v}_j)\right|. \qquad (3)$$

The energy E_{ss} is modeled as a product of Gaussians where the variances $\sigma_{w,d}$ represent the distances at which other targets will influence each other. For instance, if two targets i, j are close to each other ($\Delta\mathbf{p}_{ij}$ is small), E_{ss} will be large when $\sigma_{w,d}$ are small.

We define the parameter $\Theta_{ss} = \{\sigma_d, \sigma_w, \beta\}$ as the social sensitivity feature and interpret its dimension as follows:

- σ_d is the preferred distance a target maintains to avoid collision,
- σ_w is the distance at which a target reacts to prevent a collision (distance at which (s)he starts deviating from its linear trajectory),

– and β controls the peakiness of the weighting function.

In other words, the parameters $\{\sigma_d, \sigma_w, \beta\}$ aim at describing how targets avoid each others - i.e., their social sensitivity. We now present how we infer the parameters Θ_{ss} at training and testing time.

Training. At training time, since we observe all targets' velocities, V^{train}, we could learn a unique set of parameters, i.e., a single value for social sensitivity, that minimizes the energy potential as follows (similarly to what previous methods do [1–5]):

$$\{\sigma_d, \sigma_w, \beta\} = \underset{\{\sigma_d, \sigma_w, \beta\}}{\mathrm{argmin}} \left(\sum_{i=1}^{T-1} E_{ss}(v_i^{train}, s_i, s_{-i} | \sigma_d, \sigma_w, \beta) \right), \qquad (4)$$

where T is the number of targets in the training data. This minimization is operated with an interior-point method and is set with the following constraint on σ_d: $\sigma_d > 0.1$ (it specifies that every target can't have a "vital space" smaller than 10cm). As mentioned previously, however, we claim that learning a unique set of parameters is not suitable when one needs to deal with complex multi-class target scenarios whereby targets can have different social sensitivity. To validate this claim, we plot in Fig. 3 each target into a *social sensitivity space* where the x-axis is the σ_d values and the y-axis is the σ_w ones. These data are computed using training images from our dataset (see Sect. 6 for more details). We did not plot the third parameter β since it does not change much across targets. Even if our approach can handle an arbitrary number of classes, we cluster the points into four clusters for illustration purposes. Each cluster corresponds to what we define as a "navigation style". A navigation style describes the sensitivity of a target to its surrounding. We illustrate on the sides of Fig. 3 how targets follow different strategies in avoiding each other as different navigation styles are used.

Thanks to the above analysis of the *social sensitivity space*, at training, we solve Eq. 4 for each target to get its social sensitivity feature. We then cluster the points with K-mean clustering to have N number of clusters. Each cluster represents a navigation style. In Sect. 6, we study the impact of the number of clusters used by our method on the forecasting accuracy in Table 4.

Testing. At test time, we observe the targets until time t, and want to assign a navigation style.

In the presence of other targets, we solve Eq. 5 for each specific target i at time t:

$$\{\sigma_d(i), \sigma_w(i), \beta(i)\} = \underset{\{\sigma_d(i), \sigma_w(i), \beta(i)\}}{\mathrm{argmin}} (E_{ss}(v_i^t, s_i, s_{-i} | \sigma_d(i), \sigma_w(i), \beta(i))). \quad (5)$$

We obtain the social sensitivity feature $\Theta_{ss}(i) = \{\sigma_d(i), \sigma_w(i), \beta(i)\}$ for each target i. Given the clusters found at training, we assign each $\Theta_{ss}(i)$ to its corresponding cluster, i.e., navigation style.

In the absence of interactions, a target takes either a "neutral" navigation style (when entering a scene) or inherit the last inferred class from the previous

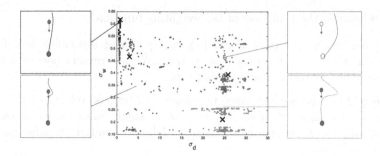

Fig. 3. Illustration of the social sensitivity space where we have illustrated how targets avoid each other with four navigation styles (from a top view). Each point in the middle plot is a target. The x-axis is the preferred distance σ_d a target keeps with its surrounding targets, and y-axis is the distance σ_w at which a target reacts to prevent a collision. Each color code represents a cluster (a navigation style). Even if our approach can handle an arbitrary number of classes, we only use 4 clusters for illustration purposes. In this plot, the green cluster represents targets with a mild behavior, willing to avoid other targets as much as possible and considering them from afar, whereas the red cluster describes targets with a more aggressive behavior and with a very small safety distance, considering others at the last moment. We illustrate on the sides of the plot examples of how targets follow different strategies in avoiding each other as different navigation styles are used. (Color figure online)

interaction. The "neutral" navigation style is the most popular one (in green in Fig. 3). In Fig. 4, we show that when the target is surrounded by other targets, its class changes with respect to its social sensitivity.

5 Forecasting and Tracking with Social Sensitivity

Our new collected dataset creates the opportunity to study methods for trajectory forecasting and multi-target tracking, and evaluate them on a large-scale broad setting, *i.e.* a space occupied by several classes of targets. Thanks to our proposed social sensitivity feature, we have more flexibility in modeling target interactions to forecast future trajectories. In the remaining of this section, we present the details behind our forecasting model driven by social sensitivity. Then, in Sect. 5.2, we show how to use our forcasting model on multi-target tracking.

5.1 Forecasting Multiple Classes of Targets

Problem formulation. Given the observed trajectories of several targets at time t, we aim to forecast their future positions over the next N time frames (where N is in seconds).

We adapt the Social Forces model [1] from single class to multiple classes. Each target makes a decision on its velocity $\mathbf{v}_i^{(t+1)}$. The energy function, E_{Θ},

Fig. 4. Illustration of the class assignment for each target. The same color represents the same navigation style (cluster) described in Fig. 3. Note that for a given target its class changes across time regardless of its physical class (*i.e.*, whether it is a pedestrian, bike, etc.). When the target is surrounded by other targets, its class changes with respect to its social sensitivity. In this scene, first we can observe a cyclist (shown as label 1 in the images) belonging to a black cluster, *i.e.*, being aggressive in his moves, then belonging to some milder clusters (purple and green). We also can see the evolution of a group of pedestrians (shown as labels 2,3) in the images), initially "mild" (green at $T = 1$), who become red at time $T = 3$ at which they decide to overtake another group and accelerate. (Color figure online)

associated to every single target is defined as:

$$
\begin{aligned}
E_\Theta(\mathbf{v}^{t+1}; s_i, \mathbf{s}_{-i}) &= \lambda_0(c)E_{damp}(\mathbf{v}^{t+1}; s_i) + \lambda_1(c)E_{speed}(\mathbf{v}^{t+1}; s_i) \\
&+ \lambda_2(c)E_{dir}(\mathbf{v}^{t+1}; s_i) + \lambda_3(c)E_{att}(\mathbf{v}^{t+1}; s_i) + \lambda_4(c)E_{group}(\mathbf{v}^{t+1}; s_i, \mathbf{s}_{A_i}) \\
&+ E_{ss}(\mathbf{v}^{t+1}; s_i, \mathbf{s}_{-i} | \sigma_d(v^t), \sigma_w(v^t), \beta)
\end{aligned}
\tag{6}
$$

where $\Theta = \{\lambda_0(c), \lambda_1(c), \lambda_2(c), \lambda_3(c), \lambda_4(c), \sigma_d(v^t), \sigma_w(v^t), \beta\}$ and c is the navigation class. More details on the definition of each of the energy terms can be found in [1].

In our work, we propose to compute σ_d, and σ_w directly from the observed velocity v^t using Eq. 5. Both distances σ_d, and σ_w will then be used to identify the navigation class c. For each class c, the parameter Θ can be learned from training data by minimizing the energy in Eq. 6.

Time Complexity. At test time, we only need to infer 3 parameters instead of few dozen at training time. Once these 3 parameters are inferred, we use the result from our k-means clustering to get the remaining parameters. Consequently, the computation cost went from 1 min (to infer all parameters) to 0.1 sec (to infer three parameters) (per frame and agent with a matlab implementation).

There is an additional computational complexity of $\mathcal{O}(nkdi)$ for k-means which comes at negligible computational cost (less than 1 ms), where n is the number of d-dimensional vectors (in this application 2), k the number of clusters (number of behavioral classes) and i the number of iterations needed until convergence which is not more than 10 iterations.

5.2 Multi-target Tracking

Problem formulation. Given the detected targets at each time frame (using for instance a target detector [43], or a background subtraction method [44]), we want to link the detection results across time to form trajectories, commonly referred to as tracking-by-detection.

As mentioned in Sect. 2, we modify the Multi-target Tracking (MTT) algorithm from Xiang *et al.* [39] to utilize our multi-class forecasting model based on social sensitivity. They formulate the MTT problem as a Markov Decision Process (MDP), which seeks to model the trajectory of targets according to a set of valid states (*e.g.*, $s_{tracked}, s_{lost}$) and transitions. They construct an approach to data association by computing a feature vector ϕ_i^t that describes the appearance of the targets in each of these possible states. They furthermore use a linear motion prior to reason on the navigation of targets, to thus determine a heuristic as to where a target should generally lie in future frames.

In order to evaluate the effectiveness of social sensitivity, we replace their linear motion prior with our multi-class forecasting method. More specifically, we modify ϕ_i^t, the feature vector for target i at time t as follows: Given the coordinates x_i^t, y_i^t of the target, we first apply our social force model to obtain a prediction x_i^{t+1}, y_i^{t+1} of the target at the next timestep. Then, given a list of candidate detections D^{t+1} for data association, we compute a normalized Euclidean distances $\{d_1, d_2, \ldots\}$ between each detection and the predicted coordinates, and append e^{-d_j} to ϕ_i^t, where d_j is the distance to detection j. In Sect. 6, we show the gain in performance from applying this method to our dataset.

6   Experiments

We run two sets of experiments: First, we study the performance of our method on trajectory forecasting problem. Then, we demonstrate the effectiveness of our proposed social sensitivity feature on state-of-the-art multi-target tracking - whereby the learnt forecasting models help the data association step.

6.1   Forecasting Accuracy

Datasets and metrics. We evaluate our multi-class forecasting framework on our new collected dataset as well as previous existing pedestrian-only ones [11,18]. Our dataset has two orders of magnitude more targets than the combined pedestrian-only datasets. We evaluate the performance of forecasting methods with the following measures: average prediction error over (i) the full estimated trajectory, (ii) the final estimated point, and (iii) the average displacement during collision avoidance's. Similar to [11,18], we observe trajectories for 2.4 s and predict for 4.8 s. We sub-sample a trajectory every 0.4 s. We also focus our evaluation when non-linear behaviors occur in the trajectories to not be affected by statistically long linear behaviors.

Quantitative and qualitative results. We evaluate our proposed multi-class forecasting framework against the following baselines: (i) single class forecasting methods such as SF [1] and IGP [45], (ii) physical class based forecasting (SF-pc), *i.e.*, using the ground truth physical class, and (iii) our proposed method

Table 2. Pedestrian Only dataset - Our 3 main evaluation methods, ordered as: Mean Average Displacement on all trajectories | Mean Average Displacement on collisions avoidance | Average displacement of the predicted final position (after 4.8 s).

Methods	Lin			LTA			SF [1]			IGP [45]			Our SF-mc		
ETH	0.80	0.95	1.31	0.54	0.70	0.77	0.41	0.49	0.59	**0.20**	**0.39**	**0.43**	0.41	0.46	0.59
HOTEL	0.39	0.55	0.63	0.38	0.49	0.64	0.25	0.38	0.37	**0.24**	0.34	0.37	**0.24**	**0.32**	**0.37**
ZARA 1	0.47	0.56	0.89	0.37	0.39	0.66	0.40	**0.41**	0.60	0.39	0.54	**0.39**	**0.35**	**0.41**	0.60
ZARA 2	0.45	0.44	0.91	0.40	0.41	0.72	0.40	0.40	0.68	0.41	0.43	0.42	**0.39**	**0.39**	0.67
UCY	0.57	0.62	1.14	0.51	0.57	0.95	0.48	0.54	0.78	0.61	0.62	1.82	**0.45**	**0.51**	**0.76**
AVERAGE	0.54	0.62	0.97	0.44	0.51	0.75	0.39	0.44	**0.60**	**0.37**	0.46	0.69	**0.37**	**0.42**	0.60

Table 3. Campus Dataset - Our 3 main evaluation methods, ordered as: Mean Average Displacement on all trajectories | Mean Average Displacement on collisions avoidance | Average displacement of the predicted final position (after 4.8 s).

Methods	Lin			SF			IGP [45]			SF-Physical			Our SF-mc		
ISENGARD	1.69	1.00	2.84	1.60	0.99	2.32	1.57	1.14	2.64	1.56	0.86	1.83	**1.53**	**0.84**	1.81
HOBBITON	1.17	1.01	1.81	**1.11**	0.82	1.70	**1.11**	**0.81**	2.25	1.12	**0.81**	**1.70**	1.12	0.83	1.70
EDORAS	0,91	0.83	1.03	0.80	**0.81**	0.89	1.33	0.85	2.61	0.79	**0.81**	0.89	**0.78**	0.82	0.89
MORDOR	1.72	1.10	3.80	1.38	0.89	2.30	**0.95**	0.69	**1.78**	1.37	0.65	2.30	1.37	**0.60**	2.30
FANGORN	1.02	0.75	2.00	0.94	0.41	1.66	0.96	0.69	1.67	0.90	0.40	**1.51**	**0.89**	**0.36**	1.51
VALLEY	1.38	0.86	2.45	1.29	0.87	2.02	1.20	0.75	2.46	1.01	**0.65**	**1.65**	**0.99**	0.66	1.65
AVERAGE	1.32	0.93	2.32	1.29	0.79	1.82	1.19	0.82	2.24	1.14	0.70	1.65	**1.11**	**0.69**	1.64

inferring navigation style of the targets referred to as SF-mc. We present our quantitative results in Tables 2 and 3:

On pedestrian-only dataset. (Table 2), our SF-mc performs the same as the single class Social Forces model in ETH dataset, and outperforms other methods in UCY datasets. This result can be justified by the fact that the UCY dataset is considerably more crowded, with more collisions, and therefore presenting different types of behaviors. Non-linear behaviors such as people stopping and talking to each other, walking faster, or turning around each others are more common in UCY than in ETH. Our forecasting model is able to infer these navigation patterns hence better predict the trajectories of pedestrians. We also report the performance of the IGP model on these pedestrian-only datasets for completeness. While IGP performs better on the less crowded dataset, it does not do well on the crowded ones. Notice that IGP uses the destination and time of arrival as additional inputs (which our method don't use).

On our multi-class dataset. (Table 3), we can see that our approach is more accurate on every scenes when a large amount of different classes are present. Our highest gain in performance is visible on the last three scenes, rich in classes and collisions (see Table 1). In HOBBITON and EDORAS scenes, our algorithm, trained on a multi-class dataset, matches the single class Social Forces. This happens because the social sensitivity feature stays the same across targets. In a scene with less number of classes, this could become a drawback, but yet our algorithm can perform with the same accuracy.

Table 4. Forecasting error with respect to the number of clusters in our new campus dataset.

	1 [1]	2	4	7	12	18
Mean error	1.14	1.16	1.15	**1.11**	1.12	1.20
Collision error	0.72	**0.68**	0.69	0.69	0.73	0.75
Final position error	1.84	1.74	1.70	**1.64**	1.69	1.80

Table 5. MTT tracking results.

	Rcll	Prcn	MT	ML	MOTA	MOTP	MOTAL
MDP [39] + Lin	74.1	80.1	44.18 %	**20.9 %**	51.5	74.2	55.4
MDP [39] + SF [1]	84.4	91.5	58.13 %	25.5 %	73.5	77.1	76.3
MDP [39] + our SF-mc	**86.1**	**92.6**	**60 %**	23.2 %	**75.6**	**78.2**	**79.3**

In Sect. 5.1, we present our method to forecast multiple classes of targets where we use the learned navigation styles as classes. One can argue that instead of using the navigation styles, we could use target's class (*e.g.* pedestrian, bicyclist, etc.). Table 3 compares the performance of using navigation style against targets' class (e.g. one parameter per pedestrian, bicyclist, and so on...), referred to as SF-Physical. We use the ground truth class label to associate each target to their corresponding physical class - this gives an upper bound accuracy. Interestingly, both multi-class strategies perform almost the same although our method does not require ground truth physical class labels as it automatically assign the navigation style class to each target as described in Sect. 5.1.

We further study the impact of the number of navigation styles (clusters) used by our method on the forecasting accuracy in Table 4. The optimal performance is obtained with 7 navigation styles which coincidentally, is very similar to the number of target's class (6 in our dataset). All experiments results in Table 3 are given considering 7 clusters.

Once a target is associated to one of the navigation styles, the corresponding parameter θ from Eq. 6 is used to predict the trajectory of the target. We can visualize the impact of the navigation style on the prediction. In Fig. 5, we show the predicted trajectories when several navigation styles are used to perform the forecasting. This shows the need to assign targets into specific classes.

Finally, in Fig. 6, we show more examples of our predicted trajectories and compare them with previous works. Our proposed multi-class framework outperforms previous methods in crowded scenes. However, in the absence of interactions, all methods perform the same.

6.2 Multi-target Tracking Evaluation

Dataset and metrics. We evaluate the impact of our social sensitivity feature on multi-target tracking using our newly collected dataset which contain images

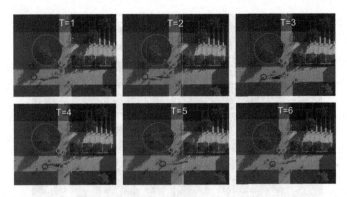

Fig. 5. We show the predicted trajectory of a given target (red circle) in which four different navigation styles are used to perform the prediction. The corresponding predicted trajectories are overlaid on one other and shown with different color codes (the same as those used for depicting the clusters in Fig. 3). The ground truth is represented in blue. Predicted trajectories are shown for 6 subsequent frames indicated by $T = 1, ..., 6$ respectively. Interestingly, when the target is far away from other targets (no interactions are taking place) the predicted trajectories are very similar to each other (they almost overlap and show a linear trajectory). However, when the red target gets closers to other targets (e.g. the ones indicated in yellow), the predicted trajectories start showing different behaviors depending on the navigation style: a conservative navigation style activates trajectories' prediction that keep large distances to the yellow targets in order to avoid them (green trajectory) whereas an aggressive navigation style activates trajectories' prediction that are not too distant from the yellow targets (red trajectory). Notice that our approach is capable to automatically associate the target to one of the 4 clusters based on the characteristics in the social sensitivity space that have been observed until present. In this example, our approach selects the red trajectory which is the closest to the ground truth's predicted trajectory (in blue). (Color figure online)

from crossing roads, sidewalks, and many other types of scene semantics with roughly 30 people observed per frame. We use the same evaluation metric as the MTT challenge [40], such as the multi object tracking accuracy (MOTA), or mostly tracked (MT) objects. In details the multiple object tracking accuracy (MOTA) takes into account false positives, missed targets and identity switches, multiple object tracking precision (MOTP) is simply the average distance between true and estimated targets. The other metrics such as mostly tracked (MT) and mostly lost (ML) counts the number of mostly tracked trajectories (more than 80 % of the frames) and mostly lost (was not able to track more than 20 % of the frames). The full list of metrics can be found in [40].

Quantitative results. We evaluate our proposed MTT algorithm against the following baselines: (i) Xiang's MDP algorithm [39] with a linear motion prior, (ii) [39] with single class forecasting model [1], (iii) [39] with our proposed multi-class forecasting model based on social sensitivity. We show that using our proposed

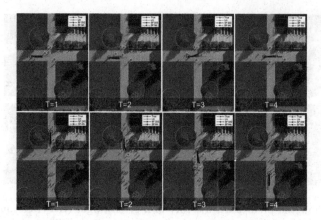

Fig. 6. Illustration of the predicted trajectories by our SF-mc method (in red) across time. Predicted trajectories are shown for 4 subsequent frames indicated by $T = 1, ..., 4$ respectively. We compare them with previous work [1]. The ground truth is represented in blue. Our proposed multi-class framework outperforms previous methods when targets start interacting with other target ($t = 2, 3, 4$). However, in the absence of interactions ($t = 1$), all methods perform the same. (Color figure online)

MTT with social sensitivity feature outperforms previous work. Our quantitative results are shown in Table 5.

7   Conclusions

We have presented our efforts to study human navigation at a new scale. We have contributed the first large-scale dataset of aerial videos from multiple classes of targets interacting in complex outdoor spaces. We have presented our work on predicting the trajectories of several classes of targets without explicitly solving the target classification task. We further demonstrate the impact of our forecasting model on multi-target tracking. Future work will study other forecasting methods such as Long Short-Term Memory (LSTM) to jointly solve the prediction task. Finally, by sharing our dataset, we hope that researchers will push the limits of existing methods in modeling human interactions, learning scene specific human motion, or detecting and tracking tiny targets from UAV data.

References

1. Yamaguchi, K., Berg, A.C., Ortiz, L.E., Berg, T.L.: Who are you with and where are you going? In: 2011 IEEE Conference on Computer Vision and Pattern Recognition (CVPR), pp. 1345–1352. IEEE (2011)
2. Pellegrini, S., Ess, A., Van Gool, L.: Improving data association by joint modeling of pedestrian trajectories and groupings. In: Daniilidis, K., Maragos, P., Paragios, N. (eds.) ECCV 2010, Part I. LNCS, vol. 6311, pp. 452–465. Springer, Heidelberg (2010)

3. Leal-Taixé, L., Fenzi, M., Kuznetsova, A., Rosenhahn, B., Savarese, S.: Learning an image-based motion context for multiple people tracking. In: CVPR, pp. 3542–3549. IEEE (2014)
4. Choi, W., Savarese, S.: A unified framework for multi-target tracking and collective activity recognition. In: Fitzgibbon, A., Lazebnik, S., Perona, P., Sato, Y., Schmid, C. (eds.) ECCV 2012, Part IV. LNCS, vol. 7575, pp. 215–230. Springer, Heidelberg (2012)
5. Smeulders, A.W., Chu, D.M., Cucchiara, R., Calderara, S., Dehghan, A., Shah, M.: Visual tracking: an experimental survey. IEEE Trans. Pattern Anal. Mach. Intell. **36**(7), 1442–1468 (2014)
6. Xie, D., Todorovic, S., Zhu, S.C.: Inferring dark matter and dark energy from videos. In: 2013 IEEE International Conference on Computer Vision (ICCV), pp. 2224–2231. IEEE (2013)
7. Choi, W., Savarese, S.: Understanding collective activitiesof people from videos. IEEE Trans. Pattern Anal. Mach. Intell. **36**(6), 1242–1257 (2014)
8. Lan, T., Wang, Y., Yang, W., Mori, G.: Beyond actions: discriminative models for contextual group activities. In: Advances in Neural Information Processing Systems, pp. 1216–1224 (2010)
9. Choi, W., Shahid, K., Savarese, S.: What are they doing? Collective activity classification using spatio-temporal relationship among people. In: 2009 IEEE 12th International Conference on Computer Vision Workshops (ICCV Workshops), pp. 1282–1289. IEEE (2009)
10. Kitani, K.M., Ziebart, B.D., Bagnell, J.A., Hebert, M.: Activity forecasting. In: Fitzgibbon, A., Lazebnik, S., Perona, P., Sato, Y., Schmid, C. (eds.) ECCV 2012, Part IV. LNCS, vol. 7575, pp. 201–214. Springer, Heidelberg (2012)
11. Lerner, A., Chrysanthou, Y., Lischinski, D.: Crowds by example. In: Computer Graphics Forum, vol. 26, pp. 655–664. Wiley Online Library (2007)
12. Trautman, P., Ma, J., Murray, R.M., Krause, A.: Robot navigation in dense human crowds: the case for cooperation. In: 2013 IEEE International Conference on Robotics and Automation (ICRA), pp. 2153–2160. IEEE (2013)
13. Cucchiara, R., Grana, C., Tardini, G., Vezzani, R.: Probabilistic people tracking for occlusion handling. In: 2004 Proceedings of the 17th International Conference on Pattern Recognition, ICPR 2004, vol. 1, pp. 132–135. IEEE (2004)
14. Hughes, R.L.: The flow of human crowds. Annu. Rev. Fluid Mech. **35**(1), 169–182 (2003)
15. Helbing, D., Molnar, P.: Social force model for pedestrian dynamics. Phys. Rev. E **51**(5), 4282 (1995)
16. Boyle, P., Frean, M.: Dependent gaussian processes. Adv. Neural Inf. Process. Syst. **17**, 217–224 (2005)
17. Tay, M.K.C., Laugier, C.: Modelling smooth paths using gaussian processes. In: Laugier, C., Siegwart, R. (eds.) Field and Service Robotics. Springer Tracts in Advanced Robotics, vol. 42, pp. 381–390. Springer, Heidelberg (2008)
18. Pellegrini, S., Ess, A., Schindler, K., Van Gool, L.: You'll never walk alone: modeling social behavior for multi-target tracking. In: 2009 IEEE 12th International Conference on Computer Vision, pp. 261–268. IEEE (2009)
19. Treuille, A., Cooper, S., Popović, Z.: Continuum crowds. ACM Trans. Graph. (TOG) **25**(3), 1160–1168 (2006)
20. Antonini, G., Venegas, S., Thiran, J.P., Bierlaire, M.: A discrete choice pedestrian behavior model for pedestrian detection in visual tracking systems. In: Advanced Concepts for Intelligent Vision Systems, ACIVS 2004. Number EPFL-CONF-87109. IEEE (2004)

21. Antonini, G., Bierlaire, M., Weber, M.: Discrete choice models of pedestrian walking behavior. Transp. Res. Part B Methodological **40**(8), 667–687 (2006)
22. Wang, J.M., Fleet, D.J., Hertzmann, A.: Gaussian process dynamical models for human motion. IEEE Trans. Pattern Anal. Mach. Intell. **30**(2), 283–298 (2008)
23. Ziebart, B.D., Ratliff, N., Gallagher, G., Mertz, C., Peterson, K., Bagnell, J.A., Hebert, M., Dey, A.K., Srinivasa, S.: Planning-based prediction for pedestrians. In: 2009 IEEE/RSJ International Conference on Intelligent Robots and Systems, IROS 2009, pp. 3931–3936. IEEE (2009)
24. Henry, P., Vollmer, C., Ferris, B., Fox, D.: Learning to navigate through crowded environments. In: 2010 IEEE International Conference on Robotics and Automation (ICRA), pp. 981–986. IEEE (2010)
25. Ziebart, B.D., Maas, A.L., Bagnell, J.A., Dey, A.K.: Maximum entropy inverse reinforcement learning. In: AAAI, pp. 1433–1438 (2008)
26. Levine, S., Popovic, Z., Koltun, V.: Nonlinear inverse reinforcement learning with gaussian processes. In: Advances in Neural Information Processing Systems, pp. 19–27 (2011)
27. Thompson, S., Horiuchi, T., Kagami, S.: A probabilistic model of human motion and navigation intent for mobile robot path planning. In: 2009 4th International Conference on Autonomous Robots and Agents, ICARA 2009, pp. 663–668. IEEE (2009)
28. Luber, M., Stork, J.A., Tipaldi, G.D., Arras, K.O.: People tracking with human motion predictions from social forces. In: 2010 IEEE International Conference on Robotics and Automation (ICRA), pp. 464–469. IEEE (2010)
29. Mehran, R., Oyama, A., Shah, M.: Abnormal crowd behavior detection using social force model. In: 2009 IEEE Conference on Computer Vision and Pattern Recognition, CVPR 2009, pp. 935–942. IEEE (2009)
30. Leal-Taixé, L., Pons-Moll, G., Rosenhahn, B.: Everybody needs somebody: modeling social and grouping behavior on a linear programming multiple people tracker. In: 2011 IEEE International Conference on Computer Vision Workshops (ICCV Workshops), pp. 120–127. IEEE (2011)
31. Alahi, A., Ramanathan, V., Fei-Fei, L.: Socially-aware large-scale crowd forecasting. In: CVPR (2014)
32. Kretzschmar, H., Kuderer, M., Burgard, W.: Learning to predict trajectories of cooperatively navigating agents. In: 2014 IEEE International Conference on Robotics and Automation (ICRA), pp. 4015–4020. IEEE (2014)
33. Yi, S., Li, H., Wang, X.: Understanding pedestrian behaviors from stationary crowd groups. In: Proceedings of the IEEE Conference on Computer Vision and Pattern Recognition, pp. 3488–3496 (2015)
34. Fleuret, F., Berclaz, J., Lengagne, R., Fua, P.: Multicamera people tracking with a probabilistic occupancy map. IEEE Trans. Pattern Anal. Mach. Intell. **30**(2), 267–282 (2008)
35. Pirsiavash, H., Ramanan, D., Fowlkes, C.C.: Globally-optimal greedy algorithms for tracking a variable number of objects. In: CVPR (2011)
36. Alahi, A., Boursier, Y., Jacques, L., Vandergheynst, P.: A sparsity constrained inverse problem to locate people in a network of cameras. In: 2009 16th International Conference on Digital Signal Processing, pp. 1–7. IEEE (2009)
37. Alahi, A., Jacques, L., Boursier, Y., Vandergheynst, P.: Sparsity driven people localization with a heterogeneous network of cameras. J. Math. Imaging Vis. **41**(1), 1–20 (2011)

38. Roshan Zamir, A., Dehghan, A., Shah, M.: GMCP-tracker: global multi-object tracking using generalized minimum clique graphs. In: Fitzgibbon, A., Lazebnik, S., Perona, P., Sato, Y., Schmid, C. (eds.) ECCV 2012, Part II. LNCS, vol. 7573, pp. 343–356. Springer, Heidelberg (2012)
39. Xiang, Y., Alahi, A., Savarese, S.: Learning to track: online multi-object tracking by decision making. In: International Conference on Computer Vision (ICCV), pp. 4705–4713 (2015)
40. Leal-Taixé, L., Milan, A., Reid, I., Roth, S., Schindler, K.: MOTChallenge 2015: towards a benchmark for multi-target tracking. [cs], April 2015. arXiv:1504.01942
41. Amer, M.R., Xie, D., Zhao, M., Todorovic, S., Zhu, S.-C.: Cost-sensitive top-down/bottom-up inference for multiscale activity recognition. In: Fitzgibbon, A., Lazebnik, S., Perona, P., Sato, Y., Schmid, C. (eds.) ECCV 2012, Part IV. LNCS, vol. 7575, pp. 187–200. Springer, Heidelberg (2012)
42. Shu, T., Xie, D., Rothrock, B., Todorovic, S., Chun Zhu, S.: Joint inference of groups, events and human roles in aerial videos. In: The IEEE Conference on Computer Vision and Pattern Recognition (CVPR), June 2015
43. Alahi, A., Bierlaire, M., Vandergheynst, P.: Robust real-time pedestrians detection in urban environments with low-resolution cameras. Transp. Res. Part C Emerg. Technol. 39, 113–128 (2014)
44. Alahi, A., Bierlaire, M., Kunt, M.: Object detection and matching with mobile cameras collaborating with fixed cameras. In: Workshop on Multi-camera and Multi-modal Sensor Fusion Algorithms and Applications-M2SFA2 2008 (2008)
45. Trautman, P., Krause, A.: Unfreezing the robot: navigation in dense, interacting crowds. In: 2010 IEEE/RSJ International Conference on Intelligent Robots and Systems (IROS), pp. 797–803. IEEE (2010)

Bayesian Image Based 3D Pose Estimation

Marta Sanzari[✉], Valsamis Ntouskos[✉], and Fiora Pirri[✉]

ALCOR Lab, DIAG, Sapienza University of Rome, Rome, Italy
{sanzari,ntouskos,pirri}@diag.uniroma1.it

Abstract. We introduce a 3D human pose estimation method from single image, based on a hierarchical Bayesian non-parametric model. The proposed model relies on a representation of the idiosyncratic motion of human body parts, which is captured by a subdivision of the human skeleton joints into groups. A dictionary of motion snapshots for each group is generated. The hierarchy ensures to integrate the visual features within the pose dictionary. Given a query image, the learned dictionary is used to estimate the likelihood of the group pose based on its visual features. The full-body pose is reconstructed taking into account the consistency of the connected group poses. The results show that the proposed approach is able to accurately reconstruct the 3D pose of previously unseen subjects.

Keywords: Human pose estimation · Hierarchical non-parametric Bayes

1 Introduction

Human pose estimation from images has been considered since the early days of computer vision and many approaches have been proposed to face this quite challenging problem. A large part of the literature has concentrated on identifying a 2D description of the pose mainly by trying to estimate the positions of the human joints in the images. Recently, attention has been shifted to the problem of recovering the full 3D pose of a subject either from a single frame or from a video sequence. Despite this is an ill-posed problem due to the ambiguities emerging by the projection operation, the constraints induced by both human motion kinematics and dynamics have facilitated the recovery of some accurate 3D human pose estimation.

In this work we approach the problem of 3D pose estimation from a single image building a hierarchical framework based on Bayesian non-parametric estimation. A schema of the framework is shown in (Fig. 3). Following the schema flow, we divide the human body into different parts and we study the idiosyncratic motion behavior of each part independently from the others. In this way

Electronic supplementary material The online version of this chapter (doi:10.1007/978-3-319-46484-8_34) contains supplementary material, which is available to authorized users.

© Springer International Publishing AG 2016
B. Leibe et al. (Eds.): ECCV 2016, Part VIII, LNCS 9912, pp. 566–582, 2016.
DOI: 10.1007/978-3-319-46484-8_34

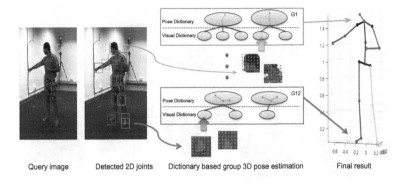

Query image   Detected 2D joints   Dictionary based group 3D pose estimation   Final result

Fig. 1. Method overview; 3D pose estimation given a query image.

we learn the principal motion modes of each part. Each body part is specified by a group of joints, and its motion is represented by pose features obtained by the principal motion direction on the $SE(3)$ manifold with respect to a reference pose. As a natural reference pose we consider the "Vitruvian man" pose presented in Fig. 2 together with the selected groups.

The visual features for each group are the PHOG features of [1], which are computed using the state-of-the-art approach of [2]. Assuming a correspondence between the visual and pose features both the space of visual features and pose features are partitioned, in such a way that from the visual features it is possible to accede to the non observed pose features. These nested partitions are built up for each group with a hierarchical non-parametric Bayesian model, designed purposefully to deal with the inverse projection problem, from 2D to 3D. Indeed, the goal is to recover the unknown human poses just from the available visual features, since visual features are the only available observations.

Fig. 2. "Vitruvian" pose with defined groups.

The hierarchical model is based on two nested countably infinite mixtures of normal distributions. The first level builds a dictionary of 3D human poses by considering various examples of 3D human poses taken from a large number of motion sequences, while the second level takes into account the corresponding images obtained from a number of view points. Indeed, the dictionary is built by partitioning the space of 3D poses with a Dirichlet process mixture model (DPM). The partition is defined on the space of poses specified by the principal motion directions on the $SE(3)$ manifold. The nested part of the model builds the visual dictionary on top of the pose dictionary, and it is also based on Dirichlet process mixture models. Here the mixture processes the PHOG [1] features extracted from a window centered at the 2D position of each joint in the given image.

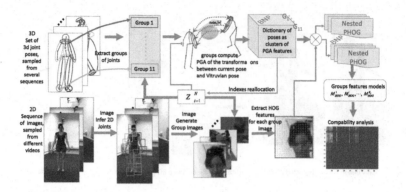

Fig. 3. Schematic representation of the proposed hierarchical model.

Based on the learned dictionary 3D pose estimation is performed as follows (Fig. 1). Given a query image we extract the 2D positions of the joint in the image using a state-of-the-art approach [2] and compute the corresponding PHOG features for each group. From these features we infer the most likely cluster of the visual dictionary, which in turns indicates the cluster of 3D poses with the highest probability for the given group. The final 3D pose is reconstructed by assembling together the most representative poses of the selected clusters for each group. Clusters are selected considering also the compatibility between the group poses.

In the following, Sect. 2 discusses related work and Sect. 3 the structure of the training and testing data, and preliminaries. Section 4 presents the architecture of the proposed model and how pose estimation is performed. In Sect. 5 we present the results obtained with our method in comparison with state-of-the-art 3D pose estimation approaches. Finally, Sect. 6 discusses conclusions and future work.

2   Related Work

Human pose estimation (HPE) has been extensively studied during the years by considering videos, 2D images and depth data, [3–5]. There exist several open problems; among them we mention variations in human appearance, clothing and background, arbitrary camera view-point, self-occlusions and obstructed visibility, ambiguities and inconsistency in the estimated poses.

Different features can be chosen to describe the different types of data. Focusing on 2D input data, some works assume the 2D body joints locations already given [6], while others extract features from silhouettes such as HOG [7], PHOG [1], SIFT [8] and shape context [9], or dense trajectories [10].

In detail, concerning 3D HPE from videos, very recently [10] introduced a spatio-temporal matching (STM) among 3D Motion Capture (MoCap) data and 2D feature trajectories providing the estimated camera view-point and a selected subset of tracked trajectories. In our approach, instead, as in [11,12], body parts in 2D are detected by using the algorithm introduced in [2].

In the last years many works have approached the estimation of the poses via deep learning as in [13–16]. In Zhou et al. [17] a convolutional neural network is used to estimate the 2D joint locations in the image. 3D pose sequences are then estimated via an EM algorithm over the entire video by considering a sparse model of 3D human pose in input where each 3D body pose is represented by a linear combination of a predefined basis of poses. Wang et al. [12] propose an overcomplete dictionary of poses learned from 3D human poses and HPE is managed by minimizing an L_1 norm error between the projection of the 3D pose and the corresponding 2D detection, optimizing via alternating direction method. In [18], body part detectors provide proposals for the location of 2D pose of visible limbs. The 2D pose is then refined via non-parametric belief propagation and the corresponding 3D pose is estimated by learning the parameters of a mixture of experts model.

In [19] a relevance vector machine is proposed to learn a reconstruction function that is a linear combination over a set of basis functions. The authors extract shape descriptors from a set of 2D images and the corresponding 3D poses. [20] store a set of different images and full body poses, both in 2D, together with the corresponding viewpoint. A test image is directly matched with all the training images via the shape context matching procedure. The 3D positions are then estimated via the Taylor's approach [21]. Differently from ours, their methods is instance-based, which is not feasible for a real-time application, without also the possibility of generalizing over the training images.

Assuming that joint positions are already given in 2D with the corresponding image, [6] propose to learn pose-dependent joint angle limits from a MoCap dataset, to form a prior for estimating the 3D poses, together with the camera parameters. A tracking-by-detection technique is used in [22] to collect a small number of consecutive video frames. A novel class of descriptors, called tracklets, is defined and 3D poses are recovered from them. In [23], human pose is estimated via a non-parametric Bayesian network and structure learning, considering the dependencies of body parts. In our approach, instead, nested non-parametric clustering is considered to find relations among the appearance and the 3D pose of each body part. As in [23], our approach is able to generalize over the observed data so as to generate new poses never seen before.

In [24], besides the construction of a large dataset, a benchmark among various HPE approaches is performed. [25] use boolean relationships between body components, called posebits, for training an SVM for retrieving the 3D body pose. Finally, [26] consider annotated 2D images and MoCap data as independent input data to first obtain an initial pose model which is then refined iteratively.

3   Description of Input Data

Human 3.6 M Dataset. The dataset we consider for the development of our HPE algorithm is Human 3.6 M [24], which includes about 3.6 million video frames with associated labelled joints and poses of different human subjects performing actions. Relevant for us are the motion capture (MoCap) data (provided as joints rotations and translations) acquired with the Vicon MoCap System; data of 11 subjects performing 15 different actions are available. The 3D joint poses are provided as transformation matrices evaluated with respect to a fixed world origin as described in the next subsection.

Additionally, we consider the corresponding video frames captured from high resolution RGB cameras from 4 different viewpoints. This is done to ensure that we take in consideration a sufficiently varied set of poses captured from different view points. We consider the 4 views of each pose as distinct instances. Furthermore, we are given also the positions of the MoCap skeleton mapped into the image domain. This is used for the 2D joints inference in images, as explained in the following. As in [17], we use 5 subjects (S1, S5, S6, S7, S8) for the training stages, and 2 subjects (S9, S11) for testing. Moreover, we consider only 18 out of the entire set of 32 3D joints by excluding joints corresponding to fingers and toes and by merging together joints corresponding to the same 3D position in order to avoid redundancy in the data. Therefore, for each video frame we have the association among the image, the 3D joint poses, and the 2D joints mapped in the image.

PGA-Based Features. We now describe the basic principles used for extracting features representing the pose of each group. A MoCap sequence amounts to the poses of a subject at regular time instances. At each time instant the pose of the subject is represented by a given configuration of its joints. In detail, a skeleton $\mathcal{J}$ is specified by 18 joints, where the first one is the index of the root joint. Each joint has a single parent joint, except from the root joint. The configuration of the i-th joint is represented by a homogeneous transformation matrix $T_i \in SE(3)$, a *Lie Group* with identity element defined by the 4×4 identity matrix. By defining a proper metric the Lie Group is a Riemannian manifold, on which we can define (via the exponential mapping) the notion of geodesic between two elements on the manifold (see [27–29]), which is locally the shortest path that connects two group elements. Henceforth each joint is considered as a rigid body moving in space with respect to some coordinate system. Note that this coordinate system may change according to the MoCap system used for acquiring the data.

We breakdown the skeleton into 11 sub-body groups G_s, with $s = 1, \ldots, 11$. Each group contains M_s joints and is defined as $G_s = \{J_{\psi(1)}, \ldots, J_{\psi(M_s)}\} \subseteq \mathcal{J}$, with $\psi(\cdot)$ providing the relation of the group joint indices with respect to the skeleton indexes. All joints belonging to a group have a parent within the same group, except the root of the group, which is included in at least one other group, whenever it is not the root of the entire skeleton, this proviso is required by the reconstruction of the full-body pose (Algorithm 2).

Breaking down the skeleton into groups is motivated by the idiosyncratic motion of body parts, and to appraise this fact we use the Da Vinci's Vitruvian pose as the reference skeleton configuration, adapting an idea of [30]. The Vitruvian pose and the joint groups considered here are shown in Fig. 2. Now, given

Table 1. Average geodesic distance between the Karcher mean and the rotations of each joints for each group over the whole dataset.

	G_1	G_2	G_3	G_4	G_5	G_6	G_7	G_8	G_9	G_{10}	G_{11}
J_1	1.102	1.152	1.152	1.149	1.144	1.143	1.108	1.145	1.106	1.110	1.141
J_2	1.102	1.521	1.521	1.521	1.524	1.518	1.108	1.535	1.106	1.110	1.510
J_3	-	1.520	1.519	1.519	1.540	1.521	-	1.530	-	-	1.519

a pose, we find the transformation between the current pose configuration and the Vitruvian pose, for each group G_s, $s = 1, \ldots, 11$. Then, the pose feature set for each group is obtained from the principal direction, computed via *Principal Geodesic Analysis* [31] from these transformations.

More specifically, for each G_s, $s = 1, \ldots, 11$ the transformation matrices mapping the joints from a current arbitrary pose to the Vitruvian pose are computed, taking into account the dependencies from the parent pose. We compute the Karcher mean [32] μ of the group transformations, following the algorithm of Afsari [33]. In particular, regarding rotation averaging, the center of mass should be within a geodesic distance no larger than $\pi/2$ in order to be unique, and thus well defined [33–35]. Table 1 shows the average geodesic distance between the intrinsic mean and the rotations of the individual joints for each group over the whole dataset, suggesting that the Karcher mean computation is well defined for this particular choice of groups.

Hence we compute the tangent space of SE(3) at μ and select the principal direction. This direction is the one that best interprets the variability of the motion that the group of joints performs in order to return to the configuration of joints of that sub-body group, in the Vitruvian rest pose. The actual computation of the principal direction in SE(3) is given in [36], and for the transformation considered here the whole computation is resumed in Algorithm 1.

2D Joints Estimation from Monocular Images. In both learning and testing stages we extract PHOG visual features for each considered group. For this purpose, given an image sampled from a video of the dataset in Human 3.6 M, the first step is the estimation of the 2D joints together with suitable surrounding boxes in the image domain.

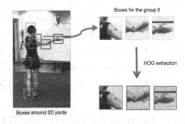

In detail, since we have considered the 3D skeleton subdivided into 11 groups we recover 11 boxes (or windows), one for each imaged group. From each of these boxes we extract the most

Fig. 4. Left: 2D joints estimation using [2]; **Right:** HOG descriptor extraction for a group of joints.

suitable image descriptors for our purpose, that are the Pyramid Histogram of Oriented Gradients (PHOG) [1,7]. We have decided to consider a pyramid with levels equal to 0 and 1 and 8 bins spanning an angle of 360°, for each joint in the group, this choice leads to feature vectors of size m, $m \in \{16, 24, 32\}$.

Data: The pose of the group G_s given by the corresponding set of
   homogeneous transformations $\{T_{\psi(1)}, \ldots, T_{\psi(M_s)}\}$; the Vitruvian
   joints configuration $\{T_{\psi(1)}^V, \ldots, T_{\psi(M_s)}^V\}$.

Result: Feature vector for the pose of the group G_s

1. Move the root of G_s to the root of the corresponding group in
   Vitruvian pose.
2. Compute the "disparity" between each joint current pose and the
   Vitruvian pose as $\hat{G}_s = \{\hat{T}_{\psi(1)}, \ldots, \hat{T}_{\psi(M_s)}\}$, taking into account the
   dependency of each joint pose from its parent pose.
3. Compute the Karcher mean as in [33], extending it to translation.
4. Compute the variance S as in [31], but using the twist
   $\mathbf{u}^\vee = (\omega^\top, \mathbf{v}^\top)^\top$, obtained from the Lie algebra of the given
   transformations, to extend the PGA to SE(3), with ω and $\mathbf{v}$ the
   instantaneous angular and linear velocities, as in [36].
5. Compute the eigenvector and eigenvalues of S and return the first
   principal direction in the Lie algebra $se(3)$.
6. Build the feature vector in $\mathbb{R}^7$ using the instantaneous angular and
   linear velocities from the principal direction, forming a twist, together
   with the norm of the instantaneous linear velocity [36].

Algorithm 1. Feature extraction for the pose of a group G_s of joints

The estimation of the 2D joints from images is performed using the state-of-the-art approach [2]. This approach is particularly suitable for the estimation of the sought-after boxes surrounding joints of human body. We train a model using the algorithm described in [2] using images sampled from the videos in the Human 3.6 M dataset. In particular, we used 61750 images for training taken by the 5 different subjects (S1, S5, S6, S7, S8) performing all the actions, provided together with the 2D joints positions. We used 24700 images for testing taken from the remaining subjects (S9, S11) performing the same actions. From the boxes obtained we consider the central points being the 2D joints. Note that we know the ordering of the parts and so of the joints. Figure 4 shows the result of the boxes extraction for two different testing images and the process of PHOG extraction from an image of a group when the PHOG level is set to 0.

4   Features to Poses Mapping: A Hierarchical Model

In this section we present the hierarchical model connecting 3D poses and visual features, which make it possible to infer a human pose from the visual features. The hierarchical model takes care of the main aspects of this inference process. First of all it generates a dictionary of poses, for each group. The dictionary collects poses in clusters, where the similarity within a cluster is defined according to the parameters of the underlying distribution. In particular, the dictionary for the poses is a list of indexes specifying for each pose the set of poses sharing the same partition block – or the same parameters. Because a set of similar poses admits several views, the visual features indexed in the same partition generate a mixture of features too. Finally, a principle of compatibility amid clusters of different groups is defined.

In this section we consider $(X_1, X_2, \ldots, X_N)$, $(Y_1, Y_2, \ldots, Y_N)$ sets of real valued random variables; with $\mathbf{X} = (\mathbf{x}_1, \ldots, \mathbf{x}_N)$ and $\mathbf{Y} = (\mathbf{y}_1, \ldots \mathbf{y}_N)$ their realization. In particular, we consider here a multivariate $\mathbf{X}$, for the principal direction of the poses of a group of joints, such that a random sample of observations $\mathbf{x}_i \in \mathbb{R}^7$. We consider also a multivariate $\mathbf{Y}$ for the PHOG features, with $\mathbf{y}_i \in \mathbb{R}^m$, $m \in \{16, 24, 32\}$. To simplify reading we sometimes talk about poses, though in fact we consider the twists obtained by the principal direction of the set of rototranslations of the joints of a group, with respect to the same joints in the Vitruvian pose, as explained in Sect. 3.

Given the training sets $D_s^X = \{\mathbf{x}_i | \mathbf{x}_i \in \mathbb{R}^7,$ $i = 1, \ldots, N\}$ and $D_s^Y = \{\mathbf{y}_i | \mathbf{y}_i \in \mathbb{R}^m, i = 1, \ldots, N,$ $m \in \{16, 24, 32\}\}$ as the sampled pose and visual features for a group $G_s, s = 1, \ldots, 11$ (a subset of joints as specified in Fig. 2), we want to partition these sets, though neither the partition dimensions nor the specific allocations are known. Hence we resort to the Bayesian nonparametric perspective on mixtures with countably infinite number of components. In this perspective we are given a measurable space $\mathbb{X}$, a discrete measure μ on this space, a collection of continuous observations, latent variables $(\theta_1, \ldots, \theta_K)$ admitting a distribution, with K a random number $\leq N$, and a probability distribution function $F(\cdot | \theta_i)$, parametrized by the random vari-

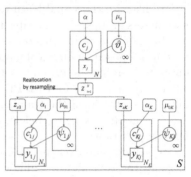

Fig. 5. Plate representation of $S = 1, \ldots, 11$ fold replication of the stacked DPM for pose and visual features. Inner plates are replicated for each DPM.

ables θ_i. This setting leads to the popular Dirichlet process mixture model, where $F(\cdot | \theta_i)$ is the kernel of the mixture, here the normal distribution, and $\mu \sim DP(\alpha, \mu_0)$, is the mixing measure, with concentration parameter α and mean $E\{\mu\} = \mu_0$. This is usually expressed in a hierarchical representation as:

$$X_i | \theta_i = F(\cdot | \theta_i), \qquad i = 1, \ldots, K$$
$$\theta_1, \ldots, \theta_N | \mu \sim_{iid} \mu \text{ and } \mu \sim DP(\alpha, \mu_0). \tag{1}$$

Then $X \sim \int F(X | \theta) d\mu(\theta)$ is a mixture of distributions with countably infinite number of components [37,38]. Since the measure μ is discrete, each pair of latent random variables can take the same value with probability $p > 0$. Where the taken value is precisely that of a mixture component. Hence the observations will be allocated by the latent variables to a random number of components.

Different representations have been given of the DPM since [39] and several methods have been devised to sample the mixture parameters from the

$DP(\alpha, \mu_0)$ (see [40,41]). Recently a number of contributions have explored advanced methods to obtain a parallel implementation [42,43], and to obtain a distribution on the partition of the tangent space to the sphere [44], introducing mixture models for data lying on the sphere, and on Riemaniann manifolds [45]. In this work we did not consider our data as placed on a curved manifold. Despite features data for poses are obtained from the principal direction on SE(3), each twist extended with the velocity norm, as described in Sect. 3 is independent of the others and forms an exchangeable set. As we do not consider any trajectory between the pose feature vectors we may not consider them on a curved manifold, though we are exploring the interesting modeling that a manifold representation could lead to. Several approaches have also considered different forms of hierarchical and nested NPB models. Though here we could not use the hierarchical model of [46], since the pose clusters of the same group, likewise the visual features, do not share any element. Neither could be used across groups, since groups have different ranges of PHOG variates and the number of clusters depends on the number of poses of a specific body part.

Our proposed hierarchical model relies on the hypothesis that for the training datasets there exists an index set $\{Z\}_{i=1}^N$, with a bijective mapping h between any two datasets. So, for each PHOG feature vector $\mathbf{y}_i$ there exists a corresponding pose vector $\mathbf{x}_i$ in the training set. This fact does not affects generality nor exchangeability, as we see below, since the index set labels the sampled features not the partitions.

To generate an exchangeable random partition for the mixture of poses, we consider the well known Chinese restaurant process (CRP) [47]. On the other hand, to compute the parameter α we followed the approach of [48], defining the prior of α as coming from the class of mixtures of gamma distributions, with small initial scale and shape parameters. For inference we resort to Gibbs sampling [49,50] with conjugate priors.

Given the distribution on the partition induced by the mixture model, a finite set of parameters $\hat{\theta}_1, \ldots, \hat{\theta}_K$ is obtained, together with a cluster indexing $\mathbf{c} = (c_1, \ldots, c_N)$ for each element in the training set. The prediction of a new pose $\mathbf{x}_{N+1}$ is defined by the posterior predictive distribution:

$$p(\mathbf{x}_{N+1}|\mathbf{X}) = \sum_{c_1, \ldots c_{N+1}} \int p(\mathbf{x}_{N+1}|c_{N+1}, \theta)p(c_{N+1}|\mathbf{c})p(\mathbf{c}, \theta|\mathbf{X})d\theta \qquad (2)$$

Here:

$$p(\mathbf{c}, \theta|\mathbf{X}) = \frac{1}{H} \prod_{k=1}^{K} \mu_0(\theta_k) \prod_{j=1}^{n} F(x_j|\theta_{c_j})P(c_j), \qquad (3)$$

where H is the marginal likelihood of the mixture of Normals given the computed parameters. And, according to the sampling process induced by the CRP, $p(c_{N+1}|\mathbf{c})$ is:

$$p(c_{N+1} = k|\mathbf{c}) = \begin{cases} \dfrac{n_k}{N-1+\alpha} & k \leq K \\ \dfrac{\alpha}{N-1+\alpha} & \text{otherwise} \end{cases} \qquad (4)$$

Here n_k is the size of the set of elements in $\mathbf{c}$ having value k. Since poses are continuous and somehow unpredictable, the case that a new pose asks for the initialization of a new cluster has probability greater than zero. However, once the partition is specified, we make it available to the visual inference, recovering the association between the index set $\{Z\}_{i=1}^{N}$, and each element in each cluster of the dictionary. Because of the label switching problem we prefer to reallocate the indexes $\{Z\}_{i=1}^{N}$ to the clusters. Hence, for each pair $\hat{\theta}_{c_i} = (\eta_{c_i}, \Sigma_{c_i})$ we sample a number of pose vectors $\{\mathbf{u}\}_{|\mathbf{c}_i|}$, proportional to the current ones from $(\eta_{c_i}, \beta D)$, with $\Sigma_{c_i} = U D U^{\top}$, and β a filtering parameter. Given the sampled set we find, in the training set D_s^X, the pose vectors $\mathbf{x}$ which minimize the square error, w.r.t. some specific threshold, i.e. $\{\mathbf{x} \in \mathbf{X} \mid \|\mathbf{x} - \mathbf{u}\|_2 \leq \epsilon, \epsilon > 0\}$. This fact allows, at the same time, to regularize the clusters around their mean, and to reallocate the observations into the clusters together with the observation index set $\{Z\}_{i=1}^{N}$. Therefore according to the model, the induced partition, and the reallocation, given elements $s = \{\mathbf{x}_{s1}, \ldots, \mathbf{x}_{sk}\} \mid \hat{\theta}_{c_j}$ we have that $h^{-1}(s) = z_{sj}$, a subindex set $z_{sj} \in \{Z\}_{i=1}^{N}$, such that $h(z_{sj}) = \{\mathbf{y}_{s1}, \ldots, \mathbf{y}_{sk}\}$, namely it returns a choice of visual features. The subindex z_{sj} specifies which set of features, having index in $\{Z\}_{i=1}^{N}$ should be allocated to the cluster generated by parameters θ_{c_j}, due to the bijection between the training data. Repeating this for all parameters $\hat{\theta}_{c_j}$, $j = 1, \ldots K$, and for each group, a CRP process is computed for each feature set indexed by z_{sj}. The probability measures generating these new set of DPM, are obviously specific for each PHOG feature set. The structure of the hierarchical model is illustrated in Fig. 5. Each feature set indexed by z_{sj} can specify different views of the same pose, and possibly under different lighting conditions. Further, we expect that similar poses of different people, yet belong to the same cluster, and the PHOGs might capture this, when represented by a mixture distribution. Thus we induce a new partition exploiting the Gamma additive property. For each cluster of poses, generated by each group, there exists a set of models $\mathbb{M}_s = (\mathcal{M}_{PHOG}^1, \ldots, \mathcal{M}_{PHOG}^{K_s})$, with K varying according to the group $s, s = 1, \ldots, 11$.

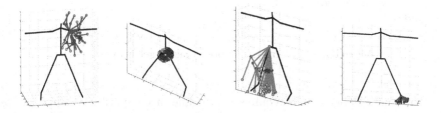

Fig. 6. Most representative poses of the learned dictionary for the groups *Left Arm, Hips, Right Leg, Left Foot*, with respect to the "Vitruvian pose".

Now, given a new observation $\mathbf{y}^\star$, this could be either a query or a new measure. Then the posterior predictive of Eq. (2) should integrate with respect to the parameters of the feature set indexed by z_{sj}, for $j = 1, \ldots, K$ and with respect to each feature set $\mathbf{Y}_{z_{sj}}$, collected in the training. Without loss of generality we can do this into two steps. In the first step we compute the density, finding the model that best fits $\mathbf{y}^\star$. We can do this because the index set for the visual features is not required for this step:

$$\arg\max_{\mathcal{M}_{PHOG}} p(\mathbf{y}^\star|\xi) = \sum_h \sum_j \pi_{hj}\varphi_h(\mathbf{y}^\star|\xi_{hj}, \mathcal{M}_{PHOG}^h). \tag{5}$$

Here the πs are the mixing proportion and $\varphi(\cdot|\xi)$ is the Normal density with parameters ξ for the specific PHOG features set. Once the model is chosen, hence the cluster, the predictive distribution in Eq. (2), can be applied to the PHOG feature $\mathbf{y}^\star$. Note that if a new component is generated, this now will have its reference pose being the mean of the cluster it is hooked to. Note that if the subindexes of the clusters generated by the visual features $\mathbf{y}$ with subindex z_{sj} are needed, to identify a particular feature and its connection to a particular pose, then a resampling is necessary, as we did with the poses. Otherwise the mean pose can be used. We can see this process as a funnel guiding visual features into the small opening of the pose set, and possibly widening the opening as new observations come in.

Data: Pairwise group compatibility probabilities r_{ij} (Eq. 6).
Result: Most likely set of consistent pose clusters.
Find the most likely pose cluster for the root group (G_8);
Add all the connected groups of G_8 (denoted $children(G_8)$) in the set $\mathcal{G}_{open}$;
while $\mathcal{G}_{open}$ *is not empty* **do**
    for *Each group* $G_s \in \mathcal{G}_{open}$ **do**
        Find its most likely pose cluster taking into account the
        compatibilities $\{r_{ij}\}_{i\in\{1,M_s\}}$ with respect to the selected cluster j
        of its parent group $parent(G_s)$
    end
    Remove (G_s) from $\mathcal{G}_{open}$;
    Add $children(G_s)$ in $\mathcal{G}_{open}$
end

Algorithm 2. Consistent pose cluster selection.

The final inference step requires a principle of compatibility amid groups from which derive the consistent pose selection summarized in Algorithm 2. We define the intergroup clusters compatibility as follows. Let i, j, be two clusters from groups q and s. Let $W_{ij} = |z_{qj} \cap z_{si}|$ with $|\cdot|$ the cardinality and let $D_{ij} = z_{qj} \cup z_{si}$ and $p(m_{ij} = 1) = W_{ij}/|D_{ij}|$.

The probability that the two intergroup clusters are compatible is given as:

$$r_{ij} = \frac{p(D_{ij}|m_{ij}=1)p(m_{ij}=1)}{p(D_{ij}|m_{ij}=1)p(m_{ij}=1) + p(D_{ij}|m_{ij}=0)(1-p(m_{ij}=1))} \tag{6}$$

With

$$p(D_{ij}|m_{ij} = 1) = \gamma \sum_{D_{ij}} \pi_i \delta_{D_{ij}}(\mathbf{x}) + (1 - \gamma) \sum_{D_{ij}} \pi_j \delta_{D_{ij}}(\mathbf{x}) \tag{7}$$

Where $\delta_{D_{ij}}(\mathbf{x}) = 1$ if $\mathbf{x} \in D_{ij}$ and zero otherwise, π_i and π_j are the mixing proportions of the DPM of the two clusters, and $0 \leq \gamma \leq 1$ balances the contribution from the two clusters. While, where the two clusters are completely uncorrelated:

$$p(D_{ij}|m_{ij} = 0) = \prod_{D_{ij}} \pi_i \pi_j \tag{8}$$

5   Results

Dictionary Learning. As described in Sect. 3, we consider the dataset Human 3.6 M [24] to evaluate our 3D pose estimation algorithm. In order to obtain the dictionaries of the 3D poses we first apply the decomposition of the joints in groups according to Fig. 2 and then compute PGA-based features for each group joints, as described in Sect. 3. As the dataset contains 3D poses synchronized with video frames at a high rate (50 Hz), we subsample with a factor of 12 in order to remove redundant data. Further we compute the PHOG features as described in Sect. 3. The number of clusters generated for each group by the DPM models are reported in Table 2.

Table 2. Number of clusters generated by the DPM models for the PHOG and the PGA-based features for each group of joints.

Groups	1	2	3	4	5	6	7	8	9	10	11	12
Nr. of pose clusters	56	155	38	85	20	49	90	88	58	49	52	16
Avg. nr. of visual components	18	31	31	25	22	22	4	22	22	11	18	13

The significance of pose clusters is shown in Fig. 6, where the mean poses are visualized for the groups *Left Arm, Hips, Right Leg, Left Foot*.

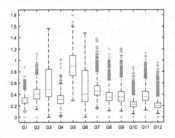 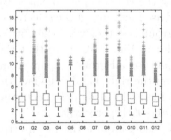

Fig. 7. Error distribution for the PHOG (left) and the PGA (right) features.

3D Pose Estimation. Using the learned dictionary of poses and visual features we perform 3D pose estimation for the testing part of the dataset, namely for the actions performed by subjects S9 and S11. For each query image, the 2D joint positions in the image are estimated by using [2], and they are grouped together forming the groups of Fig. 2. For each group, the PHOG features are then extracted, as described in Sect. 3, and the corresponding cluster of the visual dictionary is selected as the most likely one according to the learned hierarchical model. We calculate the error of the visual features as the euclidean distance of the extracted features with respect to the most representative visual features of the selected cluster. The mean of this error together with the 25th and 75th percentiles for each group, are shown in the left box-plot of Fig. 7. Note that as the errors refer to distances, we expect that they follow a χ^2 distribution instead of a normal one. We observe that the errors of the PHOG features are low in average for most of the groups. The groups corresponding to the hands and the arms (G_3, G_4, G_5, G_6) show higher errors, mainly because of the high variability of their appearance.

The 3D pose of the whole body is obtained according to Algorithm 2.

Table 3. Average per joint error between the estimated 3D pose and the ground truth in mm. Best values in bold.

	Directions	Discussion	Eating	Greeting	Phoning	Photo	Posing	Purchases
LinKDE [24]	132.71	183.55	132.37	164.39	162.12	205.94	150.61	171.31
Li et al. [13]	-	136.88	96.94	124.74	-	168.68	-	-
Tekin et al. [51]	102.39	158.52	87.95	126.83	118.37	185.02	114.69	107.61
Zhou et al. [17]	87.36	109.31	**87.05**	103.16	116.18	143.32	106.88	**99.78**
Ours	**48.82**	**56.31**	95.98	**84.78**	**96.47**	**105.58**	**66.30**	107.41
	Sitting	SittingDown	Smoking	Waiting	WalkDog	Walking	WalkTogether	**Average**
LinKDE [24]	151.57	243.03	162.14	170.69	177.13	96.60	127.88	162.14
Li et al. [13]	-	-	-	-	132.17	69.97	-	-
Tekin et al. [51]	136.15	205.65	118.21	146.66	128.11	**65.86**	**77.21**	125.28
Zhou et al. [17]	124.52	199.23	107.42	118.09	**114.23**	79.39	97.70	113.01
Ours	**116.89**	**129.63**	**97.84**	**65.94**	130.46	92.58	102.21	**93.15**

Examples of the recovered poses for query images of the subjects S9 and S11 are shown in Fig. 8. We calculate the euclidean distance of the PGA-based features of the true 3D pose of the subject, with respect to the most representative PGA-based features of the selected cluster for each group. The mean distance for each group together with the 25th and 75th percentiles, are shown in the right box-plot of Fig. 7. We note that the average errors of the PGA-based features are small for all groups, apart from G_5 and G_6 which correspond to the right arm and the right hand. The fact that the PGA features reside in a deeper level of the hierarchical model affects the presence of an increased number of errors above the 95th percentile.

We also compute the mean error of the joint positions of the recovered 3D pose with respect to the ground truth 3D pose of the subject. This error, compared to the error of other state of the art approaches is reported in Table 3.

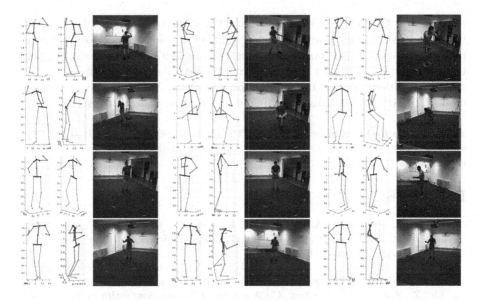

Fig. 8. Examples of query images and the recovered 3D pose. More results are reported in the supplementary material.

The results show that our method gives slightly worse results only with respect to [17] for the 'Eating' and 'Purchases' actions, and for the walking actions with respect to [51] and [17]. In summary, the proposed method outperforms other recently proposed state of the art 3D pose estimation methods both in average and also for the vast majority of actions considered in the Human 3.6 M dataset.

Efficiency of the Method. For the 2D joints estimation training uses 61750 frames of the Human 3.6 M dataset taking about 10^4 s, [2] does not report efficiency. For the hierarchical DPM we consider a training set of 130272 frames, asking for $\sim 8.5 \times 10^5$ s for the poses partitioning and $\sim 7 \times 10^4$ s for the visual features partitioning. This considering main Gibbs cycles of 1800 iterations. Full-pose consistency takes around 0.05 s for a single query, and the total percentage of queries not satisfying it are around 23 %. Once parameters are learned pose computation takes around 0.96 s, with PGA and group computation taking around 0.07 s. These results are obtained with a computer equipped with four Xeon E5-2643, 3.70 GHz CPUs and 64 GB RAM.

6   Conclusions

We present a novel method for 3D human pose estimation from a single image based on a hierarchical Bayesian non-parametric model. The proposed model captures idiosyncratic variations of the motion and the appearance of different body parts, identified by groups of joints. The decomposition in groups avoids redundant configurations, obtaining a more concise dictionary of poses and visual appearances. Given the learned model a 3D pose query can be resolved in real-time. The results show that the proposed model is able to generalize and accurately reconstruct the 3D pose of previously unseen subjects. Our results improve the current state of the art though we aim to further ameliorate them, by considering additional constraints of the pose structure. We shall also consider to move the NBP on the Riemann manifold for the pose features considered.

Acknowledgement. Supported by EU FP7 TRADR (609763) and EU H2020 SecondHands (643950) projects. The authors thank the anonymous reviewers for their comments.

References

1. Bosch, A., Zisserman, A., Munoz, X.: Representing shape with a spatial pyramid kernel. In: Proceedings of the International Conference on Image and Video Retrieval, pp. 401–408. ACM (2007)
2. Yang, Y., Ramanan, D.: Articulated human detection with flexible mixtures of parts. IEEE Trans. Pattern Anal. Mach. Intell. **35**(12), 2878–2890 (2013)
3. Liu, Z., Zhu, J., Bu, J., Chen, C.: A survey of human pose estimation: the body parts parsing based methods. J. Vis. Commun. Image Represent. **32**, 10–19 (2015)
4. Hen, Y.W., Paramesran, R.: Single camera 3D human pose estimation: a review of current techniques. In: Proceedings of the International Conference for Technical Postgraduates (TECHPOS), pp. 1–8. IEEE (2009)
5. Poppe, R.: Vision-based human motion analysis: an overview. Comput. Vis. Image Underst. **108**(1), 4–18 (2007)
6. Akhter, I., Black, M.J.: Pose-conditioned joint angle limits for 3D human pose reconstruction. In: Proceedings of the IEEE Conference on Computer Vision and Pattern Recognition, pp. 1446–1455 (2015)
7. Dalal, N., Triggs, B.: Histograms of oriented gradients for human detection. In: Proceedings of the IEEE Conference on Computer Vision and Pattern Recognition, vol. 1, pp. 886–893. IEEE (2005)
8. Lowe, D.G.: Object recognition from local scale-invariant features. In: Proceedings of the International Conference on Computer Vision, vol. 2, pp. 1150–1157. IEEE (1999)
9. Belongie, S., Malik, J., Puzicha, J.: Shape matching and object recognition using shape contexts. IEEE Trans. Pattern Anal. Mach. Intell. **24**(4), 509–522 (2002)
10. Zhou, F., Torre, F.: Spatio-temporal matching for human detection in video. In: Fleet, D., Pajdla, T., Schiele, B., Tuytelaars, T. (eds.) ECCV 2014. LNCS, vol. 8694, pp. 62–77. Springer, Heidelberg (2014). doi:10.1007/978-3-319-10599-4_5
11. Simo-Serra, E., Ramisa, A., Alenyà, G., Torras, C., Moreno-Noguer, F.: Single image 3D human pose estimation from noisy observations. In: Proceedings of the IEEE Conference on Computer Vision and Pattern Recognition, pp. 2673–2680. IEEE (2012)
12. Wang, C., Wang, Y., Lin, Z., Yuille, A., Gao, W.: Robust estimation of 3D human poses from a single image. In: Proceedings of the IEEE Conference on Computer Vision and Pattern Recognition, pp. 2361–2368 (2014)
13. Li, S., Chan, A.B.: 3D human pose estimation from monocular images with deep convolutional neural network. In: Cremers, D., Reid, I., Saito, H., Yang, M.-H. (eds.) ACCV 2014. LNCS, vol. 9004, pp. 332–347. Springer, Heidelberg (2015). doi:10.1007/978-3-319-16808-1_23

14. Tompson, J.J., Jain, A., LeCun, Y., Bregler, C.: Joint training of a convolutional network and a graphical model for human pose estimation. In: Advances in Neural Information Processing Systems, pp. 1799–1807 (2014)
15. Ouyang, W., Chu, X., Wang, X.: Multi-source deep learning for human pose estimation. In: Proceedings of the IEEE Conference on Computer Vision and Pattern Recognition, pp. 2329–2336 (2014)
16. Toshev, A., Szegedy, C.: DeepPose: human pose estimation via deep neural networks. In: Proceedings of the IEEE Conference on Computer Vision and Pattern Recognition, pp. 1653–1660 (2014)
17. Zhou, X., Zhu, M., Leonardos, S., Derpanis, K., Daniilidis, K.: Sparseness meets deepness: 3D human pose estimation from monocular video. In: Proceedings of the IEEE Conference on Computer Vision and Pattern Recognition. IEEE (2016)
18. Sigal, L., Black, M.J.: Predicting 3D People from 2D Pictures. In: Perales, F.J., Fisher, R.B. (eds.) AMDO 2006. LNCS, vol. 4069, pp. 185–195. Springer, Heidelberg (2006). doi:10.1007/11789239_19
19. Agarwal, A., Triggs, B.: Recovering 3D human pose from monocular images. IEEE Trans. Pattern Anal. Mach. Intell. 28(1), 44–58 (2006)
20. Mori, G., Malik, J.: Recovering 3D human body configurations using shape contexts. IEEE Trans. Pattern Anal. Mach. Intell. 28(7), 1052–1062 (2006)
21. Taylor, C.J.: Reconstruction of articulated objects from point correspondences in a single uncalibrated image. In: Proceedings of the IEEE Conference on Computer Vision and Pattern Recognition, vol. 1, pp. 677–684. IEEE (2000)
22. Andriluka, M., Roth, S., Schiele, B.: Monocular 3D pose estimation and tracking by detection. In: Proceedings of the IEEE Conference on Computer Vision and Pattern Recognition, pp. 623–630. IEEE (2010)
23. Lehrmann, A.M., Gehler, P.V., Nowozin, S.: A non-parametric Bayesian network prior of human pose. In: Proceedings of the IEEE International Conference on Computer Vision (2013)
24. Ionescu, C., Papava, D., Olaru, V., Sminchisescu, C.: Human 3.6m: large scale datasets and predictive methods for 3D human sensing in natural environments. IEEE Trans. Pattern Anal. Mach. Intell. 36(7), 1325–1339 (2014)
25. Pons-Moll, G., Fleet, D., Rosenhahn, B.: Posebits for monocular human pose estimation. In: Proceedings of the IEEE Conference on Computer Vision and Pattern Recognition, pp. 2337–2344 (2014)
26. Yasin, H., Iqbal, U., Krüger, B., Weber, A., Gall, J.: 3D pose estimation from a single monocular image. arXiv preprint arXiv:1509.06720 (2015)
27. Flaherty, F., do Carmo, M.: Riemannian Geometry. Mathematics: Theory and Applications. Birkhäuser, Boston (2013)
28. Zefran, M., Kumar, V., Croke, C.: On the generation of smooth three-dimensional rigid body motions. IEEE Trans. Robot. Autom. 14, 576–589 (1998)
29. Duan, X., Sun, H., Peng, L.: Riemannian means on special euclidean group and unipotent matrices group. Sci. World J. 2013 (2013). doi:10.1155/2013/292787
30. Taylor, J., Shotton, J., Sharp, T., Fitzgibbon, A.: The vitruvian manifold: inferring dense correspondences for one-shot human pose estimation. In: Proceedings of the IEEE Conference on Computer Vision and Pattern Recognition, pp. 103–110. IEEE (2012)
31. Fletcher, P., Lu, C., Pizer, S., Joshi, S.: Principal geodesic analysis for the study of nonlinear statistics of shape. IEEE Trans. Med. Imaging 23, 995–1005 (2004)
32. Karcher, H.: Riemannian center of mass and mollifier smoothing. Commun. Pure Appl. Math. 30(5), 509–541 (1977)

33. Afsari, B., Tron, R., Vidal, R.: On the convergence of gradient descent for finding the riemannian center of mass. SIAM J. Control Optim. **51**(3), 2230–2260 (2013)
34. Kendall, W.S.: Probability, convexity, and harmonic maps with small image. I: uniqueness and fine existence. Proc. Lond. Math. Soc. **3**(2), 371–406 (1990)
35. Hartley, R., Trumpf, J., Dai, Y., Li, H.: Rotation averaging. Int. J. Comput. Vis. **103**(3), 267–305 (2013)
36. Natola, F., Ntouskos, V., Pirri, F., Sanzari, M.: Bayesian non-parametric inference for manifold based MoCap representation. In: Proceedings of the International Conference on Computer Vision (ICCV), pp. 4606–4614 (2015)
37. Lo, A.Y.: On a class of Bayesian nonparametric estimates. I: density estimate. Ann. Statist. **12**, 351–357 (1984)
38. Ferguson, T.: Bayesian density estimation by mixtures of normal distributions. Recent Adv. Stat. **1**, 287–302 (1983)
39. Ferguson, T.: A Bayesian analysis of some nonparametric problems. Ann. Stat. **1**, 209–230 (1973)
40. Gorür, D.: Nonparametric Bayesian discrete latent variable models for unsupervised learning. Ph.D. thesis, Max Planck Institute for Biological Cybernetics (2007)
41. Sudderth, E.B.: Graphical models for visual object recognition and tracking. Ph.D. thesis, MIT (2006)
42. Lovell, D., Adams, R.P., Mansingka, V.: Parallel markov chain monte carlo for Dirichlet process mixtures. In: Workshop on Big Learning, NIPS (2012)
43. Chang, J., Fisher III., J.W.: Parallel sampling of DP mixture models using subcluster splits. In: Advances in Neural Information Processing Systems, pp. 620–628 (2013)
44. Straub, J., Chang, J., Freifeld, O., Fisher III., J.W.: A Dirichlet process mixture model for spherical data. In: AISTATS (2015)
45. Kim, H.J., Xu, J., Vemuri, B.C., Singh, V.: Manifold-valued Dirichlet processes. In: Proceedings of the 2015 International Conference on Machine Learning, vol. 2015, pp. 1199–1208 (2015)
46. Teh, Y.W., Jordan, M.I., Beal, M.J., Blei, D.M.: Hierarchical Dirichlet processes. J. Am. Stat. Assoc. **101**, 1566–1581 (2012)
47. Pitman, J.: Combinatorial Stochastic Processes: Ecole D'Eté de Probabilités de Saint-Flour XXXII-2002. Springer, Heidelberg (2006)
48. West, M.: Hyperparameter estimation in Dirichlet process mixture models. ISDS discussion paper# 92–A03, Duke University (1992)
49. Neal, R.M.: Markov chain sampling methods for Dirichlet process mixture models. J. Comput. Graph. Stat. **9**(2), 249–265 (2000)
50. Jain, S., Neal, R.M.: A split-merge Markov chain monte carlo procedure for the Dirichlet process mixture model. J. Comput. Graph. Stat. **13**, 158–182 (2012)
51. Tekin, B., Sun, X., Wang, X., Lepetit, V., Fua, P.: Predicting people's 3D poses from short sequences. arXiv preprint arXiv:1504.08200 (2015)

Efficient and Robust Semi-supervised Learning Over a Sparse-Regularized Graph

Hang Su[1]([✉]), Jun Zhu[1], Zhaozheng Yin[2], Yinpeng Dong[1], and Bo Zhang[1]

[1] State Key Lab of Intelligent Technology and Systems,
Tsinghua National Lab for Information Science and Technology,
Department of Computer Science and Technology,
Center for Bio-Inspired Computing Research, Tsinghua University, Beijing, China
{suhangss,dcszj,dcszb,dongyp13}@tsinghua.edu.cn
[2] Department of Computer Science,
Missouri University of Science and Technology, Rolla, USA
yinz@mst.edu

Abstract. Graph-based Semi-Supervised Learning (GSSL) has limitations in widespread applicability due to its computationally prohibitive large-scale inference, sensitivity to data incompleteness, and incapability on handling time-evolving characteristics in an open set. To address these issues, we propose a novel GSSL based on a batch of informative beacons with sparsity appropriately harnessed, rather than constructing the pairwise affinity graph between the entire original samples. Specifically, (1) beacons are placed automatically by unifying the consistence of both data features and labels, which subsequentially act as indicators during the inference; (2) leveraging the information carried by beacons, the sample labels are interpreted as the weighted combination of a subset of characteristics-specified beacons; (3) if unfamiliar samples are encountered in an open set, we seek to expand the beacon set incrementally and update their parameters by incorporating additional human interventions if necessary. Experimental results on real datasets validate that our algorithm is effective and efficient to implement scalable inference, robust to sample corruptions, and capable to boost the performance incrementally in an open set by updating the beacon-related parameters.

Keywords: Semi-supervised learning · Beacon · Sparse representation · Online learning

1 Introduction

In the era of information deluge, Semi-Supervised Learning (SSL) [1,2], which implements inference by combining a limited amount of labeled data and abundant unlabeled data in open sources, is a promising direction to cope with the

This research is partly supported by the National Basic Research Program (973 Program) of China (Nos. 2013CB329403, 2012CB316301), National Natural Science Foundation of China (Nos. 61571261, 61322308, 61332007), China Postdoctoral Science Foundation (No. 2015M580099). Zhaozheng Yin is supported by NSF CAREER Award IIS-1351049 and NSF EPSCoR grant IIA-1355406.

© Springer International Publishing AG 2016
B. Leibe et al. (Eds.): ECCV 2016, Part VIII, LNCS 9912, pp. 583–598, 2016.
DOI: 10.1007/978-3-319-46484-8_35

flood of big data. Among various SSL methods, Graph-based Semi-Supervised Learning (GSSL) [3,4] is an appealing paradigm thanks to the prevalence of graph data and its good capability in exploiting intrinsic manifold structures.

Recent years have witnessed significant advances in GSSL, including Mincut [5], Random Walk [6,7], Manifold Regularization [8], Gaussian Fields and Harmonic Functions (GFHF) [9], and Learning with Local and Global Consistency (LLGC) [10]. Nevertheless, the algorithms are often sensitive to data noise and improper parameter settings [11,12], i.e., the graph structures may be changed dramatically due to the corruption of features or shift of global hyperparameters. To address these issues, Cheng et al. [11] proposed an ℓ_1-graph, which is robust to data noise and adaptive to graph structures. However, these algorithms are actually designed for small or medium sized data; the high computational complexity blocks their widespread applicability to real-life problems.

To temper the time complexity, a lot of efforts have been made during the past years, e.g., Nystrom approximation [13], the eigenfunction approximation [14], ensemble projection [15], etc. Among these works, anchor-based algorithms are attractive [16,17], which construct a tractable large graph by coupling anchor-based label prediction and adjacency matrix design. However, anchors in these methods are obtained in two separate steps—anchors are placed in the feature domain only based on the feature information but neglecting the useful knowledge in labels; the anchor labels are then estimated by propagating the labels of human-annotated samples whose locations in the feature domain are already fixed. We would expect that these two steps can mutually enhance each other if they are properly unified and learned jointly.

Above all, the aforementioned algorithms assume that queries are drawn from a closed pool and the properties of training and testing samples are the same. Unfortunately, this assumption may not be valid in many real-world scenarios, where the training and testing data may be collected under different experimental conditions and therefore often exhibit differences in their statistics; and properties of samples may gradually change over time thus incomplete knowledge is present at the training phase. In this case, a classifier learned from the initial labeling tends to result in more and more misclassifications if no further knowledge is provided or no update paradigm is applied.

1.1 Our Proposal

To address the above issues (i.e., *data noise, time complexity and statistics shift*), we propose an ℓ_1-Beacon Graph based semi-supervised algorithm, which places a batch of characteristic-specific beacons in the feature domain, and represent the original samples with a subset of beacons. Prediction on missing labels can be implemented with label fusion of the corresponding beacons.

To mitigate the computational bottleneck, the label prediction is implemented by weighted averaging the soft labels of a subset of *beacons*, which is a concept in large-scale network analysis [18]. In this paper, we use *beacons* to represent the super-nodes whose characteristics are propagated from the human specified information, and ultimately facilitate the sample inference. Specifically, the beacons are generated automatically by minimizing the sample-to-beacon reconstruction error while preserving the label consistence jointly. The resultant beacons therefore behave as indicators to guide the inference procedure, i.e., the information provided by human annotations is propagated to the beacons and "lights" their indications or soft labels. Different from the orthogonal anchor planes in [19], our method does not requires orthogonal planes to represent/code samples.

In the testing phase with voluminous or streaming data to handle, the label inference is implemented by setting up a relational connection between the original samples and the most relevant beacons, which are identified by enforcing the sparsity. The ℓ_1-regularization also offers robustness to the corrupted or incomplete sample features [11], which is an inevitable nightmare [20] for the large-scale data analysis. The main reason is because the sample-to-beacon relationship can be estimated appropriately by making use of the abundant information embedded in the uncorrupted feature entries under the sparsity constraint.

When unfamiliar samples are encountered in the *open-set* inference, e.g., the reconstruction error is above a user-specified threshold, we seek to expand the beacon set and update their characteristic parameters dynamically by incorporating additional human interventions. Consequently, the performance is boosted incrementally with a small amount of computation for the unseen data with time-evolving statistics.

Compared with the anchor-based algorithms in [16,17], the proposed algorithm has the major novelties below

- To address the beacon construction, we propose to learn the beacons by utilizing both the label information and feature information jointly, which generalizes the K-means clustering anchors in [16,17] and provides a more flexible representation for data lying in a complex manifold.
- To explore the sample-to-beacon relationship, we derive the neighboring beacons of a sample and the corresponding relationship weights automatically by solving an ℓ_1-norm regularized problem, which yields an adaptive and flexible representation especially for data in a complex high-dimensional manifold. In contrast, the samples are represented with s neighboring anchors in [16], which may incur significant performance degeneration if the global parameter "s" is set improperly. With sparsity properly harnessed, our method also offers adaptations of local neighborhood structures and robustness for the corrupted sample features.
- To address the issues in the open-set inference, we propose to expand the beacon set and update their characteristics incrementally, which offers advantages to handle the mismatch between training and testing data.

In summary, the proposed algorithm is much more robust to data noise, provides a more adaptive and stable graph construction to local neighborhood structures, needs fewer beacons to realize the comparable performance, and boosts the performance incrementally when unfamiliar samples appear.

2   Construction of ℓ_1-Beacon Graph

Semi-supervised learning typically involves a dataset that consists of N_l labeled data $\mathcal{L} \triangleq \{(\mathbf{x}_l, \mathbf{y}_l)\}_{l=1}^{N_l}$ and N_u unlabeled data $\mathcal{U} \triangleq \{\mathbf{x}_u\}_{u=1}^{N_u}$, where $N_u \gg N_l$ and $N = N_l + N_u$. Label propagation algorithms [9,10] entangle all these samples, and build a huge graph to model the pairwise similarity between samples in the entire dataset, which require to calculate the inverse of a large Laplacian matrix with the cubic time complexity $O(N^3)$. Therefore, it becomes an unbearable computational burden for processing gigantic even medium-sized datasets.

In this case, it is desirable to develop more efficient algorithms by taking advantage of both the labeled and a portion of the unlabeled data to build a training dataset $\mathcal{X}^{\text{train}}$, and train a classification model to handle unseen data outside the training data set. Much fewer training samples are used for these models and thus more efficient for the label prediction.

In this paper, we propose to generate a batch of "beacons", which behave as indicators to guide the inference. Original samples are represented by a linear combination of the beacons, resulting in a sample-to-beacon relationship matrix. The predicted labels of samples are inferred as the weighted combination of a subset of beacons as,

$$\mathbf{Y} = \mathbf{F}\mathbf{Z}, \text{ with } \mathbf{Z} \in \mathbb{R}^{M \times N}, \ M \ll N, \tag{1}$$

where $\mathbf{Y}$ is the prediction label matrix with each column being the label of a specific sample; $\mathbf{B} = [\mathbf{b}_1, \cdots, \mathbf{b}_M]$ is a beacon set and $\mathbf{F} = [f(\mathbf{b}_1), \cdots, f(\mathbf{b}_M)]$ is the label matrix with each column corresponding to the label of a beacon; and $\mathbf{Z} = [\mathbf{z}_1, \cdots, \mathbf{z}_N]$ is the weight matrix in which each column indicates the sample-to-beacon relationship for a specific sample. To solve the problem in Eq. (1), we need to

- Determine the informative beacons $\mathbf{B}$ along with their labelling characteristics $\mathbf{F}$ effectively; and
- Calculate the sample-to-beacon relationship matrix $\mathbf{Z}$ efficiently despite the incompleteness and corruption existing in data.

2.1   Design of Informative Beacons

In [16,17], the authors proposed to generate K anchors using the clustered centers by K-means, and estimate the corresponding relationship matrix by representing samples as linear combinations of s nearest neighboring anchors. However, it is difficult to determine the optimal parameters of K and s in advance. For instance, the distribution of samples and their neighboring anchors may vary at different areas in the feature domain, which results in distinctive neighborhood structures for each sample. In this case, the graph generated via local anchor embedding [16] may introduce unreasonable neighborhood structures due to the improper parameters. In many cases, these unfavorable structures incur a significant performance degeneration since the labels may be propagated via those edges across samples belonging to different classes.

To address these issues, we seek a beacon set that yields a flexible and adaptive representation by utilizing the ℓ_1-norm regularization. Additionally, the beacon generation and their corresponding characteristic estimations are unified within a framework with both the features and label information harnessed, thereby encouraging their mutual enhancements.

With a unified representation, we denote the beacon-related parameters as $\Psi = [\mathbf{B}; \mathbf{F}]$ with each column corresponding to a specific beacon embedding its related characteristic information. Therefore, $\mathbf{B} = \mathbf{S}_b \Psi$ with $\mathbf{S}_b = [\mathbf{I}_d, \mathbf{0}] \in \mathbb{R}^{d \times (d+c)}$, and $\mathbf{F} = \mathbf{S}_f \Psi$ with $\mathbf{S}_f = [\mathbf{0}, \mathbf{I}_c] \in \mathbb{R}^{c \times (d+c)}$. d and c are the sample dimension and corresponding numbers of classes, respectively; and $\mathbf{I}_d$ and $\mathbf{I}_c$ are the identity matrices with proper sizes.

By taking both the feature and label information into account, the beacon generation can be derived by minimizing the risk functions for both labeled and unlabeled data and also preserving the global graph smoothness as

$$(\Psi^*, \mathbf{Z}^*) = \arg \min_{\Psi, \mathbf{Z}} R_{\mathcal{L}}(\Psi, \mathbf{Z}) + R_{\mathcal{U}}(\Psi, \mathbf{Z}) + \lambda R_{\mathbf{Y}}(\Psi, \mathbf{Z}),$$

$$\text{s.t. } \forall i \in [1, N], \|\mathbf{z}_i\|_1 \leq T, \ \mathbf{z}_i \geq \mathbf{0}, \ \mathbf{y}_i = \mathbf{S}_f \Psi \mathbf{z}_i. \tag{2}$$

Specifically, the risk function on the labeled set is defined as

$$R_{\mathcal{L}}(\Psi, \mathbf{Z}) = \sum_{i=1}^{N_l} \left\| \begin{bmatrix} \mathbf{x}_i \\ \mathbf{y}_i \end{bmatrix} - \Psi \mathbf{z}_i \right\|_2^2, \tag{3}$$

which jointly penalizes the reconstruction error in the feature domain and preserves the consistence in the label domain; the risk function on the unlabeled set is defined as

$$R_{\mathcal{U}}(\Psi, \mathbf{Z}) = \sum_{i=1}^{N_u} \|\mathbf{x}_i - \mathbf{S}_b \Psi \mathbf{z}_i\|_2^2, \tag{4}$$

which is the residual error on all unlabeled samples; and the graph smoothness regularization is defined as

$$R_{\mathbf{Y}}(\Psi, \mathbf{Z}) = \sum_{i,j}^{N} \|\mathbf{y}_i - \mathbf{y}_j\|_2^2 w_{ij}, \tag{5}$$

where $\mathbf{y}_i$ and $\mathbf{y}_j$ are encouraged to be similar if $\mathbf{x}_i$ and $\mathbf{x}_j$ are close in the intrinsic geometry of the feature domain.

In Eq. (2), $\mathbf{Z} = [\mathbf{z}_1, \cdots, \mathbf{z}_N]$ is the weight matrix with each column corresponding to the sample-to-beacon relationship of a specific sample; T is the sparsity level, which is related to the number of beacons that are chosen for the representation; $w_{ij} = \mathbf{z}_i^T \mathbf{z}_j$ is the pairwise affinity between $\mathbf{x}_i$ and $\mathbf{x}_j$, which is measured in terms of correlation (inner product).

When deriving the problem in Eq. (2), the beacons are placed in the feature domain and lightened up simultaneously by providing its label characteristics.

By incorporating the feature and label information together, the generated beacons are therefore consistent with both labels and features. Additionally, the results are also benefited from the graph smoothness, which favors the label consistence when samples share similar features.

By introducing the ℓ_1-norm regularization on the sample-to-beacon relationship $\mathbf{z}_i$, the most relevant beacons are selected automatically to represent the samples. Therefore, it provides a more adaptive representation for data lying in a complex manifold by reducing the spurious connections between the dissimilar sample-to-beacon connections. The nonnegative property on $\mathbf{z}_i$ further guarantees a positive semi-definite Laplacian matrix when inferring the sample-to-sample affinity via the sample-to-beacon mapping, which is of importance to ensure a global optimum of Graph-based Semi-Supervised Learning [1].

2.2   Optimization Algorithm

The problem in Eq. (2) is convex with respect to each of the two variables Ψ and $\mathbf{Z}$ when the other one is fixed. It can be solved by alternately minimizing one variable while keeping the other one fixed.

We construct an affinity matrix $\mathbf{W} = [w_{ij}] = \mathbf{Z}^T\mathbf{Z}$ which characterizes the pairwise similarity between samples in the training set, resulting in a similarity graph $\mathcal{G}$ with the affinity matrix $\mathbf{W}$. In this case, the corresponding Laplacian matrix is $\mathbf{L} = \mathbf{D} - \mathbf{W}$ with $\mathbf{D}$ being the diagonal degree matrix as $\mathbf{D}(j,j) = \sum_{i=1}^{N} \mathbf{W}(i,j)$. Therefore, the graph smoothness term in Eq. (5) can be rewritten as

$$R_{\mathbf{Y}}(\Psi, \mathbf{Z}) = \sum_{i=1}^{N} \mathbf{y}_i^T \mathbf{L} \mathbf{y}_i = \sum_{i=1}^{N} \mathbf{z}_i^T \mathbf{F}^T \mathbf{L} \mathbf{F} \mathbf{z}_i \tag{6}$$

$$= \mathrm{tr}(\mathbf{Y}\mathbf{L}\mathbf{Y}^T) = \mathrm{tr}(\mathbf{F}\mathbf{Z}\mathbf{L}\mathbf{Z}^T\mathbf{F}^T). \tag{7}$$

Using Eqs. (6) and (7), the problem in Eq. (2) can be solved by alternately solving the following two problems as

P1: Solving $\mathbf{Z}$ by fixing Ψ:

$$\mathbf{Z}^* = \underset{\mathbf{Z}=[\mathbf{z}_i]}{\arg\min} \left\{ \sum_{i=1}^{N_l} \| [\mathbf{x}_i; \mathbf{y}_i] - \Psi\mathbf{z}_i \|_2^2 + \sum_{i=1}^{N_u} \|\mathbf{x}_i - \mathbf{B}\mathbf{z}_i\|_2^2 + \lambda \sum_{i=1}^{N} \mathbf{z}_i^T \mathbf{F}^T \mathbf{L} \mathbf{F} \mathbf{z}_i \right\},$$

s.t. $\forall i, \|\mathbf{z}_i\|_1 \leq T, \mathbf{z}_i \geq \mathbf{0}$, \hfill (8)

where $\mathbf{B}$ and $\mathbf{F}$ are the sub-matrices of Ψ corresponding to the feature and label domains, respectively; and

P2: Solving Ψ by fixing $\mathbf{Z}$:

$$\Psi^* = \underset{\Psi}{\arg\min} \left\{ \| [\mathbf{X}_l; \mathbf{Y}_l] - \Psi\mathbf{Z}_l \|_2^2 + \|\mathbf{X}_u - \mathbf{B}\mathbf{Z}_u\|_2^2 + \lambda \mathrm{tr}(\mathbf{F}\mathbf{Z}\mathbf{L}\mathbf{Z}^T\mathbf{F}^T) \right\}$$

s.t. $\mathbf{B} = \mathbf{S}_b\Psi, \mathbf{F} = \mathbf{S}_f\Psi$, \hfill (9) where $\mathbf{X}_l = [\mathbf{x}_1, \cdots, \mathbf{x}_{N_l}]$ and $\mathbf{X}_u = [\mathbf{x}_1, \cdots, \mathbf{x}_{N_u}]$ are corresponding to the labeled and unlabeled samples, respectively; $\mathbf{Y}_l = [\mathbf{y}_1, \cdots, \mathbf{y}_{N_l}]$ is the indicator matrix by stacking sample labels in column; $\mathbf{Z}_l$ and $\mathbf{Z}_u$ are corresponding to the sub-matrix of $\mathbf{Z}$ related to the labeled and unlabeled subsets, respectively.

In order to solve $P1$, we propose to calculate $\mathbf{z}_i$ iteratively using the efficient interior-point method [21], which jointly preserves consistence of both the feature and label information. Afterwards, the Laplacian matrix $\mathbf{L}$ in Eq. (9) is updated with the corresponding sample-to-beacon relationship matrix $\mathbf{Z}$. Moreover, the objective function in $P2$ can be rewritten as

$$(\mathbf{B}^*, \mathbf{F}^*) = \arg\min_{\mathbf{B},\mathbf{F}} g(\mathbf{B}, \mathbf{F}) = \arg\min_{\mathbf{B},\mathbf{F}} \|\mathbf{X} - \mathbf{B}\mathbf{Z}\|_2^2 + \|\mathbf{Y}_l - \mathbf{F}\mathbf{Z}_l\|_2^2 + \lambda \text{tr}(\mathbf{F}\mathbf{Z}\mathbf{L}\mathbf{Z}^T\mathbf{F}^T). \quad (10)$$

Applying the cyclic property of trace and differentiating Eq. (10) with respect to $\mathbf{B}$ and $\mathbf{F}$, the partial derivatives of Eq. (10) is

$$\frac{\partial g}{\partial \mathbf{B}} = -2(\mathbf{X} - \mathbf{B}\mathbf{Z})\mathbf{Z}^T, \ \frac{\partial g}{\partial \mathbf{F}} = -2(\mathbf{Y}_l - \mathbf{F}\mathbf{Z}_l)\mathbf{Z}_l^T + 2\lambda\mathbf{F}\mathbf{Z}\mathbf{L}\mathbf{Z}^T. \quad (11)$$

Setting the derivatives in Eq. (11) to zeros yields the optimal solution as

$$\mathbf{B}^* = \mathbf{X}\mathbf{Z}^T(\mathbf{Z}\mathbf{Z}^T)^{-1}, \ \mathbf{F}^* = \mathbf{Y}_l\mathbf{Z}_l^T(\mathbf{Z}_l\mathbf{Z}_l^T + \lambda\mathbf{Z}\mathbf{L}\mathbf{Z}^T)^{-1}. \quad (12)$$

Hereby, the optimum of Ψ in $P2$ is obtained as $\Psi^* = [\mathbf{B}^*; \mathbf{F}^*]$. We alternately optimize the $P1$ in Eq. (8) and $P2$ in Eq. (9) until convergence. It is noted that, in Eq. (12), the inversion is computed on a rather small matrix sized $M \times M$ efficiently, rather than a huge matrix sized $N \times N$ in the previous GSSLs [9,10].

3   Inductive Inference

After obtaining the M beacons $\mathbf{B}$ along with their characteristics $\mathbf{F}$, the scalable inference in the testing data is implemented by label fusion of those beacons that are linked to the test data. For any testing sample $\tilde{\mathbf{x}}_i$, we propose to determine its neighborhood structure along with the strength of sample-to-beacon association by solving the following optimization problem with the sparsity constraint as

$$\tilde{\mathbf{z}}^* = \arg\min_{\tilde{\mathbf{z}}_i} \|\tilde{\mathbf{x}}_i - \mathbf{B}\tilde{\mathbf{z}}_i\|_2^2, \ \text{s.t.} \ \|\tilde{\mathbf{z}}_i\|_1 \leq T, \ \tilde{\mathbf{z}}_i \geq \mathbf{0}, \quad (13)$$

where $\tilde{\mathbf{z}}_i$ denotes the relationship between sample i and beacons. After solving $\tilde{\mathbf{z}}_i$ iteratively using the efficient interior-point method [21], the identity of sample i is obtained via label fusion by plugging $\mathbf{F}$ and $\tilde{\mathbf{z}}_i$ into Eq. (1) as

$$\tilde{\mathbf{y}}_i^* = \mathbf{F}\tilde{\mathbf{z}}_i^*. \quad (14)$$

The hard label vector can be obtained simply by converting the maximum value in each $\mathbf{y}_i^*$ into 1 and the others into 0.

With sparsity appropriately harnessed in Eq. (13), the most relevant beacons are chosen to describe the samples, which improves the performance in terms of efficiency, accuracy and robustness to noise. By introducing the beacons to the feature domain, it is not necessary to estimate the pairwise sample affinity in the sheer volume of testing data [11,12], which reduces the time cost significantly. Additionally, the beacon-based inference can be conducted via distributed computing by sharing beacon information across different servers, which is of practical value in large-scale data analysis.

4   Incremental Update of Beacons in Open-Set

To address the characteristics-evolving issue in the open-set inference, it is worth to consider how to further update the model to boost the performance with a small amount of incremental computation with new data. Specifically, when the model encounters a set of "unfamiliar" samples with new, novel or unknown characteristics that cannot be reconstructed using the existing beacons well (e.g., the reconstruction error is above a threshold as $r(\mathbf{x}_i) = \|\mathbf{x}_i - \mathbf{B}\mathbf{z}_i\|_2^2 > th$), we propose to expand the beacon set by incrementally adding k new beacons $\mathbf{B}_k = [\mathbf{b}_k]$ as $\bar{\mathbf{B}} \triangleq [\mathbf{B}, \mathbf{B}_k]$.

Since the beacon set $\mathbf{B}$ is obtained by solving the problem in Eq. (2), the intuitive way to conduct the beacon update would be to learn the beacons from scratch using the set of identified unfamiliar data $\bar{\mathcal{X}}$ along with the training samples, i.e., substituting $\mathcal{X}^{\text{train}}$ with $\mathcal{X}^{\text{train}} \cup \bar{\mathcal{X}}$ in Eq. (2). Nevertheless, it is inefficient to re-build the model from scratch and it would be nice if the model could be updated incrementally.

In this case, we propose to improve the on-hand beacon set $\mathbf{B}$ incrementally by feeding the unfamiliar samples to handle the time-evolving characteristics. Specifically, we initialize the newly-created k beacons as $\mathbf{B}_k = [\epsilon \mathbf{I}_{d \times k}]$ with ϵ being a positive number that is close to zero; afterwards, the $\mathbf{B}_k$ is updated gradually with the stochastic gradient descent (SGD) algorithm [22] until convergence. We derive the incremental updating algorithm below.

Similarly to Eq. (15), the partial derivatives with respect to the beacon parameter $\bar{\mathbf{B}}$ and its corresponding characteristic parameter $\bar{\mathbf{F}}$ in the unfamiliar sample set are

$$\frac{\partial g}{\partial \bar{\mathbf{B}}} = -2(\bar{\mathbf{X}} - \bar{\mathbf{B}}\bar{\mathbf{Z}})\bar{\mathbf{Z}}^T, \quad \frac{\partial g}{\partial \bar{\mathbf{F}}} = -2(\mathbf{Y}_l - \bar{\mathbf{F}}\mathbf{Z}_l)\mathbf{Z}_l^T + \lambda \bar{\mathbf{F}}\bar{\mathbf{Z}}\bar{\mathbf{L}}\bar{\mathbf{Z}}^T, \quad (15)$$

where $\bar{\mathbf{X}} = [\bar{\mathbf{x}}_i]$ represents the samples that are detected to be unfamiliar to the initial beacon set; and $\bar{\mathbf{Z}} = [\bar{\mathbf{z}}_i]$ is the sample-to-beacon relationship matrix with each column corresponding to a specific sample; $\mathbf{Z}_l$ is the sub-matrix of $\bar{\mathbf{Z}}$ related to the labeled subset, which is updated when more human annotations are provided by users on the unfamiliar samples.

In order to update the parameters iteratively, we denote $\bar{\mathbf{X}}_t$ as the novel samples drawn at iteration t, and the beacon set can be updated using the Stochastic Gradient Descent (SGD) as

$$\bar{\mathbf{B}}_t = \bar{\mathbf{B}}_{t-1} - \delta \frac{\partial g}{\partial \bar{\mathbf{B}}_{t-1}} = \bar{\mathbf{B}}_{t-1} + 2\delta (\bar{\mathbf{X}}_t \bar{\mathbf{Z}}_t^T - \bar{\mathbf{B}}_{t-1} \bar{\mathbf{Z}}_t \bar{\mathbf{Z}}_t^T),$$

$$\bar{\mathbf{F}}_t = \bar{\mathbf{F}}_{t-1} - \delta \frac{\partial g}{\partial \bar{\mathbf{F}}_{t-1}} = \bar{\mathbf{F}}_{t-1} + \delta \left(2(\mathbf{Y}_l - \bar{\mathbf{F}}_{t-1} \mathbf{Z}_l) \mathbf{Z}_l^T - \lambda \bar{\mathbf{F}}_{t-1} \bar{\mathbf{Z}}_t \mathbf{L}_t \bar{\mathbf{Z}}_t^T \right), \quad (16)$$

where $\bar{\mathbf{B}}_t$ is the update of the beacon set $\bar{\mathbf{B}}_{t-1}$ at the t_{th} iteration; $\bar{\mathbf{Z}}_t$ is the sample-to-beacon relationship for the labeled samples in the t_{th} iteration; and δ is the learning rate. When the algorithm converges, the optimal beacon-related parameter $\bar{\Psi}$ is obtained as $\bar{\Psi} = [\bar{\mathbf{B}}; \bar{\mathbf{F}}]$. In this paper, we use the original beacon-related parameters $\mathbf{B}$ and $\mathbf{F}$ in Eq. (12) as a warm start.

5   Experiments

In this section, we evaluate the proposed ℓ_1-Beacon Graph based Semi-Supervised Learning algorithm against alternative algorithms in terms of accuracy, time complexity, robustness to data corruption and data incompleteness, and the performance in the open-set inference.

5.1   Datasets

To verify the effectiveness of our algorithm on graph construction and scalable inference, we implement image classification and image segmentation with three real-world benchmark datasets in our experiments. To evaluate our method, we conduct image classification on **MNIST**[1] and **CIFAR**[2], and image segmentation on **CELL**[3].

5.2   Sample Results

Figure 1 shows some examples of image classification. In each experiment, we use intensity of images as visual features, and annotate a small portion of samples in each dataset (1 % for MNIST and 5 % for CIFAR) as seeds for subsequential estimation of beacon characteristics and inference on categories of unlabeled samples. The images with green and red boundaries in Fig. 1 denote the true and false recognitions, respectively. As is observed, most of the images are classified into confident categories except for samples with odd morphological features. False classifications for CIFAR occur when the dominant object does not occupy significant areas in the image.

---

[1] **MNIST** consists of 70,000 handwritten digits sized 28×28 with 60,000 training ones, http://yann.lecun.com/exdb/mnist/.

[2] **CIFAR** consists of 60,000 32×32 color images in 10 classes, with 6000 images per class, http://www.cs.toronto.edu/~kriz/cifar.html.

[3] **CELL** contains different types of muscle stem cells of a progeroid mouse in time-lapse microscopy sequences, in which each frame contains 50~800 cells, http://www.celltracking.ri.cmu.edu/downloads.html.

Fig. 1. Sample results of image classification, in which the image with green and red boundaries indicates the true and false recognition, respectively. (Color figure online)

Figure 2 shows some sample results for cell segmentation. For each sequence, each image is first partitioned into superpixels [23]. Cell segmentation is realized by classifying the superpixels into specific classes based on a small portion of annotated superpixels (around 1.5 % in our experiments). As is demonstrated in the results, superpixels corresponding to different cells with different visual characteristics are classified into specific categories, resulting in a cell segmentation with high qualities.

5.3   Comparison Methods

In order to evaluate the proposed algorithm, we compare our ℓ_1-*Beacon graph* based algorithm against alternative learning algorithms with respect to beacon-based and sample-based methods.

- **Beacon**-based algorithms. We generate beacons **B** using the centers of K-means clustering, and then calculate the sample-to-beacon relationship matrix by the Local Anchor Embedding (LAE) (K-means LAE) [16], and Nadaraya-Watson Kernel regression (K-means Kernel) [17], respectively.
- **Sample**-based algorithms. Besides the beacon-based algorithms, we also implement the classification based on the sample-based algorithms. Specifically, we construct the *KNN graph* [1] and the ϵ-*graph* [2], based on which the classification is implemented with the label propagation algorithm [9]. Additionally, the label propagation is also conducted on the ℓ_1-*graph* in [11].

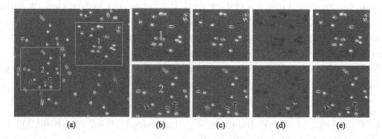

Fig. 2. Sample results of image segmentation. (a) Input phase contrast microscopy images; (b) Zoom-in sub-images; (c) Sample selection and annotation over the superpixels; (d) Soft classification results based on label propagation with human annotations. (e) Cell segmentation by finding the labels with the maximum likelihood, and grouping the neighboring superpixels with the same labels.

To reduce the bias in evaluation, the results are averaged over 10 trials on the testing dataset based on different subsets of seed labels.

5.4 Quantitative Evaluation

Classification Accuracy. In this section, we evaluate the performance against alternative methods after setting the percentage of beacons over samples as 5 % for MNIST, 30 % for CIFAR and 2.5 % for CELL. The optimal essential parameters for each algorithm (e.g., T^* for ℓ_1-Beacon, k_n^* for K-means LAE, ϵ^* for ϵ-graph) are obtained via grid-search. The performance in terms of classification accuracy is reported in Table 1, which demonstrates that all the approaches are comparable in each dataset with the optimal parameters. In some cases, the ϵ-Graph and KNN graph methods outperform other methods mainly because they perform transductive inference and predict the labels by taking all the unlabeled samples into account; however, they lack the capability to handle the samples outside the training datasets, and result in an unbearable burden for large-scale applications.

Table 1. Quantitative comparison in terms of accuracy (%)

	Our ℓ_1-Beacon	K-means LAE	K-means Kernel	ℓ_1-Graph	KNN Graph	ϵ-Graph
MNIST	94.87	91.86	92.12	92.78	93.99	95.06
CIFAR	72.53	65.72	65.34	70.21	70.61	73.04
CELL	95.13	92.33	92.87	94.33	95.46	94.90

Robustness to Improper Parameter. In this section, we demonstrate that the proposed algorithm is more robust to the sub-optimal parameters. In each experiment, we sample a batch of sub-optimal parameters by deviating from the optimal ones (T^* for ℓ_1-Beacon, k_n^* for K-means LAE, ϵ^* for ϵ-graph) with up-to 50 % offset, i.e., the sub-optimal parameters $\phi^- = (\epsilon^-, k^-, T^-)$ with four alternative options as $\phi^- = (0.5, 0.75, 1.25, 1.5)\phi^*$, and repeat the experiments with the sub-optimal parameters. The results of mean and standard deviation based on the sub-optimal parameters are reported in Table 2. Compared to the optimal results in Table 1, performance degeneration for the ℓ_1-Beacon graph is not obvious and the deviation is small when the critical parameters are not set optimally. The main reason is because our algorithm still searches for the most informative beacons in the training dataset regarding to the suboptimal parameter setting and links individual samples to their most relevant beacons by a sample-to-beacon relationship matrix. However, the performance degenerates significantly with a larger deviation for alternative methods since noisy information is involved and graph structures are changed due to improper parameters. The property of parameter robustness offers advantages to practical applications, since the parameter sensitiveness is an essential issue for graph-based semi-supervised learning algorithms.

Table 2. Comparison of accuracy with sub-optimal parameters (%)

	Our ℓ_1-Beacon	K-means LAE	K-means Kernel	ℓ_1-Graph	KNN Graph	ϵ-Graph
MNIST	93.62 ± 1.17	89.17 ± 2.23	88.16 ± 3.77	89.83 ± 1.38	84.45 ± 6.75	85.46± 8.09
CIFAR	70.86 ± 2.01	61.65 ± 2.89	60.11 ± 5.66	67.03 ± 2.93	65.26 ± 8.66	63.23 ± 9.75
CELL	92.99 ± 2.14	87.01± 4.02	84.96 ± 4.98	89.76± 2.73	85.07± 7.75	84.22± 9.33

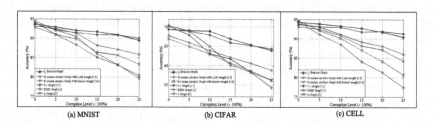

(a) MNIST   (b) CIFAR   (c) CELL

Fig. 3. Performance comparison on corrupted data. (Color figure online)

Robustness to Corrupted Samples. To test the robustness of algorithms regarding to sample corruption, we randomly corrupt a portion of entries of the feature vector in the testing samples (i.e., replace their values with random values drawn from a uniform distribution).

As shown in Fig. 3, the performance of our algorithm degrades around 5%, when 25% entries of feature vectors are corrupted (red curves). A reasonable explanation is that noise corrupts only a fraction of the feature vector and is therefore sparse in the standard beacons. In this case, the information provided by the uncorrupted entries still offers a good opportunity to estimate the relationship between the samples and beacons. Due to the same reason, ℓ_1-graph [11] is also robust to the noisy features (blue curves with star markers). As a comparison, if ℓ_2 minimization is used to represent corrupted samples, most of the sample-to-beacon relationship matrix may be corrupted [11,17], which will lead to a significant performance degeneration (green curves). Moreover, the performance for the transductive inference based on GFHF [1,2] (blue curves with circle and cross markers) undergoes a significant performance degeneration since the noisy samples introduce too much misleading information and the graph structure is changed greatly if no error suppression paradigm is involved.

Time Complexity. We summarize the time complexity of all methods in Table 3. The label propagation based on KNN and ϵ-graph is of high computational cost due to the matrix inversion operation with complexity $O(N^3)$, where N is the sample number. Our proposed ℓ_1-Beacon is comparable to the K-means anchor-based methods with time complexity $O(M^2N)$ [16], since the ℓ_1 optimization can be implemented efficiently with an empirically complexity $O(M^2N^{1.3})$ [21], where M is the number of beacons ($M \ll N$). However, three sample-based methods are infeasible for larger dataset, e.g., MNIST, since the time cost is rather expensive. For example, in ℓ_1-graph, if pairwise ℓ_1

Table 3. Comparison of time complexity (second)

	ℓ_1-Beacon	K-means LAE	K-means Kernel	ℓ_1-Graph	KNN Graph	ϵ-Graph
MNIST	1103.27	607.32	652.55	4367.90	3616.35	3435.23
CIFAR	2480.35	1932.67	1733.62	8237	9970.52	10322.83
CELL	54.10	48.35	41.36	138.22	1324.71	1237.64

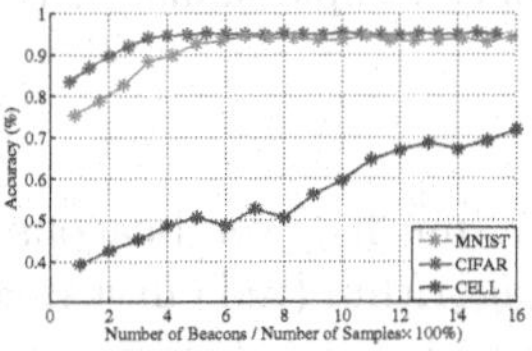

Table 4. Comparison of accuracy

Fig. 4. Accuracy vs. Number of updated beacons

	MNIST	CIFAR	CELL
ℓ_1-Beacon Update	93.14	72.03	95.04
ℓ_1-Beacon	82.50	39.06	76.13
K-means LAE [16]	80.17	36.45	72.06
K-means Kernel [17]	78.31	37.13	73.93
ℓ_1-Graph [11]	84.01	39.61	75.03
KNN [1]	84.99	39.13	77.31
ϵ-Graph [2]	83.30	38.29	78.60

optimization between all samples is implemented, resulting in $O(N^{3.3})$ complexity by particularly setting $M = N$ for ℓ_1-Beacon Graph.

Classification in Open Set. In order to validate the performance of the proposed algorithm in open set, we use only 10 % of the samples in total for the initial beacon training. Therefore, it is expected that there exist some "unfamiliar" samples with high probability due to the incomplete coverage of the feature space, which shares similar properties with the open-set inference. The results are shown in Fig. 4. As is expected and observed, the accuracies are improved as the beacon set expanding and updating, since more informative beacons are involved to handle the samples whose statistics are not present during the initial training phrase.

The comparison in terms of the converged optimal accuracy is reported in Table 4, which demonstrates that the performance benefits substantially from the updating of beacon set. The main reason is that the initial beacons learnt from the initial samples cannot cover the entire feature space, and may lead to improper sample-beacon couplings during the inference. It is also noted that the proposed algorithm allows to load only a small portion of data, and implement the inference incrementally by updating the characteristics of beacons dynamically as data arrive continuously. Therefore, it is useful when analyzing an enormous volume of data in a limited memory.

Performance Versus Beacon Number. Finally, we study the performance versus the number of beacons (M) which is the most critical parameter for the beacon-based algorithms. Figure 5 reveals that the performance is significantly

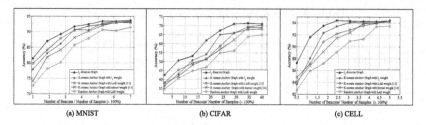

(a) MNIST   (b) CIFAR   (c) CELL

Fig. 5. The classification accuracy versus (beacon number/sample number). (Color figure online)

improved as the beacon number increases. However, much fewer beacons are needed to realize a comparable performance for our algorithm (red curves) compared to the K-means centers (blue curves) and random beacons (green curves). The main reason is that the beacons obtained via our algorithm generalizes the K-means centers to adapt to the complex manifold structures, and the weight matrix optimized via ℓ_1 regularization (curves with star markers) also reduces unreasonable neighborhood structures by avoiding the artificial parameters, e.g., number of neighboring beacons of each sample "k_n" for LAE (curves with circle markers) [16] and kernel regression (curves with cross markers) [17].

5.5   Discussions

Comprehensive experiments demonstrate that our proposed algorithm is attractive in practical applications. When parameters are set properly, the accuracy is comparable to state-of-the-art [17]. Furthermore, our algorithm offers robustness to sub-optimal parameter and corrupted data, which are essential issues in graph-based semi-supervised learning. Compared with the sample-based algorithms, our proposed algorithm is orders of magnitudes more efficient by omitting the inverse of huge matrices. Besides, we also provide a paradigm to handle statistics shift for time-evolving data by updating the beacon set incrementally.

6   Conclusions

We propose an ℓ_1-Beacon Graph algorithm for graph-based semi-supervised learning, in which the scalable inference is implemented by coupling the design of an informative beacon set and estimation of the sample-to-beacon relationship. Compared with the transductive algorithms [1,2], the proposed algorithm is orders of magnitude more efficient in computation and offers a solution to handle unfamiliar data; moreover, it needs fewer beacons to realize comparable results, since it generalizes the clustered centers by K-means [16,17] and provides more flexible representations. With sparsity and graph smoothness properly harnessed, the algorithm is more robust to corrupted samples. Once unfamiliar samples are encountered, the algorithm is capable of handling novel and unseen data with time-evolving statistics by expanding the beacon set and updating the beacon-related parameters incrementally.

References

1. Chapelle, O., Schlkopf, B., Zien, A.: Semi-Supervised Learning, 1st edn. The MIT Press, Cambrdige (2010)
2. Zhu, X., Goldberg, A.B., Brachman, R., Dietterich, T.: Introduction to Semi-Supervised Learning. Morgan and Claypool Publishers, Cambrdige (2009)
3. Zhu, X.: Semi-supervised learning literature survey. Technical report 1530, Computer Sciences, Carnegie Mellon University (2005)
4. Subramanya, A., Talukdar, P.: Graph-Based Semi-Supervised Learning. Synthesis Lectures on Artificial Intelligence and Machine Learning. Morgan & Claypool Publishers, San Rafael (2014)
5. Blum, A., Chawla, S.: Learning from labeled and unlabeled data using graph mincuts. In: Proceedings of the Eighteenth International Conference on Machine Learning (ICML), pp. 19–26 (2001)
6. Grady, L.: Random walks for image segmentation. IEEE Trans. Pattern Anal. Mach. Intell. **28**(11), 1768–1783 (2006)
7. Couprie, C., Grady, L., Najman, L., Talbot, H.: Power watershed: a unifying graph-based optimization framework. IEEE Trans. Pattern Anal. Mach. Intell. **33**(7), 1384–1399 (2011)
8. Belkin, M., Niyogi, P., Sindhwani, V.: Manifold regularization: a geometric framework for learning from labeled and unlabeled examples. J. Mach. Learn. Res. **7**, 2399–2434 (2006)
9. Zhu, X., Ghahramani, Z., Lafferty, J.: Semi-supervised learning using Gaussian fields and harmonic functions. In: Twentieth International Conference on Machine Learning (ICML), pp. 912–919 (2003)
10. Zhou, D., Bousquet, O., Lal, T.N., Weston, J., Schölkopf, B.: Learning with local and global consistency. In: Advances in Neural Information Processing Systems (NIPS), pp. 321–328. MIT Press (2004)
11. Cheng, B., Yang, J., Yan, S., Fu, Y., Huang, T.S.: Learning with ℓ_1-graph for image analysis. IEEE Trans. Image Process. **19**(4), 858–866 (2010)
12. Yang, Y., Wang, Z., Yang, J., Wang, J., Chang, S., Huang, T.S.: Data clustering by Laplacian regularized ℓ_1-graph. In: Twenty-Eighth AAAI Conference on Artificial Intelligence (AAAI), pp. 3148–3149 (2014)
13. Talwalkar, A., Kumar, S., Rowley, H.: IEEE Conference on Large-scale manifold learning. In: Computer Vision and Pattern Recognition (CVPR), pp. 1–8. IEEE (2008)
14. Fergus, R., Weiss, Y., Torralba, A.: Semi-supervised learning in gigantic image collections. In: Advances in Neural Information Processing Systems (NIPS), pp. 522–530 (2009)
15. Dai, D., Van Gool, L.: Ensemble projection for semi-supervised image classification. In: 2013 IEEE International Conference on Computer Vision (CVPR), pp. 2072–2079. IEEE (2013)
16. Liu, W., He, J., Chang, S.F.: Large graph construction for scalable semi-supervised learning. In: Proceedings of the 27th International Conference on Machine Learning (ICML), pp. 679–686 (2010)
17. Chen, X., Cai, D.: Large scale spectral clustering with landmark-based representation. In: The 25th AAAI Conference on Artificial Intelligence (AAAI), pp. 313–318 (2011)
18. Kleinberg, J., Slivkins, A., Wexler, T.: Triangulation and embedding using small sets of beacons. In: Proceedings of the 45th Annual IEEE Symposium on Foundations of Computer Science, pp. 444–453, October 2004

19. Zhang, Z., Ladicky, L., Torr, P., Saffari, A.: Learning anchor planes for classification. In: Advances in Neural Information Processing Systems (NIPS), pp. 1611–1619 (2011)
20. Globerson, A., Roweis, S.: Nightmare at test time: robust learning by feature deletion. In: Proceedings of the 23rd international conference on Machine learning (ICML), pp. 353–360 (2006)
21. Kim, S.J., Koh, K., Lustig, M., Boyd, S., Gorinevsky, D.: An interior-point method for large-scale ℓ_1-1-regularized least squares. IEEE J. Sel. Top. Sig. Process. **1**(4), 606–617 (2007)
22. Mairal, J., Bach, F., Ponce, J., Sapiro, G.: Online dictionary learning for sparse coding. In: Proceedings of the 26th Annual International Conference on Machine Learning (ICML), pp. 689–696 (2009)
23. Su, H., Yin, Z., Huh, S., Kanade, T.: Cell segmentation in phase contrast microscopy images via semi-supervised classification over optics-related features. Med. Image Anal. **17**, 746–765 (2013)

Novel Coplanar Line-Points Invariants for Robust Line Matching Across Views

Qi Jia, Xinkai Gao, Xin Fan$^{(\boxtimes)}$, Zhongxuan Luo, Haojie Li, and Ziyao Chen

School of Software, Dalian University of Technology, Dalian, China
{jiaqi,xin.fan,zxluo,hjli}@dlut.edu.cn,
{gaoxinkai,2013czy}@mail.dlut.edu.cn

Abstract. Robust line matching across wide-baseline views is a challenging task in computer vision. Most of the existing methods highly depend on the positional relationships between lines and the associated textures. These cues are sensitive to various image transformations especially perspective deformations, and likely to fail in the scenarios where few texture present. In this paper, we construct a new coplanar line-points invariant upon a newly developed projective invariant, named characteristic number, and propose a line matching algorithm using the invariant. The construction of this invariant uses intersections of coplanar lines instead of endpoints, rendering more robust matching across views. Additionally, a series of line-points invariant values generate the similarity metric for matching that is less affected by mismatched interest points than traditional approaches. Accurate homography recovered from the invariant allows all lines, even those without interest points around them, a chance to be matched. Extensive comparisons with the state-of-the-art validate the matching accuracy and robustness of the proposed method to projective transformations. The method also performs well for image pairs with few textures and similar textures.

Keywords: Line matching · Projective invariant · Characteristic number

1 Introduction

Feature matching is such a fundamental task in computer vision that it has found wide applications in photogrammetry, image mosaicking, and object tracking *etc.* [2,7]. Points and lines are prone to be mismatched due to illumination and viewpoint changes. In the last two decades, point matching methods have been well studied [11,14], while lines are not so popular as points due to the higher geometric complexity. Lines usually incorporate more semantic and structural information than points, and thus it is quite important to match lines in the scenarios where lines are abundant. The scenarios include 3D modeling and robot navigation in manmade scenes [6,13].

Most of existing line matching methods use texture information near lines as descriptors. Wang *et al.* [17] proposed a SIFT-like descriptor, the mean-standard

© Springer International Publishing AG 2016
B. Leibe et al. (Eds.): ECCV 2016, Part VIII, LNCS 9912, pp. 599–611, 2016.
DOI: 10.1007/978-3-319-46484-8_36

deviation line descriptor (MSLD). In many images, the textures in the vicinity of line segments are not rich enough to assemble an effective descriptor. These textures are also quite similar, possibly generating a less distinctive descriptor. Moreover, MSLD is sensitive to scale changes that is quite common in feature matching. Zhang et al. [18] utilize both local appearance and geometric attributes of lines in order to construct the line band descriptor (LBD). This method requires a global rotation angle between images, which is not always accurate. Texture based methods are typically sensitive to various image transformations, and may fail on images of low texture images and similar textures.

Some methods match a group of lines instead of giving each line a descriptor in order to obtain better performance in low texture images. In [15], line groups are matched through a feature named line signature (LS), and a multi-scale scheme is used to enhance the performance under scale changes. Unfortunately, this process is computationally expensive. López et al. [9] combined geometric properties with local appearance of a pair of lines and the structural context of their neighboring segments. Nevertheless, both methods highly rely on the endpoints of line segments. These endpoints are prone to be mismatched when their locations are not accurate due to various image transformations and partial occlusions.

Different from generating descriptors for lines or line groups, researchers resort to epipolar constraints or geometric invariants for line matching. Similar textures and inaccurate endpoints have less effects on these constraints or invariants. Lourakis et al. [10] used two lines and two points to build a projective invariant to match lines. However, this method can only work on images with a single plane. Al-Shahri et al. [1] exploited the epipolar geometry and coplanarity constraints between pairs of lines. This method performs well in wide-baseline images, but needs to estimate the fundamental matrix via the interest point correspondences. This estimation relies on the accuracy of the point correspondences, resulting in the chicken-and-egg dilemma. Fan et al. [4,5] provide two kinds of invariants based on the distance between matched feature points and lines. This method performs well under various image transformations. Again, it highly depends on the accuracy of the matched interest points.

In this paper, we propose a novel line matching method based on a newly developed projective invariant, named characteristic number (CN) [12]. Figure 1 sketches the work flow of the algorithm. As Fig. 2 shows, the line-points geometries in the neighborhood of each line construct our new line-points invariant upon CN robust to projective transformations. Hence, we are able to obtain well-matched neighborhoods as well as the homography between these neighborhoods. Finally, we incorporate more matched line pairs using this homography for line matching. The main contributions are:

(1) a new line-points projective invariant constructed on the intersections of coplanar lines that are more robust than those interest points matched upon textural information;
(2) a similarity metric between line neighborhoods given by a series of line-points invariant values less affected by mis-matched interest points;

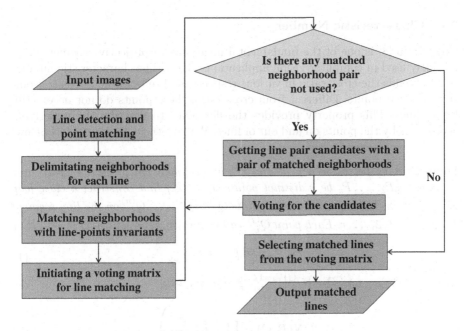

Fig. 1. Architecture of the proposed method

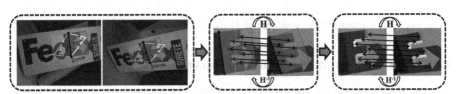

Fig. 2. Overview of matching neighborhoods and selecting line pair candidates. l and l' are a pair of lines; red dots represent the interest points (Color figure online)

(3) accurate homography between matched line neighborhoods recovered by the intrinsic coplanar attributes of the new line-points invariant. All the lines in image pairs have a chance to be matched. Thus, this strategy makes it possible to exploit more potential matched line pairs without interest points around them.

The rest of this paper is organized as follows. Section 2 introduces the projective invariant of characteristic numbers and from which the line-points invariant is derived. The line matching method is deliberated in Sect. 3. Experiments and results are reported in Sect. 4. Section 5 concludes the paper.

2   Line-Points Projective Invariant

In this section, a newly developed projective invariant characteristic number (CN) [12] is introduced into the construction of line-points invariant due to its geometric flexibility, and a new line-points invariant is constructed based on it.

2.1 Characteristic Number

Cross ratio [8] is one of the fundamental invariants in projective geometry and is widely used in computer vision applications [3,13]. The characteristic number (CN) extends the cross ratio in various respects, and reflects the intrinsic geometry of given points. Different from cross ratio, these points do not necessarily lie on lines. This property provides the flexibility to describe the underlying geometries by the points on and out of lines. We give the definition of CN below.

Definition 1. *Let $\mathbb{K}$ be a field and $\mathbb{P}^m$ be m-dimension projective space over $\mathbb{K}$, and $P_1, P_2, \ldots, P_r$ be r distinct points in $\mathbb{P}^m(\mathbb{K})$ that construct a close loop $(P_{r+1} = P_1)$. There are n distinct points $Q_i^{(1)}, Q_i^{(2)}, \ldots, Q_i^{(n)}$ on the line segment $P_i P_{i+1}, i = 1, 2, \ldots, r$. Each point $Q_i^{(j)}$ can be linearly represented by P_i and P_{i+1} as*

$$Q_i^{(j)} = a_i^{(j)} P_i + b_i^{(j)} P_{i+1} \qquad (1)$$

Let $\mathcal{P} = \{P_i\}_{i=1}^r$ and $\mathcal{Q} = \{Q_i^{(j)}\}_{i=1,\ldots,r}^{j=1,\ldots,n}$, the quantity

$$CN(\mathcal{P}, \mathcal{Q}) = \prod_{i=1}^r \left(\prod_{j=1}^n \frac{a_i^{(j)}}{b_i^{(j)}} \right) \qquad (2)$$

is called the characteristic number of $\mathcal{P}$ and $\mathcal{Q}$.

2.2 Construction of Line-Points Projective Invariant

Interest points and lines are used to construct the line-points projective invariant. Generally, the most representative points of a line are the endpoints, but due to various changes between images, the line extraction methods usually cannot provide accurate endpoints. However, if two lines are located on the same plane, the location of their intersection to the object remains unchanged under projective transformation. We make a rough hypothesis that if the intersection of two lines is very close to one of the endpoints, the two lines are likely to be coplanar. Given a line l, suppose e is one of its endpoints. For all the intersections on line l, if o is the nearest intersection to e and the distance between o and e is smaller than $0.1 * length(l)$, o is chosen to substitute e as a key point of l. Only in the case that there is no such intersection available near an endpoint, the endpoint itself will be a key point. Further, in order to reduce pseudo intersections produced by collinear and parallel lines, we set a threshold for the angle between two lines. In our experiment, if the angle is not greater than $\pi/8$, their intersection will be abandoned. We also define the gradient of a line as the average gradient of all points on it. As shown in Fig. 3, two black arrows illustrate the gradient directions of lines a and b respectively. In order to keep rotation invariant, for line a, the area directed by the line gradient is denoted as $Right(a)$, and the other side is $Left(a)$. In a clockwise direction, the key point on the edge from $Left(a)$ to $Right(a)$ is denoted as KP_a^1 and the other is KP_a^2.

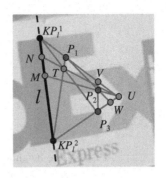

Fig. 3. The gradient directions and sides of lines

Fig. 4. Construction of line-points invariant.

We use five points to construct the line-points projective invariant. As shown in Fig. 4, KP_l^1 and KP_l^2 are two key points on line l, P_1, P_2, and P_3 are three non-collinear interest points on the same side of l. We denote the line through two points, P_i and P_j, as $\overline{P_iP_j}$ and the intersection of two lines, $\overline{P_iP_j}$, and $\overline{P_kP_m}$, as $<\overline{P_iP_j}, \overline{P_kP_m}>$. We can obtain several intersection points (blue dots), including $U = <\overline{KP_l^1P_1}, \overline{KP_l^2P_3}>$, $V = <\overline{KP_l^1P_1}, \overline{P_3P_2}>$, $W = <\overline{P_1P_2}, \overline{KP_l^2P_3}>$, $T = <\overline{KP_l^1P_3}, \overline{P_1KP_l^2}>$, $M = <\overline{KP_l^1KP_l^2}, \overline{UP_2}>$, and $N = <\overline{KP_l^1KP_l^2}, \overline{UT}>$. Thus we have $\triangle KP_l^1UKP_l^2$ with two points on every side. Thereafter, we are able to calculate CN with $\mathcal{P} = \{KP_l^1, U, KP_l^2\}$ and $\mathcal{Q} = \{P_1, V, W, P_3, M, N\}$. We denote the CN constructed in this way as $FCN(KP_l^1, KP_l^2, P_1, P_2, P_3)$.

3 Line Matching

In this section, a two-stage line matching algorithm is designed to obtain as many matched line pairs as possible with high accuracy. In the first stage, the similarities between line neighborhoods are calculated. In the second stage, the homography transformations between matched coplanar neighborhoods are calculated, creating some bases on which more matched line pairs can be exploited.

3.1 Similarity Between Line Neighborhoods

Neighborhood Definition. Line neighborhoods provide structural information around each line. In this paper, the neighborhood is determined by the length of the line to keep invariant to scale changes. As shown in Fig. 5, in the neighborhood of line l, the distance from any interest point to l is less than $\alpha*length(l)$ and less than $\beta*length(l)$ to the perpendicular bisector line. If point p is in the neighborhood of l, it is denoted as $p \in \mathcal{LPS}_l$. In our experiments, α is set as 2.0 while β is set as 0.5.

As many lines are formed by the intersection of planes, points located on different sides of a line may not be coplanar. Hence, the neighborhood is split

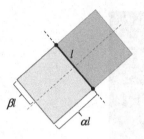

Fig. 5. The neighborhood of a line (Color figure online)

into left one and right one according to the gradient direction, which is detailed in Sect. 2.2 and Fig. 5. The left neighborhood is denoted as $\mathcal{LPS}_l^L$ and the right one is $\mathcal{LPS}_l^R$, which are represented in Fig. 5 in red and blue, respectively.

Neighborhood-to-Neighborhood Similarity Measure. Suppose there are two images, I and I', of the same subject from different views. The set of lines detected in each image is denoted as $\mathcal{L} = \{a_1, a_2, \ldots, a_n\}$ and $\mathcal{L}' = \{b_1, b_2, \ldots, b_m\}$. The matched interest points set in the two images is denoted as $\mathcal{C} = \{(x_i, y_i), i = 1, 2, \ldots\}$(some matches are not correct), where x_i and y_i are matched interest points in I and I' respectively.

The similarity between line neighborhoods is measured by the line-points invariant with matched interest points in the neighborhood. For line l, $\mathcal{LPS}_l^L$ and $\mathcal{LPS}_l^R$ are evaluated separately. We take $\mathcal{LPS}_l^R$ as the example in the following steps.

Given a pair of lines $a \in \mathcal{L}$ and $b \in \mathcal{L}'$, the matched interest points in $\mathcal{LPS}_a^R$ and $\mathcal{LPS}_b^R$ compose a set: $\{(x_i, y_i) | x_i \in \mathcal{LPS}_a^R, y_i \in \mathcal{LPS}_b^R, (x_i, y_i) \in \mathcal{C}, i = 1, 2, \ldots, N\}$, where N is the number of matched interest points. If $N < 5$, we set the similarity between the two neighborhoods as 0. Otherwise, we select one pair of points (x_i, y_i) as the ith base point pair each time, giving us N base point pairs. For each base point pair, another two pairs (x_j, y_j) and (x_k, y_k) in the remaining $N-1$ pairs can be used to calculate $FCN(KP_a^1, KP_a^2, x_i, x_j, x_k)$ and $FCN(KP_b^1, KP_b^2, y_i, y_j, y_k)$. We have C_{N-1}^2 choices, which means we have C_{N-1}^2 FCN values to represent the relationships between each base point and the line. The rth $(r = 1, 2, \ldots, C_{N-1}^2)$ FCN value for the ith base point pair is denoted as $FCN_i^a(r)$ and $FCN_i^b(r)$, respectively, and the similarity between the two values is calculated by:

$$S(r) = e^{-||FCN_i^a(r) - FCN_i^b(r)||}.$$

Then we can get C_{N-1}^2 similarities for the ith base point pair, and the median value is used as the similarity of the ith base point pair to reduce the effect of mismatched points.

$$SIM(x_i, y_i) = median\{S(r)\}, r = 1, 2, \ldots, C_{N-1}^2.$$

Finally, the similarity of $\mathcal{LPS}_a^R$ and $\mathcal{LPS}_b^R$ is denoted as the base point pair with the max similarity:

$$SIM_R(a,b) = max\{SIM(x_i, y_i)\}, i = 1, 2, \ldots, N.$$

Finally, if in image I', for all the neighborhoods of lines on the right side, $\mathcal{LPS}_b^R$ has the max similarity with $\mathcal{LPS}_a^R$, and in image I, $\mathcal{LPS}_a^R$ has the max similarity with $\mathcal{LPS}_b^R$ as well, then we take $\mathcal{LPS}_a^R$ and $\mathcal{LPS}_b^R$ as a pair of matched line neighborhoods on the right side. The same method can be used to get matched line neighborhoods on the left side.

3.2   Matching Lines by Homography Transformation

The property of line-points invariant indicates that if the similarity between two neighborhoods of lines is very high, most of the interest points in the neighborhoods are very likely to locate on the same plane area. Thus, the homography **H** between the two neighborhoods can be calculated by matched points with Random Sample Consensus (RANSAC). Then for each line $a \in \mathcal{L}$ in image I and $b \in \mathcal{L}'$ in image I', we can map a to a' via $a' = \mathbf{H}a$, and map b to b' via $b' = \mathbf{H}^{-1}b$.

We then use two constrains to screen the potential matching lines, taking the line a and the mapped line b' in image I for example.

1. **Vertical distance constraint:** As illustrated in Fig. 6(a), d_1 and d_3 are the distances from the endpoints of line a to line b', while d_2 and d_4 are the distances from the endpoints of line b' to line a. The distance between line a and line b' is denoted as $d_v(a, b') = max(d_1, d_2, d_3, d_4)$. If $d_v(a, b') < \gamma$, then a and b' satisfy the vertical distance constraint. This constraint ensures two lines are vertically near to each other, where γ is set to 3 pixels in our experiment.
2. **Horizontal distance constraint:** As illustrated in Fig. 6(b), the distance between the midpoint of line a and line b' is denoted as d_h. If $d_h < (length(a) + length(b'))/2$, then the two lines satisfy the horizontal constraint. This constraint ensures two lines are horizontally near to each other.

If a and b' satisfy both constraints while the corresponding lines a' and b also satisfy both constraints, then line a and b are regarded as a pair of candidates. In practice, there may be one line in one image satisfying the constraints with several lines in another image, and the candidates calculated from different matched neighborhoods may also be different. In order to pick out the best-matched line pairs, a weighted voting strategy is used.

We construct a voting matrix **V** with size $n * m$, where n and m are the number of lines in images I and I', respectively. All elements are initialized by 0, which will be updated by the matched neighborhoods.

For a pair of matched neighborhoods $\mathcal{LPS}_a^R$ and $\mathcal{LPS}_b^R$, we suppose they are well matched with similarity $SIM_R(a, b)$. As the accuracy of the candidate selection is affected by the accuracy of **H**, and **H** is calculated by the matched

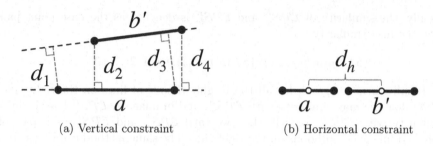

(a) Vertical constraint   (b) Horizontal constraint

Fig. 6. Two constraints to obtain matching lines

points in $\mathcal{LPS}_a^R$ and $\mathcal{LPS}_b^R$, we take the similarity between two matched neighborhoods into account. For example, if $a_i \in \mathcal{L}$ and $b_j \in \mathcal{L}'$ are regarded to be a pair of candidates based on $\mathbf{H}$ as calculated from $\mathcal{LPS}_a^R$ and $\mathcal{LPS}_b^R$, then $\mathbf{V}$ is updated by $\mathbf{V}_{i,j} = \mathbf{V}_{i,j} + SIM_R(a,b)$.

After all the matching neighborhoods in image I and I' are used to update $\mathbf{V}$, if $\mathbf{V}_{i,j}$ is greater than 0.9 and is the maximum between both the ith row and the jth column, then line a_i and line b_j are regarded as matched lines.

4   Experiments

To evaluate the performance of our method, another two state-of-the-art line matching methods are used for comparison: LP [4,5] and CA [9]. Both implementations are provided by their authors, and they are selected due to their good performance dealing with a wide range of image transformations. In order to follow the same protocol, we use the line detection method LSD [16] when comparing with LP, while taking the detector used in [9] when comparing with CA. In addition, the interest points used in our method and in LP are detected and matched by SIFT [11]. We test the proposed method in four conditions to verify its robustness to different changes: rotation, scaling, occlusion, and viewpoint changing. Most of the images used in our experiments are the same as [4,5]. In the viewpoint change experiment, we test the proposed method on both low texture images and high but similar texture images to illustrate the robustness of our methods to interest points changing on number and quantity.[1]

The results of the proposed method are shown in Figs. 7, 8, 9, 10, 11 and 12, where the matched lines are labeled in red with the same number. The statistical results are listed in Tables 1 and 2. The first column is the label of image pairs, and the second column is the number of lines detected from the image pair. The last two columns show the correct matched lines/total matched lines, and the correct rates of our method and the compared method. Besides the correct rates, the count of total matches also weighs the performance as more candidates of matched lines are likely to render robustness to subsequent processing such

---

[1] The source code of the proposed method is available at https://github.com/dlut-dimt/LineMatching.

(a)   (b)

Fig. 7. Results under rotation changes (Color figure online)

as stereo reconstruction and panorama stitching. Also, the more total matches there are, the more difficult it is to generate correct matches.

Rotation changes: In rotation transformation, the length of lines, angles and relative positions between lines are kept. Our result is shown in Fig. 7, and the details are shown in the first row of Tables 1 and 2. We can see that the matching precision of the three methods are all 100 % for all the methods are rotation invariant. However, the proposed method gets 4 more correct matched pairs than LP, and 53 more correct matched pairs than CA.

Scale changes: As shown in Fig. 8, the length of lines are changed in scale changes, resulting in some lines disappearing. Both LP and our method perform well with the number of correct matched lines are 121 and 131, respectively. The accuracy for both the proposed method and LP are more than 98 %, while the accuracy for CA is less than 70 % for CA depends on the position relationship between lines. The lines may disappear in large scale changes which badly affects the result.

Further, we test our method on the images with both rotation and scale changes, as shown in Fig. 9. As shown in Tables 1 and 2, our method outperforms other methods with accuracy of 93 %, while the accuracy of LP drops to 88.9 % and CA cannot get any correct matches for most lines disappear, as shown in Fig. 9. The results indicate that our method is robust in sever image transformations with the number of lines and interest points changing.

Occlusion: In the condition of occlusion, the endpoints and the length of lines are greatly changed, and methods based on such attributes may fail. We give our result in Fig. 10 and the 4th rows of Tables 1 and 2. The proposed method has a matching precision of 100 %, while LP and CA are 98.6 % and 95.8 %, respectively. The proposed method gets 9 and 24 more correct matches than LP and CA, respectively. In particular, the correct matched lines are twice that of CA. This result validates the robustness of our method as regards endpoints changing.

Viewpoint changes: Viewpoint changes are very common in reality. We test two groups with three images in each group. In each group, the first image is regarded as the reference image and the other two are query images, thus

Fig. 8. Results under scale changes (Color figure online)

Fig. 9. Results under scale changes plus rotation (Color figure online)

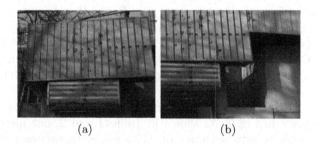

Fig. 10. Results under occlusion (Color figure online)

providing us two pairs of images for each group. The first group contains three
low texture images, while the second group has high texture images, and many
local parts of which are similar. Both groups are very challenging.

Our results on the first group are shown in Fig. 11 and are detailed in the
5th and 6th rows of Tables 1 and 2. The proposed method and LP get all the
matches correct, but CA gets only 91.1 % in the first pair and failed to get any
matches again in the second pair under larger viewpoint changes. We also get
26 and 16 more correct pairs than LP, and 19 and 22 more pairs than CA. Our
results on the second group are shown in Fig. 12 and are detailed in the last two
rows of Tables 1 and 2. The matching precision of LP and CA are about the

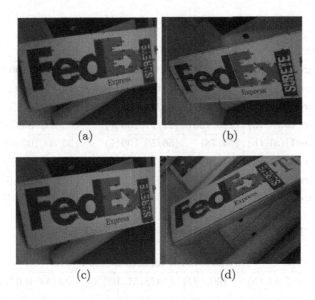

Fig. 11. Results on low texture images with viewpoint changes (Color figure online)

same as the proposed method, however, we get 25 and 28 more correct matches than LP and get 35 and 38 more correct matches than CA.

The experiments show that the proposed method is robust in projective transformation. In addition, LP [4,5] used an affine invariant with 1 line and 2 points in [4], while [5] used an additional projective invariant with 1 line and 4 points. Let N is the number of lines and M is the number of points in both images, the complexity of LP is $O(N^2M^2)$ to be invariant to affine transformations and is $O(N^2M^4)$ to be invariant to projective transformations. The proposed method is invariant to projective transformations with complexity $O(N^2M^3)$ only. Although LP can also be projective invariant, it depends on the accuracy of matched interest points. When there are few interest points in low texture

Fig. 12. Results on high texture images with viewpoint changes (Color figure online)

Table 1. Comparison of the proposed method and LP

Images	Extracted	Proposed method	LP
Figure 7(a)–(b)	(272, 237)	(194/194, 100 %)	(190/190, 100 %)
Figure 8(a)–(b)	(315, 225)	(131/133, 98.5 %)	(121/122, 99.2 %)
Figure 9(a)–(b)	(540, 202)	(53/57, 93.0 %)	(40/45, 88.9 %)
Figure 10(a)–(b)	(210, 153)	(77/77, 100 %)	(68/69, 98.6 %)
Figure 11(a)–(b)	(94, 78)	(56/56, 100 %)	(30/30, 100 %)
Figure 11(c)–(d)	(94, 101)	(38/38, 100 %)	(22/22, 100 %)
Figure 12(a)–(b)	(247, 234)	(148/154, 96.1 %)	(123/126, 97.6 %)
Figure 12(c)–(d)	(247, 233)	(126/141, 89.3 %)	(98/112, 87.5 %)

Table 2. Comparison of the proposed method and CA

Images	Extracted	Proposed method	CA
Figure 7(a)–(b)	(196, 181)	(137/137, 100 %)	(84/84, 100 %)
Figure 8(a)–(b)	(241, 202)	(97/101, 96.0 %)	(41/59, 69.5 %)
Figure 9(a)–(b)	(386, 123)	(18/20, 90.0 %)	(0/0, 0 %)
Figure 10(a)–(b)	(169, 134)	(47/47, 100 %)	(23/24, 95.8 %)
Figure 11(a)–(b)	(92, 87)	(50/50, 100 %)	(41/45, 91.1 %)
Figure 11(c)–(d)	(92, 101)	(22/22, 100 %)	(0/0, 0 %)
Figure 12(a)–(b)	(217, 219)	(93/99, 93.9 %)	(58/62, 93.5 %)
Figure 12(c)–(d)	(217, 209)	(91/95, 95.8 %)	(53/55, 96.4 %)

images or a large number of mismatched interest points in high texture images with similar parts, the accuracy significantly declines.

5 Conclusion

In this paper, a new line-points projective invariant is proposed, which is used to compute the similarities between line neighborhoods. An extending matching strategy is also adopted to exploit more potential matching lines. Experiment results show that the proposed method is robust against many distortions, and can achieve better performance than some existing state-of-the-art methods, especially in images with low texture and large viewpoint changes. Moreover, the proposed method is based on the planar projective invariant, so the performance for non-planar scenes may not be as good as planar scenes.

References

1. Al-Shahri, M., Yilmaz, A.: Line matching in wide-baseline stereo: a top-down approach. IEEE Trans. Image Process. **23**(9), 4199–4210 (2014)
2. Albarelli, A., Rodolà, E., Torsello, A.: Loosely distinctive features for robust surface alignment. In: Daniilidis, K., Maragos, P., Paragios, N. (eds.) ECCV 2010. LNCS, vol. 6315, pp. 519–532. Springer, Heidelberg (2010). doi:10.1007/978-3-642-15555-0_38
3. Bergamasco, F., Albarelli, A., Torsello, A.: Pi-Tag: a fast image-space marker design based on projective invariants. Mach. Vis. Appl. **24**(6), 1295–1310 (2013)
4. Fan, B., Wu, F., Hu, Z.: Line matching leveraged by point correspondences. In: 2010 IEEE Conference on Computer Vision and Pattern Recognition (CVPR), pp. 390–397. IEEE (2010)
5. Fan, B., Wu, F., Hu, Z.: Robust line matching through line-point invariants. Pattern Recogn. **45**(2), 794–805 (2012)
6. Jain, A., Kurz, C., Thormahlen, T., Seidel, H.P.: Exploiting global connectivity constraints for reconstruction of 3D line segments from images. In: 2010 IEEE Conference on Computer Vision and Pattern Recognition (CVPR), pp. 1586–1593. IEEE (2010)
7. Lemaire, T., Lacroix, S.: Monocular-vision based SLAM using line segments. In: 2007 IEEE International Conference on Robotics and Automation, pp. 2791–2796. IEEE (2007)
8. Li, L., Tan, C.: Recognizing planar symbols with severe perspective deformation. IEEE Trans. Pattern Anal. Mach. Intell. **32**(4), 755–762 (2010)
9. López, J., Santos, R., Fdez-Vidal, X.R., Pardo, X.M.: Two-view line matching algorithm based on context and appearance in low-textured images. Pattern Recogn. **48**(7), 2164–2184 (2015)
10. Lourakis, M.I., Halkidis, S.T., Orphanoudakis, S.C.: Matching disparate views of planar surfaces using projective invariants. Image Vis. Comput. **18**(9), 673–683 (2000)
11. Lowe, D.G.: Distinctive image features from scale-invariant keypoints. Int. J. Comput. Vis. **60**(2), 91–110 (2004)
12. Luo, Z., Zhou, X., Gu, D.X.: From a projective invariant to some new properties of algebraic hypersurfaces. Sci. Chin. Math. **57**(11), 2273–2284 (2014)
13. Ramalingam, S., Antunes, M., Snow, D., Lee, G.H., Pillai, S.: Line-sweep: cross-ratio for wide-baseline matching and 3D reconstruction. In: 2015 IEEE Conference on Computer Vision and Pattern Recognition (CVPR), pp. 1238–1246, June 2015
14. Rublee, E., Rabaud, V., Konolige, K., Bradski, G.: ORB: an efficient alternative to SIFT or SURF. In: 2011 IEEE International Conference on Computer Vision (ICCV), pp. 2564–2571. IEEE (2011)
15. Wang, L., Neumann, U., You, S.: Wide-baseline image matching using line signatures. In: 2009 IEEE 12th International Conference on Computer Vision, pp. 1311–1318. IEEE (2009)
16. Wang, L., You, S., Neumann, U.: Supporting range and segment-based hysteresis thresholding in edge detection. In: 15th IEEE International Conference on Image Processing, ICIP 2008, pp. 609–612. IEEE (2008)
17. Wang, Z., Wu, F., Hu, Z.: MSLD: a robust descriptor for line matching. Pattern Recogn. **42**(5), 941–953 (2009)
18. Zhang, L., Koch, R.: An efficient and robust line segment matching approach based on LBD descriptor and pairwise geometric consistency. J. Vis. Commun. Image Represent. **24**(7), 794–805 (2013)

Sparse Representation Based Complete Kernel Marginal Fisher Analysis Framework for Computational Art Painting Categorization

Ajit Puthenputhussery[✉], Qingfeng Liu, and Chengjun Liu

Department of Computer Science,
New Jersey Institute of Technology, Newark, USA
{avp38,ql69,cliu}@njit.edu

Abstract. This paper presents a sparse representation based complete kernel marginal Fisher analysis (SCMFA) framework for categorizing fine art images. First, we introduce several Fisher vector based features for feature extraction so as to extract and encode important discriminatory information of the painting image. Second, we propose a complete marginal Fisher analysis method so as to extract two kinds of discriminant information, regular and irregular. In particular, the regular discriminant features are extracted from the range space of the intraclass compactness using the marginal Fisher discriminant criterion whereas the irregular discriminant features are extracted from the null space of the intraclass compactness using the marginal interclass separability criterion. The motivation for extracting two kinds of discriminant information is that the traditional MFA method uses a PCA projection in the initial step that may discard the null space of the intraclass compactness which may contain useful discriminatory information. Finally, we learn a discriminative sparse representation model with the objective to integrate the representation criterion with the discriminant criterion in order to enhance the discriminative ability of the proposed method. The effectiveness of the proposed SCMFA method is assessed on the challenging Painting-91 dataset. Experimental results show that our proposed method is able to (i) achieve the state-of-the-art performance for painting artist and style classification, (ii) outperform other popular image descriptors and deep learning methods, (iii) improve upon the traditional MFA method as well as (iv) discover the artist and style influence to understand their connections in different art movement periods.

1 Introduction

Fine art painting categorization and analysis is an emerging research area in computer vision, which is gaining increasing popularity in the recent years. Pioneer works in cognitive psychology [1,2] believe that the analysis of visual art is a complex cognitive task and requires involvement of multiple centers in the human brain in order to process different elements of visual art such as color, shapes, boundaries and brush strokes.

© Springer International Publishing AG 2016
B. Leibe et al. (Eds.): ECCV 2016, Part VIII, LNCS 9912, pp. 612–627, 2016.
DOI: 10.1007/978-3-319-46484-8_37

From the computer vision point of view, unlike conventional image classification tasks, computational painting categorization exhibits two important issues for artist classification and style classification respectively. First, as for the artist classification, there are large variations in appearance, topics and styles within the paintings of the same artist. Second, as for the style classification, the inherent similarity gap between paintings within the same style is much larger compared to other image classification tasks such as object recognition and face recognition where the images of the same class have a lower variance in similarity. Painting art images are different from photographic images due to the following reasons: (i) Texture, shape and color patterns of different visual classes in art images (say, a multicolored face or a disproportionate figure) are inconsistent with regular photographic images. (ii) Some artists have a very distinctive style of using specific colors (for ex: dark shades, light shades etc.) and brush strokes resulting in art images with diverse background and visual elements. As a result, conventional features, such as LBP [3], PHOG [4], GIST [5], SIFT [6], complete LBP [7], CN-SIFT [8] etc., which are applied to conventional image classification, independently cannot capture the key aspects of computational painting categorization. A comparative evaluation of different conventional features by Khan et al. [8] for computational fine art painting categorization clearly suggests the need of designing more powerful visual features and learning methods in order to effectively capture complex discriminative information from fine art painting images.

To address the issues raised above, we first present DAISY Fisher vector (D-FV), WLD-SIFT Fisher vector (WS-FV) and color fused Fisher vector (CFFV) features for feature extraction so as to encode the local, color, spatial, relative intensity and gradient orientation information. We then propose a complete marginal Fisher analysis method so as to overcome the limitation of the traditional marginal Fisher analysis (MFA) [9] method. The initial step of the traditional MFA method is the principal component analysis (PCA) projection which projects the data into the PCA subspace. A potential problem with the PCA step is that it may discard the null space of the intraclass compactness which may contain useful discriminatory information since the PCA criterion is not compatible with the MFA criterion. In our proposed method, we extract two kinds of discriminatory information, regular and irregular so as to overcome the drawback of the PCA projection step. Specifically, we extract the regular discriminant features from the range space of intraclass compactness using marginal Fisher discriminant criterion whereas the irregular discriminant features are extracted from its null space using the marginal interseparability criterion. Finally, we apply a discriminative sparse model by adding a discriminant term to the sparse representation criterion so as to have correspondence between the dictionary atoms and class labels for improving the pattern recognition performance. In particular, we utilize the intrinsic structure of sparse representation in order to define new discriminative within-class and between-class matrices for learning the discriminative dictionary efficiently using a discriminative sparse optimization criterion. Our proposed method is evaluated on the challenging Painting-91 dataset [8] and experimental results show that our framework achieves the state-of-the-art performance for fine art painting categorization, outperforms other popular image descriptors and deep learning methods and discover the artist influence and style influence.

The rest of this paper is organized as follows. In Sect. 2, we briefly review some related work on painting categorization, feature extraction and learning methods. In Sect. 3, we present the feature extraction step using the proposed Fisher vector features. Section 4 describes the motivation and theoretical formulation of the sparse representation based kernel MFA framework. Section 5 conducts extensive experiments and analysis of results. Finally, we conclude the paper in Sect. 6.

2   Related Work

Painting Categorization. Recently, several research efforts have been invested on developing techniques for fine art categorization using computer vision methods. Sablatnig et al. [10] examined the structural characteristics of a painting and introduced a classification scheme based on color, shape of region and structure of brush strokes in painting images. Shamir et al. [11] showed a method to automatically categorize paintings using low level features and find common elements between painters and artistic styles. A statistical model for combining multiple visual features was proposed by Shen [12] for automatic categorization of classical western paintings. Shamir and Tarakhovsky [13] presented an image analysis method inspired from cell biology for analysis of art painting based on painters, different artistic movements, artistic styles, and provide similar elements and influential links between painters. The work of Zujovic et al. [14] proposed an approach to classify paintings by analyzing different features in order to capture salient aspects of a painting. Siddique et al. [15] developed a framework for learning multiple kernels efficiently by greedily selecting data instances for each kernel using AdaBoost followed by SVM learning.

Feature Extraction. Local, color, spatial and intensity information are the cues based on which the visual cortex of the human brain can find discriminative elements in different images, and hence these cues are necessary for precise fine art painting categorization. Guo et al. [7] proposed a complete modeling of the local binary pattern descriptor to extract the image local gray level and the sign and magnitude features of local difference. The work of van de Sande et al. [16] showed the effectiveness of color invariant features for categorization tasks to increase the illumination invariance and the discriminative power. Shechtman and Irani [17] presented an approach to measure similarity between images using a self-similarity descriptor by capturing self-similarities of color, edges, repetitive patterns and complex textures.

Learning Methods. Several manifold learning methods such as marginal Fisher analysis (MFA) [9], locality preserving projections [18], locality sensitive discriminant analysis (LSDA) [19] etc. have been widely used to preserve data locality in the embedding space. The MFA method [9] proposed by Yan et al.

overcomes the limitations of the traditional linear discriminant analysis method and uses a graph embedding framework for supervised dimensionality reduction. Cai et al. [19] proposed the LSDA method that discovers the local manifold structure by finding a projection which maximizes the margin between data points from different classes at each local area.

In visual recognition applications, sparse representation methods focus on developing efficient learning algorithms [20,21] and exploring data manifold structures for representation [22,23]. Zhou et al. [24] proposed a novel joint dictionary learning (JDL) algorithm to exploit the visual correlation within a group of visually similar object categories for dictionary learning. Mairal et al. [25] proposed to co-train the discriminative dictionary, sparse representation as well as the linear classifier using a combined objective function.

3   Feature Extraction Using Fused Fisher Vector Features

In this section, we present a set of image features that encode the local, color, spatial, relative intensity and gradient orientation information of fine art painting images.

3.1   Fisher Vector

We briefly review the Fisher vector which is widely applied for different visual recognition problems such as face detection and recognition [26], object classification [27,28], etc. Theoretical analysis [27] shows that Fisher vector features describes an image by what makes it different from other images. In particular, let $\mathbf{X} = \{\mathbf{f}_t, t = 1, 2, \ldots, T\}$ be the set of T local descriptors extracted from the image, then the Fisher kernel is defined as: $K(\mathbf{X}, \mathbf{Y}) = (\mathbf{G}_\lambda^X)^T \mathbf{F}_\lambda^{-1} \mathbf{G}_\lambda^Y$ where μ_λ is the probability density function of $\mathbf{X}$ with parameter λ and $\mathbf{F}_\lambda$ is the Fisher information matrix of μ_λ. The gradient vector of the log-likelihood that indicates the contribution of the parameters to the generation process can be represented as: $\mathbf{G}_\lambda^X = \frac{1}{T} \nabla_\lambda \log_{\mu_\lambda}(\mathbf{X})$. Since $\mathbf{F}_\lambda^{-1}$ is symmetric and positive definite, it has a Cholesky decomposition as $\mathbf{F}_\lambda^{-1} = \mathbf{L}_\lambda^T \mathbf{L}_\lambda$. Therefore, the kernel $K(\mathbf{X}, \mathbf{Y})$ can be written as a dot product between normalized vectors $\mathbf{G}_\lambda$, obtained as $\mathbf{G}_\lambda^X = \mathbf{L}_\lambda \mathbf{G}_\lambda^X$ where $\mathbf{G}_\lambda^X$ is the Fisher vector of $\mathbf{X}$.

3.2   DAISY Fisher Vector (D-FV)

In this section, we present a DAISY Fisher vector (D-FV) feature where Fisher vectors are computed on densely sampled DAISY descriptors. DAISY descriptors consists of values computed from the convolved orientation maps located on concentric circles centered on each pixel location. The DAISY descriptor [29] $\mathcal{D}(u_0, v_0)$ for location (u_0, v_0) is represented as:

$$\mathcal{D}(u_0, v_0) = [\tilde{\mathbf{h}}_{\Sigma_1}^T(u_0, v_0),$$
$$\tilde{\mathbf{h}}_{\Sigma_1}^T(\mathbf{I}_1(u_0, v_0, R_1)), \ldots, \tilde{\mathbf{h}}_{\Sigma_1}^T(\mathbf{I}_T(u_0, v_0, R_1)), \ldots, \tag{1}$$
$$\tilde{\mathbf{h}}_{\Sigma_Q}^T(\mathbf{I}_1(u_0, v_0, R_Q)), \ldots, \tilde{\mathbf{h}}_{\Sigma_Q}^T(\mathbf{I}_T(u_0, v_0, R_Q)))]^T$$

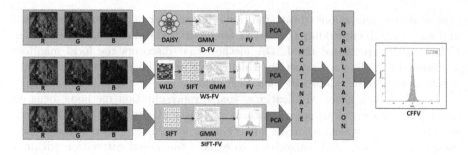

Fig. 1. Framework of the feature extraction process.

where $\mathbf{I}_j(u, v, R)$ is the location with distance R from (u, v) in the direction given by j, Q represents the number of circular layers and $\tilde{\mathbf{h}}_\Sigma(u, v)$ is the unit norm of vector containing Σ-convolved orientation maps in different directions. DAISY descriptors are suitable for dense computation and offers precise localization and rotational robustness, therefore provides improved performance and better accuracy for classification relative to other local descriptors such as GLOH, SURF and NCC [29]. We fit the sampled DAISY descriptors to a Gaussian Mixture Model (GMM) with 256 parameters and the GMM is trained for each component of the image separately in order to encode the color information. The Fisher vectors are then encoded as derivatives of log-likelihood of the model based on the parameters.

3.3 Weber-SIFT Fisher Vector (WS-FV)

We introduce a Weber-SIFT Fisher vector (WS-FV) feature that integrates the Weber local descriptor along with SIFT features so as to encode the color, local, relative intensity and gradient orientation information from an image. The Weber local descriptor (WLD) [30] is based on the Weber's law [31] which states that the ratio of increment threshold to the background intensity is a constant. The descriptor contains two components differential excitation [30] and orientation [30] which are defined as:

$$\xi(x_c) = \arctan\left[\frac{\nu_s^{00}}{\nu_s^{01}}\right] \; and \; \theta(x_c) = \arctan\left(\frac{\nu_s^{11}}{\nu_s^{10}}\right) \tag{2}$$

where $\xi(x_c)$ is the differential excitation and $\theta(x_c)$ is the orientation of the current pixel x_c, $x_i(i = 0, 1, ...p - 1)$ denotes the i-th neighbours of x_c and p is the number of neighbors, ν_s^{00}, ν_s^{01}, ν_s^{10} and ν_s^{11} are the output of filters f_{00}, f_{01}, f_{10} and f_{11} respectively. The WLD descriptor is based on a biological model and its feature extraction process simulates how humans perceive the environment. WLD provides robustness to illumination changes and noise in the image [30], therefore acts as a good descriptor for painting images.

In order to encode important discriminatory information of the painting image, we compute the WLD for every component of the image to form the color WLD. SIFT features are then densely sampled and the process is repeated separately for the three components of the image resulting in color WLD-SIFT feature. We train a parametric model [32,33], in our case, Gaussian Mixture Model (GMM) by fitting it to the sampled color WLD-SIFT features. The spatial information is also encoded by augmenting the visual features derived by SIFT with their spatial co-ordinates [34]. The Fisher vectors are then extracted by capturing the average first order and second order differences between the computed features and each of the GMM centers.

3.4   Color Fused Fisher Vector (CFFV)

In this section, we present a fused Fisher vector feature (FFV) that combines the most expressive features of the D-FV, WS-FV and SIFT-FV features. In the SIFT-FV feature, we compute Fisher vectors on densely sampled SIFT features using a GMM [26,33] for every component of the image. The most expressive features are then extracted by means of principal component analysis (PCA) [35].

To derive the proposed FFV feature, we first compute the D-FV, WS-FV and the color SIFT-FV for all the components of the image separately. The D-FV features of R, G and B components of the image are concatenated and normalized to zero mean and unit standard deviation. The dimensionality of the D-FV feature is then reduced by using PCA, which derives the most expressive features with respect to the minimum square error. The above process is then repeated for the WS-FV and SIFT-FV features. Finally, the computed D-FV, WS-FV and the SIFT FV features are further concatenated and normalized to create the FFV feature. Figure 1 shows the component images, the process of computation of D-FV, WS-FV and the SIFT-FV features, the PCA process and the CFFV feature derived from the concatenation and subsequent normalization of the computed features. The color cue provides powerful discriminating information in pattern recognition in general [36,37], therefore we also incorporate color information to our proposed feature. We repeat the above steps and compute the FFV in different color spaces namely YCbCr, YIQ, LAB, oRGB, XYZ, YUV and HSV. The CFFV feature is derived by fusing the FFV features in the different color spaces listed above.

4   Sparse Representation Based Complete Kernel Marginal Fisher Analysis Framework

In this section, we build a theoretical framework for sparse representation based complete kernel marginal Fisher analysis (SCMFA) based on two phase MFA framework. In SCMFA, we capture two kinds of important discriminant information namely the regular and irregular discriminant features from the range space and null space of intraclass compactness of the MFA method. We then use a discriminative sparse representation model with the objective of integrating representation criterion such as sparse coding with discriminative criterion so as to enhance the discriminative ability of the proposed method.

4.1   Motivation

The linear discriminant analysis (LDA) method assumes that the data of each class is of Gaussian distribution which is not always satisfied in real world problems. The separability of different classes cannot be well characterized by the interclass scatter if the above property is not satisfied [9]. This limitation of LDA is overcome by the marginal Fisher analysis (MFA) [9] which develops a new criteria that characterizes the intraclass compactness and interclass separability using an intrinsic and a penalty graph respectively.

Given the sample data matrix $\mathbf{X} = [\mathbf{x}_1, \mathbf{x}_2, ..., \mathbf{x}_m] \in \mathbb{R}^{n \times m}$ that consists of m samples each with dimension n, the intraclass compactness is characterized from the intrinsic graph by the term

$$\tilde{\mathbf{S}}_c = \sum_i \sum_{i \in N_{k_1}^+(j) \, or \, j \in N_{k_1}^+(i)} ||\mathbf{W}^T \mathbf{x}_i - \mathbf{W}^T \mathbf{x}_j||^2 = 2\mathbf{W}^T \mathbf{X}(\mathbf{D} - \mathbf{A})\mathbf{X}^T \mathbf{W} \tag{3}$$

where $\mathbf{A}_{ij}$ is 1 if $i \in N_{k_1}^+(j)$ or $j \in N_{k_1}^+(i)$ and 0 otherwise, $N_{k_1}^+(i)$ denotes the set of k_1 nearest neighbors of the sample x_i of the same class. The interclass separability is characterized by the following penalty graph:

$$\tilde{\mathbf{S}}_p = \sum_i \sum_{(i,j) \in P_{k_2}(c_i) \, or \, (i,j) \in P_{k_2}(c_j)} ||\mathbf{W}^T \mathbf{x}_i - \mathbf{W}^T \mathbf{x}_j||^2 = 2\mathbf{W}^T \mathbf{X}(\mathbf{D}^p - \mathbf{A}^p)\mathbf{X}^T \mathbf{W} \tag{4}$$

where $\mathbf{A}_{ij}^p$ is 1 if $(i,j) \in P_{k_2}(c_i)$ or $(i,j) \in P_{k_2}(c_j)$ and 0 otherwise, $P_{k_2}(c)$ denotes the set that are k_2 nearest neighbors among the set $\{(i,j), i \in \pi_c, j \notin \pi_c\}$. As a result, the marginal Fisher criterion [9] is given as follows:

$$\mathbf{T} = \arg\max_W \frac{\mathbf{tr}(\mathbf{W}^T \mathbf{X}(\mathbf{D}^p - \mathbf{A}^p)\mathbf{X}^T \mathbf{W})}{\mathbf{tr}(\mathbf{W}^T \mathbf{X}(\mathbf{D} - \mathbf{A})\mathbf{X}^T \mathbf{W})} = \arg\max \frac{\mathbf{tr}(\tilde{\mathbf{S}}_p)}{\mathbf{tr}(\tilde{\mathbf{S}}_c)} \tag{5}$$

The initial step of the MFA method is the PCA projection which projects the data into the PCA subspace where the dimensionality is reduced. A potential problem with the PCA step is that it may discard dimensions that contain important discriminative information as the PCA criterion is not compatible with the MFA criterion. Previous works of research by [38,39] for the linear discriminant analysis method prove that the null space of the within-class scatter matrix contain important discriminative information whereas the null space of the between-class scatter matrix contain no useful discriminatory information. We apply the same motivation for the intraclass compactness and the interclass separability of the MFA method.

In the complete kernel marginal Fisher analysis method, the strategy is to split the intraclass compactness $\mathbf{S}_c^k$ into two subspaces namely the range space $\mathbf{C}_r$ and null space $\mathbf{C}_n$ so as to extract two kinds of discriminant features: regular and irregular discriminant features. The regular discriminant features are extracted from the range space using the marginal Fisher discriminant criterion whereas the irregular discriminant features are extracted from the null space using the marginal interclass separability criterion.

In our proposed method, the kernel trick is used so as to increase the separation ability. Specifically, we use the Fisher kernel [32] with the kernel function $\phi(\mathbf{x}) : \mathbb{R}^n \rightarrow \mathbb{R}^h$ and $\mathbf{K}$ is the kernel gram matrix where $K_{ij} = K(x_i, x_j)$. The kernel marginal Fisher criterion is represented as:

$$\mathbf{T}^* = \arg\max_J \frac{\mathrm{tr}(\mathbf{J}^T \mathbf{K}(\mathbf{D}^p - \mathbf{A}^p)\mathbf{K}^T \mathbf{J})}{\mathrm{tr}(\mathbf{J}^T \mathbf{K}(\mathbf{D} - \mathbf{A})\mathbf{K}^T \mathbf{J})} = \arg\max \frac{\mathrm{tr}(\mathbf{S}_p^k)}{\mathrm{tr}(\mathbf{S}_c^k)} \tag{6}$$

4.2 Extraction of Regular and Irregular Discriminant Features

Suppose $\beta_1, \beta_2, ..., \beta_h$ be the eigenvectors of $\mathbf{S}_c^k$ then we define the range space as $\mathbf{C}_r = [\beta_1, ..., \beta_p]$ corresponding to the nonzero eigenvalues and the null space as $\mathbf{C}_n = [\beta_{p+1}, ..., \beta_h]$ where $p < h$. We extract the regular discriminant features from the range space of $\mathbf{S}_c^k$. As a result, the objective function is to maximize the marginal Fisher discriminant criterion which can be expressed as:

$$\mathbf{T}^r = \arg\max \frac{\mathrm{tr}(\mathbf{C}_r^T \mathbf{S}_p^k \mathbf{C}_r)}{\mathrm{tr}(\mathbf{C}_r^T \mathbf{S}_c^k \mathbf{C}_r)} \tag{7}$$

The criterion in Eq. (7) can be maximized directly by calculating the eigenvectors of the following eigen-equation:

$$\mathbf{S}_p^k \mathbf{C}_r = \lambda \mathbf{S}_c^k \mathbf{C}_r \tag{8}$$

Let $\boldsymbol{\xi} = [\boldsymbol{\xi}_1, \boldsymbol{\xi}_2, \ldots, \boldsymbol{\xi}_p]$ be the solutions of Eq. 8 ordered according to their eigenvalues, then the regular discriminant features are given as follows:

$$\mathbf{U}^r = \boldsymbol{\xi}^T \mathbf{C}_r^T \mathbf{K} \tag{9}$$

In order to compute the irregular discriminant features, the strategy is to remove the null space of interclass separability $\mathbf{S}_p^k$ and keep the null space of intraclass compactness $\mathbf{S}_c^k$. The null space of $\mathbf{S}_c^k$ is defined above as: $\mathbf{C}_n = [\beta_{p+1}, ..., \beta_h]$. We will diagonalize the $\mathbf{S}_p^k$ in the null space of $\mathbf{S}_c^k$ so as to project the data to the null space of $\mathbf{S}_c^k$.

$$\hat{\mathbf{S}}_p^k = \mathbf{C}_n^T \mathbf{S}_p^k \mathbf{C}_n \tag{10}$$

As a result, the objective function is to maximize the marginal interclass separability criterion which can be expressed as:

$$\mathbf{T}^{ir} = \arg\max \mathrm{tr}(\mathbf{C}_n^T \mathbf{S}_p^k \mathbf{C}_n) = \arg\max \mathrm{tr}(\hat{\mathbf{S}}_p^k) \tag{11}$$

We then have to remove the null space of $\hat{\mathbf{S}}_p^k$ since it has no useful discriminatory information. We maximize the criterion in Eq. 11 by eigenvalue analysis. Let $\zeta = [\zeta_1, \ldots, \zeta_{h-p}]$ be the eigen vectors ordered according to their eigenvalues, then we select $\zeta_{ir} = [\zeta_1, \ldots, \zeta_l]$ corresponding to the nonzero eigenvalues where $l < (h - p)$. Therefore, we define the irregular discriminant features as:

$$\mathbf{U}^{ir} = \zeta_{ir}^T \mathbf{C}_n^T \mathbf{K} \tag{12}$$

In order to obtain the final set of features, the regular and irregular discriminant features are fused and normalized to zero mean and unit standard deviation.

$$U = \begin{bmatrix} U^r \\ U^{ir} \end{bmatrix} \tag{13}$$

4.3 Discriminative Sparse Representation Model

In this section, we use a discriminative sparse representation criterion with the rationale to integrate the representation criterion such as sparse coding with the discriminative criterion so as to improve the classification performance. Given the feature matrix $U = [u_1, u_2, \ldots, u_l] \in \mathbb{R}^{l \times m}$ learned from the complete marginal Fisher analysis method, which contains m samples in a l dimensional space, let $D = [d_1, d_2, \ldots, d_r] \in \mathbb{R}^{l \times m}$ denote the dictionary that represents r basis vectors and $S = [s_1, s_2, \ldots, s_m] \in \mathbb{R}^{r \times m}$ denote the sparse representation matrix which represents the sparse representation for m samples. Each coefficient a_i correspond to the items in the dictionary D.

In our proposed discriminative sparse representation model, we optimize a sparse representation criterion and a discriminative analysis criterion to derive the dictionary D and sparse representation S from the training samples. We use the representation criterion of the sparse representation to define new discriminative within-class matrix $\hat{H}_w$ and discriminative between-class matrix $\hat{H}_b$ by considering only the k nearest neighbors. Specifically, using the sparse representation criterion the descriminative within class matrix is defined as $\hat{H}_w = \sum_{i=1}^{m} \sum_{(i,j) \in N_k^w(i,j)} (s_i - s_j)(s_i - s_j)^T$, where $(i,j) \in N_k^w(i,j)$ represents the (i,j) pairs where sample u_i is among the k nearest neighbors of sample u_j of the same class or vice versa. The discriminative between class matrix is defined as $\hat{H}_b = \sum_{i=1}^{m} \sum_{(i,j) \in N_k^b(i,j)} (s_i - s_j)(s_i - s_j)^T$, where $(i,j) \in N_k^b(i,j)$ represents k nearest (i,j) pairs among all the (i,j) pairs between samples u_i and u_j of different classes.

As a result, we define the new optimization criterion as:

$$\min_{D,S} \sum_{i=1}^{m} \{\|u_i - Ds_i\|^2 + \lambda\|s_i\|_1\} + \alpha \mathbf{tr}(\beta \hat{H}_w - (1-\beta)\hat{H}_b)$$

$$s.t. \|d_j\| \leq 1, (j = 1, 2, \ldots, r) \tag{14}$$

where the parameter λ controls the sparseness term, the parameter α controls the discriminatory term, the parameter β balances the contributions of the discriminative within class matrix $\hat{H}_w$ and between class matrix $\hat{H}_b$ and $\mathbf{tr}(.)$ denotes the trace of a matrix.

In order to derive the discriminative sparse representation for the test data, as the dictionary D is already learned, we only need to optimize the following criterion: $\min_B \sum_{i=1}^{t} \{\|y_i - Db_i\|^2\} + \lambda\|b_i\|_1$ where $y_1, y_2, \ldots, y_t$ are the test samples and t is the number of test samples. The discriminative sparse representation for the test data is defined as $B = [b_1, \ldots, b_t] \in \mathbb{R}^{r \times t}$. Since the dictionary **D** is learned from the training optimization process, it contains both sparseness and discriminative information, therefore the derived representation **B** is the discriminative sparse representation for the test set.

5 Experiments

In this section, we evaluate the performance of our proposed method for fine art painting categorization using the challenging Painting-91 dataset [8]. There are 4266 painting images by 91 artists in the dataset covering different eras ranging from the early renaissance period to the modern art period. The images are collected from the internet and every artist has atleast 31 images. The dataset classifies 50 painters to 13 style categories with style labels as follows: abstract expressionism (1), baroque (2), constructivism (3), cubbism (4), impressionism (5), neoclassical (6), popart (7), post-impressionism (8), realism (9), renaissance (10), romanticism (11), surrealism (12) and symbolism (13).

5.1 Artist Classification

In this section, we make a comparative assessment of our proposed method with other popular image descriptors and deep learning methods on the task of artist classification. Artist classification is the task wherein we determine the artist for a painting. In order to follow the experimental protocol and have a fair comparison with other methods, we use the fixed train/test split provided in the dataset containing 2275 training and 1991 test images. MSCNN is the abbreviation for multi-scale convolutional neural networks. Experimental results in Table 1 show that our proposed SCMFA method achieves the state-of-the-art classification performance of 65.78 % for artist classification and outperforms other popular image descriptors and deep learning methods.

5.2 Style Classification

In this section, we evaluate our proposed method on style classification wherein a painting is classified to its respective style out of the thirteen style categories defined in the dataset. The fourth column in Table 1 shows the results obtained using different features and learning methods for style classification. The experimental results demonstrate that our proposed SCMFA method achieves the state-of-the-art results compared to other popular image descriptors and deep learning methods for style classification.

Figure 2 shows the confusion matrix for the style categorization where the rows show the true style categories and the columns show the assigned categories. It can be seen from Fig. 2 that style categories 1 (abstract expressionism), 13 (symbolism), 4 (cubbism) and 8(post-impressionism) give the best accuracy with classification rates of 93 %, 89 %, 81 % and 80 % respectively. The style category with the lowest accuracy is category 6 (neoclassical) as there are large confusions

Table 1. Comparison of the proposed SCMFA method with other popular image descriptors and deep learning methods on the Painting-91 dataset.

No.	Method	Artist classification	Style classification
1	LBP [3,8]	28.50	42.20
2	Color-LBP [8]	35.00	47.00
3	PHOG [4,8]	18.60	29.50
4	Color-PHOG [8]	22.80	33.20
5	GIST [5,8]	23.90	31.30
6	Color-GIST [8]	27.80	36.50
7	SIFT [6,8]	42.60	53.20
8	CLBP [7,8]	34.70	46.40
9	CN [8,40]	18.10	33.30
10	SSIM [8,17]	23.70	37.50
11	OPPSIFT [8,16]	39.50	52.20
12	RGBSIFT [8,16]	40.30	47.40
13	CSIFT [8,16]	36.40	48.60
14	CN-SIFT [8]	44.10	56.70
15	Combine(1–14) [8]	53.10	62.20
16	MSCNN-1 [41]	58.11	69.67
17	MSCNN-2 [41]	57.91	70.96
18	CNN F_3 [42]	56.40	68.57
19	CNN F_4 [42]	56.35	69.21
20	**SCMFA**	**65.78**	**73.16**

Table 2. Art movement associated with different art styles.

Art movement	Art style
Renaissance	Renaissance
Post renaissance	Baroque, neoclassical, realism, romanticism
Modern art	Popart, impressionism, post impressionism, symbolism, constructivism, surrealism, cubbism, abstract expressionism

between the style categories baroque : neoclassical and renaissance : neoclassical. Similarly, the other style category pair that have large similarities is style renaissance : baroque due to evolution of the baroque style from the renaissance style.

5.3   Comprehensive Analysis of Results

We now evaluate the relation between the art painting styles and the art movement periods. An art movement period is a movement wherein a group of artists

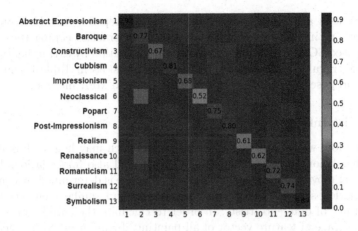

Fig. 2. The confusion matrix for 13 style categories of the Painting-91 dataset.

follow a common philosophy or goal in art during a specific period of time. Table 2 shows the different art styles that were practiced in different art movement periods. Important patterns can be deduced by correlating the confusion diagram in Fig. 2 and the results of Table 2. We can observe that the art styles practiced in the same art movement period show higher similarity compared to art styles between different art movement periods. It can be seen from Fig. 2 that the style baroque has large confusions with styles neoclassical, romanticism and realism. These style categories belong to the same art movement period - post renaissance. Similarly, popart paintings have high similarities with styles surrealism and post impressionism within the same art movement period - modern art. The only exception to the above observation is the style categories renaissance and baroque as even though they belong to different art movement period, there are large confusions between them. The renaissance and baroque art paintings have high similarity as the baroque style evolved from the renaissance style resulting in few discriminating aspects between them [43].

5.4   Comparison with the MFA Method

In this section, we compare our proposed SCMFA method with the traditional marginal Fisher analysis (MFA) method. In order to have a fair comparison, the same experimental settings and Fisher vectors features are used for comparison.

Table 3. Comparison of the proposed method with marginal Fisher analysis method.

No.	Method	Artist classification	Style classification
1	MFA [9]	59.57	66.79
2	**SCMFA**	**65.78**	**73.16**

The MFA uses a PCA projection in the initial step due to which important discriminatory information in the null space of intraclass compactness is lost. Our proposed SCMFA method overcomes this limitation by extracting two kinds of features, regular and irregular. Experimental results in Table 3 demonstrate that our proposed SCMFA method outperforms the MFA method.

5.5 Artist Influence

In this section, we analyze the artist influence which may help us link different artists that belong to an art movement period and also find relations between different art movement periods. The artist influence is determined by computing the correlation score of every artist in order to find similar elements between the paintings of different artists. In order to calculate the correlation score, we find the average of feature vector of all paintings by an artist. In particular, let $\mathbf{F}_p$ denote the average feature vector of all painting images by artist p. We then find the relation between the average feature vector of all artists by computing the correlation matrix. Finally, different artists are grouped together to form clusters based on the correlation score. Figure 3(a) shows the artist influence cluster graph with correlation threshold of 0.70.

Interesting observations can be deduced from Fig. 3(a). A particular art style and time period can be associated with every cluster. Cluster 1 shows artists with major contributions to the styles realism and romanticism and they belong to the post renaissance art movement period. Cluster 2 has the largest number of artists associated with the styles renaissance and baroque. Cluster 3 represents artists for the style Italian renaissance that took place in the 16th century. And cluster 4 shows artists associated with style abstract expressionism in the modern art movement period.

5.6 Style Influence

In this section, we study the style influence so as to find common elements between different art styles and understand the evolution of art styles in different art movement periods. In order to calculate the style influence, we compute the average feature vector of all paintings for a style similar to the artist influence. The k-means clustering method is then applied with k set as 3 so as to form clusters of similar art styles. We finally plot a style influence graph using the first two principal components of the average feature vector.

Figure 3(b) shows the style influence graph clusters with k set as 3. Cluster 1 contains the styles of the post renaissance art movement period with the only exception of style renaissance. The reason for this may be due the high similarity between styles baroque and renaissance as the style baroque evolved from the style renaissance [43]. The styles impressionism, post impressionism and symbolism in cluster 2 show that there are high similarities between these styles in the modern art movement period as the three styles have a common french and belgian origin. Similarly, styles constructivism and popart in cluster 3 show high similarity in the style influence cluster graph.

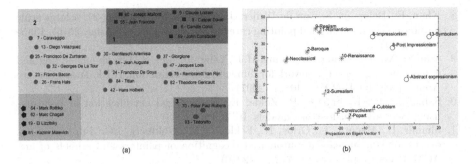

Fig. 3. (a) Shows the artist influence graph (b) shows the style influence graph.

6   Conclusion

This paper presents a sparse representation based complete kernel marginal Fisher analysis (SCMFA) framework for categorizing fine art painting images. First, we perform hybrid feature extraction by introducing the D-FV, WS-FV and CFFV features to extract and encode important discriminatory information of the art painting images. We then propose a complete marginal Fisher analysis method so as to extract regular and irregular discriminant features in order to overcome the limitation of the traditional MFA method. The regular features are extracted from the range space of the intraclass compactness whereas the irregular features are extracted from the null space of the intraclass compactness. Finally, we learn a sparse representation model so as to integrate the representation criterion with the discriminative criterion. Experimental results show that our proposed method outperforms other popular methods in the artist and style classification task of the challenging Painting-91 dataset.

References

1. Solso, R.L.: Cognition and the Visual Arts. MIT Press, Cambridge (1996)
2. Zeki, S.: Inner Vision: An Exploration of Art and the Brain. Oxford University Press, Oxford (1999)
3. Ojala, T., Pietikainen, M., Maenpaa, T.: Multiresolution gray-scale and rotation invariant texture classification with local binary patterns. IEEE Trans. Pattern Anal. Mach. Intell. **24**(7), 971–987 (2002)
4. Bosch, A., Zisserman, A., Munoz, X.: Representing shape with a spatial pyramid kernel. In: Proceedings of the 6th ACM International Conference on Image and Video Retrieval. In: CIVR 2007, pp. 401–408 (2007)
5. Oliva, A., Torralba, A.: Modeling the shape of the scene: a holistic representation of the spatial envelope. Int. J. Comput. Vis. **42**(3), 145–175 (2001)
6. Lowe, D.: Distinctive image features from scale-invariant keypoints. Int. J. Comput. Vis. **60**(2), 91–110 (2004)
7. Guo, Z., Zhang, D., Zhang, D.: A completed modeling of local binary pattern operator for texture classification. IEEE Trans. Image Process. **19**(6), 1657–1663 (2010)

8. Khan, F., Beigpour, S., van de Weijer, J., Felsberg, M.: Painting-91: a large scale database for computational painting categorization. Mach. Vis. Appl. **25**(6), 1385–1397 (2014)
9. Yan, S., Xu, D., Zhang, B., Zhang, H.J., Yang, Q., Lin, S.: Graph embedding and extensions: a general framework for dimensionality reduction. IEEE Trans. Pattern Anal. Mach. Intell. **29**(1), 40–51 (2007)
10. Sablatnig, R., Kammerer, P., Zolda, E.: Hierarchical classification of paintings using face- and brush stroke models. In: ICPR (1998)
11. Shamir, L., Macura, T., Orlov, N., Eckley, D.M., Goldberg, I.G.: Impressionism, expressionism, surrealism: automated recognition of painters and schools of art. ACM Trans. Appl. Percept. **7**(2), 8 (2010)
12. Shen, J.: Stochastic modeling western paintings for effective classification. Pattern Recognit. **42**(2), 293–301 (2009). Learning Semantics from Multimedia Content
13. Shamir, L., Tarakhovsky, J.A.: Computer analysis of art. J. Comput. Cult. Herit. **5**(2), 7 (2012)
14. Zujovic, J., Gandy, L., Friedman, S., Pardo, B., Pappas, T.: Classifying paintings by artistic genre: an analysis of features and classifiers. In: IEEE International Workshop on Multimedia Signal Processing (MMSP 2009), pp. 1–5, October 2009
15. Siddiquie, B., Vitaladevuni, S., Davis, L.: Combining multiple kernels for efficient image classification. In: 2009 Workshop on Applications of Computer Vision (WACV), pp. 1–8 (2009)
16. van de Sande, K., Gevers, T., Snoek, C.: Evaluating color descriptors for object and scene recognition. IEEE Trans. Pattern Anal. Mach. Intell. **32**(9), 1582–1596 (2010)
17. Shechtman, E., Irani, M.: Matching local self-similarities across images and videos. In: CVPR, pp. 1–8, June 2007
18. He, X., Yan, S., Hu, Y., Niyogi, P., Zhang, H.J.: Face recognition using laplacianfaces. IEEE Trans. Pattern Anal. Mach. Intell. **27**(3), 328–340 (2005)
19. Cai, D., He, X., Zhou, K., Han, J., Bao, H.: Locality sensitive discriminant analysis. In: Proceedings of the 20th International Joint Conference on Artifical Intelligence (IJCAI 2007), pp. 708–713. Morgan Kaufmann Publishers Inc., San Francisco (2007)
20. Mairal, J., Bach, F., Ponce, J., Sapiro, G.: Online dictionary learning for sparse coding. In: Proceedings of the 26th Annual International Conference on Machine Learning, pp. 689–696. ACM (2009)
21. Lee, H., Battle, A., Raina, R., Ng, A.Y.: Efficient sparse coding algorithms. In: Advances in Neural Information Processing Systems, pp. 801–808 (2006)
22. Wang, J., Yang, J., Yu, K., Lv, F., Huang, T., Gong, Y.: Locality-constrained linear coding for image classification. In: 2010 IEEE Conference on Computer Vision and Pattern Recognition (CVPR), pp. 3360–3367, June 2010
23. Zheng, M., Bu, J., Chen, C., Wang, C., Zhang, L., Qiu, G., Cai, D.: Graph regularized sparse coding for image representation. IEEE Trans. Image Process. **20**(5), 1327–1336 (2011)
24. Zhou, N., Shen, Y., Peng, J., Fan, J.: Learning inter-related visual dictionary for object recognition. In: 2012 IEEE Conference on Computer Vision and Pattern Recognition (CVPR), pp. 3490–3497, June 2012
25. Mairal, J., Ponce, J., Sapiro, G., Zisserman, A., Bach, F.R.: Supervised dictionary learning. In: Advances in Neural Information Processing Systems, pp. 1033–1040 (2009)
26. Simonyan, K., Parkhi, O.M., Vedaldi, A., Zisserman, A.: Fisher vector faces in the wild. In: BMVC (2013)

27. Jegou, H., Perronnin, F., Douze, M., Sanchez, J., Perez, P., Schmid, C.: Aggregating local image descriptors into compact codes. IEEE Trans. Pattern Anal. Mach. Intell. **34**(9), 1704–1716 (2012)

28. Perronnin, F., Sánchez, J., Mensink, T.: Improving the Fisher Kernel for large-scale image classification. In: Daniilidis, K., Maragos, P., Paragios, N. (eds.) ECCV 2010, Part IV. LNCS, vol. 6314, pp. 143–156. Springer, Heidelberg (2010)

29. Tola, E., Lepetit, V., Fua, P.: Daisy: an efficient dense descriptor applied to wide-baseline stereo. IEEE Trans. Pattern Anal. Mach. Intell. **32**(5), 815–830 (2010)

30. Chen, J., Shan, S., He, C., Zhao, G., Pietikainen, M., Chen, X., Gao, W.: WLD: a robust local image descriptor. IEEE Trans. Pattern Anal. Mach. Intell. **32**(9), 1705–1720 (2010)

31. Jain, A.K.: Fundamentals of Digital Image Processing. Prentice-Hall Inc., Upper Saddle River (1989)

32. Jaakkola, T., Diekhans, M., Haussler, D.: Using the Fisher Kernel method to detect remote protein homologies. In: Proceedings of the Seventh International Conference on Intelligent Systems for Molecular Biology, pp. 149–158. AAAI Press (1999)

33. Perronnin, F., Dance, C.: Fisher Kernels on visual vocabularies for image categorization. In: CVPR, June 2007

34. Snchez, J., Perronnin, F., de Campos, T.: Modeling the spatial layout of images beyond spatial pyramids. Pattern Recognit. Lett. **33**(16), 2216–2223 (2012)

35. Fukunaga, K.: Introduction to Statistical Pattern Recognition. Academic Press Professional Inc., San Diego (1990)

36. Sinha, A., Banerji, S., Liu, C.: New color GPHOG descriptors for object and scene image classification. Mach. Vis. Appl. **25**(2), 361–375 (2014)

37. Liu, C.: Extracting discriminative color features for face recognition. Pattern Recognit. Lett. **32**(14), 1796–1804 (2011)

38. Chen, L.F., Liao, H.Y.M., Ko, M.T., Lin, J.C., Yu, G.J.: A new LDA-based face recognition system which can solve the small sample size problem. Pattern Recognit. **33**(10), 1713–1726 (2000)

39. Yu, H., Yang, J.: A direct LDA algorithm for high-dimensional data with application to face recognition. Pattern Recognit. **34**(10), 2067–2070 (2001)

40. van de Weijer, J., Schmid, C., Verbeek, J., Larlus, D.: Learning color names for real-world applications. IEEE Trans. Image Process. **18**(7), 1512–1523 (2009)

41. Peng, K.C., Chen, T.: A framework of extracting multi-scale features using multiple convolutional neural networks. In: 2015 IEEE International Conference on Multimedia and Expo (ICME), pp. 1–6, June 2015

42. Peng, K.C., Chen, T.: Cross-layer features in convolutional neural networks for generic classification tasks. In: 2015 IEEE International Conference on Image Processing (ICIP), pp. 3057–3061, September 2015

43. Rathus, L.: Foundations of Art and Design. Wadsworth Cengage Learning, Boston (2008)

3D-R2N2: A Unified Approach for Single and Multi-view 3D Object Reconstruction

Christopher B. Choy$^{(\boxtimes)}$, Danfei Xu, JunYoung Gwak, Kevin Chen, and Silvio Savarese

Stanford University, Stanford, USA
{chrischoy,danfei,jgwak,kchen92,ssilvio}@stanford.edu

Abstract. Inspired by the recent success of methods that employ shape priors to achieve robust 3D reconstructions, we propose a novel recurrent neural network architecture that we call the 3D Recurrent Reconstruction Neural Network (3D-R2N2). The network learns a mapping from images of objects to their underlying 3D shapes from a large collection of synthetic data [13]. Our network takes in one or more images of an object instance from arbitrary viewpoints and outputs a reconstruction of the object in the form of a 3D occupancy grid. Unlike most of the previous works, our network does not require any image annotations or object class labels for training or testing. Our extensive experimental analysis shows that our reconstruction framework (i) outperforms the state-of-the-art methods for single view reconstruction, and (ii) enables the 3D reconstruction of objects in situations when traditional SFM/SLAM methods fail (because of lack of texture and/or wide baseline).

Keywords: Multi-view · Reconstruction · Recurrent neural network

1 Introduction

Rapid and automatic 3D object prototyping has become a game-changing innovation in many applications related to e-commerce, visualization, and architecture, to name a few. This trend has been boosted now that 3D printing is a democratized technology and 3D acquisition methods are accurate and efficient [15]. Moreover, the trend is also coupled with the diffusion of large scale repositories of 3D object models such as ShapeNet [13].

Most of the state-of-the-art methods for 3D object reconstruction, however, are subject to a number of restrictions. Some restrictions are that: (i) objects must be observed from a dense number of views; or equivalently, views must have a relatively small baseline. This is an issue when users wish to reconstruct

---

D. Xu and J. Gwak—Equal contribution.

Electronic supplementary material The online version of this chapter (doi:10.1007/978-3-319-46484-8_38) contains supplementary material, which is available to authorized users.

B. Leibe et al. (Eds.): ECCV 2016, Part VIII, LNCS 9912, pp. 628–644, 2016.
DOI: 10.1007/978-3-319-46484-8_38

the object from just a handful of views or ideally just one view (see Fig. 1(a)); (ii) objects' appearances (or their reflectance functions) are expected to be Lambertian (i.e. non-reflective) and the albedos are supposed be non-uniform (i.e., rich of non-homogeneous textures).

These restrictions stem from a number of key technical assumptions. One typical assumption is that features can be matched across views [4,18,21,35] as hypothesized by the majority of the methods based on SFM or SLAM [22,24]. It has been demonstrated (for instance see [37]) that if the viewpoints are separated by a large baseline, establishing (traditional) feature correspondences is extremely problematic due to local appearance changes or self-occlusions. Moreover, lack of texture on objects and specular reflections also make the feature matching problem very difficult [9,43].

In order to circumvent issues related to large baselines or non-Lambertian surfaces, 3D volumetric reconstruction methods such as space carving [5,23,33,45] and their probabilistic extensions [12] have become popular. These methods, however, assume that the objects are accurately segmented from the background or that the cameras are calibrated, which is not the case in many applications.

A different philosophy is to assume that prior knowledge about the object appearance and shape is available. The benefit of using priors is that the ensuing reconstruction method is less reliant on finding accurate feature correspondences across views. Thus, shape prior-based methods can work with fewer images and with fewer assumptions on the object reflectance function as shown in [6,16,25]. The shape priors are typically encoded in the form of simple 3D primitives as demonstrated by early pioneering works [34,39] or learned from rich repositories of 3D CAD models [11,41,52], whereby the concept of fitting 3D models to images of faces was explored to a much larger extent [10,31,38]. Sophisticated mathematical formulations have also been introduced to adapt 3D shape models to observations with different degrees of supervision [40] and different regularization strategies [42].

This paper is in the same spirit as the methods discussed above, but with a key difference. Instead of trying to match a suitable 3D shape prior to the observation of the object and possibly adapt to it, we use deep convolutional neural networks to learn a mapping from observations to their underlying 3D shapes of objects from a large collection of training data. Inspired by early works that used machine learning to learn a 2D-to-3D mapping for scene understanding [29,44], data driven approaches have been recently proposed to solve the daunting problem of recovering the shape of an object from just a single image [20,30,47,50] for a given number of object categories. In our approach, however, we leverage for the first time the ability of deep neural networks to automatically learn, in a mere end-to-end fashion, the appropriate intermediate representations from data to recover approximated 3D object reconstructions from as few as a single image with minimal supervision.

Inspired by the success of Long Short-Term Memory (LSTM) [28] networks [48,49] as well as recent progress in single-view 3D reconstruction using Convolutional Neural Networks [17,36], we propose a novel architecture that we

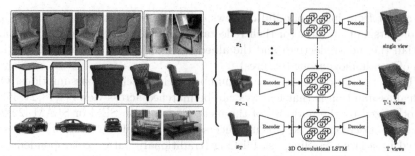

(a) Images of objects we wish to reconstruct (b) Overview of the network

Fig. 1. (a) Some sample images of the objects we wish to reconstruct - notice that views are separated by a large baseline and objects' appearance shows little texture and/or are non-lambertian. (b) An overview of our proposed **3D-R2N2**: The network takes a sequence of images (or just one image) from arbitrary (uncalibrated) viewpoints as input (in this example, 3 views of the armchair) and generates voxelized 3D reconstruction as an output. The reconstruction is incrementally refined as the network sees more views of the object.

call the 3D Recurrent Reconstruction Neural Network (3D-R2N2). The network takes in one or more images of an object instance from different viewpoints and outputs a reconstruction of the object in the form of a 3D occupancy grid, as illustrated in Fig. 1(b). Note that in both training and testing, our network does not require any object class labels or image annotations (i.e., no segmentations, keypoints, viewpoint labels, or class labels are needed).

One of the key attributes of the 3D-R2N2 is that it can selectively update hidden representations by controlling *input* gates and *forget* gates. In training, this mechanism allows the network to adaptively and consistently learn a suitable 3D representation of an object as (potentially conflicting) information from different viewpoints becomes available (see Fig. 1).

The main contributions of this paper are summarized as follows:

– We propose an extension of the standard LSTM framework that we call the 3D Recurrent Reconstruction Neural Network which is suitable for accommodating multi-view image feeds in a principled manner.
– We unify single- and multi-view 3D reconstruction in a single framework.
– Our approach requires minimal supervision in training and testing (just bounding boxes, but no segmentation, keypoints, viewpoint labels, camera calibration, or class labels are needed).
– Our extensive experimental analysis shows that our reconstruction framework outperforms the state-of-the-art method for single-view reconstruction [30].
– Our network enables the 3D reconstruction of objects in situations when traditional SFM/SLAM methods fail (because of lack of texture or wide baselines).

An overview of our reconstruction network is shown in Fig. 1(b). The rest of this paper is organized as follows. In Sect. 2, we give a brief overview of LSTM and GRU networks. In Sect. 3, we introduce the 3D Recurrent Reconstruction Neural Network architecture. In Sect. 4, we discuss how we generate training data and give details of the training process. Finally, we present test results of our approach on various datasets including PASCAL 3D and ShapeNet in Sect. 5.

2   Recurrent Neural Network

In this section we provide a brief overview of Long Short-Term Memory (LSTM) networks and a variation of the LSTM called Gated Recurrent Units (GRU).

Long Short-Term Memory Unit. One of the most successful implementations of the hidden states of an RNN is the Long Short Term Memory (LSTM) unit [28]. An LSTM unit explicitly controls the flow from input to output, allowing the network to overcome the vanishing gradient problem [7,28]. Specifically, an LSTM unit consists of four components: memory units (a memory cell and a hidden state), and three gates which control the flow of information from the input to the hidden state (*input gate*), from the hidden state to the output (*output gate*), and from the previous hidden state to the current hidden state (*forget gate*). More formally, at time step t when a new input x_t is received, the operation of an LSTM unit can be expressed as:

$$i_t = \sigma(W_i x_t + U_i h_{t-1} + b_i) \tag{1}$$

$$f_t = \sigma(W_f x_t + U_f h_{t-1} + b_f) \tag{2}$$

$$o_t = \sigma(W_o x_t + U_o h_{t-1} + b_o) \tag{3}$$

$$s_t = f_t \odot s_{t-1} + i_t \odot \tanh(W_s x_t + U_s h_{t-1} + b_s) \tag{4}$$

$$h_t = o_t \odot \tanh(s_t) \tag{5}$$

i_t, f_t, o_t refer to the input, output, and forget gate, respectively. s_t and h_t refer to the memory cell and the hidden state. We use $\odot$ to denote element-wise multiplication and the subscript t to refer to an activation at time t.

Gated Recurrent Unit. A variation of the LSTM unit is the Gated Recurrent Unit (GRU) proposed by Cho et al. [14]. An advantage of the GRU is that there are fewer computations compared to the standard LSTM. In a GRU, an update gate controls both the input and forget gates. Another difference is that a *reset gate* is applied before the nonlinear transformation. More formally,

$$u_t = \sigma(W_u T x_t + U_u * h_{t-1} + b_f) \tag{6}$$

$$r_t = \sigma(W_i T x_t + U_i * h_{t-1} + b_i) \tag{7}$$

$$h_t = (1 - u_t) \odot h_{t-1} + u_t \odot \tanh(W_h x_t + U_h(r_t \odot h_{t-1}) + b_h) \tag{8}$$

u_t, r_t, h_t represent the update, reset, and hidden state respectively.

3   3D Recurrent Reconstruction Neural Network

In this section, we introduce a novel architecture named the 3D Recurrent Reconstruction Network (3D-R2N2), which builds upon the standard LSTM and GRU.

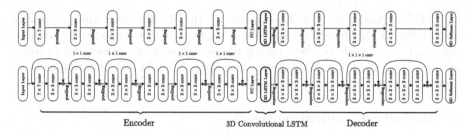

Fig. 2. Network architecture: Each 3D-R2N2 consists of an encoder, a recurrence unit and a decoder. After every convolution layer, we place a LeakyReLU nonlinearity. The encoder converts a 127 × 127 RGB image into a low-dimensional feature which is then fed into the 3D-LSTM. The decoder then takes the 3D-LSTM hidden states and transforms them to a final voxel occupancy map. After each convolution layer is a LeakyReLU. We use two versions of 3D-R2N2: (top) a shallow network and (bottom) a deep residual network [26].

The goal of the network is to perform both single- and multi-view 3D reconstructions. The main idea is to leverage the power of LSTM to retain previous observations and incrementally refine the output reconstruction as more observations become available.

The network is made up of three components: a 2D Convolutional Neural Network (2D-CNN), a novel architecture named 3D Convolutional LSTM (3D-LSTM), and a 3D Deconvolutional Neural Network (3D-DCNN) (see Fig. 2). Given one or more images of an object from arbitrary viewpoints, the 2D-CNN first encodes each input image x into low dimensional features $\mathcal{T}(x)$ (Sect. 3.1). Then, given the encoded input, a set of newly proposed 3D Convolutional LSTM (3D-LSTM) units (Sect. 3.2) either selectively update their cell states or retain the states by closing the input gate. Finally, the 3D-DCNN decodes the hidden states of the LSTM units and generates a 3D probabilistic voxel reconstruction (Sect. 3.3).

The main advantage of using an LSTM-based network comes from its ability to effectively handle object self-occlusions when multiple views are fed to the network. The network selectively updates the memory cells that correspond to the visible parts of the object. If a subsequent view shows parts that were previously self-occluded and mismatch the prediction, the network would update the LSTM states for the previously occluded sections but retain the states of the other parts (Fig. 2).

3.1 Encoder: 2D-CNN

We use CNNs to encode images into features. We designed two different 2D-CNN encoders as shown in Fig. 2: A standard feed-forward CNN and a deep residual variation of it. The first network consists of standard convolution layers, pooling layers, and leaky rectified linear units followed by a fully-connected layer. Motivated by a recent study [26], we also created a deep residual variation

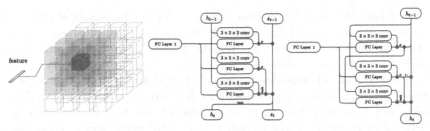

(a) inputs for each LSTM unit (b) 3D Convolutional LSTMs (c) 3D Convolutional GRUs

Fig. 3. (a) At each time step, each unit (purple) in the 3D-LSTM receives the same feature vector from the encoder as well as the hidden states from its neighbors (red) by a $3 \times 3 \times 3$ convolution ($W_s * h_{t-1}$) as inputs. We propose two versions of 3D-LSTMs: (b) 3D-LSTMs without output gates and (c) 3D Gated Recurrent Units (GRUs). (Color figure online)

of the first network and report the performance of this variation in Sect. 5.2. According to the study, adding residual connections between standard convolution layers effectively improves and speeds up the optimization process for very deep networks. The deep residual variation of the encoder network has identity mapping connections after every 2 convolution layers except for the 4th pair. To match the number of channels after convolutions, we use a 1×1 convolution for residual connections. The encoder output is then flattened and passed to a fully connected layer which compresses the output into a 1024 dimensional feature vector.

3.2   Recurrence: 3D Convolutional LSTM

The core part of our 3D-R2N2 is a recurrence module that allows the network to retain what it has seen and to update the memory when it sees a new image. A naive approach would be to use a vanilla LSTM network. However, predicting such a large output space ($32 \times 32 \times 32$) would be a very difficult task without any regularization. We propose a new architecture that we call 3D-Convolutional LSTM (3D-LSTM). The network is made up of a set of structured LSTM units with restricted connections. The 3D-LSTM units are spatially distributed in a 3D grid structure, with each unit responsible for reconstructing a particular part of the final output (see Fig. 3(a)). Inside the 3D grid, there are $N \times N \times N$ 3D-LSTM units where N is the spatial resolution of the 3D-LSTM grid. Each 3D-LSTM unit, indexed (i, j, k), has an independent hidden state $h_{t,(i,j,k)} \in \mathbb{R}^{N_h}$. Following the same notation as in Sect. 2 but with f_t, i_t, s_t, h_t as 4D tensors ($N \times N \times N$ vectors of size N_h), the equations governing the 3D-LSTM grid are

$$f_t = \sigma(W_f \mathcal{T}(x_t) + U_f * h_{t-1} + b_f) \tag{9}$$

$$i_t = \sigma(W_i \mathcal{T}(x_t) + U_i * h_{t-1} + b_i) \tag{10}$$

$$s_t = f_t \odot s_{t-1} + i_t \odot \tanh(W_s \mathcal{T}(x_t) + U_s * h_{t-1} + b_s) \tag{11}$$

$$h_t = \tanh(s_t) \tag{12}$$

We denote the convolution operation as $*$. In our implementation, we use $N = 4$. Unlike a standard LSTM, we do not have output gates since we only extract the output at the end. By removing redundant output gates, we can reduce the number of parameters.

Intuitively, this configuration forces a 3D-LSTM unit to handle the mismatch between a particular region of the predicted reconstruction and the ground truth model such that each unit learns to reconstruct one part of the voxel space instead of contributing to the reconstruction of the entire space. This configuration also endows the network with a sense of locality so that it can selectively update its prediction about the previously occluded part of the object. We visualize such behavior in the appendix[1].

Moreover, a 3D Convolutional LSTM unit restricts the connections of its hidden state to its spatial neighbors. For vanilla LSTMs, all elements in the hidden layer h_{t-1} affect the current hidden state h_t, whereas a spatially structured 3D Convolutional LSTM only allows its hidden states $h_{t,(i,j,k)}$ to be affected by its neighboring 3D-LSTM units for all i, j, and k. More specifically, the neighboring connections are defined by the convolution kernel size. For instance, if we use a $3 \times 3 \times 3$ kernel, an LSTM unit is only affected by its immediate neighbors. This way, the units can share weights and the network can be further regularized.

In Sect. 2, we also described the Gated Recurrent Unit (GRU) as a variation of the LSTM unit. We created a variation of the 3D-Convolutional LSTM using Gated Recurrent Unit (GRU). More formally, a GRU-based recurrence module can be expressed as

$$u_t = \sigma(W_{fx}\mathcal{T}(x_t) + U_f * h_{t-1} + b_f) \tag{13}$$

$$r_t = \sigma(W_{ix}\mathcal{T}(x_t) + U_i * h_{t-1} + b_i) \tag{14}$$

$$h_t = (1 - u_t) \odot h_{t-1} + u_t \odot \tanh(W_h\mathcal{T}(x_t) + U_h * (r_t \odot h_{t-1}) + b_h) \tag{15}$$

3.3   Decoder: 3D Deconvolutional Neural Network

After receiving an input image sequence $x_1, x_2, \cdots, x_T$, the 3D-LSTM passes the hidden state h_T to a decoder, which increases the hidden state resolution by applying 3D convolutions, non-linearities, and 3D unpooling [3] until it reaches the target output resolution.

As with the encoders, we propose a simple decoder network with 5 convolutions and a deep residual version with 4 residual connections followed by a final convolution. After the last layer where the activation reaches the target output resolution, we convert the final activation $\mathcal{V} \in \mathbb{R}^{N_{vox} \times N_{vox} \times N_{vox} \times 2}$ to the occupancy probability $p_{(i,j,k)}$ of the voxel cell at (i, j, k) using voxel-wise softmax.

3.4   Loss: 3D Voxel-Wise Softmax

The loss function of the network is defined as the sum of voxel-wise cross-entropy. Let the final output at each voxel (i, j, k) be Bernoulli distributions

---

[1] http://cvgl.stanford.edu/3d-r2n2/

$[1 - p_{(i,j,k)}, p_{(i,j,k)}]$, where the dependency on input $\mathcal{X} = \{x_t\}_{t \in \{1,...,T\}}$ is omitted, and let the corresponding ground truth occupancy be $y_{(i,j,k)} \in \{0,1\}$, then

$$L(\mathcal{X}, y) = \sum_{i,j,k} y_{(i,j,k)} \log(p_{(i,j,k)}) + (1 - y_{(i,j,k)}) \log(1 - p_{(i,j,k)}) \qquad (16)$$

4   Implementation

Data augmentation: In training, we used 3D CAD models for generating input images and ground truth voxel occupancy maps. We first rendered the CAD models with a transparent background and then augmented the input images with random crops from the PASCAL VOC 2012 dataset [19]. Also, we tinted the color of the models and randomly translated the images. Note that all viewpoints were sampled randomly.

Training: In training the network, we used variable length inputs ranging from one image to an arbitrary number of images. More specifically, the input length (number of views) for each training example within a single mini-batch was kept constant, but the input length of training examples across *different* mini-batches varied randomly. This enabled the network to perform both single- and multi-view reconstruction. During training, we computed the loss only at the end of an input sequence in order to save both computational power and memory. On the other hand, during test time we could access the intermediate reconstructions at each time step by extracting the hidden states of the LSTM units.

Network: The input image size was set to 127×127. The output voxelized reconstruction was of size $32 \times 32 \times 32$. The networks used in the experiments were trained for 60,000 iterations with a batch size of 36 except for [Res3D-GRU-3] (See Table 1), which needed a batch size of 24 to fit in an NVIDIA Titan X GPU. For the LeakyReLU layers, the slope of the leak was set to 0.1 throughout the network. For deconvolution, we followed the unpooling scheme presented in [3]. We used Theano [8] to implement our network and used Adam [32] for the SGD update rule. We initialized all weights except for LSTM weights using MSRA [27] and 0.1 for all biases. For LSTM weights, we used SVD to decompose a random matrix and used an unitary matrix for initialization.

5   Experiments

In this section, we validate and demonstrate the capability of our approach with several experiments using the datasets described in Sect. 5.1. First, we show the results of different variations of the 3D-R2N2 (Sect. 5.2). Next, we compare the performance of our network on the PASCAL 3D [51] dataset with that of a state-of-the-art method by Kar et al. [30] for single-view real-world image reconstruction (Sect. 5.3). Then we show the network's ability to perform multi-view reconstruction on the ShapeNet dataset [13] and the Online Products dataset [46] (Sects. 5.4 and 5.5). Finally, we compare our approach with a Multi View Stereo method on reconstructing objects with various texture levels and viewpoint sparsity (Sect. 5.6).

5.1   Dataset

ShapeNet: The ShapeNet dataset is a collection of 3D CAD models that are organized according to the WordNet hierarchy. We used a subset of the ShapeNet dataset which consists of 50,000 models and 13 major categories (see Fig. 5(c) for a complete list). We split the dataset into training and testing sets, with 4/5 for training and the remaining 1/5 for testing. We refer to these two datasets as the ShapeNet training set and testing set throughout the experiments section.

PASCAL 3D: The PASCAL 3D dataset is composed of PASCAL 2012 detection images augmented with 3D CAD model alignment [51].

Online Products: The dataset [46] contains images of 23,000 items sold online. MVS and SFM methods fail on these images due to ultra-wide baselines. Since the dataset does not have the ground-truth 3D CAD models, we only used the dataset for qualitative evaluation.

MVS CAD Models: To compare our method with a Multi View Stereo method [2], we collected 4 different categories of high-quality CAD models. All CAD models have texture-rich surfaces and were placed on top of a texture-rich paper to aid the camera localization of the MVS method.

Metrics: We used two metrics in evaluating the reconstruction quality. The primary metric was the voxel Intersection-over-Union (IoU) between a 3D voxel reconstruction and its ground truth voxelized model. More formally,

$$IoU = \sum_{i,j,k} \left[I(p_{(i,j,k)} > t) I(y_{(i,j,k)}) \right] / \sum_{i,j,k} \left[I \left(I(p_{(i,j,k)} > t) + I(y_{(i,j,k)}) \right) \right] \quad (17)$$

where variables are defined in Sect. 3.4. $I(\cdot)$ is an indicator function and t is a voxelization threshold. Higher IoU values indicate better reconstructions. We also report the cross-entropy loss (Sect. 3.4) as a secondary metric. Lower loss values indicate higher confidence reconstructions.

Table 1. Reconstruction performance of 3D-LSTM variations according to cross-entropy loss and IoU using 5 views.

	Encoder	Recurrence	Decoder	Loss	IoU
3D-LSTM-1	simple	LSTM	simple	0.116	0.499
3D-GRU-1	simple	GRU	simple	0.105	0.540
3D-LSTM-3	simple	LSTM	simple	0.106	0.539
3D-GRU-3	simple	GRU	simple	0.091	0.592
Res3D-GRU-3	residual	GRU	residual	**0.080**	**0.634**

5.2   Network Structures Comparison

We tested 5 variations of our 3D-R2N2 as described in Sect. 3. The first four
networks are based on the standard feed-forward CNN (top Fig. 2) and the fifth
network is the residual network (bottom Fig. 2). For the first four networks, we
used either GRU or LSTM units and and varied the convolution kernel to be
either $1 \times 1 \times 1$ [3D-LSTM/GRU-3] or $3 \times 3 \times 3$ [3D-LSTM/GRU-3]. The residual
network used GRU units and $3 \times 3 \times 3$ convolutions [Res3D-GRU-3]. These
networks were trained on the ShapeNet training set and tested on the ShapeNet
testing set. We used 5 views in the experiment. Table 1 shows the results. We
observe that (1) the GRU-based networks outperform the LSTM-based networks,
(2) that the networks with neighboring recurrent unit connections ($3 \times 3 \times 3$
convolutions) outperform the networks that have no neighboring recurrent unit
connection ($1 \times 1 \times 1$ convolutions), and (3) that the deep residual network
variation further boosts the reconstruction performance.

5.3   Single Real-World Image Reconstruction

We evaluated the performance of our network in single-view reconstruction using
real-world images, comparing the performance with that of a recent method
by Kar et al. [30]. To make a quantitative comparison, we used images from
the PASCAL VOC 2012 dataset [19] and its corresponding 3D models from the

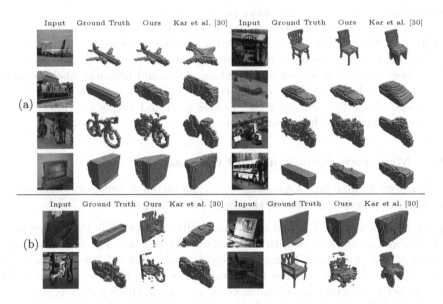

Fig. 4. (a) Reconstruction samples of PASCAL VOC dataset. (b) Failed reconstructions on the PASCAL VOC dataset. Note that Kar et al. [30] is trained/tested per
category and takes ground-truth object segmentation masks and keypoint labels as
additional input.

Table 2. Per-category reconstruction of PASCAL VOC compared using voxel Intersection-over-Union (IoU). Note that the experiments were ran with the same configuration except that the method of Kar et al. [30] took ground-truth object segmentation masks and keypoint labels as additional inputs for both training and testing.

	Aero	Bike	Boat	Bus	Car	Chair	Mbike	Sofa	Train	Tv	Mean
Kar et al. [30]	0.298	0.144	0.188	0.501	0.472	0.234	0.361	0.149	0.249	0.492	0.318
Ours [LSTM-1]	0.472	0.330	0.466	0.677	0.579	0.203	0.474	0.251	0.518	0.438	0.456
Ours [Res3D-GRU-3]	**0.544**	**0.499**	**0.560**	**0.816**	**0.699**	**0.280**	**0.649**	**0.332**	**0.672**	**0.574**	**0.571**

PASCAL 3D+ dataset [51]. We ran the experiments with the same configuration as Kar et al. except that we allow the Kar et al. method to have ground-truth object segmentation masks and keypoint labels as additional inputs for both training and testing.

Training. We fine-tuned a network trained on the ShapeNet dataset with PASCAL 3D+. We used the PASCAL 3D+ validation set to find hyperparameters such as the number of fine-tuning iterations and the voxelization threshold.

Results. As shown in Table 2, our approach outperforms the method of Kar et al. [30] in every category. However, we observe that our network has some difficulties reconstructing thin legs of chairs. Moreover, the network often confuses thin flat panels with thick CRT screens when given a frontal view of the monitor. Yet, our approach demonstrates a competitive quantitative performance. For the qualitative results and comparisons, please see Fig. 4.

Aside from better performance, our network has several advantages over Kar et al. [30]. First, we do not need to train and test per-category. Our network trains and reconstructs without knowing the object category. Second, our network does not require object segmentation masks and keypoint labels as additional inputs. Kar et al. does demonstrate the possibility of testing on a wild unlabeled image by estimating the segmentation and keypoints. However, our network outperforms their method tested with ground truth labels.

5.4   Multi-view Reconstruction Evaluation

In this section, we report a quantitative evaluation of our network's performance in multi-view reconstruction on the ShapeNet testing set.

Experiment setup. We used the [Res3D-GRU-3] network in this experiment. We evaluated the network with the ShapeNet testing set. The testing set consisted of 8725 models in 13 major categories. We rendered five random views for each model, and we applied a uniform colored background to the image. We report both softmax loss and intersection over union (IoU) with a voxelization threshold of 0.4 between the predicted and the ground truth voxel models.

Overall results. We first investigate the quality of the reconstructed models under different numbers of views. Figure 5(a) and (b) show that reconstruction quality improves as the number of views increases. The fact that the marginal

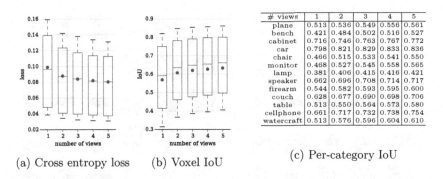

# views	1	2	3	4	5
plane	0.513	0.536	0.549	0.556	0.561
bench	0.421	0.484	0.502	0.516	0.527
cabinet	0.716	0.746	0.763	0.767	0.772
car	0.798	0.821	0.829	0.833	0.836
chair	0.466	0.515	0.533	0.541	0.550
monitor	0.468	0.527	0.545	0.558	0.565
lamp	0.381	0.406	0.415	0.416	0.421
speaker	0.662	0.696	0.708	0.714	0.717
firearm	0.544	0.582	0.593	0.595	0.600
couch	0.628	0.677	0.690	0.698	0.706
table	0.513	0.550	0.564	0.573	0.580
cellphone	0.661	0.717	0.732	0.738	0.754
watercraft	0.513	0.576	0.596	0.604	0.610

(a) Cross entropy loss   (b) Voxel IoU

(c) Per-category IoU

Fig. 5. (a), (b): Multi-view reconstruction using our model on the ShapeNet dataset. The performance is reported in median (red line) and mean (green dot) cross-entropy loss and intersection over union (IoU) values. The box plot shows 25 % and 75 %, with caps showing 15 % and 85 %. (c): Per-category reconstruction of the ShapeNet dataset using our model. The values are average IoU. (Color figure online)

gain decreases accords with our assumption that each additional view provides less information since two random views are very likely to have partial overlap.

Per-category results. We also report the reconstruction IoUs on each of the 13 major categories in the testing set in Fig. 5. We observed that the reconstruction quality improved for every category as the number of views increased, but the quality varied depending on the category. Cabinets, cars, and speakers had the highest reconstruction performance since the objects are bulky-shaped and have less (shape) variance compared to other classes. The network performed worse on the lamp, bench, and table categories. These classes have much higher shape variation than the other classes. For example, a lamp can have a slim arm or a large lampshade which may move around, and chairs and tables have various types of supporting structures.

Qualitative results. Figure 6(a) shows some sample reconstructions from the ShapeNet testing set. One exemplary instance is the truck shown in row 2. In the initial view, only the front part of the truck is visible. The network took the safest guess that the object is a sedan, which is the most common shape in the car category. Then the network produced a more accurate reconstruction of the truck after seeing more views. All other instances show similar improvements as the network sees more views of the objects. Fig. 6(b) shows two failure cases.

5.5   Reconstructing Real World Images

In this experiment, we tested our network on the Online Products dataset for qualitative evaluation. Images that were not square-shaped were padded with white pixels.

Figure 6(c) shows some sample reconstructions. The result shows that the network is capable of reconstructing real world objects using only synthetic data

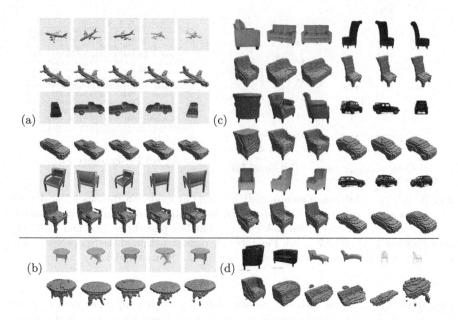

Fig. 6. Sample reconstructions on (a) the ShapeNet [13] testing set and (c) the Online Products dataset [46]. Top rows are input image sequences (from left to right). Bottom rows are the reconstructions at each time step. (b), (d): Failure cases on each dataset.

as training samples. It also demonstrates that the network improves the reconstructions after seeing additional views of the objects. One exemplary instance is the reconstruction of couch as shown in row 1. The initial side view of the couch led the network to believe that it was a one-seater sofa, but after seeing the front of the couch, the network immediately refined its reconstruction to reflect the observation. Similar behaviors are also shown in other samples. Some failure cases are shown in Fig. 6(d).

5.6 Multi View Stereo(MVS) vs. 3D-R2N2

In this experiment, we compare our approach with a MVS method on reconstructing objects that are of various texture levels with different number of views. MVS methods are limited by the accuracy of feature correspondences across different views. Therefore, they tend to fail reconstructing textureless objects or images from sparsely positioned camera viewpoints. In contrast, our method does not require accurate feature correspondences or adjacent camera viewpoints. Please refer to the supplementary material for the detailed experiment setup.

Results. The results are shown in Fig. 7(a) and (b). We observed (1) that our model worked with as few as one view, whereas the MVS method failed completely when the number of views was less than 20 (IoU = 0), and (2) that our

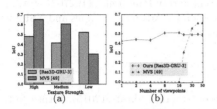
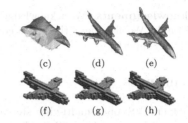

Fig. 7. Reconstruction performance of MVS [1] compared with that of our network. (a) shows how texture strengths affect the reconstructions of MVS and our network, averaged over 20, 30, 40, and 50 input views of all classes. (b) compares the quality of the reconstruction across the number of input images, averaged over all texture levels of all classes. (c–e) show the reconstruction result of MVS and (f–h) show the reconstruction results from our method [Res3D-GRU-3] on a high-texture airplane model with 20, 30, and 40 input views respectively.

model worked regardless of the objects' texture level, whereas the MVS method frequently failed to reconstruct objects that had low texture level even when a large number of views were provided. This shows that our method works in situations where MVS methods would perform poorly or completely fail. Note that the reconstruction performance of our method decreased after the number of views passed 24. This is because we only fine-tuned our network on samples with a maximum of 24 views. Also, our method could not reconstruct as many details as the MVS method did when given more than 30 different views of the model, since 3D-R2N2 used 127×127 resolution images (compared to 640×480)and a low resolution voxel grid. However, a larger network could easily overcome such limitation. Finally, our method performed worse in reconstructing objects with high texture levels. This is largely because most models in the ShapeNet training set have low texture level.

6   Conclusion

In this work, we proposed a novel architecture that unifies single- and multi-view 3D reconstruction into a single framework. Even though our network can take variable length inputs, we demonstrated that it outperforms the method of Kar et al. [30] in single-view reconstruction using real-world images. We further tested the network's ability to perform multi-view reconstruction on the ShapeNet dataset [13] and the Online Products dataset [46], which showed that the network is able to incrementally improve its reconstructions as it sees more views of an object. Lastly, we analyzed the network's performance on multi-view reconstruction, finding that our method can produce accurate reconstructions when techniques such as MVS fail. In summary, our network does not require a minimum number of input images in order to produce a plausible reconstruction and is able to overcome past challenges of dealing with images which have insufficient texture or wide baseline viewpoints.

Acknowledgments. We acknowledge the support of Panasonic (1192707-1-GWMSX) and Baidu. We also thank the Korea Foundation for Advanced Studies and NSF GRFP for their support.

References

1. OpenMVS: open multi-view stereo reconstruction library (2015). https://github.com/cdcseacave/openMVS. (Accessed 14 Mar 2016)
2. Cg studio (2016). https://www.cgstud.io/ (Accessed 14 Mar 2016)
3. Dosovitskiy, A., Springenberg, J.T., Brox, T.: Learning to generate chairs with convolutional neural networks. In: IEEE International Conference on Computer Vision and Pattern Recognition (CVPR) (2015)
4. Agarwal, S., Snavely, N., Simon, I., Seitz, S.M., Szeliski, R.: Building rome in a day. In: 2009 IEEE 12th International Conference on Computer Vision. IEEE (2009)
5. Anwar, Z., Ferrie, F.: Towards robust voxel-coloring: handling camera calibration errors and partial emptiness of surface voxels. In: Proceedings of the 18th International Conference on Pattern Recognition, ICPR 2006, vol. 1. IEEE Computer Society, Washington, DC, USA (2006). doi:10.1109/ICPR.2006.1129
6. Bao, Y., Chandraker, M., Lin, Y., Savarese, S.: Dense object reconstruction using semantic priors. In: Proceedings of the IEEE International Conference on Computer Vision and Pattern Recognition (2013)
7. Bengio, Y., Simard, P., Frasconi, P.: Learning long-term dependencies with gradient descent is difficult. IEEE Trans. Neural Netw. **5**(2), 157–166 (1994)
8. Bergstra, J., Breuleux, O., Bastien, F., Lamblin, P., Pascanu, R., Desjardins, G., Turian, J., Warde-Farley, D., Bengio, Y.: Theano: a CPU and GPU math expression compiler. In: Proceedings of the Python for Scientific Computing Conference (SciPy), June 2010
9. Bhat, D.N., Nayar, S.K.: Ordinal measures for image correspondence. IEEE Trans. Pattern Anal. Mach. Intell. **20**(4), 415–423 (1998)
10. Blanz, V., Vetter, T.: Face recognition based on fitting a 3D morphable model. IEEE Trans. Pattern Anal. Mach. Intell. **25**(9), 1063–1074 (2003)
11. Bongsoo Choy, C., Stark, M., Corbett-Davies, S., Savarese, S.: Enriching object detection with 2D–3D registration and continuous viewpoint estimation. In: The IEEE Conference on Computer Vision and Pattern Recognition (CVPR), June 2015
12. Broadhurst, A., Drummond, T.W., Cipolla, R.: A probabilistic framework for space carving. In: Eighth IEEE International Conference on Computer Vision, ICCV 2001, Proceedings, vol. 1. IEEE (2001)
13. Chang, A.X., Funkhouser, T., Guibas, L., Hanrahan, P., Huang, Q., Li, Z., Savarese, S., Savva, M., Song, S., Su, H., Xiao, J., Yi, L., Yu, F.: ShapeNet: an information-rich 3D model repository. Technical report, Stanford University, Princeton University, Toyota Technological Institute at Chicago (2015)
14. Cho, K., van Merrienboer, B., Gulcehre, C., Bahdanau, D., Bougares, F., Schwenk, H., Bengio, Y.: Learning phrase representations using RNN encoder-decoder for statistical machine translation. ArXiv e-prints arXiv:1406.1078 (2014)
15. Choi, S., Zhou, Q.Y., Miller, S., Koltun, V.: A large dataset of object scans. arXiv preprint arXiv:1602.02481 (2016)
16. Dame, A., Prisacariu, V.A., Ren, C.Y., Reid, I.: Dense reconstruction using 3D object shape priors. In: 2013 IEEE Conference on Computer Vision and Pattern Recognition (CVPR) (2013)

17. Eigen, D., Puhrsch, C., Fergus, R.: Depth map prediction from a single image using a multi-scale deep network. Adv. Neural Inf. Process. Syst. **27**, 11:1–11:15 (2014)

18. Engel, J., Schöps, T., Cremers, D.: LSD-SLAM: large-scale direct monocular SLAM. In: Fleet, D., Pajdla, T., Schiele, B., Tuytelaars, T. (eds.) ECCV 2014, Part II. LNCS, vol. 8690, pp. 834–849. Springer, Heidelberg (2014)

19. Everingham, M., Van Gool, L., Williams, C., Winn, J., Zisserman, A.: The pascal visual object classes challenge 2012 (2011)

20. Firman, M., Mac Aodha, O., Julier, S., Brostow, G.J.: Structured prediction of unobserved voxels from a single depth image. In: CVPR (2016)

21. Fitzgibbon, A., Zisserman, A.: Automatic 3D model acquisition and generation of new images from video sequences. In: 9th European Signal Processing Conference (EUSIPCO 1998). IEEE (1998)

22. Fuentes-Pacheco, J., Ruiz-Ascencio, J., Rendón-Mancha, J.M.: Visual simultaneous localization and mapping: a survey. Artif. Intell. Rev. **43**(1), 55–81 (2015)

23. Slabaugh, G.G., Culbertson, W.B., Malzbender, T., Stevens, M.R., Schafer, R.W.: Methods for volumetric reconstruction of visual scenes. Int. J. Comput. Vis. **57**(3), 179–199 (2004)

24. Häming, K., Peters, G.: The structure-from-motion reconstruction pipeline-a survey with focus on short image sequences. Kybernetika **46**(5), 926–937 (2010)

25. Häne, C., Savinov, N., Pollefeys, M.: Class specific 3D object shape priors using surface normals. In: IEEE Conference on Computer Vision and Pattern Recognition (CVPR) (2014)

26. He, K., Zhang, X., Ren, S., Sun, J.: Deep residual learning for image recognition. ArXiv e-prints arXiv:1512.03385 (2015)

27. He, K., Zhang, X., Ren, S., Sun, J.: Delving deep into rectifiers: surpassing human-level performance on imagenet classification. In: Proceedings of the IEEE International Conference on Computer Vision, pp. 1026–1034 (2015)

28. Hochreiter, S., Schmidhuber, J.: Long short-term memory. Neural Comput. **9**(8), 1735–1780 (1997)

29. Hoiem, D., Efros, A.A., Hebert, M.: Automatic photo pop-up. ACM Trans. Graph. (TOG) **24**(3), 577–584 (2005)

30. Kar, A., Tulsiani, S., Carreira, J., Malik, J.: Category-specific object reconstruction from a single image. In: 2015 IEEE Conference on Computer Vision and Pattern Recognition (CVPR). IEEE (2015)

31. Kemelmacher-Shlizerman, I., Basri, R.: 3D face reconstruction from a single image using a single reference face shape. IEEE Trans. Pattern Anal. Mach. Intell. **33**(2), 394–405 (2011)

32. Kingma, D., Ba, J.: Adam: a method for stochastic optimization. ArXiv e-prints arXiv:1412.6980 (2014)

33. Kutulakos, K.N., Seitz, S.M.: A theory of shape by space carving. Int. J. Comput. Vis. **38**(3), 199–218 (2000)

34. Lawrence, G.R.: Machine perception of three-dimensional solids. Ph.D. thesis (1963)

35. Lhuillier, M., Quan, L.: A quasi-dense approach to surface reconstruction from uncalibrated images. IEEE Trans. Pattern Anal. Mach. Intell. **27**(3), 418–433 (2005)

36. Liu, F., Shen, C., Lin, G.: Deep convolutional neural fields for depth estimation from a single image. In: Proceedings of IEEE Conference Computer Vision and Pattern Recognition (2015)

37. Lowe, D.G.: Distinctive image features from scale-invariant keypoints. Int. J. Comp. Vis. **60**(2), 145–166 (2004)

38. Matthews, I., Xiao, J., Baker, S.: 2D vs. 3D deformable face models: representational power, construction, and real-time fitting. Int. J. Comput. Vis. **75**(1), 93–113 (2007)
39. Nevatia, R., Binford, T.O.: Description and recognition of curved objects. Artif. Intell. **8**(1), 77–98 (1977)
40. Prisacariu, V.A., Segal, A.V., Reid, I.: Simultaneous monocular 2D segmentation, 3D pose recovery and 3D reconstruction. In: Lee, K.M., Matsushita, Y., Rehg, J.M., Hu, Z. (eds.) ACCV 2012, Part I. LNCS, vol. 7724, pp. 593–606. Springer, Heidelberg (2013)
41. Rock, J., Gupta, T., Thorsen, J., Gwak, J., Shin, D., Hoiem, D.: Completing 3D object shape from one depth image. In: Proceedings of the IEEE Conference on Computer Vision and Pattern Recognition (2015)
42. Sandhu, R., Dambreville, S., Yezzi, A., Tannenbaum, A.: A nonrigid kernel-based framework for 2D–3D pose estimation and 2D image segmentation. IEEE Trans. Pattern Anal. Mach. Intell. **33**(6), 1098–1115 (2011)
43. Saponaro, P., Sorensen, S., Rhein, S., Mahoney, A.R., Kambhamettu, C.: Reconstruction of textureless regions using structure from motion and image-based interpolation. In: 2014 IEEE International Conference on Image Processing (ICIP). IEEE (2014)
44. Saxena, A., Sun, M., Ng, A.Y.: Make3D: learning 3D scene structure from a single still image. IEEE Trans. Pattern Anal. Mach. Intell. **31**(5), 824–840 (2009)
45. Seitz, S.M., Dyer, C.R.: Photorealistic scene reconstruction by voxel coloring. Int. J. Comput. Vis. **35**(2), 151–173 (1999)
46. Song, H.O., Xiang, Y., Jegelka, S., Savarese, S.: Deep metric learning via lifted structured feature embedding. ArXiv e-prints arXiv:1511.06452 (2015)
47. Su, H., Huang, Q., Mitra, N.J., Li, Y., Guibas, L.: Estimating image depth using shape collections. ACM Trans. Graph. **33**(4) (2014). Article No. 37 http://dl.acm.org/citation.cfm?id=2601159
48. Sundermeyer, M., Schlüter, R., Ney, H.: LSTM neural networks for language modeling. In: INTERSPEECH (2012)
49. Sutskever, I., Vinyals, O., Le, Q.V.: Sequence to sequence learning with neural networks. In: Advances in Neural Information Processing Systems (2014)
50. Vicente, S., Carreira, J., Agapito, L., Batista, J.: Reconstructing PASCAL VOC. In: The IEEE Conference on Computer Vision and Pattern Recognition (CVPR) (2014)
51. Xiang, Y., Mottaghi, R., Savarese, S.: Beyond pascal: A benchmark for 3D object detection in the wild. In: 2014 IEEE Winter Conference on Applications of Computer Vision (WACV). IEEE (2014)
52. Zia, M.Z., Stark, M., Schiele, B., Schindler, K.: Detailed 3D representations for object modeling and recognition. In: TPAMI (2013)

Cascaded Continuous Regression for Real-Time Incremental Face Tracking

Enrique Sánchez-Lozano[✉], Brais Martinez, Georgios Tzimiropoulos,
and Michel Valstar

Computer Vision Laboratory, University of Nottingham, Nottingham, UK
{psxes1,yorgos.tzimiropoulos,michel.valstar}@nottingham.ac.uk

Abstract. This paper introduces a novel real-time algorithm for facial landmark tracking. Compared to detection, tracking has both additional challenges and opportunities. Arguably the most important aspect in this domain is updating a tracker's models as tracking progresses, also known as incremental (face) tracking. While this should result in more accurate localisation, how to do this online and in real time without causing a tracker to drift is still an important open research question. We address this question in the cascaded regression framework, the state-of-the-art approach for facial landmark localisation. Because incremental learning for cascaded regression is costly, we propose a much more efficient yet equally accurate alternative using continuous regression. More specifically, we first propose cascaded continuous regression (CCR) and show its accuracy is equivalent to the Supervised Descent Method. We then derive the incremental learning updates for CCR (iCCR) and show that it is an order of magnitude faster than standard incremental learning for cascaded regression, bringing the time required for the update from seconds down to a fraction of a second, thus enabling real-time tracking. Finally, we evaluate iCCR and show the importance of incremental learning in achieving state-of-the-art performance. Code for our iCCR is available from http://www.cs.nott.ac.uk/~psxes1.

1 Introduction

The detection of a sparse set of facial landmarks in still images has been a widely-studied problem within the computer vision community. Interestingly, many face analysis methods either systematically rely on video sequences (e.g., facial expression recognition [1]) or can benefit from them (e.g., face recognition [2]). It is thus surprising that facial landmark tracking has received much less attention in comparison. Our focus in this paper is on one of the most important problems in model-specific tracking, namely that of updating the tracker using previously tracked frames, also known as incremental (face) tracking.

The standard approach to face tracking is to use a facial landmark detection algorithm initialised on the landmarks detected at the previous frame. This

Electronic supplementary material The online version of this chapter (doi:10. 1007/978-3-319-46484-8_39) contains supplementary material, which is available to authorized users.

© Springer International Publishing AG 2016
B. Leibe et al. (Eds.): ECCV 2016, Part VIII, LNCS 9912, pp. 645–661, 2016.
DOI: 10.1007/978-3-319-46484-8_39

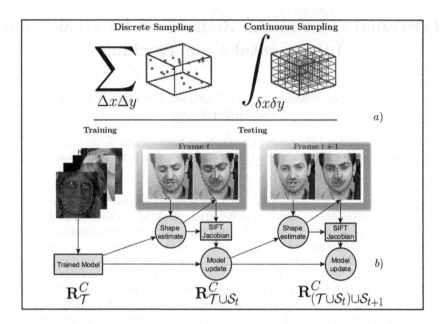

Fig. 1. Overview of our incremental cascaded continuous regression algorithm (iCCR). (a) shows how continuous regression uses all data in a point's neighbourhood, whereas sampled regression uses a finite subset. (b) shows how the originally model $\mathbf{R}_{\mathcal{T}}$ learned offline is updated with each new frame.

exploits the fact that the face shape varies smoothly in videos of sufficiently high framerates: If the previous landmarks were detected with acceptable accuracy, then the initial shape will be close enough for the algorithm to converge to a "good" local optimum for the current frame too. Hence, tracking algorithms are more likely to produce highly accurate fitting results than detection algorithms that are initialised by the face detector bounding box.

However, in this setting the tracker still employs a generic deformable model of the face built offline using a generic set of annotated facial images, which does not include the subject being tracked. It is well known that person-specific models are far more constrained and easier to fit than generic ones [3]. Hence one important problem in tracking is how to improve the generic model used to track the first few frames into an increasingly person-specific one as more frames are tracked.

This problem can be addressed with incremental learning, which allows for the smart adaptation of pre-trained generic appearance models. Incremental learning is a common resource for generic tracking, being used in some of the state-of-the-art trackers [4,5], and incremental learning for face tracking is by no means a new concept, please see Ross et al. [6] for early work on the topic. More recently, incremental learning within cascaded regression, the state-of-the-art approach for facial landmark localisation, was proposed by Xiong and De la

Torre [7] and independently by Asthana et al. [8]. However, in both [7,8] the model update is far from being sufficiently efficient to allow real-time tracking, with [8] mentioning that the model update requires 4.7 s per frame. Note that the actual tracking procedure (without the incremental update) is faster than 25 frames per second, clearly illustrating that the incremental update is the bottleneck impeding real-time tracking.

If the model update cannot be carried out in real time, then incremental learning might not be the best option for face tracking - once the real-time constraint is broken in practice one would be better off creating person-specific models in a post-processing step [9] (e.g., re-train the models once the whole video is tracked and then track again). That is to say, without the need and capacity for real-time processing, incremental learning is sub-optimal and of little use.

Our main contribution in this paper is to propose the first incremental learning framework for cascaded regression which allows real-time updating of the tracking model (Fig. 1). To do this, we build upon the concept of continuous regression [10] as opposed to standard sampling-based regression used in almost all prior work, including [7,8]. We note that while we tackle the facial landmark tracking problem, cascaded regression has also been applied to a wider range of problems such as pose estimation [11], model-free tracking [5] or object localisation [12], thus making our methodology of wider interest. We will release code for training and testing our algorithm for research purposes.

1.1 Contributions

Our main contributions are as follows:

- We propose a complete **new formulation for Continuous Regression**, of which the original continuous regression formulation [10] is a special case. Crucially, our method is now formulated by means of a **full covariance matrix capturing real statistics** of how faces vary between consecutive frames rather than on the shape model eigenvalues. This makes our method particularly suitable for the task of tracking, something the original formulation cannot deal with.
- We incorporate continuous regression in the Cascaded Regression framework (coined Cascaded Continuous Regression, or **CCR**) and demonstrate its performance is equivalent to sampling-based cascaded regression.
- We derive the **incremental learning for continuous regression**, and show that it **is an order of magnitude faster** than its standard incremental SDM counterpart.
- We evaluate the incremental Cascaded Continuous Regression (**iCCR**) on the 300VW data set [13] and show the importance of incremental learning in achieving state-of-the-art performance, especially for the case of very challenging tracking sequences.

1.2   Prior Work on Face Alignment

Facial landmark tracking methods have often been adaptations of facial land-mark detection methods. For example, Active Appearance Models (AAM) [14,15], Constrained Local Models (CLM) [16] or the Supervised Descent Method (SDM) [17] were all presented as detection algorithms. It is thus natural to group facial landmark tracking algorithms in the same way as the detection algorithms, i.e. splitting them into discriminative and generative methods [8].

On the generative side, AAMs have often been used for tracking. Since the model fitting relies on gradient descent, it suffices to start the fitting from the last solution[1]. Tracking is particularly useful to AAMs since they are considered to have frequent local minima and a small basin of attraction, making it important that the initial shape is close to the ground truth. AAMs have further been regarded as very reliable for person specific tracking, but not for generic tracking (i.e., tracking faces unseen during training) [3]. Recently [19] showed however that an improved optimisation procedure and the use of in-the-wild images for training can lead to well-behaving person independent AAM. Eliminating the piecewise-affine representation and adopting a part-based model led to the Gauss-Newton Deformable Part Model (GN-DPM) [20], which is the AAM state of the art.

Historically, discriminative methods relied on the training of local classifier-based models of appearance, with the local responses being then constrained by a shape model [16,21,22]. These algorithms can be grouped into what is called the Constrained Local Models (CLM) framework [16]. However, the appearance of discriminative regression-based models quickly transformed the state-of-the-art for face alignment. Discriminative regressors were initially used within the CLM framework substituting classifiers, showing improved performance [23,24]. However, the most important contributions came with the adoption of cascaded regression [11] and direct estimation of the full face shape rather than first obtaining local estimates [17,25]. Successive works have further shown the impressive efficiency [26,27] and reliable performance [28,29] of face alignment algorithms using cascaded regression. However, how to best exploit discriminative cascaded regression for tracking and, in particular, how to best integrate incremental learning, is still an open problem.

2   Linear Regression Models for Face Alignment

In this section we revise the preliminary concepts over which we build our method. In particular, we describe the methods most closely related to ours, to wit the incremental supervised descent method [8] and the continuous regressor [10], and motivate our work by highlighting their limitations.

---

[1] Further "implementation tricks" can be found in [18], which provides a very detailed account of how to optimise an AAM tracker.

2.1   Linear Regression

A face image is represented by $\mathbf{I}$, and a face shape is a $n \times 2$ matrix describing the location of the n landmarks considered. A shape is parametrised through a Point Distribution Model (PDM) [30]. In a PDM, a shape $\mathbf{s}$ is parametrised in terms of $\mathbf{p} = [\mathbf{q}, \mathbf{c}] \in \mathbb{R}^m$, where $\mathbf{q} \in \mathbb{R}^4$ represents the rigid parameters and $\mathbf{c}$ represents the flexible shape parameters, so that $\mathbf{s} = t_{\mathbf{q}}(\mathbf{s}_0 + \mathbf{B}_s \mathbf{c})$, where t is a Procrustes transformation parametrised by $\mathbf{q}$. $\mathbf{B}_s \in \mathbb{R}^{2n \times m}$ and $\mathbf{s}_0 \in \mathbb{R}^{2n}$ are learned during training and represent the linear subspace of flexible shape variations. We will sometimes use an abuse of notation by referring treating shape $\mathbf{s}$ also as function $\mathbf{s}(\mathbf{p})$. We also define $\mathbf{x} = f(\mathbf{I}, \mathbf{p}) \in \mathbb{R}^d$ as the feature vector representing shape $\mathbf{s}(\mathbf{p})$. An asterisk represents the ground truth, e.g., $\mathbf{s}_j^*$ is the ground truth shape for image j.

Given a test image $\mathbf{I}$, and a current shape prediction $\mathbf{s}(\mathbf{p}^* + \delta\mathbf{p})$, the goal of Linear Regression for face alignment is to find a mapping matrix $\mathbf{R} \in \mathbb{R}^{m \times d}$ able to infer $\delta\mathbf{p}$, the increment taking directly to the ground truth, from $f(\mathbf{I}, \mathbf{p}^* + \delta\mathbf{p})$. By using M training images, and K perturbations per image, the mapping matrix $\mathbf{R}$ is typically learned by minimising the following expression w.r.t. $\mathbf{R}$:

$$\sum_{j=1}^{M} \sum_{k=1}^{K} \| \delta\mathbf{p}_{j,k} - \mathbf{R}f(\mathbf{I}_j, \mathbf{p}_j^* + \delta\mathbf{p}_{j,k}) \|_2^2, \tag{1}$$

where the bias term is implicitly included by appending a 1 to the feature vector[2].

In order to produce K perturbed shapes $\mathbf{s}(\mathbf{p}_j^* + \delta\mathbf{p}_{j,k})$ per image, it suffices to draw the perturbations from an adequate distribution, ideally capturing the statistics of the perturbations encountered at test time. For example, during detection, the distribution should capture the statistics of the errors made by using the face detection bounding box to provide a shape estimation.

The minimisation in Eq. 1 has a closed-form solution. Given M images and K perturbed shapes per training image, let $\mathbf{X} \in \mathbb{R}^{d \times KM}$ and $\mathbf{Y} \in \mathbb{R}^{2n \times KM}$ represent the matrices containing in its columns the input feature vectors and the target output $\delta\mathbf{p}_{j,k}$ respectively. Then, the optimal regressor $\mathbf{R}$ can be computed as:

$$\mathbf{R} = \mathbf{Y}\mathbf{X}^T \left(\mathbf{X}\mathbf{X}^T\right)^{-1}. \tag{2}$$

Given a test shape $\mathbf{s}(\mathbf{p})$, the predicted shape is computed as $\mathbf{s}(\mathbf{p} - \mathbf{R}f(\mathbf{I}, \mathbf{p}))$.

2.2   Continuous Regression

Continuous Regression (CR) [10] is an alternative solution to the problem of linear regression for face alignment. The main idea of Continuous Regression is to treat $\delta\mathbf{p}$ as a continuous variable and to use *all samples* within some finite

---

[2] It is in practice beneficial to include a regularisation term, although we omit it for simplicity. All of the derivations in this paper hold however for ridge regression.

limits, instead of sampling a handful of perturbations per image. That is to say, the problem is formulated in terms of finite integrals as:

$$\min_{\mathbf{R}} \sum_{j=1}^{M} \int_{-r_1\sqrt{\lambda_1}}^{r_1\sqrt{\lambda_1}} \cdots \int_{-r_{|c|}\sqrt{\lambda_{|c|}}}^{r_{|c|}\sqrt{\lambda_{|c|}}} \|\delta\mathbf{c} - \mathbf{R}f(\mathbf{I}_j, \mathbf{c}_j^* + \delta\mathbf{c})\|_2^2 d\delta\mathbf{c}, \qquad (3)$$

where λ_i is the eigenvalue associated to the i-th flexible parameter of the PDM, $|\mathbf{c}|$ represent the number of flexible parameters, and r_i is a parameter determining the number of standard deviations considered in the integral.

Unfortunately, this formulation does not have a closed-form solution. However, it is possible to solve it approximately in a very efficient manner by using a first order Taylor expansion of the loss function. Following the derivations in [10], we denote $\mathbf{J}_j^*$ as the Jacobian of the image features with respect to the shape parameters evaluated at the ground truth $\mathbf{p}_j^*$, which can be calculated simply as $\mathbf{J}_j^* = \frac{\partial f(\mathbf{I}_j,\mathbf{s})}{\partial \mathbf{s}} \frac{\partial \mathbf{s}}{\partial \mathbf{p}}|_{(\mathbf{p}=\mathbf{p}_j^*)}$. A solution to Eq. 3 can then be written as:

$$\mathbf{R}(\mathbf{r}) = \boldsymbol{\Sigma}(\mathbf{r})(\sum_{j=1}^{M} \mathbf{J}_j^{*T}) \left(\sum_{j=1}^{M} \mathbf{x}_j^* \mathbf{x}_j^{*T} + \mathbf{J}_j^* \boldsymbol{\Sigma}(\mathbf{r})\, \mathbf{J}_j^{*T} \right)^{-1}, \qquad (4)$$

where $\boldsymbol{\Sigma}(\mathbf{r})$ is a diagonal matrix whose i-th entries are defined as $\frac{1}{3}r_i^2\lambda_i$. CR formulated in this manner has the following practical limitations:

1. It does not account for correlations within the perturbations. This corresponds to using a fixed (not data-driven) diagonal covariance to model the space of shape perturbations, which is a harmful oversimplification.
2. Because of 1, it is not possible to incorporate CR within the popular cascaded regression framework in an effective manner.
3. Derivatives are computed over image pixels, so more robust features, e.g., HOG or SIFT, are not used.
4. The CR can only account for the flexible parameters, as the integral limits are defined in terms of the eigenvalues of the PDM's PCA space.

In Sect. 3.1 we will solve all of these shortcomings, showing that it is possible to formulate the cascaded continuous regression and that, in fact, its performance is equivalent to the SDM.

2.3   Supervised Descent Method

The main limitation of using a single Linear Regressor to predict the ground truth shape is that the training needs to account for too much intra-class variation. That is, it is hard for a single regressor to be simultaneously accurate and robust. To solve this, [31] successfully adapted the cascaded regression of framework of Dollár et al. [11] to face alignment. However, the most widely-used form of face alignment is the SDM [17], which is a cascaded linear regression algorithm.

At **test time**, the SDM takes an input $s(\mathbf{p}^{(0)})$, and then for a fixed number of iterations computes $\mathbf{x}^{(i)} = f(\mathbf{I}, \mathbf{p}^{(i)})$ and $\mathbf{p}^{(i+1)} = \mathbf{p}^{(i)} - \mathbf{R}^{(i)}\mathbf{x}^{(i)}$. The key idea is to use a different regressor $\mathbf{R}^{(i)}$ for each iteration. The input to the **training** algorithm is a set of images $\mathbf{I}_j$ and corresponding perturbed shapes $\mathbf{p}_{j,k}^{(0)}$. The training set i is defined as $\mathbf{X}^{(i)} = \{\mathbf{x}_{j,k}^{(i)}\}_{j=1:M,k=1:K}$, with $\mathbf{x}_{j,k}^{(i)} = f(\mathbf{I}_j, \mathbf{p}_{j,k}^{(i)})$, and $\mathbf{Y}^{(i)} = \{\mathbf{y}_{j,k}^{(i)}\}_{j=1:M,k=1:K}$, with $\mathbf{y}_{j,k}^{(i)} = \mathbf{p}_{j,k}^{(i)} - \mathbf{p}_j^*$. Then regressor i is computed using Eq. 2 on training set i, and a new training set $\{\mathbf{X}^{(i+1)}, \mathbf{Y}^{(i+1)}\}$ is created using the shape parameters $\mathbf{p}_{j,k}^{(i+1)} = \mathbf{p}_{j,k}^{(i)} - \mathbf{R}^{(i)}\mathbf{x}_{j,k}^{(i)}$.

2.4   Incremental Learning for SDM

Incremental versions of the SDM have been proposed by both Xiong and De la Torre [7] and Asthana et al. [8]. The latter proposed the *parallel SDM*, a modification of the original SDM which facilitates the incremental update of the regressors. More specifically, they proposed to alter the SDM training procedure by modelling $\{\mathbf{p}_{j,k}^{(i)} - \mathbf{R}^{(i)}\mathbf{x}_{j,k}^{(i)}\}_{j,k}$ as a Normal distribution $\mathcal{N}(\boldsymbol{\mu}^{(i)}, \boldsymbol{\Sigma}^{(i)})$, allowing training shape parameters to be sampled for the next level of the cascade as:

$$\mathbf{p}_{j,k}^{(i+1)} \sim \mathcal{N}(\mathbf{p}_j^* + \boldsymbol{\mu}^{(i)}, \boldsymbol{\Sigma}^{(i)}) \tag{5}$$

Once the parallel SDM is defined, its incremental extension is immediately found. Without loss of generality, we assume that the regressors are updated in an on-line manner, i.e., the information added is extracted from the fitting of the last frame. We thus define $\mathcal{S} = \{\mathbf{I}_j, \{\mathbf{p}_{j,k}\}_{k=1}^K\}$, arrange the matrices $\mathbf{X}_\mathcal{S}$ and $\mathbf{Y}_\mathcal{S}$ accordingly, and define the shorthand $\mathbf{V}_\mathcal{T} = (\mathbf{X}_\mathcal{T}\mathbf{X}_\mathcal{T}^T)^{-1}$, leading to the following update rules [8]:

$$\mathbf{R}_{\mathcal{T}\cup\mathcal{S}} = \mathbf{R}_\mathcal{T} - \mathbf{R}_\mathcal{T}\mathbf{Q} + \mathbf{Y}_\mathcal{S}\mathbf{X}_\mathcal{S}^T\mathbf{V}_{\mathcal{T}\cup\mathcal{S}} \tag{6}$$

$$\mathbf{Q} = \mathbf{X}_\mathcal{S}\mathbf{U}\mathbf{X}_\mathcal{S}^T\mathbf{V}_\mathcal{T} \tag{7}$$

$$\mathbf{U} = \left(\mathbb{I}_K + \mathbf{X}_\mathcal{S}^T\mathbf{V}_\mathcal{T}\mathbf{X}_\mathcal{S}\right)^{-1} \tag{8}$$

$$\mathbf{V}_{\mathcal{T}\cup\mathcal{S}} = \mathbf{V}_\mathcal{T} - \mathbf{V}_\mathcal{T}\mathbf{Q} \tag{9}$$

where $\mathbb{I}_K$ is the K-dimensional identity matrix.

The cost for these incremental updates is dominated by the multiplication $\mathbf{V}_\mathcal{T}\mathbf{Q}$, where both matrices have dimensionality $d \times d$, which has a computational complexity of $\mathcal{O}(d^3)$. Since d is high-dimensional (> 1000), the cost of updating the models becomes prohibitive for real-time performance. Once real time is abandoned, offline techniques that do not analyse every frame in a sequential manner can be used for fitting, e.g., [9]. We provide a full analysis of the computational complexity in Sect. 4.

3   Incremental Cascaded Continuous Regression (iCCR)

In this section we describe the proposed Incremental Cascaded Continuous Regression, which to the best of our knowledge is the first cascaded regression tracker with **real-time incremental learning** capabilities. To do so, we

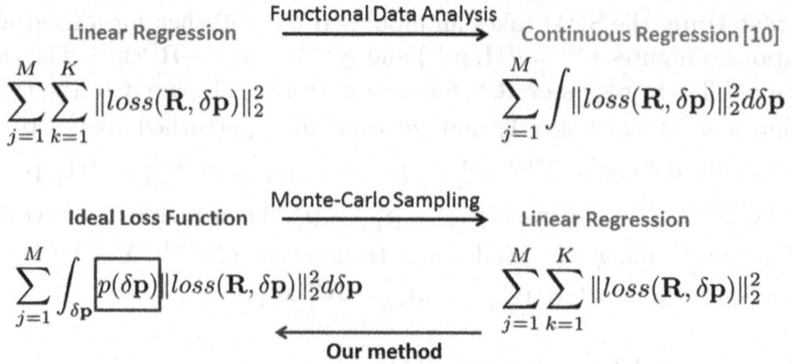

Functional Data Analysis

Linear Regression ⟶ Continuous Regression [10]

$$\sum_{j=1}^{M}\sum_{k=1}^{K}\|loss(\mathbf{R},\delta\mathbf{p})\|_2^2 \qquad \sum_{j=1}^{M}\int\|loss(\mathbf{R},\delta\mathbf{p})\|_2^2 d\delta\mathbf{p}$$

Monte-Carlo Sampling

Ideal Loss Function ⟶ Linear Regression

$$\sum_{j=1}^{M}\int_{\delta\mathbf{p}} \boxed{p(\delta\mathbf{p})}\|loss(\mathbf{R},\delta\mathbf{p})\|_2^2 d\delta\mathbf{p} \qquad \sum_{j=1}^{M}\sum_{k=1}^{K}\|loss(\mathbf{R},\delta\mathbf{p})\|_2^2$$

⟵
Our method

Fig. 2. Main difference between original Continuous Regression [10] and our method.

first extend the Continuous Regression framework into a fully fledged cascaded regression algorithm capable of performance on par with the SDM (see Sects. 3.1 and 3.2). Then, we derive the incremental learning update rules within our Cascaded Continuous Regression formulation (see Sect. 3.3). We will show in Sect. 4 that our newly-derived formulas have complexity of one order of magnitude less than previous incremental update formulations.

3.1 Continuous Regression Revisited

We first modify the original formulation of Continuous Regression. In particular, we add a "data term", which is tasked with encoding the probability of a certain perturbed shape, allowing for the modelling of correlations in the shape dimensions. Plainly speaking, the previous formulation assumed an i.i.d. uniform sampling distribution. We instead propose using a data-driven full covariance distribution, resulting in regressors that model the test-time scenario much better. In particular, we can see the loss function to be optimised as:

$$\arg\min_{\mathbf{R}} \sum_{j=1}^{M} \int_{\delta\mathbf{p}} p(\delta\mathbf{p})\|\delta\mathbf{p} - \mathbf{R}f(\mathbf{I}_j, \mathbf{p}_j^* + \delta\mathbf{p})\|_2^2 d\delta\mathbf{p}. \tag{10}$$

It is interesting to note that this equation appears in [17], where the SDM equations are interpreted as a MCMC sampling-based approximation of this equation. Contrariwise, the Continuous Regression proposes to use a different approximation based on a first-order Taylor approximation of the *ideal loss function* defined in Eq. 10. However, the Continuous Regression proposed in [10] extends the Functional Data Analysis [32] framework to the imaging domain, without considering any possible data correlation. Instead, the "data term" in Eq. 10 (which defines how the data is sampled in the MCMC approach), will serve to correlate the different dimensions in the Continuous Regression. That is to say, the "data term" does not play the role of how samples are taken, but rather helps to find an analytical solution in which dimensions can be correlated. These differences are illustrated in Fig. 2.

The first-order approximation of the feature vector is given by:

$$f(\mathbf{I}_j, \mathbf{p}_j^* + \delta\mathbf{p}) \approx f(\mathbf{I}_j, \mathbf{p}_j^*) + \mathbf{J}_j^*\delta\mathbf{p} \tag{11}$$

where $\mathbf{J}_j^*$ is the Jacobian of the feature representation of image $\mathbf{I}_j$ at $\mathbf{p}_j^*$. While [10] used a pixel-based representation, the Jacobian under an arbitrary representation can be computed empirically as:

$$\mathbf{J}_x = \frac{\partial f(\mathbf{I}, \mathbf{s})}{\partial x} \approx \frac{f(\mathbf{I}, [\mathbf{s}_x + \Delta x, \mathbf{s}_y]) - f(\mathbf{I}, [\mathbf{s}_x - \Delta x, \mathbf{s}_y])}{2\Delta x} \tag{12}$$

where $\mathbf{s}_x$ are the x coordinates of shape $\mathbf{s}$, and $\mathbf{s}_x + \Delta x$ indicates that Δx is added to each element of $\mathbf{s}_x$ (in practice, Δx is the smallest possible, 1 pixel). $\mathbf{J}_y$ can be computed similarly. Then $\mathbf{J}_j^* = [\mathbf{J}_x, \mathbf{J}_y]\frac{\partial \mathbf{s}}{\partial \mathbf{p}_j^*}$. Equation 10 has a closed form solution as[3]:

$$\mathbf{R}_{\mathcal{T}} = \left(\sum_{j=1}^{M} \mu \mathbf{x}_j^{*T} + (\boldsymbol{\Sigma} + \boldsymbol{\mu}\boldsymbol{\mu}^T)\mathbf{J}_j^{*T}\right) \cdot$$

$$\left(\sum_{j=1}^{M} \mathbf{x}_j^*\mathbf{x}_j^{*T} + 2\mathbf{x}_j^*\boldsymbol{\mu}^T\mathbf{J}_j^{*T} + \mathbf{J}_j^*(\boldsymbol{\Sigma} + \boldsymbol{\mu}\boldsymbol{\mu}^T)\mathbf{J}_j^{*T}\right)^{-1} \tag{13}$$

where $\boldsymbol{\mu}$ and $\boldsymbol{\Sigma}$ are the mean and covariance of the data term, $p(\delta\mathbf{p})$.

Finally, we can see that Eq. 13 can be expressed in a more compact form. Let us first define the following shorthand notation: $\mathbf{A} = [\boldsymbol{\mu}, \boldsymbol{\Sigma} + \boldsymbol{\mu}\boldsymbol{\mu}^T]$, $\mathbf{B} = \begin{pmatrix} 1 & \boldsymbol{\mu}^T \\ \boldsymbol{\mu} & \boldsymbol{\Sigma}+\boldsymbol{\mu}\boldsymbol{\mu}^T \end{pmatrix}$, $\mathbf{D}_j^* = [\mathbf{x}_j^*, \mathbf{J}_j^*]$ and $\bar{\mathbf{D}}_{\mathcal{T}}^* = [\mathbf{D}_1^*, \dots, \mathbf{D}_M^*]$. Then:

$$\mathbf{R}_{\mathcal{T}} = \mathbf{A}\left(\sum_{j=1}^{M} \mathbf{D}_j^*\right)^T \left(\bar{\mathbf{D}}_{\mathcal{T}}^*\hat{\mathbf{B}}(\bar{\mathbf{D}}_{\mathcal{T}}^*)^T\right)^{-1} \tag{14}$$

where $\hat{\mathbf{B}} = \mathbf{B} \otimes \mathbb{I}_M$. Through this arrangement, the parallels with the sampling-based regression formula are clear (see Eq. 2).

It is interesting that, while the standard linear regression formulation needs to sample perturbed shapes from a distribution, the Continuous Regression training formulation only needs to extract the features and the Jacobians on the ground-truth locations. This means that once these features are obtained, re-training a new model under a different distribution takes seconds, as it only requires the computation of Eq. 14.

---

[3] A full mathematical derivation is included in the Supplementary Material.

3.2   Cascaded Continuous Regression (CCR)

Now that we have introduced a new formulation with the Continuous Regression capable of incorporating a data term, it is straightforward to extend the CR into the cascade regression formulation: we take the distribution in Eq. 5 as the *data term* in Eq. 10.

One might argue that due to the first-order Taylor approximation required to solve Eq. 10, CCR might not work as well as the SDM. One of the main experimental contributions of this paper is to show that in reality this is not the case: in fact CCR and SDM have equivalent performance (see Sect. 5). This is important because, contrary to previous works on Cascaded Regression, incremental learning within CCR allows for real time performance.

3.3   Incremental Learning Update Rules for CCR

Once frame j is tracked, the incremental learning step updates the existing training set $\mathcal{T}$ with $\mathbf{S} = \{\mathbf{I}_j, \hat{\mathbf{p}}_j\}$, where $\hat{\mathbf{p}}_j$ denotes the predicted shape parameters for frame j. Note that in this case $\mathbf{S}$ consists of only one example compared to K examples in the incremental SDM case.

The update process consists of computing matrix $\mathbf{D}_j$, which stores the feature vector and its Jacobian at $\hat{\mathbf{p}}_j$ and then, using the shorthand notation $\mathbf{V}_{\mathcal{T}} = \bar{\mathbf{D}}_{\mathcal{T}}^* \hat{\mathbf{B}} (\bar{\mathbf{D}}_{\mathcal{T}}^*)^T$, updating continuous regressor as:

$$\mathbf{R}_{\mathcal{T} \cup \mathcal{S}} = \mathbf{A} \left(\sum_{j=1}^{M} \mathbf{D}_j^* + \mathbf{D}_{\mathcal{S}}^* \right)^T (\mathbf{V}_{\mathcal{T} \cup \mathcal{S}})^{-1} \tag{15}$$

In order to avoid the expensive re-computation of $\mathbf{V}_{\mathcal{T}}^{-1}$, it suffices to update its value using the Woodbury identity [32]:

$$\mathbf{V}_{\mathcal{T} \cup \mathcal{S}}^{-1} = \mathbf{V}_{\mathcal{T}}^{-1} - \mathbf{V}_{\mathcal{T}}^{-1} \mathbf{D}_{\mathcal{S}}^* \left(\mathbf{B}^{-1} + \mathbf{D}_{\mathcal{S}}^{*T} \mathbf{V}_{\mathcal{T}}^{-1} \mathbf{D}_{\mathcal{S}}^* \right)^{-1} \mathbf{D}_{\mathcal{S}}^{*T} \mathbf{V}_{\mathcal{T}}^{-1} \tag{16}$$

Note that $\mathbf{D}_{\mathcal{S}}^* \in \mathbb{R}^{d \times (m+1)}$, where m accounts for the number of shape parameters. We can see that computing Eq. 16 requires computing first $\mathbf{D}_{\mathcal{S}}^{*T} \mathbf{V}_{\mathcal{T}}^{-1}$, which is $\mathcal{O}(md^2)$. This is a central result of this paper, and reflects a property previously unknown. We will examine in Sect. 4 its practical implications in terms of real-time capabilities.

4   Computational Complexity

In this section we first detail the computational complexity of the proposed iCCR, and show that it is real-time capable. Then, we compare its cost with that of incremental SDM, showing that our update rules are an order of magnitude faster.

iCCR update complexity: Let us note the computational cost of the feature extraction as $\mathcal{O}(q)$. The update only requires the computation of the feature vector at the ground truth, and in two adjacent locations to compute the Jacobian, thus resulting in $\mathcal{O}(3q)$ complexity. Interestingly, this is independent from the number of cascade levels.

Then, the update equation (Eq. 16), has a complexity dominated by the operation $\mathbf{D}_{\mathcal{S}}^T \mathbf{V}_{\mathcal{T}}^{\mathcal{C}^{-1}}$, which has a cost of $\mathcal{O}(d^2 m)$. It is interesting to note that $\mathbf{B}^{-1} + \mathbf{D}_{\mathcal{S}}^T \mathbf{V}_{\mathcal{T}}^{\mathcal{C}^{-1}} \mathbf{D}_{\mathcal{S}}$ is a matrix of size $(m+1) \times (m+1)$ and thus its inversion is extremely efficient. The detailed cost of the incremental update is:

$$\mathcal{O}(3md^2) + \mathcal{O}(3m^2 d) + \mathcal{O}(m^3). \tag{17}$$

Incremental SDM update complexity: Incremental learning for SDM requires sampling at each level of the cascade. The cost per cascade level is $\mathcal{O}(qK)$, where K denotes the number of samples. Thus, for L cascade levels the total cost of sampling is $\mathcal{O}(LKq)$. The cost of the incremental update equations (Eqs. (6–9)), is in this case dominated by the multiplication $\mathbf{V}_{\mathcal{T}}\mathbf{Q}$, which is $\mathcal{O}(d^3)$. The detailed computational cost is:

$$\mathcal{O}(d^3) + \mathcal{O}((3m + k)d^2) + \mathcal{O}((2K^2 + mk)d) + \mathcal{O}(K^3). \tag{18}$$

Detailed comparison and timing: One advantage of iCCR comes from the much lower number of feature computations, being as low as 3 vs. the LK computations required for incremental SDM. However, the main difference is the $\mathcal{O}(d^3)$ complexity of the regressor update equation for the incremental SDM compared to $\mathcal{O}(d^2 m)$ for the iCCR. In our case, $d = 2000$, while $m = 24$. The feature dimensionality results from performing PCA over the feature space, which is a standard procedure for SDM. Note that if we avoided the use of PCA, the complexity comparison would be even more in our favour. A detailed summary of the operations required by both algorithms, together with their computational complexity and the execution time on our computer are given in Algorithm 1. Note that $\mathcal{O}(D)$ is the cost of projecting the output vector into the PCA space. Note as well that for incremental SDM, the "Sampling and Feature extraction" step is repeated L times.

5 Experimental Results

This section describes the experimental results. First, we empirically demonstrate the performance of CCR is equivalent to SDM. In order to do so, we assess both methods under the same settings, avoiding artefacts to appear, such as face detection accuracy. We follow the VOT Challenge protocol [33]. Then, we develop a fully automated system, and we evaluate both the CCR and iCCR in the same settings as the 300VW, and show that our fully automated system achieves state of the art results, illustrating the benefit of incremental learning to achieve it.

Algorithm 1. Computational costs for iCCR and incremental SDM [8] updates

---

iCCR update (Total: 72 ms.):
precompute: Feature and Jacobian extraction : $\langle \mathcal{O}(3q) : 9$ ms.$\rangle$

for $i \leftarrow 1$ **to** $L = 3$ *cascade levels* **do**
  | PCA Projection   : $\langle \mathcal{O}(Dm) : 6$ ms.$\rangle$;
  | Update **R** (Eq. 16)   : $\langle \mathcal{O}(md^2) : 15$ ms.$\rangle$;
end

---

iSDM [8] update (Total: 705 ms.):
for $i \leftarrow 1$ **to** $L = 3$ *cascade levels* **do**
  | Sampling and Feature extraction : $\langle \mathcal{O}(Kq) : 30$ ms.$\rangle$;
  | PCA Projection   : $\langle \mathcal{O}(DK) : 5$ ms.$\rangle$;
  | Update **R** (Eqs. 6–9)   : $\langle \mathcal{O}(d^3) : 200$ ms.$\rangle$;
end

5.1 Experimental Set-Up

Training Data: We use data from different datasets of static images to construct our training set. Specifically, we use Helen [34], LFPW [35], AFW [36], IBUG [37], and a subset of MultiPIE [38]. The training set comprises ~ 7000 images. We have used the facial landmark annotations provided by the 300 faces in the wild challenge [37], as they offer consistency across datasets. The *statistics* are computed across the training sequences, by computing the differences of ground-truth shape parameters between consecutive frames. Given the easiness of the training set with respect to the test set, we also included differences of several frames ahead. This way, higher displacements are also captured.

Features: We use the SIFT [39] implementation provided by Xiong and De la Torre [17]. We apply PCA on the output, retaining 2000 dimensions. We apply the same PCA to all of the methods, computed during our SDM training.

Test Data: All the methods are evaluated on the test partition of the 300 Videos in the Wild challenge (300VW) [13]. The 300VW is the only publicly-available large-scale dataset for facial landmark tracking. Its test partition has been divided into categories 1, 2 and 3, intended to represent increasingly unconstrained scenarios. In particular, category 3 contains videos captured in totally unconstrained scenarios. The ground truth has been created in a semi-supervised manner using two different methods [29,40].

Error Measure: To compute the error for a specific frame, we use the error measure defined in the 300VW challenge [13]. The error is computed by dividing the average point-to-point Euclidean error by the inter-ocular distance, understood as the distance between the two outer eye corners.

5.2   CCR vs. SDM

In order to demonstrate the performance capability of our CCR method against SDM, we followed the protocol established by the Visual Object Tracking (VOT) Challenge organisers for evaluating the submitted tracking methods [33]. Specifically, if the tracker error exceeds a certain threshold (0.1 in our case, which is a common definition of alignment failure), we proceed by re-initialising the tracker. In this case, the starting point will be the ground truth of the previous frame. This protocol is adopted to avoid the pernicious influence on our comparison of some early large failure from which the tracker is not able to recover, which would mean that successive frames would yield a very large error. Results are shown in Fig. 3 (**Left**). We show that the CCR and the SDM provide similar performance, thus ensuring that the CCR is a good starting point for developing an incremental learning algorithm. It is possible to see from the results shown in Fig. 3 that the CCR compares better and even sometimes surpasses the SDM on the lower levels of the error, while the SDM systematically provides a gain for larger errors with respect to the CCR. This is likely due to the use of first-order Taylor approximation, which means that larger displacements are less accurately approximated. Instead, the use of *infinite* shape perturbations rather than a handful of sampled perturbations compensates this problem for smaller errors, and even sometimes provides some performance improvement.

5.3   CCR vs. iCCR

We now show the benefit of incremental learning with respect to generic models. The incremental learning needs to filter frames to decide whether a fitting is suitable or harmful to update the models. That is, in practice, it is beneficial to filter out badly-tracked frames by avoiding performing incremental updates in these cases. We follow [8] and use a linear SVM trained to decide whether a particular fitting is "correct", understood as being under a threshold error. Despite its simplicity, this tactic provides a solid performance increase. Results on the test set are shown in Fig. 3 (**Right**).

5.4   Comparison with State of the Art

We developed a fully automated system to compare against state of the art methods. Our fully automated system is initialised with a standard SDM [41], and an SVM is used to detect whether the tracker gets lost. We assessed both our CCR and iCCR in the most challenging category of the 300VW, consisting of 14 videos recorded in unconstrained settings. For a fair comparison, we have reproduced the challenge settings (a brief description of the challenge and submitted methods can be found in [13]). We compare our method against the top two participants [42,43]. Results are shown in Fig. 4. The influence of the incremental learning to achieve state of the art results is clear. Importantly, as shown in the paper, our iCCR allows for real-time implementation. That is to say, our iCCR reports state of the art results whilst working in near real-time,

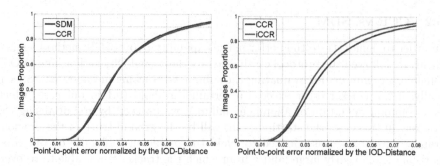

Fig. 3. Left: Accumulated graph across all three categories for SDM and CCR methods. In both cases, the Area Under the Curve (AUC) is 0.49, meaning that CCR shows better capabilities for lower errors, whereas SDM fits better in higher errors. **Right**: Accumulated graph across all three categories for CCR and iCCR methods. The contribution of incremental learning is clear.

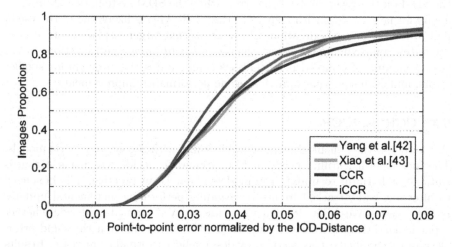

Fig. 4. Results given by our fully automated system in the most challenging category of the 300VW benchmark. Results are shown for the 49 inner points. The contribution of Incremental Learning in challenging sequences, and in a fully automated system, is even higher.

something that could not be achieved by previous works on Cascaded Regression. Code for our fully automated system is available for download at www.cs.nott.ac.uk/~psxes1.

6   Conclusion

In this article we have proposed a novel facial landmark tracking algorithm that is capable of performing on-line updates of the models through incremental learning. Compared to previous incremental learning methodologies, it can produce much faster incremental updates without compromising on accuracy. This was achieved by firstly extending the Continuous Regression framework [10], and then incorporating it into the cascaded regression framework to lead to the CCR method, which we showed provides equivalent performance to the SDM. We then derived the incremental learning update formulas for the CCR, resulting in the iCCR algorithm. We further show the computational complexity of the incremental SDM, demonstrating that iCCR is an order of magnitude simpler computationally. This removes the bottleneck impeding real-time incremental cascaded regression methods, and thus results in the state of the art for real-time face tracking.

Acknowledgments. The work of Sánchez-Lozano, Martinez and Valstar was supported by the European Union Horizon 2020 research and innovation programme under grant agreement No 645378, ARIA-VALUSPA. The work of Sánchez-Lozano was also supported by the Vice-Chancellor's Scholarship for Research Excellence provided by the University of Nottingham. The work of Tzimiropoulos was supported in part by the EPSRC project EP/M02153X/1 Facial Deformable Models of Animals. We are also grateful for the given access to the University of Nottingham High Performance Computing Facility, and we would like to thank Jie Shen and Grigoris Chrysos for their insightful help in our tracking evaluation.

References

1. Dhall, A., Goecke, R., Joshi, J., Sikka, K., Gedeon, T.: Emotion recognition in the wild challenge 2014: Baseline, data and protocol. In: International Conference on Multimodal Interaction, pp. 461–466 (2014)
2. Zhou, S., Krueger, V., Chellappa, R.: Probabilistic recognition of human faces from video. Comput. Vis. Image Underst. **91**(12), 214–245 (2003)
3. Gross, R., Matthews, I., Baker, S.: Generic vs. person specific active appearance models. Image Vis. Comput. **23**(11), 1080–1093 (2005)
4. Hare, S., Golodetz, S., Saffari, A., Vineet, V., Cheng, M.M., Hicks, S., Torr, P.: Struck: Structured output tracking with kernels. Trans. Pattern Anal. Mach. Intell. (2016). doi:10.1109/TPAMI.2015.2509974
5. Wang, X., Valstar, M., Martinez, B., Khan, M.H., Pridmore, T.: Tric-track: tracking by regression with incrementally learned cascades. In: International Conference on Computer Vision (2015)
6. Ross, D.A., Lim, J., Lin, R.S., Yang, M.H.: Incremental learning for robust visual tracking. Int. J. Comput. Vis. **77**(1–3), 125–141 (2008)
7. Xiong, X., la Torre, F.D.: Supervised descent method for solving nonlinear least squares problems in computer vision. arXiv abs/1405.0601 (2014)
8. Asthana, A., Zafeiriou, S., Cheng, S., Pantic, M.: Incremental face alignment in the wild. In: IEEE Conference on Computer Vision and Pattern Recognition (2014)
9. Sagonas, C., Panagakis, Y., Zafeiriou, S., Pantic, M.: RAPS: Robust and efficient automatic construction of person-specific deformable models. In: IEEE Conference on Computer Vision and Pattern Recognition (2014)
10. Sánchez-Lozano, E., De la Torre, F., González-Jiménez, D.: Continuous regression for non-rigid image alignment. In: European Conference on Computer Vision, pp. 250–263 (2012)

11. Dollár, P., Welinder, P., Perona, P.: Cascaded pose regression. In: IEEE Conference on Computer Vision and Pattern Recognition, pp. 1078–1085 (2010)

12. Yan, J., Lei, Z., Yang, Y., Li, S.: Stacked deformable part model with shape regression for object part localization. In: European Conference on Computer Vision, pp. 568–583 (2014)

13. Shen, J., Zafeiriou, S., Chrysos, G.S., Kossaifi, J., Tzimiropoulos, G., Pantic, M.: The first facial landmark tracking in-the-wild challenge: benchmark and results. In: International Conference on Computer Vision - Workshop (2015)

14. Cootes, T.F., Edwards, G.J., Taylor, C.J.: Active appearance models. Trans. Pattern Anal. Mach. Intell. **23**(6), 681–685 (2001)

15. Matthews, I., Baker, S.: Active appearance models revisited. Int. J. Comput. Vis. **60**(2), 135–164 (2004)

16. Saragih, J.M., Lucey, S., Cohn, J.F.: Deformable model fitting by regularized landmark mean-shift. Int. J. Comput. Vis. **91**(2), 200–215 (2011)

17. Xiong, X., De la Torre, F.: Supervised descent method and its applications to face alignment. In: IEEE Conference on Computer Vision and Pattern Recognition (2013)

18. Tresadern, P., Ionita, M., Cootes, T.: Real-time facial feature tracking on a mobile device. Int. J. Comput. Vis. **96**(3), 280–289 (2012)

19. Tzimiropoulos, G., Pantic, M.: Optimization problems for fast AAM fitting in-the-wild. In: International Conference on Computer Vision (2013)

20. Tzimiropoulos, G., Pantic, M.: Gauss-newton deformable part models for face alignment in-the-wild. In: IEEE Conference on Computer Vision and Pattern Recognition, pp. 1851–1858 (2014)

21. Cootes, T.F., Taylor, C.J., Cooper, D.H., Graham, J.: Active shape models-their training and application. Comput. Vis. Image Underst. **61**(1), 38–59 (1995)

22. Cristinacce, D., Cootes, T.: Feature detection and tracking with constrained local models. In: British Machine Vision Conference, pp. 929–938 (2006)

23. Cootes, T.F., Ionita, M.C., Lindner, C., Sauer, P.: Robust and accurate shape model fitting using random forest regression voting. In: European Conference on Computer Vision, pp. 278–291 (2012)

24. Valstar, M.F., Martinez, B., Binefa, X., Pantic, M.: Facial point detection using boosted regression and graph models. In: IEEE Conference on Computer Vision and Pattern Recognition, pp. 2729–2736 (2010)

25. Cao, X., Wei, Y., Wen, F., Sun, J.: Face alignment by explicit shape regression. Int. J. Comput. Vis. **107**(2), 177–190 (2014)

26. Ren, S., Cao, X., Wei, Y., Sun, J.: Face alignment at 3000 FPS via regressing local binary features. In: IEEE Conference on Computer Vision and Pattern Recognition, pp. 1685–1692 (2014)

27. Kazemi, V., Sullivan, J.: One millisecond face alignment with an ensemble of regression trees. In: IEEE Conference on Computer Vision and Pattern Recognition (2014)

28. Yan, J., Lei, Z., Yi, D., Li, S.: Learn to combine multiple hypotheses for accurate face alignment. In: Internation Conference on Computer Vision - Workshop, pp. 392–396 (2013)

29. Tzimiropoulos, G.: Project-out cascaded regression with an application to face alignment. In: IEEE Conference on Computer Vision and Pattern Recognition, pp. 3659–3667 (2015)

30. Cootes, T.F., Taylor, C.J.: Statistical models of appearance for computer vision (2004)

31. Cao, X., Wei, Y., Wen, F., Sun, J.: Face alignment by explicit shape regression. In: IEEE Conference on Computer Vision and Pattern Recognition, pp. 2887–2894 (2012)
32. Brookes, M.: The matrix reference manual (2011)
33. Kristan, M., Matas, J., Leonardis, A., Vojir, T., Pflugfelder, R., Fernandez, G., Nebehay, G., Porikli, F., Čehovin, L.: A novel performance evaluation methodology for single-target trackers. arXiv (2015)
34. Le, V., Brandt, J., Lin, Z., Bourdev, L.D., Huang, T.S.: Interactive facial feature localization. In: European Conference on Computer Vision, pp. 679–692 (2012)
35. Belhumeur, P.N., Jacobs, D.W., Kriegman, D.J., Kumar, N.: Localizing parts of faces using a consensus of exemplars. In: IEEE Conference on Computer Vision and Pattern Recognition, pp. 545–552 (2011)
36. Zhu, X., Ramanan, D.: Face detection, pose estimation, and landmark localization in the wild. In: IEEE Conference on Computer Vision and Pattern Recognition, pp. 2879–2886 (2012)
37. Sagonas, C., Tzimiropoulos, G., Zafeiriou, S., Pantic, M.: A semi-automatic methodology for facial landmark annotation. In: IEEE Conference on Computer Vision and Pattern Recognition - Workshops (2013)
38. Gross, R., Matthews, I., Cohn, J., Kanade, T., Baker, S.: Multi-pie. Image Vis. Comput. 28(5), 807–813 (2010)
39. Lowe, D.G.: Distinctive image features from scale-invariant keypoints. Int. J. Comput. Vis. 60(2), 91–110 (2004)
40. Chrysos, G.S., Antonakos, E., Zafeiriou, S., Snape, P.: Offline deformable face tracking in arbitrary videos. In: International Conference on Computer Vision - Workshop (2015)
41. Sánchez-Lozano, E., Martinez, B., Valstar, M.: Cascaded regression with sparsified feature covariance matrix for facial landmark detection. Pattern Recogn. Lett. 73, 19–25 (2016)
42. Yang, J., Deng, J., Zhang, K., Liu, Q.: Facial shape tracking via spatio-temporal cascade shape regression. In: Internationl Conference on Computer Vision - Workshop (2015)
43. Xiao, S., Yan, S., Kassim, A.: Facial landmark detection via progressive initialization. In: International Conference on Computer Vision - Workshop (2015)

Real-Time Visual Tracking: Promoting the Robustness of Correlation Filter Learning

Yao Sui[1(✉)], Ziming Zhang[2], Guanghui Wang[1], Yafei Tang[3], and Li Zhang[4]

[1] Department of EECS, University of Kansas, Lawrence, KS 66045, USA
suiyao@gmail.com, ghwang@ku.edu
[2] Department of ECE, Boston University, Boston, MA 02215, USA
zzhang14@bu.edu
[3] China Unicom Research Institute, Beijing 100032, China
tangyf24@chinaunicom.cn
[4] Department of EE, Tsinghua University, Beijing 100084, China
chinazhangli@tsinghua.edu.cn

Abstract. Correlation filtering based tracking model has received lots of attention and achieved great success in real-time tracking, however, the lost function in current correlation filtering paradigm could not reliably response to the appearance changes caused by occlusion and illumination variations. This study intends to promote the robustness of the correlation filter learning. By exploiting the anisotropy of the filter response, three sparsity related loss functions are proposed to alleviate the overfitting issue of previous methods and improve the overall tracking performance. As a result, three real-time trackers are implemented. Extensive experiments in various challenging situations demonstrate that the robustness of the learned correlation filter has been greatly improved via the designed loss functions. In addition, the study reveals, from an experimental perspective, how different loss functions essentially influence the tracking performance. An important conclusion is that the sensitivity of the peak values of the filter in successive frames is consistent with the tracking performance. This is a useful reference criterion in designing a robust correlation filter for visual tracking.

Keywords: Visual tracking · Correlation filtering · Sparsity regularization · Loss function · Robustness

1 Introduction

In recent years, there is a significant interest in correlation filtering based tracking. Under this paradigm, a correlation filter is efficiently learned online from previously obtained target regions, and the target is located according to the magnitude of the filter response over a large number of target candidates. The main strength of this paradigm is its high computational efficiency, because the target and the candidate regions can be represented in frequency domain and manipulated by fast Fourier transform (FFT), which yields $\mathcal{O}\left(n\log n\right)$

© Springer International Publishing AG 2016
B. Leibe et al. (Eds.): ECCV 2016, Part VIII, LNCS 9912, pp. 662–678, 2016.
DOI: 10.1007/978-3-319-46484-8_40

computational complexity for a region of $\sqrt{n} \times \sqrt{n}$ pixels. For this reason, extensive real-time trackers [1–9] have been proposed within the correlation filtering paradigm.

Specifically, a correlation filter is learned from previously obtained target regions to approximate an expected filter response, such that the peak of the response is located at the center of the target region. The response used in previous methods is often assigned to be of Gaussian shaped, which is treated as a continuous version of an impulse signal. For this reason, the learned filter is encouraged to produce Gaussian shaped response. The candidate region with the strongest filter response is determined as the target.

(a)   (b)

Fig. 1. Illustration of the cyclic shift method. (a) The base image. (b) The cyclic shifts of the base image with ±15 pixels in horizontal and vertical directions, respectively.

Note that the Gaussian shaped response, from a signal processing perspective, is *isotropic*, *i.e.*, all the regions that deviate the same distance away from the center of the target are assigned to the same response values. However, it has been demonstrated that the anisotropic response values can significantly improve the tracking performance from a regression point of view [10,11][1], *e.g.*, using the overlap rates between the training image samples and the target as the response values. Figure 1 illustrates a popular approach for samples generation adopted by previous correlation filtering based trackers [2,7]. It is evident from Fig. 1(b) that the regions of interest are not continuous. This will bring challenges to the correlation filter learning if the response values of the four significantly different regions are enforced to be the same, easily leading to an overfitting.

In addition, from a loss function point of view, the correlation filter is always learned under the squared loss (*i.e.*, ℓ_2-loss) in the previous methods. The choice for the squared loss is limited by the Parseval's identity, by which the learning problem can be exactly transferred into frequency domain. Moreover, the squared loss can lead to a closed-form solution, which guarantees the high computational efficiency. Nevertheless, the target appearance may change significantly during tracking in various challenging situations, such as occlusion and illumination variation. A robust loss function is required to reliably respond to these appearance changes, and avoid the overfitting. The squared loss allows the filter response to fit the expected response with small errors, *i.e.*, stochastically yields Gaussian errors with a small variance. In the presence of significant appearance

---

[1] The exact equivalence between regression and correlation filtering is proved in [7].

changes, the errors may be extremely large in some feature dimensions, leading to an instability of the squared loss.

Inspired by the previous success, an *anisotropy* of the filter response is exploited in this work by means of an adaptive learning approach via robust loss functions, including ℓ_1-, $\ell_1\ell_2$-, and $\ell_{2,1}$-loss functions. These loss functions will increase the robustness, since they allow large errors in the filter learning in the presence of significant appearance changes. As a result, three real-time trackers are proposed in this study, and it is demonstrated how the loss functions essentially influence the tracking performance. An interesting observation is obtained from the experimental results, which can be taken as a reference criterion in designing a robust correlation filter for visual tracking: the sensitivity of the peak values of the filter in successive frames is consistent with the tracking performance. The proposed algorithms are evaluated by extensive experiments on a popular benchmark [12], and they outperform the competing counterparts.

2   Related Work

Recently, correlation filtering [1] has received much attention in visual tracking. It achieves state-of-the-art tracking performance in terms of both accuracy and running speed. By exploiting the circulant structure [2], visual tracking can be described as a correlation filtering problem, which is also demonstrated to be equivalent to a ridge regression problem [2]. In this paradigm, the cyclic shifts of the latest target region (a base image) is utilized to generate a large number of training samples, essentially as the dense sampling method does, as illustrated in Fig. 1. The cyclic shifts lead to the fact that the sample matrix has a circulant structure. To efficient solve the correlation filtering, the tracking is conducted in frequency domain by fast Fourier transform (FFT) under the Parseval's identity. Because the filter response is considered to be of Gaussian shaped, there is a closed-form solution to the problem of the correlation filter learning. This is why the correlation filtering based tracking methods significantly improve the tracking speed.

There is extensive literature on correlation filtering based tracking methods in recent years. Henriques *et al.* [7] proposed to incorporating the kernel trick with the correlation filter learning, leading to kernelized version of [2]. Since the scale variations of the target appearance between successive frames are not considered in [7], Danelljan *et al.* [4] and Li and Zhu [5] integrated adaptive scale estimations with the correlation filter learning, respectively. An approach leveraging adaptive color attributes [3] was proposed for real-time visual tracking within the correlation filtering framework. Ma *et al.* [13] developed a long-term correlation tracking method by decomposing visual tracking into translation and scale estimations. Liu *et al.* [8] designed an adaptive correlation filter to exploit the part-based information of the target. Tang and Feng [14] proposed a multi-kernel correlation filter for visual tracking, which fully takes advantage of the invariance-discriminative power spectrums of various features. Danelljan *et al.* [9] leveraged a spatial regularization for correlation filter learning, leading to an impressive tracking performance.

Beyond the correlation filter based method, extensive tracking approaches were proposed and achieved state-of-the-art performance, such as structural learning [11,15,16], sparse and low-rank learning [17–20], subspace learning [21–23], and deep learning [24,25]. Readers are recommended to refer to [26,27] for a thorough review of visual tracking.

3   Proposed Approach

3.1   Formulation

The typical correlation filtering based model focuses on solving the following ridge regression problem

$$\min_{\mathbf{w}} \sum_i \left(f\left(\mathbf{x}_i\right) - y_i\right)^2 + \lambda \left\|\mathbf{w}\right\|_2^2, \tag{1}$$

where a regression function $f\left(\mathbf{x}_i\right) = \mathbf{w}^T \varphi\left(\mathbf{x}_i\right)$ is trained with a feature-space projector $\varphi\left(\cdot\right)$; the objective values y_i are specified to be of Gaussian shaped; and $\lambda > 0$ is a weight parameter. The training samples $\{\mathbf{x}_i\}$ consists of the cyclically shifted image patches of the base image (i.e., the latest target). With the learned regression model, the target is localized by selecting the candidate with the largest regression value (filter response in the frequency domain) from a set of target candidates that are generated by the cyclically shifted patches of the latest target region in the current frame.

The goal of the proposed approach is to promote the robustness of the correlation filter learning. An anisotropy of the filter response, from a signal processing perspective, is exploited for visual tracking, and the robust loss functions, from a overfitting point of view, are utilized to deal with the significant appearance changes. To this end, an adaptive approach is leveraged in this work, which employs different sparsity related loss functions to adaptively fit the Gaussian shaped objective values. Similar to the previous work [2,7], the proposed approach is modeled from the regression perspective and solved via the correlation filtering method. Generally, the regression in this work is defined as

$$\min_{\mathbf{w}} \sum_i \ell\left(f\left(\mathbf{x}_i\right) - y_i\right) + \lambda \left\|\mathbf{w}\right\|_2^2, \tag{2}$$

where $\ell\left(\cdot\right)$ is a loss function, and the regularization $\left\|\mathbf{w}\right\|_2^2$ is reserved to make the regression stable. In order to promote the robustness of the above model against the significant target appearance changes, the sparsity related loss function [28] is encouraged. Three loss functions, ℓ_1-, $\ell_1\ell_2$- and $\ell_{2,1}$-loss, are leveraged in this work, which exploit the sparsity, elastic net and group sparsity structures of the loss values. Note that the problem in Eq. (1) is also described via the above model when the loss function is set as ℓ_2-loss.

3.2   Evaluation Algorithm

The problem in Eq. (2) is NP-hard [28] because the sparsity related constraints on the data fitting term are involved. For this reason, it is equivalently reformulated as

$$\min_{\mathbf{w},\mathbf{e}} \sum_i \ell(e_i) + \lambda \|\mathbf{w}\|_2^2, \quad s.t. \ e_i = y_i - f(\mathbf{x}_i), \tag{3}$$

where e_i denotes the difference between the regression values $f(\mathbf{x}_i)$ and the objective values y_i, and y_i is of Gaussian shaped. Notice that the reformulated problem is convex with respect to either $\mathbf{w}$ or $\mathbf{e}$. However, it is still NP-hard with respect to both $\mathbf{w}$ and $\mathbf{e}$. As a result, an iterative algorithm is required to approximate the solution. First, an equivalent form is employed to represent the above problem as

$$\min_{\mathbf{w},\mathbf{e}} \sum_i (f(\mathbf{x}_i) + e_i - y_i)^2 + \lambda \|\mathbf{w}\|_2^2 + \tau \sum_i \ell(e_i), \tag{4}$$

where τ is a weight parameter. Note that Eq. (4) can be split into two subproblems:

$$\min_{\mathbf{w}} \|\mathbf{f}(\mathbf{X}) + \mathbf{e} - \mathbf{y}\|_2^2 + \lambda \|\mathbf{w}\|_2^2 \tag{5}$$

$$\min_{\mathbf{e}} \|\mathbf{f}(\mathbf{X}) + \mathbf{e} - \mathbf{y}\|_2^2 + \tau \ell(\mathbf{e}), \tag{6}$$

where $\mathbf{X}$ denotes the sample matrix, of which each row denotes a sample. Both the above two subproblems have globally optimal solutions. The problem in Eq. (4) can be solved by alternately optimizing the two subproblems until the objective function values converged.

The dual space is leveraged to solve Eq. (5). The dual conjugate of $\mathbf{w}$, denoted by $\boldsymbol{\alpha}$, is introduced, such that $\mathbf{w} = \sum_i \alpha_i \varphi(\mathbf{x}_i)$. The problem with respect to $\boldsymbol{\alpha}$ is squared. It indicates that there is a closed-form solution

$$\hat{\boldsymbol{\alpha}} = \frac{\hat{\mathbf{y}} - \hat{\mathbf{e}}}{\hat{\mathbf{k}}_1 + \lambda}, \tag{7}$$

where $\mathbf{k}_1$ denotes the first row of the kernel matrix $\mathbf{K}$ whose element $k_{ij} = \varphi^T(\mathbf{x}_i)\varphi(\mathbf{x}_j)$, the fraction means element-wise division, and the hat $\hat{}$ stands for the discrete Fourier transform (DFT) and hereafter. Note that because the sample matrix $\mathbf{X}$ denotes all the training samples that are generated by cyclically shifting the latest target, some kernels, such as Gaussian, and polynomial, can lead to a circulant kernel matrix, as demonstrated in [7]. Based on such a circulant structure, the kernel matrix $\mathbf{K}$ can be diagonalized as

$$\mathbf{K} = \mathbf{D} diag\left(\hat{\mathbf{k}}_1\right) \mathbf{D}^H, \tag{8}$$

where $\mathbf{D}$ denotes the DFT matrix, $\mathbf{k}_1$ denotes the first row[2] of the kernel matrix $\mathbf{K}$, and $\mathbf{D}^H$ denotes the Hermitian transpose of $\mathbf{D}$. Note that the above diagonalization significantly improves the computational efficiency.

---

[2] The rows of the kernel matrix $\mathbf{K}$ are actually obtained from the cyclic shifts of the vector $\mathbf{k}_1$.

Three algorithms are employed to solve Eq. (6), corresponding to the three loss functions used in Eq. (4).

(1) ℓ_1-*loss*. In this case, the sparsity constraint is imposed on $\mathbf{e}$. By using the shrinkage thresholding algorithm [29], the globally optimal solution of $\mathbf{e}$ can be obtained from

$$\mathbf{e} = \sigma \left(\frac{1}{2}\tau, \mathcal{F}^{-1} \left(\hat{\mathbf{y}} - \hat{\alpha} \odot \hat{\mathbf{k}}_1 \right) \right), \tag{9}$$

where $\mathcal{F}^{-1}(\cdot)$ denotes the inverse Fourier transform, and $\odot$ denotes the element-wise multiplication, and the function σ is a shrinkage operator, defined as

$$\sigma\left(\varepsilon, x\right) = sign\left(x\right) \max\left(0, |x| - \varepsilon\right). \tag{10}$$

(2) $\ell_1\ell_2$-*loss*. In this case, the elastic net constraint is enforced on $\mathbf{e}$. By completing the square, Eq. (6) can be solved in a similar way as using ℓ_1-loss. The globally optimal solution of $\mathbf{e}$ is obtained from

$$\mathbf{e} = \sigma \left(\frac{\tau}{4 + 2\tau}, \frac{2}{2 + \tau}\mathcal{F}^{-1} \left(\hat{\mathbf{y}} - \hat{\alpha} \odot \hat{\mathbf{k}}_1 \right) \right). \tag{11}$$

The coefficients of the ℓ_1- and ℓ_2-regularization terms in the elastic net constraint are set to be equal in the experiments.

(3) $\ell_{2,1}$-*loss*. In this case, the variables are considered to be two-dimensional (*i.e.*, matrix variables). Under the $\ell_{2,1}$-loss, the group sparsity of $\mathbf{e}$ is exploited. By using the accelerated proximal gradient method [30], the globally optimal solution of $\mathbf{e}$ is obtained from

$$\mathbf{e}_j = \begin{cases} \left(1 - \frac{1}{\tau\|\mathbf{q}_j\|_2}\right) \mathbf{q}_j, & \frac{1}{\tau} < \|\mathbf{q}_j\|_2 \\ \mathbf{0}, & otherwise, \end{cases} \tag{12}$$

where $\mathbf{e}_j$ denotes the j-th column of the matrix $\mathbf{e}$, and $\mathbf{q} = \mathcal{F}^{-1}\left(\hat{\mathbf{y}} - \hat{\alpha} \odot \hat{\mathbf{k}}_1\right)$. In addition, considering the symmetry of the matrix $\mathbf{e}$, the j-th row of $\mathbf{e}$ is also zeroed for all $j \in \{k | \mathbf{e}_k = \mathbf{0}\}$.

The computational cost in each iteration comes from the Fourier and the inverse Fourier transforms of $\mathbf{e}$, which yield $\mathcal{O}\left(n \log n\right)$ complexity. The empirical results in this work show that the algorithm converges within tens of iterations. Thus, the efficiency of the proposed approach can be satisfied for a real-time tracker.

3.3   Target Localization

In each frame, a large number of training samples are generated by cyclically shifting the latest target region (a base image), essentially as the dense sampling method does. Given a target candidate $\mathbf{x}'$, the regression value of this candidate is computed in the frequency domain from

$$\hat{\mathbf{f}}\left(\mathbf{x}'\right) = \hat{\mathbf{k}}' \odot \hat{\alpha}, \tag{13}$$

where $\hat{\mathbf{k}}' = \varphi^T(\mathbf{x})\,\varphi(\mathbf{x}')$ denotes the kernel correlation of the latest target region $\mathbf{x}$ and the candidate region $\mathbf{x}'$. The candidate with the largest regression value (filter response) f is determined as the current target. Note that the above operation in Eq. (13) is actually a spatial correlation filtering over $\mathbf{k}'$ using the filter $\boldsymbol{\alpha}$ in frequency domain, because the frequency representation can lead to significant improvement in the running speed.

3.4 Explanation on the Loss Functions

The different sparsity related loss functions are leveraged in this work, in order to promote the robustness of the filter learning. The ℓ_1-loss allows the errors $\mathbf{e}$ to be extremely large but sparse, such that the learned filter $\boldsymbol{\alpha}$ may ignore the significant appearance changes of the target. The $\ell_1\ell_2$-loss appends an additional ℓ_2-loss to the ℓ_1-loss. Note that because the ℓ_2-loss always leads to small and dense errors, the globally uniform appearance changes, *e.g.*, in the case of illumination variation, can be dealt with effectively. For this reason, the $\ell_1\ell_2$-loss allows for both the abrupt and the slow appearance changes. The $\ell_{2,1}$-loss exploits the relationship between the errors, such that the appearance changes in local patches can be well handled.

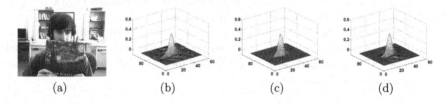

| (a) | (b) | (c) | (d) |

Fig. 2. The anisotropy of the expected filter response exploited in the frame shown in (a) with respect to the ℓ_1-loss (b), the $\ell_1\ell_2$-loss (c), and the $\ell_{2,1}$-loss (d).

As discussed above, the three loss functions can tolerate the large errors during the filter learning, leading to promoted robustness. Referring to Eq. (3), it indicates that the difference e_i between the filter response $f(\mathbf{x}_i)$ and the Gaussian shaped response y_i can be large, leading to an anisotropic expected response $y_i - e_i$. In fact, such an anisotropy essentially facilitates tracking. Figure 2 illustrates the anisotropic expected filter response adaptively learned via the three loss functions in a representative frame. It is evident that the three loss functions result in relatively larger filter responses in the horizontal direction. It suggests that because the distractive object (the book) moves vertically, the loss functions punish the regions vertically deviating away from the target region more severely.

3.5 Implementation Details

The training samples $\mathbf{X}$ in each frame are the fully cyclic shifts of the image region centered at the current target region with the size of 1.5 times of the target. A cosine window is leveraged in the based image to avoid the discontinuity caused by the cyclic shifts. Histogram of orientation gradient (HOG) feature is employed to describe the samples. Gaussian kernel is adopted to map the samples into a non-linear high-dimensional feature space. The above operations are also imposed on the target candidates in each frame, which cyclically shifted from the image centered at the latest target region. As recommended in [7], the parameter λ in Eq. (4) is set to 10^{-4}. Another parameter τ in Eq. (4) is set to be equal to λ in the experiments.

4 Experiments

Three trackers are implemented, corresponding to the ℓ_1-, $\ell_1\ell_2$- and $\ell_{2,1}$-loss functions, denoted by $Ours_S$ (sparsity), $Ours_{EN}$ (elastic net), and $Ours_{GS}$ (group sparsity), respectively. The proposed trackers were evaluated on a popular benchmark [12], which contains 51 video sequences with various challenging situations, such as illumination change, non-rigid deformation, and occlusion. The target region in each frame of the 51 video sequences is labeled manually and used as the ground truth. Although many real-time trackers [31–39] have been proposed recently, the 12 most related state-of-the-art trackers, which are publicly provided by the authors, were compared in the experiments. Two criteria of performance evaluation were used in the comparisons, which are defined as follows.

– *Precision*. The percentage of frames where the center location errors (CLE) are less than a predefined threshold. The CLE in each frame is measured by the Euclidean distance between the centers of the tracking and the ground truth regions.
– *Success Rate*. The percentage of frames where the overlap rates (OR) are greater than predefined threshold. The OR in each frame is computed from $\frac{A_t \cap A_g}{A_t \cup A_g}$ for A_t and A_g are the areas of the tracking and the ground truth regions, respectively.

4.1 Comparison with the State-of-the-Art Trackers

We compared the proposed trackers to the top five trackers in [12], including Struck [11], SCM [40], TLD [41], ASLA [42], and CXT [43]. Figure 3 shows the precision plots and success rate plots of the proposed and the top five trackers in [12] on the 51 video sequences. It is evident that the proposed trackers significantly outperform the top five trackers, yielding the improvements of 14 % in precision ($\rho = 20$) and 5 % in success rate (average). This is attributed to the advantage of the correlation filtering paradigm.

4.2 Comparison with Trackers Within Correlation Filter Learning

It is also desired to investigate the performance of the proposed trackers within the correlation filtering based methods. 7 popular correlation filtering based

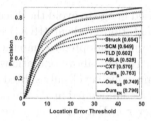 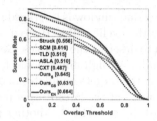

Fig. 3. Tracking performance of the proposed and the top ten trackers in [12] on the 51 video sequences.

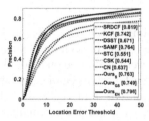 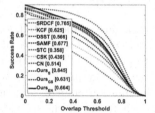

Fig. 4. Tracking performance of the proposed and the popular correlation filtering based trackers on the 51 video sequences.

trackers are referred to for the comparisons. Figure 4 shows the precision plots and success rate plots of the proposed and the 7 correlation filtering based trackers on the 51 video sequences.

It is evident that the proposed tracker, Ours$_{EN}$, obtains the second best results in terms of precisions. This is attributed to the robustness of the $\ell_1\ell_2$-loss used in the correlation filter learning. Because the scale variation is not considered, the performance of the proposed trackers is inferior to the SMAF tracker and the SRDCF tracker in terms of success rate, which adopt ad hoc strategies to deal with the scale change. It is also necessary to note that the success rate of the proposed trackers are still superior to other five competing counterparts (except for SMAF and SRDCF), because of the improved accuracy on the target localization.

The computational efficiency should be compared within the correlation filtering based methods for a fair evaluation. Table 1 shows the running speeds (in frames per second) of the proposed and the popular correlation filtering based trackers. Because the iterative algorithm can converge within tens of iterations, the proposed trackers run faster than their counterparts like SRDCF, SMAF, and DSST.

4.3   Evaluations in Various Situations

The tracking performance in various challenging situations is analyzed to thoroughly evaluate the proposed trackers. In order to investigate the effectiveness of

Table 1. Running speeds (in frames per second) of the proposed and the popular correlation filtering based trackers.

Tracker	Ours	SRDCF [9]	SAMF [5]	DSST [4]	KCF [7]	CN [44]	CSK [2]	STC [6]
FPS	37	5	15	25	172	135	154	181

the three (ℓ_1-, $\ell_1\ell_2$- and $\ell_{2,1}$-) loss functions, the KCF tracker (ℓ_2-loss) is referred to as the base line method. Figure 5 shows the results in the six challenging situations, respectively.

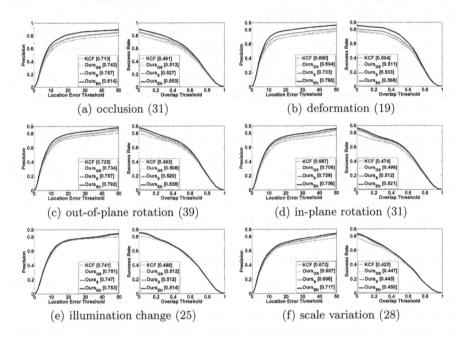

Fig. 5. Tracking performance of the three proposed trackers and the KCF tracker on various challenging situations. In the caption of each sub-figure, the number in parentheses denotes the number of the video sequences in the corresponding situation.

Occlusion. In the case of occlusion, the target is occluded by the other objects, leading to abrupt appearance changes. It is evident that the three proposed trackers significant outperform the KCF tracker in this case. This is attributed to that the sparsity related loss functions of the proposed trackers are more robust to the abrupt appearance changes than the squared loss, resulting in more reliable filter response.

Deformation. The target suffers from the non-rigid deformation in some complicated factors, like motion, pose change, and viewpoint variation. In this case, the target appearance often partially changes significantly. Note that the sparsity related loss functions work more robustly in the presence of significant appearance change, while the squared loss is more effective to deal with globally uniform appearance change. It is evident from the results that the proposed tracker, Ours$_{EN}$, achieves the best results in this case, because the significant changes are well handled by its sparsity constraint and the small changes are dealt with by its squared regularization. Ours$_S$ also obtains better results than KCF. In contrast, the $\ell_{2,1}$-loss (Ours$_{GS}$) does not improve the results obviously because of its sensitivity to this complicated situation.

In-Plane/Out-of-Plane Rotation. This challenge is often caused by the target motion and/or viewpoint change. It is evident that the three proposed trackers improve the KCF tracker to different extent. This benefits from the robustness of the sparsity based loss functions.

Illumination Change. In this case, the target appearance changes as the lighting condition of the scene varies. This challenge often causes uniform changes in target appearance, *i.e.*, the illumination change influences in the entire target appearance. For this reason, the squared loss is very efficient to deal with this case. As a result, the proposed approach does not improve the KCF tracker significantly.

Scale Variation. During tracking, the scale of the target appearance is inevitably changed. If the tracker does not adjust the size of the target window appropriately, tracking failure will be possibly caused because more background information is unexpectedly acquired by the tracker. Unfortunately, considering the efficiency, the KCF and the proposed trackers does not deal with the scales. It can be seen from the results that the proposed trackers improve the precisions but obtain similar success rates as the KCF tracker in this situation.

4.4   Analysis of the Proposed Approach

The goal of the proposed approach is to improve the robustness of the correlation filter learning by means of different loss functions. The different loss functions lead to different anisotropic filter responses. In this section, we interpret how the different loss functions essentially influence the tracking performance via the anisotropic filter responses.

Intuitively, the peak value of an online learned correlation filter, which is responsible for the accuracy of the target localization in each frame, should be stable enough between successive frames in the presence of various challenges. To this end, we analyze the peak values of the filter on three representative video sequences, which include the challenges of occlusion, illumination change, and deformation, respectively. Because there are also other challenges on the video sequences of *faceocc2* and *david*, only the first 200 and 100 frames are selected, respectively. For the convenience of discussion, we use the KCF tracker [7] as a baseline method in the analysis.

Qualitatively, Fig. 6 plots the peak value of the correlation filter and the filter responses, respectively, in each frame of the three video sequences with respect to the KCF and the proposed trackers. Note that the abrupt changes of the peak values correspond to the significant appearance changes in the corresponding

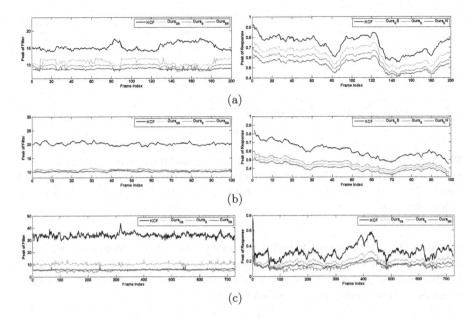

(a)

(b)

(c)

Fig. 6. Peak values of the online learned filters (left column) and the responses (right column) with respect to the four trackers in different challenging cases. The curves are expected to be as smooth as possible. (a) occlusion (first 200 frames of *faceocc2*); (b) illumination change (first 100 frames of *david*); and (c) deformation (all the 725 frames of *basketball*).

frames. If the peak values are sensitive in successive frames, the corresponding filter responses will be unstable, leading to lower accuracy of target location.

In the case of occlusion, as shown in Fig. 6(a), the peak values of the filter with respect to the $\ell_1\ell_2$-loss (Ours$_{EN}$) varies the most slowly between the frames. The ℓ_1-loss (Ours$_S$) also achieves smoother plot of the peak values than the $\ell_{2,1}$- (Ours$_{GS}$) and the ℓ_2-loss (the KCF tracker). The analysis results on the sensitivity of the peak values in the successive frames are consistent with the tracking performance evaluations shown in Fig. 5(a).

In the case of illumination change, it is evident in Fig. 6(b) that the peak values of the filter with respect to the four trackers have the similar sensitivities in the successive frames. It is also verified in Fig. 5(e) that the four trackers achieve similar tracking performance.

When non-rigid deformation is involved, as shown in Fig. 6(c), the proposed tracker, Ours$_{EN}$, produces the most stable filter peak values, achieving the best tracking performance, as shown in Fig. 5(b). In contrast, the peak values of the filter with respect to the KCF tracker are very sensitive between the frames, resulting in the interior tracking performance, as evaluated in Fig. 5(b).

Quantitatively, a metric is required to measure the sensitivity of the filter. It is discussed in [1] that, from a signal processing perspective, a good correlation filter often has a large peak-to-sidelobe ratio (PSR) value. The PSR only

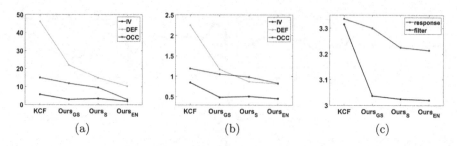

Fig. 7. Sensitivity of the peak values of the filters (a) and the responses (b) with respect to the four trackers in different challenging cases. (c) Average sensitivity of the peak values of the filters and the responses with respect to the four trackers on all the 51 video sequences.

considers the performance of the filter in one frame, while a measurement focusing on the performance in successive frames is more desired for tracking analysis. To this end, the following metric is defined, from a visual tracking point of view, to measure the sensitivity of a correlation filter:

$$s = \sum_{i=1}^{n} (p_i - p_m)^2, \tag{14}$$

where p_i denotes the peak value of the correlation filter in the i-th frame, p_m denotes the mean of the peak values in the n frames, and the n peak values are normalized by their squared norm. As discussed above, the value of s is expected to be small for a good correlation filter.

Figures 7(a) and (b) plot the sensitivity s of the learned correlation filters and the filter responses with respect to the four trackers in the above three challenging situations, respectively. To thoroughly verify the sensitivity, in Fig. 7(c), we show the average sensitivity of the filter and the response on all the 51 video sequences. It is evident that the sensitivity analysis of the correlation filter in successive frames is consistent with the tracking performance evaluations (refer to the results shown in Fig. 5).

From both the qualitative and the quantitative analysis, a conclusion can be drawn to explain how the loss functions essentially influence the tracking performance: the lower the sensitivity s of the learned correlation filter in successive frames is, the higher the tracking performance is achieved. This also can be used as a criterion to design a robust correlation filter for visual tracking.

Revisiting the proposed approach, because the sparsity related loss functions allow large errors in the correlation filter learning, the appearance changes will not cause the significant changes in filter peak values, leading to low sensitivity values. In contrast, the squared loss used by the KCF tracker enforces small errors in the correlation filter learning, such that the filter is always adjusted to fit all the small appearance changes, leading to high sensitivity values. This explains why the proposed trackers perform better than the KCF tracker from the sensitivity perspective.

Fig. 8. Representative frames with 5 %, 10 % , 15 % and 20 % corrupted pixels (from left to right).

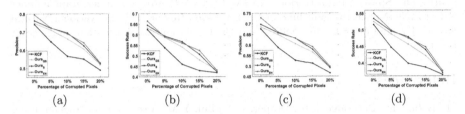

Fig. 9. Tracking performance of the three proposed trackers and the KCF tracker in the presence of noise with different amounts on the 51 video sequences. (a) precision plots with $\theta = 20$; (b) success plot with $\rho = 0.5$; (c) precision plots in average; and (d) success plot in average.

4.5 Tracking in Noise Contaminated Frames

In the practical applications, the quality of the video sequences cannot be guaranteed, *i.e.*, the frames are often corrupted by noise. Thus, a visual tracker is expected to be robust to the noise contaminated frames. For this reason, to thoroughly evaluate the robustness of the proposed approach, the tracking is investigated in the noise contaminated frames. The representative noise contaminated frames are shown in Fig. 8. Figure 9 shows the tracking performance of the three proposed trackers and the KCF tracker in the presence of noise with different amounts. It is evident that, in the case that even small number of pixels are corrupted, the performance of the KCF tracker decreases significantly. In contrast, the proposed trackers are not influenced by the noise so drastically as the KCF tracker. The performance of the proposed trackers decreases sharply until a relative large number of pixels (20 %) are corrupted. As a result, it can be observed that the proposed trackers perform more robustly than the KCF tracker in the noise contaminated frames. This also suggests that the proposed approach is closer to the practical applications.

5   Conclusion

Three real-time trackers have been proposed in this work within the correlation filtering paradigm. The robustness of the filter learning has been successfully promoted by employing three sparsity related loss functions. It has been shown that the tracking performance in various challenging situations has been improved via the proposed approach. Through analyzing how the different loss functions essentially influenced the tracking performance, we have found that the analysis result on the sensitivity of the peak values of the filter is consistent with the tracking performance evaluations. This is a very useful reference criterion to design a robust correlation filter for tracking.

Acknowledgment. This work is partly supported by the National Natural Science Foundation of China (NSFC) under grants 61573351 and 61132007, the National Aeronautics and Space Administration (NASA) LEARN II program under grant number NNX15AN94N, and the joint fund of Civil Aviation Research by the National Natural Science Foundation of China (NSFC) and Civil Aviation Administration under grant U1533132.

References

1. Bolme, D., Beveridge, J.R., Draper, B.A., Lui, Y.M.: Visual object tracking using adaptive correlation filters. In: IEEE Computer Society Conference on Computer Vision and Pattern Recognition (CVPR) (2010)
2. Henriques, J.F., Caseiro, R., Martins, P., Batista, J.: Exploiting the circulant structure of tracking-by-detection with kernels. In: Fitzgibbon, A., Lazebnik, S., Perona, P., Sato, Y., Schmid, C. (eds.) ECCV 2012, Part IV. LNCS, vol. 7575, pp. 702–715. Springer, Heidelberg (2012)
3. Danelljan, M., Khan, F.S., Felsberg, M., Weijer, J.V.D.: Adaptive color attributes for real-time visual tracking. In: IEEE Computer Society Conference on Computer Vision and Pattern Recognition (CVPR), pp. 1090–1097 (2014)
4. Danelljan, M., Häger, G., Khan, F.S., Felsberg, M.: Accurate scale estimation for robust visual tracking. In: British Machine Vision Conference (BMVC) (2014)
5. Li, Y., Zhu, J.: A Scale adaptive kernel correlation filter tracker with feature integration. In: European Conference on Computer Vision Workshop (2014)
6. Zhang, K., Zhang, L., Liu, Q., Zhang, D., Yang, M.-H.: Fast visual tracking via dense spatio-temporal context learning. In: Fleet, D., Pajdla, T., Schiele, B., Tuytelaars, T. (eds.) ECCV 2014, Part V. LNCS, vol. 8693, pp. 127–141. Springer, Heidelberg (2014)
7. Henriques, J., Caseiro, R., Martins, P., Batista, J.: High-speed tracking with kernelized correlation filters. IEEE Trans. Pattern Anal. Mach. Intell. (TPAMI) 37(3), 583–596 (2015)
8. Liu, T., Wnag, G., Yang, Q.: Real-time part-based visual tracking via adaptive correlation filters. In: IEEE Computer Society Conference on Computer Vision and Pattern Recognition (CVPR), pp. 4902–4912 (2015)
9. Danelljan, M., Gustav, H., Khan, F.S., Felsberg, M.: Learning spatially regularized correlation filters for visual tracking. In: IEEE International Conference on Computer Vision (ICCV), pp. 4310–4318 (2015)
10. Zhang, S., Zhao, S., Sui, Y., Zhang, L.: Single object tracking with fuzzy least squares support vector machine. IEEE Trans. Image Process. (TIP) 24(12), 5723–5738 (2015)
11. Hare, S., Saffari, A., Torr, P.: Struck: structured output tracking with kernels. In: IEEE International Conference on Computer Vision (ICCV), pp. 263–270 (2011)
12. Wu, Y., Lim, J., Yang, M.H.: Online object tracking: a benchmark. In: IEEE Computer Society Conference on Computer Vision and Pattern Recognition (CVPR), pp. 2411–2418 (2013)

13. Ma, C., Yang, X., Zhang, C., Yang, M.h.: Long-term correlation tracking. In: IEEE Computer Society Conference on Computer Vision and Pattern Recognition (CVPR), pp. 5388–5396 (2015)
14. Tang, M., Feng, J.: Multi-kernel correlation filter for visual tracking. In: IEEE International Conference on Computer Vision (ICCV), pp. 3038–3046 (2015)
15. Kalal, Z., Mikolajczyk, K., Matas, J.: Tracking-learning-detection. IEEE Trans. Pattern Anal. Mach. Intell. (TPAMI) 34(7), 1409–1422 (2012)
16. Zhang, T., Liu, S., Xu, C., Yan, S., Ghanem, B., Ahuja, N., Yang, M.H.: Structural sparse tracking. In: IEEE Computer Society Conference on Computer Vision and Pattern Recognition (CVPR), pp. 150–158 (2015)
17. Mei, X., Ling, H.: Robust visual tracking and vehicle classification via sparse representation. IEEE Trans. Pattern Anal. Mach. Intell. (TPAMI) 33(11), 2259–2272 (2011)
18. Zhang, T., Ghanem, B., Liu, S., Ahuja, N.: Low-rank sparse learning for robust visual tracking. In: Fitzgibbon, A., Lazebnik, S., Perona, P., Sato, Y., Schmid, C. (eds.) ECCV 2012, Part VI. LNCS, vol. 7577, pp. 470–484. Springer, Heidelberg (2012)
19. Sui, Y., Tang, Y., Zhang, L.: Discriminative low-rank tracking. In: IEEE International Conference on Computer Vision (ICCV), pp. 3002–3010 (2015)
20. Sui, Y., Zhang, L.: Robust tracking via locally structured representation. Int. J. Comput. Vis. (IJCV) 119(2), 110–144 (2016)
21. Kwon, J., Lee, K.: Visual tracking decomposition. In: IEEE Computer Society Conference on Computer Vision and Pattern Recognition (CVPR), pp. 1269–1276 (2010)
22. Wang, D., Lu, H., Yang, M.H.: Least soft-thresold squares tracking. In: IEEE Computer Society Conference on Computer Vision and Pattern Recognition (CVPR), pp. 2371–2378 (2013)
23. Sui, Y., Zhang, S., Zhang, L.: Robust visual tracking via sparsity-induced subspace learning. IEEE Trans. Image Process. (TIP) 24(12), 4686–4700 (2015)
24. Ma, C., Huang, J.b., Yang, X., Yang, M.H.: Hierarchical convolutional features for visual tracking. In: IEEE International Conference on Computer Vision (ICCV), pp. 3074–3082 (2015)
25. Wang, L., Ouyang, W., Wang, X., Lu, H.: Visual tracking with fully convolutional networks. In: IEEE International Conference on Computer Vision (ICCV), pp. 3119–3127 (2015)
26. Yilmaz, A., Javed, O., Shah, M.: Object tracking: a survey. ACM Comput. Surv. 38(4), 13–57 (2006)
27. Smeulders, A.W.M., Chu, D.M., Cucchiara, R., Calderara, S., Dehghan, A., Shah, M.: Visual tracking: an experimental survey. IEEE Trans. Pattern Anal. Mach. Intell. (TPAMI) 36(7), 1442–1468 (2014)
28. Wright, J., Ma, Y., Mairal, J., Sapiro, G.: Sparse representation for computer vision and pattern recognition. Proc. IEEE 98(6), 1031–1044 (2010)
29. Beck, A., Teboulle, M.: A fast iterative shrinkage-thresholding algorithm for linear inverse problems. SIAM J. Imaging Sci. 2(1), 183–202 (2009)
30. Bach, F., Jenatton, R., Mairal, J., Obozinski, G.: Convex optimization with sparsity-inducing norms. In: Optimization for Machine Learning, pp. 1–35 (2011)
31. Grabner, H., Grabner, M., Bischof, H.: Real-time tracking via on-line boosting. Br. Mach. Vis. Conf. (BMVC) 6(1–6), 10 (2006)
32. Zhang, K., Zhang, L., Yang, M.H.: Real-time object tracking via online discriminative feature selection. IEEE Trans. Image Process. (TIP) 22(12), 4664–4677 (2013)

33. Zhang, K., Zhang, L., Yang, M.-H.: Real-time compressive tracking. In: Fitzgibbon, A., Lazebnik, S., Perona, P., Sato, Y., Schmid, C. (eds.) ECCV 2012, Part III. LNCS, vol. 7574, pp. 864–877. Springer, Heidelberg (2012)

34. Li, H., Shen, C., Shi, Q.: Real-time visual tracking using compressive sensing. In: IEEE Computer Society Conference on Computer Vision and Pattern Recognition (CVPR) (2011)

35. Hall, D., Perona, P.: Online, real-time tracking using a category-to-individual detector. In: Fleet, D., Pajdla, T., Schiele, B., Tuytelaars, T. (eds.) ECCV 2014, Part I. LNCS, vol. 8689, pp. 361–376. Springer, Heidelberg (2014)

36. Wu, Y., Cheng, J., Wang, J., Lu, H.: Real-time visual tracking via incremental covariance tensor learning. In: IEEE International Conference on Computer Vision (ICCV) (2009)

37. Bao, C., Wu, Y., Ling, H., Ji, H.: Real time robust L1 tracker using accelerated proximal gradient approach. In: IEEE Computer Society Conference on Computer Vision and Pattern Recognition (CVPR), pp. 1830–1837, June 2012

38. Holzer, S., Pollefeys, M., Ilic, S., Tan, D.J., Navab, N.: Online learning of linear predictors for real-time tracking. In: Fitzgibbon, A., Lazebnik, S., Perona, P., Sato, Y., Schmid, C. (eds.) ECCV 2012, Part I. LNCS, vol. 7572, pp. 470–483. Springer, Heidelberg (2012)

39. Hager, G.D., Belhumeur, P.N.: Real-time tracking of image regions with changes in geometry and illumination. In: IEEE Computer Society Conference on Computer Vision and Pattern Recognition (CVPR), pp. 403–410 (1996)

40. Zhong, W., Lu, H., Yang, M.H.: Robust object tracking via sparsity-based collaborative model. In: IEEE Computer Society Conference on Computer Vision and Pattern Recognition (CVPR), pp. 1838–1845 (2012)

41. Kalal, Z., Matas, J., Mikolajczyk, K.: P-N learning: Bootstrapping binary classifiers by structural constraints. In: IEEE Computer Society Conference on Computer Vision and Pattern Recognition (CVPR). 49–56., June 2010

42. Jia, X., Lu, H., Yang, M.H.: Visual tracking via adaptive structural local sparse appearance model. In: IEEE Computer Society Conference on Computer Vision and Pattern Recognition (CVPR), pp. 1822–1829 (2012)

43. Dinh, T.B., Vo, N., Medioni, G.: Context tracker: exploring supporters and distracters in unconstrained environments. In: IEEE Computer Society Conference on Computer Vision and Pattern Recognition (CVPR), pp. 1177–1184, June 2011

44. Danelljan, M., Khan, F.S., Felsberg, M., Weijer, J.V.D.: Adaptive color attributes for real-time visual tracking. In: IEEE Computer Society Conference on Computer Vision and Pattern Recognition (CVPR) (2014)

Deep Self-correlation Descriptor for Dense Cross-Modal Correspondence

Seungryong Kim[1], Dongbo Min[2], Stephen Lin[3], and Kwanghoon Sohn[1(✉)]

[1] Yonsei University, Seoul, South Korea
{srkim89,khsohn}@yonsei.ac.kr
[2] Chungnam National University, Daejeon, South Korea
dbmin@cnu.ac.kr
[3] Microsoft Research, Beijing, China
stevelin@microsoft.com

Abstract. We present a novel descriptor, called deep self-correlation (DSC), designed for establishing dense correspondences between images taken under different imaging modalities, such as different spectral ranges or lighting conditions. Motivated by local self-similarity (LSS), we formulate a novel descriptor by leveraging LSS in a deep architecture, leading to better discriminative power and greater robustness to non-rigid image deformations than state-of-the-art descriptors. The DSC first computes self-correlation surfaces over a local support window for randomly sampled patches, and then builds hierarchical self-correlation surfaces by performing an average pooling within a deep architecture. Finally, the feature responses on the self-correlation surfaces are encoded through a spatial pyramid pooling in a circular configuration. In contrast to convolutional neural networks (CNNs) based descriptors, the DSC is training-free, is robust to cross-modal imaging, and can be densely computed in an efficient manner that significantly reduces computational redundancy. The state-of-the-art performance of DSC on challenging cases of cross-modal image pairs is demonstrated through extensive experiments.

Keywords: Cross-modal correspondence · Deep architecture · Self-correlation · Local self-similarity · Non-rigid deformation

1 Introduction

In many computer vision and computational photography applications, images captured under different imaging modalities are used to supplement the data provided in color images. Typical examples of other imaging modalities include near-infrared [1–3] and dark flash [4] photography. More broadly, photos taken under different imaging conditions, such as different exposure settings [5], blur levels [6,7], and illumination [8], can also be considered as cross-modal [9,10].

Establishing dense correspondences between cross-modal image pairs is essential for combining their disparate information. Although powerful global optimizers may help to improve the accuracy of correspondence estimation to some

This work was done while Seungryong Kim was an intern at Microsoft Research.

© Springer International Publishing AG 2016
B. Leibe et al. (Eds.): ECCV 2016, Part VIII, LNCS 9912, pp. 679–695, 2016.
DOI: 10.1007/978-3-319-46484-8_41

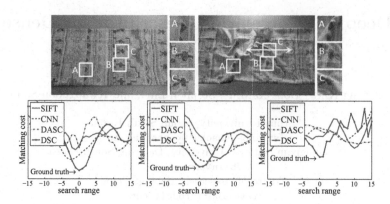

Fig. 1. Examples of matching cost profiles, computed with different descriptors along the scan lines of A, B, and C for image pairs under severe non-rigid deformations and illumination changes. Unlike other descriptors, DSC yields reliable global minima.

extent [11,12], they face inherent limitations without the help of suitable matching descriptors [13]. The most popular local descriptor is scale invariant feature transform (SIFT) [14], which provides relatively good matching performance when there are small photometric variations. However, conventional descriptors such as SIFT often fail to capture reliable matching evidence in cross-modal image pairs due to their different visual properties [9,10].

Recently, convolutional neural networks (CNNs) based features [15–19] have emerged as a robust alternative with high discriminative power. However, CNN-based descriptors cannot satisfactorily deal with severe cross-modality appearance differences, since they use shared convolutional kernels across images which lead to inconsistent responses similar to conventional descriptors [19,20]. Furthermore, they do not scale well for dense correspondence estimation due to their high computational complexity. Though recent works [21] propose an efficient method that extracts dense outputs through the deep CNNs, they do not extract dense CNN features for all pixels individually. More seriously, their methods are usually designed to perform a specific task only, *e.g.*, semantic segmentation, not to provide a general purpose descriptor like ours.

To address the problem of cross-modal appearance changes, feature descriptors have been proposed based on local self-similarity (LSS) [22], which is motivated by the notion that the geometric layout of local internal self-similarities is relatively insensitive to imaging properties. The state-of-the-art descriptor for cross-modal dense correspondence, called dense adaptive self-correlation (DASC) [10], makes use of LSS and has demonstrated high accuracy and speed on cross-modal image pairs. However, DASC suffers from two significant shortcomings. One is its limited discriminative power due to a limited set of patch sampling patterns used for modeling internal self-similarities. In fact, the matching performance of DASC may fall well short of CNN-based descriptors on images that share the same modality. The other major shortcoming is that the DASC descriptor does not provide the flexibility to deal with non-rigid deformations, which leads to lower robustness in matching.

In this paper, we introduce a novel descriptor, called deep self-correlation (DSC), that overcomes the shortcomings of DASC while providing dense cross-modal correspondences. This work is motivated by the observation that local self-similarity can be formulated in a deep architecture to enhance discriminative power and gain robustness to non-rigid deformations. Unlike the DASC descriptor that selects patch pairs within a support window and calculates the self-similarity between them, we compute self-correlation surfaces that more comprehensively encode the intrinsic structure by calculating the self-similarity between randomly selected patches and all of the patches within the support window. These self-correlational responses are aggregated through spatial pyramid pooling in a circular configuration, which yields a representation less sensitive to non-rigid image deformations than the fixed patch selection strategy used in DASC. To further enhance the discriminative power and robustness, we build hierarchical self-correlation surfaces resembling a deep architecture used in CNN, together with nonlinear and normalization layers. For efficient computation of DSC over densely sampled pixels, we calculate the self-correlation surfaces through fast edge-aware filtering.

DSC resembles a CNN in its deep, multi-layer, and convolutional structure. In contrast to existing CNN-based descriptors, DSC requires no training data for learning convolutional kernels, since the convolutions are defined as the local self-similarity between pairs of image patches, which provides robustness for cross-modal imaging. Figure 1 illustrates the robustness of DSC for image pairs across non-rigid deformations and illumination changes. In the experimental results, we show that the DSC outperforms existing area-based and feature-based descriptors on various benchmarks.

2   Related Work

Feature Descriptors. Conventional gradient-based descriptors, such as SIFT [14] and DAISY [23], as well as intensity comparison-based binary descriptors, such as BRIEF [24], have shown limited performance in dense correspondence estimation between cross-modal image pairs. Besides these handcrafted features, several attempts have been made using machine learning algorithms to derive features from large-scale datasets [15,25]. A few of these methods use deep CNNs [26], which have revolutionized image-level classification, to learn discriminative descriptors for local patches. For designing explicit feature descriptors based on a CNN architecture, immediate activations are extracted as the descriptor [15–19], and have been shown to be effective for this patch-level task. However, even though CNN-based descriptors encode a discriminative structure with a deep architecture, they have inherent limitations in cross-modal image correspondence because they are derived from convolutional layers using shared patches or volumes [19,20]. Furthermore, they cannot in practice provide dense descriptors in the image domain due to their prohibitively high computational complexity.

To estimate cross-modal correspondences, variants of the SIFT descriptor have been developed [27], but these gradient-based descriptors maintain an

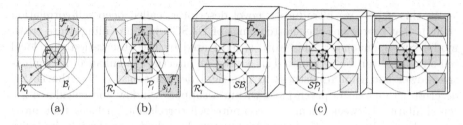

Fig. 2. Illustration of (a) LSS [22] using center-biased dense max pooling, (b) DASC [10] using patch-wise receptive field pooling, and (c) our DSC. Boxes, formed by solid and dotted lines, depict source and target patches. DSC incorporates a circular spatial pyramid pooling on hierarchical self-correlation surfaces.

inherent limitation similar to SIFT in dealing with image gradients that vary differently between modalities. For illumination invariant correspondences, Wang *et al.* proposed the local intensity order pattern (LIOP) descriptor [28], but severe radiometric variations may often alter the relative order of pixel intensities. Simo-Serra *et al.* proposed the deformation and light invariant (DaLI) descriptor [29] to provide high resilience to non-rigid image transformations and illumination changes, but it cannot provide dense descriptors in the image domain due to its high computational time.

Schechtman and Irani introduced the LSS descriptor [22] for the purpose of template matching, and achieved impressive results in object detection and retrieval. By employing LSS, many approaches have tried to solve for cross-modal correspondences [30–32]. However, none of these approaches scale well to dense matching in cross-modal images due to low discriminative power and high complexity. Inspired by LSS, Kim *et al.* recently proposed the DASC descriptor to estimate cross-modal dense correspondences [10]. Though it can provide satisfactory performance, it is not able to handle non-rigid deformations and has limited discriminative power due to its fixed patch pooling scheme.

Area-Based Similarity Measures. A popular measure for registration of cross-modal medical images is mutual information (MI) [33], based on the entropy of the joint probability distribution function, but it provides reliable performance only for variations undergoing a global transformation [34]. Although cross-correlation based methods such as adaptive normalized cross-correlation (ANCC) [35] produce satisfactory results for locally linear variations, they are less effective against more substantial modality variations. Robust selective normalized cross-correlation (RSNCC) [9] was proposed for dense alignment between cross-modal images, but as an intensity based measure it can still be sensitive to cross-modal variations. Recently, DeepMatching [36] was proposed to compute dense correspondences by employing a hierarchical pooling scheme like CNN, but it is not designed to handle cross-modal matching.

3   Background

Let us define an image as $f_i : \mathcal{I} \to \mathbb{R}$ for pixel i, where $\mathcal{I} \subset \mathbb{N}^2$ is a discrete image domain. Given the image f_i, a dense descriptor $\mathcal{D}_i : \mathcal{I} \to \mathbb{R}^L$ with a feature dimension of L is defined on a local support window $\mathcal{R}_i$ of size $M_\mathcal{R}$.

Unlike conventional descriptors, relying on common visual properties across images such as color and gradient, LSS-based descriptors provide robustness to different imaging modalities since internal self-similarities are preserved across cross-modal image pairs [10,22]. As shown in Fig. 2(a), the LSS discretizes the correlation surface on a log-polar grid, generates a set of bins, and then stores the maximum correlation value of each bin. Formally, it generates an $L^{\mathrm{LSS}} \times 1$ feature vector $\mathcal{D}_i^{\mathrm{LSS}} = \bigcup_l d_i^{\mathrm{LSS}}(l)$ for $l \in \{1, ..., L^{\mathrm{LSS}}\}$, with $d_i^{\mathrm{LSS}}(l)$ computed as

$$d_i^{\mathrm{LSS}}(l) = \max_{j \in \mathcal{B}_i(l)} \{\exp(-\mathcal{S}(\mathcal{F}_i, \mathcal{F}_j)/\sigma_c)\}, \tag{1}$$

where log-polar bins are defined as $\mathcal{B}_i = \{j | j \in \mathcal{R}_i, \rho_{r-1} < |i - j| \leq \rho_r, \theta_{a-1} < \angle(i - j) \leq \theta_a\}$ with a log radius ρ_r for $r \in \{1, \cdots, N_\rho\}$ and a quantized angle θ_a for $a \in \{1, \cdots, N_\theta\}$ with $\rho_0 = 0$ and $\theta_0 = 0$. $\mathcal{S}(\mathcal{F}_i, \mathcal{F}_j)$ is a correlation surface between a patch $\mathcal{F}_i$ and $\mathcal{F}_j$ of size $M_\mathcal{F}$, computed using the sum of square differences. Each pair of r and a is associated with a unique index l. Though LSS provides robustness to modality variations, its significant computation does not scale well for estimating dense correspondences in cross-modal images.

Inspired by the LSS [22], the DASC [10] encodes the similarity between patch-wise receptive fields sampled from a log-polar circular point set $\mathcal{P}_i$ as shown in Fig. 2(b). It is defined such that $\mathcal{P}_i = \{j | j \in \mathcal{R}_i, |i - j| = \rho_r, \angle(i - j) = \theta_a\}$, which has a higher density of points near a center pixel, similar to DAISY [23]. The DASC is encoded with a set of similarities between patch pairs of sampling patterns selected from $\mathcal{P}_i$ such that $\mathcal{D}_i^{\mathrm{DASC}} = \bigcup_l d_i^{\mathrm{DASC}}(l)$ for $l \in \{1, ..., L^{\mathrm{DASC}}\}$:

$$d_i^{\mathrm{DASC}}(l) = \exp(-(1 - |\mathcal{C}(\mathcal{F}_{s_{i,l}}, \mathcal{F}_{t_{i,l}})|)/\sigma_c), \tag{2}$$

where $s_{i,l}$ and $t_{i,l}$ are the lth selected sampling pattern from $\mathcal{P}_i$ at pixel i. The patch-wise similarity is computed with an exponential function with a bandwidth of σ_c, which has been widely used for robust estimation [37]. $\mathcal{C}(\mathcal{F}_{s_{i,l}}, \mathcal{F}_{t_{i,l}})$ is computed using an adaptive self-correlation measure. While the DASC descriptor has shown satisfactory results for cross-modal dense correspondence [10], its randomized receptive field pooling has limited descriptive power and does not accommodate non-rigid deformations.

4   The DSC Descriptor

4.1   Motivation and Overview

Inspired by DASC [10], our DSC descriptor also measures an adaptive self-correlation between two patches. We, however, adopt a different strategy for selecting patch pairs, and build self-correlation surfaces that more comprehensively encode self-similar structure to improve the discriminative power and the

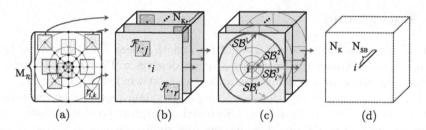

Fig. 3. Computation of single self-correlation (SSC) descriptor. (a) A local support window $\mathcal{R}_i$ of size $M_{\mathcal{R}}$ with N_K random samples. (b) For each random patch, a self-correlation surface is computed using an adaptive self-correlation measure. (c) A self-correlation response is then obtained through circular spatial pyramid pooling (C-SPP). (d) The response from C-SPP is concatenated as 1-D feature vector.

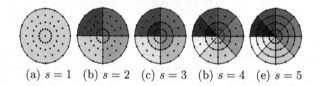

(a) $s = 1$ (b) $s = 2$ (c) $s = 3$ (b) $s = 4$ (e) $s = 5$

Fig. 4. Examples of the circular spatial pyramidal bins $\mathcal{SB}_i$. The total number of bins is $N_{SB} = \sum_{s=2}^{N_S} 2^s + 1$, where N_S represents the pyramid level.

robustness to non-rigid image deformation (Sect. 4.2). Motivated by the deep architecture of CNN-based descriptors [19], we further build hierarchical self-correlation surfaces to enhance the robustness of the DSC descriptor (Sect. 4.4). Densely sampled descriptors are efficiently computed over an entire image using a method based on fast edge-aware filtering (Sect. 4.3). Figure 2(c) illustrates the DSC descriptor, which incorporates a circular spatial pyramid pooling on hierarchical self-correlation surfaces.

4.2   SSC: Single Self-correlation

To simultaneously leverage the benefits of self-similarity in DASC [10] and the deep architecture of CNNs while overcoming the limitations of each method, our approach builds self-correlation surfaces. Unlike DASC [10], the feature response is obtained through circular spatial pyramid pooling. We start by describing a single-layer version of DSC, which we denote as SSC.

Self-correlations. To build a self-correlation surface, we randomly select N_K points from a log-polar circular point set $\mathcal{P}_i$ defined within a local support window $\mathcal{R}_i$. We convolve a patch $\mathcal{F}_{r_{i,k}}$ centered at the k-th point $r_{i,k}$ with all patches $\mathcal{F}_j$, which is defined for $j \in \mathcal{R}_i$ and $k \in \{1, ..., N_K\}$ as shown in Fig. 3(b). Similar to DASC [10], the similarity $\mathcal{C}(\mathcal{F}_{r_{i,k}}, \mathcal{F}_j)$ between patch pairs is measured

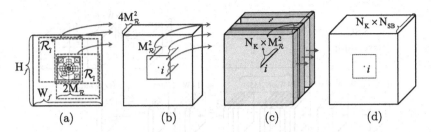

Fig. 5. Efficient computation of self-correlation surfaces on the image. (a) An image f_i with a doubled support window $\mathcal{R}_i^*$ and random samples. (b) 1-D vectorial self-correlation surface. (c) Self-correlation surfaces. (d) Self-correlation responses after C-SPP. With an efficient edge-aware filtering and response reformulation, self-correlation responses are computed efficiently in a dense manner.

using an adaptive self-correlation, which is known to be effective in addressing cross-modality. With (i, k) omitted for simplicity, $\mathcal{C}(\mathcal{F}_r, \mathcal{F}_j)$ is computed as follows:

$$\mathcal{C}(\mathcal{F}_r, \mathcal{F}_j) = \frac{\sum_{r',j'} \omega_{r,r'} (f_{r'} - \mathcal{G}_{r,r})(f_{j'} - \mathcal{G}_{r,j})}{\sqrt{\sum_{r'} \omega_{r,r'} (f_{r'} - \mathcal{G}_{r,r})^2} \sqrt{\sum_{r',j'} \omega_{r,r'} (f_{j'} - \mathcal{G}_{r,j})^2}}, \tag{3}$$

for $r' \in \mathcal{F}_r$ and $j' \in \mathcal{F}_j$. $\mathcal{G}_{r,r} = \sum_{r'} \omega_{r,r'} f_{r'}$ and $\mathcal{G}_{r,j} = \sum_{r',j'} \omega_{r,r'} f_{j'}$ represent weighted averages of $f_{r'}$ and $f_{j'}$. Similar to DASC [10], the weight $\omega_{r,r'}$ represents how similar two pixels r and r' are, and is normalized, $i.e.$, $\sum_{r'} \omega_{r,r'} = 1$. It may be defined using any form of edge-aware weighting [38,39].

Circular Spatial Pyramid Pooling. To encode the feature responses on the self-correlation surface, we propose a circular spatial pyramid pooling (C-SPP) scheme, which pools the responses within each hierarchical spatial bin, similar to a spatial pyramid pooling (SPP) [20,40,41] but in a circular configuration. Note that many existing descriptors also adopt a circular pooling scheme thanks to its robustness based on a higher pixel density near a central pixel [22–24]. We further encode more structure information with a C-SPP.

The circular pyramidal bins $\mathcal{SB}_i(u)$ are defined from log-polar circular bins $\mathcal{B}_i$, where u indexes all pyramidal levels $s \in \{1, ..., N_S\}$ and all bins in each level s as in Fig. 4. The circular pyramidal bin at the top of pyramid, $i.e.$, $s = 1$, encompasses all of bins $\mathcal{B}_i$. At the second level, $i.e.$, $s = 2$, it is defined by dividing $\mathcal{B}_i$ into quadrants. For lower pyramid levels, $i.e.$, $s > 2$, the circular pyramidal bins are defined differently according to whether s is odd or even. For an odd s, the bins are defined by dividing bins in the upper level into two parts along the radius. For an even s, they are defined by dividing bins in the upper level into two parts with respect to the angle. The set of all circular pyramidal bins $\mathcal{SB}_i$ is denoted such that $\mathcal{SB}_i = \bigcup_u \mathcal{SB}_i(u)$ for $u \in \{1, ..., N_{SB}\}$, where the number of circular spatial pyramid bins is defined as $N_{SB} = \sum_{s=2}^{N_S} 2^s + 1$.

As illustrated in Fig. 3(c), the feature responses are finally max-pooled on the circular pyramidal bins $\mathcal{SB}_i(u)$ of each self-correlation surface $\mathcal{C}(\mathcal{F}_{r_{i,k}}, \mathcal{F}_j)$, yielding a feature response

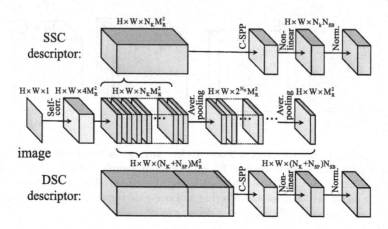

Fig. 6. Visualization of SSC and DSC descriptor. Our architecture consists of a hierarchical self-correlational layer, circular spatial pyramid pooling layer, non-linear gating layer, and normalization layer.

$$h_i(k, u) = \max_{j \in SB_i(u)} \{C(\mathcal{F}_{r_{i,k}}, \mathcal{F}_j)\}, \quad u \in \{1, ..., N_{SB}\}. \tag{4}$$

This pooling is repeated for all $k \in \{1, ..., N_K\}$, yielding accumulated correlation responses $\hat{h}_i(l) = \bigcup_{\{k,u\}} h_i(k, u)$ where l indexes for all k and u.

Interestingly, LSS [22] also uses the max pooling strategy to mitigate the effects of non-rigid image deformation. However, max pooling in the 2-D self-correlation surface of LSS [22] loses fine-scale matching details as reported in [10]. By contrast, DSC employs circular spatial pyramid pooling in a 3-D self-correlation surface that provides a more discriminative representation of self-similarities, thus maintaining fine-scale matching details as well as providing robustness to non-rigid image deformations.

Non-linear Gating and Nomalization. The final feature responses are passed through a non-linear and normalization layer to mitigate the effects of outliers. With accumulated correlation responses $\hat{h}_i$, the single self-correlation (SSC) descriptor $\mathcal{D}_i^{SSC} = \bigcup_l d_i^{SSC}(l)$ is computed for $l \in \{1, ..., L^{SSC}\}$ through a non-linear gating layer:

$$d_i^{SSC}(l) = \exp(-(1 - |\hat{h}_i(l)|)/\sigma_c), \tag{5}$$

where σ_c is a Gaussian kernel bandwidth. The size of features obtained from the SSC becomes $L^{SSC} = N_K N_{SB}$. Finally, $d_i^{SSC}(l)$ for each pixel i is normalized with an L-2 norm for all l.

4.3 Efficient Computation for Dense Description

The most time-consuming part of DSC is in constructing self-correlation surfaces $C(\mathcal{F}_{r_{i,k}}, \mathcal{F}_j)$ for k and j, where $N_K M_R^2$ computations of (3) are needed for each pixel i. Straightforward computation of a weighted summation using ω in (3) would require considerable processing with a computational complexity of $O(IM_{\mathcal{F}}N_KM_{\mathcal{R}}^2)$, where $I = H_fW_f$ represents the image size (height H_f and width W_f). To expedite processing, we utilize fast edge-aware filtering [38,39] and propose a pre-computation scheme for self-correlation surfaces.

Similar to DASC [10], we compute $\mathcal{C}(\mathcal{F}_{r_{i,k}}, \mathcal{F}_j)$ efficiently by first rearranging the sampling patterns $(r_{i,k}, j)$ into reference-biased pairs $(i, j_r) = (i, i+r_{i,k}-j)$. $\mathcal{C}(\mathcal{F}_i, \mathcal{F}_{j_r})$ can then be expressed as

$$\mathcal{C}(\mathcal{F}_i, \mathcal{F}_{j_r}) = \frac{\mathcal{G}_{i,ij_r} - \mathcal{G}_{i,i} \cdot \mathcal{G}_{i,j_r}}{\sqrt{\mathcal{G}_{i,i^2} - (\mathcal{G}_{i,i})^2} \cdot \sqrt{\mathcal{G}_{i,j_r^2} - (\mathcal{G}_{i,j_r})^2}}, \qquad (6)$$

where $\mathcal{G}_{i,ij_r} = \sum_{i',j'_r} \omega_{i,i'} f_{i'} f_{j'_r}$, $\mathcal{G}_{i,j_r^2} = \sum_{i',j'_r} \omega_{i,i'} f_{j'_r}^2$, and $\mathcal{G}_{i,i^2} = \sum_{i'} \omega_{i,i'} f_{i'}^2$. $\mathcal{C}(\mathcal{F}_i, \mathcal{F}_{j_r})$ can be efficiently computed using any form of fast edge-aware filter [38,39] with a complexity of $O(IN_KM_{\mathcal{R}}^2)$. $\mathcal{C}(\mathcal{F}_{r_{i,k}}, \mathcal{F}_j)$ is then simply obtained from $\mathcal{C}(\mathcal{F}_i, \mathcal{F}_{j_r})$ by re-indexing sampling patterns.

Though we remove the computational dependency on patch size $M_{\mathcal{F}}$, $N_KM_{\mathcal{R}}^2$ computations of (6) are still needed to obtain the self-correlation surfaces, where many sampling pairs are repeated. To avoid such redundancy, we first compute self-correlation surface $\mathcal{C}(\mathcal{F}_i, \mathcal{F}_j)$ for $j \in \mathcal{R}_i^*$ with a doubled local support window $\mathcal{R}_i^*$ of size $2M_{\mathcal{R}}$. A doubled local support window is used because (6) is computed with patch $\mathcal{F}_{j_r}$ and the minimum support window size for $\mathcal{R}_i^*$ to cover all samples within $\mathcal{R}_i$ is $2M_{\mathcal{R}}$ as shown in Fig. 5(b). After the self-correlation surface for $\mathcal{R}_i^*$ is computed once over the image domain, $\mathcal{C}(\mathcal{F}_{r_{i,k}}, \mathcal{F}_j)$ can be extracted through an index mapping process, where the indexes for $\mathcal{R}_{i-r_{i,k}}$ are estimated from $\mathcal{R}_i^*$. Finally, the computational complexity of constructing the 3-D self-correlation surfaces becomes $O(I4M_{\mathcal{R}}^2)$, which is smaller than $O(IN_kM_{\mathcal{R}}^2)$ as $N_k \gg 4$.

Algorithm 1: Deep Self-Correlation (DSC) Descriptor

Input : image f_i, random samples $r_{i,k}$.
Output : DSC descriptor $\mathcal{D}_i^{\mathrm{DSC}}$.
Parameters : The number of circular pyramidal bins (point sets) $N_{\mathcal{SB}}(N_{\mathcal{SP}})$.
1 : Compute $\mathcal{C}(\mathcal{F}_i, \mathcal{F}_j)$ for a doubled support window $\mathcal{R}_i^*$ by using (6).
2 : Estimate $\mathcal{C}(\mathcal{F}_{r_{i,k}}, \mathcal{F}_j)$ from $\mathcal{C}(\mathcal{F}_i, \mathcal{F}_j)$ according to the index mapping process.
    for $v = 1 : N_{\mathcal{SP}}$ **do** /* **hierarchical aggregation using average pooling** */
3 : | Determine a circular pyramidal point $\mathcal{SP}_i(v)$.
4 : | Compute $\mathcal{C}(\mathcal{F}_v, \mathcal{F}_j)$ by using an average pooling for $\mathcal{SP}_i(v)$ on $\mathcal{C}(\mathcal{F}_{r_{i,k}}, \mathcal{F}_j)$.
    end for
    for $u = 1 : N_{\mathcal{SB}}$ **do** /* **hierarchical spatial aggregation using C-SPP** */
6 : | Determine a circular pyramidal bin $\mathcal{SB}_i(u)$.
7 : | Compute $h_i(k, u)$ and $h_i(v, u)$ by using C-SPP on each $\mathcal{SB}_i(u)$
   | from $\mathcal{C}(\mathcal{F}_{r_{i,k}}, \mathcal{F}_j)$ and $\mathcal{C}(\mathcal{F}_v, \mathcal{F}_j)$, respectively.
    end for
8 : Build hierarchical self-correlation responses $\hat{h}_i(l)$ from $h_i(k, u)$ and $h_i(v, u)$.
9 : Compute a DSC descriptor $\mathcal{D}_i^{\mathrm{DSC}} = \bigcup_l d_i^{\mathrm{DSC}}(l)$, followed by L-2 normalization.

4.4   DSC: Deep Self-correlation

So far, we have discussed how to build the self-correlation surface on a single level. In this section, we extend this idea by encoding self-similar structures at multiple levels in a manner similar to a deep architecture widely adopted in CNNs [26]. DSC is defined similarly to SSC, except that an average pooling is executed before C-SPP (see Fig. 6). With self-correlation surfaces, we perform the average pooling on circular pyramidal point sets. In comparison to the self-correlations just from a single patch, the spatial aggregation of self-correlation responses is clearly more robust, and it requires only marginal computational overhead over SSC. The strength of such a hierarchical aggregation has also been shown in [36].

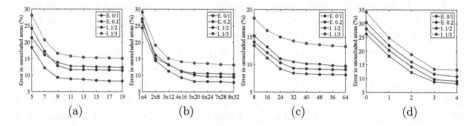

(a)   (b)   (c)   (d)

Fig. 7. Component analysis of DSC on the Middlebury benchmark [42] for varying parameter values, such as (a) support window size $M_{\mathcal{R}}$, (b) number of log-polar circular point $N_\rho \times N_\theta$, (c) number of random samples N_K, and (d) level of circular spatial pyramid N_S. In each experiment, all other parameters are fixed to the initial values.

To build the hierarchical self-correlation surface using an average pooling, we first define the circular pyramidal point sets $\mathcal{SP}_i(v)$ from log-polar circular point sets $\mathcal{P}_i$, where v associates all pyramidal levels $o \in \{1, ..., N_O\}$ and all points in each level o. In the average pooling, the circular pyramidal bins $\mathcal{SB}_i(u)$ used in C-SPP are re-used such that $\mathcal{SP}_i(v) = \{j | j \in \mathcal{P}_i, j \in \mathcal{SB}_i(u)\}$, thus $N_S = N_O$. Deep self-correlation surfaces are defined by aggregating $\mathcal{C}(\mathcal{F}_{r_{i,k}}, \mathcal{F}_j)$ for all $r_{i,k}$ patches determined on each $\mathcal{SP}_i(v)$ such that

$$\mathcal{C}(\mathcal{F}_v, \mathcal{F}_j) = \sum\nolimits_{r_{i,k} \in \mathcal{SP}_i(v)} \mathcal{C}(\mathcal{F}_{r_{i,k}}, \mathcal{F}_j)/N_v, \tag{7}$$

which is defined for all v, and N_v is the number of $r_{i,k}$ patches within $\mathcal{SP}_i(v)$. The hierarchical surfaces are sequentially aggregated using average pooling from the bottom to the top of the circular pyramidal point set $\mathcal{SP}_i(v)$. After computing hierarchical self-correlational aggregations, the DSC employs C-SPP as well as non-linear and normalization layer, similar to SSC as presented in Sect. 4.2. A hierarchical self-correlation response $h_i(v, u)$ is computed using the C-SPP as

$$h_i(v, u) = \max_{j \in \mathcal{SB}_i(u)} \{\mathcal{C}(\mathcal{F}_v, \mathcal{F}_j)\}. \tag{8}$$

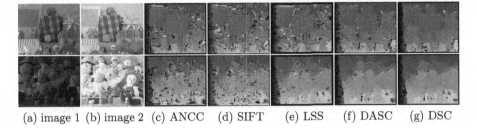

(a) image 1 (b) image 2 (c) ANCC   (d) SIFT   (e) LSS   (f) DASC   (g) DSC

Fig. 8. Comparison of disparity estimations for *Moebius* and *Dolls* image pairs across illumination combination '1/3' and exposure combination '0/2', respectively. Compared to other methods, DSC estimates more accurate and edge-preserved disparity maps.

Accumulated self-correlation responses are built from $h_i(k, u)$ in (4) and $h_i(v, u)$ in (8) such that $\hat{h}_i(l) = \bigcup_{\{k,v,u\}} \{h_i(k, u), h_i(v, u)\}$. Our DSC descriptor $d_i^{\mathrm{DSC}}(l)$ is then passed through a non-linear layer. $\mathcal{D}_i^{\mathrm{DSC}} = \bigcup_l d_i^{\mathrm{DSC}}(l)$ is built for $l \in \{1, ..., L^{\mathrm{DSC}}\}$ with $L^{\mathrm{DSC}} = (N_K + N_{\mathcal{SP}})N_{\mathcal{SB}}$. Finally, $d_i^{\mathrm{DSC}}(l)$ for each pixel i is normalized with an L-2 norm for all l.

5   Experimental Results and Discussion

5.1   Experimental Settings

In our experiments, the DSC was implemented with the following fixed parameter settings for all datasets: $\{\sigma_c, M_{\mathcal{F}}, M_{\mathcal{R}}, N_K, N_S\} = \{0.5, 5, 9, 32, 3\}$, and $\{N_\rho, N_\theta\} = \{4, 16\}$. The dimension of SSC and DSC are fixed to 416 and 585, respectively. We chose the guided filter (GF) for edge-aware filtering in (6), with a smoothness parameter of $\epsilon = 0.03^2$. We implemented the DSC in C++ on an Intel Core i7-3770 CPU at 3.40 GHz. We will make our code publicly available. The DSC was compared to other state-of-the-art descriptors (SIFT [14], DAISY [23], BRIEF [24], LIOP [28], DaLI [29], LSS [22], and DASC [10]), as well as to area-based approaches (ANCC [35] and RSNCC [9]). Furthermore, to evaluate the performance gain with a deep architecture, we compared SSC and DSC.

5.2   Parameter Evaluation

The performance of DSC is exhibited in Fig. 7 for varying parameter values, including support window size $M_{\mathcal{R}}$, number of log-polar circular points $N_\rho \times N_\theta$, number of random samples N_K, and levels of the circular spatial pyramid N_S. Note that $N_O = N_S$. Figure 7(c) and (d) demonstrate the effectiveness of self-correlation surfaces and deep architectures. For a quantitative analysis, we measured the average bad-pixel error rate on the Middlebury benchmark [42]. With a larger support window $M_{\mathcal{R}}$, the matching quality improves rapidly until about 9×9. $N_\rho \times N_\theta$ influences the performance of circular pooling, which is found to plateau at 4×16. Using a larger number of random samples N_K yields better

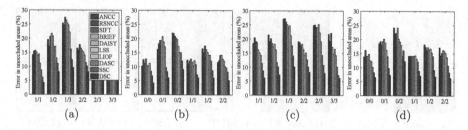

(a)   (b)   (c)   (d)

Fig. 9. Average bad-pixel error rate on the Middlebury benchmark [42] with illumination and exposure variations. Optimization was done by GC in (a), (b), and by WTA in (c), (d). DSC descriptor shows the best performance with the lowest error rate.

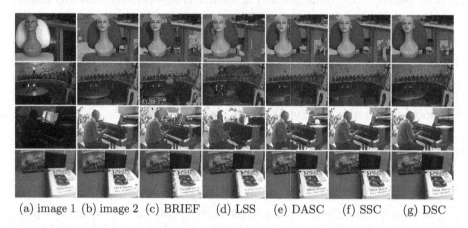

(a) image 1 (b) image 2 (c) BRIEF   (d) LSS   (e) DASC   (f) SSC   (g) DSC

Fig. 10. Dense correspondence evaluations for (from top to bottom) RGB-NIR, flash-noflash, different exposures, and blurred-sharp images. Compared to others, DSC estimates more reliable dense correspondences for challenging cross-modal pairs.

performance since DSC encodes more information. The level of circular spatial pyramid N_S also affects the amount of encoding. Based on these experiments, we set $N_K = 32$ and $N_S = 3$ in consideration of efficiency and robustness.

5.3   Middlebury Stereo Benchmark

We evaluated DSC on the Middlebury stereo benchmark [42], which contains illumination and exposure variations. In the experiments, the illumination (exposure) combination '1/3' indicates that two images were captured under the 1st and 3rd illumination (exposure) conditions. For a quantitative evaluation, we measured the bad-pixel error rate in non-occluded areas of disparity maps [42].

Figure 8 shows the disparity maps estimated under severe illumination and exposure variations with winner-takes-all (WTA) optimization. Figure 9 displays the average bad-pixel error rates of disparity maps obtained under illumination or exposure variations, with graph-cut (GC) [43] and WTA optimization. Area-based approaches (ANCC [35] and RSNCC [9]) are sensitive to severe radiometric

Table 1. Comparison of quantitative evaluation on cross-modal benchmark.

Methods	WTA optimization				SF optimization [11]			
	RGB-NIR	flash-noflash	diff. expo.	blur-sharp	RGB-NIR	flash-noflash	diff. expo.	blur-sharp
ANCC [35]	23.21	20.42	25.19	26.14	18.45	14.14	11.96	19.24
RSNCC [9]	27.51	25.12	18.21	27.91	13.41	15.87	9.15	18.21
SIFT [14]	24.11	18.72	19.42	27.18	18.51	11.06	14.87	20.78
DAISY [23]	27.61	26.30	20.72	27.41	20.42	10.84	12.71	22.91
BRIEF [24]	29.14	18.29	17.13	26.43	17.54	9.21	9.54	19.72
LSS [22]	27.82	19.18	18.21	26.14	16.14	11.88	9.11	18.51
LIOP [28]	24.42	16.42	14.22	20.42	15.32	11.42	10.22	17.12
DASC [10]	14.51	13.24	10.32	16.42	13.42	7.11	7.21	11.21
SSC	10.12	10.12	8.22	14.22	9.12	6.18	5.22	9.12
DSC	8.12	8.22	6.72	13.28	7.62	5.12	4.72	8.01

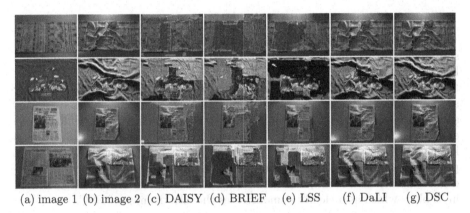

(a) image 1 (b) image 2 (c) DAISY (d) BRIEF (e) LSS (f) DaLI (g) DSC

Fig. 11. Dense correspondence comparisons for images with different illumination conditions and non-rigid image deformations [29]. Compared to other approaches, DSC provides more accurate dense correspondence estimates with reduced artifacts.

variations, especially when local variations occur frequently. Feature descriptor-based methods (SIFT [14], DAISY [23], BRIEF [24], LSS [22], and DASC [10]) perform better than the area-based approaches, but they also provide limited performance. Our DSC achieves the best results both quantitatively and qualitatively. Compared to SSC, the performance of DSC is highly improved, where the performance benefits of the deep architecture are apparent.

5.4 Cross-Modal and Cross-Spectral Benchmark

We evaluated DSC on a cross-modal and cross-spectral benchmark [10] containing various kinds of image pairs, namely RGB-NIR, different exposures, flash-noflash, and blurred-sharp. Optimization for all descriptors and similarity measures was done using WTA and SIFT flow (SF) with hierarchical dual-layer belief propagation [11], for which the code is publicly available. Sparse ground truths for those images are used for error measurement as done in [10].

Table 2. Average error rates on the DaLI benchmark.

Methods	Def.	Illum.	Def./Illum.	Aver.
DAISY [23]	43.98	42.72	43.42	43.37
BRIEF [24]	41.51	37.14	41.35	40
LSS [22]	40.81	39.54	40.11	40.12
LIOP [28]	28.72	31.72	30.21	30.22
DaLI [29]	27.12	27.31	27.99	27.47
DASC [10]	26.21	24.83	27.51	26.18
SSC	**23.42**	**22.21**	**24.17**	**23.27**
DSC	**20.14**	**20.72**	21.87	**20.91**

Figure 10 provides a qualitative comparison of the DSC descriptor to other state-of-the-art approaches. As already described in the literature [9], gradient-based approaches such as SIFT [14] and DAISY [23] have shown limited performance for RGB-NIR pairs where gradient reversals and inversions frequently appear. BRIEF [24] cannot deal with noisy regions and modality-based appearance differences since it is formulated on pixel differences only. Unlike these approaches, LSS [22] and DASC [10] consider local self-similarities, but LSS is lacking in discriminative power for dense matching. DASC also exhibits limited performance. Compared to those methods, the DSC displays better correspondence estimation. We also performed a quantitative evaluation with results listed in Table 1, which also clearly demonstrates the effectiveness of DSC.

5.5   DaLI Benchmark

We also evaluated DSC on a recent, publicly available dataset featuring challenging non-rigid deformations and very severe illumination changes [29]. Figure 11 presents dense correspondence estimates for this benchmark [29]. A quantitative evaluation is given in Table 2 using ground truth feature points sparsely extracted for each image, although DSC is designed to estimate dense correspondences. As expected, conventional gradient-based and intensity comparison-based feature descriptors, including SIFT [14], DAISY [23], and BRIEF [24], do not provide reliable correspondence performance. LSS [22] and DASC [10] exhibit relatively high performance for illumination changes, but are limited on non-rigid deformations. LIOP [28] provides robustness to radiometric variations, but is sensitive to non-rigid deformations. Although DaLI [29] provides robust correspondences, it requires considerable computation for dense matching. DSC offers greater discriminative power as well as more robustness to non-rigid deformations in comparison to the state-of-the-art cross-modality descriptors.

Table 3. Computation speed of DSC and other state-of-the-art local and global descriptors. The brute-force and efficient implementations of DSC are denoted by * and †, respectively.

Image size	SIFT	DAISY	LSS	DaLI	DASC	DSC*	DSC†
463 × 370	130.3s	2.5s	31s	352.2s	2.7s	193.2s	**9.2s**

5.6 Computational Speed

In Table 3, we compared the computational speed of DSC to the state-of-the-art local descriptor, namely DaLI [29], and dense descriptors, namely DAISY [23], LSS [22], and DASC [10]. Even though DSC needs more computational time compared to some previous dense descriptors, it provides significantly improved matching performance as described previously.

6 Conclusion

The deep self-correlation (DSC) descriptor was proposed for establishing dense correspondences between images taken under different imaging modalities. Its high performance in comparison to state-of-the-art cross-modality descriptors can be attributed to its greater robustness to non-rigid deformations because of its effective pooling scheme, and more importantly its heightened discriminative power from a more comprehensive representation of self-similar structure and its formulation in a deep architecture. DSC was validated on an extensive set of experiments that cover a broad range of cross-modal differences. In future work, thanks to the robustness to non-rigid deformations and high discriminative power, DSC can potentially benefit object detection and semantic segmentation.

Acknowledgement. This work was supported by Institute for Information and communications Technology Promotion (IITP) grant funded by the Korea government (MSIP) (No. R0115-15-1007, High quality 2d-to-multiview contents generation from large-scale RGB+D database).

References

1. Brown, M., Susstrunk, S.: Multispectral sift for scene category recognition. In: CVPR (2011)
2. Yan, Q., Shen, X., Xu, L., Zhuo, S.: Cross-field joint image restoration via scale map. In: ICCV (2013)
3. Hwang, S., Park, J., Kim, N., Choi, Y., Kweon, I.: Multispectral pedestrian detection: benchmark dataset and baseline. In: CVPR (2015)
4. Krishnan, D., Fergus, R.: Dark flash photography. In: SIGGRAPH (2009)
5. Sen, P., Kalantari, N.K., Yaesoubi, M., Darabi, S., Goldman, D.B., Shechtman, E.: Robust patch-based HDR reconstruction of dynamic scenes. In: SIGGRAPH (2012)

6. HaCohen, Y., Shechtman, E., Lishchinski, E.: Deblurring by example using dense correspondence. In: ICCV (2013)
7. Lee, H., Lee, K.: Dense 3d reconstruction from severely blurred images using a single moving camera. In: CVPR (2013)
8. Petschnigg, G., Agrawals, M., Hoppe, H.: Digital photography with flash and no-flash iimage pairs. In: SIGGRAPH (2004)
9. Shen, X., Xu, L., Zhang, Q., Jia, J.: Multi-modal and multi-spectral registration for natural images. In: Fleet, D., Pajdla, T., Schiele, B., Tuytelaars, T. (eds.) ECCV 2014. LNCS, vol. 8692, pp. 309–324. Springer, Heidelberg (2014). doi:10.1007/978-3-319-10593-2_21
10. Kim, S., Min, D., Ham, B., Ryu, S., Do, M.N., Sohn, K.: DASC: dense adaptive self-correlation descriptor for multi-modal and multi-spectral correspondence. In: CVPR (2015)
11. Liu, C., Yuen, J., Torralba, A.: Sift flow: dense correspondence across scenes and its applications. IEEE Trans. PAMI 33(5), 815–830 (2011)
12. Kim, J., Liu, C., Sha, F., Grauman, K.: Deformable spatial pyramid matching for fast dense correspondences. In: CVPR (2013)
13. Pinggera, P., Breckon, T., Bischof, H.: On cross-spectral stereo matching using dense gradient features. In: BMVC (2012)
14. Lowe, D.: Distinctive image features from scale-invariant keypoints. IJCV 60(2), 91–110 (2004)
15. Simonyan, K., Vedaldi, A., Zisserman, A.: Learning local feature descriptors using convex optimisation. IEEE Trans. PAMI 36(8), 1573–1585 (2014)
16. Gong, Y., Wang, L., Guo, R., Lazebnik, S.: Multi-scale orderless pooling of deep convolutional activation features. In: Fleet, D., Pajdla, T., Schiele, B., Tuytelaars, T. (eds.) ECCV 2014. LNCS, vol. 8695, pp. 392–407. Springer, Heidelberg (2014). doi:10.1007/978-3-319-10584-0_26
17. Fischer, P., Dosovitskiy, A., Brox, T.: Descriptor matching with convolutional neural networks: a comparison to sift arXiv:1405.5769 (2014)
18. Donahue, J., Jia, Y., Vinyals, O., Hoffman, J., Zhang, N., Tzeng, E., Darrell, T.: DeCAF: a deep convolutional activation feature for generic visual recognition. In: ICML (2014)
19. Simo-Serra, E., Trulls, E., Ferraz, L., Kokkinos, I., Fua, P., Moreno-Noguer, F.: Discriminative learning of deep convolutional feature point descriptors. In: ICCV (2015)
20. Dong, J., Soatto, S.: Domain-size pooling in local descriptors: DSP-SIFT. In: CVPR (2015)
21. Long, J., Shelhamer, E., Darrell, T.: Fully conovlutional networks for semantic segmentation. In: CVPR (2015)
22. Schechtman, E., Irani, M.: Matching local self-similarities across images and videos. In: CVPR (2007)
23. Tola, E., Lepetit, V., Fua, P.: Daisy: an efficient dense descriptor applied to wide-baseline stereo. IEEE Trans. PAMI 32(5), 815–830 (2010)
24. Calonder, M.: Brief: computing a local binary descriptor very fast. IEEE Trans. PAMI 34(7), 1281–1298 (2011)
25. Trzcinski, T., Christoudias, M., Lepetit, V.: Learning image descriptor with boosting. IEEE Trans. PAMI 37(3), 597–610 (2015)
26. Alex, K., Ilya, S., Geoffrey, E.H.: Imagenet classification with deep convolutional neural networks. In: NIPS (2012)
27. Saleem, S., Sablatnig, R.: A robust sift descriptor for multispectral images. IEEE SPL 21(4), 400–403 (2014)

28. Wang, Z., Fan, B., Wu, F.: Local intensity order pattern for feature description. In: ICCV (2011)
29. Simo-Serra, E., Torras, C., Moreno-Noguer, F.: DaLI: deformation and light invariant descriptor. IJCV 115(2), 136–154 (2015)
30. Heinrich, P., Jenkinson, M., Bhushan, M., Matin, T., Gleeson, V., Brady, S., Schnabel, A.: MIND: modality indepdent neighbourhood descriptor for multi-modal deformable registration. MIA 16(3), 1423–1435 (2012)
31. Torabi, A., Bilodeau, G.: Local self-similarity-based registration of human rois in pairs of stereo thermal-visible videos. PR 46(2), 578–589 (2013)
32. Ye, Y., Shan, J.: A local descriptor based registration method for multispectral remote sensing images with non-linear intensity differences. JPRS 90(7), 83–95 (2014)
33. Pluim, J., Maintz, J., Viergever, M.: Mutual information based registration of medical images: a survey. IEEE Trans. MI 22(8), 986–1004 (2003)
34. Heo, Y., Lee, K., Lee, S.: Joint depth map and color consistency estimation for stereo images with different illuminations and cameras. IEEE Trans. PAMI 35(5), 1094–1106 (2013)
35. Heo, Y., Lee, K., Lee, S.: Robust stereo matching using adaptive normalized cross-correlation. IEEE Trans. PAMI 33(4), 807–822 (2011)
36. Weinzaepfel, P., Revaud, J., Harchaoui, Z., Schmid, C.: Deepflow: large displacement optical flow with deep matching. In: ICCV (2013)
37. Black, M.J., Sapiro, G., Marimont, D.H., Heeger, D.: Robust anisotropic diffusion. IEEE Trans. IP 7(3), 421–432 (1998)
38. Gastal, E., Oliveira, M.: Domain transform for edge-aware image and video processing. In: SIGGRAPH (2011)
39. He, K., Sun, J., Tang, X.: Guided image filtering. IEEE Trans. PAMI 35(6), 1397–1409 (2013)
40. Seidenari, L., Serra, G., Bagdanov, A.D., Bimbo, A.D.: Local pyramidal descriptors for image recognition. IEEE Trans. PAMI 36(5), 1033–1040 (2014)
41. He, K., Zhang, X., Ren, S., Sun, J.: Spatial pyramid pooling in deep convolutional networks for visual recognition. IEEE Trans. PAMI 37(9), 1904–1916 (2015)
42. http://vision.middlebury.edu/stereo/
43. Boykov, Y., Yeksler, O., Zabih, R.: Fast approximation enermgy minimization via graph cuts. IEEE Trans. PAMI 23(11), 1222–1239 (2001)

Structured Matching for Phrase Localization

Mingzhe Wang[✉], Mahmoud Azab, Noriyuki Kojima,
Rada Mihalcea, and Jia Deng

Computer Science and Engineering, University of Michigan, Ann Arbor, USA
{mzwang,mazab,kojimano,mihalcea,jiadeng}@umich.edu

Abstract. In this paper we introduce a new approach to phrase localization: grounding phrases in sentences to image regions. We propose a
structured matching of phrases and regions that encourages the semantic relations between phrases to agree with the visual relations between
regions. We formulate structured matching as a discrete optimization
problem and relax it to a linear program. We use neural networks to
embed regions and phrases into vectors, which then define the similarities (matching weights) between regions and phrases. We integrate
structured matching with neural networks to enable end-to-end training.
Experiments on Flickr30K Entities demonstrate the empirical effectiveness of our approach.

Keywords: Vision · Language

1 Introduction

This paper addresses the problem of phrase localization: given an image and a
textual description, locate the image regions that correspond to the noun phrases
in the description. For example, an image may be described as "a man wearing a
tan coat signs papers for another man wearing a blue coat". We wish to localize,
in terms of bounding boxes, the image regions for the phrases "a man", "tan
coat", "papers", "another man", and "blue coat". In other words, we wish to
ground these noun phrases to image regions.

Phrase localization is an important task. Visual grounding of natural language is a critical cognitive capability necessary for communication, language
learning, and the understanding of multimodal information. Specifically, understanding the correspondence between regions and phrases is important for natural language based image retrieval and visual question answering. Moreover,
by aligning phrases and regions, phrase localization has the potential to improve
weakly supervised learning of object recognition from massive amounts of paired
images and texts.

Recent research has brought significant progress on the problem of phrase
localization [1–3]. Plummer et al. introduced the Flickr30K Entities dataset,
which includes images, captions, and ground-truth correspondences between
regions and phrases [1]. To match regions and phrases, Plummer et al. embedded

© Springer International Publishing AG 2016
B. Leibe et al. (Eds.): ECCV 2016, Part VIII, LNCS 9912, pp. 696–711, 2016.
DOI: 10.1007/978-3-319-46484-8_42

regions and phrases into a common vector space through Canonical Correlation Analysis (CCA) and pick a region for each phrase based on the similarity of the embeddings. Subsequent works by Wang et al. [2] and Rohrbach et al. [3] have since achieved significant improvements by embedding regions and phrases using deep neural networks.

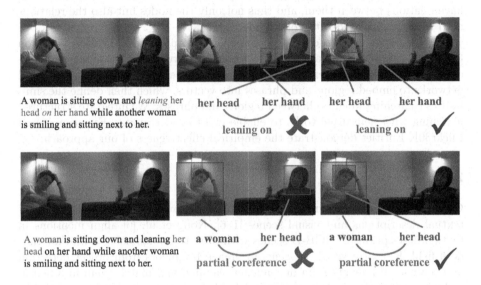

Fig. 1. Structured matching is needed for phrase localization: it is not enough to just match phrases and regions individually; the relations between phrases also need to agree with the relations between regions.

But existing works share a common limitation: they largely localize each phrase independently, ignoring the semantic relations between phrases. The only constraint used in previous research was that different phrases should describe different regions, i.e., that each region should be matched to no more than one phrase [3]. But phrases have more complex semantic relations between each other, and phrase localization is often impossible without a deep understanding of those semantic relations. For example, in Fig. 1, an image from Flickr30K Entities is captioned as "a woman is sitting down and leaning her head on her hand while another woman is smiling and sitting next to her." Consider the localization of "her head" and "her hand" from "leaning her head on her hand". There are two women, two heads, and two hands visible in the image, but only one head and one hand have a "leaning on" relation. So "her head" and "her hand" cannot be localized independently without verifying whether the head is actually leaning on the hand.

This brings forward the problem of *structured matching* of regions and phrases, that is, finding an optimal matching of regions and phrases such that not only does the visual content of each individual region agree with the meaning of its corresponding phrase (e.g. the regions must individually depict "head" and "hand"), but the visual relation between each pair of regions also agrees with the semantic relation between the corresponding pair of phrases (e.g. the pair of regions together must depict "leaning her head on her hand"). The problem of structured matching is closely related to the standard (maximum weighted) bipartite matching, although significantly harder: the nodes on the same side have relations between them, and thus not only the nodes but also the relations need to be matched with the other side.

In this paper we introduce a new approach to phrase localization based on the idea of structured matching. We formulate structured matching as a discrete optimization problem and relax it to a linear program. We use neural networks to embed regions and phrases into vectors, which then define the similarities (matching weights) between regions and phrases. We integrate structured matching with neural networks to enable end-to-end training. Experiments on Flickr30K Entities demonstrate the empirical effectiveness of our approach.

2   Related Work

Grounding image descriptions. Many works have studied the alignment of textual descriptions and visual scenes [1–6]. Kong et al. [6] align mentions in textual descriptions of RGB-D scenes with object cuboids using a Markov random field. Karpathy et al. [4] generate image fragments from object detection and sentence fragments from dependency parsing, and match them in a neural embedding framework. Karpathy and Fei-Fei [5] use a similar framework but replace dependency parsing with bidirectional recurrent neural networks in order to generate image descriptions. It is worth noting that Karpathy et al. [4] and Karpathy and Fei-Fei [5] only evaluate the performance on proxy tasks (image retrieval and captioning) and do not evaluate the quality of matching.

Plummer et al. [1] introduced the Flickr30K Entities dataset, making it possible to directly evaluate image-sentence alignments. Using this dataset, Wang et al. [2] learn neural embeddings of phrases and regions under a large-margin objective and localize each phrase by retrieving the closest region in the embedding space. Instead of producing explicit embeddings, Rohrbach et al. [3] train a neural network to directly predict the compatibility of a region and a phrase; their framework also allows unsupervised training when ground truth correspondences are unavailable.

All these works differ from ours because when they align sentences and images, they do not explicitly consider how relations between parts of a sentence match the relations between parts of an image.

Object retrieval using natural language. The task of object retrieval using natural language is to locate visual objects based on natural language queries. Guadarrama et al. [7] generate textual descriptions for each region proposal and retrieval objects by matching a query with the descriptions. In contrast, Arandjelovic and Zisserman [8] convert a query into multiple query images using Google image search and retrieve objects by matching the query images with

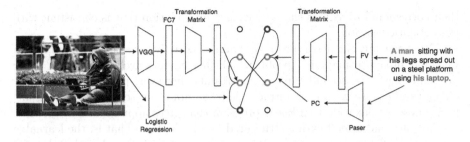

Fig. 2. We embed regions and phrases into a common vector space and perform structured matching that encourages not only the individual agreement of regions with phrases but also the agreement of phrase-phrase relations with region-region relations. In particular, we consider "partial match coreference" (PC) relations—the relation between phrases such as "a man" and "his legs".

images in a database. Hu et al. [9] use a recurrent neural network to score each object proposal given an input text query and an input image, and retrieve the objects with the highest score. The difference between object retrieval using natural language and phrase localization is that the former aims to match an image region to a whole sentence whereas the latter aims to match an image region to only one part of a sentence.

Image captioning and retrieval. There has been a large body of prior work on image captioning or retrieval [2,4,5,10–19]. Typical approaches include recurrent neural networks [4,5,14,16,17], Canonical Correlation Analysis [10], encoder-decoder architectures [13], and Discriminative Component Analysis [12]. These works differ from ours in that the emphasis of learning and evaluation is placed on matching images and sentences as a whole rather than matching their individual components such as regions and phrases.

3 Approach

Figure 2 illustrates our approach. Given an image and a description, our goal is to localize the image region that corresponds to each phrase in the description. Following prior work [1], we assume that short noun phrases ("a man", "tan coat") have already been extracted from the description. We also assume that pronouns and non-visual phrases have been removed. Also following prior work [1], we generate a set of region proposals in the form of bounding boxes.

Given these phrases and regions, the next step is to match them. To this end we adopt the same approach by Wang et al. [2]: we extract visual and phrasal features, embed them into a common vector space using neural networks, and measure region-phrase similarities in this common vector space. Using these similarities we then solve a structured matching problem: finding the optimal matching subject to two types of constraints: (1) a region can be matched to no more than one phrase, and (2) if two phrases have a certain semantic relation, their corresponding regions should have a visual relation that is consistent with the semantic relation.

If we have only the first type of constraints, we arrive at a standard maximum weighted bipartite matching problem, which can be solved exactly by linear programming. The second type of constraints, however, pose significant new difficulties because it appears intractable to obtain exact solutions. As a result, we propose a relaxation to a linear program that gives approximate solutions.

We learn end to end with a structured prediction loss. That is, the learnable parameters of our framework are jointly optimized with the objective that for each image-sentence pair in the training set the ground truth matching should have a higher score than all other possible matchings. It is worth noting that although prior work on phrase localization has considered the constraint that a region should be matched to no more than one phrase [3], they have only used it as a post-processing heuristic, whereas we integrate this constraint into end-to-end training.

3.1 Representing Regions and Phrases

We generate regions proposals using Edgebox [20]. These regions serve as the candidates to be matched with phrases. To represent each region, we use Fast-RCNN [21] features, that is, features from a 16-layer VGG convolutional network that is pre-trained on the ImageNet [22] classification dataset and fine-tuned on the VOC2007 detection dataset [23]. In particular, we extract the fc7 layer activations to represent each region with a $4,096$ dimensional feature vector.

To represent phrases, we use Fisher vectors [10]. Following [10], we extract Fisher Vectors of 18,000 dimensions by first applying ICA on the 300-dimensional word2vec [24] word vectors and then constructing a codebook with 30 centers from a Hybrid Gaussian-Laplacian mixture model (HGLMM). Similar to [2], to save time during training, we apply PCA to reduce the dimensionality of the Fisher vectors from 18,000 to 6,000.

Next, we apply a linear transformation to the fc7 activations of the regions and another linear transformation to the Fisher Vectors of the phrases in order to embed them in the same vector space. That is, given for a phrase p and a region r and their feature vectors x_p and x_r, we compute the embedded features $\tilde{x}_p$ and $\tilde{x}_r$ as

$$\begin{aligned}\tilde{x}_p = M_1 x_p + b_1,\\ \tilde{x}_r = M_2 x_r + b_2,\end{aligned} \tag{1}$$

where M_1, M_2, b_1, b_2 are learnable parameters. We define the similarity w_{ij} between a phrase p and a region r as

$$\cos(x_p, x_r) = \frac{<x_p, x_r>}{\|x_p\|\|x_r\|}, \tag{2}$$

i.e. the cosine similarity between the embedded vectors.

Given phrases $p_1, p_2 \ldots p_n$ and regions $r_1, r_2 \ldots r_m$, we obtain a similarity matrix $W_\theta = \{w_{ij}\}$, where

$$w_{ij} = \cos(x_{p_i}, x_{r_j}) \tag{3}$$

and θ represents the learnable parameters M_1, M_2, b_1, b_2.

3.2   Bipartite Matching

Given the similarities between regions and phrases, we are ready to solve the matching problem. We first consider bipartite matching, matching with only the constraint that each region should be matched to no more than one phrase. We refer to this constraint as the exclusivity constraint.

It is worth noting that in the most general case, this constraint is not always valid. Two phrases can refer to the same region: for example, "a man" and "he", "a man" and "the man". In these cases we need to perform coreference resolution and group the coreferences before phrase localization. Here we assume that this step has been done. This is a valid assumption for the Flickr30K Entities dataset we use in our experiments—coreferences such as "he" and "she" have been removed.

Given phrases $p_1, p_2, \ldots, p_n$, regions $r_1, r_2, \ldots, r_m$, and their similarity matrix W_θ, we have a standard bipartite matching problem if we consider only the exclusivity constraints. We first formulate this problem as an integer program.

We define a binary variable $y_{ij} \in \{0, 1\}$ for each potential region-phrase pair $\{p_i, r_j\}$ to indicate whether r_j is selected as a match for p_i in a matching y. Let $S(W, y)$ be a score that measures the goodness of a matching y, computed as the sum of similarities of the matched pairs:

$$S(w, y) = \sum_{i=1}^{n} \sum_{j=1}^{m} w_{ij} y_{ij}. \tag{4}$$

The best matching maximizes this score and can be found by a linear program that relaxes y_{ij} to continuous variables in $[0, 1]$.

$$
\max_{y} S(W_\theta, y)
$$

$$
\text{s.t.} \sum_{j=1}^{m} y_{ij} = 1, \; i = 1, 2, \ldots, n
$$

$$
\sum_{i=1}^{n} y_{ij} \leq 1, \; j = 1, 2, \ldots, m \tag{5}
$$

$$
0 \leq y_{ij} \leq 1, \; i = 1, \ldots, n, j = 1, \ldots, m.
$$

Here, the first constraint guarantees that each phrase is matched with exactly one region, and the second constraint guarantees that each region is matched with no more than one phrase. This linear program is guaranteed to have an integer solution because all of its corner points are integers and this integer solution can be found by the simplex method.

To learn the embedding parameters, we optimize an objective that encourages the ground truth matching to have the best matching score. Let $y^{(l)}$ be the ground truth matching for the lth image-sentence pair in a training set, and let $W_\theta^{(l)}$ be the region-phrase similarities. We define the training loss L as

$$L(\theta) = \sum_l \max(0, \max_{y'} S(W_\theta^{(l)}, y') - S(W_\theta^{(l)}, y^{(l)})), \qquad (6)$$

where θ represents the learnable parameters. Note that although this loss involves a max operator that ranges over all possible matchings, computing the gradient of L with respect to θ only involves the best matching, which we can find by solving a linear program. It is also worth noting that this loss function is a simplified version of the structured SVM loss [25] with a margin of zero: although the ground truth matching needs to have the highest score among all possible matchings, the score does not need to be higher by a fixed positive margin than that of the best non-ground-truth matching. With no margin requirement, this loss is not as stringent as the original structured SVM formulation but is significantly easier to implement.

3.3   Partial Match Coreference

We now address the matching of relations. In this work, we consider "partial match coreference"(PC) relations, a specific type of sematnic relations between phrases. Partial match coreference is composed of a noun phrase and another noun phrase including a possessive pronoun such as "his" or "her". Such relations indicate that the second phrase refers to an entity that belongs to the first phrase. For instance, the following are examples of partial match coreference:

1. **A woman** is dressed in Asian garb with a basket of goods on **her hip**.
2. **An instructor** is teaching **his students** how to escape a hold in a self-defense class.

Partial match coreference points to a strong connection between the two noun phrases, which places constraints on the visual relation between their corresponding regions. In particular, partial match coreference relations can give strong cues about the appearance and spatial arrangement of the corresponding regions. We thus use PC relations in the task of phrase localization and study if it can bring any improvements.

We extract partial match coreference relations using the Stanford CoreNLP library [26]. Since a partial match coreference is indicated by possessive pronouns such as "his" or "her", we first extract coreference relations between entity mentions in each image caption.

Among the extracted coreferences, some are "full matches", such as "he" as a coreference of "a man" where the entire phrase "he" and the entire phrase "a man" are mutual coreferences. The rest are "partial matches" such as "her hip" as a coreference of "a woman" where only a part of the phrase "her hip", i.e. the possessive pronoun "her", is a coreference of "a woman". We discard all "full match" coreferences and keep only the "partial match" coreferences. Note that full match coreference is also useful because it indicates that two phrases should be matched to the same region. We discard them only because in Flickr30K Entities, the dataset we use for experiments, all pronouns that are full match coreferences are annotated as non-visual objects and excluded in evaluation.

3.4   Structured Matching with Relation Constraints

Given a certain type of semantic relations between phrases, we would like to enforce the constraint that the visual relations between regions should agree with these semantic relations. In the rest of this paper we use the partial coreference relation as an example.

Formally, consider two arbitrary phrases p_i, p_s. Let r_j, r_t be two arbitrary regions, which are potential matches for the two phrases. Given a matching y, let $z_{ijst} \in \{0, 1\}$ be a binary variable indicating whether phrases p_i and p_s are simultaneously matched to regions r_j and r_t. In other words,

$$z_{ijst} = y_{ij} \wedge y_{st}. \tag{7}$$

Let $g(r_j, r_t)$ be a non-negative function that measures whether two regions r_j, r_t have a visual relation that agrees with the partial match coreference (PC) relation, that is, whether the the two regions have a "visual PC" relation.

We can now modify our matching objective to encourage the agreement between relations:

$$\max_y \sum_{i=1}^{n} \sum_{j=1}^{m} w_{ij} y_{ij} + \lambda \sum_{(i,s) \in Q} \sum_{j,t} z_{ijst} g(r_j, r_t), \tag{8}$$

where Q is the set of all pairs of phrases with PC relations. The term $z_{ijst} g(r_j, r_t)$ makes a matching y more desirable if whenever a pair of phrases have a PC relation the corresponding pair of regions have a visual PC relation.

This new objective poses additional challenges for finding the best matching. It is an integer program that appears difficult to solve directly, and it is not obvious how to relax it to a linear program with the Boolean term $z_{ijst} = y_{ij} \wedge y_{st}$.

We propose a linear program relaxation by introducing a probabilistic interpretation. We relax the binary variables y and z into real values in $[0, 1]$. We imagine that the matching is generated through a probabilistic procedure where each phrase p_i chooses, not necessarily independently, a region from all regions according to a multinomial distribution parametrized by the relaxed, continuous variables y_{ij}. That is, we interpret y_{ij} as $\Pr(R(p_i) = r_j)$, where $R(p_i)$ represents the region chosen by phrase p_i. This interpretation naturally requires that

$$\sum_j y_{ij} = \sum_j \Pr(R(p_i) = r_j) = 1, \tag{9}$$

which is the same constraint used earlier in bipartite matching that requires a phrase to match with exactly one region. We also add the exclusivity constraint that each region is matched to no more than one phrase:

$$\sum_i y_{ij} = \sum_i \Pr(R(p_i) = r_j) \leq 1. \tag{10}$$

We treat z_{ijst} as the joint probability $\Pr(R(p_i) = r_j, R(p_s) = r_t)$, that is, the probability that we match p_i to r_j and p_s to r_t simultaneously. It follows from the rule of marginalization that

$$\sum_{t=1}^m z_{ijst} = \sum_t \Pr(R(p_i) = r_j, R(p_s) = r_t) = \Pr(R(p_i) = r_j) = y_{ij}$$
$$\sum_{j=1}^m z_{ijst} = \sum_j \Pr(R(p_i) = r_j, R(p_s) = r_t) = \Pr(R(p_s) = r_t) = y_{st}. \tag{11}$$

Putting all the constraints together we have the following linear program for structured matching:

$$\max_{y \in \mathcal{Y}} \sum_{i=1}^n \sum_{j=1}^m w_{ij} y_{ij} + \lambda \sum_{(i,s) \in Q} \sum_{j,t} z_{ijst} g(r_j, r_t)$$

$$\text{s.t.} \ \sum_{j=1}^m y_{ij} = 1, \text{ for } i = 1, 2, \ldots, n$$

$$\sum_{i=1}^n y_{ij} \leq 1, \text{ for } j = 1, 2, \ldots, m$$

$$\sum_{t=1}^m z_{ijst} = y_{ij} \text{ for any } i, j, s \tag{12}$$

$$\sum_{j=1}^m z_{ijst} = y_{st} \text{ for any } i, s, t$$

$$0 \leq y_{ij} \leq 1, \text{ for all } i, j$$
$$0 \leq z_{ijst} \leq 1, \text{ for all } i, j, s, t.$$

In this linear program, each pair of phrases with a partial match coreference relation p_i, p_s will lead to n^2 instances of z and g. This means that the linear program may have too many variables to be solved in a reasonable amount of time. To remedy this issue we adopt a heuristic that only applies the relation constraints to a subset of regions that are the most likely to be matched to phrases. Specifically, for a pair of phrases p_i and p_s, we only introduce z variables for the top 10 regions of p_i and the top 10 regions of p_s as measured by the cosine similarity. That is, the index j in z_{ijst} ranges over only the top 10 most similar regions of p_i and the index t ranges over only the top 10 most similar regions of p_s. This heuristic helps avoid a bloated linear program.

This linear program is easy to solve but is not guaranteed to produce an integer solution. A fractional solution indicates multiple possible regions for some phrases. In such cases we run a depth first search to enumerate all feasible solutions contained in this fractional solution and find the best matching. Since we limit the number of z variables, the search space is usually small and our approach remains efficient.

To learn or fine-tune parameters for structured matching we use the same loss function as defined in Eq. 6, except that the matching score S is given by the solution value of this new linear program.

We implement the "visual PC" scoring function $g(r_j, r_t)$ as a logistic regressor. For a pair of regions r_j, r_t, we concatenate their fc7 feature vectors and pass the longer feature into the logistic regressor. The parameters of this logistic regressor can be learned jointly with all other parameters of our method.

4 Experiments

Setup. We evaluate our approach using the Flickr30k Entities dataset [1]. Flickr30k Entities is built on Flickr30K, which contains 31,783 images, each annotated with five sentences. In each sentence, the noun phrases are provided along with their corresponding bounding boxes in the image. These region-to-phrase correspondences enable the evaluation of phrase localization. There are more than 500k noun phrases (a total of 70k unique phrases) matched to 275k bounding boxes. Following [1], we divide these 31,783 image into three subsets, 1,000 images for validation, 1,000 for testing, and the rest for training. Also following [1], if a phrase is matched with multiple ground truth bounding boxes, we merge them into a new enclosing box. After this merging, every phrase has one and only one ground truth bounding box.

Following prior work [1-3], we generate 100 region proposals for each image using Edgebox [20] and localize each phrase by selecting from these regions. We select one region for each phrase and the selection is deemed correct if the region overlaps with the ground truth bounding box with an IoU (intersection over union) over 0.5. We evaluate the overall performance in terms accuracy, the percentage of phrases that are correctly matched to regions. Note that some prior works [1,2] have reported performance in terms of recall@K: each phrase can select K regions; recall@K is 1 if one of them overlaps with the ground truth and 0 otherwise. Our definition of accuracy is the same as recall@1. We do not report recall@K with a K larger than 1 because it is unclear what it means to select more than one region for each phrase when we jointly localize phrases subject to the exclusivity constraints and relation constraints.

We use the same evaluation code released by [1]. It is also worth noting that since each phrase can only be localized to one of the region proposals, the quality of the region proposals establishes an upperbound of performance. Consistent with prior work, with EdgeBox the upperbound in our implementation is 76.91 %.

Implementation. We implement the following approaches:

1. *CCA+Fast-RCNN*: We produce CCA embeddings using the code from Klein et al. [10] except we replace the VGG features pretrained on ImageNet with

the Fast-RCNN features (VGG features pretrained on ImageNet and fine-tuned on the VOC2007 detection dataset).
2. *Bipartite Matching*: using the same features as CCA+Fast-RCNN, we embed the features into a common vector space through (shallow) neural networks and perform bipartite matching with exclusivity constraints.
3. *Structure Matching*: Same as Bipartite Matching except we perform structured matching with relation constraints.

In training we modify the set of candidate regions: for each image we start with the 100 region proposals from EdgeBox; then we remove those with an IoU larger than 0.5 and add ground truth bounding boxes. The reason for this modification is that the EdgeBox region proposals may not contain the ground truth matches for all phrases. This modification ensures that all ground truth matches are included and each phrase has only one ground truth region.

For all training we use Stochastic Gradient Descent (SGD) with a learning rate of 1e-4. We decrease the learning rate slightly after each epoch. We use a momentum of 0.9 and a weight decay of 0.0005. The hyperparameter λ in the matching loss (Eq. 6) is selected on the validation set. For bipartite matching, we initialize the embedding matrices M_1, M_2 with Canonical Correlation Analysis(CCA) [27] and fine-tune all parameters end to end for 3 epochs, optimizing the matching loss defined in Eq. 6. Since CCA provides a good initialization, the matching loss converges quickly.

For structured matching, we pre-train the "visual PC" logistic regressor using the 10,325 pairs of regions in the training set that have a ground truth "visual PC" relation and an equal number of negative pairs of regions. This pre-trained logistic regressor has an accuracy of 78 % on the validation set. Then we initialize all other parameters using the pre-trained bipartite matching model and fine-tune all parameters (including those of the logistic regressor) for 2 epochs optimizing the structured matching loss with relation constraints.

Table 1. Accuracy (Recall@1) of our approach compared to other methods. Results in parentheses were released after the submission of this paper for peer review and are concurrent with our work.

Methods	Accuracy (Recall@1)
CCA [1]	25.30
NonlinearSP [2]	26.70 (43.89)
SCRC [9]	27.80
GroundR [3]	29.02 (47.70)
MCB [28]	(48.69)
CCA [29]	(50.89)
Ours: CCA+Fast-RCNN	39.44
Ours: Matching	41.78
Ours: Structured Matching	42.08

Table 2. Performance of bipartite matching and structured matching on only phrases with partial match corerference (PC) relations.

Methods	Accuracy (Recall@1) on PC phrases only
Bipartite Matching	47.8
Structured Matching	49.3

Results. Table 1 summarizes our results and compares them with related work. It is worth noting that some of the results from related work are concurrent with ours as they were released after the submission of this paper for peer review. Table 3 provides accuracy of phrase localization for different categories of phrases. Figures 3 and 4 show qualitative results including success and failure cases.

Our results show that Fast-RCNN features leads to a large boost of performance, as can been seen by comparing the CCA result from [1] with our CCA+Fast-RCNN result. Similar results have also been reported in [29] and the latest version of [2].

Also we see that Bipartite Matching further improves CCA+Fast-RCNN, which demonstrates the effectiveness of end-to-end training with our matching based loss function. Structured Matching with relation constraints provides a small additional improvement over Bipartite Matching. It is worth noting that the improvement from Structured Matching appears small partly because in the test set only 694 phrases out of a total of 17519 are involved in partial match coreference relations, limiting the maximum possible improvement when averaged over all phrases. If we consider only these 694 phrases and their accuracy as shown in Table 2, we see that Structured Matching achieves a more significant improvement over Bipartite Matching.

Table 3. Performance within categories. "Upperbound" is the maximum accuracy (recall@1) possible given the region proposals. Results in parentheses were released after the submission of this paper for peer review.

Methods	Person	Clothing	Body parts	Animals	Vehicles	Instruments	Scene	Other
CCA [1]	29.58	24.20	10.52	33.40	34.75	35.80	20.20	20.75
GroundR [3]	44.24	9.93	1.91	45.17	46.00	20.99	30.20	16.12
	(53.80)	(34.04)	(7.27)	(49.23)	(58.75)	(22.84)	(52.07)	(24.13)
CCA [29]	(64.73)	(46.88)	(17.21)	(65.83)	(68.75)	(37.65)	(51.39)	(31.77)
Ours: CCA+FRCN	55.39	32.78	16.25	53.86	48.50	19.14	28.97	23.56
Ours: Bipartite	57.94	34.43	16.44	56.56	51.50	27.16	33.42	26.23
Ours: Structured	57.89	34.61	15.87	55.98	52.25	23.46	34.22	26.23
Upperbound	89.36	66.48	39.39	84.56	91.00	69.75	75.05	67.40

(a) A man with a helmet is using an ATM. (b) Two women and a man discuss notes in a classroom.

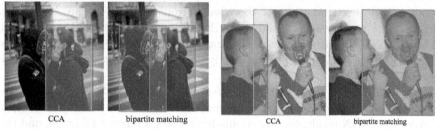

(c) A man wearing a black jacket with a woman wearing a black jacket are standing close to each other.

(d) A man and a boy holding microphones.

(e) A young boy shows his brown and green bead necklace.

(f) A man is working on his house by repairing the windows.

(g) This lady is wearing a pink shirt and tuning her guitar.

(h) A baby with red hat sit in his stroller.

Fig. 3. Qualitative results. The first two rows compare CCA with bipartite matching. The rest compare bipartite matching with structured matching. (Color figure online)

(a) A black man wearing a white suit and hat is holding a paper cup.

(b) A boy wearing an orange shirt is playing on a swing.

(c) A blond woman speaks at a podium labeled Holiday Stars Projectin front of a blue wall.

(d) A man is walking his horse on a racetrack.

(e) A dark-haired bearded man wearing a turquoise shirt with a yellow peace sign on it.

(f) A womanwearing a black helmet riding on a bike.

(g) A clown in red plaid overalls relaxes in the back of his tent.

(h) A man at a podium is speaking to a group of men at a conference.

(i) A man in a green shirt is jumping a ramp on his skateboard.

(j) Several people are standing on a street corner watching a cartoonist with glasses draw on his sketch pad.

Fig. 4. Qualitative results. The first two rows compare CCA with bipartite matching. The rest compare bipartite matching with structured matching. (Color figure online)

5   Conclusion

In this paper we have introduced a new approach to phrase localization. The key idea is a structured matching of phrases and regions that encourages the relations between phrases to agree with the relations between regions. We formulate structured matching as a discrete optimization problem and relax it to a linear program. We integrate structured matching with neural networks to enable end-to-end training. Experiments on Flickr30K Entities have demonstrated the empirical effectiveness of our approach.

References

1. Plummer, B.A., Wang, L., Cervantes, C.M., Caicedo, J.C., Hockenmaier, J., Lazebnik, S.: Flickr30k entities: collecting region-to-phrase correspondences for richer image-to-sentence models. In: Proceedings of the IEEE International Conference on Computer Vision, pp. 2641–2649 (2015)
2. Wang, L., Li, Y., Lazebnik, S.: Learning deep structure-preserving image-text embeddings. arXiv preprint arXiv:1511.06078 (2015)
3. Rohrbach, A., Rohrbach, M., Hu, R., Darrell, T., Schiele, B.: Grounding of textual phrases in images by reconstruction. arXiv preprint arXiv:1511.03745 (2015)
4. Karpathy, A., Joulin, A., Li, F.F.F.: Deep fragment embeddings for bidirectional image sentence mapping. In: Advances in Neural Information Processing Systems, pp. 1889–1897 (2014)
5. Karpathy, A., Fei-Fei, L.: Deep visual-semantic alignments for generating image descriptions. In: Proceedings of the IEEE Conference on Computer Vision and Pattern Recognition, pp. 3128–3137 (2015)
6. Kong, C., Lin, D., Bansal, M., Urtasun, R., Fidler, S.: What are you talking about? text-to-image coreference. In: IEEE Conference on Computer Vision and Pattern Recognition (CVPR), 2014, pp. 3558–3565 (2014)
7. Guadarrama, S., Rodner, E., Saenko, K., Zhang, N., Farrell, R., Donahue, J., Darrell, T.: Open-vocabulary object retrieval. In: Robotics: Science and Systems (2014)
8. Arandjelovic, R., Zisserman, A.: Multiple queries for large scale specific object retrieval. In: BMVC, pp. 1–11 (2012)
9. Hu, R., Xu, H., Rohrbach, M., Feng, J., Saenko, K., Darrell, T.: Natural language object retrieval. arXiv preprint arXiv:1511.04164 (2015)
10. Klein, B., Lev, G., Sadeh, G., Wolf, L.: Fisher vectors derived from hybrid gaussian-laplacian mixture models for image annotation. arXiv preprint arXiv:1411.7399 (2014)
11. Gong, Y., Wang, L., Hodosh, M., Hockenmaier, J., Lazebnik, S.: Improving image-sentence embeddings using large weakly annotated photo collections. In: Fleet, D., Pajdla, T., Schiele, B., Tuytelaars, T. (eds.) ECCV 2014, Part IV. LNCS, vol. 8692, pp. 529–545. Springer, Heidelberg (2014)
12. Hoi, S.C., Liu, W., Lyu, M.R., Ma, W.Y.: Learning distance metrics with contextual constraints for image retrieval. In: IEEE Computer Society Conference on Computer Vision and Pattern Recognition, 2006, vol. 2. IEEE pp. 2072–2078 (2006)
13. Kiros, R., Salakhutdinov, R., Zemel, R.S.: Unifying visual-semantic embeddings with multimodal neural language models. arXiv preprint arXiv:1411.2539 (2014)

14. Vinyals, O., Toshev, A., Bengio, S., Erhan, D.: Show and tell: a neural image caption generator. arXiv preprint arXiv:1411.4555 (2014)
15. Kulkarni, G., Premraj, V., Dhar, S., Li, S., Choi, Y., Berg, A.C., Berg, T.L.: Baby talk: understanding and generating image descriptions. In: Proceedings of the 24th CVPR, Citeseer (2011)
16. Mao, J., Xu, W., Yang, Y., Wang, J., Yuille, A.: Deep captioning with multimodal recurrent neural networks (m-RNN). arXiv preprint arXiv:1412.6632 (2014)
17. Donahue, J., Hendricks, L.A., Guadarrama, S., Rohrbach, M., Venugopalan, S., Saenko, K., Darrell, T.: Long-term recurrent convolutional networks for visual recognition and description. arXiv preprint arXiv:1411.4389 (2014)
18. Young, P., Lai, A., Hodosh, M., Hockenmaier, J.: From image descriptions to visual denotations: new similarity metrics for semantic inference over event descriptions. Trans. Assoc. Comput. Linguist. 2, 67–78 (2014)
19. Socher, R., Karpathy, A., Le, Q.V., Manning, C.D., Ng, A.Y.: Grounded compositional semantics for finding and describing images with sentences. Trans. Assoc. Comput. Linguist. 2, 207–218 (2014)
20. Zitnick, C.L., Dollár, P.: Edge boxes: locating object proposals from edges. In: Fleet, D., Pajdla, T., Schiele, B., Tuytelaars, T. (eds.) ECCV 2014. LNCS, vol. 8693, pp. 391–405. Springer, Heidelberg (2014). doi:10.1007/978-3-319-10602-1_26
21. Girshick, R.: Fast R-CNN. In: Proceedings of the IEEE International Conference on Computer Vision, pp. 1440–1448 (2015)
22. Deng, J., Dong, W., Socher, R., Li, L.J., Li, K., Fei-Fei, L.: Imagenet: a large-scale hierarchical image database. In: IEEE Conference on Computer Vision and Pattern Recognition, CVPR 2009, pp. 248–255. IEEE (2009)
23. Everingham, M., Van Gool, L., Williams, C.K.I., Winn, J., Zisserman, A.: The PASCAL Visual Object Classes Challenge 2007 (VOC 2007) Results(2007). http://www.pascal-network.org/challenges/VOC/voc2007/workshop/index.html
24. Mikolov, T., Sutskever, I., Chen, K., Corrado, G.S., Dean, J.: Distributed representations of words and phrases and their compositionality. In: Advances in Neural Information Processing Systems, pp. 3111–3119 (2013)
25. Tsochantaridis, I., Joachims, T., Hofmann, T., Altun, Y.: Large margin methods for structured and interdependent output variables. J. Mach. Learn. Res. 6(Sep), 1453–1484 (2005)
26. Clark, K., Manning, C.D.: Entity-centric coreference resolution with model stacking. In: Association for Computational Linguistics (ACL) (2015)
27. Hardoon, D.R., Szedmak, S., Shawe-Taylor, J.: Canonical correlation analysis: an overview with application to learning methods. Neural Comput. 16(12), 2639–2664 (2004)
28. Fukui, A., Park, D.H., Yang, D., Rohrbach, A., Darrell, T., Rohrbach, M.: Multimodal compact bilinear pooling for visual question answering and visual grounding. arXiv preprint arXiv:1606.01847 (2016)
29. Plummer, B.A., Wang, L., Cervantes, C.M., Caicedo, J.C., Hockenmaier, J., Lazebnik, S.: Flickr30k entities: Collecting region-to-phrase correspondences for richer image-to-sentence models. arXiv preprint arXiv:1505.04870v3 (2015)

Crossing-Line Crowd Counting with Two-Phase Deep Neural Networks

Zhuoyi Zhao[1], Hongsheng Li[1(✉)], Rui Zhao[2,3], and Xiaogang Wang[1(✉)]

[1] Department of Electronic Engineering,
The Chinese University of Hong Kong, Shatin, Hong Kong
{zyzhao,hsli,xgwang}@ee.cuhk.edu.hk
[2] SenseNets Technology Limited, Shenzhen, China
zhaorui@sensenets.com
[3] SenseTime Group Limited, Shatin, Hong Kong

Abstract. In this paper, we propose a deep Convolutional Neural Network (CNN) for counting the number of people across a line-of-interest (LOI) in surveillance videos. It is a challenging problem and has many potential applications. Observing the limitations of temporal slices used by state-of-the-art LOI crowd counting methods, our proposed CNN directly estimates the crowd counts with pairs of video frames as inputs and is trained with pixel-level supervision maps. Such rich supervision information helps our CNN learn more discriminative feature representations. A two-phase training scheme is adopted, which decomposes the original counting problem into two easier sub-problems, estimating crowd density map and estimating crowd velocity map. Learning to solve the sub-problems provides a good initial point for our CNN model, which is then fine-tuned to solve the original counting problem. A new dataset with pedestrian trajectory annotations is introduced for evaluating LOI crowd counting methods and has more annotations than any existing one. Our extensive experiments show that our proposed method is robust to variations of crowd density, crowd velocity, and directions of the LOI, and outperforms state-of-the-art LOI counting methods.

Keywords: Intelligent surveillance · Crowd counting · Deep learning

1 Introduction

Automatically counting crowds in surveillance scenes with large population density, such as train stations, shopping malls, and tourist attractions, has escalating demands in intelligent surveillance industry. It has drawn increasing attention from the computer vision community in recent years and can provide vital information for the management departments of public spaces to make crucial decisions. Nearly all major stampedes resulted from the failure of controlling crowd density and traffic flow in public spaces. Such problems could be effectively mitigated by intelligent surveillance systems with crowd counting capabilities. Whenever the crowd number of a public space exceeds an alarming threshold,

© Springer International Publishing AG 2016
B. Leibe et al. (Eds.): ECCV 2016, Part VIII, LNCS 9912, pp. 712–726, 2016.
DOI: 10.1007/978-3-319-46484-8_43

the management departments can be automatically alerted to control crowd density by either opening new exits, closing entrances, or sending extra staffs to guide the crowd traffic flows. However, the crowd counting problem is challenging, especially for scenes with high crowd density and low viewing angles. The pedestrians might heavily occlude each other, which prevent pedestrian tracking methods from being used to solve this problem.

The existing crowd counting algorithms either count the number of people in a region-of-interest (ROI) or count the number of people crossing a line-of-interest (LOI) (see Fig. 1(a)). Although most algorithms focus on the former ROI counting problem, solving the latter LOI counting problem has more practical uses. For instance, in order to count the number of people in a public space by ROI counting algorithms, all locations of the space should be monitored by cameras, which might not be practical for places like large squares and metro stations. In the contrary, the LOI counting systems only need to monitor the entrances and exits of a space. By counting the number of people across the lines of interest, the total number of people within the space can be easily inferred.

State-of-the-art methods for solving the crossing-line crowd counting problem require generating 2D temporal slices by temporally concatenating video frame lines at the LOI (see Fig. 1(b) for examples). The number of people across the line is then estimated based on the temporal slices. When the scene is not crowded and pedestrians walks in normal speed (Fig. 1(b, row 1)), people can be well recognized in the temporal slices. However, we observe that temporal slices are not robust to scenes with high crowd density, slow walking speed, and low camera viewing angles. In Fig. 1(b, row2), the temporal slice shows excess jitters and people in it are no longer recognizable.

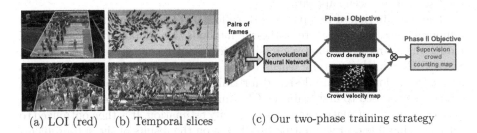

(a) LOI (red)   (b) Temporal slices   (c) Our two-phase training strategy

Fig. 1. (a) The problem of counting people crossing a line-of-interest (red) in both directions. (b) Temporal slices generated from (a), which are used by state-of-the-art LOI counting methods. (Row 1) When the scene is not crowded and pedestrians' walking speed is not too slow, people could be distinguished from the temporal slices. (Row 2) The temporal slices are heavily degenerated when the scenes are very crowded. (c) Our proposed Convolutional Neural Network (CNN) is trained to solve the crossing-line people counting problem with rich pixel-level supervision maps in two phases. In the first phase, the CNN learns to predict the crowd density map and crowd velocity map. In the second phase, the CNN learns to predict crowd counting map in an end-to-end manner. (Color figure online)

In this paper, we propose a deep Convolutional Neural Network (CNN) for counting the number of people across the line of interest by directly using video frames as input. Deep learning models usually learn better if rich supervision information is provided. We therefore generate rich pixel-level supervision from annotated pedestrian trajectories for training our CNN. Three types of supervision maps are generated, crowd density maps, crowd velocity maps, and crossing-line crowd counting maps. Based on the new learning objectives, a two-phase training scheme is designed (Fig. 1(c)). Our network is first trained to simultaneously estimate the crowd density map and crowd velocity map, where the two tasks share the same bottom neural layers. As shown by our experiments, sharing the same bottom neural layers helps learn more effective feature representations for each of the tasks. The estimated crowd density and crowd velocity maps are then elementwisely multiplied to generate the crowd counting maps and trained with only the supervision crowd counting maps in an end-to-end manner.

In comparison, existing methods utilize only the number of crossing-line people as ground truth for training. Much spatial information is ignored and the mapping from features to final counts is treated as a black box. In contrast, the three types of our supervision are all of pixel-level and help better train the deep model. Each of our two learning phases has specific physical meanings: the first step is to learn pixel-level crowd density and crowd velocity, and the second step is to learn pixel-level crossing-line crowd counts. Such a strategy can be viewed as decomposing the original crowd counting problem to two easier sub-problems and optimizing our model to solve them first. This strategy avoids directly recovering complex and highly non-linear relations between video frames and final per-pixel crowd counts. In addition, by learning to estimate pixel-level crossing-line counting maps for different scenes, our proposed model is robust to the variations of scene appearances.

The contribution of this paper is three-fold. (1) Observing the limitations of temporal slices used by state-of-the-art methods, we propose training a CNN model that directly estimates crossing-line crowd counts from video frames. Since CNN models generally learns better with rich supervision signals, pixel-level supervision maps are designed for training. (2) A two-phase optimization scheme is proposed to first train the CNN model on the two easier sub-problems of crowd density estimation and crowd velocity estimation. It is then optimized to solve crossing-line crowd counting task based on the results of the sub-problems in an end-to-end manner. (3) We contribute a large-scale dataset for evaluating crossing-line crowd counting algorithms, which includes 5 different scenes, 3,100 annotated frames and 5,900 annotated pedestrians. Compared with existing datasets, our dataset has more scenes and provides trajectory annotations for each pedestrian instead of crowd counts of fixed lines. Counting ground truth at different LOIs could be easily obtained for our dataset.

2   Related Work

The learning-based crowd counting algorithms can be generally categorized into two types: the first type of methods focus on counting the number of people in a region-of-interest (ROI), and the second type of methods learn to count the number of people across a line-of-interest (LOI).

ROI Counting. Most existing ROI counting methods extract features from the ROI and learn a regression function to predict the number of people within it. Chan *et al.* [3] identified pedestrian foreground by motion segmentation. A Gaussian process regression function is trained to predict the counts based on the shape, edge, and texture features of the pedestrian foreground. In [4], the same features as those in [3] were used, but a Bayesian Poisson regression function is trained to predict the crowd counts. In [13], linear regression functions are learned to predict the number of people in small blobs with low-level features, and the overall number is obtained by summing up the numbers of all small blobs.

There were also methods that learn to estimate pixel-level density maps for a ROI instead of just predicting a single count number. The counting number could be obtained by integrating over the estimated density values in the ROI. Lempitsky and Zisserman [8] proposed to generate ground truth density maps with Gaussian functions and learn linear regression functions for estimating per-pixel density with a specially designed loss function. Zhang *et al.* [18] proposed a CNN for cross-scene crowd counting, which is trained alternatively to learn the crowd density map and the crowd counting numbers.

LOI counting. To the best of our knowledge, all state-of-the-art methods [2,5,10] only use the numbers of crossing-line pedestrians as supervision. Where and how fast a pedestrian has crossed the LOI are ignored. In addition, all the methods require to create temporal slices before counting, which are created by temporally concatenating the intensity values on the LOI. The limitations of such temporal slices are illustrated in Fig. 1(b). When creating temporal slices, the flow mosaicking method [5] assigns different thickness at different locations of the LOI based on the traffic flow velocity. Pedestrians with different velocities could be "normalized" to generate images of similar appearance. A quadratic regression function is then trained to predict the final crossing-line counts. However, the major limitation of flow mosaicking is that the flow velocity at LOI might not be reliably obtained for complex scenes. Ma and Chan [10] proposed an integer programming method for estimating crossing-line crowd counts. Local HOG features are extracted from moving foreground regions of the temporal slices to train a Gaussian process regression function. In [2], deep learning models are trained for the LOI counting problem. Given the image temporal slices and optical flow temporal slices, three CNNs are trained to estimate the number of people in a temporal slice, the type of a temporal slice, and the ratio of the numbers of people crossing the LOI in the two directions, respectively. By combining the results of the three CNNs, the number of pedestrians across the LOI in both directions can be obtained.

Multi-person tracking. The crowd counting problem might also be solved by multi-person tracking methods, such as [1,11,12], if the scene is not crowded and people do not heavily occlude each other. The number of people across a LOI in both directions can be easily obtained by counting the number of pedestrian trajectories that crossed the LOI. However, such pedestrian tracking methods do not work well when the scene is crowded. Pedestrian-to-pedestrian occlusions severely affected the tracking performance and led to poor counting results.

Deep learning. Deep convolutional neural networks have achieved great success on image classification [14] and object detection [15]. For surveillance applications, various deep learning methods were proposed for tasks including person re-identification [9], pedestrian detection [16] and object tracking [17]. The only deep learning method for LOI crowd counting [2] is based on temporal slices and is therefore unreliable when the scene is too crowded or the camera has a too low viewing angle. The FlowNet [6] was proposed to estimate optical flow from pairs of images, which is used as the base model for our proposed CNN model.

3   Method

3.1   Pixel-Level Supervision Maps

Deep Convolutional Neural Networks (CNN) learn more discriminative features when rich supervision information is provided. For instance, pre-training a CNN for 1,000-class image classification on the ImageNet dataset is able to boost the performance of 200-class object detection task by a large margin [7].

Unlike exiting LOI counting methods that utilize single crossing-line counting numbers on an LOI as training supervision signals, the learning goal for our CNN is designed as pixel-level crossing-line crowd counting map C_t at each time t, where each location of the map records a two-dimensional vector representing how many people pass this location along x and y directions respectively between t and $t+1$ (see Fig. 2(b) for illustration). Note that the values of each entry are generally smaller than 1, which denotes that a fraction of a person have passed this location at time t. When an LOI is provided, the crossing-line crowd counts at each time t could be obtained by first transforming each location's x- and y-directional crowd counts to the normal direction of the LOI and then integrating the normalized values on the LOI as the final count.

However, raw crowd counting map directly obtained from pedestrian annotations (Fig. 2(a)) would not be suitable for training the CNN because of its high annotation sparsity. We therefore model the crossing-line crowd counting map as elementwise multiplication of a crowd density map D_t and a crowd velocity map V_t, $i.e.$ $C_t = D_t \otimes V_t$. This decomposition assumes that pedestrians' velocity and density on the LOI remain constant between time t and $t+1$. Since our proposed algorithm works on videos of frame rate greater than 25 fps, the time interval is small enough for generating accurate crowd counting map with such crowd density and crowd velocity maps.

Given dot pedestrian annotations $\mathbf{P}_t = \{P_t^1, \cdots, P_t^n\}$ at time t (Fig. 2(a)), the crowd density map D_t (Fig. 2(c)) can be generated by applying a kernel density estimation function based on the annotated pedestrian locations as

$$D_t(p) = \sum_{P \in \mathbf{P}_t} \mathcal{N}(p; P, \sigma_P^2), \qquad (1)$$

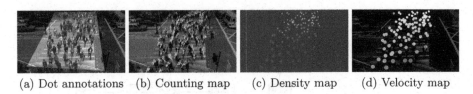

(a) Dot annotations   (b) Counting map   (c) Density map   (d) Velocity map

Fig. 2. (a) Dot annotations on pedestrians. (b) Illustration of the crossing-line crowd counting map, where each entry stores how many people pass this location along x and y directions. (c) The supervision crowd density map generated based on (a). Hotter color denotes higher crowd density. (d) The supervision crowd velocity map generated based on (a). (Color figure online)

where $D_t(p)$ denotes the density value at location p, $\mathcal{N}(p; P, \sigma_P^2)$ denotes a normalized 2D Gaussian kernel evaluated at p, with a mean value at location P and a bandwidth σ_P. For each scene, a perspective map could be obtained following [3]. The bandwidth σ_P is perspectively normalized based on the dot location P to represent objects at different distances to the camera. The sum of such density values in any region would be the same as counting the crowd within it. The generated crowd density map is similar to those in [8,18].

To generate the crowd velocity maps V_t (Fig. 2(d)) from dot pedestrian annotations $\mathbf{P}_t$ and $\mathbf{P}_{t-1}$, we first calculate the x- and y-displacements between corresponding pedestrian annotations $v_t^{P^i} = P_t^i - P_{t-1}^i$. The crowd velocity map V_t is then created as

$$V_t(p) = \sum_{P \in \mathbf{P}_t} K(p; P, r_P) \cdot v_t^P, \tag{2}$$

where $V_t(p)$ stores the crowd velocity at location p along x and y directions. $K(p; P, r_P)$ is a disk-shape masking function with a perspectively normalized radius threshold r_P that assigns each dot annotation's displacement values v_t^P to the small neighborhood around it.

$$K(p; P, r_P) = \mathbf{1} \left(p \le \|P - r_P\|^2 \right), \tag{3}$$

where $\mathbf{1}(\cdot)$ represents the indicator function. Note that our crowd velocity map is different from the general optical flow maps and only has non-zero flow values at pedestrian locations.

To obtain a crowd counting map for training our CNN, one could first generate the crowd density map and crowd velocity map as (2) and (3) based on the ground truth dot annotations. The crowd counting map can then be obtained as the elementwise multiplication of the density and velocity maps. In Sect. 4.3, we show that the supervision counting map obtained in this way is accurate. Therefore, we choose to use those pixel-level maps as supervision signals for training our CNN model.

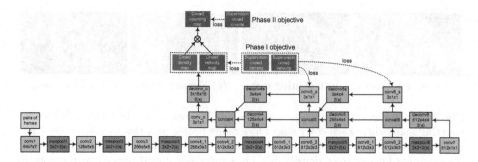

Fig. 3. Illustration of our proposed CNN model for crossing-line crowd counting. "conv", "maxpool", "deconv", and "concat" represent convolution, max pooling, deconvolutional, and channel-wise concatenation layers, respectively. "$c \times k \times k + m(s)$" denotes that a layer has c kernels of size $k \times k$ with a stride m. The output of each convolution layer is activated by a Rectified Linear Unit (ReLU) function. In the first phase, the learning supervisions for our CNN model are the crowd density map and crowd velocity map introduced in Sect. 3.1. In the second phase, the learning supervision is the final crowd counting map. The dashed arrows represent training supervision signals. (Color figure online)

3.2 Deep Convolutional Neural Network for LOI Crowd Counting

CNN models have shown great capabilities on learning discriminative feature representations for various computer vision tasks. An overview of our LOI crowd counting CNN model is shown in Fig. 3, which consists of convolutional layers, max pooling layers and deconvolutional layers. The network structure is similar to that of the FlowNetSimple network in [6] but with max pooling layers. The input of the CNN is pairs of consecutive video frames to take necessary temporal information into account. As shown by the lower part of Fig. 3, the bottom layers of our CNN are conventional CNN layers that extract spatio-temporal visual features for describing the contents of the pair of frames. Since the max pooling layers decrease spatial resolutions of the input, learnable deconvolutional layers "deconv4"-"deconv6" are added to "upsample" the feature maps of decreased resolutions. In the topmost part of the network, a convolution layer with 1×1 kernels ("conv_o") act as a regressor to output the estimated density, flow, or counting values. Similar to the GoogLeNet [15], two loss short-cuts are added to "conv5_s" and "conv6_s" for directly providing training supervision to lower layers. The upper part of Fig. 3 shows the proposed learning supervision of two different training phases, which will be introduced in the following paragraphs.

We propose to train the CNN in two phases. In the first training phase, the network is trained to predict the crowd density map D_t and the crowd velocity map V_t simultaneously. These two tasks are easier than directly predicting crossing-line crowd counting map and can therefore be better trained. The loss functions for the two tasks are designed as the L_2 distances between the estimated crowd density map $\widetilde{D}_t$ and crowd velocity map $\widetilde{V}_t$, and their ground truth,

$$L_D = \sum_p \left\| \widetilde{D}_t(p) - D_t(p) \right\|^2, \tag{4}$$

$$L_V = \sum_p \left\| \widetilde{V}_t(p) - V_t(p) \right\|^2, \tag{5}$$

and the overall loss function for the first phase is then defined as

$$L_{first} = L_D + L_V. \tag{6}$$

The joint learning of the crowd density and crowd velocity maps is illustrated by the red and blue boxes in Fig. 3. Because learning the two maps are related tasks, we let them share the feature representations by the same bottom layers. By simultaneously learning the two related task, each of the two tasks can be better trained with much fewer parameters (see experiments in Sect. 4.4).

Although we could directly multiply the estimated crowd density and crowd velocity map to predict the crossing-line crowd counting map, there might be spatial mis-matches between the two maps. The multiplication of them might deviate from the desired counting map. Illustration of density and velocity mismatching is shown in Fig. 4. The reason is that there is no term to regularize the interactions between the two maps during training. In addition, we observe that the crowd counting map instead of the density and velocity maps is closer to our true objectives.

We therefore further fine-tune the trained network in the second phase with supervision of the crossing-line crowd counting map C_t, which is generated by multiplying the supervision maps of crowd density and crowd velocity respectively. As shown by the "$\otimes$" symbol in Fig. 3, the estimated density map and velocity map are multiplied to predict the crowd counting map (illustrated as the red box in Fig. 3), while the supervision signals used in the first phase are discarded. The network is then fine-tuned in an end-to-end manner by minimizing the L_2 distance between the estimated crossing-line crowd counting map $\widetilde{C}_t$ and the corresponding ground truth C_t,

$$L_{second} = \sum_p \left\| \widetilde{C}_t(p) - C_t(p) \right\|^2. \tag{7}$$

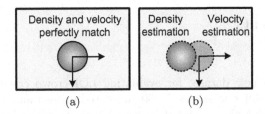

Fig. 4. (a) In an ideal case, the estimated crowd density and crowd velocity should be spatially matched. (d) Illustration of spatial mismatching between the estimated crowd density region (red) and estimated crowd velocity region (yellow). (Color figure online)

The proposed two-phase training scheme can be viewed as first dividing the original counting problem into two easier sub-problems with clear semantic meanings, *i.e.* estimating crowd density and estimating crowd velocity. Although there is no way to regularize the pairwise relations between the estimated density map and velocity map in the first phase, the trained network could serve as a good initial point for training towards the crowd counting map in the second phase, which is our desired results. In the second phase, the two maps are elementwisely multiplied and the adaptation between them are automatically optimized. Our experiments in Sect. 4.4 demonstrate that such a two-phase training strategy outperform directly learning the counting map in an end-to-end manner.

3.3   From Crowd Counting Map to LOI Counts

After our CNN model is trained, an instantaneous crossing-line crowd counting map can be predicted for every video frame by the trained counting CNN, where each entry records the estimated numbers of people passing this location along x and y directions respectively. Given an LOI, the x and y directional counting values on the LOI could be projected to its normal direction. Integrating over all the projected counting values on the LOI locations p leads to the instantaneous LOI counting numbers $c_{1,t}$ and $c_{2,t}$ in the two directions at time t,

$$c_{1,t} = \sum_{\{p|cos(\theta_p) \geq 0\}} \sqrt{C_{t,x}(p)^2 + C_{t,y}(p)^2} \cdot \cos(\theta_p), \qquad (8)$$

$$c_{2,t} = \sum_{\{p|cos(\theta_p) < 0\}} \sqrt{C_{t,x}(p)^2 + C_{t,y}(p)^2} \cdot (-\cos(\theta_p)), \qquad (9)$$

where θ_p is the angle between the normal direction of the LOI and the crowd counting vector $(C_{t,x}(p), C_{t,y}(p))$ at each location p. For certain period of time T, we can then integrate the instantaneous counting numbers to generate the final crossing line counts within the period as,

$$c_1 = \sum_{\{t|t \in T\}} c_{1,t}, \quad c_2 = \sum_{\{t|t \in T\}} c_{2,t}. \qquad (10)$$

4   Experiments

4.1   Datasets

We contribute a new dataset for evaluating LOI crowd counting algorithms, which includes 5 different scenes, 5,900 annotated pedestrians (each one with an ID specified), and 3,100 annotated frames. A comparison with existing datasets can be seen in Table 1. As shown by the table, our dataset has more scenes and more detailed annotations (pedestrian locations vs. single counting numbers) than any existing dataset. Since we provide complete trajectory annotations for

Table 1. Statistics of existing crossing-line crowd counting datasets. [a]This dataset is not publicly available at the time of publication.

Dataset	Proposed	UCSD [3]	LHI [5]	TS-CNN[a] [2]
# of scenes	5	1	5	7
Data type	video	video	video	temporal slices
Annotation type	trajectory	trajectory	none	total counts
# of annotations	5,900	153	0	n/a
Frame resolution	1280×720	238×158	352×288	n/a

Scene 1: Street   Scene 2: Alley   Scene 3: Alley

Scene 4: Square   Scene 5: Alley

Fig. 5. Illustration of the 5 scenes and the LOIs in our datasets.

each pedestrian in our dataset, we can generate ground truth counts for arbitrary LOIs. We manually defined 1 LOI perpendicular to the traffic flow direction for each scene. Some example frames and LOIs from the 5 scenes are shown in Fig. 5. The training set is created as the first 70 % continuous frames of the 5 scenes, and the remaining 30 % frames are used as the test set. We also evaluate our proposed CNN model on the UCSD crossing-line counting dataset [10].

4.2   Experimental Setup

We compared our proposed method with the temporal-slice-based CNN model in [2] and the integer programming based method [10]. For our proposed CNN model, we randomly cropped video frame patches of size 224×224 as our training samples. Our CNN model was randomly initialized and trained with the training set of our proposed dataset. The network parameters were optimized by Stochastic Gradient Descent (SGD) with a batch size of 96. We gradually decreased the learning rate until the training is converged. During testing, pairs of whole video frames were input into our CNN to estimate the crowd counting maps. On an NVIDIA TITAN GPU, our proposed CNN model achieves a near real-time processing speed of 10 frames per second. For the temporal-slice-based CNN method [2], we generated training temporal slices of 12 s from our dataset at the pre-defined LOIs, which result in a total of more than 50,000 temporal slices. We implemented their 3 networks following the description in [2].

To evaluate the accuracy of LOI crowd counting methods, we divided the test frames into short video clips of 10 s. The accuracy of crossing-line crowd counting was then calculated as the Mean Windowed Relative Absolute Errors (MWRAE) between the ground truth cumulative counts and the estimated cumulative counts for all short clips:

$$MWRAE = \frac{1}{N} \sum_{i=1}^{N} \frac{\|u_i - \widetilde{u}_i\|}{u_i} \times 100\%, \tag{11}$$

where u_i and $\widetilde{u}_i$ represent the ground truth and estimated cumulative crowd counts of ith test video clip, and N is the total number of test clips. The reason we chose this metric instead of the Mean Absolute Errors (MAE) and Mean Windowed Absolute Errors (MWAE) in existing literatures [10] is because the MAE would be sensitive to one single frame's large error while the MWAE favors video clips with fewer pedestrians. They are not comparable across different scenes and provide no information on the difficulties of different scenes. Therefore, we argue the MWRAE is a more reasonable evaluation metric for crossing-line people counting. However, when evaluating our proposed model's performance on the UCSD dataset [10], we still report the MAE and MWAE to make fair comparison with existing methods.

In addition to the methods from existing literature, we also designed multiple baseline models for comparison, which investigate the effects of different components of our proposed algorithm and other plausible solutions. (1) *Phase I*: this baseline network has the same structure as our proposed one but is only trained with phase I learning objectives, *i.e.*, the crowd density map and crowd velocity map. The crowd counting map is obtained by elementwisely multiplying the estimated density and velocity maps. (2) *Direct-training-A*: instead of training the proposed CNN using the proposed two-phase scheme with different learning objectives at each stage, this CNN was directly trained towards the crowd counting map. The short-cut loss signals were also modified so that they back-propagate from the crowd counting map to "conv5_s" and "conv6_ s". (3) *Direct-training-B*: this network is the same as *Direct-training-A* but "conv_o" and "deconv_o" directly output the 2-channel crowd counting map without the two elementwise multiplication branches. (4) *Two-separate*: two separated CNN models of the same structure as our proposed one were trained for estimating the crowd density map and the crowd velocity respectively. The counting map is obtained by multiplying the results of the two CNNs.

4.3 Evaluation on the Accuracy of Supervision Crowd Counting Maps

Since we generate the pixel-level crowd counting map by elementwisely multiplying a crowd density map with Gaussian density functions and a crowd velocity

Table 2. The MWRAE (%) between the ground truth crowd counts and the counts calculated by performing count mapping in Sect. 3.3 on our supervision crowd counting maps.

Scene 1	Scene 2	Scene 3	Scene 4	Scene 5	**All**
Down/Up	Down/Up	Down/Up	Down/Up	Down/Up	Down/Up
0.82/1.03	2.68/2.36	1.67/2.31	2.49/2.90	4.16/3.00	2.47/2.25

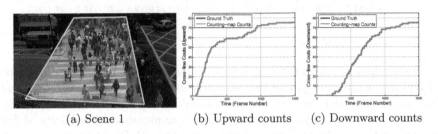

(a) Scene 1   (b) Upward counts   (c) Downward counts

Fig. 6. (a) Scene 1 with its LOI. (b-c) The ground-truth LOI cumulative counts (red) and the LOI cumulative counts from our supervision counting maps (green) for the LOI in (a). (Color figure online)

map, we evaluated if such supervision counting map provides accurate approximations for calculating the correct counting numbers with our proposed evaluation metric (see Table 2). For each LOI in our dataset, the crowd counts from our supervision counting maps are generated as introduced in Sect. 3.3. The MWRAEs between the ground truth counts and counts from our counting map for all scenes are reported in Table 2. The small MWRAEs show the way of generating crowd counting maps is able to obtain accurate enough crowd counting numbers for different LOIs and the generated supervision maps are suitable for training our CNN model. In Fig. 6, we show one example LOI's ground truth crowd counts and the counts from our supervision counting maps. The count curves from our counting map closely follow those of the ground truth.

4.4 Results on the Proposed Dataset

For our proposed dataset, we evaluated the MWRAE of the cumulative counts by our proposed CNN and other compared methods. The results are reported in Table 3, which show that our proposed CNN achieves the lowest errors for most scenes.

The TS-CNN [2] is based on temporal slices of both frames and optical flow maps. Since our dataset has many crowded scenes, the temporal slices are heavily degenerated (see Fig. 1(b) for examples). TS-CNN cannot output satisfactory crowd counts based on these temporal slices. The IP-based method [10] performs worst on this dataset, because it is based on hand-crafted features and cannot effectively adapt to such complex scenes.

Table 3. MWRAE (%) by our proposed method and other compared ones on the proposed dataset.

Method	Proposed	TS-CNN [2]	IP-based [10]	*Phase I*	*Direct-A*	*Direct-B*	*Two-separate*
	Down/Up	Down/Up	Down/Up	Down/Up	Down/Up	Down/Up	Down/Up
Scene 1	**4.01/5.59**	55.9/53.2	479/895	5.17/6.99	5.11/10.1	12.4/22.6	4.84/8.06
Scene 2	**7.21/14.6**	17.9/31.6	398/569	10.3/18.5	7.75/13.9	7.39/**13.4**	11.5/19.1
Scene 3	**4.82/5.82**	19.4/23.3	505/471	6.19/9.36	13.3/8.57	6.25/7.83	6.58/10.8
Scene 4	13.4/15.1	20.3/33.5	254/362	18.5/14.9	**11.8/12.4**	12.9/ 14.6	20.2/16.6
Scene 5	20.7/**13.7**	**17.8/28.0**	518/646	24.4/16.7	22.5/19.3	22.7/17.7	27.4/21.7
All	**11.2/10.7**	29.5/36.0	454/648	14.0/13.0	13.0/13.7	14.0/17.7	15.3/15.3

For the baseline deep CNN models, the (1) *Phase I* model was trained only with phase I learning objective and was not finetuned with the final crowd counting map. This model has lower accuracy than our CNN model trained with the proposed two-phase training scheme, which demonstrates the necessity of fine-tuning our CNN with the phase II objective. The (2) *Direct-training-A* model learns to directly output the two-channel crowd counting map by training with only the phase II learning objectives. The network structure remains the same as that of the proposed network. The accuracy of this training scheme is lower than that of our two-phase training strategy. Since our strategy decomposes the original problem into two easier sub-problems with clear semantic meanings, the bottom layers can learn more powerful feature representations. The (3) *Direct-training-B* model also directly outputs the two-channel crowd counting map but without the elementwise multiplication layer in the top layer. It actually generates better result than the *Direct-training-A* model, which demonstrates that it is our proposed two-phase training strategy instead of the elementwise multiplication operation that contributes to the increase of the counting accuracy. For the (4) *Two-separate* model that learns two independent networks for predicting crowd density and crowd velocity separately, we compare it with our *Phase I* model, which shows that the jointly learning crowd density and crowd velocity is able to assist the learning of both tasks and results in accurate results. Note that the *Two-separate* model has twice the parameters compared with *Phase I* model and is also twice slower for evaluation.

4.5   Results on the UCSD Dataset

We also evaluated our proposed method on the UCSD dataset [3], which contains only 1 video, and the results are reported in Table 4. The IP-based method [10] based on temporal slices has very good performance on this dataset because the video has relatively low crowd density (Fig. 7), and the training and testing samples are all from the same video. Because of the small number of the training frames in the dataset, our proposed CNN model was first trained with our proposed dataset and then fine-tuned on the UCSD dataset. The size of the video in the dataset is four times smaller than the ones in our training set. We enlarge the video frames and then input into our network for evaluation. Although with

Table 4. The results on the UCSD dataset by our proposed method and the IP-based method [10].

Method	Left		Right	
	MAE	MWAE	MAE	MWAE
Proposed CNN	1.1833	0.5964	0.6285	0.4719
IP-based [10]	0.6040	0.7231	0.6883	0.5105

| (a) | (b) |

Fig. 7. (a) Example frame of the UCSD dataset and the pre-defined LOI for the dataset. (b) Example temporal slice generated from the LOI. The shape and appearance of pedestrians could be well recognized because of the low crowd density of the dataset.

such difficulties, our proposed CNN show better accuracy compared with the integer-programming-based method in [10].

5   Conclusion

The problem of counting people crossing a line-of-interest is of great interest to the intelligent surveillance industry. In this paper, we present a deep Convolutional Neural Network for solving this problem. We observe that temporal slices used by state-of-the-art methods are sensitive to high crowd density, slow walking speed and different orientations of the LOI. A CNN model is therefore proposed to directly process pairs of video frames and predict pixel-level crossing-line crowd counting map. The proposed CNN model is trained with counting maps with rich supervision information and a novel two-phase training scheme. Such a training scheme decomposes the original problem into two easier ones with clear semantic meanings, which helps the CNN learn more discriminative feature representations. A new dataset for evaluating crossing-line crowd counting is proposed and would benefit related research along this direction.

Acknowledgments. This work is partially supported by the General Research Fund sponsored by the Research Grants Council of Hong Kong (Project Nos. CUHK14206114, CUHK14205615, CUHK419412, CUHK14203015), the Hong Kong Innovation and Technology Support Programme (No. ITS/221/13FP), National Natural Science Foundation of China (Nos. 61371192, 61301269), and Ph.D programs foundation of China (No. 20130185120039).

References

1. Bae, S.H., Yoon, K.J.: Robust online multi-object tracking based on tracklet confidence and online discriminative appearance learning. In: IEEE Conference Computer Vision and Pattern Recognition (2014)
2. Cao, L., Zhang, X., Ren, W., Huang, K.: Large scale crowd analysis based on convolutional neural network. Pattern Recogn. **48**(10), 3016–3024 (2015)
3. Chan, A.B., Liang, Z.S.J., Vasconcelos, N.: Privacy preserving crowd monitoring: Counting people without people models or tracking. In: IEEE Conference Computer Vision and Pattern Recognition (2008)
4. Chan, A.B., Vasconcelos, N.: Bayesian poisson regression for crowd counting. In: International Conference Computer Vision (2009)
5. Cong, Y., Gong, H., Zhu, S.C., Tang, Y.: Flow mosaicking: real-time pedestrian counting without scene-specific learning. In: IEEE Conference Computer Vision and Pattern Recognition (2009)
6. Fischer, P., Dosovitskiy, A., Ilg, E., Häusser, P., Hazırbaş, C., Golkov, V., van der Smagt, P., Cremers, D., Brox, T.: FlowNet: learning optical flow with convolutional networks. In: International Conference Computer Vision (2015)
7. Girshick, R., Donahue, J., Darrell, T., Malik, J.: Rich feature hierarchies for accurate object detection and semantic segmentation. In: IEEE Conference Computer Vision and Pattern Recognition (2014)
8. Lempitsky, V., Zisserman, A.: Learning to count objects in images. In: International Conference Advances in Neural Information Processing Systems (2010)
9. Li, W., Zhao, R., Xiao, T., Wang, X.: Deep-reID: Deep filter pairing neural network for person re-identification. In: IEEE Conference Computer Vision and Pattern Recognition (2014)
10. Ma, Z., Chan, A.: Counting people crossing a line using integer programming and local features. IEEE Trans. Circuits Syst. Video Technol. **PP**(99), 1 (2016)
11. Milan, A., Leal-Taixé, L., Schindler, K., Reid, I.: Joint tracking and segmentation of multiple targets. In: IEEE Conference Computer Vision and Pattern Recognition (2015)
12. Possegger, H., Mauthner, T., Roth, P.M., Bischof, H.: Occlusion geodesics for online multi-object tracking. In: IEEE Conference Computer Vision and Pattern Recognition (2014)
13. Ryan, D., Denman, S., Fookes, C., Sridharan, S.: Crowd counting using multiple local features. In: International Confernce Digital Image Computing Techniques and Applications (2009)
14. Simonyan, K., Zisserman, A.: Very deep convolutional networks for large-scale image recognition. In: International Confernce Learning Representations (2014)
15. Szegedy, C., Liu, W., Jia, Y., Sermanet, P., Reed, S., Anguelov, D., Erhan, D., Vanhoucke, V., Rabinovich, A.: Going deeper with convolutions. In: IEEE Confernce Computer Vision and Pattern Recognition (2015)
16. Tian, Y., Luo, P., Wang, X., Tang, X.: Pedestrian detection aided by deep learning semantic tasks. In: IEEE Conference Computer Vision and Pattern Recognition (2015)
17. Wang, L., Ouyang, W., Wang, X., Lu, H.: Visual tracking with fully convolutional networks. In: International Conference Computer Vision (2015)
18. Zhang, C., Li, H., Wang, X., Yang, X.: Cross-scene crowd counting via deep convolutional neural networks. In: IEEE Conference Computer Vision and Pattern Recognition (2015)

Revisiting Visual Question Answering Baselines

Allan Jabri[(⊠)], Armand Joulin, and Laurens van der Maaten

Facebook AI Research, New York, USA
{ajabri,ajoulin,lvdmaaten}@fb.com

Abstract. Visual question answering (VQA) is an interesting learning setting for evaluating the abilities and shortcomings of current systems for image understanding. Many of the recently proposed VQA systems include attention or memory mechanisms designed to perform "reasoning". Furthermore, for the task of multiple-choice VQA, nearly all of these systems train a multi-class classifier on image and question features to predict an answer. This paper questions the value of these common practices and develops a simple alternative model based on binary classification. Instead of treating answers as competing choices, our model receives the answer as input and predicts whether or not an image-question-answer triplet is correct. We evaluate our model on the Visual7W Telling and the VQA Real Multiple Choice tasks, and find that even simple versions of our model perform competitively. Our best model achieves state-of-the-art performance of 65.8 % accuracy on the Visual7W Telling task and compares surprisingly well with the most complex systems proposed for the VQA Real Multiple Choice task. Additionally, we explore variants of the model and study the transferability of the model between both datasets. We also present an error analysis of our best model, the results of which suggest that a key problem of current VQA systems lies in the lack of visual grounding and localization of concepts that occur in the questions and answers.

Keywords: Visual question answering · Dataset bias

1 Introduction

Recent advances in computer vision have brought us close to the point where traditional object-recognition benchmarks such as Imagenet are considered to be "solved" [1,2]. These advances, however, also prompt the question how we can move from object recognition to *visual understanding*; that is, how we can extend today's recognition systems that provide us with "words" describing an image or an image region to systems that can produce a deeper semantic representation of the image content. Because benchmarks have traditionally been a key driver for progress in computer vision, several recent studies have proposed methodologies to assess our ability to develop such representations. These proposals include modeling relations between objects [3], visual Turing tests [4], and visual question answering [5–8].

© Springer International Publishing AG 2016
B. Leibe et al. (Eds.): ECCV 2016, Part VIII, LNCS 9912, pp. 727–739, 2016.
DOI: 10.1007/978-3-319-46484-8_44

What color is the jacket?	How many cars are parked?	What event is this?	When is this scene taking place?
-Red and blue.	-Four.	-A wedding.	-Day time.
-Yellow.	-Three.	-Graduation.	-Night time.
-Black.	-Five.	-A funeral.	-Evening.
-Orange.	-Six.	-A picnic.	-Morning.

Fig. 1. Four images with associated questions and answers from the Visual7W dataset. Correct answers are typeset in green. (Color figure online)

The task of Visual Question Answering (VQA) is to answer questions—posed in natural language—about an image by providing an answer in the form of short text. This answer can either be selected from multiple pre-specified choices or be generated by the system. As illustrated by the examples from the Visual7W dataset [9] in Fig. 1, VQA naturally combines computer vision with natural language processing and reasoning, which makes it a good way to study progress on the path from computer vision to more general artificially intelligent systems.

VQA seems to be a natural playground to develop approaches able to perform basic "reasoning" about an image. Recently, many studies have explored this direction by adding simple memory or attention-based components to VQA systems. While in theory, these approaches have the potential to perform simple reasoning, it is not clear if they do actually reason, or if they do so in a human-comprehensible way. For example, Das *et al.* [10] recently reported that "machine-generated attention maps are either negatively correlated with human attention or have positive correlation worse than task-independent saliency". In this work, we also question the significance of the performance obtained by current "reasoning"-based systems. In particular, this study sets out to answer a simple question: are these systems better than baselines designed to solely capture the dataset bias of standard VQA datasets? We limit the scope of our study to multiple-choice tasks, as this allows us to perform a more controlled study that is not hampered by the tricky nuances of evaluating generated text [11,12].

We perform experimental evaluations on the Visual7W dataset [8] and the VQA dataset [5] to evaluate the quality of our baseline models. We: (1) study and model the bias in the Visual7W Telling and VQA Multiple Choice datasets, (2) measure the effect of using visual features from different CNN architectures, (3) explore the use of a LSTM as the system's language model, and (4) study transferability of our model between datasets.

Our best model outperforms the current state-of-the-art on the Visual7W telling task with a performance of 65.8%, and competes surprisingly well with the most complex systems proposed for the VQA dataset. Furthermore, our models perform competitively even with missing information (that is, missing images, missing questions, or both). Taken together, our results suggests that the performance of current VQA systems is not significantly better than that of systems designed to exploit dataset biases.

2   Related Work

The recent surge of studies on visual question answering has been fueled by the release of several visual question-answering datasets, most prominently, the VQA dataset [5], the DAQUAR dataset [13], the Visual Madlibs Q&A dataset [7], the Toronto COCO-QA dataset [6], and the Visual7W dataset [8]. Most of these datasets were developed by annotating subsets of the COCO dataset [14]. Geman *et al.* [4] proposed a visual Turing test in which the questions are automatically generated and require no natural language processing. Current approaches to visual question answering can be subdivided into "generation" and "classification" models:

Generation Models. Malinowski *et al.* [15] train a LSTM model to generate the answer after receiving the image features (obtained from a convolutional network) and the question as input. Wu *et al.* [16] extend a LSTM generation model to use external knowledge that is obtained from DBpedia [17]. Gao *et al.* [18] study a similar model but decouple the LSTMs used for encoding and decoding. Whilst generation models are appealing because they can generate arbitrary answers (also answers that were not observed during training), in practice, it is very difficult to jointly learn the encoding and decoding models from the question-answering datasets of limited size. In addition, the evaluation of the quality of the generated text is complicated in practice [11,12].

Classification Models. Zhou *et al.* [9] study an architecture in which image features are produced by a convolutional network, question features are produced by averaging word embeddings over all words in the question, and a multi-class logistic regressor is trained on the concatenated features; the top unique answers are treated as outputs of the classification model. Similar approaches are also studied by Antol *et al.* [5] and Ren *et al.* [6], though they use a LSTM to encode the question text instead of an average over word embeddings. Zhu *et al.* [8] present a similar method but extend the LSTM encoder to include an attention mechanism for jointly encoding the question with information from the image. Ma *et al.* [19] replace the LSTM encoder by a one-dimensional convolutional network that combines the word embeddings into a question embedding. Andreas *et al.* [20] use a similar model but perform the image processing using a compositional network whose structure is dynamically determined at run-time based on a parse of the question. Fukui *et al.* [21] propose the use of "bilinear pooling" for combining multi-modal information. Lu *et al.* [22] jointly learn a hierarchical attention mechanism based on parses of the question and the image which they call "question-image co-attention".

Our study is most closely related to a recent study by Shih *et al.* [23], which also considers models that treat the answer as an input variable and predicts

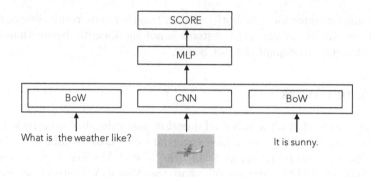

Fig. 2. Overview of our system for visual question answering. See text for details.

whether or not an image-question-answer triplet is correct. However, their study develops a substantially more complex pipeline involving image-region selection.

3   System Overview

Figure 2 provides an overview of the architecture of our visual question answering system. The system takes an image-question-answer feature triplet as input. Unless otherwise stated (that is, in the LSTM experiment of Sect. 4), both the questions and the answers are represented by averaging word2vec embeddings over all words in the question or answer, respectively. The images are represented using features computed by a pre-trained convolutional network. Unless otherwise stated, we use the penultimate layer of Resnet-101 [2]. The word2vec embeddings are 300-dimensional and the image features are 2,048-dimensional. The three feature sets are concatenated and used to train a classification model that predicts whether or not the image-question-answer triplet is correct.

The classification models we consider are logistic regressors and multilayer perceptrons (MLP) trained on the concatenated features, and bilinear models that are trained on the answer features and a concatenation of the image and question features. The MLP has 8,192 hidden units unless otherwise specified. We use dropout [24] after the first layer. We denote the image, question, and answer features by $\mathbf{x}_i$, $\mathbf{x}_q$, and $\mathbf{x}_a$, respectively. Denoting the sigmoid function $\sigma(x) = 1/(1 + \exp(-x))$ and the concatenation operator $\mathbf{x}_{iq} = \mathbf{x}_i \oplus \mathbf{x}_q$, we define the models as follows:

$$\textbf{Linear:} \quad y = \sigma(\mathbf{W}\mathbf{x}_{iqa} + b)$$
$$\textbf{Bilinear:} \quad y = \sigma(\mathbf{x}_{iq}^\top \mathbf{W}\mathbf{x}_a + b)$$
$$\textbf{MLP:} \quad y = \sigma(\mathbf{W}_2 \max(0, \mathbf{W}_1 \mathbf{x}_{iqa}) + b).$$

The parameters of the classifier are learned by minimizing the binary logistic loss of predicting whether or not an image-question-answer triplet is correct using stochastic gradient descent. During training we sampled two negative examples

Table 1. Comparison of our models with the state-of-the-art for the Visual7W telling task [8]. Human accuracy on the task is 96.0 %. Higher values are better.

Method	What	Where	When	Who	Why	How	Overall
LSTM (Q + I) [15]	48.9	54.4	71.3	58.1	51.3	50.3	52.1
LSTM-Att [8]	51.5	57.0	75.0	59.5	55.5	49.8	55.6
MCB [21]	60.3	70.4	79.5	69.2	58.2	**51.1**	62.2
MLP (A)	47.1	57.8	73.6	63.3	57.6	36.3	50.7
MLP (A + Q)	54.9	60.0	76.0	65.9	63.8	40.2	56.1
MLP (A + I)	60.0	73.9	80.0	70.3	63.9	36.6	61.0
MLP (A + Q + I)	**64.4**	**76.2**	**82.3**	**72.8**	**69.5**	40.9	**64.8**

Table 2. Comparison of our models with the state-of-the-art single models for the VQA Real Multiple Choice task [5]. Results are reported on the test2015-standard split. Human accuracy on the task is 83.3 %. Higher values are better.

Method	Yes/No	Number	Other	All
Two-layer LSTM [5]	80.6	37.7	53.6	63.1
Region selection [23]	77.2	33.5	56.1	62.4
Question-image co-attention [22]	80.0	**39.5**	59.9	**66.1**
MLP (A + Q + I)	**80.8**	17.6	**62.0**	65.2

from the multiple choices for each positive example, for a maximum of 300 epochs. The convolutional networks were pre-trained on the Imagenet dataset, following [25], and were not further finetuned. We used pre-trained word2vec [26] embeddings, which we did not finetune on VQA data either.

4   Experiments

We perform experiments on the following two datasets:

Visual7W Telling [8]. The dataset includes 69, 817 training questions, 28, 020 validation questions, and 42, 031 test questions. Each question has four answer choices. The negative choices are human-generated on a per-question basis. The performance is measured by the percentage of correctly answered questions.

VQA Real Multiple Choice [5]. The dataset includes 248, 349 questions for training, 121, 512 for validation, and 244, 302 for testing. Each question has 18 answer choices. The negative choices are randomly sampled from a predefined set of answers. Performance is measured following the metric proposed by [5].

4.1   Comparison with State-of-the-Art

We first compare the MLP variant of our model with the state-of-the-art. Table 1 shows the results of this comparison on Visual7W, using three variants of our

Table 3. Accuracy of models using either a *softmax* or a *binary* loss. Results are presented for different models using answer, question and image. On VQA, we use the test2015-dev split. Higher values are better.

Dataset	Model	Softmax	Binary
Visual7W	Linear	41.6	42.7
	Bilinear	–	61.8
	MLP	50.2	**64.8**
VQA	MLP	61.1	**64.9**

Table 4. The five most similar answers in the Visual7W dataset for three answers appearing in that dataset (in terms of cosine similarity between their feature vectors).

During the daytime	On the bus stop bench	On a tree branch
During daytime	Bus bench	On the tree branch
Outside, during the daytime	In front of the bus stop	The tree branch
Inside, during the daytime	The bus stop	Tree branch
In the daytime	At the bus stop	A tree branch
In the daytime	The sign on the bus stop	Tree branches

baseline with different inputs: (1) answer and question $(A + Q)$; (2) answer and image $(A + I)$; (3) and all three inputs $(A + Q + I)$. The model achieves state-of-the-art performance when it has access to all the information. Interestingly, as shown by the results with the $A + Q$ variant of our model, simply exploiting the most frequent question-answer pairs obtains competitive performance. Surprisingly, even a variant of our model that is trained *on just the answers* already achieves a performance of 50.7 %, simply by learning biases in the answer distribution.

In Table 2, we also compare our models with the published state-of-the-art on the VQA dataset. Despite its simplicity, our baseline achieves comparable performance with state-of-the-art models. We note that recent work [21] obtained 70.1 %, but used an ensemble of 7 models trained on additional data (the Visual Genome dataset [3]). Nonetheless, [21] performs only 5 % better than our model whilst being substantially more complex.

4.2   Additional Experiments

In the following, we present the results of additional experiments to understand why our model performs relatively well, and when it fails. All evaluations are conducted on the Visual7W Telling dataset unless stated otherwise.

Does It Help to Consider the Answer as an Input? In Table 3, we present the results of experiments in which we compare the performance of our (binary) baseline model with variants of the model that predict softmax probabilities over

Table 5. Accuracy on the Visual7W Telling task using visual features produced by five different convolutional networks. Higher values are better.

Model	AlexNet	GoogLeNet	ResNet-34	ResNet-50	ResNet-101
(dim.)	(4,096)	(1,792)	(512)	(2,048)	(2,048)
Linear	42.7	42.9	42.7	42.7	42.8
Bilinear	54.9	57.0	58.5	60.7	61.8
MLP	61.6	62.1	63.9	64.2	**64.8**

a discrete set of the 5,000 most common answers, as is commonly done in most prior studies, for instance, [9].

The results in the table show a substantial advantage of representing answers as inputs instead of outputs for the Visual7W Telling task and the VQA Real Multiple Choice task. Taking the answer as an input allows the system to model the similarity between different answers. For example, the answers "two people" and "two persons" are modeled by disjoint parameters in a softmax model; instead, the binary model will generally assign similar scores to these answers because they have similar bag-of-words word2vec representations.

To illustrate this, Table 4 shows examples of the similarities that can be captured by the binary model. For a given answer, the table shows the five most similar answers in the dataset based on cosine similarity between the feature vectors. The binary model can readily exploit these similarities, whereas a softmax model has to learn them from the (relatively small) Visual7W training set.

Interestingly, the gap between the binary and softmax models is smaller on the VQA datasets. This result may be explained by the way the incorrect-answer choices were produced in both datasets: the choices are human-generated for each question in the Visual7W dataset, whereas in the VQA dataset, the choices are randomly chosen from a predefined set that includes irrelevant correct answers.

What is the Influence of Convolutional Network Architectures? Nearly all prior work on VQA uses features extracted using a convolutional network that is pre-trained on Imagenet to represent the image in an image-question pair. Table 5 shows to what extent the quality of these features influences the VQA performance by comparing five different convolutional network architectures: AlexNet [27], GoogLeNet [1], and residual networks with three different depths [2]. While the performance on Imagenet is correlated with performance in visual question answering, the results show this correlation is quite weak: a reduction in the Imagenet top-5 error of 18 % corresponds to an improvement of only 3 % in question-answering performance. This result suggests that the performance on VQA tasks is limited by either the fact that some of the visual concepts in the questions do not appear in Imagenet, or by the fact that the convolutional networks are only trained to recognize object presence and not to predict higher-level information about the visual content of the images.

Table 6. Accuracy on Visual7W Telling dataset of a bag-of-words (*BoW*) and a *LSTM* model. We did not use image features to isolate the difference between language models. Higher values are better.

Model	BoW	LSTM
Bilinear	51.5	52.5
MLP	**56.1**	51.0

Table 7. Accuracy on Visual7W of models (1) trained from *scratch*, (2) *transfer*ed from the VQA dataset, and (3) *finetune*d after transferring. Higher values are better.

Model	Method	What	Where	When	Who	Why	How	Overall
MLP (A + Q)	Scratch	54.9	60.0	76.0	65.9	63.8	40.2	56.1
	Transfer	44.7	38.9	32.9	49.6	45.0	27.3	41.1
MLP (A + I)	Scratch	60.0	73.9	80.0	70.3	63.9	36.6	61.0
	Transfer	28.4	26.6	44.1	37.0	31.7	25.2	29.4
MLP (A + Q + I)	Scratch	64.4	76.2	**82.3**	72.8	**69.5**	40.9	64.8
	Transfer	58.7	61.7	41.7	60.2	53.2	29.1	53.8
	Finetune	**66.4**	**76.3**	81.6	**73.1**	68.7	**41.7**	**65.8**

Do Recurrent Networks Improve Over Bag of Words? Our baseline uses a simple bag-of-words (BoW) model to represent the questions and answers. Recurrent networks (in particular, LSTMs [28]) form a popular alternative for BoW models. We perform an experiment in which we replace our BoW representations by a LSTM model. The LSTM was trained on the Visual7W Telling training set, using a concatenation of one-hot encodings and pre-trained word2vec embeddings as input for each word in the question.

We experimented with using the average over time of the hidden states as feature representation for the text, as well as using only the last hidden state. We observed little difference between the two; here, we report the results using the last-state representation.

Table 6 presents the results of our experiment comparing BoW and LSTM representations. To study just the difference between the language models, we did not use images features as input in this experiment. The results show that despite their greater representation power, LSTMs actually do not outperform BoW representations on the Visual7W Telling task, presumably, because the dataset is quite small and the LSTM overfits easily. This may also explain why attentional LSTM models [8] perform poorly on the Visual7W dataset.

Can We Transfer Knowledge from VQA to Visual7W? An advantage of the presented model is that it can readily be transfered between datasets: it does not suffer from out-of-vocabulary problems nor does it require the set of answers to be known in advance. Table 7 shows the results of a transfer-learning experiment in which we train our model on the VQA dataset, and use it to answer questions in the Visual7W dataset. We used three different variants of our model, and experimented with three different input sets. The table presents three sets of results: (1) baseline results in which we trained on Visual7W from *scratch*, (2) *transfer* results in which we train on VQA but test on Visual7W, and (3) results in which we train on VQA, *finetune* on Visual7W, and then test on Visual7W.

The poor performance of the A + I transfer-learning experiment suggests that there is a substantial difference in the answer distribution between both datasets, especially since both use images from [14]. Transferring the full model from VQA to Visual7W works surprisingly well: we achieve 53.8 % accuracy, which is less than 2 % worse than LSTM-Att [8], even though the model never learns from Visual7W training data. If we finetune the transferred model on the Visual7W dataset, it actually outperforms a model trained from scratch on that same dataset, obtaining an accuracy of **65.8 %**. This additional boost likely stems from the model adjusting to the biases in the Visual7W dataset.

5   Error Analysis

To better understand the shortcomings and limitations of our models, we performed an error analysis of the best model we obtained in Sect. 4 on six types of questions, which are illustrated in Figs. 3, 4 and 5.

What is the color of the tree leaves?	What is the color of the train?	What shape is this sign?	What shape is the clock?
-Green.	-Green.	-Octagon.	-Cube.
-Brown.	-Yellow.	-Oval.	-Circle.
-Orange.	-Black.	-Hexagon.	-Oval.
-Red.	-Red.	-Square.	-Rectangle.

Fig. 3. Examples of good and bad predictions by our visual question answering model on color and shape questions. Correct answers are typeset in green; incorrect predictions by our model are typeset in red. See text for details. (Color figure online)

Colors and Shapes. Approximately 5,000 questions in the Visual7W test set are about colors and approximately 200 questions are about shapes. While colors and shapes are fairly simple visual features, our models only achieve around 55 % accuracy on these types of questions. For reference, our (A + Q) baseline already achieves 50 % in accuracy. This means that our models primarily learn the bias in the dataset. For example, for shape, it predicts either "circle", "round", or "octagon" when the question is about a "sign". For color questions, even though the

How many clouds are in the sky?	How many giraffes sitting?	What is behind the photographer?	What color leaves are on the tree behind the elephant on the left of the photo?
-None.	-Three.	-A bus.	-Red.
-Three.	-One.	-A dump truck.	-Orange.
-Five.	-Two.	-A duck.	-Green.
-Seven.	-Four.	-A plate of food.	-Brown.

Fig. 4. Examples of good and bad predictions by our visual question answering model on counting and spatial reasoning. Correct answers are typeset in green; incorrect predictions by our model are typeset in red. See text for details. (Color figure online)

performances are similar, it appears that the image-based models are able to capture additional information. For example, Fig. 3 shows that the model tends to predict the most salient color, but fails to capture color coming from small objects, which constitute a substantial number of questions in the Visual7W dataset. This result highlights the limits of using global image features in visual question answering.

Counting. There are approximately 5,000 questions in the Visual7W test set that involve counting the number of objects in the image ("how many ...?"). On this type of questions, our model achieves an accuracy of 36%. This accuracy is hardly better than that the 35% achieved by the (Q + A) baseline. Again, this implies that our model does not really extract information from the image that can be used for counting. In particular, our model has a strong preference for answers such as: "none", "one", or "two".

Spatial Reasoning. We refer to any question that refers to a relative position ("left", "right", "behind", *etc.*) as questions about "spatial reasoning". There are approximately 1,500 such questions in the Visual7W test set. On questions requiring spatial reasoning, our models achieve an accuracy of approximately 50%, whereas a purely text-based model achieves an accuracy 40%. This suggests that our models, indeed, extract some information from the images that can be used to make inferences about spatial relations.

Actions. We refer to any question that asks what an entity is "doing" as an "action" question. There are approximately 1,200 such questions in the Visual7W test set. Our models achieve an accuracy of roughly 75% on action questions. By contrast, a purely text-based model achieves an accuracy of around 65%. This result suggests that our model does learn to exploit image features in recognizing actions. This result is in line with results presented in earlier studies that show image features transfer well to simple action-recognition tasks [29,30].

What is the man doing?
-Surfing.
-Singing.
-Working.
-Playing.

What is the man doing?
-Golfing.
-Playing tennis.
-Walking.
-Biking.

Why is the ground white?
-Snow.
-Sand.
-Stones.
-Concrete.

Why is his arm up?
-To serve the tennis ball.
-About to hit the ball.
-Reaching for the ball.
-Swinging his racket.

Fig. 5. Examples of good and bad predictions by our visual question answering model on action and causality. Correct answers are typeset in green; incorrect predictions by our model are typeset in red. See text for details. (Color figure online)

Causality. "Why" questions test the model's ability to capture a weak form of causality. There are around 2,600 of them. Our model has an accuracy of 68% on such questions, but a simple text-based model already obtains 62%. This means that most "why" questions can be answered by looking at the text. This is unsurprising, as many of these questions refer to common sense that is encoded in the text. For example, in Fig. 5, one hardly needs the image to correctly predict that the ground is "white" because of "snow" instead of "sand".

6 Discussion and Future Work

This paper presented a simple alternative model for visual question answering multiple choice, explored variants of this model, and experimented with transfer between VQA datasets. Our study produced stronger baseline systems than those presented in prior studies. In particular, our results demonstrate that featurizing the answers and training a binary classifier to predict correctness of an image-question-answer triplet leads to substantial performance improvements over the current state-of-the-art on the Visual7W Telling task: our best model obtains an accuracy of 64.8% when trained from scratch, and 65.8% when transferred from VQA and finetuned on the Visual7W. On the VQA Real Multiple Choice task, our model outperforms models that use LSTMs and attention mechanisms, and is close to the state-of-the-art despite being very simple.

Our error analysis demonstrates that future work in visual question answering should focus on grounding the visual entities that are present in the images, as the "difficult" questions in the Visual7W dataset cannot be answered without such grounding. Whilst global image features certainly help in visual question answering, they do not provide sufficient grounding of concepts of interest. More precise grounding of visual entities, as well as reasoning about the relations between these entities, is likely to be essential in making further progress.

Furthermore, in order to accurately evaluate future models, we need to understand the biases in VQA datasets. Many of the complex methods in prior work perform worse than the simple model presented in this paper. We hypothesize that one of two things (or both) may explain these results: (1) it may be that, currently, the best-performing models are those that can exploit biases in VQA datasets the best, *i.e.*, models that "cheat" the best; (2) it may be that current, early VQA models are unsuitable for the difficult task of visual question answering, as a result of which all of them hit roughly the same ceiling in experiments and evaluations. In some of our experiments, we have seen that a model that appears qualitatively better may perform worse quantitatively, because it captures dataset biases less well. To address such issues, it may be necessary to consider alternative evaluation criterions that are less sensitive to dataset bias.

Finally, the results of our transfer-learning experiments suggest that exploring the ability of VQA systems to generalize across datasets may be an interesting alternative way to evaluate such systems in future work.

References

1. Szegedy, C., Liu, W., Jia, Y., Sermanet, P., Reed, S., Anguelov, D., Erhan, D., Vanhoucke, V., Rabinovich, A.: Going deeper with convolutions. In: Proceedings of the IEEE Conference on Computer Vision and Pattern Recognition (2015)
2. He, K., Zhang, X., Ren, S., Sun, J.: Deep residual learning for image recognition. In: Proceedings of the IEEE Conference on Computer Vision and Pattern Recognition (2016)
3. Krishna, R., Zhu, Y., Groth, O., Johnson, J., Hata, K., Kravitz, J., Chen, S., Kalanditis, Y., Li, L.J., Shamma, D., Bernstein, M., Fei-Fei, L.: Visual genome: connecting language and vision using crowdsourced dense image annotations. arXiv:1602.07332 (2016)
4. Geman, D., Geman, S., Hallonquist, N., Younes, L.: Visual turing test for computer vision systems. Proc. Natl. Acad. Sci. **112**(12), 3618–3623 (2015)
5. Antol, S., Agrawal, A., Lu, J., Mitchell, M., Batra, D., Zitnick, C., Parikh, D.: VQA: visual question answering. In: Proceedings of the International Conference on Computer Vision (2015)
6. Ren, M., Kiros, R., Zemel, R.: Exploring models and data for image question answering. In: Advances in Neural Information Processing Systems (2015)
7. Yu, L., Park, E., Berg, A., Berg, T.: Visual madlibs: fill in the blank image generation and question answering. arXiv:1506.00278 (2015)
8. Zhu, Y., Groth, O., Bernstein, M., Fei-Fei, L.: Visual7W: grounded question answering in images. arXiv:1511.03416 (2015)
9. Zhou, B., Tian, Y., Sukhbaatar, S., Szlam, A., Fergus, R.: Simple baseline for visual question answering. arXiv:1512.02167 (2015)
10. Das, A., Agrawal, H., Zitnick, C.L., Parikh, D., Batra, D.: Human attention in visual question answering: do humans and deep networks look at the same regions? arXiv:1606.03556 (2016)
11. Koehn, P.: Statistical significance tests for machine translation evaluation. In: EMNLP, pp. 388–395 (2004)
12. Callison-Burch, C., Osborne, M., Koehn, P.: Re-evaluation the role of BLEU in machine translation research. In: EACL, vol. 6, pp. 249–256 (2006)
13. Malinowski, M., Fritz, M.: A multi-world approach to question answering about real-world scenes based on uncertain input. CoRR abs/1410.0210 (2014)

14. Lin, T.Y., Maire, M., Belongie, S., Hays, J., Perona, P., Ramanan, D., Dollar, P., Zitnick, C.: Microsoft COCO: common objects in context. In: Proceedings of the European Conference on Computer Vision (2014)

15. Malinowski, M., Rohrbach, M., Fritz, M.: Ask your neurons: a neural-based approach to answering questions about images. In: Proceedings of the Internation Conference on Computer Vision(2015)

16. Wu, Q., Shen, C., van den Hengel, A., Wang, P., Dick, A.: Image captioning and visual question answering based on attributes and their related external knowledge. arXiv:1603.02814 (2016)

17. Auer, S., Bizer, C., Kobilarov, G., Lehmann, J., Cyganiak, R., Ives, Z.: DBpedia: a nucleus for a web of open data. In: Aberer, K., Choi, K.-S., Noy, N., Allemang, D., Lee, K.-I., Nixon, L., Golbeck, J., Mika, P., Maynard, D., Mizoguchi, R., Schreiber, G., Cudré-Mauroux, P. (eds.) ASWC/ISWC -2007. LNCS, vol. 4825, pp. 722–735. Springer, Heidelberg (2007). doi:10.1007/978-3-540-76298-0_52

18. Gao, H., Mao, J., Zhou, J., Huang, Z., Wang, L., Xu, W.: Are you talking to a machine? Dataset and methods for multilingual image question answering. In: Advances in Neural Information Processing Systems (2015)

19. Ma, L., Lu, Z., Li, H.: Learning to answer questions from image using convolutional neural network. arXiv:1506.00333 (2015)

20. Andreas, J., Rohrbach, M., Darrell, T., Klein, D.: Deep compositional question answering with neural module networks. arXiv:1511.02799 (2015)

21. Fukui, A., Huk Park, D., Yang, D., Rohrbach, A., Darrell, T., Rohrbach, M.: Multimodal compact bilinear pooling for visual question answering and visual grounding (2016)

22. Lu, J., Yang, J., Batra, D., Parikh, D.: Hierarchical question-image co-attention for visual question answering (2016)

23. Shih, K.J., Singh, S., Hoiem, D.: Where to look: Focus regions for visual question answering. arXiv:1511.07394 (2016)

24. Srivastava, N., Hinton, G., Krizhevsky, A., Sutskever, I., Salakhutdinov, R.: Dropout: a simple way to prevent neural networks from overfitting. J. Mach. Learn. Res. 15(1), 1929–1958 (2014)

25. Gross, S., Wilber, M.: Training and investigating residual nets (2016)

26. Mikolov, T., Chen, K., Corrado, G., Dean, J.: Efficient estimation of word representations in vector space. arXiv:1301.3781 (2013)

27. Krizhevsky, A., Sutskever, I., Hinton, G.: Imagenet classification with deep convolutional neural networks. In: Advances in Neural Information Processing Systems (2012)

28. Hochreiter, S., Schmidhuber, J.: Long short-term memory. Neural Comput. 9(8), 1735–1780 (1997)

29. Joulin, A., van der Maaten, L., Jabri, A., Vasilache, N.: Learning visual features from large weakly supervised data. arXiv:1511.0225 (2015)

30. Razavian, A.S., Azizpour, H., Sullivan, J., Carlsson, S.: CNN features off-the-shelf: an astounding baseline for recognition. arXiv:1403.6382 (2014)

Unsupervised CNN for Single View Depth Estimation: Geometry to the Rescue

Ravi Garg[✉], Vijay Kumar B.G., Gustavo Carneiro, and Ian Reid

The University of Adelaide, Adelaide, SA 5005, Australia
{ravi.garg,vijay.kumar,gustavo.carneiro,ian.reid}@adelaide.edu.au

Abstract. A significant weakness of most current deep Convolutional Neural Networks is the need to train them using vast amounts of manually labelled data. In this work we propose a unsupervised framework to learn a deep convolutional neural network for single view depth prediction, without requiring a pre-training stage or annotated ground-truth depths. We achieve this by training the network in a manner analogous to an autoencoder. At training time we consider a pair of images, source and target, with small, known camera motion between the two such as a stereo pair. We train the convolutional encoder for the task of predicting the depth map for the source image. To do so, we explicitly generate an inverse warp of the target image using the predicted depth and known inter-view displacement, to reconstruct the source image; the photometric error in the reconstruction is the reconstruction loss for the encoder. The acquisition of this training data is considerably simpler than for equivalent systems, requiring no manual annotation, nor calibration of depth sensor to camera. We show that our network trained on less than half of the KITTI dataset gives comparable performance to that of the state-of-the-art supervised methods for single view depth estimation.

1 Introduction

The availability of very large human annotated datasets like Imagenet [6] has led to a surge of deep learning approaches successfully addressing various vision problems. Trained initially on tasks such as image classification, and fine-tuned to fit other tasks, supervised CNNs are now state-of-the-art for object detection [14], per-pixel image classification [28], depth and normal prediction from single image [22], human pose estimation [9] and many other applications. A significant and abiding weakness, however, is the need to accrue labeled data for the supervised learning. Providing per-pixel segmentation masks on large datasets like CoCo [23], or classification labels for Imagenet requires significant human effort and is prone to error. Supervised training for single view depth estimation for outdoor scenes requires expensive hardware and careful acquisition [8,21,24,29].

Electronic supplementary material The online version of this chapter (doi:10.
1007/978-3-319-46484-8_45) contains supplementary material, which is available to authorized users.

B. Leibe et al. (Eds.): ECCV 2016, Part VIII, LNCS 9912, pp. 740–756, 2016.
DOI: 10.1007/978-3-319-46484-8_45

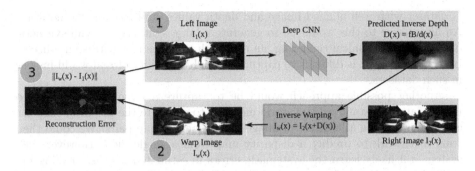

Fig. 1. We propose a stereopsis based auto-encoder setup: the encoder (Part 1) is a traditional convolutional neural network with stacked convolutions and pooling layers (See Fig. 2) and maps the left image (I_1) of the rectified stereo pair into its depth map. Our decoder (Part 2) explicitly forces the encoder output to be disparities (scaled inverse depth) by synthesizing a backward warp image (I_w) by moving pixels from right image I_2 along the scan-line. We use the reconstructed output I_w to be matched with the encoder input (Part 3) via a simple loss. For end-to-end training, we minimize the reconstruction loss with a simple smoothness prior on disparities which deals with the aperture problem, while at test time our CNN performs single-view disparity (inverse depth) prediction, up to the scene scale given in form of fB at the time of training.

For example, despite using state-of-the-art 3D sensors, multiple calibrated cameras and inertial sensors, a dataset like KITTI [13] provides sparse depthmaps with less than 5 % density on the captured image resolutions and with only a limited reliable depth range. A significant challenge now is to develop unsupervised training regimes that can train networks that perform either as well as, or better than those trained used using these supervised methods. This will be a major step towards realizing in-situ learning, in which we can retrain or tune a network for specific circumstances, and towards life-long learning, in which continuous acquisition of data leads to improved performance over time.

In this paper we are particularly concerned with the task of single-view depth estimation, in which the goal is to learn a non linear prediction function which maps an image to its depth map. CNNs have achieved the state-of-the-art performance on this task due to their ability to capture the complex and implicit relationships between scene depth and the corresponding image textures, scene semantics, and local and global context in the image. State-of-the-art supervised learning methods for this task train a CNN to minimize a loss based on either the scale invariant RMS [8], or the log RMS [24] of the depth predictions from ground-truth. These networks have been trained using datasets that provide both RGB images and corresponding depthmaps such as NYUv2 and KITTI.

However as noted in [24], the networks learned by these systems do not generalize well outside their immediate domain of application. For example, [24] trained two separate networks, one for indoors (using NYUv2) and one for street scenes (using KITTI), because the weights learned in one do not work well in the other. To transfer the idea of single-view depth estimation into yet another domain would require indulging in the expensive task of acquiring a new RGB-

D dataset with well aligned image and depth values, and re-train the network. An alternative to this would be to generate a large synthetic or semi-synthetic dataset using graphical rendering, an approach that has met with some success in [15]. However it is difficult to capture the full variability of real-world images in such datasets.

Another possible approach would be to capture a large dataset of stereo images, and use standard geometric methods to compute the disparity map for each pair, yielding a large set of image-plus-disparity-map pairs. We could then train a network to predict a disparity map from a single view. However such system will likely learn the systematic errors in estimated depths, "baking in" the failure modes of the stereo algorithm. Factors such as sensor flare, motion blur, lighting changes, shadows, etc. are present in real images and rarely dealt with adequately by standard stereo algorithms.

We adopt a different approach that moves towards a system capable of in-situ training or even lifelong learning, using real un-annotated imagery. We take inspiration from the idea of autoencoders, and leverage well-understood ideas in visual geometry. The result is a convolutional neural network for single-view depth estimation, the first of its kind that can be trained end-to-end from scratch, in a fully unsupervised fashion, simply using data captured using a stereo rig.

2   Approach

In this section we give more detail of our approach. Figure 1 explains our idea graphically. To train our network, we make use of pairs of images with a known camera motion between the two, such as stereo pairs. Such data are considerably more easily acquired than calibrated depthmaps and aligned images. In our case we use large numbers of stereo pairs, but the method applies equally to data acquired from a moving SLAM system in an otherwise static scene.

We learn a CNN to model the complex non-linear transformation which converts the image to a depth-map. The loss we use for learning this CNN is the photometric difference between the input – or source – image, and the inverse-warped target image (the other image in the stereo pair). This loss is both differentiable (to facilitate back-propagation) and is highly correlated with the prediction error - i.e. can be used to accurately rank two different depth-maps without using ground-truth labels.

This approach can be interpreted in the context of convolutional autoencoders. The task of the standard autoencoder is to encode the input with a series of non-linear operations to a compressed code that captures sufficient core information so that a decoder can reconstruct the input with minimal reconstruction error. In our case we replace the decoder with a standard geometric image warp, based on the predicted depth map and the relative camera positions. This has two advantages: first, the decoder in our case does not need to be learned, since it is already a well-understood geometric operation; second, our reconstruction loss naturally encourages the code to be the correct depth image.

2.1   Autoencoder Loss

Every training instance $i \in \{1 \cdots N\}$ in our setup is a rectified stereo pair $\{I_1^i, I_2^i\}$ captured by a single pre-calibrated stereo rig with two cameras having focal length f each which are separated horizontally by a distance B.[1] Assuming that the predicted depth of a pixel x for the left image of the rig via CNN is $d^i(x)$, the motion of the pixel along the scan-line $D^i(x)$ is then $fB/d^i(x)$. Thus, using the right image I_2^i, a warp I_w^i can be synthesized as $I_2^i(x + fB/d^i(x))$.

With this explicit parameterization of the warp, we propose to minimize standard color constancy (photometric) error between the reconstructed image I_w^i and the left image I_1^i:

$$E_{recons}^i = \int_\Omega \|I_w^i(x) - I_1^i(x)\|^2 dx = \int_\Omega \|I_2^i(x + \underbrace{D^i(x)}_{fB/d^i(x)}) - I_1^i(x)\|^2 dx \qquad (1)$$

It is well known that this photometric loss function is non-informative in homogeneous regions of the scene. Thus multiple disparities can generate equally good warps I_w's and a prior on the disparities is needed to get a unique depthmap. We use very simple $L2$ regularization on the disparity discontinuities as our prior to deal with the aperture problem:

$$E_{smooth}^i = \|\nabla D^i(x)\|^2 \qquad (2)$$

This regularizer is known to over-smooth the estimated motion, however a vast literature of more sophisticated edge preserving regularizers with robust penalty functions like [2,33] for which gradients can be computed are at our disposal and can be easily used with our setup to get sharper depthmaps. As the main purpose of our work is to prove that end-to-end training of the proposed autoencoder is feasible and helpful for depth prediction, we choose to minimize the simplest suitable loss summed over all training instances:

$$E = \sum_{i=1}^{N} E_{recons}^i + \gamma E_{smooth}^i \qquad (3)$$

where γ is the strength of the regularization forcing the estimated depthmaps to be smooth.

Our loss function as described in (3) is similar to the standard Horn and Schunck optic flow cost [17] for every frame. However, the major difference is that our disparity maps D^i's are parametrized to be a non-linear function of the input image and unknown weights of the CNN which are shared for estimating the motion between every stereo pair. This parameter sharing enforces consistency in the estimated depths over 1000's of correlated training images of a large dataset like KITTI. Our autoencoder's reconstruction loss can be seen as a generalization

---

[1] All training images are assumed to be taken with a fixed rectified stereo setup as is the case in KITTI for simplicity but our method is generalizable to work with instances taken by different calibrated stereos.

of the multi-frame optic flow methods like [11,12]. The difference is, instead of modeling the correlations in the estimated motions for a shorter video sequence with a predefined linear subspace [11], our autoencoder learns (and models) valid flows which are consistent throughout the dataset non-linearly.

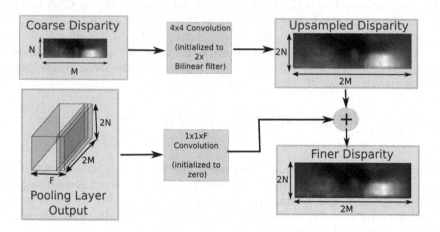

Fig. 2. Coarse-to-fine stereo with CNN with results on a sample validation instance: We adapt the convolution based upsampling architecture proposed in [26] to mimic the coarse-to-fine stereo estimations. Our upsampling filter is initialized with simple bilinear interpolation kernel and we initialize the corresponding pooling layer contribution by setting both bias and 1×1 convolution filter to be zero. The figure shows how features coming from previous layers of the CNN (L3) combined with finer resolution loss function generate better depthmaps at 44×172 from our bilinear upsampled initial estimate of coarser prediction at 22×76.

3   Coarse-to-Fine Training with Skip Architecture

To compute the gradient for standard back-propagation on our cost (1), we need to linearize the warp image at the current estimate of the disparities using Taylor expansion:

$$I_2(x + D^n(x)) = I_2(x + D^{n-1}(x)) + (D^n(x) - D^{n-1}(x))I_{2h}(x + D^{n-1}(x)) \quad (4)$$

where I_{2h} represents the horizontal gradient of the warp image computed at the current disparity D^{n-1} at iteration n.[2] This linearization is valid only for small values of $D^n(x) - D^{n-1}(x)$ limiting the magnitude of estimated disparities in the image. To estimate larger motions (smaller depths) accurately, a coarse-to-fine strategy with iterative warping is well established in the stereo and optic flow literature which facilitates gradient descent-based continuous optimization. We

---

[2] We have dropped the training instance index i for simplicity.

refer the readers to [30] for more detailed discussion of the requirements of this linearization, its limitations and existing alternatives.

However, our disparities are a non-linear function of the CNN parameters and the input image. To move from coarse-to-fine level, we not only need a good disparity initialization at the finer resolutions to linearize the warps but also the corresponding CNN parameters which predict these initial disparities for each training instance. Fortunately, the recent fully-convolutional architecture with upsampling, proposed in [26], is a suitable choice to enable coarse-to-fine warping for our system. As depicted in Fig. 2, given a network which predicts an $M \times N$ disparities, we can use a simple bilinear upsampling filter to initialize upscaled disparities (to get $2M \times 2N$ depthmaps) keeping the other network parameters fixed. It has been shown that the finer details of the images are captured in the previous layers of CNN, and fusing back such information is helpful for refining a coarse CNN prediction. We use 1×1 convolution with the filter and bias both initialized to zero and the convolved output is then fused with the upscaled depths with an element-wise sum layer for refinement.

4 Network Architecture

The network architecture for our deep convolutional encoder is shown in Fig. 3 which is similar to the Alexnet architecture [19] up to the C5 layer. We replace the fully connected layer of Alexnet by a fully convolutional layer with 2048 convolution filters of size 5×5 each.[3] This reduces the number of parameters in the network and allows for the network to accept variable size inputs at test time. More importantly, it preserves the spatial information present in the image and allows us to upsample the predictions in a stage-wise manner in the layers that follow the L7 output of the figure, which is a requirement for our stereopsis based autoencoder. Inspired by the observations from [26], that the finer details in the images are lost in the last few layers of the deep convolutional network we employ the "skip architecture" that combines the coarser depth prediction with the local image information to get finer predictions. The effect of this is illustrated using an example from the validation set in Fig. 2. The layers following the L9 output (22×76 depthmap) in our network are simple 4×4 convolutions each converting a coarser low resolution depth map to a higher resolution output.

5 Experiments

We evaluate our method on the publicly available KITTI dataset [13] that comprises several outdoor scenes captured using a stereo camera mounted on a moving vehicle. We employ the same train/test split used in [8]: from the 56 scenes belonging to the categories "city", "residential" and "road", we choose 28 for training and the remaining 28 for testing. We downsample the left images by a

---

[3] A 5×18 convolution can be used instead to increase network capacity and replicate the effect of a fully connected layer of [19].

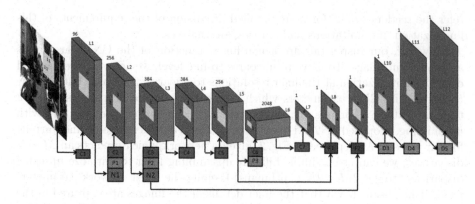

Fig. 3. Network architecture: The blocks C (red), P (yellow), L (dark blue), F (green), D (blue) correspond to convolution, pooling, local response normalization, FCN and upsampling layers respectively. The FCN blocks F1 and F2 upsample the predictions from layers (L7, L8) and combine it with the input of the pooling layers P3 and P2 respectively. (Color figure online)

factor of 2 to bring them to 188×620, and at this resolution they are used as input to the network. Each corresponding right image in a stereo pair is used at the resolution of the predicted depthmap at each stage of our coarse-to-fine training to generate the warp and match it with a resized left image.

The training set consists of 23488 stereo pairs out of which we use 22600 for training and the remaining for validation. Neither the right to left stereo nor any data augmentation are used for the coarse-to-fine training in multiple stages. For testing, we use the 697 images provided by [8]. We do not use any ground-truth depths for training the network. To evaluate all the results produced by our network we use simple upscaling of the low resolution disparity predictions to the resolution at which the stereo images were captured. Using the stereo baseline of 0.54 m, we convert the upsampled disparities to generate depthmaps at KITTI resolution using $d = fB/D$.

For fair comparison with state-of-the-art single view depth prediction, we evaluate our results on the same cropped region of interest as [8]. Since the supervised methods are trained using the ground-truth depth that ranges between 1 and 50 m whereas we can predict larger depths, we clamp the predicted depth values for our method between 1 and 50 for evaluation. i.e. setting the depths bigger than 50 m to 50. We evaluate our method using the error measures reported in [8,24]:

$$\text{RMS}: \sqrt{\tfrac{1}{T}\sum_{i\in T}\|d_i - d_i^{gt}\|^2} \qquad \text{log RMS}: \sqrt{\tfrac{1}{T}\sum_{i\in T}\|log(d_i) - log(d_i^{gt})\|^2}$$

$$\text{abs. relative}: \tfrac{1}{T}\sum_{i\in T}\frac{|d_i - d_i^{gt}|}{d_i^{gt}} \qquad \text{sq. relative}: \tfrac{1}{T}\sum_{i\in T}\frac{\|d_i - d_i^{gt}\|^2}{d_i^{gt}}$$

$$\text{Accuracies}: \% \text{ of } d_i \text{ s.t. } max\left(\frac{d_i}{d_i^{gt}}, \frac{d_i^{gt}}{d_i}\right) = \delta < thr$$

Table 1. Performance of the proposed framework at various stages of training.

Methods	Resolution	RMS	*log* RMS	Absolute relative	Square relative	$\delta < 1.25$	Accuracies $\delta < 1.25^2$	$\delta < 1.25^3$
Ours L9	22 × 76	5.740	0.310	0.205	1.353	0.660	0.872	0.948
Ours L10 + skip[a]	46 × 154	5.850	0.338	0.246	1.673	0.607	0.842	0.937
Ours L10	44 × 152	5.434	0.292	0.189	1.214	0.705	0.889	0.955
Ours L11	88 × 304	5.326	0.285	0.179	1.177	0.721	0.892	0.958
Ours L12	176 × 608	5.285	0.282	0.177	1.169	0.727	0.896	0.958
Ours L12, Aug. 8x		5.104	0.273	0.169	1.08	0.740	0.904	0.962

[a] Layer 10 result while using 3rd skip-connection.

Input Image	Results without aug.	Results with aug.

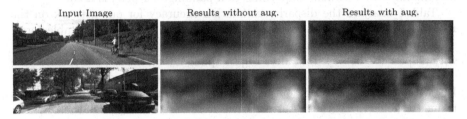

Fig. 4. Data augmentation improves the predicted disparities for smaller objects. Look at the biker in the first and the bottom right car in the second example.

5.1 Implementation Details

We train our network using the CNN toolbox MatConvnet [31]. We use SGD for optimization with momentum 0.9 and weight decay of 0.0005. Our network weights are initialized randomly for the first 5 layers of the Alexnet and we append the 5 × 5 fully convolutional layer initialized with zero weights to get zero disparity estimates. We subtract every pixel's color by 128 and divide it by 255 to have both left and right images $\in [-0.5, 0.5]$. The smoothness prior strength γ was set to 0.01.

Due to the linearization of the loss function as explained in Sect. 3, we learn the network proposed in Fig. 3 in multiple stages, starting from the coarsest level (L7 in Fig. 3), and iteratively adding upsampling layers one at a time. The learning rate for the network which predicts depths at the coarsest resolution is initialized to 0.01 and gradually decreased after each epoch using the factor $1/(1 + \alpha * n)^{(n-1)}$ where n is the index of current epoch and $\alpha = 0.0005$. The smoothness prior strength γ was set to 0.01. We train this coarse depth prediction network (L1-L7) for 100 epochs.

5.2 Effect of Upsampling

Having the coarser depth estimates for the training-set, we iteratively add upsampling layers which increases the resolution of the predictions by a factor of ≈ 2.[4] Since the number of pixels in the images are increased by a factor of 4, the cost approximately increases by the same factor when moving from coarser to finer level training. Hence we decrease the initial learning rate by a factor of 4 for training the finer networks. Starting from the coarsest predictions (L7) we progressively add upsampling layers L8 to L12 to get depths at resolutions $10 \times 37, 22 \times 76, 44 \times 152, 88 \times 304$ and 176×608 respectively. We train each of the finer networks for 100 epochs with the decaying learning rate as described in previous section. While adding the upsampling layers, we crop and pad the layers such that the resolution of predictions in L8 and L9 matches the resolution of the input to the pooling layers P3 and P2 respectively. For the upsampling layers without skip-connection padding of 1 pixel is used.

Table 1 analyses the disparity estimation accuracy for our network on the KITTI test-set at various stages of the training. Row 1 and 2 of our table correspond to our L9 and L10 output with 2 and 3 FCN blocks respectively. Consistent with [26] we also observe that after 2 upsampling layers, the skipped architecture starts to give diminishing returns. As evident from the third row in Table 1 layer L10 without skip-connection outperforms the counterpart. We believe that this is due to the fact that the features learned in the first few layers of the CNN are more relevant to ordinary photometric images than to the depth images. Thus, a simple weighted sum of these features with that of the depth map does not work well. However, higher resolution images still have richer information for image correspondences which can be back-propagated via our loss function for better predictions. The gradual improvement in disparity estimations using high resolution images is evident in Table 1.

5.3   Fine Tuning with Augmentation

Once we have our base network trained in the stage-wise manner described above, we further fine-tune this network (without coarse-to-fine training) for another 100 epochs with following augmentations:

- Color (2×): Color channels are multiplied by a factor $c \in [0.9, 1.1]$ randomly.
- Scale (2×): We scale the input image by a factor of $s \in [1, 1.6]$ and randomly crop the images to match the network input size.
- Left-Right flips (2×): We flip left and right images horizontally and swap them to get new training pair with positive disparities to keep consistency.

Consistent with other CNNs, fine tuning our network with this new augmented dataset leads to noticeable improvements in depth prediction. Figure 4 illustrates how 8× data for the fine tuning improves the reconstructions. Notice in particular the improved localization of object edges. This is particularly encouraging for our stereopsis loss based unsupervised training procedure as its fine tuning only requires a cheap stereo-rig to collect new data in the wild. For example, we can resort to much larger road scene understanding dataset like cityscapes [5]

---

[4] Alexnet uses uneven padding for some convolutions leading to change in the aspect ratio and the image size.

Table 2. Comparison with state-of-the-art methods on KITTI dataset.

Methods	Resolution	RMS	logRMS	Absolute relative	Square relative	$\delta < 1.25$	Accuracies $\delta < 1.25^2$	$\delta < 1.25^3$
Ours L12	176 × 608	5.285	0.282	0.177	1.169	0.727	0.896	0.958
Ours L12, Aug 8x		**5.104**	0.273	**0.169**	**1.080**	**0.740**	**0.904**	0.962
Mean	-	9.635	0.444	0.412	5.712	0.556	0.752	0.870
Make3D [29]	Dense	8.734	0.361	0.280	3.012	0.601	0.820	0.926
Eigen et al. (c[a]) [8]	28 × 144	7.216	0.273	0.194	1.531	0.679	0.897	**0.967**
Eigen et al. (f) [8]	27 × 142	7.156	**0.270**	0.190	1.515	0.692	0.899	**0.967**
Fayao et al. (pt) [24]	superpix	7.421	-	-	-	0.613	0.858	0.949
Fayao et al. (ft) [24]	superpix	7.046	-	-	-	0.656	0.881	0.958

[a] c and f indicates the coarse and fine networks of [8]. Also pt and ft indicates the pre-trained and fine-tuned networks of [24]

Input Image	L9 predictions 27 × 76	Final predictions 176 × 608	Eigen etal 27 × 144*

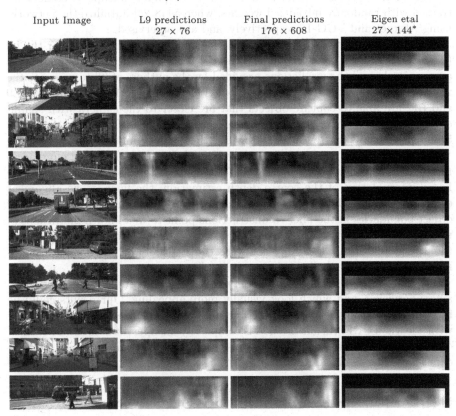

Fig. 5. Inverse Depths visualizations. Brighter color means closer pixel.

(captured without laser sensor) or a vast collection of 3D movies much like recently published work Deep3D [32] to repeat this fine-tuning experiment for single view depth prediction in the wild.

5.4   Comparison with State-of-the-Art Methods on KITTI Dataset

In Table 2, we compare the performance our network with state-of-the-art single view depth prediction methods [8,24,29]. Errors for other methods are taken from [8,24]. Our method achieves the lowest RMS and Square relative error on the dataset and significantly outperforms other methods for these measures. It performs on par with the state-of-the-art methods on all other evaluation measures. Eigen *et al.* [8] obtains slightly lower error in terms of *log* RMS compared to ours. However, as [8,24] are trained by minimizing *log* RMS error with respect to the true depths, we expect the best performance of these methods under same metric.

The most noteworthy point is that our is a completely unsupervised network trained with randomly initialized weights, whereas [8,24] initialize the networks using Alexnet and VGG-16 respectively, and are supervised.

Figure 5 compares the output inverse depthmaps (scaled to [0 1]) for the L9 (2nd column) and L12 (3rd column) layers of the proposed method and [8]. We appropriately pad the predictions provided by the authors of [8] to generate the visualizations at the correct scale. It is evident from the figure that both L9 and L12 are able to capture objects that are closer to the camera with significantly more details. For example, notice the traffic light in Row 4, truck in Row 5 and pedestrians in Row 6 and Row 10; these important scene elements are "washed out" in the predictions generated by [8]. Edges are localized more accurately in L12 results compared to L9. This depicts that even with the simple linear interpolation of the coarse depth estimation, the finer image alignment errors are correctly back-propagated leading to the performance boost. Blurred object boundaries in the finer reconstructions point to well-known limitations of upsampling based approaches which to a certain extent can be addressed with the atrous algorithm [3], a fully connected CRF [18,35] or polynomial interpolations replacing simple linear interpolation layers.

In summary, our simple, skinnier network than [8] gives on par results without any supervision, and which look visually more appealing. Our results could be further refined using better loss functions and replacing linear interpolation filter with a learned CRF. As our method is completely unsupervised, it can be trained on theoretically limitless data with deeper networks to capture variation and give depthmaps at full image resolutions.

5.5   Comparisons with Baseline Supervised Networks and Stereo

As discussed in Sect. 1, an alternative to our proposal of directly minimizing the loss (3), would be to train with a standard "depth loss" using the output of an off-the-shelf stereo algorithm to generate proxy ground-truth depth for

Table 3. Comparison of proposed auto-encoder framework with a supervised CNN trained on stereo data, and stereo baselines on the KITTI dataset.

Methods	Coverage	RMS	log RMS	Absolute relative	Square relative	$\delta < 1.25$	Accuracies $\delta < 1.25^2$	$\delta < 1.25^3$
Ours L12	100 %	**5.285**	**0.282**	**0.177**	**1.169**	**0.727**	**0.896**	**0.958**
HS→ CNN,$\gamma = .01$	100 %	6.691	0.385	0.309	2.657	0.476	0.750	0.891
HS→ CNN	100 %	6.292	0.338	0.238	1.639	0.573	0.841	0.941
SGM→ CNN	100 %	5.680	0.300	0.185	1.370	0.703	0.886	0.955
HS-Stereo, $\gamma = .01$	**100 %**	6.077	0.381	0.299	3.264	0.677	0.822	0.90
HS-Stereo	**100 %**	6.760	0.366	0.254	4.040	0.754	0.872	0.928
SGM-Stereo	87 %	3.030	0.150	0.064	0.506	0.955	0.979	0.989

training. In this section, we substantiate that the proposed autoencoder framework is superior to this alternative approach (which we denote as Stereo → CNN). For this purpose, we train the network described in Fig. 3, end-to-end, with least square loss on the disparity difference between CNN prediction and stereo prediction.[5]

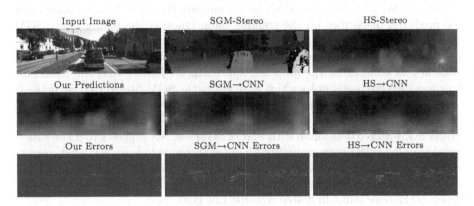

Fig. 6. Comparing depth predictions baseline stereo methods (top row), with the proposed unsupervised CNN (left column-middle row) and Stereo→CNN approaches (center/right column-middle row). Bottom row shows the depth estimation errors as heatmaps for the corresponding methods in middle row.

To generate the stereo prediction, we use a variational Horn-Schunck algorithm. While this is clearly not a state-of-the-art stereo algorithm, it is a fair baseline since this is the same loss on which we train our photometric loss network. We use the OpenCV implementation, with 6 coarse-to-fine pyramid levels with scale factor 0.5. To make sure the algorithm converges properly, we

---

[5] Much like the log depth, inverse depth parametrization is less prone to the higher depth errors at very distant points and is used successfully in many stereo [13] and SLAM frameworks [27].

increased the number of warp iterations to 1000. We additionally tried HS → CNN with the disparity regularization strength $\gamma = 0.01$ as well, but the results were less accurate.

As shown in Table 3, depth prediction accuracy of this HS → CNN baseline falls significantly short of the proposed framework on all accuracy measures. We also incorporate the test-set depth estimation accuracies for the baseline HS-stereo method (which uses both left and right image) for the reference. A very surprising observation is that our single view depth prediction network works on par with even HS-stereo thanks to the common structure present in the road scenes that our network successfully learns. Having access to two images, HS-stereo was able to estimate disparity of the closer points with much more precision but over-reliance on the depth regularization and unawareness of the scene context results in wrong depths near edges – where the single view depth estimation even outperforms the HS Stereo.

In addition to HS-Stereo, we also used Semi Global Matching (SGM) algorithm [16] to supervise the CNN. Semi Global matching is known to produce more accurate depths and is an integral part of many of the state-of-the-art stereo algorithms on KITTI stereo dataset [13]. This stereo method gave very accurate results on the test-set for 87 % of the pixels but left holes in the reconstructions. We train SGM → CNN by minimizing the sum of least square error for predicted disparities on the training data, ignoring the points where SGM gave no disparity. We observed SGM → CNN performed on par with the state-of-the-art fully supervised single view depth estimation algorithm but the results were not as accurate as the proposed approach. We believe that the reason for this was the systematic holes which were left in the SGM-Stereo reconstructions.

To validate this, in Fig. 6 we analyze if regions with lower depth accuracy of SGM→CNN coincide with the holes left by SGM-Stereo. The correlation in errors SGM-Stereo depthmap with that of SGM →CNN suggests that the supervised training with proxy ground-truth indeed is prone to learn systematic errors in the proxy ground truth and advocates need for a more principled integration of a state-of-the-art stereo method with deep learning. The proposed autoencoder setup is the reasonable first step towards this goal.

6   Related Work

In this work we have proposed a geometry-inspired unsupervised setup for visual learning, in particular addressing the problem of single view depth estimation. Our main objective was to address the downsides of training deep networks with large amount of labeled data. Another body of work which attempts to address this issue is the set of methods like [7, 15, 20] which rely mainly on generating synthetic/semi-synthetic training data with the aim to mimic the real world and use it to train deep network in a *supervised* fashion. For example, in [7], CNN is used to discriminate a set of surrogate classes where the data for each class is generated automatically from unlabeled images. The network thus learned is shown to perform well on the task image classification. Handa *et al.* [15] learn a network for semantic segmentation using synthetic data of indoor scenes and show that the network can generalize well on the real-world scenes. Similarly, [20] employs a CNN to learn local image descriptors where the correspondences between the patches are obtained using a multi-view stereo algorithm.

Recently, many methods have used CNN to learn good visual features for matching patches which are sampled from stereo datasets like KITTI [4,34], and match these features while doing classical stereo to achieve state-of-the-art depth estimation. These methods are reliant on local matching and lose global information about the scene; furthermore they use ground-truth. But their success is already an indicator that a joint visual learning and depth estimation approach like ours could be extended at the test time to use a pair of images.

There have been few works recently that approach the problem of novel view synthesis with CNN [10,32]. Deep stereo [10] uses a large set of posed images to learn a CNN that can interpolate between the set of input views that are separated by a wide baseline. A concurrent work with ours, [32] addresses the problem of generating 3D stereo pairs from 2D images. It employs a CNN to infer a soft disparity map from a single view image which in turn is used to render the second view. Although, these methods generate depth-like maps as an intermediate step in the pipeline, their goal however is to generate new views and hence do not evaluate the computed depth maps

Using camera motion as the information for visual learning is also explored in the works like [1,25] which directly regress over the 6DOF camera poses to learn a deep network which performs well on various visual tasks. In contrast to that work, we train our CNN for a more generic task of synthesizing image and get the state-of-the-art single view depth estimation. It will be of immense interest to evaluate the quality of the features learned with our framework on other semantic scene understand tasks.

7   Conclusions

In spite of the enormous growth and success of deep neural networks for a variety of visual tasks, an abiding weakness is the need for vast amounts of annotated training data. We are motivated by the desire to build systems that can be trained relatively cheaply without the need for costly manual labeling or even trained on the fly. To this end we have presented the first convolutional neural network for single-view depth estimation that can be trained end-to-end from scratch, in a fully unsupervised fashion, simply using data captured using a stereo rig. We have shown that our network trained on less than half of the KITTI dataset gives comparable performance to the current state-of-the-art supervised methods for single view depth estimation.

Various natural extensions to our work present themselves. Instead of training on KITTI data (which is nevertheless convenient because it provides a clear baseline) we aim to train on a continuous feed from a stereo rig "in the wild", and to explore the effect on accuracy by augmenting the KITTI data with new stereo pairs. Furthermore, as intimated in the Introduction, our method is not restricted to stereo pairs, and a natural extension is to use a monocular SLAM system to compute camera motion, and use this known motion within our autoencoder framework; here the warp function is slightly more complex than for rectified stereo, but still well understood. The resulting single-view depth estimation system could be used for bootstrapping structure, or generating useful priors on the scene structure that capture much richer information than typical continuity or smoothness assumptions. It also seems likely that the low-level features learned by our system will prove effective for other tasks such as classification, in a manner analogous to [1,7], but this hypothesis remains to be proven experimentally.

Acknowledgments. This research was supported by the Australian Research Council through the Centre of Excellence in Robotic Vision, CE140100016, and through Laureate Fellowship FL130100102 to IDR.

References

1. Agrawal, P., Carreira, J., Malik, J.: Learning to see by moving. In: IEEE International Conference on Computer Vision (ICCV) (2015)
2. Brox, T., Bruhn, A., Papenberg, N., Weickert, J.: High accuracy optical flow estimation based on a theory for warping. In: Pajdla, T., Matas, J.G. (eds.) ECCV 2004. LNCS, vol. 3024, pp. 25–36. Springer, Heidelberg (2004)
3. Chen, L.C., Papandreou, G., Kokkinos, I., Murphy, K., Yuille, A.L.: Semantic image segmentation with deep convolutional nets and fully connected CRFs. In: International Conference on Learning Representations (ICLR) (2015)
4. Chen, Z., Sun, X., Wang, L., Yu, Y., Huang, C.: A deep visual correspondence embedding model for stereo matching costs. In: IEEE International Conference on Computer Vision (ICCV) (2015)
5. Cordts, M., Omran, M., Ramos, S., Rehfeld, T., Enzweiler, M., Benenson, R., Franke, U., Roth, S., Schiele, B.: The cityscapes dataset for semantic urban scene understanding. In: IEEE Conference on Computer Vision and Pattern Recognition (CVPR) (2016)
6. Deng, J., Dong, W., Socher, R., Li, L.J., Li, K., Fei-Fei, L.: ImageNet: a large-scale hierarchical image database. In: IEEE Conference on Computer Vision and Pattern Recognition (CVPR) (2009)
7. Dosovitskiy, A., Springenberg, J.T., Riedmiller, M., Brox, T.: Discriminative unsupervised feature learning with convolutional neural networks. In: Advances in Neural Information Processing Systems (NIPS) (2014)
8. Eigen, D., Puhrsch, C., Fergus, R.: Depth map prediction from a single image using a multi-scale deep network. In: Advances in Neural Information Processing Systems (NIPS) (2014)
9. Fan, X., Zheng, K., Lin, Y., Wang, S.: Combining local appearance and holistic view: dual-source deep neural networks for human pose estimation. In: IEEE Conference on Computer Vision and Pattern Recognition (CVPR) (2015)
10. Flynn, J., Neulander, I., Philbin, J., Snavely, N.: Deepstereo: learning to predict new views from the world's imagery (2016)
11. Garg, R., Pizarro, L., Rueckert, D., Agapito, L.: Dense multi-frame optic flow for non-rigid objects using subspace constraints. In: Kimmel, R., Klette, R., Sugimoto, A. (eds.) ACCV 2010, Part IV. LNCS, vol. 6495, pp. 460–473. Springer, Heidelberg (2011)

12. Garg, R., Roussos, A., Agapito, L.: Dense variational reconstruction of non-rigid surfaces from monocular video. In: IEEE Conference on Computer Vision and Pattern Recognition (CVPR) (2013)
13. Geiger, A., Lenz, P., Stiller, C., Urtasun, R.: Vision meets robotics: the KITTI dataset. Int. J. Robot. Res. (IJRR) **32**, 1229–1235 (2013)
14. Girshick, R., Donahue, J., Darrell, T., Malik, J.: Rich feature hierarchies for accurate object detection and semantic segmentation. In: IEEE Conference on Computer Vision and Pattern Recognition (CVPR) (2014)
15. Handa, A., Patraucean, V., Badrinarayanan, V., Stent, S., Cipolla, R.: Scenenet: understanding real world indoor scenes with synthetic data. arXiv preprint (2015). arXiv:1511.07041
16. Hirschmuller, H.: Accurate and efficient stereo processing by semi-global matching and mutual information. In: IEEE Conference on Computer Vision and Pattern Recognition (CVPR) (2005)
17. Horn, B.K., Schunck, B.G.: Determining optical flow. In: 1981 technical symposium east, pp. 319–331. International Society for Optics and Photonics (1981)
18. Koltun, V.: Efficient inference in fully connected CRFs with Gaussian edge potentials. In: Neural Information Processing Systems (NIPS) (2011)
19. Krizhevsky, A., Sutskever, I., Hinton, G.E.: Imagenet classification with deep convolutional neural networks. In: Advances in Neural Information Processing Systems (NIPS) (2012)
20. Vijay Kumar, B.G., Carneiro, G., Reid, I.: Learning local image descriptors with deep siamese and triplet convolutional networks by minimising global loss functions. In: IEEE Conference on Computer Vision and Pattern Recognition (CVPR) (2016)
21. Ladicky, L., Shi, J., Pollefeys, M.: Pulling things out of perspective. In: IEEE Conference on Computer Vision and Pattern Recognition (CVPR) (2014)
22. Li, B., Shen, C., Dai, Y., van den Hengel, A., He, M.: Depth and surface normal estimation from monocular images using regression on deep features and hierarchical CRFs. In: IEEE Conference on Computer Vision and Pattern Recognition (CVPR) (2015)
23. Lin, T.-Y., Maire, M., Belongie, S., Hays, J., Perona, P., Ramanan, D., Dollár, P., Zitnick, C.L.: Microsoft COCO: common objects in context. In: Fleet, D., Pajdla, T., Schiele, B., Tuytelaars, T. (eds.) ECCV 2014, Part V. LNCS, vol. 8693, pp. 740–755. Springer, Heidelberg (2014)
24. Liu, F., Shen, C., Lin, G., Reid, I.: Learning depth from single monocular images using deep convolutional neural fields. In: IEEE Transactions on Pattern Analysis and Machine Intelligence (2016)
25. Long, G., Kneip, L., Alvarez, J.M., Li, H.: Learning image matching by simply watching video. CoRR abs/1603.06041 (2016). http://arxiv.org/abs/1603.06041
26. Long, J., Shelhamer, E., Darrell, T.: Fully convolutional networks for semantic segmentation. In: IEEE Conference on Computer Vision and Pattern Recognition (CVPR) (2015)
27. Newcombe, R.A., Lovegrove, S.J., Davison, A.J.: Dtam: dense tracking and mapping in real-time. In: IEEE International Conference on Computer Vision (ICCV) (2011)
28. Noh, H., Hong, S., Han, B.: Learning deconvolution network for semantic segmentation. In: IEEE International on Computer Vision (ICCV) (2015)
29. Saxena, A., Sun, M., Ng, A.: Make3d: learning 3d scene structure from a single still image. IEEE Trans. Pattern Anal. Mach. Intell. (PAMI) **31**, 824–840 (2009)

30. Steinbrücker, F., Pock, T., Cremers, D.: Large displacement optical flow computation withoutwarping. In: IEEE International Conference on Computer Vision (ICCV) (2009)
31. Vedaldi, A., Lenc, K.: Matconvnet - convolutional neural networks for matlab (2015)
32. Xie, J., Girshick, R., Farhadi, A.: Deep. 3d: fully automatic 2d-to-3d video conversion with deep convolutional neural networks. arXiv preprint (2016). arXiv:1604.03650
33. Zach, C., Pock, T., Bischof, H.: A duality based approach for realtime TV-L^1 optical flow. In: Hamprecht, F.A., Schnörr, C., Jähne, B. (eds.) Pattern Recognition, vol. 4713, pp. 214–223. Springer, Heidelberg (2007)
34. Zbontar, J., LeCun, Y.: Computing the stereo matching cost with a convolutional neural network. In: IEEE Conference on Computer Vision and Pattern Recognition (CVPR) (2015)
35. Zheng, S., Jayasumana, S., Romera-Paredes, B., Vineet, V., Su, Z., Du, D., Huang, C., Torr, P.H.S.: Conditional random fields as recurrent neural networks. In: IEEE International Conference on Computer Vision (ICCV) (2015)

A Continuous Optimization Approach for Efficient and Accurate Scene Flow

Zhaoyang Lv[1]($\boxtimes$), Chris Beall[1], Pablo F. Alcantarilla[3], Fuxin Li[4],
Zsolt Kira[2], and Frank Dellaert[1]

[1] Georgia Institute of Technology, Atlanta, USA
{zlv30,cbeal3}@gatech.edu, dellaert@cc.gatech.edu
[2] Georgia Tech Research Institute, Atlanta, USA
zkira@gatech.edu
[3] iRobot Corporation, London, UK
palcantarilla@irobot.com
[4] Oregon State University, Corvallis, USA
lif@eecs.oregonstate.edu

Abstract. We propose a continuous optimization method for solving dense 3D scene flow problems from stereo imagery. As in recent work, we represent the dynamic 3D scene as a collection of rigidly moving planar segments. The scene flow problem then becomes the joint estimation of pixel-to-segment assignment, 3D position, normal vector and rigid motion parameters for each segment, leading to a complex and expensive discrete-continuous optimization problem. In contrast, we propose a purely continuous formulation which can be solved more efficiently. Using a fine superpixel segmentation that is fixed a-priori, we propose a factor graph formulation that decomposes the problem into photometric, geometric, and smoothing constraints. We initialize the solution with a novel, high-quality initialization method, then independently refine the geometry and motion of the scene, and finally perform a global non-linear refinement using Levenberg-Marquardt. We evaluate our method in the challenging KITTI Scene Flow benchmark, ranking in third position, while being 3 to 30 times faster than the top competitors (x37 [10] and x3.75 [24]).

Keywords: Scene flow · Stereo · Optical flow · Factor graph · Continuous optimization

1 Introduction

Understanding the geometry and motion within urban scenes, using either monocular or stereo imagery, is an important problem with increasingly relevant applications such as autonomous driving [15], urban scene understanding

Electronic supplementary material The online version of this chapter (doi:10.1007/978-3-319-46484-8_46) contains supplementary material, which is available to authorized users.

© Springer International Publishing AG 2016
B. Leibe et al. (Eds.): ECCV 2016, Part VIII, LNCS 9912, pp. 757–773, 2016.
DOI: 10.1007/978-3-319-46484-8_46

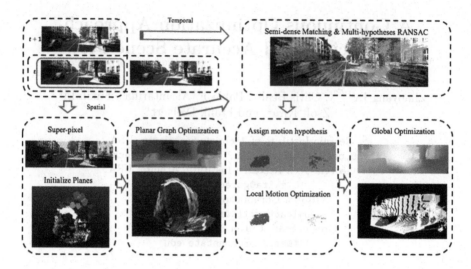

Fig. 1. An overview of our system: we estimate the 3D scene flow w.r.t. the reference image (the red bounding box), a stereo image pair and a temporal image pair as input. Image annotations show the results at each step. We assign a motion hypothesis to each superpixel as an initialization and optimize the factor graph for more accurate 3D motion. Finally, after global optimization, we show a projected 2D flow map in the reference frame and its 3D scene motion (static background are plotted in white). (Color figure online)

[13,15,26], video analysis [7], dynamic reconstruction [12,14], etc. In contrast to separately modeling 3D geometry (stereo) and characterizing the movement of 2D pixels in the image (optical flow), the scene flow problem is to characterize the 3D motion of points in the scene [20] (Fig. 1). Scene flow in the context of stereo sequences was first investigated by Huguet et al. [6]. Recent work [10,19,23] has shown that explicitly reasoning about the scene flow can in turn improve both stereo and optical flow estimation.

Early approaches to scene flow ranged from directly estimating 3D displacement from stereo [30], using volumetric representations [20,21] in a many-camera setting, to re-casting the problem as a 2D disparity flow [6,8] in motion stereo settings. A joint optimization is often leveraged to solve an energy model with all spatio-temporal constraints, e.g. [1,6,10,23], but [19] argues for solving scene and camera motion in an alternating fashion. [25] claims that a decomposed estimation of disparity and motion field can be advantageous as each step can use a different optimization technique to solve the problem more efficiently. A real-time semi-dense scene flow can be achieved without loss of accuracy.

However, efficient and accurate estimation of scene flow is still an unsolved problem. Both dense stereo and optical flow are challenging problems in their own right, and reasoning about the 3D scene must still cope with an equivalent aperture problem [20]. In particular, in scenarios where the scene scale is much larger than the stereo camera baseline, scene motion and depth are hardly distinguishable. Finally, when there is significant motion in the scene there is a large displacement association problem, an unsolved issue for optical flow algorithms.

Recently, approaches based on a rigid moving planar scene assumption have achieved impressive results [10, 22, 23]. In these approaches, the scene is represented using planar segments which are assumed to have consistent motion. The scene flow problem is then posed as a discrete-continuous optimization problem which associates each pixel with a planar segment, each of which has continuous rigid 3D motion parameters to be optimized. Vogel et al. [23] view scene flow as a discrete labeling problem: assign the best label to each super-pixel plane from a set of moving plane proposals. [22] additionally leverages a temporal sequence to achieve consistency both in depth and motion estimation. Their approach casts the entire problem into a discrete optimization problem. However, joint inference in this space is both complex and computationally expensive. Menze and Geiger [10] partially address this by parameter-sharing between multiple planar segments, by assuming the existence of a finite set of moving objects in the scene. They solve the candidate motion of objects with continuous optimization, and use discrete optimization to assign the label of each object to each superpixel. However, this assumption does not hold for scenes with non-rigid deformations. Piece-wise continuous planar assumption is not limited to 3D description. [29] achieves state-of-art optical flow results using planar models.

In contrast to this body of work, we posit that it is better to solve for the scene flow in the continuous domain. We adopt the same rigid planar representation as [23], but solve it more efficiently with high accuracy. Instead of reasoning about discrete labels, we use a fine superpixel segmentation that is fixed a-priori, and utilize a robust nonlinear least-squares approach to cope with occlusion, depth and motion discontinuities in the scene. A central assumption is that once a fine enough superpixel segmentation is used as a priori, there is no need to jointly optimize the superpixel segmentation within the system. The rest of the scene flow problem, being piecewise continuous, can be optimized entirely in continuous domain. A good initialization is obtained by leveraging *DeepMatching* [27]. We achieve fast inference by using a sparse nonlinear least squares solver and avoid discrete approximation. To utilize Census cost for fast robust cost evaluation in continuous optimization, we proposes a differentiable Census-based cost, similar to but not same as the approach in [2].

This work makes the following contributions: first, we propose a factor-graph formulation of the scene flow problem that exposes the inherent sparsity of the problem, and use a state of the art sparse solver that directly optimizes over the manifold representations of the continuous unknowns. Compared to the same representation in [23], we achieve better accuracy and faster inference. Second, instead of directly solving for all unknowns, we propose a pipeline to decompose geometry and motion estimation. We show that this helps us cope with the highly nonlinear nature of the objective function. Finally, as initialization is crucial for nonlinear optimization to succeed, we use the DeepMatching algorithm from [27] to obtain a semi-dense set of feature correspondences from which we initialize the 3D motion of each planar segment. As in [10], we initialize planes from a restricted set of motion hypotheses, but optimize them in the continuous domain to cope with non-rigid objects in the scene.

2   Scene Flow Analysis

We follow [23] in assuming that our 3D world is composed of locally smooth and rigid objects. Such a world can be represented as a set of rigid planes moving in 3D, $\mathcal{P} = \{\bar{n}, \mathcal{X}\}$, with parameters representing the plane normal $\bar{n}$ and motion $\mathcal{X}$. In the ideal case, a slanted plane projects back to one or more superpixels in the images, inside of which the appearance and geometry information are locally similar. The inverse problem is then to infer the 3D planes (parameters $\bar{n}$ and $\mathcal{X}$), given the images and a set of pre-computed superpixels.

3D Plane. We denote a plane as $\bar{n}$ in 3-space, specified by its normal coordinates in the reference frame. For any 3D point $x \in \mathbf{R}^3$ on $\bar{n}$, the plane equation holds as $\bar{n}^\top x + 1 = 0$. We choose this parameterization for ease of optimization on its manifold (refer to Sect. 2.3.)

Plane Motion. A rigid plane transform $\mathcal{X} \in \mathbf{SE}(3)$ comprising rotation and translation is defined by

$$\mathcal{X} = \begin{bmatrix} R & t \\ 0 & 1 \end{bmatrix}, R \in \mathbf{SO}(3), t \in \mathbf{R}^3 \tag{1}$$

Superpixel Associations. We assume each superpixel S_i is a one-to-one mapping from the reference frame to a 3D plane. The boundary between adjacent superpixels S_i and S_j is defined as $\mathcal{E}_{i,j} \in \mathbf{R}^2$.

2.1   Transformation Induced by Moving Planes

For any point x on $\bar{n}$, its homogeneous representation is $[x^\top, -\bar{n}^\top x]$. From x_0 in the reference frame, its corresponding point x_1 in an observed frame is:

$$\begin{bmatrix} x_1 \\ 1 \end{bmatrix} = \begin{bmatrix} R_0^1 & t_0^1 \\ 0 & 1 \end{bmatrix} \begin{bmatrix} R_i & t_i \\ 0 & 1 \end{bmatrix} \begin{bmatrix} x_0 \\ -\bar{n}^T x_0 \end{bmatrix} \tag{2}$$

where $[R_0^1 | t_0^1]$ is the transform from reference frame to the observed image frame (referred to as $\mathcal{T}_0^1$) and $[R_i | t_i]$ is the plane motion in the reference frame (referred to as $\mathcal{X}_i$). Suppose the camera intrinsic matrix as K, A homography transform can thus be induced as:

$$H(\mathcal{P}_i, \mathcal{T}_0^1) = K[A - a\bar{n}]K^{-1}$$
$$\begin{bmatrix} A & a \\ 0 & 1 \end{bmatrix} = \begin{bmatrix} R_0^1 & t_0^1 \\ 0 & 1 \end{bmatrix} \begin{bmatrix} R_i & t_i \\ 0 & 1 \end{bmatrix} \tag{3}$$

In stereo frames where planes are static, the homography from reference frame to the right frame is simply:

$$H(\bar{n}, \mathcal{T}_0^r) = K(R_0^r - t_0^r \bar{n})K^{-1} \tag{4}$$

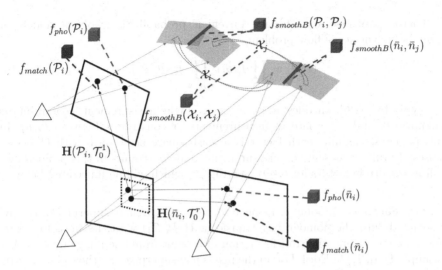

Fig. 2. The proposed factor graph for this scene flow problem. The unary factors are set up based on the homography transform relating two pixels, given $\mathcal{P}$. Binary factors are set up based on locally smooth and rigid assumptions. In this graph, a three-view geometry is used to explain factors for simplicity. Any other views can be constrained by incorporating the same temporal factors in this graph.

We will only use $\mathcal{T}_0^r$ to represent the transform of reference frame to the other stereo frame, while $\mathcal{T}_0^1$ is applicable from reference frame to any other frames, whether the planes are static or moving.

2.2 A Factor Graph Formulation for Scene Flow

For all images $I' : \Omega \to \mathbf{R}$ relative to the reference image $I : \Omega \to \mathbf{R}$, we want to estimate all of the planes $\Theta = \{\bar{\mathbf{n}}_{\{1...N\}}, \mathcal{X}_{\{1...N\}}\}$ observed in I. Besides raw image measurements, we also assume that a set of sparsely matched point pairs $M \in \mathbf{R}^2$ is available. As mentioned above, we assume an a-priori fixed superpixel segmentation S, along with its boundaries $\mathcal{E}$. We denote these as our measurements $\mathcal{M} = \{I, I', M, S, \mathcal{E}\}$.

We begin by defining parameters $\theta = \{\bar{\mathbf{n}}, \mathcal{X}\}$, in which $\bar{\mathbf{n}}$ and $\mathcal{X}$ are independent to each other. We also assume dependencies only exist between superpixels across common edges. The joint probability distribution of Θ can then be:

$$
\begin{aligned}
\mathbf{P}(\Theta, \mathcal{M}) &\propto \prod_{i \in N} \mathbf{P}(\theta_i | \mathcal{M}) \prod_{j \in N \setminus \{i\}} \mathbf{P}(\theta_i, \theta_j | \mathcal{M}) \\
\mathbf{P}(\theta_i | \mathcal{M}) &\propto \mathbf{P}(I', M | \bar{\mathbf{n}}_i, \mathcal{X}_i, S_i, I) \mathbf{P}(\bar{\mathbf{n}}_i) \mathbf{P}(\mathcal{X}_i) \\
\mathbf{P}(\theta_i, \theta_j | \mathcal{M}) &= \mathbf{P}(\bar{\mathbf{n}}_i, \bar{\mathbf{n}}_j | S_i, S_j, \mathcal{E}_{i,j}) \mathbf{P}(\mathcal{X}_i, \mathcal{X}_j | S_i, S_j, \mathcal{E}_{i,j}),
\end{aligned}
\tag{5}
$$

Factor graphs (see e.g., [9]) are convenient probabilistic graphical models for formulating the scene flow problem:

$$G(\Theta) = \prod_{i \in N} f_i(\theta_i) \prod_{i,j \in N} f_{ij}(\theta_i, \theta_j), \tag{6}$$

Typically $f(\theta_i)$ encodes a prior or a single measurement constraint at unknown θ, and $f_{i,j}$ relate to measurements or constraints between θ_i, θ_j. In this paper, we assume each factor is a least-square error term with Gaussian noises. To fully represent the measurements and constraints in this problem, we will use multiple factors for $G(\Theta)$ (see Fig. 2), which will be illustrated below.

Unary Factors. A point p, associated with a particular superpixels, can be associated with the homography transform $\mathbf{H}(\mathcal{P}_i, \mathcal{T}_s)$ w.r.t. its measurements. For a stereo camera, the transformation of a point from one image to the other is simply $\mathbf{H}(\bar{\mathbf{n}}, \mathcal{T}_s)$ in Eq. 4. For all the pixels p in superpixel S_i, their photometric costs given $\mathcal{P}\{\bar{\mathbf{n}}_i, \mathcal{X}_i\}$ is described by factor $f_{pho}(\mathcal{P}_i)$:

$$f_{pho}(\mathcal{P}_i) \propto \prod_{p \in S_i} f\big(C(p'), C(\mathbf{H}(\mathcal{P}_i, \mathcal{T}_0^1)p)\big), \tag{7}$$

where $C(\cdot)$ is the Census descriptor. This descriptor is preferred over intensity error for its robustness against noise and edges. Similarly, using the homography transform and with sparse matches we can estimate the geometric error of match m by measuring its consistency with the corresponding plane motion:

$$f_{match}(\mathcal{P}_i) \propto \prod_{p \in S_i} f\big(p + m, \mathbf{H}(\mathcal{P}_i, \mathcal{T}_0^1)p\big), \tag{8}$$

Pairwise Factors. The pairwise factors relate the parameters based on their constraints. $f_{smoothB}(\cdot, \cdot)$ describes the locally smooth assumption that adjacent planes should share similar boundary connectivity:

$$f_{smoothB}(\bar{\mathbf{n}}_i, \bar{\mathbf{n}}_j) \propto \prod_{p \in \mathcal{E}_{i,j}} f\big(D^{-1}(\bar{\mathbf{n}}_i, p), D^{-1}(\bar{\mathbf{n}}_j, p)\big), \tag{9}$$

where $D^{-1}(\bar{\mathbf{n}}, p)$ represents the inverse depth of pixel p on $\bar{\mathbf{n}}$. This factor describes the distance of points over the boundary of two static planes. After plane motion, we expect the boundary to still be connected after the transformation:

$$f_{smoothB}(\mathcal{P}_i, \mathcal{P}_j) \propto \prod_{p \in \mathcal{E}_{i,j}} f\big(D^{-1}(\mathcal{P}_i, p), D^{-1}(\mathcal{P}_j, p)\big), \tag{10}$$

With our piece-wise smooth motion assumption, we also expect that two adjacent superpixels should share similar motion parameters, described by $f_{smoothM}$, which is a *Between* operator of $\mathbf{SE}(3)$:

$$f_{smoothM}(\mathcal{X}_i, \mathcal{X}_j) \propto f(\mathcal{X}_i, \mathcal{X}_j). \tag{11}$$

Each factor is created as a Gaussian noise model: $f(x; m) = \exp(-\rho(h(x) - m)_\Sigma)$ for unary factor and $f(x_1, x_2) = \exp(-\rho(h_1(x_1) - h_2(x_2))_\Sigma)$ for binary factor. $\rho(\cdot)_\Sigma$ is the Huber robust cost which measures the Mahalanobis norm. It incorporates the noise effect of each factor and down-weights the effect of outliers. Given a decent initialization, this robust kernel helps us to cope with occlusions, depth and motion discontinuities properly.

2.3 Continuous Optimization of Factor Graph on Manifold

The factor graph in Eq. 5 can be estimated via maximum a posteriori (MAP) as a non-linear least square problem, and solved with standard non-linear optimization methods. In each step, we linearize all the factors at $\theta = \{\bar{n}_\theta, \mathcal{X}_\theta\}$. On manifold, the update is a *Retraction* $\mathcal{R}_\theta$. The retraction for $\{\bar{n}, \mathcal{X}\}$ is:

$$\mathcal{R}_\theta(\delta\bar{n}, \delta\mathcal{X}) = (\bar{n} + \delta\bar{n}, \mathcal{X}\mathrm{Exp}(\delta x)), [\delta\bar{n} \in \mathbf{R}^3, \delta x \in \mathbf{R}^6] \tag{12}$$

For $\bar{n} \in \mathbf{R}^3$, it has the same value of its tangent space at any value $\hat{n}$. This explains our choice of plane representation: it is the most convenient for manifold optimization in all of its families in 3-space. For motion in $\mathbf{SE}(3)$, the retraction is an exponential map.

Although the linearized factor graph can be thought of as a huge matrix, it is actually quite sparse in nature: pairwise factors only exist between adjacent superpixels. Sparse matrix factorization can solve this kind of problem very efficiently. We follow the same sparse matrix factorization which is discussed in detail in [4].

2.4 Continuous Approximation for Census Transform

In Eq. 7, there are two practical issues: first, we cannot get a sub-pixel Census Transform; and second, the Hamming distance between the two descriptors is not differentiable. To overcome these problems, we use bilinear interpolated distance as the census cost (see Fig. 3). The bilinear interpolation equation is differentiable w.r.t. the image coordinate, from which we can approximately get the Jacobian of Census Distance w.r.t. to a sub-pixel point. We use a 9×7 size Census, and set up Eq. 7 over a pyramid of images. In evaluation, we will discuss how this process helps us to achieve better convergence purely with a data-cost.

3 Scene Flow Estimation

The general pipeline of our algorithms consists of five steps (see Fig. 1). We summarize each step and provide detailed descriptions in the subsections below.

Initialization. We initialize the superpixels for the reference frame. For both of the stereo pairs, we estimate a depth map as priors. The 3D plane is initialized from the depth map using RANSAC.

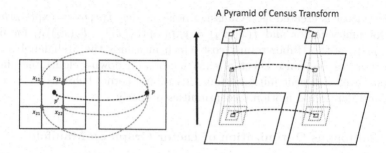

Fig. 3. The left figure shows how to use bilinear interpolation to achieve a differentiable cost of Census Transform. In the right figure, a census descriptor is extracted at different pyramid levels of the images. When evaluating its distance w.r.t. another pixel, we also use bilinear interpolation to evaluate census cost at lower resolution images.

Planar Graph Optimization. We solve the factor graph composed of factors in Eqs. 7, 8 and 9. The result is the estimation of plane geometry parameter $\bar{n}$ w.r.t. reference frame.

Estimation of Motion Hypotheses. We first estimate a semi-dense matching from reference frame to the next temporal frame and associate them with our estimated 3D plane to get a set of 3D features. We use RANSAC to heuristically find a set of motion hypothesis. In each RANSAC step, we find the most likely motion hypothesis of Eq. 3 by minimizing the re-projection errors of 3D features in two temporally consecutive frames. A set of motion hypotheses are generated by iterating this process.

Local Motion Graph Optimization. We initialize the motion of superpixels from the set of motion hypotheses, framed as a Bayesian classification problem. For all of the superpixels assigned to one single motion hypothesis, we estimate both the plane $\bar{n}$ and its motion $\mathcal{X}$, by incorporating factors in Eqs. 7, 10 and 11.

Global Graph Optimization. In this step, the set of all unknowns $\mathcal{P}$ is estimated globally. All factors from Eqs. 7–11 are used.

3.1 Initialization

The superpixels in the reference frame are initialized with the sticky-edge superpixels introduced in [31]. Since the urban scene is complex in appearance, the initialized superpixel number needs to be large to cope with tiny objects, while too many superpixels can cause an under-constrained condition for some plane parameters. Empirically, we find generating 2,000 superpixels is a good balance (refer to our superpixel discussion in supplement materials.)

We use the stereo method proposed in [28] to generate the stereo prior, and initialize the 3D planes with a plane-fitting RANSAC algorithm. The plane is initialized as frontal parallel if the RANSAC inlier percentage is below a certain threshold (50 % in our setting), or the plane induces a degenerated homography transform (where the plane is parallel to the camera focal axis).

We sample robust matches $\mathcal{M}$ from the disparity map, and use it to set up the matching factor in Eq. 8. The samples are selected from the Census Transform which share a maximum distance of 3 bits, given the disparity matching.

3.2 Planar Graph Optimization

In the stereo factor graph, we only estimate the planes $\bar{n}$ from the factors in Eq. 7, i.e. we constrain the motion $\mathcal{X}$ to be constant (Eqs. 8 and 9). Suppose for each Gaussian noise factor, r is its residual: $f(x) = \exp(-r(x))$. We can obtain the maximum a posterior (MAP) of the factor graph by minimizing the residuals in the least-square problem:

$$
\begin{aligned}
\bar{n}^\star &= \text{argmax}_{\bar{n}} \prod f_{pho}(\bar{n}_i) \cdot \prod f_{match}(\bar{n}_i) \cdot \prod f_{smoothB}(\bar{n}_i, \bar{n}_j) \\
&= \text{argmin}_{\bar{n}} \sum r_{pho}(\bar{n}_i) + \sum r_{match}(\bar{n}_i) + \sum r_{smoothB}(\bar{n}_i, \bar{n}_j)
\end{aligned}
\tag{13}
$$

Levenberg-Marquardt can be used to solve this equation as a more robust choice (e.g. compared to Gauss-Newton), trading off efficiency for accuracy.

3.3 Semi-dense Matching and Multi-hypotheses RANSAC

We leverage the state-of-art matching method [27] to generate a semi-dense matching field, which has the advantage of being able to associate across large displacements in the image space. To estimate the initial motion for superpixels, we chose RANSAC similar to [10]. We classify putatives as inliers based on their re-projection errors. The standard-deviation $\sigma = 1$ is small to ensure that bad hypotheses are rare. All hypotheses with more than 20 % inliers in each step are retained. Compared to the up-to-5 hypotheses in [10], we found empirically that our RANSAC strategy can retrieve 10–20 hypotheses in complex scenes, which ensures a high recall of even small moving objects, or motion patterns on non-rigid objects (e.g. pedestrians and cyclists). This process can be quite slow when noisy matches are prominent and inliers ratios are low. To cope with this effect, we use superpixels as a prior in RANSAC. We evaluate the inlier superpixels (indicated by inlier feature matches through non-maximum suppression), and reject conflicting feature matches as outliers. This prunes the number of motion hypotheses, and substantially speeds up this step. See Fig. 4 for an illustration of the motion hypotheses.

Since the most dominant transform in the scene is induced by the camera transform, we can get an estimate of the incremental camera transform in the first iteration. After each iteration, the hypothesis is refined by a weighted least squares optimization, solved efficiently by Levenberg-Marquardt.

Fig. 4. A visualization of motion hypothesis (left), optical flow (middle), and scene motion flow (right). Camera motion is explicitly removed from scene motion flow. In the image of the cyclist we show that although multiple motion hypotheses are discovered by RANSAC (in two colors), a final smooth motion over this non-rigid entity is estimated with continuous optimization. (Color figure online)

3.4 Local Motion Estimation

After estimation of the plane itself, we initialize the motion $\mathcal{X}_i$ of each individual plane from the set of motion hypotheses. At this step, given the raw image measurements $I_{0,1}$, a pair of estimated depth maps in both frames $D_{0,1}$, and the sparse point-matching field F, the goal is to estimate the most probable hypothesis $l^\star$ for each individual superpixel. We assume a set of conditional independencies among $I_{0,1}$, $D_{0,1}$, and F, given the superpixel. The label l for each superpixel can therefore be inferred from the Bayes rule:

$$
\begin{aligned}
P(l|F, I_{0,1}, D_{0,1}) &\propto P(F, I_{0,1}, D_{0,1}|l)P(l) \\
&\propto P(I_{0,1}|l)P(D_{0,1}|l)P(F, I_0, D_0|l)P(l),
\end{aligned}
\tag{14}
$$

Assuming each motion hypothesis has equally prior information, a corresponding MAP estimation to the above equation can be presented as:

$$
l^\star = \mathrm{argmax}_{l^\star} \; \mathbf{E}_{depth}(l) + \alpha\mathbf{E}_{photometric}(l) + \beta\mathbf{E}_{cluster}(l),
\tag{15}
$$

where $\mathbf{E}_{depth}(l)$ represents the depth error between the warped depth and transformed depth, given a superpixel and its plane; $\mathbf{E}_{photometric}(l)$ represents the photometric error between the superpixel and its warped superpixel; $\mathbf{E}_{cluster}(l)$ represents the clustering error of a superpixel, w.r.t. its neighborhood features:

$$
\mathbf{E}_{depth}(l) = \sum_{p_i \in S} (D_1(\mathbf{H}p_i) - z(\mathbf{H}p_i))^2,
$$

$$
\mathbf{E}_{photometric}(l) = \sum_{p_i \in S} (I(p_i) - I(\mathbf{H}p_i))^2,
\tag{16}
$$

$$
\mathbf{E}_{cluster}(l) = \sum_{p_i \in S} \sum_{p_k \in F_l} \exp(-\frac{\bigtriangledown I_{i,k}^2}{\sigma_i^2}) \exp(-\frac{\bigtriangledown D_{i,k}^2}{\sigma_D^2}),
$$

where $\mathbf{H}$ is the homography transform and $z(p)$ is the depth at pixel p. $\bigtriangledown I_{i,k}^2$ and $\bigtriangledown D_{i,k}^2$ describes the color and depth difference of a pixel $p_i \in S$ to a feature point $p_k \in F_l$ belonging to hypothesis l. σ_I and σ_D are their variances.

A local motion optimization is done for each hypothesis by incorporating the factors 7, 8, 10, 11 with pre-estimated planes values as:

$$\mathcal{X}^* = \underset{\mathcal{X}}{\operatorname{argmin}} \sum r_{pho}(\mathcal{X}_i) + \sum r_{match}(\mathcal{X}_i) + \sum r_{smoothB}(\mathcal{X}_i, \mathcal{X}_j)$$
$$+ \sum r_{smoothM}(\mathcal{X}_i, \mathcal{X}_j) + \sum r_{prior}(\mathcal{M}). \tag{17}$$

Similar to Eq. 13, r is the residual for each factor. We add a prior factor $f_{prior}(\cdot)$ to enforce an L_2 prior centered at 0. It works as a diagonal term to improve the condition numbers in the matrix factorization. The prior factor has small weights and in general do not affect the accuracy or speed significantly.

3.5   Global Optimization

Finally, we estimate the global factor graph, with the complete set of parameters $\mathcal{P} = \{\bar{n}, \mathcal{X}\}$ in the reference frame. The factors in this stage are set using measurements in all of the other three views, w.r.t. reference image.

$$\mathcal{P}^* = \underset{\mathcal{P}}{\operatorname{argmin}} \sum r_{pho}(\mathcal{P}_i) + \sum r_{match}(\mathcal{P}_i) + \sum r_{smoothB}(\mathcal{P}_i, \mathcal{P}_j)$$
$$+ \sum r_{smoothM}(\mathcal{P}_i, \mathcal{P}_j) + \sum r_{prior}(\mathcal{P}_i) \tag{18}$$

4   Experiments and Evaluations

Our factors and optimization algorithm are implemented using GTSAM [3]. As input to our method, we use super-pixels generated from [31], a fast stereo prior from [28], and the DeepMatching method in [27]. The noise models and robust kernel thresholds of the Gaussian factors are selected based on the first 100 training images in KITTI. In the next subsections, we discuss the results as well as optimization and individual factor contribution to the results.

4.1   Evaluation over KITTI

We evaluate our algorithm on the challenging KITTI Scene Flow benchmark [10], which is a realistic benchmark in outdoor environments. In the KITTI benchmark, our method ranks *3rd in Scene Flow test* while being significantly faster than close competitors, as well as *3nd in the KITTI Optical Flow test* and 11th in the stereo test which we did not explicitly target. We show our quantitative scene flow results in Table 1 and qualitative visualizations in Fig. 6.

Table 1 shows a comparison of our results against the other top 4 publicly-evaluated scene flow algorithms. In addition, we also added [6] (which proposed the four-image setting in scene flow) as a general comparison. In all of these results, the errors in disparity and flow evaluation are counted if the disparity or flow estimation exceeds 3 pixels and 5 % of its true value. In the Scene Flow evaluation, the error is counted if any pixel in any of the three estimates (two

Table 1. Quantitative Results on KITTI Scene Flow Test Benchmark. We show the disparity errors reference frame (D1) and second frame (D2), flow error (Fl), and the scene flow (SF) in 200 test images on KITTI. The errors are reported as background (bg), foregound (fg), and all pixels (bg+fg), OCC for errors over all areas, NOC only for errors non-occluded areas.

Method	Occlusion (OCC) error												time
	D1			D2			Fl			SF			
	bg %	fg %	all %	bg %	fg %	all %	bg %	fg %	all %	bg %	fg %	all %	
PRSM [24]	**3.02**	**10.52**	**4.27**	**5.13**	**15.11**	**6.79**	**5.33**	**17.02**	**7.28**	**6.61**	**23.60**	**9.44**	300 s
OSF [10]	4.54	12.03	5.79	5.45	19.41	7.77	5.62	22.17	8.37	7.01	28.76	10.63	50 min
PRSF [23]	4.74	13.74	6.24	11.14	20.47	12.69	11.73	27.73	14.39	13.49	33.72	16.85	150 s
SGM+SF [5]	5.15	15.29	6.84	14.10	23.13	15.60	20.91	28.90	22.24	23.09	37.12	25.43	45 min
SGM+C+NL [18]	5.15	15.29	6.84	28.77	25.65	28.25	34.24	45.40	36.10	38.21	53.04	40.68	4.5 min
VSF [6]	27.73	21.72	26.38	59.51	44.93	57.08	50.06	47.57	49.64	67.69	64.03	67.08	125 min
Ours	4.57	13.04	5.98	7.92	20.76	10.06	10.40	30.33	13.71	12.21	36.97	16.33	**80 s**
Method	Non-Occlusion (NOC) error												time
	D1			D2			Fl			SF			
	bg %	fg %	all %	bg %	fg %	all %	bg %	fg %	all	bg %	fg %	all	
PRSM [24]	**2.93**	**10.00**	**4.10**	**4.13**	**12.85**	**5.69**	4.33	**14.15**	**6.11**	**5.54**	**20.16**	**8.16**	300 s
OSF [10]	4.14	11.12	5.29	4.49	16.33	6.61	**4.21**	18.65	6.83	5.52	24.58	8.93	50 min
PRSF [23]	4.41	13.09	5.84	6.35	16.12	8.10	6.94	23.64	9.97	8.35	28.45	11.95	150 s
SGM+SF [5]	4.75	14.22	6.31	8.34	18.71	10.20	13.36	25.21	15.51	15.28	32.33	18.33	45 min
SGM+C+NL [18]	4.75	14.22	6.31	15.72	20.79	16.63	23.03	41.92	26.46	26.22	48.61	30.23	4.5 min
VSF [6]	26.38	19.88	25.31	52.30	40.83	50.24	41.15	44.16	41.70	61.14	60.38	61.00	125 min
Ours	4.03	11.82	5.32	6.39	16.75	8.25	8.72	26.98	12.03	10.26	32.58	14.26	**80 s**

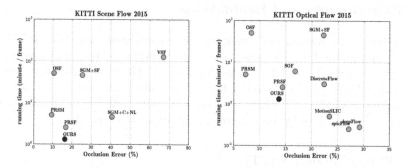

Fig. 5. Occlusion error-vs-time on KITTI. The running time axis is plotted in log scale. Our method is highlighted as green, which achieves top performance both in accuracy and computation speed. (Color figure online)

stereo frame disparity images and flow image) exceed the criterion. We plot a error-vs-time figure in Fig. 5, which shows that our method achieves state-of-art performance, when considering both efficiency and accuracy.

Our results show a small difference in occlusion-errors, although occlusion is not directly handled as discrete labels. We follow the same representation in [23] and achieved better performance in overall pixel errors and faster inference.

Compared to all of these methods, our method is the fastest. Detailed test results are presented in our supplementary materials.

Table 2. Quantitative Results on KITTI Optical Flow 2015 Dataset. The errors are reported as background error(Fl-bg), foreground error (Fl-fg), and all pixels (Fl-bg+Fl-fg), NOC for non-occluded areas error and OCC for errors over all pixels. Methods that use stereo information are shown as *italic*.

Method	OCC error			NOC error			time
	Fl-bg %	Fl-fg %	all %	Fl-bg %	Fl-fg %	all %	
PRSM [24]	**5.33**	**17.02**	**7.28**	4.33	**14.15**	**6.11**	300 s
OSF [10]	5.62	22.17	8.37	**4.21**	18.65	6.83	50 min
PRSF [23]	11.73	27.32	14.39	6.94	23.64	9.97	150 s
SOF [17]	14.63	27.73	16.81	8.11	23.28	10.86	6 min
SGM SF[5]	20.91	28.90	22.24	13.36	25.21	15.51	45 min
DiscreteFlow [11]	21.53	26.68	22.38	9.96	22.17	12.18	3 min
MotionSLIC [28]	14.86	66.21	23.40	6.19	64.82	16.83	30 s
epicFlow [16]	25.81	33.56	27.10	15.00	29.39	17.61	**15 s**
deepFlow [27]	27.96	35.28	29.18	16.47	31.25	19.15	17s
ours	10.40	30.33	13.71	8.72	26.98	12.03	80 s

Table 2 shows our method compared to state-of-art optical flow methods. Methods using stereo information are shown in italic. The deepFlow [27] and epicFlow [16] methods are also presented; these also leverage DeepMatching for data-association. Our method is third best for all-pixels estimation.

4.2 Parameter Discussions

In Table 3, we evaluate the choice of each factor and their effects in the results. During motion estimation, we see that multi-scale Census has an important positive effect in improving convergence towards the optima. Note that the best choice of weights for each factor was tuned by using a similar analysis. A more detailed parameter analyses is presented in the supplement materials.

5 Conclusions

We present an approach to solve the scene flow problem in continuous domain, resulting in a high accuracy (3rd) on the KITTI Scene Flow benchmark at a large computational speedup. We show that faster inference is achievable by rethinking the solution as a non-linear least-square problem, cast within a factor graph formulation. We then develop a novel initialization method, leveraging a multi-scale differentiable Census-based cost and DeepMatching. Given this

Table 3. Evaluation over factors. The non-occlusion error are used from 50 images of KITTI training set. The corresponding factors (in braces) are in Sect. 2.2

Stereo error % (Noc)				Flow error % (Noc)			
Factors	D1-bg %	D1-fg %	D1-all %	Factors	F-bg %	F-fg %	F-all %
Census (7)	9.21	19.22	12.31	Census raw only (7)	10.9	34.25	14.20
Matching (8)	5.95	15.20	7.62	Census multi-scale (7)	9.3	30.13	12.45
Census + matching (7, 8)	5.66	15.01	6.93	Matching only (8)	10.5	33.40	13.20
Census + continuity (7, 9)	4.85	14.22	5.94	Census + piecewise motion (7, 11)	9.0	29.01	12.45
All (7, 8, 9)	4.13	10.20	4.85	Census + continuity (7, 10)	9.2	30.15	12.44
				All (7, 8, 11, 10)	8.92	28.92	12.31

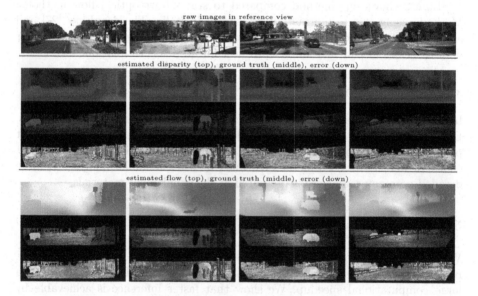

raw images in reference view

estimated disparity (top), ground truth (middle), error (down)

estimated flow (top), ground truth (middle), error (down)

Fig. 6. Qualitative Results in KITTI. We show the disparity and flow estimation against the ground truth results in Kitti Scene Flow training set.

initialization, we individually optimize geometry (stereo) and motion (optical flow) and then perform a global refinement using Levenberg-Marquardt. Analysis shows the positive effects of each of these contributions, ultimately leading to a fast and accurate scene flow estimation.

The proposed method has already achieved significant speed and accuracy, and several enhancements are possible. For example, there are several challenging points and failure cases that we do not cope with so far, such as photometric inconsistency in scenes and areas with aperture ambiguity. To address these problems, we expect to explore more invariant constraints than the current unary factors, and more prior knowledge to enforce better local consistency. Finally, it is possible that additional speed-ups could be achieved through profiling and optimization of the code. Such improvements in both accuracy and speed would enable a host of applications related to autonomous driving, where both are crucial factors.

Acknowledgments. This work was supported by the National Science Foundation and National Robotics Initiative (grant # IIS-1426998). Fuxin Li was partially supported by NSF # 1320348.

References

1. Basha, T., Moses, Y., Kiryati, N.: Multi-view scene flow estimation: a view centered variational approach. Int. J. Comput. Vis. **101**, 6–21 (2012)
2. Vogel, C., Roth, S., Schindler, K.: An evaluation of data costs for optical flow. In: Weickert, J., Hein, M., Schiele, B. (eds.) GCPR 2013. LNCS, vol. 8142, pp. 343–353. Springer, Heidelberg (2013)
3. Dellaert, F.: Factor graphs and GTSAM: a hands-on introduction. Technical report, GT-RIM-CP&R-2012-002, Georgia Institute of Technology, September 2012
4. Dellaert, F., Kaess, M.: Square Root SAM: simultaneous localization and mapping via square root information smoothing. Intl. J. Robot. Re. **25**(12), 1181–1203 (2006)
5. Hornacek, M., Fitzgibbon, A., Rother, C.: SphereFlow: 6 DOF scene flow from RGB-D pairs. In: IEEE Conference on Computer Vision and Pattern Recognition (CVPR), June 2014
6. Huguet, F., Devernay, F.: A variational method for scene flow estimation from stereo sequences. In: International Conference on Computer Vision (ICCV). IEEE (2007)
7. Hung, C.H., Xu, L., Jia, J.: Consistent binocular depth and scene flow with chained temporal profiles. Intl. J. Comput. Vis. **102**(1–3), 271–292 (2013)
8. Isard, M., MacCormick, J.: Dense motion and disparity estimation via loopy belief propagation. In: Narayanan, P.J., Nayar, S.K., Shum, H.-Y. (eds.) ACCV 2006. LNCS, vol. 3852, pp. 32–41. Springer, Heidelberg (2006)
9. Kschischang, F., Frey, B., Loeliger, H.A.: Factor graphs and the sum-product algorithm. IEEE Trans. Inf. Theor. **47**(2), 498–519 (2001)
10. Menze, M., Geiger, A.: Object scene flow for autonomous vehicles. In: IEEE Conference on Computer Vision and Pattern Recognition (CVPR) (2015)

11. Menze, M., Heipke, C., Geiger, A.: Discrete optimization for optical flow. In: Gall, J., Gehler, P., Leibe, B. (eds.) GCPR 2015. LNCS, vol. 9358, pp. 16–28. Springer, Heidelberg (2015). doi:10.1007/978-3-319-24947-6_2

12. Newcombe, R.A., Fox, D., Seitz, S.M.: Dynamicfusion: reconstruction and tracking of non-rigid scenes in real-time. In: IEEE Conference on Computer Vision and Pattern Recognition (CVPR), June 2015

13. Pfeiffer, D., Franke, U.: Efficient representation of traffic scenes by means of dynamic stixels. In: Proceedings of the IEEE Intelligent Vehicles Symposium, San Diego, CA, pp. 217–224, June 2010

14. Pons, J.P., Keriven, R., Faugeras, O.: Multi-view stereo reconstruction and scene flow estimation with a global image-based matching score. Intl. J. Comput. Vis. **72**(2), 179–193 (2007)

15. Rabe, C., Müller, T., Wedel, A., Franke, U.: Dense, robust, and accurate motion field estimation from stereo image sequences in real-time. In: Daniilidis, K., Maragos, P., Paragios, N. (eds.) ECCV 2010, Part IV. LNCS, vol. 6314, pp. 582–595. Springer, Heidelberg (2010)

16. Revaud, J., Weinzaepfel, P., Harchaoui, Z., Schmid, C.: EpicFlow: edge-preserving interpolation of correspondences for optical flow. In: IEEE Conference on Computer Vision and Pattern Recognition (CVPR) (2015)

17. Sevilla-Lara, L., Sun, D., Jampani, V., Black, M.J.: Optical flow with semantic segmentation and localized layers. In: IEEE Conference on Computer Vision and Pattern Recognition (CVPR) (2016)

18. Sun, D., Roth, S., Black, M.J.: A quantitative analysis of current practices in optical flow estimation and the principles behind them. Intl. J. Comput. Vis. **106**(2), 115–137 (2014). doi:10.1007/s11263-013-0644-x

19. Valgaerts, L., Bruhn, A., Zimmer, H., Weickert, J., Stoll, C., Theobalt, C.: Joint estimation of motion, structure and geometry from stereo sequences. In: Daniilidis, K., Maragos, P., Paragios, N. (eds.) ECCV 2010, Part IV. LNCS, vol. 6314, pp. 568–581. Springer, Heidelberg (2010)

20. Vedula, S., Baker, S., Rander, P., Collins, R., Kanade, T.: Three-dimensional scene flow. In: International Conference on Computer Vision (ICCV), vol. 2, pp. 722–729 (1999)

21. Vedula, S., Baker, S., Rander, P., Collins, R.T., Kanade, T.: Three-dimensional scene flow. IEEE Trans. Pattern Anal. Machine Intell. **27**(3), 475–480 (2005)

22. Vogel, C., Roth, S., Schindler, K.: View-consistent 3D scene flow estimation over multiple frames. In: Fleet, D., Pajdla, T., Schiele, B., Tuytelaars, T. (eds.) ECCV 2014, Part IV. LNCS, vol. 8692, pp. 263–278. Springer, Heidelberg (2014)

23. Vogel, C., Schindler, K., Roth, S.: Piecewise rigid scene flow. In: International Conference on Computer Vision (ICCV), pp. 1377–1384 (2013)

24. Vogel, C., Schindler, K., Roth, S.: 3D scene flow estimation with a piecewise rigid scene model. Intl. J. Comput. Vis. **115**(1), 1–28 (2015)

25. Wedel, A., Brox, T., Vaudrey, T., Rabe, C., Franke, U., Cremers, D.: Stereoscopic scene flow computation for 3D motion understanding. Intl. J. Comput. Vis. **95**(1), 29–51 (2011)

26. Wedel, A., Rabe, C., Vaudrey, T., Brox, T., Franke, U., Cremers, D.: Efficient dense scene flow from sparse or dense stereo data. In: Forsyth, D., Torr, P., Zisserman, A. (eds.) ECCV 2008, Part I. LNCS, vol. 5302, pp. 739–751. Springer, Heidelberg (2008)

27. Weinzaepfel, P., Revaud, J., Harchaoui, Z., Schmid, C.: DeepFlow: large displacement optical flow with deep matching. In: International Conference on Computer Vision (ICCV) (2013)

28. Yamaguchi, K., McAllester, D., Urtasun, R.: Efficient joint segmentation, occlusion labeling, stereo and flow estimation. In: Fleet, D., Pajdla, T., Schiele, B., Tuytelaars, T. (eds.) ECCV 2014, Part V. LNCS, vol. 8693, pp. 756–771. Springer, Heidelberg (2014)
29. Yang, J., Li, H.: Dense, accurate optical flow estimation with piecewise parametric model. In: IEEE Conference on Computer Vision and Pattern Recognition (CVPR), pp. 1019–1027 (2015)
30. Zhang, Z., Faugeras, O.D.: Estimation of displacements from two 3-D frames obtained from stereo. IEEE Trans. Pattern Anal. Mach. Intell. **14**(12), 1141–1156 (1992). http://dx.doi.org/10.1109/34.177380
31. Zitnick, C.L., Dollár, P.: Edge boxes: locating object proposals from edges. In: Fleet, D., Pajdla, T., Schiele, B., Tuytelaars, T. (eds.) ECCV 2014, Part V. LNCS, vol. 8693, pp. 391–405. Springer, Heidelberg (2014)

Improving Multi-frame Data Association with Sparse Representations for Robust Near-online Multi-object Tracking

Loïc Fagot-Bouquet[1]([⊠]), Romaric Audigier[1],
Yoann Dhome[1], and Frédéric Lerasle[2,3]

[1] CEA, LIST, Vision and Content Engineering Laboratory,
Point Courrier 173, 91191 Gif-sur-Yvette, France
{loic.fagot-bouquet,romaric.audigier,yoann.dhome}@cea.fr
[2] CNRS, LAAS, 7, Avenue du Colonel Roche, 31400 Toulouse, France
[3] Université de Toulouse, UPS, LAAS, 31400 Toulouse, France
lerasle@laas.fr

Abstract. Multiple Object Tracking still remains a difficult problem due to appearance variations and occlusions of the targets or detection failures. Using sophisticated appearance models or performing data association over multiple frames are two common approaches that lead to gain in performances. Inspired by the success of sparse representations in Single Object Tracking, we propose to formulate the multi-frame data association step as an energy minimization problem, designing an energy that efficiently exploits sparse representations of all detections. Furthermore, we propose to use a structured sparsity-inducing norm to compute representations more suited to the tracking context. We perform extensive experiments to demonstrate the effectiveness of the proposed formulation, and evaluate our approach on two public authoritative benchmarks in order to compare it with several state-of-the-art methods.

Keywords: Multiple Object Tracking · Tracking by detection · Multiple frame data association · Sparse representation · MCMC sampling

1 Introduction

Multiple Object Tracking (MOT) aims to estimate the trajectories of several targets in a scene. It is still a challenging problem in computer vision and has a large number of potential applications from video-surveillance to embedded systems. Thanks to the recent advances in object detection, MOT community has strongly focused on the *tracking-by-detection* technique where object detections are grouped in order to estimate the correct tracks. However, despite this data

---

Electronic supplementary material The online version of this chapter (doi:10.1007/978-3-319-46484-8_47) contains supplementary material, which is available to authorized users.

B. Leibe et al. (Eds.): ECCV 2016, Part VIII, LNCS 9912, pp. 774–790, 2016.
DOI: 10.1007/978-3-319-46484-8_47

association formulation of the problem, tracking multiple objects remains a challenging problem due to frequent occlusions and interactions of targets, similar appearances between targets, pose variations, and object detection failures.

In the literature, the problem is addressed by a large variety of approaches, from *online* (or single-scan) techniques [1–4] where only the previous frames are considered, to *offline* approaches using past and future frames. Among offline techniques, global approaches perform the data association over all the frames simultaneously or by batch [5–15], whereas *sliding window* (a.k.a. multi-scan, near-online, or online with delay) methods optimize only a few recent frames at the same time [16–20].

The large variety of approaches in the literature is justified by the variety of contexts and applications that encounters the MOT problem. Online approaches are well-suited for time-critical applications but are more prone to specific errors such as identity switches. On the other hand, global tracking approaches offer the advantage of dealing with all the available information at the cost of a major temporal delay. Finally, sliding window approaches offer an interesting compromise, having a relative time to understand the situation at the cost of a slight temporal delay. By delaying the final tracking results by only a few frames, these methods are able to correct association mistakes occurring inside the sliding window and generally yield more robust results with fewer identity switches and fragmented tracks.

Recently, many online or sliding window approaches have gained in performances by incorporating more complex appearance models [1,4,17]. These models, inspired by the recent improvements in Single Object Tracking (SOT), can be updated online to take into account changes in appearance or pose variations and help better distinguish targets, for more robust tracking results.

In particular, *sparse representation*-based models have been employed successfully in SOT [21–26]. The main idea is to model the target appearance in a linear subspace defined by a small number of templates grouped in a dictionary. Each candidate for the new target location is then represented by a sparse linear combination of the dictionary elements, the best reconstruction error being used as the selection criterion. However, only a few recent methods have considered extending these models for online MOT systems [3,27,28].

We propose two contributions in this paper. The first one consists of improving multi-frame data association by using sparse representation-based appearance models. To the best of our knowledge, we are the first to combine such concepts and so their aforementioned advantages. Our second contribution is to use structured sparse representations, derived from a weighted $l_{\infty,1}$ norm, that are more suited in this context. Comparisons with the l_1 norm and more basic appearance models without sparse representations support the effectiveness of this approach. Our method was evaluated on two public benchmarks and compares well with recent state-of-the-art approaches.

2   Related Work

2.1   Object Tracking with Sparse Representations

Appearance models based on sparse representations were first proposed by [21] in a SOT framework before being extended by many other authors [26]. In contrast to standard approaches that use a dictionary composed solely by target views, some approaches tried to handle occlusions by better discriminating the target from its background. To this end, they considered a dictionary incorporating boundary elements that mix object and its surrounding background [24]. Others employed a description based on local patches of the target and used spatial considerations when reconstructing the patches from a candidate location [23]. Initially, these tracking methods induced a significant CPU cost until optimization techniques based on accelerated proximal gradient descent led to real-time approaches [22].

Due to their success in SOT context, these appearance models have been recently used in a few MOT frameworks. In [28], such models are used in an online tracking method based on a particle filter. However, as many specific and independent models as the number of targets are necessary. In contrast, in [3,27], a single dictionary is shared by all targets and collaborative representations are used to better discriminate them. All these MOT approaches are using a two-frame data association in an online fashion and thus cannot reconsider wrong associations when further information comes and contradicts them.

In this work, we propose a new approach that improves a standard sliding window method by exploiting sparse representations of the detections. Our approach is inspired by [3,27,28], but instead of relying on sparse representations induced by the standard l_1 norm, we design a sparsity-inducing norm, based on a weighted $l_{\infty,1}$ norm, more suited for a multi-frame data association problem.

2.2   Multi-frame Data Association

Offline MOT approaches consider the data association either globally over the whole sequence [5–15] or over a sliding window dealing with a few frames [16–20]. In all cases, this leads to formulate a multi-frame data association problem solved most of the time by an energy minimization procedure.

In some approaches, the multi-frame data association problem has been formulated in a more specific class of problems, like for example minimum cost flow problems [5–7,12], binary integer programming [14], maximum weighted clique [13] or independent set [15]. The main advantage of such approaches is that efficient optimization methods designed for these problems can be directly employed to find the data association solution. However, particular constraints must be satisfied by the energy formulation which makes it difficult to correctly model important aspects of the MOT problem like target interactions and dynamics.

On the other hand, some state-of-the-art approaches focused on designing more complex energies that better model the MOT problem. However, the non-convex energy formulation puts out of reach any possibility of global minimization. It is still possible to get approximate solutions using non-exact optimization

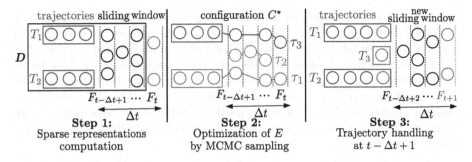

Fig. 1. Steps followed by the proposed approach. Firstly, sparse representations of the detections (symbolized by circles) from the last frame are computed. Then, the global energy E is optimized by MCMC sampling, yielding a configuration C^*. Finally, the trajectories (symbolized by rectangles) are definitively estimated in the first frame of the sliding window, following configuration C^*.

techniques that do not require a specific energy formulation, as done in Multiple Hypothesis Tracking [17] using a breadth-first search with branch pruning or in Markov Chain Monte Carlo Data Association (MCMCDA) with MCMC sampling [20,29]. Despite the non-optimality of the found solution, these methods can fully exploit the use of more appropriate interaction and dynamic models and can therefore cope with more difficult tracking issues.

In this work, we formulate a multi-frame data association with an energy that exploits sparse representations through its appearance model and that can be minimized efficiently using an MCMCDA approach.

3 System Overview

We propose a MOT system based on a sliding window and tracking-by-detection mechanisms. At each new frame, we seek for the best association between the detections over the current sliding window and the already estimated trajectories beyond this window. This multi-frame data association problem is formulated as an energy minimization solved by an MCMCDA approach in the vein of [29]. We design an energy function E assigning low values to solutions with tracks that are both close to the given detections and consistent with some appearance, motion and interaction models.

In the case of visually distinctive targets, taking into account appearances can lead to a significant improvement of the tracking performances. To this aim, we propose an appearance model that considers sparse representations of the detections in the sliding window. The main concept behind our work is that a target should be best represented by the detections of its own track rather than using detections from other targets. Our appearance model is thus formulated to promote the solutions that are the most consistent with these representations.

Our system performs the following steps (cf. Fig. 1). Firstly, sparse representations of the detections from a new frame are computed over a dictionary that includes all the detections inside a sliding window of Δt frames and some from the latterly estimated trajectories. Secondly, the data association problem is solved using an MCMCDA approach that yields an approximate solution C^*. Thirdly, this solution is used to propagate the trajectories at the first frame of the sliding window, possibly initializing new ones or terminating some of them. Finally, the sliding window is shifted by one frame. While the associations remaining inside the sliding window can still be modified, the ones beyond it are definitive. Therefore, the proposed method outputs results with a slight delay limited to Δt frames.

4　Multi-frame Data Association Formulation

4.1　Notations

We consider a sliding window over the last Δt frames, $\{F_{t-\Delta t+1}, F_{t-\Delta t+2}, ..., F_t\}$. At each frame F_t the detector yields a set of n_t detections $\{d_t^1, d_t^2, ..., d_t^{n_t}\}$. Each detection d is associated to a specific bounding box x_d, with height h_d and width w_d, and a detection score s_d. The trajectories, definitively fixed beyond the sliding window and still active, are denoted by $T_1, T_2, ..., T_N$.

The multi-frame data association requires to find a set $\{\tau_1, \tau_2, ..., \tau_M\}$ of tracks where each track τ is composed by the detections and, possibly, the trajectory related to the same target. A feasible solution for the multi-frame data association is called a configuration. A configuration C is a set of tracks in which (i) each detection and trajectory is included in at most one track, (ii) each track includes at most a single trajectory, and (iii) a single detection by frame. Furthermore, two consecutive detections d and d' linked in a track, spaced by δt frames, have to satisfy (i) $\delta t \leq \delta t_l$, (ii) $dist(x_d, x_{d'}) \leq (1 + \delta t) \frac{w_d + w_{d'}}{2} d_l$, and (iii) $|h_d - h_{d'}| \leq (1 + \delta t) \frac{h_d + h_{d'}}{2} h_l$, where $dist(x_d, x_{d'})$ is the Euclidean distance between the two bounding box centers and $\delta t_l, d_l, h_l$ are fixed parameters.

For each track τ, we denote by x_τ the set of bounding boxes resulting from a linear interpolation between the detections in τ. Therefore, $x_\tau(t)$ stands for the location of the track τ at time t which is either a bounding box from a detection in τ or one resulting from a linear interpolation to fill a gap between two consecutive detections in τ. We denote respectively by b_τ and e_τ the time of the first and last element in the track τ.

4.2　Proposed Energy

The proposed energy is formulated as a linear combination of four terms:

$$E(C) = \theta_{Ob}Ob(C) + \theta_{App}App(C) + \theta_{Mot}Mot(C) + \theta_{Int}Int(C). \quad (1)$$

Each one of these terms handles a specific aspect of the MOT problem while the θ values allow to ponderate them.

The objective of the *observation model* is to keep the tracks close to both the given detections and the trajectories already estimated outside the sliding window. To that end, our observation model is written as:

$$Ob(C) = -\sum_{\tau \in C} \sum_{d \in \tau} [\alpha_{Ob} + \beta_{Ob} s_d] - \sum_{\tau \in C} \sum_{T \in \tau} \gamma_{Ob} , \tag{2}$$

where α_{Ob}, β_{Ob} and γ_{Ob} are fixed positive parameters. The first term of Eq. 2 rewards the inclusion of detections with a high detection score s_d in the tracks while the second favors the extension of the latterly estimated trajectories.

Our *appearance model App(C)* uses sparse representations of the detections and promotes the configurations in which each detection achieves a small residual error over its own track. More details on this term are given in Sect. 5.

Assuming a constant velocity model, we consider the here below *motion model*:

$$Mot(C) = \sum_{\tau \in C} \sum_{t=b_\tau+1}^{e_\tau-1} ||x_\tau(t+1) + x_\tau(t-1) - 2x_\tau(t)||_2^2 . \tag{3}$$

This term favors smooth and constant motion by penalizing the acceleration over the tracks. A constant velocity model, despite its simplicity, already helps limit identity switches in the case of occlusions or collisions between targets.

Lastly, our *interaction model* takes the following form:

$$Int(C) = \sum_{\tau_1 \in C} \sum_{\tau_2 \in C \setminus \{\tau_1\}} \sum_{t=max(b_{\tau_1},b_{\tau_2})}^{min(e_{\tau_1},e_{\tau_2})} IOU(x_{\tau_1}(t), x_{\tau_2}(t))^2 . \tag{4}$$

This term avoids collisions between estimated targets, using a two bounding box Intersection-Over-Union (IOU) criterion.

4.3   MCMC Optimization and Trajectory Handling

Inspired by some recent works [20, 29] we use an MCMC sampling method based on the Metropolis-Hastings approach. It finds a good approximate solution of our energy minimization problem by exploring efficiently the space of possible configurations. Such an approach estimates the probability distribution:

$$\pi(C) = \frac{1}{Z} e^{-E(C)/\sigma^2} , \tag{5}$$

where Z is a normalization constant, not necessary to compute as only probability ratios are considered in the Metropolis-Hastings approach, and where σ can be chosen to make the distribution more or less peaked. In practice, a suited σ makes an appropriate trade-off between the exploration of the search space and the exploitation of the current state in the Markov Chain, and thus avoids being kept inside a local minimum/maximum of E/π respectively.

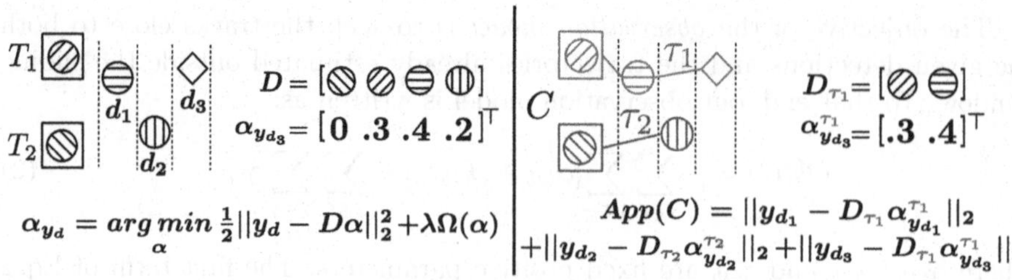

$$T_1 \boxed{\oslash} \quad \ominus \quad \diamondsuit \quad D = [\oslash \oslash \ominus \oplus] \quad \Big| \quad C \quad \quad \quad D_{T_1} = [\oslash \ominus]$$
$$\quad \quad \quad d_1 \quad d_3 \quad \quad \alpha_{y_{d_3}} = [0 \ .3 \ .4 \ .2]^{\mathsf{T}} \quad \quad \quad \quad \alpha_{y_{d_3}}^{T_1} = [.3 \ .4]^{\mathsf{T}}$$
$$T_2 \boxed{\oslash} \quad \quad \oplus$$
$$\quad \quad \quad d_2$$

$$\alpha_{y_d} = arg\,min_{\alpha} \tfrac{1}{2} ||y_d - D\alpha||_2^2 + \lambda\Omega(\alpha)$$

$$App(C) = ||y_{d_1} - D_{T_1}\alpha_{y_{d_1}}^{T_1}||_2$$
$$+ ||y_{d_2} - D_{T_2}\alpha_{y_{d_2}}^{T_2}||_2 + ||y_{d_3} - D_{T_1}\alpha_{y_{d_3}}^{T_1}||_2$$

Fig. 2. Proposed appearance model with sparse representations. Left: current sliding window and sparse representations computed for detections in the new frame. Right: configuration C considered and related appearance model value $App(C)$.

We use the approach proposed in [29] with minor differences. In our method, the types of moves are limited to the following ones: birth and death, merge and split, update and switch. We allow these moves to be done not only forward in time, as in [29], but also in a backward manner in order to explore more efficiently the space of configurations.

This method gives an approximate solution C^* of the minimization problem of the energy E. Once this configuration is found, any trajectory T_i that belongs to a track τ in C^* is extended to the first frame of the sliding window accordingly to τ (cf. Fig. 1, Step 3). Any trajectory not included in C^* is terminated while a track τ at the beginning of the sliding window with no associated trajectory possibly leads to the creation of a new trajectory. A new trajectory is indeed created if we are confident enough on the track τ, requiring that τ includes at least N_c detections with a mean detection score value above s_c.

5   Sparse Representations Using an $l_{\infty,1}$ Penalty

5.1   Proposed Appearance Model

We define here the appearance model $App(C)$ that we use in the energy E described previously (Eq. 1). Our approach model takes benefit from the efficient sparse representation-based models in SOT [26].

We propose an appearance model which exploits sparse representations of the detections in the sliding window. Each detection d_t^i is associated to a normalized feature vector $y_{d_t^i}$ and we use a dictionary D that includes all the feature vectors of the detections in the current sliding window. The dictionary D also includes the feature vectors of the N_{tr} last detections assigned to each trajectory T_i. A sparse representation for a given detection d is defined by:

$$\alpha_{y_d} = \arg\min_{\alpha} \frac{1}{2} ||y_d - D\alpha||_2^2 + \lambda\Omega(\alpha), \tag{6}$$

where $\Omega(\alpha)$ is a penalty that promotes solutions α with a few non-zero elements.

When one needs to perform multiclass classification and assign a label or a class L^* to the vector y_d, sparse representations can be used to estimate this class based on its related residual error:

$$L^* = \arg\min_L ||y_d - D_L \alpha_{y_d}^L||_2, \tag{7}$$

where D_L is the restriction of D to its elements from class L, and $\alpha_{y_d}^L$ is the restriction of α_{y_d} to the dimensions related to those elements [30]. In SOT, a common approach is to classify a candidate location either in a target or background class [24]. We propose an appearance model for multi-object tracking based on the same technique. This leads to consider:

$$App(C) = \sum_{\tau \in C} \sum_{d \in \tau} ||y_d - D_\tau \alpha_{y_d}^\tau||_2, \tag{8}$$

where $||y_d - D_\tau \alpha_{y_d}^\tau||_2$ is the residual error of detection d with respect to track τ. This model promotes the configurations C that achieve the smallest residual errors for all the detections with respect to the assigned tracks (cf. Fig. 2).

In practice, evaluating the value of $App(C)$ for each state of an MCMC sampling framework is computationally expensive due to the estimation of a significant number of residual errors. Instead of using residual errors, some approaches in classification and SOT, as for example in [23], directly use:

$$L^* = \arg\max_L \sum_i \alpha_{y_d}^L(i), \tag{9}$$

where the summation takes into account all coefficients $\alpha_{y_d}^L(i)$ of the vector $\alpha_{y_d}^L$. In order to speed up the MCMC sampling, we use this same approach and finally consider as appearance model:

$$App(C) = \sum_{\tau \in C} \sum_{d \in \tau} [1 - \sum_i \alpha_{y_d}^\tau(i)]. \tag{10}$$

5.2   Desired Sparsity Structure

In Eq. 6, a large number of penalties $\Omega(\alpha)$ can be employed to favor different sparsity structures in the representations. A simple choice is to consider $\Omega(\alpha) = ||\alpha||_1$, promoting a strict sparsity with an l_1 norm. More complex sparsity structures can be induced, notably by considering groups of dictionary elements. For example, an $l_{1,2}$ or $l_{1,\infty}$ norm can easily promote representations where only a few groups are non-zero with a uniform participation of the elements inside these groups. These penalties have been used in SOT approaches to produce sparse representations more suited to efficiently handle multiple features or to consider jointly all candidate locations.

This leads us to wonder which penalty will be the most appropriate for the MOT problem. Ideally, all detections should be represented by elements from their own trajectories. Therefore, a well-suited sparsity structure should promote

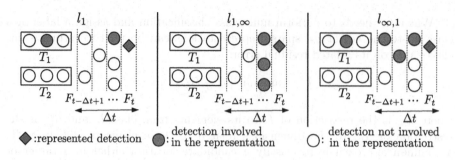

Fig. 3. Sparsity structures induced by different penalties over the sliding window.

a few non-zero elements in each frame, as two detections in a frame F_j cannot be related to the same target. It should as well favor the participation of only a few elements from trajectories $T_1, ..., T_N$ as a detection should be related to a single trajectory at most. Thus, considering for $i = [1...\Delta t - 1]$ a group G_i composed of the elements related to frame F_{t-i} and a group $G_{\Delta t}$ that includes all elements from trajectories $T_1, ..., T_N$, we want to impose a strict sparsity within each individual group. As a target should be located at each frame, we also want to promote a uniform participation of these groups. In this way, each detection should be represented by all the other detections relative to the same target.

Neither the l_1 norm nor group norms like the $l_{1,2}$ or $l_{1,\infty}$ norms induce the described structure. So we propose to use instead a weighted $l_{\infty,1}$ defined by:

$$||\alpha||_{\infty,1}^w = \max_{i=1..\Delta t} w_i ||\alpha^{G_i}||_1 ,$$ (11)

where α^{G_i} is the restriction of α to the elements related to G_i. The values w are positive weights balancing the participation of the groups. We use in practice $w_{\Delta t} = \frac{1}{\Delta t - 1}$ and $w_i = 1$ for $i < \Delta t$ in order to allow a greater participation of the elements inside the trajectories in $G_{\Delta t}$. This norm induces the desired sparsity structure, as it imposes a strict sparsity inside the groups while favoring that all the groups are involved in the representation (cf. Fig. 3).

5.3   Computing $l_{\infty,1}$-based Sparse Representations

Computing sparse representations induced by a weighted $l_{\infty,1}$ norm requires to solve:

$$\alpha_y = \arg\min_\alpha \frac{1}{2} ||y - D\alpha||_2^2 + \lambda ||\alpha||_{\infty,1}^w .$$ (12)

This is a convex and non-differentiable problem, which can be efficiently solved using an accelerated proximal gradient descent (APG or FISTA) algorithm described by Algorithm 1. This method achieves a global optimization with a quadratic rate of convergence [31] but relies on a proximal operator defined by:

$$prox_{\lambda ||\cdot||_{\infty,1}^w}(u) = \arg\min_v \frac{1}{2} ||u - v||_2^2 + \lambda ||v||_{\infty,1}^w .$$ (13)

input: D, y, w
$k = 1$, $\alpha_{k-1} = \alpha_k = 0$;
repeat

   | $\mu_k = \frac{k}{k+3}$;
   | $\beta = \alpha_k + \mu_k(\alpha_k - \alpha_{k-1})$;
   | find ρ by line search [31];
   | $\gamma = \beta - \rho D^{\top}(D\beta - y)$;
   | $\alpha_{k+1} = prox_{\rho\lambda\|.\|^w_{\infty,1}}(\gamma)$;
   | $k = k + 1$;

until *convergence*;
return α_k;

Algorithm 1. FISTA optimization for $l_{\infty,1}$-based sparse representation.

input: D, y, w
$\mathcal{A} = \varnothing$, $\alpha_{\mathcal{A}} = 0$;
repeat

   $\mathcal{S} = \mathcal{S}(\alpha_{\mathcal{A}})$;
   using $\alpha_{\mathcal{A}}$ as a warm start, find
   the optimal solution $\alpha_{\mathcal{A}\cup\mathcal{S}}$ of
   the problem Eq. 12 restricted to
   $\mathcal{A} \cup \mathcal{S}$;
   $\mathcal{A} = \mathcal{A} \cup \mathcal{S}$;

until $\|D^{\top}(D\alpha_{\mathcal{A}} - y)\|^{1/w}_{1,\infty} \leq \lambda$;
return $\alpha_{\mathcal{A}}$;

Algorithm 2. Active set strategy for $l_{\infty,1}$-based sparse representation.

When Ω is a norm, its proximal can be derived from a Euclidean projection on the unit ball of its dual norm Ω^* [31]:

$$prox_{\lambda\Omega}(u) = u - \lambda\Pi_{\Omega^*\leq 1}(u/\lambda). \tag{14}$$

In fact, the dual norm of the $l_{\infty,1}$ norm is exactly the $l_{1,\infty}$ norm. In the case of a weighted $l_{\infty,1}$ norm, the dual norm is also a weighted $l_{1,\infty}$ norm (see supplementary material for detail):

$$\|\alpha\|^w_{\infty,1}{}^* = \|\alpha\|^{1/w}_{1,\infty} = \sum_{i=1..\Delta t} \frac{1}{w_i}\|\alpha^{G_i}\|_\infty. \tag{15}$$

Therefore, Eq. 12 reduces to compute the Euclidean projection on the unit ball of a weighted $l_{1,\infty}$ norm:

$$prox_{\lambda\|.\|^w_{\infty,1}}(u) = u - \lambda\Pi_{\|.\|^{1/w}_{1,\infty}\leq 1}(u/\lambda). \tag{16}$$

An efficient algorithm for computing Euclidean projections on the unit ball of the $l_{1,\infty}$ norm was proposed in [32] and can be easily extended to handle the case of weighted $l_{1,\infty}$ norms. We use the implementation given on the authors' website to compute those projections for the proximal operators.

This optimization process can be sped up by using an active set strategy as explained in [33]. A necessary condition, based on the dual norm, for a representation α to be an optimal solution of Eq. 12 is:

$$\|D^{\top}(D\alpha - y)\|^{1/w}_{1,\infty} = \sum_{i=1..\Delta t} \frac{1}{w_i}\|D_{G_i}{}^{\top}(D\alpha - y)\|_\infty \leq \lambda. \tag{17}$$

An active set strategy optimizes Eq. 12 on a small set of active variables $\mathcal{A}$, yielding a solution $\alpha_{\mathcal{A}}$, and makes it progressively grow by adding a set of non-active variables $\mathcal{S}(\alpha_{\mathcal{A}})$ until the condition Eq. 17 is satisfied. This process, described in Algorithm 2, yields a global solution of Eq. 12 [33]. In practice, we set $\mathcal{S}(\alpha_{\mathcal{A}})$ to K non-active variables that have the highest $|d_i^{\top}(D\alpha_{\mathcal{A}} - y)|$ value with at most one variable by group to avoid focusing on a single one.

6 Evaluations and Discussion

6.1 Benchmarks, Metrics, and Parameter Tuning

We use the *MOTChallenge* benchmarks, *2DMOT2015* and *MOT16* [34,35], to evaluate the performances of the proposed approach. These benchmarks are composed of training and testing sets [36–41] with public detections, given by Aggregate Channel Features (ACF) pedestrian detector [42] in the case of the *2DMOT2015* and a Deformable Part Model (DPM) [43] for the *MOT16*.

The metrics employed by these benchmarks are based on the widely accepted CLEARMOT metrics [44]. MOT accuracy (MOTA) takes jointly into account false positives (FP), false negatives (FN) and identity switches (IDS). MOT precision (MOTP) measures the overlap distance between the found pedestrians' locations and the ground truth. We also indicate track fragmentations (FM), false alarms by frame (FAF) and the mostly tracked and mostly lost targets percentages (MT and ML). Furthermore, we report the IDS ratio (IR), defined by $\frac{IDS}{Recall}$, to measure the IDS more independently from the false negatives (FN).

As our method depends on several parameters, notably in the formulation of the energy E, manual tuning of these free parameters on the training set is out of reach. We use a hyper-optimization procedure (see the public implementation of [45]) to explore efficiently the space of parameters within 1000 runs of our algorithm. Thus, we automatically find the best set of parameters by optimizing the MOTA value, which is the main metric used to compare MOT approaches.

6.2 Comparison with *l*1 Norm and Basic Appearance Models

To validate our approach with $l_{\infty,1}$-based sparse representations, we implement three variants that only differ by considering different appearance models $App(C)$. We denote by LINF1 the proposed approach using $App(C)$ defined by Eq. 10 with $l_{\infty,1}$-based sparse representations. A first variant, called L1, uses the model $App(C)$ defined by Eq. 10 with l_1-based sparse representations to demonstrate the effectiveness of the weighted $l_{\infty,1}$ norm compared to the l_1 norm.

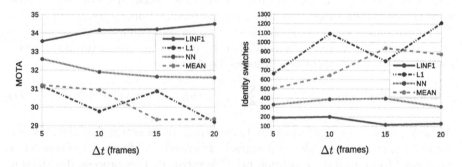

Fig. 4. MOTA (best higher↑) and identity switches (best lower↓) of our approach (LINF1) and other appearance models for different windows of size Δt frames, evaluated on the *2DMOT2015* training set.

Two variants without sparse representations are also evaluated to verify that using appropriate sparse representations effectively increases performances compared to more basic appearance models. These two baselines, denoted by NN and $MEAN$, differ from the proposed approach by respectively using the appearance models $App_{NN}(C)$ and $App_{MEAN}(C)$ defined by:

$$App_{NN}(C) = \sum_{\tau \in C} \sum_{d \in \tau} ||y_d - NN_\tau(y_d)||_2 , \tag{18}$$

$$App_{MEAN}(C) = \sum_{\tau \in C} \sum_{d \in \tau} ||y_d - y_\tau||_2 , \tag{19}$$

where $NN_\tau(y_d)$ stands for the nearest neighbor of y_d among the features of the other detections in track τ, and y_τ stands for the mean of the features of all detections in τ.

6.3   Comparison Between the Proposed Variants

Our approach and the three variants described previously are compared on the *2DMOT2015* training set, with sliding windows of size $\Delta t \in \{5, 10, 15, 20\}$. Similarly to [21–24], we do not use any complex features and simply use for y_d color intensity values of the templates resized to 32×32. To fairly compare these variants, we use for each variant and Δt value the hyper-optimization procedure discussed previously to find the best set of parameters.

MOTA values and IDS are indicated in Fig. 4. First of all, they show that the proposed LINF1 variant outperforms the other variants both in terms of MOTA

Table 1. Results of our approach, with windows of Δt frames, on the *2DMOT2015* training set (best values in bold and red, second best ones underlined in blue).

Method	Δt	MOTA (%)↑	IDS ↓	IR ↓	FM ↓	FAF ↓	MOTP (%) ↑	FP ↓	FN ↓	MT (%) ↑	ML (%) ↓
LINF1	5	33.6	188	4.4	413	0.6	72.8	3346	22980	16.5	57.8
	10	34.2	199	4.5	444	0.7	72.6	3740	22330	17.8	59.7
	15	34.2	116	2.6	410	0.7	72.7	3829	22307	18.4	58.8
	20	34.5	129	2.9	385	0.7	72.8	3931	22073	18.0	57.1
	25	34.1	163	3.3	470	1.1	72.4	6200	19942	22.2	50.6
	30	33.8	155	3.3	446	1.0	72.6	5260	20997	20.8	53.2
	35	33.6	141	3.0	446	1.0	72.7	5455	20909	20.4	51.4

Table 2. Best parameter set for LINF1, with a sliding window of 20 frames, found on the *2DMOT2015* and *MOT16* training set using a hyper-optimisation procedure.

Benchmark	θ_{Ob}	θ_{App}	θ_{Mot}	θ_{Int}	α_{Ob}	β_{Ob}	γ_{Ob}	σ	λ	N_c	s_c	δt_l	d_l	h_l	N_{tr}
2DMOT2015	0.50	0.39	0.77	0.08	0.60	0.004	0.99	0.14	3.1	5	29	6	0.28	0.24	11
MOT16	0.33	0.40	0.77	0.41	1.3	0.99	1.3	0.15	7.7	5	0.13	18	0.29	0.30	18

and IDS. L1 variant performs poorly in our multi-frame data association context, especially concerning IDS. When using these representations, each detection is represented by only a few similar detections. It leads to promote short tracks of highly similar detections rather than long tracks through the whole sliding window. The two other appearance models, App_{NN} and App_{MEAN}, yield more acceptable results. However, they rapidly deteriorate in performance when the number of frames in the sliding window increases.

The proposed approach, LINF1, is the only one able to leverage a larger sliding window, gaining slightly in MOTA and track fragmentations, and reducing more significantly the number of IDS (cf. Table 1). As it promotes representations where each frame is involved, even distant ones, the $l_{\infty,1}$ norm succeeds in efficiently exploiting the additional information provided by larger sliding windows. The optimal sliding window size is about 20 frames and the performances deteriorate slightly for larger windows. The search space for the MCMCDA is rapidly growing with the sliding window size, making the optimization more difficult, which possibly explains this slight decrease in performances.

6.4 Evaluations on the MOTChallenge Benchmarks

The results of the proposed LINF1 approach on the *2DMOT2015* test dataset are shown in Table 3 with all the other published methods that use the public detections given by the benchmark. Following the benchmark policy, we use the best set of parameters found on the training set, as indicated in Table 2.

In terms of MOTA, our method is superior or comparable to most of recent approaches. However, our method distinguishes itself by achieving *the smallest number of IDS* on the benchmark. This indicates a greater ability in discriminating similar targets, especially compared to methods achieving a similar or greater false negative number (FN) as increasing this number can naturally lead to decrease the number of IDS. IDS ratios (IR) can be considered to compare IDS more independently of the false negative number, and the proposed method is still *the best one in terms of IDS ratios*. Our approach is also *the first one in terms of false alarm by frame (FAF) and false positive (FP)*, and is *the second one in terms of track fragmentations (FM)*. The proposed method yields very confident results due to the use of $l_{\infty,1}$-based sparse representations. Indeed, these representations are still sparse over the elements of a same frame and thus exhibit a high discriminative power to differentiate the targets, leading to a small number of IDS. Furthermore, inducing a sparsity structure that promotes the participation of all the frames creates more links between temporally distant elements and helps handle occlusions or gaps between detections, reducing again the number of IDS and track fragmentations. Our approach is therefore well-suited for applications where the precision is a more important concern than the recall and where maintaining the identities of the targets is a crucial need.

Our method can process the *2DMOT15* benchmark around 7.5 fps using a 8 cores CPU at 2.7 GHz, running near real-time. Some results are shown in Fig. 5, and entire trajectories are visible on the benchmark website.

Table 3. Results for LINF1 on the test set of the *2DMOT2015* and *MOT16* benchmarks (accessed on 14/03/2016), compared to other recent state-of-the-art methods (best values in bold and red, second best ones underlined in blue). Third column: method type with O standing for online, G for global and S for sliding window.

2DMOT2015			MOTA	IDS	IR	FM	FAF	MOTP	FP	FN	MT	ML
Method	Ref.	T.	(%)↑	↓	↓	↓	↓	(%)↑	↓	↓	(%)↑	(%)↓
NOMT	[16]	S	33.7	442	9.4	823	1.3	71.9	7762	32547	12.2	44.0
MHT_DAM	[17]	S	32.4	435	9.1	826	1.6	71.8	9064	32060	16.0	43.8
MDP	[1]	O	30.3	680	14	1500	1.7	71.3	9717	32422	13.0	38.4
LP_SSVM	[5]	G	25.2	646	16	849	1.4	71.7	8369	36932	5.8	53.0
ELP	[6]	G	25.0	1396	36	1804	1.3	71.2	7345	37344	7.5	43.8
LINF1	-	S	24.5	298	8.6	744	1.0	71.3	5864	40207	5.5	64.6
JPDA_m	[18]	S	23.8	365	11	869	1.1	68.2	6373	40084	5.0	58.1
MotiCon	[7]	G	23.1	1018	24	1061	1.8	70.9	10404	35844	4.7	52.0
SegTrack	[19]	S	22.5	697	19	737	1.4	71.7	7890	39020	5.8	63.9
DCO_X	[8]	G	19.6	521	14	819	1.8	71.4	10652	38232	5.1	54.9
CEM	[9]	G	19.3	813	19	1023	2.5	70.7	14180	34591	8.5	46.5
RMOT	[2]	O	18.6	684	17	1282	2.2	69.6	12473	36835	5.3	53.3
SMOT	[10]	G	18.2	1148	33	2132	1.5	71.2	8780	40310	2.8	54.8
ALExTR.	[46]	S	17.0	1859	53	1872	1.6	71.2	9233	39933	3.9	52.4
TBD	[11]	G	15.9	1939	45	1963	2.6	70.9	14943	34777	6.4	47.9
GSCR	[3]	O	15.8	514	18	1010	1.3	69.4	7597	43633	1.8	61.0
TC_ODAL	[4]	O	15.1	637	17	1716	2.2	70.5	12970	38538	3.2	55.8
DP_NMS	[12]	G	14.5	4537	105	3090	2.3	70.8	13171	34814	6.0	40.8
MOT16			MOTA	IDS	IR	FM	FAF	MOTP	FP	FN	MT	ML
Method	Ref.	T.	(%)↑	↓	↓	↓	↓	(%)↑	↓	↓	↑	↓
LINF1	-	S	40.5	426	9.4	953	1.4	74.9	8401	99715	10.7	56.1
DP_NMS	[12]	G	31.9	969	29	941	0.2	76.4	1343	121813	4.8	65.2
SMOT	[10]	G	29.2	3072	75	4437	3.0	75.2	17929	108041	4.9	53.3

Venice1 #100   ADL-Rundle-3 #300

Fig. 5. Tracklets inferred by our approach on the *2DMOT2015* test set.

The results on the *MOT16* benchmark are also reported at the bottom of Table 3. As this benchmark was recently released, the results from only two other tracking approaches are available. Our method outperforms these approaches with the best MOTA score and the lowest number of IDS.

7   Conclusion

In this paper, we have proposed a new MOT approach by combining a sparse representation-based appearance model with a sliding window tracking method. We have designed a weighted $l_{\infty,1}$ norm in order to induce a sparsity structure more suited to a MOT problem compared to the usual l_1 norm. Besides, we have proposed an efficient optimization to compute the $l_{\infty,1}$-based sparse representations using accelerated proximal gradient descent techniques. Combining $l_{\infty,1}$-based sparse representations with a sliding window approach results in a robust tracking method less prone to association errors like identity switches or track fragmentations due to its ability to efficiently correct previous association mistakes. Our method was tested on the *MOTChallenge* benchmarks, comparing well with the majority of competitors in terms of MOTA and achieving the best results in terms of identity switches and false alarms.

Several ideas developed in this paper can be extended as future work. For example, the representations are defined independently for each detection whereas one could consider computing them jointly with an appropriate penalty.

References

1. Xiang, Y., Alahi, A., Savarese, S.: Learning to track: online multi-object tracking by decision making. In: ICCV (2015)
2. Yoon, J.H., Yang, M.H., Lim, J., Yoon, K.J.: Bayesian multi-object tracking using motion context from multiple objects. In: WACV (2015)
3. Fagot-Bouquet, L., Audigier, R., Dhome, Y., Lerasle, F.: Online multi-person tracking based on global sparse collaborative representations. In: ICIP (2015)
4. Bae, S.H., Yoon, K.J.: Robust online multi-object tracking based on tracklet confidence and online discriminative appearance learning. In: CVPR (2014)
5. Wang, S., Fowlkes, C.C.: Learning optimal parameters for multi-target tracking. In: BMVC (2015)
6. McLaughlin, N., Del Rincon, J.M., Miller, P.: Enhancing linear programming with motion modeling for multi-target tracking. In: WACV (2015)
7. Leal-Taix, L., Fenzi, M., Kuznetsova, A., Rosenhahn, B., Savarese, S.: Learning an image-based motion context for multiple people tracking. In: CVPR (2014)
8. Milan, A., Schindler, K., Roth, S.: Multi-target tracking by discrete-continuous energy minimization. TPAMI (2016). doi:10.1109/TPAMI.2015.2505309
9. Milan, A., Roth, S., Schindler, K.: Continuous energy minimization for multitarget tracking. TPAMI **36**(1), 58–72 (2014)
10. Dicle, C., Sznaier, M., Camps, O.: The way they move: tracking targets with similar appearance. In: ICCV (2013)
11. Geiger, A., Lauer, M., Wojek, C., Stiller, C., Urtasun, R.: 3D traffic scene understanding from movable platforms. TPAMI **36**(5), 1012–1025 (2014)
12. Pirsiavash, H., Ramanan, D., Fowlkes, C.C.: Globally-optimal greedy algorithms for tracking a variable number of objects. In: CVPR (2011)

13. Zamir, A.R., Dehghan, A., Shah, M.: GMCP-tracker: global multi-object tracking using generalized minimum clique graphs. In: Fitzgibbon, A., Lazebnik, S., Perona, P., Sato, Y., Schmid, C. (eds.) ECCV 2012, Part II. LNCS, vol. 7573, pp. 343–356. Springer, Heidelberg (2012)
14. Dehghan, A., Assari, S.M., Shah, M.: GMMCP-tracker: globally optimal generalized maximum multi clique problem for multiple object tracking. In: CVPR (2015)
15. Brendel, W., Amer, M.R., Todorovic, S.: Multiobject tracking as maximum weight independent set. In: CVPR (2011)
16. Choi, W.: Near-online multi-target tracking with aggregated local flow descriptor. In: ICCV (2015)
17. Kim, C., Li, F., Ciptadi, A., Rehg, J.M.: Multiple hypothesis tracking revisited. In: ICCV (2015)
18. Rezatofighi, S.H., Milan, A., Zhang, Z., Shi, Q., Dick, A.R., Reid, I.D.: Joint probabilistic data association revisited. In: ICCV (2015)
19. Milan, A., Leal-Taix, L., Schindler, K., Reid, I.: Joint tracking and segmentation of multiple targets. In: CVPR (2015)
20. Benfold, B., Reid, I.: Stable multi-target tracking in real-time surveillance video. In: CVPR (2011)
21. Mei, X., Ling, H.: Robust visual tracking and vehicle classification via sparse representation. TPAMI 33(11), 2259–2272 (2011)
22. Bao, C., Wu, Y., Ling, H., Ji, H.: Real time robust L1 tracker using accelerated proximal gradient approach. In: CVPR (2012)
23. Jia, X., Lu, H., Yang, M.: Visual tracking via adaptive structural local sparse appearance model. In: CVPR (2012)
24. Zhong, W., Lu, H., Yang, M.: Robust object tracking via sparsity-based collaborative model. In: CVPR (2012)
25. Hong, Z., Mei, X., Prokhorov, D., Tao, D.: Tracking via robust multi-task multi-view joint sparse representation. In: ICCV (2013)
26. Zhang, S., Yao, H., Sun, X., Lu, X.: Sparse coding based visual tracking: review and experimental comparison. Pattern Recogn. 46(7), 1772–1788 (2013)
27. Fagot-Bouquet, L., Audigier, R., Dhome, Y., Lerasle, F.: Collaboration and spatialization for an efficient multi-person tracking via sparse representations. In: AVSS (2015)
28. Naiel, M.A., Ahmad, M.O., Swamy, M.N.S., Wu, Y., Yang, M.: Online multi-person tracking via robust collaborative model. In: ICIP (2014)
29. Oh, S., Russell, S.J., Sastry, S.: Markov chain Monte Carlo data association for multi-target tracking. Trans. Autom. Control 54(3), 481–497 (2009)
30. Wright, J., Yang, A., Ganesh, A., Sastry, S., Ma, Y.: Robust face recognition via sparse representation. TPAMI 31(2), 210–227 (2009)
31. Parikh, N., Boyd, S.: Proximal algorithms. Found. Trends Optim. 1(3), 123–231 (2013)
32. Quattoni, A., Carreras, X., Collins, M., Darrell, T.: An efficient projection for l1, infinity regularization. In: ICML (2009)
33. Bach, F., Jenatton, R., Mairal, J., Obozinski, G.: Optimization with sparsity-inducing penalties. Found. Trends Mach. Learn. 4(1), 1–106 (2012)
34. Leal-Taixé, L., Milan, A., Reid, I., Roth, S., Schindler, K.: MOTChallenge 2015: Towards a Benchmark for Multi-Target Tracking. arXiv:1504.01942 [cs] (2015)
35. Milan, A., Leal-Taixé, L., Reid, I., Roth, S., Schindler, K.: MOT16: A Benchmark for Multi-Object Tracking. arXiv:1603.00831 [cs] (2016)
36. Ess, A., Leibe, B., Gool, L.V.: Depth and appearance for mobile scene analysis. In: ICCV (2007)

37. Andriluka, M., Roth, S., Schiele, B.: Monocular 3D pose estimation and tracking by detection. In: CVPR (2010)
38. Andriluka, M., Roth, S., Schiele, B.: People-tracking-by-detection and people-detection-by-tracking. In: CVPR (2008)
39. Ferryman, J., Shahrokni, A.: Pets 2009: dataset and challenge. In: Performance Evaluation of Tracking and Surveillance (PETS-Winter) (2009)
40. Geiger, A., Lenz, P., Urtasun, R.: Are we ready for autonomous driving? The KITTI vision benchmark suite. In: CVPR (2012)
41. Benfold, B., Reid, I.: Guiding visual surveillance by tracking human attention. In: BMVC (2009)
42. Dollar, P., Appel, R., Belongie, S., Perona, P.: Fast feature pyramids for object detection. TPAMI 36(8), 1532–1545 (2014)
43. Felzenszwalb, P.F., Girshick, R.B., McAllester, D., Ramanan, D.: Object detection with discriminatively trained part-based models. TPAMI 32(9), 1627–1645 (2010)
44. Bernardin, K., Stiefelhagen, R.: Evaluating multiple object tracking performance: the CLEAR MOT metrics. EURASIP J. Image Video Process. 2008(1), 1–10 (2008). doi:10.1155/2008/246309
45. Hutter, F., Hoos, H.H., Leyton-Brown, K.: Sequential model-based optimization for general algorithm configuration. In: Coello, C.A.C. (ed.) LION 2011. LNCS, vol. 6683, pp. 507–523. Springer, Heidelberg (2011)
46. Bewley, A., Ott, L., Ramos, F., Upcroft, B.: ALExTRAC: affinity learning by exploring temporal reinforcement within association chains. In: ICRA (2016)

Gated Siamese Convolutional Neural Network Architecture for Human Re-identification

Rahul Rama Varior, Mrinal Haloi, and Gang Wang[(✉)]

School of Electrical and Electronic Engineering,
Nanyang Technological University, Singapore, Singapore
{rahul004,mhaloi,wanggang}@ntu.edu.sg

Abstract. Matching pedestrians across multiple camera views, known as human re-identification, is a challenging research problem that has numerous applications in visual surveillance. With the resurgence of Convolutional Neural Networks (CNNs), several end-to-end deep Siamese CNN architectures have been proposed for human re-identification with the objective of projecting the images of similar pairs (i.e. same identity) to be closer to each other and those of dissimilar pairs to be distant from each other. However, current networks extract fixed representations for each image regardless of other images which are paired with it and the comparison with other images is done only at the final level. In this setting, the network is at risk of failing to extract finer local patterns that may be essential to distinguish positive pairs from hard negative pairs. In this paper, we propose a gating function to selectively emphasize such fine common local patterns by comparing the mid-level features across pairs of images. This produces flexible representations for the same image according to the images they are paired with. We conduct experiments on the CUHK03, Market-1501 and VIPeR datasets and demonstrate improved performance compared to a baseline Siamese CNN architecture.

Keywords: Human re-identification · Siamese Convolutional Neural Network · Gating function · Matching gate · Deep Convolutional Neural Networks

1 Introduction

Matching pedestrians across multiple camera views, also known as human re-identification, is a research problem that has numerous potential applications in visual surveillance. The goal of the human re-identification system is to retrieve a set of images captured by different cameras (gallery set) for a given query image (probe set) from a certain camera. Human re-identification is a very challenging task due to the variations in illumination, pose and visual appearance

Electronic supplementary material The online version of this chapter (doi:10. 1007/978-3-319-46484-8_48) contains supplementary material, which is available to authorized users.

B. Leibe et al. (Eds.): ECCV 2016, Part VIII, LNCS 9912, pp. 791–808, 2016.
DOI: 10.1007/978-3-319-46484-8_48

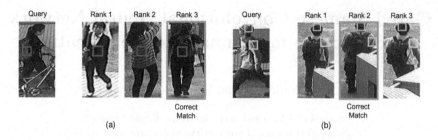

Fig. 1. Example case: Results obtained using a S-CNN. Red, Blue and Yellow boxes indicate some sample corresponding patches extracted from the images along the same horizontal row. See text for more details. **Best viewed in color** (Color figure online)

across different camera views. With the resurgence of Convolutional Neural Networks (CNNs), several deep learning methods [1,21,49] were proposed for human re-identification. Most of the frameworks are designed in a siamese fashion that integrates the tasks of feature extraction and metric learning into a single framework.

The central idea behind a Siamese Convolutional Neural Network (S-CNN) is to learn an embedding where similar pairs (i.e. images belonging to the same identity) are close to each other and dissimilar pairs (i.e. images belonging to different identities) are separated by a distance defined by a parameter called 'margin'. In this paper, we first propose a baseline S-CNN architecture that can outperform majority of the deep learning architectures as well as other handcrafted approaches for human re-identification on challenging human re-identification datasets, the CUHK03 [21], the Market-1501 [57] and the VIPeR [10] dataset.

The major drawback of the S-CNN architecture is that it extract fixed representations for each image without the knowledge of the paired image. This setting results in a risk of failing to capture and propagate the local patterns that are necessary to increase the confidence level (i.e., reducing the distances) in identifying the correct matches. Figure 1(a) and (b) shows two queries and the retrieved matches at the top 3 ranks using a S-CNN architecture. Even though there are obvious dissimilarities among the top 3 matches for a human observer in both the cases, the network fails to identify the correct match at Rank 1. For example, the patches corresponding to the 'bag' (indicated by red boxes) in Fig. 1(a) and the patches corresponding to the 'hat' (indicated by blue boxes) in Fig. 1(b) could be helpful to distinguish between the top retrieved match and the actual positive pairs. However, a network that fails to capture and propagate such finer details may not perform well in efficiently distinguishing positives from hard-negatives.

CNNs extract low-level features at the bottom layers and learn more abstract concepts such as the parts or more complicated texture patterns at the mid-level. Since the mid-level features are more informative compared to the higher-level features, the finer details that may be necessary to increase the similarity for positive pairs can be more evident at the middle layers. Hence, we propose a gating function to compare the extracted local patterns for an image pair starting from the mid-level and promote (i.e. to amplify) the local similarities along the higher layers so that the network propagates more relevant features to the higher layers of the network. Additionally, during training phase, the mechanisms inside the gating function also boost the back propagated gradients corresponding to the amplified local similarities. This encourages the lower and middle layers to learn filters to extract more locally similar patterns that discriminate positive pairs from negative pairs. Hereafter, we refer to the proposed gating function as 'the Matching Gate' (MG).

The primary challenge in developing the matching gate is that it should be able to compare the local features across two views effectively and select the common patterns. Due to pose change across two views, features appearing at one location may not necessarily appear in the same location for its paired image. Since all the images are resized to a fixed scale, it is reasonable to assume a horizontal row-wise correspondence. Therefore, the matching gate first summarizes the features along each horizontal stripe for a pair of images and compares it by taking the Euclidean distance along each dimension of the obtained feature map. Once the distances between each individual dimensions are obtained, a Gaussian activation function is used to output a similarity score ranging from 0–1 where 0 indicates that the stripe features are dissimilar and 1 indicating that the stripe features are similar. These values are used to gate the stripe features and finally, the gated features are added to the input features to boost them thus giving more emphasis to the local similarities across view-points. Our approach does not require any part-level correspondence annotation between image pairs during the training phase as it directly compares the extracted mid-level features along corresponding horizontal stripes. Additionally, the proposed matching gate is formulated as a differentiable parametric function to facilitate the end-to-end learning strategy of typical deep learning architectures. To summarize, the major contributions of the proposed work are:

– We propose a baseline siamese convolutional neural network architecture that can outperform majority of the existing deep learning frameworks for human re-identification.
– To incorporate run time feature selection and boosting into the S-CNN architecture, we propose a novel matching gate that can boost the common local features across two views. This encourages the network to learn filters that can extract subtle patterns to discriminate hard-negatives from positive pairs. The proposed matching gate is differentiable to facilitate end-to-end training of the S-CNN architecture.
– We conduct experiments on the CUHK03 [21], Market-1501 [57] and the VIPeR [10] datasets for human re-identification and prove the effectiveness of our approach. The proposed framework also achieves promising results compared to the state-of-the-art algorithms.

2   Related Works

2.1   Human Re-identification

Existing research on human re-identification mainly concentrates on two aspects: (1) Developing a new feature representation [5,19,23,28,41,47,48,52] and (2) Learning a distance metric [20,22–24,31,32,38,46]. Novel feature representations were proposed [23,28,41] to address the challenges such as variations in illumination, pose and view-point. Scale Invariant Feature Transforms [27,53,54], Scale Invariant Local Ternary Patterns [23,25], Local Binary Patterns [30,46], Color Histograms [23,46,53,54] or Color Names [48,57] etc. are the basis of the majority of these feature representations developed for human re-identification. Several Metric Learning algorithms such as Locally adaptive Decision Functions (LADF) [22], Cross-view Quadratic Discriminant Analysis (XQDA) [23], Metric Learning with Accelerated Proximal Gradient (MLAPG) [24], Local Fisher Discriminant Analysis (LFDA) [31] and its kernel variant (k-LFDA) [46] were proposed for human re-identification achieving remarkable performance in several benchmark datasets. However, different from all the above works, our approach is modeled based on the Siamese Convolutional Neural Networks (S-CNN) [2,12] that can learn an embedding where similar instances are closer to each other and dissimilar images are distant from each other from raw pixel values.

Deep Learning for Human Re-identification: Convolutional Neural Networks have achieved phenomenal results on several computer vision tasks [13, 35,36,39]. In the recent years, several CNN architectures [1,4,21,40,43,45,49] have been proposed for human re-identification. The first Siamese CNN (S-CNN) architecture for human re-identification was proposed in [49]. The system (DML) consists of a set of 3 S-CNNs for different regions of the image and the features are combined by using a cosine similarity as the connection function. Finally a binomial deviance is used as the cost function to optimize the network end-to-end. Local body-part based features and the global features were modeled using a Multi-Channel CNN framework in [4]. Deep Filter Pairing Neural Network (FPNN) was introduced in [21] to jointly handle misalignment, photometric and geometric transformations, occlusion and cluttered background. In [1], a cross-input neighborhood difference module was proposed to extract the cross-view relationships of the features and have achieved impressive results in several benchmark datasets. A recent work [43] also attempts to model the cross-view relationships by jointly learning subnetworks to extract the single image as well as the cross image representations. In [45], domain guided dropout was introduced for selecting the appropriate neuron for the images belonging to a given domain. A Long-Short Term Memory (LSTM) based architecture was proposed in [40] to model the contextual dependencies and selecting the relevant contexts to improve the discriminative capabilities of the local features. Different from all the above works, the proposed matching gate aims at comparing features at multiple levels (different layers) to boost the local similarities and enhance the discriminative capability of the propagated local features. The proposed gating

Table 1. Proposed Baseline Siamese Convolutional Neural Network architecture.

Input	Conv Block - P2	Max Pool	Conv Block - P1	Max Pool	Conv Block - P1	Max Pool	Conv Block	Conv Block	Conv Block	Conv Block
128 × 64	5 × 5 × 3 × 32	2 × 2	3 × 3 × 32 × 50	2 × 2	3 × 3 × 50 × 32	2 × 2	1 × 4 × 32 × 32	1 × 3 × 32 × 32	1 × 3 × 32 × 32	16 × 1 × 32 × 150

ConvBlock - Convolution -> Batch Normalization -> Parametric Rectified Linear Unit

P2 and P1 - zero padding the input with 2 pixels and 1 pixel on all sides respectively before convolution

function is flexible (in architecture) and differentiable to facilitate end-to-end learning strategy of deep neural networks.

2.2 Gating Functions

Gating functions have been proven to be an important component in deep neural networks [15,37]. Gating mechanisms such as the input gates and output gates were proposed in Long-Short Term Memory (LSTM) [15] cells for regulating the information flow through the network. Further, LSTM unit with forget gate [9] was proposed to reset the internal states based on the inputs. Inspired by the LSTM, Highway Networks [37] were proposed to train very deep neural networks by introducing gating functions into the CNN architecture. More recently, 'Trust Gates' were introduced in [26] to handle the noise and occlusion in 3D skeleton data for action recognition. However, the proposed matching gate is modeled entirely in a different context in terms of its architecture and purpose; i.e., the goal of the matching gate is to compare the local feature similarities of input pairs from the mid-level through the higher layers and weigh the common local patterns based on the similarity scores. This will enable the lower layers of the network to learn filters that can discriminate the local patterns of positive pairs from negative pairs. Additionally, to the best of our knowledge, the proposed work is the first of its nature to introduce differentiable gating functions in siamese architecture for human re-identification.

3 Proposed Model

In this section, we first describe our baseline S-CNN architecture and further introduce the Matching Gate to address the limitations of the baseline S-CNN architecture.

3.1 Model Architecture

Baseline Siamese CNN Architecture: The fundamental CNN architecture is modeled in a siamese fashion optimized by the contrastive loss function proposed in [12]. Table 1 summarizes the proposed Siamese CNN architecture. All the inputs are resized to a resolution of 128 × 64 and the mean image computed on the training set is subtracted from all the images. The description of the proposed S-CNN layers is as follows. First, we limit the number of pooling layers to only 3 so that it results in less information loss as the features propagate through the network. Second, we also use asymmetric filtering in layers 4–6 to preserve the number of rows at the output of the third layer while reducing the number of 'columns' progressively to 1. This strategy is inspired by the technique introduced in [23] in which the features along a single row is pooled to make the final feature map to a shape (number of rows) × 1. It also helps to reduce the number of parameters compared to symmetric filters. Further, this feature map is fed into a fully connected layer which is the last layer of our network. Finally, we also incorporate some of the established state-of-the-art techniques to the proposed S-CNN architecture. As suggested in VGG-Net [36], we use smaller convolutional filters to reduce the number of parameters to be learned while making the framework deeper. We also employ Batch Normalization [16] for standardizing the distribution of the inputs to each layer which helps in accelerating the training procedure. Parametric rectified linear unit (PReLU) [14] was used as the non-linear activation function as it has shown better convergence properties and performance gains with little risk of over-fitting. More results and analysis about the design choices are given in the supplementary material. The proposed S-CNN architecture outperforms majority of the existing approaches for human re-identification. However, as discussed in Sect. 1, the S-CNN model is not capable of adaptively emphasizing the local features that may be helpful to distinguish the correct matches from hard-negative pairs during run time. Therefore, we propose a matching gate to address this drawback. Below we give the details of the proposed module.

Matching Gate: The proposed matching gate (MG) receives input activations from the previous convolutional block, compares the local features along a horizontal stripe and outputs a gating mask indicating how much more emphasis should be paid to each of the local patterns. Figure 2 illustrates the proposed final architecture with the gating function. The various components of the proposed MG are given below.

1. **Feature summarization:** The feature summarization unit aggregates the local features along a horizontal stripe in an image. This is necessary due to the pose changes of the pedestrian images across different views. For instance, as shown in Fig. 1, the local features (indicated by red, blue and yellow boxes) appearing in one view may not be exactly at the same position in the other view, but it is very likely to be along the same horizontal region.

   Let $\mathbf{x_{r1}} \in \mathbb{R}^{1 \times c \times h}$ be the input stripe features from the rth row of a feature map at the input of the MG from one view point and $\mathbf{x_{r2}} \in \mathbb{R}^{1 \times c \times h}$ be the corresponding input stripe features from the other view point. Here, c denotes the number of columns and h denotes the depth of the input feature map. Given $\mathbf{x_{r1}}$ and $\mathbf{x_{r2}}$, we propose to use a convolution strategy followed by the parametric rectified linear unit activation (PReLU) to summarize the features along the row resulting in feature vectors $\mathbf{y_{r1}}$ and $\mathbf{y_{r2}}$ respectively with dimensions $\mathbb{R}^{1 \times 1 \times h}$. The input features $\mathbf{x_{r1}}$ and $\mathbf{x_{r2}}$, are convolved with

Final Siamese CNN Architecture

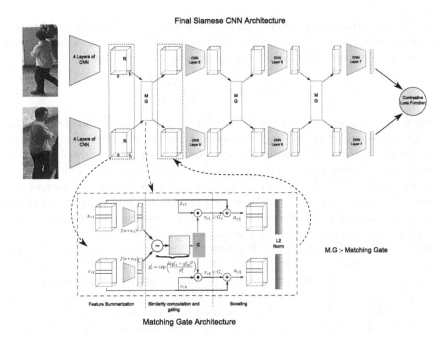

Matching Gate Architecture

Fig. 2. Proposed architecture: The proposed architecture is a modified version of our baseline S-CNN proposed in Table 1. The matching gate is inserted between layers 4–5, 5–6 and 6–7. The detailed architecture of the gating function is also shown in the figure. See text for details. **Best viewed in color** (Color figure online)

filters $\mathbf{w} \in \mathbb{R}^{1 \times c \times h \times h}$ without any padding. This will compute the combination of different extracted patterns along each of the feature maps of $\mathbf{x_{r1}}$ and $\mathbf{x_{r2}}$.

Mathematically, it can be expressed as

$$\mathbf{y_{r1}} = f(\mathbf{w} * \mathbf{x_{r1}}); \quad \mathbf{y_{r2}} = f(\mathbf{w} * \mathbf{x_{r2}}) \tag{1}$$

where '$*$' denotes the convolution operation and $f(.)$ denotes the PReLU activation function. The bias is omitted in Eq. (1) for brevity. The parameters $\mathbf{w}$ and bias of the summarization unit can be learned along with the other parameters of the matching gate through back-propagation.

2. **Feature Similarity computation:** Once the features along a horizontal stripe are summarized across the two views, the similarity between them is computed. The similarity is computed by calculating the Euclidean distance along each dimension 'h' of the summarized features. Computing the distance between each dimension is important as the gating function must have the flexibility to smoothly turn 'on' or turn 'off' each of the extracted patterns in the feature map. Once the distance is computed, a Gaussian activation function is used to obtain the gate values. The value of the Gaussian activation function varies from 0–1 and acts as a smooth switch for the input features.

It also helps the function to be differentiable which is essential for end-to-end training of the S-CNN framework. Mathematically the gating value for each of the dimensions along row 'r' can be obtained as given below;

$$\mathbf{g_r}^i = exp\left(\frac{-(\mathbf{y_{r1}}^i - \mathbf{y_{r2}}^i)^2}{\mathbf{p}_i^2}\right) \tag{2}$$

where $\mathbf{g_r}^i, \mathbf{y_{r1}}^i$ and $\mathbf{y_{r2}}^i$ denotes the ith ($i = \{1, 2, \ldots, h\}$) dimension of the gate values ($\mathbf{g_r}$), $\mathbf{y_{r1}}$ and $\mathbf{y_{r2}}$ respectively for the rth row. The parameter $\mathbf{p}_i$ decides the variance of the Gaussian function and the optimal value can be learned during the training phase. It is particularly important to set a higher initial value for $\mathbf{p}_i$ to ensure smooth flow of feature activations and gradients during forward and backward pass in the initial iterations of the training phase. Further, the network can decide the variance of the Gaussian function for each dimension by learning an optimal $\mathbf{p}_i$.

3. **Filtering and Boosting the features:** Once the gate values ($\mathbf{g_r}$) are computed, each dimension along a row of the input is gated with the corresponding dimension of $\mathbf{g_r}$. The computed gate values will be of dimensions $\mathbb{R}^{1 \times 1 \times h}$ and is repeated c times horizontally to obtain $\mathbf{G_r} \in \mathbb{R}^{1 \times c \times h}$ matrix and further an element wise product is computed with the input stripe features $\mathbf{x_{r1}}$ and $\mathbf{x_{r2}}$. This will 'select' the common patterns along a row from the images appearing in both views. To boost these selected common patterns, the input is again added to these gated values. Mathematically, each dimension of the boosted output can be written as

$$\mathbf{a_{r1}}^i = \mathbf{x_{r1}}^i + \mathbf{x_{r1}}^i \odot \mathbf{G_r}^i \tag{3}$$

$$\mathbf{a_{r2}}^i = \mathbf{x_{r2}}^i + \mathbf{x_{r2}}^i \odot \mathbf{G_r}^i \tag{4}$$

$$\mathbf{G_r}^i = [\mathbf{g_r}^i, \mathbf{g_r}^i, \ldots, \mathbf{g_r}^i]_{repeated \; c \; times} \tag{5}$$

where $\mathbf{a_{r1}}^i, \mathbf{a_{r2}}^i, \mathbf{x_{r1}}^i, \mathbf{x_{r2}}^i, \mathbf{G_r}^i \in \mathbb{R}^{1 \times c \times 1}$. Once the boosted output $\mathbf{a_{r1}}$ and $\mathbf{a_{r2}}$ are obtained, we perform an $L2$ normalization across channels and the obtained features are propagated to the rest of the network. From Eqs. (3) and (4), we can understand that the gradients with respect to the 'selected' $\mathbf{x_{r1}}$ and $\mathbf{x_{r2}}$ will also be boosted during the backward pass. This will encourage the lower layers of the network to learn filters that can extract patterns that are more similar for positive pairs.

The key advantages of the proposed MG is that it is flexible in its architecture as well as differentiable. If the optimal variance factor $\mathbf{p}$ is learned to be high, it facilitates maximum information flow from the input to output and conversely if it is learned to be a low value, it allows only very similar patches to be boosted. The network learns to identify the optimal $\mathbf{p}$ for each dimension from the training data which results in a matching gate that is flexible in its functioning. Alongside learning an optimal $\mathbf{p}$, the network also learns the parameter $\mathbf{w}$ and the bias in Eq. (1) to summarize the features along a horizontal stripe. Additionally, the MG can be inserted in between any layers or multiple layers in the network as it is a differentiable function. This will also facilitate end-to-end learning strategy in deep networks.

Final Architecture: The final architecture of the proposed system is shown in Fig. 2. The baseline network is designed in such a way as to reduce the width of the feature map progressively without reducing the height from layers 4–6. This is essential to address the pose change of the human images across cameras while preserving the finer row-wise characteristics. As shown in the Fig. 2, we inserted the proposed MG between the last 4 layers once the number of rows of the propagated feature maps is fixed.

3.2   Training and Optimization

Input Preparation: Siamese networks take image pairs as inputs. Therefore, we first pair all the images in the training set with a label '1' indicating negative pairs and '0' indicating the positive pairs. For large datasets, the number of negative image pairs will be orders of magnitude higher than the number of positive pairs. To alleviate this bias in the training set, we sample approximately 5 times the number of positive image pairs, as negative image pairs, for each subject. The mean image computed from all the training images is subtracted from all the images and the input pairs are fed to the network.

Training: Both the baseline S-CNN model and the proposed architecture (Fig. 2) are trained from scratch in an end-to-end manner with a batch size of 100 pairs in an iteration. The weight parameters (i.e. filters) of the networks are initialized uniformly following [14]. The gradients with respect to the feature vectors at the last layer are computed from the contrastive loss function and back-propagated to the lower layers of the network. Once all the gradients are computed at all the layers, we use mini batch stochastic gradient descent (SGD) to update the parameters of the network. Specifically, we use the adaptive per-parameter update strategy called the RMSProp [6] to update the weights. The decay parameter for RMSProp is fixed to 0.95 following previous works [17] and the margin for the contrastive loss function is kept as 1. Training is done for 20 epochs with an early stopping strategy based on the saturation of the validation set performance. The initial learning rate is set to 0.002 and reduced by a factor of 0.9 after each epoch. The main hyper-parameter of the MG is the initial value of $\mathbf{p}$. We set this value to 4 initially and the network discovers the optimal value during learning. More details on parameter tuning and validation are given in the supplementary material.

Testing: During testing, each query image has to be paired with all the gallery images and passed to the network. The gating function can selectively boost the common patterns in each image pair. The Euclidean distance between the feature vectors obtained at the last layer is used to compare two input images. Once the distance between the query image and all the images in the gallery set are obtained, it is sorted in ascending order to find the top matches. The above procedure is done for all the query images and the final results are obtained. For an identity with multiple query images, the distances obtained for each query are rescaled in the range of 0–1 and then averaged.

4   Experiments

We provide a comprehensive evaluation of the proposed S-CNN architecture with the matching gate by comparing it against the baseline S-CNN architecture as well as other state-of-the-art algorithms for human re-identification. Majority of the human re-identification systems are evaluated based on the Cumulative Matching Characteristics by treating human re-identification as a ranking problem. However, in [57], human re-identification is treated as a retrieval problem and the mean average precision (mAP) is also reported along with the Rank - 1 accuracy (R1 Acc). For a fair comparison, we report both mAP as well as the performance at different ranks for CUHK03 dataset and mAP and R1 Acc for Market-1501 dataset. For VIPeR dataset, we report only the CMC as it is the relevant measure [57]. All the implementations are done in MATLAB-R2015b and we use the MatConvNet package [42] for implementing all the proposed frameworks. Experiments were run on NVIDIA-Tesla K40 GPU and it took approximately 40–50 minutes per epoch on the CUHK03 dataset.

4.1   Datasets and Settings

Experiments were conducted on challenging benchmark datasets for human re-identification, the Market-1501 [57] dataset, the CUHK03 [21] dataset and the VIPeR [10] dataset. Below, we give the details of the datasets.

Market-1501: The Market-1501 dataset contains 32668 annotated bounding boxes of 1501 subjects captured from 6 cameras and is currently the largest dataset for human re-identification. The bounding boxes for the pedestrian images are obtained by using deformable parts model detectors. Therefore, the bounding boxes are not as ideal as the ones generated by human annotators and there are also several mis-detections which make the dataset very challenging. Following the standard evaluation protocols in [57], the dataset is split into 751 identities for training and 750 identities for testing. We report the single-query (SQ) as well as the multi-query (MQ) evaluation results for this dataset. For multi-query evaluation, the matching scores obtained for each of the query images per identity are rescaled from 0–1 and averaged to obtain the final matching score.

CUHK03: CUHK03 dataset contains 13164 images of 1360 subjects collected on the CUHK campus. Authors of [21] provide two different settings for evaluating on this dataset, 'detected' with automatically generated bounding boxes and 'labeled' with human annotated bounding boxes. All the experiments presented in this paper follow the 'detected' setting as this is closer to the real-world scenario. Following the splitting settings provided in [21], evaluation is conducted 20 times with 100 test subjects and the average result obtained at different ranks is reported. We also use 100 identities from the training set for cross-validation leaving out 1160 identities for training the network.

Table 2. Performance Comparison of state-of-the-art algorithms for the Market-1501 dataset. Proposed baseline S-CNN architecture outperforms the previous works for Market-1501 dataset. The S-CNN architecture with the gating function advances the state-of-the-art results on the Market-1501 dataset.

Method	Rank 1	mAP
SDALF [8]	20.53	8.20
eSDC [54]	33.54	13.54
BoW [57] - (SQ)	34.40	14.09
DNS [50] - (SQ)	61.02	35.68
Ours - Baseline - S-CNN - (SQ)	**62.32**	**36.23**
Ours - With Matching Gate - (SQ)	**65.88**	**39.55**
BoW [57] - (MQ)	42.14	19.20
BoW + HS [57] - (MQ)	47.25	21.88
S-LSTM [40] - (MQ)	61.60	35.31
DNS [50] - (MQ)	71.56	46.03
Ours - Baseline - S-CNN - (MQ)	**72.92**	**45.39**
Ours - With Matching Gate - (MQ)	**76.04**	**48.45**

VIPeR: VIPeR dataset consists of 1264 images belonging to 632 subjects captured using 2 cameras. The dataset is relatively small and the number of distinct identities as well as positive pairs per identity for training are very less compared to the other datasets. Therefore, we conduct data augmentation as well as transfer learning from Market-1501 and CUHK03 datasets. For transfer learning, we remove the last fully connected layer in our baseline S-CNN architecture and then fine-tune the network using the VIPeR dataset. Removing the last fully connected layer was to avoid over-fitting by reducing the number of parameters. For the gated S-CNN framework, the MGs are inserted between layers 4–5 and 5–6. Other experimental settings are kept the same as in [1].

4.2 Results and Discussion

The results for the Market-1501, CUHK03 and VIPeR datasets are given in Tables 2, 3 and 4 respectively. The proposed baseline S-CNN architecture outperforms all the existing approaches for human re-identification for Market-1501 and CUHK03 datasets at Rank 1. We believe that the baseline S-CNN architecture sets a strong baseline for comparison of supervised techniques in future works for both datasets. However, for VIPeR dataset, even though our baseline S-CNN does not achieve the best results, it outperforms several other CNN based architectures [1,43,49]. Our final architecture with the MG improves over the baseline architecture by a margin of 4.2 % and 1.6 % at Rank 1 for CUHK03 and VIPeR datasets respectively. For Market-1501 dataset, our approach outperforms the baseline by a margin of 3.56 % at Rank 1 for single query (SQ) setting and 3.12 % at Rank 1 for multi query (MQ) setting.

Table 3. Performance Comparison of state-of-the-art algorithms for the CUHK03 dataset on the 'detected' setting. Proposed baseline S-CNN architecture outperforms all the previous state-of-the-art methods for CUHK03 dataset at Rank 1. The proposed variant of the S-CNN architecture with the gating function achieves the state-of-the-art results on CUHK03 benchmark dataset. In addition to the results at various ranks, we also provide the mean average precision to analyze the retrieval performance.

Method	Rank 1	Rank 5	Rank 10	mAP
SDALF [8]	4.9	21.0	31.7	-
ITML [7]	5.14	17.7	28.3	-
LMNN [44]	6.25	18.7	29.0	-
eSDC [54]	7.68	22.0	33.3	-
LDML [11]	10.9	32.3	46.7	-
KISSME [18]	11.7	33.3	48.0	-
FPNN [21]	19.9	49.3	64.7	-
BoW [57]	23.0	45.0	55.7	-
BoW + HS [57]	24.3	-	-	-
ConvNet [1]	45.0	75.3	55.0	-
LX [23]	46.3	78.9	88.6	-
MLAPG [24]	51.2	83.6	92.1	-
SS-SVM [51]	51.2	80.8	89.6	-
SI-CI [43]	52.2	84.3	92.3	-
DNS [50]	54.7	84.8	**94.8**	-
S-LSTM [40]	57.3	80.1	88.3	46.3
Ours - Baseline - S-CNN	**63.9**	**86.7**	92.6	**55.57**
Ours - With Matching Gate	**68.1**	**88.1**	94.6	**58.84**

For multi-camera networks, the mean average precision is a better measure for performance compared to the Rank - 1 accuracy [57] as it signifies how many of the correct matches are retrieved from various camera views. Therefore, compared to the improvement in Rank 1 accuracy, the mean average precision which indicates the retrieval accuracy may be more interesting for real-world applications with camera networks. Even though the mean average precision is not particularly important for CUHK03 dataset as it contains only two views, we report the mAP to compare the retrieval results of the proposed final architecture with the baseline S-CNN architecture. It can be seen that our final architecture with MG outperforms the mean average precision obtained by the baseline S-CNN by a margin of 3.32 %, 3.06 % and 3.27 % for Market-1501-Single Query, Market-1501-Multi Query and CUHK03 datasets respectively.

The visualization of the gating mechanism in the proposed matching gate is shown in Fig. 3. Figure 3(a) shows a query image and a hard negative image (example shown in Fig. 1(b)). The middle row shows the average feature

Table 4. Performance Comparison of state-of-the-art algorithms using an individual method for the VIPeR dataset. Proposed S-CNN framework outperforms several previous deep learning approaches for human re-identification [1,49]. Our S-CNN with MG achieves promising results compared to other approaches.

Method	Rank 1	Rank 5	Rank 10
LFDA [31]	24.1	51.2	67.1
eSDC [54]	26.9	47.5	62.3
Mid-level [55]	29.1	52.3	65.9
SVMML [22]	29.4	63.3	76.3
VWCM [52]	30.7	63.0	76.0
SalMatch [53]	30.2	52.3	65.5
QAF [56]	30.2	51.6	62.4
DML [49]	28.2	59.3	73.5
ConvNet [1]	34.8	63.7	75.8
CMWCE [47]	37.6	68.1	81.3
SCNCD [48]	37.8	68.5	81.2
LX [23]	40.0	68.1	80.5
PRCSL [33]	34.8	68.7	82.3
MLAPG [24]	40.7	69.9	82.3
MT-LORAE [38]	42.3	**72.2**	81.6
Semantic [34]	41.6	71.9	**86.2**
S-LSTM [40]	42.4	68.7	79.4
DGDropout [45]	38.6	-	-
SI-CI [43]	35.8	67.4	83.5
SS-SVM [51]	42.7	-	84.3
MCP-CNN [4]	47.8	74.7	84.8
HGD [29]	49.7	79.7	88.7
DNS [50]	51.7	82.1	90.5
SCSP [3]	**53.5**	**82.6**	**91.5**
Ours - Baseline - S-CNN	36.2	65.1	76.3
Ours - With Matching Gate	37.8	66.9	77.4

activations at the output of the 4th convolutional block which is the input to the proposed gating function and the third row shows the obtained gate values using the proposed gating function. It can be seen that for the first few rows where the subject in the query is wearing a hat, the gate activations are low indicating lower similarity where as for a few middle rows, the gate activations are high indicating higher similarity. In Fig. 3(b), we show the image paired with its true positive, the layer 5 inputs and the gate values. It can be seen that for majority of the patches, the gate values are high indicating high similarity between the

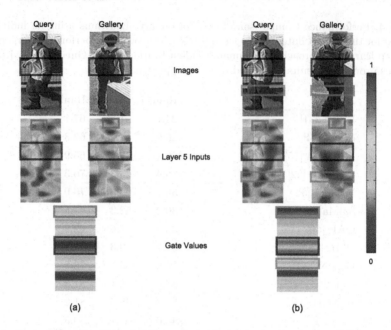

Fig. 3. Gate Visualization: (a) Query paired with its hard-negative (b) Query paired with its positive. Middle row shows the layer 5 input values of all the 4 images and last row shows the corresponding gate values obtained for both pairs. Boxes of same color indicates corresponding regions in the images. **Best viewed in color** (Color figure online)

image patches. This indicates that the gating function can efficiently extract relevant common information from the feature maps of both the images and boost them.

5 Conclusion and Future Works

We have proposed a baseline siamese CNN and a learnable Matching Gate function for siamese CNN that can vary the network behavior during training and testing for the task of human re-identification. The Matching Gate can compare the local features along a horizontal stripe for an input image pair during run-time and adaptively boost local features for enhancing the discriminative capability of the propagated features. The gating function is also designed to be a differentiable one with learnable parameters for adjusting the variance of the gate values as well as for summarizing the horizontal stripe features. This is essential for adjusting the amount of filtering at each stage of the network as well as to facilitate end-to-end learning of deep networks. We have conducted experiments on the Market-1501 dataset, the CUHK03 dataset and the VIPeR dataset to evaluate how run-time feature selection can enable the network to learn more discriminative features for extracting meaningful similarity information for an input pair. The introduction of the gating function in between convolutional layers results in significant improvement of performance over the baseline S-CNN. Our S-CNN model with the matching gate achieves promising results compared to the state-of-the-art algorithms on the above datasets.

Acknowledgments. The research is supported by Singapore Ministry of Education (MOE) Tier 2 ARC28/14, and Singapore A*STAR Science and Engineering Research Council PSF1321202099.

This research was carried out at the Rapid-Rich Object Search (ROSE) Lab at Nanyang Technological University. The ROSE Lab is supported by the National Research Foundation, Singapore, under its Interactive Digital Media (IDM) Strategic Research Programme.

We thank NVIDIA Corporation for their generous GPU donation to carry out this research.

References

1. Ahmed, E., Jones, M., Marks, T.K.: An improved deep learning architecture for person re-identification. In: IEEE Conference on Computer Vision and Pattern Recognition (CVPR) (2015)
2. Bromley, J., Guyon, I., LeCun, Y., Säckinger, E., Shah, R.: Signature verification using a "siamese" time delay neural network. In: Advances in Neural Information Processing Systems, vol. 6 (1994)
3. Chen, D., Yuan, Z., Chen, B., Zheng, N.: Similarity learning with spatial constraints for person re-identification. In: The IEEE Conference on Computer Vision and Pattern Recognition (CVPR) (2016)
4. Cheng, D., Gong, Y., Zhou, S., Wang, J., Zheng, N.: Person re-identification by multi-channel parts-based CNN with improved triplet loss function. In: The IEEE Conference on Computer Vision and Pattern Recognition (CVPR) (2016)
5. Cheng, D.S., Cristani, M., Stoppa, M., Bazzani, L., Murino, V.: Custom pictorial structures for re-identification. In: Proceedings of the British Machine Vision Conference (BMVC) (2011)
6. Dauphin, Y.N., de Vries, H., Chung, J., Bengio, Y.: RMSProp and equilibrated adaptive learning rates for non-convex optimization. CoRR abs/1502.04390 (2015). http://arxiv.org/abs/1502.04390
7. Davis, J.V., Kulis, B., Jain, P., Sra, S., Dhillon, I.S.: Information-theoretic metric learning. In: Proceedings of the International Conference on Machine Learning (ICML) (2007)
8. Farenzena, M., Bazzani, L., Perina, A., Murino, V., Cristani, M.: Person re-identification by symmetry-driven accumulation of local features. In: IEEE Conference on Computer Vision and Pattern Recognition (CVPR) (2010)
9. Gers, F., Schmidhuber, J., Cummins, F.: Learning to forget: continual prediction with LSTM. In: International Conference on Artificial Neural Networks, ICANN 1999 (1999)
10. Gray, D., Brennan, S., Tao, H.: Evaluating appearance models for recognition, reacquisition, and tracking. In: IEEE International Workshop on Performance Evaluation of Tracking and Surveillance (PETS) (2007)
11. Guillaumin, M., Verbeek, J., Schmid, C.: Is that you? Metric learning approaches for face identification. In: IEEE 12th International Conference on Computer Vision, ICCV 2009 (2009)

12. Hadsell, R., Chopra, S., LeCun, Y.: Dimensionality reduction by learning an invariant mapping. In: Proceedings of the IEEE Conference on Computer Vision and Pattern Recognition, CVPR 2006 (2006)
13. He, K., Zhang, X., Ren, S., Sun, J.: Deep residual learning for image recognition. CoRR abs/1512.03385 (2015). http://arxiv.org/abs/1512.03385
14. He, K., Zhang, X., Ren, S., Sun, J.: Delving deep into rectifiers: surpassing human-level performance on imagenet classification. CoRR abs/1502.01852 (2015). http://arxiv.org/abs/1502.01852
15. Hochreiter, S., Schmidhuber, J.: Long short-term memory. Neural Comput. **9**, 1735–1780 (1997)
16. Ioffe, S., Szegedy, C.: Batch normalization: accelerating deep network training by reducing internal covariate shift. CoRR abs/1502.03167 (2015). http://arxiv.org/abs/1502.03167
17. Karpathy, A., Johnson, J., Li, F.: Visualizing and understanding recurrent networks. CoRR abs/1506.02078 (2015). http://arxiv.org/abs/1506.02078
18. Kostinger, M., Hirzer, M., Wohlhart, P., Roth, P., Bischof, H.: Large scale metric learning from equivalence constraints. In: IEEE Conference on Computer Vision and Pattern Recognition (CVPR) (2012)
19. Kviatkovsky, I., Adam, A., Rivlin, E.: Color invariants for person reidentification. IEEE Trans. Pattern Anal. Mach. Intell. (TPAMI) **35**, 1622–1634 (2013)
20. Li, W., Zhao, R., Wang, X.: Human reidentification with transferred metric learning. In: Lee, K.M., Matsushita, Y., Rehg, J.M., Hu, Z. (eds.) ACCV 2012, Part I. LNCS, vol. 7724, pp. 31–44. Springer, Heidelberg (2013). doi:10.1007/978-3-642-37331-2_3
21. Li, W., Zhao, R., Xiao, T., Wang, X.: DeepReID: deep filter pairing neural network for person re-identification. In: 2014 IEEE Conference on Computer Vision and Pattern Recognition (CVPR), pp. 152–159, June 2014
22. Li, Z., Chang, S., Liang, F., Huang, T.S., Cao, L., Smith, J.R.: Learning locally-adaptive decision functions for person verification. In: IEEE Conference on Computer Vision and Pattern Recognition (CVPR) (2013)
23. Liao, S., Hu, Y., Zhu, X., Li, S.Z.: Person re-identification by local maximal occurrence representation and metric learning. In: The IEEE Conference on Computer Vision and Pattern Recognition (CVPR) (2015)
24. Liao, S., Li, S.Z.: Efficient PSD constrained asymmetric metric learning for person re-identification. In: Proceedings of the IEEE International Conference on Computer Vision, pp. 3685–3693 (2015)
25. Liao, S., Zhao, G., Kellokumpu, V., Pietikainen, M., Li, S.: Modeling pixel process with scale invariant local patterns for background subtraction in complex scenes. In: IEEE Conference on Computer Vision and Pattern Recognition (CVPR) (2010)
26. Liu, J., Shahroudy, A., Xu, D., Wang, G.: Spatio-temporal LSTM with trust gates for 3D human action recognition. In: European Conference on Computer Vision (ECCV) (2016)
27. Lowe, D.G.: Distinctive image features from scale-invariant keypoints. Int. J. Comput. Vis. (IJCV) **60**, 91–110 (2004)
28. Ma, B., Su, Y., Jurie, F.: BiCov: a novel image representation for person re-identification and face verification. In: Proceedings of the British Machive Vision Conference (BMVC) (2012)
29. Matsukawa, T., Okabe, T., Suzuki, E., Sato, Y.: Hierarchical Gaussian descriptor for person re-identification. In: The IEEE Conference on Computer Vision and Pattern Recognition (CVPR) (2016)

30. Ojala, T., Pietikainen, M., Maenpaa, T.: Multiresolution gray-scale and rotation invariant texture classification with local binary patterns. IEEE Trans. Pattern Anal. Mach. Intell. (TPAMI) **24**, 971–987 (2002)
31. Pedagadi, S., Orwell, J., Velastin, S., Boghossian, B.: Local fisher discriminant analysis for pedestrian re-identification. In: IEEE Conference on Computer Vision and Pattern Recognition (CVPR) (2013)
32. Rama Varior, R., Wang, G.: Hierarchical invariant feature learning with marginalization for person re-identification. ArXiv e-prints (2015)
33. Shen, Y., Lin, W., Yan, J., Xu, M., Wu, J., Wang, J.: Person re-identification with correspondence structure learning. In: The IEEE International Conference on Computer Vision (ICCV) (2015)
34. Shi, Z., Hospedales, T.M., Xiang, T.: Transferring a semantic representation for person re-identification and search. In: IEEE Conference on Computer Vision and Pattern Recognition (CVPR) (2015)
35. Shuai, B., Wang, G., Zuo, Z., Wang, B., Zhao, L.: Integrating parametric and non-parametric models for scene labeling. In: 2015 IEEE Conference on Computer Vision and Pattern Recognition (CVPR), pp. 4249–4258, June 2015
36. Simonyan, K., Zisserman, A.: Very deep convolutional networks for large-scale image recognition. CoRR abs/1409.1556 (2014). http://arxiv.org/abs/1409.1556
37. Srivastava, R.K., Greff, K., Schmidhuber, J.: Training very deep networks. In: Cortes, C., Lawrence, N.D., Lee, D.D., Sugiyama, M., Garnett, R. (eds.) Advances in Neural Information Processing Systems, vol. 28, pp. 2377–2385. Curran Associates, Inc. (2015). http://papers.nips.cc/paper/5850-training-very-deep-networks.pdf
38. Su, C., Yang, F., Zhang, S., Tian, Q., Davis, L.S., Gao, W.: Multi-task learning with low rank attribute embedding for person re-identification. In: The IEEE International Conference on Computer Vision (ICCV), December 2015
39. Szegedy, C., Vanhoucke, V., Ioffe, S., Shlens, J., Wojna, Z.: Rethinking the inception architecture for computer vision. CoRR abs/1512.00567 (2015). http://arxiv.org/abs/1512.00567
40. Varior, R.R., Shuai, B., Lu, J., Xu, D., Wang, G.: A siamese long short-term memory architecture for human re-identification. In: European Conference on Computer Vision (ECCV) (2016)
41. Varior, R.R., Wang, G., Lu, J., Liu, T.: Learning invariant color features for person re-identification. IEEE Trans. Image Process. **PP**(99), 1 (2016)
42. Vedaldi, A., Lenc, K.: Matconvnet – convolutional neural networks for matlab (2015)
43. Wang, F., Zuo, W., Lin, L., Zhang, D., Zhang, L.: Joint learning of single-image and cross-image representations for person re-identification. In: The IEEE Conference on Computer Vision and Pattern Recognition (CVPR) (2016)
44. Weinberger, K.Q., Saul, L.K.: Distance metric learning for large margin nearest neighbor classification. J. Mach. Learn. Res. (JMLR) **10**, 207–244 (2009)
45. Xiao, T., Li, H., Ouyang, W., Wang, X.: Learning deep feature representations with domain guided dropout for person re-identification. In: The IEEE Conference on Computer Vision and Pattern Recognition (CVPR) (2016)
46. Xiong, F., Gou, M., Camps, O., Sznaier, M.: Person re-identification using kernel-based metric learning methods. In: Fleet, D., Pajdla, T., Schiele, B., Tuytelaars, T. (eds.) ECCV 2014, Part VII. LNCS, vol. 8695, pp. 1–16. Springer, Heidelberg (2014). doi:10.1007/978-3-319-10584-0_1
47. Yang, Y., Liao, S., Lei, Z., Yi, D., Li, S.Z.: Color models and weighted covariance estimation for person re-identification. In: Proceedings of International Conference on Pattern Recognition (ICPR) (2014)

48. Yang, Y., Yang, J., Yan, J., Liao, S., Yi, D., Li, S.Z.: Salient color names for person re-identification. In: Fleet, D., Pajdla, T., Schiele, B., Tuytelaars, T. (eds.) ECCV 2014, Part I. LNCS, vol. 8689, pp. 536–551. Springer, Heidelberg (2014). doi:10. 1007/978-3-319-10590-1_35

49. Yi, D., Lei, Z., Liao, S., Li, S.Z.: Deep metric learning for person re-identification. In: Proceedings of International Conference on Pattern Recognition (ICPR) (2014)

50. Zhang, L., Xiang, T., Gong, S.: Learning a discriminative null space for person re-identification. In: The IEEE Conference on Computer Vision and Pattern Recognition (CVPR) (2016)

51. Zhang, Y., Li, B., Lu, H., Irie, A., Ruan, X.: Sample-specific SVM learning for person re-identification. In: The IEEE Conference on Computer Vision and Pattern Recognition (CVPR) (2016)

52. Zhang, Z., Chen, Y., Saligrama, V.: A novel visual word co-occurrence model for person re-identification. In: European Conference on Computer Vision Workshop on Visual Surveillance and Re-identification (ECCV Workshop) (2014)

53. Zhao, R., Ouyang, W., Wang, X.: Person re-identification by salience matching. In: IEEE International Conference on Computer Vision (ICCV) (2013)

54. Zhao, R., Ouyang, W., Wang, X.: Unsupervised salience learning for person re-identification. In: IEEE Conference on Computer Vision and Pattern Recognition (CVPR) (2013)

55. Zhao, R., Ouyang, W., Wang, X.: Learning mid-level filters for person re-identfiation. In: IEEE Conference on Computer Vision and Pattern Recognition (CVPR) (2014)

56. Zheng, L., Wang, S., Tian, L., He, F., Liu, Z., Tian, Q.: Query-adaptive late fusion for image search and person re-identification. In: IEEE Conference on Computer Vision and Pattern Recognition (CVPR) (2015)

57. Zheng, L., Shen, L., Tian, L., Wang, S., Wang, J., Bu, J., Tian, Q.: Scalable person re-identification: a benchmark. In: IEEE International Conference on Computer Vision (2015)

Saliency Detection via Combining Region-Level and Pixel-Level Predictions with CNNs

Youbao Tang and Xiangqian Wu[⊠]

Harbin Institute of Technology, Harbin 150001, China
{tangyoubao,xqwu}@hit.edu.cn

Abstract. This paper proposes a novel saliency detection method by combining region-level saliency estimation and pixel-level saliency prediction with CNNs (denoted as CRPSD). For pixel-level saliency prediction, a fully convolutional neural network (called pixel-level CNN) is constructed by modifying the VGGNet architecture to perform multi-scale feature learning, based on which an image-to-image prediction is conducted to accomplish the pixel-level saliency detection. For region-level saliency estimation, an adaptive superpixel based region generation technique is first designed to partition an image into regions, based on which the region-level saliency is estimated by using a CNN model (called region-level CNN). The pixel-level and region-level saliencies are fused to form the final salient map by using another CNN (called fusion CNN). And the pixel-level CNN and fusion CNN are jointly learned. Extensive quantitative and qualitative experiments on four public benchmark datasets demonstrate that the proposed method greatly outperforms the state-of-the-art saliency detection approaches.

Keywords: Saliency detection · Convolutional neural network · Region-level saliency estimation · Pixel-level saliency prediction · Saliency fusion

1 Introduction

Visual saliency detection, which is an important and challenging task in computer vision, aims to highlight the most important object regions in an image. Numerous image processing applications incorporate the visual saliency to improve their performance, such as image segmentation [1] and cropping [2], object detection [3], and image retrieval [4], etc.

The main task of saliency detection is to extract discriminative features to represent the properties of pixels or regions and use machine learning algorithms to compute salient scores to measure their importances. A large number of saliency detection approaches [5–36] have been proposed by exploiting different salient cues recently. They can be roughly categorized as pixel based approaches and region based approaches. For the pixel based approaches, the local and global features, including edges [5], color difference [36], spatial information [6], distance transformation [30], and so on, are extracted from pixels for saliency detection.

© Springer International Publishing AG 2016
B. Leibe et al. (Eds.): ECCV 2016, Part VIII, LNCS 9912, pp. 809–825, 2016.
DOI: 10.1007/978-3-319-46484-8_49

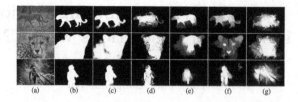

Fig. 1. Three examples of saliency detection results estimated by the proposed method and the state-of-the-art approaches. (a) The input images. (b) The ground truths. (c) The salient maps detected by the proposed method. (d)-(g) The salient maps detected by the state-of-the-art approaches MC [26], MDF [21], LEGS [28], and MB+ [30].

Generally, these approaches highlight high contrast edges instead of the salient objects, or get low contrast salient maps. That is because the extracted features are unable to capture the high-level and multi-scale information of pixels. As we know that convolutional neural network (CNN) is powerful for high-level and multi-scale feature learning and has been successfully used in many applications of computer vision, such as semantic segmentation [37,38], edge detection [39,40], etc. This work will employ CNN for pixel-level saliency detection.

For the region based approaches, they first segment an image into a number of regions, and then many different kinds of hand-designed features [7–10, 17,18,23,25,27,32–35] and CNN based features [21,26,28] are extracted to compute the salienies from these regions. Compared with the pixel based approaches, these regions based approaches are more effective to detect the saliency since more sophisticated and discriminative features can be extracted from regions. The approaches based on CNN learned features have gotten better performance than the ones based on hand-designed features. That is because CNN is able to extract more robust and discriminative features with considering the global context information of regions. Therefore, this work also employs CNN for region-level saliency estimation. Recently, the best region based saliency detection approach proposed by Zhao et al. [26] extracts superpixels as regions, then estimates the saliency for each superpixel based on CNN. In their work, an inevitable problem is that it is hard to decide the number of superpixels. If there are too few superpixels, the regions belonging to salient objects may be under-segmented. If there are too many superpixels, the regions belonging to saliency objects or backgrounds may be over-segmented, which may cause that the saliencies are not uniform in salient objects or backgrounds, and the superpixels around the boundaries of background and salient objects may get wrong saliencies. Furthermore, the number of superpixels should be different according to the complexity of images. In this paper, we follow their work and propose an adaptive superpixel based region generation technique, which can automatically determine the number of generated regions for different images to solve the above-mentioned problems and improve the performance of saliency detection.

Since pixel-level and region-level saliency detection approaches make use of different information of images, these two salient maps are complementary.

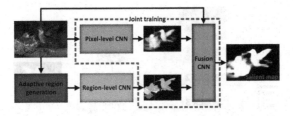

Fig. 2. The framework of the proposed method.

Hence, we propose a CNN network to fuse the pixel-level and the region-level saliencies to improve the performance. Figure 1 shows some results of the proposed method, which are very close to the ground truths.

Figure 2 shows the framework of proposed method, which consists of three stages, i.e. pixel-level saliency prediction, region-level saliency estimation, and the salient map fusion. For pixel-level saliency prediction, a pixel-level CNN is constructed by modifying the VGGNet [41] and finetuning from the pre-trained VGGNet model for pixel-level saliency prediction. For region-level saliency estimation, the input image is first segmented into a number of regions by using an adaptive superpixel based region generation technique. Then for each region, a salient score is estimated based on a region-level CNN. For salient map fusion, the pixel-level and region-level salient maps are fused to form the final salient map by using a fusion CNN which is jointly trained with the pixel-level CNN.

The main contributions of this paper are summarized as follows. (1) A novel multiple CNN framework is proposed to extract and combine pixel and region information of images for saliency detection. (2) A pixel-level CNN is devised for pixel-level saliency prediction. (3) An adaptive region generation technique is developed to generate regions and based on which a region-level CNN is used for region-level saliency estimation. (4) A fusion-level CNN is proposed to fuse the pixel-level and region-level saliencies.

2 Pixel-Level Saliency Prediction

CNN has achieved a great success in various applications of computer vision, such as classification and segmentation. Here, we proposed a CNN (denoted as pixel-level CNN) to predict the saliency for each pixel. Pixel-level CNN takes the original image as the input and the salient map as the output. To get an accurate saliency prediction, the CNN architecture should be deep and have multi-scale stages with different strides, so as to learn discriminative and multi-scale features for pixels. Training such a deep network from scratch is difficult when the training samples is not enough. However, there are several networks which have achieved the state-of-the-art results in the ImageNet challenge, such as VGGNet [41] and GoogleNet [42]. So it is an effective way to use these excellent models trained on the large-scale dataset as the pre-trained model for finetuning.

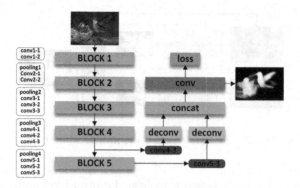

Fig. 3. The architecture of the pixel-level CNN network.

In this work, we construct a deep CNN architecture based on VGGNet for pixel-level saliency prediction. The VGGNet consists of six blocks. The first five blocks contain convolutional layers and pooling layers, as shown in Fig. 3. The last block contains one pooling layer and two fully connected layer, which are used to form the final feature vector for image classification. While for saliency prediction, we need to modify the VGGNet to extract dense pixel-level features. Therefore, the last block is removed in this work. There are two main reasons for this modification. The first one is that the fully connected layers cost much time and memory during training and testing. The second one is that the output of the last pooling layer is too small compared with the original image, which will reduce the accuracy of fullsize prediction. In order to capture the multi-scale information, we combine the outputs of the last two blocks of the modified VGGNet for the multi-scale feature learning. The benefits of doing such combination is two-fold. The first one is that the receptive field size becomes larger when the output size of blocks becomes smaller. Therefore, the output combination of multiple blocks can automatically learn the multi-scale features. The second one is that the shallow blocks mainly learn the local features, such as edges and parts of objects, which are not very useful for saliency detection since we hope to capture the global information of whole salient objects. Therefore, the outputs of the last two blocks are combined for multi-scale feature learning.

Since the output sizes of the last two blocks are different and smaller than the size of the input image. To make the whole CNN network automatically learn the multi-scale features for pixel-level saliency prediction, we first perform the deconvolutional operation for the outputs of the last two blocks to make them have the same size with the input image, and concatenate them in the channel direction. Then a convolutional kernel with size of 1×1 is used to map the concatenation feature maps into a probability map, in which larger values mean more saliencies. For testing, the probability map actually is a salient map of the input image. For training, a loss function is needed to compute the errors between the probability map and the ground truth. For most of the images, the numbers of salient and non-salient pixels are heavily imbalanced. Therefore,

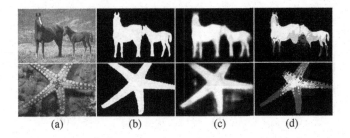

Fig. 4. Examples of pixel-level saliency prediction results. (a) Original images. (b) Ground truths. (c) Pixel-level saliency prediction results. (d) Salient maps estimated by the state-of-the-art approach MC [26].

given an image X and its ground truth Y, a cross-entropy loss function is used to balance the loss between salient and non-salient classes as follows:

$$L\left(\mathbf{W}\right) = -\alpha \sum_{i=1}^{|Y_+|} \log P\left(y_i = 1 | X, \mathbf{W}\right) - (1 - \alpha) \sum_{i=1}^{|Y_-|} \log P\left(y_i = 0 | X, \mathbf{W}\right) \quad (1)$$

where $\alpha = |Y_-| / (|Y_+| + |Y_-|)$, $|Y_+|$ and $|Y_-|$ mean the number of salient pixels and non-salient pixels in ground truth, and $\mathbf{W}$ denotes the parameters of all network layers. Here and now, the whole pixel-level CNN architecture is constructed as shown in Fig. 3. The standard stochastic gradient descent algorithm is used to minimize the above loss function during training. After training, given an image, we can use the trained CNN model to predict a pixel-level salient map. Figure 4 shows two examples of pixel-level saliency prediction results.

3   Region-Level Saliency Estimation

Inspired by the successful application of CNN in salient object detection [21, 26, 28], all of which are based on regions (e.g. superpixels [26] and multi-scale regions [21]), this work also employs CNN for the region-level saliency estimation.

3.1   Adaptive Region Generation

During the region-level saliency estimation, the first step is to generate a number of regions from the input image. Wang et al. [28] use the regions in sliding windows to estimate their saliencies, which may result in the salient object and background in the same sliding window having the same saliency. Li et al. [21] use multi-scale hierarchical regions, which consumes much time to perform the region segmentation and some generated regions are under-segmented. Zhao et al. [26] use superpixels as the regions to estimate their saliencies, which is difficult to decide the number of superpixels. If there are too few superpixels, the regions belonging to salient objects may be under-segmented. If there are too many superpixels, the regions belonging to saliency objects or backgrounds

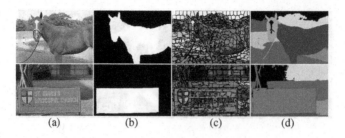

| (a) | (b) | (c) | (d) |

Fig. 5. Examples of our adaptive region generation technique. (a) Original images. (b) Ground truths. (c) Superpixel segmentation results. (d) Region generation results.

may be over-segmented. Both over-segmentation and under-segmentation may make the saliencies are not uniform in salient objects or backgrounds. Different images should be segmented into different number of superpixels because of their different properties.

Since the superpixels based approach [26] gets the state-of-the-art performance, this work proposes an adaptive region generation technique based on this approach to segment the images and solve the above mentioned problems.

Given an input image I, it is first over-segmented into n superpixels by using SLIC algorithm [43]. Here, we set $n = 300$ with considering both of effectiveness and efficiency. Then for each superpixel, a simple feature vector including its average colors in L*a*b color space and average spatial coordinates is computed. Then a graph-based agglomerative clustering algorithm (called Graph Degree Linkage) [44], which takes the superpixel as nodes and assigns each node with k edges whose weights are computed according to the Euclidean distances between the feature vectors of the current node and its k nearest neighbor nodes, is used to cluster the superpixels into different regions. The clustering process is stopped when the least affinity between two clusters is larger than a given threshold t. Therefore, for different images, the numbers of clustered regions are different and are much less than n. The superpixels which are adjacent and have similar colors are usually clustered into the same regions. The whole clustering process has two important parameters k and t, which are set as $k = 15$ and $t = -0.04$ through experiments in this work. Figure 5 shows two examples of region generation results.

3.2 Region Saliency Estimation

After obtaining the regions, the next step is to estimate the regions saliencies. This work employs CNN for region-level saliency estimation. The Clarifai model [45], which is the winning model in the classification task of ImageNet 2013, is used as our CNN model as done by [26]. It contains five convolutional layers and two fully connected layers. For more detail information about this model, please refer to the reference [45]. In this work, we use the CNN model provided by the authors of [26] as the pre-trained model and finetune for the region-level saliency estimation.

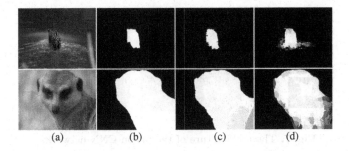

Fig. 6. Examples of region-level saliency estimation results. (a) Original images. (b) Ground truths. (c) Salient maps estimated by the proposed region-level saliency estimation method. (d) Salient maps estimated by superpixel based region saliency estimation method.

In [26], the region in a superpixel-centered large context window is resized and fed into the CNN model to estimate the saliency of current superpixel. If we follow the same way except using region-centered instead of superpixel-centered, a problem will be introduced, that is some background regions may have large saliencies, because the centers of some background regions may belong to or close to the salient objects. To solve this problem, we randomly choose m superpixels around the centerline of each region at first. Then we set these m superpixels centers as the windows centers to construct m large context windows including the full image as done by [26]. We choose superpixels around the regions centerline to make the windows centers far away from the regions boundaries as much as possible, and the constructed windows from different regions are different as much as possible. Here, we set $m = 5$ if the number of superpixels in a region is larger than 5. Otherwise, we set m as the number of superpixels. Through experiments, we find that the performances of saliency detection vary little when $m > 5$.

For each region, we can construct m window images and feed them into the CNN model to obtain m saliencies. In this work, the mean saliency is computed as the regions saliency due to its robustness to noises. Compared with the superpixel-centered saliency estimation approach, the proposed region-level saliency estimation method has three advantages described as follows. (1) More efficiency, because the constructed images are much less than the superpixels. (2) Less boundary effect, which is that the salient regions around the boundaries of salient objects and backgrounds may have small saliencies while the background regions around the boundaries may have large saliencies, as shown in Fig. 6. (3) More uniform salient map, since the pixels in a region are assigned the same salient values, as shown in Fig. 6.

4   Salient Map Fusion

Given an input RGB image, the proposed saliency detection method efficiently produces two salient maps, i.e. region-level salient map and the pixel-level salient

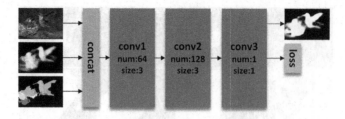

Fig. 7. The architecture of the fusion CNN network.

map. These two salient maps are computed by using different information of images, hence they are complementary and can be fused to further improve the performance.

There are many fusion strategies, such as establishing some measures to select a better individual salient map [11] or combining salient maps with weighted values [7]. They don't use the information of all salient maps or only linearly combine them. In this work, we sufficiently dig their complementary information with a nonlinear manner to improve the performance by using a CNN network. The CNN network contains one concatenation layer, three convolutional layers, and a loss layer, as shown in Fig. 7. The input image and its two salient maps are concatenated into a 5-channel image, and then through three convolutional layers whose configures are given in Fig. 7. For testing, the output of the last convolutional layer is the prediction salient map. For training, the loss layer is used to compute the errors between the output of the last convolutional layer and the ground truth with the cross-entropy loss function described before. It is needed to be noticed that the original image also is used for fusion except two salient maps. That's because richer information of original images is incorporated to correct some errors which cannot be solved by only using the salient maps.

The fusion CNN network can be trained separately. But as we know that joint training multiple sub-networks can gain the performance improvement. In this work, the region-level salient estimation needs to generate a number of regions at the beginning and the region-level CNN has a big different with the pixel-level CNN and fusion CNN. So it is hard to treat all of these three CNN network as an end-to-end network for joint training. Finally, the region-level CNN is trained alone, and after that, the pixel-level CNN and fusion CNN are jointly trained to get the final salient map as shown in Fig. 2. Based on the final salient maps, some post-processings, such as fully connected CRF [46], can be used to further improve the performance. But in this work, to focus on the performance of saliency detection models, we don't conduct any post-processing.

5   Experiments

5.1   Implementation

We use the popular Caffe library [47] to implement the proposed saliency detection framework. The THUS-10000 dataset [34] contains 10,000 images and their corresponding ground truths, which is used for CNN model training. For the region-level CNN network training, we use the Clarifai model trained by [26] as the pre-trained model to finetune on the training dataset. Before joint training the pixel-level CNN and fusion CNN network, we separately train them to get the initial models. For the pixel-level CNN network, since it is a fully convolutional network, arbitrary images don't need to be resized. And the weights of the first five blocks of VGGNet model trained on ImageNet are used to do the weight initialization, based on which the modified VGGNet is finetuned for pixel-level saliency prediction. For the fusion CNN network, we train the model from scratch. After obtaining the initial models of pixel-level and fusion CNN network, we use the weights of these models as weight initialization of the joint CNN network and use the training dataset to do the end-to-end training. The above training process costs about 49 h for 30,000 iterations on a PC with an Intel i7-4790k CPU, a TESLA k40c GPU, and 32 G RAM. For testing on an image with the size of 300 × 400, the region-level saliency estimation takes about 0.5 s, the process of pixel-level saliency prediction and saliency fusion takes about 0.38 s. Therefore, the whole process time of our saliency detection method is about 0.88 s.

5.2   Datasets and Evaluation Criteria

Datasets. We evaluate the proposed method on four standard benchmark datasets: SED [48], ECSSD [7], PASCAL-S [19], and HKU-IS [21].

SED [48] contains 200 images with one or two salient object, in which objects have largely different sizes and locations. This dataset is the combination of SED1 and SED2 dataset.

ECSSD [7] contains 1,000 images with complex backgrounds, which makes the detection tasks much more challenging.

PASCAL-S [19] is constructed on the validation set of the PASCAL VOC 2012 segmentation challenge. This dataset contains 850 natural images with multiple complex objects and cluttered backgrounds. The PASCAL-S data set is arguably one of the most challenging saliency data sets without various design biases (e.g., center bias and color contrast bias).

HKU-IS [21] contains 4447 challenging images, which is newly developed by considering at least one of the following criteria: (1) there are multiple disconnected salient objects, (2) at least one of the salient objects touches the image boundary, (3) the color contrast (the minimum Chi-square distance between the color histograms of any salient object and its surrounding regions) is less than 0.7.

All datasets provide the corresponding ground truths in the form of accurate pixel-wise human-marked labels for salient regions.

Evaluation Criteria. The standard precision-recall (PR) curves are used for performance evaluation. Precision corresponds to the percentage of salient pixels correctly assigned, while recall corresponds to the fraction of detected salient pixels in relation to the ground truth number of salient pixels. The PR curves are obtained by binarizing the saliency map in the range of 0 and 255. The F-measure (F_β) is the overall performance measurement computed by the weighted harmonic of precision and recall:

$$F_\beta = \frac{\left(1 + \beta^2\right) \times Precision \times Recall}{\beta^2 \times Precision + Recall} \tag{2}$$

where we set $\beta^2 = 0.3$, as done by other approaches.

The mean absolute error (MAE), which is the average per-pixel difference between the ground truth GT and the saliency map S, is also evaluated. Here, GT and S are normalized to the interval $[0, 1]$. MAE is defined as

$$MAE = \frac{\sum\limits_{x=1}^{W} \sum\limits_{y=1}^{H} |S(x,y) - GT(x,y)|}{W \times H} \tag{3}$$

where W and H are the width and height of the image.

We also adopt the weighted F_β metric [49] (denoted as wF_β) for evaluation, which suffers less from curve interpolation flaw, improper assumptions about the independence between pixels, and equal importance assignment to all errors. We use the code and the default setting of wF_β provided by the authors of [49].

5.3   Performance Comparisons with State-of-the-Art Approaches

We compare the proposed method (denoted as CRPSD) and the two submodules (pixel-level saliency prediction, denoted as PSD, and region-level saliency estimation, denoted as RSD) with seventeen existing state-of-the-art saliency detection approaches on four datasets, including MC [26], MDF [21], LEGS [28], CPISA [31], MB+ [30], SO [17], BSCA [25], DRFI [10], DSR [9], LPS [32], MAP [33], MR [8], RC [34], RRWR [27], SGTD [35], BL [23], and HS [7]. For fair comparison, the source codes of these state-of-the-art approaches released by the authors are used for test with recommended parameter settings in this work.

According to Fig. 8 and Table 1, the proposed method (CRPSD) significantly outperforms all of the state-of-the-art approaches on all test datasets in terms of all evaluation criterions, which convincingly demonstrates the effectiveness of the proposed method. In these four test datasets, the most complex one is PASCAL-S. Therefore, all methods get the worst performance on this dataset. For all datasets, our method gets the largest gain on PASCAL-S dataset compared with the best state-of-the-art approach (MC) or our PSD, which demonstrates that our method can better deal with the complex cases than other approaches.

From the experimental results, three benefits of our method can be confirmed. (1) Although only the submodule region-level saliency estimation is used, it still gets the best performance compared with the state-of-the-art approaches on four datasets. Compared with MC [26], the RSD estimates the region saliency based on the regions generated by the proposed adaptive region generation technique while MC is based on superpixels, and the RSD uses a different strategy to form the context windows. The good performance of the RSD demonstrates the effectiveness of these improvements. (2) The submodule PSD also gets the best performance compared with the state-of-the-art approaches, which validates that the pixel-level CNN modified from VGGNet can well extract the multi-scale deep features for pixels to decide its saliency. (3) The proposed CRPSD by using the fusion network and joint training with the pixel-level CNN network can greatly improve the performance of the submodules, which demonstrates that CRPSD can well dig the complementary information of saliencies estimated by RSD and PSD for saliency detection.

Also, we qualitatively compare the salient maps detected by different approaches, as shown in the first ten rows of Fig. 9. Obviously, the proposed method is able to highlight saliencies of salient objects and suppress the saliencies

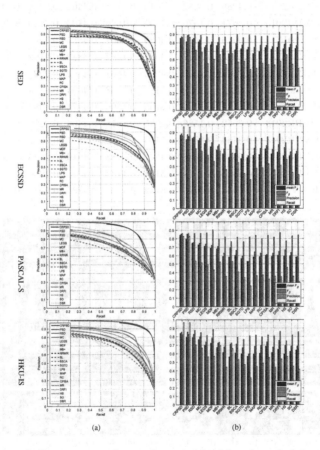

Fig. 8. Results of all test approaches on four standard benchmark datasets, i.e. SED, ECSSD, PASCAL-S, and HKU-IS. (a) presents the PR curves, (b) presents the mean F_β and the adaptive F_β/precision/recall which are computed from the binary images obtained by using Otsu algorithm on the salient maps.

Table 1. The wF_β and MAE of different saliency detection method on different test datasets (red, blue, and green texts respectively indicate rank 1, 2, and 3).

Method	Year	SED		ECSSD		PASCAL-S		HKU-IS	
		wF_β	MAE	wF_β	MAE	wF_β	MAE	wF_β	MAE
CRPSD	/	0.8292	0.0509	0.8485	0.0455	0.7761	0.0636	0.8209	0.0431
PSD	/	0.7590	0.0758	0.7572	0.0798	0.7113	0.1057	0.7371	0.0693
RSD	/	0.7759	0.0922	0.7569	0.0915	0.6195	0.1338	0.7286	0.0813
MC	CVPR2015	0.7387	0.1032	0.7293	0.1019	0.6064	0.1422	0.6899	0.0914
LEGS	CVPR2015	0.6498	0.1279	0.6722	0.1256	0.5791	0.1593	0.5911	0.1301
MDF	CVPR2015	0.6748	0.1196	0.6194	0.1377	0.5386	0.1633	0.6135	0.1152
MB+	ICCV2015	0.6555	0.1364	0.5632	0.1717	0.5307	0.1964	0.5438	0.1497
RRWR	CVPR2015	0.6117	0.1547	0.5026	0.1850	0.4435	0.2262	0.4592	0.1719
BL	CVPR2015	0.4986	0.1887	0.4615	0.2178	0.4464	0.2478	0.4119	0.2136
BSCA	CVPR2015	0.5671	0.1576	0.5159	0.1832	0.4703	0.2220	0.4643	0.1760
SGTD	TIP2015	0.6216	0.1475	0.4689	0.2007	0.4385	0.2269	0.4785	0.1627
LPS	TIP2015	0.5976	0.1477	0.4585	0.1877	0.3882	0.2162	0.4252	0.1635
MAP	TIP2015	0.5567	0.1621	0.4953	0.1861	0.4361	0.2222	0.4533	0.1717
RC	TPAMI2015	0.5652	0.1588	0.5118	0.1868	0.4694	0.2253	0.4768	0.1714
CPISA	TIP2015	0.6174	0.1474	0.5735	0.1596	0.4478	0.1983	0.5575	0.1374
MR	CVPR2013	0.6052	0.1586	0.4985	0.1875	0.4406	0.2288	0.4556	0.1740
DRFI	CVPR2013	0.6464	0.1360	0.5433	0.1658	0.4817	0.2042	0.5180	0.1444
HS	CVPR2013	0.5828	0.1948	0.4571	0.2283	0.4516	0.2625	0.4213	0.2151
SO	CVPR2014	0.6568	0.1351	0.5134	0.1733	0.4723	0.1986	0.5162	0.1426
DSR	ICCV2013	0.6055	0.1476	0.5162	0.1728	0.4385	0.2043	0.5079	0.1429

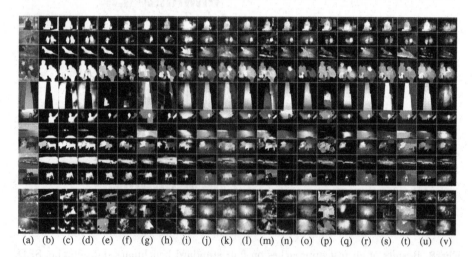

(a) (b) (c) (d) (e) (f) (g) (h) (i) (j) (k) (l) (m) (n) (o) (p) (q) (r) (s) (t) (u) (v)

Fig. 9. Visual Comparisons of different saliency detection approaches in various challenging scenarios. (a) Original images, (b) Ground truths, (c) CRPSD, (d) PSD, (e) RSD, (f) MC, (g) LEGS, (h) MDF, (i) MB+, (j) RRWR, (k) BL, (l) BSCA, (m) SGTD, (n) LPS, (o) MAP, (p) RC, (q) CPISA, (r) MR, (s) DRFI, (t) HS, (u) SO, (v) DSR.

of background better than other approaches, and the salient maps of the proposed method are much close to the ground truths in various challenging scenarios.

The last three rows of Fig. 9 show some cases in which the proposed method fails. For example, the colors of salient objects and backgrounds are very similar, the salient objects are too small, and the backgrounds are too complex. In these cases, the other approaches also cannot correctly detect the salient objects and it is not easy to accurately locate the salient objects even for human eyes.

5.4 Performance Comparisons with Baselines

As pixel labeling task, saliency detection and semantic segmentation are very similar. And recently, many CNN models [37,38,50] have been proposed for semantic segmentation. In order to test their performance on saliency detection, the most powerful model of deeplab [50], i.e. the DeepLab-MSc-LargeFOV model (DML), is chosen as a baseline, which is trained on THUS-10000 dataset for saliency detection. And its pretrained DeepLab-LargeFOV-COCO-MSC model (pre-DML) on semantic image segmentation is used as another baseline, which is directly used for saliency detection by summing up the probability predictions across all 20 object classes and using these sumed-up probabilities as a salient map. And to demonstrate the benefit of joint training of our method, we also test the performance of our method with separate training (sep-CRPSD).

Table 2. The wF_β of baselines and our methods on all test datasets.

Method	SED	ECSSD	PASCAL-S	HKU-IS
pre-DML	0.5140	0.6530	0.7322	0.6755
DML	0.7439	0.7482	0.6948	0.7258
sep-CRPSD	0.8109	0.8249	0.7621	0.7942
CRPSD	**0.8292**	**0.8485**	**0.7761**	**0.8209**

Table 2 lists the wF_β of baselines and our methods on all test datasets. According to Table 2, three conclusions can be summarized: (1) The performance of pre-DML is very good on PASCAL-S, while dramatically drops on other datasets. Because many salient objects in other datasets don't belong to the trained classes, and hence are considered as non-salient objects during saliency detection. (2) The DML trained for saliency detection gets better results than pre-DML on all datasets except PASCAL-S, but still much worse than our method, which further demonstrates that our method with multiple CNNs is powerful for saliency detection. (3) Our method with joint training (CRPSD) gets better performance than separate training (sep-CRPSD), which demonstrates the effectiveness of joint training.

Table 3. The mean shuffled-AUC of different fixation prediection methods on test datasets.

Dataset	PSD	Mr-CNN [51]	SDAE [55]	BMS [54]
MIT	**0.7587**	0.7184	0.7095	0.7105
Toronto	**0.7606**	0.7221	0.7230	0.7243

5.5 Performance of Fixation Prediction with Pixel-Level CNN

The model (PSD) for pixel-level saliency prediction also can be used for fixation prediction. To validate its performance for fixation prediction, we use the same experimental setting with Mr-CNN [51] to test our model on MIT [52] and Toronto [53] datasets. The evaluation metric is mean shuffled-AUC [54]. Table 3 lists the experimental results of our model and the other three state-of-the-art fixation prediction approaches on these two datasets. According to Table 3, PSD gets the best performance, which means that our model has powerful ability of fixation prediction. Above experimental results further demonstrate the effectiveness of our pixel-level CNN model.

6   Conclusions

This paper proposes a novel saliency detection method by combining region-level saliency estimation and pixel-level saliency prediction (denoted as CRPSD). A multiple CNN framework, composed of pixel-level CNN, region-level CNN and fusion CNN, is proposed for saliency detection. The pixel-level CNN, which is a modification of VGGNet, can predict the saliency at pixel-level by extracting multi-scale features of images. The region-level CNN can effectively estimate the saliencies of these regions generated by the proposed adaptive region generation technique. The fusion CNN can take full advantage of the original image, the pixel-level and region-level saliencies for final saliency detection. The proposed method can effectively detect the salient maps of images in various scenarios and greatly outperform the state-of-the-art saliency detection approaches.

Acknowledgments. This work was supported by the Natural Science Foundation of China under Grant 61472102. The authors would like to thank the founders of the publicly available datasets and the support of NVIDIA Corporation with the donation of the Tesla K40 GPU used for this research.

References

1. Jung, C., Kim, C.: A unified spectral-domain approach for saliency detection and its application to automatic object segmentation. IEEE Trans. Image Process. **21**(3), 1272–1283 (2012)
2. Rother, C., Bordeaux, L., Hamadi, Y., Blake, A.: Autocollage. ACM Trans. Graph. **25**(3), 847–852 (2006)

3. Luo, P., Tian, Y., Wang, X., Tang, X.: Switchable deep network for pedestrian detection. In: IEEE Conference on Computer Vision and Pattern Recognition, pp. 899–906 (2014)
4. Gao, Y., Wang, M., Zha, Z.J., Shen, J., Li, X., Wu, X.: Visual-textual joint relevance learning for tag-based social image search. IEEE Trans. Image Process. **22**(1), 363–376 (2013)
5. Rosin, P.L.: A simple method for detecting salient regions. Pattern Recogn. **42**(11), 2363–2371 (2009)
6. Liu, T., Yuan, Z., Sun, J., Wang, J., Zheng, N., Tang, X., Shum, H.Y.: Learning to detect a salient object. IEEE Trans. Pattern Anal. Mach. Intell. **33**(2), 353–367 (2011)
7. Yan, Q., Xu, L., Shi, J., Jia, J.: Hierarchical saliency detection. In: IEEE Conference on Computer Vision and Pattern Recognition, pp. 1155–1162 (2013)
8. Yang, C., Zhang, L., Lu, H., Ruan, X., Yang, M.H.: Saliency detection via graph-based manifold ranking. In: IEEE Conference on Computer Vision and Pattern Recognition, pp. 3166–3173 (2013)
9. Li, X., Lu, H., Zhang, L., Ruan, X., Yang, M.H.: Saliency detection via dense and sparse reconstruction. In: International Conference on Computer Vision, pp. 2976–2983 (2013)
10. Jiang, H., Wang, J., Yuan, Z., Wu, Y., Zheng, N., Li, S.: Salient object detection: A discriminative regional feature integration approach. In: International Conference on Computer Vision, pp. 2083–2090 (2013)
11. Cheng, M.M., Warrell, J., Lin, W.Y., Zheng, S., Vineet, V., Crook, N.: Efficient salient region detection with soft image abstraction. In: International Conference on Computer Vision, pp. 1529–1536 (2013)
12. Zhang, J., Sclaroff, S.: Saliency detection: a boolean map approach. In: International Conference on Computer Vision, pp. 153–160 (2013)
13. Jiang, B., Zhang, L., Lu, H., Yang, C., Yang, M.H.: Saliency detection via absorbing markov chain. In: International Conference on Computer Vision, pp. 1665–1672 (2013)
14. Li, X., Li, Y., Shen, C., Dick, A., Van Den Hengel, A.: Contextual hypergraph modeling for salient object detection. In: International Conference on Computer Vision, pp. 3328–3335 (2013)
15. Liu, R., Cao, J., Lin, Z., Shan, S.: Adaptive partial differential equation learning for visual saliency detection. In: IEEE Conference on Computer Vision and Pattern Recognition, pp. 3866–3873 (2014)
16. Lu, S., Mahadevan, V., Vasconcelos, N.: Learning optimal seeds for diffusion-based salient object detection. In: IEEE Conference on Computer Vision and Pattern Recognition, pp. 2790–2797 (2014)
17. Zhu, W., Liang, S., Wei, Y., Sun, J.: Saliency optimization from robust background detection. In: IEEE Conference on Computer Vision and Pattern Recognition, pp. 2814–2821 (2014)
18. Kim, J., Han, D., Tai, Y.W., Kim, J.: Salient region detection via high-dimensional color transform. In: IEEE Conference on Computer Vision and Pattern Recognition, pp. 883–890 (2014)
19. Li, Y., Hou, X., Koch, C., Rehg, J.M., Yuille, A.L.: The secrets of salient object segmentation. In: IEEE Conference on Computer Vision and Pattern Recognition, pp. 280–287 (2014)
20. Tang, Y., Wu, X., Bu, W.: Saliency detection based on graph-structural agglomerative clustering. In: ACM International Conference on Multimedia, pp. 1083–1086 (2015)

21. Li, G., Yu, Y.: Visual saliency based on multiscale deep features. In: IEEE Conference on Computer Vision and Pattern Recognition, pp. 5455–5463 (2015)

22. Frintrop, S., Werner, T., Martin Garcia, G.: Traditional saliency reloaded: a good old model in new shape. In: IEEE Conference on Computer Vision and Pattern Recognition, pp. 82–90 (2015)

23. Tong, N., Lu, H., Ruan, X., Yang, M.H.: Salient object detection via bootstrap learning. In: IEEE Conference on Computer Vision and Pattern Recognition, pp. 1884–1892 (2015)

24. Gong, C., Tao, D., Liu, W., Maybank, S.J., Fang, M., Fu, K., Yang, J.: Saliency propagation from simple to difficult. In: IEEE Conference on Computer Vision and Pattern Recognition, pp. 2531–2539 (2015)

25. Qin, Y., Lu, H., Xu, Y., Wang, H.: Saliency detection via cellular automata. In: IEEE Conference on Computer Vision and Pattern Recognition, pp. 110–119 (2015)

26. Zhao, R., Ouyang, W., Li, H., Wang, X.: Saliency detection by multi-context deep learning. In: IEEE Conference on Computer Vision and Pattern Recognition, pp. 1265–1274 (2015)

27. Li, C., Yuan, Y., Cai, W., Xia, Y., Dagan Feng, D.: Robust saliency detection via regularized random walks ranking. In: IEEE Conference on Computer Vision and Pattern Recognition, pp. 2710–2717 (2015)

28. Wang, L., Lu, H., Ruan, X., Yang, M.H.: Deep networks for saliency detection via local estimation and global search. In: IEEE Conference on Computer Vision and Pattern Recognition, pp. 3183–3192 (2015)

29. Li, N., Sun, B., Yu, J.: A weighted sparse coding framework for saliency detection. In: IEEE Conference on Computer Vision and Pattern Recognition, pp. 5216–5223 (2015)

30. Zhang, J., Sclaroff, S., Lin, Z., Shen, X., Price, B., Mech, R.: Minimum barrier salient object detection at 80 fps. In: International Conference on Computer Vision, pp. 1404–1412 (2015)

31. Wang, K., Lin, L., Lu, J., Li, C., Shi, K.: Pisa: Pixelwise image saliency by aggregating complementary appearance contrast measures with edge-preserving coherence. IEEE Trans. Image Process. **24**(10), 3019–3033 (2015)

32. Li, H., Lu, H., Lin, Z., Shen, X., Price, B.: Inner and inter label propagation: salient object detection in the wild. IEEE Trans. Image Process. **24**(10), 3176–3186 (2015)

33. Sun, J., Lu, H., Liu, X.: Saliency region detection based on markov absorption probabilities. IEEE Trans. Image Process. **24**(5), 1639–1649 (2015)

34. Cheng, M.M., Mitra, N.J., Huang, X., Torr, P.H., Hu, S.M.: Global contrast based salient region detection. IEEE Trans. Pattern Anal. Mach. Intell. **37**(3), 569–582 (2015)

35. Scharfenberger, C., Wong, A., Clausi, D.A.: Structure-guided statistical textural distinctiveness for salient region detection in natural images. IEEE Trans. Image Process. **24**(1), 457–470 (2015)

36. Achanta, R., Hemami, S., Estrada, F., Susstrunk, S.: Frequency-tuned salient region detection. In: IEEE Conference on Computer Vision and Pattern Recognition, pp. 1597–1604. IEEE (2009)

37. Zheng, S., Jayasumana, S., Romera-Paredes, B., Vineet, V., Su, Z., Du, D., Huang, C., Torr, P.H.: Conditional random fields as recurrent neural networks. In: International Conference on Computer Vision, pp. 1529–1537 (2015)

38. Long, J., Shelhamer, E., Darrell, T.: Fully convolutional networks for semantic segmentation. In: IEEE Conference on Computer Vision and Pattern Recognition, pp. 3431–3440 (2015)

39. Xie, S., Tu, Z.: Holistically-nested edge detection. In: International Conference on Computer Vision, pp. 1395–1403 (2015)
40. Bertasius, G., Shi, J., Torresani, L.: Deepedge: A multi-scale bifurcated deep network for top-down contour detection. In: IEEE Conference on Computer Vision and Pattern Recognition, pp. 4380–4389 (2015)
41. Simonyan, K., Zisserman, A.: Very deep convolutional networks for large-scale image recognition. arXiv preprint (2014). arXiv:1409.1556
42. Szegedy, C., Liu, W., Jia, Y., Sermanet, P., Reed, S., Anguelov, D., Erhan, D., Vanhoucke, V., Rabinovich, A.: Going deeper with convolutions. In: IEEE Conference on Computer Vision and Pattern Recognition, pp. 1–9 (2015)
43. Achanta, R., Shaji, A., Smith, K., Lucchi, A., Fua, P., Süsstrunk, S.: Slic superpixels compared to state-of-the-art superpixel methods. IEEE Trans. Pattern Anal. Mach. Intell. **34**(11), 2274–2282 (2012)
44. Zhang, W., Wang, X., Zhao, D., Tang, X.: Graph degree linkage: agglomerative clustering on a directed graph. In: Fitzgibbon, A., Lazebnik, S., Perona, P., Sato, Y., Schmid, C. (eds.) ECCV 2012. LNCS, vol. 7572, pp. 428–441. Springer, Heidelberg (2012). doi:10.1007/978-3-642-33718-5_31
45. Zeiler, M.D., Fergus, R.: Visualizing and understanding convolutional networks. In: Fleet, D., Pajdla, T., Schiele, B., Tuytelaars, T. (eds.) ECCV 2014. LNCS, vol. 8689, pp. 818–833. Springer, Heidelberg (2014). doi:10.1007/978-3-319-10590-1_53
46. Koltun, V.: Efficient inference in fully connected crfs with gaussian edge potentials. Neural Inf. Process. Syst. (2011)
47. Jia, Y., Shelhamer, E., Donahue, J., Karayev, S., Long, J., Girshick, R., Guadarrama, S., Darrell, T.: Caffe: Convolutional architecture for fast feature embedding. In: ACM International Conference on Multimedia, pp. 675–678. ACM (2014)
48. Alpert, S., Galun, M., Brandt, A., Basri, R.: Image segmentation by probabilistic bottom-up aggregation and cue integration. IEEE Trans. Pattern Anal. Mach. Intell. **34**(2), 315–327 (2012)
49. Margolin, R., Zelnik-Manor, L., Tal, A.: How to evaluate foreground maps? In: IEEE Conference on Computer Vision and Pattern Recognition, pp. 248–255 (2014)
50. Chen, L.C., Papandreou, G., Kokkinos, I., Murphy, K., Yuille, A.L.: Deeplab: semantic image segmentation with deep convolutional nets, atrous convolution, and fully connected crfs. arXiv preprint (2016). arXiv:1606.00915
51. Liu, N., Han, J., Zhang, D., Wen, S., Liu, T.: Predicting eye fixations using convolutional neural networks. In: IEEE Conference on Computer Vision and Pattern Recognition, pp. 362–370 (2015)
52. Judd, T., Ehinger, K., Durand, F., Torralba, A.: Learning to predict where humans look. In: International Conference on Computer Vision, pp. 2106–2113. IEEE (2009)
53. Bruce, N.D., Tsotsos, J.K.: Saliency, attention, and visual search: an information theoretic approach. J. Vis. **9**(3), 5–5 (2009)
54. Zhang, J., Sclaroff, S.: Exploiting surroundedness for saliency detection: a Boolean map approach. IEEE Trans. Pattern Anal. Mach. Intell. **38**(5), 889–902 (2016)
55. Han, J., Zhang, D., Wen, S., Guo, L., Liu, T., Li, X.: Two-stage learning to predict human eye fixations via SDAEs. IEEE Trans. Cybern. **46**(2), 487–498 (2016)

Author Index